Addictions Counseling Today

Perhaps only now I realize that flowers blossom in spring.
Perhaps to believe otherwise is just denial.

To Scott Read

July 29, 1980 – January 13, 2014

Perhaps

I never knew you well,
But I knew you,
Your grace and charm warmed the rooms you entered,
Perhaps I entered a few.

Your smile was radiant,
It lit sparks wherever it traveled,
And perhaps it traveled far,
Because I kept hearing about you.

When I heard news of your departure,
I sat stunned, trying to understand,
As someone special had left this earth,
Perhaps for all the wrong reasons.

Perhaps if I had known you better,
Perhaps I could have got through to you,
Perhaps I could have helped you,
Perhaps.

Sara Miller McCune founded SAGE Publishing in 1965 to support the dissemination of usable knowledge and educate a global community. SAGE publishes more than 1000 journals and over 600 new books each year, spanning a wide range of subject areas. Our growing selection of library products includes archives, data, case studies and video. SAGE remains majority owned by our founder and after her lifetime will become owned by a charitable trust that secures the company's continued independence.

Los Angeles | London | New Delhi | Singapore | Washington DC | Melbourne

Addictions Counseling Today

Substances and Addictive Behaviors

Kevin G. Alderson
University of Calgary

Los Angeles | London | New Delhi
Singapore | Washington DC | Melbourne

FOR INFORMATION:

SAGE Publications, Inc.
2455 Teller Road
Thousand Oaks, California 91320
E-mail: order@sagepub.com

SAGE Publications Ltd.
1 Oliver's Yard
55 City Road
London EC1Y 1SP
United Kingdom

SAGE Publications India Pvt. Ltd.
B 1/I 1 Mohan Cooperative Industrial Area
Mathura Road, New Delhi 110 044
India

SAGE Publications Asia-Pacific Pte. Ltd.
18 Cross Street #10-10/11/12
China Square Central
Singapore 048423

Acquisitions Editor: Abbie Rickard
Editorial Assistant: Elizabeth Cruz
Production Editor: Rebecca Lee
Copy Editor: Celia McCoy
Typesetter: C&M Digitals (P) Ltd.
Proofreader: Caryne Brown
Indexer: Sylvia Coates
Cover Designer: Dally Verghese
Marketing Manager: Zina Craft

Printed in the United States of America

Library of Congress Cataloging-in-Publication Data

Names: Alderson, Kevin, author.
Title: Addictions counseling today : substances and addictive behaviors / Kevin Alderson, University of Calgary.
Description: Los Angeles : SAGE, [2020] | Includes bibliographical references and index.
Identifiers: LCCN 2019028128 | ISBN 978-1-4833-0826-5 (paperback) | ISBN 978-1-5443-9231-8 (epub) | ISBN 978-1-5443-9233-2 (pdf)
Subjects: LCSH: Substance abuse—Treatment. | Substance abuse—Patients—Counseling of.
Classification: LCC RC564 .A42 2020 | DDC 362.29—dc23
LC record available at https://lccn.loc.gov/2019028128

This book is printed on acid-free paper.

19 20 21 22 23 10 9 8 7 6 5 4 3 2 1

Contents

12 Nicotine Addiction 320

13 Other Drug Addictions 354

18 Food Addiction 530

19 Exercise Addiction 558

21 Work Addiction 602

PART V: SUMMARY AND CONCLUSIONS 622

22 Summary and Conclusions 624

Preface

I am an addict. I now understand why, as much as any of us truly knows ourselves. Perhaps these four words seem unsavory, but the flavors of our lives are not something we randomly pick from a smorgasbord. But here's the thing: I am flawed, and so are you. We are but imperfect human beings living our lives among a myriad of problems and issues. Given a particular set of circumstances, you could be the next one to sit in a counseling office.

Some of you are also addicts. Your drug or behavior of addiction may be different, but as in the lyrics to "I Am... I Said" by Neil Diamond, "The story's the same one." We were not born as perfect slates. Like me, your suffering may have gone unnoticed – even by you – for years. The power of our unconscious minds to keep the obvious from becoming hurtful is truly remarkable.

If you *are* an addict, two sayings may be particularly pertinent to you in your developing awareness:

1. "The unexamined life is not worth living" (attributed to the philosopher Socrates).
2. "Be the change that you wish to see in the world" (an abridged quote from Mohandas K. Gandhi).

These two sayings remind us that (a) self-awareness is critical if we want to get better and (b) we cannot hope for a better existence if we are not prepared to work at changing ourselves.

Some scholars and counselors today do not use the word *addict*. This is a semantic endeavor to adopt English Prime (i.e., E-Prime), which is an adaptation of the English language that removes all versions of the word, "to be." Semantically, E-Prime makes sense because we are *more than* any word(s) used to describe us. For example, addicts are more than addicted persons. They enact many roles in life, and the addict is only one of them. Surprisingly little research has been done anywhere in the world that explores drinker's self-identification, let alone regarding those addicted to other substances or addictive behaviors (Callinan, Pennay, & Livingston, 2017).

However, no one raises an eyebrow when I say, "I am a counseling psychologist," "I am a father," or "I am married." When eyebrows are raised, it usually concerns a stigmatized identity label, and the word *addict* certainly falls into this category, and so do all of the other mental disorders labeled in the *Diagnostic and Statistical Manual of Mental Disorders, Fifth Edition* (*DSM–5*; American Psychiatric Association, 2013). Although we can E-Prime *out* particular identities, those of us who are addicts understand what this word means to us. With over 40 years of on-off dysregulation, I know that if I return to using, I will insidiously return to my previous levels of use within no time. Nonetheless, in most places in this book, you will find that I use the word addict as an adjective instead of as a noun.

I would be remiss not to reveal that my counseling heroes are humanists like Carl Rogers and Abraham Maslow and existentialists like Viktor Frankl, and, although my journey toward becoming harmonious, real, and genuine has felt like an eternity, writing this text represents my most authentic expression of self-actualization. As an existential humanist, I think that the personal is political, and I believe that self-disclosure is appropriate if it helps you in some way.

An appropriate subtitle for this textbook might have been *The Book That Almost Didn't Happen*. When the contract to write this text appeared, my mind was as closed as the front door. How could I relate to this topic? That soon changed. Nothing had prepared me for the ensuing horror.

I should have seen the signs. I should have understood. I should have known. When I was 22 years old, I fell in love for the first time. I also began smoking weed daily until the relationship ended, concurrently ending the puffs of smoke with its demise. The clinical depression that followed landed me in a hospital for a week, but the suffering continued for the next nine months. I often felt hopeless. I quit my job amid that torturous hell called depression. Thinking I might never work again was ridiculous; depression runs its course, and the light of spring eventually relit my torch.

When I was 39, I started doctoral study along with a new 10-year relationship. It went up in smoke eventually as well. Few days went by without puffs from my familiar dragon, not to mention the consumption of copious amounts of alcohol. My use continued into the next relationship, and then into the next. My reprieve began in 2008, soon after my partner asked that I stop smoking marijuana altogether. Within a few weeks, depression again visited me, and one antidepressant after another did not conquer the sinking feeling. Months later, I was again admitted for a brief stay in a hospital, but, gratefully, that too eventually passed.

Allow me to switch into present tense as I continue. I receive the book contract for this text in January 2013, and, by early March, my spouse leaves our relationship. The next day I do not know how to feel, so, before I feel anything, I phone a trusted source and get a joint. This unlocks the pattern, and, 18 months later, I realize I have written nothing. Daily use of cannabis leaves me numb, but also irritable, impulsive, and emotionally labile. I stop cold turkey, and my ability to sleep becomes compromised as depression again revisits me for months.

I never knew what it meant to live one day at a time until I was living it. I am stronger now, but I am not fully healed . . . I am in recovery. I am doing the best I can, living this day knowing that this is all I have for sure. Our lives can be over in the twinkling of an eye, but for so long as I breathe, I plan to *really* live. After all, I belong here, so do you, and so do the frail addicted individuals who muster enough courage to find their way to your doorstep, possibly still thinking that the contrived reality lived in is still better than the more painful one long avoided.

No one is immune to the potentiality of addiction. For me, it was predominantly cannabis. For others, it might be alcohol, street drugs, sex, the Internet, gambling, gaming, or food. Whatever we stuff ourselves with, eventually we will find ourselves looking at the disgraceful image we created in the mirror. As with the Johari window (Luft, & Ingham, 1955), there are those areas that we do not yet see but are evident to others. We wait until something breaks our cosmic egg so that our denial can shatter before us. Hopefully, it fractures before it is too late.

*****

I hope this book is the most exciting, provocative, enlightening, and practical text you ever read on the subject. In every chapter, I have included a section called *personal reflections*. You may wonder why I added it. I am a retired professor of counseling psychology, and most of my research was qualitative. I have also been the editor-in-chief of a Canadian journal for over 10 years. All research is situated in preconceptions. In quantitative research, we call these preconceptions hypotheses. Before a quantitative study is conducted, researchers need to state what they expect to find by stating their hypotheses.

In qualitative research, on the other hand, a technique called "bracketing" (Tufford & Newman, 2010), "reflexive bracketing" (Ahern, 1999), or simply "reflexivity" (Ahern, 1999) is utilized to help mitigate the potentially adverse effects of having preconceptions. Bracketing is the process whereby researchers state their assumptions regarding the topic they will study. Even though I've used hundreds of references to support what I write in this textbook, I still have biases that affect my perceptions and the research that captures my foci. For example, you would be astute to know that, when I write about cannabis, I may not sound as enthusiastic as many young people today. Given my experience that I have shared in this preface, you will understand the birth of my trepidations.

*****

This book is intended for counseling students, whether specialists or generalists in addiction counseling, and for those already in practice. You will not find another textbook on this subject that is more thorough in its coverage of what matters to an addiction counselor.

Addictions to both substances and behaviors are covered in depth. Many names have attempted to capture the essence of these mind-altering experiences. You will hear and read terms like abuse, misuse, dependency, addiction, disorder, compulsive or problematic behavior, process addiction, or the "isms" (e.g., alcoholism, workaholism). Does it matter what you name them? In this book, all terms will be used synonymously to create some variety. The definition of addiction is in Chapter 1, which will establish the common ground for our understanding.

At least four aspects make this text a unique contribution to the literature. First, this text addresses every accreditation standard for addiction counseling as outlined by the Council for Accreditation of Counseling and Related Educational Programs ([CACREP], 2016). Turn to Appendix A to see where precisely each standard is included in this textbook. This was no easy feat to accomplish, but the result is a text that could be used for several of your classes in a CACREP-accredited addictions program.

Second, the primary behavioral addictions are covered in separate chapters. Your addiction course might cover only substance use disorders, in which case these behavioral addictions will provide you a valuable resource for later application. The neuroscience underlying substance use disorders and behavioral addictions is similar. Furthermore, behavioral addictions are increasing in prevalence, and many of them co-occur with substance use disorders. Consequently, you are going to be working with individuals who have multiple addictions, some of which are behavioral addictions (also referred to as *process* addictions).

Third, Chapters 9 through 21 are stand-alone chapters. This means that you can turn to any of those chapters and know the best of what we know about that particular addiction. Everything you need is right there in that one chapter! Once you are in practice, you will appreciate having this textbook as the ultimate resource.

Fourth, the intention is to bring you, the reader, into the heart of addictive thinking. This will be facilitated by a section in Chapters 9 through 21 called "Inside an Addicted Person's Mind." You will also find an interesting section in several of the substance chapters that provide a first-person portrayal of what it is like to be high on specific drugs. But the unique features of this book do not stop there. Chapters 9 through 21 include the following:

1. *Challenging Your Assumptions About This Addiction* – Designed to help readers become aware of their assumptions before reading the chapter.
2. *Personal Reflections* – My bracketing/reflexivity.
3. *Inside an Addicted Person's Mind* – A first-person narrative to help the reader gain a sense of what it would feel like and be like to have the addiction.
4. *Roleplay Scenarios* – Two scenarios are offered that can be roleplayed in class in dyads.
5. *How Would an Addiction Counselor Help This Person?* – This is a longer, more complicated case that is meant for class discussion or personal reflection.
6. *Working With Diverse Populations* – A separate section in the addiction chapters that focuses on the empirical literature regarding what we know that applies explicitly to work with sex differences, adolescents, ethnically/racially diverse clients, disabled clients, and lesbian, gay, bisexual, transgender, and queer (LGBTQ) clients.
7. *Counseling Scenario* (also found in Chapter 7) – A typical scenario where the client sees a counselor for addiction but encounters a counselor who makes several mistakes or errors in working with the client. We learn what we should do and what we should avoid. One reviewer of the chapters found this sometimes to be a humorous "release valve" from the intensity found in many of the content sections. Indeed, I tried to make the mistakes visible. The saddest part is knowing that I have made some of these mistakes at one time or another! I read an online review of a counselor, and the ex-client wrote that the therapist told her that she looked constipated. Well, at least I never said that to a client, even if it was meant to be metaphorical.
8. *Individual Exercises* – Exercises that students can do if interested (or if assigned) outside of class to increase their knowledge and/or skills in working with the addiction.
9. *Classroom Exercises* – Exercises that can be done in class.

Now it is time to introduce you to a faction of the population that is frequently unconventional, at times frightening, and always fascinating. Turn this page and begin your journey into the mind-altering world of addiction.

References

Ahern, K. J. (1999). 10 tips for reflexive bracketing. *Qualitative Health Research*, *9*(3), 407–411.

American Psychiatric Association. (2013). *Diagnostic and statistical manual of mental disorders* (5th ed.). Washington, DC: Author.

Buckingham, S. A., Frings, D., & Albery, I. P. (2013). Group membership and social identity in addiction recovery. *Psychology of Addictive Behaviors*, *27*(4), 1132–1140.

Callinan, S., Pennay, A., & Livingston, M. (2017). Decreasing prevalence of social drinkers in Australia. *Addictive Behaviors*, *67*, 20–25.

Council for Accreditation of Counseling and Related Educational Programs (CACREP). (2016). Section 5: Entry-level specialty areas – Addiction counseling (pp. 20–21). *2016 CACREP standards*. Alexandria, VA: Author. Retrieved from http://www.cacrep.org/wp-content/uploads/2018/05/2016-Standards-with-Glossary-5.3.2018.pdf

Grubbs, J. B., Grant, J. T., & Engelman, J. (2019). Self-identification as a pornography addict: Examining the roles of pornography use, religiousness, and moral incongruence. *Sexual Addiction & Compulsivity*, *26*, 1–24.

Luft, J., & Ingham, H. (1955). The Johari window, a graphic model of interpersonal awareness. *Proceedings of the western training laboratory in group development*. Los Angeles, CA: University of California, Los Angeles.

Tufford, L., & Newman, P. A. (2010). Bracketing in qualitative research. *Qualitative Social Work*, *11*(1), 80–96.

Valencia-Payne, M. A. (2018). My name is alcoholic and I am your identity: An exploration of an individual's self-identification process as an alcoholic. *Dissertation Abstracts International: Section B: The Sciences and Engineering*, *79*(8-B(E)), No Pagination Specified.

Acknowledgments

Without the incredible support of people working at SAGE Publishing, this book would only reside somewhere in my mind. Special thanks are extended to Abbie Rickard, Acquisitions Editor for the Psychology and Counseling division of SAGE. You saw me through North and South and East and West. Your support was deeply valued while my life fell in every direction. I am glad this eagle has finally landed.

Thank you to my daughter, Shauna Alderson. You helped me immensely with the contribution you made to three chapters. Your creative and mental abilities dazzle me. They still do today.

The most special thanks go to Gerry Beriault. I couldn't have done this without your constant help and dedication. You brought Dickens into my life, and every day the spirits of Christmas shine over you. You helped make the tale of two cities become the tale of one.

SAGE wishes to thank the following reviewers for their valuable feedback during the development of this book:

R. Trent Codd, III, EdS, LPC, LCAS
Lenoir-Rhyne University and Cognitive-Behavioral Therapy Center of Western North Carolina

Dr. Brenda J. Edwards
Mercer University/Penfield College

Natalie F. Spencer
NC A&T State University

Dr. Betsy St. Pierre, LPC
Nicholls State University

Scott Tracy
Kutztown University

Laurie Walker
Yavapai College

Kevin Curtin
Alfred University

Daniel G. Duryea
University of Detroit Mercy

Joshua C. Watson
Texas A&M University-Corpus Christi

Genevieve Weber, PhD
Hofstra University

Caroline S. Booth
North Carolina A & T State University

Valerie McGaha
Oklahoma State University

Michael Roadhouse
University of the Cumberlands

Dr. Shawn L. Spurgeon
The University of Tennessee, Knoxville

For Instructors

There is a great deal of information and resources within this textbook. The text addresses every accreditation standard for addiction counseling as outlined by the Council for Accreditation of Counseling and Related Educational Programs ([CACREP], 2016). Turn to Appendix A to see where precisely each standard is included in this textbook.

This text was designed to be used potentially in more than one course in an addictions program. It arguably covers counseling for behavioral addictions in substantially greater depth than any other addiction counseling textbook on the market. Chapters 9 through 21 can also act as standalone chapters. They provide the latest synopsis of research and practice in the specific addiction each covers. My hope is that students will cherish this book and use it for many years. After graduation, they need a thorough text like this one to act as a refresher for how to work with clients experiencing the many substance and behavioral addictions included.

If the intent is to cover most of the content of this textbook in a single course, I suggest the following sequence for a course that has 13 actual weeks of class time.

Teaching Sequence in a 13-Term Semester

Week	Chapters
1	Preface, Chapter 1, Chapter 2
2	Chapters 3 and 4
3	Chapter 5
4	Chapter 6
5	Chapter 7
6	Chapter 8
7	Chapter 9
8	Chapter 10
9	Chapter 11
10	Chapter 12
11	Chapter 13
12	Chapters 14 and 15
13	Include one of Chapters 16 to 21; -AND- Chapter 22, Epilogue

About the Author

Kevin G. Alderson, PhD, is Professor Emeritus of counseling psychology from the University of Calgary. He has been a counselor for 40 years and a registered psychologist since 1986. He is serving a 3-year term as president-elect, president, and past president, respectively, for the College of Alberta Psychologists, the body that regulates psychology in Alberta, Canada. Dr. Alderson is a professional member of the Association for Addiction Professionals, and currently sits on the editorial board for the *Journal of Alcoholism, Drug Abuse & Substance Dependence* and the *Austin Journal of Drug Abuse and Addiction*. He also holds membership in the American Counseling Association, the American Psychological Association, the Canadian Counselling and Psychotherapy Association, and the Canadian Psychological Association. Since 2008, Dr. Alderson has been the editor-in-chief of the *Canadian Journal of Counselling and Psychotherapy*, which is the only national peer-reviewed journal in the counseling and psychotherapy field in Canada. He currently works half-time for Yorkville University as its director for a proposed online doctor of counseling and psychotherapy degree program.

Dr. Alderson has authored nine previous books and several scholarly articles and book chapters. He completed a MSc in clinical, school, and community psychology from the University of Calgary and a PhD in counseling psychology at the University of Alberta. Dr. Alderson is married and is the father of two adult children. Outside of counseling, he enjoys racket sports, dancing, hiking, camping, and weight training.

1 Introduction

iStock.com/abl

Learning Objectives

1. Learn about the percentage of Americans addicted to substances and addictive behaviors, and the costs of addiction to both the public and the users of illegal substances.
2. Understand the definitions of abnormal psychology, addiction, addicted individuals, counseling, and addiction counseling as they are used throughout this textbook.
3. Summarize the history of drugs, addictions, and addiction counseling.
4. Become familiar with relapse rates and individuals who stop their addictions without professional help.
5. Discover details pertaining to becoming a certified addiction counselor.

CHALLENGING YOUR ASSUMPTIONS ABOUT ADDICTIONS

1. What images come to your mind when you think about someone who is addicted to alcohol? How does this image shift when you think about a person addicted to illegal drugs?
2. How do you respond to addicted individuals who are asking for money as you pass them by on the sidewalk or when they approach your vehicle window? To what extent is your response conditioned by the images you have of individuals who abuse alcohol and/or drugs (i.e., pertaining to the previous question)?
3. What do you believe will be most challenging part of becoming an addiction counselor? What will be easiest?
4. What personal theory do you have about why some people become addicted to a substance and/or behavior (i.e., how do addicted individuals become addicted)? Why don't *all* people become addicted to something?
5. If you could make nicotine, alcohol, and illegal drugs entirely unavailable for Americans, would you support this standpoint? If "yes," why, and if "no," why not?

PERSONAL REFLECTIONS

Today I see the sun shining through the trees, but it is not like this every day for everyone. For many addicted individuals, a day that feels hopeless is a day to use more. Even for those in recovery, without light, there is dark. In the darkness, one needs to use relapse prevention strategies to hope that tomorrow brings back yesterday's lightness.

This is the beginning of a long journey for both of us. You can likely tell that by the thickness of this textbook! Addiction consumes afflicted individuals in important life areas (e.g., relationships with lovers, friends, and family; free time; leisure time; lifestyle; personal identity). The hurdle before them to become "clean" can feel not only as intimidating as reading this entire book; rather, it can feel like actually writing it. Addiction *becomes* your life, your lifestyle, and your preoccupation. When you decide to stop doing addiction, the void it creates is enormous.

My priority is to teach you well and to bring you in as much as possible to the lived experience of addicted persons. The challenge before me is unlike any that I have faced. As I begin writing this textbook, I wonder how I will finish it without losing my mind. But it doesn't matter. There is no turning back now, whatever the cost.

Introduction

> *"Where have all the flowers gone?"* (Song written by Pete Seeger and Joe Hickerson).

We are amid a worldwide addiction crisis. Using more accurate research methods than was available in the past, the United Nations Office on Drugs and Crime (2019a) stated on their home page that "the adverse health consequences of drug use are more severe and widespread than previously thought" (para. 1). The *World Drug Report 2019* (United Nations Office on Drugs and Crime, 2019b) estimates that, worldwide, the number of opioid users is currently at 53 million, which is up 56% from previous estimates.

America itself is in crisis. Car crashes are no longer the leading cause of accidental deaths in the United States: Drug overdoses have tragically accelerated to first place (Katz, 2017). Nearly 64,000 Americans died of drug overdoses in 2016. Fentanyl deaths went up 540% between 2013 and 2016 (Katz, 2017), and the numbers continue to rise. In August 2018, for example, the 12-month prevalence of deaths due to drug overdoses was 67,360 (National Center for Health Statistics, 2019) and traffic deaths were estimated at 40,000 in the same year (National Safety Council, 2019). Substance addictions affect at least one in every four American families (Milkman & Sunderwirth, 2010).

According to the Surgeon General's Report (U.S. Department of Health & Human Services Office of the Surgeon General [HHSOSG], 2016), 8% of the population meets the diagnostic criteria for a substance use disorder (SUD) (ages 12 and older). Although 20.8 million people (7.8% of the population) met the diagnostic criteria in 2015 for an SUD, only about 2.2 million of these individuals (10.4%) received any treatment (HHSOSG, 2016). "Abuse of tobacco, alcohol, and illicit drugs is costly to our Nation, exacting more than $740 billion annually in costs related to crime, lost work productivity and health care" (National Institute on Drug Abuse, 2017, para. 2).

That sum of money does not include what Americans spend on illegal drugs. Kilmer et al. (2014) estimated that, between 2000 and 2010, Americans spent about $1 trillion on illegal substances (or $100 billion each year). At the same time, the

U.S. government spent between $40 billion and $50 billion in the continuing war on drugs to little avail; the amount spent on illegal substances annually remained the same over the 10 years (Kilmer et al., 2014). Globally, the war on drugs is not working. After Australia prohibited heroin in 1953, for example, "overdose deaths increased 55-fold between 1964 and 1997" (Wodak, 2018).

Alcohol and/or illicit drugs have always prevailed in American society. In 2017, half of Americans (49.5%), ages 12 and older, had used an illicit drug in their lifetime and 19.0% in the past year (National Survey on Drug Use and Health [NSDUH], 2018). Americans continue to "turn on, tune in, drop out," borrowing Timothy Leary's phrase spoken at the Human Be-In, a gathering of about 30,000 hippies in Golden Gate Park in San Francisco in 1967 (Ott & Joseph, 2017). This gathering, a prelude to San Francisco's Summer of Love, turned the Haight-Ashbury district into America's symbol of a psychedelic counterculture (Barusch, 2017). Although hallucinogens and barbiturates were the craze in the 1960s and 1970s, each generation has embraced some drugs more than others. Drugabuse.com (2019) analyzed NSDUH data between 1978 and 2013. The NSDUH is a national annual survey that has been conducted in the United States since 1971 (see https://nsduhweb.rti.org/respweb/homepage.cfm for details).[1]

Drugabuse.com (2019) compared the substance-taking habits of Millennials (born 1983–2002), Generation X (born 1963–1982), Baby Boomers (born 1943–1962), and the generation called "The Lucky Few" (born 1923–1942). Unsurprisingly, alcohol has always been the most commonly used substance, and this remains true of adults and adolescents (Office of Adolescent Health [OAH], 2017). Across the generations, marijuana was the second most-used drug (Drugabuse.com, 2019). Of the four generations analyzed, Baby Boomers led the pack, with nearly 50% reporting use of marijuana within the last year.

Unfortunately, prescription painkiller abuse has become more common among Millennials compared to the previous three generations. At their peak, less than 8% of Baby Boomers and Generation X abused painkillers in the past year compared to over 12% of Millennials ages 19 to 20. The OAH (2017) stated that, when surveyed in 2016, 3.6% of adolescents aged 12–17 reported using opioids over the past year. The rate is twice as high for youth aged 18–25. OAH reported that, although opioid misuse is diminishing, the rate of overdose deaths among teenagers is increasing.

Although the use of illegal drugs by adolescents is decreasing, "vaping" (i.e., inhaling and exhaling vapors produced by electronic cigarettes and similar devices) is increasing (Lindstrom & Rosvall, 2018; Miech et al., 2018). Nicotine, marijuana, and neither (i.e., just flavoring) can be vaped. In 2017, levels of nicotine vaping for students in grades 8, 10, and 12 were 8%, 16%, and 19%, respectively (Miech et al., 2018), and it remains unknown if these percentages have peaked (Miech et al., 2018). Vaping was the most common use of a tobacco product among adolescents in 2017 (Miech et al., 2018). Not only that, adolescents are not inhaling nicotine from electronic cigarettes in most cases to help them quit smoking. The most common reasons for vaping by adolescents include taste and entertainment (63.4%), experimentation (29.4%), and only 7.3% to replace cigarettes (Miech et al., 2018).

But substance addictions are only the first chapter of the American addiction story. When the behavioral addictions are included (e.g., gambling, Internet-based, romantic relationship, sex, exercise, work), the percentage of U.S. adults addicted to something over 12 months explodes into a walloping 47% by some estimates (Carnes, 1991; Sussman, Lisha, & Griffiths, 2011). Figures from Canada are comparable (Thege, Hodgins, & Wild, 2016). As Greenfield (2011) contemplated, it seems that "the more choices we seem to have, the less healthy we seem to become. The more choices we have, the more stress we have" (p. 141).

Definitions

Abnormal Psychology

Abnormal psychology is defined as "the scientific study of abnormal behavior aiming to describe, predict, explain and change abnormal patterns of functioning" (Flood, 2016, p. 154). According to Comer (2013), the field of abnormal psychology includes four Ds: (a) *deviance*, which is being different and displaying extreme or bizarre behaviors compared to others; (b) *distress*, either to oneself or others; (c) *dysfunction*, which involves having difficulty performing daily tasks constructively; and (d) *danger*, which includes a threat to self, others, or society. Substance and addictive behaviors qualify on all four counts. In other words, addictions fit within the four Ds, and, unsurprisingly, most of them are found in the *Diagnostic and Statistical Manual of Mental Disorders, Fifth Edition* (*DSM-5*; American Psychiatric Association [APA], 2013). The *DSM-5* is the primary classification system used by psychiatrists and psychologists in North America to diagnose mental disorders (note that the dominant system used in most other countries is the *International Classification of Diseases, 11th Revision*; see https://icd.who.int/).

Addiction

Ask researchers, counselors, and laypeople regarding their definition of addiction, and they will come up with many conflicting answers (Drugabuse.com, 2018). Individuals' definitions of addiction often imply something about their belief regarding etiology. Answers to the following five controversial aspects of addiction might also have an impact on the definition of it (Drugabuse.com, 2018):

1. Is It a Disease or a Choice? This is an ongoing debate that began when addictions were first recognized.
2. Are Addicted Individuals Bad People? As you will read in Chapter 3, some people continue to believe that addiction is a moral failing.
3. Should They Be Treated or Punished? Both are options as using, manufacturing, or selling illegal drugs are punishable in courts of law. At the same time, there are many addiction treatments available to addicted individuals.
4. Do They Need to Hit "Rock Bottom" Before They Can Be Helped? Hitting rock bottom is a colloquial expression

[1]Web links often change. If a link provided in this textbook does not work, type the name of what you are looking for in your browser. Likely, its location has moved, or it is available from another source.

meaning that addicted individuals have lost nearly everything and have suffered horrible consequences from their addiction. Although hitting bottom may get some addicted people into treatment, it can also be traumatic, damaging, or even life-threatening. Nonetheless, there are still some who believe this today.

5. Should We Invest in Sober Living Homes? Although advocates stress the importance of sober living homes for addiction recovery, many people do not want these homes in their neighborhood.

Let's consider some of the definitions of addiction that have been suggested. Milkman and Sunderwirth (2010), for example, highlighted the craving for ecstasy in their *description* of addiction as follows: "Addiction results from failed attempts to achieve extended ecstasy (extreme and prolonged pleasure) from experiences that are, by their very nature, impermanent and short-lived" (p. xx). Their *definition* of addiction was as follows: "self-induced changes (psychology) in neurotransmission (biology) that result in problem behaviors (sociology)" (p. 6). In writing the American Society of Addiction Medicine Handbook of Addiction Medicine, unsurprisingly, Rastegar and Fingerhood (2016) stressed its biological aspects by referring to it as "a chronic disease.... that involves a complex interplay of genetics, physiology, environment, and behavior" (p. 4).

A definition of drug addiction by Koob (2012) focused on some of its diagnostic features. His definition was "a chronically relapsing disorder characterized by (1) compulsion to seek and take the drug, (2) loss of control in limiting intake, and (3) emergence of a negative emotional state (e.g., dysphoria, anxiety, irritability) when access to the drug is prevented" (p. 3).Tarman and Werdell (2014) stressed a hallmark feature of addiction: "the inability to stop using, despite repeated efforts" (pp. 71–72). Tarman and Werdell (2014) considered it "the disease, while excessive drinking, drug use, eating, spending, even excessive indulgence in recovery activities, are only the symptoms" (p. 188). A definition of addictions based on behavioral theory is "as reward-seeking behavior that is pursued despite the emergence of various problems and that is characterized by progressive loss of self-control" (Dakwar, 2015, p. 30). Another behavioral definition is

> A chronic condition involving a repeated powerful motivation to engage in a rewarding behavior, acquired as a result of engaging in that behavior, that has significant potential for unintended harm. Someone is addicted to something to the extent that they experience this repeated powerful motivation. (West & Brown, 2013, pp. 15, 18)

Alternatively, if one believes in the moral/choice model (see Chapter 3), the definition would include something about the choice that some people make who insist on repeating and indulging themselves in excessive, harmful behaviors (Heather, 2017). The problem with creating a definition based on a given theory is that there are multiple pathways to addiction, and, although each theory explains addiction for some people, they do not apply to all addicted individuals. Some argue that addiction can affect any person under the right circumstances (Fisher, 2011). Although theories continue to contradict one another, as Flanagan (2017) wrote, "the debate about whether addiction is a disease is much ado about nothing, since all parties agree it is 'unquestionably destructive'" (p. 91).

Heather (2017) wrote an entire chapter looking at the various ways that addiction can be defined, and it is an adaptation of his definition that will be adopted in this textbook. ***Addiction*** is involvement in specific behaviors that individuals repeat continually, but who fail when they attempt to reduce or stop, despite the adverse consequences such behaviors create for them. The definition is inclusive of both substance and addictive behaviors (also referred to as process addictions or behavioral addictions). The strength of this definition is that it neither presupposes the reasons that addictive behavior occurs nor specifies much in the way of specific criteria. Why is this a good thing? Fisher (2011), for example, wrote that the loss of control, which is often the hallmark in many definitions of addiction, is contentious. Fingarette (as cited in Fisher, 2011) indicated that, if individuals with alcohol use disorder (AUD) lack control after only their first drink, they should not have any difficulty abstaining altogether. Instead, individuals with AUD could simply exert their willpower and self-control. Studies have shown that even individuals with severe AUD can control their drinking but that it depends on circumstances and the environment (Fisher, 2011).

Similarly, critics of the disease model argue that addictions do not follow an inevitable and entirely predictable sequence or stages of symptoms; neither do they experience a consistent loss of control (Fisher, 2011). Lastly, even the criteria for addictions in *DSM-5* provide a lot of "legroom" for which symptoms addicted individuals exhibit. In other words, addiction looks different for every addicted individual.

Addicted Individuals

The controversy surrounding this term was addressed in the Preface, and the pros and cons of labeling theory are discussed later in this chapter. The definition of addicted individuals used in this text is as follows: ***Addicted individuals*** are people who become involved in specific behaviors that are continually repeated, despite unsuccessful attempts to reduce or stop the behavior, despite the adverse consequences such behaviors create for them. The word "addict" is used as a synonym for "individuals with a substance use disorder and/or a behavioral addiction." Furthermore, its usage will generally be restricted to those people who are still engaged in their addictive behavior. For these addicted individuals, addictive behavior truly is front-and-center in their lives presently.

Counseling

The American Counseling Association's definition of counseling will be adopted. Their consensus definition is as follows: "***Counseling*** [boldface added] is a professional relationship that empowers diverse individuals, families, and groups to accomplish mental health, wellness, education, and career goals" (Kaplan, Tarvydas, & Gladding, 2014, p. 366). The definition of counseling implies a strengths-based perspective; this contrasts with clinical psychology, which emphasizes diagnoses based on peoples' weaknesses (i.e., their diagnoses).

Addiction Counseling

Addiction counseling is counseling aimed at helping individuals, couples, and families in individual or group modalities to manage or overcome varying degrees of involvement with substances or addictive behaviors.

History of Drugs, Addictions, and Addiction Counseling

History of Drugs

Substance use occurs in most cultures with origins early in humanity's history (Wanigaratne, Salas, & Strang, 2007). Beer was being brewed about 20,000 years ago, and fermentation of grape juice into wine is nearly as ancient (Guidot & Mehta, 2014). Cannabis is one of the earliest crops, with records indicating it was used 6,000 years ago (Sawler et al., 2015). Evidence also suggests that the Incas chewed coca leaves (which contains cocaine) before 2500 BC (Van Dyke & Byck, 1983). Hernán Cortés traveled to Mexico in the early 16th century and found that the Aztecs used psychedelic plants such as psilocybin mushrooms (commonly known as "magic mushrooms") and the peyote cactus (which contains mescaline) in their religious ceremonies (Milkman & Sunderwirth, 2010).

Depressants.

As noted previously, alcoholic beverages have the longest history, but many other drugs act as central nervous system depressants. Sedative-hypnotics are depressants that reduce anxiety and induce sleep, and these were introduced with bromides in 1826. Barbiturates hit the scene in 1903 with barbital, followed by chloral hydrate in 1932 and meprobamate in 1955. Quaaludes also belong to the barbiturate class (Rastegar & Fingerhood, 2016). Barbiturates have high addiction potential, so researchers went in search of a different class of sedative.

The benzodiazepines were subsequently discovered, beginning with Librium in 1960 and Valium in 1963 (Ashton, n.d.). There are many benzodiazepines such as chlordiazepoxide, diazepam, flurazepam, flunitrazepam, clorazepate, lorazepam, oxazepam, alprazolam, and triazolam (Rastegar & Fingerhood, 2016). Zopiclone, a sedative, was introduced in 1998, and Lunesta (eszopiclone) appeared in 2005 (Ashton, n.d.).

Amphetamines.

The WGBH Educational Foundation ([WGBHEF], 1995–2014) provided an excellent history of many drugs, and only a summary will be provided. Amphetamines were first synthesized in 1887, but they did not become popular in the medical community until the 1920s. Abuse of these drugs began during the 1930s when they were sold under the brand name Benzedrine and sold in over-the-counter inhalers. Injecting amphetamines became popular in the 1960s, a practice known as *amphetamine mainlining*. Crystal methamphetamine (crystal meth) became popular during the 1990s, which is a smokable form of methamphetamine. Since 1995, Mexico-based traffickers now dominate the trade of crystal meth in the United States.

Cocaine.

The medical effects of cocaine were not realized until the 1880s. In July 1884, Sigmund Freud published his use and praise of cocaine in Über Cola (Freud, 1884). Cocaine is extracted from coca leaves. Even today, chewing coca leaves and drinking coca tea remains legal in Argentina, Peru, Bolivia, and Chile (Metaal, 2014; Rubio et al., 2019).

Some of you might know the famous story of John Pemberton, who lived in Atlanta, GA. In 1886, John marketed Coca-Cola, the refreshing soft drink made from coca leaves and African kola nuts. Pemberton was rumored to have used up to 5 ounces of coca leaves per gallon of syrup, which Metaal (2014) described as "quite a significant dose" (p. 40). Although its alkaloid content is now suppressed, coca leaves are still used to produce Coca-Cola syrup (Metaal, 2014).

Crack.

Crack, the freebase version of cocaine, is made by heating cocaine powder, water, and baking soda until it forms a solid. It first appeared in large cities like Los Angeles, Miami, and New York around 1985. Because it is less expensive than cocaine, it became more common in working-class and poor neighborhoods. Although White and Hispanic individuals primarily used crack, the United States Sentencing Commission in 1994 found that 84.5% of individuals convicted of crack possession were Black, revealing racial profiling in sentencing (WGBHEF, 1995–2014).

LSD.

Dr. Albert Hofmann was a Swiss chemist who accidentally discovered and ingested lysergic acid diethylamide (LSD) in 1943. During the 1950s, the U.S. military and CIA researched LSD in hopes it could be used as a "truth drug." As the military's interest in LSD waned as they discovered better drugs for their purposes, psychiatry began to investigate its potential therapeutic value. Individuals started using LSD throughout the late 1950s and 1960s merely to get high. Before 1962, however, LSD was only available to a select group of medical personnel or others who had connections to these individuals. The drug was not difficult to produce in the laboratory, and it soon began flourishing (WGBHEF, 1995–2014).

Marijuana.

Cultivation of marijuana in the United States began around 1600 with the Jamestown settlers. Their primary purpose was to grow hemp, known as a strong fiber used in making rope, sails, and clothing. Nonetheless, some began noting its psychedelic properties (WGBHEF, 1995–2014).

Cannabis as a species remains poorly understood. Sawler et al. (2015), for example, described how *Cannabis sativa, indica*, and *ruderalis* had been thought of as both three distinct species by some but as monotypic by others. In the vernacular, *sativa* plants (these have tall and narrow leaves) are thought to produce marijuana with a stimulating and cerebral effect, whereas *indica* plants (these have short and wide leaves) are reported to produce marijuana that is sedating and relaxing (Sawler et al., 2015). In truth, the species have become cross-bred to a point where there is now considerable genetic overlap between them. Although marijuana and hemp are closely related, legal hemp regulations (at least in the European Union and Canada) only permit cultivators of hemp to grow plants that contain less than 0.3% delta-9-tetrahydrocannabinol (THC) (Sawler et al., 2015). Marijuana, on the other hand, is rich in THC (see Chapter 10 for details).

Marijuana plantations thrived in Mississippi, Georgia, California, South Carolina, Nebraska, New York, and Kentucky during the 19th century. Between 1850 and 1937, marijuana was readily available in pharmacies and general stores in the United States because it was viewed as a medicinal drug (WGBHEF, 1995–2014). After the Mexican Revolution of 1910, Mexican immigrants to the Unites States were largely credited with introducing recreational use of marijuana. The drug became especially attractive after the Volstead Act of 1920 raised the price of alcohol. Arguably, the most significant deterrent to using marijuana was when President Reagan signed the Anti-Drug Abuse Act in 1986. This act reintroduced federal penalties for possessing and distributing cannabis. Today, most foreign marijuana enters the United States through Mexico, but other countries, including Thailand and Cambodia, also provide a supply (WGBHEF, 1995–2014).

Opium and heroin.

Opiates became popular during the 19th century, particularly among women. One just needed to go to the drugstore to buy tonics and elixirs that contained opium. Morphine injection began during the American Civil War due to its fast-acting properties of relieving pain. Heroin was synthesized in 1895 by Heinrich Dreser, who at the time worked for the Bayer company in Germany. Bayer started selling heroin in 1898.

Interestingly, heroin was welcomed as an alternative to morphine addiction (WGBHEF, 1995–2014)! Another wave of opiate addiction emerged as part of the "hipster" identity in the 1930s and 1940s and later with the Beatnik subculture of the 1950s. Use of heroin increased substantially in the 1990s. Increasingly, South American drug groups have expanded from the cocaine market into selling heroin. Before then, heroin was mostly imported into the United States through the "French Connection," which was a collaborative effort between Corsican gangs in Marseille and the Sicilian Mafia (WGBHEF, 1995–2014).

History of Addictions

The term addiction entered the English language during the 16th century, borrowed from the Latin word *addictionem* (Westermeyer, 2013). However, reference had been made much earlier in ancient Egyptian and Greek writings, which revealed that the societies understood addiction (West & Brown, 2013).

18th-century perspectives.

Benjamin Franklin wrote about the mischief that drunkenness created, including theft and violence, as far back as 1736 (Freed, 2012). Benjamin Rush, a prominent physician who advised George Washington and Thomas Jefferson and who also cosigned the Declaration of Independence, warned about the dangerous consequences associated with chronic drinking in 1784 in his book *An Inquiry into the Effects of Ardent Spirits on the Human Body and Mind* (Freed, 2012). Rush (1812), who is also known as the founder of the American Psychiatric Association, wrote about individuals with excessive sexual desire (Rosenberg & Feder, 2014). The DSM system, however, did not include behavioral addictions until its fifth edition (APA, 2013).

19th-century perspectives.

Early in the 19th century, Americans viewed alcohol as something really good. For example, by 1810, there were 14,191 distilleries in the United States (Henninger & Sung, 2014). Alcohol was drunk for many celebrations, and some Americans drank all day, every day, and they drank to get drunk (Freed, 2012). In 1830, for example, the annual per capita consumption of distilled spirits was 5 gallons compared to 0.73 gallons in 2009 (Freed, 2012). Although the 19th-century temperance movement gathered steam and eventually came to view chronic drunkards as people who had lost control of their drinking, the Washingtonian movement, founded in 1840, offered the first organized method of addiction treatment (Freed, 2012). The movement, however, ended in the late 1840s.

During the second half of the 19th century, the Civil War took the focus away from the temperance movement. Inebriety specialists began looking at chronic drunkenness as a disease late in the 19th century (Freed, 2012). Inebriety specialists started sending individuals with alcohol and drug problems to asylums.

20th-century perspectives.

The word *addict* began referring to opioid use disorders only in the early 20th century (Davis & Carter, 2009). A businessman with no training in addictions, Charles B. Towns, opened a private facility in New York City to treat alcohol and drug problems in 1901. Towns believed he had found the cure for addiction, which consisted of small doses of the hallucinogenic belladonna, together with some extract from hyoscyamus plants and xanthoxylum shrubs (Freed, 2012). The sale of "miracle cures" continued well into the mid-20th century (Henninger & Sung, 2014).

By 1902, there were about 100 facilities in the United States to treat alcohol addiction (Henninger & Sung, 2014). It would be a mistake, however, to believe that "treatment" was anything compared with what it is today. For example, Henninger and Sung (2014) mentioned that, during the first half of the 20th century, treatments for both AUD and drug addiction included extremely invasive techniques such as "insulin-induced comas, electroconvulsive therapy (ETC), aversion therapy, psychosurgery (i.e., lobotomy), and serum therapy" (p. 2261). Serum therapy involved withdrawing serum from blisters that were raised on the abdomen of an individual and then reinjected (Henninger & Sung, 2014).

The Harrison Narcotics Tax Act (HNTA) was signed by President Wilson in 1914, which criminalized opiate and cocaine use for nonmedical purposes in the United States. Before then, pharmacies openly sold products containing opiates and cocaine (Redford & Powell, 2016). Redford and Powell (2016) stated that the HNTA is widely considered in the published literature to begin the U.S. government's "war on drugs" (p. 509). Alcohol prohibition soon followed the HNTA with the adoption of the 18th Amendment to the Constitution in 1920. By 1925, all morphine maintenance clinics had been closed (Henninger &

Sung, 2014). Prohibition continued until 1933, when the 21st Amendment to the Constitution was enacted (Henninger & Sung, 2014). The beginnings of Alcoholics Anonymous (AA) are described in Chapter 7. AA began in 1935 soon after William Griffith Wilson (*Bill W.*) met Dr. Robert Holbrook Smith (*Dr. Bob*) (White, 2004).

In 1937, the Research Council on Problems of Alcohol hired E. M. Jelinek, an individual with no experience in alcohol studies, to compose its literature review. Jellinek managed to catalog and abstract 3,000 works regarding alcohol. He was rewarded for his great efforts when he was named the section director for the Research Council's Section on Alcohol Studies in 1943 (Freed, 2012). Jellinek (1960) wrote *The Disease Model of Alcoholism*, which became influential.

After World War II, at a time when the awareness of addiction increased, other drugs like cocaine, amphetamine, and nicotine were also added to the rubric of addictive substances (Davis & Carter, 2009). Social and behavioral theories developed in the second half of the 20th century, and now social and cultural factors were being looked at as contributing to chronic alcohol and drug use (Freed, 2012). Some social scientists have wholly rejected the disease model of alcoholism, suggesting that it is, in fact, a "moral judgment" (Seeley, as cited in Freed, 2012, p. 37). The social and behavioral theories are reviewed in Chapter 3 (Westermeyer [2013] provided a thorough history regarding addiction theories).

In the DSM system, the American Psychiatric Association stigmatized addiction in both DSM-I and DSM-II (Wanigaratne, 2011). In DSM-I (APA, 1952; available from http://www.turkpsikiyatri.org/arsiv/dsm-1952.pdf) and DSM-II (APA, 1968; available from https://www.madinamerica.com/wp-content/uploads/2015/08/DSM-II.pdf), both alcoholism and drug addiction (dependence was the word used in DSM-II) were classified together with personality disorders.

History of Addiction Counseling

Substance abuse treatment, which includes addiction counseling, began about 300 years ago in the United States. Treatment was always affected by the public perception people had of addiction but also by social and political movements (Henninger & Sung, 2014). During the colonial period, "treatment" might include, if you were a heavy or addicted drinker, being placed in wooden stocks (also called pillories) to encourage public humiliation (Westermeyer, 2013). Being locked into a stock would have been extremely uncomfortable as well, given that the drunkard would be left there for hours in a bent-forward position. Similar treatments today include, at least in some jurisdictions, having your name published if arrested for public intoxication or driving under the influence (Westermeyer, 2013).

The field of addiction counseling and addiction treatment is relatively new. In the 1930s, many individuals with AUD were treated in state mental hospitals (McCrady, Ladd, & Hallgren, 2012). Most treatment programs for substance addictions developed from the Hazelden Foundation, which began in the 1940s and 1950s (Fisher, 2011). The leaders of AA did not want drug-addicted individuals to become part of their group, so a new version of AA sprung up first called "Addicts Anonymous," but the name was soon changed to Narcotics Anonymous to ensure that people did not confuse the two "AAs" (Henninger & Sung, 2014).

In 1958, Charles Dederich experimented with helping addicted individuals in his home and decided to try a new treatment modality. This developed into Synanon I, Synanon II, and Synanon III in 1974, when it became declared a religion (Henninger & Sung, 2014). Therapeutic communities, which were initially residences where both clients and counselors lived together (today they are more typically day units), grew out of Synanon. By 1975, there were 500 therapeutic communities based on the earlier ideas of Synanon in the United States. Therapeutic communities continue today, but residence times tend to be shorter with less intimidating confrontational tactics used as compared to the past (Henninger & Sung, 2014). These communities are often associated with the criminal justice system and outpatient treatment centers.

Fisher (2011) noted that addiction treatment began as only focused on individuals with AUD, but, during the Vietnam War, there was concern among both the American government and the military. Many returning soldiers were addicted to heroin (Fisher, 2011). Jerry Jaffee, a physician in Chicago, began treating the veterans and attracted residents who were also interested in working with drug-addicted individuals. This beginning roused academics to research substance addictions. In 1993, Jaffee became an administrator during the Nixon administration. Before then, almost all addiction counselors were themselves recovering individuals, most of whom lacked formal education and training (Fisher, 2011).

Legislated in July 2016, the Comprehensive Addiction and Recovery Act was the first legislation in 40 years that authorized the spending of $181 million to fight the opioid crisis (Greenfield & Weiss, 2017). Later, in December 2016, Congress passed the 21st Century Cures Act. This legislation provided $1 billion for states to offer treatment for opioid use disorders (Greenfield & Weiss, 2017).

According to White (2004), four beliefs have historically defined addiction counselors as distinct from other helping professionals. They include the following views:

1. Addictions are primary disorders.
2. Life problems of addicted individuals are only resolvable through recovery and maintenance.
3. Addicted individuals with complex problems and with few protective factors (i.e., internal assets, support from others) cannot achieve stable recovery without professional help.
4. Professional help is best offered by individuals having specialized knowledge and expertise in addictions recovery.

Historically, other helping professionals assumed that addiction resulted from other problems and untreated mental disorders (White, 2004). The field of addictions introduced the concept of "wounded healer," and individuals in the field have most arguably respected the idea that addiction counseling is a "calling" (White, 2004). As you will witness throughout this text, White (2004) wrote about the "greater emphasis on mutual vulnerability, mutual self-disclosure and mutual honesty . . . in addiction counseling" (p. 45).

Spinzy and Cohen-Rappaport (2016) stated that, before 1939, addictions were viewed in psychoanalytic literature as resulting from moral deficiencies, aggressive impulses, or repressed homosexuality. These authors opined that "drug addicts are seen as the unwanted children of psychiatry and psychoanalysis" (Spinzy & Cohen-Rappaport, 2016, p. 121). Although this opinion may be refutable, addiction counselors will not find themselves out of work any day soon given the enormous problems caused by both substance and behavioral addictions. There is a shortage of addiction counselors in the United States (Crawford, 2017).

Labeling Theory

Labels have meaning in people's lives, and many labels change over time. As one label becomes sufficiently stigmatized, it generally morphs into a name that is considered nonderogatory. West and Brown (2013) pointed out that, when the American Psychiatric Association was deciding on the classification scheme for DSM-III, committee members disagreed on what label should be used for addiction. The term *dependence* won by only a single vote! Labels can be as much a political decision as one based on social change. In Chapter 5, you will discover that the word *addict* or *addiction* does not appear in *DSM-5* (APA, 2013); *DSM-5* is the version that psychiatrists and psychologists currently use to diagnose mental disorders, including addiction.

Although identifying as an addict has been found in some research to act as a negative self-fulfilling prophecy (Walters, 1996), it can also serve as a positive label by those who are seeking help (e.g., "I am an addict in recovery") (Valencia-Payne, 2018). Using a word(s) to describe one's identity can also act to indicate group membership (Buckingham, Frings, & Albery, 2013), such as by saying, "I am an alcoholic," at an AA meeting. Often, a *DSM-5* diagnosis is required for an individual to qualify for specialized treatment (e.g., getting admitted to a residential addiction treatment facility). Consequently, medical labels open treatment doors.

An adverse effect of labeling, however, is that some labels were never meant to last forever. For example, take *DSM-5* diagnoses as an example of labeling. Also, most diagnoses do not specify a period at which point one can stop using the label (e.g., is having major depressive disorder forever, even if the specifier "in full remission" is added?). Furthermore, as addictive behaviors become recognized in the DSM system (which is already the case for gambling disorder), how might these labels affect people in a court of law? A common legal problem already noted in the literature is in dealing with a pedophile who repeatedly downloads child pornography but who has also been diagnosed with an Internet-based addiction (Sadoff, Drogin, & Gurmu, 2015). The perplexing question then becomes, does having an Internet-based addiction become a mediating factor in pedophiliac behavior? Remember that the DSM is titled the book of "mental disorders." If Internet-based addiction becomes a diagnosis in the next DSM (gaming disorder is already included in ICD-11), how might this play out in court for the pedophile example? Perhaps Fisher (2011) has already answered this question when he wrote that "court rulings have rarely allowed the defense of addiction for criminal behavior" (p. 27).

Furthermore, will having a behavioral addiction diagnosis deny afflicted parents' equal rights/access to their children in cases of separation and divorce? Willick (2014) wrote that the "mental illness" (which is typically used as a synonym for mental disorders) of a parent could create child custody issues. So, there are both pros and cons of labeling. Spin the labeling coin, and you will find both heads (i.e., advantages) and tails (i.e., disadvantages). Regardless of which side eventually wins, many people continue to refer to themselves as addicted individuals (Grubbs, Grant, & Engelman, 2019; Valencia-Payne, 2018).

In counseling practice, you are always wisest to use the word(s) that your clients use to describe themselves. In some segments or communities in society (perhaps especially in underserved communities), words matter. Terms describing individuals involved in same-sex relationships as "gay" or "lesbian" or individuals questioning gender as "transgender," for example, may not be the terms they use. Pronouns are also variable; some individuals refer to themselves as "they" and not "he" or "she." Respectful practice in counseling is to use our clients' terms to describe themselves.

Repeating Harmful Addictive Behaviors

Most of our clients will remain addicted individuals (Maté, 2008), but why? As expounded in Chapter 3, the answer to this question depends largely on one's theoretical orientation. Is it based on humankind's search for ecstasy combined with feeling discomfort and living a life that lacks meaning (Milkman & Sunderwirth, 2010)? Does it "always originate in pain" (Maté, 2008)? Maybe addiction is rooted in apprehension, negative beliefs, and cognitive distortions (Young, Yue, & Ying, 2011)? Are addictions a way of life (May, 1988)?

This text includes many examples of possible causes and the unique aspects of each addiction, but it also includes the commonalities of addiction. What seems clear is that addicted individuals continue using or doing their behavior(s) for multiple reasons, but these reasons also vary across specific addictions. For example, thinking that one must continue gambling to "win back" what one has lost and believing that one's chances of winning improve with each loss (Xian et al., 2008) are experienced frequently by addicted gamblers, but they are not common beliefs held by other addicted individuals. A consistent finding in the research is salient, however, when it comes to explaining addictions. That is, addicted individuals were commonly maltreated in childhood. This maltreatment includes child abuse (physical, mental, verbal, sexual, spiritual) or neglect (Fernandez-Montalvo, Lopez-Goni, & Arteaga, 2015; Lu, Wen, Deng, & Tang, 2017; Sarvet & Hasin, 2016; Wardell, Strang, & Hendershot, 2016).

There are few truisms in addiction or psychology for that matter. A general principle found by Brooks and McHenry (2009), however, is that "clients do not ingest drugs with the intention of becoming addicted" (p. 35). Instead, their behavior begins with a desire to experience pleasure, indulge curiosity, or escape painful emotions (Brooks & McHenry, 2009).

Treatment and "Maturing Out"

Between 40% and 60% of substance-addicted individuals relapse during the 1st year following treatment (Kwon, 2011). Lassiter, Czerny, and Williams (2015) suggested even a more extensive range for relapse 1 year after treatment (i.e., 20–80%). Consequently, we know that relapse rates are high in addicted individuals who receive professional help for addictions. However, as Miller (2016) indicated, based on 40 years of research, clients have an incredible ability to change without help from professionals. "Most recovery happens without any professional treatment" (Miller, 2016, p. 103). Given this, it is not surprising that lack of control cannot be said to apply to everyone who is addicted. Nonetheless, perhaps those who receive treatment are more severely addicted or cajoled more than most to seek it. Whatever the reason, addiction is a broad concept that does not apply the same way to everyone.

It was Winick (1962) who founded the term "maturing out." Winick, using statistical files from the Federal Bureau of Narcotics (5553 men, 1681 women), discovered that the average duration of addiction was 8.6 years. Some, however, had been addicted for up to 50 years. From these findings, Winick hypothesized that either addicted individuals mature out of addiction because of where they are in their life cycle or because of the duration of their addiction. Earleywine (2016) noted that approximately two thirds of individuals with an SUD no longer meet the criteria after 3 years, despite most never having received formal treatment. Earleywine hypothesized that we might think of addictions only as chronic relapsing disorders because these are the people who seek help. Similarly, Heilig (2015) reported on research that found individuals in the general population who had ever received a diagnosis of AUD and who were interviewed 5 years later. In that sample, two thirds of the women and one third of the men no longer had an AUD diagnosis.

Heyman and Mims (2017) concluded that, in every American survey that asks for the prevalence and correlates of psychiatric disorders, most who meet the DSM criteria for addiction are in remission. Remission from SUDs generally occurs by age 30, whereas nicotine addiction and AUDs often continue well into the 40s. Given that most addicted individuals do not receive professional help, it must be something within these nontreated individuals that results in their stopping of substance use.

Breidenbach and Tse (2016) wrote about what they called the natural recovery from alcohol and/or drug addiction in English-speaking Hong Kong residents. In their exploratory qualitative study, they suggested that some addicted individuals have "an awakening experience" where they develop greater insight into their addictive behaviors and consequently stop using their substance.

Becoming a Certified Addiction Counselor

The median pay for substance abuse, behavioral disorder, and mental health counselors in 2017 was $43,300 per year ($20.82 per hour) (U.S. Bureau of Labor Statistics, 2019; check website for the most current details: https://www.bls.gov/cpi/). Many states require that you have a master's degree, supervised clinical experience, and passing of licensure exams (i.e., state and national) to practice as an addiction counselor (Psychology School Guide, 2018). Psychology School Guide (2018) noted that, in some cases, individuals with a bachelor's degree or less might qualify to become licensed if they have extensive experience in addiction counseling. It is essential that you check the requirements of your particular state because each state regulates credentials for addiction counselors (Yalisove, 2010).

Links to the agencies in each state that regulate credentials for substance abuse counseling can be found at the Addiction Treatment Technology Transfer Center (ATTC) website (https://attcnetwork.org/). Quoting from the website,

> Established in 1993 by the Substance Abuse and Mental Health Services Administration (SAMHSA), the ATTC Network is comprised of 10 Domestic Regional Centers, 6 International HIV Centers (funded by PEPFAR), 2 National Focus Area Centers, and a Network Coordinating Office. Together the Network serves the 50 U.S. states, the District of Columbia, Puerto Rico, the U.S. Virgin Islands, and the Pacific Islands of Guam, American Samoa, Palau, the Marshall Islands, Micronesia, and the Mariana Islands. The International HIV ATTCs serve Vietnam, Southeast Asia, South Africa, and Ukraine. (under the About icon)

There are between 1 and 18 certifications available among the states for addiction professionals.

The International Certification & Reciprocity Consortium ([IC&RC]; https://internationalcredentialing.org/) "promotes public protection by offering internationally-recognized credentials and examinations for prevention, substance use treatment, and recovery professionals" (para. 1). Although standards vary from state to state, many states follow the Consortium's standards. IC&RC offers six reciprocal credentials: (a) alcohol and drug counselor, (b) advanced alcohol and drug counselor, (c) clinical supervisor, (d) prevention specialist, (e) certified criminal justice addictions professional, and (f) peer recovery.

Addiction counselors can become members of the Association for Addiction Professionals ([NAADAC]; visit https://www.naadac.org/ for details), and they can also become certified through their National Certification Commission for Addiction Professionals (NCC AP) program. As they note on their website, having NAADAC membership is not the same as having NCC AP certification (visit https://www.naadac.org/certification for details).

Three foundational credentials are available as follows:

1. National Certified Addiction Counselor, Level I.
2. National Certified Addiction Counselor, Level II.
3. Master Addiction Counselor.

Also, NCC AP offers four specialization credentials as follows:

1. Nicotine Dependence Specialist.
2. National Certified Adolescent Addiction Counselor.
3. National Peer Recovery Support Specialist.
4. National Clinical Supervision Endorsement.

The American Counseling Association (ACA), the International Association of Addiction and Offenders Counselors (IAAOC), and the National Board for Certified Counselors (NBCC) jointly offer a credential called Master Addiction Counselor (MAC). Individuals who have this credential become eligible to become Substance Abuse Professionals (SAPs) through the U.S. Department of Transportation (USDOT). Visit https://www.nbcc.org/Certification/MAC for details.

Roles and Settings of Addiction Counselors

Doukas (2015) underlined that contemporary addiction counselors, including counselors in recovery, are "fully integrated members of the counseling profession" (p. 244). They are respected and valued members, often working within interprofessional teams in both residential and in various nonresidential and community settings. Addiction counselors work with individuals experiencing alcohol, drug, and addictive behaviors. Depending on the setting, they may work in any of several modalities including individual, couples, family, and group counseling with children, teenagers, and adults of all ages. They assess, diagnose, and treat individuals with addiction issues (Crawford, 2017).

The National Association for Alcoholism and Drug Abuse Counselors (NAADAC, 2019) estimated that the addiction workforce comprises more than 100,000 individuals in the Unites States, which includes counselors, educators, and other addiction-focused healthcare professionals. NAADAC (2019) estimates that most addiction professionals work in the following settings:

1. Outpatient care centers.
2. Residential mental retardation, mental health, and substance abuse facilities.
3. Individual and family services.
4. Local government.
5. General medical and surgical hospitals.
6. Psychiatric and substance abuse hospitals.
7. Private practice.
8. Prisons.
9. Probation or parole agencies.
10. Juvenile detention facilities.
11. Halfway houses.
12. Detox centers.
13. Employee assistance programs.

All Psychology Schools (n.d.) also wrote, if you are working with children or teenagers, you might work in a school or after-school program.

Addiction counselors develop strong positive working relationships with clients, provide emotional support to individuals, offer individual counseling sessions, administer drug tests, develop treatment plans, assist clients in creating an aftercare program, and offer group counseling that often includes family members or other clients (AddictionCenter.com, 2019; Wake Forest University, n.d.). They help clients both in crisis and in long-term addiction management (Wake Forest University, n.d.). Addiction counselors also refer clients to outside resources such as mutual support groups (Wake Forest University, n.d.). They may assist clients in finding jobs or reestablishing their career (All Psychology Schools, n.d.). Some will provide updates and progress reports in court (All Psychology Schools, n.d.).

Bach-Sterling (2014) noted that counseling is only one of the roles of addiction counselors. They are also interventionists, mediators, advocates, change agents, advisors, and facilitators. "The approaches include harm reduction, coping skills training, life-skills training, motivational interviewing, cognitive-behavioral therapy, social skills training, and behavior therapy. These approaches are included in the direct effect strategies as well as [the] broad spectrum strategies" (Bach-Sterling, 2014, para. 1).

In SAMHSA-Center for Substance Abuse Treatment (SAMHSA-CSAT, 2012), the best addiction counselors demonstrate warmth, friendliness, genuineness, respect, empathy, and affirmation of clients. Addiction counselors do better when they focus on client strengths rather than on their weaknesses. In other words, confrontational approaches actually lead clients to become less motivated. The goal is to help clients recognize their problematic behaviors and guide them into recovery. As noted earlier, this role fits nicely into what all counselors do, which is to empower clients by focusing on their strengths.

VIDEOS

To view these videos, search their titles on YouTube.

1. *Lesson 1 – Introduction to Drug, Alcohol and Addiction Counseling* – L. Jasmine Harris.
2. *Substance Use Disorders/Addictions – Clinical Overview* – Dr. Jeffrey DeVido.
3. *The Rise of Fentanyl: Drug Addiction on the I-95 – Two Years On.* BBC Three.
4. *Overview of Behavioral Addictions* – Dr. Dawn-Elise Snipes.
   - *Part 1.*
   - *Part 2.*
   - *Part 3.*
5. *Mark Griffiths - Behavioural addiction: A brief personal overview.*

INDIVIDUAL EXERCISES

1. Read about one of the names found near the beginning of this book called *Tribute to the Fallen*. Pick one of these famous individuals and spend some time reading about their life using an Internet search engine. Was alcohol or drugs the primary cause of this famous person's death? If not, how might substance abuse have contributed to an early grave?
2. Interview someone in your family who has an addiction issue, either past or present. First, write out a list of questions that you would want to ask him or her. A few examples include
   a. "How old were you when you first started using (or doing) . . .?" "What was the precipitating event that led to an increase in your using (or doing) . . .?"
   b. "In what ways do you see this activity as a blessing, and in what ways do you see it as a curse?"
   c. "If you ever decided to stop, how would you go about doing so?" or (if he or she has already stopped) "What did you do to stop your addictive behavior?"
3. Perhaps most people engage in some form of excessive behavior at least at some point in their lives. If you were to develop (or already have) an addiction, which one would it be? Why would this one be the most likely in your case?

CLASSROOM EXERCISES

1. Show any of the videos suggested earlier in the chapter. After the video ends, lead a discussion with your students regarding its content.
2. Assign a brief essay assignment. Two ideas follow:
   a. Ask students to write a two-page essay outlining the reasons that they choose to enter the addiction counseling field. As a second step, consider having them develop their credo artistically. For example, they could write a poem, create a collage, write a brief theatrical play, etc.
   b. Have students write a brief essay regarding personal behaviors that could be construed either as an addiction or at least as some kind of excessive behavior. Include in the assignment how the student would go about changing their excessive behavior.
3. Use a guided imagery exercise. You could either read a guided imagery that takes the class into what it would be like to experience addiction (several are available on the Internet or in books focused on guided imagery) or use an example from YouTube (one example is https://www.youtube.com/watch?v=a8_ENeZ2x28).

CHAPTER SUMMARY

Drug overdoses have now taken first place as the leading cause of accidental deaths in the United States. Fentanyl deaths alone rose 540% between 2013 and 2016. Approximately 8% of the population meets diagnostic criteria for SUD, but, when combined with behavioral addictions, some researchers estimate that 47% of adult Americans have experienced one or more forms of addiction within the past year.

The cost of addictions is enormous. The National Institute on Drug Abuse estimated that tobacco, alcohol, and illicit drugs cost American taxpayers about $740 billion annually. Even more staggering are figures estimating that, between 2000 and 2010, Americans paid $1 trillion to purchase illegal drugs. Alcohol and illicit drugs have always existed in American society, but each generation has used and abused different drugs to varying degrees. Many of today's youth, for example, are into "vaping," a practice that was unheard of in generations before the marketing of electronic cigarettes.

Definitions for abnormal psychology, addiction, addicted individuals, counseling, and addiction counseling were included in this chapter. A history of drugs, addictions, and addiction counseling followed. The next section on labeling theory highlighted both its advantages and disadvantages. Addicted individuals continue engaging in harmful behaviors for many reasons. No two addicted individuals are precisely alike. What they have in common is that our clients do not become addicted intentionally.

Next, Chapter 1 looked at the high relapse rates of addicted individuals leaving treatment. Nonetheless, most addicted individuals never receive professional help, yet a good percentage of these individuals stop their addictions without external intervention. It seems that, for many addicted people, addiction runs its course. Most Americans with SUDs find remission by about age 30, whereas nicotine addiction and AUDs often continue well into their 40s.

The chapter ended by looking at details pertaining to becoming a certified addiction counselor and the role of addiction counselors. Addiction counselors work in diverse settings using several counseling modalities. They emphasize clients' strengths, not their weaknesses. Addiction counselors will not find themselves out of work any day soon.

REFERENCES

AddictionCenter.com. (2019). *Addiction counselors*. Retrieved on April 18, 2019, from https://www.addictioncenter.com/treatment/addiction-counselors/

All Psychology Schools. (n.d.). *Substance abuse counseling job description: What you'll do*. Retrieved on April 18, 2019, from https://www.allpsychologyschools.com/substance-abuse-counseling/job-description/

American Psychiatric Association (APA). (1952). *Diagnostic and statistical manual of mental disorders*. Washington, DC: Author.

American Psychiatric Association (APA). (1968). *Diagnostic and statistical manual of mental disorders* (2nd ed.). Washington, DC: Author.

American Psychiatric Association (APA). (2013). *Diagnostic and statistical manual of mental disorders* (5th ed.). Washington, DC: Author.

Ashton, H. (n.d.). *History of benzodiazepines: What the textbooks may not tell you* (PowerPoint presentation). Retrieved on March 21, 2019, from http://www.benzosupport.org/History%20of%20Benzodiazepines.htm

Bach-Sterling, A. M. (2014, February 23). *Roles of an addiction counselor*. Retrieved on April 18, 2019, from https://www.studymode.com/essays/Roles-Of-An-Addiction-Counselor-47845677.html

Barusch, A. (2017). Love, in retrospect. *Generations*, *41*(2), 48–54.

Breidenbach, S., & Tse, S. (2016). Exploratory study: Awakening with natural recovery from alcohol or drug addiction in Hong Kong. *Journal of Humanistic Psychology*, *56*(5), 483–502.

Brooks, F., & McHenry, B. (2009). *A contemporary approach to substance abuse and addiction counseling: A counselor's guide to application and understanding*. Alexandria, VA: American Counseling Association.

Buckingham, S. A., Frings, D., & Albery, I. P. (2013). Group membership and social identity in addiction recovery. *Psychology of Addictive Behaviors*, *27*, 1132–1140.

Bureau of Labor Statistics. (2019, February 15). *Occupational Outlook handbook: Substance abuse, behavioral disorder, and mental health counselors*. Retrieved on March 21, 2019, from https://www.bls.gov/ooh/community-and-social-service/substance-abuse-behavioral-disorder-and-mental-health-counselors.htm

Carnes, P. (1991). *Don't call it love: Recovery from sexual addiction*. Toronto, ON: Bantam Books.

Comer, R. J. (2013). *Abnormal psychology* (8th ed.). Basingstoke, England: Palgrave Macmillan.

Crawford, T. J. (2017, February 9). Issues related to the shortage of addiction/substance abuse counselors in the United States. *Counselor-Education.com*. Retrieved on April 22, 2019, from https://www.counselor-education.com/issues-related-shortage-addiction-substance-abuse-counselors-united-states/

Dakwar, E. (2015). Problematic exercise: A case of alien feet. In M. S. Ascher & P. Levounis (Eds.), *The behavioral addictions* (pp. 29–42). Washington, DC: American Psychiatric.

Davis, C., & Carter, J. C. (2009). Compulsive overeating as an addiction disorder. A review of theory and evidence. *Appetite*, *3*, 1–8.

Doukas, N. (2015). A contemporary new role for counselors in recovery: Recovery coaches in communities of recovery. *Alcoholism Treatment Quarterly*, *33*(2), 244–247.

Drugabuse.com. (2018). *Five controversial thoughts we have about addiction*. Retrieved on December 15, 2018, from https://drugabuse.com/5-controversial-thoughts-addiction/

Drugabuse.com. (2019). *Drug use across the generations: Comparing the drug taking habits of Millennials, Gen Xers, Baby Boomers, and the Lucky Few*. Retrieved on March 18, 2019, from https://drugabuse.com/featured/drug-and-alcohol-abuse-across-generations/

Earleywine, M. (2016). *Substance use problems* (2nd ed.). Ashland, OH: Hogrefe.

Fernandez-Montalvo, J., Lopez-Goni, J. J., & Arteaga, A. (2015). Psychological, physical, and sexual abuse in addicted patients who undergo treatment. *Journal of Interpersonal Violence*, *30*(8), 1279–1298.

Fisher, G. L. (2011). *Understanding why addicts are not all alike: Recognizing the types and how their differences affect intervention and treatment*. Santa Barbara, CA: Praeger/ABC-CLIO.

Flanagan, O. (2017). Addiction doesn't exist, but it is bad for you. *Neuroethics*, *10*(1), 91–98.

Flood, C. (2016). Abnormal cyberpsychology and cybertherapy. In I. Connolly, M. Palmer, H. Barton, & G. Kirwan (Eds.), *An introduction to cyberpsychology* (pp. 153–166). New York, NY: Routledge.

Freed, C. R. (2012). Historical perspectives on addiction. In H. J. Shaffer, D. A. LaPlante, & S. E. Nelson (Eds.), *APA addiction syndrome handbook, Vol. 1: Foundations, influences, and expressions of addiction* (pp. 27–47). Washington, DC: American Psychological Association.

Freud, S. (1884). "Über coca," Centralblatt für die ges. *Therapie*, *2*, 289–314. Retrieved on March 20, 2019, from http://www.heretical.com/freudian/coca1884.html

Greenfield, D. (2011). The addictive properties of Internet usage. In K. S. Young & C. Nabuco de Abreu (Eds.), *Internet addiction: A handbook and guide to evaluation and treatment* (pp. 135–153). Hoboken, NJ: John Wiley & Sons.

Greenfield, S. F., & Weiss, R. D. (2017). Addiction—25 years later. *Harvard Review of Psychiatry*, *25*, 97–100.

Grubbs, J. B., Grant, J. T., & Engelman, J. (2019). Self-identification as a pornography addict: Examining the roles of pornography use, religiousness, and moral incongruence. *Sexual Addiction & Compulsivity*, 1–24 [no volume indicated].

Guidot, D. M., & Mehta, A. J. (2014). A brief history of alcohol use and abuse in human history. In D. M. Guidot & A. J. Mehta (Eds.), *Alcohol use disorders and the lung: A clinical and pathophysiological approach* (pp. 3–6). Totowa, NJ: Humana Press.

Heather, N. (2017). On defining addiction. In N. Heather & G. Segal (Eds.), *Addiction and choice: Rethinking the relationship* (pp. 3–25). New York, NY: Oxford University Press.

Heilig, M. (2015). *The thirteenth step: Addiction in the age of brain science*. New York, NY: Columbia University Press.

Henninger, A., & Sung, H.-E. (2014). History of substance abuse treatment. In G. Bruinsma & D. Weisburd (Eds.), *Encyclopedia of criminology and criminal justice* (pp. 2257–2269). New York, NY: Springer.

Heyman, G. M., & Mims, V. (2017). What addicts can teach us about addiction: A natural history. In N. Heather & G. Segal (Eds.), *Addiction and choice: Rethinking the relationship* (pp. 385–408). New York, NY: Oxford University Press.

Jellinek, E. M. (1960). *The disease concept of alcoholism*. New Haven, CT: Hillhouse Press.

Kaplan, D. M., Tarvydas, V. M., & Gladding, S. T. (2014). 20/20: A vision for the future of counseling: The new consensus definition of counseling. *Journal of Counseling & Development, 92*(3), 366–372.

Katz, J. (2017, September 2). The first count of fentanyl deaths in 2016: Up 540% in three years. *New York Times*. Retrieved on March 19, 2019, from https://www.nytimes.com/interactive/2017/09/02/upshot/fentanyl-drug-overdose-deaths.html

Kilmer, B., Everingham, S., Caulkins, J., Midgette, G., Pacula, R., Reuter, P., . . . Lundberg, R. (2014, February). What America's users spend on illegal drugs: 2000–2010. *RAND Corporation*. Retrieved on November 14, 2018, from https://obamawhitehouse.archives.gov/sites/default/files/ondcp/policy-and-research/wausid_results_report.pdf

Koob, G. F. (2012). Animal models of drug addiction. In K. D. Brownell & M. S. Gold (Eds.), *Food and addiction: A comprehensive handbook* (pp. 3–13). New York, NY: Oxford University Press.

Kwon, J.-H. (2011). Toward the prevention of adolescent Internet addiction. In K. S. Young & C. N. de Abreu (Eds.), *Internet addiction: A handbook and guide to evaluation and treatment* (pp. 223–243). Hoboken, NJ: John Wiley & Sons.

Lassiter, P. S., Czerny, A. B., & Williams, K. S. (2015). Working with addictions in family therapy. In D. Capuzzi & M. D. Stauffer (Eds.), *Foundations of couples, marriage, and family counseling* (pp. 389–417). Hoboken, NJ: John Wiley & Sons.

Lindstrom, M., & Rosvall, M. (2018). Addictive behaviors, social and psychosocial factors, and electronic cigarette use among adolescents: A population-based study. *Public Health, 155*, 129–132.

Lu, F.-Y., Wen, S., Deng, G., & Tang, Y.-L. (2017). Self-concept mediate the relationship between childhood maltreatment and abstinence motivation as well as self-efficacy among drug addicts. *Addictive Behaviors, 68*, 52–58.

Maté, G. (2008). *In the realm of hungry ghosts: Close encounters with addiction*. Toronto, ON: Vintage Books.

May, G. G. (1988). *Addiction and grace: Love and spirituality in the healing of addictions*. New York, NY: HarperCollins.

McCrady, B. S., Ladd, B. O., & Hallgren, K. A. (2012). Theoretical bases of family approaches to substance abuse treatment. In S. T. Walters & F. Rotgers (Eds.), *Treating substance abuse: Theory and technique* (3rd ed., pp. 224–255). New York, NY: Guilford Press.

Metaal, P. (2014). Coca in debate: The contradiction and conflict between the UN Drug Conventions and the real world. In B. C. Labate & C. Cavnar (Eds.), *Prohibition, religious freedom, and human rights: Regulating traditional drug use* (pp. 25–44). Berlin, Germany: Springer.

Miech, R. A., Johnston, L. D., O'Malley, P. M., Bachman, J. G., Schulenberg, J. E., & Patrick, M. E. (2018, June). *Monitoring the future: National survey results on drug use, 1975–2017:Vol. I. Secondary school students*. Ann Arbor, MI: University of Michigan Institute for Social Research. Retrieved on March 19, 2019, from http://monitoringthefuture.org/pubs/monographs/mtf-vol1_2017.pdf

Milkman, H. B., & Sunderwirth, S. G. (2010). *Craving for ecstasy and natural highs: A positive approach to mood alteration*. Thousand Oaks, CA: SAGE.

Miller, W. R. (2016). Sacred cows and greener pastures: Reflections from 40 years in addiction research. *Alcoholism Treatment Quarterly, 34*, 92–115.

National Association for Alcoholism and Drug Abuse Counselors (NAADAC). (2019). *What is an addiction professional?* Retrieved on April 18, 2019, from https://www.naadac.org/what-is-an-addiction-professional

National Center for Health Statistics. (2019, February 13). *NVSS vital statistics rapid release: Provisional drug overdose death counts*. Retrieved on March 19, 2019, from https://www.cdc.gov/nchs/nvss/vsrr/drug-overdose-data.htm

National Institute on Drug Abuse. (2017, April). *Trends & statistics*. Retrieved on March 19, 2019, from https://www.drugabuse.gov/related-topics/trends-statistics

National Safety Council. (2019). *Vehicle deaths estimated at 40,000 for third straight year*. Retrieved on March 19, 2019, from https://www.nsc.org/road-safety/safety-topics/fatality-estimates

National Survey on Drug Use and Health (NSDUH). (2018, September 7). *Results from the 2017 National Survey on Drug Use and Health: Detailed tables*. Retrieved on March 24, 2019, from https://www.samhsa.gov/data/report/2017-nsduh-detailed-tables

Office of Adolescent Health. (2017, November 29). *Opioids and adolescents*. Retrieved on March 18, 2019, from https://www.hhs.gov/ash/oah/adolescent-development/substance-use/drugs/opioids/index.html

Ott, B. D., & Joseph, L. S. (2017). Mysticism, technology, and the music of the summer of love. *Generations, 41*(2), 27–33.

Psychology School Guide. (2018). *What are the requirements for addiction counselor certification?* Retrieved on March 22, 2019, from https://www.psychologyschoolguide.net/guides/requirements-for-addiction-counselor-certification/

Rastegar, D., & Fingerhood, M. (2016). *The American Society of Addiction Medicine handbook of addiction medicine*. New York, NY: Oxford University Press.

Redford, A., & Powell, B. (2016). Dynamics of intervention in the War on Drugs: The buildup to the Harrison Act of 1914. *Independent Review, 20*(4), 509–530.

Rosenberg, K. P., & Feder, L. C. (2014). An introduction to behavioral addictions. In K. P. Rosenberg & L. C. Feder (Eds.), *Behavioral addictions: Criteria, evidence, and treatment* (pp. 1–17). San Diego, CA: Academic Press.

Rubio, N. C., Krumbiegel, F., Pragst, F., Thurmann, D., Nagel, A., Zytowski, E., et al. (2019). Discrimination between chewing of coca leaves or drinking of coca tea and smoking of "paco" (coca paste) by hair analysis. A preliminary study of possibilities and limitations. *Forensic Science International, 297*, 171–176.

Rush, B. (1812). *Medical inquiries and observations upon the diseases of the mind*. Philadelphia, PA: Kimber & Richardson.

Sadoff, R. L., Drogin, E. Y., & Gurmu, S. (2015). Forensic implications of behavioral addictions. In M. S. Ascher & P. Levounis (Eds.), *The behavioral addictions* (pp. 9–26). Arlington, VA: American Psychiatric.

Sarvet, A. L., & Hasin, D. (2016). The natural history of substance use disorders. *Current Opinion in Psychiatry, 29*(4), 250–257.

Sawler, J., Stout, J. M., Gardner, K. M., Hudson, D., Vidmar, J., Butler, L., . . . Myles, S. (2015). The genetic structure of marijuana and hemp. *PLoS ONE, 10*(8), 1–9.

Spinzy, Y., & Cohen-Rappaport, G. (2016). Heaven and earth: Dual-diagnosis group therapy on a closed psychiatric ward. *Group, 40*(2), 121–128.

Substance Abuse and Mental Health Services Administration, Center for Substance Abuse Treatment (SAMHSA-CSAT). (2012). *Treatment Improvement Protocol (TIP) Series #35 Enhancing motivation for change in substance abuse treatment*. Retrieved on April 19, 2019, from https://www.ncbi.nlm.nih.gov/books/NBK64967/pdf/Bookshelf_NBK64967.pdf

Sussman, S., Lisha, N., & Griffiths, M. (2011). Prevalence of the addictions: A problem of the majority or the minority? *Evaluation & the Health Professions, 34*(1), 3–56.

Tarman, V., & Werdell, P. (2014). *Food junkies: The truth about food addiction.* Toronto, ON: Dundurn.

Thege, B. K., Hodgins, D. C., & Wild, T. (2016). Co-occurring substance-related and behavioral addiction problems: A person-centered, lay epidemiology approach. *Journal of Behavioral Addictions, 5*(4), 614–622.

United Nations Office on Drugs and Crime. (2019a, June). *Home page.* Retrieved on July 18, 2019, from https://www.unodc.org/unodc/en/frontpage/2019/June/world-drug-report-2019_-35-million-people-worldwide-suffer-from-drug-use-disorders-while-only-1-in-7-people-receive-treatment.html

United Nations Office on Drugs and Crime. (2019b, June). *World Drug Report 2019: Booklet 1, Executive Summary* (United Nations publication, Sales No. E.19.XI.8). Retrieved on July 18, 2019, from https://wdr.unodc.org/wdr2019/prelaunch/WDR19_Booklet_1_EXECUTIVE_SUMMARY.pdf

U.S. Department of Health and Human Services (HHS), Office of the Surgeon General. (2016, November). Facing addiction in America: *The Surgeon General's Report on alcohol, drugs, and health.* Washington, DC: HHS. Retrieved on September 29, 2017, from https://addiction.surgeongeneral.gov/surgeon-generals-report.pdf

Valencia-Payne, Marisol A. (2018). My name is alcoholic and I am your identity: An exploration of an individual's self-identification process as an alcoholic. *Dissertation Abstracts International: Section B: The Sciences and Engineering, 79*(8-B(E)). No Pagination Specified.

Van Dyke, C., & Byck, R. (1983). Cocaine use in man. *Advances in Substance Abuse, 3,* 1–24.

Wake Forest University. (n.d.). *The role of the counselor in addiction recovery.* Retrieved on April 18, 2019, from https://counseling.online.wfu.edu/blog/the-role-of-the-counselor-in-addiction-recovery/

Walters, G. D. (1996). Addiction and identity: Exploring the possibility of a relationship. *Psychology of Addictive Behaviors, 10*(1), 9–17.

Wanigaratne, S. (2011). Cultural issues in group work. In R. Hill & J. Harris (Eds.), *Principles and practice of group work in addictions* (pp. 153–164). New York, NY: Routledge/Taylor & Francis.

Wanigaratne, S., Salas, S., & Strang, J. (2007). Substance misuse. In D. Bhugra & K. Bhui (Eds.), *Textbook of cultural psychiatry* (pp. 242–254). Cambridge, MA: Cambridge University Press.

Wardell, J. D., Strang, N. M., & Hendershot, C. S. (2016). Negative urgency mediates the relationship between childhood maltreatment and problems with alcohol and cannabis in late adolescence. *Addictive Behaviors, 56,* 1–7.

West, R., & Brown, J. (2013). *Theory of addiction* (2nd ed.). Hoboken, NJ: Wiley Blackwell.

Westermeyer, J. (2013). Historical understandings of addiction. In P. M. Miller, S. A. Ball, M. E. Bates, A. W. Blume, K. M. Kampman, D. J. Kavanagh, M. E. Larimer, N. M. Petry, & P. De Witte (Eds.), *Comprehensive addictive behaviors and disorders, Vol. 1: Principles of addiction* (pp. 3–12). San Diego, CA: Elsevier Academic Press.

WGBH Educational Foundation. (1995–2014). A social history of America's most popular drugs. *Frontline.* Retrieved on March 19, 2019, from https://www.pbs.org/wgbh/pages/frontline/shows/drugs/buyers/socialhistory.html

White, W. (2004). The historical essence of addiction counseling. *Counselor, 5*(3), 43–48.

Willick, D. H. (2014). Behavioral addiction in American law: The future and the expert's role. In K. P. Rosenberg & L. C. Feder (Eds.), *Behavioral addictions: Criteria, evidence, and treatment* (pp. 361–372). San Diego, CA: Academic Press.

Winick, C. (1962). Maturing out of narcotic addiction. *Bulletin on Narcotics, 14*(1), 1–7.

Wodak, A. (2018). From failed global drug prohibition to regulating the drug market. *Addiction, 113,* 1225–1226.

Xian, H., Shah, K. R., Phillips, S. M., Scherrer, J. F., Volberg, R., & Eisen, S. A. (2008). The association of cognitive distortions with problem and pathological gambling in adult male twins. *Psychiatry Research, 160*(3), 300–307.

Yalisove, D. (2010). *Developing clinical skills for substance abuse counseling.* Alexandria, VA: American Counseling Association.

Young, K. S., Yue, X. D., & Ying, L. (2011). Prevalence estimates and etiologic models of Internet addiction. In K. S. Young & C. Nabuco de Abreu (Eds.), *Internet addiction: A handbook and guide to evaluation and treatment* (pp. 3–17). Hoboken, NJ: John Wiley & Sons.

2 Ethical, Legal, and Professional Issues in Addiction Counseling

iStock.com/george

Learning Objectives

1. Learn about the most important aspects of ethical practice.
2. Become familiar with the six ethical principles of autonomy, nonmaleficence, beneficence, justice, fidelity, and veracity.
3. Become informed about the ethical standards in counseling, which include confidentiality and privacy, privileged communication, relationship boundaries with clients, informed consent, and professional responsibility and competence.
4. Discover the ethical and legal issues specific to addiction counseling, whether it is focused on individuals, groups, couples, or families.
5. Summarize the important information concerning record-keeping, third-party and private practice reimbursement, and the advantages and disadvantages of being a counselor in recovery.

PERSONAL REFLECTIONS

Half of my practice today is focused on working with addicted individuals. My client "Luc" came to see me a few months ago. He told me his fascinating story of growing up in a large city in eastern Canada. Luc came from a multigenerational crime family, and his description was not unlike what you would expect to hear from someone involved in the Mafia. One of their involvements was selling drugs, and, like many young people, he was curious to find out what it would be like to try some of his product. After becoming deeply involved in using cocaine and serving some time in prison, he decided to change his life and moved west. Luc began several legitimate businesses, met his fiancée, Celine, but continued to struggle with intense cravings to use again. Celine found out about some of his relapses and threatened not to marry him if he kept using. Luc took her threat seriously, and that is why he made his first appointment to see me.

After three or four sessions, I received a lengthy email from Celine. Based on reports from Luc, she was worried that I was befriending him instead of helping him. She also suspected that I was not taking his problem with cocaine seriously. Little did she know that I had strongly discouraged him from returning to his home city for Christmas holidays, given the high likelihood that he would relapse and then become dishonest with Celine again by first denying it.

I thought briefly about what kind of response was appropriate. What is the answer based on our ethics code? The answer is no response at all. If I had replied to Celine, it would have breached confidentiality. I did not have a signed release form to talk to her. Instead, I emailed Luc and told him that I had heard from her but that I could not reply to her email because of confidentiality. I invited him to bring her to a session if that were something that he wanted to do at some point. I never did hear from Luc again.

Upon reflection, I wondered if Luc interpreted my building of a strong and positive working alliance as an overture of friendship. Using motivational interviewing techniques can create a strong bond between counselors and clients. As in my example, there is often a consequence to behaving ethically (and legally for that matter), but the alternative of not acting in accord with ethics and laws creates even more substantial adverse consequences.

What are the ethics that underlie our work with addicted clients? Find out as you get into reading this chapter.

This chapter begins by overviewing ethical practice regarding all services that fall under the rubric of mental health counseling. In other words, the first major section of this chapter concerns *counseling in general.* These are ***not*** specific to addiction counseling, which is the topic explored in the second major section. Regarding general codes of ethics governing counseling practice, only the American Counseling Association's (ACA, 2014) *Code of Ethics* will be highlighted. The Council for Accreditation of Counseling and Related Educational Programs (CACREP), which is the accrediting body for addiction counseling programs in the United States, grew out of concern for standards by the organization now called ACA. A copy of ACA's code of ethics and other relevant documents can be easily downloaded from https://www.counseling.org/knowledge-center/ethics. I suggest you download a copy now to supplement the material covered in this first major section. Following this review, the ethical, legal, and professional issues pertaining to addiction counseling specifically are covered.

Although there are some differences between the ethical codes of various professional bodies that encompass counseling practice (e.g., ACA, American Psychological Association [APA], National Association of Social Workers), there are more similarities. Individuals who belong to more than one professional body must adhere to the ethical principles and standards of *all* groups to which they belong.

After reading this chapter, you might find it useful to complete the Ethical and Legal Issues in Counseling Self-Efficacy Scale (ELICSES; Mullen, Lambie, & Conley, 2014). Mullen et al. (2014) recommended that the total score on the ELICSES is a psychometrically sound measure of students' and practitioners' self-efficacy regarding ethical and legal issues.

General Discussion of Ethics (ACA's 2014 Code of Ethics)[1]

Why do we need ethics? Counseling, like psychology, is a noble profession. We are expected to have exemplary personal qualities and act according to higher-order moral principles and ideals. Clients come to trust us (that is, if we develop a strong and positive working alliance), and they tell us some of their most profound and sometimes darkest secrets. Occasionally you will hear your client tell you, "I have never told anyone this before you." This can be both an honor and a curse. It is an honor to know that your client is seeking help from *you*, but it can be a curse if you have not provided earlier sufficient signed informed consent. For example, some things could be told to you that you cannot ethically and/or legally keep confidential. If your client tells you, "I have been sexually abusing my 6-year-old son, but, thanks to you, I stopped doing so a month ago," or "I am going to kill myself when I leave your office," or "I am going to kill my wife when I get home," you cannot keep this information confidential. You need to ensure that the times you need to breach confidentiality are included in your informed consent form, which is signed by the client as soon as he or she sits down in your office (and sometimes even sooner).

You might think, "Would it *not* be better if these times you need to breach confidentiality were excluded in the informed consent form? That way, for example, you might be more likely to *catch* a child abuser or someone who is imminently suicidal or homicidal." Although that may be true, professional counselors play a specific

[1]Note that much of this discussion is adapted from Cottone and Tarvydas (2016).

role in society, and role boundaries are needed. We are not the police, for example. It is not our job to investigate alleged crimes or misconduct. To preserve the integrity of counseling relationships and to build strong and positive working alliances, we need to be honest with our clients from the beginning of our work with them.

There is sometimes a tension between ethics and the law. Just as the law does not dictate what is ethical (instead, it dictates what is legal and illegal), there are some actions performed (or not performed) that are legal but not ethical (Geppert, 2013). Sometimes the law needs to "catch up" with ethical practice. For example, the regulatory body for psychologists in Alberta, Canada, is currently awaiting approval of its continuing education program by the government. Most psychologists would agree, however, that it is important to remain current in their knowledge regarding the areas in which they practice. Consequently, although it is ethical for psychologists to stay current, modern practices do not always conform to laws on the books.

Six Ethical Principles

Cottone and Tarvydas (2016) suggested that there are six ethical principles, which include autonomy, nonmaleficence, beneficence, justice, fidelity, and veracity. These principles are defined as follows:

1. Autonomy. Counselors respect their clients' freedom of choice and self-determination. They believe that clients have a right to make their own decisions.
2. Nonmaleficence. Counselors do not inflict harm. This is similar to the Hippocratic Oath taken by physicians, "Primun non nocere," which in Latin means, "First, do no harm" (Shmerling, 2015, para. 1). As counselors, we might not always be helpful to clients, but it is especially important that we do not cause them additional hurt or suffering.
3. Beneficence. Counselors do their best to help clients and be of benefit to them. We work to help relieve and lessen harm.
4. Justice. Counselors strive to be fair and egalitarian in their work with clients.
5. Fidelity. Counselors are honest and faithful, and they honor commitments to their clients. Abandoning a client would be a breach of fidelity (e.g., If you are taking a vacation or cannot work with a particular client, you need to ensure that the client has another counselor to see temporarily or permanently, respectively).
6. Veracity. Counselors remain truthful in relationships with clients and with other involved parties or stakeholders.

Now let's have a closer look at each principle (for greater depth, please see Cottone and Tarvydas, 2016).

Respecting Autonomy

There is often a difference between our freedom to make choices and our freedom to act on them (from Kitchener, as cited in Cottone & Tarvydas, 2016). For example, although a client might think of killing someone, it is ethical to prevent this from occurring if possible (within the constraints of our standards of practice). This was tested in a well-known case, *Tarasoff v. Regents* (VandeCreek & Knapp, 1993), where a student at the University of California told his psychologist of his intent to kill his ex-girlfriend, Tatiana Tarasoff, and later did so. Although the psychologist had notified the police, he failed to inform the intended victim.

In another court case (*Ewing v. Goldstein*), the California State Supreme Court (CSSC) extended the duty to warn when a therapist, David Goldstein, was provided information from his client's parents that their son (LAPD officer Geno Colello) was going to hurt another individual (Keith Ewing). Goldstein notified neither the police nor Ewing. Colello subsequently killed Ewing before killing himself. The CSSC ruled that Goldstein was at fault, thus introducing the new requirement that even third-party information regarding homicidal intent needs to be reported (Smith, 2006).

Some clients, in their anger, will threaten killing someone they know but it is said without intent. How do you know when someone is serious about murdering someone and when it is only an uttered threat? Cottone and Tarvydas (2016) agreed that suicidal or homicidal ideation is not necessarily a warning sign, so they suggested that counselors look for additional signs such as (a) they have an organized plan, (b) they know when they are going to enact the plan, and/or (c) they have the means by which to enact the plan (e.g., access to weapons). However, assessing risk for violence does not reduce it (Large & Ryan, 2015), and there is no preferred measure or approach for counselors to use to evaluate it (Nicholls, Pritchard,

AUTONOMY CASE EXAMPLE: WHAT WOULD *YOU* DO?

Imagine that you are the counselor in the case examples in this chapter. Frances is your client, and she knows that you are a trained hypnotherapist. Frances is convinced that hypnotherapy is the only method that will help her break free of her gambling disorder. She has seen other counselors before you, and she has tried cognitive-behavioral therapy (CBT) and behavioral methods. None of these has worked sufficiently.

You do not believe, however, that hypnotherapy is the best approach, so you tell Frances that you will not offer her hypnotherapy because you do not think it will be helpful to her. It appears that Frances receives your refusal rather well. However, she fails to attend her next scheduled session.

1. What ethical issues are embedded in this scenario?
2. Hypnotherapy is not an evidence-based treatment for gambling disorder. In what ways could you talk to Frances differently so that it would not take away her ability to choose?
3. How does an addiction counselor provide informed consent when working with someone like Frances?

Reeves, & Hilterman, 2013). Tips for assessing both suicide and homicide risk with clients can be found in Chapter 6.

Respecting autonomy, then, involves not interfering unnecessarily in the decisions made by our clients. To help set the stage for informed decision-making, we provide all the necessary information to our clients in ways that they can understand. Assuming our clients can carry out their decisions, we stand aside (or help them if needed or asked) and let them proceed.

Nonmaleficence

Nonmaleficence and beneficence are related concepts. Although beneficence represents a more active way of helping our clients, nonmaleficence is about *not* taking actions that might harm our clients. Nonmaleficence is about doing no harm. It is often viewed as one of the most important obligations for professionals because their work has the potential to be either helpful or hurtful. Diagnosis, for example, can have either effect on an individual. Some diagnoses, once given, "stick around" far longer than they should, in which case they may cause more harm than good. For example, if individuals were given the diagnosis of gender dysphoria before they transitioned, this diagnosis may be required so that they can proceed with the needed medical interventions. However, if the diagnosis continued or they were treated differently posttransition, this could be harmful if the clients had been married with children and were now fighting in court to have custody of their children.

NONMALEFICENCE CASE EXAMPLE: WHAT WOULD *YOU* DO?

You are a counselor who practices only person-centered therapy. Jeanette is your client, and she is experiencing moderate depression that was triggered when she stopped long-term use of cocaine. Her depression has already persisted for 12 months since becoming clean from cocaine. You know that CBT has demonstrated effectiveness with depression, whereas person-centered therapy can make it worse. Nonetheless, you are not trained in CBT, and you need more sessions because you are in private practice and have bills to pay. After 10 sessions, Jeanette tells you that her depression is worsening. You tell her that, if she does not improve after the next two sessions, you will refer her to someone else.

1. What ethical issues are embedded in this scenario?
2. What would be a better way to deal with Jeanette?
3. Counselors in private practice are also running a business. How can you ethically operate a practice that has an insufficient number of clients to cover expenses while at the same time maintain professional ethics?

Beneficence

The existence of a profession is based on society recognizing that the professional has special skills and knowledge in which to help individuals who are struggling. Among other things, this requires that professionals become competent in their work. It is critical that counselors do not assume a paternalistic or authoritative attitude toward their clients. Instead, competence must be weighed with knowing that clients come from diverse backgrounds, classes, races, religions, abilities, etc. In postmodern counseling approaches, for example, counselors assume the position of not knowing, meaning that, despite having expert knowledge, they do not have expert knowledge of this particular individual sitting before them.

Justice

It is essential that counselors treat their clients fairly and without discrimination. Furthermore, they must avoid making prejudicial decisions and "picking favorites." If counselors are working for someone else including agencies, if they determine that serious inequities exist, they must find ways to be advocates for clients and address injustice.

BENEFICENCE CASE EXAMPLE: WHAT WOULD *YOU* DO?

You know that CBT has the greatest likelihood of helping Rodney reduce his Internet gaming disorder. He is your last client of the day, however, and you are feeling exhausted. Instead of offering CBT, you decide to just listen to him talk about his problems as you did the week before because it takes less energy.

1. What ethical issues are embedded in this scenario?
2. What would be a better way to deal with Rodney?
3. What if you simply were too tired to be effective with Rodney. What would be the ethical thing to do?

JUSTICE CASE EXAMPLE: WHAT WOULD *YOU* DO?

Your agency offers a group for clients with substance use disorders (SUDs) who have difficulties maintaining close intimate relationships. Your client, Bernard, is gay. You are aware that the other group members are straight, and you also know that at least one is deeply homophobic. Consequently, you do not tell Bernard about the group, even though you have every reason to believe that group treatment would be most helpful for him.

1. What ethical issues are embedded in this scenario?
2. What would be a better way to deal with Bernard?
3. There might be some truth in believing that Bernard would face some prejudice and discrimination if he were to attend the group treatment. What actions could you take before you unilaterally decide not to invite Bernard to participate (hint: think about interventions at the agency level)?

Fidelity

Counselors need to uphold the promises they make to clients and remain loyal to them. Counseling practices that are outgrowths of fidelity include informed consent, confidentiality, professional disclosure, and avoiding harmful relationships (these will be discussed shortly).

Veracity

Honesty is the primary characteristic underlying veracity. Counselors neither misrepresent information nor withhold the truth from clients or stakeholders (i.e., other individuals legitimately involved in working with the client). Often beginning counselors find it difficult to be entirely honest with clients out of concern that they might offend them. It is important that we find ways to be tactful with our truth. For example, if you had a client with schizophrenia who did not practice personal hygiene, you might find that your office continues to smell bad for an extended period after the client leaves. The smell affects both you and clients who enter subsequently. You might begin with saying something like, "To what extent are you familiar with ways to practice personal hygiene daily?" If the client is unaware of what this looks like, you may need to play an instructional role and instruct him or her. Alternatively, if the client is aware of how to practice personal hygiene but fails to do so, you might follow up with, "Walk me through the personal hygiene steps that you take each day." The client may well ask you why you are asking these questions. It is incumbent on you to be tactfully honest (e.g., "Every session, I have noticed that you have an unpleasant odor. I have wondered what steps you might need to take to eliminate the smell").

Ethical Standards

"Ethical standards are specific profession-relevant directives or guidelines that reflect the best ethical practice of professionals" (Cottone & Tarvydas, 2016, p. 103). By having ethical standards, counselors find it easier to understand what is specifically required of them in frequently encountered situations.

Confidentiality and Privacy

Although these are related concepts, they are also different. Privacy refers to the rights of individuals to have information about them kept from being divulged to others. For example, if you are working with a client over the age of 18 and a parent or relative phones you to ask if she or he is attending counseling sessions with you, unless you have a signed release of information form from your client, you cannot divulge that you are counseling this client. Clients

FIDELITY CASE EXAMPLE: WHAT WOULD *YOU* DO?

Leroy's parents, Niles and Texra, accompanied him to his first counseling appointment. Leroy is a 17-year-old African American. His parents expressed deep concern that Leroy was becoming an alcoholic. Texra has tried to wake him up many mornings, but Leroy has been so drunk that it has taken him a long time to get out of bed. He has skipped college many times because he says he is too ill to attend.

During your second session, Leroy tells you that he typically drinks several ounces of bourbon before complementing this with one or two 10-mg Valium pills. You know that this is a dangerous combination and tell Leroy accordingly. Leroy says that his tranquilizer use is none of your business as he is only seeing you for alcohol abuse. You decide not to confront Leroy any further because you think it will hamper developing a strong working alliance with him. Nonetheless, as soon as he leaves your office, you phone Texra to tell her about the danger regarding Leroy's concurrent use of two central nervous system depressants.

1. What ethical issues are embedded in this scenario?
2. What would be a better way to deal with Leroy?
3. What wording needs to be in your informed consent form before you call his parents? How can you ascertain if Leroy understood and remembers the information contained in your informed consent form?

VERACITY CASE EXAMPLE: WHAT WOULD *YOU* DO?

Your client, Edward, is a 33-year-old self-confessed sex-addicted person (note that sex addiction is not included in *DSM-5*). As you write down his history, you learn that Edward has been married to Leah for the last 9 years. Although he defines as heterosexual, he has secretly been engaging in sex with other men for several months. He tells you that he never wears condoms because he always takes the penetrator role and consequently views his risk of contracting sexually transmitted diseases (STDs) as very low. You are aware, however, that his risk of contracting STDs is quite high, and this includes risk of contracting the HIV virus. As this is your first session with him, you decide that it would only negatively impact your working alliance if you were to begin a conversation regarding the risk of contracting STDs and spreading these to his wife. You think this conversation would be better suited for a later session when a positive therapeutic relationship has already become established.

1. What ethical issues are embedded in this scenario?
2. What would be a better way to deal with Edward?
3. What ethical obligations are there, if any, regarding informing Leah of the risk that Edward is creating for her?

have the right to keep their counseling relationships with you a secret from others, perhaps especially family members. Special rules apply to counseling those under the age of 18, and you will need to find out what those rules are in the jurisdiction in which you practice.

Confidentiality, on the other hand, is more specific than privacy. It refers to keeping information gleaned within the counseling session to oneself. It is like an "anti-gossip guarantee" (Cottone & Tarvydas, 2016, p. 108). As stated by ACA (2014), counselors must safeguard the information provided to them about a "client's identity, identifying characteristics, and private communications" (p. 20). A client must first sign a release of information form that stipulates to whom and for how long you can release information to another person or agency. Except under exceptional circumstances (i.e., child abuse, imminent suicidal risk, and/or homicidal risk in all states), confidentiality cannot be broken except by written permission of the client.

In states that do *not* have laws restricting privileged communications (see next section), confidentiality must also be broken if your client intends to engage in a serious illegal act or if records are subpoenaed by a court order. Regarding subpoenas, under federal confidentiality laws (explained later), addiction counselors cannot submit or reproduce case records and submit these to the court. Instead, addiction counselors must ask the court for a special closed-court hearing (Ward, 2002). Breaching confidentiality can lead to both legal consequences and to consequences with one's regulatory body in other circumstances where written permission is not provided. When working within a "team" (e.g., you work for a counseling agency where records are accessible by all staff who work there), information can be shared among staff members, but this practice of sharing records and information among staff members must be communicated to the client within the informed consent form that is signed at the beginning of the first session.

The Health Insurance Portability and Accountability Act (HIPAA) of 1996 was designed to provide greater confidentiality in the use of health records. In 2001, the U.S. Department of Health and Human Services brought in rules related to HIPAA such as psychotherapy notes cannot be released with clients' permission unless they sign a release form that explicitly includes the release of psychotherapy notes (Cottone & Tarvydas, 2016). Under HIPAA, clients themselves cannot obtain a copy of their psychotherapy notes (however, some state laws do afford clients this information as well; Hecker & Edwards, 2014). The central purpose of these laws is to ensure that only the minimal and necessary amount of information is provided in disclosures of information.

HIPAA has distinguished between the clinical record and "psychotherapy notes" (often called "process or case notes" by counselors; Hecker & Edwards, 2014). Clients can request and receive a copy of their clinical record in all states. Psychotherapy notes contain counselors' impressions about the client and details about the counseling session considered inappropriate for the clinical record. They are typically kept separate from the clinical record because they contain sensitive information that is pertinent only to the counselor. "Psychotherapy notes are not to be disclosed and are highly protected under HIPAA" (Hecker & Edwards, 2014, p. 100). Again, it is important to know that some states do have laws that provide access to psychotherapy notes from clients.

Psychotherapy notes should exclude clients' current state, the treatment plan, symptoms, progress, diagnoses, prognosis, when the session began and ended, the types of treatment provided, and the results of clinical tests. They should also exclude details regarding the theme of the session, medications prescribed, and any additional information regarding treatment or payment. These notes should not be disclosed except in legal proceedings brought against the individual or to prevent "a serious and imminent threat to public health or safety, to a health oversight agency for lawful oversight of the originator of the psychotherapy notes, for the lawful activities of coroner or medical examiner or as required by law" (Hecker & Edwards, 2014, pp. 100–101). Counselors should be aware that both state and/or federal laws may be more stringent than HIPAA, and these laws trump HIPAA (Hecker & Edwards, 2014).

Under HIPAA is the Health Information Technology for Economic and Clinical Health Act (HITECH) of 2009. HITECH requires that electronic data must be password protected and the clinical files encrypted (Haley, 2015). If counselors discover that a breach of confidential information has occurred, they must follow the requirements under HITECH or face financial penalties that can run into millions of dollars. Counselors should get further details regarding HIPAA and other requirements through the website for the Centers for Medicare and Medicaid Services (https://www.cms.gov/Regulations-and-Guidance/Regulations-and-Guidance.html).

Note that federal confidentiality and privacy laws for individuals receiving substance abuse treatment are more stringent than HIPAA. These are covered in the section of this chapter entitled Specific Discussion of Ethical, Legal, and Professional Issues.

Privileged Communication

A client's right to privileged communication is contained in state and/or federal statutes. If the privilege is upheld in court, the counselor cannot be forced to testify on the client's behalf. Privileged communication is a legal right, and it is not found in professional codes of ethics. However, there are limits to it. In many states, for example, privileged communication can be overturned in instances of suspected or substantiated child abuse or neglect (Cottone & Tarvydas, 2016). If the counselor receives a court subpoena regarding either a criminal or civil matter, if the state does not have laws protecting privileged communication, the counselor would need to comply. If the subpoena occurs in a state that has laws protecting privileged communication, the counselor must refuse to provide information. When in doubt, consult with the ethics committee of your state counseling association or licensure board.

CONFIDENTIALITY CASE EXAMPLE: WHAT WOULD *YOU* DO?

Ivan is a recent immigrant from Russia. He has found it difficult acculturating into his life in the United States. Ivan works as a radiology technologist, and at times other staff have found his behavior to be somewhat erratic and unprofessional. He tells you in the first session that he frequently uses illegal stimulants. In the following sessions, the topic never comes up again. Instead, Ivan becomes more focused on his problems understanding American culture, and he claims that the hospital he works at has provided no help at all in his acculturation process. Ivan has developed a close relationship with you over 10 sessions, and he has come to trust you like family, perhaps partly because he is alone here, and he currently has no friends. You are Russian yourself, and you have seen Ivan at a few cultural events.

After the 10th session, Ivan's employment at the hospital is terminated. He can no longer afford to see you, and counseling ends abruptly. About 2 months later, you receive a letter from his union that includes a release of information form that Ivan has signed. The union is building a case for wrongful dismissal, suggesting in the letter that the hospital had some responsibility for providing Ivan a thorough orientation and assistance with acculturation. They have asked for a report from you. You believe in fact that Ivan forgot that he told you about his stimulant use in the first session. Do you include this information in the report to the union?

1. What ethical issues are embedded in this scenario?
2. What actions might you take before sending the union a letter?
3. In a professional relationship, how would you distinguish between becoming friends in contrast to acting in a friendly manner so that this is clear to the client?

PRIVILEGED COMMUNICATION CASE EXAMPLE: WHAT WOULD *YOU* DO?

You have a hostile client, Bruno, whom you have seen for 20 sessions. Bruno has an addiction to crystal meth. Most counselors would refuse to work with this type of client, but, given that this is your specialty, you are the one to whom many counselors refer. He has uttered violent threats against his estranged wife several times, particularly when high on crystal meth, and you have notified the police and his wife on each occurrence. Your client has a restraining order that prevents him from being within half a mile of his wife, but that hasn't stopped him from making threats in your office. You are aware of many of his disturbed, violent, and crazy thoughts.

Before the case goes to trial, you receive a subpoena from the judge commanding you to release information concerning Bruno. You have reason to believe that no one else really understands Bruno's thought processes, but, because of your expertise, you know him arguably better than anyone. Nonetheless, you are living in a state that has laws protecting privileged communication.

1. What ethical issues are embedded in this scenario?
2. What would be a better way to deal with Bruno?
3. What if you have substantial evidence that Bruno is going to kill his wife very soon? What would be the ethical thing to do? What would you do if the ethical thing to do is actually illegal in your state?

Relationship Boundaries With Clients

You may have heard of the terms "dual" or "multiple" relationships regarding counselors having one or more other relationships with the client besides the counseling one. The other roles were always considered harmful in ethics codes. The terms dual and multiple relationships have lost favor recently because they are unclear and sometimes misleading. For example, counselors in private practice act as counselors, "collectors" of payment, and maintainers of records. That involves three roles. You can add a fourth role if you happen to belong to a nondominant group (e.g., LGBTQ), and perhaps add a fifth role if you are part of a small or rural community. Ethics codes today acknowledge that you are not an individual who must hide secretly at home to avoid running into current or past clients. What is in common with ethics codes is banning harmful, potentially harmful, or exploitive relationships with clients.

Sexual relationships with clients, or other students or counselors that you might be supervising, are unethical, and, in states where counseling practice is regulated, also illegal. Such relationships are psychologically damaging to clients (Sonne, 2012). It is important that you check the requirements in the jurisdiction in which you live. In some cases, after a certain number of years have passed since the last counseling interaction, counselors can become sexually or romantically involved with past clients, but there are always several caveats attached. It is critical that you look into the legalities and the ethics code or codes that regulate your practice (i.e., some counselors may belong to more than one regulatory body). Our society is rightly concerned about sexual improprieties, which are increasingly in the spotlight due to the #MeToo movement. (Known by different names internationally, this phrase represents a social movement against sexual harassment and sexual assault; Jaffe, 2018.) Sexual impropriety with a current client (or counselor or counseling student you are supervising) could easily lead to loss of license to practice for life.

The issue of whether counselors should touch their clients is controversial. It is vital that, if counselors use touch, they should do so cautiously and appropriately. Although we as counselors might be very comfortable with touch, we don't know how touch may trigger our clients, as we do not know how they may have been traumatized. For that matter, clients may not remember how they have been traumatized! A substantial percentage of clients with addictive disorders have a history of childhood trauma, and touch may well be a trigger for them. A good practice is to let the client be the one who initiates (e.g., a handshake or hug). Touching the knee or thigh of a client for *any* reason is generally contraindicated. This would be crossing a boundary.

RELATIONSHIP BOUNDARIES CASE EXAMPLE: WHAT WOULD *YOU* DO?

Your name is Nora, and you are a 26-year-old female addiction counselor. You are out one Saturday at your favorite nightclub, and, after having several drinks, a man comes up to you and introduces himself as Mark. He says that he saw you for addiction counseling regarding a problem he had with hallucinogenic drugs about 3 or 4 years ago. You do not have any recollection of him. He can see that from your expression, and he tells you that he only saw you for two sessions. The two of you have a great conversation while Mark keeps buying you drinks. By the end of the night, you take a taxi home and feel quite hungover the next day. You forget that you gave Mark your telephone number, and you notice he has already texted you to say he had a great time and would like to see you again. You are uncertain whether to reply.

1. What ethical issues are embedded in this scenario?
2. Is it okay to date Mark? Why or why not?
3. Would it be okay to become friends with him? Why or why not?

Informed Consent

In many ways, this is a process similar to what occurs when a physician or medical specialist prescribes either medications or procedures, most of which carry some risk. You have likely seen the television commercials promoting certain medications, but, toward the end of the ad, they list all of the adverse effects that occur for some people. In counseling practice, assessment, and other procedures in which a counselor might be involved, informed consent consists of ensuring that clients understand the potential benefits and potential drawbacks of the said procedure. Before offering a counseling technique, let your clients know whether or not it is empirically validated but also let them know that the method does not work with all clients.

Furthermore, it is important that they understand (a) how the technique works and (b) the potential benefits and risks regarding it. Let them know about the expected outcomes from the treatment that you are proposing. Additionally, let clients know about other techniques that could be used so that they understand there is a choice. As the cliché goes, "one size does not fit all." Because of the principle of autonomy, clients need to choose the treatment that they will receive, and there should be no sense that they were coerced in the process. Remember that the choice of therapy is a collaborative decision. Informed consent begins with having clients sign your informed consent form at the beginning of counseling. But it doesn't stop there. Informed consent occurs throughout counseling when either you or your client indicate a change of direction.

Mandatory clients also need to be provided informed consent. Usually, information from compulsory counseling needs to be reported back to the referring party (e.g., a probation officer, lawyer, judge). Clients maintain the right to refuse services.

Whoever will be the recipient of information needs to be included in the informed consent form. For counselors intending to conduct research, providing informed consent is also critical.

Children and teenagers under the age of 18 are unable to provide consent for counseling services. Instead, their parents or legal guardians must consent for them. In some states, minors are permitted to receive certain kinds of counseling without parental consent (Cottone & Tarvydas, 2016). Please refer to your jurisdiction for details regarding what is permissible in working with juveniles. In work with minors, it is still prudent to attain their agreement (and collaboration wherever possible) regarding the treatment plan. This is called *assent*, which is agreeing to participate in counseling, assessment, or research by those who are otherwise not authorized to provide formal informed consent. Appendix 2A provides an example of a document designed to encourage assent and Appendices 2B and 2C reflect examples of an initial clinical record and a subsequent clinical record, respectively.

INFORMED CONSENT CASE EXAMPLE: WHAT WOULD *YOU* DO?

Erica comes to you for counseling because, now that she has stopped drinking alcohol altogether, she has become intensely aware of the trauma that she experienced as a child. You advertise that you have expertise in dealing with posttraumatic stress disorder (PTSD) and trauma. After Erica provides some details about her childhood, you ask her to recline back in your chair, and you begin making suggestions that she is getting very tired and drowsy. After 10 minutes or so, you start reading an already prepared script that you use with clients who have experienced childhood trauma. After a few more minutes, Erica opens her eyes, appearing quite startled. You ask her if there is anything wrong. She replies, "Was that some kind of hypnosis you were doing with me?" "Yes, it was," you reply, "I was trained in hypnotherapy several years back." Erica retorts, "In my religion, that is considered a form of mind control. It is not allowed." You come back with, "It is a potent method of helping people get over the trauma. It is not mind control at all." Erica becomes defensive and it takes you the rest of the session to calm her down so that you can better explore her fears.

1. What ethical issues are embedded in this scenario?
2. What would be a better way to deal with Erica?
3. If you advertise that you specialize in PTSD and trauma, in what other methods besides hypnotherapy should you be trained? If hypnotherapy were considered the best treatment for childhood trauma (which it is not), is it still ethical to offer it as your first-line treatment?

Professional Responsibility and Competence

Professional responsibility refers to the obligations that counselors have toward their clients and the counseling profession. Our job is to promote the welfare of our clients. This means that counselors cannot become involved in discriminatory practices toward those who seek their services. It also means that they cannot shirk their responsibilities to clients for the sake of rewards, financial or otherwise. If clients can no longer afford to see you, it is your duty to help them find a suitable low-cost or free counseling service. ACA's Code of Ethics (2014) encourages counselors to provide some service "for which there is little or no financial return" (p. 8), which is often called "pro bono" work. Counselors also maintain an obligation to end counseling if it is not helping their clients. When that occurs, it is also essential that the counselor refer the client to someone else.

Another aspect of professional responsibility is to oneself. Counselors are expected to take care of their own emotional, physical, mental, and spiritual well-being. If counselors are not looking after themselves, they become more likely to burn out or become incapacitated. When counselors become mentally, cognitively, or emotionally impaired, they must take a break from providing counseling until they are well.

Professional responsibility also encompasses competence. If counselors lack the necessary competence to deal with a particular client issue, they are obligated to refer to a counselor or other professional who does have this competence. Counselors are required to work within the limits of their training, experience, and practice. When counselors want to increase their competence in an area, they need to receive sufficient further training or hire a consultant who is paid to provide supervision. Counselors today are also expected to be multiculturally competent (see Sue, Arredondo, & McDavis, 1992, for the expected competencies). Despite the call to the profession by Sue et al. (1992), across various students, most clients (53–81%) report experiencing at least one racial-ethnic microaggression from their therapist, and this has lowered ratings of the working alliance and therapy outcomes (Owen et al., 2018).

Today's counselor will likely need to become competent in providing alternative service deliveries that involve technology. Examples here include providing counseling by phone, email, and Internet (Collone & Tarvydas, 2016). ACA's attention to this has grown substantially.

If there is a conflict between counselors' professional responsibility and their employers, they are expected to try to remedy the situation. If a resolution cannot be negotiated or found, counselors are expected to terminate their employment rather than persist and possibly compound the problem.

PROFESSIONAL RESPONSIBILITY CASE EXAMPLE: WHAT WOULD *YOU* DO?

Jay and Kristin have been married for 5 years. Jay has a serious addiction to heroin, and, while he was receiving methadone until a few months ago, he relapsed and is still injecting street heroin when the two of them come to you for couples counseling. Kristin is afraid that Jay will overdose and possibly die from fentanyl. Furthermore, she feels that Jay has moved away from her emotionally. Now that he is back into using heroin, he is again spending time with the junkies he used to call his friends. Jay is aware of the dangers of his return to heroin, but he does not want to resume methadone maintenance treatment. He tells both of you that methadone does not give him a high and that is what he craves when he is not getting heroin.

You decide that it is critical that you work on helping Jay and Kristin develop greater emotional intimacy so that Jay becomes likelier to listen to Kristin's desire for him to stop using street-grade heroin.

1. What ethical issues are embedded in this scenario?
2. Given that Jay does not want to stop using his drug of choice, what is the likelihood that helping the two of them create greater emotional intimacy will have an impact on Jay's heroin use?
3. What other approach could you take with Jay and Kristin?

TABLE 2.1 Principles Outlined in the NAADAC Code Alongside the Sections of ACA Code

NAADAC	ACA
Introduction to NAD/NCC AP Ethical Standards	ACA Code of Ethics Preamble; ACA Code of Ethics Purpose
Principle I: The Counseling Relationship	Section A. The Counseling Relationship
Principle II: Confidentiality and Privileged Communication	Section B. Confidentiality and Privacy
Principle III: Professional Responsibilities and Workplace Standards	Section C. Professional Responsibility
Principle IV: Working in a Culturally Diverse World	Section D. Relationships With Other Professionals
Principle V: Assessment, Evaluation, and Interpretation	Section E. Evaluation, Assessment, and Interpretation
Principle VI: E-Therapy, E-Supervision, and Social Media	Section F. Supervision, Training, and Teaching
Principle VII: Supervision and Consultation	Section G. Research and Publication
Principle VIII: Resolving Ethical Concerns	Section H. Distance Counseling, Technology, and Social Media
Principle IX: Publication and Communications	Section I. Resolving Ethical Issues

Specific Discussion of Ethical, Legal, and Professional Issues[2]

National Association for Addiction Professionals' (2016) Code of Ethics

Most addiction counselors will become members of the National Association for Addiction Professionals[3] (NAADAC), and their ethics code (NAADAC, 2016) will need to be upheld (download a copy from https://www.naadac.org/code-of-ethics). A comparison of NAADAC's code with that of ACA's can be found in Table 2.1.

NAADAC (2016) recommends that addiction counselors consider the following when making ethical decisions:

1. Autonomy: To allow others the freedom to choose their own destiny.
2. Obedience: The responsibility to observe and obey legal and ethical directives.
3. Conscientious Refusal: The responsibility to refuse to carry out directives that are illegal and/or unethical.
4. Beneficence: To help others.

[2]Note that much of this discussion is adapted from Cottone and Tarvydas (2016).

[3]This organization is usually known simply as the Association for Addiction Professionals.

5. Gratitude: To pass along the good that we receive to others.
6. Competence: To possess the necessary skills and knowledge to treat the clientele in a chosen discipline and to remain current with treatment modalities, theories, and techniques.
7. Justice: Fair and equal treatment, to treat others in a just manner.
8. Stewardship: To use available resources in a judicious and conscientious manner, to give back.
9. Honesty and Candor: Tell the truth in all dealing with clients, colleagues, business associates, and the community.
10. Fidelity: To be true to your word, keeping promises and commitments.
11. Loyalty: The responsibility to not abandon those with whom you work.
12. Diligence: To work hard in the chosen profession, to be mindful, careful, and thorough in the services delivered.
13. Discretion: Use of good judgment, honoring confidentiality and the privacy of others.
14. Self-improvement: To work on professional and personal growth to be the best you can be.
15. Nonmalfeasance: Do no harm to the interests of the client.
16. Restitution: When necessary, make amends to those who have been harmed or injured.
17. Self-interest: To protect yourself and your personal interests. (pp. 1–2)

NAADAC's (2016) code, in contrast to ACA's (2014), is explicit regarding sharing and giving back to others, and making amends (point 16) in a manner similar to 12-step programs. NAADAC makes it clear that, if clients are working with another behavioral health professional, they should request that clients sign a release of information so that a collaborative professional relationship can be established with the other professional helpers. Their code of ethics makes it clear that engaging in any form of sexual or romantic relationship with a current or former client is prohibited. If a court orders a NAADAC member to release confidential and privileged information, the member will obtain written and informed consent from the client or take steps to prohibit the disclosure or at least keep it limited as narrowly as possible. There is also a proviso that, if addiction professionals become aware of "inappropriate, illegal, discriminatory, and/or unethical policies, procedures and practices at their agency, organization, or practice, they shall alert their employers" (p. 11). There is a great deal more information contained in the NAADAC code of ethics, and it is a responsibility incumbent on all members to be highly familiar with its contents.

Cottone and Tarvydas's (2016) Discussion of Ethics in Addiction Counseling

Confidentiality and Privacy

Confidentiality provisions regarding addiction counseling are included in both state and federal laws and regulations. As in other areas of counseling, addiction counselors must keep client records confidential and release information only with the signed consent of the client. Cottone and Tarvydas (2016) reported that these laws are complex and recommended addiction counselors become familiar with these rules (e.g., https://www.hhs.gov/regulations/find-rules-by-operating-division.html; https://www.integration.samhsa.gov/operations-administration/the_confidentiality_of_alcohol_and_drug_abuse.pdf; https://pubs.niaaa.nih.gov/publications/Social/Module9Legal&EthicalIssues/Module9.html).

Federal laws in the substance abuse field govern confidentiality (42 U.S.C. § 290dd-2) and regulations (42 CFR Part 2) (Kunkel, 2012). A final rule was implemented on March 21, 2017, that facilitated exchange of information for treatment and health integration within new models of healthcare and that further ensured confidentiality of individuals seeking help for SUDs (Murow Klein & Yeung, 2018).

A Part 2 consent to release information may be revoked orally, whereas HIPAA consents may be revoked only in writing (Murow Klein & Yeung, 2018). A Part 2 consent must include the following elements:

1. Name or general designation of the program or person permitted to make the disclosure.
2. Name or title of the individual or name of the organization to which disclosure is to be made.
3. Name of the patient.
4. Purpose of the disclosure.
5. How much and what kind of information is to be disclosed.
6. Signature of patient or personal representative.
7. Date on which consent is signed.
8. Statement that the consent is subject to revocation at any time except to the extent that the program has already acted on it.
9. Date, event, or condition upon which consent will expire if not previously revoked. (Murow Klein & Yeung, 2018, p. 21)

The federal restrictions provide for *strict* confidentiality of information regarding persons receiving treatment for substance abuse prevention and treatment. The intent was to encourage individuals with SUDs to seek help without fear of repercussion (Murow Klein & Yeung, 2018). The restrictions are more stringent than are communications between physicians and patients and attorneys and their clients. For example, federal confidentiality codes prevent staff from confirming that a particular person is a client, even if the person calling is a family member. If a counselor leaves a phone or text message for a client, it is important that the message does not implicate the person as a client. Further, police cannot be provided access to client records unless they have a valid court order.

Ward (2002) provided a gripping and real example regarding the strictness of 42 CFR Part 2. A social worker was told by a male client in an inpatient facility that he had murdered his ex-girlfriend's new boyfriend out of jealousy while being high. Under Part 2, the social worker was not permitted to release this information, despite having concerns for the family of the murdered victim.

Group counseling is a specific instance whereby counselors must keep what is said in the group confidential, but there is no legal protection regarding confidentiality for what group members say outside of the group. Counselors need to make this clear at the beginning of a group as part of the informed consent process. If the group has minors in it, parents are technically entitled to see case file information that may have reference to other group members. Consequently, if minors are in the group, all members must be informed regarding the additional means by which confidentiality could be compromised. Group counselors are required to write case notes for every individual in the group, so information about other group members should be deleted or omitted. Regardless of whether minors are in the group or not, group case notes should not refer to individuals specifically. Cottone and Tarvydas (2016) recommended that counselors should not see clients in an individual counselor role and as a group facilitator at the same time. The intent is to avoid contamination of information gleaned in individual sessions that could be shared inadvertently in group sessions.

Privileged Communication

What is considered privileged communication varies by state, and addiction counselors need to become aware of regulations in their jurisdiction. Laws governing privileged communication would also apply to addiction counselors running groups.

Relationship Boundaries With Clients

The ethics code of the Association for Addiction Professionals (NAADAC; note that the same code of ethics applies to the National Certification Commission for Addiction Professionals [NCC AP]. The 2016 code is available from https://www.naadac.org/assets/2416/naadac-nccap-code-of-ethics11-04-16.pdf and stipulates that addiction professionals can *never* engage in sexual or romantic relationships with current or former clients. Counselors who are themselves in recovery may face unique ethical dilemmas. These are outlined in a later section of this chapter.

According to the Association for Specialists in Group Work Best Practice Guidelines (available at https://www.ncbi.nlm.nih.gov/books/NBK64220/pdf/Bookshelf_NBK64220.pdf), counselors running groups should discourage group members from establishing romantic or other dual relationships among themselves. Outside relationships may have adverse effects on the group process and create negative personal outcomes. Nonetheless, there is nothing that group leaders can do if group members establish external relationships.

Informed Consent

The caution here is that some clients, due to the enduring cognitive deficits that may occur with someone who has been abusing drugs for some period, might not be in a condition or state to make informed decisions regarding their treatment. Providing a routine mental status exam (see Chapter 6) will help in ascertaining this possibility. Scott (2000) noted evidence suggesting that individuals with alcohol use disorder entering treatment experience varying degrees of cognitive dysfunction due to prolonged consumption of alcohol. This dysfunction affects their ability to absorb and benefit from the treatment interventions administered during the early weeks following detoxification.

There is an important caveat regarding substance abuse treatment for minors. In some states, minors can receive substance abuse counseling without the consent of parents or guardians in cases where the child or teenager is eligible for mature minor status (Cottone & Tarvydas, 2016). Ensure that you are familiar with the laws governing substance abuse treatment of minors in your state.

In the case of mandatory clients, clients maintain the right to refuse treatment. It is not the counselor's role to persuade compulsory clients to receive help. If counseling does not commence, the counselor has no ethical responsibility to maintain confidentiality and therefore can let the referral sources know that the individual has refused services. Given that some mandatory clients may begin counseling but then withdraw after a period, counselors should include in their informed consent form that the counselor has the right to contact referral sources if the client either terminates counseling or remains noncompliant with treatment. Several studies have found that clients with SUDs are less likely to follow recommended treatments compared with clients having other issues (Rastegar & Fingerhood, 2016).

Furthermore, it is not uncommon that clients struggling with addiction will display inappropriate behaviors and a tendency toward relapse (Walton, 2018). If a counselor is discharging a client from addiction treatment, it is important that a thorough assessment of the situation occur first (Walton, 2018). Morgan, Schackman, Leff, Linas, and Walley (2018) found that, among those receiving evidence-based medication therapies for opioid use disorder, for example, discontinuation rates after 30 days are high:

> At 30 days after initiation, 52% for individuals treated with injectable naltrexone, 70% for individuals treated with oral naltrexone, 31% for individuals treated with sublingual or oralmucosal buprenorphine/naloxone, 58% for individuals treated with sublingual buprenorphine, and 51% for individuals treated with transdermal buprenorphine discontinued treatment. (p. 90)

Regarding group counseling, potential group members should be screened to ensure their suitability for the group. They should not be coerced into participating in group counseling either. Informed consent in a group includes providing group members information about the counselor's credentials and background, the rules and procedures that will be followed in the group, the purpose of the group, the counselor's expectations regarding how clients behave in the group, and the rights, responsibilities, and risks of belonging to the group.

Professional Responsibility and Competence

Counselors should familiarize themselves with NAADAC's code of ethics noted in the previous section entitled Relationship Boundaries With Clients. Addiction counselors must be aware of conflicting or multiple responsibilities, which may be particularly salient when clients are mandated to treatment. When there are conflicts between a counselor's duty to a client and a third party, the counselor must attempt to rectify the conflict.

It is essential that counselors running groups remember that their responsibilities are to both individual members and to the group itself. For example, if the group is scapegoating a member, counselors are obligated to protect the individual participant despite the possible impact on group membership and process. Group leaders must also watch for and intervene when other serious and personal challenges to group members occur that may have detrimental effects.

Addiction counselors need to be competent. If counselors have received general training in counseling that is not specific to addiction's work, they will need to obtain additional training and specialized supervision. The core competencies for addiction counseling can be found in the downloadable 223-page document published by the U.S. Department of Health and Human Services (DHHS, also known simply as the HHS) called *Addiction Counseling Competencies: The Knowledge, Skills, and Attitudes of Professional Practice* (download from https://aspirace.com/wp-content/uploads/2015/09/Addiction-Counseling-Competencies-CEU-Continuing-Education-Course-1.pdf). Addiction counselors engage in stressful work. They must remain aware that, if they find themselves becoming impatient or uncompromising with clients, this may indicate signs that they are becoming burned out. That is a time to particularly engage in self-care and to take a leave from addictions work if self-care strategies are insufficient. To help you assess this, consider completing the Counselor Burnout Inventory (Lee et al., 2007).

Addiction counselors running groups require specific training in group dynamics, group leadership, group counseling theories, group counseling methods and techniques, ethical considerations, and the different types of groups. As Cottone and Tarvydas (2016) stated, group counseling is "a technically sophisticated mode of treatment requiring special training" (p. 230). Addiction counselors should also lead groups under supervision until they have developed sufficient competence.

Revisiting Child Abuse

Some states have expanded the definition of child abuse to include excessive alcohol use and/or illegal drug use. In most states and the U.S. Virgin Islands, criminal statutes now exist regarding exposing children to illicit drug activity (Child Welfare Information Gateway, 2016). Exposing children to the possession of illegal drugs is considered child endangerment in 11 states, and exposing them to illicit drugs or drug paraphernalia is a crime in eight states and the Virgin Islands (Child Welfare Information Gateway, 2016).

Furthermore, Rastegar and Fingerhood (2016) reported that, in some states, counselors must report pregnant women with an SUD. According to the Guttmacher Institute (see https://www.guttmacher.org/state-policy/explore/substance-use-during-pregnancy), 24 states and the District of Columbia require healthcare professionals to report suspected prenatal drug use.

Honoring Diverse Values

Addiction counselors demonstrate respect for their clients, and part of this is honoring diversity. Counselors need to be aware of the extent to which their values influence the process of counseling (Herring, 2017). They cannot assume that everyone sees the world the same way that they do. In multicultural training, for example, it is stressed that our worldviews often differ from those of our clients and that individuals are unique. For example, two individuals who share the same sect or denomination within a religion still view many things differently from each other, including the degree to which they believe and practice the various tenets and doctrine of their faith. The important practice is to help our clients understand their attitudes, beliefs, and values (ABVs) and for them to understand the impact that inconsistencies among these may have in their lives. If clients want to change one or more of their ABVs, that is their choice to make.

Working With the Legal System and Court-Referred Clients

Working With the Legal System

"The courtroom can be a daunting arena" (Clement, 2017, p. 123). Different vocabulary is used, and professional norms are often unclear (Clement, 2017). To make matters worse, counselors are often unprepared when they find themselves in the courtroom (Francis, Oswald, & Flamez, 2018). Furthermore, research has found that counselor training often provides graduates with inadequate ethical and legal knowledge for application within court settings (Francis et al., 2018).

Ethical codes speak to the role of the expert witness in courtroom involvement. An essential aspect of court testimony is record-keeping, providing informed consent to clients, and the implications of changing from a nonforensic role to a forensic one as required in the process of court expert testimony (Francis et al., 2018).

DIFFERING WORLDVIEWS CASE EXAMPLE: WHAT WOULD *YOU* DO?

Neera, age 21, comes to see you for counseling. Although she was born in Los Angeles, her parents grew up in India. Neera's parents have decided that it is time for her to marry. Five months ago, they introduced her to Ajay, whom they think is an appropriate suitor. Ajay is 35 years old, and Neera soon found out that he smokes cannabis several times a day. Although he has maintained employment in a high-paying job, Neera finds him to be very forgetful, especially of things she has told him that she believes are important. After she tells you her story of how much she does not want to marry Ajay, you side with her and find it hard to understand why her parents would be forcing this marriage in the first place. Before the session ends, you do your best to empower Neera to make the right choice for herself.

1. What ethical issues are embedded in this scenario?
2. What would be a better way to deal with Neera?
3. Neera is not in love with Ajay; instead, she has great reservations about marrying him. What would need to happen for Neera to put an end to her parents' plans to marry her to Ajay?

If receiving a subpoena is involved, this can be both intimidating and frightful (Francis et al., 2018). Attorneys represent their clients exclusively, and counselors need to remember that they have no allegiance or care about the ethical or legal limitations that affect counselors (Francis et al., 2018).

As Marini (2016) explained, before 1993, expert witnesses could give opinions based solely on their education, training, and experience. In a 1993 decision (i.e., *Daubert v. Merrill Dow Pharmaceuticals*), however, the testimony of an expert witness was disqualified. This decision impacted the federal court system whereby expert testimony henceforth had to be empirically supported, and theories or techniques expressed within court had to be generally accepted within a profession and to have been subjected to peer review. As of 2016, 26 states have also adopted this as the standard. Another court decision in 1999 (*Kumho Tire Co. v. Carmichael*) addressed witness qualifications and under what conditions opinions could be considered in rendering conclusions.

If you are called as an expert witness, you will likely be required to give a *deposition* before a potential court appearance. There are two types of depositions: *evidentiary* and a *discovery*. In an evidentiary deposition, experts provide testimony in the same way they would in court except the setting is typically a conference room. A discovery is where the opposing attorney asks most of the questions to learn about the expert's qualifications, to review what and how conclusions were made, and to observe the credibility of the potential witness in court. In both cases, the expert is usually subpoenaed weeks before the deposition and is required to bring certain materials to it, which are each marked as exhibits (Marini, 2016).

If court work is likely going to be part of your job or career, securing a copy of Irmo Marini's (2016) chapter is recommended as well as the latest copy of Wheeler and Bertram's guide, *The Counselor and the Law: A Guide to Legal and Ethical Practice*. There are numerous strategies that counselors can use in delivery of their testimony. Marini addressed physical appearance (e.g., dress, demeanor), visual aids, language, and the style one adopts in explaining findings. Marini concluded, "The most credible and trustworthy expert is one who is confident and can remain calm under duress, stay objective, and educate the jury using nontechnical terms" (p. 583).

Taylor (2017) recommended that counselors talk clearly and politely to others in the courtroom. Furthermore, it is suggested that counselors refrain from having or developing an argumentative or defensive demeanor or tone of voice if challenged by the opposing attorney (Taylor, 2017). Cross-examination is intended to be confrontational, so it is important that you learn not to take challenges personally. "Exhibit grace under pressure" (Taylor, 2017, para. 36). Learn to stay calm under all circumstances.

Robertson (2016) interviewed Deirdra Ward, who worked as an assistant district attorney, for advice concerning how family counselors and attorneys can work together in child abuse and neglect cases. Dr. Ward's doctorate is in jurisprudence. She said that she frequently heard from counselors who stated that they were not given enough time to prepare for court. She said that a counselor "should be prepared to give testimony at any time and your documentation should be up to date and current, allowing for short notice court appearances" (p. 191). She also recommended that, before going to court, counselors should

> Review the ethical and legal boundaries of your counseling license. . . . [as] most attorneys frankly don't know the scope of practice of your licenses. . . . Unless you are trained as a psychologist and have conducted projective tests on the client, I know that your licenses do not allow you to predict the future behavior of clients. (p. 192)

Lawyers also have their own set of "trade secrets," and Dr. Ward revealed one of them:

> Many attorneys, myself included, use a technique of questioning in which we ask a series of three or four questions which have obvious yes or no answers. In this technique, all of the questions have the same consistent and very evident affirmative or negative answer. Then, following the series of questions in which you have answered "yes" 3 or 4 times or "no" 3 or 4 times, we quickly pose a question to you that we want answered yes or no, just as you have answered the previous questions. For example we might ask, "You would agree that the sky is blue," "You would agree that October is in the fall," "You would agree that counselors must have at least a master's degree," and then the zinger, "You would agree that this parent does not understand safety of the children." Based upon the previous affirmative answers, we hope the witness will simply automatically say "yes." Of course, we want the truth; however, this is a technique to extract what we sometimes see as a difficult answer regarding something that will support our argument. Thus, the lesson for you as a counselor is to think before simply answering a question. If you are not comfortable providing an answer, say so or ask the questioning attorney to clarify the question. (Robertson, 2016, pp. 192–193)

Dr. Ward also advised counselors to avoid creating an appearance of having a conflict of interest. Instead, tell the court if they might perceive or that there is a conflict of interest. For example, when a court requires that individuals receive counseling and they report they are already seeing a counselor, the court will often tell them to continue seeing their regular counselor. In this instance, it is important that the counselor immediately write to the judge and the attorneys to tell them that they are forbidden due to conflict of interest. Ethics codes state that you cannot change roles from a general counselor to a forensic counselor (Robertson, 2016). Lastly, if you don't have an answer to a question posed to you, simply make that clear. It is better to say that you don't know something than to testify "yes" or "no." Also, do not say "yes" to a question when the answer is really a "maybe." Under all circumstances, tell only the truth, and do not embellish statements. Simplicity is sacrosanct (Taylor, 2017).

Ordway and Moore (2015) provided counselors 10 simple guidelines to follow when dealing with families engaged in high-conflict divorce, separation, and custody litigation. Although most of these pertain to court work, some of them can also be implemented in the next section entitled Working With Court-Referred Clients. Addiction counselors can benefit from being aware of these guidelines, and the examples provided all pertain to addiction work:

1. Remain mindful of possible ulterior motives. An attorney may refer a client for counseling with hopes of arguing that the addicted client is receiving appropriate care, and, consequently, say that he or she is at lesser risk regarding the legal matter. Also, clients may intentionally lie to make themselves look better in court.

2. Be familiar with your role and avoid dual or multiple relationships. For example, you might be asked questions that would be better answered by someone who has conducted an impartial assessment. The role of counseling is *always* in conflict with the purpose of unbiased evaluation.

3. Maintain familiarity with the latest ethical codes, legal statutes, and best practices. When in doubt, always consult with the ethical codes that guide your practice. For most addiction counselors, this will include the ethics codes from ACA and NAADAC. Also, become familiar with relevant federal laws, state laws, and regulations. Always refer clients to attorneys when legal advice is required.

4. Obtain written consent and document all contacts. Ensure that your consent form contains information pertaining to legal matters such as the possibility that your records could be subpoenaed and other requirements if your clients are court referred.

5. Maintain objectivity. There is usually more than one side to the "truth." Given that clients will likely have a vested interest in not sharing incriminating evidence, it is important that, in the documentation or court, it is clear what clients have *reported* being true and what has been *substantiated* to be true.

6. Maintain neutrality. Particularly regarding children, it is often easier to believe the person that you have listened to or heard from the most. Remain aware of the bias that this can create.

7. Refrain from offering opinions regarding individuals that you have never met. Instead, stick with what you know. If you have not met an individual that you are being questioned about, you do not (in a courtroom or any other legal matter) have an opinion to share about this person.

8. Assume that you will need to appear in court at some time in your career. A subpoena can trump whatever agreement you may have with clients to the contrary (i.e., stating you will not appear in court on their behalf).

9. Consult when necessary. Consult with your state licensing board, an attorney, or your liability insurance carrier when needed. If you are subpoenaed, consulting with an attorney before releasing documents or providing testimony is recommended.

10. Pick your words carefully. Speak only to that which you know because words can mean everything in court. Avoid supposition and assumption. Support recommendations and opinions with facts, best practices, and empirical evidence.

Working With Court-Referred Clients

Research has found that, whereas less than 7% of offenders experience schizophrenia, estimates range between 50% and 100% regarding the proportion that would receive a mental health diagnosis (Simourd, 2016). Also, most of these individuals would be diagnosed with antisocial personality disorder and/or substance abuse disorders. As Simourd (2016) stated, "they are more likely to be 'bad' rather than 'mad'" (p. 434). Results from meta-analyses indicate that individuals in custody who do not receive any treatment experience a 7% *increase* in recidivism, those receiving insight-oriented therapy experience a 5% *increase* in recidivism, those receiving unstructured skill-based therapy have a 14% *reduction* in recidivism, whereas those who receive structured skill-based therapy (of a cognitive-behavioral type) have a 30% *reduction* in recidivism (Simourd, 2016). Although these statistics refer to individuals serving time in jail, they nonetheless indicate that CBT is especially effective even when clients are mandatory.

Simourd (2016) stated that most criminal justice clients experience multiple problems in managing life areas, not all of which are related to their criminality. Consequently, the key to working with these clients is to focus on the factors that are most responsible for their criminal behavior (Simourd, 2016). In the work of addiction counseling, this often means dealing with SUDs and other behavioral addictions.

Like all counselors, addiction counselors need to stay focused on helping clients achieve goals. In working with non-court-referred clients, the goal is often to improve their well-being. When working with court-referred clients, Simourd (2016) stated that the primary goal is to reduce reoffending. Simourd suggested that a useful way to improve counseling outcomes is to address the clients' deficits that are linked to their criminal risk potential.

Meta-analyses have also revealed that there are eight typical and relevant risk factors that lead individuals to recidivate (Simourd, 2016). These are as follows, in diminishing order of importance, including suggestions by Simourd for decreasing their likelihood:

#	Risk Factor	Counselors Should Focus on Helping Clients
1	Having a history of antisocial behavior	Develop alternative behaviors to their high-risk situations
2	Having a diagnosis of antisocial personality disorder	Develop general self-management and problem-solving skills
3	Antisocial cognitions	Enhance prosocial thinking and reduce procriminal thinking
4	Having antisocial associates	Reduce contact with these individuals
5	Family/marital problems	Enhance positive relationships and reduce conflict
6	School/work problems	Enhance rewards for improvements in performance
7	Low involvement in leisure/recreation	Enhance rewards for increasing involvement
8	Substance abuse	Enhance alternatives to drug use and reduce substance abuse

For her dissertation, Ragas (2018) interviewed 11 counselors who had reputations of being successful at managing resistance from court-mandated clients. Six themes emerged from her interviews:

1. Resistance. Participants noted that the perception of resistance is subjective. For example, resistance might be perceived as fighting against change or wanting clients to do something with which they are not in agreement. Resistance was not regarded as necessarily a negative quality in working with mandated clients.
2. Managing Resistance. Participants recommended not fighting resistance. One recommended in fact "getting in front of the client's punches" (p. 48). It is important not to take resistance personally. Let clients know that you are not there to hurt them.
3. Progress Versus Stagnation. Clients may resist counseling by fighting against change. Participants stated the change occurs in different stages and that it often occurs over time. It is essential to be patient when working with mandated clients.
4. Judicial System's Receptiveness. Most of the participants (10 out of 11) said that the courts were receptive to their recommendations for treatment.
5. Identifying Barriers. Participants commented on how several factors like gender and race/ethnicity can create barriers. Some of the male clients presented a "tough guy" attitude. White counselors might experience resistance with Black clients and Hispanic males. One participant stated that people of color in Louisiana, for example, "don't view counseling as a good thing – whether it's mandated or they volunteer for it" (p. 62). Cognitive functioning and language skills were also noted as potential barriers.
6. Determining Success. Determining success might be based on body language and clients' eagerness to reveal themselves to counselors. One participant stated that progress didn't have to be something big. Being satisfied with clients gaining even a few insights constituted progress. Success occurs when clients are working toward reaching their goals. It is also recognizable when they are no longer exhibiting or displaying the behaviors that led to their court referral in the first place.

Special Considerations in Offering Couples, Marriage, and Family Counseling

Marriage and family therapy (which will be referred to herein as couples, marriage, and family counseling [CMFC]), began in the mid-1950s, and, by 1970, had become its own counseling specialty. Since the 1970s, there has been a dramatic increase in the number of individuals practicing CMFC (Haley, 2015). CMFC is its own specialty, but counselors trained in related fields also practice it. Training in CMFC includes theories related to couples and families, family and relationship dynamics including issues of power and hierarchy, decision-making, communication patterns and skills, family roles, and the family life cycle. Those who train specifically as CMFCs will likely want to pursue membership in the American Association for Marriage and Family Therapy (AAMFT). The AAMFT has its own ethical code, the most recent version of which came into effect on January 1, 2015 (the version is available from https://www.aamft.org/Legal_Ethics/Code_of_Ethics.aspx). Licensed AAMFT members focus on a strength-based approach (as opposed to a medical model), using methods that are usually brief and solution focused aimed at specific and attainable goals (Haley, 2015).

The AAMFT includes primarily the same ethical considerations that are included in other ethical codes. An area that came under scrutiny was that the CMFC profession was focused mostly on preparing masters-level counselors and not researchers. The AAMFT code beginning in 2012 addressed the importance of scholarship (Haley, 2015). Interestingly, there remains a lack of diversity among CMFC counselors. Two studies reported by Haley (2015) found that most are Caucasian (91%) and female (60%) with a mean age of 54 years.

An AAFMT task force created a list of 128 competencies, which can be found on their website (https://www.aamft.org/). Haley (2015) mentioned that many training programs have based their curriculum on these core competencies. CMFC programs can be accredited through either the Commission on Accreditation for Marriage and Family Therapy Education (COAMFTE) or the Council for Accreditation of Counseling and Related Programs (CACREP). Although accreditation is a voluntary process, students often benefit from graduating from an accredited program in most if not all fields of practice.

Working with couples and families can be very challenging (Sobhana, Saxena, & Daimari, 2016). According to Hecker and Murphy (2015), some family therapists (FTs) have developed what Hecker and Murphy referred to as "defensive clinical practice" (p. 469), which is where FTs have become overconcerned with the increasing litigiousness of American society and have based their treatment decisions solely on having fears of litigation. Hecker and Murphy made several other key points in their article, one of which they called "relational ethics." They provided Shaw's (as cited in Hecker & Murphy, 2015) definition as follows:

> Relational ethics encompasses the territory in which people come to reflect on, think about, and decide on their obligations and responsibilities to self and others. The reflections take into account personal and community values, morals, and preferences. A process of ethical reflection requires rationality, attunement to feelings and intuitions, and attention to care-in-relationships. (p. 468)

Hecker and Murphy stated that relational ethics is beginning to appear in the field of family counseling. A critical component of relational ethics is to understand people in the context of not only their families but also in their communities.

Another key point made by Hecker and Murphy (2015) was their belief that e-therapy will likely be the future of family counseling. They included some preliminary research suggesting that the working alliance is sometimes stronger in online counseling than in face-to-face counseling. Family counseling is also struggling regarding how to use relational ethics in counseling LGBTQ clients. Although counselors are expected to become multiculturally competent, some counselors are reluctant to work with LGBTQ clients because of their personal or faith-related beliefs. This creates a schism regarding the intent of ethics codes.

Regarding work with minors, Sori and Hecker (2015) commented on how the issues of privacy, confidentiality, and legal privilege can be difficult because parents, children, and other stakeholders often have competing interests. Counselors need to be aware of several considerations before sharing information from a minor with parents. Although parents usually have the right to know what is happening during their child's counseling, this varies among states. In most cases, information should be shared with parents "when it is in the *best interest of the child*" (italics included in the quote; Sori & Hecker, 2015, p. 455).

Four positions that a counselor can take in sharing information to parents are (a) complete confidentiality (with exceptions covered earlier in the chapter), (b) limited confidentiality (this requires the minor to waive in advance what will and will not be revealed to parents or guardians), (c) informed forced consent (the child has no say in what is disclosed, but he or she is notified before the disclosure occurs), and (d) no guarantee of confidentiality (where the counselor believes that "secrets" could negatively impact individual and family counseling) (Sori & Hecker, 2015). Whichever approach is taken must be disclosed to both children and parents.

I would encourage counselors to use a collaborative approach wherever possible so that all parties are in agreement. Notwithstanding the previous approaches, one is still obligated by state and federal laws to disclose to parents where stipulated. Sori and Hecker also reminded readers that laws typically supersede ethical codes, and they often vary from state to state and from country to country. Consequently, it is critical that counselors be aware of the laws in their jurisdiction.

The ethical concerns that typically arise in family counseling include informed consent for all family members, multiple relationships, confidentiality, and legal issues (e.g., custody) (Lambert, Carmichael, & Williams, 2016). Lambert et al. (2016) recommended that counselors become trained in family counseling approaches before attempting to use them in session, and they should also seek supervision to gain experience in providing this service. The same applies to offering couples and marriage counseling.

Resolving Ethical Issues

Levitt, Farry, and Mazzarella (2015) reported that more than 30 different ethical decision-making models have arisen in the counseling literature over the past 3 decades. Despite this plethora of choices, Cottone and Claus (2000) stated that few of the available models have been tested empirically, and few are grounded either theoretically or philosophically. These models have covered several foci, including "multiculturalism, collaboration, counselor education, and counselor settings" (Levitt et al., 2015, p. 84). Levitt et al. found in their qualitative study ($N = 6$; 5 White women, 1 White man) that a counselor's ethical decision-making was based on four themes: (a) counselors' personal values, (b) clients' best interests, (c) transparency in making decisions, and (d) how they perceived their formal training and practice.

Canter, Bennett, Jones, and Nagy (1994) created a seven-step decision-making model that is easy to follow:

1. Know the applicable code of ethics.
2. Know the state and federal laws and regulations that are applicable.
3. Know the rules and regulations of your employer.
4. Engage in continuing your education in ethics.
5. Identify the potential ethical problem.
6. Learn how to analyze complex ethical obligations.
7. Consult with senior addiction professionals.

Other steps that could be included as part of point 6 are (a) generate potential courses of action, (b) consider the potential consequences of each action by evaluating the rights, responsibilities, and welfare of all people impacted, and (c) determine a course of action. Regarding point 7, one can also get feedback from peers and one's supervisor (Cottone & Claus, 2000).

Bradley and Hendricks (2008) suggested that, when counselors are in an ethical dilemma, they should consider asking themselves the following questions:

- What is the core dilemma?
- If you were consulting with the counselor, what would your potential course(s) of action be?
- If you were a member of a disciplinary board taking action against this counselor, what would your potential course of action be to ensure client welfare?
- What course of action (if any) would you take regarding disciplinary action against the counselor?
- Would you suggest that the counselor become more familiar with an ethics code even though the code may not directly address the situation?
- As a disciplinary board member, would you suggest supervision for this counselor? If so, what would the justification be for this supervision? (p. 263)

Record-Keeping Standards

All mental health professionals must keep thorough written records of their work with clients. Marino (as cited in Fisher & Harrison, 2013, p. 95) wrote

> By keeping good records, counselors can ensure that their clients and their own best interests are served. . . . Without proper records, there is no way another counselor can intervene when the assigned counselor is not available, no way to defend themselves in a lawsuit and no way to verify a payable service.

But the reasons are more inclusive than what Marino has stated. Mitchell (2007), in his publication about record-keeping published by the ACA, wrote that the number of lawsuits and allegations made against counselors is increasing. He stated that counselors' vulnerability is heightened if they do not provide adequate documentation or if they fail to adhere to the ACA Code of Ethics (or other ethics code specific to addiction counselors). Mitchell stated that the legal system relies heavily on documentation that assists it in making decisions about involuntary hospitalization, child custody issues, and many other situations.

Symons (2004) offered a few helpful suggestions regarding record-keeping. His ideas include (a) maintain all entries in chronological order, (b) record information as soon as possible,

ETHICAL DECISION-MAKING CASE EXAMPLE: WHAT WOULD *YOU* DO?

Use the aforementioned suggestions in thinking through what ethical decision you should make regarding how you would deal with the following example. You are in private practice, and a 14-year-old girl named Emma finds herself in your waiting room. You were not expecting her, but you can see that she is highly distraught. She caught you at an appropriate time as you have the next hour free, but you ask her while she is seated, "What is wrong?" Emma replies, "A friend told me to take some LSD. I have never tried drugs before, but I feel so awful, and a voice in my head keeps telling me to kill myself. I saw the sign outside that says you are a licensed counselor. I really need your help right now." What action should you take, given that she is only 14 and you do not have consent from a parent or guardian?

1. Besides the fact that she is a minor, what other ethical issues are embedded in this scenario?
2. If you decide to bring her into your office, what might you say to her?
3. Let's say you decided to try contacting one of her parents to get consent, but Emma refuses to let you because she believes that her parents will possibly strike out at her physically because of their reported view on illegal drug use. What do you do?

(c) if writing notes, make alterations with a straight line, date it, and initial it, (d) stick to providing concise descriptions of behaviors, (e) refrain from including diagnoses and interpretation (unless qualified and expected to do so), and (f) limit records to directly relevant information. Notes of contacts with family members, friends, or others should be kept separately to protect their confidentiality. Records need to be stored securely and not accessible to unauthorized individuals. APA also provides some valuable insights regarding record-keeping (available at https://www.apa.org/monitor/2012/02/ce-corner.aspx).

Dierdre Ward, JD, stated the following regarding notes (this advice was given in the instance where you may need to testify in court):

> Clearly written documentation is vital. You don't have to write down everything, but if something important happens, you have to write it down. The old adage is true that if something isn't documented, it didn't happen. Don't depend solely on your memory when you are testifying. In your notes, document the content of sessions, behavioural observations, treatment plan, and treatment goals. Document the progress toward goals. Finally, please remember to document missed appointments and why a client says they missed an appointment. (Robertson, 2016, p. 194)

In the addictions field, regulations by accrediting bodies and state agencies often specify the form and content of both treatment plans and progress notes. They also specify how often written documentation must occur (Fisher & Harrison, 2013). Agencies will often have their way of recording written documentation, but those in private practice might need to rely on their judgment. Fisher and Harrison (2013) recommended that you ensure that your clinical record notes would be defensible in a courtroom. How do you do that? Make entries brief and mostly factual. Clearly label when you are stating opinions and conclusions. Avoid using terms that are not generally used by professionals (e.g., inner child work). Clearly document any reports of child abuse and neglect, including the name and title of the person providing the information. Carefully document any incidents that involve the health, safety, or security of the client. An example of headings for clinical record notes completed in the first session and subsequent sessions can be found in Appendices 2B and 2C.

Third-Party and Private Practice Reimbursement

Current Initiative of the American Counseling Association

One of the top priorities of the Government Affairs team with ACA (2019) is to get a proposed federal law passed that would allow licensed professional counselors to obtain reimbursement for services through Medicare. ACA (2019) reported that Medicare, established in 1965, is the most extensive health insurance program in the United States. It covers more than 43 million Americans, ages 65 and older, and another 10 million individuals with disabilities. Although the plan has covered services provided by psychologists and clinical social workers since 1989, it does not cover those provided by Licensed Professional Counselors (LPCs). LPCs are licensed to practice counseling in all 50 states. Furthermore, they *are* covered by private health plans.

Managed Care

Today, many counselors either are employed by managed care companies or are under contract with them (Fisher & Harrison, 2013). *Managed care* is a system of healthcare whereby individuals agree to receive health-related services only from specific counselors, agencies, doctors, hospitals, etc. This means that counseling services are paid for by the managed care company after they receive invoices. Some ethical issues have arisen through the practice of managed care. Fisher and Harrison (2013) outlined some of the ethical dilemmas that can result, such as a client who does not have benefits that cover SUDs but whose plan will cover other mental disorder diagnoses.

Another example would be if you believe a client needs inpatient treatment, but their managed healthcare covers only outpatient services for a limited number of sessions. What do you do? Some managed healthcare companies will also stipulate what kinds of counseling intervention you can offer if you expect to get paid. This will frequently rule in cognitive-behavioral, behavioral, or short-term, solution-focused approaches while ruling out other forms of treatment in which you may be trained.

Private Practice Clients

Another situation that can affect counselors in private practice is that their livelihood depends on having a sufficient number of paying clients. What do you do if you find that, during the warmer months, your client base greatly diminishes and your current clients want to finish in fewer numbers of sessions? Another issue might be whether you offer packages for a certain number of sessions, or how you collect payment if the client fails to pay in a timely fashion.

Summary of Reimbursement Issues

Here is a summary of the issues that you may need to resolve:

1. Loss of personal autonomy. Either the managed care company tells you how to do your job (e.g., what treatment approach you will take, how many sessions they will cover, how much they pay per session) or private practice clients tell you the approach they want or the number of sessions they can afford.
2. Keeping a business afloat or following the highest level of ethical practice? What do you do when these are at odds with each other? We all know what would be ethical in these situations but, in actual practice, at what cost?

Counselor Recovery Status

Addiction counseling began as a true anomaly in mental health practice. The historical roots of addiction counseling were based more on the experience of recovering counselors than on empirical findings in the field (Crabb, 2003). As Doukas (2015) aptly noted, recovering volunteers and counselors in the addictions field "have a long and distinguished history as agents of treatment" (p. 244).

The advantages and disadvantages of addiction counselors in recovery versus those who are not has been studied for decades (Robinson, 2018). Individuals who have successfully dealt with their addiction often have a profound understanding and deep empathy for their clients, and clients often appreciate their experience (Herring, 2017). For some clients, having a counselor with similar experience increases their credibility (Toriello & Strohmer, 2004). Research by Stoffelmayr, Mavis, and Kasim (1998) found that recovering counselors helped clients pursue more diverse goals and used more treatment techniques compared with nonrecovering counselors. The counselor's personal experience with addiction may provide hope to clients that change is possible. It may help reduce the shame that binds most addicted clients (Herring, 2017).

Nonetheless, there are some important considerations and cautions:

1. *Insufficient recovery*. Recovering counselors need to have sustained abstinence from their addictive behaviors before working with clients. Otherwise, they may have (a) some degree of cognitive impairment (e.g., some drugs such as cannabis are fat-soluble and can create insidious effects that last for weeks beyond abstinence; see Chapter 10), (b) some loss of objectivity (e.g., overidentifying with the client's struggles), and (c) a higher likelihood of relapsing themselves. Sustained abstinence is an ethical requirement for working in the field (Herring, 2017). When recovering counselors relapse, they must decide whether to reduce, suspend, or end their clinical duties (Herring, 2017). In a study of 657 male, 580 female, and 2 transgender addiction counselors (ages 18–70), the overall relapse rate was nearly 38% (Jones, Sells, & Rehfuss, 2009).
2. *Rigidity regarding therapeutic approach or goals*. Recovering counselors need to be careful that they are not overly committed to the treatment approach that worked for them. For example, counselors who found a 12-step program effective may find it difficult to accept that nonabstinence may be attainable by some individuals with SUDs or behavioral addictions (Herring, 2017).
3. *Excessive self-disclosure*. When counselors have had a similar experience to their clients, they run the risk of sharing too much information about themselves. Too much self-disclosure takes the focus off the client and places it on the counselor. When counselors self-disclose, they need to remain self-aware as to whether the disclosure is helping clients explore their issues with greater depth or if it is alienating them from this process. This includes disclosure of one's sexual or affectional orientation. Schneider and Levinson (2006) quoted a gay therapist who aptly recommended, "Disclose only that which is in the service of the client and only when it is in the service of the client" (p. 34).
4. *Compromised confidentiality and anonymity* (Cottone & Tarvydas, 2016). Ethical issues are raised if recovering counselors are attending the same mutual support groups as current or former clients. It is ethically inappropriate if these counselors sponsor their clients or lead 12-step meetings where they are employed (Herring, 2017). In what ways are clients' rights to confidentiality compromised when their counselor is attending the same meeting? How is the counselor's anonymity at risk? What are appropriate ways for the recovering counselors to deal with the social relationships that often form in these meetings? If recovering counselors can attend meetings that are not frequented by their clients, that resolves this issue, but that will not be possible in smaller locales or with some addictions (e.g., some places might only have one Marijuana Anonymous meeting). It is essential that counselors remain cognizant of these potential dual roles and that they do their best to avoid them (Doyle, 1997).

RESOURCES AND VIDEOS

Resources

1. National Association for Addiction Professionals (NAADAC). https://www.naadac.org/
2. ACA Code of Ethics (2014). https://www.counseling.org/resources/aca-code-of-ethics.pdf
3. Ethical Principles of Psychologists and Code of Contact. American Psychological Association (APA). https://www.apa.org/ethics/code/index.aspx
4. American Psychological Association Record Keeping Guidelines. https://www.apa.org/practice/guidelines/record-keeping.aspx
5. Ethical and Legal Issues in Counseling / Ethical Standards and Laws. https://www.sulross.edu/sites/default/files/sites/default/files/users/docs/education/counseling-ethics_6.pdf
6. A Matter of Law: Patient Record Keeping, Part 1. (APA). https://www.apaservices.org/practice/business/legal/professional/records and A Matter of Law: Patient Record Keeping, Part 2. (APA). https://www.apaservices.org/practice/business/legal/professional/records2

Videos

To view these videos, search their titles on YouTube.

1. *Legal and Ethical Standards for Addiction Counseling | Confidentiality | Self Care* by Addiction Professional Lena Schefeild, LMHC, CAP, MAC, CEDS. Published on Nov 7, 2016.
2. *Law vs. Ethics - Dr. Dean Aslinia.* Published on Sep 7, 2016.
3. *NCYI Free Training—Legal & Ethical Issues for School Counselors with Dr. Carolyn Stone.* Published on Mar 18, 2014.
4. *NAADAC and NBCC Ethics for Counselors.* AllCEUs Counseling Education. Published on Jan 10, 2013.
5. *Counseling: Confidentiality.* Mometrix Academy.

JOURNALS AND CONFERENCES

Journals

There is no peer-reviewed journal specifically dedicated to the ethics, legal, or professional (ELP) issues involved in addiction counseling. The following list contains more generic journals regarding ethics in counseling practice. Most, if not all, journals in the addictions field publish articles on ELP issues, so the journals listed in Chapters 9 through 21 will be relevant to you as well.

1. *Journal of Addictions and Offender Counseling.* ACA also publishes this journal on behalf of the International Association of Addictions and Offender Counselors (IAAOC). IAAOC's website: http://www.iaaoc.org/

   Journal information: https://onlinelibrary.wiley.com/journal/21611874

2. *Counseling and Values.* A journal published by ACA on behalf of the Association for Spiritual, Ethical, and Religious Values in Counseling (ASERVIC). ASERVIC's website: https://www.counseling.org/about-us/governance-bylaws/candidate-profiles/divisions-and-regions/association-for-spiritual-ethical-and-religious-values-in-counseling

   Journal information: https://onlinelibrary.wiley.com/journal/2161007X

3. *Journal of Mental Health Counseling.* http://amhcajournal.org/

   Quoted from website:

   "The quarterly *Journal of Mental Health Counseling* (JMHC) provides clinical mental health counselors and researchers with practical knowledge and illuminating background from in-depth research on clinical studies and counseling practice. Published since 1978, *JMHC* articles address all aspects of practice, theory, professionalism, and research related to clinical mental health counseling."

4. *Journal of Ethics in Mental Health.* https://jemh.ca/index.html

   Quoted from website:

   "The Journal of Ethics in Mental Health is an international, peer-reviewed, web-based journal, available free on-line worldwide. The journal was developed in association with The Ontario Shores Centre for Mental Health Sciences and McMaster University (Canada). PURPOSE: The journal aims at providing a useful forum for sharing ideas and experiences among all who are committed to improving ethical standards, behaviors, and choices in mental health care giving."

Conferences

1. National Association of Alcoholism and Drug Abuse Counselors (NAADAC) Annual Conference. This organization is generally called the Association for Addiction Professionals, and it is the largest professional organization for addiction counselors. Check https://www.naadac.org/annualconference for details.
2. Annual Law and Ethics in Counseling Conference. Check www.aascb.org/ for details.
3. Law and Ethics in Counseling Conference. Check Google to find out if an upcoming conference has been scheduled.
4. National Counseling Advances Conference. Check Google to find out if an upcoming conference has been scheduled.
5. Check annual conferences for ACA, American Mental Health Counselors Association, and other national or state counseling associations. Large addiction organizations also have annual conferences (e.g., American Society of Addictive Medicine, National Institute on Drug Abuse, Substance Abuse and Mental Health Services Administration; see others listed in the Conferences sections of Chapters 9–21). Although these conferences do not deal specifically with ethical, legal, and professional issues, they will often have one or more presentations on these topics.

INDIVIDUAL EXERCISES

1. Check with a counseling regulatory body in your state and ask if it could provide you with information regarding the nature of the ethics violations that have occurred with its members over the past year. This information is generally available in the annual report. Take note of which violations are most common and which occur infrequently.
2. Have a careful look at the six ethical principles and the five ethical standards that are described in this chapter. Which ones do you believe would be most comfortable for you to follow, and which ones would be more difficult for you? Also, ask yourself what makes adhering to some of these challenging for you.
3. Because of the growing litigiousness of American society, some counselors change their practice so that treatments become based more on protecting oneself than on what is in the best interests of the client. Hecker and Murphy (2015) referred to this as "defensive clinical practice." What other way could responsible counselors operate that would provide them protection from legal intervention while at the same time promote the best interests of the client? If you get stuck answering this question, pull up a copy of Hecker and Murphy's article.

CLASSROOM EXERCISES

1. Separate the class into two groups. Have one group take the position that alcohol treatment programs have the right to discharge clients if found drinking while in the program, and the other group take the view that treatment programs have a duty to care despite the struggles that some clients have with maintaining sobriety during treatment. Provide each side 10 minutes to develop their positions. Follow this with either a debate or a class discussion (adapted from National Institute on Alcohol Abuse and Alcoholism [NIAAA], 2005).
2. Break the class into small groups of three or four. Have them discuss the various aspects of today's technology and how different devices can affect, both positively and negatively, addiction counseling practice. Some topics include how technology affects confidentiality, the maintenance and security of records, informed consent, sharing information both within and between agencies, service delivery without face-to-face contact, how to protect the identity of clients, clients' ability to access information over the Internet, and clients' access to alternative treatments (adapted from NIAAA, 2005).
3. One aspect of professional ethics that was not discussed in this chapter involves fellow addiction counselors who become impaired in their ability to counsel clients or who engage in one or more unethical practices. Lead a discussion regarding what students believe should occur when peers are either impaired or act unethically. Follow this discussion by referring to ACA's (2014) Code of Ethics or another respected ethics code (adapted from NIAAA, 2005; have a look at this resource for additional discussion topics).

CHAPTER SUMMARY

Chapter 2 began by looking at the ethics and legalities that encompass general counseling practice. Although many ethics codes guide counseling, this chapter highlighted those addressed in ACA's (2014) Code of Ethics. Ethical dilemmas are sometimes complicated and occasionally result in tension between what is legal and what is ethical. Although counselors must follow a code of ethics, state and federal laws supersede whatever is contained in ethics codes. Counselors need to be aware of applicable laws in their jurisdiction.

The six ethical principles are autonomy, nonmaleficence, beneficence, justice, fidelity, and veracity. Each of these was defined followed by a case example to provide greater clarity and understanding. Ethical standards specific to the profession were then considered. These offer directives and/or guidelines to counselors. The ethical standards described included confidentiality and privacy, privileged communication, relationship boundaries with clients, informed consent, and professional responsibility and competence. A case example also followed the discussion of each.

The next major section focused on issues specific to addiction counseling, described under the same headings as those used under the ethical standards. The ethics of group counseling were included under these headings as well. Some discussion then followed regarding child abuse and honoring diverse values. Then the ethics underlying couples, marriage, and family counseling were addressed. Resolving ethical issues followed.

Record-keeping standards were covered, and several tips were offered aimed at improving the notes kept by addiction counselors. Third-party and private practice reimbursement issues were then reviewed. Finally, a special section called Counselor Recovery Status highlighted some of the advantages and disadvantages of counselors who are themselves in recovery from addiction.

REFERENCES

American Counseling Association (ACA). (2014). *2014 ACA code of ethics*. Retrieved from file:///C:/Users/Owner-PC/Desktop/aca-code-of-ethics.pdf

American Counseling Association (ACA). (2019). *Medicare reimbursement*. Retrieved on January 17, 2019, from https://www.counseling.org/government-affairs/federal-issues/medicare-reimbursement

Bradley, L. J., & Hendricks, C. B. (2008). Ethical decision making: Basic issues. *Family Journal, 16*, 261–263.

Canter, M. B., Bennett, B. E., Jones, S. E., & Nagy, T. F. (1994). *Ethics for psychologists: A commentary on the APA Ethics Code*. Washington, DC: American Psychological Association.

Child Welfare Information Gateway. (2016). *Parental drug use as child abuse*. Washington, DC: U.S. Department of Health and Human Services, Children's Bureau. Retrieved on January 14, 2019, from https://www.childwelfare.gov/pubpdfs/drugexposed.pdf

Clement, L. (2017). Navigating legal issues and serving your client. In T. A. Sartor, B. McHenry, & J. McHenry (Eds.), *Ethical and legal issues in counseling children and adolescents* (pp. 123–133). New York, NY: Routledge/Taylor & Francis.

Cottone, R. R., & Claus, R. E. (2000). Ethical decision-making models: A review of the literature. *Journal of Counseling and Development, 78*(3), 275–283.

Cottone, R. R., & Tarvydas, V. (2016). *Ethics and decision making in counseling and psychotherapy* (4th ed.). New York, NY: Springer.

Crabb, A. E. (2003). Substance abuse treatment: Substance abuse counselors' belief systems and how these beliefs impact treatment. *Dissertation Abstracts International: Section B: The Sciences and Engineering, 63*(9-B), 4364. Retrieved from http://ovidsp.ovid.com/ovidweb.cgi?T=JS&PAGE=reference&D=psyc4&NEWS=N&AN=2003-95006-279

Doukas, N. (2015). A contemporary new role for counselors in recovery: Recovery coaches in communities of recovery. *Alcoholism Treatment Quarterly, 33*, 244–247.

Doyle, K. (1997). Substance abuse counselors in recovery: Implications for the ethical issue of dual relationships. *Journal of Counseling & Development, 75*, 428–432.

Fisher, G. L., & Harrison, T. C. (2013). *Substance abuse information for school counselors, social workers, therapists, and counselors* (5th ed.). Upper Saddle River, NJ: Pearson.

Francis, J. D., Oswald, G. R., & Flamez, B. (2018). Reducing ethical complaints through professional counselor competency in court testimony. *Family Journal, 26*, 64–72.

Geppert, C. M. A. (2013). Legal and ethical issues. In B. S. McCrady & E. E. Epstein (Eds.), *Addictions: A comprehensive guidebook* (2nd ed., pp. 625–640). New York, NY: Oxford University Press.

Haley, M. (2015). Legal, ethical, and professional issues. In D. Capuzzi & M. D. Stauffer (Eds.), *Foundations of couples, marriage, and family counseling* (pp. 101–126). Hoboken, NJ: John Wiley & Sons.

Hecker, L. L., & Edwards, A. B. (2014). The impact of HIPAA and HITECH: New standards for confidentiality, security, and documentation for marriage and family therapists. *American Journal of Family Therapy, 42*(2), 95–113.

Hecker, L. L., & Murphy, M. J. (2015). Contemporary and emerging ethical issues in family therapy. *Australian and New Zealand Journal of Family Therapy, 36*(4), 467–479.

Herring, B. (2017). *A basic set of core ethical guidelines for addiction treatment professionals*. Retrieved on January 14, 2019, from http://billherring.com/basic-set-core-ethical-guidelines-addiction-treatment-professionals

Jaffe, S. (2018). The collective power of #me too. *Dissent, 65*(2), 80–87.

Jones, T., Sells, J. N., & Rehfuss, M. (2009). How wounded the healers? The prevalence of relapse among addiction counselors in recovery from alcohol and other drugs. *Alcoholism Treatment Quarterly, 27*, 389–408.

Kunkel, T. (2012). *Substance abuse and confidentiality: 42CFR Part 2*. Retrieved on April 22, 2019, from https://www.ncsc.org/

sitecore/content/microsites/future-trends-2012/home/Privacy-and-Technology/Substance-Abuse.aspx

Lambert, S. F., Carmichael, A. R., & Williams, L. (2016). Guidelines in counseling families. In I. Marini & M. A. Stebnicki (Eds.), *The professional counselor's desk reference* (2nd ed., pp. 351–355). New York, NY: Springer.

Large, M. M., & Ryan, C. J. (2015). Violence risk assessment has not been shown to reduce violence. *Australian and New Zealand Journal of Psychiatry*, *49*, 91.

Lee, S. M., Baker, C. R., Cho, S. H., Heckathorn, D. E., Holland, M. W., Newgent, R. A., . . . Yu, K. (2007). Development and initial psychometrics of the Counselor Burnout Inventory. *Measurement and Evaluation in Counseling and Development*, *40*(3), 142–154.

Levitt, D. H., Farry, T. J., & Mazzarella, J. R. (2015). Counselor ethical reasoning: Decision-making practice versus theory. *Counseling and Values*, *60*, 84–99.

Marini, I. (2016). Testifying issues and strategies as an expert witness. In I. Marini & M. A. Stebnicki (Eds.), *The professional counselor's desk reference* (2nd ed., pp. 579–583). New York, NY: Springer.

Mitchell, R. W. (2007). *Documentation in counseling records: An overview of ethical, legal, and clinical issues* (3rd ed.). Alexandria, VA: American Counseling Association.

Morgan, J. R., Schackman, B. R., Leff, J. A., Linas, B. P., & Walley, A. Y. (2018). Injectable naltrexone, oral naltrexone, and buprenorphine utilization and discontinuation among individuals treated for opioid use disorder in a United States commercially insured population. *Journal of Substance Abuse Treatment*, *85*, 90–96.

Mullen, P. R., Lambie, G. W., & Conley, A. H. (2014). Development of the Ethical and Legal Issues in Counseling Self-Efficacy Scale. *Measurement and Evaluation in Counseling and Development*, *47*(1), 62–78.

Murow Klein, R., & Yeung, L. (2018, March 7). *42 C.F.R. Part 2: Understanding the new final rules and where we go from here*. Retrieved on April 22, 2019, from https://www.naadac.org/assets/2416/understanding_cfr_part_2_webinarslides.pdf

National Association for Addiction Professionals (NAADAC). (2016). *Code of ethics*. Retrieved on April 22, 2019, from https://www.naadac.org/code-of-ethics

National Institute on Alcohol Abuse and Alcoholism (NIAAA). (2005, March). *Social work education for the prevention and treatment of alcohol use disorders*. Retrieved on January 14, 2019, from https://pubs.niaaa.nih.gov/publications/Social/Module9Legal&EthicalIssues/Module9.html

Nicholls, T. L., Pritchard, M. M., Reeves, K. A., & Hilterman, E. (2013). Risk assessment in intimate partner violence: A systematic review of contemporary approaches. *Partner Abuse*, *4*, 76–168.

Ordway, A. M., & Moore, R. O. (2015, October 21). Stuck in the middle. *Counseling Today*. Retrieved on April 19, 2019, from https://ct.counseling.org/2015/10/stuck-in-the-middle/

Owen, J., Drinane, J. M., Tao, K. W., DasGupta, D. R., Zhang, Y. S. D., & Adelson, J. (2018). An experimental test of microaggression detection in psychotherapy: Therapist multicultural orientation. *Professional Psychology: Research and Practice*, *49*(1), 9–21.

Ragas, C. (2018). Counselor experiences with successfully managing resistance with court-mandated clients. *Dissertation Abstracts International: Section B: The Sciences and Engineering, 79*(9-B(E)). No Pagination Specified.

Rastegar, D., & Fingerhood, M. (2016). *The American Society of Addiction Medicine handbook of addiction medicine*. New York, NY: Oxford University Press.

Robertson, D. L. (2016). Collaboration strategies between family counselors and attorneys in child abuse and neglect cases, child custody cases and reporting: An interview with Deirdra Ward, JD. *Family Journal*, *24*(2), 190–194.

Robinson, S. R. (2018). Moral reasoning and authenticity in paraprofessional and professional and recovering and non-recovering addiction counselors. *Dissertation Abstracts International: Section B: The Sciences and Engineering, 79*(9-B(E)). No Pagination Specified. Retrieved from http://ovidsp.ovid.com/ovidweb.cgi?T=JS&PAGE=reference&D=psyc14&NEWS=N&AN=2018-30618-091

Schneider, J. P., & Levinson, B. (2006). Ethical dilemmas related to disclosure issues: Sex addiction therapists in the trenches. *Sexual Addiction & Compulsivity*, *13*(1), 1–39.

Scott, C. G. (2000). Ethical issues in addition counseling. *Rehabilitation Counseling Bulletin*, *43*(4), 209–214.

Shmerling, R. H. (2015, October 13). *First, do no harm*. Retrieved on January 10, 2019, from https://www.health.harvard.edu/blog/first-do-no-harm-201510138421

Smith, G. F. (2006). *Ewing v. Goldstein* and the therapist's duty to warn in California. *Golden Gate University Law Review*, *36*(2), 1–27.

Sobhana, H., Saxena, P., & Daimari, B. N. (2016). Ethical issues in working with couples and families. In P. Bhola & A. Raguram (Eds.), *Ethical issues in counselling and psychotherapy practice: Walking the line* (pp. 87–104). New York, NY: Springer Science + Business Media.

Sonne, J. L. (2012). Sexualized relationships. In S. J. Knapp, M. C. Gottlieb, M. M. Handelsman, & L. D. VandeCreek (Eds.), *APA handbook of ethics in psychology, Vol 1: Moral foundations and common themes* (pp. 295–310). Washington, DC: American Psychological Association.

Sori, C. F., & Hecker, L. L. (2015). Ethical and legal considerations when counselling children and families. *Australian and New Zealand Journal of Family Therapy*, *36*(4), 450–464.

Stoffelmayr, B. E., Mavis, B. E., & Kasim, R. M. (1998). Substance abuse treatment staff: Recovery status and approaches to treatment. *Journal of Drug Education*, *28*, 135–145.

Sue, D. W., Arredondo, P., & McDavis, R. J. (1992). Multicultural counseling competencies and standards: A call to the profession. *Journal of Counseling and Development*, *20*, 64–68.

Symons, C. (2004). Record-keeping: Ideas for counsellors. In G. Sheppard (Ed.), *Notebook on ethics, legal issues, and standards for counsellors*. Ottawa, ON: Canadian Counselling and Psychotherapy Association.

Taylor, M. (2017, May 10). Counselors in the courtroom. *Counseling Today*. Retrieved on April 19, 2019, from https://ct.counseling.org/2017/05/counselors-in-the-courtroom/

Toriello, P. J., & Strohmer, D. C. (2004). Addictions counselors' credibility: The impact of interactional style, recovery status, and nonverbal behavior. *Journal of Addictions & Offender Counseling*, *25*, 43–57.

VandeCreek, L., & Knapp, S. (1993). *Tarasoff and beyond: Legal and clinical considerations in the treatment of life-endangering patients*. Sarasota, FL: Professional Resource Press.

Walton, M. T. (2018). Administrative discharges in addiction treatment: Bringing practice in line with ethics and evidence. *Social Work*, *63*, 85–90.

Ward, K. (2002). Confidentiality in substance abuse counseling. *Journal of Social Work Practice in the Addictions*, *2*(2), 39–52.

APPENDIX 2A. CONFIDENTIALITY AGREEMENT WITH MINORS ("ASSENT")

Counseling sessions are confidential, meaning that information about you is **not** provided to anyone besides myself, [COUNSELOR'S NAME], without your signed consent. The only exception to this practice is where you or another person is at imminent risk of serious harm or where admission of child abuse or child neglect is disclosed. It is important for you to be aware that any information obtained in treatment may be subpoenaed by a court of law; this, of course, would only occur in serious situations where you become involved in the judicial system (e.g., charged with a serious criminal offense).

As you, the client, are under 18 years of age, further conditions apply. Although legal guardian(s) have a legal right to know what occurs within a counseling session with a minor, counselors are obligated to maintain confidentiality, once the limits of this are established among the minor, the guardian(s), and the counselor. Once established, this means that the only way a counselor can provide information to the guardian(s) is if a court order forces the counselor to do so [ENSURE THAT THIS IS TRUE IN YOUR JURISDICTION].

My preferred style of operating is that the guardian(s) is/are only entitled to information from me if I assess that there is **moderate** risk to the well-being of the minor or another person. Moderate risk includes such things as having frequent and serious suicidal thoughts, making suicidal gestures, continuing use of dangerous illicit drugs (note: dangerous drugs do not include marijuana, but do include heroin, crack, and crystal meth, for example), or having a strong desire to hurt someone else.

Your signature and that of your legal guardian(s) below indicate that you have read and understand the contents of this form and that you agree with this confidentiality agreement:

______________________________ __________
Signature of Minor Date

______________________________ __________
Signature of Guardian #1 Date

______________________________ __________
Signature of Guardian #2 Date

APPENDIX 2B. INITIAL CLINICAL RECORD

INITIAL CLINICAL RECORD

NAME: DATE:

PHONE: (CELL): (DAY): (EVENING):

ADDRESS: CITY OR TOWN:

ZIP CODE:

REFERRAL SOURCE (if applicable):

REASON FOR REFERRAL:

RELEVANT BACKGROUND HISTORY:

PRESENTING ISSUES:

GOALS/EXPECTATIONS REGARDING THERAPY:

ASSESSMENT (include assessing suicidal/homicidal risk and possible children at risk; medical—possible somatopsychic—disorder, drugs/alcohol):

TREATMENT PLAN:

HOMEWORK (if assigned):

FEE ARRANGEMENT (if applicable): PAYMENT MADE ($):

APPENDIX 2C. SUBSEQUENT CLINICAL RECORDS

SUBSEQUENT CLINICAL RECORD

NAME: DATE: SESSION #:

SESSION FOCUS:

PROGRESS INDICATORS:

INTERVENTIONS (include treatment plan if changing):

HOMEWORK (if assigned):

PAYMENT MADE ($):

3 Theories of Addiction

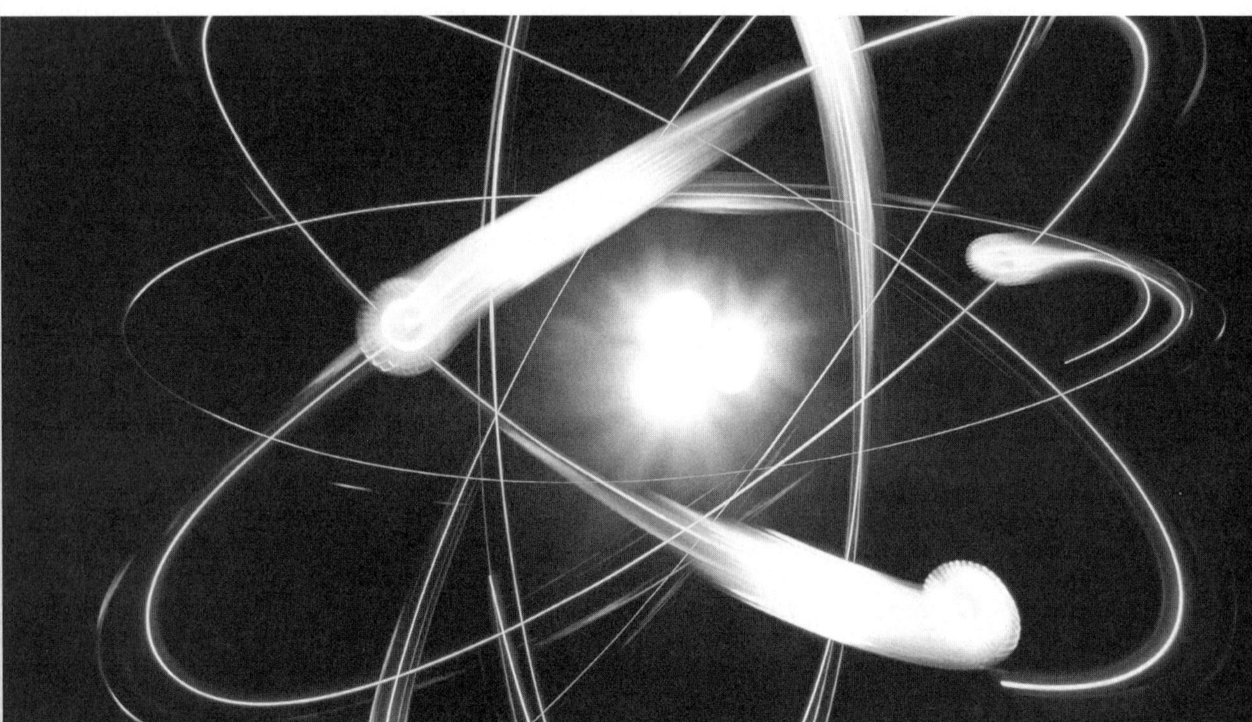

iStock.com/zoom-

Learning Objectives

1. Become familiar with what constitutes a theory.
2. Learn about common theories of addiction, including the moral/choice model, biological/disease theories, psychological theories, family models, sociocultural theories, postmodern theories, and the biopsychosocial model.
3. Compare and contrast the theories according to their strengths and limitations.
4. Apply these theories by practicing roleplays that highlight each theory.
5. Become informed of some different ways that theory informs the practice of addiction counselors.

PERSONAL REFLECTIONS

I often think about my clients and my family members. In Chapter 13, my personal reflection is about "George," a family member raised in a middle-class home. George became addicted to crack over the last few years even though he is now in his 50s. His story is the classic one of "prince" to "pauper." A few years ago, George was worth $2 million, but, when he moved to a different city 18 months ago, he was receiving welfare or social insurance benefits, as it might be called in some jurisdictions.

Why and how did George become addicted to crack, and why does he continue to use even now? Is it because he was raised by parents who were reportedly unloving in many of their actions during his childhood and adolescence? Did he just find crack to be so enticing and rewarding because of the intense high it provides? Maybe he became addicted to crack because of his personality, which was possibly already predisposed to addiction. How about the possibility that the real dysfunction began with the unhappy relationship between his parents and that his addiction is mostly an expression of their dysfunction? Perhaps he became addicted to crack because he was raised in a very blue-collar family with lower socioeconomic attitudes and beliefs in a subculture that values drugs and alcohol. As I've thought about him periodically, I have wondered if he is merely a victim of the disease we call addiction or, even worse, that he simply freely chooses to keep using crack rather than face his loneliness and his other problems. Lastly, could it be due to several of the previous reasons?

As you read about theories in this chapter, think about George. Even more relevant, however, would be if you know a George, or *are* a George. What has led you, him, or her to become an addict?

Why should we be interested in theory? As suggested in Chapter 1, the way we view addiction (i.e., our theory) will largely determine our definition of it. The converse is also true: Our definition of addiction is mostly based upon our theory of it. If we believe in the biological or "disease" model, our definition will read something like, "Addiction is a chronic, relapsing disease." If we believe in the choice model, our definition might instead look like the following: "Addiction is a choice that some individuals make to repeatedly and eagerly indulge themselves in excessive and harmful behaviors." See the difference?

So, what then is a theory? You would think that this would be an easy question to answer. Merriam-Webster's (2019b) first definition of a *theory* is "a plausible or scientifically acceptable general principle or body of principles offered to explain phenomena." Merriam-Webster's (2019a) 11th definition of a *model* is "a description or analogy used to help visualize something (such as an atom) that cannot be directly observed." Although often the terms theory and model are used interchangeably, strictly speaking, a theory is explanatory, and a model is descriptive (West, 2001). A theory then ought to answer *Why* and *How* questions, whereas models are better suited to answer *What, When*, and *Where* questions. In this chapter, the convention will be to use the words theory and model according to the way they are used in the published literature (i.e., as synonyms).

Westmeyer (2013) stated that, over the last century, the number of new addiction models has increased at a rate much higher than ever before in history. Unfortunately, although the newer theories capture important aspects regarding the phenomenon of addiction, the theories do not build upon what was addressed earlier by other theories (West & Brown, 2013).

The need to understand addictions is fueled by the enormous cost that addiction creates in nearly every society on earth. How does addiction develop, why does it not affect everyone similarly, and why do addicted individuals return to their addictive behaviors when they know that these have already caused them adverse consequences? Recalling a blooper once made by George W. Bush, the corrected idiom used was, "Fool me once, shame on you: fool me twice, shame on me" (McGraw-Hill, 2002). Yet addicted individuals continue to "fool" themselves ad nauseam as they become lost in their compulsive behaviors. *Why? How?*

Naim-Feil, Arunogiri, Spagnolo, and Lubman (2017) began their chapter on addictions by stating that, although the physical symptoms of dependence are what bring many substance users into treatment, it is not what leads to relapse because physical symptoms are short-lived. Instead, the psychological components of addiction are what bring both substance and behavioral addicted individuals back to their addictive behaviors. Not everyone agrees, however. A lot of neuroscience and neurobiology is occurring in our central nervous systems, affecting the way we think, feel, and act. It is possible that neurons "call" addicted individuals back to their addictive substance or behavior. Is there really an escape from ourselves (or our "neuro-activations," as a neuroscientist might put it)?

How do we ever prove a theory to be true? In science, we never do. The best we can do is to *disprove* the viability of a theory. Nonetheless, a good theory is one that has *not* been disproven, one that demonstrates predictive power, and one that continues to withstand the scrutiny of empirical research aimed at disproving it (West & Brown, 2013). This is the reason that a theory gathers moss as increasing amounts of research provide support for the "possibility" that it is true. If a research finding is not replicated, the theory loses credibility. If the results are replicated many times, the theory gains momentum. A good theory, according to West and Brown (2013), should bode well under the scrutiny of four questions:

1. Is it contradicted by observations?
2. Does it fail to encompass important relevant observations?
3. Does it have more elements than are needed?
4. Is it misleading? (p. 23)

If an observation can be found in the real world that contradicts a theory, a "theory must be wrong" (West & Brown, 2013, p. 26).

Our theoretical stance should also be what informs our practice. The most defensible interventions will always be those that

CAN YOU GUESS WHICH THEORY/IES EXPLAIN THE COUNSELOR'S BEHAVIOR?

Before reading the remainder of the chapter, test yourself regarding which theory or theories listed below would provide the best explanation for the counselor's behavior exemplified with each case. Provide your answers in the column on the right. The answers are found in Appendix 3A.

Theories

- Moral/Choice Model
- Biological/Disease Theories
- Psychological Theories
  - a) Psychodynamic Theories
  - b) Behavioral/Learning Theories
  - c) Cognitive-Behavioral Theories
  - d) Personality Theories
- Family Models (systems theory)
- Sociocultural Theories
- Postmodern Theories
- Biopsychosocial Model

Scenario	Theory/ies?
Chester, age 29, drinks heavily before committing breaking and entering and sometimes commits worse offenses when drunk. If you asked him, he would tell you he needs the alcohol to gain the necessary confidence to do these crimes. Chester does not use other drugs, but he does often have two or three drinks a night. After Chester gets caught one night, he asks you, his counselor, to write him a note for court. You refuse, telling him that he is entirely to blame for his criminal behavior. You let him know that, after he serves his time in jail, you would be prepared to help him use classical conditioning to break his connection between drinking and crime, and operant conditioning to reward himself for engaging in constructive, noncriminal activities.	Example 1
Meadow, age 62, was raised in a hippie commune in Canada. Her earliest memories were of regularly seeing her parents and other members of the commune smoking marijuana. By the time she was 12, she was smoking it regularly herself. She emigrated to Shoal Creek, a small town in Alabama, 3 years ago. Its population is approximately 1500. Meadow was surprised at how conservative it felt to live there. She smokes marijuana from morning to night, 7 days a week, and thinks nothing of it. Nonetheless, she makes an appointment to see you because of concerns expressed by her neighbors. After completing your assessment of Meadow, you conclude that she smokes marijuana because it is her cultural heritage.	Example 2
Walter, age 16, lives in his mother's basement. His father died 15 years ago. Walter spends nearly 20 hours a day in his room. Daytime and evening hours are mostly spent playing video games. Although he tells his mother that he is training for a competition, he never enrolls in one. After you meet with Walter and collect a thorough history, you conclude that Walter's addiction is due to early deprivation resulting from his father's death. You also note that Walter is very unassertive, and you attribute this to the lack of a male role model in his life. Furthermore, his mother is a highly stressed individual, and you believe that Walter has anger toward his mom but projects his repressed emotions into the video games that he plays.	Example 3
Sylvia, age 34, has lived on the street for the last 8 years. She injects heroin daily. After you collect a history from her, you arrange for her to begin a methadone maintenance program and conclude your work with her.	Example 4

Scenario	Theory/ies?
Tim is a 23-year-old gay circuit party-goer. Circuit parties are large all-night raves held regularly in various cities (which constitute the "circuit"), attended primarily by gay men. Tim attends as many circuit parties as he can afford. Additionally, he dances at a local bar Friday and Saturday nights. While at these events, Tim drinks and then uses several drugs such as ecstasy, cannabis, cocaine, crystal meth, and crack. He is consistent in his drug use, and, if ever asked, he denies that he has a substance abuse problem. After your assessment, you conclude that he is using drugs as a way of breaking free from a family that is itself toxic.	Example 5
Naomi, age 47, is very devoted to her Mormon faith. Nearly every day, she sees alcoholics and drug-addicted individuals on her way to work downtown as an addiction counselor. She deeply believes that drug-addicted individuals choose to continue using of their own free will. She also thinks that the only real cure is for these individuals to believe in God.	Example 6
Anton, age 41, moved to Portland, Oregon, from Moscow a few months ago. He drinks at least a 13-ounce bottle of vodka every night and more on weekends. A friend has brought him in to get assessed by you because of his concern regarding the quantity of alcohol Anton consumes. The first thing he says to you in session is, "We all drink like this in Russia." After gathering more details, you conclude that Anton's drinking is mostly attributable to his culture of origin. However, you also believe he now has a severe addiction to alcohol due to his altered biochemistry.	Example 7
Amitola, age 18, is Native American. Her friend Lucille is shocked at how often Amitola uses peyote and gets drunk. She drinks heavily every day, whereas her use of peyote is restricted to weekends. Finding Amitola without impairment from alcohol is rare. Through some coercion and deception, Amitola ends up in your office. She tells you in no uncertain terms to mind your own business. After the interview, you conclude that, although Amitola began her peyote use as a cultural ritual, what is maintaining her current level of use of both peyote and alcohol is the sexual abuse she experienced as a child. Furthermore, her parents are frequent drug users, and you consider this a contributing factor. You also acknowledge that Amitola may have a genetic or biological component to her addictive behaviors.	Example 8
Jay, age 43, was diagnosed with paranoid schizophrenia when he was in his 20s. He frequently experiences a delusion that people are watching him electronically through hidden cameras that he believes are located nearly everywhere. Jay thinks that, over time, these videos will be edited by someone intending to do him harm. However, most of the time Jay can work and fit in reasonably well. His coworkers find him to be a bit odd, but there are two guys at work who have struck up a friendship with him. One night after being coaxed by his friends, the three of them each take a hit of LSD. Jay becomes increasingly uncomfortable being around others and decides to leave his friends. His delusions worsen, and, as he waits in the subway, he believes that he is looking at the man who will edit the videos. Approaching from behind, Jay begins choking the stranger, and, if it were not for bystanders pulling Jay off, the stranger would have died. You have seen Jay for counseling before, and you offer to write him a letter for court suggesting that Jay is not criminally responsible due to insanity, together with the moderating factor of LSD use, reportedly taken on this one occasion only.	Example 9
Brandy, age 72, has always been an impulsive risk-taker in her life. If she had been diagnosed earlier in her life, she likely would have been on medications for ADHD. She recently received a nearly $100,000 inheritance after her sister died. Brandy had always liked gambling, so she walked into the casino and began playing at high-limit crap tables. Five hours later, Brandy has spent half of her inheritance, and she is now more determined than ever to win it back. After losing another $45,000, she leaves the casino, feeling defeated. After your assessment, you determine that the primary causal factor is Brandy's continuing belief that she deserves to live a rich person's life now that she is retired. You also conclude that she is extraverted, agreeable, and open to experience but also neurotic and lacking conscientiousness.	Example 10

are empirically validated (also called empirically supported or evidence-based) and those that fit within a theoretical orientation. If you believe our thoughts are what primarily determine our feelings and guide our actions, for example, your theoretical orientation is cognitive-behavioral. That does not mean that you view every client through a cognitive-behavioral lens or that you only offer cognitive-behavioral therapy. However, it does mean that, much of the time, this is the theory you are most likely to adopt and use for treatment planning.

Smith (2015) wrote that "the addictive process is complex" (p. 14) and that it includes several causative factors such as biological, environmental, and psychological components. That is *his* theory, and not everyone in the field would agree with him. Nonetheless, he asked some important questions:

- Why is one individual able to drink in moderation, whereas another needs to remain abstinent?
- Why are addictions intergenerational in nature but only with certain members of a family?
- To what degree does the specific substance or behavior play a role in determining whether one will become addicted? (p. 1)

Although Maté (2008) strongly argued that "addiction always originates in pain" (p. 34), this overgeneralization does not stand up to scrutiny. Although some addicted individuals do use substances or addictive behaviors to self-medicate, we know that addiction develops from many different trajectories, only two of which result from physical or psychological pain (West & Brown, 2013). Some drugs are inherently highly addictive, such as heroin, methadone, and nicotine (West & Brown, 2013). Additionally, some addicted individuals come from healthy households, but, because of their impulsivity and high risk-taking attitudes, they begin using a drug that enhances their experience with others (e.g., at parties, nightclubs) and continue doing so even when it leads to negative consequences such as addiction.

Anytime one makes a global claim in psychology (e.g., "all people do this or that"), the statement is overgeneralized. For example, we could state that no addicted individuals begin using alcohol or a drug wanting to become addicted, but, once an exception is found, the entire statement loses credibility. As West and Brown (2013) stated, there is often no intention to make a substance or behavior into "a regular thing" (p. 33). The key phrase that keeps their statement believable is that there is "often no intention." Students interested in reading about the plethora of theories applied to addiction are referred to three books: (a) Pagliaro and Pagliaro's (2019) *Theories of Addiction: Why People Use Drugs and Substances of Abuse*, (b) Kopetz and Lejuez's (2016) *Addictions: A Social Psychological Perspective*, and (c) West and Brown's (2013) *Theory of Addiction*. This chapter will focus on the moral/choice model, biological/disease theories, psychological theories, family models, sociocultural theories, postmodern theories, and the biopsychosocial model.

Before reading the remainder of this chapter, you might want to complete the Public Attitudes About Addiction Survey (Broadus & Evans, 2015) found in Appendix 3B. Based on three studies, the survey measures your affinity regarding five models of addiction: (a) moral model, (b) nature model, (c) psychological model, (d) sociological model, and (e) disease model. Although this chapter is not organized according to these five models, the survey will provide you with a good sense of the type of model (or theory) that you most strongly endorse currently.

Moral or "Choice" Model

Strictly speaking, the moral model explained the cause of addiction as residing within the sinful nature of fallible human beings (McNeece & DiNitto, 2012). The model itself has little support today because the concept of sin is a value judgment that is not empirically verifiable. However, historically, the moral model was likely the first "choice" model.

Choice models espouse the view that addiction occurs through personal choice. Addicted individuals are *not* seen as suffering from an incurable disease but instead are perceived as free agents who lack the intestinal fortitude to practice appropriate behavior. Heyman (2009) argued, for example, that addictive behavior is voluntary and that it results from making a series of poor choices. Peele (2016), himself an advocate of addiction as a choice, noted that the epidemic increases in opiate addiction corresponded with the rise in popularity of the disease model! West and Brown (2013) described a version of this theory called the rational informed choice model, which advocates that individuals should make choices regarding substances and/or addictive behaviors and accept their consequences.

Thomas Szasz, famous for his critique of psychiatry (Szasz, 1961), supported the moral model regarding addictions (Szasz, 2013). Always known for his controversial and nonconventional views, Szasz (2013) recommended that all drugs be made legal and available to all adults in the United States. He stated that drugs like barbiturates, codeine, and other drugs are freely available for purchase in Lebanon. Such practices of providing easy access, however, also have their consequences. For example, "Benzodiazepine use in Lebanon is particularly high" (Naja, Pelissolo, Haddad, Baddoura, & Baddoura, 2000, p. 429), and drug abuse and addiction are serious problems among Lebanese youth (Arevian, 2010).

Certain religious groups have adopted the moral or choice model (Fisher & Harrison, 2013), as has the American legal system (Morse, 2017). Advocates of the choice model believe that addiction can be cured (Faulkner, 2013).

Capuzzi and Stauffer (2012) opined that believers of the moral/choice model might be the reason that needle/syringe exchange programs have often been opposed in the United States. Similarly, Fisher and Harrison (2013) suggested that the moral/choice model has been an important contributor in creating the stigma around addiction and addicts.

Role of the Counselor

A counselor who endorses a choice model might adopt a humanistic approach that emphasizes taking personal responsibility for one's choices. Three examples include person-centered counseling, Gestalt therapy, or reality therapy. Behavioral methods might also be used to "teach coping skills, mobilize community forces, and instill values toward prosocial behavior" (Peele, 1990–1991, p. 1409). Peele (1990–1991) stated that behavioral methods help addicted individuals develop a deeper sense of self-efficacy.

Alternatively, the counselor might take a faith-based approach that involves seeking help from a higher power. Concurrently, the addicted individual would receive social support from members of the congregation and possibly financial aid and/or accommodation during the early stages of recovery.

Strengths of This Approach

Perhaps the greatest strength of the moral/choice model is that it reminds addicted individuals that, despite the hold that their addiction has on them, they continue to have free will and can exercise it whenever they develop adequate resolve. The approach refuses to accept the idea that addicted individuals are victims; instead, they are victimizing themselves by continuing to engage in harmful behavior.

Limitations of This Approach

The moral/choice model has been held largely accountable for the stigma that addicted individuals continue to experience, and such stigma acts more like a self-fulfilling prophecy than as an agent of hope. The approach focuses exclusively on one's own ability to stop the addictive behavior, thereby relying extensively on "willpower." The model also fails to consider biological factors and the impact of the environment (Faulkner, 2013).

As Morse (2017) concluded, although the American justice system is based on the moral/choice model, "current doctrine and practice are probably too unforgiving and harsh" (p. 426). West and Brown (2013) criticized the rational informed choice model for not accounting for the many addicted individuals who attempt to exercise restraint yet fail miserably at it despite spending substantial amounts of time, effort, and money.

Biological and "Disease" Theories

Without question, the biological/disease theories have ruled the nest regarding the theory and treatment of substance and behavioral addictions. Perhaps, by the way, with good reason. Looking back at the history of addictions beginning with the moral/choice models, addicted individuals were stigmatized. As we know from a plethora of research, stigma helps produce the very problem in individuals for which they are stigmatized (Alderson, 2013). A devastating example of this is the stigma experienced by Indigenous individuals, both historically and today, which has contributed to collective and intergenerational trauma (Yellow Horse Brave Heart, Chase, Elkins, & Altschul, 2011).

As MacKillop and Ray (2018) indicated, the biological/disease models mostly focus today on neuroscience and genetic research. Research suggests, for example, that about 50% of an individual's likelihood of developing a substance addiction is related to genetic factors (Smith, 2015). Epigenetic research has also glaringly boomed in popularity (Palmisano & Pandey, 2017; see Chapter 4 for an explanation of epigenetics). Given that the next chapter is about neuroscience and genetics, and Chapters 9 through 21 contain ample coverage of the biological/disease theories, little will be restated here. The primary belief underlying these theories is that addiction is "primary, progressive, [and] chronic" (McNeece & DiNitto, 2012, p. 25). It is viewed and treated as a brain disease and, as regards substance addictions, is often fatal.

The research base underlying the biological/disease theories is massive, and it continues growing daily (e.g., Berkel & Pandey, 2017; Vadigepalli & Hoek, 2018; Williams & Holmes, 2017). It also remains the prevailing theory behind the work in most treatment centers and Alcoholics Anonymous (AA)–based mutual help groups (White, 2014).

Role of the Counselor

Those who subscribe to the biological/disease theories believe that abstinence is the only option for addicted individuals. Counselors operating from this perspective share that goal and help their clients to learn that it is their *best* option. Nonetheless, as counseling practice is based on a collaborative relationship with clients, that will not always be the choice by addicted individuals themselves. Adherents of these theories also support the use of medication and other medical treatments. A new field of counseling has emerged as well called neurocounseling. Chapter 6 has details concerning how some counselors have incorporated research from neuroscience into their practices.

ROLEPLAY SCENARIO

The following roleplay provides an example of a client situation wherein the moral/choice model might be appropriate to use. If roleplay is not possible, write out a few lines of what you could say to the client that might be helpful. Do not be concerned if you do not know enough about the moral/choice model to demonstrate this approach competently. The goal here is merely to help anchor or enhance your learning so that you remember this approach is a possibility to use with some clients in actual addiction counseling practice.

You are working as an addiction counselor. You have already seen Rachel, age 25, for a few sessions. Rachel tells you that, when she goes to a nightclub with friends, she has four or five drinks during the first 3 hours upon arrival, which negatively impairs her judgment. On more than one occasion, Rachel has awakened in a stranger's bed, which is disturbing to her as she wants to stop having casual sex. The two of you collaboratively decide that the target of intervention is not for Rachel to reduce her drinking but instead to help her make better decisions when approached by willing men.

Strengths of This Approach

Counselors who subscribe to the biological/disease theories will not be alone. These remain the predominant theories used today in designing medical and biological treatments for clients with addictive disorders. Laypersons (often more than practitioners) understand the need for addicted individuals to give up their addictive behavior(s) entirely, whenever possible (obviously clients cannot stop eating if they identify as food addicts). These theories have also helped reduce the stigma of having an addictive disorder.

Limitations of This Approach

The biological/disease models do not sufficiently answer the question of why some individuals do *not* become addicted (MacKillop & Ray, 2018). Peele (2015) and others have harshly criticized these theories. Carter and Hall (2013), for example, stated that the problem with the disease model is that abnormal behavior and biological changes in the brain will occur simultaneously. This does not demonstrate that the brain changes constitute a disease of biological origin, however. Carter and Hall went on to argue that proponents of disease models need to accept that drug-dependent individuals still maintain some degree of autonomy in deciding whether to continue their drug use. Peele argued that these models are inaccurate and that treatments based on them have been "predictably disastrous" (Peele, 2007, p. 153). Peele (2015) wrote that these models fail to account for person–environment interactions. Furthermore, Peele stated that psychiatric medications damage addicts' brains.

ROLEPLAY SCENARIO

The following roleplay provides an example of a client situation wherein biological/disease theories might be appropriate to use. If roleplay is not possible, write out a few lines of what you could say to the client that might be helpful. Do not be concerned if you do not know enough about the biological/disease theories to demonstrate this approach competently. The goal here is merely to help anchor or enhance your learning so that you remember this approach is a possibility to use with some clients in actual addiction counseling practice.

You are working as an addiction counselor. Max, age 59, has abused drugs and alcohol since he first started using at age 21. He tells you that, from the first drink, he was an alcoholic. Despite the physical toll that drugs and alcohol have had on him (e.g., he experiences short-term memory difficulties, and his physician told him his liver enzymes are elevated), Max seems unable to stop using. This is his first attempt at getting help from a professional counselor.

Psychological Theories

"The one who merely flees is not yet free. In fleeing he is still conditioned by that from which he flees" (Georg Wilhelm Friedrich Hegel, source unknown).

Many psychological theories and models have evolved to explain addictions. The main metatheories will be considered here, including psychodynamic, behavioral (learning), cognitive-behavioral, and personality theories. A thorough review of psychological and sociocultural models can be found in Kopetz and Lejuez (2016) and West and Brown (2013).

Psychodynamic Theories

Many mental health professionals and the lay public see addiction as resulting from deeper, psychological issues or problems, often with their origins in childhood. Subscribers of such thinking either wittingly or unknowingly espouse a psychodynamic approach. Psychodynamic theories grew out of Sigmund Freud's psychoanalysis and today include several approaches. Capuzzi and Stauffer (2012) linked psychodynamic explanations of addiction with "ego deficiencies, inadequate parenting, attachment disorders, hostility, homosexuality, [and] masturbation" (p. 7). Besides these linkages, McNeece and DiNitto (2012) also noted that other psychodynamic theorists have viewed alcoholics, for example, as orally fixated, narcissistic, and self-destructive. One theorist noted by McNeece and DiNitto blamed alcoholism on a mother's failure to provide milk!

Core beliefs underlying the psychodynamic approach include the difficulties that addicted individuals face in regulating their emotions and disturbed object relations (Capuzzi & Stauffer, 2012). The three prominent names in the object relations field are Melanie Klein, Ronald Fairbairn, and Donald Winnicott (Pizer, 2018). Object relations theory refers to several psychodynamic approaches, all of which stress the belief that the way adults relate to others and situations are shaped by experiences in their families during the first 3 years of life, especially the mother–infant bond. In other words, inadequate parenting (along with a child's constitution) leads to maladaptive attachment to one's mother, which, in turn, creates a lasting effect that projects into future close/intimate relationships (McNeece & DiNitto, 2012).

It appears that, when children experience trauma, abuse, and/or neglect, or insecure attachments to their parents, they become vulnerable to mental health disorders of nearly every type, including addiction (Fletcher, Nutton, & Brend, 2015). There is a great deal of research that documents that many addicted individuals have experienced trauma in childhood or have endured abuse and/or neglect during their childhood years (Bailey & Stewart, 2014; Brents, Tripathi, Young, James, & Kilts, 2015; Fernandez-Montalvo, Lopez-Goni, & Arteaga, 2015; Lu, Wen, Deng, & Tang, 2017). Severe childhood trauma is associated with injection drug use (Hammersley et al., 2016). Behavioral addictions are also associated with traumatic experiences in childhood (Schwaninger et al., 2017). Addiction itself continues the enactment of trauma (Pintus, 2017).

Addicted parents might inadvertently set the stage for their children to become addicted individuals later themselves. Rutherford and Mayes (2017) described how, neurologically, addicted parents become compromised in their ability to act effectively as parents. Parolin and Simonelli (2016) wrote about the negative influence that maternal substance abuse has on parenting, thus compromising the attachment bond between mother and infant.

Role of the counselor.

Depending on the specific psychoanalytic or psychodynamic perspective of the counselor, the main focus of treatment will be on helping clients develop insight into the root causes of their addictions. The belief in psychodynamic models is that insight is sufficient to effect change. Today's psychodynamic counselor may use a host of eclectic techniques, however, that extend beyond insight alone. Fletcher et al., (2015) encouraged counselors to use an attachment-focused approach in treating substance use disorders (SUDs), as did Flores (2004) in his book entitled *Addiction as an Attachment Disorder*. Lu et al. (2017) recommended that counselors focus on improving their clients' self-worth and self-concept as a way of helping them overcome the adverse influence caused by childhood mistreatment.

Strengths of this approach.

As McNeece and DiNitto (2012) noted, many counselors use psychodynamic approaches. Studies, albeit with small sample sizes, have found that psychodynamic approaches help treat SUDs (Craparo, 2017; Dodes & Dodes, 2017; Gottdiener, 2013). Woods (2013) used group analytic therapy with compulsive users of Internet pornography. Nyhuis et al. (2018) compared psychoanalytical group therapy to behavioral group therapy and concluded that both were equally effective for relapse prevention in individuals with alcohol use disorder (AUD). Gibbons, Crits-Christoph, and Hearon (2008) reviewed psychodynamic therapy over the previous decade. Their review suggested that the treatment of opiate use disorder might be facilitated through a psychodynamic approach. Counselors interested in learning more about psychodynamic approaches are directed to a book edited by Weegmann and Cohen (2008) called *The Psychodynamics of Addiction*.

Limitations of this approach.

The efficacy and effectiveness of psychodynamic approaches are difficult to substantiate empirically because the concepts are challenging to operationalize (Capuzzi & Stauffer, 2012). Also, childhood maltreatment (CM) does not always predict addiction, as CM also leads to many other potential mental disorders. Furthermore, CM is only one of several pathways toward addictive behavior.

McNeece and DiNitto (2012) suggested that possibly the biggest criticism of the psychodynamic approaches is that they are generally nondirective. Although these approaches focus mostly on helping clients develop insight, addictive substances and behaviors often create powerful cravings that usurp insight and rational decision-making. Lastly, the empirical support for psychodynamic theory remains minimal compared to most of the other approaches that are used in addiction counseling today.

Behavioral or "Learning" Theories

Following the moral/choice model and the psychodynamic theories, behavioral/learning theories regarding addiction were the next to develop. According to Coplan (2010), the founding fathers of American behaviorism were Edward Thorndike (his work with

ROLEPLAY SCENARIO

The following roleplay provides an example of a client situation wherein a psychodynamic theory might be appropriate to use. If roleplay is not possible, write out a few lines of what you could say to the client that might be helpful. Do not be concerned if you do not know enough about a psychodynamic theory to demonstrate this approach competently. The goal here is merely to help anchor or enhance your learning so that you remember this approach is a possibility to use with some clients in actual addiction counseling practice.

You are working as an addiction counselor. Keith, age 39, has finally stayed clean from his regular use of cocaine for 3 months. Like having a flashback, memories from his past have begun emerging. Keith experiences them as fleeting thoughts, but he knows these things really happened. His anger toward his parents had begun seething as he remembers an incident when he was about 10 years old. Keith was not buckled in the back seat of the family car, and, for some reason, Keith recalls that, when his dad turned a corner sharply a block from their house, the rear door opened and Keith fell onto the pavement. Instead of stopping, his parents continued driving home. Keith was not injured. This memory had become forgotten over the years of Keith's cocaine use (note: this incident actually happened to one of my clients). As you soon discover in talking to Keith, this is only one of several memories that he begins recalling that are examples of child abuse.

animals focused on reinforcement theory and behavior analysis) and John Watson (his work with children explained human behavior as responses to stimuli). Malone (2014), however, explained that Thorndike would be considered more of the founder of behaviorism. In 1913, Watson argued that psychology should be viewed as a natural science; behaviorism was already clearly established (Malone, 2014). Also, near the beginning of the 20th century, Russian physiologist Ivan Pavlov became known as the founder of *classical conditioning* (learning that occurs when reinforcement and stimuli occur almost simultaneously). Behaviorism's most well-known figure (Coplan, 2010) was Burrhus Frederic Skinner (commonly known as B. F. Skinner). Skinner's theory, which he called *operant conditioning* (learning that occurs when reinforcement follows a stimulus), was based on the earlier work of Thorndike.

All behaviorists believe that behavior is learned, and thus it can also be unlearned (Faulkner, 2013). Besides classical and operant conditioning, behaviorists focus on a third type of learning that occurs through *modeling*, which results from observing and imitating others. Modeling forms the central concept within social learning theory (SLT). SLT was developed by Albert Bandura (1977). Some readers may be familiar with his classic Bobo doll experiments with children. Children who observed adults striking bobo dolls were more likely to imitate this behavior when left alone with the Bobo dolls compared to children who did not witness adults hitting the dolls (Bandura & Huston, 1961; Bandura, Ross, & Ross, 1961, 1963).

According to behaviorism, addiction occurs as a learned behavior in some individuals because of classical conditioning (West & Brown, 2013), operant conditioning (Foddy, 2017), and SLT/modeling (Fisher & Harrison, 2013; McNeece & DiNitto, 2012). Addiction might occur in some individuals who have insufficient coping abilities to deal with stressors (Faulkner, 2013). McNeece and DiNitto (2012) explained that, in the behavioral approach, addiction could result from efforts to decrease negative emotions such as stress, anxiety, and tension. McCarthy, Curtin, Piper, and Baker (2010) concurred that many addicted individuals "crave and use drugs to escape various forms of distress" (p. 15). The behavioral term for this is *negative reinforcement* (reinforcement that occurs after responding to an unpleasant stimulus, thereby increasing the likelihood of repeating [i.e., reinforcing] that behavior when again confronted with the same or similar negative stimuli; George, Koob, & Vendruscolo, 2014).

Foddy (2017) suggested that addiction is "a possibility for any human being" (p. 49) because of the cascade of rewards that substances or addictive behaviors deliver. Cho et al. (2019) used longitudinal data (N = 2556) and found that the association between negative reinforcement and alcohol consumption increased with the presence of alcohol dependence. The association between positive reinforcement and alcohol consumption, however, did not differ significantly with alcohol dependence. These results suggest that, in individuals with AUD, negative reinforcement becomes more important than positive reinforcement, which likely occurs to avoid withdrawal symptoms and other sequelae.

Alan Marlatt, a leading proponent of SLT, believed that addiction is a composite of "bad habits" (Fisher & Harrison, 2013, p. 41). In Marlatt's view, addiction results from either environmental stressors or through modeling others with perceived status. SLT is widely used in developing relapse prevention strategies (Fisher & Harrison, 2013).

Lamb and Ginsburg (2018) viewed addiction as a "behavioral allocation disorder" (p. 62). This expression referred to addicted individuals picking behaviors (i.e., allocation) that are harmful to them instead of picking adaptive choices. In this way, drug use becomes habitual. Lamb and Ginsburg did not see these maladaptive choices as deliberate; instead, they result from automatic thinking processes. The authors suggested that, although difficult, for addicted individuals to improve, they need to become more deliberate in making better choices.

Role of the counselor.

Behavioral counselors (BCs) have a large arsenal of techniques that they use in helping others (see Chapter 6). These techniques are also applicable to helping addicts. BCs are directive in their approach. They work hard at educating their clients about their methods and having them do "homework" outside of session (homework often involves practicing prosocial behaviors and refraining from maladaptive behaviors). Recent developments in behavioral approaches to treating addictions can be found in Chapters 9 through 21. For example, Chesworth and Corbit (2017) summarized developments regarding the extinction of drug seeking. Their techniques included various forms of extinction training that included relapse prevention, cue exposure therapy, and counterconditioning.

Strengths of this approach.

The behavioral approach deals directly with symptoms. Given that most clients seek our help for specific problems, BCs can assist

ROLEPLAY SCENARIO

The following roleplay provides an example of a client situation wherein behavioral/learning theories might be appropriate to use. If roleplay is not possible, write out a few lines of what you could say to the client that might be helpful. Do not be concerned if you do not know enough about behavioral/learning theories to demonstrate this approach competently. The goal here is merely to help anchor or enhance your learning so that you remember this approach is a possibility to use with some clients in actual addiction counseling practice.

You are working as an addiction counselor. Sherry, age 20, has come to see you for the first time regarding what she perceives as addiction to her cell phone. Her typical pattern of use includes answering every phone call and reading every text message as soon as her phone alerts her. She is also regularly using Facebook, Instagram, and Twitter. Last week, she totaled the amount of time that she spent on her cell phone to be nearly 25 hours. She would like to reduce her usage to not more than 5 hours each week.

clients immediately. Behaviorism also focuses on the here-and-now, so clients do not need to explore their pasts to get help in the present. As you will read in later chapters, behavioral methods have a great deal of empirical validation, and they also offer counselors many techniques (Gladding & Alderson, 2012).

Limitations of this approach.

Faulkner (2013) concluded that the major disadvantage of this approach concerns its lack of directly addressing intergenerational, family, and biological factors. For long-lasting change to occur, a shift in the way families interact and attention to the biological aspects of addictions are typically needed. Critics have also argued that BCs do not deal with the total person but instead focus only on specific behaviors (Gladding & Alderson, 2012). Furthermore, the approach is sometimes applied mechanically, it ignores clients' past histories, and it often focuses on helping clients reach only a minimal or tolerable level of behaving (Gladding & Alderson, 2012).

Cognitive-Behavioral Theories

A detailed section about cognitive-behavioral theory and therapy (CBT[1]) can be found in Chapter 6. CBT is based on the idea that it is our cognitions (i.e., processes involving thinking, knowing, and/or remembering) that determine how we feel about things and not the things themselves. For example, whether a divorce is seen as a blessing or a tragedy depends on how a person is currently viewing their marriage.

The cognitive-behavioral model includes several motivations and reinforcers for using drugs (Capuzzi & Stauffer, 2012). For example, individuals might use drugs for escapism, variety, self-exploration, mood alteration, spiritual or religious exploration, relieving boredom or other negative emotions, enhancing positive emotions, creativity, and pleasure. Milkman and Sunderwirth (2010) hypothesized that addictive behavior occurs because individuals are struggling with handling discomfort and/or lack meaning in their lives.

For the most part, behavior in CBT is motivated by the reasons that underlie it. For example, individuals addicted to gaming might have convinced themselves that their self-worth is contingent on becoming one of the best players in the United States. Playing games for endless hours each day becomes justifiable in their thinking despite the adverse consequences this commitment is causing them. There are many different reasons that individuals continue engaging in substance use or behaviors until and beyond the point at which addiction occurs.

A growing body of research is finding that metacognitive beliefs might play a role in several addictions. Hamonniere and Varescon (2018) reviewed 38 studies, all of which found a significant positive association between metacognitive beliefs and addictive behaviors. However, Hamonniere and Varescon reported that there are few longitudinal studies or experimental designs. Consequently, causal connections cannot be ascertained currently.

Hamonniere and Varescon (2018) stated that there are three subtypes of metacognitive beliefs. These include those that pertain to (a) control of internal cognitive-affective experiences (e.g., "I must always have control of my thoughts"), (b) "positive" beliefs that troubling thoughts are helpful (e.g., "If I continue worrying, I will be better able to cope when something happens"), and (c) negative beliefs that mental events cannot be controlled (e.g., "I cannot stop thinking about the mistake I made"). All three subtypes of beliefs lead to the continuance of psychological distress, and much research has found a strong relationship between these subtypes of metacognitive beliefs and mental disorders (Hamonniere & Varescon, 2018).

Role of the counselor.

As Granillo, Perron, Gutowski, and Jarman (2013) indicated, CBT represents many interventions and strategies, including such approaches as "rational emotive therapy, multimodal therapy, cognitive therapy, behavioral therapy, contingency management, and applied behavioral analysis" (p. 101). As with behavioral approaches, CBT counselors are active and direct in their sessions with clients. A primary focus is on teaching and correcting clients' cognitions and providing them homework to continue as repetition is important for maladaptive thoughts to become replaced with healthier cognitions (Gladding & Alderson, 2012).

[1]CBT will be used interchangeably as an acronym for cognitive-behavioral theory and cognitive-behavioral therapy.

ROLEPLAY SCENARIO

The following roleplay provides an example of a client situation wherein cognitive-behavioral theories might be appropriate to use. If roleplay is not possible, write out a few lines of what you could say to the client that might be helpful. Do not be concerned if you do not know enough about cognitive-behavioral theories to demonstrate this approach competently. The goal here is merely to help anchor or enhance your learning so that you remember this approach is a possibility to use with some clients in actual addiction counseling practice.

You are working as an addiction counselor. Romeo, age 48, is attending his first session with you. For the past 20 years, Romeo has gambled compulsively to the point where his wife is currently considering leaving him. He estimates that he has lost $150,000 or more playing blackjack and slot machines. As you talk to him, you discover that he firmly believes the following:

1. Slot machines will eventually provide a high payout. If I continue playing on the same machine, there is a good chance I will become rich eventually.
2. If I start losing money, I should place larger bets to win back what I have lost.
3. If I do not become well-off, I am a worthless human being.

Strengths of this approach.

The strengths of CBT are comparable to those of behavioral approaches. CBT is transparent and quickly learned by clients. Most clients can easily understand its principles. Research has consistently demonstrated CBT's effectiveness in addictions work (see Chapters 9 through 21).

Limitations of this approach.

CBT practitioners need to be careful that they do not become overzealous given the directedness of these approaches. Another caution is that helping clients change their thinking may not be the simplest way of changing their emotions. CBT requires clients to be active, which generally includes completing homework assignments. If the homework is not completed before the next session, clients may feel reluctant to return for their next session. Given that the approach is cognitive, it is likely not the best approach for individuals who are intellectually challenged or unmotivated to change. Lastly, CBT has been harshly criticized by some feminists and multicultural counselors because its worldview is patriarchal and Euro-American (Gladding & Alderson, 2012).

Personality Theories

Is there a personality type that is most prone to developing an addiction? Capuzzi and Stauffer (2012) stated that persons with an alcoholic personality were often described by traits such as "dependent, immature, impulsive, highly emotional, having low frustration tolerance, unable to express anger, confused about their sexual orientation, etc." (p. 7). For the most part, efforts directed at finding an "addictive personality" have been unsuccessful (McNeece & DiNitto, 2012). Consequently, most who work in the addictions field do not attribute much importance to personality traits (Capuzzi & Stauffer, 2012). This, however, may be changing due to continuing research efforts.

Although Amodeo (2015) suggested that the term "addictive personality" (p. 1031) should be eliminated, researchers continue their search for addictive personality traits. A scale with good psychometric properties was developed by Anderson, Barnes, and Murray (2011) called the Addiction-Prone Personality (APP) Scale.

Since McCrae and Costa's (1987) five-factor model of personality (sometimes referred to as the "big five") became well-established as a personality theory, several researchers appear to have developed a fresh interest to find traits associated with addictions. The five-factor theory has a great deal of empirical support behind it. The five factors are as follows, and besides these are the opposite traits:

- Openness to new experience versus closed to experience.
- Conscientiousness versus lack of conscientiousness.
- Extraversion versus introversion.
- Agreeableness versus disagreeableness.
- Neuroticism versus emotional stability (adapted from https://www.psychestudy.com/general/personality/big-five).

Zilberman, Yadid, Efrati, Neumark, and Rassovsky (2018) compared the personality profiles (using several personality and sociodemographic questionnaires) of 216 addicted individuals and 78 controls. The addictions represented included drug and alcohol addiction and gambling and sex addiction. Zilberman et al. found "notable personality distinctions" (p. 174) among the different addictions. Impulsivity and neuroticism were higher among all the addicted individuals studied compared to the control group. The specific differences found were as follows:

1. Alcohol use disorder. This sample scored lower on extraversion, agreeableness, and openness to experience.
2. Drug use disorders and compulsive sexual behavior. These two groups were surprisingly similar and scored lowest on the traits of agreeableness and conscientiousness.
3. Gambling disorder. Their personality profile was similar to the control group.

A host of other studies have also found interesting results. Some of the more recent studies include

- Heroin use disorder (HUD). Delic, Kajdiz, and Pregelj (2017) reported that several studies have shown that individuals with HUD tend to be high on neuroticism and high on extraversion, but they are also more impulsive and less sociable compared to controls. Those who are successful at maintaining abstinence are higher in agreeableness and conscientiousness compared with those who are unsuccessful (Delic et al., 2017).
- Cocaine use disorder (CUD). Brents et al. (2015) studied 95 participants (ages 18–50, mean age = 38 years) who had CUD together with early life stress (CUD-ELS group), no CUD but ELS (ELS), CUD but no ELS (CUD), or no CUD and no ELS (NCE). The CUD-ELS group was the unhealthiest psychologically. They were also more neurotic than the CUD group, suggesting (as a hypothesis) that it might be early life stress that predisposes individuals with CUD to becoming neurotic. ELS also predicted agreeableness.
- Gambling disorder. Mackinnon, Lambe, and Stewart (2016) conducted a longitudinal study of 679 emerging adults (mean age = 18.90 years; 51.8% female). Note that these individuals were not individuals with a gambling disorder. The participants completed self-report questionnaires across four occasions, each between 12 and 18 months apart. The most robust finding was that extraversion and agreeableness predicted social motives as a reason for gambling (i.e., gambling to increase social affiliation). In a large study of 10,081 (51.5% female) Norwegians, Brunborg, Hanss, Mentzoni, Molde, and Pallesen (2016) compared non-problem gamblers and those with low, moderate, and severe gambling problems. Higher levels of problem gambling were associated with higher scores on neuroticism, and with lower scores on conscientiousness and agreeableness.
- Internet addiction (IA). Kayis et al. (2016) performed a meta-analysis based on 12 studies of IA. They found that all big-five personality traits were related to IA. Although neuroticism was positively associated with IA, openness to new experiences, conscientiousness, extraversion,

and agreeableness were negatively associated with it. In another study, Braun, Stopfer, Muller, Beutel, and Egloff (2016) compared gaming addicts, regular gamers, and nongamers in a total sample of 2891 participants. The individuals with gaming addiction were found to have high neuroticism. The regular gamers who preferred action games were high on extraversion and low on neuroticism.

- Work addiction (WA). Andreassen et al. (2016) conducted a longitudinal study of 1267 nurses who participated in 2012, 2013, and 2014. Their results indicated that neuroticism was correlated positively with increases in workaholism.

In Chapters 9 through 21, you will find that many addictions are also correlated with certain personality disorders. For example, individuals with antisocial personality disorder have a higher likelihood of experiencing an AUD compared with the general population (McNeece & DiNitto, 2012).

Role of the counselor.

How a counselor might begin, if using personality theory, would depend on the particular personality theory the counselor is using. Presumably, a common starting place would be to assess the personality traits in question. If using the big-five theory, for example, one could use either the NEO Personality Inventory-Revised (Costa & McCrae, 1992) or the 44-item Big Five Inventory (BFI; John, Donahue, & Kentle, 1991; see also John, Naumann, & Soto, 2008; John & Srivastava, 1999). There are free versions of the BFI that self-score (see https://www.truity.com/test/big-five-personality-test or https://www.psychologistworld.com/influence-personality/five-factor-test/). Given that the BFI was created 25 plus years ago, Soto and John (2017), using advanced statistical techniques, developed the 60-item BFI-2 (take the test for free from the Colby Personality Lab, available at http://www.personalitylab.org/). After assessing personality, a counselor would then need to develop interventions aimed at reducing problematic traits while accentuating adaptive ones.

Strengths of this approach.

It appears that research exploring the relationships between personality theories and addiction is here to stay. Correlations are being found, particularly with the big-five theory.

Limitations of this approach.

Counselors in practice are advised to use empirically validated treatments. To date, available research does not provide sufficient rationale to use personality theory in working with addicts.

Family or "Systems Theory" Models

Historically, addiction counselors worked only with addicted individuals while family members were kept on the sideline. It didn't take long, however, for counselors to realize that family members could play a substantial role in motivating clients to get treatment (Capuzzi & Stauffer, 2012; McCrady, Ladd, & Hallgren, 2012).[2] Stemming from the work of Bertalanffy (1968) regarding systems theory, all family counseling approaches have subsequently been based on it (Stevens, 2013).

Systems theory suggests that a change in one aspect of a system will affect the other aspects of the system. For example, if one part of a machine stops working, likely the entire operation of the machine will be affected. If enough crucial parts are not working, the machine stops functioning altogether. Similarly, as you will read throughout this textbook, if children are raised in dysfunctional families, they are likely to become vulnerable to addictions and most types of mental disorders. The effect of parents on raising their children is enormous (both positively and negatively) (Watt, Weber, Davies, & Forster, 2017).

As Capuzzi and Stauffer (2012) noted, there are three predominant family models: behavioral, family systems, and family disease. In the behavioral family model, one or more members reinforce the addictive behavior of the *client*.[3] For example, some family members might actually prefer that our clients are involved in their addictive behavior. Why is that? Addicted individuals may demonstrate more desirable qualities when they are actively engaged in their addiction because, when they are not, they are experiencing some degree of withdrawal.

In the family systems model, the belief is that clients become the scapegoat or exemplar of problems within the family. In other words, the "identified" client is merely the person who most expresses the family dysfunction, at least in the form of an addiction. Other family members may express family problems differently (e.g., mental disorder).

Counselors who subscribe to the family disease model view the entire family as having a disorder or a disease (Capuzzi & Stauffer, 2012). For counseling to be effective then, the whole family is believed to require counseling simultaneously (i.e., family counseling). In other words, the entire family *must* be present for sessions (Capuzzi & Stauffer, 2012). Members of the family are viewed as being *codependent*, which is described by Cermak (as cited in McCrady et al., 2012, p. 229) as a "recognizable pattern of personality traits, predictably found within most members of chemically dependent families." Behaviors that perpetuate addictive behaviors in the family are known as *enabling* (McCrady et al., 2012).

Randle, Stroink, and Nelson (2015) concluded that addiction occurs within a complex family system that undergoes cyclical patterns of stability and change. They suggested that interventions and research should consider addiction as involving three separate but related adaptive cycles: "the addictive cycle itself, a transitory cycle, and a final cycle in which the individual is actively responsible for the maintenance of his or her own recovery" (p. 81).

Role of the Counselor

The role of the counselor will vary depending on which "school" of family counseling one is practicing. Common schools of practice include Bowen systems theory (BST), structural family counseling (SFC), strategic counseling (SC), and emotion-focused family therapy (EFT) (Gladding & Alderson, 2012). In BST, counselors coach and teach their clients to be more

[2]See Chapter 7 for an in-depth look at family counseling for addictions.

[3]The word client is placed in italics because, in systems theory, the client is often viewed as the scapegoat of family problems. In other words, it is the entire family system that shares the problem.

ROLEPLAY SCENARIO

The following roleplay provides an example of a client situation wherein family/systems theory models might be appropriate to use. If roleplay is not possible, write out a few lines of what you could say to the client that might be helpful. Do not be concerned if you do not know enough about family/systems theory models to demonstrate this approach competently. The goal here is merely to help anchor or enhance your learning so that you remember this approach is a possibility to use with some clients in actual addiction counseling practice.

You are working as an addiction counselor. Lily, age 19, has been upgrading high school for the past year. She has plans to enter a college in the fall, but her parents, Bradley and Marion, are concerned that she will not succeed because of her alcohol and drug use. Only her parents are attending this first session with you. Given your systems orientation, you take a complete history from Bradley and Marion concerning everyone in the immediate and extended family who has played a role in Lily's life. In doing so, you discover that Bradley has experienced severe alcohol use disorder (SAUD) for most of his adult life and that Marion was a hippie through the 1960s and 1970s and has retained few memories of this time due to her extensive drug use. Lily is also close to her Aunt Vera, who is only 10 years older than Lily. Vera has worked as a sex worker for several years now, and, as far as Marion, her sister, is aware, Vera smokes a lot of crack.

cognitive in their dealings with others. The approach is similar to Socratic dialogue where the counselor calmly asks questions until the family members can think for themselves. In SFC, counselors act as both observers and experts in making interventions to change the underlying structure of how a family operates. They also create clear boundaries among family members. In SC, counselors focus on the process rather than on the content of dysfunctional interactions in the family. Their role is to get clients to try new behaviors because the old behaviors are not working. Counselors in the SC approach are active, direct, goal-oriented, problem-focused, and pragmatic. In EFT, counselors focus on creating a stronger and healthier emotional bond among family members. The counselors' goal is to help clients identify their primary emotions and express them to others.

Strengths of This Approach

The effectiveness of each approach varies, particularly by the disorder. Overall, family-based therapies have demonstrated some effectiveness in addictions work (Carra, Clerici, Ghodse, Poldrugo, & el-Guebaly, 2009).

Limitations of This Approach

What are family counseling techniques for treating AUDs? Even with behavioral interventions, counselors have complained about a lack of administrative guidelines and procedures (Chan, 2003). There is no agreed-upon theory of alcoholism in the field of family therapy (Chan, 2003). Furthermore, family therapy has been criticized for minimizing the importance of individual factors in AUD (Chan, 2003). Also, often family therapists do not include children despite the recommendation of many theorists (Gladding & Alderson, 2012).

Sociocultural Theories

"In explaining substance abuse and addiction, it is important to examine the individual's unique perspective and their sociocultural context" (Thakker, 2013, p. 51).

Sociocultural theories focus on the influence that cultural, social, and societal factors have on individuals' relationships to substances and addictive behaviors. Nearly every culture in the world has discovered alcohol as a beverage, for example, but each culture has set boundaries regarding its use. Drinking alcohol is illegal in several Muslim countries (particularly, consumption by Muslims). Prophet Muhammad described drinking as "the mother of all vices" (Okon, 2014, p. 232), and the prescribed punishment for alcoholism and public intoxication as set out in the *Hadith* (i.e., a record of the words, actions, and habits of Prophet Muhammed) is 80 lashes (Okon, 2014). Given the religious and societal proscriptions against drinking, these countries have a low prevalence of alcohol consumption (Al-Ansari1, Thow, Day1, & Conigrave1, 2016).

Although there are many similarities between French and Italian cultures (e.g., both are primarily Catholic and high producers of alcoholic beverages), there are also some stark differences in their use of alcohol (McNeece & DiNitto, 2012). The French drink wine and spirits at home and elsewhere, they do not strongly oppose public drunkenness, and it is considered rude to refuse a drink. Italians, on the other hand, usually drink wine and mostly at family meals. They also strongly disfavor drunkenness. The result of this cultural difference? The World Health Organization (WHO, 2019) provides information on substance abuse in various countries around the world. From their Country Profiles 2014, Table 3.1 reveals differences between the two countries and the United States for comparison.

As indicated in Table 3.1, the rate of AUD in France for males is nearly seven times higher compared with Italy, whereas, for females, it is about three times higher. The rate was even higher for males and females, 15 years of age and higher, in the United States in 2010. The gender differences in alcohol consumption among the three countries are also apparent in Table 3.1.

McNeece and DiNitto (2012) noted that the Irish have high percentages of both abstainers and problem drinkers, whereas Jews have low rates of both. The Irish are more accepting of drunkenness, and Jews condemn it.

Bales (1946) hypothesized that cultures that condone alcohol use but also suppress aggression and sexuality, thereby inducing guilt, are likelier to have higher rates of alcoholism compared with more libertarian societies. Furthermore, individuals who drink for

TABLE 3.1 **Alcohol Consumption Patterns in France, Italy, and the United States**

France					
Liters#		Heavy*		AUD^	
2003–2005	2008–2010	Males	Females	Males	Females
13.0	11.8	42.2	17.7	8.8	2.5
Italy					
Liters#		Heavy*		AUD^	
2003–2005	2008–2010	Males	Females	Males	Females
8.1	6.5	8.0	0.7	1.3	0.8
United States					
Liters#		Heavy*		AUD^	
2003–2005	2008–2010	Males	Females	Males	Females
8.5	8.7	23.2	10.9	10.7	4.2

Source: All information extracted from reports with WHO (2019).

\# Liters of pure alcohol consumed per capita.

* Prevalence of heavy episodic drinking (at least 60 grams of pure alcohol on at least one occasion in the past 30 days in 2010, by population (ages 15+).

^ 12-month prevalence of AUDs in 2010 (ages 15+).

personal self-interest reasons (e.g., coping with stress) are also likelier to develop difficulties related to alcohol use.

Conversely, Bales suggested that individuals in societies that favor abstinence, ritual use for religious practices, and/or drinking within an amiable social situation are less likely to develop alcohol problems.

Cigarette smoking varies greatly between the genders among nations. For example, although smoking is common for males in many south and southeast countries, it is much less common for females compared to the United States, where the percentage of male and female smokers is substantially more comparable (Sreeramareddy, Pradhan, Mir, & Sin, 2014; see Chapter 12 for details).

Individuals living in communities that are disorganized demonstrate higher rates of substance use. For example, inner-city drug use is more common than in the suburbs (McNeece & DiNitto, 2012). Furthermore, drug use varies among specific subcultures. Heroin addiction is common among jazz musicians, for example, whereas sniffing glue is more common among inner-city youth than it is in other groups. Getting high on gasoline fumes also more frequently occurs on some Native American reservations (McNeece & DiNitto, 2012).

Social perceptions also characterize drug use. Although morphine and heroin are similar pharmacologically and biochemically, morphine is exalted as an opiate with great therapeutic value, whereas heroin is denounced with great contempt, disapproval, and fear. Recreational use of peyote is illegal in all states and territories by federal law. However, because some Indigenous groups have used it in religious ceremonies for thousands of years, its use is permitted for this purpose within the Native American Church. Interestingly, McNeece and DiNitto (2012) reported that, when peyote is taken merely to get high, it does not usually produce religious or mystical experiences for the user.

Even the concept of addiction varies "cross-culturally and historically in significant ways" (Peele, 2000, p. 599). Peele (2000, 2010) argued that how people view addiction influences the way some individuals become addicted, and it also influences their likelihood of becoming addicted. Adams (2016) suggested that social approaches to addiction might increase the effectiveness of treatment.

A social influence that affects addiction is called the *social network perspective* (MacKillop & Ray, 2018). This perspective refers to the finding that substance users and addicted individuals are likely to associate with users who demonstrate similar levels of use of the same substance or addictive behavior. In other words, individuals with SAUD tend to associate with others with SAUD. Heroin-addicted individuals spend time with other heroin addicts, and so on. Associating with others who engage in a similar level of use creates social and sometimes romantic bonds. It is common, for example, that couples will share the same addiction, which is unfortunately associated with higher levels of intimate partner violence and poor parenting (MacKillop & Ray, 2018). When bonds are created with others who share the same (or a similar) addiction, treatment is often compromised. Giving up an addiction also means, in many if not most instances, that addicted individuals need to give up friends and lovers as well (MacKillop & Ray, 2018).

Role of the Counselor

Counselors operating within a sociocultural model need to understand how substances and potentially addictive behaviors fit within the sociocultural realities of their clients (Nielsen & Mai, 2017). We know, for example, that different ethnic groups are

ROLEPLAY SCENARIO

The following roleplay provides an example of a client situation wherein sociocultural theories might be appropriate to use. If roleplay is not possible, write out a few lines of what you could say to the client that might be helpful. Do not be concerned if you do not know enough about sociocultural theories to demonstrate this approach competently. The goal here is merely to help anchor or enhance your learning so that you remember this approach is a possibility to use with some clients in actual addiction counseling practice.

You are working as an addiction counselor. Jean-Pierre, age 31, is in your office because his employer sent him to talk to you about his alcohol use. His employer's referral letter informed you that, nearly every day, Jean-Pierre comes to work still smelling of wine and is frequently irritable with his peers. You find out that Jean-Pierre drinks about one and a half bottles of white wine every night. He is quick to point out that, back in France, everyone he knows drinks at least this much if not more every day. Living in Salt Lake City for the past 6 months, he has encountered a great deal of intolerance toward his alcohol intake.

affected differently by problematic gambling (Richard, Baghurst, Faragher, & Stotts, 2017). Rowan et al. (2014) wrote about cultural interventions that are appropriate for Indigenous populations. The counselors' role is to design interventions that are appropriate given the clients' various sociocultural contexts. Sociocultural models begin from the broader perspective (the sociocultural context) to the individual's positioning within that context. For example, knowing that alcohol consumption is high within Irish culture does not mean that the Irish client before you is a heavy drinker. By remaining sensitive and interested in sociocultural issues, counselors can provide appropriate treatment.

Strengths of This Approach

A major strength of sociocultural models is their emphasis on understanding people in context. By doing so, counselors can gain a much better understanding of how clients come to the place where they are now. Such knowledge also provides the opportunity to develop interventions that are culturally relevant.

Limitations of This Approach

The emphasis, comparable to the systems approaches, is on external factors or influences that affect clients' relationships with substances and addictive behaviors. Clearly, this is only part of the puzzle of addictions. If this were not true, all individuals from within the same sociocultural position would experience addictions similarly. Furthermore, clients may assume the identity of a heavy user of a substance or addictive behavior by attributing this to their culture, thereby absolving themselves of responsibility for their difficulties.

Postmodern Theories

"There is no absolute reality except as a social product" (Gladding & Alderson, 2012, p. 279).

What is a postmodern approach? Well, imagine waking up one morning and finding that the reality that you have been living in until now has disappeared while you slept. What would you care about, what would give your life meaning, and what would be the point of any of it? What if all the knowledge you have ever gained was now in question? Something comparable happened in the field of psychology. Paul Pedersen (1990) wrote about his conception of four forces having occurred in counseling practice. The first force was psychoanalysis, the second was behaviorism, third was humanism, and the fourth force (which we are living in now) is multiculturalism. The force of multiculturalism can be viewed as a subset of postmodernism (Gladding & Alderson, 2012). As Gladding and Alderson (2012) wrote, the basic tenets of postmodern thought as applied to counseling practice include the following:

1. Accept that no one has privileged knowledge.
2. Be aware of the counselor's position of power.
3. Recognize that psychology itself is a set of power practices and narratives.
4. Assume a "not-knowing" position.
5. Remember that clients already hold knowledge about how to be successful.
6. Know that the focus on some themes means deemphasizing other possibilities.
7. Avoid all interpretations and reframes of clients' thoughts, feelings, and actions. (headings quoted from p. 278)

According to the postmodern perspective, there is no single reality but rather multiple realities regarding the beliefs that people hold and the ways they live their lives. Reality as we know it is shaped by historical, social, societal, political, and linguistic realities. Although the modern theories (e.g., psychoanalysis, behaviorism, humanism) regarding counseling are primarily developed and applicable to White individuals living in Western society, multicultural approaches focus on the different worldviews that other people have in different cultures and in different parts of the world. One of the most fundamental distinguishing features is the difference between having an individualistic worldview (life's purpose is to fulfill oneself), exemplified in the United States and most Western nations, and having a collectivist view (life's purpose is to uphold the importance of family), exemplified in Mexico, Central and South America, Arab-dominant countries, South Asia, East Asia, and Southeast Asian countries (Gladding & Alderson, 2012).

Two postmodern approaches have become popular in counseling practice today: narrative therapy (founders: Michael White and David Epston) and solution-focused therapy (founders: Steve de Shazer and Insoo Kim Berg). A third one that has not gained the same degree of popularity is collaborative therapy (founders: Harold Goolishian and Harlene Anderson) (Gladding & Alderson, 2012).

Young (2017) provided an exemplary overview of the techniques used in narrative therapy in addictions practice. These techniques and those of solution-focused therapy are included in Chapter 6. Young argued that many studies have found that traditional substance abuse treatment is not nearly as effective as once thought (Currie, 1993; Foote, Wilkens, Kosanke, & Higgs, 2014; Glaser, 2013, 2015). Looking at narrative therapy as a strengths-based perspective, Young, and the title of his article, even refused to call this perspective a "recovery" movement because recovery implies that something was initially missing or absent (i.e., something needs to be recovered). His title began with a word he called "uncovery" to suggest that the necessary attributes to overcoming addiction were always within the individual. As Young noted, most models, including the ever-popular biological/disease model, are pathology-based approaches that stand in inherent conflict with the strengths-based approaches (which are synonymous with postmodern approaches).

Providing a diagnosis, in Young's (2017) view, is "inherently disempowering" (p. 56). When professionals name the problem, the power is taken away from clients. It places clients into a separate group, one that distinguishes them from those who do not have the problem. Young viewed diagnostic labeling as reductionist because it fails to account for several factors that underlie the struggle, the strengths, and the environmental factors that help tell the story of a person's challenge with addictive behavior(s). As Currie (1993) highlighted, most people who have an SUD never receive treatment, and yet substantial numbers quit using without getting any professional assistance.

Young (2017) suggested that AA is disempowering to individuals as it creates a dominant narrative that alcoholics must surrender themselves to a higher power to overcome their addiction. In fairness, Young wrote that AA might have been designed for chronic individuals with SAUD and that it was never meant to be applied to such a broad group as to whom it is now being promoted. Even Jellinek (1960), who is generally considered the father of the disease model of addiction, identified only two of five drinking patterns as indicative of the "disease" often referred to as alcoholism.

The recovery movement was viewed by Young (2017) as inherently strengths-based. He provided an example at the community level with the check-up phone calls that the Connecticut Community for Addiction Recovery initiated. Those in Connecticut leaving a treatment facility are asked if they would like a weekly follow-up phone call from a peer, also in recovery, for the next 12 weeks. The vast majority agreed to having these calls, and many wanted them to continue beyond the initial 12 weeks. This small initiative has yielded sobriety rates of 88%, and, for those who have relapsed, a 60% re-engagement rate in treatment. Within a strengths-based perspective, clients are empowered to take responsibility for the long-term management of their disorder. Medical terms like "*patient, diagnosis, disease*, and *prognosis*" are never used (Young, 2017, p. 60).

ROLEPLAY SCENARIO

The following roleplay provides an example of a client situation wherein postmodern theories might be appropriate to use. If roleplay is not possible, write out a few lines of what you could say to the client that might be helpful. Do not be concerned if you do not know enough about postmodern theories to demonstrate this approach competently. The goal here is merely to help anchor or enhance your learning so that you remember this approach is a possibility to use with some clients in actual addiction counseling practice.

You are working as an addiction counselor. Genesis, age 47, tells you in the first session that she has been addicted to food since she was a child. Her parents let her eat whatever she wanted, and now she weighs more than 300 pounds. She tells you that she has gone through many programs and has seen many counselors. Genesis has learned so much about different counseling approaches that she has become an expert consumer of counseling services. In telling you her story, she talks of many counseling sessions where she felt disempowered by the counselor who tried to take control of how "therapy" was going to look. Her last counselor told her that she would have to attend weekly sessions for at least a year if she were serious about permanently losing weight. As a staunch feminist, Genesis has taken offense to these approaches. She has asked you to provide her with either solution-focused therapy or narrative therapy.

Role of the Counselor

The first role of a postmodern counselor is to determine how active and committed clients are to making a change. Postmodern counselors view themselves as collaborators and masters of asking questions. Clients are always considered to be the experts on their lives. Symptoms are perceived as not serving a function; instead, they are oppressive. Consequently, efforts are made to eliminate problems as quickly as possible. Counselors also act as facilitators by helping clients access resources and strengths that they already possess. There is no blaming or asking "why." Particularly in solution-focused therapy, counselors are not interested in how the problem arose. They are concerned only with helping their clients arrive at a solution.

Strengths of This Approach

Some of the strengths are that blame is alleviated, and dialogue is mostly focused on resolving the problem, exceptions to problems are highlighted, and clients are prepared ahead of time for possible setbacks. Most postmodern approaches emphasize brevity and empowerment. The approach is of a positive nature in working with all clients. The collaborative nature creates a less hierarchical and more egalitarian and respectful approach to working with clients. Although the approaches focus on change, small changes in behavior are acknowledged. Furthermore, clients attend as many sessions as they choose compared to some other approaches where they are expected to attend a certain number of sessions (Gladding & Alderson, 2012).

Limitations of This Approach

Because postmodern approaches do not adhere to a single reality, no norms are dictating what clients should become by the end of counseling. The history of clients' problems is minimized, which may leave some clients feeling that they have not been sufficiently heard. Little attention is given to focusing on insight. Although these approaches are popular today, they continue to lack sufficient empirical validation, particularly in rigorously controlled quantitative studies (Gladding & Alderson, 2012).

Biopsychosocial Model

It should be evident by now that what is lacking in the theories and models already described is an integration of approaches. Skewes and Gonzalez (2013) noted that the biopsychosocial model occurred following criticisms of the ever-popular biomedical theories. Furthermore, Skewes and Gonzalez stated that research does not support the medical model of addiction; instead, the biopsychosocial model better fits the data. First, illness is not merely the result of biochemical changes or neurological abnormalities. Second, some people become sick in the absence of any "abnormality or dysfunction" (Skewes & Gonzales, 2013, p. 62). MacKillop and Ray (2018) concurred, remarking that none of the available theories has provided a widely accepted account explaining why some people develop addictions and others do not. What we have are several empirically supported theoretical approaches that MacKillop and Ray suggested fall into three overarching categories: biological, psychological, and social models. Collectively, these form the biopsychosocial model (MacKillop & Ray, 2018).

Give these three categories, what should be the role of theory in addiction theory? MacKillop and Ray (2018) suggested that it should play a major role, and, for a treatment to be considered evidence-based, it needs to be rooted in interventions, practices, and techniques that are theoretically informed.

MacKillop and Ray (2018) described the biological, psychological, and social models individually. What emerged

ROLEPLAY SCENARIO

The following roleplay provides an example of a client situation wherein the biopsychosocial model might be appropriate to use. If roleplay is not possible, write out a few lines of what you could say to the client that might be helpful. Do not be concerned if you do not know enough about the biopsychosocial model to demonstrate this approach competently. The goal here is merely to help anchor or enhance your learning so that you remember this approach is a possibility to use with some clients in actual addiction counseling practice.

You are working as an addiction counselor. Romina, age 17, was sent to see you from her high school counselor. The accompanying referral letter from the counselor indicated that Romina was born in Uruguay and lived there prior to a year ago. The letter reports that Romina is coming to school high on crystal meth most days of the week, and it is having a serious impact on her academic performance. She is currently headed toward getting consistent F grades. You are now meeting with Romina for her first counseling session. In her words, "Mi consejero es estúpido (my counselor is stupid). She knows nothing about my country. Everyone my age uses drugs, all my friends, y toda mi familia (and all my family)." As you talk with Romina, you discover that she comes from a family lineage that has used a lot of drugs, and she recounts many relatives (recent and distant) becoming cocaine and heroin addicts. It soon becomes apparent that Romina has no intention of quitting her use of crystal meth.

from their review is that the answer to the question of why some people develop addictions is complex. There is no single answer. Skewes and Gonzales (2013) concluded that treatment programs would glean benefit by taking a biopsychosocial view of addiction.

Role of the Counselor

Using this model, counselors need to consider the complex interaction of all the factors that potentially contribute to addiction (Capuzzi & Stauffer, 2012). Treatment is likely to also be multimodal with consideration given to as many biological, psychological, social, and sociocultural influences as possible.

Strengths of This Approach

The strength of the biopsychosocial model is its comprehensiveness. Instead of subscribing to one school of thought, counselors embrace every approach that offers potential therapeutic value.

Limitations of This Approach

In MacKillop and Ray's (2018) critique of the biopsychosocial model, they stated that the model has never created a true synthesis. Instead, those who write about the model continue to describe the three categories of theory separately (as did MacKillop & Ray, 2018). Addiction counselors await a true integration of theory and approaches for their work with clients.

RESOURCES AND VIDEOS

Resources

1. The Genetics of Drug and Alcohol Addiction. https://addictionsandrecovery.org/is-addiction-a-disease.htm
2. Alternative Models of Addiction. https://www.ncbi.nlm.nih.gov/pmc/articles/PMC4327176/
3. The Meaning of Addiction / Theories of Addiction. https://www.peele.net/lib/moa3.html
4. Addiction / Substance Abuse. https://www.psychologytoday.com/us/basics/addiction
5. Theories of addiction: Causes and maintenance of addiction. https://www.open.edu/openlearn/ocw/pluginfile.php/629967/mod_resource/content/1/addictionarticle1teeson.pdf
6. What causes addiction? (Recovery.org). https://www.recovery.org/topics/what-causes-addiction/

Videos

To view these videos, search their titles on YouTube.

1. *Addiction is a disease. We should treat it like one | Michael Botticelli.*
2. *What is Addiction? [Gabor Maté].*
3. *(2) The 5 Models of Addiction* by Cameron Haslehurst.
4. *Drug Addiction is a Learning Disorder, says Maia Szalavitz.*
5. *The Roots of Addiction.* The Agenda with Steve Paikin.

JOURNALS AND CONFERENCES

Journals

Although there do not appear to be journals that deal specifically with theories of addiction, with perhaps the exception of the first one cited here, each chapter of this textbook lists journals that deal with addictions. Most of these journals will publish manuscripts on one or more theories. Here are a few likely choices:

1. *Addiction Research and Theory.* https://www.researchgate.net/journal/1606-6359_Addiction_Research_and_Theory
2. *Journal of Addiction Research & Therapy.* https://www.omicsonline.org/addiction-research-therapy.php
3. *Journal of Addictive Behaviors, Therapy & Rehabilitation.* https://www.scitechnol.com/addictive-behaviors-therapy-rehabilitation.php
4. *Journal of Addiction Medicine.* https://www.asam.org/resources/publications/journal-of-addiction-medicine
5. *Journal of Addiction.* https://www.hindawi.com/journals/jad/
6. *Addiction.* http://addictionjournal.org/

Conferences

Although there do not appear to be conferences that deal specifically with theories of addiction, each chapter of this textbook lists conferences that deal with addictions. Most of these conferences will include presentations on one or more theories. Here are a few likely choices:

1. Global Conference on Addiction and Behavioral Health. Do an Internet search for details regarding the next conference.
2. National Counseling Advances Conference. Do an Internet search for details regarding the next conference.
3. American Society of Addictive Medicine Annual Conference. https://www.asam.org/
4. National Institute on Drug Abuse. https://www.drugabuse.gov/
5. World Congress on Advances in Addiction Science and Medicine. https://addiction.cmesociety.com/

INDIVIDUAL EXERCISES

1. Spend an afternoon or evening in a safe environment for you where one or more individuals are smoking cigarettes, drinking alcohol, or doing both. Focus on one individual that draws your attention. After noticing this person periodically, imagine how each theory in this chapter would explain this person's behavior. How do you feel toward this person's smoking and/or alcohol use as you imagine each theory explaining it? Which theory sits best with you, and why? Additionally, which theory is the worst fit for you, and why?
2. Learn about theories that explain a specific mental disorder such as bipolar disorder, schizophrenia spectrum disorder, dissociative identity disorder, or autism spectrum disorder. How do the theories that explain this disorder compare and contrast with theories that explain addictions?
3. Imagine that you are responsible for developing a treatment program for individuals with moderate or severe AUD that does not use the biological/disease model. What would your program look like? Which other theory or theories would you utilize in developing the treatment program, and why? Why would you exclude one or more theories in developing the program?

CLASSROOM EXERCISES

1. Assign a theory to different groups of students. Then offer a case that can be conceptualized through each model. Once the groups have had time to create their conceptualization, have them offer theirs to the class in any of several ways (e.g., written on the board, class discussion, class debate where each group stays within their conceptualization). An example you could use in class is as follows:

   Miguel is a 21-year-old Mexican American. His parents emigrated to the United States when he was 10 years old. Consequently, he has developed a bicultural identity. He has been indoctrinated into the collectivist views shared by most Mexican families, and he has learned to be more cooperative than competitive in his approach to life. Since he turned 21, he has been drinking and using several stimulants regularly. His parents do not know about his alcohol and drug use, but Miguel tells you that his papa drinks between one half and an entire 26er (26 ounces) of tequila every night. On numerous occasions, he has physically struck his mama after getting drunk. Miguel tells you that he believes that he uses alcohol and drugs because he feels unable to stand up to his papa regarding the abuse of his mama. When you ask him about his friends, you find out that he mostly hangs out with other Hispanic youth who also drink excessively and use stimulants periodically. Miguel tells you that he has become concerned about his drinking because of what it has done to his papa. For some reason, however, he cannot seem to stop the intense cravings for alcohol that he experiences daily. When he has tried to stop drinking, he begins shaking so much that he gets scared, and this causes him to resume imbibing alcoholic beverages.

2. Given the importance of theory in the treatment of addictions, have students write a reflective paper on their preferred theory, describing the theory, the strengths of the theory in practice, and the weaknesses of the theory in practice. The emphasis in the paper would explain why the student chose this theory over other theories.
3. Have an addiction counselor present to your class. Find out ahead of time which theory he or she most subscribes to or uses in treating addicted clients. Have your class prepare a few questions in advance to ensure a lively and vibrant learning experience.

CHAPTER SUMMARY

This chapter began by defining and describing the concept of a *theory*, which is used synonymously in this textbook with the term *model*. Over the past century, addiction models have flourished, but each has failed to build upon what was addressed earlier by other theories. Theory ought to inform treatment, and a good theory coexists with empirically validated treatments.

The theories described in this chapter include the moral/choice model, biological/disease theories, psychological theories, family models, sociocultural theories, postmodern theories, and the biopsychosocial model. A brief discussion followed each theory with a look at the role of the counselor using each approach, the strengths of the approach, and its limitations.

The moral/choice model was the first pervasive addiction theory, which stigmatized addicted individuals as it focused on their sinful nature. Eventually, this view morphed by some into viewing addicted individuals as people with free will who continued making bad choices despite their self-evident maladaptive behaviors.

Chronologically, the ever-popular biological/disease theories followed, which fortunately helped remove the stigma as addicted individuals were now seen as ordinary people who experienced a disease comparable to others with physical diseases. Genetic and neuroscience research continues to support this view of addictions.

Four psychological theories were considered, including the (a) psychodynamic theories that focus on clients' pasts in explaining their addictions, (b) behavioral/learning theories that contend that addictions are learned behaviors that can be unlearned, (c) cognitive-behavioral theories that provide several reasons (i.e., cognitions) that perpetuate addictive behaviors, and (d) personality theories that purport that people become dependent because they have "addictive personalities." Each theory helps explain the mystery of addictions.

Other researchers and counselors subscribe to a family/systems theory perspective. In this approach, the "identified" client represents an endemic problem shared with other family members. The three predominant models that use a systems approach are the behavioral, family systems, and family disease models. Each model advocates different approaches for helping families improve and possibly heal from addiction (and other problems that originate from the family dysfunction).

Sociocultural theories focus on the context (environment) in which addictions become situated. If counselors can understand the dynamic interplay among the cultural, social, and societal factors that affect clients, addictions become better understood. Such understanding also informs treatment possibilities.

Many contemporary counselors have been exposed to postmodern theories. These theories postulate that reality is only in the eyes of the beholder. Instead of a single truth, there are multiple realities. No single truth is philosophically better than any other. Counselors endorsing this view empower their clients by not imposing their "expert" status. Instead, they help clients embrace their strengths that are already there.

The biopsychosocial model acknowledges that the three broad categories represented by the biological, psychological, and social models each contributes to our understanding of addictions. Although advocates of the model purport to offer a synthesis of approaches, to date, they have failed to provide an integration of the theories that already exist. Instead, each of the three categories is described by researchers and writers as separate theories. Counselors applying the biopsychosocial model attempt to include as many factors as possible in their understanding, assessment, and treatment of clients with addictive behaviors.

REFERENCES

Adams, P. J. (2016). Switching to a social approach to addiction: Implications for theory and practice. *International Journal of Mental Health and Addiction, 14*(1), 86–94.

Al-Ansari1, B., Thow, A.-M., Day1, C. A., & Conigrave1, K. M. (2016). Extent of alcohol prohibition in civil policy in Muslim majority countries: The impact of globalization. *Addiction, 111*, 1703–1713.

Alderson, K. (2013). *Counseling LGBTI clients*. Thousand Oaks, CA: SAGE.

Amodeo, M. (2015). The addictive personality. *Substance Use & Misuse, 50*, 1031–1036.

Anderson, R. E., Barnes, G. E., & Murray, R. P. (2011). Psychometric properties and long-term predictive validity of the Addiction-Prone Personality (APP) scale. *Personality and Individual Differences, 50*, 651–656.

Andreassen, C. S., Bjorvatn, B., Moen, B. E., Waage, S., Mageroy, N., & Pallesen, S. (2016). A longitudinal study of the relationship between the five-factor model of personality and workaholism. *TPM-Testing, Psychometrics, Methodology in Applied Psychology, 23*(3), 285–298.

Arevian, M. (2010). Training trainees, young activists, to conduct awareness campaigns about prevention of substance abuse among Lebanese/Armenian young people. *Journal of Interprofessional Care, 24*(2), 173–182.

Bailey, K. M., & Stewart, S. H. (2014). Relations among trauma, PTSD, and substance misuse: The scope of the problem. In

P. Ouimette & J. P. Read (Eds.), *Trauma and substance abuse: Causes, consequences, and treatment of comorbid disorders* (2nd ed., pp. 11–34). Washington, DC: American Psychological Association.

Bales, B. F. (1946). Cultural differences in rates of alcoholism. *Quarterly Journal of Studies on Alcohol, 6*, 480–499.

Bandura, A. (1977). *Social learning theory*. Englewood Cliffs, NJ: Prentice-Hall.

Bandura, A., & Huston, A. C. (1961). Identification as a process of incidental learning. *Journal of Abnormal and Social Psychology, 63*(2), 311–318.

Bandura, A., Ross, D., & Ross, S. A. (1961). Transmission of aggression through the imitation of aggressive models. *Journal of Abnormal and Social Psychology, 63*(3), 575–582.

Bandura, A., Ross, D., & Ross, S. A. (1963). Imitation of film-mediated aggressive models. *Journal of Abnormal and Social Psychology. 66*(1), 3–11.

Berkel, T. D. M., & Pandey, S. C. (2017). Emerging role of epigenetic mechanisms in alcohol addiction. *Alcoholism: Clinical and Experimental Research, 41*, 666–680.

Bertalanffy, L. V. (1968). *General systems theory: Foundation, development, applications*. New York, NY: Braziller.

Braun, B., Stopfer, J. M., Muller, K. W., Beutel, M. E., & Egloff, B. (2016). Personality and video gaming: Comparing regular gamers, non-gamers, and gaming addicts and differentiating between game genres. *Computers in Human Behavior, 55*(Part A), 406–412.

Brents, L. K., Tripathi, S. P., Young, J., James, G., & Kilts, C. D. (2015). The role of childhood maltreatment in the altered trait and global expression of personality in cocaine addiction. *Journal of Psychiatric Research, 64*, 23–31.

Broadus, A. D., & Evans, W. P. (2015). Developing the public attitudes about addiction instrument. *Addiction Research & Theory, 23*(2), 115–130.

Brunborg, G. S., Hanss, D., Mentzoni, R. A., Molde, H., & Pallesen, S. (2016). Problem gambling and the five-factor model of personality: A large population-based study. *Addiction, 111*(8), 1428–1435.

Capuzzi, D., & Stauffer, M. D. (2012). History and etiological models of addiction. In D. Capuzzi & M. D. Stauffer (Eds.), *Foundations of addictions counselling* (2nd ed., pp. 1–15). Upper Saddle River, NJ: Pearson Education.

Carra, G., Clerici, M., Ghodse, H., Poldrugo, F., & el-Guebaly, N. (2009). Family issues in the field of addiction treatment. In A. Browne-Miller (Ed.), *The Praeger international collection on addictions, Vol 3: Characteristics and treatment perspectives* (pp. 129–139). Santa Barbara, CA: Praeger/ABC-CLIO.

Carter, A., & Hall, W. (2013). Ethical issues in the treatment of drug dependence. In P. M. Miller, S. A. Ball, M. E. Bates, A. W. Blume, K. M. Kampman, D. J. Kavanagh, M. E. Larimer, N. M. Petry, & P. De Witte (Eds.), *Comprehensive addictive behaviors and disorders, Vol. 3: Interventions for addiction* (pp. 611–620). San Diego, CA: Elsevier Academic Press.

Chan, J. G. (2003). An examination of family-involved approaches to alcoholism treatment. *Family Journal, 11*(2), 129–138.

Chesworth, R., & Corbit, L. H. (2017). Recent developments in the behavioural and pharmacological enhancement of extinction of drug seeking. *Addiction Biology, 22*, 3–43.

Cho, S. B., Su, J., Kuo, S. I.-C., Bucholz, K. K., Chan, G., Edenberg, H. J., . . . Dick, D. M. (2019). Positive and negative reinforcement are differentially associated with alcohol consumption as a function of alcohol dependence. *Psychology of Addictive Behaviors, 33*(1), 58–68.

Coplan, J. (2010, August 29). Thorndike and Watson: Founding fathers of behaviorism. *Psychology Today*. Retrieved on February 25, 2019, from https://www.psychologytoday.com/us/blog/making-sense-autistic-spectrum-disorders/201008/020-thorndike-watson-founding-fathers

Costa, P. T., & McCrae, R. R. (1992). *NEO PI-R professional manual*. Odessa, FL: Psychological Assessment Resources.

Craparo, G. (2017). Unrepressed unconscious and *unsaid* in addictive symptomatology. *Psychodynamic Practice: Individuals, Groups and Organisations, 23*, 282–292.

Currie, E. (1993). *Reckoning: Drugs, the cities, and the American future*. New York, NY: Hill and Wang.

Delic, M., Kajdiz, K., & Pregelj, P. (2017). Association of the five-factor model personality traits and opioid addiction treatment outcome. *Psychiatria Danubina, 29*(Suppl 3), 289–291.

Dodes, L. M., & Dodes, J. (2017). The case study method in psychodynamic psychology: Focus on addiction. *Clinical Social Work Journal, 45*, 215–226.

Faulkner, C. A. (2013). Etiology of substance abuse: Why people use. In P. Stevens & R. L. Smith (Eds.), *Substance abuse counselling: Theory and practice* (5th ed., pp. 98–121). Upper Saddle River, NJ: Pearson Education.

Fernandez-Montalvo, J., Lopez-Goni, J. J., & Arteaga, A. (2015). Psychological, physical, and sexual abuse in addicted patients who undergo treatment. *Journal of Interpersonal Violence, 30*(8), 1279–1298.

Fisher, G. L., & Harrison, T. C. (2013). *Substance abuse: Information for school counselors, social workers, therapists, and counselors* (5th ed.). Upper Saddle River, NJ: Pearson Education.

Fletcher, K., Nutton, J., & Brend, D. (2015). Attachment, a matter of substance: The potential of attachment theory in the treatment of addictions. *Clinical Social Work Journal, 43*, 109–117.

Flores, P. J. (2004). *Addictions as an attachment disorder*. New York, NY: Jason Aronson.

Foddy, B. (2017). Addiction: The pleasures and perils of operant behavior. In N. Heather & G. Segal (Eds.), *Addiction and choice: Rethinking the relationship* (pp. 49–65). New York, NY: Oxford University Press.

Foote, J., Wilkens, C., Kosanke, N., & Higgs, S. (2014). *Beyond addiction: How science and kindness help people change*. New York, NY: Scribner.

George, O., Koob, G. F., & Vendruscolo, L. F. (2014). Negative reinforcement via motivational withdrawal is the driving force behind the transition to addiction. *Psychopharmacology, 231*(19), 3911–3917.

Gibbons, M. B. C., Crits-Christoph, P., & Hearon, B. (2008). The empirical status of psychodynamic therapies. *Annual Review of Clinical Psychology, 4*, 93–108.

Gladding, S. T., & Alderson, K. G. (2012). *Counselling: A comprehensive profession* (Canadian ed.). Toronto, ON: Pearson Canada.

Glaser, G. (2013). *Her best-kept secret: Why women drink—And how they regain control*. New York, NY: Simon & Schuster.

Glaser, G. (2015, April). The false gospel of Alcoholics Anonymous. *Atlantic, 315*(3), 50–60.

Gottdiener, W. H. (2013). Assimilative dynamic addiction psychotherapy. *Journal of Psychotherapy Integration, 23*, 39–48.

Granillo, M. T., Perron, B. E., Gutowski, S. M., & Jarman, C. (2013). Cognitive behavioral therapy with substance use disorders: Theory, evidence, and practice. In M. G. Vaughn & B. E. Perron (Eds.), *Social work practice in the addictions* (pp. 101–118). New York, NY: Springer Science + Business Media.

Hammersley, R., Dalgarno, P., Mccollum, S., Reid, M., Strike, Y., Smith, A., . . . Liddell, D. (2016). Trauma in the childhood stories of people who have injected drugs. *Addiction Research & Theory, 24*(2), 135–151.

Hamonniere, T., & Varescon, I. (2018). Metacognitive beliefs in addictive behaviours: A systematic review. *Addictive Behaviors, 85*, 51–63.

Henden, E. (2017). Addiction, compulsion, and weakness of the will: A dual-process perspective. In N. Heather & G. Segal (Eds.), *Addiction and choice: Rethinking the relationship* (pp. 116–132). New York, NY: Oxford University Press.

Heyman, G. M. (2009). *Addiction: A disorder of choice*. Cambridge, MA, Harvard University Press.

Jellinek, E. M. (1960). *The disease concept of alcoholism*. New Haven, CT: Hillhouse Press.

John, O. P., Donahue, E. M., & Kentle, R. L. (1991). *The Big Five Inventory—Versions 4a and 54*. Berkeley, CA: University of California, Berkeley, Institute of Personality and Social Research.

John, O. P., Naumann, L. P., & Soto, C. J. (2008). Paradigm shift to the integrative Big-Five trait taxonomy: History, measurement, and conceptual issues. In O. P. John, R. W. Robins, & L. A. Pervin (Eds.), *Handbook of personality: Theory and research* (3rd ed., pp. 114–158). New York, NY: Guilford Press.

John, O. P., & Srivastava, S. (1999). The Big Five trait taxonomy: History, measurement, and theoretical perspectives. In L. A. Pervin & O. P. John (Eds.), *Handbook of personality: Theory and research* (2nd ed., pp. 102–138). New York, NY: Guilford Press.

Kayis, A. R., Satici, S. A., Yilmaz, M. F., Simsek, D., Ceyhan, E., & Bakioglu, F. (2016). Big five-personality trait and internet addiction: A meta-analytic review. *Computers in Human Behavior, 63*, 35–40.

Kopetz, C. E., & Lejuez, C. W. (2016). *Addictions: A social psychological perspective. In Addictions: A social psychological perspective* (pp. x, 289). New York, NY: Routledge/Taylor & Francis Group.

Lamb, R. J., & Ginsburg, B. C. (2018). Addiction as a BAD, a behavioral allocation disorder. *Pharmacology, Biochemistry and Behavior, 164*, 62–70.

Lu, F.-Y., Wen, S., Deng, G., & Tang, Y.-L. (2017). Self-concept mediate the relationship between childhood maltreatment and abstinence motivation as well as self-efficacy among drug addicts. *Addictive Behaviors, 68*, 52–58.

MacKillop, J., & Ray, L. A. (2018). The etiology of addiction: A contemporary biopsychosocial approach (pp. 32–53). In J. MacKillop, G. A. Kenna, L. Leggio, & L. A. Ray (Eds.), *Integrating psychological and pharmacological treatments for addictive disorders: An evidence-based guide*. New York, NY: Routledge/Taylor & Francis Group.

Mackinnon, S. P., Lambe, L., & Stewart, S. H. (2016). Relations of five-factor personality domains to gambling motives in emerging adult gamblers: A longitudinal study. *Journal of Gambling Issues, 34*, 179–200.

Malone, J. C. (2014). Did John B. Watson really "found" behaviorism? *Behavior Analyst, 37*(1), 1–12.

Maté, G. (2008). *In the realm of hungry ghosts: Close encounters with addiction*. Toronto, ON: Vintage Books.

McCarthy, D. E., Curtin, J. J., Piper, M. E., & Baker, T. B. (2010). Negative reinforcement: Possible clinical implications of an integrative model. In J. D. Kassel (Ed.), *Substance abuse and emotion* (pp. 15–42). Washington, DC: American Psychological Association.

McCrady, B. S., Ladd, B. O., & Hallgren, K. A. (2012). Theoretical bases of family approaches to substance abuse treatment. In S. T. Walters & F. Rotgers (Eds.), *Treating substance abuse: Theory and technique* (3rd ed., pp. 224–255). New York, NY: Guilford Press.

McCrae, R. R., & Costa, P. T. (1987). Validation of the five-factor model of personality across instruments and observers. *Journal of Personality and Social Psychology, 52*(1), 81–90.

McGraw-Hill. (2002). *Dictionary of American idioms and phrasal verbs*. Retrieved from https://idioms.thefreedictionary.com/Fool+me+once%2c+shame+on+you%3b+fool+me+twice%2c+shame+on+me

McNeece, C. A., & DiNitto, D. M. (2012). *Chemical dependency: A systems approach* (*4th ed.*). Upper Saddle River, NJ: Pearson Education.

Merriam-Webster. (2019a). *Definition of model*. Retrieved from https://www.merriam-webster.com/dictionary/model

Merriam-Webster. (2019b). *Definition of theory*. Retrieved from https://www.merriam-webster.com/dictionary/theory

Milkman, H. B., & Sunderwirth, S. G. (2010). *Craving for ecstasy and natural highs: A positive approach to mood alteration*. Thousand Oaks, CA: SAGE.

Morse, S. J. (2017). Addiction, choice, and criminal law. In N. Heather & G. Segal (Eds.), *Addiction and choice: Rethinking the relationship* (pp. 426–445). New York, NY: Oxford University Press.

Naim-Feil, J., Arunogiri, S., Spagnolo, P. A., & Lubman, D. I. (2017). Addiction. In N. J. Rinehart, J. L. Bradshaw, & P. G. Enticott (Eds.), *Developmental disorders of the brain* (2nd ed., pp. 208–230). New York, NY: Routledge.

Naja, W. J., Pelissolo, A., Haddad, R. S., Baddoura, R., & Baddoura, C. (2000). A general population survey on patterns of benzodiazepine use and dependence in Lebanon. *Acta Psychiatrica Scandinavica, 102*(6), *2000*, 429–431.

Nielsen, A. S., & Mai, A.-M. (2017). Alcohol and culture: An introduction. *Nordic Studies on Alcohol and Drugs, 34*, 285–288.

Nyhuis, P. W., Niederhofer, E., Scherbaum, N., Schifano, F., Bonnet, U., Dembski, N., . . . Tenbergen, M. (2018). Effectiveness of psychoanalytic-interactional group therapy vs. behavioral group therapy in routine outpatient treatment of alcohol-dependent patients. *Substance Use & Misuse, 53*, 426–431.

Okon, E. E. (2014). Hudud punishments in Islamic criminal law. *European Scientific Journal, 14*, 227–238.

Pagliaro, A. M., & Pagliaro, L. A. (2019). *Theories of addiction: Why people use drugs and substances of abuse*. Hoboken, NJ: Wiley.

Palmisano, M., & Pandey, S. C. (2017). Epigenetic mechanisms of alcoholism and stress-related disorders. *Alcohol, 60*, 7–18.

Parolin, M., & Simonelli, A. (2016). Attachment theory and maternal drug addiction: The contribution to parenting interventions. *Frontiers in Psychiatry, 7*, 1–14.

Pedersen, P. (1990). The multicultural perspective as a fourth force in counseling. *Journal of Mental Health Counseling, 12*(1), 93–95.

Peele, S. (1990–1991). What works in addiction treatment and what doesn't: Is the best therapy no therapy? *International Journal of the Addictions, 25*, 1409–1419.

Peele, S. (2000). What addiction is and is not: The impact of mistaken notions of addiction. *Addiction Research, 8*, 599–607.

Peele, S. (2007). Addiction as disease: Policy, epidemiology, and treatment consequences of a bad idea. In J. E. Henningfield, P. B. Santora, & W. K. Bickel (Eds.), *Addiction treatment: Science and policy for the twenty-first century* (pp. 153–164). Baltimore, MD: Johns Hopkins University Press.

Peele, S. (2010). Alcohol as evil—Temperance and policy. *Addiction Research & Theory, 18*, 374–382.

Peele, S. (2015). Why neurobiological models can't contain mental disorder and addiction. *Behavior Therapist, 38*(7), 218–222.

Peele, S. (2016). People control their addictions: No matter how much the "chronic" brain disease model of addiction indicates otherwise, we know that people can quit addictions—With special reference to harm reduction and mindfulness. *Addictive Behaviors Reports, 4*, 97–101.

Pintus, G. (2017). Addiction as persistent traumatic experience: Neurobiological processes and good contact. *Gestalt Review, 21*, 221–232.

Pizer, S. A. (2018). "Where all the ladders start": A clinical account of object relations legacies, self-states and analytic process. *Psychoanalytic Dialogues, 28*, 679–686.

Randle, J. M., Stroink, M. L., & Nelson, C. H. (2015). Addiction and the adaptive cycle: A new focus. *Addiction Research & Theory, 23*(1), 81–88.

Richard, K., Baghurst, T., Faragher, J. M., & Stotts, E. (2017). Practical treatments considering the role of sociocultural factors on problem gambling. *Journal of Gambling Studies, 33*, 265–281.

Rowan, M., Poole, N., Shea, B., Gone, J. P., Mykota, D., Farag, M., . . . Dell, C. (2014). Cultural interventions to treat addictions in Indigenous populations: Findings from a scoping study. *Substance Abuse Treatment, Prevention, and Policy, 9*(34), 1–27.

Rutherford, H. J. V., & Mayes, L. C. (2017). Parenting and addiction: Neurobiological insights. *Current Opinion in Psychology, 15*, 55–60.

Schwaninger, P. V., Mueller, S. E., Dittmann, R., Poespodihardjo, R., Vogel, M., Wiesbeck, G. A., . . . Petitjean, S. A. (2017). Patients with non-substance-related disorders report a similar profile of childhood trauma experiences compared to heroin-dependent patients. *American Journal on Addictions, 26* (3), 215–220.

Skewes, M. C., & Gonzalez, V. M. (2013). The biopsychosocial model of addiction. In P. M. Miller, S. A. Ball, M. E. Bates, A. W. Blume, K. M. Kampman, D. J. Kavanagh, M. E. Larimer, N. M. Petry, & P. De Witte (Eds.), *Comprehensive addictive behaviors and disorders, Vol. 1: Principles of addiction* (pp. 61–70). San Diego, CA: Elsevier Academic Press.

Smith, R. L. (2015). Addictions: An overview. In R. L. Smith (Ed.), *Treatment strategies for substance abuse and process addictions* (pp. 1–31). [Kindle version]. Retrieved from Amazon.ca

Soto, C. J., & John, O. P. (2017). The next Big Five Inventory (BFI-2): Developing and assessing a hierarchical model with 15 facets to enhance bandwidth, fidelity, and predictive power. *Journal of Personality and Social Psychology, 113*, 117–143.

Sreeramareddy, C. T., Pradhan, P. M. S., Mir, I. A., & Sin, S. (2014). Smoking and smokeless tobacco use in nine South and Southeast Asian countries: Prevalence estimates and social determinants from demographic and health surveys. *Population Health Metrics, 12*, —1–16.

Stevens, P. W. (2013). Family treatment. In P. Stevens & R. L. Smith (Eds.), *Substance abuse counseling: Theory and practice* (5th ed., pp. 240–260). New York, NY: Pearson.

Szasz, T. S. (1961). *The myth of mental illness: Foundations of a theory of personal conduct*. New York, NY: Harper & Row.

Szasz, T. S. (2013). The ethics of addiction. In D. A. Sisti, A. L. Caplan, & H. Rimon-Greenspan (Eds.), *Applied ethics in mental health care: An interdisciplinary reader* (pp. 201–210). Cambridge, MA: MIT Press.

Thakker, J. (2013). International perspectives on addiction. In P. M. Miller, S. A. Ball, M. E. Bates, A. W. Blume, K. M. Kampman, D. J. Kavanagh, M. E. Larimer, N. M. Petry, & P. De Witte (Eds.), *Comprehensive addictive behaviors and disorders, Vol. 1: Principles of addiction* (pp. 51–59). San Diego, CA: Elsevier Academic Press.

Vadigepalli, R., & Hoek, J. B. (2018). Alcohol and epigenetic regulation: Do the products of alcohol metabolism drive epigenetic control of gene expression in alcohol-related disorders? *Alcoholism: Clinical and Experimental Research, 42*, 845–848.

Watt, M. J., Weber, M. A., Davies, S. R., & Forster, G. L. (2017). Impact of juvenile chronic stress on adult cortico-accumbal function: Implications for cognition and addiction. *Progress in Neuro-Psychopharmacology & Biological Psychiatry, 79*, 136–154.

Weegmann, M., & Cohen, R. (2008). *The psychodynamics of addiction*. Hoboken, NJ: Wiley.

West, R. (2001). Theories of addiction. *Addiction, 96*, 3–13.

West, R., & Brown, J. (2013). *Theory of addiction (2nd ed.)*. Hoboken, NJ: Wiley Blackwell.

Westmeyer, J. (2013). Historical understandings of addiction. In P. M. Miller, S. A. Ball, M. E. Bates, A. W. Blume, K. M. Kampman, D. J. Kavanagh, M. E. Larimer, N. M. Petry, & P. De Witte (Eds.), *Comprehensive addictive behaviors and disorders, Vol. 1: Principles of addiction* (pp. 3–12). San Diego, CA: Elsevier Academic Press.

White, W. L. (2014). *Slaying the dragon: The history of addiction treatment and recovery in America (2nd ed.)*. Bloomington, IL: Chestnut Health Systems/Lighthouse Institute.

Williams, R. W., & Holmes, A. (2017). Preface to a special issue on genetic models of alcoholism and alcohol-stress interactions. *Alcohol, 58*, 23–24.

Woods, J. (2013). Group analytic therapy for compulsive users of internet pornography. *Psychoanalytic Psychotherapy, 27*, 306–318.

World Health Organization (WHO). (2019). *Management of substance abuse: Country profiles 2014.* Retrieved on February 28, 2019, from https://www.who.int/substance_abuse/publications/global_alcohol_report/profiles/en/

Yellow Horse Brave Heart, M., Chase, J., Elkins, J., & Altschul, D. B. (2011). Historical trauma among Indigenous peoples of the Americas: Concepts, research, and clinical considerations. *Journal of Psychoactive Drugs, 43*(4), 282–290.

Young, A. (2017). Uncovery: Beneath the monolith of addiction there remains a human being. In J. K. Edwards, A. Young, & H. J. Nikels (Eds.), *Handbook of strengths-based clinical practices: Finding common factors* (pp. 53–69). New York, NY: Routledge/Taylor & Francis Group.

Zilberman, N., Yadid, G., Efrati, Y., Neumark, Y., & Rassovsky, Y. (2018). Personality profiles of substance and behavioral addictions. *Addictive Behaviors, 82*, 174–181.

APPENDIX 3A. ANSWERS TO CAN YOU GUESS WHICH THEORY/IES EXPLAIN THE COUNSELOR'S BEHAVIOR?

Example 1. Moral/Choice Model, Behavioral/Learning Theories.

Example 2. Sociocultural Theories.

Example 3. Psychodynamic Theory.

Example 4. Biological/Disease Theories.

Example 5. Family Models.

Example 6. Moral/Choice Model.

Example 7. Sociocultural Theories, Biological/Disease Theories.

Example 8. Biopsychosocial Model.

Example 9. Biological/Disease Theories.

Example 10. Cognitive-Behavioral Theories, Personality Theories.

APPENDIX 3B. PUBLIC ATTITUDES ABOUT ADDICTION SURVEY

Public Attitudes About Addiction Survey

Please check the response that most closely aligns with your beliefs.	Strongly Disagree	Somewhat Disagree	Disagree	Neither Disagree nor Agree	Agree	Somewhat Agree	Strongly Agree
1. "Once an addict, always an addict" is a true statement.							
2. A person can be addicted to anything from drugs to video games.							
3. Marijuana is accepted in some communities, so there is nothing wrong with using it while there.							
4. Individuals engage in risky behaviors that might lead to addiction because they are depressed.							
5. It is easy to tell if someone has an addiction.							
6. Addicts cannot control their addictive behavior.							
7. Addiction is a form of wrongdoing.							
8. As long as no one else is harmed, people should have the right to engage in whatever behaviors they want.							
9. Addiction is a choice.							
10. Addicts are immature people.							
11. If an addict fails to recover in treatment, it is because they are not motivated to quit.							
12. The instant reward a person feels from certain behaviors leads to addiction.							
13. There are people who have significant problems with alcohol but who are not alcoholics.							
14. Even in religious communities, there are addicts.							
15. Daily use of small amounts of substances like marijuana is not necessarily harmful.							

Public Attitudes About Addiction Survey							
16. Drug use changes the brain after a few exposures and causes addiction.							
17. Poor people are less motivated to obey laws about risky behaviors like drug use.							
18. People often outgrow drug and alcohol addiction.							
19. A person's environment influences attitudes about addiction.							
20. Addiction is best seen as a habit, not as a disease.							
21. Genetics, not psychology, determines whether one drinker will become addicted to alcohol and another will not.							
22. People fail to consider that some addictive behaviors may be positive.							
23. Addiction does not always result in a negative outcome.							
24. Although risky behavior is a choice, the person is influenced in that choice by their upbringing and education.							
25. Addicts use drugs to escape from bad family situations.							
26. Addicts are low-life people.							
27. Individuals engage in risky behaviors that might lead to addiction because they lack self-confidence.							
28. If a person's neighborhood supports drug use, a person is more likely to use drugs.							
29. Personal use of drugs should be legal in the confines of one's own home.							
30. An inability to gain pleasure from life may lead to addiction.							
31. Saying that addiction is a disease implies a lack of personal responsibility.							
32. Addicts have a carefree attitude toward life.							
33. Pain can cause addiction.							
34. Religious beliefs influence attitudes about addiction.							
35. Traumatic events may lead to addiction.							
36. Beliefs about addiction influence attitudes about addiction.							
37. Addicts are failures.							
38. Addicts continue to use even when they know the cost of their behavior.							
39. The media (e.g., news, television, movies) influence attitudes about addiction.							
40. A person's culture influences their attitudes toward addiction.							
41. Individuals engage in risky behaviors that might lead to addiction because they are avoiding personal problems.							
42. Addicts can learn to control their use.							
43. It is their own fault if an addict relapses.							

Public Attitudes About Addiction Survey							
44. Individuals engage in risky behaviors that might lead to addiction in order to feel better about themselves.							
45. Addiction is caused by unhappiness in a person's life, marriage, or job.							
46. Addictive behavior is a choice, and the person is influenced in that choice by their moral values.							
47. Addicts are not capable of solving their addiction on their own.							
48. You can tell a person is an addict by their appearance.							
49. Addicts lack moral standards.							
50. Individuals engage in risky behaviors that might lead to addiction because they do not respect authority.							
51. Anyone can become an addict.							
52. Children who lack emotional support may choose to use drugs as an adult.							
53. Addicts cannot use pain medicine. They would become addicted to it.							
54. Some people use drugs but never become addicted.							

Source: Reproduced with permission from the author.

Code	Public Attitudes About Addiction—Item by Model
P	Psychology
1	Traumatic events may lead to addiction.
2	An inability to gain pleasure from life may lead to addiction.
3	Individuals engage in risky behaviors that might lead to addiction because they are depressed.
4	Addicts use to escape from bad family situations.
5	Individuals engage in risky behaviors that might lead to addiction because they are avoiding personal problems.
6	Addicts continue to use even when they know the cost of their behavior.
7	A person can be addicted to anything from drugs to video games.
8	Individuals engage in risky behaviors that might lead to addiction because they lack self-confidence.
9	Individuals engage in risky behaviors that might lead to addiction in order to feel better about themselves.
10	What causes addiction? Children who lack emotional support may choose to use drugs as an adult.
11	Even in religious communities, there are addicts.
12	Anyone can become an addict.
13	What causes addiction? Pain can cause addiction.
14	What causes addiction? Addiction is caused by unhappiness in a person's life, marriage, or job.
15	What causes addiction? The instant reward a person feels from certain behaviors leads to addiction.

Code	Public Attitudes About Addiction—Item by Model
M	**Moral**
1	Addicts lack moral standards.
2	Addicts are low-life people.
3	Addicts are failures.
4	Addicts are immature people.
5	Addicts have a carefree attitude toward life.
6	If addicts fail to recover in treatment, it is because they are not motivated to quit.
7	You can tell a person is an addict by their appearance.
8	It is easy to tell if someone has an addiction.
9	Addiction is best seen as a habit, not as a disease.
10	Saying that addiction is a disease implies a lack of personal responsibility.
11	Addiction is a choice.
12	It is their own fault if an addict relapses.
13	Individuals engage in risky behaviors that might lead to addiction because they do not respect authority.
14	Addiction is a form of wrongdoing.
15	Poor people are less motivated to obey laws about risky behaviors like drug use.
16	Addictive behavior is a choice, and the person is influenced in that choice by their moral values.
N	**Nature**
1	Daily use of small amounts of substances like marijuana is not necessarily harmful.
2	Marijuana is accepted in some communities, so there is nothing wrong with using it while there.
3	Personal use of drugs should be legal in the confines of one's own home.
4	As long as no one else is harmed, people should have the right to engage in whatever behaviors they want.
5	Some people use drugs, but never become addicted.
6	Addiction does not always result in a negative outcome.
7	People fail to consider that some addictive behaviors may be positive.
8	People often outgrow drug and alcohol addiction.
9	There are people who have significant problems with alcohol but who are not alcoholics.
10	Addicts can learn to control their use.
S	**Sociology**
1	What factors influence attitudes about addiction? Beliefs about addiction.
2	What factors influence attitudes about addiction? Religious beliefs.
3	A person's culture influences their attitudes toward addiction.
4	What causes addiction? If a person's neighborhood supports drug use, a person is more likely to use drugs.
5	What factors influence attitudes about addiction? A person's environment.

Code	Public Attitudes About Addiction—Item by Model
S	**Sociology**
6	What factors influence attitudes about addiction? The media (e.g., news, television, movies).
7	Although risky behavior is a choice, the person is influenced in that choice by upbringing and education.
D	**Disease/Biological**
1	Addicts cannot control their addictive behavior.
2	Addicts cannot use pain medicine. They would become addicted to it.
3	Addicts are not capable of solving their addiction on their own.
4	What causes addiction? Genetics, not psychology, determines whether one drinker will become addicted to alcohol and another will not.
5	Drug use changes the brain after a few exposures and causes addiction.
6	"Once an addict, always an addict" is a true statement.

Source: Reproduced with permission from the author.

4 The Neuroscience of Addictions

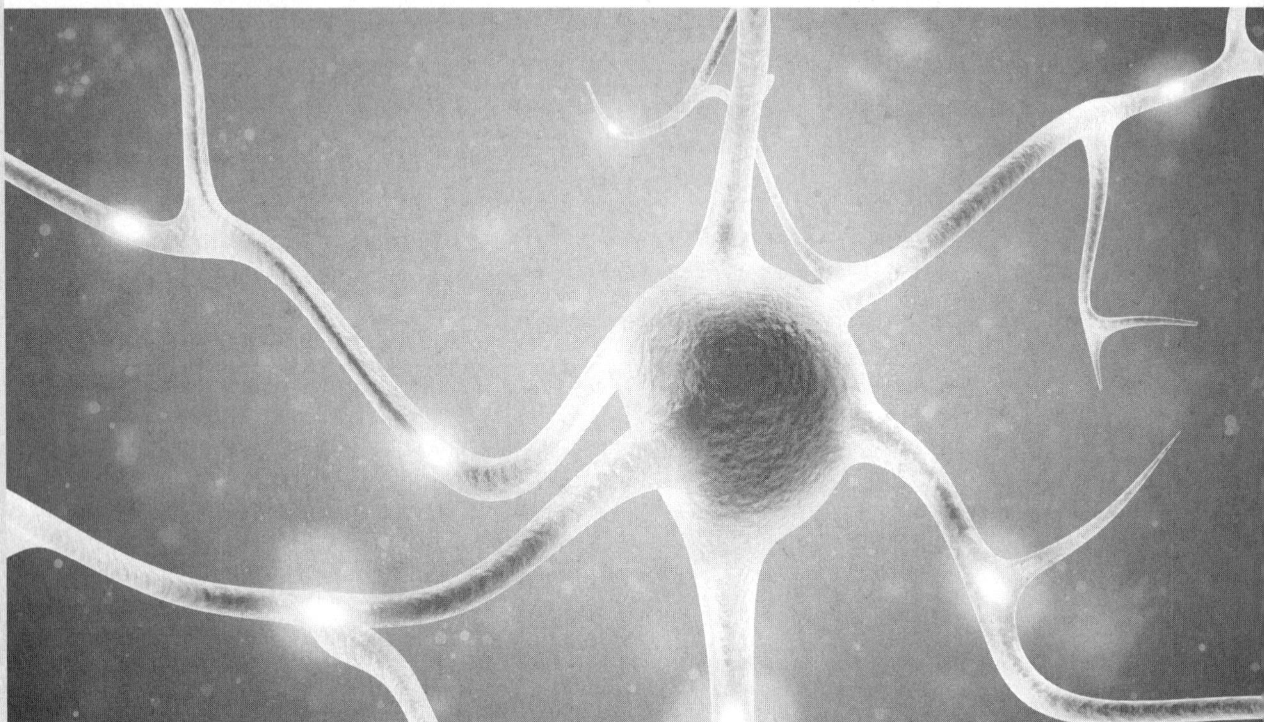

iStock.com/zoom-

Learning Objectives

1. Become familiar with the heritability of addictions and the study of neurogenetics.
2. Learn about the basics of neuroscience, including neurons, the nervous system, the three regions of the brain, and the important brain parts and systems that are most implicated in addictions.
3. Describe the effect that psychoactive substances have on the brain.
4. List some of the effects that psychoactive drugs have on adolescent development.
5. Understand some of the treatment implications emanating from neuroscience but also some of the criticisms of this approach.

PERSONAL REFLECTIONS

I began university in pre-med. The courses in biology and chemistry were interesting, albeit tedious, but the course that really scared me was calculus. By the end of the term, I still seemed clueless when I received my final grade of C–. Thankfully, a new interest in psychology was growing rapidly at that time, and I pursued it. But calculus seemed like a subject beyond my capabilities.

I felt equally intimidated to write this chapter on neuroscience. Perhaps it was because my goals of becoming a medical doctor were thwarted due to many marks in the natural sciences that were in the C and B range. Alternatively, it might have been that the readings I did in this area reminded me that biology is not my greatest strength. Seriously, that same old fear I had of calculus returned as I began preparing to write this chapter. I do not want you to have that experience reading it. Consequently, I have written it in a way that I believe you will appreciate. You are becoming a specialist in addictions and possibly in addiction counseling, and you will find hardcore neuroscience in a different textbook that, clearly, I did not write.

The neuroscience research that applies to specific addictions will be found in a separate section in Chapters 9 through 21. The intent here is to take you into a fascinating journey into the brain. If I am successful in doing so, you might just be the one who picks up that hardcore neuroscience textbook and enjoys reading it. In the meantime, what does neuroscience have to do with addiction anyway? Let's find out.

Neurogenetic and Genetic Studies

In 2016, the National Institute on Drug Abuse (NIDA) awarded a 5-year grant totaling nearly $12 million to the Jackson Laboratory to create a new Center for Systems Neurogenetics of Addiction (CSNA; Peterson, 2016). The researchers intend to identify ways in which some individuals are more likely than others to begin using drugs or to become addicted to them. Furthermore, the intent is to understand better how the brain responds to drugs so that better treatments for compulsive drug-seeking behavior may follow. **Neurogenetics** looks at the role that genetics plays in the development and function of the nervous system. It is hoped that the 5-year neurogenetics studies will lead to greater precision in assessing addiction risk.

Family, twin, and adoption studies have shown that substance use disorders (SUDs) have a high degree of hereditability. Addictive potential can be passed down through our genes (Bennett & Petrash, 2014). NIDA (2016) estimated that up to 50% of people's risk of becoming addicted to psychoactive substances, including nicotine and alcohol, depends on their genetic makeup. However, it is impossible to generalize genetic research from one family to the next as there are hundreds if not thousands of genes that directly or indirectly contribute to addictions (Pihl & Stewart, 2013).

Of course, genes are not the only factor that determines addictive potential. The old saying "nature or nurture" is more accurately phrased as "nature *and* nurture" because there is a dynamic interplay between genes and individuals' environments (NIDA, 2016).

Basics of Neuroscience

Neuroscience is the study of the brain and nervous system.[1] **Neurobiology**, on the other hand, is a subdivision of both biology and neuroscience that specifically studies neurons and their organization into functional circuits. The field of neuroscience is important in understanding addictions because it situates addictions as a health disorder instead of placing it in the domain of morality (Bedendo, Andrade, & Noto, 2016). Historically, it was believed that many addictions occurred because the individuals afflicted were morally weak or inferior, the type of people who did not exercise self-restraint and instead overindulged in substance abuse of their own free will (Stolberg, 2006). Neuroscience has provided answers regarding how, and in what ways, the brain changes in response to repeated engagement in addictive behavior.

The main methods that scientists use to study the nervous system include (a) animal studies, (b) examining autopsy tissue, (c) testing the behavior of individuals with brain damage, (d) recording electrical brain activity (EEG or ERP), and (e) neuroimaging techniques that show visual images in awake humans. The three most common neuroimaging techniques are computerized axial tomography (i.e., the CAT scan), magnetic resonance imaging (i.e., the MRI scan), and diffusion tensor imaging (i.e., the DTI scan). The MRI scan has been key to opening the door to understanding what occurs at the microscopic and mesoscopic neurobiological levels (Suckling & Nestor, 2017). MRIs together with positron emission tomography (i.e., the PET scan), single photon emission computed tomography (i.e., the SPECT scan), molecular genetics, and neurophysiological methods have revealed the structural and functional impairments that occur with individuals with Internet use disorders (Park, Han, & Roh, 2017). Nonetheless, much of this research is in its infancy stage (Park et al., 2017).

The Body's Nervous System, Neurons, and Glial Cells

Central Nervous System

The central nervous system (CNS) includes both the brain and spinal cord. The CNS is the control center for bodily functions, acting as both a transmitter and receiver of information. Both the brain and spinal cord are encased in sheaths called meninges, and, if these become infected, it creates a potentially lethal disease called meningitis. The CNS has its own nutritional supply called cerebral spinal fluid (CSF), which both nourishes the brain and acts as a cushion. CSF is produced in hollow cavities within the brain called ventricles.

[1]Much of the Basics of Neuroscience section has been adapted from Comer, Ogden, Boyes, and Gould (2018).

Peripheral Nervous System

There are two main systems within the peripheral nervous system: the somatic nervous system and the autonomic nervous system. We are in control of the somatic nervous system. Through it, we can regulate voluntary movements and move our bodies. The autonomic nervous system, on the other hand, regulates involuntary responses; consequently, we have only indirect control of some aspects of its functioning. It comprises two subsystems known as the sympathetic nervous system and the parasympathetic nervous system. The sympathetic nervous system mobilizes us toward what many call the "fight or flight" response. People who are anxious have an overactive sympathetic nervous system. The parasympathetic nervous system operates oppositely: it acts to conserve our energy. When we practice relaxation, for example, we activate the parasympathetic nervous system.

Neurons and Glial Cells

There are two kinds of cells within the CNS: neurons and glial cells. Glial (glia means "glue") cells provide a supportive and protective function for neurons. In the neuroscience of addictions, we are mostly concerned about neurons. They are sometimes called nerve cells, and they are specialized to carry messages to and receive messages from other neurons. The human brain has nearly 100 billion neurons (86 billion is a more accurate estimate; Bedendo et al., 2016), and each neuron is connected to about 10,000 other neurons. This means there are approximately 1000 trillion connections in your brain!

Neurons have responsibility for communications within the nervous system. The main parts of a neuron are the **soma** or **cell body**, which provides energy for the neuron; the **dendrites**, which receive messages from other neurons; the **axon**, which carries information away from the cell body; the **axon terminals** or **terminal buttons**, which relay signals to the dendrites of the next neuron; and the **myelin sheath**, which speeds up firing of the neuron. The myelin sheath is not named in the diagram but is represented by what appears to be each "sausage" (i.e., the thicker segments along the axon). The space between each thicker portion is called the **node of Ranvier**). See Figure 4.1.

Once a **nerve impulse** (which is mostly a chemical signal in mammals but is sometimes electrical) begins, it travels down the axon until it activates the terminal buttons to release **neurotransmitters** (NTs), which are the chemical messengers that relay the impulse to several other neurons. The **synapse** is the area between two neurons comprising three constituents: the presynaptic terminal, the postsynaptic terminal, and the 20- to 50-nanometer gap between them called the **synaptic cleft**. Figure 4.2 shows the NTs flowing across the synaptic cleft to the next neuron.

Although many NTs have been identified in the human brain, the main ones are acetylcholine, norepinephrine (also called noradrenaline), dopamine, glutamate, GABA, serotonin, and the endogenous opioids, which are commonly called endorphins. It is important to understand that NTs cannot bind to just any region of the accompanying dendrite. Like a lock and key, most keys can open only a specific lock (Bedendo et al., 2016). Similarly, each NT has its own particular binding sites called receptors (e.g., dopamine has to be received by dopamine receptors in the next neuron) (Bedendo et al., 2016).

Acetylcholine serves several functions, but, for our purposes, it regulates attention, arousal, and memory. Some acetylcholine synapses are stimulated by nicotine. Norepinephrine is released in the brain in response to stress, and it helps to regulate mood and anxiety. Cocaine and amphetamines increase activity at the norepinephrine synapses. Dopamine plays a role in creating the experience of pleasure, plus it is the primary NT that produces "wanting" or "craving." Dopamine helps give us a natural, enthusiastic, excited feeling, like the feeling we might have on a first date (Tarman & Werdell, 2014). Dopamine is a mobilizing NT; it makes us want to do things. Drugs that create the greatest surge in dopamine are the stimulants (Tarman & Werdell, 2014). Persons living with schizophrenia have increased levels of dopamine in their brains, whereas those with Parkinson's disease have decreased levels. Serotonin is

FIGURE 4.1 **Parts of the neuron.**

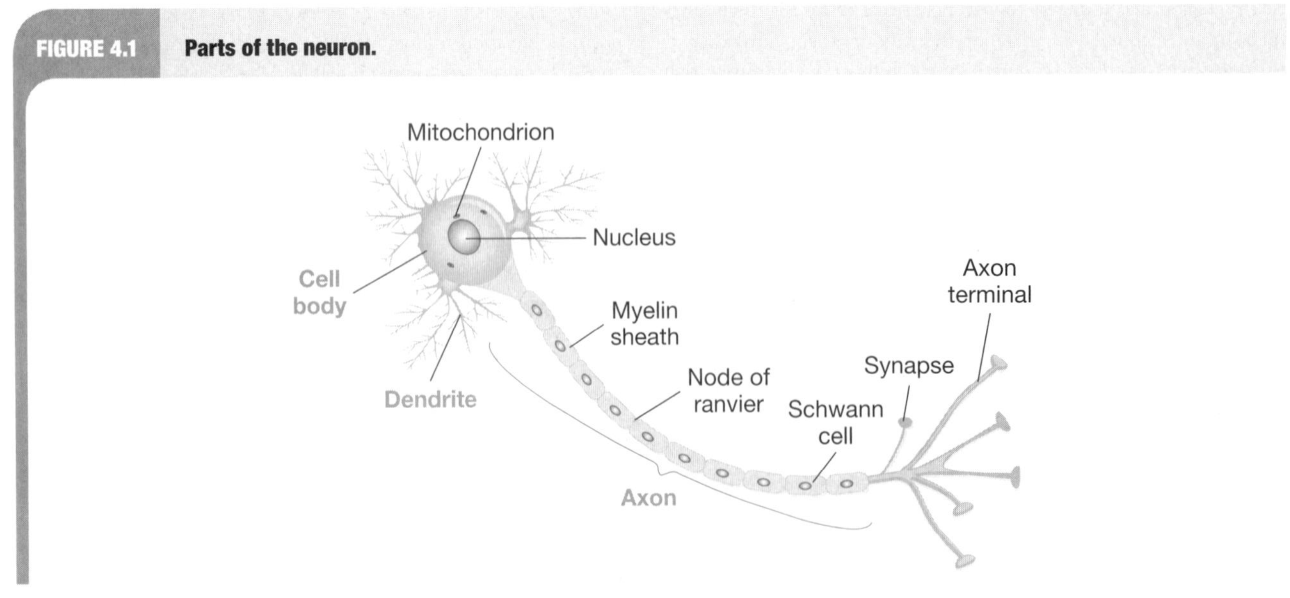

Source: iStock.com/ttsz

FIGURE 4.2 **Communication across the synapse.**

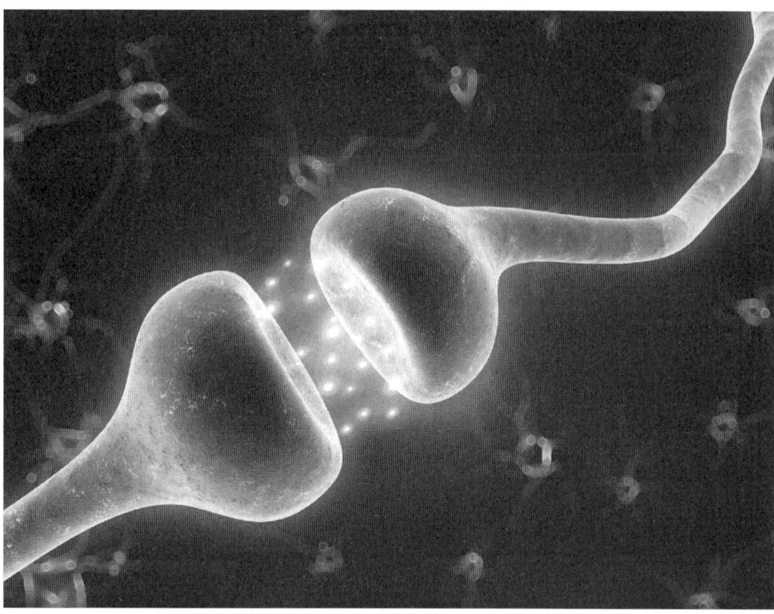

Source: iStock.com/Eraxion

important in regulating sleep and arousal, but it is also important in regulating mood and pleasure. Serotonin helps us feel calm, satisfied, and contented; an abundance of it makes us feel grateful, but it can also become demotivating (Tarman & Werdell, 2014). The drugs that increase serotonin are primarily the hallucinogens (Tarman & Werdell, 2014). You can see from this that serotonin, like dopamine, is involved in the pleasure cycle.

Both GABA and glutamate are involved in nearly all CNS functions. GABA is an antagonistic (or inhibitory) NT, meaning that it inhibits CNS functioning. It is the major inhibitory NT in mammals (Gipson & Kalivas, 2016). Valium and antianxiety medications, for example, bind to GABA receptors, thereby creating relaxation. Glutamate, on the other hand, is an excitatory NT. It is also the most abundant NT in vertebrates. Endogenous opioids, the endorphins, are the most important NT in creating feelings of pleasure. Endorphins are the body's natural pain relievers. They also provide energy when we need to leave dangerous situations (Tarman & Werdell, 2014). Tarmen and Werdell (2014) provided the example of a mother who becomes able to lift concrete blocks to save her infant during a bombing raid. Too many endorphins can lead people to search for stressful practices such as physical fighting or self-mutilating behavior (Tarman & Werdell, 2014). Drugs that resemble endorphins are the opioids (Tarman & Werdell, 2014). Alcohol often creates a surge in serotonin, dopamine, and endorphins, which explains why drinkers may experience an enhanced sense of safety, sociability, excitement, numbness, and analgesia (Tarman & Werdell, 2014). Anesthesia can also develop from consuming a large and unsafe quantity of alcohol (Wong, Fong, Tauck, & Kendig, 1997).

Another important NT when it comes to creating pleasure is oxytocin. Its release builds intimacy and trust. Both men and women release it during orgasm, and mothers release it during childbirth and breastfeeding. It is sometimes referred to as the "cuddle hormone" (note: oxytocin can act as both an NT and a hormone in the body). Paul Zak, a world expert on oxytocin, reported that one of the simplest ways to release oxytocin is to hug someone (Burkeman, 2012).

Divisions and Structures of the Brain

Figures 4.3 and 4.4 show many parts of the brain. Several of the relevant structures will be described in this section. The brain can be viewed as having three major divisions: the hindbrain, the midbrain, and the forebrain.

Hindbrain

The hindbrain is closest to the spinal cord. Its purpose is to regulate basic life functions. It consists of the medulla, the pons, and the cerebellum (see Figure 4.4). It is also where the reticular formation begins, which then extends into the midbrain.

Medulla.

The medulla (also called the medulla oblongata) mostly controls basic processes in the body, but it also regulates some reflexes. More specifically, it regulates our heartbeat, breathing, and reflexes like sneezing and coughing. It is about 1.5 inches in length.

Pons.

The pons sends signals to and from the forebrain and the cerebellum. It plays an important function in sleeping, breathing, swallowing, facial sensations and expressions, and eye movements.

FIGURE 4.3 **The dopamine pathway.**

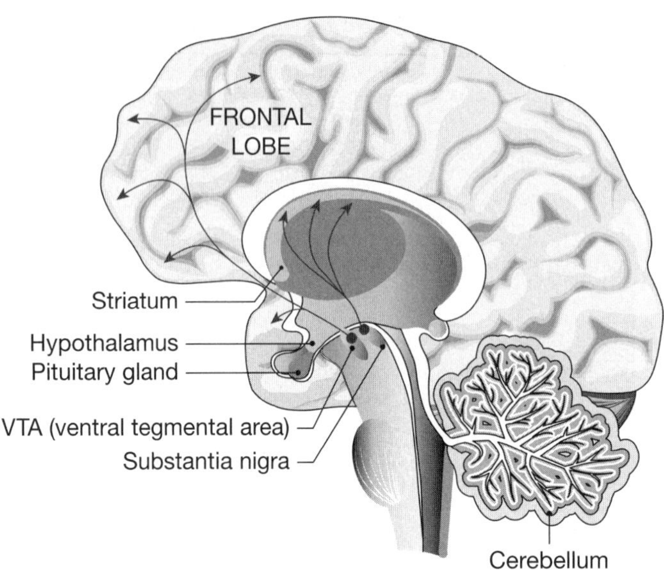

Source: iStock.com/ttsz

FIGURE 4.4 **Parts of the brain—I.**

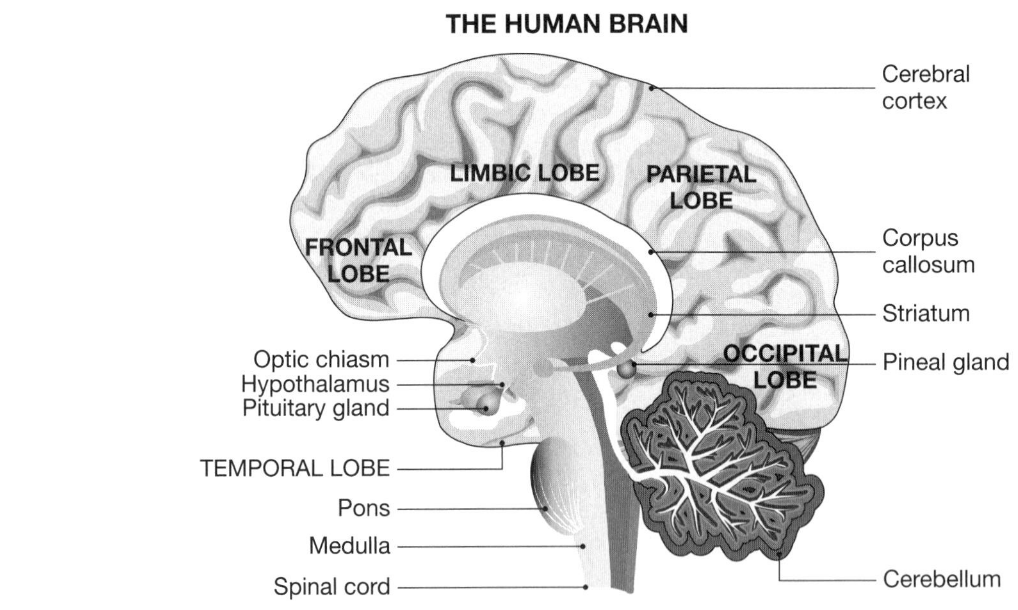

Source: iStock.com/ttsz

Cerebellum.

This part of the brain is near the back of the head. It is most important for motor coordination, but it also plays a role in movements that require learning (e.g., learning to ride a bicycle). THC, which is the active ingredient in cannabis, affects the cerebellum, and this explains why it can create incoordination and loss of balance (Csiernik, 2016).

Reticular formation.

The reticular formation is a complex, neural network that extends from the hindbrain into the midbrain. It regulates both consciousness and arousal (e.g., the sleep–wake cycle). It is also the primary source for creating serotonin.

WHAT WOULD HAPPEN IF PARTS OF THE HINDBRAIN WERE DAMAGED IN HUMANS?

1. What do you think would happen if the medulla were damaged?
2. What do you think would happen if the pons were damaged?
3. What do you think would happen if the cerebellum were damaged?
4. What do you think would happen if the reticular formation were damaged?

Midbrain

Situated above the pons is the midbrain. The midbrain coordinates reflex responses to visual, tactile, and auditory input. It contains several different nuclei, two of which are called the substantia nigra and the ventral tegmental area (shown in Figure 4.3).

Substantia nigra (SN).

The SN is considered part of the basal ganglia (note: the basal ganglia is located at the top of the midbrain and is considered part of the forebrain). It plays an important role not only in activating and inhibiting movements but also in creating fluidity of movement. It also produces dopamine.

Ventral tegmental area (VTA).

The VTA is adjacent to the SN. It is known as part of the reward system in the brain and, like the SN, it is involved with dopamine. The VTA is believed to be involved with various cognitive and emotional processes, but it is best known for its role in motivation, reward, and addiction (Saunders & Richard, 2011).

WHAT WOULD HAPPEN IF PARTS OF THE MIDBRAIN WERE DAMAGED IN HUMANS?

1. What do you think would happen if the SN were damaged?
2. What do you think would happen if the VTA were damaged?

Forebrain, Four Lobes, and Limbic System

The forebrain is the largest division of the human brain in humans. It controls complex cognitive, emotional, sensory, and motor functions. The forebrain has two main parts: the diencephalon (the posterior part of the forebrain) and the telencephalon (the anterior part of the forebrain, which is the most highly developed part and consists mostly of the cerebrum, which comprises the two cerebral hemispheres and the corpus callosum, which connects the two sides). The cerebrum is the largest and most highly developed part of our brain. For 99% of right-handers (and 70% of left-handers), the left hemisphere controls (for the most part) verbal processing, language, speech, reading, and writing. The right hemisphere is more specialized for nonverbal processing (e.g., spatial, musical, visual recognition).

The outer part of the cerebrum is called the cerebral cortex, a layer that is 0.06–0.20 in. thick. The cortex is divided into four lobes: (a) frontal lobes, (b) parietal lobes, (c) temporal lobes, and (d) occipital lobes. Remember that there are two sides to each lobe corresponding with the two cerebral hemispheres (see Figure 4.4 for their locations). The **insula** (also called the insular cortex) is a small region of the cerebral cortex. The insula maintains our body temperature and influences cognitive function and motor control. Some have speculated that it is associated with "understanding what it feels like to be human" (Blakeslee, 2007, para. 4). Craig (2009) reported that it likely facilitates our concept of self-awareness. To date, however, the insula remains somewhat mysterious.

Within most people, the left frontal lobe contains a region called **Broca's area**, which is critical for speech production. Speech comprehension, on the other hand, located in the left temporal lobe for 90% of humans, is **Wernicke's area**. Damage to these areas will result in an inability to speak sensibly and grammatically or to understand what others are saying, respectively.

The **prefrontal cortex** is important for memory, morality, mood, and planning functions. You likely remember hearing of a procedure called a prefrontal lobotomy that was used in the 1940s and 1950s as a treatment for thousands of individuals experiencing severe mental illness, nonconformity, and rebelliousness. This resulted in apathy, difficulty responding emotionally, personality changes, irresponsibility, and seizures.

Other terms that you will encounter in Chapters 9 through 21 are the two components of the **mesocorticolimbic system**: the **mesolimbic** and **mesocortical pathways**, sometimes called "circuits" (note that the prefix "meso" means the middle-tissue layer in biology). The pathway that extends from the VTA into the nucleus accumbens is the mesolimbic pathway, which also contains the amygdala. This pathway is associated with reinforcement, pleasure, and memories. Neurons that extend from the VTA into the prefrontal cortex form the mesocortical pathway. This pathway is associated with the compulsive aspects of drug use, reduced inhibitory control, and the emotional valence of the drug's effect (Bedendo et al., 2016).

The parietal lobe is responsible for touch perception and understanding complex visual information. Damage to the left parietal lobe can result in Gerstmann's Syndrome. The symptoms of this disorder include right–left confusion, difficulty with writing, and problems in doing mathematics. It can also create disorders of language such as aphasia and the inability to perceive objects normally.

The occipital lobe contains the center of visual perception. Although the eyes see objects, making sense of what we see occurs in the occipital lobe. Damage to one occipital lobe may make it difficult to recognize familiar objects, whereas damage to both occipital lobes will render the individual incapable of seeing anything despite normal functioning of the eyes. Occasionally damage or stimulation of the occipital lobes results in visual hallucinations.

For our purposes, the most important structures contained in the forebrain make up the limbic system (which arguably includes the thalamus, hypothalamus, the pituitary gland, amygdala, hippocampus, basal ganglia, and several other areas). Not all researchers agree on the structures that make up the limbic system. Consequently, this discussion of what belongs there may be contentious by some researchers. Overall, the **limbic system** consists of brain structures that deal with emotions and memories.

Thalamus.

The thalamus works to relay incoming sensory information. All of our sensory systems, except for the sense of smell, have major pathways located in the thalamus.

Hypothalamus.

This structure is important for motivation and our basic drives. Furthermore, it controls the endocrine system. It also produces two hormones: oxytocin (which is also used in the brain as an NT) and vasopressin.

Pituitary gland.

This gland, located just below the hypothalamus (see Figure 4.5), regulates hormones in the body. It releases eight hormones, six of which it produces. It is often named the "master gland" of the body because it controls nearly all activity regarding hormones.

Amygdala.

The amygdala is located deep within the brain in the temporal lobe. It is involved in processing information about emotions, especially fear, but it can also process information concerning positive emotions.

Hippocampus.

The hippocampus is a brain region that is important for some types of learning and memory. It is important for the formation of new autobiographical and fact memories. THC affects the hippocampus, which explains why cannabis affects memory (Csiernik, 2016).

Basal ganglia.

The basal ganglia represents a group of nuclei that work together cohesively. It is located at the base of the forebrain and the top of the midbrain (see Figure 4.5). It includes the caudate nucleus and the putamen (together these form the striatum), the globus pallidus, SN, and nucleus accumbens.

FIGURE 4.5 Parts of the brain—II.

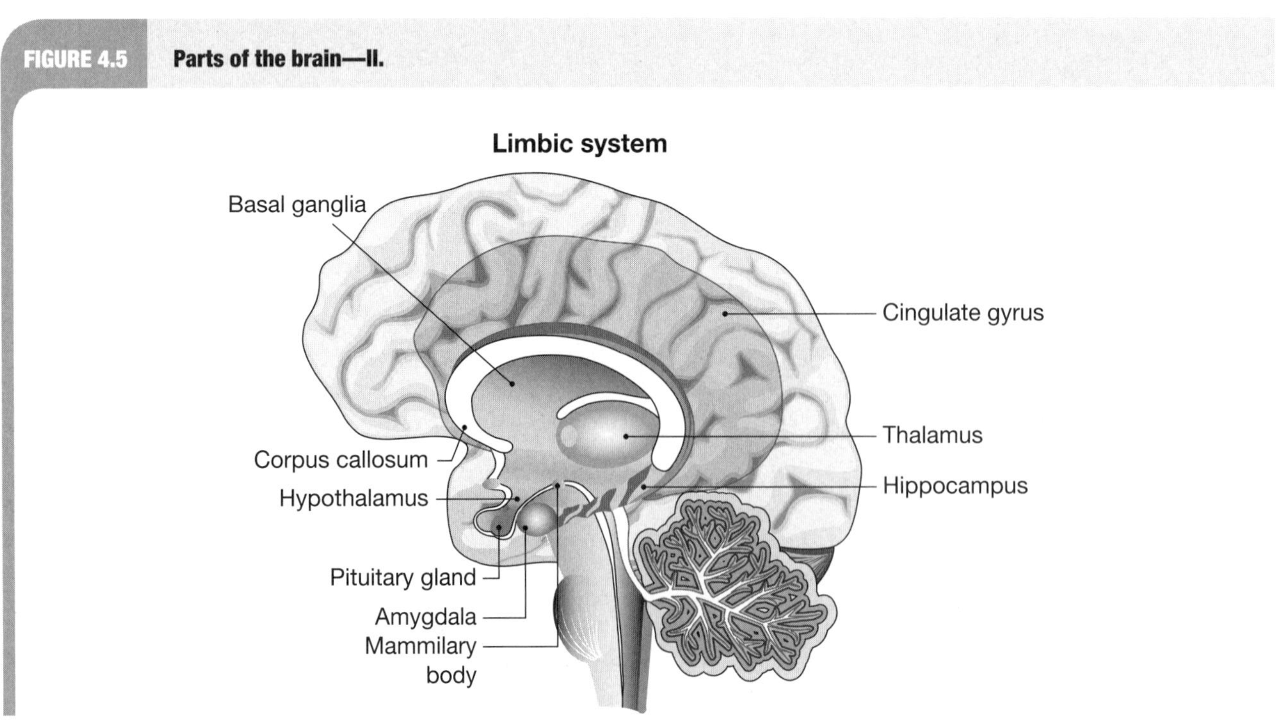

Source: Stock.com/ttsz.

Note: The basal ganglia is not fully represented in the diagram because it contains groups of nuclei across the base of the forebrain and the top of the midbrain.

Striatum. The striatum receives glutamate and dopamine from different sources. It is a critical component of the reward system as it serves as the primary input to the rest of the basal ganglia.

Globus pallidus. The globus pallidus is involved in regulating voluntary movement.

Nucleus accumbens. The nucleus accumbens is the "primary reward center of the human brain" (Milkman & Sunderwirth, 2010, p. 1). It is important for motivation and reward learning. It receives information from other neurons in the midbrain that use dopamine to transmit messages. Dopamine release in the nucleus accumbens has been associated with both reward learning and drug abuse. Recent evidence suggests that glutamate may play an even larger role than dopamine in individuals' transitioning from engaging in recreational use to engaging in drug addiction (Gipson & Kalivas, 2016).

WHAT WOULD HAPPEN IF PARTS OF THE FOREBRAIN WERE DAMAGED IN HUMANS?

1. What do you think would happen if the insula were damaged?
2. What do you think would happen if the thalamus were damaged?
3. What do you think would happen if the hypothalamus were damaged?
4. What do you think would happen if the pituitary gland were damaged?
5. What do you think would happen if the amygdala were damaged?
6. What do you think would happen if the hippocampus were damaged?
7. What do you think would happen if the basal ganglia were damaged?
8. What do you think would happen if the striatum were damaged?
9. What do you think would happen if the globus pallidus were damaged?
10. What do you think would happen if the nucleus accumbens were damaged?

Neuroscience of Addictions

Research focused on the neuroscience behind particular addictions is covered separately in Chapters 9 through 21. Here will be a more general discussion of important aspects of addiction neuroscience.

Effects of Psychoactive Drugs in the Brain

As Sherman (2017) explained, drugs can alter the way people think, feel, and behave by disrupting neurotransmission in the brain. Many studies have established that drug addiction (i.e., drug dependence) is an organic brain disorder caused by the drug's cumulative effect on neurotransmission (Sherman, 2017). The action of a psychoactive drug in the brain, including medications, can do the following to neurotransmission (Bedendo et al., 2016):

1. Increase the *amount* of an NT released into the synaptic cleft.
2. Increase the *time* the NT is available in the synaptic cleft.
3. Release enzymes that *break down* the NT (e.g., acetylcholine can release a special enzyme called acetylcholinesterase).
4. *Change* the action of an NT.
5. *Prevent absorption* of the NT by its receiving receptors.
6. *Activate absorption* of the NT by its receiving receptors.
7. *Prevent reabsorption* of the NT by the neuron that released it (in which case the drug itself may bind to the receptor or even bind to an entirely different NT receptor).
8. *Activate reabsorption* of the NT by the neuron that released it (this is called **reuptake**). Through the process of reuptake (note: norepinephrine, dopamine, and serotonin are terminated mostly by reuptake), the reabsorption by the releasing neuron results in more of the NT becoming available at the synapse. Depression, for example, is associated with low levels of serotonin in the CNS, which has led selective serotonin reuptake inhibitors (SSRIs) to become a major class of antidepressant medications.

To put it simply, psychoactive drugs "mess up" our neurotransmission, which in turn affects our neurons, which in turn affects our functioning. Although some drugs affect mostly one NT, other drugs affect more than one NT. Opioids mostly affect two NTs: endorphins and enkephalins. Both endorphins and enkephalins are referred to as opioid peptides, and both naturally occur in the body. Working together, these two NTs produce analgesia, decreased alertness, and slowed respiration. Opioids act by mimicking the effect of endorphins and enkephalins, but, because they stimulate many more receptors than what natural NTs can do, the effect is substantially magnified. Cocaine increases dopamine activity and at the same time affects norepinephrine and glutamate, which together produce feelings of euphoria. The club drug MDMA damages axons that release serotonin. The disruption of serotonin release may underlie the memory problems sometimes experienced by heavy MDMA users. All psychoactive drugs create a common dramatic increase in dopamine in the nucleus accumbens, which in turn leads to euphoria and a desire to repeat the experience (Sherman, 2017).

Allostasis is a term that refers to the body's ability to adjust its "setpoints" to maintain homeostasis. **Homeostasis** is the body's tendency to create balance and internal stability while dealing with changes originating from within or outside itself. For example, the body's withdrawal reaction to a stimulant is to produce physiological depression to bring itself back to balance; the opposite is true if withdrawing from a depressant (i.e., the body becomes stimulated to reestablish homeostasis). The idea behind allostasis is that chronic drug use may create a new and long-standing setpoint. Consequently, the individual needs more of the drug to get the same effect as earlier (i.e., tolerance) (Hall & Walker, 2017). Research regarding alcohol use disorder (AUD), for example, has found that chronic alcohol consumption affects allostasis such that it results in nonpermanent **downregulation** (i.e., the process whereby cells decrease the quantity of a cellular component) of dopamine and GABA, a permanent **upregulation** (i.e., the process whereby cells increase the amount of a cellular component) in the glutamate system, and dysregulation of the stress systems (corticotropin-releasing hormone and serotonin) (Esel & Dinc, 2017).

Eventually, following repeated drug use, changes occur in the structure and functioning of neurons, which can create long-lasting and sometimes permanent neuron and neurotransmission abnormalities. For example, the brain will respond to massive dopamine surges from a drug by reducing its number of dopamine receptors. The reduced number of these receptors results in the reward circuits becoming desensitized, and this results in a diminished ability to feel pleasure (i.e., anhedonia), decreased motivation to pursue everyday activities, increased stress reactivity that results in increased craving for alcohol and other drugs, increased experience of negative emotions when the cravings are not heeded, and weakening of the brain regions involved in executive functioning such as decision-making, controlling inhibitions, and self-regulation (Volkow, Koob, & McLellan, 2016). Anhedonia is known to follow cocaine, amphetamine, tobacco, alcohol, cannabis, and especially opioid SUDs, although its occurrence and intensity vary from person to person (Hatzigiakoumis, Martinotti, Di Giannantonio, & Janiri, 2011).[2]

Furthermore, neural motivational pathways are altered in response to chronic drug use, which in turn makes the drug more compelling (Renard, Rosen, Rushlow, & Laviolette, 2017). Regarding individuals with AUD, longitudinal research provides convincing evidence that, following sustained sobriety, brain structure and function improve considerably (Sullivan, 2017). Nonetheless, if an individual with AUD relapses, the brain has already been "primed" or "kindled" (this refers to the observation that, when abstinent drug users return to using, they often experience a rapid return to drug use at high levels). After just a few days, this individual is quickly able to drink copious amounts of alcohol and experience severe withdrawal again if attempts are made to quickly become abstinent (Rastegar & Fingerhood, 2016).

Will the brains of addicted individuals eventually make a complete recovery once the psychoactive drugs are stopped permanently? This is currently unknown. Some research suggests that both former (those who have not used for anywhere between 4 and 6 years) and current cocaine users showed less activation in most reward circuits compared with healthy control subjects, suggesting that some changes may be long-lasting or permanent (Patel et al., 2013). As Patel et al. (2013) noted, longitudinal studies will need to be undertaken before the permanence of these changes can be clearly established. Anhedonia may persist for more than a year into recovery from a substance addiction, and this appears to be due to neurobiological changes (Begun & Brown, 2014).

There is evidence that *some* areas of the brain, including the hippocampus, the cerebellum, and the prefrontal cortex, can grow (at least sometimes) new brain cells to replace lost ones, and this growth occurs even into older adulthood. We also know that the brain can develop new neural pathways resulting from experience or following an injury. This regenerative ability of the brain is called **neuroplasticity**. An example provided by Comer et al. (2018) is that children raised in homes where they learned two languages have brains that are different regarding certain structures compared to the brains of children who learned only one language.

Although psychoactive drugs do not change a person's genes, if repeated and chronic use leads to structural and functional changes in the neurons, some of these changes can be passed on to the next generation. This process whereby neurons are altered and passed down to offspring is known as **epigenesis**.

Although deoxyribonucleic acid (DNA) contains genetic instructions, ribonucleic acid (RNA) is involved in transmitting genetic information and expression of genes. Through epigenesis, messenger RNA (mRNA) becomes converted to protein products, and a group of these are called the "Fos family" by Hall and Walker (2017, p. 152). Of these, ΔFosB has received notable attention in addiction research. It is thought that ΔFosB creates behavior change by altering the *expression* of genes. Why do they believe this? Mainly because the other protein products have brief effects on gene expression, whereas ΔFosB is uniquely stable, and it is hypothesized that its effects may be more enduring. Evidence also suggests that chronic drug use creates an accumulation of ΔFosB in the nucleus accumbens, the dorsal striatum, and to some extent in the prefrontal cortex. It may be that ΔFosB produces long-term effects on neuroplasticity (Hall & Walker, 2017).

It is also believed that ΔFosB increases drug sensitivity and compulsive behavior temporarily (after 1 or 2 months, ΔFosB is no longer detectable following drug withdrawal) (Hall & Walker, 2017). Accumulating evidence also indicates that the insula may play a role in addiction. Abnormal activity in the insula during addiction may increase impulsivity and diminish the addict's ability to identify risky situations (Hall & Walker, 2017).

Bedendo et al. (2016) suggested that, neurobiologically, continually consuming drugs can be viewed as a learning process whereby the drug acts as a reinforcement. In other words, the basic concepts of behaviorism are important for understanding the neurobiological bases of drug use! These include the concepts of stimulus, response, operant conditioning, punishment, positive and negative reinforcement, and classical conditioning. If individuals use a psychoactive drug (the stimulus) and they subsequently feel euphoric (response), it increases the chance that the behavior will be repeated. That means they are operantly conditioned (which occurs when a reward follows either a positive or a negative behavior) to use more of the drug. If they experience withdrawal and stop

[2] Hatzigiakoumis et al. (2011) recommended pharmacological interventions for anhedonia, specifically, medications that activate the dopaminergic reward system. These include psychostimulants, dopamine agonists, and the norepinephrine ring/dopamine reuptake inhibitor bupropion. In clinical practice, bupropion is used most widely.

using the drug, they will experience negative consequences (punishment), but, by again taking the drug, the negative consequences disappear (when you are rewarded for removing a negative consequence, it is called negative reinforcement). Over time, many cues become associated with using the drug such as having the thought of using the drug, seeing paraphernalia used with the drug, hanging out with friends who use the drug, smelling the drug, and so forth. Remember Pavlov's dogs who salivated when they heard the bell. Similarly, these associations (cues) of drug use have become classically conditioned. So now we have both operant and classical conditioning at work to increase the likelihood of continuing drug use.

The lack of inhibition of craving and drug-seeking behavior peaks when the drug user is exposed to memory cues, which often trigger relapse (Renard et al., 2017). Both drug craving and preoccupation involve circuits in the prefrontal cortex, the amygdala, the hippocampus, and other areas involved in conditioned reinforcement (NIDA, 2016). The dysphoria that occurs during withdrawal is known to be affected by circuits in the basal ganglia and the extended amygdala (NIDA, 2016).

Although most adults report having used drugs at some point in their lives (Suzuki & Kober, 2018), it is reassuring to know that, despite the powerful influence of operant conditioning, classical conditioning, and the neurological underpinnings of addiction, most users do not become addicted. Bedendo et al. (2016) provided the example of Brazilians. Although 74% drink, only about 12% meet the criteria for AUD. The way a drug is consumed (e.g., sniffed, snorted, inhaled, swallowed, smoked, intramuscular, intravenous, oral, anal) is also correlated with the likelihood of developing dependency. The quicker a drug reaches the brain, the higher its dependency potential (e.g., using a drug intravenously compared with swallowing it). Further, the faster a drug enters the brain, the faster its effects wear off (e.g., smoking crack is more addictive than snorting cocaine).

The feeling of pleasure from drug use appears to depend on the release of dopamine into the nucleus accumbens and is also related to the compulsive behavior and increased motivation to find more of the substance (Bedendo et al., 2016). Regions of the prefrontal cortex are also believed to be involved in drug addiction, areas that appear to regulate decision-making regarding approach toward or avoidance of a substance (Bedendo et al., 2016).

Neurobiological Theories of Drug Dependence

Bedendo et al. (2016) stated that Roy Wise first presented the first substantial neurobiological theory about drugs in 1980. His theory was that several types of reinforcement would activate the reward pathway in the brain. Although drugs like cocaine and amphetamine would act directly in the reward pathway (i.e., the dopaminergic system), drugs like opioids, benzodiazepines, ethanol, and barbiturates would act by exciting or inhibiting signals from within the body (called afferences). In 1987, in work with Michael Bozarth, the two authors suggested that *all* drugs with potential to cause addiction could create psychomotor stimulation (Bedendo et al., 2016). In this revised theory, Wise suggested that opioids would function similarly to stimulants by promoting psychomotor activity. Depressants would act by directly stimulating dopaminergic fibers or via circuits associated with it. About 20 years later, the theory was again revised to suggest that it is the dopaminergic mesolimbic pathway that is the key to explaining the reinforcing effects from psychoactive drugs.

Another theory was offered by George Koob to explain the common action of drugs on the brain (Bedendo et al., 2016). He also focused on the reinforcement and pleasure produced by drugs with three key systems involved in creating pleasure: the endogenous opioid system,[3] the GABAergic system, and the dopaminergic system. The difference between his theory and that of Wise is that Koob did not believe that dopamine plays a critical role in creating the reinforcing effects from *all* drugs. Nutt, Lingford-Hughes, Erritzoe, and Stokes (2015) opined that the dopamine theory (i.e., that the release of dopamine underlies all addictive disorders) applies to stimulants, but they argued it does not equally apply to individuals with opiate, nicotine, or cannabis dependence. For example, studies have shown that abusing alcohol, cannabis, and ketamine do not always induce dopamine release in humans (Nutt et al., 2015).

According to Bedendo et al. (2016), Koob suggested that drug dependence results from (a) compulsive searching for the drug, (b) loss of control of its use, and (c) the occurrence of negative emotional states when the drug is unavailable. Koob's theory, then, also considered the importance of negative reinforcement in maintaining dependency (i.e., getting rid of withdrawal effects by again taking the drug). We now understand that negative reinforcement is as important as positive reinforcement in SUDs (NIDA, 2016).

Bedendo et al. (2016) reminded the reader that, whereas neurobiological factors are at work in addictive processes, addiction should be viewed as a biopsychosocial disorder. Neuroscience does not provide us with the entire explanation for how drug dependence either begins or ends.

Developmental Concerns During Adolescence

The adolescent brain is vulnerable. More than half of all mental illnesses emerge during adolescence, and one in five adolescents will have a mental illness that persists into adulthood. It is the prime period in which anxiety disorders, bipolar disorder, depression, eating disorders, psychosis, and SUDs emerge (Giedd, 2015).

Adolescence is a very active time for brain development, which includes development of the sex hormones, white and grey matter in the limbic system, and the cortex and other brain regions (Meruelo, Castro, Cota, & Tapert, 2017). In their literature review, Meruelo et al. (2017) concluded that alcohol and cannabis have a significant impact on adolescent brain development. Both cannabis and alcohol users show less brain volumes in several brain areas compared to nonusers. "Lifetime cannabis use has been associated with thinner temporal and frontal cortices. While heavy drinkers have been found to have poorer attention and executive function long term, though [*sic*] emotional reactivity and distress tolerance are recovered with abstinence" (Meruelo et al., 2017, p. 49). A central goal of intervention with adolescents is to delay their onset of using psychoactive drugs (Begun & Brown, 2014). Substance use during adolescence and young adulthood may compromise identity development and consolidation, career development, self-esteem, emotional maturity, development of intimate relationships, and cognitive capacities (Begun & Brown, 2014). Other concerns regarding adolescent development are found in Chapters 9 through 21.

[3]This system consists of neurons that create three naturally occurring opioids in the body, including beta-endorphin, the met- and leu-enkephalins, and the dynorphins (Holden, Jeong, & Forrest, 2005).

Behavioral Addictions

Behavioral addictions have not been considered up to this point in the chapter. As you will read in Chapters 14–21, research in neuroscience is showing us that all addictions are similar neurobiologically. The same brain regions are affected, the same NTs are implicated, and the reward pathway is much the same (Rosenberg & Curtiss Feder, 2014). Research is showing us that addiction *is* addiction, regardless of the object of that addiction (Milkman & Sunderwirth, 2010). Furthermore, "any drug or activity repeated specifically for pleasure has the potential to become addicting" (Milkman & Sunderwirth, 2010, p. 141).

For example, both structural and functional changes occur in the reward circuitry of people experiencing Internet gaming disorder (Weinstein, 2017). There are many similarities between the neurobiological correlates of Internet gaming disorder and gambling addiction (Fauth-Buhler & Mann, 2017). The same changes in the dopamine D2 receptors that occur with those experiencing AUD also are found in obese individuals (Sinha, 2012; Tarman & Werdell, 2014). Individuals addicted to exercise experience the dopamine rush that individuals with SUDs experience (Dakwar, 2015). Dopamine rush is also experienced by individuals addicted to sex (Cohen, 2015) and gambling (Clark, 2015).

Treatment Implications Emanating from Neuroscience

Neuroscience findings have led to the development of medications that target neurocircuitry at different stages of addiction regarding AUD (Harris & Koob, 2017). Other techniques that have demonstrated some efficacy for reducing long-term withdrawal and reinforcing abstinence regarding SUDs include meditation, biofeedback, and mindfulness treatments (Begun & Brown, 2014).

The American Counseling Association recently published a book called *Neurocounseling: Brain-Based Clinical Approaches*, edited by Field, Jones, and Russell-Chapin (2017). The field of neurocounseling only entered our vocabulary in December 2013 (Field et al., 2017). It represents the integration of neuroscience research into the counseling profession. Because it is a new field, much is still to be learned regarding how counselors can apply this research in their practice. Furthermore, studies done to date have mostly revealed transient changes resulting from applications of neuroscience. For example, Naim-Feil, Arunogiri, Spagnolo, and Lubman (2017) reported experimental research showing that noninvasive brain stimulation techniques are being investigated as possible treatment approaches for substance dependence. They offered preliminary results suggesting that these techniques can create transient reductions and craving levels in drug consumption, but they also noted that further large-scale studies are needed to evaluate their clinical efficacy conclusively. Additionally, efficacy as measured in a laboratory is not the same as effectiveness as measured in clinical practice. Sometimes interventions are found to be efficacious experimentally but not nearly so effective in real-life settings. Lastly, given the multifaceted nature of addiction, researchers remain unclear in predicting who will be most vulnerable to addiction and the best treatment approaches that should be provided for any particular individual (Naim-Feil et al., 2017).

Satel and Lilienfeld (2010) argued that neuroscience researchers sing "the brain disease blues" (p. 46). Why, they suggested, is addiction a brain disease as opposed to a molecular disease or a psychological or sociocultural disease? Satel and Lilienfeld suggested that all are equally valid perspectives depending on the purpose. They argued that calling addictions a brain disease is seductive, yet addicted individuals do not spend all their time "in the throes of an intense neurochemical siege" (p. 46). Most individuals addicted to heroin have jobs, cocaine-addicted individuals decide whether to attend a Narcotics Anonymous meeting, and so forth. "Users perform their own mental calculations all the time" (p. 46).

Stanton Peele (2015) emphatically stated that neurobiological models cannot explain addiction. He remarked that a study by Oslin and colleagues found no difference between alcohol-dependent subjects who received either naltrexone or placebo regarding the number of heavy drinking days, drinking days per week, and weekly cravings, but, despite these results, the authors concluded that pharmacotherapy holds great promise to improve treatment response. Peele argued in favor of a nonreductionist view of human behavior.

Racine, Sattler, and Escande (2017) titled their article about free will that included the phrase "the not so seductive allure of neuroscience." Racine et al. argued that the proponents of neuroscience suggest that the brain-disease model of addiction re-attributes the cause of the disorder "to the brain rather than to the person" (p. 1). Furthermore, these authors pondered whether this assault on free will might lead drug-addicted individuals to become less responsible (e.g., "I couldn't help myself"). In their web-based experiment of 2378 German participants, Racine et al. found that those who knew about neuroscience were more likely to decrease attribution of responsibility to the person regarding addiction (thereby supporting the brain-disease model instead).

Philosophical questions remain: "To what extent is an individual's free will affected by becoming dependent on a substance or behavior?" "Will the answer be found through psychology, spirituality, neuroscience, or a combination?"

WHAT DO YOU THINK?

As you think about the previous two questions, how would you answer them right now based on your values? To what extent do you believe that the answers to these questions will never be found and that, instead, answers will always be values-based?

As you think about these questions, also ask yourself, "Is this a different issue from whether individuals high on psychoactive drugs are responsible for the crimes that they commit while under the influence?" Alternatively, "Are crimes committed while under the influence of a psychoactive drug more akin to someone who is found not guilty for reasons of insanity?"

RESOURCES AND VIDEOS

Resources

1. Free Will and Neuroscience: From Explaining Freedom Away to New Ways of Operationalizing and Measuring It (Andrea Lavazza, 2016). https://www.ncbi.nlm.nih.gov/pmc/articles/PMC4887467/
2. Neuroscience of Psychoactive Substance Abuse and Dependence published by World Health Organization (WHO) 2004. https://www.who.int/substance_abuse/publications/en/Neuroscience.pdf
3. The Neurobiology of Drug Addiction. https://www.drugabuse.gov/publications/teaching-packets/neurobiology-drug-addiction/section-i-introduction-to-brain
4. Pathological Choice: The Neuroscience of Gambling and Gambling Addiction (Luke Clark et al., 2013). http://www.jneurosci.org/content/33/45/17617
5. Neuroscience of Addiction: Relevance to Prevention and Treatment (Nora Volkow, 2018). https://www.uniad.org.br/images/2018/articles/VOLKOW_NEUROSCIENCE_OF_ADDICTION.pdf

Videos

To view these videos, search their titles on YouTube.

1. *Why do our brains get addicted?* Neuroscientist Nora Volkow, director of the National Institute on Drug Abuse at the NIH, applies a lens of addiction to the obesity epidemic.
2. *The Brain and Recovery: An Update on the Neuroscience of Addiction.*
3. *Addiction Neuroscience 101.*
4. *The Neuroscience of Addiction - with Marc Lewis.*
5. *Neurobiology of Addiction.* Hosted by Dr. Frank R. George, compelling speaker and leading expert on drugs, addiction and the brain.

JOURNALS AND CONFERENCES

Journals

1. *Neuroscience.* https://www.journals.elsevier.com/neuroscience/
2. *Journal of Neuroscience.* http://www.jneurosci.org/
3. *Neuroscience Journal.* https://www.hindawi.com/journals/neuroscience/
4. *Frontiers in Neuroscience.* https://www.frontiersin.org/journals/neuroscience#
5. *Journal of Neurology and Neuroscience.* http://www.jneuro.com
6. *Schimago Journal & Country Rank.* They provide a list that ranks 50 of the top journals in neuroscience. https://www.scimagojr.com/journalrank.php?category=2801

Conferences

Society for Neuroscience. They both offer conferences and other training (see www.sfn.org/).

Conferenceseries.com. Neuroscience conferences can be found at https://www.conferenceseries.com/neuroscience-meetings

Another site for neuroscience conferences. https://neuroscience.conferenceseries.com/

Noldus Information Technology. They list several international conferences on neuroscience. https://www.noldus.com/blog/neuroscience-conferences (or use https://www.noldus.com and search from there)

World Congress on Neurology and Neuroscience. https://neuroscience.neurologyconference.com/ or https://world.neurologyconference.com/

INDIVIDUAL EXERCISES

1. Use flashcards to learn the parts of the brain better. On one card, print hindbrain on the front and list the four parts of the hindbrain on the back. Then create a separate card for each of these four parts. Do the same

with the midbrain (two parts) and the forebrain (10 parts beginning with the insula). On the back of each of the cards that have the separate parts, print the functions of that part of the brain.

2. Interview someone who experiences an SUD. Ask him or her about both what he or she liked about the drug but also disliked about using the drug. From the list of likes and dislikes, cross-reference these with what happens to the brains of individuals who use that particular drug. You may need to do a Google search to learn more about that specific substance.

3. Teach a family member or friend what you have learned about neuroscience. This will help you see what you have learned well and what is still unclear to you.

CLASSROOM EXERCISES

1. Neuron Transmission Exercise.

   A. **Organize the Neurons**. First, have 12 students stand at the front of the class (in a smaller class, use six students at the front and create only one line for neurotransmission).

      (a) ***Forming the Axons***. Have the remainder of the class form two equal lines, facing the front of the class. Each student should be arms-length away from the student behind and in front of him or her. In one line (the line on the left facing the front of the class), have the students outstretch their left arm and lightly grip the left shoulder of the student ahead. In the other line (the one on the right facing the front of the class), have the students outstretch their right arm and lightly grip the right shoulder of the student ahead.

      (b) ***One Dendrite***. Take one student off the back of one line (the shorter one if there is an unequal number of students in your class). Have this student outstretch his left arm, lightly gripping the right shoulder of the student in the left line while also outstretching his right arm to grasp the left shoulder of the student in the right line.

      (c) ***Four Axon Terminals***. Now take four of the 12 students at the front of the class. Two of them stand in front of one line and the other two at the front of the other line. The student behind each of the two students places their left arm on the right shoulder of one and right arm on the left shoulder of the other. Also, do this for the second line. Now you should have four axon terminals.

      (d) ***Four NTs***. Now add another student at the front of each of four axon terminals. These are the four NTs.

      (e) ***Four Dendrites of the Next Neuron***. Have the remaining four students at the front of the class face the two lines, standing directly in front of the four students who will act as NTs.

      (f) ***The Synapses***. Create a 6-foot gap between the four students facing their counterpart.

   B. **Sending Transmissions**. Have the four dendrites of the next neuron (the ones facing the rest of the class) outstretch their arms with one of their hands clenched in a fist. This means they are ready to receive the NTs.

   C. **Begin the Transmission**. The one dendrite at the back of the class now squeezes the two shoulders. The students relay the message by squeezing the shoulder in front of them, then that student transmits the message to the next student, and so forth. Once the message reaches the dendrites at the front, the students playing the part of the NTs detach and, using an outstretched hand facing upward, touches the fist of the dendrite in front of them. The goal is to see which line can most quickly transmit the message to the receiving dendrites. As the exercise proceeds, have two of the receiving dendrites drop their arms so that there are only two dendrites capable of receiving a transmission. This provides an example of having an insufficient number of receiving dendrites. Alternatively, you could keep the four receiving dendrites but take two of the NTs away from the front of the class (i.e., now you only have one terminal per line). This provides an example where there is not enough of the NT in the synapse.

2. Invite a neuroscience researcher to your class to provide a presentation. Beforehand, have your students prepare questions that they can ask that pertain particularly to addictions.

3. Break the students into 16 groups and assign each of them one of the four parts of the hindbrain noted in this chapter, the two parts of the midbrain, or the 10 parts of the forebrain (include the insula). Have each group spend time doing a Google search to learn more about the functions of their brain part, and then have them look further into what happens if that part is damaged. Have each group then present to the class.

CHAPTER SUMMARY

The National Institute on Drug Abuse (2016) estimated that up to 50% of people's risk of becoming addicted to psychoactive substances, including nicotine and alcohol, depends on their genetic makeup. Nonetheless, it remains impossible to generalize genetic research from one family to the next as there are hundreds if not thousands of genes that directly or indirectly contribute to addictions. Neurogenetics is a more specific field that looks at the role that genetics plays in the development and function of the nervous system. Studies in neurogenetics will, it is hoped, lead to greater precision in assessing addiction risk.

Neuroscience is the study of the brain and nervous system, whereas neurobiology is a subdivision of both biology and neuroscience that specifically studies neurons and their organization into functional circuits. Scientists study the nervous system through animal studies, examining autopsy tissue, testing the behavior of people with brain damage, recording electrical brain activity, and using neuroimaging techniques that show visual images in awake humans.

There are two main nervous systems in the body: the CNS and the peripheral nervous system. The peripheral nervous system is broken down into the somatic nervous system, which we have control over, and the autonomic nervous system, which we can exert some control over indirectly. The two kinds of cells within the CNS include neurons and glial cells. The parts of the neuron were reviewed followed by a closer look at NTs.

The brain comprises the hindbrain (which includes the medulla, pons, cerebellum, and reticular formation), the midbrain (which contain several nuclei, including the SN and the VTA), and the forebrain. The two main parts of the forebrain include the diencephalon and the telencephalon. The telencephalon consists mostly of the cerebrum, which consists of the two cerebral hemispheres, and the corpus callosum, which connects the two sides. The outer part of the cerebrum is called the cerebral cortex. The mesolimbic and mesocortical pathways were also described. Parts of the forebrain include the thalamus, hypothalamus, pituitary gland, amygdala, hippocampus, and basal ganglia (which consists of the striatum, the globus pallidus, the nucleus accumbens, and the SN, which is part of the midbrain).

Drugs affect NTs in different ways and over time affect allostasis, which is the body's ability to adjust its setpoints to maintain homeostasis. Over repeated drug use, changes occur in both the structure and functioning of neurons. These changes create long-lasting and sometimes permanent neuron and neurotransmission abnormalities. The resulting changes create several symptoms, one of which is anhedonia (the inability to experience pleasure). Some regions of the brain can regenerate, a process called neuroplasticity. It is unknown, however, if some of the brain alterations resulting from excessive drug use remain permanent. The process of epigenesis involves altered neurons being passed down to future generations, which may increase the likelihood of offspring developing addiction problems and/or other mental health issues.

Neuroscientists are concerned that, because the adolescent brain is vulnerable, substance use during adolescence may compromise identity development and consolidation, career development, self-esteem, emotional maturity, development of intimate relationships, and cognitive capacities. Research is showing that addiction *is* addiction, regardless of the object of that addiction. Consequently, behavioral addictions are similar to substance addictions neurobiologically.

Treatment implications emanating from neuroscience research require further study. Current research suggests that the results are sometimes transitory. Furthermore, efficacious treatments discovered in a laboratory are not always effective in real-life settings. Some researchers have argued that the reductionist perspective taken by neuroscientists is inappropriate. They remind us that addictions are mostly considered to be a biopsychosocial problem, and this does not mean that addicted individuals lose their free will.

REFERENCES

Bedendo, A., Andrade, A. L. M., & Noto, A. R. (2016). Neurobiology of substance abuse. In A. L. M. Andrade & D. D. Micheli (Eds.), *Innovations in the treatment of substance addiction* (pp. 17–34). Cham, Switzerland: Springer International.

Begun, A., & Brown, S. (2014). Neurobiology of substance use disorders and implications for treatment. In S. L. A. Straussner (Ed.), *Clinical work with substance-abusing clients* (3rd ed., pp. 39–66). New York, NY: Guilford Press.

Bennett, S., & Petrash, P. (2014). The neurobiology of substance use disorders: Information for assessment and clinical treatment. *Smith College Studies in Social Work, 84*(2–3), 273–291.

Blakeslee, S. (2007, February 6). A small part of the brain, and its profound effects. *New York Times*. Retrieved on January 4, 2019, from https://www.nytimes.com/2007/02/06/health/psychology/06brain.html

Burkeman, O. (2012, July 15). Meet "Dr. Love," the scientist exploring what makes people good or evil. *Guardian*. Retrieved on January 2, 2019, from https://www.theguardian.com/science/2012/jul/15/interview-dr-love-paul-zak's

Clark, L. (2015). Neurobiology of pathological gambling. In H. Bowden-Jones & S. George (Eds.), *A clinician's guide to working with problem gamblers* (pp. 53–74). New York, NY: Routledge/Taylor & Francis Group.

Cohen, L. J. (2015). Sex addiction: The fire down below. In M. S. Ascher & P. Levounis (Eds.), *The behavioral addictions* (pp. 137–152). Washington, DC: American Psychiatric Association.

Comer, R., Ogden, N., Boyes, M., & Gould, E. (2018). *Psychology around us* (3rd Canadian ed.). Toronto, ON: John Wiley & Sons Canada.

Craig, A. D. (2009). How do you feel—now? The anterior insula and human awareness. Nature reviews. *Neuroscience, 10*(1), 59–70.

Csiernik, R. (2016). *Substance use and abuse: Everything matters* (2nd ed.). Toronto, ON: Canadian Scholar's Press.

Dakwar, E. (2015). Problematic exercise: A case of alien feet. In M. S. Ascher & P. Levounis (Eds.), *The behavioral addictions* (pp. 29–42). Washington, DC: American Psychiatric.

Esel, E., & Dinc, K. (2017). Neurobiology of alcohol dependence and implications on treatment. *Turk Psikiyatri Dergisi, 28*(1), 1–10.

Fauth-Buhler, M., & Mann, K. (2017). Neurobiological correlates of internet gaming disorder: Similarities to pathological gambling. *Addictive Behaviors, 64*, 349–356.

Field, T. A., Jones, L. K., & Russell-Chapin, L. A. (Eds.). (2017). *Neurocounseling: Brain-based clinical approaches* (pp. 149–164). Alexandria, VA: American Counseling Association.

Giedd, J. N. (2015). Adolescent neuroscience of addiction: A new era. *Developmental Cognitive Neuroscience, 16*, 192–193.

Gipson, C. D., & Kalivas, P. W. (2016). Neural basis of drug addiction. In D. D. Micheli, A. L. Monezi Andrade, E. A. da Silva, & M. L. Oliveira de Souza Formigoni (Eds.), *Drug abuse in adolescence: Neurobiological, cognitive, and psychological issues* (pp. 37–56). Cham, Switzerland: Springer International.

Hall, S. B., & Walker, K. D. (2017). Clinical neuroscience of substance use disorders. In T. A. Field, L. K. Jones, & L. A. Russell-Chapin (Eds.), *Neurocounseling: Brain-based clinical approaches* (pp. 149–164). Alexandria, VA: American Counseling Association.

Harris, R. A., & Koob, G. F. (2017). The future is now: A 2020 view of alcoholism research. *Neuropharmacology, 122*, 1–2.

Hatzigiakoumis, D. S., Martinotti, G., Di Giannantonio, M., & Janiri, L. (2011). Anhedonia and substance dependence: Clinical correlates and treatment options. *Frontiers in Psychiatry, 2*, 1–12.

Holden, J. E., Jeong, Y., & Forrest, J. M. (2005). The endogenous opioid system and clinical pain management. *AACN Clinical Issues, 16*(3), 291–301.

Meruelo, A. D., Castro, N., Cota, C. I., & Tapert, S. F. (2017). Cannabis and alcohol use, and the developing brain. *Behavioural Brain Research, 325*(Part A), 44–50.

Milkman, H. B., & Sunderwirth, S. G. (2010). *Craving for ecstasy and natural highs: A positive approach to mood alteration*. Thousand Oaks, CA: SAGE.

Naim-Feil, J., Arunogiri, S., Spagnolo, P. A., & Lubman, D. I. (2017). Addiction. In N. J. Rinehart, J. L. Bradshaw, & P. G. Enticott (Eds.), *Developmental disorders of the brain* (2nd ed., pp. 208–230). New York, NY: Routledge/Taylor & Francis Group.

National Institute on Drug Abuse (NIDA). (2016). Neurobiology of addiction—From reward to relief: The complex neuroadaptations underlying addiction. In P. Levounis, E. Zerbo, & R. Aggarwal (Eds.), *Pocket guide to addiction assessment and treatment* (pp. 3–6). Washington, DC: American Psychiatric.

Nutt, D. J., Lingford-Hughes, A., Erritzoe, D., & Stokes, P. R. A. (2015). The dopamine theory of addiction: 40 years of highs and lows. *Nature Reviews Neuroscience, 16*(5), 305–312.

Park, B., Han, D. H., & Roh, S. (2017). Neurobiological findings related to Internet use disorders. *Psychiatry and Clinical Neurosciences, 71*(7), 467–478.

Patel, K. T., Stevens, M. C., Meda, S. A., Muska, C., Thomas, A. D., Potenza, M. N., & Pearlson, G. D. (2013). Robust changes in reward circuitry during reward loss in current and former cocaine users during performance of a monetary incentive delay task. *Biological Psychiatry, 74*, 529–537.

Peele, S. (2015). Why neurobiological models can't contain mental disorder and addiction. *Behavior Therapist, 38*(7), 218–222.

Peterson, J. (2016, August 8). NIH grant to fund new Center for Systems Neurogenetics of Addiction. *Jackson Laboratory*. Retrieved on January 6, 2019, from https://www.jax.org/news-and-insights/2016/august/nih-grant-to-fund-new-center-for-systems-neurogenetics-of-addiction

Pihl, R., & Stewart, S. (2013). Substance use disorders. In L. Castonguay & T. Oltmanns (Eds.), *Psychopathology: From science to clinical practice* (pp. 241–274). New York, NY: Guilford Press.

Racine, E., Sattler, S., & Escande, A. (2017). Free will and the brain disease model of addiction: The not so seductive allure of neuroscience and its modest impact on the attribution of free will to people with an addiction. *Frontiers in Psychology, 8*, 1–17.

Rastegar, D., & Fingerhood, M. (2016). *The American Society of Addiction Medicine handbook of addiction medicine*. New York, NY: Oxford University Press.

Renard, J., Rosen, L., Rushlow, W. J., & Laviolette, S. R. (2017). Role of the prefrontal cortex in addictive disorders. In D. Cechetto & N. Weishaupt (Eds.), *The cerebral cortex in neurodegenerative and neuropsychiatric disorders: Experimental approaches to clinical issues* (pp. 289–309). San Diego, CA: Elsevier Academic Press.

Rosenberg, P. R., & Curtiss Feder, L. (2014). An introduction to behavioral addictions. In K. P. Rosenberg & L. Curtiss Feder (Eds.), *Behavioral addictions: Criteria, evidence, and treatment* (pp. 1–17). San Diego, CA: Elsevier Academic Press.

Satel, S., & Lilienfeld, S. O. (2010). Singing the brain disease blues. *AJOB Neuroscience, 1*(1), 46–47.

Saunders, B. T., & Richard, J. M. (2011). Shedding light on the role of ventral tegmental area dopamine in reward. *Journal of Neuroscience, 31*(50), 18195–18197.

Sherman, C. (2017, March 9). Impacts of drugs on neurotransmission. *National Institute on Drug Abuse*. Retrieved on January 4, 2019, from https://www.drugabuse.gov/news-events/nida-notes/2017/03/impacts-drugs-neurotransmission

Sinha, R. (2012). Stress and addiction: A brief overview. In K. D. Brownell & M. S. Gold (Eds.), *Food and addiction: A comprehensive handbook* (pp. 59–66). New York, NY: Oxford University Press.

Stolberg, V. B. (2006). A review of perspectives on alcohol and alcoholism in the history of American health and medicine. *Journal of Ethnicity in Substance Abuse, 5*, 39–106.

Suckling, J., & Nestor, L. J. (2017). The neurobiology of addiction: The perspective from magnetic resonance imaging present and future. *Addiction, 112*, 360–369.

Sullivan, E. V. (2017). Contributions to understanding the neuropsychology of alcoholism: An INS legacy. *Journal of the International Neuropsychological Society, 23*, 843–859.

Suzuki, S., & Kober, H. (2018). Substance-related and addictive disorders. In J. N. Butcher & J. M. Hooley (Eds.), *APA handbook of psychopathology. Vol. 1, Psychopathology: Understanding, assessing, and treating adult mental disorders* (pp. 481–506). Washington, DC: American Psychological Association.

Tarman, V., & Werdell, P. (2014). *Food junkies: The truth about food addiction.* Toronto, ON: Dundurn.

Volkow, N. D., Koob, G. F., & McLellan, A. T. (2016). Neurobiologic advances from the brain disease model of addiction. *New England Journal of Medicine, 374*, 363–371.

Weinstein, A. M. (2017). An update overview on brain imaging studies of Internet gaming disorder. *Frontiers in Psychiatry, 8*, 1–13.

Wong, S. M. E., Fong, E., Tauck, D. L., & Kendig, J. J. (1997). Ethanol as a general anesthetic: Actions in spinal cord. *European Journal of Pharmacology, 329*(2–3), 121–127.

PART I

General Treatment Considerations

5 *DSM-5*, Polyaddictions, and Comorbidity

iStock.com/KatarzynaBialasi

Learning Objectives

1. Describe the fundamentals of the DSM system, *DSM-5*, and controversies surrounding diagnoses.
2. Become aware of some aspects of personality disorders, psychosis, and schizophrenia.
3. Learn about the prevalence of polyaddictions and comorbidity regarding both substance use disorders (SUDs) and behavioral addictions.
4. Apply lessons regarding *DSM-5*, polyaddictions, and comorbidity.
5. Become familiar with recent findings regarding comorbidities and addictions.

PERSONAL REFLECTIONS

I remember my friend "Gary" (not his real name) with both fondness and disdain. We were friends for more than 30 years, but, eventually, I could not continue the friendship. Gary became increasingly verbally abusive. His father had severe alcohol use disorder (AUD), and Gary turned out much the same. Most of all, I remember the day he told me that his doctor had diagnosed him with borderline personality disorder (BPD). I was already a counseling psychologist by this point, and, in the field of counseling generally, we do not embrace labels the same way that medical doctors, psychiatrists, and clinical psychologists frequently do.

I told him, "Gary, if you have a label, then I must find one for myself as well. Only in that way can we continue as equal friends." He seemed satisfied with that, and so was I. After our conversation, I immediately turned to the DSM to read about BPD. Indeed, it did seem that Gary fulfilled the criteria. However, I could not find an appropriate diagnosis for myself. I knew that I had experienced bouts of major depression, but these were transitory. And, back then, I did not see my cannabis use as problematic. I vividly remember the night he left a scathing voicemail because I was beginning to pull away from our friendship. He threatened to tell my boss everything that I had ever done for which I should be ashamed, and, in that moment of listening to his message, I indeed felt ashamed. But, more than that, I was angry, and I felt betrayed and manipulated.

Given that I was an untenured professor then, however, I was unwilling to take the chance. Soon after that, while he sat at home unemployed, he got himself extremely drunk before driving to buy more hard liquor. During his departure from the store, he fell on ice (we get a lot of snow and ice in our winters), lost consciousness, and awakened to two police officers standing over him. He was charged with a DUI, but, before this ever went to court, his fall had led to bleeding in his brain. This required surgery, and, after that was finished, he was unable to talk sensibly for several weeks. I visited him once in hospital and knew that, after doing so, this would be the last time I would ever see Gary again.

I understand personality disorders much better today than I did back then. They are, by definition, enduring dysfunctions that often never have an ending. What I also understand is that he was experiencing comorbidity, which in the addictions field means having an addictive disorder and a psychiatric one at the same time.

Counselors and researchers are faced with some interesting questions when it comes to comorbidity. The same applies when one is experiencing more than one addiction. As you will discover in this chapter, the validity and reliability of diagnoses are also troublesome, regardless of which classification system is utilized. These are just some of the topics covered in this chapter.

DSM-5

More than 90% of psychologists using *DSM-5* are dissatisfied with numerous aspects regarding it, which was also true of the DSM system 30 years ago (Raskin & Gayle, 2015). Furthermore, a study conducted by Gayle and Raskin (2017) found that counselors have conflicting attitudes regarding *DSM-5*. Counselors believed that the DSM places a higher priority on diagnosis than treatment, and many were in support of developing an alternative to the DSM system.

Diagnosis in psychiatry has always been a controversial topic (Kinderman, Allsopp, & Cooke, 2017). According to Kinderman et al. (2017), this was particularly evident in the release of *DSM-5* (American Psychiatric Association, 2013). Elkins (2017) argued that a paradigm shift is occurring in psychotherapy away from a medical to a nonmedical view of helping others.

From a social constructionist perspective, diagnostic criteria are considered to be historical artifacts situated in the current social, political, and economic context. Psychiatric diagnoses are dynamic social constructs that are continually shifting and changing (Miller, 2016). If this were not the case regarding the DSM system, we would not have witnessed the developments of DSM-I, DSM-II, DSM-III, DSM-III-R, DSM-IV, DSM-IV-TR, and now *DSM-5*.

Miller (2016) provided an interesting example regarding the social construction of addictive disorders. Prohibition ended in 1933, making alcohol again freely available throughout the United States. It was in the interests of the alcohol industry to make alcohol appear to be a substance that was only a risk to those "rare" individuals who were "alcoholics." This suggested a qualitative difference between "them" and "us" (i.e., the nonalcoholics), and the treatment of choice flowing from this view was that only alcoholics needed to become abstinent but not the rest of us. *DSM-5* no longer includes the terms *alcoholic, abuse, dependence*, or *addiction*. What happened to the alcoholics of yesteryear? *DSM-5* has erased them from existence in principle and on paper.

Nonetheless, Cooper (2018) commented that the *DSM-5* is very similar to DSM-IV. Cooper argued that this suggests that DSM has become static, "locked-in" (p. 49), and increasingly challenging to change.

DSM-I and DSM-II were developed in the context of the U.S. Veterans Administration following World War II. DSM-III and DSM-IV arose in response to psychiatry's crisis of legitimacy (Kinderman et al., 2017). The diagnosis of posttraumatic stress disorder (PTSD) was also introduced in DSM-III following the Vietnam War. Although some diagnoses such as hysteria and homosexuality have been removed in the DSM system, others like gender dysphoria and hearing voices are seen as pathological today *only* if they are upsetting to the individual experiencing them (Kinderman et al., 2017).

The British Psychological Society (BPS, as cited by Kinderman et al., 2017) responded to the spring 2011 draft of *DSM-5* by writing about their concern regarding the public's "continued and continuous medicalization of their natural and normal responses to their experiences" (p. 630). The BPS went on to address the "putative diagnoses" that were largely based on social norms (p. 630). Aggarwal (2017), in his editorial, highlighted the ethnic and racial bias of *DSM-5*. Hartung and Lefler (2019) concluded that sex and gender ratios in *DSM-5* are unsystematic. Padmanabhan (2017) provided an excellent example of cultural bias. In *DSM-5*, the possession form of dissociative identity disorder turns this normalized practice in Kerala, South India, into a disease.

The Society for Humanistic Psychology, which represents Division 32 of the American Psychological Association, also raised concerns regarding "the lowering of diagnostic thresholds for multiple disorder categories" (Kinderman et al., 2017, p. 632). Some psychiatrists advocated a boycott of *DSM-5*. To that point, the "Statement of Concern" written by the International *DSM-5* Response Committee in October 2012 stated the following:

> We believe that there is now overwhelming evidence that *DSM-5*
>
> - is the result of a secretive, closed, and rushed process that put publishing profits ahead of public welfare;
> - is in many places scientifically unsound and statistically unreliable, and did not receive a much needed and widely requested external scientific review;
> - is clinically risky because of many new and untested diagnoses and lowered diagnostic thresholds;
> - will result in the mislabeling of mental illness in people who will do better without a psychiatric diagnosis;
> - will result in unnecessary and potentially harmful treatment with psychiatric medication;
> - will divert precious mental health resources away from those who most need them.
>
> For these reasons, we have serious concerns about the new *DSM-5* scheduled for publication by the APA on 20th May, 2013. (Kinderman et al., 2017, p. 635)

The previous concerns should be particularly disconcerting to counselors. Counselors, in general, have never valued labeling because counseling focuses on people's strengths more than their weaknesses (and diagnosis emphasizes their shortcomings). This concern with labeling is especially problematic for counselors who identify with the humanistic or postmodern perspective because of their strong antidiagnosis beliefs. Nonetheless, it is generally recognized that psychiatry trumps the psychological or counseling fields regarding practices within the mental health profession. Consequently, many if not most addiction counselors will find themselves needing to adhere to and understand diagnoses as outlined in *DSM-5* if practicing in the United States. In many other parts of the world, the *International Classification of Diseases, 11th Revision* (ICD-11), may be used instead of *DSM-5* (visit https://icd.who.int/ for details regarding ICD-11, which is published by the World Health Organization).

Although the DSM and ICD systems dominate psychiatric discourse, other classification systems have been advanced in the literature. For example, Gordon and Bornstein (2018) wrote about the *Psychodynamic Diagnosis Manual* (PDM) and its updated version, PDM-2. Gordon and Bornstein suggested that this approach offered a "person-centered perspective" (p. 280). In their article, Gordon and Bornstein discussed the development, structure, format, scoring, and interpretation of the psychodiagnostic chart that they developed for use with the PDM and PDM-2.

Another proposed alternative is what Rubin (2018) suggested should be called the Classification and Statistical Manual of Mental Health Concerns (CSM). Rubin believed that naming problems as mental health concerns instead of mental disorders would be less stigmatizing. He also stressed that it would be more practical, which, in turn, would improve mental health services.

In the United Kingdom, Johnstone (2018) recommended a practice supported by the BPS. She suggested that "psychological formulation" (p. 30) is a credible alternative to diagnosis. Formulation was defined as "the process of co-constructing a hypothesis or 'best guess' about the origins of a person's difficulties" (p. 32). Johnstone also stated that formulations include the context of a person's difficulties.

DSM-5 is arranged in three sections and includes seven appendices. Three of the appendices list *DSM-5* diagnoses and codes for ICD-9 and ICD-10, which has now been replaced by ICD-11. The three main sections of *DSM-5* are included in Table 5.1.[1]

The DSM system had already abandoned using the term *addiction* in favor of *abuse* and *dependence* before *DSM-5* (Stein et al., 2018). *DSM-5* has also removed the words *abuse* and *dependence*, instead rating severity as *mild* (presence of two or three symptoms), *moderate* (presence of four or five symptoms), or *severe* (presence of six or more symptoms). Each SUD includes a total of 11 possible symptoms (these 11 symptoms are listed in Chapters 9 through 13). The convention in *DSM-5* is to name particular SUDs (e.g., AUD, cannabis use disorder) and specific substance-induced disorders (e.g., alcohol intoxication, alcohol withdrawal, other alcohol-induced disorders). Despite *DSM-5*'s position of not using the word *addiction*, it remains in the vernacular and most peer-reviewed publications.

Diagnoses of SUDs have also fallen under scrutiny. A study by Verges, Ellingson, Schroder, Slutske, and Sher (2018) found that daily drinkers are a highly heterogeneous group, and AUD as defined by both DSM-IV and *DSM-5* did not diagnose more than 68% of daily binge drinkers (past-year use). Their representative sample was based on research conducted by the National Institute on Alcohol Abuse and Alcoholism in 2001 and 2002 (Wave 1) and 2004 and 2005 (Wave 2). In Wave 1, 43,093 respondents were interviewed, and 34,653 of these same respondents were interviewed in Wave 2. Data analysis of Verges et al. was based on 26,946 past-year alcohol users.

Wu et al. (2017) used data from a multisite validation study using a screening instrument with 2000 adults (over age 18) in four states to establish the prevalence of 12-month *DSM-5* SUDs. The participants were primary care patients. Wu et al. found that, overall, 75.5% of the sample used any substance over the past year. This included "alcohol (62.0%), tobacco (44.1%), or illicit drugs/nonmedical medications (27.9%) in the past 12 months (marijuana 20.8%, cocaine 7.3%, opioids 4.8%, sedatives 4.1%, heroin 3.9%)" (p. 42). Furthermore, among those who used over the last 12 months,

[1]For details of these disorders, please refer to *DSM-5*. The criteria for SUDs, however, are included in Chapters 9 through 13. Note that the headings are not numbered in DSM-5 as they are in Table 5.1.

TABLE 5.1 Sections and Headings in *DSM-5* Not Including Appendices

Section I
1. Introduction
2. Use of the Manual
3. Cautionary Statement for Forensic Use of *DSM-5*
Section II
1. Neurodevelopmental Disorders
2. Schizophrenia Spectrum and Other Psychotic Disorders
3. Bipolar and Related Disorders
4. Depressive Disorders
5. Anxiety Disorders
6. Obsessive-Compulsive and Related Disorders
7. Trauma- and Stressor-Related Disorders
8. Dissociative Disorders
9. Somatic Symptom and Related Disorders
10. Feeding and Eating Disorders
11. Elimination Disorders
12. Sleep-Wake Disorders
13. Sexual Dysfunctions
14. Gender Dysphoria
15. Disruptive, Impulse-Control, and Conduct Disorders
16. Neurocognitive Disorders
17. Personality Disorders
18. Paraphilia Disorders
19. Other Mental Disorders
20. Medication-Induced Movement Disorders and Other Adverse Effects of Medication
21. Other Conditions That May Be a Focus of Clinical Attention
Section III
1. Assessment Measures
2. Cultural Formulation
3. Alternative *DSM-5* Model for Personality Disorders
4. Conditions for Further Study

a high proportion met criteria for tobacco use disorder (57.4% total: 26.1% mild, 31.3% moderate/severe) and any drug use disorder (50.2% total: 14.3% mild, 35.8% moderate/severe). The findings of Wu et al. highlight the high prevalence of SUDs in primary care.

Besides SUDs, behavioral addictions, which are the subject of Chapters 14–21, came into discussion in the published literature about 3 decades ago (Stein et al., 2018). Gambling disorder is the first behavioral addiction introduced into *DSM-5*, and Internet gaming disorder is included as a condition requiring further study in Section III. Gaming disorder has already been added to ICD-11.

Grzegorzewska (2017) reviewed the research regarding behavioral addictions in children and adolescents. She noted that the research base is far larger regarding behavioral addictions in adults. Nonetheless, she concluded that early signs of behavioral addiction constitute a substantial threat to the mental well-being of children and adolescents both now and in the future.

The diagnosis of Internet gaming disorder, despite *DSM-5*'s having placed it under conditions requiring further study, has already been scrutinized by Hajela and Love (2017). Hajela and Love argued that the American Psychiatric Association ought to have called it Internet addiction instead of "a fabricated diagnosis based on one of its subtypes" (p. 11). Deleuze et al. (2017) suggested that the evidence regarding the validity of this diagnosis remains scarce.

HOW WOULD AN ADDICTION COUNSELOR HELP THIS CLIENT (RE: *DSM*)?

You are working as a professional counselor. Your client, Talon, age 38, has seen you for two sessions to deal with his alcohol use. He has attended Alcoholics Anonymous for 5 years. During the first session, you administer some questionnaires and collect personal history. Your assessment of Talon's drinking would place him in the mild range of AUD. In the second session, you focus on helping Talon look at the different areas of his life regarding the ways that alcohol has affected them. A few days later, he calls you and tells you that he has been experiencing a relapse that has affected him for the past few weeks. He never told you this in session. On the telephone, he informs you that he physically assaulted his girlfriend during his relapse. He wants you to write a note for court saying he is a full-blown alcoholic. He believes this will help act as a mitigating factor in sentencing. You are caught off guard and tell him that you will get back to him within 24 hours.

1. If you agree to write the letter, what would you include in it?
2. If you don't write the letter, how would you maintain a positive working alliance with Talon?
3. Some clients come to us for reasons other than what they disclose initially. You might feel deceived and wonder if he only booked sessions with you to get a supporting letter. Nonetheless, what other possible explanations could there be for him to ask for a letter after only two sessions?

Personality Disorders, Psychosis, and Schizophrenia

Although it is beyond the scope of this chapter to describe every mental disorder found in *DSM-5*, personality disorders will be overviewed in a general sense as they are commonly comorbid with SUDs. Additionally, psychosis and schizophrenia will be reviewed. Working with individuals experiencing psychosis is most likely outside of your training and expertise, and, when these symptoms are present, a psychiatric consult is indicated.

Personality disorders.

Tyrer (2017) emphatically stated his opinion regarding the current classification of personality disorders in *DSM-5*. It is "complicated, unprincipled and useless. It is disliked by almost everybody, even experts in the field, is not diagnosed clinically even when it is clearly present, and has an evidence base that is patently unacceptable, that of expert opinion only" (p. 1077). Given that caveat, the personality disorders that are diagnosable in *DSM-5* include paranoid personality disorder, schizoid personality disorder, schizotypal personality disorder, antisocial personality disorder (APD), BPD, histrionic personality disorder, narcissistic personality disorder (NPD), avoidant personality disorder, dependent personality disorder, obsessive-compulsive personality disorder, personality change due to another medical condition, and other specified personality disorder and unspecified personality disorder. If you do not have a copy of *DSM-5* (which I strongly suggest you purchase), you can find the DSM diagnostic criteria for mental disorders as follows:

> If you know the exact name of the diagnosis as it appears in *DSM-5*, you can pull up both the DSM-IV and *DSM-5* criteria for the disorder by going to http://dsm.wikia.com/wiki/Name of Disorder, each word separated by an underscore. For example, to find the DSM-IV and *DSM-5* criteria for AUD, type http://dsm.wikia.com/wiki/Alcohol_Use_Disorder
>
> For generalized anxiety disorder, type http://dsm.wikia.com/wiki/Generalized_Anxiety_Disorder, and so forth.

For the first time in the DSM system, *DSM-5* offers an alternative model for personality disorders (AMPD). One can still use the current clinical practice of diagnosing each personality disorder separately, which has typically shown that people end up being diagnosed with more than one personality disorder (APA, 2013). In the alternative model, personality disorders are characterized according to impairments in personality *functioning* and personality *traits* that are assessed as pathological. A personality disorder in the alternative model is characterized by the following features (adapted from APA, 2013, p. 761):

1. *Impairment*. Personality functioning must be impaired to at least a moderate level.
2. *Pathological traits*. One or more pathological personality traits must be evident.
3. *Inflexibility and pervasiveness*. The impairments in both functioning and traits must be relatively inflexible and pervasive across many situations.
4. *Stability*. The impairments must be relatively long-lasting.
5. *Impairments not explained by a different mental disorder*. For example, an individual with delusional disorder might be incorrectly diagnosed as having paranoid personality disorder.

6. *Not caused by an SUD or a medical condition.* For example, individuals with active SUDs often display maladaptive personality characteristics that can be mistaken for a personality disorder.

7. *Not resulting from normal development or one's environment.* Maladaptive traits or dysfunction is not better explained by a person's developmental stage or by their social or cultural environment.

The AMPD explains in detail APD, avoidant personality disorder, BPD, NPD, obsessive-compulsive personality disorder, schizotypal personality disorder, and personality disorder-trait specified. A meta-analysis provided some support for the AMPD model except for obsessive-compulsive personality disorder (Watters, Bagby, & Sellbom, 2018). Evidence for the discriminant validity, however, was dubious for several of the personality disorders (Watters et al., 2018). A new questionnaire that measures personality disorders in the alternative model is the *DSM-5* Levels of Personality Functioning Questionnaire (DLOPFQ; Huprich et al., 2018). The DLOPFQ demonstrates reliability and validity, but the authors suggested that the instrument warrants further study.

Remember that SUDs can mimic (or create, at least temporarily) other *DSM-5* diagnoses. The only way mental health professionals can ascertain the extent to which the SUD plays a role in the expression of the other diagnosis is for the client to stop using the drug in question for as long as the drug continues producing its effects (e.g., THC from cannabis is fat soluble, and its effects may continue for weeks following cessation of use). Aside from this, personality disorders are often comorbid with SUDs (see the Comorbidity section of this chapter). Following are exemplars of one personality disorder that many are fascinated by.

It is often difficult for providers-in-training to understand the experiences of someone with a mental disorder. The following passage, a composite adapted from individual stories found online, is intended to provide an "insider's" perspective on APD (also referenced in popular media as *psychopathy* or *sociopathy*). Each person's experience is unique; this portrayal is not indicative of every experience with the disorder. The composite was adapted from

- https://www.businessinsider.com/what-its-like-to-have-antisocial-personality-disorder-2014-4
- https://bipolar1blog.com/2016/10/01/antisocial-personality-disorder/
- https://www.quora.com/What-Does-It-Feel-Like-to-have-antisocial-personality-disorder
- https://www.healthyplace.com/personality-disorders/sociopath/can-sociopaths-love-or-even-fall-in-love
- https://www.healthguideinfo.com/personality-disorders/p91074/
- https://www.quora.com/What-is-it-like-to-be-a-psychopath

What Is It *Really* Like to Experience Antisocial Personality Disorder?

I was given the label antisocial personality disorder (APD) because I exhibit many symptoms associated with it. In childhood, I was stubborn and had difficulty maintaining friendships. My parents described me as cold and distant. Perhaps there was some truth in this, as I had zero sense of loyalty and I used people for what I could get from them.

Not everyone with APD will become involved in criminal activity. Although I've had a few minor encounters with the law, I am not a criminal, and I have no desire to become involved in criminal behavior. Contrary to what you might think, I *do* experience emotions; it is just that they are substantially less intense than what I think most people feel. It is often difficult for me to identify what I am feeling, and sometimes they are inappropriate given the situation.

If you think that I have no empathy, you are correct. I do not feel sorrow or grief when people that are close to me die. I have learned to exhibit the emotions that I know that I am supposed to feel so that others do not see how little I *actually* feel. Having APD is alienating, and this is often the only emotion that individuals with APD genuinely understand. If I permit the alienation to define me, I become less able to fight antisocial urges. It is these antisocial actions that cause people with APD to break the law and/or hurt others.

[Another example] I was violent between 10 and 12 years of age. Anger would surge in me at the drop of a hat. For example, I choked someone for throwing a ball at me. My fantasies are often very violent, and they typically involve someone who has ever wronged me some way. I am not going to be a serial killer, however, so don't worry.

Having reassured you, you should know that I have wanted to kill people and get away with it. So, I joined the infantry during the height of our recent wars. I killed one man, and I enjoyed it a lot. I discovered, however, that killing is not really my thing. To me, the losers that end up in prison are impulsive, unevolved dullards. I am not one of them.

If you want to hear good stories, I have them, and they are all true. One time, I beat up five grown men who wanted cash, another time I escaped a 10-minute police chase, and I convinced a husband to let me have sex with his wife. I made him sleep on the floor while I cuddled her like we had been married for 30 years. I can get almost everything I want. I had a lover cry to me because I acted so cold toward her. I laughed for an hour straight. Later that evening, I had sex with her and forced her to have her best friend join us. They still call me to this day, and that's my point.

Although I am no longer violent, I am verbally brutal and ruthless, even if you are a very close friend. Things like death and sickness that bother other people do not bother me at all. Emotion is like a small breeze that ends quickly.

(Continued)

(Continued)

After ripping off several companies in business, I decided it was easier to make money by keeping clients instead of continually needing new ones. I am now close to becoming a millionaire. I always need to be on guard to not break too many of society's laws.

[Another example] Most of the time I feel absolutely nothing. Every day is an exercise in restraint. Constantly I need to control my impulses, and it doesn't get easier. I enjoy f#%king with people and seeing them get emotional. I enjoy dominating men and the thrill of a good fight. Desires I have I can never fulfill, mostly because they are morbid. They are so wicked that I cannot discuss them here, but they gnaw at me, and I have to push them out of my head because I do not want to go to prison. Take it from me, we are not good people.

The way I am both sucks yet feels awesome and exhilarating at the same time. My self-esteem is through the roof. It's like I always know what to do in a situation. I love it. It is likely that because so many people with APD are confident that we can easily come across as charming and charismatic. It is nearly impossible for us to get our feelings hurt. I have virtually no anxiety, and, if I do, it's like a fly landing on you. Although it might be annoying, it goes away almost immediately. I don't really care about other people and their feelings, which makes it easy to do things and get what I want. I do not refrain from pursuing sex (interested, ladies? message me!). Seriously, though, I screw up every relationship. For a while, I had the perfect woman, but I cheated on her because I couldn't stop wanting other women, too. I will not tell you how many illegal things I've done in my life. The thrill is doing it and not getting caught.

Anyone who puts all psychopaths and people with APD into the same category are plain ignorant. Psychopathy and APD are on a continuum. Some people exhibit more factor 1 traits, and others experience more factor 2 traits (if you do not know what I mean by this, it takes 2 seconds to Google what I'm talking about). Remember that psychopaths are people too, and they are all different. Plenty of us are not in prison and haven't murdered anyone . . . yet. Yes, that was just a joke, though I suspect the only people laughing are others like myself.

Getting into a relationship with someone who has APD can leave you with no idea what happened, but it's almost definite that you will be damaged. Like getting struck by a Mack truck, you will likely be the one who feels that you are all wrong and crazy. We are the masters of manipulation, and, before long, we will have you eating out of our hands.

Can psychopaths fall in love? If you truly know and understand us, this question is almost laughable. Although we can act like we are in love and others will believe us, we do not feel empathy. If love means manipulating people, I guess we qualify. If love means saying things but not feeling them in the heart, then we qualify. If love is the same thing as sex (knowing that sex is a momentary and meaningless physical pleasure), we qualify even further. When you think that we love you, you better know that we are playing a role to gain something for ourselves. Psychopaths constantly need thrills and stimulation, so, generally, we drop the charade and move on. Our love is manipulative, uncaring, and unemotional.

I have no shame, guilt, fear, or empathy. I have an irresistible need to dominate other people. I am cold, calculating, and view others as either tools for my pleasure or as obstacles to be crushed. I sleep with as many women as possible. The flipside of our personality, of course, is that we can be full of laughter and fun. Are you interested yet?

Some people confuse us with those who have narcissistic personality disorder (NPD). The truth is, we are way worse than them. Although narcissists think unrealistically high of themselves (known as grandiosity), they also have a high need for admiration. They typically exhibit behavior that is rude or condescending, and they look down on others. So, although people with NPD exaggerate their accomplishments to a theatrical level, people with APD are content with just lying regularly. But our intent in lying is to take advantage of somebody.

All those with NPD want others to see them as superior to feel better about themselves, we [i.e., individuals with APD] do not think that we are special, and we will engage in risky behavior even if we might end up incarcerated or seriously injured. We are into manipulation and personal gain, not an inflated self-appraisal. We do not need excessive approval, but we are also not into disparaging other people publicly. We are impulsive, and we do not think much about our future, but those with NPD are *very* concerned about their future. So, as you can see from this, we have different motives and behaviors than them. They build themselves up while tearing others down, all to increase their feelings of superiority. Although we might display some arrogance and lack of remorse, it is because of our desire for personal gain and our lack of respect for authority.

Psychosis.

Individuals experiencing psychosis are, to one extent or another (i.e., on a spectrum), out of touch with reality. The most common symptoms of psychosis are hallucinations and delusions. Hallucinations represent sensations that are not real, such as hearing voices that do not exist or hearing sounds that are misinterpreted (e.g., hearing air-conditioning but interpreting the sounds as something else). Hallucinations can affect any sense (i.e., hearing, sight, smell, taste, touch). Delusions, on the other hand, are strong beliefs that cannot possibly be true. Common delusions include believing that someone is following or monitoring you, believing that you have extraordinary abilities, or thinking that you have extraordinary powers. Besides hallucinations and delusions, other common psychotic symptoms include having racing thoughts or a flight of ideas, extreme difficulty concentrating, and extreme inability to complete tasks or make decisions.

Recent evidence has demonstrated that childhood trauma is a risk factor for developing psychosis (Abajobir et al., 2017; Bailey et al., 2018). Bailey et al. (2018) conducted a systematic review and meta-analysis of research in this area. They identified 6667 studies, but, of these, only 41 met their inclusion criteria. Only 29 studies, however, were meta-analyzed with a combined sample size of 4680 participants. Their findings established that trauma in childhood sometimes leads to hallucinations and delusions as part of a psychotic disorder.

Abajobir et al. (2017) conducted a longitudinal study of 3752 participants. Their study examined relationships between substantiated child maltreatment between ages 0 and 14 years of age and reports of hallucinations and delusions at 21 years after birth. Those children who were emotionally abused and neglected were more likely to report hallucinations, lifetime delusional experiences, and lifetime psychosis compared with their nonabused counterparts.

Some common delusions center on (a) other people making hints about something or implying double meanings, (b) being persecuted, (c) victimization by conspiracy, (d) having special or unusual abilities, (e) having an unusually close relationship with God, (f) having sinned more than the average person, (g) being looked at oddly, and (h) believing that one's thoughts are being echoed back (Verdoux & van Os, 2002). Surprisingly, hallucinations are not always pathological (Wilkinson & Alderson-Day, 2016). For example, a common experience is hearing one's name called aloud or hearing a person's voice without anyone being present. Some individuals experience hearing a comforting voice, or one that advises them, at some point in their lives. Recently bereaved widows and widowers might not only hear their dead spouse but also see their deceased spouse as a ghost or spirit (Chaudhury, 2010). Another common hallucination is hearing voices conversing (Verdoux & van Os, 2002). In a longitudinal study, even insomnia was shown to precipitate hallucinations in some individuals (Sheaves et al., 2016).

Interestingly, the types of voices that people hear are shaped by local culture. Luhrmann, Padmavati, Tharoor, and Osei (2015) conducted a study wherein participants from the United States, India, and Ghana were interviewed. Americans were more likely to report experiencing violent commands, whereas those in India and Ghana were more likely to report rich relationships that involved their voices.

If a psychoactive drug causes hallucinations, they are typically visual hallucinations (Chaudhury, 2010). Ingesting some substances such as hallucinogens or psychoactive stimulants may result in psychosis. Withdrawing from severe physical dependency on alcohol or other depressants may result in a temporary psychotic state (see Chapters 9–13 for details).

Lim et al. (2016) suggested that there are 14 sensory modalities within hallucinations. Their list included the following: (a) visual, (b) auditory, (c) olfactory (i.e., smell), (d) gustatory (i.e., taste), (e) tactile (i.e., touch), (f) somatic (i.e., sensory), (g) proprioceptive (i.e., posture), (h) kinaesthetic (i.e., body movement), (i) vestibular (a feeling of vertigo such as dizziness, light-headedness, floating, or falling), (j) cenesthetic (i.e., unusual body awareness such as feeling a propeller inside one's stomach), (k) algesic (i.e., hypersensitivity to pain), (l) sexual, (m) thermal, and/or (n) temporal (i.e., time distortion). "Auditory verbal hallucinations (AVH) are sensory experiences that occur in the absence of external stimulation" (Rosen et al., 2018, p. 281). Some believe that persons with AVH are simply talking to themselves without realizing it (Rosen et al., 2018).

Regardless, hallucinations are experienced by 60%–80% of all patients diagnosed with a schizophrenia spectrum disorder (Lim et al., 2016). The most common type of hallucination in people with schizophrenia is auditory, followed next by visual (Chaudhury, 2010). In their sample of 750 patients diagnosed with a schizophrenia spectrum disorder, Lim et al. (2016) found that 27% reported unimodal hallucinations, whereas 53% experienced multimodal hallucinations. Although the predominant finding with schizophrenic individuals has been that most experience AVH, the results of Lim et al. suggest multimodal hallucinations are more common. AVHs are also sometimes experienced by people with major depression disorder, postpartum psychosis, bipolar disorder, BPD, PTSD, anorexia, and delirium and in individuals with neurological or organic mental disorders (Chaudhury, 2010; Wilkinson & Alderson-Day, 2016)

Schizophrenia.

Schizophrenia is an illness that creates psychosis, but it also has other symptoms. It "is characterized by a wide range of symptoms which lead to cognitive, social, and functional impairment" (Haro et al., 2018, p. 56). The symptoms of schizophrenia are often divided into three domains:

1. Positive symptoms. These include delusions, hallucinations, and disorganization of thoughts and/or bizarre behavior.
2. Negative symptoms. These include anhedonia, lessened ability to think or speak, reduced motivation, and withdrawal from others both emotionally and socially.
3. Cognitive impairment. Impairment is particularly experienced in memory, attention, and executive functioning (Haro et al., 2018).

Although it was generally believed that blunted or flat affect was the predominant negative symptom for individuals with schizophrenia, recent research suggests that anhedonia (i.e., inability to feel pleasure or joy) is actually more central (Mohn, Olsson, & Helldin, 2018). Even after 2 years of receiving antipsychotic medication, about two thirds of patients with schizophrenia continue to experience significant positive symptoms, and one third will continue to have the symptoms 6 years following diagnosis (Haro et al., 2018). Many patients will continue to experience persistent negative symptoms as well, which makes it difficult for them to live independently, perform the usual activities of daily living, engage in socializing, maintain personal relationships, and participate in either work or study. Across all eight countries that Haro et al. (2018) studied, between 70% and 90% experienced either positive symptoms or negative symptoms at 12-month follow-up.

It is often difficult for providers-in-training to understand the experiences of someone with a mental disorder. The following passage, a composite adapted from individual stories found online, is intended to provide an "insider's" perspective on schizophrenia. Each person's experience is unique; this portrayal is not indicative of every experience with the disorder. The composite was adapted from

- https://www.mentalhealth.org.uk/a-to-z/h/hearing-voices
- https://www.jnj.com/personal-stories/mother-daughter-bariatric-weight-loss-surgery-success-story
- https://psychcentral.com/blog/what-its-like-to-live-with-schizophrenia/
- https://academic.oup.com/schizophreniabulletin/article/32/2/209/1899556
- https://www.quora.com/What-is-it-like-to-have-schizophrenia-1

What Is It *Really* Like to Experience Schizophrenia?

If you have never heard voices before, it is a difficult experience to describe. Some people have said it is like hearing the voice of someone standing beside them, and others have said that the voices are more like thoughts. Still others have described voices as a combination of both. Voices might tell you to do things that are harmful, or they may be highly critical of your behavior, but in other instances, they may build you up with compliments or are simply neutral in content. Some voices engage you in conversation. The voices might be present all day and keep you from doing things in your life. Some people cannot talk about their voices and consequently become isolated and withdrawn.

I was diagnosed with schizophrenia when I was 27. My personality has always been bubbly and happy. I enjoy fashion, cookouts with my family, shopping, and other activities. I am also a peaceful person, but you would not have got that impression if you had met me in 2010. That was the year I spent time in jail for getting into a physical confrontation with a neighbor over a parking spot. By then, I was already feeling paranoid, seeing things, and hearing voices. The last thing I wanted to do was get dressed or get out of bed, and I had no idea why. In the summer of 2008, I was hospitalized. Doctors thought I had a mood disorder, which they labeled as bipolar.

They gave me many drugs in the hospital that I stopped taking as soon as I was released. After all, my symptoms had disappeared, so, by late summer, I started working again. Shortly after that, I had another breakdown, and, after a few weeks of hospitalization, I left with medications that caused me to twitch. I had been working as a server in a restaurant, but you cannot serve food and drinks when you're twitching! I stopped taking the prescribed medications again. It was only a few months after that when I fought with my neighbor.

After getting out of jail, I decided to be honest with my psychiatrist. I told him about the voices and the paranoia. After answering several of his questions, he said, "You are experiencing schizophrenia." I had no idea what that meant. After he explained it, I took medications for the next few months. Nonetheless, I stopped taking them, thinking that I was now better.

I started believing that I was a prophet, and I began receiving secret messages from the TV and the radio. At the same time as this was occurring, a voice was coming into my ear telling me to do nasty things. I didn't listen to these voices. One day, however, I began experiencing terrible confusion and agitation. I thought I must be in hell. My insides were on fire, my mind was on fire, my outsides were on fire, and I was stricken with panic. Why was I so terrified?

I began to think less of daily life and more about the fantasy that was building in my mind. Deep down, I knew I was going to find a way to transform the universe. The thought was there every day and all day long. I knew I would become famous, I was a genius, and the world was waiting for me to speak. But then my ideas began to turn as feelings of vulnerability and helplessness surfaced. Did you ever *know* that someone was going to kill you? I knew it, but I was afraid to tell my family in case one of them would become the perpetrator. You see, I didn't know exactly who was going to take me out, but I knew that he or she needed to before I transformed the universe and the way that everyone would live on earth. I was just too dangerous in their minds.

Is there more than one? How many are there? Who can I still trust? The answer is obviously no one. Who is trying to infect me with HIV? I was not dating anyone. Why are people watching me whenever I go out? I hear their whispers as I walk by, and the conspiracy against me is growing by leaps and bounds. I am beginning to realize there are many people behind this plot to end my life. I see their snickers, I feel their wrath, but I am ready for them.

Whoever they are, they were watching me . . . all the time. I sometimes wondered, "How is any of this possible?" Some part of me knew that something about my thinking was off. It did not matter! The awareness kept returning that I was going to die at the hands of one of these conspirators. They were trying to control my thoughts. "GET AWAY!" I screamed, while I walked downtown. People stared at me and crossed the street if I tried to make eye contact. They knew that I knew what they were thinking. I couldn't take much more of this. I knew I had to get home and barricade myself and my family. Let me tell you in present tense what happened next.

The family is out, likely at work. A man comes to the door carrying other people's mail in a large bag. I know what is in that bag! I open the door with a revolver in each hand, my guns are loaded, and I scream, "DROP THE GOD DAMN BAG NOW!!!" He does what he is told, and no one is hurt. A few minutes later, police surround my home. I am done for. I cannot hold them off . . . too many. I come walking out with my hands above my head, doing what I am told. The fear is overwhelming, gripping, my limbs are numb, I fall, and my trembling hands are placed in handcuffs. I know they are going to kill me. During the entire drive to the gas chamber, I am screaming at the top of my lungs. All of my knowledge will be extracted before they kill me. I have never been more scared in my entire life. I am no more. Who is talking to me now, right now? "Satan, please; please NO!!! . . ."

The next few days are a blur. I think a couple of weeks have passed, but I am unsure. A few of my friends are sending me messages, asking about how I'm doing now, and I'm doing great! I am back in the hospital. I find out that there are no charges against me. My psychiatrist visits and says, "I will soon be able to release you. You must promise to keep taking your medications and to keep your appointments with your regular psychiatrist. Are you in agreement with this?" It dawns on me that I have been experiencing a psychotic breakdown, and the seriousness of this has finally sunk in. I reply, "Absolutely. I now understand how much I need to keep taking medications regularly."

I came to accept that I have schizophrenia and that I will need treatment for the rest of my life. Cognitive-behavioral therapy and medication have been critical to my success. In the past, I had refused to accept that schizophrenia is a forever thing. I am not going to outgrow it.

Months later, I have returned to university, and, of course, I am studying psychology. Most people will never understand what I went through, but I hope that, in describing this experience, some of you will find the compassion that you need to work with those of us who have gone through hell but returned from it to live another day.

The voices often return, by the way, but the medications allow me to know that they are not real. Some days it is honestly an internal fight to keep them from taking over. My life, though, is too important to listen to evil when I have my heart focused on doing good. Thank you for hearing me out. It was important for me to tell you my story.

Misdiagnosis, Underdiagnosis, and Overdiagnosis

Khan and Shaikh (2008) indicated that "A major source of clinical errors is inaccurate diagnosis" (p. 67). Diagnostic errors made with prison inmates has been estimated at between 10% and 15% (Martin, Hynes, Hatcher, & Colman, 2016). Bipolar disorder is frequently misdiagnosed (Rakofsky & Dunlop, 2015) and overdiagnosed, whereas BPD is underdiagnosed (Morgan & Zimmerman, 2015). Morgan and Zimmerman (2015) surmised that this occurs because psychiatric reports are based on clinical phenomenology and patient self-report. Unfortunately, these sources are often "inconsistent, unclear, or limited in scope" (p. 65).

Attention deficit hyperactivity disorder (ADHD) is overdiagnosed in children (Haber, 2000). Rimm (2011) indicated that there can be many causes of ADHD-like symptoms in a child who does not actually have ADHD. Rimm suggested that dramatic or toxic family situations and families who inconsistently apply family rules can create symptoms in children that mimic ADHD. Children who are stressed and fatigued, or those with neurological or emotional problems, may also experience ADHD symptoms (Wright & National Institute of Mental Health, Bethesda, MD, 2010). Also, children with bipolar II disorder are frequently misdiagnosed as having major depressive disorder (MDD) (Raman et al., 2007).

King (2016) wrote about how psychiatry as a profession is blind regarding its impact on African American men. He described this unawareness of the impact of Whiteness as a form of "cultural schizophrenia" (p. 69). The overdiagnosis or misdiagnosis of schizophrenia in African American clients has been a long-standing issue in mental health services (Barnes, 2008).

MDD in African Americans is often underdiagnosed, misdiagnosed, and undertreated (Sohail, Bailey, & Richie, 2014). Beljan (2011) stated that Hispanic and African American children attending public schools in the United States are often underidentified as gifted, which can lead to misdiagnosis.

Some evidence suggests that ethnic minority youth are misdiagnosed regarding their emotional and behavioral problems (Liang, Matheson, & Douglas, 2016). Liang et al. (2016) concluded that misdiagnoses might be due to cultural and contextual factors. Paniagua (2013) recommended that clinicians use cross-cultural assessment strategies together with traditional psychiatric/psychological evaluations to reduce the overdiagnosis, underdiagnosis, and misdiagnosis of culturally diverse clients.

Mobile Apps for *DSM-5* Diagnoses

Van Ameringen, Turna, Khalesi, Pullia, and Patterson (2017) described the current mobile applications (apps) that can be used for individuals experiencing mental health disorders. Some of these apps allow healthcare professionals to track data from patients, treatment apps, multipurpose apps (these may include assessment, tracking, psychoeducation, and treatment), and assessment apps (read their article for details regarding these apps in each category). Studies have not validated most of the assessment apps. Three exceptions, however, include the following:

1. MDD. The Patient Health Questionnaire (PHQ-9) is one of the few apps that have been validated for assessing MDD. Scores equal to or greater than 11 suggest high risk.
2. PTSD. The mobile version of the PTSD Checklist-Civilian (PCL-C) version has good reliability. The 17-item instrument can also be downloaded at https://www.mirecc.va.gov/docs/visn6/3_PTSD_CheckList_and_Scoring.pdf
3. Multiple conditions. The WhatsMyM3 app is free through iTunes. The 27-item tool can also be taken online at https://whatsmym3.com/

A multipurpose app with published evidence for anxiety disorders, obsessive-compulsive disorder, and PTSD is the AnxietyCoach (the Mayo Clinic developed this app, available from iTunes for a small cost). Other apps exist but currently lack evidence. These include MoodTools (for MDD), Pacifica (for nonspecific anxiety), MindShift (for anxious adolescents), and Self-Help Anxiety (for anxiety) (Van Ameringen et al., 2017).

Polyaddictions

Polyaddiction is synonymous with *multiple addictions*, and both terms remain in current usage (Meziou et al., 2019). Polyaddiction refers to (a) switching from one addiction to another and/or (b) having more one addiction concurrently. Regarding the first definition, switching from one addiction to another is often unintentional, but it is sometimes planned. Maharajh, Ali, and Maharaj (2014) wrote about transition drug use, for example, which they defined explicitly as replacing AUD with using cannabis.

Polyaddictions are common. Individuals with cannabis use disorder frequently experience other SUDs concurrently (Kerridge, Pickering, Chou, Saha, & Hasin, 2018). Common associations are found between cigarette smoking and cannabis dependence (Hindocha et al., 2015; McClure et al., 2018) and between cigarette smoking and alcohol use (Tarren & Bartlett, 2017).

McCabe, West, Jutkiewicz, and Boyd (2017) used data from interviews conducted during the 2012–2013 National Epidemiologic Survey on Alcohol and Related Conditions. The sample comprised 36,309 adults (51.9% women, 66.2% White, 14.7% Hispanic, 11.8% African American, 5.7% Asian, and 1.6% Native American or other racial category). Most individuals with past-year nonalcohol *DSM-5* SUDs had at least one other past-year SUD with a range of 56.8% (past-year prescription opioid use disorder [OUD]) to 97.5% (past-year hallucinogen use disorder). By comparison, only 15.0% of individuals with past-year AUD had at least one other SUD. McCabe et al. concluded that clinical assessment and diagnosis should screen for multiple SUDs (i.e., polysubstance addictions).

Having multiple SUDs is associated with greater severity of both AUD and/or tobacco use disorder (John et al., 2018). In the study by John et al. (2018), individuals who were male, ages 26–34, less educated, and unemployed had increased likelihood of experiencing multiple SUDs compared to only one SUD. Adolescents who have experienced childhood maltreatment are also more likely to become polydrug users when compared to non-polydrug users (Alvarez-Alonso et al., 2016).

American reproductive-age women (N = 4498) reporting nonmedical opioid use also experience a high rate of polysubstance use disorders (Jarlenski et al., 2017). In Reitan's (2017) study of pregnant women who abused substances in Sweden and were forced into compulsory care between 2000 and 2009 (N = 119), the average number of drugs used concurrently was 2.65. Injection drugs were recorded in 73% of the pregnancies. Opiates and amphetamines were most commonly consumed, followed by alcohol.

Bobashev, Tebbe, Peiper, and Hoffer (2018) conducted a face-to-face survey in 2016 of 200 non-in-treatment heroin users in Cleveland. Their analysis revealed five clusters of polydrug use: (a) heroin with alcohol and occasionally crack, (b) heroin and crack daily, (c) heroin daily and nearly exclusively, (d) heroin and marijuana daily, and (e) part-time drug users.

Morley, Ferris, Winstock, and Lynskey (2017) used data from the Global Drug Survey in five countries (United States, N = 1334; United Kingdom, N = 1199; France, N = 1258; Germany, n = 866; and Australia, N = 1013). Individuals who misused or abused prescribed opioids were more likely to be polysubstance users compared to non-opioid users. Individuals receiving opioid maintenance treatment (OMT) are also known to abuse other drugs concurrently, but Heikman, Muhonen, and Ojanpera (2017) found that this was much more widespread when individuals addicted to opioids received inadequate amounts of OMT. Heikman et al. recommended that physicians adjust OMT doses as needed.

Liu, Williamson, Setlow, Cottler, and Knackstedt (2018) found in their meta-analysis that the prevalence of cocaine users who also used alcohol simultaneously and concurrently was 74% and 77%, respectively. The prevalence of cocaine users who also used cannabis simultaneously and concurrently was 38% and 64%, respectively. Liu et al. noted that consuming cocaine with alcohol or cannabis enhances the subjective response to cocaine. Particularly in the case of combining cocaine and alcohol, a psychoactive metabolite called cocaethylene is produced. Cocaethylene is a harmful by-product that may result in liver damage, cardiovascular events (e.g., heart attack, stroke), and sudden death in cocaine users.

The 3-year persistence rate of alcohol, drug, and polysubstance use disorders varies by gender and race/ethnicity (31–81%; N = 1025 women and 1835 men) (Evans, Grella, Washington, & Upchurch, 2017). For example, Hispanic women with AUD were less likely to persist than White women, Hispanic men with drug use disorders were less likely to persist than White men, Black men with alcohol or drug use disorder were less likely to persist than White men, and Black men with polysubstance use disorder were less likely to persist than Hispanic men.

Dermody (2018) analyzed data from the cross-sectional 2015 CDC's Youth Risk Behavior Surveillance System (N = 15,624). She focused her analysis on polysubstance use among gay/lesbian and bisexual youth compared to heterosexual youth. Dermody concluded that youth with nondominant sexualities, and particularly bisexual youth, were at increased risk of polysubstance use compared to heterosexual youth. An earlier study arrived at similar conclusions, particularly regarding younger female youth with nondominant sexualities (Kecojevic, Jun, Reisner, & Corliss, 2017).

Adolescent smokers are also more likely to engage in polysubstance use than nonsmoking peers (McKelvey, Ramo, Delucchi, & Rubinstein, 2017). Schepis, West, Teter, and McCabe (2016) found that, in a nationally representative sample of 11,444 grade 12 students, 5.3% were found to take nonmedical tranquilizers. Of this group, 72.6% had also ingested another psychoactive substance within the past year.

In a study of 1298 young adults (ages 18–35) in England and Denmark, researchers Ostergaard, Ostergaard, and Fletcher (2016) found that young adults who used drugs in England preferred mixing alcohol with cocaine (65%), whereas in Denmark, the preference was to mix alcohol and cannabis (78%). In the United States, the most commonly used substances used concurrently by adolescents are alcohol and cannabis (Biggar, Forsyth, Chen, & Burstein, 2017; Patrick et al., 2018).

Chan, Kelly, Hides, Quinn, and Williams (2016) found that, in their Australian study of 5412 secondary school students under 16 years of age, 7.52% and 2.55% of the teenagers reported having sex and unprotected sex before age 16, respectively. For the females involved in polydrug use, they were more likely to engage in unprotected sex, whereas for the males, the findings were not significant.

Using a substance today sometimes predicts later use of a different substance, with the first drug referred to as a "gateway drug." For example, cannabis use in adults is associated with AUD 3 years later (Weinberger, Platt, & Goodwin, 2016). In a longitudinal study of 11,996 U.S. youth (ages 12–17), having ever used tobacco was predictive of subsequent substance use (Silveira et al., 2018). Similarly, cannabis is often viewed as a gateway drug to "harder drugs" (see Chapter 10 for details).

SUDs also co-occur with behavioral addictions. A few examples of the relationships that have been studied include AUD and problematic Internet use (Bibbey, Phillips, Ginty, & Carroll, 2015), stimulant use and gambling (Geisner et al., 2016), drinking and gambling (Hodgins & Racicot, 2013), SUDs and sex addiction (Beveridge, 2015; Rawson, Washton, Domier, & Reiber, 2002), SUDs and romantic relationship addiction (Acevedo & Aron, 2014), SUDs and exercise addiction (Freimuth, Moniz, & Kim, 2011), SUDs and Internet addiction (Moore, 2017; Wang, Yao, Zhou, Liu, & Lv, 2017), SUDs and shopping addiction (Zhang, Brook, Leukefeld, & Brook, 2016), and heroin use disorder and food addiction (Canan, Karaca, Sogucak, Gecici, & Kuloglu, 2017).

HOW WOULD AN ADDICTION COUNSELOR HELP THIS CLIENT (RE: POLYADDICTIONS)?

You are working as a professional counselor. Beverly, age 26, used many different illicit drugs as a youth. Since she stopped using all drugs at age 22, she reported to you that she has become unable to get excited about anything. You recognize the symptoms as anhedonia. Beverly has tried every antidepressant on the market, and nothing has helped sufficiently to end this symptom. You ask her if anything gives her pleasure, and she tells you that she feels some contentment only after playing video games for upwards of 10 hours a day. This level of gaming, she tells you, prevents her from working. She reports that gaming for this many hours exhausts her mentally and emotionally. She currently lives in her parents' basement.

1. What do you think would help Beverly?
2. Should her video game use be considered a harm reduction approach (i.e., less harmful than abusing drugs and alcohol)? Why or why not? Should her video game use become a target for intervention?
3. What are your views regarding substituting one addiction for a less harmful one?

Comorbidity

> *"How can one decide with certainty which of two coexistent phenomena is the cause and which the effect, whether one of them is the cause at all instead of both being effects of a third cause, or even whether both are effects of two entirely unrelated causes?"* (A quote from 160 years ago; Virchow, as cited in Anthony, 2013, p. 83).

As evident from the quote, one of the most challenging aspects of comorbidity is deciding which condition occurs first and whether there is a causal relationship between it and another condition. In a medical sense, comorbidity occurs when a patient experiences two or more diseases or events concurrently. *Comorbidity* in addictions can also refer to the same concept, but here it will be defined as occurring when a client experiences one or more SUDs (or addictive behaviors) and one or more non-addiction-related mental disorders concurrently. A great deal of research has been published since 1990 concerning comorbidity between psychiatric conditions and SUDs (Anthony, 2013).

Nearly half of people with severe mental disorders also have a co-occurring SUD, and recovery from both is a critical objective for healthcare services (Hides, 2013). The pathologies of mood and anxiety disorders together with SUDs are the most common comorbidities in the substance abuse field (Torrens & Rossi, 2015; Turner, Mota, Bolton, & Sareen, 2018). Common mood disorders experienced by substance-addicted individuals include especially major depression but also bipolar disorder and dysthymic disorder (Rastegar & Fingerhood, 2016). Anxiety disorders are common among individuals with active *or* recent substance use, and this is especially true with depressants including alcohol (Rastegar & Fingerhood, 2016).

Regarding comorbidity with personality disorders, the most strongly correlated are with BPD and APD (Rastegar & Fingerhood, 2016). Many of the features of personality disorders decline over one's lifetime. Studies have found that, for APD, criminology particularly begins dropping by age 27 (Rastegar & Fingerhood, 2016). In a methadone program, 34.8% had personality disorders with higher rates experienced by men than women (40.5% and 28.4%, respectively). There were higher rates of APD among men, whereas there were higher rates of BPD among women (Rastegar & Fingerhood, 2016). In another study of inpatients reported by Rastegar and Fingerhood (2016), 57 of 100 patients had a personality disorder.

The most widely cited comorbidity study ever undertaken in the United States, according to Anthony (2013), was the National Comorbidity Survey conducted between 1990 and 1992 ($N = 8098$; age range = 15–54; Kessler et al., 1994). Kessler et al. (1994) found in their analysis of the data that comorbid psychiatric conditions were far more prevalent than previously thought.

Nearly 50% of the respondents reported at least one lifetime mental disorder, 30% reported at least one 12-month disorder, and almost one in six reported having three or more disorders in their lifetime using DSM-III-R criteria. Although Kessler et al. did not report comorbidity between SUDs and psychiatric disorders, they did report the lifetime prevalence[3] of SUDs at 25%. The 12-month prevalence of SUDs for males and females was 16.1% and 6.6%, respectively.

Nonetheless, comorbidity between psychiatric disorders and SUDs is common (Hodgson et al., 2016; Milkman & Sunderwirth, 2010). Enez, Nurmedov, Noyan, Yilmaz, and Dilbaz (2015) found in their study of 323 records of patients who were hospitalized between January 2012 and December 2013 in an addictions clinic that, using DSM-IV-TR criteria, 74.3% were diagnosed with an Axis I disorder and 73.7% with an Axis II disorder (note that *DSM-5* no longer uses a multiaxial diagnostic system; in DSM-IV-TR, an Axis I disorder included the primary diagnoses that required immediate attention, whereas Axis II disorders included pervasive conditions such as personality disorders and intellectual disability). Excessive anger, although not given a diagnosis per se in *DSM-5*, is highly prevalent in individuals with addictive disorders (Enright & Firtzgibbons, 2015). Dobmeier and Stevens (2013) reported that over five million Americans experience co-occurring substance abuse and mental health disorders.

Dual disorders of all kinds are common, and they are associated with more severe conditions and worse outcomes, including higher suicide risk, less adherence to treatment strategies, and more frequent relapses (Roncero, Grau-Lopez, & Casas, 2017). Chapters 9 through 21 go into greater detail with the comorbid conditions that are associated with each of the addictions covered, so the following is meant only as a quick summary of these comorbidities so you have this information in one place. The research regarding comorbidity is extensive.

Comorbidity With Alcohol Addiction

AUD is comorbid with virtually every psychiatric disorder. This list includes mood and anxiety disorders (Turner et al., 2018), bipolar disorder (Banach et al., 2018), schizophrenia (Subramaniam et al., 2017), BPD (Margolis & Zweben, 2011), APD (Sher et al., 2015), gambling (Suomi, Dowling, & Jackson, 2014), PTSD (Dworkin, Wanklyn, Stasiewicz, & Coffey, 2018), ADHD (Margolis & Zweben, 2011), and intimate partner violence (Oberleitner, Mandel, & Easton, 2013).

Comorbidity With Cannabis Addiction

Similarly, cannabis use disorder shares comorbidity with several disorders. This list includes mood and anxiety disorders (Atkinson, 2016; Curran et al., 2016), nicotine (Grant et al., 2015), psychotic disorders like schizophrenia (Aggarwal, Banerjee, Singh, Mattoo, & Basu, 2012; Hides, 2013), and externalizing disorders such as ADHD, conduct disorder, and oppositional defiant disorder (Atkinson, 2016).

Comorbidity With Opioid Addiction

OUDs are comorbid with several disorders. As one would expect, OUDs are frequently comorbid with pain conditions (Dennis et al., 2014; Lin et al., 2015). The list also includes mood and anxiety disorders (Fink et al., 2015; Wilson et al., 2018), personality disorders (Kerridge et al., 2015), PTSD (Fareed et al., 2013), and viral infections (Schulte et al., 2015). Heroin use disorder specifically has comorbidity with psychiatric comorbidity (Uchtenhagen, 2015), bipolar I disorder (Maremmani et al., 2013), ADHD (Liao et al., 2017), eating disorders, and food addiction in men (Canan et al., 2017).

Comorbidity With Nicotine Addiction

Smokers often experience comorbidity with other conditions. For example, tobacco use disorder is comorbid with psychiatric disorders (Lasser et al., 2000), MDD (Cohn et al., 2014), schizophrenia (Moran, Sampath, Kochunov, & Hong, 2013), nicotine withdrawal and psychotic symptoms (Rastegar & Fingerhood, 2016), conduct disorder (Grant et al., 2015), and ADHD (Ohlmeier et al., 2007).

Comorbidity With Other Drug Addictions

In general, SUDs are comorbid with psychiatric disorders such as mood and anxiety disorders (Earleywine, 2016), personality disorders (Earleywine, 2016), and psychotic disorders (Rastegar & Fingerhood, 2016). Research has also shown that each drug class has associated comorbidity.

Comorbidity with stimulants.

Stimulants are comorbid with psychiatric disorders (Pavon et al., 2013), APD (Earleywine, 2016), PTSD (Earleywine, 2016), ADHD (Earleywine, 2016), and chest pain (Earleywine, 2016).

Comorbidity with depressants (including sedative hypnotics).

Depressant disorders are comorbid with mood and anxiety disorders (APA, 2013) and possibly APD (APA, 2013).

Comorbidity with hallucinogens (psychedelics).

Hallucinogen-related disorders are comorbid with mood and anxiety disorders (APA, 2013), psychosis (Pechnick, Cunningham, & Danovitch, 2014), and APD (APA, 2013). Hallucinogen persisting perception disorder is comorbid with panic disorder or MDD (APA, 2013).

Comorbidity with inhalants.

Inhalant use disorder is comorbid with conduct disorder, APD (APA, 2013), and suicidality (APA, 2013).

---

[3]Lifetime prevalence means at any point in one's lifetime, *not* throughout one's lifetime.

Comorbidity With Gambling Addiction

Several disorders co-occur with gambling disorder. This list includes psychiatric disorders (Cowlishaw, Hakes, & Dowling, 2016), mood and anxiety disorders (Edgerton, Keough, & Roberts, 2018; Pilszyk, Silczuk, Habrat, & Heitzman, 2018), psychological distress (Pfund et al., 2017), schizophrenia (Yakovenko, Fortgang, Prentice, Hoff, & Potenza, 2018), personality disorders (Dowling et al., 2015; Vaddiparti & Cottler, 2017), obsessive-compulsive personality disorder (Medeiros & Grant, 2018), food addiction (Jimenez-Murcia et al., 2017), Internet addiction (Rumpf et al., 2015), ADHD (Tackett et al., 2017), and suicidality (Bischof et al., 2016).

Comorbidity With Internet-Based Addiction

Internet-based addictions also experience their share of comorbidity. They co-occur with psychiatric disorders (Floros, Siomos, Stogiannidou, Giouzepas, & Garyfallos, 2014; Ho et al., 2014), bipolar disorder (Wolfling, Beutel, Dreier, & Muller, 2015), personality disorders (Zadra et al., 2016), ADHD (Evren, Evren, Dalbudak, Topcu, & Kutlu, 2018; Lemenager et al., 2018), and mood and anxiety disorders, somatoform disorders, sleep disturbances, and suicidality in Korea (Kim et al., 2016).

Comorbidity With Sex Addiction

Research has found sex addiction to be comorbid with several disorders as well. These include mood and anxiety disorders (Kafka & Hennen, 1999), other mental disorders (Raymond, Coleman, & Miner, 2003), personality disorders (Campbell & Stein, 2016), PTSD (Delmonico & Griffin, 2015), ADHD (Rosenberg, Carnes, & O'Connor, 2014), and aggression (Elmquist, Shorey, Anderson, & Stuart, 2016).

Comorbidity With Romantic Relationship Addiction

Romantic relationship addiction is comorbid with mood and anxiety disorders (Sussman, 2010), separation anxiety disorder (APA, 2013), dependent personality disorder (APA, 2013), and BPD (APA, 2013).

Comorbidity With Food Addiction

Food addiction shares comorbidity with mood disorders (Hardy, Fani, Jovanovic, & Michopoulos, 2018; Nunes-Neto et al., 2018), eating disorders (de Vries & Meule, 2016; Zmuda, 2014), probable relationship to obesity and binge eating (Davis, Edge, & Gold, 2014), and ADHD (Karaca, Saleh, Canan, & Potenza, 2017).

Comorbidity With Exercise Addiction

As one might expect, exercise addiction is comorbid with eating disorders (Lichtenstein, Hinze, Emborg, Thomsen, & Hemmingsen, 2017). It also shares comorbidity with depression and anxiety (Berczik et al., 2014) and muscle dysmorphia (Foster, Shorter, & Griffiths, 2015).

Comorbidity With Shopping Addiction

Shopping addiction has comorbidity with mood and anxiety disorders (Platania, Castellano, Santisi, & Di Nuovo, 2017; Zhang, Brook, Leukefeld, & Brook, 2016), eating disorders (Zhang et al., 2016), and personality disorders (Zhang et al., 2016).

Comorbidity With Work Addiction

Work addiction is commonly called workaholism. It is comorbid with psychiatric disorders (Andreassen, Griffiths, Sinha, Hetland, & Pallesen, 2016), mood and anxiety disorders (Griffiths, 2016), and ADHD (Griffiths, 2016).

Comorbidity With Posttraumatic Stress Disorder

It is worthy of mention that individuals experiencing PTSD often have comorbid conditions. SUDs are common, including alcohol and drug use disorders (Coffey et al., 2016; Haller & Chassin, 2013). Milkman and Sunderwirth (2010) estimated that about 8% of men and 20% of women would develop PTSD following the experience of a traumatic event, particularly sexual assault. PTSD is also commonly associated with anxiety-related disorders in individuals with SUDs (Rastegar & Fingerhood, 2016).

Comorbidity With Attention Deficit Hyperactivity Disorder

SUDs are common in individuals with ADHD (Rastegar & Fingerhood, 2016). ADHD is also associated with the severity of an SUD (Fatseas et al., 2016). ADHD is often comorbid with AUD and tobacco use disorder (Ohlmeier et al., 2007), cocaine, cannabis, crystal meth, gambling, and other behavioral addictions (Karaca et al., 2017; Maté, 2008).

Comorbidity With Adolescents and Addiction

Comorbidity is also common with adolescents. For example, teenagers experience comorbidity between alcohol and depression (Stewart, Arlt, Felleman, Athenour, & Arger, 2015); AUDs and conduct disorder (Greenfield, Sittner, Forbes, Walls, & Whitbeck, 2017); PTSD and addiction, especially in girls and Latinos (Chasser, 2016); Internet gaming disorder and SUDs and ADHD (Van Rooij et al., 2014; Yen et al., 2017); Internet addiction, oppositional defiant disorder/conduct disorder, and ADHD (Chou, Liu, Yang, Yen, & Hu, 2015; Gunes et al., 2018); and Internet addiction and aggression (Lim et al., 2015).

HOW WOULD AN ADDICTION COUNSELOR HELP THIS CLIENT (RE: COMORBIDITY)?

You are working as a professional counselor. Your client, Shayla, is 39 years old. She was diagnosed by a psychiatrist recently as experiencing schizophrenia. Shayla is coming to you for counseling regarding her alcohol use, however. You find her very difficult to understand. Shayla changes topics abruptly but provides no transitions, leaving you confused most of the time. What is she talking about now? You attribute the symptoms to having a flight of ideas, which occurs for some people with schizophrenia. You also notice that Shayla is typically jittery, shaky, and twitching while she talks to you. You assume this is directly related to the antipsychotic medications that she takes daily. Leaving one afternoon from work, you witness Shayla smoking crack with several other individuals. She does not notice you, however.

1. How would you go about bringing up Shayla's crack use at the next session?
2. If she stopped using crack and became able to communicate effectively, could you conclude her crack use caused her flight of ideas? Why or why not?
3. If Shayla were indeed addicted to crack but she never told her psychiatrist, to what extent do you believe this could have affected the psychiatrist's diagnosis of schizophrenia?
4. What is the main lesson you can learn about diagnoses from this scenario?

RESOURCES AND VIDEOS

Resources

1. *DSM-5*. American Psychiatric Association. https://www.psychiatry.org/psychiatrists/practice/dsm/educational-resources/assessment-measures
2. Comorbidity: Substance Use Disorders and Other Mental Illnesses. Revised August 2018.
3. https://www.drugabuse.gov/publications/drugfacts/comorbidity-substance-use-disorders-other-mental-illnesses
4. Co-occurring Disorders (Mental Health America MHA). http://www.mentalhealthamerica.net/conditions/co-occurring-disorders
5. The *DSM-5*: Classification and criteria changes. Published online 2013 Jun 4. https://www.ncbi.nlm.nih.gov/pmc/articles/PMC3683251/
6. Comorbidity of Alcoholism and Psychiatric Disorders. https://pubs.niaaa.nih.gov/publications/arh26-2/81-89.htm

Videos

To view these videos, search their titles on YouTube.

1. *Overview of How to Diagnose Substance Use Disorders Using DSM-5*. Published on Feb 15, 2017.
2. *Introduction to Addiction DSM 5 changes.*
3. *What really happens when you mix medications?* | Russ Altman. Published on Mar 23, 2016.
4. *Drug Abuse, Mental Illness And Co-Occurring Disorders.* Published on Jun 16, 2013.
5. *Drug use problems and mental health: Comorbidity explained.* Published on May 31, 2016.

JOURNALS AND CONFERENCES

Journals

1. *Journal of Addiction Research & Therapy.* https://www.omicsonline.org/addiction-research-therapy.php

   Quoted from website:

   "Addiction Journal is an official peer reviewed journal for the rapid publication of innovative research covering all aspects of addiction and its related disorders. Addiction Journal with highest journal impact factor offers Open Access option to meet the needs of authors and maximize article visibility."

2. *Journal of Substance Abuse Treatment.* https://www.journals.elsevier.com/journal-of-substance-abuse-treatment/

   Quoted from website:

   "The *Journal of Substance Abuse Treatment (JSAT)* features original research, systematic reviews and reports on meta-analyses and, with editorial approval, special articles on the assessment and treatment of substance use and addictive disorders, including alcohol, illicit and prescription drugs, and nicotine."

3. *Journal of Addiction Medicine.* https://journals.lww.com/journaladdictionmedicine/Pages/aboutthejournal.aspx

   Quoted from website:

   "The mission of *Journal of Addiction Medicine*, the official peer-reviewed journal of the American Society of Addiction Medicine, is to promote excellence in the practice of addiction medicine and in clinical research as well as to support Addiction Medicine as a mainstream medical sub-specialty."

4. *Journal of Dual Diagnosis.* https://www.augusta.edu/mcg/psychiatry/dual-diagnosis.php

   Quoted from website:

   "The *Journal of Dual Diagnosis* (JDD – also with subtitle "research and practice in substance abuse comorbidity") is a quarterly, peer-reviewed international Journal that publishes all research of relevance to the comorbidity of drug and alcohol substance abuse disorders with psychiatric disorders. The anticipated readership is that of clinicians, research neuroscientists, mental health services researchers, and mental health trainees whose interest is in the specialty topic of substance abuse comorbidity. The *Journal* may also be of interest to health service administrators who oversee dual diagnosis services."

5. *International Journal of Mental Health & Psychiatry.* https://publons.com/journal/32505/international-journal-of-mental-health-psychiatry

   Quoted from the journal's website:

   "*International Journal of Mental Health & Psychiatry* (IJMHP) is a hybrid open access international journal which is distributed all over the globe. The journal provides the choice of both open access and subscription mode of publication to the authors and publishes almost all types of write-ups like research articles, review, case reports, case study, commentary, letter to editor, mini review, opinion, short communication, book review, editorials, etc."

Conferences

Depending on the addiction that you are interested in, you will find a list of conferences pertaining to that addiction in each of Chapters 9 through 21. Additionally, the following conferences will typically have sessions on the subject matter of this chapter (especially the first two conferences listed):

1. Annual International Conference on Dual Diagnosis Disorders. For details, visit https://dualdiagnosis-disorders.neurologyconference.com/
2. Annual International DSM Conference. Check the Internet for details.
3. Global Conference on Addiction and Behavioral Health. Check the Internet for details.
4. Annual Addictions and Mental Health Conference. Check the Internet for details.
5. International Conference on Addiction Research and Therapy. Check the Internet for details.
6. Annual International Congress on Addictions. Check the Internet for details.
7. Annual International Society of Addiction Annual Meeting. Check the Internet for details.
8. Annual Addictive Disorders and Alcoholism Conference. Check the Internet for details.

9. Annual Addictive Disorders and Addiction Therapy Conference. Check the Internet for details.
10. Annual International Conference on Addiction Psychiatry and Mental Health. Check the Internet for details.
11. International Conference on Trauma and Addiction. Check the Internet for details.
12. Canadian Centre on Substance Use and Addiction (CCSA) Issues of Substance Conference. Check the Internet for details.

INDIVIDUAL EXERCISES

1. Interview someone you know who has a dual or multiple diagnoses (where one of these diagnoses is an addiction). How does this individual see one condition contributing to the other? How do you see one condition contributing to the other?
2. Attend a Narcotics Anonymous meeting. For most meetings, you might need to ask permission to attend first. After the meeting ends, approach someone who has abused more than one drug at the same time (e.g., many individuals with cocaine use disorder also abuse alcohol; opioid users often use other drugs). Ask him or her if it would be okay if you asked a few questions. Does this person have a drug of choice? If so, what makes it the preferred drug? What interaction effects has this person noticed when taking both drugs at the same time? Create a list of other questions that interest you.
3. Arrange an information interview with a clinical psychologist. Information interviews are generally conducted when an individual is considering that profession as a possible career choice. Create a list of 10–15 questions in advance of the interview. Performing an Internet search for information interviews will provide you with a list of many such questions. Be sure to include questions such as the following, "What do you like and dislike about the *DSM-5*? Have you ever looked at the ICD-11 system? What comments would you make about the ICD system in comparison to the DSM system, which is more typically used in the United States and Canada?"

CLASSROOM EXERCISES

1. Invite a speaker to the class who experiences either a polyaddiction or an addiction comorbid with a mental health disorder. Ensure that the students have prepared a list of questions in advance for the speaker.
2. Lead a debate where half the class defends the position that Internet gaming disorder should be included in the DSM system and half takes the opposite view and defends why it should not be included. List the arguments on the board for and against as students bring these up in class.
3. Assign a different addiction to small groups of three or four students per group. Have each group review the pertinent section of this chapter that lists the comorbid conditions associated with it. Have the class answer the question, "Do these comorbid conditions have 'face validity' (i.e., does it make sense that they co-occur) given the particular addiction assigned to your group? Why or why not?" Share these with the rest of the class in a large group discussion.
4. If possible, arrange a field trip to an inpatient addiction facility. Have your students prepare questions in advance that pertain to each of the three areas covered in this chapter (i.e., *DSM-5*, polyaddictions, and comorbid conditions).

CHAPTER SUMMARY

This chapter focused on *DSM-5*, polyaddictions, and comorbidity. Both psychologists and counselors have expressed dissatisfaction with the DSM system of classifying mental disorders. For that matter, the entire practice of diagnosis has remained a controversial topic in psychiatry.

Counselors appreciate that a diagnostic system is a social construction and is, therefore, amenable to change. This change has been witnessed through the developments of DSM-I, DSM-II, DSM-III, DSM-III-R, DSM-IV, DSM-IV-TR, and now *DSM-5*. *DSM-5* is arranged in three sections and includes seven appendices. It no longer contains the terms *addiction, abuse*, or *dependence* regarding SUDs. SUDs are now diagnosed according to severity (i.e., *mild, moderate*, or *severe*). Gambling disorder is the first behavioral addiction to be included in the DSM system. Internet gaming disorder has also been introduced but placed in a conditional section called conditions requiring further study.

The other primary diagnostic system used in many places around the world is the *International Classification of Diseases, 11th revision*, which was released in 2018. Other classification systems have been advanced in the literature.

Counselors, in general, have never valued labeling because counseling focuses on people's strengths more than their weaknesses (and diagnosis emphasizes their shortcomings). Counselors who identify with the humanistic or postmodern perspectives may be especially opposed to labeling practices. The DSM section of the chapter also provided a brief overview of personality disorders, psychosis, schizophrenia, and mobile apps that can assist in diagnoses and treatment.

The next major section of the chapter focused on polyaddictions. Polyaddiction refers to (a) switching from one addiction to another and/or (b) having more one addiction concurrently. Polyaddictions are common among individuals with SUDs and need to be routinely assessed.

The last major section of the chapter focused on comorbidity. Although the term *comorbidity* can also include polyaddictions, here it is defined as occurring when a client experiences one or more SUDs (or addictive behaviors) and one or more non-addiction-related mental disorders concurrently. A great deal of research has been published since 1990 concerning comorbidity between psychiatric conditions and SUDs. Roughly half of the people with severe mental disorders also experience a co-occurring SUD, and recovery from both is a critical objective for healthcare services. Mood disorders are particularly common with substance-addicted individuals. Anxiety disorders are common among individuals with active *or* recent substance use, and this is especially true with depressants, including alcohol. The final component of this section focused on a list of recent research regarding comorbidity anchored to Chapters 9 through 21 in this textbook.

REFERENCES

Abajobir, A. A., Kisely, S., Scott, J. G., Williams, G., Clavarino, A., Strathearn, L., . . . Moses, A. (2017). Childhood maltreatment and young adulthood hallucinations, delusional experiences, and psychosis: A longitudinal study. *Schizophrenia Bulletin*, *43*, 1045–1055.

Acevedo, B. P., & Aron, A. P. (2014). Romantic love, pair-bonding, and the dopaminergic reward system. In M. Mikulincer & P. R. Shaver (Eds.), *Mechanisms of social connection: From brain to group* (pp. 55–69). Washington, DC: American Psychological Association.

Aggarwal, M., Banerjee, A., Singh, S. M., Mattoo, S. K., & Basu, D. (2012). Substance-induced psychotic disorders: 13-year data from a de-addiction centre and their clinical implications. *Asian Journal of Psychiatry*, *5*(3), 220–224.

Aggarwal, N. K. (2017). Culture, communication, and *DSM-5* diagnostic reliability. *Journal of the National Medical Association*, *109*, 150–152.

Alvarez-Alonso, M. J., Jurado-Barba, R., Martinez-Martin, N., Espin-Jaime, J. C., Bolanos-Porrero, C., Ordonez-Franco, A., . . . Ribio, G. (2016). Association between maltreatment and polydrug use among adolescents. *Child Abuse & Neglect*, *51*, 379–389.

American Psychiatric Association (APA). (2013). *Diagnostic and statistical manual of mental disorders* (5th ed.). Washington, DC: Author.

Andreassen, C. S., Griffiths, M. D., Sinha, R., Hetland, J., & Pallesen, S. (2016). The relationships between workaholism and symptoms of psychiatric disorders: A large-scale cross-sectional study. *PLoS ONE*, *11*(5), 1–19.

Anthony, J. C. (2013). Understanding psychiatric comorbidities and addictions. In J. MacKillop & H. de Wit (Eds.), *The Wiley-Blackwell handbook of addiction psychopharmacology* (pp. 83–109). New York, NY: John Wiley & Sons.

Atkinson, D. L. (2016). Marijuana's effects on the mind: Intoxication, effects on cognition and motivation, and addiction. In M. T. Compton (Ed.), *Marijuana and mental health* (pp. 11–37). Arlington, VA: American Psychiatric.

Bailey, T., Alvarez-Jimenez, M., Garcia-Sanchez, A. M., Hulbert, C., Barlow, E., & Bendall, S. (2018). Childhood trauma is associated with severity of hallucinations and delusions in psychotic disorders: A systematic review and meta-analysis. *Schizophrenia Bulletin*, *44*, 1111–1122.

Banach, E., Pawlak, J., Kapelski, P., Szczepankiewicz, A., Rajewska-Rager, A., Skibinska, M., . . . Dmitrzak-Weglarz, M. (2018). Clock genes polymorphisms in male bipolar patients with comorbid alcohol abuse. *Journal of Affective Disorders*, *241*, 142–146.

Barnes, A. (2008). Race and hospital diagnoses of schizophrenia and mood disorders. *Social Work*, *53*, 77–83.

Beljan, P. (2011). Misdiagnosis of culturally diverse students. In J. A. Castellano & A. D. Frazier (Eds.), *Special populations in gifted education: Understanding our most able students from diverse backgrounds* (pp. 317–332). Waco, TX: Prufrock Press.

Berczik, K., Griffiths, M. D., Szabo, A., Kurimay, T., Urban, R., & Demetrovics, Z. (2014). Exercise addiction. In K. P. Rosenberg & L. Curtiss Feder (Eds.), *Behavioral addictions: Criteria, evidence, and treatment* (pp. 317–342). San Diego, CA: Elsevier Academic Press.

Beveridge, J. (2015). A tangled web: Internet pornography, sexual addiction, and the erosion of attachment. In L. Cundy (Ed.), *Love in the age of the Internet: Attachment in the digital era* (pp. 31–52). London, England: Karnac Books.

Bibbey, A., Phillips, A. C., Ginty, A. T., & Carroll, D. (2015). Problematic Internet use, excessive alcohol consumption, their comorbidity and cardiovascular and cortisol reactions to acute psychological stress in a student population. *Journal of Behavioral Addictions, 4*(2), 44–52.

Biggar, R. W., Jr., Forsyth, C. J., Chen, J., & Burstein, K. (2017). The poly-drug user: Examining associations between drugs used by adolescents. *Deviant Behavior, 38*, 1186–1196.

Bischof, A., Meyer, C., Bischof, G., John, U., Wurst, F. M., Thon, N., . . . Rumpf, H.-J. (2016). Type of gambling as an independent risk factor for suicidal events in pathological gamblers. *Psychology of Addictive Behaviors, 30*(2), 263–269.

Blumenthal, D. M., & Gold, M. S. (2012). Relationships between drugs of abuse and eating. In K. D. Brownell & M. S. Gold (Eds.), *Food and addiction: A comprehensive handbook* (pp. 254–265). New York, NY: Oxford University Press.

Bobashev, G., Tebbe, K., Peiper, N., & Hoffer, L. (2018). Polydrug use among heroin users in Cleveland, OH. *Drug and Alcohol Dependence, 192*, 80–87.

Campbell, M. M., & Stein, D. J. (2016). Hypersexual disorder. In N. Petry (Ed.), *Behavioral addictions: DSM-5 and beyond* (pp. 101–123). New York, NY: Oxford University Press.

Canan, F., Karaca, S., Sogucak, S., Gecici, O., & Kuloglu, M. (2017). Eating disorders and food addiction in men with heroin use disorder: A controlled study. *Eating and Weight Disorders, 22*(2), 249–257.

Chan, G. C. K., Kelly, A. B., Hides, L., Quinn, C., & Williams, J. W. (2016). Does gender moderate the relationship between polydrug use and sexual risk-taking among Australian secondary school students under 16 years of age? *Drug and Alcohol Review, 35*, 750–754.

Chasser, Y. M. (2016). Profiles of youths with PTSD and addiction. *Journal of Child & Adolescent Substance Abuse, 25*(5), 448–454.

Chaudhury, S. (2010). Hallucinations: Clinical aspects and management. *Industrial Psychiatry Journal, 19*(1), 5–12.

Chou, W.-J., Liu, T.-L., Yang, P., Yen, C.-F., & Hu, H.-F. (2015). Multi-dimensional correlates of Internet addiction symptoms in adolescents with attention-deficit/hyperactivity disorder. *Psychiatry Research, 225*(1–2), 122–128.

Coffey, S. F., Schumacher, J. A., Nosen, E., Littlefield, A. K., Henslee, A. M., Lappen, A., & Stasiewicz, P. R. (2016). Trauma-focused exposure therapy for chronic posttraumatic stress disorder in alcohol and drug dependent patients: A randomized controlled trial. *Psychology of Addictive Behaviors, 30*(7), 778–790.

Cohn, A. M., Cobb, C., Hagman, B. T., Cameron, A., Ehlke, S., & Mitchell, J. N. (2014). Implicit alcohol cognitions in risky drinking nicotine users with and without co-morbid major depressive disorder. *Addictive Behaviors, 39*(4), 797–802.

Cooper, R. (2018). Understanding the *DSM-5*: Stasis and change. *History of Psychiatry, 29*, 49–65.

Cowlishaw, S., Hakes, J., & Dowling, N. (2016). Gambling problems in treatment for affective disorders: Results from the National Epidemiologic Survey on Alcohol and Related Conditions (NESARC). *Journal of Affective Disorders, 202*, 110–114.

Csiernik, R. (2016). *Substance use and abuse: Everything matters* (2nd ed.). Toronto, ON: Canadian Scholar's Press.

Curran, H., Freeman, T. P., Mokrysz, C., Lewis, D. A., Morgan, C. J., & Parsons, L. H. (2016). Keep off the grass? Cannabis, cognition and addiction. *Nature Reviews Neuroscience*, 17(5), 293–306.

Davis, A. A., Edge, P. J., & Gold, M. S. (2014). New directions in the pharmacological treatment of food addiction, overeating, and obesity. In K. P. Rosenberg & L. Curtiss Feder (Eds.), *Behavioral addictions: Criteria, evidence, and treatment* (pp. 185–213). San Diego, CA: Academic Press.

Deleuze, J., Nuyens, F., Rochat, L., Rothen, S., Maurage, P., & Billieux, J. (2017). Established risk factors for addiction fail to discriminate between healthy gamers and gamers endorsing *DSM-5* Internet gaming disorder. *Journal of Behavioral Addictions, 6*, 516–524.

Delmonico, D. L., & Griffin, E. J. (2015). Sexual compulsivity: Diagnosis, assessment, and treatment. In K. M. Hertlein, G. R. Weeks, & N. Gambescia, Nancy (Eds.), *Systemic sex therapy* (2nd ed.). (pp. 235–254). New York, NY: Routledge/Taylor & Francis.

Dennis, B. B., Samaan, M., Bawor, M., Paul, J., Plater, C., Pare, G., . . . Samaan, Z. (2014). Evaluation of clinical and inflammatory profile in opioid addiction patients with comorbid pain: Results from a multicenter investigation. *Neuropsychiatric Disease and Treatment, 10*, ArtID 2239–2247.

Dermody, S. S. (2018). Risk of polysubstance use among sexual minority and heterosexual youth. *Drug and Alcohol Dependence, 192*, 38–44.

de Vries, S.-K., & Meule, A. (2016). Food addiction and bulimia nervosa: New data based on the Yale Food Addiction Scale 2.0. *European Eating Disorders Review, 24*(6), 518–522.

Dobmeier, R. A., & Stevens, P. S. (2013). Retaining sobriety: Relapse prevention strategies. In P. Strevens & R. L. Smith (Eds.), *Substance abuse counseling: Theory and practice* (5th ed., pp. 261–286). Upper Saddle River, NJ: Pearson.

Dowling, N. A., Cowlishaw, S., Jackson, A., Merkouris, S., Francis, K., & Christensen, D. (2015). The prevalence of comorbid personality disorders in treatment-seeking problem gamblers: A systematic review and meta-analysis. *Journal of Personality Disorders, 29*(6), 735–754.

Dworkin, E. R., Wanklyn, S., Stasiewicz, P. R., & Coffey, S. F. (2018). PTSD symptom presentation among people with alcohol and drug use disorders: Comparisons by substance of abuse. *Addictive Behaviors, 76*, 188–194.

Earleywine, M. (2016). *Substance use problems* (2nd ed.). Ashland, OH: Hogrefe.

Edgerton, J. D., Keough, M. T., & Roberts, L. W. (2018). Co-development of problem gambling and depression symptoms in emerging adults: A parallel-process latent class growth model. *Journal of Gambling Studies, 34*, 949–968.

Elkins, D. N. (2017). The paradigm shift in psychotherapy: Implications for the DSM. *Journal of Humanistic Psychology, 57*, 667–674.

Elmquist, J., Shorey, R. C., Anderson, S., & Stuart, G. L. (2016). The relation between compulsive sexual behaviors and aggression in a substance-dependent population. *Journal of Aggression, Maltreatment & Trauma, 25*(1), 110–124.

Enez, D. A., Nurmedov, S., Noyan, C. O., Yilmaz, O., & Dilbaz, N. (2015). Psychiatric comorbidity among inpatients in an addiction clinic and its association with the process of addiction. *Journal of Psychiatry and Neurological Sciences, 28*(3), 196–203.

Enright, R. D., & Fitzgibbons, R. P. (2015). *Forgiveness therapy in addictive disorders*. Washington, DC: American Psychological Association.

Evans, E. A., Grella, C. E., Washington, D. L., & Upchurch, D. M. (2017). Gender and race/ethnic differences in the persistence of alcohol, drug, and poly-substance use disorders. *Drug and Alcohol Dependence*, *174*, 128–136.

Evren, B., Evren, C., Dalbudak, E., Topcu, M., & Kutlu, N. (2018). Relationship of internet addiction severity with probable ADHD and difficulties in emotion regulation among young adults. *Psychiatry Research*, *269*, 494–500.

Fareed, A., Eilender, P., Haber, M., Bremner, J., Whitfield, N., & Drexler, K. (2013). Comorbid posttraumatic stress disorder and opiate addiction: A literature review. *Journal of Addictive Diseases*, *32*(2), 168–179.

Fatseas, M., Hurmic, H., Serre, F., Debrabant, R., Daulouede, J.-P., Denis, C., & Auriacombe, M. (2016). Addiction severity pattern associated with adult and childhood Attention Deficit Hyperactivity Disorder (ADHD) in patients with addictions. *Psychiatry Research*, *246*, 656–662.

Fink, D. S., Hu, R., Cerda, M., Keyes, K. M., Marshall, B. D., Galea, S., & Martins, S. S. (2015). Patterns of major depression and nonmedical use of prescription opioids in the United States. *Drug and Alcohol Dependence*, *153*, 258–264.

Floros, G., Siomos, K., Stogiannidou, A., Giouzepas, I., & Garyfallos, G. (2014). Comorbidity of psychiatric disorders with Internet addiction in a clinical sample: The effect of personality, defense style and psychopathology. *Addictive Behaviors*, *39*(12), 1839–1845.

Foo, J. C., Streit, F., Treutlein, J., Ripke, S., Witt, S. H., Strohmaier, J., . . . Frank, J. (2018). Shared genetic etiology between alcohol dependence and major depressive disorder. *Psychiatric Genetics*, *28*(4), 66–70.

Foster, A. C., Shorter, G. W., & Griffiths, M. D. (2015). Muscle dysmorphia: Could it be classified as an addiction to body image? *Journal of Behavioral Addictions*, *4*(1), 1–5.

Freimuth, M., Moniz, S., & Kim, S. R. (2011). Clarifying exercise addiction: Differential diagnosis, co-occurring disorders, and phases of addiction. *International Journal of Environmental Research and Public Health*, *8*, 4069–4081.

Frohlich, J. R., Rapinda, K. K., O'Connor, R. M., & Keough, M. T. (2018). Examining co-patterns of depression and alcohol misuse in emerging adults following university graduation. *Addictive Behaviors Reports*, *8*, 40–45.

Gayle, M. C., & Raskin, J. D. (2017). *DSM-5*: Do counselors really want an alternative? *Journal of Humanistic Psychology*, *57*, 650–666.

Geisner, I. M., Huh, D., Cronce, J. M., Lostutter, T. W., Kilmer, J., & Larimer, M. E. (2016). Exploring the relationship between stimulant use and gambling in college students. *Journal of Gambling Studies*, *32*(3), 1001–1016.

Gordon, R. M., & Bornstein, R. F. (2018). Construct validity of the Psychodiagnostic Chart: A transdiagnostic measure of personality organization, personality syndromes, mental functioning, and symptomatology. *Psychoanalytic Psychology*, *35*, 280–288.

Grant, J., Lynskey, M., Madden, P., Nelson, E., Few, L., Bucholz, K., . . . Agrawal, A. (2015). The role of conduct disorder in the relationship between alcohol, nicotine and cannabis use disorders. *Psychological Medicine*, *45*(16), 3505–3515.

Greenfield, B. L., Sittner, K. J., Forbes, M. K., Walls, M. L., & Whitbeck, L. B. (2017). Conduct disorder and alcohol use disorder trajectories, predictors, and outcomes for Indigenous youth. *Journal of the American Academy of Child & Adolescent Psychiatry*, *56*(2), 133–139.

Griffiths, M. D. (2016, December 1). *Workaholism and psychiatric disorders: Is there a relationship between work addiction and OCD, ADHD and depression?* Retrieved on June 3, 2018, from https://www.psychologytoday.com/us/blog/in-excess/201612/workaholism-and-psychiatric-disorders

Grzegorzewska, I. (2017). Behavioural addictions in children and adolescents. *Current Issues in Personality Psychology*, *5*(3), 206–214.

Gunes, H., Tanidir, C., Adaletli, H., Kilicoglu, A. G., Mutlu, C., Bahali, M. K., . . . Uneri, O. S. (2018). Oppositional defiant disorder/conduct disorder co-occurrence increases the risk of Internet addiction in adolescents with attention-deficit hyperactivity disorder. *Journal of Behavioral Addictions*, *7*, 284–291.

Haber, J. S. (2000). *ADHD: The great misdiagnosis*. Dallas, TX: Taylor Trade.

Hajela, R., & Love, T. (2017). Addiction beyond substances—What's up with the DSM? *Sexual Addiction & Compulsivity*, *24*, 11–22.

Haller, M., & Chassin, L. (2013). The influence of PTSD symptoms on alcohol and drug problems: Internalizing and externalizing pathways. *Psychological Trauma: Theory, Research, Practice, and Policy*, *5*(5), 484–493.

Hardy, R., Fani, N., Jovanovic, T., & Michopoulos, V. (2018). Food addiction and substance addiction in women: Common clinical characteristics. *Appetite*, *120*, 367–373.

Haro, J. M., Altamura, C., Corral, R., Elkis, H., Evans, J., Krebs, M.-O., et al. (2018). Understanding the course of persistent symptoms in schizophrenia: Longitudinal findings from the pattern study. *Psychiatry Research*, *267*, 56–62.

Hartung, C. M., & Lefler, E. K. (2019). Sex and gender in psychopathology: *DSM-5* and beyond. *Psychological Bulletin*. No pagination specified.

Heikman, P. K., Muhonen, L. H., & Ojanpera, I. A. (2017). Polydrug abuse among opioid maintenance treatment patients is related to inadequate dose of maintenance treatment medicine. *BMC Psychiatry*, *17*(1). No pagination specified.

Hides, L. (2013). Diagnostic dilemmas in comorbidity. In P. M. Miller (Ed.), *Interventions for addiction: Comprehensive addictive behaviors and disorders*, Vol. *3* (pp. 309–315). San Diego, CA: Elsevier Academic Press.

Hindocha, C., Shaban, N. D., Freeman, T. P., Das, R. K., Gale, G., Schafer, G., . . . Curran, H. (2015). Associations between cigarette smoking and cannabis dependence: A longitudinal study of young cannabis users in the United Kingdom. *Drug and Alcohol Dependence*, *148*, 165–171.

Ho, R. C., Zhang, M. W. B., Tsang, T. Y., Toh, A. H., Pan, F., Lu, Y., . . . Mak, K.-K. (2014). The association between Internet addiction and psychiatric co-morbidity: A meta-analysis. *BMC Psychiatry*, *14*, ArtID 183.

Hodgins, D. C., & Racicot, S. (2013). The link between drinking and gambling among undergraduate university students. *Psychology of Addictive Behaviors*, *27*(3), 885–892.

Hodgson, K., Almasy, L., Knowles, E., Kent, J., Curran, J., Dyer, T., . . . Glahn, D. (2016). Genome-wide significant loci for addiction and anxiety. *European Psychiatry*, *36*, 47–54.

Huprich, S. K., Nelson, S. M., Meehan, K. B., Siefert, C. J., Haggerty, G., Sexton, J., . . . Baade, L. (2018). Introduction of the *DSM-5* levels of Personality Functioning Questionnaire. *Personality Disorders: Theory, Research, and Treatment*, *9*, 553–563.

Jarlenski, M., Barry, C. L., Gollust, S., Graves, A. J., Kennedy-Hendricks, A., & Kozhimannil, K. (2017). Polysubstance use among US women of reproductive age who use opioids for nonmedical reasons. *American Journal of Public Health, 107*, 1308–1310.

Jimenez-Murcia, S., Granero, R., Wolz, I., Bano, M., Mestre-Bach, G., Steward, T., . . . Fernandez-Aranda, F. (2017). Food addiction in gambling disorder: Frequency and clinical outcomes. *Frontiers in Psychology, 8*. No pagination specified.

John, W. S., Zhu, H., Mannelli, P., Schwartz, R. P., Subramaniam, G. A., & Wu, L.-T. (2018). Prevalence, patterns, and correlates of multiple substance use disorders among adult primary care patients. *Drug and Alcohol Dependence, 187*, 79–87.

Johnstone, L. (2018). Psychological formulation as an alternative to psychiatric diagnosis. *Journal of Humanistic Psychology, 58*, 30–46.

Kafka, M. P., & Hennen, J. (1999). The paraphilia-related disorders: An empirical investigation of nonparaphilic hypersexuality disorders in 206 outpatient males. *Journal of Sex and Marital Therapy, 25*, 305–319.

Karaca, S., Saleh, A., Canan, F., & Potenza, M. N. (2017). Comorbidity between behavioral addictions and Attention Deficit/Hyperactivity Disorder: A systematic review. *International Journal of Mental Health and Addiction, 15*(3), 701–724.

Kecojevic, A., Jun, H.-J., Reisner, S. L., & Corliss, H. L. (2017). Concurrent polysubstance use in a longitudinal study of US youth: Associations with sexual orientation. *Addiction, 112*, 614–624.

Kerridge, B. T., Pickering, R., Chou, P., Saha, T. D., & Hasin, D. S. (2018). *DSM-5* cannabis use disorder in the National Epidemiologic Survey on Alcohol and Related Conditions—III: Gender-specific profiles. *Addictive Behaviors, 76*, 52–60.

Kerridge, B. T., Saha, T. D., Chou, S. P., Zhang, H., Jung, J., Ruan, W. J., . . . Hasin, D. S. (2015). Gender and nonmedical prescription opioid use and *DSM-5* nonmedical prescription opioid use disorder: Results from the National Epidemiologic Survey on Alcohol and Related Conditions—III. *Drug and Alcohol Dependence, 156*, 47–56.

Kessler, R. C., McGonagle, K. A., Zhao, S., Nelson, C. B., Hughes, M., Eshleman, S., . . . Kendler, K. S. (1994). Lifetime and 12-month prevalence of DSM-III-R psychiatric disorders in the United States: Results from the National Comorbidity Survey. *Archives of General Psychiatry, 51*(1), 8–19.

Khan, A. Y., & Shaikh, M. R. (2008). Challenging the established diagnosis in psychiatric practice: Is it worth it? *Journal of Psychiatric Practice, 14*, 67–72.

Kim, B.-S., Chang, S. M., Park, J. E., Seong, S. J., Won, S. H., & Cho, M. J. (2016). Prevalence, correlates, psychiatric comorbidities, and suicidality in a community population with problematic Internet use. *Psychiatry Research, 244*, 249–256.

Kinderman, P., Allsopp, K., & Cooke, A. (2017). Responses to the publication of the American Psychiatric Association's *DSM-5*. *Journal of Humanistic Psychology, 57*, 625–649.

King, C. (2016). Whiteness in psychiatry: The madness of European misdiagnoses. In J. Russo & A. Sweeney (Eds.), *Searching for a rose garden: Challenging psychiatry, fostering mad studies* (pp. 69–76). Ross-on-Wye, England: PCCS Books.

Lasser, K., Boyd, J. W., Woohandler, S., Himmelstein, D. U., McCormick, D., & Bor, D. H. (2000). Smoking and mental illness: A population-based prevalence study. *JAMA, 284*(20), 2606–2610.

Lemenager, T., Hoffmann, S., Dieter, J., Reinhard, I., Mann, K., & Kiefer, F. (2018). The links between healthy, problematic, and addicted Internet use regarding comorbidities and self-concept-related characteristics. *Journal of Behavioral Addictions, 7*, 31–43.

Liang, J., Matheson, B. E., & Douglas, J. M. (2016). Mental health diagnostic considerations in racial/ethnic minority youth. *Journal of Child and Family Studies, 25*, 1926–1940.

Liao, Y.-T., Chen, C.-Y., Ng, M.-H., Huang, K.-Y., Shao, W.-C., Lin, T.-Y., . . . Gossop, M. (2017). Depression and severity of substance dependence among heroin dependent patients with ADHD symptoms. *American Journal on Addictions, 26*(1), 26–33.

Lichtenstein, M. B., Hinze, C. J., Emborg, B., Thomsen, F., & Hemmingsen, S. D. (2017). Compulsive exercise: Links, risks and challenges faced. *Psychology Research and Behavior Management, 10*, 85–95.

Lim, A., Hoek, H. W., Deen, M. L., Blom, J. D., Bruggeman, R., Cahn, W., . . . Wiersma, D. (2016). Prevalence and classification of hallucinations in multiple sensory modalities in schizophrenia spectrum disorders. *Schizophrenia Research, 176*, 493–499.

Lim, J.-A., Gwak, A. R., Park, S. M., Kwon, J.-G., Lee, J.-Y., Jung, H. Y., . . . Choi, J.-S. (2015). Are adolescents with Internet addiction prone to aggressive behavior? The mediating effect of clinical comorbidities on the predictability of aggression in adolescents with Internet addiction. *Cyberpsychology, Behavior, and Social Networking, 18*(5), 260–267.

Lin, L., Bohnert, A. S., Price, A. M., Jannausch, M., Bonar, E. E., & Ilgen, M. A. (2015). Pain acceptance and opiate use disorders in addiction treatment patients with comorbid pain. *Drug and Alcohol Dependence, 157*, 136–142.

Liu, Y., Williamson, V., Setlow, B., Cottler, L. B., & Knackstedt, L. A. (2018). The importance of considering polysubstance use: Lessons from cocaine research. *Drug and Alcohol Dependence, 192*, 16–28.

Luhrmann, T. M., Padmavati, R., Tharoor, H., & Osei, A. (2015). Differences in voice-hearing experiences of people with psychosis in the USA, India and Ghana: Interview-based study. *British Journal of Psychiatry, 206*, 41–44.

Maharajh, H. D., Ali, J. K., & Maharaj, M. (2014). Transitional drug use: Switching from alcohol disability to marijuana creativity. In J. Merrick & A. Tenenbaum (Eds.), *Public health concern: Smoking, alcohol and substance use* (pp. 137–147). Hauppauge, NY: Nova Biomedical Books.

Maremmani, A. G. I., Rovai, L., Bacciardi, S., Rugani, F., Pacini, M., Pani, P. P., . . . Maremmani, I. (2013). The long-term outcomes of heroin dependent-treatment-resistant patients with bipolar 1 comorbidity after admission to enhanced methadone maintenance. *Journal of Affective Disorders, 151*(2), 582–589.

Margolis, R. D., & Zweben, J. E. (2011). *Treating patients with alcohol and other drug problems: An integrated approach* (2nd ed.). Washington, DC: American Psychological Association.

Martin, M. S., Hynes, K., Hatcher, S., & Colman, I. (2016). Diagnostic error in correctional mental health: Prevalence, causes, and consequences. *Journal of Correctional Health Care, 22*, 109–117.

Maté, G. (2008). *In the realm of hungry ghosts: Close encounters with addiction*. Toronto, ON: Vintage Books.

McCabe, S. E., West, B. T., Jutkiewicz, E. M., & Boyd, C. J. (2017). Multiple *DSM-5* substance use disorders: A national study of US adults. *Human Psychopharmacology: Clinical and Experimental, 32*, 1–10.

McClure, E. A., Baker, N. L., Sonne, S. C., Ghitza, U. E., Tomko, R. L., Montgomery, L., . . . Gray, K. (2018). Tobacco use during cannabis cessation: Use patterns and impact on abstinence in a National Drug Abuse Treatment Clinical Trials Network study. *Drug and Alcohol Dependence, 192*, 59–66.

McKelvey, K. L., Ramo, D. E., Delucchi, K., & Rubinstein, M. L. (2017). Polydrug use among urban adolescent cigarette smokers. *Addictive Behaviors, 66*, 145–150.

Medeiros, G. C., & Grant, J. E. (2018). Gambling disorder and obsessive-compulsive personality disorder: A frequent but understudied comorbidity. *Journal of Behavioral Addictions, 7*, 366–374.

Meziou, O., Ghali, F., Khelifa, E., Maamri, A., Ben Saadi, S., Mrizak, J., & Zalila, H. (2019). Alexithymia, impulsivity and sensation seeking in buprenorphine addiction: A comparative study. *Journal of Substance Use, 24*(1), 101–104.

Milkman, H. B., & Sunderwirth, S. G. (2010). *Craving for ecstasy and natural highs: A positive approach to mood alteration*. Thousand Oaks, CA: SAGE.

Miller, W. R. (2016). Sacred cows and greener pastures: Reflections from 40 years in addiction research. *Alcoholism Treatment Quarterly, 34*, 92–115.

Mohn, C., Olsson, A.-K., & Helldin, L. (2018). Positive and negative affect in schizophrenia spectrum disorders: A forgotten dimension? *Psychiatry Research, 267*, 148–153.

Moore, D. (2017). Internet and gaming addiction in youth on the autism spectrum: A particularly vulnerable population. In K. S. Young & C. N. de Abreu (Eds.), *Internet addiction in children and adolescents: Risk factors, assessment, and treatment* (pp. 83–100). New York, NY: Springer.

Moran, L. V., Sampath, H., Kochunov, P., & Hong, L. (2013). Brain circuits that link schizophrenia to high risk of cigarette smoking. *Schizophrenia Bulletin, 39*(6), 1373–1381.

Morgan, T. A., & Zimmerman, M. (2015). Is borderline personality disorder underdiagnosed and bipolar disorder overdiagnosed? In L. W. Choi-Kain & J. G. Gunderson (Eds.), *Borderline personality and mood disorders: Comorbidity and controversy* (pp. 65–78). New York, NY: Springer Science + Business Media.

Morley, K. I., Ferris, J. A., Winstock, A. R., & Lynskey, M. T. (2017). Polysubstance use and misuse or abuse of prescription opioid analgesics: A multi-level analysis of international data. *Pain, 158*, 1138–1144.

Nunes-Neto, P. R., Kohler, C. A., Schuch, F. B., Solmi, M., Quevedo, J., Maes, M., . . . Carvalho, A. F. (2018). Food addiction: Prevalence, psychopathological correlates and associations with quality of life in a large sample. *Journal of Psychiatric Research, 96*, 145–152.

Oberleitner, L. M., Mandel, D. L., & Easton, C. J. (2013). Treatment of co-occurring alcohol dependence and perpetration of intimate partner violence: The role of anger expression. *Journal of Substance Abuse Treatment, 45*(3), 313–318.

Ohlmeier, M. D., Peters, K., Kordon, A., Seifert, J., Te Wildt, B., Wiese, B., . . . Schneider, U. (2007). Nicotine and alcohol dependence in patients with comorbid attention-deficit/hyperactivity disorder (ADHD). *Alcohol and Alcoholism, 42*(6), 539–543.

Ostergaard, J., Ostergaard, S. V., & Fletcher, A. (2016). Preferences for simultaneous polydrug use: A comparative study of young adults in England and Denmark. *Contemporary Drug Problems: An Interdisciplinary Quarterly, 43*, 350–368.

Padmanabhan, D. (2017). From distress to disease: A critique of the medicalisation of possession in *DSM-5*. *Anthropology & Medicine, 24*, 261–275.

Paniagua, F. A. (2013). Culture-bound syndromes, cultural variations, and psychopathology. In F. A. Paniagua & A.-M. Yamada (Eds.), *Handbook of multicultural mental health: Assessment and treatment of diverse populations* (2nd ed., pp. 25–47). San Diego, CA: Elsevier Academic Press.

Patrick, M. E., Kloska, D. D., Terry-McElrath, Y. M., Lee, C. M., O'Malley, P. M., & Johnston, L. D. (2018). Patterns of simultaneous and concurrent alcohol and marijuana use among adolescents. *American Journal of Drug and Alcohol Abuse, 44*, 441–451.

Pavon, F. J., Araos, P., Pastor, A., Calado, M., Pedraz, M., Campos-Cloute, R., . . . de Fonseca, F. R. (2013). Evaluation of plasma-free endocannabinoids and their congeners in abstinent cocaine addicts seeking outpatient treatment: Impact of psychiatric comorbidity. *Addiction Biology, 18*(6), 955–969.

Pechnick, R. N., Cunningham, K. A., & Danovitch, I. (2014). Hallucinogen-related disorders. In G. O. Gabbard (Ed.), *Gabbard's treatments of psychiatric disorders* (5th ed., pp. 829–839). Arlington, VA: American Psychiatric.

Pfund, R. A., Whelan, J. P., Greenburg, J. E., Peter, S. C., Wilson, K. K., & Meyers, A. W. (2017). Psychological distress as an indicator of co-occurring psychopathology among treatment-seeking disordered gamblers. *Journal of Gambling Studies, 33*, 907–918.

Pilszyk, A., Silczuk, A., Habrat, B., & Heitzman, J. (2018). Difficulties to differentiate mood disorders co-occurring with compulsive gambling. Discussion based on a case study. *Psychiatria Polska, 52*, 45–54.

Platania, S., Castellano, S., Santisi, G., & Di Nuovo, S. (2017). Personality correlates of the tendency to compulsive shopping. [Italian]. Correlati di personalita della tendenza allo shopping compulsivo. *Giornale Italiano di Psicologia, 44*(1), 137–155.

Rakofsky, J. J., & Dunlop, B. W. (2015). The over-under on the misdiagnosis of bipolar disorder: A systematic review. *Current Psychiatry Reviews, 11*, 222–234.

Raman, R. P. B., Sheshadri, S. P., Reddy, Y. C. J., Girimaji, S. C., Srinath, S., & Raghunandan, V. N. G. P. (2007). Is bipolar II disorder misdiagnosed as major depressive disorder in children? *Journal of Affective Disorders, 98*(3), 263–266.

Raskin, J. D., & Gayle, M. C. (2015). *DSM-5*: Do psychologists really want an alternative? *Journal of Humanistic Psychology, 56*, 439–456.

Rastegar, D., & Fingerhood, M. (2016). *The American Society of Addiction Medicine handbook of addiction medicine*. New York, NY: Oxford University Press.

Rawson, R. A., Washton, A., Domier, C. P., & Reiber, C. (2002). Drugs and sexual effects: Role of drug type and gender. *Journal of Substance Abuse Treatment, 22*(2), 103–108.

Raymond, N. C. C., Coleman, E., & Miner, M. H. (2003). Psychiatric comorbidity and compulsive/impulsive traits in compulsive sexual behavior. *Comprehensive Psychiatry, 44*, 370–380.

Reitan, T. (2017). Patterns of polydrug use among pregnant substance abusers. *NAT Nordisk alkohol & narkotikatidskrift, 34*(2), 145–159.

Rimm, S. (2011). Attention deficit/hyperactivity disorder: A difficult diagnosis. In J. L. Jolly, D. J. Treffinger, T. F. Inman, J. F. Smutny

(Eds.), *Parenting gifted children: The authoritative guide from the National Association for Gifted Children* (pp. 399–404). Waco, TX: Prufrock Press.

Roncero, C., Grau-Lopez, L., & Casas, M. (2017). Dual disorders: A clinical perspective. *Addictive Disorders & Their Treatment, 16*, 175–179.

Rosen, C., McCarthy-Jones, S., Chase, K. A., Humpston, C. S., Melbourne, J. K., Kling, L., . . . Sharma, R. P. (2018). The tangled roots of inner speech, voices and delusions. *Psychiatry Research, 264*, 281–289.

Rosenberg, K. P., Carnes, P., & O'Connor, S. (2014). Evaluation and treatment of sex addiction. *Journal of Sex & Marital Therapy, 40*(2), 77–91.

Rubin, J. (2018). The classification and statistical manual of mental health concerns: A proposed practical scientific alternative to the DSM and ICD. *Journal of Humanistic Psychology, 58*, 93–114.

Rumpf, H.-J., Bischof, A., Wolfling, K., Lemenager, T., Thon, N., Moggi, F., . . . Wurst, F. M. (2015). Non-substance-related disorders: Gambling disorder and Internet addiction. In G. Dom & F. Moggi (Eds.), *Co-occurring addictive and psychiatric disorders: A practice-based handbook from a European perspective* (pp. 221–236). New York, NY: Springer-Verlag.

Salani, D. A., Zdanowicz, M., & Joseph, L. (2016). Heroin use. *Journal of Psychosocial Nursing and Mental Health Services, 54*(6), 31–37.

Schepis, T. S., West, B. T., Teter, C. J., & McCabe, S. E. (2016). Prevalence and correlates of co-ingestion of prescription tranquilizers and other psychoactive substances by U.S. high school seniors: Results from a national survey. *Addictive Behaviors, 52*, 8–12.

Schulte, M., Hser, Y., Saxon, A., Evans, E., Li, L., Huang, D., . . . Ling, W. (2015). Risk factors associated with HCV among opioid-dependent patients in a multisite study. *Journal of Community Health, 40*(5), 940–947.

Sheaves, B., Bebbington, P. E., Goodwin, G. M., Harrison, P. J., Espie, C. A., Foster, R. G., & Freeman, D. (2016). Insomnia and hallucinations in the general population: Findings from the 2000 and 2007 British Psychiatric Morbidity Surveys. *Psychiatry Research, 241*, 141–146.

Sher, L., Siever, L. J., Goodman, M., McNamara, M., Hazlett, E. A., Koenigsberg, H. W., & New, A. S. (2015). Gender differences in the clinical characteristics and psychiatric comorbidity in patients with antisocial personality disorder. *Psychiatry Research, 229*(3), 685–689.

Silveira, M. L., Conway, K. P., Green, V. R., Kasza, K. A., Sargent, J. D., Borek, N., . . . Compton, W. (2018). Longitudinal associations between youth tobacco and substance use in waves 1 and 2 of the Population Assessment of Tobacco and Health (PATH) Study. *Drug and Alcohol Dependence, 191*, 25–36.

Sohail, Z., Bailey, R. K., & Richie, W. D. (2014). Misconceptions of depression in African Americans. *Frontiers in Psychiatry, 5*, 1–3.

Stein, D. J., Billieux, J., Bowden-Jones, H., Grant, J. E., Fineberg, N., Higuchi, S., . . . Poznyak, V. (2018). Balancing validity, utility and public health considerations in disorders due to addictive behaviours. *World Psychiatry, 17*, 363–364.

Stewart, D. G., Arlt, V. K., Felleman, B., Athenour, D. R., & Arger, C. (2015). Mechanisms of alcohol use disorder severity in adolescents with co-occurring depressive symptoms: Findings from a school-based substance use intervention. *School Mental Health, 7*(2), 147–159.

Subramaniam, M., Mahesh, M. V., Peh, C. X., Tan, J., Fauziana, R., Satghare, P., . . . Chong, S. A. (2017). Hazardous alcohol use among patients with schizophrenia and depression. *Alcohol, 65*, 63–69.

Suomi, A., Dowling, N. A., & Jackson, A. C. (2014). Problem gambling subtypes based on psychological distress, alcohol abuse and impulsivity. *Addictive Behaviors, 39*(12), 1741–1745.

Sussman, S. (2010). Love addiction: Definition, etiology, treatment. *Sexual Addiction & Compulsivity, 17*(1), 31–45.

Tackett, J. L., Krieger, H., Neighbors, C., Rinker, D., Rodriguez, L., & Edward, G. (2017). Comorbidity of alcohol and gambling problems in emerging adults: A bifactor model conceptualization. *Journal of Gambling Studies, 33*, 131–147.

Tarren, J. R., & Bartlett, S. E. (2017). Alcohol and nicotine interactions: Pre-clinical models of dependence. *American Journal of Drug and Alcohol Abuse, 43*, 146–154.

Torrens, M., & Rossi, P. (2015). Mood disorders and addiction. In G. Dom & F. Moggi (Eds.), *Co-occurring addictive and psychiatric disorders: A practice-based handbook from a European perspective* (pp. 103–117). New York, NY: Springer-Verlag.

Turner, S., Mota, N., Bolton, J., & Sareen, J. (2018). Self-medication with alcohol or drugs for mood and anxiety disorders: A narrative review of the epidemiological literature. *Depression & Anxiety, 35*(9), 851–860.

Tyrer, P. (2017). Personality disorder: Good reasons to reclassify. *Australian and New Zealand Journal of Psychiatry, 51*(11), 1077–1078.

Uchtenhagen, A. A. (2015). Psychiatric comorbidity in heroin maintenance and methadone maintenance treatments. In G. Dom & F. Moggi (Eds.), *Co-occurring addictive and psychiatric disorders: A practice-based handbook from a European perspective* (pp. 363–373). New York, NY: Springer-Verlag.

Vaddiparti, K., & Cottler, L. B. (2017). Personality disorders and pathological gambling. *Current Opinion in Psychiatry, 30*, 45–49.

Van Ameringen, M., Turna, J., Khalesi, Z., Pullia, K., & Patterson, B. (2017). There is an app for that! The current state of mobile applications (apps) for *DSM-5* obsessive-compulsive disorder, posttraumatic stress disorder, anxiety and mood disorders. *Depression and Anxiety, 34*, 526–539.

Van Rooij, A. J., Kuss, D. J., Griffiths, M. D., Shorter, G. W., Schoenmakers, T. M., & Van De Mheen, D. (2014). The (co-)occurrence of problematic video gaming, substance use, and psychosocial problems in adolescents. *Journal of Behavioral Addictions, 3*(3), 157–165.

Verdoux, H., & van Os, J. (2002). Psychotic symptoms in non-clinical populations and the continuum of psychosis. *Schizophrenia Research, 54*, 59–65.

Verges, A., Ellingson, J. M., Schroder, S. A., Slutske, W. S., & Sher, K. J. (2018). Intensity of daily drinking and its relation to alcohol use disorders. *Alcoholism: Clinical and Experimental Research, 42*, 1674–1683.

Wang, B.-q., Yao, N.-q., Zhou, X., Liu, J., & Lv, Z.-t. (2017). The association between attention deficit/hyperactivity disorder and Internet addiction: A systematic review and meta-analysis. *BMC Psychiatry, 17*, 1–12.

Watters, C. A., Bagby, R. M., & Sellbom, M. (2018). Meta-analysis to derive an empirically based set of personality facet criteria for the alternative *DSM-5* model for personality disorders. *Personality*

Disorders: Theory, Research, and Treatment. No Pagination Specified.

Weinberger, A. H., Platt, J., & Goodwin, R. D. (2016). Is cannabis use associated with an increased risk of onset and persistence of alcohol use disorders? A three-year prospective study among adults in the United States. *Drug and Alcohol Dependence, 161*, 363–367.

Wilkinson, S., & Alderson-Day, B. (2016). Voices and thoughts in psychosis: An introduction. *Review of Philosophy and Psychology, 7*, 529–540.

Wilson, M., Gogulski, H. Y., Cuttler, C., Bigand, T. L., Oluwoye, O., Barbosa-Leiker, C., & Roberts, M. A. (2018). Cannabis use moderates the relationship between pain and negative affect in adults with opioid use disorder. *Addictive Behaviors, 77*, 225–231.

Wolfling, K., Beutel, M. E., Dreier, M., & Muller, K. W. (2015). Bipolar spectrum disorders in a clinical sample of patients with Internet addiction: Hidden comorbidity or differential diagnosis? *Journal of Behavioral Addictions, 4*(2), 101–105.

Wright, R. H., & National Institute of Mental Health, Bethesda, MD. (2010). Is attention-deficit hyperactivity disorder (ADHD) a real disorder? In B. Slife (Ed.), *Clashing views on psychological issues* (16th ed., pp. 250–271). New York, NY: McGraw-Hill.

Wu, L.-T., McNeely, J., Subramaniam, G. A., Brady, K. T., Sharma, G., VanVeldhuisen, P., . . . Schwartz, R. P. (2017). *DSM-5* substance use disorders among adult primary care patients: Results from a multisite study. *Drug and Alcohol Dependence, 179*, 42–46.

Yakovenko, I., Fortgang, R., Prentice, J., Hoff, R. A., & Potenza, M. N. (2018). Correlates of frequent gambling and gambling-related chasing behaviors in individuals with schizophrenia-spectrum disorders. *Journal of Behavioral Addictions, 7*, 375–383.

Yen, J.-Y., Liu, T.-L., Wang, P.-W., Chen, C.-S., Yen, C.-F., & Ko, C.-H. (2017). Association between Internet gaming disorder and adult attention deficit and hyperactivity disorder and their correlates: Impulsivity and hostility. *Addictive Behaviors, 64*, 308–313.

Zadra, S., Bischof, G., Besser, B., Bischof, A., Meyer, C., John, U., & Rumpf, H.-J. (2016). The association between Internet addiction and personality disorders in a general population-based sample. *Journal of Behavioral Addictions, 5*(4), 691–699.

Zhang, C., Brook, J. S., Leukefeld, C. G., & Brook, D. W. (2016). Associations between compulsive buying and substance dependence/abuse, major depressive episodes, and generalized anxiety disorder among men and women. *Journal of Addictive Diseases, 35*, 298–304.

Zhong, B., Xiang, Y., Cao, X., Li, Y., Zhu, J., & Chiu, H. F. (2014). Prevalence of antisocial personality disorder among Chinese individuals receiving treatment for heroin dependence: A systematic review. *Shanghai Archives of Psychiatry, 26*(5), 259–271.

Zmuda, N. (2014). Assessment and treatment of co-occurring substance use disorders and process addictions: Eating disorders, pathological gambling, and sexual addiction. In S. L. A. Straussner (Ed.), *Clinical work with substance-abusing clients* (3rd ed., pp. 520–536). New York, NY: Guilford Press.

6 Individual Counseling and Relapse Prevention

iStock.com/Niko

Learning Objectives

1. Become familiar with ways to begin a session, develop a strong and positive working alliance, and develop considerations for terminating counseling with clients.
2. Understand six evidence-based counseling approaches, suicide risk assessment, and homicide risk assessment.
3. Learn the fundamentals of solution-focused therapy.
4. Describe relapse prevention and have familiarity with many of its methods.
5. Name some of the behavioral methods that can be used with clients.

PERSONAL REFLECTIONS

I have worked with many types of people and problems over my career as a counselor and psychologist. Of all groups, I most prefer working with addicted individuals. Perhaps it is because they remind me of myself. Before recovery begins, addicted individuals seem so confident, albeit alongside their shroud of secrecy and deception. During recovery, however, they begin to reveal themselves as they truly are. Like coming out of a closet as commonly described by LGBTQ individuals, individuals with addictions emerge from their dark holes and begin to see the light again after sometimes decades of addiction-induced half-truths and lies. Perhaps I am also mesmerized by the thrill-seeking aspect and the unusual experiences that addicted individuals have had while using their drug of choice, or other drugs for that matter. Whatever the reasons, I can relate to them at a deep level.

However, there is also another side to this work. Witnessing the terrible guilt and shame when addicted individuals have relapsed is disappointing. Addicted individuals in recovery are often humble as their egos have been abused by others and by themselves more times than they can count. They are vulnerable: We all are vulnerable.

This chapter takes us into how we can help people face themselves again with dignity and respect. I keep asking the question, "What needs to happen for this individual at this juncture in their life so that lapses and relapses become only memories?" How can we help individuals deeply and permanently transform their lives?

Evidence-Based Individual Counseling for Addictions

What is counseling? The American Counseling Association reached a consensus definition of counseling as "a professional relationship that empowers diverse individuals, families, and groups to accomplish mental health, wellness, education, and career goals" (Kaplan, Tarvydas, & Gladding, 2014, p. 366). The word "*empowers*" speaks to the strength-based perspective upon which counselors base their work. This chapter reflects the collaborative stance taken by counselors as they work with their clients. We empower clients to decide on their goals and work with them toward their achievement.

There are three basic tenets to strength-based approaches in counseling practice. First, the hallmark of a strength-based intervention is *choice*. This means respecting the rights of individuals to manage their destinies and to take responsibility for their actions. Second, *providing options* is an important tenet. If the program is based solely on abstinence, clients are not provided options. Third, another tenet of strength-based approaches is to pay attention to the *readiness for change* of their clients and/or their systems (Van Wormer & Rae Davis, 2013).

Beginning Counseling Work With Clients

Regardless of which theory and techniques of counseling you intend to use, the beginning work with clients is similar. If you do the following, you are likely to find that most of your clients improve and most return for further sessions if needed. It is also the reason that, overall, all therapies boast about the same degree of effectiveness (Miller, 2016). With each client, we need to develop a strong and positive working alliance whether our work is with adults (Ardito & Rabellino, 2011; Tasca, Town, Abbass, & Clarke, 2018) or with children and adolescents (Karver, De Nadai, Monahan, & Shirk, 2018).

The working alliance has three components: (a) the bond between the counselor and the client (i.e., we work at building a positive, collaborative, and trusting relationship with our clients), (b) collaboration in establishing goals (i.e., our clients and we decide on what is to be accomplished through counseling), and (c) collaboration in deciding tasks (i.e., the method of how our clients and we are going to work on the problem together) (Bordin, 1979). Clients prefer counselors who (a) are respectful, (b) facilitate openness and are open themselves (i.e., they self-disclose), and (c) can connect on a deep level (Noyce & Simpson, 2018). They also prefer counselors who are nondefensive when hearing negative feedback (Timulak & Keogh, 2017).

The three essential components of effective counseling as theorized by Carl Rogers (1957) assist in building a positive working alliance. These three components include (a) genuineness, (b) unconditional positive regard, and (c) accurate empathy. Miller, Taylor, and West (1980), for example, found that counselors who demonstrated accurate empathy predicted two thirds of the variance regarding drinking outcomes of their clients at 6 months and one half of the variance at 12 months' follow-up. Even 2 years later, accurate empathy predicted one third of the variance in drinking outcomes (Miller & Baca, 1983).

Counselors who are themselves, who show deep acceptance of their clients, and who both feel and demonstrate an understanding of their clients' thoughts, feelings, and actions will have the highest likelihood of creating a caring and respectful environment in which clients can improve. In many ways, effective counselors emulate "loving parents" but without the important childrearing role of creating rules and setting limits on their clients' behaviors. We may help our clients, however, create their own rules and limits on their behavior.

Gladding and Alderson (2019) recommended that clients play an active role in their counseling. Early in the process, it is important that clients come to understand that they get out of counseling what they put into it. The change, after all, is what occurs within them. As counselors, we act as facilitators, guides, teachers, and catalysts for change, but clients remain the ones who make the changes in their lives. Gladding and Alderson suggested that clients be taught to come to sessions prepared. The best ways to do this are for clients to create an agenda for each session, list their goals for each session, and/or write down their expectations for each session and to share these with the counselor preferably before the session via email, text, or phone message. If that is untenable, this information should be shared at the beginning of the session.

Furthermore, counselors are not mind-readers, so it is helpful if clients are taught to tell us if they think we are missing the mark. In other words, clients ought to direct us periodically so that we can do our jobs better as counselors. This also helps to create equal power between us.

Beginning counselors often feel the imposter syndrome, meaning that they do not feel competent and so consequently believe they are "faking it." Try not to let that thought and feeling interfere with the development of a strong working alliance. Remember that most of your success will be based on the strength of this working alliance. As Jeffrey Kottler said (J. A. Kottler, personal communication, March 28, 2018; Dr. Kottler is a well-known American counselor and writer of over 100 books), even when he was making educational videotapes of some of the founders of counseling approaches doing their work, most needed, on average, three attempts to sufficiently demonstrate their techniques!

Furthermore, reflecting on over 40 years of working in the field, William R. Miller (2016) stated that, "Most recovery happens without any professional treatment" (p. 103). Clients have an amazing capacity to change on their own. Perhaps we, as counselors, provide the "value-added" dimension, and perhaps not. If we *genuinely* care about our clients without compromising our professional boundaries, however, we have every reason to believe that we will offer a value-added service to their recovery.

Brooks and McHenry (2009) reminded counselors that addicted clients might feel a degree of "shame, guilt, embarrassment, and terror . . . [that is] beyond description" (p. 2). It is helpful to thank clients for seeking help and acknowledging to them the tremendous effort that it requires. It has long struck me that most of us could use more praise, recognition, acknowledgment, and a deeper sense of belonging in our lives. We can help fill our clients' longing to belong and be accepted. Our clients often feel defeated, and our job is to instill hope and encourage them to appreciate that recovery is possible.

With new clients who have booked an appointment with you of their own volition, first ensure that they read and sign your informed consent form. Ask if they have any questions or concerns regarding the form. It is also helpful to tell them that informed consent is an ongoing process and that you encourage them to ask questions at any time. It is also important that you keep them informed at regular intervals of changes in the treatment plan.

Following signed informed consent, focus on building rapport. Imagine that you are good friends and, as you talk, find common ground. If the client initiated the session, after 2 or 3 min ask something like, "What would you like to talk about today?" or "What would you like to focus on today?" It is usually better to avoid beginning with, "What problem [or issue] would you like to talk about today?" This is because the client may not view what they want to talk to you about as a problem or issue.

If a client has been sent to you, it is important to know whether he or she is voluntary or mandatory. Voluntary clients see you because they want to be there, but you still need to begin by finding out why someone referred them to you (unless you know this already). With mandatory clients, you will want to ask why they have been sent to you. That will help you ascertain the likelihood that they are invested in the process or whether they do not want to receive counseling.

Some research has shown that mandatory clients benefit from counseling. In fact, addicted clients who are legally pressured to enter treatment sometimes improve more than those who enter treatment voluntarily (National Institute on Drug Abuse, 2014). In a recent systematic review of compulsory drug treatment, Werb et al. (2016) concluded that, on the whole, evidence does not support compulsory treatment approaches, and some studies suggest they can create potential harm. Werb et al. recommended that non-compulsory treatment be prioritized by policymakers. Countries like Malaysia are considering transitioning away from involuntary detention of people who use drugs (Khan et al., 2018). Human rights violations have occurred in Bangkok, Thailand, where they have required compulsory drug detention for individuals who inject drugs (Kerr, Small, Ayutthaya, & Hayashi, 2018).

Razzhavaikina (2007) found in her dissertation research that therapist factors are most important in creating a working alliance with mandated clients. Consequently, it may take more time to build a strong and positive working alliance. At the beginning of the first session, your client will still need to read and sign the informed consent form. In the case of mandatory clients, a third party will likely be involved who requires feedback or a report from you. It is imperative that the client understand exactly the who, what, why, and where if the information is to be provided to either someone else or an agency.

Regardless of whether the client is voluntary or mandated, you next need to establish the goals of counseling collaboratively. Once these are agreed upon, the next step is to reach consensus regarding the approach that you will take in helping your client. If you have become competent in only one approach, let the client know a few fundamentals underlying your method. Although 75% of residential treatment programs in the United States have abstinence as the only goal (Van Wormer & Rae Davis, 2013), Miller (2016) surmised that this is an example of "black-or-white thinking" (p. 96). In a study of 8389 clients across seven clinical trials, Miller, Walters, and Bennett (2001) found that 24% of clients had abstained from alcohol throughout a 12-month period. If treatment success were measured only by abstinence, that would mean 76% of these people were treatment failures. Miller et al. had also found, however, that 87% of those who continued drinking decreased their alcohol consumption from an average of 77 drinks to 10 drinks per week!

Collaborating on tasks is often given minimal importance by counselors, and clients are provided whatever counselors decide to give them. Instead, get clients' agreement on how you propose to help them. For example, if you are going to use cognitive-behavioral therapy (CBT), telling them what this entails is also a way of providing informed consent. Some clients will balk at an approach that may seem too "heady" for them. Likewise, other clients will not appreciate a solution-focused approach that gives little time for clients to tell the story behind their presenting concern. If you are offering the client a smorgasbord of approaches, negotiate with the client toward reaching an agreement as to the best approach to try initially. Help clients monitor their progress and maintain flexibility so that shifting to a different approach remains viable throughout counseling.

Addiction counselors, like other counselors, need to become comfortable in asking clients questions not only about their addictive behavior but also about other areas of their lives. Human problems occur within a context. As Miller (2016) stated, counselors need to ask clients about money, emotions, and irrational beliefs. They also need to ask about topics that may be uncomfortable for some clients, such as fantasies, family secrets, sexual behaviors, and religious beliefs (Miller, 2016). As a counselor, you do not want to be the one blushing as you ask personal questions. Here is a sage piece of advice: Before you ask clients questions that are quite personal, first find out how comfortable they are in answering these questions. I typically use scaling questions such as in the following example:

> Counselors often ask personal questions the way others might ask about the weather. The questions I ask are intended to get to know you better, but I want to ensure I remain sensitive to your comfort level. On a scale of 0 to 10, how comfortable are you in answering questions about your sex life? 0 means you are *completely uncomfortable* and 10 means you are *completely comfortable*. [I then follow this up with, "Would it be okay, then, if I ask you questions about your sex life?"].

The remainder of this chapter reviews the main evidence-based counseling approaches used in addiction counseling. The intent is to provide practical strategies and examples to assist you in your practice. There is so much that has been written about some of these methods that one can get bogged down in detail. It is reassuring to know that, as Aaron Beck and colleagues (Wright, Thase, & Beck, 2014) wrote, there is room for flexibility. Arguably, whatever approach is used, it needs to resonate with the counselor. This means that no two counselors in action will look the same even when they are using the same approach.

How Effective Are Psychosocial Approaches in Addiction Treatment?

Recent Cochrane reviews, looking at meta-analyses specifically, performed on studies looking at the effectiveness of psychosocial treatments for addictions often report effect sizes in the low to moderate range (Blodgett, Maisel, Fuh, Wilbourne, & Finney, 2014; Magill & Ray, 2009; Riper et al., 2014; Sayegh, Huey, Zara, & Jhaveri, 2017; Smedslund et al., 2011; Walter et al., 2015). Dutra et al. (2008), in their review of psychosocial treatments, reported effects sizes of low-moderate to high-moderate ranges that depended on the particular substance disorder under investigation. To make some sense of this, note that, according to Cohen (1988), a moderate effect size is about 0.5, which means half of a standard deviation higher than the effect of whatever treatment (including placebo and being on a wait-list) was given to the control group.

What Is Evidence-Based Counseling?

Larios, Manuel, Newville, and Sorensen (2013) defined evidence-based counseling as "approaches that have been found to improve patients' functioning after rigorous scientific testing" (p. 621). The intent is to provide clients with the best possible services. The type of evidence used in counseling research differs from that used in pharmacology.

In pharmacological studies, the National Institutes of Health requires four phases of research:

1. Phase I: The medication is tested on a small sample.
2. Phase II: The medication is tested on a larger sample to continue monitoring safety.
3. Phase III: The medication is tested on a still-larger sample and compared to another treatment or control condition to measure its relative efficacy.
4. Phase IV: The medication that has now been routinely administered is evaluated for its effectiveness and safety in real-life settings, and the long-term effects are assessed. (Larios et al., 2013).

In counseling research, efficacy and effectiveness studies, critical literature reviews, and meta-analyses generally constitute the research in deciding whether a counseling approach is evidence-based. The gold standard in behavioral research is randomized-controlled trials (RCTs). In an RCT, individuals are randomly assigned to the treatment condition(s) and the control group(s) to control factors that could otherwise confound the study's results. RCTs, then, are carefully controlled experiments. Interestingly, the results from RCTs might not transfer to settings outside of the experiment. Other researchers conduct effectiveness trials where interventions are carried out in real-world settings to establish whether they work or not. Meta-analyses statistically combine the results of several studies and, in doing so, measure the effect size of a treatment (generally reported as small, moderate, or large). Critical literature reviews provide a summary of research in a given area to alert readers to both what is known and what is not known in the given area (Larios et al., 2013).

The counseling approach that has demonstrated the most robust empirical support for working with addictions is CBT (Greenfield & Weiss, 2017; King et al., 2017; Larios et al., 2013; McIntosh & O'Neill, 2017). Behavior therapy is also effective, especially contingency management. Other evidence-based approaches include motivational interviewing and motivational enhancement therapy, mindfulness treatment, integrative approaches, and relapse prevention (Li, Howard, Garland, McGovern, & Lazar, 2017; Miller, 2016). Furthermore, 12-step approaches have demonstrated effectiveness (Greenfield & Weiss, 2017; Kelly, Bergman, & O'Connor, 2018). Although solution-focused therapy has not sufficiently proved itself to be considered an evidence-based approach with addictions, it offers counselors several helpful techniques, and, for that reason, it too is overviewed.

Cognitive-Behavioral Therapy and Behavior Therapy

Rational Emotive Behavior Therapy

The chapters that focus on the specific addictions (i.e., Chapters 9–21) provide ample evidence that CBT and behavior therapy are effective in counseling addicts. To avoid redundancy, this extensive research base will not be included here. The two CBT approaches that have been most researched and adopted in practice are called cognitive therapy (CT) and rational emotive behavior therapy (REBT).

Albert Ellis initiated development of the first CBT in 1955. It was first called rational therapy, then rational emotive therapy, and then finally REBT (Beck, 2006). Albert Ellis was an American psychologist (1913–2007) who was first trained as a psychoanalyst. He found psychoanalysis to be "to drawn-out, long-winded, and inefficient" (Ellis & Ellis, 2014b, p. 299). Although Ellis agreed that individuals who are seriously disturbed usually benefit from longer and more intensive therapy, he believed that many individuals could be helped to change their way of thinking about things in, on average, five to 12 sessions, and even less in some cases (Ellis & Ellis, 2014b). Ellis's beliefs were based on the words of Epictetus, a 1st century Greek philosopher: "Men are disturbed not by things, but by the views which they take of them" (see https://www.brainyquote.com/quotes/epictetus_149127 for the quote).

In other words, Ellis came to believe that it is not the things that happen to us that cause us negative consequences but rather our view of those things. Ellis differentiated between *rational beliefs*, which are those that are logically defensible, and *irrational beliefs* (IBs), which involve exaggerations or other unhealthy elements that

#	Irrational Belief	Rational Belief
1	Everyone must love me.	There will always be people who like and agree with me and those who do not. It is better to focus on enhancing my self-respect than on winning the approval of others for practical purposes.
2	I must do things perfectly if I am to consider myself worthwhile.	I have intrinsic worth like everyone else, so my worth does not depend on my performances. I will strive to become competent in those things that matter to me.
3	Some people are intrinsically evil and wicked, and they should be severely blamed, damned, and punished for their actions.	People do stupid things occasionally, myself included. Poor behavior does not constitute a rotten individual.
4	Things must work out the way I want them to or it is an awful catastrophe.	I can manage bad things that happen to me or others, albeit with negative emotions. It is better that I focus on how to improve a bad situation than to dwell on it.
5	My unhappiness is caused by others, and I cannot control how I feel.	It is my view of things that determines how I feel. I can choose to focus on the cup being half empty or view it is as half full.
6	If something fearful or dangerous happens, I should dwell on it because it might happen again.	I would do better to face it and render it nondangerous if possible. If it is inevitable, I would be better off accepting it.
7	It is better and easier if I avoid life difficulties and responsibilities.	The "easy way" is typically harder in the long run.
8	I should be dependent on others and find someone stronger or greater than myself on whom to depend.	I would do better to think and act less dependently and become a stronger person myself.
9	The past controls my present behavior, and something from the past should indefinitely affect me.	I can learn from my past experiences and not be overly attached to them.
10	There is always the best and perfect solution to problems, and it is a catastrophe if I cannot find it.	There is rarely a perfect solution to problems. I can still enjoy my life while accepting its imperfections.
11	I should become distraught by other people's problems and disturbances.	If I remain calmer and keep a clear head, I can better choose what to do with this information and help where needed.
12	The world should be a fair place, and, when it's not, it is awful, and I can't stand it.	Fairness does not always rule. I am better off changing what I can and accepting what I cannot.
13	I should always live comfortably and without pain or distress.	I would do better to accept that pain and distress may visit me as it does most everyone else. I can live without perfection.
14	I must be going crazy if I am feeling anxiety.	I can learn to deal better with anxiety so that it affects me less or ends completely.
15	I can enjoy happiness the most through my inertia and inaction.	I am more likely to enjoy my life if I am an active player in it and strive toward worthy goals.

Source: Derived from several online sources and writings about REBT: https://www.padraigomorain.com/13-irrational-beliefs-albert-ellis/; http://www.rebtnetwork.org/library/ideas.html; https://nathensmiraculousescape.com/2010/05/17/albert-elliss-15-irrational-ideas/

are nondefensible and result in psychological, emotional, and/or physical symptoms.

Through his practice, he identified several IBs commonly held by his American clients (i.e., some of these IBs might not exist or be as prominent in other cultures). The more common ones are listed on the previous page and are accompanied by examples of their rational belief counterparts.

To help teach his method to students and clients, Ellis developed the ABCs of REBT, and later added a D and an E to his model (see Ross & Ellis, 2014). You may find it helpful to have a chart that you provide to your client (e.g., see https://positivepsychologyprogram.com/albert-ellis-abc-model-rebt-cbt/).

The ABCDE model is as follows:

A →	B →	C →
Activating Event	Beliefs	Consequences (emotional, mental, behavioral)
→		
D →	E →	
Disputing	Effect (Evaluation)	

The activating event (A) could be an actual event or a stream of cognitions (thoughts or images). The client's beliefs (B) become the moderating variable that largely determines the consequences (C). The process of doing REBT is to teach clients to dispute (D) the IBs but not the rational ones. Finally, the effect (E) of the disputing process is evaluated as to whether it succeeded in helping the individual reduce or eradicate the IBs that were causing much of the emotional distress. For example, imagine that you are a woman and your spouse has left you unexpectedly. How will you react? Here are three possibilities:

A →	B →	C →	D →	E →
My spouse just left me.	I need to have him in my life because I am nothing without him. He is all I live for.	Emotional: shocked, devastated, overwhelmed, diminished self-esteem and self-worth.	Where is the evidence that you are nothing without him? How are you less of a person without him? In what ways can you grow now that he has moved out?	If the disputing is effective: Rational beliefs surface and, the more they become internalized, the less intense the feelings.

A →	B →	C →	D →	E →
My spouse just left me.	I am surprised he left me like this, but I knew this was always a possibility. It will be difficult for a while, but I will be okay.	Emotional: surprised, sad, intact self-esteem and self-worth.	The beliefs expressed in column 2 (B) are rational beliefs. They do not need to be disputed. Instead, an REBT counselor would focus on helping her grieve and plan.	

A →	B →	C →	D →	E →
My spouse just left me.	That hateful man! He should have left 5 years ago. I knew I had made a mistake marrying him within the first 2 months.	Emotional: angry, relieved, intact self-esteem and self-worth.	The beliefs expressed in column 2 (B) are rational beliefs. They do not need to be disputed. Instead, an REBT counselor would focus on helping her work through her anger and plan.	

In REBT, clients are taught to discover and then dispute their IBs. Ellis wrote that people "easily can hold rational beliefs (RBs) lightly and weakly while still holding—and devoutly believing—IBs strongly and forcefully" (Ellis, 2011, p. 115). Clients' beliefs need to be vigorously disputed in this approach. The following are 12 questions that can be asked by both counselors and clients alike regarding their IBs:

1. What proof do I have that this is true?
2. Do I have any evidence that indicates it is not true?
3. Are there any competing "truths"? Is another belief just as valid?
4. Does everyone think this way? Why not?

5. Does agreeing with the majority on this make it necessarily correct?
6. Where did I learn this message? Is it possible that the messenger was wrong?
7. What purpose is served in continuing to believe this?
8. What price do I pay for continuing to believe this?
9. What will be the advantages of believing something different?
10. Are my feelings about this providing an accurate gauge of what I should believe?
11. If I were helping someone else deal with this, what would I want him to believe?
12. If I knew I would be dead tomorrow, would I be happy believing this?

Asking these questions is not always enough. Ellis (2011) offered a powerful way to dispute IBs. These instructions could be given to a client. Using a voice recording device, record one of your strong IBs into it. Write out several disputes to this IB and then present them strongly on the same recording. Using the example of a spouse suddenly leaving you, you might write down ideas like, "I can live without him. I have lived alone before, and I can do it again. I don't need to have someone living with me to prove my self-worth. Just because he doesn't want to be with me does not mean that I will necessarily remain alone and single forever, although I do have the choice of remaining alone and single." The next step is to record these disputes strongly and emphatically (i.e., with conviction). Next, listen to your disputing. Bring the recording with you to your next counseling session and share it.

Two other methods suggested by Ellis (2011) use either rational emotive imagery (REI) or role reversal. As Thorburn (2015) explained, REI was created by Maxie Maultsby and later adopted by Albert Ellis. Clients are asked to close their eyes and re-create a problematic situation (i.e., an activating event) in their mind's eye, allowing the emotions associated with it to re-emerge (i.e., the emotional consequence, C-1). Clients are then encouraged to change the emotion (i.e., C-2) but **not** to change their image of the problematic situation. Clients are taught to identify the changed emotion. REI is then assigned as regular homework for periods of 10–30 min. Several variations of the technique exist as revealed by a standard Google search. Role reversal is where someone else rigidly plays the role of the client while the client vigorously talks the individual out of their own IBs.

Although Albert Ellis was known for his disputing techniques, most practitioners:

> Will say that disputation is not the essential piece of REBT that leads to lasting change. Instead, most, if not all REBT practitioners, will say it is practicing the alternative, more functional and effective belief that will bring behavioral, cognitive, and emotional change. (Taboas, 2018, para. 1)

COUNSELING SCENARIO USING REBT

Imagine that you are the client in this scenario.

Your name is Kathy, a 25-year-old biology student. You are hoping to get accepted into medicine eventually. School is very stressful for you, and, to relax, you drink excessively. This is your second session with your counselor.

- Counselor: Hi, Kathy. Last week we talked about how you have been using alcohol as a means of coping with stress. I also taught you the ABC model of REBT and provided you the list of common irrational beliefs. Did you have an opportunity to look at these more carefully?
- You: Yes, George, I did. I certainly can relate to some of these beliefs. I never told you that I also have perfectionistic tendencies. I need to get As to have a chance of being admitted into medicine.
- Counselor: There is little dispute that you need high marks to get into medicine. What grades have you been earning?
- You: Mostly As but a few A– grades too. I keep thinking that I am not smart enough, however, to get into medicine. My high school counselor told me my IQ was average.
- Counselor: What impact does your belief in not being smart enough have in your life?
- You: I think it is the main reason why I drink so heavily. It temporarily stops the internal critic.
- Counselor: The impact of believing this is substantial. What evidence do you have that your IQ is limiting your abilities in university?
- You: My mind sometimes goes blank when I sit down to write an exam.
- Counselor: Okay, let's work with that. What other factors besides IQ might account for blanking on a test?
- You: Well, like I said, I am a perfectionist. Maybe I expect too much of myself?
- Counselor: Possibly. Do you relate to the second irrational belief on the list I gave you?
- You: Yes, I do. Whenever I get an A– grade, I feel like a complete failure. Those are the nights I get absolutely wrecked. I usually miss school the next day because the hangover is so severe.
- Counselor: I understand. You believe that you must get straight As, yet your studying is only one factor that

determines the grade you get on a test. What other factors affect your grade?

- You: Well, I don't get to pick the questions on a test. The professor can pick easy questions or hard ones. Also, I do not create the marking scheme for the test either.
- Counselor: Exactly! So, you are not the one who determines your grade. That is the job of the professor.
- You: Yes, that is true.
- Counselor: What, then, would be a healthier belief for you to adopt regarding your perfectionism?
- You: I do not control my grades; I only control my learning.
- Counselor: Wow, you really get it, Kathy. You control how well you learn the material, but you do not control the grade you get for your efforts. If you were a competent surgeon, for example, you cannot guarantee that your patient will live during or following the surgery. The only thing you have control over is using the best surgical techniques you have available to you. If the surgeon were to believe that she could guarantee the outcome, how much internal pressure would it create for her?
- You: I get it!
- Counselor: Now I'm going to ask you to put this together into a rational belief concerning your belief that you are smart enough to get into medicine. What would be a better thought to believe about your capability?
- You: The fact that I am earning A and A– grades is telling me that I am capable, and I have enough ability to possibly get into medicine.
- Counselor: Excellent work, Kathy! You are on a roll. Now it takes a lot of consistent effort to change our irrational beliefs so that they become rational. It is one thing to *know* something and another thing to really *believe* it deep within ourselves. What would be some ways that you could begin practicing the rational beliefs that you have noted here today?
- You: I could use the ABC method to challenge my thinking. If I do this regularly, I will begin to believe that I am a capable student.

From the Client's Perspective

1. As the client, what do you think you would like about this approach, and what would you dislike?
2. REBT requires that you practice regularly the rational beliefs. How would you feel about doing so if you were Kathy?
3. What would you find more helpful from a counselor in this scenario (if anything)?

From the Counselor's Perspective

1. There are many ways to do REBT. What would you do differently if you were the counselor in the previous scenario?
2. What other methods would you use to build an even stronger working alliance?
3. As the counselor, what do you think you would like about this approach, and what would you dislike?

HOW WOULD AN ADDICTION COUNSELOR HELP THIS CLIENT USING REBT?

You are working as a professional counselor. Marek, age 38, comes to see you for counseling. Marek has not used either cocaine or crack for 2 months. He is finding, however, that he has become especially prone to taking any indication of rejection from women he would like to date very deeply. He finds that his perception of rejection is all that is required to ruin his entire day and to feel at risk of relapsing. How would you help Marek?

Here are a few suggestions to help you get started. Marek needs to be approved of by all women that he would like to date.

1. What is irrational about having this belief?
2. Similar to the example provided previously, how could you go about helping Marek to come to this conclusion himself so that he is less likely to reject it?
3. If a woman does not want to date Marek, why should he not become upset by a woman saying "No" to his overture?
4. Lastly, what could you have him practice at home before his next session with you?

Cognitive Therapy

Aaron T. Beck (1921–) founded CT, primarily based on his work with depressed patients (Waltman, Sokol, & Beck, 2017). Wright et al. (2014) provided a recent account of CT's main techniques. Although Albert Ellis focused on his ABCDE model and on disputing IBs, Beck's approach followed a slightly different model, as follows:

Event →	Cognitive Appraisal (distorted) →	Emotion (e.g., depressed and/or anxious) →	Behavioral Inclination (e.g., helplessness, avoidance) →	Behavior (maladaptive) →

Beck and his colleagues (see Wright et al., 2014) believed that there are two levels of information processing: automatic thoughts and basic beliefs incorporated in schemas. *Automatic thoughts* are cognitions that rapidly occur when a person is either in a situation or recalling an event. Although clients may not be aware of these automatic thoughts, they can be accessed through the questioning techniques used in CT. Where the logic is faulty concerning an automatic thought, these are termed *cognitive errors*. Grohol (2018) noted and described the 15 most common cognitive errors that Beck theorized and David Burns popularized. The following are examples with accompanying explanations (adapted from Grohol, 2018):

#	Cognitive Error	Explanation
1	Filtering (or "Mental Filtering")	This occurs when one magnifies the negative aspects while *filtering* out the positive details in a situation.
2	Polarized Thinking (or "Black and White Thinking")	This is all-or-nothing-thinking. Either one is perfect or else a complete and utter failure.
3	Overgeneralization	If something bad happens once, one assumes it will continue to occur repeatedly.
4	Jumping to Conclusions	This occurs when one assumes that they know exactly what another person is thinking, feeling, and will do.
5	Catastrophizing	One assumes that the very worst will happen, and this will be a disaster.
6	Personalization	One believes that what others say and do is meant to be taken personally, even when that is not the other person's intention.
7	Control Fallacies (External or Internal)	This error has two components. If one is feeling externally controlled, one becomes a helpless victim of fate. Alternatively, one believes they are responsible for other people's pain or happiness, even when that has nothing to do with oneself.
8	Fallacy of Fairness	This is where one thinks that he or she knows what is fair even when other people do not agree.
9	Blaming	This occurs when one holds others responsible for one's emotional pain.
10	Shoulds	This is where one believes there are ironclad rules as to how to behave.
11	Emotional Reasoning	Believing that, if one feels a certain way, it must be true. One's feelings or emotions take over thinking rationally. For example, I feel jealous, so my partner must be cheating on me.
12	Fallacy of Change	Expecting that others will change if one cajoles or pressures them enough.
13	Global Labeling (or "Mislabeling")	This is where people generalize one or two qualities into an overall negative judgment regarding themselves or others.
14	Always Being Right	This is where people believe that their own opinions and actions are the absolute truth.
15	Heaven's Reward Fallacy	This is where people think that, if they practice sacrifice and self-denial, this will pay off later as though a more prominent force is keeping score.

The deep beliefs that people have internalized are called *schemas* in CT (Wright et al., 2014). Examples of adaptive schemas include "I'm lovable," "I'm a survivor," and "I like to be challenged." Examples of maladaptive schemas, on the other hand, include "I'm stupid," "I am unlovable," and "Without a romantic partner, I am worth nothing."

CT will usually last from five to 20 sessions (Wright et al., 2014). There is a high degree of collaboration between the counselor and the client. Together, they develop hypotheses about the validity of their automatic thoughts and schemas. In this approach, a series of exercises or experiments is often designed to test the validity of these hypotheses, a technique Beck called *collaborative empiricism* (Wright et al., 2014).

The counselor often acts as a teacher in CT. A commonly used technique is called *Socratic questioning*. The intent is to help clients move from having a "closed mind" about their automatic thoughts toward an attitude of inquisitiveness and curiosity. The purpose of the questioning is to help clients uncover or discover their dysfunctional cognitions (Wright et al., 2014). Once these cognitions are identified, CT counselors often use six techniques with clients to help them revise these: (a) creating alternatives, (b) looking carefully at the evidence, (c) de-catastrophizing, (d) re-attribution, (e) recording thoughts, and (f) cognitive rehearsal. In *examining the evidence*, several automatic thoughts are held up as hypotheses for the counselor and client to search for evidence supporting or refuting each hypothesis. *De-catastrophizing* is about looking at feared outcomes differently in a way that encourages better coping and problem-solving. *Re-attribution* consists of looking at other reasons that something unsettling might have occurred. *Cognitive rehearsal* is a common technique in CBT. Clients are asked to use imagery or roleplay to identify possible distorted cognitions that may arise in a stressful situation. Cognitive rehearsal is also used as a way for clients to practice adaptive automatic thoughts and rational responses (Wright et al., 2014).

One method that David Burns (2012) developed for helping counselors and clients challenge maladaptive automatic thoughts and replace these with functional thoughts is called the triple column technique (TCT). It can be used in two ways as you can see in the following table:

Automatic Thought or Belief	Questioning It OR Cognitive Error(s)	Healthier Thought or Belief
"I am good for nothing. I will never do well in math."	"Why do I believe this? Just because I failed a math exam doesn't mean I am no good. In my case, it means I didn't study enough, and I didn't answer enough practice questions. I need to work harder and smarter."	"I am a worthwhile person, but I need to work harder at math if I am going to do better at it."
OR "I am good for nothing. I will never do well in math."	Filtering Polarized Thinking Catastrophizing	Just because I did poorly on some math tests does not mean I am good for nothing. Maybe it says that I do not have much aptitude in math, or perhaps, if I studied more, I could do a lot better in math. Even if I fail in math, what is the big deal? I don't need it for most careers.

This is how you use the triple column:

1. Write out the thought(s) or belief(s) that is causing you to feel bad about yourself in the first column. You might already be aware of some of these, in which case you can record them now. Another approach is to wait until something triggers you to feel bad before making an entry.
2. In the second column, challenge the logic behind your thought or belief. Use the questions below to help you do this:
   a. What proof do I have that this is true?
   b. Do I have any evidence that indicates it is not true?
   c. Are there any competing "truths"? Is another belief just as valid?
   d. Does everyone think this way? Why not?
   e. Does agreeing with the majority on this make it necessarily correct?
   f. Where did I learn this message? Is it possible that the messenger was wrong?
   g. What purpose is served in continuing to believe this?
   h. What price do I pay for continuing to believe this?
   i. What will be the advantages of believing something different?
   j. Are my feelings about this providing an accurate gauge of what I should believe?
   k. If I were helping someone else deal with this, what would I want him to believe?
   l. If I knew I would be dead tomorrow, would I be happy believing this?

   Once you have challenged your thinking, write out the challenge in the second column.
3. In the third column, write out a healthier thought(s) or belief(s) that you would like to substitute for the one written in the first column.
4. Spend time focusing on the thought(s) or belief(s) written in the third column. The more you absorb yourself in repeating the thought(s) or belief(s), the more you will internalize it.
5. Whenever you catch yourself again repeating similar negative thoughts to yourself, either again write it down and repeat steps 2 through 5 or do the work in your head by talking to yourself, either silently or out loud. Remember to do the challenge and then substitute the healthier thought or belief.

As Wright et al. (2014) stated, as is the same for REBT, much of the work of CT is about recognizing and then changing negatively distorted, illogical, or maladaptive automatic thoughts. Another helpful form is Beck's *Daily Record of Dysfunctional Thoughts* (available from http://advancedpsychcare.tripod.com/sitebuildercontent/sitebuilderfiles/dysfunc.thoughts.pdf or search in Google images). This form contains six columns where clients record the date, the situation leading to unpleasant emotions, specifying and rating the experienced emotions, documenting the automatic thoughts, providing a rational response, and rating the outcome.

COUNSELING SCENARIO USING CT

Imagine that you are the client in this scenario.

Your name is Travis, a 19-year-old who dropped out of school as soon as you turned 16. You were much more interested in using crystal meth than you were in paying attention at school. After spending the last 6 years using meth, you decided to stop 2 months ago. You go to see an addiction counselor who practices CT. This is your first session.

- Counselor: Hi Travis, come on in.
- You: Thank you. I have been looking forward to our session.
- Counselor: I am glad to hear that. What brings you to see me today?
- You: I have used a lot of meth over the years, and I am afraid I will go back to using.
- Counselor: It sounds like you have already stopped using . . . is this correct?
- You: Yes, I stopped about 8 weeks ago.
- Counselor: That is fantastic, Travis! It is not easy to make such an important change. You are concerned that you could relapse. What would be the most likely reason that might lead you back to using?
- You: I think my thoughts; that is why I came to see you.
- Counselor: What sorts of thoughts are worrisome to you?
- You: Well, I keep thinking my life will not be fun anymore. I keep thinking that my girlfriend will lose interest in me because I am not so upbeat like I was on meth. I mean, I used to have tons of energy and I could be sexually active all night!
- Counselor: Would it be okay if we deal with your thoughts one at a time?
- You: Sure.
- Counselor: Which belief would you like to focus on first?
- You: Well, my thought that I won't ever have fun again. That one is really eating me up.
- Counselor: What events have led you to think that fun will forever be vanquished from your life?
- You: Hum, just the way you said that has me thinking. Sex, for example, is not half as much fun as it used to be. I have also become much quieter, and my girlfriend has told me that she misses the "old me."
- Counselor: As you know, meth is a powerful stimulant, but also a dangerous one. If you never experienced the same intensity of high from everyday activities as you used to when taking meth, to what extent would that mean that you are no longer having fun?
- You: I see where you are going with that. I can still have fun. . . I just won't have the unnatural high to go with it that meth used to provide.
- Counselor: Right on, Travis. Precisely! Is a little bit of fun still an example of having fun?
- You: Yes, it is, but I guess I really want to have the intensity of fun like when I'm high.
- Counselor: [hands out the list of cognitive errors] You miss that intensity. Here is a sheet that lists the most common thinking errors that people make. A thinking error creates a feeling of greater hardship than a situation justifiably deserves. Please take a few moments to read through the list. Tell me if you see the errors your mind is making that makes a little fun seem like no fun at all.
- You: [after a few minutes] It looks like it is an example of overgeneralization, catastrophizing, and emotional reasoning.
- Counselor: Very good. Which error would you like to spend some time on first?
- You: Let's begin with emotional reasoning.
- Counselor: Great. Before we get into this, you need to know that, because you had been taking meth for a long time, your brain needs time to heal. A common withdrawal effect is feeling that activities that used to be pleasurable no longer provide much or any pleasure. Were you aware of this?

- You: No, I didn't know that.
- Counselor: Now that you know this, how much should you trust that your feelings are providing an accurate account of what is real?
- You: I guess it could mean that I feel like everything is less enjoyable, but, like you said, it might be because my brain is fried.
- Counselor: [chuckles] I don't mean fried, Travis. But I do mean that the neurotransmitters in your brain need time to become restored. Do you understand what I just said?
- You: I do. I learned about neurotransmitters after my girlfriend became depressed a couple of years ago.
- Counselor: Okay. Given all this, how much should you trust your emotions?
- You: Not at all apparently. I need to give myself time to heal.
- Counselor: That's right. You also mentioned overgeneralization. How does that cognitive error apply to your belief that life will never be fun again?
- You: I cannot assume that, just because I am not having fun now, it will always look and feel like this.
- Counselor: That's right. We are just about out of time. Would you like to talk about some natural ways that can promote healing of your brain and possibly stimulate greater release of neurotransmitters before we finish?
- You: I would love that!
- Counselor: [moves collaboratively into exploring mindfulness, meditation, exercise, etc.]

From the Client's Perspective

1. As the client, what do you think you would like about this approach, and what would you dislike?
2. CT requires that you keep replacing maladaptive thoughts with healthy thoughts. How would you feel about doing so if you were Travis?
3. What would you find more helpful from a counselor in this scenario (if anything)?

From the Counselor's Perspective

1. There are many ways to do CT. What would you do differently if you were the counselor in the previous scenario?
2. What other methods would you use to build an even stronger working alliance?
3. As the counselor, what do you think you would like about this approach, and what would you dislike?

HOW WOULD AN ADDICTION COUNSELOR HELP THIS CLIENT USING CT?

You are working as a professional counselor. Jillian, age 17, comes to see you for counseling. Now that she is no longer drinking, she is socially anxious. She wants to go to parties but, in the past, when she wasn't drunk, she was a "wallflower" (i.e., she did not talk to anyone but instead would hang around looking at everyone else). How would you help Jillian?

Here are a few suggestions to help you get started. Jillian believes that she "should" enjoy socializing and that it is a catastrophe when she cannot engage others at a party.

1. Which cognitive errors is Jillian making?
2. What automatic thoughts likely accompany Jillian's anxiety?
3. What rational responses would be helpful for Jillian to write down and spend time practicing regularly?
4. If Jillian were to take ministeps at getting used to talking to strangers, what experiments could she practice?

New Wave Cognitive-Behavioral Therapy

Two newer approaches are sometimes referred to as either *new wave CBT* (Csiernik, 2016) or *third wave CBT* (Thoma, Pilecki, & McKay, 2015). The first is dialectical behavior therapy (DBT), and the other is acceptance and commitment therapy (ACT). DBT was developed by Marsha Linehan and her colleagues in the early 1990s. It is typically viewed as a combination of CBT and mindfulness practices derived from Buddhist meditation (Csiernik, 2016). The main goal of DBT is to balance acceptance and change, which is a middle position common to Zen practice (Gladding & Alderson, 2012). DBT is also an empirically supported treatment for borderline personality disorder (Gladding & Alderson, 2012).

Stephen Hayes developed ACT during the 1990s. It was designed to integrate acceptance and mindfulness with commitment and behavior change strategies (Gladding & Alderson, 2012). The primary goal of ACT is to teach people to become more flexible and to experience the present moment more fully and consciously (i.e., mindfulness). Another goal is to either change or continue behavior that serves a purpose valued by the client. Counselors are active in sessions, and they work to promote values clarification and encourage clients to act according to their values.

Behavioral Therapy

One of the hallmarks of behavioral treatment is the development of individualized treatment plans that are created collaboratively with the client (Marinchak & Morgan, 2012). Studies have revealed that clients ultimately decide on their substance use goals regardless of what counselors think (Marinchak & Morgan, 2012). Progress toward goals is also continually evaluated.

Behavioral therapists have many techniques that they use. Tucker-Ladd (1996–2018) conveniently organized many of these techniques based on what stage in the behavioral process they are administered. It is organized as follows: (a) *antecedent methods* that are used before the target behavior, (b) techniques that are used *during the behavior*, and (c) *consequence methods* that are administered after the target behavior occurs (note: the author makes his clearly explained "outstanding" self-help book downloadable for free; visit https://www.psychologicalselfhelp.org/ for explanations and examples of each technique). The following is from Chapter 11 in Tucker-Ladd:

Antecedent methods.

These include the following: (a) change the environment to modify your behavior, (b) learn new behavior (e.g., use models, self-instruction), (c) use controlling or conditioned responses, (d) relapse prevention, (e) motivation training to increase drive level, (f) ensure basic needs are met, so they do not hinder progress, and (g) help clients become aware of their motives and defense mechanisms.

Techniques used during the behavior.

These include the following: (a) record behavior (self-monitor to check progress), (b) record the antecedents and consequences, which produces a behavioral analysis, (c) disrupt the unwanted habit (e.g., thought stopping), (d) substitute new behaviors to break bad habits, (e) satiate the behavior (e.g., flooding) or use paradoxical intention, (f) quiet the internal critic by changing defeatist attitudes, (g) build self-efficacy by developing positive expectations, and (h) work at increasing the intrinsic satisfaction in activities.

Consequence methods.

These include the following: (a) reward the desired behavior, (b) utilize negative reinforcement, (c) self-punishment, (d) covert conditioning, punishment, and rewards, and (e) extinction through not reinforcing the target behaviors. If Tucker-Ladd's (1996–2018) materials are being used as self-help and the client does not know which method to begin with, he recommended (a) change the environment to modify your behavior, (b) learn new behavior (e.g., use models, self-instruction), and (c) reward the desired behavior.

Contingency management.

In a large independent analysis, Dutra et al. (2008) found that contingency management was the *most* effective psychosocial intervention for substance use disorders (SUDs). Contingency management involves rearranging that contingencies in an addict's life such that refraining from the addictive substance or behavior becomes more rewarding than engaging in the problematic behavior (Larios et al., 2013). Using operant conditioning, clients are rewarded (or reward themselves) for behaviors that do not involve the addictive substance or behavior. This will include all areas of the client's life.

BUILD A SELF-HELP PROGRAM FOR YOURSELF USING TUCKER-LADD'S MATERIAL

Think of a behavior you would like to either diminish or increase. Now download Tucker-Ladd's (1996–2018) Chapter 11 from https://www.psychologicalselfhelp.org/. From the methods noted previously (which are described in simple terms in his Chapter 11) regarding antecedents, the actual behavior, and consequences, design a self-help program for yourself. For example, if you wanted to stop smoking cigarettes, how would your program look if you simply used the three methods that Tucker-Ladd highlighted [i.e., (a) change the environment to modify your behavior, (b) learn new behavior (e.g., use models, self-instruction), and (c) reward the desired behavior]? What other methods noted previously would likely prove helpful to you?

An example of a contingency management program would include creating a token economy. In a token economy program, individuals receive "tokens" that can later be turned into rewards (clients can create these as a self-help program as well). If you were developing a token economy for your child, you might give a bronze, silver, or gold star daily that your child sticks on the appropriate date on a monthly calendar. Beforehand, you establish what level of behavior is needed to earn each star (e.g., bronze = screamed twice; silver = screamed once; gold = no screams). Then, the reward can follow daily (stay up by 15, 30, or 60 min, respectively) or weekly (seven gold stars = stays up 2 hr later on Friday *and* Saturday; five gold stars = stays up 2 hr later only one night).

An excellent resource for developing a contingency management program for substance abuse treatment is written by Petry (2012). Petry (2012) stated that the three key principles of a contingency management program include (a) frequently monitoring the desired behavior, (b) providing tangible and immediate positive reinforcement each time the desired behavior occurs, and (c) withholding the positive reinforcers when the desired behavior does *not* happen. In a treatment program, reinforcers might include privileges, vouchers, and prizes (Higgins, Badger, & Budney, 2000). Social reinforcers can also be used, such as making positive statements (e.g., "You're doing a fantastic job!" or "I am really proud of you!"; Higgins et al., 2000).

Marinchak and Morgan (2012) described some additional methods that can be used specifically for SUDs. These include the following:

1. Aversion treatments. Although electrical and chemical aversion techniques were used in the past, they have demonstrated inconsistent empirical support. One method that is still used is called covert sensitization. This is where the client either verbalizes or imagines the negative aspects of their addiction (e.g., imagine you are high, and you are vomiting profusely; each vivid detail will be described).
2. Cue exposure. The intent is to extinguish conditioned behavioral responses wherein clients are exposed to their addictive substance or behavior (i.e., the stimuli) but the client is unable to execute their desired response (e.g., to partake in the addictive substance or behavior). Unfortunately, exposure alone does not create substantial long-term effects, which means other elements must be included such as self-efficacy and coping skills training.
3. Behavioral self-control training (BSCT). BSCT is one of the most widely researched treatments in the alcohol field. This is a brief, educationally oriented approach for clients to achieve their goal of either abstinence or reduce drinking. Nonetheless, clients maintain the primary responsibility for making their own decisions during treatment. BSCT usually consists of between six and 12 90-min sessions. Here are the components of the program:
    a. Set limits on the number of drinks per day.
    b. Self-monitor drinking behaviors.
    c. Change the rate of drinking.
    d. Practice refusing drinks.
    e. Reward self for achieving goals.
    f. Learn the antecedents that occur before excessive drinking.
    g. Learn additional coping skills to replace drinking.

    Marinchak and Morgan (2012) emphasized that homework, roleplaying, and practice are important aspects of BSCT.
4. Social skills training. This training focuses not only on clients' substance use but also on other problem areas associated with it. Clients are taught assertiveness, relaxation, effective communication, problem-solving skills, refusal skills, planning ahead for high-risk situations, increasing pleasant activities, developing a support network of sober individuals, etc.
5. Contingency management. Programs based on contingency management use an operant conditioning paradigm that rewards desirable behaviors while punishing undesirable ones.
6. Relapse prevention. Today, some argue that negative mood states are associated with relapse. A relapse prevention protocol, then, may incorporate mindfulness and acceptance techniques as a different way of dealing with negative effects.

Motivational Interviewing and Motivational Enhancement Therapy

Motivational Interviewing

Miller and Rollnick (2013) created motivational interviewing (MI). It is a directive, client-centered counseling style focusing on helping clients explore and resolve their ambivalence regarding change. There are five basic principles intrinsic to MI:

1. Express empathy. MI counselors work hard at active listening and demonstrating empathy with their clients.
2. Help clients recognize discrepancies between their current behavior and their future goals. MI counselors point out discrepancies between clients' current behaviors and their goals.
3. Avoid unnecessary arguments. MI counselors avoid arguments wherever possible as they often create resistance to change.
4. Accept that resistance and ambivalence are normal. MI counselors explore both resistance and ambivalence openly.
5. Support clients' self-efficacy. MI counselors help clients build their confidence toward making changes.

MI is meant for individuals who have not decided yet to make a change in their addictive behavior. In fact, Miller and Rollnick

(2013) provided evidence suggesting that, if an individual is already in the "action stage" (i.e., they are already taking steps to change), MI "can defer [their] progress" (p. 128). MI is not about giving information or advice either unless permission from the client is provided first (Miller & Rollnick, 2013). Often clients already know the advice you are thinking of providing to them, so it is usually better to first ask your clients, for example, "What do you know about the effect of alcohol on the developing fetus?" If clients respond with, "Nothing at all," then the follow-up question is, "May I provide you information on this topic?"

Some useful questions to use in MI include the following from Csiernik (2016, p. 254): (a) "What do you make of all of this?," (b) "Where does this leave you?," and (c) "What do you want to do next?" Three other good questions offered by Earleywine (2016, p. 63) include (a) "What would it take to increase the costs of not changing?," (b) "What would it take to increase the benefits of change?," and (c) "Where do you see this behavior going in the near future?"

An important aspect of change is for it to feel voluntary to clients. As Miller and Rollnick (2013) noted, "People want to have a say in changes that affect them and some time to absorb, reflect, and move on. Change without engagement often feels coercive and is likely to evoke discord" (p. 361).

There are four processes in MI, including engaging, focusing, evoking, and planning.

> *Engaging* is the process by which both parties establish a helpful connection and a working relationship. . . . *Focusing* is the process by which you develop and maintain a specific direction in the conversation about change. . . . *Evoking* involves eliciting the client's own motivations for change, and it has always been at the heart of MI. . . . *Planning* encompasses both developing commitments to change and formulating a specific plan of action. (Miller & Rollnick, 2013, pp. 26–30)

In other words, engaging is about building rapport, focusing is about creating a direction for change talk, evoking brings out the client's motivations for change, and planning is about both developing commitment to change and creating the plan of action. It might also be helpful to know what MI is *not*. Miller and Rollnick (2009) answered this question. MI is ***not*** the following:

1. The transtheoretical model of change (Not).
2. Manipulating people to get them to do what you want (Not).
3. A technique (Not).
4. A decisional balance (this is where you review the pros and cons of continuing an addictive behavior with your client) (Not).
5. Required assessment feedback (Not).
6. A form of cognitive-behavioral therapy (Not).
7. Just client-centered therapy packaged differently (Not).
8. Easy to learn (Not).
9. The same as what you were already doing (Not).
10. A panacea (Not).

Motivational Enhancement Therapy

The National Institute on Alcohol Abuse and Alcoholism (NIAAA) instituted a 5-year project called MATCH in 1989. The study involved nine different sites. The NIAAA created a brief, four-session, manual-based version of MI they called motivational enhancement therapy (MET). Their manual is available at no charge from https://pubs.niaaa.nih.gov/publications/ProjectMatch/match02.pdf Project MATCH was compared with 12-session interventions that used either CBT or 12-step facilitation. The four-session MATCH program was as efficacious as the longer programs regarding improving drinking-related outcomes (Petry, Ledgerwood, & McKay, 2014).

COUNSELING SCENARIO USING MI

Imagine that you are the client in this scenario.

Your name is Randy, and you are a rebellious 15-year-old. Nearly every night, you're drinking several ounces of alcohol and getting high from smoking marijuana. Consequently, your grades have really suffered. Your school is even thinking of kicking you out. You were sent to a counselor in fact by the principal. This is your first session.

- Counselor: Hello, Randy, nice to meet you.
- You: I wish I could say the same, but I do not want to be here. Nothing against you, however.
- Counselor: Thank you for clarifying that it was not something I did already.
- You: No, it's not your fault I was sent to see you.
- Counselor: Why were you sent to see me, Randy?
- You: My school is thinking of kicking me out because I drink too much, and I smoke too much weed.
- Counselor: I see. What effect is your alcohol and drug use having on you?

- You: Not much. Makes me popular with my classmates.
- Counselor: Smoking weed and drinking has helped you in some ways in your social circle.
- You: Yeah. I like being popular at school.
- Counselor: What other reasons do you think people like you?
- You: Not much. I think mostly because I drink and smoke pot. I'm pretty stupid when it comes to school.
- Counselor: What leads you to think that you are not very intelligent?
- You: You would know why if you saw my grades. They suck!
- Counselor: I assume you used to do better at school than you do now.
- You: I did. Before I found friends and started hanging out with cool people, my marks were a lot better.
- Counselor: So, something changed when you met your friends. What was it?
- You: I started drinking and smoking weed with them.
- Counselor: Your marks started to suffer when you began drinking and smoking weed.
- You: I guess you could say that.
- Counselor: It sounds like you are aware that these activities are hurting your school performance.
- You: Yeah, but what am I supposed to do about it?
- Counselor: I appreciate that you trust me enough to ask for my advice. What have you thought about doing differently?
- You: I have wondered if only drinking and smoking marijuana on weekends would make much difference.
- Counselor: It sounds like you have given some serious thought about how you could do better at school.
- You: I have, but my friends want to use all the time.
- Counselor: Your friends have a lot of influence in your life on the one hand, but, on the other, you see how your alcohol and drug use is affecting you negatively.
- You: I hate to admit it, but you are correct.
- Counselor: I can tell in your voice that you are discouraged and sad knowing this.
- You: I don't want to get kicked out of school. My parents won't let me stay at home if I get kicked out and the nearest school to where I attend is 5 miles away!
- Counselor: Boy, I sure understand why you want to stay in your present school!
- You: I guess I just don't know what to do.
- Counselor: It must be confusing for you wanting to do well in school yet keep your close friends.
- You: I wouldn't say they are close friends. They are just friends.
- Counselor: Sorry, you did not tell me they were close friends: I just assumed that. Do you have other friends that are closer to you?
- You: Not really. I have been a loner in school until I met this bunch. They are all I have.
- Counselor: Your need to belong is understandable, Randy. You have these friends, and every day they want to drink and smoke marijuana, yet you have found it interferes with your ability to do well at school. Did I understand you correctly?
- You: Yes [tears are forming in his eyes].
- Counselor: You have a lovely personality, Randy. Things that are getting in your way from succeeding really matter to you.
- You: I know. I am so scared.
- Counselor: I know.

From the Client's Perspective

1. As the client, what do you think you would like about this approach, and what would you dislike?
2. MI requires that the counselor maintain a warm and accepting demeanor. How would you feel about the way the counselor treated you?
3. What would you find more helpful from a counselor in this scenario (if anything)?

From the Counselor's Perspective

1. What would you do differently if you were the counselor in the previous scenario while still maintaining the perspective of MI?
2. What other methods would you use to build an even stronger working alliance?
3. As the counselor, what do you think you would like about this approach, and what would you dislike?

HOW WOULD AN ADDICTION COUNSELOR HELP THIS CLIENT USING MI?

You are working as a professional counselor. Arlene, age 29, comes to see you. Since she was 21 years old, she has been going to the casino regularly. Once she begins, she does not stop before she has spent far more than she earns in her job. Her credit cards are nearly at the top of her credit limit. She is looking really distraught as she enters your office.

Here are a few suggestions to help you get started. Arlene has shared with you the financial consequences of her problematic gambling. She is also feeling a great deal of emotion.

1. Which emotions is Arlene likely feeling?
2. How could you help Arlene create a discrepancy between her actions (i.e., excessive gambling) and her feelings (e.g., feeling distraught)?
3. Without manipulating her, how could you help Arlene decide if keeping credit cards is in her best interest right now?
4. How would you begin the session so that Arlene becomes quickly engaged?

Transtheoretical Model of Change

The transtheoretical model was developed by James Prochaska and Carlo DiClemente in the late 1970s and early 1980s (Prochaska & DiClemente, 2005). It is sometimes referred to by its abbreviation TTM, and occasionally it is called the stages of change model. The model itself is based on extensive research that revealed that people change when they are ready to change.

Before the TTM, low motivation was often considered a deficiency within the client. Some people were reportedly told, "Come back when you're motivated" or "You haven't suffered enough yet. We'll see you when you hit bottom" (Miller, 2016, p. 102). TTM and MI have provided counselors with approaches and methods by which to help clients develop a greater motivation to change.

Trying to push someone to change before they want to is like trying to make the proverbial donkey drink water because you command it. A few of the techniques in TTM are similar to those of MI. These include eliciting self-motivational statements, listening with empathy, asking open-ended questions, affirming the client, handling resistance, reframing meanings and perspectives, and summarizing content and feelings for clients.

Within the TTM, the four important constructs include the stages of change, processes of change, the pros and cons of change (also called the decisional balance), and the levels of change (Prochaska & DiClemente, 2005). Each of these will be explained.

Six Stages of Change

Because of the large research base supporting the TTM regarding addiction treatment, Chapters 9 through 21 use the first five stages to organize interventions at each stage.

1. Stage 1. Precontemplation. Individuals in the precontemplation stage are not ready to make a change. Consequently, they have no intent to change. People at this stage may be in denial that the behavior in question is causing them difficulties, or they really believe that the pros of doing their behavior outweigh the cons of stopping it. How do you help someone move to the next stage? Connors, DiClemente, Velasquez, and Donovan (2013) suggested that counselors can help clients increase awareness of the negative consequences of the behavior, create interest and concern, and assist them in evaluating whether they can indeed learn to self-regulate the behavior. They also stressed that counselors should not focus on behavior change but, instead, use motivational strategies (such as MI). According to Connors et al., the critical task during the precontemplation stage is to generate concern, interest, and hope.

2. Stage 2. Contemplation. Individuals in the contemplation stage have an awareness that their behavior is causing them some difficulty. They are thinking about changing but have not committed to it. People at this stage seek information about their problem, and they begin evaluating the pros and cons of change. Connors et al. (2013) suggested that counselors help their clients decide to act and then to engage in some preliminary action. According to Connors et al., the critical tasks during the contemplation stage are to resolve ambivalence, help clients create a risk-reward analysis, and assist in decision-making.

3. Stage 3. Preparation. Individuals in Stage 3 are getting prepared to make a change. In other words, they have decided that they want to make a change and may have taken some small steps toward it. Most people in the preparation stage plan to take action within the next month (Prochaska, Norcross, & DiClemente, 1994). Connors et al. (2013) suggested that counselors could help clients set their goals and priorities to create change (i.e., develop an acceptable and effective change plan). According to Connors et al., the critical task during the preparation stage is to work at building commitment through planning and prioritizing.

4. Stage 4. Action. Individuals in Stage 4 are now beginning their change plan. They might be both modifying their problematic behavior and acquiring new, healthier behaviors. Some of the skills learned in this stage are focused on relapse prevention (i.e., helping reduce the likelihood of lapse and relapse and, if either occurs, how to rebound back from it). Connors et al. (2013) recommended that counselors help clients apply their behavior change methods and to continue to do so for an average of 6 months. According to Connors et al., the critical tasks during the action stage are to help clients implement the plan, overcome obstacles, build self-efficacy, and revise the plan as needed.

5. Stage 5. Maintenance. Individuals move into the maintenance stage if they have sustained effective action for at least 6 months and are continuing to work at preventing relapse. People need to become aware of situations (especially stressful situations) that may tempt them to slide back into doing their problematic behavior. Connors et al. (2013) suggested that counselors could help clients integrate change into their lifestyles. According to Connors et al., the critical tasks during the maintenance stage are to help clients sustain change, prevent relapse, integrate changes into their lifestyles, and avoid becoming fatigued through their change efforts.

6. Stage 6. Termination. Stage 6 does not occur for many, perhaps most, addicts. In the termination stage, individuals have zero temptation, and they are sure that they will never return to their old, unhealthy behavior(s). Prochaska and Velicer (1997) suggested that addicts might be in the termination stage if they have maintained their new behavior for more than 5 years and that they can rate their self-efficacy to avoid their problematic behavior indefinitely at 100%.

Ten Processes of Change

The 10 processes of change are theorized to be most effective during different stages of change. These are also noted in the following regarding what counselors can do with these 10 processes (note that individuals wishing to make a change can do these processes themselves). Furthermore, when these processes are used is considered important in helping clients move forward through the stages; from Table 2.2 in Connors et al., 2013, p. 21):

1. Consciousness raising (getting the facts). Counselors help clients increase their awareness by giving them information, education, and personal feedback regarding healthy behavior. [Predominantly used from precontemplation to contemplation stages]

2. Emotional arousal (paying attention to feelings; also called dramatic relief). Counselors help clients experience and identify the fear, anxiety, grief, shame, guilt, and/or worry concerning their unhealthy behavior. Counselors can also help inspire clients and instill hope by telling them that they can change to healthy behaviors (perhaps by providing them examples of others who have done so). Csiernik (2016) suggested psychodrama and personal testimonies as ways of helping clients move forward emotionally. [Predominantly used from precontemplation to contemplation stages]

3. Self-re-evaluation (creating a new self-image). Counselors help clients realize that healthy behavior is a part of who they are and who they wish to become. Techniques to use here include values clarification, imagery, and developing healthy role models (Csiernik, 2016). [Predominantly used from precontemplation to contemplation stages; also, from contemplation to preparation stages]

4. Environmental re-evaluation (noticing your effect on others). Counselors help clients develop insights as to how their unhealthy behavior affects others and how their influence could become positive if they change. Csiernik (2016) stated that this process involves training clients to become empathic. [Predominantly used from precontemplation to contemplation stages; also, from contemplation to preparation stages]

5. Social liberation (noticing public support). Counselors help clients appreciate that society becomes more supportive when they are exemplifying healthy behavior. This can be facilitated by assisting clients in engaging in non-drug-related behaviors and by teaching them to consider the needs of others. The intent is to increase their social opportunities and behavioral alternatives (Csiernik, 2016). [Predominantly used from contemplation to preparation stages; also, throughout the maintenance stage]

6. Self-liberation (making a commitment). Counselors help clients increase their self-efficacy (i.e., their ability to change and make commitments and recommitments to being faithful to their beliefs). Csiernik (2016) added that motivation research has found that, when people have two choices/options, they become more motivated than if they only have one choice/option before them. [Used during transitions between all stages]

7. Stimulus control (managing or changing one's environment). Counselors help clients use reminders and cues to encourage them to engage in healthy behaviors instead of unhealthy ones. This also involves changing one's environment to make engaging in healthy behaviors easier (e.g., if quitting smoking, get rid of all cigarettes and ashtrays and ask other smokers in the house to not smoke in front of them; avoid others who use). [Used from preparation to action stages; from action to maintenance stages; also, throughout the maintenance stage]

8. Counterconditioning (using substitutes). Counselors help clients identify their unhealthy behaviors and find (and practice) alternative healthy ways of acting and thinking. For example, relaxation can be substituted for stress, assertion instead of succumbing to peer pressure, and nicotine replacement instead of smoking cigarettes (Csiernik, 2016). [Used from preparation to action stages; from action to maintenance stages; also, throughout the maintenance stage]

9. Reinforcement management (using rewards; also called contingency management). Counselors help clients to

reinforce or increase the rewards that come from acting positively and reducing behaviors that result in negative consequences. [Used from action to maintenance stages; also, throughout the maintenance stage]

10. Helping relationships (getting support). Counselors can help clients identify others who are currently supportive of their change and teach them how to develop new connections with other supportive individuals. [Used from preparation to action stages; from action to maintenance stages; also, throughout the maintenance stage]

Pros and Cons of Changing/Decisional Balance

Prochaska and DiClemente (2005) noted that there remain clear and consistent relationships that occur between the stages of change, and part of this is the pros and cons of changing that arise at each stage. Counselors can help clients create a decisional balance worksheet. Create a large square with four boxes. In the top left corner, print "Supporting the Status Quo" and, in the top right corner, "Promoting Change." In the bottom left, print "Positives of the Behavior" (leave space for the client to write under the heading) followed by "Negatives of the Change" (again, leave space underneath for writing). In the bottom right, print "Negatives of the Behavior" followed by "Positives of the Change."

Levels of Change

The fourth component of the TTM is the levels of change (Prochaska & DiClemente, 2005). This component comprises a hierarchy of five different but interrelated levels of psychological problems that can be addressed in counseling. The five levels are (a) symptom/situational problems, (b) maladaptive cognitions, (c) current interpersonal conflicts, (d) family/systems conflicts, and (e) intrapersonal conflicts. In the transtheoretical approach, Prochaska and DiClemente (2005) preferred to intervene initially at the symptom/situational level. This is because change tends to occur more rapidly at this level, and it is often the reason the individual entered counseling. Furthermore, change at one level is likely to create change at other levels. For example, symptom/situational problems tend to be associated with intrapersonal conflicts. The same is true for other levels.

Mindfulness Treatments

Li et al. (2017) conducted a meta-analysis of mindfulness treatments (also commonly referred to as mindfulness meditation) for substance misuse. They identified 42 pertinent studies. The meta-analysis revealed significant small-to-large effects of mindfulness treatments in reducing (a) intensity of cravings, (b) severity of stress, and (c) the frequency and severity of substance misuse. Gryczynski et al. (2018) tested transcendental meditation with 60 individuals with alcohol use disorder (AUD) (35% female, 60% White) and found that those who practiced mindfulness meditation regularly experienced less stress, psychological distress, craving, and alcohol use at 3-month follow-up.

Kabat-Zinn (2013) defined mindfulness as "the awareness that arises by paying attention on purpose, in the present moment, and non-judgmentally" (p. xxxiv). More succinctly, "mindfulness is moment-to-moment non-judgmental awareness" (Kabat-Zinn, 2013, p. xlix). Mindfulness-based stress reduction (MBSR) is situated within mindfulness practice, and it is defined as "becoming aware of what is on our minds from moment to moment, and of how our experience is transformed when we do" (Kabat-Zinn, 2013, p. xxxiii). Kabat-Zinn requires his patients to practice MSBR with CDs for 45 min per day, 6 days a week, for the 8 weeks of the program.

Tang, Tang, and Posner (2016) conducted a series of RCTs and found that, after training and mindful meditation, both smokers and nonsmokers improved their abilities in emotion regulation and stress reduction. Dicken (2016) found in her dissertation research that mindfulness-based cognitive therapy (MBCT) was significantly helpful in attenuating addictive behaviors. Hoppes (2016) reported similar results in treating co-occurring addiction and mood disorders with MBCT.

Despite the promising results of using mindfulness in treating addictions, the review by Wilson et al. (2017) suggested that there is a lack of clear empirical guidelines in several areas, including (a) required training for providers of mindfulness-based interventions (MBIs), (b) adaptations to the traditional 2-hour closed-group format, (c) how to deliver MBIs in individual formats, (d) how to provide MBIs at different stages of change, (e) how to deliver MBIs using technology, and (f) how to deliver MBIs precisely. A need for further research is indicated.

Brief Interventions

As the SAMHSA-HRSA Center for Integrated Health Solutions (n.d.) described, brief interventions are meant to motivate individuals at risk for abusing substances to change their behavior. These interventions are evidence-based, and, in primary care settings, they may last anywhere from 5 min of advice to 15–30 min of brief counseling. The brief counseling offered is often CBT or MI. The empirical research regarding brief interventions provides mixed results. Some studies suggest they are not effective (Glass et al., 2015; Petry, Rash, & Alessi, 2016), whereas other studies have found the opposite (Elzerbi, Donoghue, & Drummond, 2015; Rudzinski et al., 2012). Perhaps the safest conclusion is that "brief interventions are useful in opportunistic samples" (Moyer, Finney, Swearingen, & Vergun, 2002, p. 279).

The World Health Organization (Humeniuk, Henry-Edwards, Ali, Poznyak, & Monteiro, 2010) created the Alcohol, Smoking, and Substance Involvement Screening Test (ASSIST) and developed brief interventions to be used with it (their manual is available from http://apps.who.int/iris/bitstream/handle/10665/44321/9789241599399_eng.pdf;sequence=1). Another good resource is the SAMHSA-HRSA Center for Integrated Health Solutions (n.d.; visit https://www.integration.samhsa.gov/clinical-practice/sbirt/brief-interventions).

Integrative Therapy

Integrative therapies (ITs) combine mainstream therapies (i.e., psychological and pharmacological) with complementary and alternative therapies (Morrison, Lin, & Gersh, 2018). ITs may include acupuncture, yoga, exercise, mindfulness, hypnosis, biofeedback, neurofeedback, music and art therapy, and herbal therapies. A book by Mistral (2016) focused on integrated approaches with drug and alcohol problems.

Morrison et al. (2018) argued that an integrated approach is often preferable in working with addicted clients. Studies using integrative treatments have focused on cigarette smoking, alcohol, and opiate use disorders. Women addicted to heroin have found group music therapy helpful in changing their moods, energy level, sense of self, and level of enjoyment (Gardstrom, Klemm, & Murphy, 2017); various types of acupuncture have proven helpful with recovery (Baker & Chang, 2016; Liang, Lin, Zhang, Ungvari, & Tang, 2016; Wu, Leung, & Yew, 2016); hypnosis may assist in pain management (Bubenzer & Huang, 2014); and cue-exposure therapy combined with biofeedback therapy has shown effectiveness in reducing cravings in heroin addicts.

A meta-analysis found that IT produced the largest effect sizes in treating Korean adolescents addicted to the Internet compared with CBT and reality therapy (i.e., a therapy based on accepting responsibility for one's choices) (Chun, Shim, & Kim, 2017). Mladenovic, Lazetic, Lecic-Tosevski, and Dimitrijevic (2015) created a 10-week program for pathological gamblers that integrated family therapy and CBT together within psychodynamic therapy, existential therapy, and pharmacotherapy. Extended treatment followed for the next 2 years. At 1-year follow-up, 90% of their participants remained abstinent from gambling.

The *Journal of Psychotherapy Integration* specializes in publishing across five areas of psychotherapy integration (Quoting from website (https://www.apa.org/pubs/journals/int/index.aspx):

1. Common factors (core elements to effective psychotherapy that transcend a specific orientation).
2. Technical eclecticism (application of the best treatment for a specific population and problem).
3. Theoretical integration (combining two or more theories and their associated techniques).
4. Assimilative integration (theoretical grounding in a single orientation with value-added techniques drawn from other orientations).
5. Unification (metatheoretical approaches that place theories, techniques, and principles into holistic frameworks). (para. 1)

Solution-Focused Therapy

Solution-focused therapy (SFT) began with the ideas of Milton Erikson, who maintained a strong belief that finding a solution was more important than understanding the cause of a problem (Van Wormer & Rae Davis, 2013). The development of SFT began in 1978, when Insoo Kim Berg and her husband Steve deShaver opened their office in Milwaukee and started the Solution Focused Brief Therapy Association (see http://www.sfbta.org/). SFT has become popular in many areas of addiction treatment, such as individual counseling and group therapy in both inpatient and outpatient settings (Van Wormer & Rae Davis, 2013). SFT is future-focused, and an assumption underlying it is that the future can be created and negotiated regardless of the severity of the problem. A treatment manual is available at no cost from the Research Committee of the Solution Focused Brief Therapy Association (download from http://www.solutions-centre.org/pdf/SFBT_Revised_Treatment_Manual_2013%20(3).pdf and through other online sources).

SFT focuses on client health and strength. A major goal of SFT is to help clients engage their inner resources and to notice *exceptions* to the times they are upset or distressed. Gladding and Alderson (2012) highlighted most of their techniques. They are as follows:

1. Introductory questions. These help clients to focus on solutions instead of problems (e.g., "What will be the first indication to you that you are improving by coming here?" or "How would others know that you are improving?").
2. Looking for exceptions. Clients are asked about times when the problem was less apparent or was nonexistent (e.g., "Tell me about a time when anxiety did not visit you at all").
3. Scaling questions. These questions ask clients to rate something on a scale of either 0 (none) to 10 (high) or 1 (minimal) to 10 (high) (e.g., "On a scale of 1 to 10, how much anxiety is visiting you right now?").
4. Externalizing the problem. This technique is taught to clients so that they realize problems reside outside themselves (e.g., "What is the first thing you do when alcohol knocks at your door?").
5. Compliments and cheerleading. SFT counselors often praise their clients both verbally and in writing. They act as cheerleaders when clients attain some success.
6. Clues. Clues are intended to alert clients that some behaviors they are doing are okay to continue and they should not worry about them (e.g., "What was that action you take that you find helps you when stress comes to see you?").
7. Skeleton keys. These are the procedures that have worked before for clients and that can resolve a variety of problems (e.g., "Remind me again of how avoiding certain friends helps you reduce the amount that you drink on weekends").
8. Not-knowing stance. SFT counselors act as if they lack knowledge about the client's problem and how to resolve it (e.g., "What is it that alcohol encourages you to do?").
9. Reframing. SFT counselors use reframing as a way of encouraging resolution (e.g., "If you started seeing your drinking as a lonely soul instead of as a curse, what would you want to do differently?").
10. The miracle question. The miracle question focuses on a hypothetical situation in which a problem has disappeared. There are many variations of asking the miracle question. Hope Rehab (2018) offered a good variation that is followed up by several questions. It goes something like this: Imagine that tonight when you are sleeping a miracle happens, and your problem is resolved. When you wake up in the morning, what would be the first thing you notice has changed? What do you notice around you? What do you feel inside yourself? In what ways are you different? What would other people

in your life see, hear, and notice that is different about you? What would they think about the change that has occurred? Now look back into your memories. When did you have these positive feelings in the past? What was different about you then? How were you thinking differently at that time? How were you able to cope effectively with your challenges? Are there times when you thought you would do your problem behavior, but something helped you let it go? What advice would you give to a friend or family member who has similar problems? Repeat the miracle question exercise daily. Each day, continue imagining what your life is like after the miracle in even more detail.

Young (2017) wrote about many techniques that he uses with addicted individuals that are part of what he called a strengths-based perspective. Many of these techniques fit into a solution-focused approach and/or a narrative approach, which was alluded to in Chapter 3. The way that Young begins a session is empowering to clients, and it is consistent with a solution-focused approach and other postmodern approaches. He begins as follows:

> Let's say we meet a few times . . ." (Notice the noncoercive, almost hypothetical nature of the language.) One possibility is that you find our time useful and want to continue. I think that would be great. Another possibility is that you will find our time so useful that even after a few visits you feel like you've gotten what you need and no longer want to come in for therapy. I think that would be great too, perhaps even better. But a third possibility is that we meet for a few times and you don't really find it very useful. (p. 61)

To end the first session, Young will say something like the following: "Do you want to come back?" (p. 61). Clients have told him that they find this question empowering as it lets them decide if have found Young's work with them helpful.

Another line of questions Young (2017) uses also provides clients with a sense of personal agency. After asking, "What is it about you?" (p. 61), he allows a few moments before finishing his question with something like "that despite all the hardship you've been through, you are a survivor?" "What is it about you, that even though you relapsed over the weekend you managed to get yourself to my office today?" (p. 61).

Finally, Young (2017) offered some sage advice regarding how to answer the question, which is common for addicts, "Are you in recovery?" or "Are you an addict?" The underlying assumption is often that, unless you are an addict, you could not possibly understand them. Young stated that he is not an addict, but he has found the following response helpful yet not defensive:

> Let's say we meet for a few sessions and you find it useful. If that's the case it won't likely matter whether I am in recovery or not. Likewise, it also won't matter if after a few sessions you find meeting with me not useful. In either case, whether I'm in recovery or not, if you don't find our meetings useful we should change course. (pp. 64–65)

If you *are* in recovery, Young's (2017) advice is still relevant. One of my potential clients asked me in an email if I were in recovery, and I replied affirmatively. Having that question satisfied, she followed up with an email asking, "What are in you in recovery from?" I replied honestly that it was cannabis. There was no follow-up email from her. I suspect that, unless I had experienced exactly the same addiction as she was experiencing, my services would have been rejected. You may have already wondered about this question yourself. Imagine that you had to have experienced every addiction that a client could possibly throw at you. If that were the case, it seems doubtful that you would be ever be strong enough to help others deal with their addiction.

Strengths and contributions of the solution-focused approach are that it emphasizes brevity, empowerment, flexibility, positivity, and small changes in behavior. Clients are not expected to attend a certain number of sessions, and they choose for themselves how long they continue receiving SFT. Regarding its limitations, the approach pays almost no attention to clients' history. Many clients want to tell the story of their addiction, but SFT counselors are expected to refocus clients on the solutions. SFT lacks a focus on developing insight, and some criticize the approach as being simplistic. With its emphasis on providing compliments and cheerleading, it can come across to some clients as overly optimistic and Pollyanna-ish (i.e., naïvely optimistic). Furthermore, few controlled outcome studies have been done (Gladding & Alderson, 2012).

COUNSELING SCENARIO USING SFT

Imagine that you are the client in this scenario.

Your name is Zoey, a 19-year-old who works full-time as a sales clerk in a large department store. You are often bored, especially when you are alone at home. When bored, you tend to drink too much. Over the last year, you have been drunk at least once every weekend. Your friends are concerned about you, and you have decided to meet with an addiction counselor.

- Counselor: Hello, Zoey. It is a pleasure to meet you.
- You: Thank you, Dale. I appreciate that you got me in so quickly.
- Counselor: You're welcome. What would you like to talk about today?
- You: Well, for the past year, I have been getting drunk far too frequently, and my friends are concerned about me.
- Counselor: I see. You mentioned the past year. What was your drinking like before then?
- You: Honestly, I didn't drink before then. It has just been over this past year.
- Counselor: Okay, you have been drinking too much over the past year, and it concerns you and your friends.

- You: I think it concerns my friends more than it concerns me.
- Counselor: On a scale of 0 to 10 with zero meaning not at all and 10 meaning a great deal, how much does your drinking concern you now?
- You: I would say about a 6.
- Counselor: What would you need to do to get that down to a 1 or 2?
- You: I would need to drink less on the weekend.
- Counselor: Tell me about the last weekend where you did not drink at all.
- You: I guess that was more than a year ago when I still lived at home with my parents.
- Counselor: What then has changed for you since you moved out?
- You: I spend a lot of time at home by myself. I live with two roommates, but they both are with their boyfriends on the weekend.
- Counselor: It sounds like alcohol has become the friend to help you cope with loneliness.
- You: Yes, I would agree with you.
- Counselor: If you wanted to invite this friend into your life less frequently, what would you need to do differently?
- You: I would need to either develop more friends or develop other ways of spending time alone.
- Counselor: You believe that you need to develop more friends or become more comfortable being alone.
- You: Yes.
- Counselor: Wonderful! You already know what to do differently.
- You: I guess so, but I don't know how to feel more comfortable when I am alone. I get anxious and afraid.
- Counselor: I think you are saying that you want to learn how to spend time alone without anxiety and fear entering your home. Is this correct?
- You: Yeah. I have lots of friends already, but I don't always want to have to have them with me to feel comfortable within myself.
- Counselor: Tell me about a time when you have been comfortable being by yourself.
- You: I guess when I am doing housework I don't feel lonely.
- Counselor: So, when you are doing housework, how do you manage to cope and feel okay being alone?
- You: I don't think about the fact that I am alone then. I put all my focus on doing the housework instead.
- Counselor: Terrific! One way that has helped you deal with your loneliness is to be busy doing physical work because then you don't think about the fact that you are alone.
- You: That's right.
- Counselor: What other strategies have you learned to deal with being alone?
- You: I find that listening to music helps or having the television on in the background.
- Counselor: You are coming up with some very good ideas, Zoey. You have already found several ways in your life to cope effectively with times when you are alone.
- You: I guess so. I feel like such a loser on the weekends.
- Counselor: Instead of viewing yourself as a loser, what if, instead, you looked at yourself as a person who wants more stimulation?
- You: That sounds a lot more positive, doesn't it?
- Counselor: Absolutely! You are a person who wants greater stimulation in your life. What are some ways that could look like for you?
- You: I could take up some new activities or join a meetup group. I could start going to the gym regularly, especially on weekends.
- Counselor: Wow, you really have a lot of great ideas!
- You: Thanks, Dale. You are really getting me thinking.

From the Client's Perspective

1. As the client, what do you think you would like about this approach, and what would you dislike?
2. SFT requires that you find solutions within yourself. How would you feel about continuing to do this if you were Zoey?
3. What would you find more helpful from a counselor in this scenario (if anything)?

From the Counselor's Perspective

1. There are many ways to do SFT. What would you do differently if you were the counselor in the previous scenario?
2. What other methods would you use to build an even stronger working alliance?
3. As the counselor, what do you think you would like about this approach, and what would you dislike?

HOW WOULD AN ADDICTION COUNSELOR HELP THIS CLIENT USING SFT?

You are working as a professional counselor. Kyle, age 31, comes to see you for counseling. Kyle uses a lot of cocaine, and, when he is high, his sex drive increases sharply. He blames his increased sex drive on why he cheats on his wife, Stephanie. How would you help Kyle?

Here are a few suggestions to help you get started. Kyle blames his cheating on his use of cocaine.

1. How could you adopt the not-knowing stance with Kyle?
2. What behaviors could you imagine providing him with compliments and cheerleading?
3. What are Kyle's goals for counseling? If these are not self-evident, what questions could you ask to find out? [hint: his goals are *not* self-evident]
4. If Kyle's goal was to continue his cocaine use but stop cheating on his wife, how would you go about helping him explore exceptions to his cheating behavior?

Conducting a Mental Status Examination and Collecting Clients' Histories

As Martin (1990) described, the mental status examination (MSE) is a structured assessment of a client's cognitive and behavioral functioning. Mental status testing can be threatening to clients, and Martin suggested that it be left toward the end of an assessment. Testing is important, however, because clients whose brains have been damaged from biological conditions or SUDs may provide inaccurate histories to counselors. Individuals with Alzheimer's disease, for example, or Korsakoff's syndrome (i.e., a chronic memory disorder caused by severe thiamine deficiency in some individuals with AUD), will have difficulty in passing tests that rely on short-term memory. Martin recommended that clients be provided an explanation for why the MSE is being done to enlist client cooperation. Testing should be conducted when providers see any "hint" of decline in any of these suggested areas: (a) level of consciousness, (b) appearance and general behavior, (c) speech and motor activity, (d) affect and mood, (e) thought and perception, (f) attitude and insight, (g) examiner's reaction to the client, and (h) cognitive abilities (including attention, language, memory, constructional ability and praxis, and abstract reasoning; see Martin, 1990; his brief article with details explaining each area to assess is available at https://www.ncbi.nlm.nih.gov/books/NBK320/pdf/Bookshelf_NBK320.pdf).

Richard Lakeman (1995) has kindly provided permission for his MSE to be included in this textbook (see Appendix D). Lakeman's MSE includes the following headings: general appearance, psychomotor behavior, mood and affect, speech, cognition, thought patterns, and levels of consciousness. Although his MSE does not contain actual questions to ask clients, what it offers is a list of adjectives that can be used to describe each category. Another helpful instrument is the Mini Mental State Examination (MMSE), which is used by nurses for examining the cognitive state of their patients. It is a well-known instrument, and it includes the actual questions to ask clients (Kurlowicz & Wallace, 1999). A more recent and validated version (with norms) of a mini-exam is called the Saint Louis University Mental Status Examination (SLUMS; Tariq, Tumosa, Chibnall, Perry, & Morley, 2006; available for download from http://medschool.slu.edu/agingsuccessfully/pdfsurveys/slumsexam_05.pdf).

Getting a history from clients is also helpful in our practice. A useful questionnaire was designed by Alderson for this purpose (the questionnaire, the manual, and the pie chart are available as free downloads from https://kevinalderson.ca/). If you are in private practice, you may wish to email this to clients before you see them for the first session and either ask them to return it to you before you meet or have them bring it to the first session. This will save you and the client a substantial amount of time.

Assessment and Intervention Strategies for Suicide Risk and Prevention

Determining that someone is imminently (i.e., about to happen) suicidal is not only difficult but also largely inaccurate (Jarema, 2018). This is particularly disconcerting given that the Centers for Disease Control and Prevention (2018) reported an overall 30% increase in suicides between 1999 and 2016 throughout most American states in all age groups up to 75 years. The World Health Organization (2014) reported that 800,000 individuals commit suicide each year, and the number of attempts is 20 times higher.

A simple way to begin an assessment for suicidality is to simply ask our clients if they have been planning suicide or have recently thought about it. Giddens and Sheehan (2014) found that, in their case study, responses to the single question "Do you think that you would be better off dead?" (p. 188) are important and valuable in assessing suicidality. Nonetheless, if clients do not state or deny having suicidal thoughts or intent, this does not mean their suicide risk is zero (Jarema, 2018). Patterson, Dohn, Bird, and Patterson (1983) created a clever acronym for remembering 10 common risk factors for suicide. It is important to remember that most people who show these risk factors will never attempt suicide. The acronym is SAD PERSONS. Risk factors include the following:

1. Sex. Although more men complete suicide, more women attempt.
2. Age. Elderly individuals are at the highest risk.
3. Depression (and bipolar disorder). Each depression experienced by the same person increases their risk factor 15-fold.
4. Previous suicide attempt. This is actually the strongest risk factor of them all.
5. Ethanol abuse. Nearly half of the people who attempt suicide have used alcohol immediately preceding their attempt.
6. Rational thinking loss. Although this risk factor refers to psychosis, studies have not found it to be consistently associated with suicide.
7. Social supports lacking. Having no or few social supports increases suicide risk.
8. Organized plan. Having an organized plan increases suicide risk.
9. No spouse or child. Having a child decreases suicide risk, especially for women.
10. Sickness. People in chronic pain or suffering functional impairments are at higher risk of suicide.

As indicated in point 4, the strongest risk factor for suicide is that clients have made a previous suicidal attempt. Other factors that create substantial risk include experiencing severe depressive symptoms co-occurring with substance abuse, believing that there is no escape (i.e., entrapment), having more arguments in favor of suicide than against it, experiencing the occurrence of a traumatic life event, and actively preparing for an upcoming suicide attempt (Jarema, 2018). Indirect indications that clients may be suicidal include avoiding others; refusing to participate in therapeutic activities, meetings, or conversations; avoiding questions focused on their mental state; having no future plans; not coping well with personal or family situations; and refusing meals or becoming indifferent to nutrition (Jarema, 2018).

The risk factors for suicidality in individuals addicted to heroin include having a family history of suicidal behavior, treatment with antidepressants, and having a dual addiction (e.g., alcohol, cocaine) (Roy, 2010). Individuals with a dual diagnosis of addiction and a mental health disorder also have a higher risk of relapse, display less adherence to treatment protocols, and have a higher suicide risk than those having a single diagnosis (Roncero, Grau-Lopez, & Casas, 2017).

A large, longitudinal study of more than 5000 psychiatric outpatients conducted by Green et al. (2015) found that the responses on the Beck Depression Inventory (BDI-I) suicide item were associated with both suicide attempts and completed suicides. (Note that the BDI-II is now used in practice. It is available from http://hpc-educ.org/Files/Danz/BDII.pdf.) Items on the BDI-I are scored according to the respondents' answers. The suicide item is as follows: 0 = I don't have any thoughts of killing myself; 1 = I have thoughts of killing myself, but I would not carry them out; 2 = I would like to kill myself; and 3 = I would kill myself if I had the chance. Jarema (2018) suggested using the Beck Scale for Suicidal Ideation, which has 19 items, each scored from 0 (*absent*) to 2 (*severe*). (The scale is embedded in a 1979 open access article by Beck, Kovacs, and Weissman available from https://pdfs.semanticscholar.org/c2de/a047d5d71cd6500d92d4cdf2c6e36129d8cf.pdf.) In their review of over 2000 publications that measure attitudes toward suicide, Kodaka, Postuvan, Inagaki, and Yamada (2011) recommended that three scales deserve particular attention: the Suicide Opinion Questionnaire (Domino, 1996), the Suicide Attitude Questionnaire (Diekstra & Kerkhof, 1988), and a questionnaire simply called Attitudes Toward Suicide (Renberg & Jacobson, 2003). Note that Kodaka et al. recommended these three scales for *research* purposes. They have *not* been validated for use in clinical practice. The Columbia Lighthouse Project produces an excellent set of scales. These valid scales are free to use, and there are different ones for different settings (visit http://cssrs.columbia.edu/).

A meta-analysis and metaregression of published research on whether psychotherapy is effective in reducing suicide attempts suggest that they are helpful but more homogenous outcome measures and longer follow-up periods are needed (Calati & Courtet, 2016). A commonality among all treatment approaches is that the working alliance is primary, and counselors need to know whom they are treating (Leenaars, 2006). Similarly, Harrison, Stritzke, Fay, and Hudaib (2018) recommended that counselors take a collaborative approach with their clients in assessing the likelihood of suicide risk.

In counseling suicidal adolescents, empirically supported treatments include attachment-based family therapy, integrated CBT, and DBT (Singer, McManama O'Brien, & LeCloux, 2017). The approaches that have been successful in working with adults include CBT and DBT, problem-solving therapy, interpersonal psychotherapy, and outreach approaches (e.g., sending caring letters) (Comtois & Linehan, 2006). There is some evidence that mindfulness approaches are helpful to young people by increasing their zest for life (Collins, Stritzke, Page, Brown, & Wylde, 2018). MBCT might also help prevent suicidal behavior (Chesin et al., 2018). Additional information about suicide is available through the National Institute of Mental Health (visit https://www.nimh.nih.gov/health/topics/suicide-prevention/index.shtml).

Erford, Jackson, Bardhoshi, Duncan, and Atalay (2018) performed a meta-analysis on four commonly used measures of suicidal ideation (i.e., the Beck Scale for Suicide Ideation [BSS], the Suicide Ideation Questionnaire [SIQ], the Suicide Probability Scale [SPS], and Columbia-Suicide Severity Rating Scale [C-SSR]). They surmised that no instrument can be 100% conclusive, so their "bottom line" was that standardized assessments are best used in conjunction with a clinical interview. Furthermore, here are their overall conclusions:

> So what are the best choices for use by professional counselors? The CSSR is an excellent instrument to incorporate into a clinical interview to provide a more structured approach and its outstanding diagnostic validity results will help bolster the accuracy of decisions. When considering use of self-report instruments to supplement the clinical interview and triangulate with conclusions of the pneumonics and risk factors, the BSS is the best choice for use with adults and the SIQ (and SIQ-JR [junior high version]) is the best choice for use with adolescents. (p. 52)

Assessment Strategies for Homicide Risk

Occasionally you may have a client who threatens to kill someone, often a significant other (e.g., a dating partner, a spouse). As you may recall from Chapter 2, if the homicidal intent is imminent and serious, you need to report it to police and to the intended victim whenever possible. How do you know if the intent is serious? As Large and Ryan (2015) noted, violence risk assessments have not been shown to reduce violence. Can they help predict it, however? There is currently no preferred assessment measure or approach for counselors to use (Nicholls, Pritchard, Reeves, & Hilterman, 2013), and, furthermore, it is well known that "there are no highly effective or specific treatments that prevent future violence" (Large & Mullin, 2011, p. 132).

The Fordham Risk Screening Tool (FRST; Rosenfeld et al., 2017) has been used for psychiatric patients as an initial screening device. The FRST is intended to be only a first step before a thorough risk assessment. The questions, however, will provide counselors with a good "heads up" as to whether our client uttering threats should be reported. In any case, it is important that you ascertain for imminent (i.e., about to happen) risk, meaning that your client has stated that he or she is going to or planning to kill an identified person soon after leaving your office.

Regarding intimate partner homicide (IPH), Vatnar, Friestad, and Bjørkly (2017) studied all instances of IPH that occurred in Norway between 1990 and 2012 that had received a final legal judgement ($N = 177$). Their main findings were that (a) most IPHs were committed by men in relationships where there had been previous intimate partner violence (i.e., 70.6%), (b) marginalized groups were most at risk for IPH both as victims and perpetrators, and (c) the bereaved reported that the homicidal concerns that had been reported to police, healthcare, and support services were not treated as sufficiently serious.

Vossekuil, Fein, and Berglund (2015) studied the thinking and behavior, communications, planning strategies, target selection, and mental health histories and motives of 83 attackers that were publicly identified. Although some attackers do not make threats, many do let someone know about their intentions. Below are a few questions based on their findings (adapted here for counselors):

1. What has the client communicated about their intentions to you and others (to the possible victim, family, friends, colleagues, associates, or diary or journal)?
2. What are the client's motives and goals? Carefully examine the client's thinking and behavior.
3. Has the client shown an interest in any of the following: (a) assassins or assassinations, (b) weapons, (c) militant, radical, or extreme ideas, or belonging to such organizations, (d) workplace violence, or (e) stalking incidents?
4. Is there evidence that the client has ever been involved in attack-related behaviors? (Does the client have an attack idea or plan? Is the client making efforts to acquire or practice with weapons? Are there indications that the client is rehearsing violent behavior?)
5. Has the client ever engaged in menacing, harassing, and/or stalking-type behavior?
6. Does the client have a history of mental illness involving command hallucinations (i.e., the client believes someone, or something, is telling him or her what to do), delusional ideas, or feelings of persecution or has the client ever acted on those beliefs?
7. How organized is the client? Does the client have the ability to plan and execute a violent action?
8. Is the client experiencing feelings of hopelessness, desperation, or despair?
9. Is what the client says consistent with their actions?
10. Does the client see violence as acceptable, desirable, or the only way to solve life's problems?
11. Do others who know the client have concerns about their behavior?
12. What factors in the client's life and/or environment could change and thereby increase their risk of attacking? What factors could change and thereby decrease the potential risk?

Impermanently Ending Our Counseling Relationship With Clients

If our clients had relapsing-remitting multiple sclerosis or Crohn's disease, we would most likely see them periodically through the course of their illness. Most addictions are also chronic conditions where relapse is the norm over the exception. Besides this, we are counseling people, not diseases. Clients see us for a variety of problems, only some of which are directly related to their addiction. If you are working in a residential treatment program, you might end up saying goodbye only once to most of your clients. If you are in a community agency or private practice, however, today's goodbye will often be tomorrow's hello. When this happens, you ought not to be discouraged. Instead, be encouraged that your clients think highly enough of you that they want to return to see you again. Clients continue to struggle as do the rest of us. We do not cure the human condition; instead, we embrace its humility.

Many clients merely stop booking their next appointments with us. Particularly with short-term or brief counseling, clients may not feel the need to create a formal ending to our relationship with them. When working with longer-term clients, creating an impermanent ending is more common. Some counselors may call this the "termination stage," but generally we hope that clients will return when they need our services again. Consequently, it is important to let them know that you have an open door and that they are always welcome to book another appointment when they feel the need.

How do you know when it's time to move toward an impermanent ending with clients? Here are a couple of helpful cues:

1. They are indicating that they are ready to end counseling. Our clients often let us know directly or indirectly. They may simply tell us that they have progressed sufficiently and no longer want to return for further sessions. Alternatively, we may find that our sessions have turned into social conversation, meaning they are no longer focused on helping clients achieve a goal. This is often an indirect indication that there is little left to resolve. Another indirect indication is when clients begin missing sessions.

2. They have achieved their goals. Usually, when clients have achieved their goals, it is obvious to both the counselor and the client. When it appears evident to only the counselor, it is important to review the original goals for counseling with the client and decide collaboratively if further goals are needed. When further goals are decided, the counseling process continues until those goals are achieved.

Relapse Prevention

Relapse prevention has come to have several meanings. It represents a theory about behavior change, it is a specific treatment approach, and it is a set of intervention strategies. It has two aims: (a) prevent an initial lapse and (b) provide lapse management if a lapse does occur (Witkiewitz & Kirouac, 2016). Given that up to 90% of clients have the potential to lapse (a brief episode of return to addictive behavior) or relapse (a return to more extensive addictive behavior) (Csiernik, 2016), and most relapse happens within 90 days of sobriety (Brooks & McHenry, 2009), relapse prevention is important.

The terms "lapse" and "relapse" have considerable historical baggage as they are rooted in morality and religion and not in health and medicine (White & Ali, 2010). The terms are often viewed pejoratively. By comparison, when individuals experience other medical conditions that are chronic, a return of symptoms is viewed compassionately and without judgment. It would be preferable if a similar accepting attitude accompanied addictive behavior.

Relapse prevention was initially developed for AUD by Alan Marlatt and his colleagues in the 1970s (Han & Avery, 2016). Its effectiveness and efficacy have been repeatedly demonstrated for multiple SUDs (Han & Avery, 2016). Relapse prevention generally follows a threefold strategy: (a) identifying patterns of use, (b) avoiding or managing high-risk situations, and (c) choosing different but healthier behaviors (Cuzen & Stein, 2014). People, places, and things are often reviewed in treatment programs, so clients understand who and what to avoid early in their recovery (Zmuda, 2014).

Using CBT, Marlatt's approach was to teach clients skills in both recognizing and avoiding high-risk situations to help avoid relapse (Witkiewitz, Marlatt, & Walker, 2017). Examples of high-risk situations include emotional or cognitive states such as negative affect and diminished self-efficacy, environmental contingencies like conditioned drug cues, or physiological states such as acute physical withdrawal (Hendershot, Witkiewitz, George, & Marlatt, 2011). Cognitive factors play an important role in creating relapse liability. When clients successfully navigate high-risk situations, it generally increases their self-efficacy. Furthermore, clients' attitudes or beliefs regarding a lapse also influence whether a full relapse occurs (Hendershot et al., 2011). The abstinence violation effect, for example, can occur when clients lapse by using a small amount of the drug and then decide that, because they have failed, *they* are failures, which, in turn, justifies using much more of the drug (Earleywine, 2016). In relapse prevention, a lapse is not considered an "endpoint" but rather a learning opportunity (Csiernik, 2016).

Behavioral interventions are also used in relapse prevention. Damian and Mendelson (2017) used data from a nationally representative U.S. sample of African American and Afro-Caribbean adults ($N = 4828$), which was derived from the National Survey of American Life conducted from 2001 to 2003. Those individuals who reported being physically active had greater odds of being in 12-month remission from AUDs compared with those who were physically inactive. Damian and Mendelson concluded that longitudinal studies still need to be conducted to ascertain if exercise is a potential relapse prevention strategy for alcohol use problems. Brown, Prince, Minami, and Abrantes (2016) concluded that even single bouts of moderate-intensity exercise could potentially help individuals with AUD manage mood, anxiety, and craving, thereby assisting in reducing relapse risk.

Many relapse prevention strategies have proven helpful. Just increasing activity levels, especially those incompatible with drug use, serves to minimize lapses and improve mood (Earleywine, 2016). Negative moods (e.g., boredom, depression, anger) are the most prevalent precipitants of a relapse (Mason & Higley, 2012). Other common triggers include interpersonal conflict and social pressure (Margolis & Zweben, 2011). For adolescents, the most common trigger concerns peer interactions (Margolis & Zweben, 2011). Alcoholics Anonymous developed an easy-to-remember acronym called HALT, which stands for people are most likely to relapse when they are **H**ungry, **A**ngry, **L**onely, or **T**ired (Margolis & Zweben, 2011).

Stress increases the risk of relapse, so stress management is an important aspect of relapse prevention (Mason & Higley, 2012). Clients need to develop coping skills like requesting help from others, sharing feelings and emotions or writing them down in a journal, saying no to others when they are offered a drug or other addictive behavior, and setting limits and boundaries on their behaviors and with whom they associate (Brooks & McHenry, 2009). Having employment is positively associated with relapse prevention (Barbieri, Dal Corso, Di Sipio, De Carlo, & Benevene, 2016). Kemp, Channer, and Zahn (2016) suggested that willpower training may help reduce relapse risk by increasing self-control and self-regulation.

Anhedonia, which is a condition where one loses the ability to experience pleasure, is commonly associated with SUDs (especially in alcohol, cocaine, stimulant, and cannabis use disorders). Hatzigiakoumis, Martinotti, Di Giannantonio, and Janiri (2011) recommended that treating anhedonia is important as a relapse-prevention strategy. Pekala (2017) suggested that hypnosis might be helpful with relapse prevention as it can increase self-esteem, decrease anger and impulsivity, and improve feelings of serenity.

Technological advancements have also proven helpful. You et al. (2017), for example, tested a smartphone app with a Bluetooth breathalyzer for participants with AUDs. Participants who used the technology consistently drank fewer days and consumed less alcohol, had more abstinence days, and experienced less anxiety than the less-adherent group. Chapters 9 through 21 list several phone apps that may be helpful in reducing relapse across the addiction spectrum.

Gorski and Miller (1986) outlined nine phases that many individuals with AUD experience before relapsing. These signs might also be experienced by some people dealing with other addictive behaviors (but this has not been tested empirically). These phases are as follows:

1. Phase I: denial returns. In this first phase, individuals begin minimizing, rationalizing, justifying, and distorting their feelings. They will also respond with "I'm fine" when asked how they are doing despite feeling stressed and anxious.
2. Phase II: denial and avoidance increases. Individuals believe that they will never use again and instead focus on

others. When confronted regarding their well-being, they become defensive, which results in increasing isolation.

3. Phase III: avoiding others. Failing recovery plans may result in minor depression. Individuals disconnect further from themselves and others. Feelings of being stuck increase.
4. Phase IV: "going through the motions." Individuals feel as though they are not fully living and wish life would be different.
5. Phase V: losing faith in recovery. Individuals in this phase begin feeling confused, angry, and/or overwhelmed. They continue to refrain from talking about their feelings.
6. Phase VI: feeling depressed. The symptoms of upcoming relapse are similar to depression as individuals experience lethargy, sleep difficulties, and poor eating patterns.
7. Phase VII: depression worsens. Individuals begin rejecting help by missing treatment and support meetings. They start lying again, lose self-confidence, and develop an "I don't care" attitude. They are beginning to justify having a drink.
8. Phase VIII: feeling trapped. Feelings of being trapped become consuming while feelings of overwhelming loneliness surface.
9. Phase IX: return to using or treatment and recovery. Either individuals return to uncontrolled and compulsive use, or, following use, they get back into treatment and recovery.

If a lapse occurs, drug users can reduce the likelihood of relapse if they exit the situation (Earleywine, 2016). They are also encouraged to examine the triggers for the relapse and renew their commitment to abstinence (Connors et al., 2013). Brooks and McHenry (2009) stated that clients leaving inpatient treatment need to create a daily plan of action, or they are likely to find that their maladaptive thinking patterns and previous addictive behaviors return, perhaps following a path similar to Gorski and Miller's (1986) nine phases. It is critical that clients think ahead and plan their recovery activities (e.g., regular meetings with a counselor, spending time with their sponsor if attending 12-step).

Carnes (1991), as part of his research on sexual addiction, asked addicted individuals what they found most helpful in resisting cravings. Their advice may be generalizable to other addictions. They were as follows:

1. Develop spiritual strategies.
2. Decode feelings.
3. Avoid trigger situations.
4. Forgive yourself for slips.
5. Work on nurturing yourself.
6. Avoid keeping cravings secret.
7. Find alternative passions.
8. Acknowledge your choices. (p. 292)

Brooks and McHenry (2009) stated that, following a relapse, "it is the hope and spirit of the counselor that can make a significant difference with clients and their belief in recovery" (p. 192). Counselors play an important role in helping clients deal successfully with lapses and relapses.

Clients can use many strategies in their relapse prevention efforts. A list of these can be found in Appendix C. Additionally, several free resources are available from the Internet that may be helpful to you in your counseling practice. Here is a brief list of just some of what is available for download:

1. My Action Plan for Relapse Prevention. Available from the Montgomery County Emergency Service at https://docobook.com/workbook-for-relapse-prevention-recovery.html
2. United Nations Office on Drugs and Crime. (2007). Leaders guide: Cognitive behavioural & relapse prevention strategies. Retrieved from http://www.unodc.org/ddt-training/treatment/VOLUME%20B/Volume%20B%20-%20Module%203/1.Leaders%20Guide/Presentation%20-%20VolB_M3.pdf and http://www.unodc.org/
3. Hedges, B. A. (1999). Relapse prevention workbook. Retrieved from https://www.solanocounty.com/civicax/filebank/blobdload.aspx?blobid=14403
4. Larimer, M. E., Palmer, R. S., & Marlatt, G. A. (1999). Relapse prevention: An overview of Marlatt's cognitive-behavioral model. Alcohol Research & Health, 23(2), 151–160. Retrieved from https://pubs.niaaa.nih.gov/publications/arh23-2/151-160.pdf
5. ASI-MV Worksheets & handouts. From https://www.asi-mvconnect.com/uploadedFiles/Public/Worksheets_and_Forms/ASIMVWorksheet.pdf

Common Counseling Mistakes

In Chapters 9 through 21, there is a section called *Counseling Scenario*. One of the questions in each asks that you identify which counseling mistakes the counselor has made in the scenario. **None** of these are meant to be good counseling sessions. We learn to become good counselors by learning both what we should do with our clients and what we should avoid. The following list and explanations are adapted from several online sources (http://cebucounseling.blogspot.com/2012/08/common-counseling-mistakes-part-1.html; http://gettotheinside.blogspot.com/2009/04/common-mistakes-made-by-therapists.html; and http://biblicalcounselingcoalition.org/2014/02/21/top-10-counseling-mistakes/).

1. Giving too much advice and insufficient listening. Clients need to process their feelings by talking through them. First, giving advice can circumvent this process. Second, if the advice given is not heeded, it creates a small rift in the working alliance. Clients may feel the advice was homework, and, when not completed, they may think they will be punished or that their counselor will be angry at them. Third, if the advice is taken and the situation does not improve for clients, they may blame you or believe that your competence is diminished in their eyes. Fourth, clients are more likely to take action if they come up with the action plan themselves or in collaboration

with their counselor. Fifth, clients may resent the advice that you provide them and feel coerced if they follow it.

2. Becoming impatient. This mistake often leads to mistake #1. Although good counselors often understand rather quickly why the client is in counseling, they want to jump straight to how the client can improve. Although this has some merit (e.g., it is part of how SFT operates), clients need time to work through their process of change at a pace suitable to them.

3. Disengaging clients from their feelings. It is difficult for empathic counselors to witness their clients' pain, especially when their clients are children. It is helpful for clients to feel, however, whether it be from deferred grief or anger or from feelings they harbor toward their boss. John Bradshaw, for example, described these deep wounds as "original pain" (see https://www.johnbradshaw.com/).

4. Presenting as without fault to clients. Good counselors are genuine and acknowledge their imperfections by remaining aware that they may (or do) experience the same hurts and behaviors as their clients. Some counselors, depending on their orientation, will self-disclose when it might enhance the working alliance or help clients realize they are not alone in their struggles.

5. Ignoring boundaries. Counselors do a disservice to themselves if they regularly go over the agreed-upon session time, if they reduce their fees too much if in private practice, make promises they cannot deliver, or establish friendships instead of sustaining professionalism. Professional boundaries help prevent counselor burnout and dual relationships that may constitute an ethical violation.

6. Taking their change process personally. At the time clients see us, most are experiencing pain, and they will project these onto their counselor. If we internalize their feelings and bring these home with us, we might be heading toward burnout. Furthermore, it is our clients who must change: We are there only as a guide, facilitator, and catalyst for the change process.

7. Focusing on self-gratification. Counselors are often wounded healers (Gladding & Alderson, 2019), and seeing clients may help them fill a void in their own lives for friendship, love, and companionship. Although becoming friends with clients has short-term benefits, often the long-term consequence is dependency. Instead of becoming their friend, it's important that we help them find friends.

8. Labeling clients. In many settings, labeling is required in the form of providing a diagnosis. Labeling becomes problematic when counselors begin finding a label for everyone. It often creates a "we-they" attitude, which can easily be relayed unwittingly to the client, instead of an "us" connection (i.e., where clients and counselors share equal worth and humanity). Labels are also controversial. Some clients will take a label to mean that they cannot change and, consequently, will stop trying to improve.

9. Believing that clients' pasts should be avoided. This does not mean that one should not practice future-oriented counseling approaches like narrative and SFT. Instead, the past provides a wealth of information concerning repetitive themes and patterns that are still being enacted by clients but are unknown to them (e.g., our clients hate men [or women] because have been attracted repeatedly to mates who are abusive). The past also provides us with insights into the clients' worldview.

10. Focusing only on surface issues and their resulting consequences. Some clients return weekly with a litany of new problems and hurts that have occurred since the last session. It is important that we look at the root issues behind their crises instead of focusing only on the symptoms that continue manifesting as other symptoms.

11. Assigning homework without collaboration. Usually, the best homework assignments are those that come from clients as they then feel a sense of ownership to what they are going to do before the next session. If our clients do not have any ideas regarding homework, the next best approach is to work collaboratively with them to arrive at agreeable homework. The client needs to commit to doing the homework. Furthermore, they need to know that you will not be judging them if they do not complete it for whatever reason before the next session. Some clients remember how they perceived or were punished when they did not get homework done when they were in grade school. Uncompleted homework can easily create a rupture in the working alliance.

12. Keeping your distance from clients. It is often difficult to be around clients who are deep in their psychological or physical pain. Should we keep our professional distance from these clients? The guiding principles are to remember that none of us is immune to pain (you have likely felt some in your life already) and that we continue to be genuine and display unconditional positive regard as we empathize with the pain our clients are feeling.

13. Doing or assigning more of the same. If what we are doing is not working with a client, we need to try something different. The same applies to clients who cannot complete their homework before the next session (unless their reasons for not completing it were truly beyond their control). Often when collaborated homework is not finished, it represents either some resistance or lack of sufficient commitment to change.

14. Using clichés with clients. Clichés are stereotypical expressions. Consequently, they do not provide individual feedback to clients. Furthermore, some clients will simply not understand the metaphor within the cliché.

15. Patronizing/judging clients or acting as if you are above their issue. Judging others in our minds and hearts occurs automatically for most people. It is unfortunate, however, if our clients subtly perceive that this is happening. Instead, stay focused on viewing your client unconditionally and empathically. This may be an ideal time to share one of your struggles in the session to maintain the "us" stance instead of the "we-they."

16. Sending clients back into the abyss of loneliness. Counselors need to remember the clients are returning

to several environments, including their community, after the session concludes. It is important that we focus on helping clients create stronger bonds to others in their family, friendships, intimate relationships, and/or community. This process may include teaching clients how to make friends and build greater intimacy with their existing connections.

17. Probing and questioning too soon or often. Clients need to hear what they feel and think about their situations. Asking probing questions too early or frequently may prevent clients from expressing what is most important to them. It might also result in moving the client toward issues, problems, or insights that they are not ready to face.

18. Making inappropriate self-disclosures. Remember that appropriate self-disclosure strengthens the working alliance with clients as they create bridges that demonstrate that you understand their situation. A common counseling mistake is to self-disclose too early or too deeply. It is important that counselors do not create a role reversal with their clients, meaning that clients' attention and focus is more on us instead of on exploring themselves (e.g., Client: "My dog just died"; Counselor: "I understand. My spouse just died last week in a plane crash").

19. Using challenging skills insufficiently or poorly. Counseling needs to move to the preparation and action stages for clients to get much out of the process. Counselors can easily stay too long in the stage where clients talk about other people and situations that bother them. Clients also need to be helped to look at how they contribute to the problem. This involves using challenging skills.

20. Believing that clients always tell the truth. Many clients lie for a myriad of reasons. This can include wanting to (a) placate their counselor, (b) avoid embarrassment, (c) avoid taking responsibility for their behaviors, and (d) believe that their partner is 100% responsible for their relationship difficulties.

21. Imposing one's values on clients. Counselors need to remain self-aware and diligent. Despite this, it is easy for us to impose our strong opinions, convictions, and values on clients. Although it may seem self-evident, other people often have different worldviews than our own. Even if you share one aspect of worldview with your client (e.g., you are both Christian), even that aspect may differ between you (e.g., one of you is fundamentalist and the other is liberal). Additionally, you may differ on most other dimensions of worldview (e.g., one of you believes collectivist values and the other believes individualism is more important).

22. Failing to attain agreement on goals. Whose goals are more important: yours or your clients'? The clients' goals should nearly always be viewed as more important. If clients do not receive the service that you purport to provide, they will not return. The caveat here is that, if clients want you to help them achieve unhealthy behaviors (e.g., "I want to stop the guilt I feel for cheating on my spouse"), this may be an opportunity for providing them psychoeducation (or to tell them that you are not the right counselor for them because of your deep opposing values).

23. Failing to attain agreement on tasks. This is such a common problem that even seasoned counselors often make this mistake. Instead of discussing with clients different ways to help them solve their problems, the counselor *jumps* into using CBT, narrative therapy, or whatever. Clients need to have input regarding the counseling approach. Furthermore, ongoing informed consent requires it.

24. Working harder than clients. When we are working harder than the client, something is amuck in the counseling process. This can easily lead to burnout. Every seasoned counselor has had the client who does little talking or talks too much while lacking depth of exploration. If you find yourself working harder than the client in a session, bring it up at either the end of the session or the beginning of the next session. Clients improve when they accept responsibility for change.

25. Jumping to conclusions. It is easy to jump to conclusions before thoroughly assessing our clients' problems or issues. Assessments, for example, need to be complete, and diagnoses based on these must be accurate (e.g., believing that clients need progressive muscle relaxation because they are anxious without assessing if there is a physiological reason for their anxiety such as during depressant withdrawal or because they have an overactive thyroid). Ensure that you provide a thorough assessment of the problem or issue.

26. Not respecting cultural differences. Individuals both within and from other countries experience cultural differences. This may be particularly evident with people from visible and/or invisible minority groups (e.g., race/ethnicity, LGBTQ identified, less-known religions). When in doubt, ask clients to share with you something about their cultural positioning. The clients' environments are important contributors to their functioning.

27. Enabling minimization and/or denial. Counselors who need acceptance and approval from their clients might be more likely to enable them to continue minimizing or denying their addiction issues (or other problems/issues). If you become aware that this is happening for you with clients, have your clients complete a valid and reliable test that will provide an objective sense regarding the extent of their dependency. If this is insufficient, consult with your supervisor or another trained mental health professional.

28. Using jargon with clients. In counseling and psychology, we have come up with a lot of terms that we understand but laypeople do not. Using jargon may serve to push our clients away rather than create a stronger bridge. Instead of using the words intellectualization or reaction formation, for example, how could you instead describe these defense mechanisms to a client? Wherever possible, use clients' use of language (e.g., Client: "I know I should be upset that my father just passed away but instead I just feel numb." Counselor: "Tell me more about this feeling of emotional numbness").

Generic Addiction Apps

In Chapters 9 through 21, there is a section called Relevant Phone Apps. To reduce redundancy, only the generic ones are described here. Note that this list is not exhaustive. New apps are continually being developed. Do an Internet search to find out the latest apps available. Most are for specific addictions but some, such as the four in the following list, are generic.

Lindhiem, Bennett, Rosen, and Silk (2015) conducted a meta-analysis and found that phone apps do serve an effective adjunctive function in delivering psychotherapy and other behavioral interventions. Counselors need to be aware, however, that this does not mean that an app will be useful for any particular client and that many apps have yet to be empirically tested regarding their efficacy or effectiveness in treating addictions.

1. I Am Sober. https://play.google.com/store/apps/details?id=com.thehungrywasp.iamsober

   This app is for just about every addiction. Quoted from website: "Along with tracking your sober days, it helps you build new habits and provides ongoing motivation by connecting you to a wide network of people all striving for the same goal: staying sober one day at a time." 4.7 rating.

2. Sober Time. https://play.google.com/store/apps/details?id=com.sociosoft.sobertime

   This app is for just about every addiction. Quoted from website: "At the core of sobriety is motivation and a support structure. You'll stay motivated with daily messages, goals and simply watching your sobriety counter tick by. The built-in community provides much needed human connection, allowing you to share and learn from people with years or even decades on their sobriety clock." 4.7 rating.

3. Pocket Rehab: Get Sober & Addiction Recovery. https://play.google.com/store/apps/details?id=com.getpocketrehab.app

   This app is for just about every addiction. Quoted from website: "Connect with peers anonymously 24/7. Completely private. Get help anytime via text/call/video chat. Volunteer to help other users. Keep a private journal, find meetings nearby, explore a community Q&A, and more!" 4.7 rating.

4. Loop Habit Tracker. https://play.google.com/store/apps/details?id=org.isoron.uhabits

   This app is for just about every addiction. Quoted from website: "Loop helps you create and maintain good habits, allowing you to achieve your long-term goals. Detailed graphs and statistics show you how your habits improved over time. The app is completely ad-free and open source." 4.7 rating.

RESOURCES

This list is by no means intended to be exhaustive. Instead, it exemplifies several resources (mostly at no cost) available today on the Internet.

Substances and Treatment

Substance Abuse and Mental Health Services Administration (SAMHSA). Visit https://store.samhsa.gov/ and https://store.samhsa.gov/treatment-prevention-recovery

The Treatment Improvement Protocols—produced by the Center for Substance Abuse Treatment (CSAT), which is part of SAMHSA—are invaluable free resources. They include best practice guidelines for working with people who have substance abuse disorders. A list of these, including when they were published, is available from https://www.ncbi.nlm.nih.gov/books/NBK82999/

National Institute on Drug Abuse (NIDA). Publications at http://www.unodc.org/

National Institute on Alcohol Abuse and Alcoholism. Publications at https://www.niaaa.nih.gov/publications

University of New Mexico Center on Alcoholism, Substance Abuse, and Addictions. https://casaa.unm.edu/

Cochrane Reviews. https://www.cochrane.org/

Clinical Trials Network. http://ctndisseminationlibrary.org/

Cognitive Therapy Resources

Academy of Cognitive Therapy. https://www.academyofct.org/default.aspx

Association for Behavioral and Cognitive Therapies. http://www.abct.org/Home/

Department of Veterans Affairs South Central MIRECC. A therapist's guide to brief CBT. https://www.mirecc.va.gov/visn16/docs/therapists_guide_to_brief_cbtmanual.pdf

National Institute on Alcohol Abuse and Alcoholism Project MATCH. Cognitive-behavioral coping skills therapy manual. https://pubs.niaaa.nih.gov/publications/ProjectMatch/match03.pdf

Psychology Tools. CBT worksheets, handouts, and self-help resources. https://psychologytools.com/download-therapy-worksheets.html

https://www.infocounselling.com/cbt-worksheets-where-to-find-cbt-handouts/

www.specialtybehavioralhealth.com

https://livingcbt.com/

http://www.martincbt.com/handouts.html

https://www.cci.health.wa.gov.au/Resources/For-Clinicians

https://www.therapistaid.com/therapy-worksheets

https://excelatlife.com/

http://www.specialtybehavioralhealth.com/pdfs-cognitive-behavioral-therapy/

https://www.getselfhelp.co.uk/

https://tfcbt.org/wp-content/uploads/2014/07/Your-Very-Own-TF-CBT-Workbook-Final.pdf

https://www.hpft.nhs.uk/media/1184/cbt-workshop-booklet_web.pdf

Other Helpful Resources

Individual Counseling Manual. http://www.dronet.org/sostanze/sos_pdf/manual_3c.pdf

Integrated Recovery. http://integratedrecovery.org This site offers some excellent resources. It is currently under redesign.

Therapistaid. https://www.therapistaid.com/ They offer many great tools for counselors, including worksheets on various approaches.

Book chapter. Clinicians working with individuals with alcohol use problems, as well as clinicians in training, have found this chapter to be an extraordinarily useful resource in guiding their treatment approaches. McCrady, B. S. (2014). Alcohol use disorders. In D. H. Barlow (Ed.), *Clinical handbook of psychological disorders: A step-by-step treatment manual* (5th ed., pp. 533–587) New York, NY: Guilford Press.

Book. This book is described as the established standard for writing effective and efficient treatment plans in the treatment of addictions. Perkinson, R. R., Jongsma Jr., A. E., & Bruce, T. J. (2014). *The addiction treatment planner* (5th ed.). New York, NY: Wiley.

INDIVIDUAL EXERCISES

1. Six evidence-based counseling approaches were reviewed in this chapter. They include CBT and behavior therapy, MI and MET, TTM, mindfulness treatments, brief interventions, and IT. Which of these approaches most resonates within you? In other words, which approach are you most likely to utilize in practice? Explain why you have picked this approach over the other five.
2. Watch videotapes of competent counselors demonstrating one of the approaches. What do you like and dislike about the approach?
3. Design a simple token economy that could be used to help a 10-year-old boy who is disagreeable and does not obey when you ask him to do something around the house.

CLASSROOM EXERCISES

1. Invite a speaker to the class who is in recovery from an SUD. Have students prepare a list of questions in advance. Ask the speaker to focus on what counselors did with him or her that were most helpful and most unhelpful during recovery.
2. Divide your class into six groups. To each group, assign one of the six evidence-based counseling approaches covered in this chapter (i.e., CBT and behavior therapy, MI and MET, TTM, mindfulness treatments, brief interventions, and IT). Have the groups critique the approach assigned to them. What aspects of the approach would be most helpful to clients? What aspects of the approach might not be helpful?
3. In groups of three, have students practice the various techniques used in SFT (or pick brief interventions or suicide prevention). One student acts as a counselor, another as the client, and the third is the observer who provides feedback at the end of the roleplay.

CHAPTER SUMMARY

This chapter reviews how counselors can begin their work with clients by building a strong and positive working alliance. Clients have an amazing capacity to change on their own, but many still benefit from receiving help from counselors. The main evidence-based counseling approaches include the following:

1. CBT (e.g., REBT and CT) and behavior therapy.
2. MI and MET.
3. TTM.
4. Mindfulness treatments (mindfulness meditation).
5. Brief interventions.
6. IT.

There are 15 common IBs identified in REBT and, similarly, 15 common cognitive errors identified in CT. Both REBT and CT counselors focus on teaching and working with clients to identify how their thoughts affect their interpretation of events, which, in turn, creates either adaptive (healthy) or maladaptive (unhealthy) consequences for them.

Contingency management, which is a behavioral method, has been empirically demonstrated to be the most effective psychosocial intervention for SUDs. MI helps clients explore and resolve their ambivalence regarding change. It is a direct and client-centered approach. TTM has informed us that our clients are at various stages in the change process and we should use techniques that are most effective at helping clients move to the next stage. Mindfulness approaches have also been found helpful for individuals with SUDs. Mindfulness is moment-to-moment nonjudgmental awareness. Brief interventions of even 5 min are sometimes beneficial in helping clients begin on a change process. ITs combine psychological and pharmacological methods with complementary and alternative therapies. They are often preferable in working with addicted clients.

Although SFT does not yet have a sufficient empirical base to warrant calling it evidence-based for addictions, the approach has much to offer counselors who take a strength-based perspective in helping clients. SFT is focused on the future. There is little time spent discussing problems; instead, the time in session is spent looking at, embracing, and activating solutions.

Assessment and intervention strategies for suicide risk and prevention are considered given the increased suicidality experienced by addicted clients. A brief section on homicide risk is included as well. This is followed by a section on how we can end our counseling relationship with clients with a view that they will likely return if they are satisfied with our counseling services.

Relapse prevention has several meanings, but its main thrust is to help our clients avoid lapses and relapses. It generally involves three strategies: identifying patterns of use, avoiding or managing high-risk situations, and choosing and engaging in healthier behaviors. Appendix C contains many relapse prevention strategies to use with and provide to clients.

A compilation of 28 common counseling mistakes is outlined, and these are referred to in Chapters 9 through 21. Generic addiction apps are also briefly discussed, and four of these are described. Many resources that can help counselors and clients with nearly all aspects of recovery from addictions are available on the Internet. The resources listed are mostly free of charge.

REFERENCES

Ardito, R. B., & Rabellino, D. (2011). Therapeutic alliance and outcome of psychotherapy: Historical excursus, measurements, and prospects for research. *Frontiers in Psychology*, *2*, 1–11.

Baker, T. E., & Chang, G. (2016). The use of auricular acupuncture in opioid use disorder: A systematic literature review. *American Journal on Addictions*, *25*, 592–602.

Barbieri, B., Dal Corso, L., Di Sipio, A., De Carlo, A., & Benevene, P. (2016). Small opportunities are often the beginning of great enterprises: The role of work engagement in support of people through the recovery process and in preventing relapse in drug and alcohol abuse. *Work*, *55*(2), 373–383.

Beck, A. T. (2006). Personal reflections on Albert Ellis & REBT. *REBT Network*. Retrieved on January 3, 2019, from http://rebtnetwork.org/library/personalreflections.html

Blodgett, J. C., Maisel, N. C., Fuh, I. L., Wilbourne, P. L., & Finney J. W. (2014). How effective is continuing care for substance use disorders? A meta-analytic review. *Journal of Substance Abuse Treatment*, *46*, 87–97.

Bordin, E. S. (1979). The generalizability of the psychoanalytic concept of the working alliance. *Psychotherapy: Theory, Research & Practice*, *16*(3), 252–260.

Brooks, F., & McHenry, B. (2009). *A contemporary approach to substance abuse and addiction counseling: A counselor's guide to application and understanding*. Alexandria, VA: American Counseling Association.

Brown, R. A., Prince, M. A., Minami, H., & Abrantes, A. M. (2016). An exploratory analysis of changes in mood, anxiety and craving from pre- to post-single sessions of exercise, over 12 weeks, among patients with alcohol dependence. *Mental Health and Physical Activity*, *11*, 1–6.

Bubenzer, T., & Huang, H. (2014). Posthypnotic use of olfactory stimulus for pain management. *International Journal of Clinical and Experimental Hypnosis*, *62*, 188–194.

Burns, D. D. (2012). *Feeling good: The new mood therapy*. New York, NY: New American Library.

Calati, R., & Courtet, P. (2016). Is psychotherapy effective for reducing suicide attempt and non-suicidal self-injury rates? Meta-analysis and meta-regression of literature data. *Journal of Psychiatric Research*, *79*, 8–20.

Carnes, P. (1991). *Don't call it love: Recovery from sexual addiction*. Toronto, ON: Bantam Books.

Centers for Disease Control and Prevention. (2018, June 7). *Suicide rates rising across the U.S.: Comprehensive prevention goes beyond a focus on mental health concerns*. Retrieved on January 3, 2019, from https://www.cdc.gov/media/releases/2018/p0607-suicide-prevention.html

Chesin, M. S., Brodsky, B. S., Beeler, B., Benjamin-Phillips, C. A., Taghavi, I., & Stanley, B. (2018). Perceptions of adjunctive mindfulness-based cognitive therapy to prevent suicidal behavior among high suicide-risk outpatient participants. *Crisis: The Journal of Crisis Intervention and Suicide Prevention*, *39*, 451–460.

Chun, J., Shim, H., & Kim, S. (2017). A meta-analysis of treatment interventions for internet addiction among Korean adolescents. *Cyberpsychology, Behavior, and Social Networking*, *20*, 225–231.

Cohen, J. (1988). *Statistical power analysis for the behavioral sciences* (2nd ed.). Hillsdale, NJ: Lawrence Erlbaum.

Collins, K. R. L., Stritzke, W. G. K., Page, A. C., Brown, J. D., & Wylde, T. J. (2018). Mind full of life: Does mindfulness confer resilience to suicide by increasing zest for life? *Journal of Affective Disorders, 226*, 100–107.

Comtois, K. A., & Linehan, M. M. (2006). Psychosocial treatments of suicidal behaviors: A practice-friendly review. *Journal of Clinical Psychology, 62*, 161–170.

Connors, G. J., DiClemente, C. C., Velasquez, M. M., & Donovan, D. M. (2013). *Substance abuse treatment and the stages of change: Selecting and planning interventions* (2nd ed.). New York, NY: Guilford Press.

Csiernik, R. (2016). *Substance use and abuse: Everything matters* (2nd ed.). Toronto, ON: Canadian Scholars Press.

Cuzen, N. L., & Stein, D. J. (2014). Behavioral addiction: The nexus of impulsivity and compulsivity. In K. P. Rosenberg & L. Curtiss Feder (Eds.), *Behavioral addictions: Criteria, evidence, and treatment* (pp. 19–34). San Diego, CA: Elsevier Academic Press.

Damian, A. J., & Mendelson, T. (2017). Association of physical activity with alcohol abuse and dependence in a nationally-representative US sample. *Substance Use & Misuse, 52*(13), 1744–1750.

Dicken, L. (2016). Surfing as a mindfulness based cognitive behavioral therapy intervention for the treatment of addiction. *Dissertation Abstracts International: Section B: The Sciences and Engineering, 77*(2-B(E)). No pagination specified. Retrieved from http://ovidsp.ovid.com/ovidweb.cgi?T=JS&PAGE=reference&D=psyc13a&NEWS=N&AN=2016-31156-225

Diekstra, R. F. W., & Kerkhof, A. J. F. M. (1988). Attitudes toward suicide: The construction of a Suicide-Attitude Questionnaire (SUIATT). In H.-J. Möller, A. Schmidtke, & R. Welz (Eds.), *Current issues of suicidology* (pp. 462–476). New York, NY: Springer-Verlag.

Domino, G. (1996). Test-retest reliability of the Suicide Opinion Questionnaire. *Psychological Reports, 78*, 1001–1010.

Dutra, L., Stathopoulou, G., Basden, S. L., Leyro, T. M., Powers, M. B., & Otto, M. W. (2008). A meta-analytic review of psychosocial interventions for substance use disorders. *American Journal of Psychiatry, 165*, 179–187.

Earleywine, M. (2016). *Substance use problems* (2nd ed.). Ashland, OH: Hogrefe.

Ellis, A. (2011). Vigorous disputing of irrational beliefs in rational emotive behavior therapy (REBT). In H. G. Rosenthal (Ed.), *Favorite counseling and therapy techniques* (2nd ed., pp. 115–116). New York, NY: Routledge/Taylor & Francis Group.

Ellis, A., & Ellis, D. J. (2014b). Rational emotive behavior therapy process. In G. R. VandenBos, E. Meidenbauer, & J. Frank-McNeil (Eds.), *Psychotherapy theories and techniques: A reader* (pp. 299–306). Washington, DC: American Psychological Association.

Elzerbi, C., Donoghue, K., & Drummond, C. (2015). A comparison of the efficacy of brief interventions to reduce hazardous and harmful alcohol consumption between European and non-European countries: A systematic review and meta-analysis of randomized controlled trials. *Addiction, 110*, 1082–1091.

Erford, B. T., Jackson, J., Bardhoshi, G., Duncan, K., & Atalay, Z. (2018). Selecting suicide ideation assessment instruments: A meta-analytic review. *Measurement and Evaluation in Counseling and Development, 51*(1), 42–59.

Gardstrom, S. C., Klemm, A., & Murphy, K. M. (2017). Women's perceptions of the usefulness of group music therapy in addictions recovery. *Nordic Journal of Music Therapy, 26*, 338–358.

Giddens, J. M., & Sheehan, D. V. (2014). Is there value in asking the question "Do you think you would be better off dead?" in assessing suicidality? A case study. *Innovations in Clinical Neuroscience, 11*(9–10), 182–190.

Gladding, S. T., & Alderson, K. G. (2012). *Counselling: A comprehensive profession* (Canadian ed.). Toronto, ON: Pearson Canada.

Gladding, S. T., & Alderson, K. G. (2019). *Choosing the right counselor for you*. Alexandria, VA: American Counseling Association.

Glass, J. E., Hamilton, A. M., Powell, B. J., Perron, B. E., Brown, R. T., & Ilgen, M. A. (2015). Specialty substance use disorder services following brief alcohol intervention: A meta-analysis of randomized controlled trials. *Addiction, 110*, 1404–1415.

Gorski, T. T., & Miller, M. (1986). *Staying sober: A guide for relapse prevention*. Independence, MO: Herald Publishing House.

Green, K. L., Brown, G. K., Jager-Hyman, S., Cha, J., Steer, R. A., & Beck, A. T. (2015). The predictive validity of the Beck Depression Inventory suicide item. *Journal of Clinical Psychiatry, 76*(12), 1683–1686.

Greenfield, S. F., & Weiss, R. D. (2017). Addiction—25 years later. *Harvard Review of Psychiatry, 25*, 97–100.

Grohol, J. M. (2018, October 29). *Fifteen common cognitive distortions*. Retrieved on December 19, 2018, from https://psychcentral.com/lib/15-common-cognitive-distortions/

Gryczynski, J., Schwartz, R. P., Fishman, M. J., Nordeck, C. D., Grant, J., Nidich, S., . . . O'Grady, K. E. (2018). Integration of Transcendental Meditation (TM) into alcohol use disorder (AUD) treatment. *Journal of Substance Abuse Treatment, 87*, 23–30.

Han, B., & Avery, J. (2016). Relapse prevention. In P. Levounis, E. Zerbo, & R. Aggarwal (Eds.), *Pocket guide to addiction assessment and treatment* (pp. 273–283). Arlington, VA: American Psychiatric Association.

Harrison, D. P., Stritzke, W. G. K., Fay, N., & Hudaib, A.-R. (2018). Suicide risk assessment: Trust an implicit probe or listen to the patient? *Psychological Assessment, 30*, 1317–1329.

Hatzigiakoumis, D. S., Martinotti, G., di Giannantonio, M. D., & Janiri, L. (2011). Anhedonia and substance dependence: Clinical correlates and treatment options. *Frontiers in Psychiatry, 2*, 1–12.

Hendershot, C. S., Witkiewitz, K., George, W. H., & Marlatt, G. A. (2011). Relapse prevention for addictive behaviors. *Substance Abuse Treatment, Prevention, and Policy, 6*, 1–17.

Higgins, S. T., Badger, G. J., & Budney, A. J. (2000). Initial abstinence and success in achieving longer-term cocaine abstinence. *Experimental and Clinical Psychopharmacology, 8*, 377–386.

Hope Rehab. (2018). *Reflection questions (miracle questions): Exercise for addicts*. Retrieved on December 29, 2018, from https://www.hope-rehab-center-thailand.com/blog/addiction/reflection-miracle-question-exercise-addicts/

Hoppes, K. (2016). The application of mindfulness-based cognitive interventions in the treatment of co-occurring addictive and mood disorders. *CNS Spectrums, 11*(11), 829–851.

Humeniuk, R. E., Henry-Edwards, S., Ali, R. L., Poznyak, V., & Monteiro, M. (2010). *The ASSIST-linked brief intervention for hazardous and harmful substance use: Manual for use in primary care*. Geneva, Switzerland: World Health Organization. Retrieved on December 22, 2018, from http://apps.who.int/iris/bitstream/handle/10665/44321/9789241599399_eng.pdf;sequence=1

Jarema, M. (2018). Are we able to evaluate suicide risk? *Psychiatria Polska, 52*, 7–19.

Kabat-Zinn, J. (2013). *Full catastrophe living: Using the wisdom of your body and mind to face stress, pain, and illness* (Rev. ed.). New York, NY: Bantam.

Kaplan, D. M., Tarvydas, V. M., & Gladding, S. T. (2014). 2020: A vision for the future of counseling: The new consensus definition of counseling. *Journal of Counseling & Development, 92*, 366–372.

Karver, M. S., De Nadai, A. S., Monahan, M., & Shirk, S. R. (2018). Meta-analysis of the prospective relation between alliance and outcome in child and adolescent psychotherapy. *Psychotherapy, 55*, 341–355.

Kelly, J. F., Bergman, B. G., & O'Connor, C. L. (2018). Evidence-based treatment of addictive disorders: An overview. In J. MacKillop, G. A. Kenna, L. Leggio, & L. A. Ray (Eds.), *Integrating psychological and pharmacological treatments for addictive disorders: An evidence-based guide* (pp. 54–74). New York, NY: Routledge/Taylor & Francis Group.

Kemp, R., Channer, K., & Zahn, A. (2016). Willpower building: A new element in relapse prevention. *Health Psychology Report, 4*(4), 281–293.

Kerr, T., Small, W., Ayutthaya, P. P. N., & Hayashi, K. (2018). Experiences with compulsory drug detention among people who inject drugs in Bangkok, Thailand: A qualitative study. *International Journal of Drug Policy, 52*, 32–38.

Khan, F., Krishnan, A., Ghani, M. A., Wickersham, J. A., Fu, J. J., Lim, S. H., . . . Altice, F. L. (2018). Assessment of an innovative voluntary substance abuse treatment program designed to replace compulsory drug detention centers in Malaysia. *Substance Use & Misuse, 53*(2), 249–259.

King, D. L., Delfabbro, P. H., Wu, A. M. S., Doh, Y. Y., Kuss, D. J., Pallesen, S., . . . Sakuma, H. (2017). Treatment of Internet gaming disorder: An international systematic review and CONSORT evaluation. *Clinical Psychology Review, 54*, 123–133.

Kodaka, M., Postuvan, V., Inagaki, M., & Yamada, M. (2011). A systematic review of scales that measure attitudes toward suicide. *International Journal of Social Psychiatry, 57*(4), 338–361.

Kurlowicz, L., & Wallace, M. (1999, January). *The Mini Mental State Examination (MMSE)*. Issue 3. Retrieved on January 9, 2018, from https://www.mountsinai.on.ca/care/psych/on-call-resources/on-call-resources/mmse.pdf

Large, M., & Mullin, K. (2011). Risk assessment and screening for violence. *European Psychiatry, 26*(2), 132.

Large, M. M., & Ryan, C. J. (2015). Violence risk assessment has not been shown to reduce violence. *Australian and New Zealand Journal of Psychiatry, 49*, 91.

Larimer, M. E., Palmer, R. S., & Marlatt, G. A. (1999). Relapse prevention: An overview of Marlatt's cognitive-behavioral model. *Alcohol Research & Health, 23*(2), 151–160.

Larios, S. E., Manuel, J. K., Newville, H., & Sorensen, J. L. (2013). Evidence-based treatment. In P. M. Miller, S. A. Ball, M. E. Bates, A. W. Blume, K. M. Kampman, D. J. Kavanagh, M. E. Larimar, N. M. Petry, & P. De Witte (Eds.), *Comprehensive addictive behaviors and disorders, Vol. 3: Interventions for addiction* (pp. 621–631). San Diego, CA: Elsevier Academic Press.

Leenaars, A. A. (2006). Psychotherapy with suicidal people: The commonalities. *Archives of Suicide Research, 10*, 305–322.

Li, W., Howard, M. O., Garland, E. L., McGovern, P., & Lazar, M. (2017). Mindfulness treatment for substance misuse: A systematic review and meta-analysis. *Journal of Substance Abuse Treatment, 75*, 62–96.

Liang, H.-J., Lin, Y., Zhang, C., Ungvari, G. S., & Tang, W.-K. (2016). Drug addiction: A global challenge. *East Asian Archives of Psychiatry, 26*(2), 43–44.

Lindhiem, O., Bennett, C. B., Rosen, D., & Silk, J. (2015). Mobile technology boosts the effectiveness of psychotherapy and behavioral interventions: A meta-analysis. *Behavior Modification, 39*(6), 785–804.

Magill, M., & Ray, L. A. (2009). Cognitive-behavioral treatment with adult alcohol and illicit drug users: a meta-analysis of randomized controlled trials. *Journal of Studies on Alcohol & Drugs, 70*(4), 516–527.

Margolis, R. D., & Zweben, J. E. (2011). Individual psychotherapy. In R. D. Margolis & J. E. Zweben (Eds.), *Treating patients with alcohol and other drug problems: An integrated approach* (2nd ed., pp. 117–144). Washington, DC: American Psychological Association.

Marinchak, J. S., & Morgan, T. J. (2012). Behavioral treatment techniques for psychoactive substance use disorders. In S. T. Walters & F. Rotgers (Eds.), *Treating substance abuse: Theory and technique* (3rd ed., pp. 138–166). New York, NY: Guilford Press.

Martin, D. C. (1990). The mental status examination. In H. K. Walker, W. D. Hall, & J. W. Hurst (Eds.), *Clinical methods: The history, physical, and laboratory examinations* (3rd ed., pp. 924–929). Boston, MA: Butterworths. Retrieved on January 9, 2019, from https://www.ncbi.nlm.nih.gov/books/NBK320/pdf/Bookshelf_NBK320.pdf

Mason, B. J., & Higley, A. E. (2012). Human laboratory models of addiction. In K. D. Brownell & M. S. Gold (Eds.), *Food and addiction: A comprehensive handbook* (pp. 14–19). New York, NY: Oxford University Press.

McIntosh, C., & O'Neill, K. (2017). *Evidence-based treatments for problem gambling*. New York, NY: Springer Science + Business Media.

Miller, W. R. (2016). Sacred cows and greener pastures: Reflections from 40 years in addiction research. *Alcoholism Treatment Quarterly, 34*, 92–115.

Miller, W. R., & Baca, L. M. (1983). Two-year follow-up of bibliotherapy and therapist-directed controlled drinking training for problem drinkers. *Behavior Therapy, 14*, 441–448.

Miller, W. R., & Rollnick, S. (2009). Ten things that motivational interviewing is not. *Behavioural and Cognitive Psychotherapy, 37*(2), 129–140.

Miller, W. R., & Rollnick, S. (2013). *Motivational interviewing: Helping people change* (3rd ed.). New York, NY: Guilford.

Miller, W. R., Taylor, C. A., & West, J. C. (1980). Focused versus broad spectrum behavior therapy for problem drinkers. *Journal of Consulting and Clinical Psychology, 48*, 590–601.

Miller, W. R., Walters, S. T., & Bennett, M. E. (2001). How effective is alcoholism treatment in the United States? *Journal of Studies on Alcohol, 62*, 211–220.

Mistral, W. (Ed.) (2016). *Integrated approaches to drug and alcohol problems: Action on addiction*. New York, NY: Routledge.

Mladenovic, I., Lazetic, G., Lecic-Tosevski, D., & Dimitrijevic, I. (2015). Treatment of pathological gambling-integrative systemic model. *Psychiatria Danubina, 27*(1), 107–111.

Morrison, M. F., Lin, K., & Gersh, S. (2018). Addictions: Evidence for integrative treatment. In D. A. Monti & A. B. Newberg (Eds.), *Integrative psychiatry and brain health* (2nd ed., pp. 1–22). New York, NY: Oxford University Press.

Moyer, A., Finney, J. W., Swearingen, C. E., & Vergun, P. (2002). Brief interventions for alcohol problems: A meta-analytic review of controlled investigations in treatment-seeking and non-treatment-seeking populations. *Addiction*, *97*, 279–292.

National Institute on Drug Abuse. (2014). *Is legally mandated treatment effective?* Retrieved on January 3, 2019, from https://www.drugabuse.gov/publications/principles-drug-abuse-treatment-criminal-justice-populations/legally-mandated-treatment-effective

Nicholls, T. L., Pritchard, M. M., Reeves, K. A., & Hilterman, E. (2013). Risk assessment in intimate partner violence: A systematic review of contemporary approaches. *Partner Abuse*, *4*, 76–168.

Noyce, R., & Simpson, J. (2018). The experience of forming a therapeutic relationship from the client's perspective: A metasynthesis. *Psychotherapy Research*, *28*, 281–296.

Patterson, W. M., Dohn, H. H., Bird, J., & Patterson, G. A. (1983). Evaluation of suicidal patients: The SAD PERSONS scale. *Psychosomatics*, *24*(4), 343–349.

Pekala, R. J. (2017). Addictions and relapse prevention. In G. R. Elkins (Ed.), *Handbook of medical and psychological hypnosis: Foundations, applications, and professional issues* (pp. 443–451). New York, NY: Springer.

Petry, N. M. (2012). *Contingency management for substance abuse treatment: A guide to implementing evidence-based practice*. New York, NY: Routledge/Taylor & Francis Group.

Petry, N. M., Ledgerwood, D. M., & McKay, J. R. (2014). Treatment of substance use disorders. In H. R. Kranzler, D. A. Ciraulo, & L. R. Zindel (Eds.), *Clinical manual of addiction psychopharmacology* (2nd ed., pp. 387–412). Arlington, VA: American Psychiatric Publishing.

Petry, N. M., Rash, C. J., & Alessi, S. M. (2016). A randomized controlled trial of brief interventions for problem gambling in substance abuse treatment patients. *Journal of Consulting and Clinical Psychology*, *84*, 874–886.

Prochaska, J. O., & DiClemente, C. C. (2005). The transtheoretical approach. In J. Norcorss & M. R. Goldfried (Eds.), *Handbook of psychotherapy integration: Oxford series in clinical psychology* (2nd ed., pp. 147–171). New York, NY: Oxford University Press.

Prochaska, J. O., Norcross, J. C., & DiClemente, C. C. (1994). *Changing for good: A revolutionary six-stage program for overcoming bad habits and moving your life positively forward*. New York, NY: Avon Books.

Prochaska, J. O., & Velicer, W. F. (1997). The transtheoretical model of health behavior change. *American Journal of Health Promotion*, *12*, 38–48.

Razzhavaikina, T. I. (2007). *Mandatory counseling: A mixed methods study of factors that contribute to the development of the working alliance* (Doctoral dissertation). Retrieved on December 19, 2018, from http://digitalcommons.unl.edu/cgi/viewcontent.cgi?article=1009&context=cehsdiss

Renberg, R. S., & Jacobson, L. (2003). Development of a questionnaire on Attitudes Toward Suicide (ATTS) and its application in a Swedish population. *Suicide and Life-Threatening Behavior*, *33*(1), 52–64.

Riper, H., Andersson, G., Hunter, S. B., de Wit, J., Berking, M., & Cuijpers, P. (2014). Treatment of comorbid alcohol use disorders and depression with cognitive-behavioural therapy and motivational interviewing: a meta-analysis. *Addiction*, *109*, 394–406.

Rogers, C. (1957). The necessary and sufficient conditions of therapeutic personality change. *Journal of Consulting Psychology*, *21*(2), 95–103.

Roncero, C., Grau-Lopez, L., & Casas, M. (2017). Dual disorders: A clinical perspective. *Addictive Disorders & Their Treatment*, *16*, 175–179.

Rosenfeld, B., Foellmi, M., Khadivi, A., Wijetunga, C., Howe, J., Nijdam-Jones, A., . . . Rotter, M. (2017). Determining when to conduct a violence risk assessment: Development and initial validation of the Fordham Risk Screening Tool (FRST). *Law and Human Behavior*, *41*(4), 325–332.

Ross, W., & Ellis, A. (2014). Expanding the ABCs of rational emotive therapy. In J. Carlson & W. Knaus (Eds.), *Albert Ellis revisited* (pp. 73–85). New York, NY: Routledge/Taylor & Francis Group.

Roy, A. (2010). Risk factors for attempting suicide in heroin addicts. *Suicide and Life-Threatening Behavior*, *40*, 416–420.

Rudzinski, K., McGuire, F., Dawe, M., Shuper, P., Bilsker, D., Capler, R., . . . Fischer, B. (2012). Brief intervention experiences of young high-frequency cannabis users in a Canadian setting. *Contemporary Drug Problems: An Interdisciplinary Quarterly*, *39*, 49–72.

SAMHSA-HRSA Center for Integrated Health Solutions. (n.d.). *Brief interventions*. Retrieved on January 3, 2019, from https://www.integration.samhsa.gov/clinical-practice/sbirt/brief-interventions

Sayegh, C. S., Huey, S. J., Zara, E. J., & Jhaveri, K. (2017). Follow-up treatment effects of contingency management and motivational interviewing on substance use: A meta-analysis. *Psychology of Addictive Behaviors*, *31*, 403–414.

Singer, J. B., McManama O'Brien, K. H., & LeCloux, M. (2017). Three psychotherapies for suicidal adolescents: Overview of conceptual frameworks and intervention techniques. *Child & Adolescent Social Work Journal*, *34*, 95–106.

Smedslund, G., Berg, R. C., Hammerstrom, K. T., Steiro, A., Leiknes, K. A., Dahl, H. M., & Karlsen, K. (2011). Motivational interviewing for substance abuse. *Cochrane Database of Systematic Reviews*, *5*, CD008063.

Taboas, W. (2018). Over-disputing. *Albert Ellis Institute*. Retrieved on December 19, 2018, from http://albertellis.org/over-disputing/

Tang, Y.-Y., Tang, R., & Posner, M. I. (2016). Mindfulness meditation improves emotion regulation and reduces drug abuse. *Drug and Alcohol Dependence*, *163*, S13–S18.

Tariq, S. H., Tumosa, N., Chibnall, J. T., Perry, M. H., & Morley, J. E. (2006). Comparison of the Saint Lewis University mental status examination and mini-mental state examination for detecting dementia and mild neurocognitive disorder. *American Journal of Geriatric Psychiatry*, *14*(11), 900–910.

Tasca, G. A., Town, J. M., Abbass, A., & Clarke, J. (2018). Will publicly funded psychotherapy in Canada be evidence based? A review of what makes psychotherapy work and a proposal. *Canadian Psychology/Psychologie canadienne*, *59*, 293–300.

Thoma, N., Pilecki, B., & McKay, D. (2015). Contemporary cognitive behavior therapy: A review of theory, history, and evidence. *Psychodynamic Psychiatry*, *43*(4), 423–461.

Thorburn, R. W. (2015, April 15). *Rational emotive imagery by Robin W. Thorburn*. Retrieved on January 4, 2019, from http://www.ellisrebt.co.uk/rational-emotive-imagery/

Timulak, L., & Keogh, D. (2017). The client's perspective on (experiences of) psychotherapy: A practice friendly review. *Journal of Clinical Psychology*, *73*, 1556–1567.

Tucker-Ladd, C. E. (1996–2018). *Chapter 11: Methods for changing behaviors*. Retrieved on January 3, 2019, from https://www.psychologicalselfhelp.org/

Van Wormer, K., & Rae Davis, D. (2013). *Addiction treatment: A strengths perspective* (3rd ed.). Belmont, CA: Brooks/Cole.

Vatnar, S. K. B., Friestad, C., & Bjørkly, S. (2017). Intimate partner homicide, immigration and citizenship: Evidence from Norway 1990–2012. *Journal of Scandinavian Studies in Criminology and Crime Prevention*, *18*(2), 103–122.

Vossekuil, B., Fein, R. A., & Berglund, J. M. (2015). Threat assessment: Assessing the risk of targeted violence. *Journal of Threat Assessment and Management*, *2*(3–4), 243–254.

Walter, M., Dursteler, K. M., Petitjean, S. A., Wiesbeck, G. A., Euler, S., Sollberger, D., Lang, . . . Vogel, M. (2015). [Psychosocial treatment of addictive disorders: An overview of psychotherapeutic options and their efficacy]. *Fortschritte der Neurologie-Psychiatrie*, *83*, 201–210. doi:10.1055/s-0034-1399338, 10.1055/s-0034-1399338

Waltman, S. H., Sokol, L., & Beck, A. T. (2017). Cognitive behavior therapy treatment fidelity in clinical trials: Review of recommendations. *Current Psychiatry Reviews*, *13*, 311–315.

Werb, D., Kamarulzaman, A., Meacham, M., Rafful, C., Fischer, B., Strathdee, S., & Wood, E. (2016). The effectiveness of compulsory drug treatment: A systematic review. *International Journal of Drug Policy*, *28*, 1–9.

White, W., & Ali, S. (2010). *Lapse and relapse: Is it time for a new language*. Retrieved on December 30, 2018, from http://www.williamwhitepapers.com/pr/2010%20Rethinking%20the%20Relapse%20Language.pdf

Wilson, A. D., Roos, C. R., Robinson, C. S., Stein, E. R., Manuel, J. A., Enkema, M. C., . . . Witkiewitz, K. (2017). Mindfulness-based interventions for addictive behaviors: Implementation issues on the road ahead. *Psychology of Addictive Behaviors*, *31*, 888–896.

Witkiewitz, K., & Kirouac, M. (2016). Relapse prevention. In C. M. Nezu & A. M. Nezu (Eds.), *The Oxford handbook of cognitive and behavioral therapies* (pp. 215–228). New York, NY: Oxford University Press.

Witkiewitz, K., Marlatt, G. A., & Walker, D. (2017). Mindfulness-based relapse prevention for alcohol and substance use disorders. In B. A. Gaudiano (Ed.), *Mindfulness: Clinical applications of mindfulness and acceptance: Specific interventions for psychiatric, behavioural, and physical health conditions., Vol. III* (pp. 338–360). New York, NY: Routledge/Taylor & Francis Group.

World Health Organization. (2014). *Preventing suicide—A global imperative: Executive summary*. Retrieved on January 2, 2019, from https://www.who.int/mental_health/suicide-prevention/exe_summary_english.pdf?ua=1

Wright, J. H., Thase, M. E., & Beck, A. T. (2014). Cognitive-behavior therapy. In R. E. Hales, S. C. Yudofsky, & L. W. Roberts (Eds.), *The American Psychiatric Publishing textbook of psychiatry* (6th ed., pp. 1119–1160). Arlington, VA: American Psychiatric.

Wu, S. L. Y., Leung, A. W. N., & Yew, D. T. W. (2016). Acupuncture for detoxification in treatment of opioid addiction. *East Asian Archives of Psychiatry*, *26*(2), 70–76.

You, C.-W., Chen, Y.-C., Chen, C.-H., Lee, C.-H., Kuo, P.-H., Huang, M.-C., & Chu, H.-H. (2017). Smartphone-based support system (SoberDiary) coupled with a Bluetooth breathalyser for treatment-seeking alcohol-dependent patients. *Addictive Behaviors*, *65*, 174–178.

Young, A. (2017). Uncovery: Beneath the monolith of addiction there remains a human being. In J. K. Edwards, A. Young, & H. J. Nikels (Eds.), *Handbook of strengths-based clinical practices: Finding coming factors* (pp. 53–69). New York, NY: Routledge/Taylor & Francis.

Zmuda, N. (2014). Assessment and treatment of co-occurring substance use disorders and process addictions: Eating disorders, pathological gambling, and sexual addiction. In S. L. A. Straussner (Ed.), *Clinical work with substance-abusing clients* (3rd ed., pp. 520–536). New York, NY: Guilford Press.

7 Couples, Family, Group, and Mutual Support Groups

iStock.com/KatarzynaBialasi

Learning Objectives

1. Learn about two popular couples counseling and three family counseling approaches with substantial empirical support and others that have minimal empirical support with addictions.
2. Become familiar with the types of groups, basics of group dynamics, stages in group work, limitations of group counseling, and practical suggestions for forming and leading a group.
3. Compare and contrast 12-step mutual support groups with non-12-step mutual support groups.
4. Understand the similarities and differences among SMART Recovery, LifeRing, Secular Organizations for Sobriety, Women for Sobriety, and Moderation Management.
5. Discover some helpful tools in the appendices dealing with needs and wants of each partner in a relationship, conflict resolution, and the common mistakes made by couples and family counselors.

PERSONAL REFLECTIONS

Now and then, you have the privilege of working with a client who teaches you something that stays with you forever. Last year, a client taught me something about the expectations that clients should have of us. Before every session, she would email me her agenda for the upcoming session. That really kept me on track because I was determined to ensure that each item was addressed to her satisfaction. I incorporated this idea into a recent book (Gladding & Alderson, 2019). Furthermore, I enhanced the idea by suggesting that clients could set an agenda, write out their expectations, and/or establish their goals in measurable terms before sessions and then return this to their counselors before their next session via email or hand it to their counselors at the beginning of their next sessions.

I learned a different valuable lesson about counseling from a couple several years ago. I was working at an employee assistance program where all client files were kept in a central location. I will call the couple "Harold" and "April" (not their real names). The reason they came to see me was that Harold had been carrying on an affair with another woman at work. Harold said that the affair had ended. Both he and April wanted to work on their marriage. The problem, from Harold's perspective, was that there was no longer a spark between the two of them.

Furthermore, they had not had sex for more than 2 years. I saw them for the maximum number of sessions allowed, which was roughly eight or 10. I thought I could help Harold bring back his chemistry for April if I could get them relating to each other physically, sensually, and sexually. But nothing changed.

Months later, I was shuffling through the filing cabinet for a different client file when I came upon theirs. I noticed that they had already had a few sessions with a different counselor and I wondered what their new issue was. It was the same issue! It turns out that Harold had continued seeing this other woman throughout the work I did with them. Harold taught me to begin couples counseling differently (described in the next section).

What are the secrets that people keep when they are in relationships with others? How do these secrets affect addiction counseling? What can you do to help a couple in distress or a family that is struggling with an addiction issue? Does group counseling just provide another forum for telling still more lies? These are what I think about as I write this chapter.

Couples Counseling

Although couples counseling is uncommon in addictions treatment (Sherrell & Gutierrez, 2014), several studies have found that, when supportive partners in a stable relationship are involved in it, the likelihood of success regarding addiction goals increases (McCrady, 2014). Unsurprisingly, couples counseling has become the treatment of choice when committed couples are in distress (Sherrell & Gutierrez, 2014). A review of outcome research found that, when alcohol-dependent individuals are unwilling to get help, couples and family counseling is effective in helping families motivate clients to enter treatment (O'Farrell & Clements, 2012). Klostermann (2016) stated that marital and family counseling for substance use disorders (SUDs) is efficacious for preventing, motivating, and treating SUDs. Individuals with gambling disorder in one study preferred couples counseling over individual counseling (Tremblay et al., 2018).

However, McCrady (2014) cautioned that, if the partner has experienced severe domestic violence or is ambivalent about remaining in the relationship, couples counseling might be less appropriate, particularly in the early stages of treatment. Also, it is important to remember that dyadic relationships constitute a system, and sometimes, when one partner begins to change, even if for the better, the other person either begins or continues detaching. As Rosenberg, Carnes, and O'Connor (2014) noted, addiction may act as the "glue" (p. 85) that keeps the couple together. Some individuals may find that their addicted partners are more likable when they are "doing" their addiction (and perhaps angrier and more irritable when they are not), whereas other couples may thrive on the chaos created by the addiction (Rosenberg et al., 2014).

I recommend that the first session with couples should begin with the two of them together to go over the signed informed consent form before telling them that you will meet with each individually for a few minutes before again bringing the two of them together. During the few minutes you spend alone with each client, clarify the following:

1. Confidentiality. Establish that what you talk about will be kept confidential but that you will ask at the end of the session what is okay and not okay to share with the partner.
2. Adverse factors. Find out if there are any factors that may prevent the two of them from moving forward in couples counseling. Particularly notable is if a member of the dyad is continuing involvement in a clandestine affair.
3. Commitment. Ask the clients on a scale of 0 (*not at all*) to 10 (*completely*) how committed they are to this relationship. This helps you ascertain if both individuals see the relationship similarly. If both provide a score close to 0, you might soon be providing dissolution counseling.
4. Openness or secrets. At the end of your time alone with this client, ask if it is okay to share, if appropriate, everything that has been discussed when the three of you meet again toward the end of the session. The answer is telling as it informs you about whether this individual or this couple has open communication or if one or both keep secrets.

Collins (2018) wrote that individuals addicted to sex or porn often seek treatment when they get caught. Counseling is unlikely to be successful if one or both partners are involved in a covert affair.

There are other general suggestions regarding couples work. Birchler, Fals-Stewart, and O'Farrell (2008) suggested that couples counselors could help couples with addiction issues to avoid blaming each other. Nabuco de Abreu and Sampio Goes (2011), in writing about Internet addiction, provided a few helpful suggestions in providing couples counseling:

1. Help clients set specific goals. For example, deciding upon a specific amount of time to spend on the computer should be determined jointly.
2. Use "I" statements. This helps to avoid blaming the partner. Counselors themselves should use nonjudgmental and nonaccusatory language. "I" statements should focus on the present moment and should avoid negative words that trigger the partner. Counselors can help clients rephrase their statements. For example, if one client says, "You always ignore me," an appropriate reframe might be, "I feel alone in my relationship with you, and I would like us to have more time together."
3. Encourage empathy. Empathy is important so that partners listen to each other instead of reacting to each other. A common method is teaching clients to reflect the content. For example, using the statement, "I feel alone in my relationship with you, and I would like us to have more time together," the partner could be taught to paraphrase (e.g., "You want more time with me") and/or to reflect implied or embedded feelings (e.g., "You feel abandoned by me").

Popular Approaches With Substantial Empirical Support With Addictions

Cognitive-behavioral couples therapy (CBCT).

There are surprisingly few references to the use of CBCT in addiction treatment, despite the burgeoning empirically supported literature regarding the effectiveness of CBCT in general (Baucom, Fischer, Hahlweg, & Epstein, 2019; Mack, Lebowitz, & Silverman, 2019), traumatic stress (Monson, Wagner, Fredman, Macdonald, & Pukay-Martin, 2017), relationship distress (Fischer & Baucom, 2018), and psychopathology (Fischer & Baucom, 2018). A book called *Couple Therapy for Alcoholism: A Cognitive-Behavioral Treatment Manual* (Wakefield, Williams, Yost, & Patterson, 1996) was published in the 1990s, but no further editions have been released.

Bishop (2012) stated that rational emotive behavior therapy and CBCT are both effective in helping couples deal with addictions. Bishop is the Director of Alcohol and Substance Abuse Services at the Albert Ellis Institute. As is true of both cognitive and behavioral approaches, the counselor begins with a thorough assessment. Some irrational beliefs held by addicts include the following:

- I can't stand it anymore.
- It's awful.
- He (or she) is awful and will never change.
- I'm trapped; I'm helpless and hopeless and I'll never have a good life.
- I should know what to do; I must fix this problem.
- He (or she) shouldn't lie to me about the addiction.
- There must be something wrong with me for staying with him.
- I shouldn't have married him (or her) to begin with. (p. 172).

Bishop (2012) offered several techniques that can help clients think differently about their addictive behavior. None of these were focused explicitly on CBCT, however. He did suggest that therapists should never terminate with couples where one or both have addictive issues. Given that relapse is common, keep access available when couples need help.

Behavioral couples therapy (BCT).

BCT intends to help couples become better communicators, more cohesive, and flexible (Sherrell & Gutierrez, 2014). BCT interventions target both substance abuse and relationship functioning simultaneously. BCT counselors meet their clients for between 12 and 24 weekly couple sessions. The target behaviors are initially substance-related, and the techniques utilized are creating a recovery contract, going over drug screen results (if this is occurring), reducing the impact of triggering behaviors, and teaching them to avoid high-risk situations (Sherrell & Gutierrez, 2014).

Different techniques are used concerning relationship functioning. The focus is on helping the couple develop positive feelings, deepening their commitment to each other, and improving communication skills needed for conflict resolution (Sherrell & Gutierrez, 2014). Techniques included in Chapter 6 are used such as direct instruction, modeling, behavioral rehearsal, and roleplays. Couples are also engaged in acting more caringly toward each other, and they agree to this at the outset.

Schumm and O'Farrell (2013) outlined several of their techniques. As part of the recovery contract, Schumm and O'Farrell stressed that a daily "trust discussion" (p. 59) is important. They suggest that couples pick a specific time and place where they can talk without interruption. During the discussion, addicted partners state their intent to refrain from their substance or addictive behavior, whereas the nonaddicted partners express their support. Medications such as disulfiram or naltrexone would be swallowed while their partner watches. Couples are also encouraged to focus on the present and future and not on the past.

For improving the relationship, Schumm and O'Farrell (2013) focus on increasing the number of positive exchanges that occur within the relationship. One way in which couples are instructed to do this is to implement a daily ritual of noticing and mentioning positive relationship behaviors. Couples are also told to share rewarding activities and to plan "caring days" (p. 60). Furthermore, couples create a series of special surprises such as making their partner's favorite breakfast or emailing a love letter. They are also taught effective speaking and listening skills within the session, and they are asked to apply these skills outside of the session. Conflict resolution skills are taught as well (see Appendix 7A for an example).

For effective conflict resolution to occur, counselors can assist couples in ascertaining the nature of their conflicts. Perhaps more important (from a behavioral perspective), what behaviors do they want to see change with their partners? Also, individuals have "bottom lines" (i.e., if these behaviors do not change, they will leave the relationship) and other behaviors that are of lower priority (i.e., what they would *like* to see change). I created an exercise for doing this with couples that determines what each partner needs and wants in the relationship, but also the extent to which their partners feel able and willing to make the requested changes (Appendix 7B contains the form and instructions).

Relapse prevention is also addressed (Schumm & O'Farrell, 2013). This entails creating a well-defined and mutually agreeable continuing recovery plan. Follow-up visits are commonly planned, too. An action plan is developed should a lapse or relapse occur, including sources of support.

In offering BCT, Birchler et al. (2008) found that it helped to have couples make four promises to each other. They are as follows:

1. Attend counseling sessions and complete homework as assigned.
2. Refrain from making threats of divorce or separation.
3. Maintain a focus on the present and not on the past or future.
4. Avoid angry touching (i.e., no pushing, shoving, hitting).

BCT has strong empirical support (MacKillop, Stojek, VanderBroek-Stice, & Owens, 2018). In fact, BCT has stronger efficaciousness than individual therapy for individuals with alcohol use disorder (AUD) (O'Farrell, Schumm, Dunlap, Murphy, & Muchowski, 2016). Research has found that it is helpful in keeping couples together, increasing abstinence, reducing intimate violence, helping the couple's children adjust, and creating happier relationships (Sherrell & Gutierrez, 2014). McCrady and Epstein (2015) provide excellent step-by-step instructions for counselors wanting to implement BCT for alcohol problems. BCT is *not* as effective with couples where psychosis is involved or when the addicted individual is not committed to abstinence (Sherrell & Gutierrez, 2014).

Popular Approaches With Minimal Empirical Support With Addictions

Psychodynamic couples therapy.

There is little research supporting the use of psychodynamic couples therapy with addictive behavior. Byrne (2018) wrote about the importance of attachment theory in working with couples. She highlighted the substantial research showing that unsatisfactory attachment can lead to interpersonal difficulties and destructive behavior in oneself, which is then displaced into current intimate dyadic and family relationships. In this way, Byrne suggested that attachment theory provides an empirical method of looking at the different styles of relating used by both individuals and couples.

Wanlass (2014) used a case study to exemplify how relationships can bring up what she called "encapsulated trauma" (p. 310). Laaser (2004) wrote that people do not marry sex-addicted individuals by accident. Instead, partners intentionally choose their relationships, possibly because they are themselves abuse victims or have developed codependency in intimate relationships. Carnes (1991) defined codependency, which he called co-addiction, as "an obsessive illness in which reaction to addiction causes the loss of self" (p. 152). Laaser also suggested that individuals can heal relationship patterns only when they are in one.

Emotion-focused therapy (EFT).

Sherrell and Gutierrez (2014) highlighted EFT as a brief therapy that brings together experiential, humanistic, and family systems approaches, which is based on attachment theory. The EFT counselor works at building a strong positive working alliance, exploring the emotional responses while increasing positive ones, and reorganizing the couple's interactions to become accessible and responsive (Sherrell & Gutierrez, 2014). The focus is on the present rather than on the past. EFT utilizes individual interventions within the context of couples counseling. Sherrell and Gutierrez mentioned the work of Reid and Woolley, authors who saw the benefits of using EFT with couples where one partner is hypersexual. EFT generally lasts between 10 and 12 sessions. EFT counselors do not begin their work unless the addicted partner has their problematic behavior in remission. Clients' emotions act as a guide toward seeing the meaning behind perceptions and motivations while at the same time helping clients develop positive emotions. Roleplaying is also used in EFT.

Sherrell and Gutierrez (2014) stated that the empirical base regarding attachment theory, which forms the foundation of EFT, is considerable. According to Sherrell and Gutierrez, the founders of EFT have demonstrated that about 90% of couples significantly improve their relationships compared with untreated couples. Landau-North, Johnson, and Dalgleish (2011), however, stated that there is not much material that addresses EFT with couples dealing with addictive behaviors. For example, between 2012 and 2018, only two articles appeared in PsycINFO, one of which focused on EFT and sexual addiction (Love, Moore, & Stanish, 2016) and the other a dissertation that found that couples in addiction treatment showed improvement in addiction recovery and movement from an insecure attachment style toward a secure attachment style (Bassett, 2015).

ROLEPLAY SCENARIOS

Roleplay in dyads with one of you acting as the counselor and the other as the counselee. If roleplay is not possible, work individually in writing out a list of your suggestions.

Roleplay #1

Sean, age 34, and Hilda, age 30, have been married for the past 3 years. It didn't take long before Sean was sneaking in bottles of vodka, placing these in various locations around their house and garage. Hilda says that she had no idea that Sean was an alcoholic before their marriage. She said that, although he liked to drink, she never saw him so drunk that he would stagger but that this has occurred several times since they began living together. Sean denies that he is an alcoholic and tells you that he rarely has more than four drinks at any

(Continued)

(Continued)

one time. He also denies ever staggering and came to the session today only because Hilda said she would leave him if he bailed.

Roleplay #2

Danny, age 21, and Derek, age 21, have dated seriously since the end of high school. They see each other several times a week even though they both live with their respective parents. Danny wonders if he wants to stay in this relationship. He tells you that Derek is addicted to watching erotica, and, after he becomes sexually charged by watching it, he often leaves his house for a hookup with some other guy. Derek does not deny any of this, but he thinks that his watching erotica is really not Danny's business. Regarding his outside sexual activity, Derek tells you that he would like to stop doing this because he says that he is in love with Danny and that he does not want to lose him.

COUNSELING SCENARIO

As you are reading, imagine that you are the female client in this scenario. Note the areas in which the session could be improved on the part of the counselor.

Your name is Chastity, age 23, and your boyfriend's name is Wade, age 45. The two of you have been steady for the past 18 months, and Wade has recently proposed to you. You are conflicted, however, because you see yourself as a free spirit. Furthermore, you do not feel ready to settle down and get married. Unbeknownst to Wade, you have been having sex with several men closer to your age. This has troubled you, however, because you see this as a pattern that you have established with boyfriends since you were 14 years old. You have decided that you are going to tell Wade why you could not answer him when he proposed to you: You thought it would be safer to make the disclosure in front of Isaac, an addiction counselor. You currently view your promiscuity as a sexual addiction.

- Counselor: Welcome. Please come into my office. [After both of you signed an informed consent form, Isaac meets with each of you individually for a few minutes to find out if there are any extenuating circumstances that he should know. You tell him the issue that you want to bring up today with Wade present. Now the two of you are back in Isaac's office.]
- Counselor: I believe we can get down to work right away. Chastity, you have something that you want to disclose to Wade. Would you like to begin?
- You: [thrown slightly off guard] Ah, yeah, sure. Sorry, I was expecting that we might talk about how we have been doing as a couple first.
- Wade: Chastity, what is it that you want to tell me?
- You: Well, as you know, I was unable to give you an answer when you proposed to me. I have to say that it was completely unexpected but a very kind offer on your part just the same.
- Wade: You have me worried now, Chastity. What do you want to tell me?
- You: I do not know if I am ready to get married. I am only 23, and I find myself still checking out lots of other guys.
- Wade: I think that is natural, Chastity. I've always believed it is okay to look at others but not touch.
- You: [gulps] Um, I think that might be the problem, Wade. I also like to touch. I get together with other guys two or three times a week, and I have been doing that since we met.
- Wade: [become speechless, starts crying]
- You: I am so sorry, Wade. I never meant to hurt you.
- Counselor: Chastity, what has caused you to tramp yourself out this way? Your behavior certainly has been unfair to Wade.
- You: Ah, well, when you put it that way, I just feel ashamed and unworthy.
- Wade: I had no idea you were doing this behind my back! Why didn't you tell me?
- Counselor: Yeah, why didn't you tell Wade that you were not ready to settle down?
- You: I don't know! I thought I would outgrow it perhaps and I didn't want to lose you, Wade.
- Wade: What do you want from me? Do you want to break up with me despite how deeply I am in love with you?
- You: I really don't know. I was hoping we could talk through this today.
- Counselor: I think you know, Chastity. You are not ready to get married. Wade is too old for you anyway, and he could find much better out there.

- You: [addressing Isaac] You really know how to make me hurt inside. I thought the session might look different than this!
- Counselor: You know, Chastity, I have been happily married for 20 years. If my wife ever did to me what you have done to Wade, I would throw her out face first!
- You: I can see where this is going. I am leaving!
- Counselor: You can run from your problems all your life if you want, Chastity. But they will catch up with you.
- You: [sarcastically] I will remember that. Thank you very much!

From the Client's Perspective

1. How would you feel given the way that Isaac has talked to you?
2. What is missing for you in this dialogue?
3. What would you find more helpful from a counselor in this scenario?

From the Counselor's Perspective

1. What is interfering with developing a working alliance?
2. Turn to the Common Mistakes Made by Couples and Family Counselors list in Appendix 7C. Which mistakes is the counselor making with Chastity?
3. How did the way Isaac dealt with Chastity influence Wade's behavior in the session?

Family Counseling

The field of family counseling as an independent form of treatment emerged in the 1950s (Csiernik, 2016). Historically, family counseling for individuals with AUD developed from couples therapy, but, in the case of other substance disorders, family counseling developed from systemic family therapy (O'Farrell, 2011).

Although research in family counseling continues to grow, it appears that research focused on family counseling for addictions has paled by comparison over the past decade. For example, models of working with families where AUD is present are scarce (McCrady, 2014), as are counseling intervention strategies for substance disorders (Bradshaw et al., 2015). Between 2010 and early 2019, only 26 journal articles on this topic were found in PsycINFO.[1] Although feminist theory (Silverstein & Goodrich, 2019) and postmodern approaches (e.g., narrative, solution-focused) are well represented in the general family therapy literature today (Heatherington & Johnson, 2019), this is not occurring as much when applied to addictions work. Despite this, many studies attest to the effectiveness of family therapy in addictions work (Baharudin et al., 2014; Klostermann, 2016; O'Farrell & Clements, 2012).

"The impact of addiction on families can be devastating" (Lassiter, Czerny, & Williams, 2015). The family system can be affected legally, financially, socially, psychologically, and emotionally (Lassiter et al., 2015). Furthermore, research has found that substance abuse and family problems are frequently comorbid (Klostermann, 2016).

As Belmontes (2018) highlighted, relationships can remain part of the problem for addicted individuals or become part of the solution. It is best to have families become a healing force in addicted individuals' lives. According to Rosenberg et al. (2014), the biggest obstacle in addiction work is changing the system. In many collectivist societies, healing must occur within the family as receiving outside help is either stigmatized, unavailable, and/or unaffordable (Wanigaratne, 2011). Arguably, family therapy becomes even more important in Western societies that have emphasized individuality, sometimes at the sacrifice of familial engagement.

Some argue that successful treatment cannot occur unless the family actively participates (Potkonjak, Ivancic, Zdunic, Karlovic, & Matosic, 2006). Although this is clearly overstated (i.e., some individuals have no involvement with their families yet manage to stop or curtail their addictive behavior), it does speak to the importance of including family whenever possible.

Many addictions can be conceptualized as a "family issue" (McComb, Lee, & Sprenkle, 2009, p. 415), particularly with individuals who reside with other family members. Most and usually all family members are affected by addiction (Zmuda, 2014). Although the stereotype is that most addicted individuals are loners living on the street who have lost contact with their families, substance abusers (especially drug-addicted individuals) have more contact with their families when compared with the general population (Margolis & Zweben, 2011)!

Although one would expect that, once substance-dependent individuals stop using, the situation at home would become more settled, it rarely occurs this way (Margolis & Zweben, 2011). Often families become more chaotic and confrontational immediately after addicted individuals stop their addictive behavior. Not only are the addicted individuals likely to become more irritable, but the other family members may also fail to understand everyone's increased emotional lability (Margolis & Zweben, 2011). Also, family members might have hung onto anger and resentments for years, and sometimes these now become expressed once the addicted individual is in recovery.

A family therapist understands this emotional eruption and can help the family become restabilized (or stabilized for the first time). Margolis and Zweben (2011) recommended that this is an ideal time for family members to be referred to mutual support meetings such as Al-Anon for AUDs (other family-focused groups can be found in Chapters 9 through 21).

After stabilization, the family counselor helps families develop new coping skills now that the family system has changed. Others in the family have often created a life based on reacting to the addicted member (remember, this is called codependency) (Margolis & Zweben, 2011).

[1]The search included the following search terms: (family counseling or family therapy) × (drug addiction or sexual addiction or addiction or Internet addiction or heroin addiction). Search limited to human, English language, and all journals.

Wegscheider (1981) suggested that family members adopt one of five roles in the family: the enabler, hero, lost child, mascot, and scapegoat. The spouse most often acts as the enabler (i.e., codependent), the hero is the child (usually the eldest) who takes on a parental role, the lost child "disappears" in the family as he or she tries not to bring attention to self for the sake of the addict, the mascot adds comic relief by adding humor, and the scapegoat often acts opposite to the hero (still managing to take attention away from the addict). The scapegoat is a trouble-maker and often seems angry while other members internalize their feelings.

Several authors have suggested a stage approach when offering family therapy for addictions. Four of these are as follows (this list is by no means comprehensive). George and Bowden-Jones (2015) recommended that family counselors working with addicted gamblers follow five steps: (a) get to know the family members and the problem, (b) provide relevant information, (c) focus on coping behaviors, (d) enhance social support, and (e) end counseling but explore additional needs and resources. Chan (2003) suggested using the stages of change model (described in Chapter 6). Lewis and Allen-Byrd (2007) wrote that working with families who had an alcoholic addicted member had taught them that recovery generally followed four stages: (a) drinking stage, (b) transition stage, (c) early recovery stage, and (d) ongoing recovery stage. Lastly, Lambert, Carmichael, and Williams (2016) suggested that family counseling can be seen as occurring in phases: ongoing case conceptualization, beginning sessions, middle phase, termination, and follow-up.

What does a healthy family look like, and how does it contrast to a dysfunctional family? Lambert et al. (2016) summarized the works of several family researchers and created the following list regarding healthy families (some of these in this section and the next have been adapted):

1. Belonging. In healthy families, family members feel committed to each other, and the unit is cohesive.
2. Accountable and appreciative. Family members feel a sense of responsibility to the family unit and show appreciation to one another.
3. Flexibility. Healthy families can make compromises, maintain flexibility, and accommodate one another's needs. They are adaptable.
4. Good communication. The quality of communications is effective, occurs frequently, and is of high quality.
5. Individuation. Rather than enmeshed, family members have their own identity and individuality.
6. Boundaries. Family members respect each other's emotional boundaries.
7. Healthy. The family unit encourages physical, spiritual, and emotional well-being.
8. Spiritual. Healthy families have a religious or spiritual orientation.
9. Resilience. Healthy families can deal with conflict and move beyond it.
10. Convictions and values. These are imparted to children as they mature.
11. Fun. Healthy families want to have fun together.
12. Encouraging and respectful. Family members encourage one another, and they respect each other.
13. Role clarity. Family members know what is expected of them.

Unhealthy families, on the other hand, have the following characteristics (Lambert et al., 2016):

1. Closed communication. Family members do not communicate much with each other and, when they do, it is "surface" (i.e., lacking depth).
2. Low parental self-esteem. One or both parents do not feel good about themselves.
3. Rigidity. Family members are expected to think, feel, and act in the same way.
4. Controlling parents. Parents maintain control through fear, guilt, dominance, and/or punishment.
5. Coercions and threats. These families use coercion and threats with one another.
6. Anxious and tense. There is often tension in the household when disagreements arise.
7. Coalitions or triangulation. This occurs when one or more family members create an alliance against one or more other family members.
8. Disengagement or enmeshment. Either of these patterns is taken to an unhealthy level.
9. Rigidity or chaos. Either the rules are overly rigid, or the opposite occurs, and there are insufficient rules, resulting in chaos.

There are some general family counseling techniques suggested by experts that may be helpful in your practice. Some of these include the following:

- Family behavior loop map. During a family interview, the counselor writes a step-by-step description of thoughts, feelings, and actions of each family member, which are then drawn into a flow diagram for both the counselor and family members to review (Liepman, Flachier, & Tareen, 2008).
- Enactment. During enactment, counselors have family members talk to each other during sessions rather than talking to the counselor. As counselors observe problematic communications, they interrupt, thereby destabilizing these maladaptive patterns of interaction (O'Farrell, 2011).
- Reframing. Reframing occurs when counselors assist family members to understand how their behaviors are interrelated while highlighting how addictive behavior serves a function in the family unit (O'Farrell, 2011).
- Restructuring. Restructuring is about shifting family communication patterns and establishing healthy behaviors. A typical scenario by Salvador Minuchin, the founder of structural approaches, is to change the seating arrangements to strengthen the role of parents or to create

stronger liaisons between siblings. Problems are also restated in solvable form and conflict is avoided as much as possible (O'Farrell, 2011).

- Marking boundaries. This is achieved by helping family members become clear on individual and subsystem boundaries. For example, the relationship between the parents needs to be protected by having personal boundaries between them and their children (O'Farrell, 2011).
- Joining. Family counselors need to join with the family, thereby creating a strong positive working alliance. The intent is to have family members feel welcome and safe. There are several ways to do this. Lassiter et al. (2015) suggested that counselors match the family's mood or tone, show empathy, and use the same words that family members use to talk about their problems and challenges without making any judgments. One way to do this is to, instead of directly confronting an issue, begin with the words, "I wonder how your family would act differently if . . ." or "I wonder what would happen if . . ."
- Segmenting. Segmenting a family means not including one or more individuals for a period within a session or an entire session. If planning a segment intervention, it is important that you provide informed consent regarding its purpose. Especially with children, it is important to have the permission of the parents. Another consideration is having a policy concerning what you will do if secrets are shared with you by a family member (Lassiter et al., 2015).
- A process, not an event. Teach families that family counseling is a process that evolves over sessions: It is not a single event.
- Child abuse. Lassiter et al. (2015) suggested that, when a family member reports child abuse or neglect, it is essential for counselors to proceed by promoting a safe and empowering environment that maintains a strong positive working alliance. Depending on the nature and severity of the abuse, counselors may need to collaborate with social services in working with the family. The cardinal rule is "safety first" (Lassiter et al., 2015, p. 403).

Lassiter et al. (2015) also recommended a protocol for families dealing with the potential for violence. This involved creating a plan that might look like the following:

- Having the phone numbers for police, hotlines, friends, and family members who can help close by.
- Creating a code word with a friend or neighbor that can be used when a family member needs help or asking neighbors to call 911 if they hear angry or violent noises from the home.
- Creating a safe escape plan from the home.
- Removing weapons from the home safely.
- Having a plan on where individuals can go if they do need to escape quickly, such as a local domestic violence shelter.
- Having excuses to leave the home, such as needing to take out the trash, walk the dog, or run to the store.
- Having a copy of important documents either hidden in the vehicle or at a friend or relative's house. Keep a small bag of overnight clothes and toiletries or medication there as well.
- Teaching children how to call 911.
- Reviewing the safety plan often with your clients. (pp. 410–411)

As Klostermann (2016) noted, there is a vast number of family counseling approaches suggested in the literature to treat substance abuse. Unfortunately, most have little empirical evidence to suggest their effectiveness with addictions currently. Consequently, many of the approaches will be mentioned only briefly in the section following the approaches that do have substantial empirical support.

Popular Approaches With Substantial Empirical Support With Addictions

Cognitive-behavioral family therapy (CBFT).

Lambert et al. (2016) indicated that the goal of CBFT is to help family members change their thoughts or viewpoints to help affect change in their behavior. CBFT counselors also teach communication and problem-solving skills. Techniques include such methods as contingency contracting, roleplaying, modeling, etc. (see Chapter 6 for a more complete list).

Behavioral family therapy (BFT).

Lambert et al. (2016) indicated that BFT is intended to promote change through consequences. The BFT counselor uses learning theory (operant conditioning and social learning theories; Klostermann, 2016) to help family members "unlearn" or modify unhealthy behaviors. The assumption underlying BFT is that family interactions reinforce substance and behavioral addictions. Consequently, the BFT view is that addictions are maintained by antecedents and consequences that operate within the family system. Treatment consists of contingency management targeted at rewarding nonaddictive behavior, reducing negative reinforcement derived from addictive behavior, and increasing prosocial behaviors. As with BCT, family members are taught methods of increasing positive interactions, conflict resolution skills, and enhanced communication skills (Klostermann, 2016).

Klostermann (2016) discussed the community reinforcement training approach that focuses on reinforcement and contingencies as well as the community reinforcement and family training (CRAFT) program. CRAFT focuses on encouraging substance abusers to evaluate if drug use is problematic, encouraging sobriety and investigating treatment possibilities for substance abuse, and then actually engaging in treatment. CRAFT is typically conducted over six to eight sessions (O'Farrell, 2011). Regarding programs aimed at helping substance abusers initiate change, CRAFT is currently the most effective treatment, averaging 68% treatment engagement based on four randomized trials (O'Farrell, 2011). It is also an effective program for increasing treatment engagement and improving family cohesion (Bischof, Iwen, Freyer-Adam, & Rumpf, 2016).

Despite the empirical validation of BFT, Klostermann (2016) concluded that there are some conflicting results in outcome studies. In other words, not all outcome studies have found BFT to be that effective.

Functional family therapy (FFT).

FFT was designed to deal with juveniles who committed crimes and found themselves in the court system. The approach focuses on improving communication among family members and how family members derive reinforcement from problem behaviors. FFT uses reframing and cognitive therapy methods over 8–12 weeks on average. This approach is used by many state and community agencies that work with at-risk youth. A recent meta-analysis based on 14 studies found that FFT was effective with adolescents who displayed behavioral problems and/or substance abuse (Hartnett, Carr, Hamilton, & O'Reilly, 2017; visit https://www.fftllc.com/ for further details).

Popular Approaches With Minimal Empirical Support With Addictions

Psychodynamic family therapy.

Brabender and Fallon (2019) suggested that most treatment programs would benefit from applying a structured psychodynamic model. These models have *not* been subjected to much empirical scrutiny. Gerson (2019) examined psychoanalytic and psychodynamic theories and wrote about how maturation develops from the mother–infant dyad that over time creates object representation (i.e., object relations theory).

Multidimensional family therapy (MDFT).

MDFT looks at adolescent substance abuse as resulting from multiple interacting factors. These factors may include developmental challenges or other forms of abuse and trauma (Klostermann, 2016; see Liddle, 2009, for a good overview of the method). Filges, Andersen, and Jorgensen (2018) conducted a systematic review and meta-analysis regarding the effectiveness of MDFT for the treatment of nonopioid drug use in young people. The researchers only found five studies that met their criteria. Although MDFT was more effective than other treatments concerning drug abuse severity, the meta-analysis revealed it was helpful in the short run but not long term. It did demonstrate positive results on treatment retention.

Other approaches worthy of mention include Satir-informed family therapy (Ahmad-Abadi et al., 2017), multifamily therapy (Garrido-Fernandez, Marcos-Sierra, Lopez-Jimenez, & de Alda, 2017; Murray, Labuschagne, & Le Grange, 2014), multigenerational family counseling (Lambert et al., 2016), Bowenian theory and Mental Research Institute's (MRI) strategic family therapy (Park, Kim, & Lee, 2014; Young, 2017; Yu & Park, 2016; visit MRI's website at https://mri.org/), structural family therapy (SFT) (Ford, Durtschi, & Franklin, 2012; Lambert et al., 2016; visit http://minuchincenter.org/structural_family_therapy for details regarding this approach), solution-focused family therapy (SFFT) (Lambert et al., 2016), and narrative family therapy (Lambert et al., 2016). Regarding SFT and SFFT, Lambert et al. (2016) stated that the goals of SFT include restructuring family organization and creating boundaries (techniques include joining and accommodating), whereas the goals of SFFT involve collaboratively finding solutions (techniques include miracle question, scaling questions, and coping strategies).

ROLEPLAY SCENARIOS

Roleplay #3 requires five students: one of you acts as the counselor and the other four as the counselees. Roleplay #4 can be done with a triad with one of you acting as the counselor and the other two as the parents. If roleplay is not possible, work individually in writing out a list of your suggestions.

Roleplay #3

Madeleine, Holly, Robert, and Chris attend this session together. Madeleine, age 40, has been in a 5-year relationship with Holly, age 43. Holly tells you that she is in recovery from alcoholism, but Madeleine tells you that Holly still drinks heavily, approximately once per week. Madeleine has two sons, Robert (age 13) and Chris (age 14), from a previous marriage. Increasingly, Robert and Chris do not want to be seen out in public with their mom and Holly together. Holly believes it is because the two teenagers are homophobic, but Madeleine thinks that is nonsense. Instead, Madeleine believes they are just going through a typical adolescent period where they don't want to be seen with their parents. In the session, you find out that Robert and Chris have lost respect for Madeleine because they see her as a drunkard.

Roleplay #4

Only Kitty and Everett attend this first session together (the plan is to also include Austin and Kailey in the next session). Kitty, age 45, and Everett, age 49, were both in previous marriages. They met 2 years ago and married last month. Everett moved into Kitty's house. Kitty was reticent about living with Everett because both of them have children from previous marriages. Kitty has two daughters and one son, and Everett has two sons and one daughter. Everett has custody of his children only on every second weekend. As Kitty had predicted, it is turning into a disaster. Two of Everett's children do not want to stay at Kitty's house for undisclosed reasons.

Kitty has witnessed her eldest daughter, Kailey, and Everett's eldest son, Austin, flirting a great deal. Furthermore, Kitty discovered that much of the alcohol in her basement bar has gone missing, and she has also found a couple of *roach clips* (a small clip used for holding a marijuana joint so that it can be smoked to the end without burning the fingers) in the back yard. Kitty is convinced that Austin is getting Kailey high and drunk before he has sex with her. You find out that Kitty has good reason to believe that all of this is occurring.

COUNSELING SCENARIO

As you are reading, imagine that you are the father in this scenario. Note the areas in which the session could be improved on the part of the counselor.

Your name is Lester, age 39, and your wife is Dionne, age 39. You have also brought your two children, 18-year-old Ryan and 17-year-old Tricia, to this first counseling session with an addictions counselor. The four of you are called to Office 5 (i.e., Laura's office) over the intercom.

- Counselor: It is a pleasure to meet all of you. What would you like to focus on today?
- You: I am completely beside myself, Laura. Dionne was my high school sweetheart. We started dating in grade 10 and married when we were both 20 years of age. The last 18 years have been a complete disaster. I don't know if I can continue like this any longer.
- Counselor: Are you having thoughts of suicide, Lester?
- You: No. What I mean is, I do not think I can stay in this relationship any longer.
- Counselor: What is leading you to this conclusion?
- Dionne: [interrupts] I can tell you why, Laura. Lester is the most disrespectful man I know. He spends most of his nights out with the boys, and, for all I know, he is screwing every street whore out there!
- You: You know where you can stick it, Dionne. So, I go out with my friends. What is the big deal with that? Perhaps, if you treated me in a civil manner, I might want to be at home more.
- Dionne: Shut up! You are nothing but a . . . [calls you all kinds of derogatory names].
- Counselor: Excuse me. That is no way to talk in front of your children!
- Ryan: She talks like that all the time. She speaks like that to Tricia and me as well.
- Counselor: Is that true, Dionne?
- Dionne: Maybe the odd foul word slips out. I didn't say I was perfect.
- You: That is a real understatement! You are nothing but a cheap . . . [you call Dionne all kinds of pejorative names].
- Counselor: Both of you stop for a minute. Do neither of you have any manners at all? I am just disgusted by the way both of you talk to each other.
- Dionne: Sorry if I offended you, Miss Goody-two-shoes. I suppose you're one of those highfalutin' counselors who think you know everything. I've met your type before.
- Counselor: Dionne, you are projecting the way you talk onto me. You must've been raised by addicts yourself.
- You: When you are referring to addicts, who are you referring to?
- Counselor: To you, Lester. Unless there are other addictions in this family that you would like to raise.
- You: I am not an addict. I have a few beers with my friends, but that's it.
- Dionne: Why don't you tell Laura the truth for once? God knows what other drugs you use, but you are sure one mean ass when you come home from wherever it is that you go.
- Counselor: Can I get you to agree that there will be no more name-calling in our counseling sessions?
- You: If Dionne wasn't so ignorant, I know that I could agree.
- Dionne: Go f%&# yourself. You are the . . . [off again on a tangent of name-calling].
- Counselor: Shut up! Your filthy potty mouth is disgusting.
- You: That is no way to talk to my wife.
- Tricia: Do I get to say anything?
- Counselor: Of course.
- Tricia: I am tired of being sworn at constantly. It's not just my mother, but it's also my dad and my brother. Most days I just feel like a piece of crap.
- You: Tricia, that's a damn lie! No one puts you down at home. If you spent more time doing homework and keeping your room clean no one would have anything to complain to you about.
- Tricia: The three of you are always harping on me. I don't give a s$%#!
- Counselor: Tricia . . . shut up! Nothing is going to be accomplished here if everyone keeps swearing.
- You: I am beginning to agree with my wife. You do think you're better than us, don't you?
- Counselor: That's the silliest thing I have ever heard.

From the Client's Perspective

1. How would you feel if you were Lester?
2. What is missing for you in this dialogue?
3. What would you find more helpful from a counselor in this scenario?

From the Counselor's Perspective

1. What is interfering with developing a working alliance?
2. Turn to the Common Mistakes Made by Couples and Family Counselors list in Appendix 7C. Which mistakes is the counselor making with this family?
3. What issues are not getting addressed in the session?

Group Counseling

Group counseling is heralded as the treatment of choice for substance abuse and addiction (Van Wormer & Davis, 2013). Nonetheless, Southern and Thornton (2013) stated that "there is no conclusive evidence that group therapy is more effective than individual therapy" (p. 234). Nonetheless, because group counseling is efficient and results in cost savings, group therapy will likely continue as the preferred modality. Furthermore, using 2 years' worth of Canadian data, Csiernik and Arundel (2013) compared 135 participants who received an agreed-upon number of individual counseling sessions with 38 participants who received an agreed-upon number of group counseling sessions. Clients were twice as likely to complete group counseling compared to individual counseling.

There are several advantages to offering group therapy; it (a) is an effective and efficacious treatment, (b) is cost-effective, (c) allows addicted individuals to learn from others with similar struggles, (d) provides role models from those more experienced, (e) helps clients break denial, (f) promotes a sense of belonging, (g) allows counselors the chance to build rapport for later individual counseling, and (h) is ideal for those isolated from significant others (e.g., friends, family, intimate partner) because the facilitator and group members provide acceptance and support (McNeece & DiNitto, 2012; Neukrug, 2015; Rastegar & Fingerhood, 2016; Van Wormer & Davis, 2013).

Yalom and Leszcz (2005) stressed three advantages of group work. First, participants learn that their suffering is not unique. Second, individuals in the group develop better social skills in a safe environment. Third, group therapy has been particularly helpful when members share similar problems such as a particular type of addiction (e.g., AUD). For these reasons, groups are nearly always one aspect of inpatient addiction treatments (McNeece & DiNitto, 2012).

There is a caveat, however, with group approaches and their effectiveness. There are many types of groups. Although one might expect that educational groups (i.e., groups that focus on providing education through didactic means) are ideal, they are actually the least effective type of group (Van Wormer & Davis, 2013). Instead, those that teach coping skills and cognitive-behavioral therapy (CBT) approaches regarding relapse prevention are the most effective, and these group methods rank as useful as individual counseling, if not better (Van Wormer & Davis, 2013).

Similar to couples and family counseling, group counseling requires specialized skills. Group facilitators are encouraged to follow the most current version of the American Counseling Association's (2014) code of ethics. Also, follow the ethical guidelines developed by the American Group Psychotherapy Association (AGPA; visit https://www.agpa.org/home/practice-resources/ethics-in-group-therapy). Addiction counselors specializing in group work might consider becoming certified through AGPA's International Board for Certification of Group Psychotherapists.

Types of Groups

There are many different types of groups. The ones described here are the likelier groups in which addiction counselors may be involved (note that mutual support groups are in a separate section of this chapter, but they are run without the aid of addiction counselors).

Psychoeducational groups.

These groups are sometimes known as guidance groups or educational groups. Whatever you call them, their primary intent is to be preventive and instructional (Gladding & Alderson, 2012). One of the important processes in this type of group involves discussion among members regarding how to incorporate what is being taught into their personal lives. Psychoeducational groups are common in educational settings, but they are also used in addictions work. For example, a group might be offered four sessions aimed at teaching participants the different classes of drugs and their addictive qualities.

Task/work groups.

These groups are focused on accomplishing identified tasks. They are often used in task forces, committees, community organizations, and discussion groups (Gladding & Alderson, 2012). Individuals working in teams will often attend task/work groups.

Counseling groups.

These are sometimes known as interpersonal problem-solving groups, focused on helping participants resolve typical yet often challenging problems of living (Gladding & Alderson, 2012). Sometimes it is difficult to see the difference between a psychoeducational group and a counseling group. Whereas group counseling stresses the feelings and emotions of participants, psychoeducational groups concentrate on the cognitive (learning and understanding) components. Furthermore, counseling groups are small. whereas psychoeducational groups can include a large number of participants (Gladding & Alderson, 2012).

Psychotherapy groups.

There is a risk of "hairsplitting" when distinguishing counseling from psychotherapy groups. Throughout the text, counseling and therapy are used as synonyms. Nonetheless, there are some who make these distinctions. Where this distinction occurs, psychotherapy groups focus on in-depth psychological problems, often with the goal of personality reconstruction (Gladding & Alderson, 2012). Although counseling groups tend to have fewer sessions, psychotherapy groups may go on for years. They typically occur in hospitals with outpatient facilities and select private practices.

Connors, DiClemente, Velasquez, and Donovan (2013) suggested a somewhat different typology of groups. They stated that five types of groups are common in substance abuse treatment and a sixth type is relatively new. Their six types are as follows:

1. Psychoeducational groups. These are the same as described earlier, where education is the focus.
2. Skills development groups. These focus on teaching skills to help members change their substance use.
3. CBT groups. These focus on helping group members change their thoughts and actions that act as antecedents to substance abuse.
4. Support groups. Support groups focus on sharing information about maintaining abstinence and managing daily living without alcohol or drugs.
5. Psychotherapeutic groups. Utilizing interpersonal processes, psychotherapeutic groups focus on

developmental issues that play a role in addiction or that interfere with recovery.

6. Motivational groups. This newer type of group focuses on helping members increase their desire to change using motivational interventions (e.g., motivational interviewing).

Basic Group Dynamics

According to Hulse-Killacky, Killacky, and Donigian (2001), groups run best when the following components are embedded:

1. Purpose. The focus of the group is clear to all participants.
2. Team building. Time is taken to learn about each other and to build a sense of belonging.
3. Balanced process and content. The dynamics of the group are balanced with content, which is generally offered in the form of information.
4. Member feedback. Feedback among members is exchanged. Pietrofesa, Hofmann, and Splete (1984) suggested that, in the early stages of a group, positive feedback is more beneficial and more readily accepted than negative feedback. Feedback is most effective when it immediately follows something said (or done) and when others validate it. Furthermore, according to Pietrofesa et al., feedback is of most benefit when the receiver is open and trusts the giver.
5. Here-and-now. It is important that leaders pay attention to the here-and-now experience of the group.
6. Reflection. Time is provided by the leaders to reflect on what is happening in the group.

Here are some additional tips in running groups:

1. Address the "white elephant in the room." This is a euphemism that means you need to deal with significant issues in the group (including unspoken conflicts) that are obvious to most but that are not being discussed because of the discomfort that members have with the topic. For example, if one member was talking incessantly and, by doing so, prevented other members from sharing, this would need to be addressed. If the white elephant is not attended to, group members are likely to stop sharing and attending.
2. Model what you want to see happen in the group. Embrace and demonstrate positive personal qualities such as sensitivity, empathy, honesty, integrity, and genuineness. If you want clients to be real, show them what this looks like. Many addicted individuals have learned to lie and cover up the mistakes they make (and have made) in life.
3. Stay calm. Many group counselors feel nervous at the beginning of a group, particularly when they lack experience. Remember to practice the preceding tip. You are not in the group to show yourself to be a perfect facilitator. Your clients before you are an excellent example of individuals who have faced many failures and revealed several imperfections. Be yourself, stay real, and group members will respect you.
4. Focus on daily functioning. Unless running a psychodynamic group, the focus should mostly be on the present. In addition to the here-and-now mentioned earlier, focusing on the present includes focusing on the current, daily struggles that group members encounter and ways to better cope with these challenges.
5. Self-disclosure. During the beginning of a group, leaders do well to use self-disclosure as a means of modeling and promoting this practice (Gladding & Alderson, 2012).
6. Other factors. Yalom and Leszcz (2005), using a Q-sort methodology, determined that the most essential curative factors in psychotherapy groups are (in descending order) interpersonal input (i.e., depth of one's contribution to the group), catharsis (i.e., the feeling of relief experienced after talking about a problem), cohesiveness (i.e., a group dynamic where group members feel connected to each other and committed to the group), and insight (i.e., increased self-understanding).

Stages in Groups

Group counseling is typically broken into four or five stages, with some models suggesting as few as three stages and other models having as many as six (Gladding & Alderson, 2012). One of the earlier models included five stages: forming, storming, norming, performing, and mourning/adjourning (Tuckman, 1965; Tuckman & Jensen, 1977; Waldo, 1985). Specific tasks are believed to occur in each stage.

1. Forming. The foundation for the group begins developing while group members might express anxiety and dependency. Most of the talk will likely deal superficially with nonproblematic topics. One way to help group members feel safe is to ensure that they know what is expected of them (Gladding & Alderson, 2012).
2. Storming. Substantial amounts of turmoil and conflict often occur in this stage. Conflict results as group members work to establish their roles in the group and to deal with issues of power. The group leader is sometimes verbally attacked at this stage.
3. Norming. Gladding and Alderson (2012) likened this stage to young adulthood where, having survived the "storm" of the previous stage, the group is often feeling enthusiastic and cohesive. The goals and the ways to get there are often decided at this stage.
4. Performing. Group members are ready to "perform," meaning they are prepared to work on their issues and the collective goals of the group. This is the time the group is most productive.
5. Mourning/adjourning. At this stage, the group ends, and members say goodbye to one another. Although some group members feel fulfilled, others may feel bitter (Gladding & Alderson, 2012). A brief closure ritual is recommended such as a ceremony or celebration.

In practice, it is often difficult to differentiate between the developmental stages of a group. As in the case of most stage theories, people are not so predictable in the ways that they act in groups. Movement through the stages/steps might not be sequential, and a group's behavior may fluctuate between stages within a single session.

General Considerations in Forming and Leading a Group

Forming a group.

Before forming a group, the leaders need to decide whether the group will be homogenous (members are alike in some important respect) or heterogeneous (members are different in some salient respect). Southern and Thornton (2013) stated that it is advantageous for a group to include clients with similar backgrounds as it increases members' vicarious learning and deepens their sharing. How many sessions will the group meet, and what is the duration of each session? Van Wormer and Davis (2013) cautioned that individuals who have experienced brain damage from alcohol and other drugs might require shorter meetings and fewer sessions, for example, compared to behavioral addiction groups. Also, how long have the potential group members been clean from alcohol and drugs? Participants who have not used substances for a year can deal with deeper emotional issues better when compared to those who have been sober for only a few days (Van Wormer & Davis, 2013). How much structure in the group do the leaders want? A highly structured group will require that leaders present topics in each session and have prepared exercises. In a less structured group, leaders may ask participants to decide on the topic, usually based on whatever concerns one or more members are currently experiencing (McNeece & DiNitto, 2012). In very unstructured groups, the leaders turn control over to the group members. Also, will family members and/or children be allowed to attend one or more of the sessions?

How many people will be allowed into the group? Generally groups of six to 10 are desirable; if the group has more than 10 participants, have two leaders (Gladding & Alderson, 2012). Is it a closed group (meaning that new members cannot join once it commences) or an open group (new members can join at different times throughout the group)? What type of group is it (e.g., psychoeducational, skills-based counseling)? Whom do the leaders want in the group and whom do they not want (i.e., what are the criteria)?

It is critical that addiction counselors adequately screen and prepare for running a group. Often potential members are invited to an individual pregroup interview to ensure that they are appropriate for the group (Gladding & Alderson, 2012). Some individuals are too hostile, or perhaps they are in a different stage of change (see the transtheoretical model in Chapter 6) than other members. Furthermore, some clients might not have a goal that is compatible with the purposes of the group. For example, if the group requires abstinence from all substances of abuse and a potential group member wants to practice moderation instead, their attendance in the group will likely undermine the reasons for which other members are attending.

Once group members are invited to participate, comprehensive information about the group is provided to ensure they know its expectations and objectives (Gladding & Alderson, 2012). This information is best provided in an informed consent form that is signed and dated by the group member.

Leading a group.

Brooks and McHenry (2009) recommended that, when running an addictions group, one should begin by having the members introduce themselves to the group by saying their first name, their sobriety date (in a group for behavioral addictions, pick a meaningful date), how they feel right now, and what they want to get out of the group experience. Brooks and McHenry suggested spending about 10 min for introductions. Another suggestion that could be used in the first and subsequent sessions is to have group members select and share a number from 1 (*very depressed*) to 10 (*very happy*).

Early in the process, group leaders do their best to build a strong positive working alliance with every group member. Although this may occur readily in some groups, groups comprising homeless individuals or those who have co-occurring disorders may take months or even years for this alliance to develop (Van Wormer & Davis, 2013).

Ground rules need to be established. Will touching or hugging be allowed in the group, and who gets to decide? What are the rules governing giving other members feedback (Van Wormer & Davis, 2013)? In some groups, the only input permitted is from individuals providing feedback to link their personal experience with that just offered by the speaker. In other groups, participants may be allowed to confront each other in specific ways (e.g., only provide feedback tentatively, focus only on skills that might be helpful for this person to utilize). Is the person speaking allowed to persist in talking, even if some of the content is irrelevant or inappropriate, and no one else may interrupt until he or she is finished?

Given that some clients experience anhedonia (i.e., inability to find words for emotions or express them), having a large "feeling chart" (many different Internet versions are available) readily visible is helpful. In many groups, clients are also asked during the last few minutes to express their feeling or emotion again, or at least to give a thumbs-up if they are feeling okay, a thumbs-down if they are not, and a horizontal thumb if they are feeling neutral.

A helpful exercise is to have clients write down how their substance or behavioral addiction has impacted the different areas in their lives (Brooks & McHenry, 2009). One suggestion is to include the areas of client functioning tapped in the Personal Functioning Questionnaire (PFQ; Alderson, 2018; the questionnaire, the manual, and the pie chart are available as free downloads from https://kevinalderson.ca/). What is the impact in the following areas: (a) relationship (intimate relationship, children, friendships, parents, siblings), (b) emotional health, (c) spiritual beliefs, (d) physical health, (e) paid and/or volunteer work, and (f) recreation and leisure activities? They may also note whatever feelings or emotions are associated with these impacts.

Clients need to be made aware if this disclosure of personal information is only for their purposes, if it is to be later provided to the group counselor(s), or if they will be asked later to tell some of this information to the group. If group members give their consent to this, they can reveal these impacts to the group in whatever manner is decided by the group counselor. The PFQ also includes background and demographic information and ethnicity/diversity considerations, which can also be revealed to the group if appropriate.

Another exercise proposed by Brooks and McHenry (2009) is asking group members to complete a timeline. In a timeline exercise, clients are each given a paper with one or two long lines on it. Each client will create a unique timeline, noting only those events that are meaningful or critical in some sense (e.g., assaulted someone and went to prison). Clients write dates below the line and their associated events or incidents above the line regarding their substance or behavioral addiction (e.g., if leading a group for AUD, one event might be their age or the year when they had their first drink, the year or their age when they first got drunk, and so forth). Again, if you plan to have clients present their timeline to the group, let them know before they commence the exercise. Maintaining ongoing informed consent is the key when using any counseling modality.

Csiernik (2016) recommended that, if the purpose of a group is to change behavior (which is the primary purpose of addiction counseling), the following are important considerations:

- Stress group interaction. Plan exercises to keep group members interested in attending and engaged in the group process.
- Support and protect group members. Group members will be honest and deal with personal and challenging problems and scenarios only if they feel supported and safe.
- Sufficient compatibility. You want group members to get along and like each other.
- Include enough diversity and similarities. In this way, group members can provide each other relevant examples so that each member's strengths and resources can be tapped.
- Prepare members for participation. Group members need to be provided with clear and sufficiently thorough information about the group and the treatment process. Group rules need to be communicated.

What should you do if a client attends the group and is obviously under the influence of alcohol or other drugs? In some cases, the protocol for dealing with intoxicated clients will be driven by policy where you work. If not, Margolis and Zweben (2011) suggested that rigid policies have disadvantages given that you cannot always verify intoxication. Instead, the counselor might allow the client to remain in the group if he or she is not causing disruption or ask the client to be an observer and not participate in that specific session.

Exercises.

Sometimes it is difficult to get participants in a group to talk. Hagedorn and Hirshhorn (2009) came up with three useful activities that can be used in an addictions group. The instructions are lengthy and sufficiently detailed, so interested students are advised to read their article. Hagedorn and Hirshhorn also included contraindications for participation. The three exercises include

1. Crossing the swamp. This exercise involves movement and balance, so some participants may need to observe and not participate. The intent is to help participants understand what is required during their first year of recovery.
2. Roadblocks to recovery. This is a sand-tray activity that requires several materials, including a sand tray. The exercise is recommended for individuals who have become blocked in their recovery such as by having difficulty staying clean and sober or by having had a relapse. Participants use miniatures in the sand to create a scene symbolizing their roadblocks to recovery.
3. Navigating the blind maze of recovery. In this exercise, participants apply popular recovery slogans to their lives. Participants are blindfolded in this exercise.

Limitations

Up to this point, most of the advantages of group counseling have been highlighted. There are also some disadvantages. Gladding and Alderson (2012) stated that "some client concerns and personalities are not well-suited for groups" (p. 303). If potential group members have serious psychological problems, they are likely not suited for a group until they are in better mental health (McCrady, 2014).

Brownlee, Curran, and Tsang, (2017) studied a large sample of individuals who signed up to take five sessions of a manualized group therapy program between October 2010 and October 2013 (N = 999; 690 males and 319 females; mean age = 43; age range = 18–73). Of the 999 clients invited, only 38% completed the program, which required attending only four out of five sessions. That meant the dropout rate was 62%. Brownlee et al. also interviewed some of the clients. A regression analysis, together with qualitative data, indicated that age was the strongest predictor of group completion. That is, younger individuals were less likely to complete the sessions than older individuals. The authors also noted that some clients in the group experienced heightened levels of anxiety, some of which was attributed to the distress caused when listening to other people's stories.

Wanigaratne (2011) noted as well that counseling and psychotherapy groups assume "universality" or "culture blindness" (p. 156). Group therapy's roots are planted in the psychodynamic worldview, which is situated in Eastern European Jewish culture (Wanigaratne, 2011). Wanigaratne stated that the assumption of universality is violated in Islamic cultures, especially Arabic cultures, where talking about personal issues and family matters is not acceptable. Furthermore, many individuals in Asian cultures where "saving face, honor, shame, and guilt are strongly reinforced" (p. 157) might be reluctant to share much when attending counseling or psychotherapy groups.

Some individuals need a greater depth of personal exploration than what they can accomplish in a group where time is divided among all group members. Group pressure may encourage members to self-disclose before they are ready. If that occurs, those members may not return for further sessions. In some instances, groups digress into a group think mentality, which is where everyone begins to look at things the same way or not speak up if they think or feel differently. If members are living different lifestyles or are from different socioeconomic statuses, what they learn from the group may not be relevant for them. If conflicts in the group are not successfully navigated, they may become more aggressive and even destructive through scapegoating, group narcissism, and projection (Gladding & Alderson, 2012).

Neukrug (2015) offered a few additional disadvantages. In groups, individuals may have a greater fear of disclosure than if they were receiving individual counseling. Groups often run for a longer duration (e.g., 90–120 min) than individual counseling (e.g., 50 min), which means they require a more significant time commitment. Confidentiality cannot be assured either. Although group counselors generally have members agree to keep what occurs in the group confidential, there is no guarantee that this will happen, and there is no recourse if it does not.

Popular Approaches With Substantial Empirical Support With Addictions

Cognitive-behavioral group therapy (CBGT).

Using CBT with groups is empirically validated (Wenzel, Liese, Beck, & Friedman-Wheeler, 2012). Birchard (2018) outlined how CBGT can be used in treating compulsive sexual behavior, whereas Jimenez-Murcia et al. (2012) and Ladouceur et al. (2003) applied it to pathological gamblers. Research has shown that CBGT is effective in helping individuals with AUD comorbid with personality disorders (Martinez-Gonzalez, Vilar-Lopez, and Verdejo-Garcia, 2018). CBGT has been used successfully to improve coping skills and relapse prevention in addicted individuals (Ashouri, Mollazadeh, & Mohammadi, 2008). It is also helpful with Internet-addicted children, ages 12–17, when offered in a school setting (Du, Jiang, & Vance, 2010).

The book by Wenzel et al. (2012), *Group Cognitive Therapy for Addictions*, was highly recommended by Parker (2015) as providing an evidence-based, effective, and detailed protocol for offering CBGT. Brownlee et al., (2017) stated that *The Stages of Change Therapy Manual* (Velasquez, Maurer, Crouch, & DiClemente, 2001) is used widely by counselors. The approach is CBGT-focused. Previous research has found that following their manual has been effective in improving cognitive and behavioral change (Gramani, 2007).

Motivational interviewing (MI).

John, Veltrup, Driessen, Wetterling, and Dilling (2003) found that group-administered MI was as effective as individual MI in helping clients maintain abstinence in individuals with AUD. Krejci and Neugebauer (2015) offered several strategies for using MI in groups. Navidian, Kermansaravi, Tabas, and Saeedinezhad (2016) found that group MI decreased the craving in addicted individuals receiving methadone maintenance treatment. Foote et al. (1999) developed the Group Motivational Intervention, which is a manualized four-session group approach to addiction treatment. Other studies have also found MI to be effective in group formats (Houck, Manuel, & Moyers, 2018; LaBrie, Pederson, Lamb, Quinlan, 2007; Malat, Morrow, & Stewart, 2011; Tucker, D'Amico, Ewing, Miles, & Pedersen, 2017).

Popular Approaches With Minimal Empirical Support With Addictions

Psychodynamic group therapy (PGT).

Nyhuis et al. (2018) compared an approach they called psychoanalytic-interactional group therapy (PIT) with behavioral group therapy in an outpatient program including patients with AUD. Their sample consisted of 215 patients (mean age = 49.6; 56.7% males) with a mean duration of alcohol dependence of 16.5 years. Nyhuis et al. found that, despite the study's limitations, PIT seemed to be as effective as behavioral intervention regarding retention and relapse prevention rates. Schwartz, Nickow, Arseneau, and Gisslow (2015) recommended long-term PGT as the primary treatment for compulsive overeating. Similarly, Woods (2013) recommended PGT for compulsive users of Internet pornography.

Confrontational interventions.

These are sometimes known colloquially as an "intervention." The most well known of these is the Johnson intervention method, which Vernon Johnson developed in the 1960s. Often addiction counselors will conduct the intervention. It involves bringing family, friends, and possibly even the employer of the addicted person together for a rehearsal of how the intervention will proceed (i.e., no judgment, just observations and consequences). Either immediately following or at another session, the group uses a confrontational approach (generally reserved for alcohol and other substance disorders) when the addicted individual is invited to join the group. Csiernik (2016) reported that these interventions could take as little as 10–20 min. Following the intervention, the addiction counselor would recommend, in most cases, a residential treatment program (Csiernik, 2016).

Although this method is often popular with laypersons, research has found that only 22% of these groups were successful in getting the addicted individual into treatment (Lassiter et al., 2015). Based on the literature regarding theory and efficacy, many if not most authors would not recommend this method today (Lassiter et al., 2015; MacKillop et al., 2018).

Other approaches worthy of mention include multifamily group therapy for adolescent Internet-addicted individuals (Liu et al., 2015) and narrative group therapy (Clark, 2014; Szabo, Toth, & Pakai, 2014). Some research has also looked at utilizing meditation (Young, de Armas DeLorenzi, & Cunningham, 2011), transcendental meditation (Gryczynski et al., 2018), and mindfulness approaches (Marcus & Zgierska, 2009).

ROLEPLAY SCENARIOS

Roleplay with one student acting as the group counselor with six to eight group participants. Use as many groups as needed. Also, consider having two students act as group counselors. Given the many directions that a group can take, these two roleplays have very general instructions.

Roleplay #5

First, decide ahead of time which substance disorder you want group members to roleplay. Second, determine what stage the group is in currently (i.e., forming, storming, norming, performing, and mourning/adjourning). Now let the group begin and have participants take it wherever they want the group to go. If time permits, change the counselor(s) every 15 min.

Roleplay #6

First, decide ahead of time which addictive behavior (i.e., gambling, Internet-based [Internet, gaming, social media], sex, romantic relationship, food, exercise, shopping, or work) you want group members to roleplay. Second, decide which stage the group is in currently (i.e., forming, storming, norming, performing, and mourning/adjourning). Now let the group begin and have participants take it wherever they want the group to go. If time permits, change the counselor(s) every 15 min.

Mutual Support Groups

Lembke and Humphreys (2016) surmised that the term "self-help" became popular in 1959 when Samuel Smiles published his book, *Self-Help*. Interestingly, the first sentence in *Self-Help* is "Heaven helps those who help themselves" (Lembke & Humphreys, 2016, p. 2), which is an often-quoted saying but seldom referenced. The term self-help groups eventually became known as mutual support groups (MSGs). It is preferable given that the support is bidirectional: Both the participants and the facilitator benefit from their involvement.

Humphries (as cited in Kelly & Yeterian, 2011) defined MSGs as "groups of two or more people who share an experience or problem and who come together to provide problem-specific help and support to one another" (p. 350). A defining feature of MSGs is that they operate without professional involvement. Individuals who themselves have faced an addiction problem but have achieved a requisite period of abstinence lead these groups. In other words, a foundation of MSGs is peers helping peers.

MSGs emerged over 75 years ago, and they continue flourishing today (Kelly & Yeterian, 2011). When Americans are seeking help for drug and/or alcohol problems, entering formal treatment is not their first choice (Earleywine, 2016). Instead, they most commonly turn to MSGs (Kelly & Yeterian, 2011), particularly those that are 12-step oriented (Earleywine, 2016). As a testimonial of their attendance, there were 61,904 Alcoholics Anonymous (AA) groups and 1,297,396 members in the United States alone as of January 2018 (Alcoholics Anonymous General Service Office, 2018). Worldwide, there are more than 120,000 groups and more than 2 million members (Alcoholics Anonymous General Service Office, 2018). Milkman and Sunderwirth (2010) indicated that nearly 90% of treatment programs in the United States are at least partly based on AA principles.

AA was founded in 1935 by William Griffith Wilson (*Bill W.*) and Dr. Robert Holbrook Smith (*Dr. Bob*), two "alcoholics." Bill W. was influenced greatly by the Oxford Group, which was an American evangelical movement that arose in the 1920s (Lembke & Humphreys, 2016). The Oxford Group believed that all sin could be transcended through spiritual means. Bill W. needed to detoxify, and, during his withdrawal, he saw a bright light. He emerged from detox as a man who felt fundamentally transformed (Lembke & Humphreys, 2016). He met Dr. Bob through the Oxford Group, and the two of them had their first "AA meeting" together in Akron, Ohio.

A recommendation to addicted individuals that surfaced from AA is to not make major decisions during the first year of abstinence (Carnes, 1991). Carnes (1991) validated this advice regarding his work with individuals whom he defined as sex-addicted. The addicted individuals whom Carnes interviewed gave other helpful suggestions for recruits attending a *twelve-step mutual support group* (TS-MSG; these are programs based on AA's 12 steps), including (a) you must use the phone (i.e., call your sponsor), (b) be patient, and (c) attend meetings regularly. Melemis (2018) wrote about the many benefits of attending a TS-MSG. He emphasized that, in these meetings, attendees will find more honesty and courage than almost anywhere else in the world. Among several suggestions, Melemis recommended that addicted individuals attend meetings on the days they used to engage the most in their addictive substance or behavior, and even at the same time of day if possible. He also wrote that, when most people say "give me a call," they do not necessarily mean it, but, when it is said at a TS-MSG, it is taken seriously. Melemis' webpage is a good resource for addiction counselors who want to know what it is like to attend one of these meetings.

The AA principles, when applied to a formal treatment program, have come to be known as the *Minnesota model* or *abstinence model* (MacKillop et al., 2018). The Minnesota model began in 1949 at Hazelden. Today, the well-known center is known as the Hazelden Betty Ford Foundation (https://www.hazeldenbettyford.org/).

There are also MSGs for the spouses and children of individuals addicted to substances or behaviors. After interviewing 20 Al-Anon members, Kuuluvainen and Isotalus (2015) found that attending provided interviewees with several benefits, including a sense of belonging, a comparison group, higher self-efficacy, development of a new narrative, focus on oneself, and learning ways to help recover from the negative impacts of having addiction in their homes.

Twelve-Step Mutual Support Groups

Although AA was the first TS-MSG, many others have sprung up that focus on other substances and behavioral addictions (see Chapters 9 through 21 for a list of these 12-step groups). There is also a 12-step program for individuals with dual diagnoses (i.e., Double Trouble in Recovery).

A frequently asked question concerns the effectiveness of TS-MSGs. Most research has focused on AA and other substance-oriented TS-MSGs (Kelly & Yeterian, 2011). It is nearly impossible to conduct randomized controlled trials on most MSGs because participation is voluntary, anonymous, and self-initiated (Kelly & Yeterian, 2011). Nonetheless, researchers have measured effectiveness through longitudinal studies that look at two or more points in time. It is difficult to know, however, how much such results can be generalized because they follow treated groups rather than community-based TS-MSGs (Kelly & Yeterian, 2011).

Since then, however, according to Emrick and Beresford (2016), a study by Humphreys, Blodgett, and Wagner (2014) has provided the best evidence for the effectiveness of AA. Humphreys et al. used an innovative statistical technique that resulted in a selection bias-free estimate of AA's effectiveness. Using six data sets from five National Institutes of Health-funded randomized trials, Humphreys et al. analyzed one data set ($N = 774$) separately from the remainder of the sample ($N = 1582$) due to the heterogeneity of the samples. The researchers concluded that

> For most individuals seeking help for alcohol problems, increasing AA attendance leads to short- and long-term decreases in alcohol consumption that cannot be attributed to self-selection. However, for populations with high pre-existing AA involvement, further increases in AA attendance may have little impact. (Humphreys et al., 2014, p. 2688)

Consequently, we now have ample evidence that participation in AA is an effective intervention for AUDs (Emrick & Beresford, 2016; Humphreys et al., 2014; Medina, 2014). Attending a TS-MSG also helped increase abstinence rates with heroin-addicted individuals at 1-year and 5-year follow-up (Gamble & O'Lawrence, 2016). Several professional and health organizations, including the American Psychiatric Association, recommend that referrals be made to MSGs (Moos, 2012).

In TS-MSGs, recovery is thought to occur through a "'spiritual awakening' or 'psychic change'" (Kelly & Yeterian, 2011, p. 352). For example, the second step in AA is, "Came to believe that a Power greater than ourselves could restore us to sanity" (Alcoholics Anonymous General Service Office, 2016). Followers of AA "work" the 12 steps, secure a sponsor, develop faith in a higher power, and help others (Kelly & Yeterian, 2011). Followers are encouraged to read the book, *Alcoholics Anonymous*, which was first published in 1939. It is commonly referred to as the *Big Book* (a free version is available from http://12step.org/references/the-big-book/ or, if you prefer, you can download the book chapter by chapter from http://www.aa.org/pages/en_US/alcoholics-anonymous). Several studies have shown that an important factor in the success of TS-MSGs results from the increase in dependent individuals' social network and from an increased sense of self-efficacy as a result of becoming abstinent (Kelly & Yeterian, 2011).

Before moving to the next section, it is important to highlight that TS-MSGs remain controversial for many addiction counselors (Best, Savic, Mugavin, Manning, & Lubman, 2016). They are also viewed negatively by some groups that could arguably benefit from attending them such as homeless individuals (Grazioli, Collins, Daeppen, & Larimer, 2015). Several reasons have been advanced for this continuing distrust and/or dislike of TS-MSGs.

The philosophy underlying AA and other substance-oriented TS-MSGs is based on the disease model, and, as noted in Chapter 3, this approach remains under scrutiny by many nonmedical mental health clinicians and researchers. Their worldview is also considered derogatory for many individuals. For example, according to AA, the etiology of AUD begins with character defects and personality flaws. Alcoholics in *The Big Book* are viewed as selfish, self-centered, fearful, deprived, frustrated, and resentful individuals who have "a zealous, insatiable, and fear-based urge to satisfy one's instinctual drives for sexual relationships, financial and emotional security, and social standing" (Kelly & Yeterian, 2013, p. 505). According to AA doctrine, alcoholics are pathetic souls who suffer from "profound spiritual decay and eventual alcohol-induced annihilation" (Kelly & Yeterian, 2013, p. 505). AA also views alcoholics as having an inability to deal effectively with stress (Kelly & Yeterian, 2013).

There is considerable opposition to the spiritual or "quasireligious" terminology and concepts used in these groups (Kelly & Yeterian, 2013). TS-MSGs require that members subjugate themselves to a higher power, with the underlying notion that this is the only road out of problematic substance or addictive behaviors (Humphreys & Kaskutas, 1995). TS-MSGs provide no option to choose moderation as the goal, despite the evidence that this is possible for some individuals (Miller & Munoz, 2013).

The ideology of TS-MSGs is disharmonious with feminist theory (Bond & Csordas, 2014; Saulnier, 1996). AA, for example, is male-dominated and was established by males *for* males (Bond & Csordas, 2014; Humphreys & Kaskutas, 1995). Individuals who experience substance or behavioral excesses, even those who do not cross any scientific threshold for what might constitute addiction, are reified as addicted individuals. This can occur merely by reading the literature produced by TS-MSGs or by attending their meetings. Furthermore, being labeled as an addict or an "alcoholic" is stigmatizing (Hill & Leeming, 2014).

Some clinicians and researchers have suggested that clinicians should consider a client's religious background when considering referrals to 12-step meetings and that nonreligious people should not be referred to TS-MSGs. However, some research suggests that nonreligious people can benefit from 12-step meeting attendance as much as or more than their religious counterparts in terms of their substance use outcomes (Kelly & Yeterian, 2013).

Non-Twelve-Step Mutual Support Groups

Several non-twelve-step MSGs (NTS-MSGs) have been developed in response to the criticisms launched at TS-MSGs. The main NTS-MSGs include Self-Management and Recovery Training, LifeRing, Secular Organizations for Sobriety, and Women for Sobriety. Although these programs focus on abstinence, Moderation Management is a program for nondependent "problem drinkers" whose goal is to reduce alcohol consumption. Furthermore, in addition to face-to-face meetings, some MSGs now provide online meetings.

Self-Management and Recovery Training (SMART).

According to the SMART website (https://www.smartrecovery.org/about-us/frequently-asked-questions/), SMART is a nonprofit organization that was initially named the Rational Recovery Self-Help Network. It was then affiliated with Rational Recovery Systems (Rational Recovery for short).[2] Rational Recovery (RR) is a profit corporation owned by Jack Trimpey. SMART's affiliation with Trimpey ended in 1994 and they changed their name to SMART Recovery (SMART for short). Although the authority at SMART is their Board of Directors, the authority for RR is the owner (i.e., Jack Trimpey). The SMART website also reports that the main difference between them and RR, as of 1997 at least, is that it appeared that RR had a narrower focus.

SMART is based on CBT (Kelly, Deane, & Baker, 2015). In the study by Kelly et al. (2015) of participants attending SMART in Australia ($N = 124$), most attended it for problematic alcohol use. This NTS-MSG teaches self-empowerment and self-reliance. The meetings have a CBT orientation, are educational, and include open discussions (Kelly & Yeterian, 2013). SMART is also overt in encouraging the use of appropriate medications and psychological treatments. At meetings, tools and techniques are taught that teach attendees how to (a) increase motivation to abstain, (b) cope with urges, (c) manage thoughts, feelings, and behaviors, and (d) develop a balanced lifestyle (Kelly & Yeterian, 2013). There is no cost to attend SMART meetings (Horvath & Velten, 2000).

Compared to TS-MSGs, individuals attending SMART and LifeRing (an NTS-MSG described next) were generally less religious and more educated and had higher incomes in a convenience sample of 651 individuals who completed Web-based surveys (Zemore, Kaskutas, Mericle, & Hemberg, 2017). Also, compared to TS-MSGs, both SMART and LifeRing members were less likely to endorse abstinence as their goal. Kelly et al. (2017) measured both participant and facilitator perceptions of SMART in Australia and found that, overall, satisfaction with SMART was moderate to strong.

Guarnotta (2015) did not find any difference in self-efficacy scores between members of AA and SMART ($N = 122$). In their "scoping review," Parkman, Lloyd, and Splisbury (2015) concluded that more research is needed regarding NTS-MSGs. The systematic review of SMART by Beck et al. (2017) echoed this assertion. Beck et al. found 12 studies, most of which were of poor quality.

[2]Rational Recovery (see https://rational.org) does not offer MSGs, so this method is only mentioned here. Jack Trimpey created RR in 1986, himself a California-licensed clinical social worker. Rational Recovery is a commercial trademark, as is his method, called the Addictive Voice Recognition Technique. Individuals are taught to recognize their "addictive voice" and to modify it. RR focuses on self-control and free will (Schmidt, 1996).

Standardized assessments of nonalcohol substance use were lacking in most studies, outcomes were rarely reported, and most did not provide assessments of mental health status. Although positive effects were generally found, Beck et al. were unable to make conclusive statements regarding efficacy, suggesting that future research is needed. Humphreys et al. (2004) estimated that there were 2000 members of SMART in the United States.

LifeRing (LR; http://lifering.org/).

LR began in 1997 as LifeRing Press, a publishing company that remained separate from its parent organization, Secular Organizations for Sobriety (SOS). In 1999, it became incorporated under its present name of LifeRing. It no longer has an affiliation with SOS. Martin Nicolaus was its founder and chief executive officer from 1997 through 2010, preceding Craig Whalley as president. Their philosophy is based on the three principles of sobriety, secularity, and self-empowerment. Participants create their own program, which they tailor to their needs and circumstances.

LR is described on its website as an abstinence-based, worldwide network of individuals wishing to refrain from using alcohol or other nonprescribed substances. It offers face-to-face group meetings in the United States, Canada, and a few other select countries. It invites attendees to enter, take a seat, and enjoy the experience. It also has a vibrant online community. White and Nicolaus (2005) reported survey results from 401 members and found that most were middle-aged, White, educated, and gender ratio balanced.

Sotskova, Woodin, and St. Cyr (2016) analyzed quantitative and qualitative data from 50 participants and found that LR's participants valued its group cohesiveness. Falconer's (2015) qualitative dissertation found that participants appreciated the (a) support, (b) tolerance of ambivalence, craving, and relapse, (c) peer identification, social support, and learning from others, (d) support in working through their issues, (e) improvements in their self-image and outlook, and (f) opportunities to be of help to others.

Secular Organizations for Sobriety (SOS; http://www.sossobriety.org/).

James Christopher founded SOS in 1985. He described himself as a "sober alcoholic" (from the organization's website). Although the general principles of SOS resemble AA (and so does its languaging), it does not incorporate spiritual or religious themes (Kelly & Yeterian, 2013). Although SOS does not advocate clear and sequential steps like AA, it does promote sharing, active social involvement including spending time with other "alcoholics," and placing the highest priority on sobriety (i.e., no drinking "no matter what") (Kelly & Yeterian, 2013, p. 509). How one achieves sobriety is left up to the individual, but SOS recommends that people use the wisdom of other SOS members who have been successful in achieving sobriety. Atkins and Hawdon (2007) gleaned from their national survey (analyses were based on 924 usable surveys) that religious individuals were less likely to participate in SOS, whereas it did not impact involvement in SMART. A survey of 158 SOS members found that participants were consistently positive in their reactions to the group, and most disliked AA because of its focus on religion and a higher power (Connors & Dermen, 1996). The SOS website recommends that viewers watch the award-winning short documentary produced by Sarah Barker called *No God at the Bottom of a Glass*. It is available in several brief episodes on YouTube. Humphreys et al. (2004) estimated that there were 3000 members of SOS in the United States.

Women for Sobriety (WFS; https://womenforsobriety.org/).

Sociologist Jean Kirkpatrick founded WFS in 1975 after concluding that AA did not meet her needs. Jean concluded that women needed groups that were free from men and their role expectations (Kelly & Yeterian, 2013).

Fenner and Gifford (2012) provided a comprehensive overview of WFS for the benefit of treatment professionals. They noted that Kirkpatrick created WFS alongside the rise of the women's movement. She passed away on June 19, 2000, at the age of 77. The program is designed for women who are addicted to alcohol and/or drugs. The emphasis in the program is on empowerment, and, as with CBT approaches, an important component is that negative thoughts are believed to be at the root of women's use of alcohol and drugs. Face-to-face meetings are held weekly, and they are not open to the public. Each meeting begins with participants introducing themselves by first name and saying, "My name is ____, and I am a competent woman." Following that, 13 affirmation statements are read. Then each woman in attendance shares a positive action or feeling and relates the experience to one of the affirmations. This is followed by the discussion topic for the meeting. WFS also offers online meetings and phone support (Fenner & Gifford, 2012). Facilitators need to be certified through the WFS organization. Reading Fenner and Gifford's article provides a thorough look at the history and details of WFS.

A survey of 600 women attending WFS was conducted in 1991. Findings revealed that attending WFS was most attractive to "White, well-educated, middle-aged, middle- and upper-class women" (Kaskutas, 1996, p. 77). Humphreys et al. (2004) estimated that there were 1500 members of WFS in the United States.

Moderation Management (MM; http://www.moderation.org/).

Audrey Kishline began MM in 1994 as an alternative to AA for individuals who are not alcohol dependent (Lembke & Humphreys, 2012). Although Audrey believed that her drinking problem was less serious compared to AA members, she was unable to maintain moderation and left MM to later join AA herself (Lembke & Humphreys, 2012). Tragically, during a relapse, she killed two individuals in a car accident (Lembke & Humphreys, 2012) and spent 3.5 years of a 4.5-year sentence in jail. She died at age 59 on December 19, 2014. Although two respected addiction professionals stated publicly that she died from suicide, this was never confirmed by her family (Walker, 2015).

Although abstinence is the objective of the other substance-focused MSGs, MM is the only group that advances moderation as its goal. Its four principles include "self-management, balance, moderation, and personal responsibility" (Kelly & Yeterian, 2013, p. 509). The main method used is self-monitoring of drinking. Their daily drinking chart is intended to help problematic drinkers regain control. MM recommends that drinkers begin with an initial 30 days of abstinence and, once drinking resumes, to abstain completely for at least 3 or 4 days per week (Kelly & Yeterian, 2013). Moderation drinking is defined for women as not more than nine standard drinks (i.e., 12 ounces of beer, 5 ounces of wine, or 1.5 ounces of hard liquor) per week and no more than three standard drinks on any day. For men, the limit is no more than 14 standard drinks per week and a maximum of four on any day (Lembke & Humphreys, 2012).

According to a survey conducted in 2001 (Humphreys & Klaw, 2001), most members of MM were White, employed, educated, and more secular than the population in general. Membership in this organization is small, reportedly at about 50 in 2000 (Humphreys & Klaw, 2001). Research "tentatively" supports the idea that MM attracts mostly nondependent problem drinkers. On average, members of MM are less severely dependent than those attending AA (Lembke & Humphreys, 2012). There are no published longitudinal studies or randomized clinical trials attesting to the effectiveness of MM (Lembke & Humphreys, 2012).

RESOURCES AND VIDEOS

Resources

1. The Role of Mutual-Help Groups in Extending the Framework of Treatment by John F. Kelly, Ph.D., and Julie D. Yeterian. https://pubs.niaaa.nih.gov/publications/arh334/350-355.pdf
2. Differences Between Individual, Group, and Couples Therapy. https://www.psychologytoday.com/us/blog/the-healing-crowd/201501/differences-between-individual-group-and-couples-therapy
3. What is Professional Counseling? American Counseling Association. https://www.counseling.org/aca-community/learn-about-counseling/what-is-counseling/overview
4. What is Family Therapy? https://www.webmd.com/parenting/family-therapy-overview#1
5. How to Find the Best Non-12-Step Addiction Recovery Programs. https://www.recovery.org/drug-treatment/non-12-step/

Videos

To view these videos, search their titles on YouTube.

1. *Making Marriage Work | Dr. John Gottman.*
2. *Marriage Counselling - His Needs vs Her Needs - W.F.Harley - LESSON 1/6 - Video Study.*
3. *Family Members at Different Stages of Change | Family Systems Therapy in Addiction Treatment* by Jennifer Musselman, MA, LMFT.
4. *Group Counseling Common Mistakes* by Drs. Ed Jacobs and Chris Schimmel.
5. *Self Help and Support Groups Overview* by Dr. Dawn-Elise Snipes.

JOURNALS AND CONFERENCES

Journals

There are numerous journals focused on couples, family, and group counseling. The list below provides only a sample:

1. *Journal of Marital and Family Therapy* (formerly the *Journal of Marriage and Family Counseling*). https://onlinelibrary.wiley.com/journal/17520606
2. *Journal of Couple and Relationship Therapy* (formerly the *Journal of Couples Therapy*). https://www.tandfonline.com/toc/wcrt20/current
3. *Journal of Family Therapy.* https://onlinelibrary.wiley.com/journal/14676427
4. *Journal of GLBT Family Studies.* https://www.tandfonline.com/toc/wgfs20/current
5. *Journal of LGBT Issues in Counseling.* https://www.tandfonline.com/toc/wlco20/current
6. *Contemporary Family Therapy.* https://link.springer.com/journal/10591
7. *Journal of Marriage and Family.* https://onlinelibrary.wiley.com/journal/17413737
8. *International Journal of Group Psychotherapy.* https://www.agpa.org/home/practice-resources/international-journal-of-group-psychotherapy
9. *Journal of Child and Adolescent Group Therapy.* https://www.researchgate.net/journal/1053-0800_Journal_of_Child_and_Adolescent_Group_Therapy
10. *Journal of Psychodrama, Sociometry, and Group Psychotherapy.* https://asgppjournal.org/

Conferences

Most of the following organizations offer conferences, workshops, and/or classes focused on couples, family, and group counseling. Please see websites for details:

1. American Association for Marriage and Family Therapy. https://aamft.org/

2. International Family Therapy Association. http://www.ifta-familytherapy.org/
3. National Council on Family Relations. https://www.ncfr.org/
4. World Family Therapy Congress (note that this one is a conference). http://www.ifta-congress.org/
5. American Family Therapy Academy. https://afta.org/
6. National Institute of Relationship Enhancement. http://www.nire.org/
7. Family Dynamics Institute. https://www.familydynamicsinstitute.com/
8. American Group Psychotherapy Association. https://www.agpa.org/

INDIVIDUAL EXERCISES

1. Attend one or more TS-MSGs *and* one or more NTS-MSGs. Ensure to check with the facilitator first before attending as some meetings are closed (i.e., they are not open to the public). How did your feelings compare in attending the two different kinds of meetings? If you were an addicted individual (or *are* an addict), which type of meeting would you prefer and why?
2. Addiction counselors require specialized skills before independently practicing couples, family, or group counseling. Regardless of your training in these areas, you may be required by your employer to offer one or more of these modalities. If you could choose one of these three modalities in which to specialize, which one would you pick and why? What personal qualities do you have that would help you in offering counseling in each of these three modalities, and which personal attributes might act as disadvantages?
3. This next exercise is straightforward to do if you are currently in an intimate relationship. If you are not, it is okay to focus on a close friend or close family member. As a test of systems theory, pay attention regarding the extent to which your mood both affects and influences the mood of your partner, friend, or family member. Notice the difference in either yourself or the other person when either of you is in a positive mood and when either of you is in a negative mood. How much does one influence the other? What can you take away from this exercise and apply in your relationships with others, including clients?

CLASSROOM EXERCISES

1. Assign half of your students (either individually or in a small group) to attend a TS-MSG and the other half to attend an NTS-MSG. Ensure to have your students check with the facilitator first before attending as some meetings are closed. Upon completion, have students either write an essay about their experience or lead a class discussion/debate regarding the advantages and disadvantages of both types of MSGs.
2. Group facilitation exercise. This exercise will test up to 21 students in a course on group counseling. Use Appendix 7D for this exercise. In Appendix 7D, 21 facilitation exercises are to be completed by students in the class. If your class is small enough, have everyone sit on a chair (move aside the tables) and form a circle. If your class is large, form a circle of five chairs at the front of your class (the largest group in the exercise only has five students maximum).

   Before class, cut each exercise as a separate page. Then cut along the lines of each page without actually detaching the sections. In other words, keep a little of the paper joined together so that you can tear off the different roles for the actors just before passing them out to students (ensure that you have an uncut copy of all the exercises for yourself). Then pass out the roles to the students, one of whom will act as the facilitator of the group. Besides the facilitator, there are up to four actors in each exercise. Once you give the facilitator and actors a chance to read their roles, cue the facilitator to begin the group. If actor 1 does not speak up, ask for actor 1 to start the dialogue. Do the same if the other actors fail to follow suit.
3. Create a panel by inviting one speaker from a TS-MSG and another from an NTS-MSG to attend your class at the same time. Let them know that you are not organizing a debate but that, instead, it will be a panel discussion. Allow each speaker time to talk about the benefits of attending the group in which he or she is affiliated. Ensure that the class has prepared a list of questions in advance.

CHAPTER SUMMARY

This chapter reviewed couples, family, and group counseling and then concluded by looking at MSGs. Couples counseling is not common in addictions treatment, despite being the treatment of choice when committed couples are in distress. The couples counseling approaches that have substantial empirical support include CBCT and BCT. Approaches that have less empirical support include psychodynamic couples therapy and emotion-focused therapy.

The impact of addiction on families can be devastating, but, in recovery, families can become either part of the problem for addicted individuals or part of the solution. Many addictions can be thought of as a family issue. Characteristics of healthy families and dysfunctional families are described along with some general family counseling techniques. The approaches that have substantial empirical support once again include CBFT and behavioral family therapy. A third approach is included here called functional family therapy. The approaches that have less empirical support include psychodynamic family therapy, multidimensional family therapy, and a host of others, including postmodern therapies (i.e., SFFT and narrative therapy).

The next counseling modality discussed was group counseling. Group counseling is seen as the treatment of choice for substance abuse and addiction. It is efficient and effective and has many other advantages in addiction counseling. Groups that teach coping skills and CBT techniques, including relapse prevention, are the most effective. The types of groups that addiction counselors might lead include psychoeducational, task/work, counseling, and psychotherapy. Some basic group dynamics and tips were offered. One stage theory regarding the development of a group includes the forming, storming, norming, performing, and mourning/adjourning stages. Suggestions were provided regarding how to form and lead a group. The limitations of group counseling were considered before the two group counseling approaches that have the most empirical support were described: CBGT and motivational interviewing. Other group approaches had less empirical support. This included psychodynamic group therapy, confrontational interventions, and several other approaches.

MSGs remain popular, which began with AA and the many other TS-MSGs that later formed. Many addiction counselors are philosophically opposed to TS-MSGs for several reasons that were explained. The founders of NTS-MSGs felt similarly. The more popular of these were described, including SMART Recovery, LifeRing, Secular Organizations for Sobriety, Women for Sobriety, and Moderation Management.

REFERENCES

Ahmad-Abadi, F. K., Maarefvand, M., Aghaei, H., Hosseinzadeh, S., Abbasi, M., & Khubchandani, J. (2017). Effectiveness of Satir-informed family-therapy on the codependency of drug dependents' family members in Iran: A randomized controlled trial. *Journal of Evidence-Informed Social Work, 14*, 301–310.

Alcoholics Anonymous General Service Office. (2016, August). *The twelve steps of Alcoholics Anonymous*. Retrieved on March 13, 2019, from https://www.aa.org/assets/en_US/smf-121_en.pdf

Alcoholics Anonymous General Service Office. (2018, January 1). *Estimates of A.A. groups and members as of January 1, 2018*. Retrieved on March 13, 2019, from https://www.aa.org/assets/en_US/smf-53_en.pdf

Alderson, K. (2018). *Personal Functioning Questionnaire*. Calgary, AB: Author.

American Counseling Association. (2014). *2014 ACA code of ethics*. Retrieved from file:///C:/Users/Owner-PC/Desktop/aca-code-of-ethics.pdf

Ashouri, A., Mollazadeh, J., & Mohammadi, N. (2008). The effectiveness of cognitive-behavioral group therapy on the improvement of coping skills and relapse prevention in addicted individuals. *Iranian Journal of Psychiatry and Clinical Psychology, 14*(3), 281–288.

Atkins, R. G., & Hawdon, J. E. (2007). Religiosity and participation in mutual-aid support groups for addiction. *Journal of Substance Abuse Treatment, 33*, 321–331.

Baharudin, D. F., Mohd Hussin, A. H., Sumari, M., Mohamed, S., Zakaria, M. Z., & Sawai, R. P. (2014). Family intervention for the treatment and rehabilitation of drug addiction: An exploratory study. *Journal of Substance Use, 19*, 301–306.

Bassett, B. (2015). Emotion focused therapy for couples in addiction treatment: The relationship between quality of recovery, attachment style, and relational satisfaction. *Dissertation Abstracts International: Section B: The Sciences and Engineering, 75*(10-B(E)). No pagination specified.

Baucom, D. H., Fischer, M. S., Hahlweg, K., & Epstein, N. B. (2019). Cognitive behavioral couple therapy. In B. H. Fiese, M. Celano, K. Deater-Deckard, E. N. Jouriles, & M. A. Whisman (Eds.), *APA handbook of contemporary family psychology: Family therapy and training., Vol. 3* (pp. 257–273). Washington, DC: American Psychological Association.

Beck, A. K., Forbes, E., Baker, A. L., Kelly, P. J., Deane, F. P., Shakeshaft, A., . . . Kelly, J. F. (2017). Systematic review of SMART Recovery: Outcomes, process variables, and implications for research. *Psychology of Addictive Behaviors, 31*(1), 1–20.

Belmontes, K. C. (2018). When family gets in the way of recovery: Motivational interviewing with families. *Family Journal, 26*, 99–104.

Best, D., Savic, M., Mugavin, J., Manning, V., & Lubman, D. I. (2016). Engaging with 12-step and other mutual aid groups during and after treatment: Addressing workers' negative beliefs and attitudes through training. *Alcoholism Treatment Quarterly*, *34*(3), 303–314.

Birchard, T. (2018). Group cognitive behavioural therapy for compulsive sexual behaviour. In T. Birchard & J. Benfield (Eds.), *The Routledge international handbook of sexual addiction* (pp. 190–202). New York, NY: Routledge/Taylor & Francis.

Birchler, G. R., Fals-Stewart, W., & O'Farrell, T. J. (2008). Couple therapy for alcoholism and drug abuse. In A. S. Gurman (Ed.), *Clinical handbook of couple therapy* (4th ed., pp. 523–544). New York, NY: Guilford Press.

Bischof, G., Iwen, J., Freyer-Adam, J., & Rumpf, H.-J. (2016). Efficacy of the community reinforcement and family training for concerned significant others of treatment-refusing individuals with alcohol dependence: A randomized controlled trial. *Drug and Alcohol Dependence*, *163*, 179–185.

Bishop, F. M. (2012). Helping couples deal with addictions. In A. Vernon (Ed.), *Cognitive and rational-emotive behavior with couples: Theory and practice* (pp. 169–189). New York, NY: Springer Science + Business Media.

Bond, L. M., & Csordas, T. J. (2014). The paradox of powerlessness. *Alcoholism Treatment Quarterly*, *32*(2–3), 141–156.

Brabender, V., & Fallon, A. (2019). *Group psychotherapy in inpatient, partial hospital, and residential care settings* (pp. 109–169). Washington, DC: American Psychological Association.

Bradshaw, S., Shumway, S. T., Wang, E. W., Harris, K. S., Smith, D. B., & Austin-Robillard, H. (2015). Hope, readiness, and coping in family recovery from addiction. *Journal of Groups in Addiction & Recovery*, *10*, 313–336.

Brooks, F., & McHenry, B. (2009). *A contemporary approach to substance abuse and addiction counseling: A counselor's guide to application and understanding*. Alexandria, VA: American Counseling Association.

Brownlee, N., Curran, D., & Tsang, S. M. (2017). Client engagement with a manualized group therapy program. *Journal of Groups in Addiction & Recovery*, *12*, 45–61.

Byrne, N. (2018). Couple psychotherapy through the lens of attachment theory. In P. Jools, J. Berg, & N. Byrne (Eds.), *Working with developmental anxieties in couple and family psychotherapy: The family within* (pp. 164–175). New York, NY: Routledge/Taylor & Francis.

Carnes, P. (1991). *Don't call it love: Recovery from sexual addiction*. Toronto, ON: Bantam Books.

Chan, J. G. (2003). An examination of family-involved approaches to alcoholism treatment. *Family Journal*, *11*, 129–138.

Clark, A. A. (2014). Narrative therapy integration within substance abuse groups. *Journal of Creativity in Mental Health*, *9*, 511–522.

Collins, G. (2018). The process of couples' therapy for sex and porn addiction. In T. Birchard & J. Benfield (Eds.), *The Routledge international handbook of sexual addiction* (pp. 212–223). New York, NY: Routledge/Taylor & Francis.

Connors, G. J., & Dermen, K. H. (1996). Characteristics of participants in Secular Organizations for Sobriety (SOS). *American Journal of Drug and Alcohol Abuse*, *22*, 281–295.

Connors, G. J., DiClemente, C. C., Velasquez, M. M., & Donovan, D. M. (2013). *Substance abuse treatment and the stages of change: Selecting and planning interventions* (2nd ed). New York, NY: Guilford Press.

Csiernik, R. (2016). *Substance use and abuse: Everything matters* (2nd ed.). Toronto, ON: Canadian Scholars Press.

Csiernik, R., & Arundel, M. K. (2013). Does counseling format play a role in client retention? *Journal of Groups in Addiction & Recovery*, *8*, 262–269.

Du, Y.S., Jiang, W., & Vance, A. (2010). Longer term effect of randomized, controlled group cognitive behavioural therapy for Internet addiction in adolescent students in Shanghai. *Australian and New Zealand Journal of Psychiatry*, *44*, 129–134.

Earleywine, M. (2016). *Substance use problems* (2nd ed.). Ashland, OH: Hogrefe.

Emrick, C. D., & Beresford, T. P. (2016). Contemporary negative assessments of alcoholics anonymous: A response. *Alcoholism Treatment Quarterly*, *34*(4), 463–471.

Falconer, B. J. (2015). An exploration of participants' experiences of the LifeRing secular recovery support group model in the management of chronic alcohol dependence. *Dissertation Abstracts International: Section B: The Sciences and Engineering*, *75*(8-B(E)). No pagination specified.

Fenner, R. M., & Gifford, M. H. (2012). Women for sobriety: 35 years of challenges, changes, and continuity. *Journal of Groups in Addiction & Recovery*, *7*, 142–170.

Filges, T., Andersen, D., & Jorgensen, A.-M. K. (2018). Effects of multidimensional family therapy (MDFT) on nonopioid drug abuse: A systematic review and meta-analysis. *Research on Social Work Practice*, *28*, 68–83.

Fischer, M. S., & Baucom, D. H. (2018). Cognitive-behavioral couples-based interventions for relationship distress and psychopathology. In J. N. Butcher & J. M. Hooley (Eds.), *APA handbook of psychopathology: Psychopathology: Understanding, assessing, and treating adult mental disorders*., Vol. *1* (pp. 661–686). Washington, DC: American Psychological Association.

Foote, J., DeLuca, A., Magura, S., Warner, A., Grand, A., Rosenblum, A., & Stahl, S. (1999). A group motivational treatment for chemical dependency. *Journal of Substance Abuse Treatment*, *17*, 181–192.

Ford, J. J., Durtschi, J. A., & Franklin, D. L. (2012). Structural therapy with a couple battling pornography addiction. *American Journal of Family Therapy*, *40*, 336–348.

Gamble, J., & O'Lawrence, H. (2016). An overview of the efficacy of the 12-step group therapy for substance abuse treatment. *Journal of Health and Human Services Administration*, *39*(1), 142–160.

Garrido-Fernandez, M., Marcos-Sierra, J. A., Lopez-Jimenez, A., & de Alda, I. O. (2017). Multi-family therapy with a reflecting team: A preliminary study on efficacy among opiate addicts in methadone maintenance treatment. *Journal of Marital and Family Therapy*, *43*, 338–351.

George, S., & Bowden-Jones, H. (2015). Family interventions in gambling. In H. Bowden-Jones & S. George (Eds.), *A clinician's guide to working with problem gamblers* (pp. 163–171). New York, NY: Routledge.

Gerson, M. J. (2019). Psychodynamic theories of the family. In B. H. Fiese, M. Celano, K. Deater-Deckard, E. N. Jouriles, & M. A. Whisman (Eds.), *APA handbook of contemporary family psychology: Foundations, methods, and contemporary issues across the lifespan*., *Vol. 1* (pp. 21–35). Washington, DC: American Psychological Association.

Gladding, S. T., & Alderson, K. G. (2012). *Counselling: A comprehensive profession* (Can. ed.). Toronto, ON: Pearson Canada.

Gladding, S. T., & Alderson, K. G. (2019). *Choosing the right counselor for you*. Alexandria, VA: American Counseling Association.

Gramani, Y. (2007). *An evaluation of the stages-of-change therapy programme for substance abuse* (Unpublished doctorate thesis). University of Zululand Institutional Repository.

Grazioli, V. S., Collins, S. E., Daeppen, J.-B., & Larimer, M. E. (2015). Perceptions of twelve-step mutual-help groups and their associations with motivation, treatment attendance and alcohol outcomes among chronically homeless individuals with alcohol problems. *International Journal of Drug Policy, 26*(5), 468–474

Gryczynski, J., Schwartz, R. P., Fishman, M. J., Nordeck, C. D., Grant, J., Nidich, S., . . . O'Grady, K. E. (2018). Integration of transcendental meditation™ (TM) into alcohol use disorder (AUD) treatment. *Journal of Substance Abuse Treatment, 87*, 23–30.

Guarnotta, E. (2015). A comparison of abstinence and perceived self-efficacy for individuals attending SMART Recovery and Alcoholics Anonymous. *Dissertation Abstracts International: Section B: The Sciences and Engineering, 76*(6-B(E)). No pagination specified.

Hagedorn, W. B., & Hirshhorn, M. A. (2009). When talking won't work: Implementing experiential group activities with addicted clients. *Journal for Specialists in Group Work, 34*, 43–67.

Hartnett, D., Carr, A., Hamilton, E., & O'Reilly, G. (2017). The effectiveness of functional family therapy for adolescent behavioral and substance misuse problems: A meta-analysis. *Family Process, 56*(3), 607–619.

Heatherington, L., & Johnson, B. (2019). Social constructionism in couple and family therapy: Narrative, solution-focused, and related approaches. In B. H. Fiese, M. Celano, K. Deater-Deckard, E. N. Jouriles, & M. A. Whisman (Eds.), *APA handbook of contemporary family psychology: Foundations, methods, and contemporary issues across the lifespan., Vol. 1* (pp. 127–142). Washington, DC: American Psychological Association.

Hill, J., & Leeming, D. (2014). Reconstructing 'the alcoholic': Recovering from alcohol addiction and the stigma this entails. *International Journal of Mental Health and Addiction, 12*(6), 759–771.

Horvath, A. T., & Velten, E. (2000). SMART Recovery: Addiction recovery support from a cognitive-behavioral perspective. *Journal of Rational-Emotive & Cognitive-Behavior Therapy, 18*, 181–191.

Houck, J. M., Manuel, J. K., & Moyers, T. B. (2018). Short- and long-term effects of within-session client speech on drinking outcomes in the COMBINE study. *Journal of Studies on Alcohol and Drugs, 79*(2), 217–222.

Hulse-Killacky, D., Killacky, J., & Donigian, J. (2001). *Making task groups work in your world.* Upper Saddle River, NJ: Prentice Hall.

Humphreys, K., Blodgett, J. C., & Wagner, T. H. (2014). Estimating the efficacy of Alcoholics Anonymous without self-selection bias: An instrumental variables re-analysis of randomized clinical trials. *Alcoholism: Clinical and Experimental Research, 38*(11), 2688–2694.

Humphreys, K., & Kaskutas, L. A. (1995). World views of Alcoholics Anonymous, Women for Sobriety, and Adult Children of Alcoholics/Al-Anon mutual help groups. *Addiction Research, 3*, 231–243.

Humphreys, K., & Klaw, E. (2001). Can targeting nondependent problem drinkers and providing Internet-based services expand access to assistance for alcohol problems? A study of the moderation management self-help/mutual aid organization. *Journal of Studies on Alcohol, 62*, 528–532.

Humphreys, K., Wing, S., McCarty, D., Chappel, J., Gallant, L., Haberle, B., . . . Weiss, R. (2004). Self-help organizations for alcohol and drug problems: Toward evidence-based practice and policy. *Journal of Substance Abuse Treatment, 26*, 151–158.

Jimenez-Murcia, S., Aymami, N., Gomez-Pena, M., Santamaria, J. J., Alvarez-Moya, E., Fernandez-Aranda, F., . . . Menchon, J. M. (2012). Does exposure and response prevention improve the results of group cognitive-behavioural therapy for male slot machine pathological gamblers? *British Journal of Clinical Psychology, 51*, 54–71.

John, U., Veltrup, C., Driessen, M., Wetterling, T., & Dilling, H. (2003). Motivational intervention: An individual counselling vs a group treatment approach for alcohol-dependent in-patients. *Alcohol and Alcoholism, 38*, 263–269.

Kaskutas, L. A. (1996). A road less traveled: Choosing the "Women for Sobriety" program. *Journal of Drug Issues, 26*, 77–94.

Kelly, J. F., & Yeterian, J. D. (2011). The role of mutual-help groups in extending the framework of treatment. *Alcohol Research & Health, 33*(4), 350–355.

Kelly, J. F., & Yeterian, J. D. (2013). Mutual-help groups for alcohol and other substance use disorders. In B. S. McCrady & E. E. Epstein (Eds.), *Addictions: A comprehensive guidebook* (2nd ed., pp. 500–525). New York, NY: Oxford University Press.

Kelly, P. J., Deane, F. P., & Baker, A. L. (2015). Group cohesion and between session homework activities predict self-reported cognitive–behavioral skill use amongst participants of SMART Recovery groups. *Journal of Substance Abuse Treatment, 51*, 53–58.

Kelly, P. J., Raftery, D., Deane, F. P., Baker, A. L., Hunt, D., & Shakeshaft, A. (2017). From both sides: Participant and facilitator perceptions of SMART Recovery groups. *Drug and Alcohol Review, 36*, 325–332.

Klostermann, K. (2016). Marital and family approaches. In K. J. Sher (Ed.), *The Oxford handbook of substance use and substance use disorders, Vol. 2* (pp. 567–581). New York, NY: Oxford University Press.

Krejci, J., & Neugebauer, Q. (2015). Motivational interviewing in groups: Group process considerations. *Journal of Groups in Addiction & Recovery, 10*(1), 23–40.

Kuuluvainen, V., & Isotalus, P. (2015). Words and beyond: Members' experiences of the supportive communication and helping mechanisms of Al-Anon groups. *Journal of Groups in Addiction & Recovery, 10*(3), 204–223.

Laaser, M. R. (2004). *Healing the wounds of sexual addiction.* Grand Rapids, MI: Zondervan.

LaBrie, J. W., Pedersen, E. R., Lamb, T. F., & Quinlan, T. (2007). A campus-based motivational enhancement group intervention reduces problematic drinking in freshmen male college students. *Addictive Behaviors, 32*, 889–901.

Ladouceur, R., Sylvain, C., Boutin, C., Lachance, S., Doucet, C., & Leblond, J. (2003). Group therapy for pathological gamblers: A cognitive approach. *Behaviour Research and Therapy, 41*(5), 587–596.

Lambert, S. F., Carmichael, A. R., & Williams, L. (2016). Guidelines in counseling families. In I. Marini & M. A. Stebnicki (Eds.), *The professional counselor's desk reference* (2nd ed., pp. 351–355). New York, NY: Springer.

Landau-North, M., Johnson, S. M., & Dalgleish, T. L. (2011). Emotionally focused couple therapy and addiction. In J. Furrow, S. M. Johnson, & B. A. Bradley (Eds.), *The emotionally focused casebook: New directions in treating couples* (pp. 193–217). New York, NY: Routledge/Taylor & Francis.

Lassiter, P. S., Czerny, A. B., & Williams, K. S. (2015). Working with addictions in family therapy. In D. Capuzzi & M. D. Stauffer (Eds.), *Foundations of couples, marriage, and family counseling* (pp. 389–417). Hoboken, NJ: John Wiley & Sons.

Lembke, A., & Humphreys, K. (2012). Moderation management: A mutual-help organization for problem drinkers who are not alcohol-dependent. *Journal of Groups in Addiction & Recovery, 7*, 130–141.

Lembke, A., & Humphreys, K. (2016). Self-help organizations for substance use disorders. In K. J. Sher (Ed.), *The Oxford handbook of substance use and substance use disorders, Vol. 2* (pp. 582–593). New York, NY: Oxford University Press.

Lewis, V., & Allen-Byrd, L. (2007). Coping strategies for the stages of family recovery. *Alcoholism Treatment Quarterly, 25*, 105–124.

Liddle, H. A. (2009). Multidimensional family therapy: A science-based treatment system for adolescent drug abuse. In J. H. Bray & M. Stanton (Eds.), *The Wiley-Blackwell handbook of family psychology* (pp. 341–354). New York, NY: Wiley-Blackwell.

Liepman, M. R., Flachier, R., & Tareen, R. S. (2008). Family behavior loop mapping: A technique to analyze the grip addictive disorders have on families and to help them recover. *Alcoholism Treatment Quarterly, 26*, 59–80.

Liu, Q.-X., Fang, X.-Y., Yan, N., Zhou, Z.-K., Yuan, X.-J., Lan, J., & Liu, C.-Y. (2015). Multi-family group therapy for adolescent Internet addiction: Exploring the underlying mechanisms. *Addictive Behaviors, 42*, 1–8.

Love, H. A., Moore, R. M., & Stanish, N. A. (2016). Emotionally focused therapy for couples recovering from sexual addiction. *Sexual and Relationship Therapy, 31*, 176–189.

Mack, K. N., Lebowitz, E. R., & Silverman, W. K. (2019). Contemporary family psychotherapy: Behavioral and cognitive-behavioral theories. In B. H. Fiese, M. Celano, K. Deater-Deckard, E. N. Jouriles, & M. A. Whisman (Eds.), *APA handbook of contemporary family psychology: Foundations, methods, and contemporary issues across the lifespan, Vol. 1* (pp. 57–73). Washington, DC: American Psychological Association.

MacKillop, J., Stojek, M., VanderBroek-Stice, L., & Owens, M. M. (2018). Evidence-based treatment for alcohol use disorders: A review through the lens of the theory x efficacy matrix. In D. David, S. J. Lynn, & G. H. Montgomery (Eds.), *Evidence-based psychotherapy: The state of the science and practice* (pp. 219–252). New York, NY: Wiley-Blackwell.

Malat, J., Morrow, S., & Stewart, P. (2011). Applying motivational interviewing principles in a modified interpersonal group for comorbid addiction. *International Journal of Group Psychotherapy, 61*, 557–575.

Marcus, M. T., & Zgierska, A. (2009). Mindfulness-based therapies for substance use disorders: Part 1. *Substance Abuse, 30*(4), 263–265.

Margolis, R. D., & Zweben, J. E. (2011). Family therapy. In R. D. Margolis & J. E. Zweben (Eds.), *Treating patients with alcohol and other drug problems: An integrated approach* (2nd ed., pp. 145–172). Washington, DC: American Psychological Association.

Martinez-Gonzalez, J. M., Vilar-Lopez, R., & Verdejo-Garcia, A. (2018). Long-term effectiveness of group cognitive-behavioral therapy for alcoholism: Impact of dual diagnosis on treatment outcome. *Clinica y Salud, 29*, 1–8.

McComb, J. L., Lee, B. K., & Sprenkle, D. H. (2009). Conceptualizing and treating problem gambling as a family issue. *Journal of Marital and Family Therapy, 35*, 415–431.

McCrady, B. S. (2014). Alcohol use disorders. In D. H. Barlow (Ed.), *Clinical handbook of psychological disorders: A step-by-step treatment manual* (5th ed., pp. 533–587) New York, NY: Guilford Press.

McCrady, B. S., & Epstein, E. E. (2015). Couple therapy and alcohol problems. In A. S. Gurman, J. L. Lebow, & D. K. Snyder (Eds.), *Clinical handbook of couple therapy* (5th ed., pp. 555–584). New York, NY: Guilford Press.

McNeece, C. A., & DiNitto, D. M. (2012). Treatment: The system of care. In C. A. McNeece & D. M. DiNitto (Eds.), *Chemical dependency: A systems approach* (4th ed., pp. 121–170). Upper Saddle River, NJ: Pearson.

Medina, M. (2014). The paradox of self-surrender and self-empowerment: An investigation of the individual's understanding of the Higher Power in Alcoholics Anonymous. *Counselling Psychology Review, 29*(3), 28–42.

Melemis, S. M. (2018, September 25). *Addiction self-help groups and 12 step groups*. Retrieved on March 13, 2019, from https://www.addictionsandrecovery.org/addiction-self-help-and-12-step-groups.htm

Milkman, H. B., & Sunderwirth, S. G. (2010). *Craving for ecstasy and natural highs: A positive approach to mood alteration*. Thousand Oaks, CA: SAGE.

Miller, W. R., & Munoz, R. F. (2013). *Controlling your drinking, second edition: Tools to make moderation work for you* (2nd ed.). New York, NY Guilford Press.

Monson, C. M., Wagner, A. C., Fredman, S. J., Macdonald, A., & Pukay-Martin, N. D. (2017). Couple and family therapy for traumatic stress conditions. In S. N. Gold (Ed.), *APA handbook of trauma psychology: Trauma practice, Vol. 2* (pp. 449–466). Washington, DC: American Psychological Association.

Moos, R. H. (2012). Substance use-focused self-help groups: Processes and outcomes. In B. A. Johnson (Ed.), *Addiction medicine: Science and practice* (vols. 1 and 2; pp. 925–940). New York, NY: Springer Science + Business Media.

Murray, S. B., Labuschagne, Z., & Le Grange, D. (2014). Family and couples therapy for eating disorders, substance use disorders, and addictions. In T. D. Brewerton & A. B. Dennis (Eds.), *Eating disorders, addictions and substance use disorders: Research, clinical and treatment perspectives* (pp. 563–586). New York, NY: Springer-Verlag.

Nabuco de Abreu, C., & Sampio Goes, D. (2011). Psychotherapy for Internet addiction. In K. S. Young & C. Nabuco de Abreu (Eds.), *Internet addiction: Handbook and guide to evaluation and treatment* (pp. 155–171). Hoboken, NJ: Wiley.

Navidian, A., Kermansaravi, F., Tabas, E. E., & Saeedinezhad, F. (2016). Efficacy of group motivational interviewing in the degree of drug craving in the addicts under the Methadone Maintenance Treatment (MMT) in South East of Iran. *Archives of Psychiatric Nursing, 30*, 144–149.

Neukrug, E. S. (2015). *The world of the counselor: An introduction to the counseling profession* (5th ed.). Stamford, CT: Cengage Learning.

Nyhuis, P. W., Niederhofer, E., Scherbaum, N., Schifano, F., Bonnet, U., Dembski, N., . . . Tenbergen, M. (2018). Effectiveness of psychoanalytic-interactional group therapy vs. behavioral group therapy in routine outpatient treatment of alcohol-dependent patients. *Substance Use & Misuse, 53*, 426–431.

O'Farrell, T. J. (2011). Family therapy. In M. Galanter & H. D. Kleber (Eds.), *Psychotherapy for the treatment of substance abuse* (pp. 329–350). Arlington, VA: American Psychiatric.

O'Farrell, T. J., & Clements, K. (2012). Review of outcome research on marital and family therapy in treatment for alcoholism. *Journal of Marital and Family Therapy, 38*, 122–144.

O'Farrell, T. J., Schumm, J. A., Dunlap, L. J., Murphy, M. M., & Muchowski, P. (2016). A randomized clinical trial of group versus standard behavioral couples therapy plus individually based treatment for patients with alcohol dependence. *Journal of Consulting and Clinical Psychology, 84*, 497–510.

Park, T. Y., Kim, S., & Lee, J. (2014). Family therapy for an internet-addicted young adult with interpersonal problems. *Journal of Family Therapy, 36*, 394–419.

Parker, S. (2015). Review of group cognitive therapy for addictions. *Behavioural and Cognitive Psychotherapy, 43*, 253–254.

Parkman, T. J., Lloyd, C., & Splisbury, K. (2015). Self-help groups for alcohol dependency: A scoping review. *Journal of Groups in Addiction & Recovery*, *10*(2), 102–124.

Pietrofesa, J. J., Hoffman, A., & Splete, H. H. (1984). *Counseling: An introduction* (2nd ed.). Boston, MA: Houghton Mifflin.

Potkonjak, J., Ivancic, I., Zdunic, D., Karlovic, D., & Matosic, A. (2006). Alcoholic and his family. *Alcoholism and psychiatry research: Journal on psychiatric research and addictions*, *42*(1), 23–33.

Rastegar, D., & Fingerhood, M. (2016). *The American Society of Addiction Medicine handbook of addiction medicine*. New York, NY: Oxford University Press.

Rosenberg, K. P., Carnes, P., & O'Connor, S. (2014). Evaluation and treatment of sex addiction. *Journal of Sex & Marital Therapy*, *40*(2), 77–91.

Saulnier, C. F. (1996). Images of the twelve-step model, and sex and love addiction in an alcohol intervention group for Black women. *Journal of Drug Issues*, *26*(1), 95–123.

Schmidt, E. (1996). Rational recovery: Finding an alternative for addiction treatment. *Alcoholism Treatment Quarterly*, *14*, 47–57.

Schumm, J. A., & O'Farrell, T. J. (2013). Behavioral couples therapy for alcoholism. In P. M. Miller, S. A. Ball, M. E. Bates, A. W. Blume, K. M. Kampman, D. J. Kavanagh, M. E. Larimer, N. M. Petry, & P. De Witte (Eds.), *Comprehensive addictive behaviors and disorders, Vol. 3: Interventions for addiction* (pp. 57–65). San Diego, CA: Elsevier Academic Press.

Schwartz, D. C., Nickow, M. S., Arseneau, R., & Gisslow, M. T. (2015). A substance called food: Long-term psychodynamic group treatment for compulsive overeating. *International Journal of Group Psychotherapy*, *65*, 386–409.

Sherrell, R., & Gutierrez, D. (2014). Couples and addiction: Three effective theories. *Family Journal*, *22*, 26–34.

Silverstein, L. B., & Goodrich, T. J. (2019). Feminist theories in contemporary couple and family psychology. In B. H. Fiese, M. Celano, K. Deater-Deckard, E. N. Jouriles, & M. A. Whisman (Eds.), *APA handbook of contemporary family psychology: Foundations, methods, and contemporary issues across the lifespan, Vol. 1* (pp. 93–108). Washington, DC: American Psychological Association.

Sotskova, A., Woodin, E., & St. Cyr, K. (2016). Understanding the role of group cohesion and group alliance in a secular peer support group for recovery from substance misuse. *Journal of Groups in Addiction & Recovery*, *11*, 137–154.

Southern, S., & Thornton, B. (2013). Group treatment in the continuum of care. In P. Stevens & R. L. Smith (Eds.), *Substance abuse counseling: Theory and practice* (5th ed., pp. 203–239). New York, NY: Pearson.

Szabo, J., Toth, S., & Pakai, A. K. (2014). Narrative group therapy for alcohol dependent patients. *International Journal of Mental Health and Addiction*, *12*, 470–476.

Tarman, V., & Werdell, P. (2014). *Food junkies: The truth about food addiction*. Toronto, ON: Dundurn.

Tremblay, J., Dufour, M., Bertrand, K., Blanchette-Martin, N., Ferland, F., Savard, A.-C., . . . Cote, M. (2018). The experience of couples in the process of treatment of pathological gambling: Couple vs. individual therapy. *Frontiers in Psychology*, *8*, 1–14.

Tucker, J. S., D'Amico, E. J., Ewing, B. A., Miles, J. N. V., & Pedersen, E. R. (2017). A group-based motivational interviewing brief intervention to reduce substance use and sexual risk behavior among homeless young adults. *Journal of Substance Abuse Treatment*, *76*, 20–27.

Tuckman, B. (1965). Developmental sequence in small groups. *Psychological Bulletin*, *63*, 384–399.

Tuckman, B. W., & Jensen, M. A. (1977). Stages of small-group development revisited. *Group & Organization Management*, *2*, 419–427.

Van Wormer, K., & Davis, D. R. (2013). *Addiction treatment: A strengths perspective* (3rd ed.). Boston, MA: Cengage.

Velasquez, M. M., Maurer, G. G., Crouch, C., & DiClemente, C. C. (2001). *Group treatment for substance abuse: A stages-of-change therapy manual*. New York, NY: Guilford Press.

Wakefield, P. J., Williams, R. E., Yost, E. B., & Patterson, K. M. (1996). *Couple therapy for alcoholism: A cognitive-behavioral treatment manual*. New York, NY: Guilford Press.

Waldo, M. (1985). Curative factor framework for conceptualizing group counseling. *Journal of Counseling and Development*, *64*, 52–58.

Walker, R. (2015, January 7). Remembering Audrey Kishline, the founder of Moderation Management. *Fix*. Retrieved on March 14, 2019, from https://www.thefix.com/content/remembering-audrey-kishline

Wanigaratne, S. (2011). Cultural issues in group work. In R. Hill & J. Harris (Eds.), *Principles and practice of group work in addictions* (pp. 153–164). New York, NY: Routledge/Taylor & Francis.

Wanlass, J. (2014). But my partner "is" the problem: Addressing addiction, mood disorders, and psychiatric illness in psychoanalytic couple treatment. In D. E. Scharff & J. S. Scharff (Eds.), *Psychoanalytic couple therapy: Foundations of theory and practice* (pp. 310–322). London, England: Karnac Books.

Wegscheider, S. (1981). *Another chance: Hope and health for the alcoholic family*. Palo Alto, CA: Science and Behavior Books.

Wenzel, A., Liese, B. S., Beck, A. T., & Friedman-Wheeler, D. G. (2012). *Group cognitive therapy for addictions*. New York, NY: Guilford Press.

White, W., & Nicolaus, M. (2005). Styles of secular recovery. *Counselor*, *6*(4), 58–61.

Woods, J. (2013). Group analytic therapy for compulsive users of internet pornography. *Psychoanalytic Psychotherapy*, *27*, 306–318.

Yalom, I. D., & Leszcz, M. (2005). *Theory and practice of group psychotherapy* (5th ed.). New York, NY: Basic Books.

Young, K. S. (2017). Family therapy for adolescent and childhood internet gaming addiction. In K. S. Young & C. N. de Abreu (Eds.), *Internet addiction in children and adolescents: Risk factors, assessment, and treatment* (pp. 243–255). New York, NY: Springer.

Young, M. E., de Armas DeLorenzi, L., & Cunningham, L. (2011). Using meditation in addiction counseling. *Journal of Addictions & Offender Counseling*, *32*(1–2), 58–71.

Yu, J.-H., & Park, T.-Y. (2016). Family therapy for an adult child experiencing bullying and game addiction: An application of Bowenian and MRI theories. *Contemporary Family Therapy: An International Journal*, *38*, 318–327.

Zemore, S. E., Kaskutas, L. A., Mericle, A., & Hemberg, J. (2017). Comparison of 12-step groups to mutual help alternatives for AUD in a large, national study: Differences in membership characteristics and group participation, cohesion, and satisfaction. *Journal of Substance Abuse Treatment*, *73*, 16–26.

Zmuda, N. (2014). Assessment and treatment of co-occurring substance use disorders and process addictions: Eating disorders, pathological gambling, and sexual addiction. In S. L. A. Straussner (Ed.), *Clinical work with substance-abusing clients* (3rd ed., pp. 520–536). New York, NY: Guilford Press.

APPENDIX 7A. CONFLICT RESOLUTION

Avoid "Fighting"—Disagree Instead (Until You Find the Best Solution).

What are the possible outcomes from disagreeing about something?

1. Consensus. This is the most elegant solution. This means that both people come to the same conclusion about how to resolve the issue (e.g., both of you agree to go to church regularly).

2. Compromise. This is the second-best solution. This is where both of you arrive at a solution that is not your top choice (e.g., the one who does not want to go to church agrees to do so once a month in exchange for the other agreeing to attend a secular activity once a month).

3. Conceding (giving in). This is where one of you decides to accept the way it will be from your partner. In other words, one of you concedes to doing it the way that the other person desires. This method works so long as there is give-and-take (i.e., that your partner concedes on other issues; the end goal is to maintain a balance of power in the relationship). For example, the partner who is an atheist agrees to go to church to maintain peace and harmony.

4. Agree to disagree. This is the least desirable solution. In this approach, none of the previous solutions works. In agreeing to disagree, both of you maintain your original stance but accept that neither one of you can shift your position at all (e.g., one of you is deeply religious and attends church and the other is a strident atheist and will not set foot in a church).

How to resolve a disagreement?

1. Share feelings and content (e.g., "I feel irritated and compromised every time your mother tells me what to do").

2. Reflect feelings and content from your partner after he/she responds (e.g., "You feel embarrassed when I do not give in to your mother's demands").

3. Be assertive, neither passive or aggressive (e.g., "I am sorry, but I am not prepared to obey your mother. I am 35 and capable of making my own decisions").

4. Stay absolutely calm. If you cannot stay calm right now, defer the discussion regarding the conflict until later. Alternatively, discuss the issue in a quiet public place (e.g., a quiet coffee shop).

5. MOST IMPORTANT POINT: When you are working through a conflict, do not raise your voice, resort to name-calling, or bring up the past! Instead, stay focused on the conflict in the here-and-now; keep re-focusing (if necessary) on the issue itself and do not get sidetracked.

APPENDIX 7B. CHANGES NEEDED AND WANTED IN THIS RELATIONSHIP

Name: ______________________________

Date: ______________________________

Complete this form separately from each other and return it to your counselor individually (either via email or in person at the next session). Do not show what you have written to your partner but ensure that your counselor is provided with three copies (i.e., one for you, one for your partner, and one for your counselor). Follow these instructions:

1. Complete the third column **first** (i.e., changes you *need* and *want* to see).

2. Now, in the second column, rank all your requested changes. Place a 1 beside your highest priority, 2 beside your second highest priority, and so forth until you have ranked all your requested changes.

3. Columns 4 and 5 are completed in the session with your counselor present. Your partner and your counselor each get a copy before you rank your partner's list during the counseling session (your partner does the same with your list simultaneously).

4. Once finished, provide the three copies to your counselor.

#	Rank 1 is highest	Changes Needed and Wanted	For Partner Use *	
			COM	EFF
Changes I Must See ("Bottom Lines") [NEEDS]				
1				
2				
3				

#	Rank 1 is highest	Changes Needed and Wanted	For Partner Use *	
			COM	EFF
4				
5				
Changes I Would Like to See [WANTS]				
6				
7				
8				

#	Rank 1 is highest	Changes Needed and Wanted	For Partner Use *	
			COM	EFF
9				
10				

*FOR PARTNER USE LATER

COM = rate your commitment to making this change from 1 (*not at all committed*) to 5 (*totally committed*)

EFF = rate your level of self-efficacy (your perceived ability to make the requested change) from 1 (*cannot do this*) to 5 (*totally can do this*).

APPENDIX 7C. COMMON MISTAKES MADE BY COUPLES AND FAMILY COUNSELORS

In this chapter, there is a section called *Counseling Scenario*. One of the questions in each asks that you identify which counseling mistakes the counselor has made in the scenario. **None** of these are meant to be good counseling sessions. We learn to become good counselors by learning both what we should do with our clients and what we should avoid. The following list and explanations are adapted from several online sources (http://cebucounseling.blogspot.com/2012/08/common-counseling-mistakes-part-1.html; http://gettotheinside.blogspot.com/2009/04/common-mistakes-made-by-therapists.html; and http://biblicalcounselingcoalition.org/2014/02/21/top-10-counseling-mistakes/).

1. Avoid jargon. Instead of using jargon, focus on the here-and-now of what is happening in this couple's relationship. For example, it is not helpful to couples if they know they are in a certain stage of relationship building or stage in the human life cycle. Relationships take a lot of work and plenty of negotiation. Stay focused on what is important.
2. Do not overintellectualize relationships. Although plenty has been written about love, it is the emotions associated with it that disturb individuals in their relationships. Effective counselors help clients feel the emotions associated with being in relationship with their partner and what they mean when the couple is in conflict.
3. Give up advocating one perspective. Counselors help couples tease out what is working and what is not working for them. Each couple is unique so counseling them based on your experience of relationships or your parents is not that helpful. Instead, focus on helping the couple wrestle with finding solutions to their divergent perspectives.
4. Keep it simple. Successful relationships work because both individuals continue respecting their partners, and they do the little things that maintain the quality of their connection. If couples keep doing simple things for each other daily, it means a lot more than receiving presents at Christmas and birthdays.
5. Remain neutral in relationship disputes. It is a mistake to choose sides when couples are having a disagreement. It is one of the quickest ways to alienate the person's side that you are not taking. Consequently, it becomes likely that he or she will not want to return for another counseling session. This does not mean, however, that you encourage one or the other to be complacent. Instead, help both individuals learn to communicate assertively with each other. Maintain a stance of unconditional positive regard for both individuals.
6. Remember that not all relationships are worth salvaging. Relationships sometimes become overly dysfunctional, and past actions are no longer forgiven. Chronic and unrelenting resentment destroys a relationship's foundation, as does a continuing breach of trust. In some relationships, individuals are frankly too abusive and harmful toward their partners. Although it is not your role to decide that a relationship should end, by helping couples communicate better and by helping them break denial when an addiction issue is present, each party will need to decide whether the relationship is more helpful and healthy than not.
7. Hold back from stating personal opinions and values. It does not matter what you think is best for a couple. For example, you may disagree with one or more practices of a couple such as their involvement in *swinging* (i.e., they engage in group sex or swap sexual partners within

a group setting). There are no hard-and-fast rules for how couples are supposed to live. As counselors, our role is to help them navigate *their* lifestyles, not *ours*.

8. Be collaborative. The clients' goals are what matter. Regardless of what you might think about their decisions, clients have a right to pick goals that are meaningful to them.

9. Addiction first before relationship issues. Experts in the field mostly agree that the reverse is rarely effective. Addictions affect the way that addicts think, feel, and act. Until the addiction is addressed, it will be difficult if not impossible to counsel couples toward better functioning.

10. Breaching confidences or telling secrets. In couples and family counseling, there is an increased likelihood that you might unintentionally breach confidentiality. One or more family members might have told you something with the intent that you would keep the disclosure confidential from others in the family (or from the other in couples counseling). Depending on what was disclosed to you, this could be catastrophic. Once a secret is out of the box, it cannot be stuffed back into it.

APPENDIX 7D. GROUP FACILITATION ROLEPLAYS

#1. **FACILITATOR: A participant is subtly condescending in a sexist and/or racist way.**	
ACTOR 1: Make a statement about how many immigrants find it difficult to secure good employment in the United States.	ACTOR 2: After Actor 1 comments, say something to the effect that immigrants deserve to find it more difficult to get employment in the United States because good jobs ought to go to White citizens.
ACTOR 3: After Actor 2 comments, express your displeasure with the racist undertone and prejudice expressed.	

#2. **FACILITATOR: A participant demonstrates a distinct lack of respect for the therapist.**	
ACTOR 1: Make a comment that the facilitator rarely offers anything to the group. Instead, it is only the participants who say anything meaningful, so why not run the group by themselves so everyone can save the $40 per session it costs each member?	ACTOR 2: Agree with Actor 1's comments. Why not simply run the group elsewhere and not have a facilitator?

#3. **FACILITATOR: Open hostility between two group members arises.**	
ACTOR 1: Tell Actor 2 that you took great offense last session to being called a bitch (or an asshole). You expect an apology.	ACTOR 2: After Actor 1 confronts you, say that you are not prepared to offer an apology. You really do feel that she/he is a bitch (or an asshole).

#4. **FACILITATOR: You have a participant in the group who was mandated (i.e., Actor 1), who does not admit to their own problems, and points out everyone else's problems. This person also does not respond to group feedback. He or she is generally uncooperative, and the group starts to exclude this person. Ensure that Actor 1 is a male and that Actor 2 is a female.**	
ACTOR 1: You say to Actor 2, "I have known several women like you before. You think you are depressed, but what you really need is to get laid." After Actor 2 retorts, say, "Of course I know what it's like to be single. I'm telling you, if you get out there and screw your brains out, you will feel a lot better about yourself."	ACTOR 2: After Actor 1 comments, say, "I am insulted by what you just said. I could have sex anytime I wanted, but that doesn't mean it is what I need. I have been single for a few years now, and it is a relationship I am looking for, not sex. You don't know what it is like to be single for this long."

#4.
FACILITATOR: You have a participant in the group who was mandated (i.e., Actor 1), who does not admit to their own problems, and points out everyone else's problems. This person also does not respond to group feedback. He or she is generally uncooperative, and the group starts to exclude this person. Ensure that Actor 1 is a male and that Actor 2 is a female.

ACTOR 3: [Talk after Actor 1 replies to Actor 2 by saying she should "screw her brains out, you will feel a lot better about yourself."

Say the following to Actor 1, "You really are an ass, and it's no wonder no one in the group wants to hear your garbage anymore."

#5.
FACILITATOR: A person is abrasive in their feedback and often takes an attack approach. Despite previous feedback from the group leader/facilitator, this person continues to attack others in the group. This person starts a conflict with a group member and then makes the group member cry by the manner of the attack.

ACTOR 1: Tell the group (the class), "I really have been struggling lately. My two young children are completely out of control. They won't listen to anything I say. Instead, they run around like crazy, throw their toys wherever they want, and destroy many of my belongings.

After Actor 2 retorts, say,

"You don't even have children. What makes you think you know what is best?

After Actor 2 again retorts, pretend you are beginning to sob.

ACTOR 2: After Actor 1 comments, say in a nasty tone of voice,

"You poor thing. Didn't you ever learn to discipline a child before? God, I'm tired of your constant complaining. Give the little brats a good smack on the ass. That will stop the nonsense you keep bitching about."

After Actor 1 retorts, say,

"It's time you admit you are just a lousy mother. That's my main point, you know."

#6.
FACILITATOR: A client has been through a number of therapy groups and is constantly "correcting" you or trying to take over the leadership of the group because of their experience.
You begin the group by saying, "Welcome back everyone. Let's begin by reviewing how you did with the commitments you made last week regarding what you would do differently for the next 7 days to build greater self-esteem."
[Don't say anything else until Actor 1 makes her/his second comment.]

ACTOR 1: After the facilitator speaks, say,

"You know, asking us every week about our homework really puts us on the spot. I have been in at least 10 groups before, and no one ever did this to us. Most didn't even ask us to do homework.

After Actor 2 comments, say back to Actor 2,

"Yeah, that's right. No group expects you to report back, except this one."

ACTOR 2: After the facilitator and Actor 1 says "Most didn't even ask us to do homework," say to Actor 1,

"Is that true? I don't mind telling the group if I did what I committed to doing."

#7.
FACILITATOR: A client in the group has issues with personal hygiene that other group members begin complaining about (smell). The smell is overpowering and many others, including yourself, find it distracting. You begin the group by welcoming the members, and then you wait for Actor 2 to speak first.

ACTOR 1: [You smell really bad during most of the group sessions because you are addicted to gaming and you rarely find time to take a shower or bath. You have attitude as well. When confronted with having a bad smell, you become defensive and tell the confronter that it is he or she who smells bad.]

ACTOR 2: [You are noticing a really bad smell in the group.] After the facilitator welcomes the group and Actor 1 speaks, you are the next person to speak. You say,

#7.
FACILITATOR: A client in the group has issues with personal hygiene that other group members begin complaining about (smell). The smell is overpowering and many others, including yourself, find it distracting. You begin the group by welcoming the members, and then you wait for Actor 2 to speak first.

After the facilitator welcomes the group, say, "I managed to beat my highest score yet! I am probably the best gamer of Fortnite in this city!"	"I am sure you are the best gamer. But does anyone else smell something really foul in this group?"
ACTOR 3: After the facilitator and Actor 2 speak, say, "Yeah, and I know who it is! It is the same person as in our last group" [now point your finger at Actor 1, the Fortnite gamer].	ACTOR 4: [Wait until Actor 3 has pointed the finger at the Fortnite gamer and he or she has had a chance to respond.] Now point your finger as well at the Fortnite gamer and say, "You really should go home and take a bath. I mean really! You smell worse than a dead body!"

#8.
FACILITATOR: A group member takes things too personally.
[Do not talk until after Actor 4.] Actor 3 is the one who takes things too personally. She/he has already shown a history of doing this over the past five sessions. Begin the group by welcoming everyone.

ACTOR 1: Say to Actor 2, "I am not surprised you feel so bad after your cat just died. If I lived alone and only had a cat as company, I would be really sad as well."	ACTOR 2: Comment after Actor 1, "Thank you. It really has been difficult. I can't seem to bring myself to buy another cat. I loved my cat Gertrude more than anything in my life."
ACTOR 3: [Don't speak until Actor 2 responds to Actor 1. You are the one who takes things too personally. You already have a history of doing this in the group.] Pretend you are crying, then say, "Well, I am just devastated to hear of your cat dying. I lost mine 10 years ago, and hearing you talk about this brings it all back like it was just yesterday."	ACTOR 4: [Don't speak until after Actor 3.] "Man, you are pathetic. Every session you cry about everyone else's problems. I can't imagine how you are going to respond when you end up talking about yourself, which thankfully you haven't done up to this point."

#9.
FACILITATOR: A group member has difficulty with here-and-now disclosures.
[Do not speak until Actor 2 has replied to Actor 1.]

ACTOR 1: Tell Actor 2, "It seems that you find it hard to talk about the feelings you are having toward me right now. I get a sense that you are deeply troubled by what I just said about you needing so much attention in the group."	ACTOR 2: [after Actor 1 speaks], "Listen, I would rather not share my feelings. I never do that with anyone, so it is nothing personal about you."

#10.
FACILITATOR: Your competency is challenged due to your age.
[Your group is made up of all elderly people. Ensure that Actor 1 is a male.]
[Do not speak until after Actor 2 speaks.]

ACTOR 1: You are a 75-year-old man. Say to the facilitator, "You know, I am 75 years old. I served in the Second World War. You look like you're just out of high school. Are you sure you are qualified to do this job?"	ACTOR 2: You are a 70-year-old senior. [speak after Actor 1], "I agree with that. I was raising my grandchildren when you were born. I don't mean any disrespect, but aren't you a little young to be helping us?"

#11.
FACILITATOR: Physical harm is threatened from one member to another or to the leader.
[This group is occurring in a prison setting.]
[Do not speak until after Actor 3.]

ACTOR 1:

Say, "You know, I think I've heard enough shit from all of you. I don't care why any of you are doing time in this joint. You do the crime, you do the time. It's that simple."

ACTOR 2:

Say after Actor 1,

"I hate you, you stupid ass. You had better watch your back when I see you later in the concourse."

ACTOR 3:

Say after Actor 2,

"Yeah, I second that. Don't be surprised if today is your last. [Say in a snotty tone] It's been nice knowing ya!"

#12.
FACILITATOR: As the group facilitator, you find out that one of the group members works closely with your spouse.
[Do not speak until after Actor 1 has replied back to Actor 2.]

ACTOR 1: Say to the facilitator,

"You know, I probably should have told you before. Your spouse and I work together, and we are actually the best of friends. I hear about you all the time. Some of it is a bit shocking, to tell you the truth."

After Actor 2 speaks, reply with,

"Nah, nothing like that. It's just the facilitator's spouse been showing sexual interest in me. I find that a little strange."

ACTOR 2: Say after Actor 1 comments,

"Really? What have you heard that is so shocking? I mean, I am paying money to be in this group. I don't want to be in a group led by a pervert or something."

#13.
FACILITATOR: A group member breaks confidentially. Ensure that Actor 2 is male.
[Do not speak until after Actor 2.]

ACTOR 1: Say to the group (the class),

"I have something to confess. I was talking to my best friend 2 nights ago and she asked me how the group was going. [Now look at Actor 2.] I'm sorry, but I told my friend Samantha Stevens what you disclosed to us last week about finding prepubescent boys really hot and how much you want to have sex with one of them. I also slipped up by telling her your name. She looked petrified."

ACTOR 2: Say after Actor 1 confesses,

"You have got to be kidding!!! I have known Samantha for 12 years and I often babysit her 8-year-old son!!"

#14.
FACILITATOR: A group member (i.e., Actor 2) misses a lot of sessions but always has an excuse. It is hard to tell if the excuses are real or not.
[Do not speak after Actor 4.]

ACTOR 1:

Say to Actor 2, "Well, isn't that so sweet the way you just prance in here whenever you want. The rest of us have been waiting for 10 minutes already, just like the past four sessions since this group began!"

ACTOR 2: [You are always late for group, and you always have an excuse. The truth is, you are always at a nearby casino and you do not want to tell anyone, including the facilitator, that you have a gambling problem.]

After Actor 1 speaks, say,

"I cannot help it. You know my mom is still in the hospital, and I need to be there for her. Surely you must understand."

#14.
FACILITATOR: A group member (i.e., Actor 2) misses a lot of sessions but always has an excuse. It is hard to tell if the excuses are real or not.
[Do not speak after Actor 4.]

ACTOR 3: [Actor 2 is always late for the group. You work at the hospital where Actor 2 says his mother is, reportedly on her death bed. You checked the hospital records and found that Actor 2 is lying.] After Actor 2 says, "Surely you must understand," say to Actor 2, "That is bullshit! I work at that hospital as a staff nurse, and your mother is not even admitted there!"	ACTOR 4: After Actor 3 says, "your mother is not even admitted there!", say to Actor 2, "I knew it. You have been lying to us since the beginning of this group. If I were the facilitator, I would kick you out of this group so that we do not have to deal with your constant lies. You are pathetic!"

#15.
FACILITATOR: The group is coping with the death/serious illness/accident of a member.
Begin the group by saying,
"I have some really bad news to report. Frank, whom all of you have known for the past five sessions, committed suicide last night."

ACTOR 1: After the facilitator speaks, say, "Oh my god!! I have never heard more distressing news in my life!! I have been so depressed myself lately, and this might just push me over the edge."	ACTOR 2: Say after Actor 1, "You and me both!"

#16.
FACILITATOR: The group is having a delayed reaction. Actor 2 told the group 4 weeks ago that he (or she) killed another child when he (or she) was a child. Since then, you have not been able to get the group to engage. Now Actor 1 is finally speaking up.
[Do not speak until after Actor 2.]

ACTOR 1: Refer to Actor 2 and say, "When you told us 4 weeks ago that you killed a 10-year-old boy when you were 11, I was stunned like everyone else. Frankly, I don't know what to do about it. I feel just sick inside and I can hardly sleep at night. I know this happened 20 years ago and you are deeply remorseful. However, it just makes me sick, sick, sick!!!!"	ACTOR 2: Say after Actor 1, "I understand how you feel. I'm not proud of it either, but it happened. I served 3 years in a juvenile detention center for this as you know, so I paid for it already. You are not going to make me pay for it again, are you?"
ACTOR 3: Say whatever you want to say after Actors 1 and 2 have spoken.	ACTOR 4: Say whatever you want to say after Actors 1, 2, and 3 have spoken.

#17.
FACILITATOR: Someone expresses that the group is a "waste of time" and tells you how you should run the group to make it more productive and useful.
[Do not speak until after Actor 2.]

ACTOR 1: Say to the group (the class), "You know, I have come here five times already and it has been a complete waste of time. I should be seeing patients in the hospital instead of sitting here talking about my feelings at length."	ACTOR 2: Say after Actor 1, "I feel the same way. I work on billable hours and being here is costing me money. [Now speak to the facilitator.] "Why don't you give us homework or something to do between sessions? Just talking about my sessions feels like a complete waste."
ACTOR 3: Say whatever you want to say after Actors 1 and 2 have spoken.	ACTOR 4: Say whatever you want to say after Actors 1, 2, and 3 have spoken.

#18.
FACILITATOR: Someone criticizes other group members' experiences, for example, "one-upping" them, comparing group members' experiences to their own experiences, saying that others "have no idea." Actor 2 has complained in all five sessions to date of having more serious problems after someone discloses their own pain.
[Do not speak until after Actor 3.]

ACTOR 1: Say to the group (the class), "Since I disclosed to you last week that my marriage is ending, I have felt really down. I even had some suicidal ideation."	ACTOR 2: After Actor 1 says, "I even had some suicidal ideation," say, "Well, that's nothing compared to what I have gone through since last week. I was in a car accident on Thursday, I lost my job on Friday, and I spent the weekend in hospital because I overdosed on 20 Percocets."
ACTOR 3: After Actor 2 says, ". . . because I overdosed on 20 Perocets," say to Actor 2, "You always come back with having a worse problem than everyone else in the group. What is wrong with you?"	

#19.
FACILITATOR: No one in the group opens up or engages when presented with questions. All group members display avoidance and minimization of their issues. The members fall into the pattern of superficiality and brushing past their issues.
Begin the group by saying,
"Who would like to begin today?" [Do not say anything more until after Actor 3 speaks.]

ACTOR 1: [No one speaks for the first minute.] Then begin by saying, "I guess I will begin. My spouse finally left me. Was about time." [Do not respond to Actor 2.]	ACTOR 2: [No one speaks for the first minute.] Say after comment by Actor 1, "Lucky you. Tell me know to get rid of mine and I will give you a hundred bucks."
ACTOR 3: [No one speaks for the first minute.] Say after comment by Actor 2, "Looks like you [referring to Actor 1] could make a couple hundred today. Count me in as well."	

#20.
FACILITATOR: Many or most members in the group start crying.
[Do not speak until you see everyone's reaction after Actor 1 discloses.]

ACTOR 1: You say to the group (the class) the following: "During the time they raped me, I was helpless to fight back. Six of these men were the size of football players. I barely made it out alive. Since then, I have been unable to enjoy sex or any semblance of a normal life. I cannot leave my house either except to come here once a week for this group. Without all of your support, I think I would give up."	ACTOR 2: [After Actor 1 discloses, pretend you are crying.]
ACTOR 3: [After Actor 1 discloses, pretend you are crying.]	ACTOR 4: [After Actor 1 discloses, pretend you are crying.]

#21.
FACILITATOR: You have negative feelings toward a particular group member and notice that you don't treat him or her as you do the other group members (i.e., less sensitive, more dismissing). Others notice it, too. Someone in the group now challenges you on it. Ensure that Actor 1 is a female.
Do not speak until after Actor 1 discloses, then say [in a cutting, sarcastic tone of voice], "Well, I guess you have every right to complain. I earn $500.00 a week for running groups like this one, and it only takes 35 hours of my life each week."
[After saying this, wait until after Actor 2 and Actor 3 retort before you speak again.]

ACTOR 1: You start by saying to the group (the class), "I have been really struggling. After three nights on the street, I was able to make $900.00. This is not enough to keep me happy or to feed and clothe my 10-month-old baby. I hesitate to work four or five nights because I simply get too sore."	ACTOR 2: [Do not speak until after Actor 1 and the facilitator first speak.] Then say to the facilitator, "You know, I need to bring something up that has bothered me for the past 4 weeks. I've noticed that you are especially hard on [Actor 1]. By this I mean you often address her/him in a sarcastic tone of voice. Are you aware that you are doing this?"
ACTOR 3: [Do not speak until after Actor 1, the facilitator, and Actor 2 speak.] Then say, "I would have to agree with [Actor 2]. Maybe you are unaware of it, but I have noticed it, too. It's like you really don't like [Actor 1]."	ACTOR 4:

8 Prevention, Evaluation, and Assessment

iStock.com/Olivier Le

Learning Objectives

1. Distinguish among universal, selective, and indicated prevention.
2. Compare and contrast risk factors versus protective factors.
3. Learn about prevention interventions through legislation; individual-, parental-, and community-focused interventions; and mass media.
4. Discern the differences among prevention evaluation, program evaluation, and treatment evaluation.
5. Discover ways to evaluate your own effectiveness and outcome for your clients.

PERSONAL REFLECTIONS

When I was still married to my wife, we would read our son and daughter children's books that taught values (see https://www.trueaimeducation.com/abcs-of-values-for-children/ for an example). We hoped that these books would act in a preventative way by teaching valuable lessons when they were most suggestible to learning. They both turned out to be amazing people (I am sure most parents would say this of their adult children). Nevertheless, how could we ever prove that it was reading these bedtime stories that made the difference? What other factors may have explained the positive results? I knew then that a prevention program would need to be evaluated systematically if we wanted to establish a correlational or causal relationship.

When I oversaw a large counseling and health services center at a local community college, I introduced an evaluation that students would complete yearly as they were leaving their counseling session. The questions would ask about their counseling experience and whether their needs were met. I used a 5-point Likert scale with anchors from 1 (*poor*) to 5 (*excellent*). The average rating was a 4, which meant very good. These results would be provided to the administration with the intent that we could use our success to both maintain our existence and increase the size of our department.

Numbers, however, were ineffective in helping administration see the importance of student counseling. I then introduced a qualitative evaluation component. Students would now write a sentence that described their experience of counseling. Some examples of these might be, "My counselor saved my life. I was thinking of suicide before I met with her," or "He really helped me overcome my exam anxiety. My marks have increased substantially thanks to him." Comments like these were received especially well by the administration, and, on more than one occasion, I heard an administrator use some of these comments in a public forum.

This chapter is about prevention, evaluation, and assessment. I hope you enjoy reading this chapter as much as I did writing it.

Prevention

The next 11 chapters review the most current information we have regarding common addictions. What if we could prevent addictions from developing in the first place? Given the enormity of the costs associated with addiction that are outlined in the subsequent chapters, prevention should arguably be the highest priority. As Metzler, Eddy, and Lichtenstein (2013) stated, "The potential benefit to individuals, families, and communities, preventing the development of disorders and the benefit to society of reducing the prevalence of these costly problems cannot be overstated" (p. 839). Once addiction occurs, between 80% and 90% of individuals entering addiction treatment relapse during the first year (Kwon, 2011). Addiction for many, perhaps most, individuals is a chronic relapsing condition.

Nearly 80% of juveniles were under the influence of psychoactive drugs when they committed crimes in the United States (Finn, 2012). The cost to America is in the billions of dollars annually when one considers lost productivity and absences from work and costs associated with social service organizations, the criminal justice system, law enforcement, and healthcare costs (Finn, 2012). The National Institute on Drug Abuse (2017) estimated the annual cost in the United States to be more than $740 billion!

The old cliché "an ounce of prevention is worth a pound of cure" makes intuitive sense, but does it hold up under scrutiny? This section provides an overview of the various forms of prevention.

An early but widely accepted model of prevention distinguished among three types: primary, secondary, and tertiary prevention (Smith & Luther, 2013). Primary prevention focused on those with little or no experience with a particular form of addiction, secondary prevention targeted both novices and experienced users who were showing potential signs of addiction, and tertiary prevention was aimed at those eliciting more advanced stages of abuse and/or addiction.

Gordon (1983) wrote about a different classification scheme that has subsequently become more popular. In Gordon's classification, there are again three types: universal, selective, and indicated prevention. *Universal prevention* targets the general population, *selective intervention* focuses explicitly on at-risk populations, and *indicated prevention* is aimed at those experiencing early signs of substance abuse and related problem behaviors. The Institute of Medicine (1994) recommended the use of Gordon's classification, and it has been adopted by the National Institute on Drug Abuse (2003a).

Combining methods into a comprehensive multimodal approach has demonstrated the greatest impacts on reducing drug and alcohol use. Some of these programs have found lasting results 15 years after program delivery (Finn, 2012; Smith & Luther, 2013).

The Center for Substance Abuse Prevention (CSAP) falls under the auspices of the Substance Abuse and Mental Health Services Administration (SAMHSA). That is the federal agency that coordinates prevention efforts made across the country (Fisher & Harrison, 2013). It lists six strategies that can be targeted at the universal, selective, or indicated population level.

1. Information dissemination. This strategy is focused on providing information regarding substance use, abuse, and addiction.
2. Education. The focus here is on building or changing life and social skills such as decision-making, refusal skills, and assertiveness.
3. Alternatives. This strategy attempts to develop activities that are incompatible with substance use, such as providing "midnight basketball" (Fisher & Harrison, 2013, p. 318). Promoting leisure for young people, in general, has a positive effect on preventing addictive behaviors (Lacsan, Arany, & Farkas, 2017).

4. Problem identification and referral. This focuses on targeting populations that are at risk.
5. Community-based processes. These strategies include mobilizing communities to provide prevention services.
6. Environmental approaches. This includes changing written and unwritten norms, codes, laws, and attitudes that affect the development of addictions.

Although these six strategies are not addressed explicitly in this chapter, they are provided here for the interested reader who may be designing a prevention program. Nonetheless, programs can be classified according to whether they target universal, selective, or indicated communities, or they could be classified according to the six CSAP strategy types.

WHAT MIGHT YOUR PREVENTION PROGRAM LOOK LIKE?—PART I

Consider the six strategies listed by the CSAP previously (i.e., information dissemination, education, alternatives, problem identification and referral, community-based approaches, and environmental approaches). Decide on a specific addiction for which you will design a prevention program (see the names found in Chapters 9–21 for a list). Now decide upon the age bracket that you will target with your program and other important delimiters (e.g., for middle-school boys, for high school students at my church). Write down the primary goal of your program (i.e., abstinence, reduction in use, harm reduction). Now beside each of the six strategies, write one idea that you could implement that might have an impact on your chosen addiction. We will add to this in the next exercise (i.e., Part II).

Cultural Considerations

Before looking at universal, selective, and indicated prevention, you must consider the impact of culture (Antone & Csiernik, 2017[1]). Culture dictates what is considered required, forbidden, acceptable, and unacceptable behaviors of its members, and this is also evident in substance use and other potentially addictive behaviors. Consequently, prevention efforts need to be culturally sensitive if they are to be accepted and effective within a culture. Embedded within cultural considerations are also potential prevention ideas regarding protective factors and risk factors.

Family and one's upbringing play a substantial role in creating and upholding values, beliefs, and attitudes toward substances and addictive behaviors. For example, it is established that, if abstinence is the prevailing attitude, children and adolescents are more likely to embrace sobriety themselves. Despite the rhetoric concerning adolescent crises and such, most adolescents do care about their parents' values, beliefs, and attitudes (Antone & Csiernik, 2017). Nonetheless, peer influence does increase during adolescence (Antone & Csiernik, 2017).

Risk Factors

Risk factors increase the likelihood that individuals will become either users or addicts. Preceding addiction, five categories have been discussed in the literature: (a) individual characteristics (e.g., mental illness, school failure, antisocial behavior, criminal activity, early age of onset regarding drug use), (b) attitude factors (e.g., distrust of authority figures, anger toward parents and other adults, and enjoying acting defiantly), (c) psychosocial factors (e.g., low self-esteem, having poor social skills, wanting to fit in with peers), (d) family characteristics (e.g., family history of drug use, familial antisocial behavior), and (e) environmental characteristics (e.g., poverty, community acceptance of drug use, easy access to drugs and alcohol) (Finn, 2012).

Risk factors are evident in Indigenous communities. Colonization by White settlers led to high rates of substance abuse among First Nation individuals. This is partly attributed to the Native American boarding schools (also referred to as Indian Residential Schools) that were designed to assimilate Native Americans into White American culture.

Another risk factor is having excessive drinking norms. Men in Serbia and Russia, for example, drink large amounts of alcohol as one way of exhibiting masculinity (Antone & Csiernik, 2017). In countries like Saudi Arabia, alcohol prohibition is enforced, so drinking norms are the complete opposite.

Protective Factors

Protective factors help insulate individuals from becoming either users or addicted individuals (e.g., being resilient, having strong family support). More research is needed to establish whether teaching resilience-related skills is effective in lowering drug use with youth (McNeece & Madsen, 2012). Research does indicate that more-resilient individuals are less likely to become Internet-addicted individuals (Robertson, Yan, & Rapoza, 2018).

Strongly identifying with one's culture or ethnicity can be a protective factor. This is true of Asian Americans, African Americans,

[1]This section will focus primarily on the writing of Antone and Csiernik (2017).

Mexican Americans, Puerto Ricans, and American Jewish individuals. The importance of family regarding prevention is strongly evident in Latino culture. The Latino concept of "familismo" is characterized by three qualities: (a) strong attachment and identification among nuclear and extended families, (b) interdependence and unity in the family, and (c) high levels of social support offered by family members (Antone & Csiernik, 2017). Other features of familismo include having a strong sense of family loyalty, solidarity, and reciprocity. When these aspects of familismo are combined, numerous studies have demonstrated the protective impact that parental monitoring, family commitment, and cohesion have in Latino families (Antone & Csiernik, 2017).

In Asian cultures, the concept of familial piety (i.e., obedience to parents, provision of both financial and emotional support, and avoiding disgraceful behavior that is believed to impact family honor and respect) acts as a protective factor against addictive behavior (Antone & Csiernik, 2017). African American communities are highly interdependent with high degrees of social control and norms of abstinence. Strong Christian values and beliefs are typically present in African American communities, and a substantial body of research has shown that religion and spirituality are protective factors (Antone & Csiernik, 2017). For example, students who report religion as important to them are more likely to abstain from alcohol and other drugs compared to those with no religious affiliation (Antone & Csiernik, 2017).

WHAT MIGHT YOUR PREVENTION PROGRAM LOOK LIKE?—PART II

Now return to your list of six strategies that you wrote for Part I. From the results of the previous meta-analysis noted by Metzler et al. (2013; e.g., interactive, cognitive-behavioral, or behavioral), now add to your strategies based on these findings. For example, assume that in Part I you chose "work addiction" and beside "information dissemination" you wrote, "Provide information about what distinguishes work addiction from working hard because of passionate interest." Now include how you could interactively deliver that information. Is there a way to add in a cognitive-behavioral component by introducing some of the cognitions (thoughts) that work-addicted individuals tell themselves? How does media affect people's attitudes toward work? Is there a way to include peer leaders in delivering your message? Use what you can from the meta-analysis for each of the six strategies. You have now built the rudiments of a prevention program!

Universal Prevention

Public Policy and Legislative Interventions

Government intervention can play a substantial role in assisting prevention efforts. As Warner (as cited in Brownell & Gold, 2012) stated, "The rise and fall of smoking during the twentieth century may well prove to be one of the most significant, and fascinating, stories in the history of public health" (p. 442). The rise and fall of smoking in the United States had a great deal to do with prevention efforts and legislation enacted by the government (Brownell & Gold, 2012).

The following is an itemized compilation regarding government efforts that promote prevention and/or harm reduction (see Polcin, 2014, for a list of strategies that counselors can use to influence policies at both national and local community levels).

1. Require manufacturers to reduce addictive drug potential. This could be achieved by requiring (a) cigarette makers to produce lighter brands that are low in nicotine and tar content, (b) manufacturers of distilled spirits, beers, and wines to reduce the percentage of alcohol in their products, and (c) cannabis producers in Canada to produce products with low THC and high CBD content (see Chapter 10) (McNeece & Madsen, 2012).
2. Introduce ignition interlock device legislation for individuals convicted of driving under the influence. These devices require the offender to provide breath samples for the vehicle to start (McNeece & Madsen, 2012). Research has shown that they do reduce alcohol-impaired driving recidivism (Voas, Tippetts, Bergen, Grosz, & Marques, 2016).
3. Legislate stricter enforcement of drug laws. Examples include laws banning minors from using alcohol and nicotine products (already done throughout the United States) and setting up random checkpoints where police officers stop drivers suspected of impaired driving.
4. Require offenders to receive counseling or to attend a program for repeat offenders. This is required for impaired drivers in some states. Juvenile drug courts (JDCs) are another strategy that targets youth who are using drugs. Parole officers closely supervise juveniles in the program. Furthermore, the minors are subjected to periodic drug testing. They are also provided psychological help. JDCs are considered more humane than incarceration, and they are cost-beneficial. Incarcerating youth in 2004 cost about \$43,000 per year, whereas the JDC program costs \$5,000 per year (Finn, 2012).

5. Require bartenders not to serve intoxicated persons. These are sometimes referred to as "dram shop laws" (McNeece & Madsen, 2012, p. 185).
6. Increase taxes on legal drugs, including alcohol and nicotine products. For example, research has shown that increased prices result in a reduction in the use of alcohol (McNeece & Madsen, 2012). Increasing the price of alcohol also decreased gonorrhea rates by 24% in one study (Staras, Livingston, & Wagenaar, 2016)!
7. Increase the legal age for consuming legal drugs, including alcohol and nicotine products. Although the legal drinking age in the United States is 21, it is only 16 in Germany, Portugal, and Poland, and another 17 countries have no minimum age (McNeece & Madsen, 2012). Lower drinking ages are associated with increased automobile accidents among young people (McNeece & Madsen, 2012). It is illegal for individuals under 18 years of age to use tobacco products (Fisher & Harrison, 2013).
8. Lower the maximum acceptable blood alcohol content (BAC) levels for drivers. The current maximum BAC permissible for drivers in the United States is 0.08 (McNeece & Madsen, 2012).
9. Ban legal drug products that increase abuse potential. This could include banning cigarettes that have fruity or other pleasant flavors (McNeece & Madsen, 2012). In Canada, this could include banning cannabis products such as gummy bears and brownies containing THC.
10. Require health warnings to be placed on alcohol and tobacco products. Such warnings have already been mandated (McNeece & Madsen, 2012).
11. Legislate against the tobacco and alcohol lobby. McNeece and Madsen (2012) reported that the top three distributors for alcohol (i.e., National Beer Wholesalers Association, Anheuser-Busch, and the Wine and Spirits Wholesalers of America) contributed more than $14.5 million in donations and the top three tobacco companies (i.e., Philip Morris [a subsidiary of ALTRIA], Reynolds American, and U.S. Smokeless Tobacco) donated over $17 million to state and federal groups during the 2007–2008 election cycle. During the same election, tobacco companies contributed over $2 million directly to federal candidates. Donations accepted by both candidates and government from these companies can negatively impact legislative decisions targeted at reducing alcohol and tobacco use (Fisher & Harrison, 2013; McNeece & Madsen, 2012).
12. Restrict advertising of legal drugs. In 2016, tobacco companies in the United States alone spent $9.5 billion on advertising and promotion (Centers for Disease Control and Prevention, 2018), and, in 2011, alcohol companies reported $3.45 billion in marketing expenditures (Federal Trade Commission, 2014). There is currently inadequate evidence, however, regarding the effect of alcohol advertising on consumption among heavy drinkers (Stautz, Frings, Albery, Moss, & Marteau, 2017).
13. Promote anti-drug use media campaigns. This can include advertisements that educate viewers regarding the harmful effects of nicotine products, excessive alcohol use, cannabis, and other drugs. This also includes designated-driver publicity campaigns (Fisher & Harrison, 2013).
14. Ban tobacco use in workplace settings and other public environments. For example, in 2015, only 16 states still allowed smoking in bars and restaurants (Huston, 2015).
15. Establish stricter guidelines for prescribing opioid medications. Many opioid-addicted individuals were first introduced to opioids through prescriptions for pain management (Cicero, Ellis, & Kasper, 2017; Rastegar & Fingerhood, 2016).
16. Legislate national screening days. Young (2017) recommended that the United States adopt national screening days regarding Internet addiction following the lead of Korea. National screening days could be introduced for other addictions as well.

In some instances, government intervention is ineffective in curbing drug use. Federal attempts to decrease the illegal drug supply, for example, have mostly increased the prices of street drugs and the profits for drug dealers (McNeece & Madsen, 2012). Instead of reducing drug use for those who are addicted, these legislative attempts have increased the crime rate because of the increased cost, and little change in drug use patterns has occurred (McNeece & Madsen, 2012). Conversely, it is true that criminals are likelier to be heavier drug and alcohol users than the general public (McNeece & Madsen, 2012).

Reducing the hours of operation of establishments that sell alcohol has not proven effective in reducing its consumption. In fact, Sunday closing laws increased sales (McNeece & Madsen, 2012).

Community-Based Interventions

Community-based interventions focus on changing "community systems" that pertain to substance abuse (Treno & Lee, 2013, p. 871). Changing community systems can involve attempts to change formal institutions (e.g., reduce hours in efforts to reduce consumption) and informal systems (e.g., breaking up drug markets) (Treno & Lee, 2013). Many evidence-based prevention programs for alcohol and drug use have proven effectiveness (Metzler et al., 2013). Two of the projects described by Treno and Lee (2013) to reduce and prevent alcohol problems are

1. **The Saving Lives Project.** This Massachusetts program was designed primarily to decrease the number of alcohol-impaired drivers. The program included a range of activities such as media campaigns, information programs delivered to businesses, awareness days for speeding and drinking, telephone hotlines, police training, peer-led education in high schools, the inclusion of Students Against Drunk Driving chapters, and prevention programs in colleges.

   The program produced favorable results, including a reduction in fatal crashes (25%–42%) and a 47% reduction in the number of fatally injured drivers who had consumed alcohol. There was also an 8% reduction in the number of accidents among 15- to 25-year-olds.

2. **Communities Mobilizing for Change on Alcohol (CMCA) Project.** This project was conducted in Minnesota and western Wisconsin. It intended to make alcohol less available to youth under the age of 21 years. The program focused on several components, including creating community policies, engaging in community practices, making alcohol less accessible to youth, reducing youth alcohol consumption, and reducing the number of youth alcohol problems. Youth who were 18- to 20-year-olds were contacted by telephone and participants reported fewer attempts to purchase alcohol, reduced use of alcohol, and reduced likelihood of providing alcohol to other adolescents. The study also reported more infrequent drinking and driving arrests among 18- to 20-year-olds and a reduction in disorderly conduct violations among 15- to 17-year-olds.

Other effective projects focused on reducing and preventing alcohol problems include the Community Trials Project (Holder et al., 2000), the Sacramento Neighborhood Alcohol Prevention Project (Treno, Gruenewald, Lee, & Remer, 2007), the Operation Safe Crossing Project (Voas, Tippetts, Johnson, Lange, & Baker, 2002), and the Safer California Universities Project (Saltz, Paschall, McGaffigan, & Nygaard, 2010).

The National Institute on Drug Abuse (2003d) also lists 10 universal programs on its website (for details, visit https://www.drugabuse.gov/publications/preventing-drug-abuse-among-children-adolescents/chapter-4-examples-research-based-drug-abuse-prevention-progr-0): (a) Caring School Community Program, (b) Classroom-Centered (CC) and Family-School Partnership (FSP) Intervention, (c) Guiding Good Choices (GGC), (d) Life Skills Training (LST) Program, (e) Lions-Quest Skills for Adolescents (SFA), (f) Project ALERT, (g) Project STAR, (h) Promoting Alternative Thinking Strategies (PATHS), (i) Skills, Opportunity, and Recognition (SOAR), and (j) the Strengthening Families Program: Four Parents and Youth 10-14 (FSP 10-14).

Metzler et al. (2013) provided examples of top evidence-based programs focused on children. The authors used several criteria for screening, including (a) the program is preventive and not treatment-focused, (b) focus on developing competencies in children/youth or their parents, (c) evidence provided they reduce levels of future substance use during adolescence or later, and (d) meets at least two of four "best practices" lists; this list includes being rated as a model or promising program, rated as proven or promising for outcomes and substance use or externalizing behaviors, included in the report of the National Research Council and Institute of Medicine, or had a positive cost-to-benefit ratio in reports by Aos and colleagues (as cited in Metzler et al., 2013). Each program selected included home visits during pregnancy and infancy, parenting skills offered during their child's childhood and adolescence, and/or school-based programs. Their list consists of 19 programs that met their criteria, as noted in Table 8.1.

TABLE 8.1 Child/Youth-Based Prevention Programs That Are Evidence-Based Described in Metzler et al. (2013)

1. Triple P-Positive Parenting Program.
2. Nurse-Family Partnership (NFP).
3. Raising Healthy Children (RHC).
4. Linking the Interests of Families and Teachers (LIFT).
5. Incredible Years Series.
6. Fast Track.
7. Good Behavior Game.
8. Promoting Alternate Thinking Strategies (PATHS).
9. Carolina Icebedarian Project.
10. Strengthening Families Program for Parents and Youth 10–14.
11. Families That Care: Guiding Good Choices.
12. Ecological Approach to Family Intervention and Treatment (EcoFIT).
13. Strong African American Families.
14. Life Skills Training.
15. Big Brothers Big Sisters of America.
16. Brief Alcohol Screening and Intervention for College Students (BASICS).
17. Alcohol-Related Cognitive-Behavioral Skills Training.
18. Alcohol-Related Social Norms Re-Education.
19. Alcohol-Related Expectancy Challenge.

Programs targeted at athletes and mandated students have not demonstrated positive results. However, programs aimed at first-year students, fraternity/sorority members, and those who report heavy drinking on screening tests have shown promise (Metzler et al., 2013).

Metzler et al. (2013) noted that the biggest problem with the evidence-based studies that they described is the lack of replication of findings. Most of the studies have been small-scale and suggest *promising* results instead of *definitive* conclusions. Many of the studies have also been conducted by the same investigator, a factor that may bias the results. Evidence-based programs have neither been widely implemented nor maintained in community and school settings. Furthermore, there is little evidence that the interventions are effective for diverse populations. The programs have limited reach, especially those that involve parents, and this continues to create a barrier for widespread participation in prevention programs.

Fisher and Harrison (2013) surmised that the effectiveness of prevention efforts would increase if contradictory messages were decreased. It is difficult "to counteract creative and funny beer commercials, cigarette smoking and youth-oriented movies, and mom and dad smoking a joint with their friends in the living room" (Fisher & Harrison, 2013, p. 321).

Unsurprisingly, not all programs are effective. For example, Drug Abuse Awareness and Resistance Education (DARE) is a well-known program offered in schools. Researchers found, however, that the program had only a minimal effect on preventing drug use in adolescence and that the initial positive effects decayed over time (Finn, 2012). DARE is only used here as an exemplar. Werch and Owen (2002), for example, reported on 17 programs that increased substance abuse.

Selective Prevention

Selective interventions target subgroups of the populations that are determined to be at substantially higher risk for developing an addictive disorder (Metzler et al., 2013). Interventions aimed at a population might include a focus on a specific age bracket (e.g., at-risk adolescents), a particular region (e.g., a Northern community, a poverty-stricken district), a specific ethnicity or race (e.g., Indigenous populations, Russian immigrants), or any other group that is known to face increased problems with one or more addictions (e.g., college students). Examples include developing special groups for children who have parents or siblings that are addicts, targeting students having academic difficulties, children displaying behavioral problems, or developing programs for people who live in high-crime neighborhoods.

> Meta-analyses have shown that, as a general rule, these child/youth-focused programs are most efficacious when they (a) are interactive, (b) cognitive-behavioral or behavioral in focus, (c) teach drug refusal skills, (d) teach life skills in general, (d) focus on media influences on use of drugs, (d) emphasize norms for and social commitment not to use drugs, (e) use peer leaders, and (f) are skill focused (rather than merely instructional) and use modelling, rehearsal, feedback on performance, and reinforcement to build skills. (Metzler et al., 2013, p. 843)

When is the best time to intervene with children? The earlier, the better. Selective prevention can target preschool children or during the transition to elementary school, middle school, high school, or college (Metzler et al., 2013).

The National Institute on Drug Abuse (2003c) lists four selective programs on its website:

1. **Adolescents Training and Learning to Avoid Steroids (ATLAS).** This program is targeted for male high school athletes. It is designed to help reduce risk factors for using anabolic steroids and other drugs.
2. **Coping Power.** This is a multicomponent child and parent preventive intervention aimed at pre-adolescent children who are at high risk for acting aggressively and developing later drug abuse and delinquency.
3. **Focus on Families (FOF).** This is a program for parents receiving methadone treatment and their children. The program intends to reduce parents' use of illegal drugs while teaching family management skills to reduce the likelihood that their children will later use drugs.
4. **The Strengthening Families Program (SFP).** This program is used both as a universal and as a selective multicomponent family-focused prevention program. It provides support for families with 6- to 11-year-olds. The program aims to improve parenting skills and consequently reduce the children's risk for subsequent problems.

Indicated Prevention

Indicated interventions target individuals who have already displayed early signs of substance abuse and related problem behaviors. Interventions may include abstinence as the goal, harm reduction, or reduction in use. An examples of an indicated prevention program is a substance abuse program aimed at high school students who are already displaying problematic behaviors such as failing grades, suicidal thoughts, truancy, or early signs of abusing alcohol or other drugs (Texas Health and Human Services, 2016).

Metzler et al. (2013) claimed that most developmental models of prevention are based on Bronfenbrenner's ecological framework, an approach that looks at the various environments that affect individuals. Regarding environmental impacts, children are in families, families are in neighborhoods, neighborhoods are in communities, and communities are in cultures. Preventive interventions can be designed at any level. Although we might assume that most parents attempt to do their best in rearing their children, various hardships can get in the way, such as mental instability, substance abuse, financial problems, and other stresses. Most children coming from a dysfunctional family will exhibit behavior problems or emotional issues, which may express themselves as passively withdrawing, irritability, aggressiveness, abusiveness, being demanding, and noncompliance (Metzler et al., 2013). As these children enter adolescence, they are more likely to become involved in early alcohol and substance use, high-risk sexual behavior, and delinquent behavior. Although there are other pathways to developing substance and behavioral difficulties, what is clear is that children who are experimenting with alcohol and other drugs and externalizing troublesome behaviors become more likely to have problems that are serious by mid- to late adolescence (Metzler et al., 2013).

In other words, these children become increasingly vulnerable to developing addictions. The sooner these behaviors are recognized, the earlier intervention can occur. From an ecological perspective, interventions can focus both on the individual and on the various environments in which the individual is situated (e.g., family, peers, school). Metzler et al. (2013) wrote that parents and other adults need to reinforce desirable behaviors while at the same time remaining warm and nurturant. At the same time, they need structure and rules that are consistent and fair in homes that are predictable, secure, and stable.

A recent meta-analysis has shown that even brief alcohol interventions are effective in reducing self-reported alcohol use among adolescents and young adults (Tanner-Smith & Risser, 2016). Furthermore, effectiveness does not differ across geographical regions (Elzerbi, Donoghue, & Drummond, 2015).

The National Institute on Drug Abuse (2003b) lists two indicated programs on its website:

1. **Project Towards No Drug Abuse (Project TND).** This program targets high school age youth attending alternative or traditional high schools. The program intends to prevent the transition from drug use to drug abuse through considering developmental issues that older teens face.

2. **Reconnecting Youth Program (RY).** This is a school-based prevention program for high school students who are doing poorly in school and have the potential for dropping out. The program focuses on increasing school performance, reduction of drug use, and learning skills to better manage moods and emotions.

Finn (2012) acknowledged that some adolescents and youth are thrill-seekers, and abstaining may be viewed more as a challenge to do the opposite. Instead, harm-reduction strategies may be more beneficial. Csiernik, Rowe, and Watkin (2017) emphasized the importance of harm reduction even further. They wrote that, for most drug users, "harm reduction, not abstinence, is the only chance to survive" (Csiernik et al., 2017, p. 28). This may be overstated. Although it applies to many adults who have become dependent on a substance, it does not include most who use illegal drugs recreationally. *Harm reduction* is defined as the strategies or behaviors that individuals use to reduce the potential harm of continuing their substance use or abuse.

Psychoactive drug use, by definition, constitutes a high-risk behavior. Harm reduction intends to minimize or eradicate risk from using a psychoactive drug. Even when abstinence is the ultimate goal, it is overwhelming for many addicted individuals to consider before smaller steps have been achieved successfully. Although counselors may be convinced that abstinence is the correct goal for a particular client, remember that goals need to be negotiated collaboratively with clients. To not do so is to take away the free choice of the person sitting before you.

What are some harm-reduction strategies? Harm reduction may involve (a) using safer methods of administration (e.g., orally ingesting a drug instead of smoking or injecting it, using needle exchange or safe injection sites for heroin use), (b) reducing use of the problematic drug (e.g., reduce the number of joints smoked in a day), (c) using less potent varieties of the drug (e.g., switch to a cannabis product with a lesser percentage of THC, using a vape device from a licensed distributor instead of smoking cigarettes), (d) allowing longer periods between uses of the drug (e.g., smoke marijuana only on the weekend), (e) alternating drugs used to reduce addictive potential (e.g., snort cocaine one day and use cannabis for the next two days), (f) switching to a similar drug with lesser addictive potential (e.g., methadone instead of heroin), (g) acting responsibly while high on a drug (e.g., do not drive after drinking or getting high from other drugs), (h) using devices to prevent driving while impaired (e.g., installing ignition interlock devices on cars owned by convicted impaired drivers), and (i) providing the illegal drug "legally" to those who are addicted (e.g., providing medicinal heroin to heroin addicts) (Csiernik et al., 2017).

As you rightfully suspect, some of these harm-avoidance methods are considered highly controversial (Csiernik et al., 2017). Some believe that it is another way to enable and support drug use as opposed to reducing or eradicating it. Nonetheless, the literature supports these methods as ways of either minimizing use or minimizing the harm that results from use (Csiernik et al., 2017).

Vancouver, Canada, began operating North America's first legal, safe injection site in the downtown eastside in 2003. This district is considered the most impoverished area in Canada, primarily because of its large population of addicts. The program is called Insight, and there were concerns that it would lead to an increase in the number of injection drug users and decrease the likelihood that they would seek treatment. Research has shown, however, that having a safe injection site leads to an increase in addiction treatment and detoxification services. Vancouver also witnessed a reduction of public drug use and publicly discarded syringes and needles (Wood, Tyndall, Montaner, & Kerr, 2006).

The following are some potential benefits that result from harm-avoidance strategies:

1. Improved physical and psychological health (e.g., fewer harmful effects from safer administration of the drug, less stigma when the healthcare system and clinicians support harm-reduction strategies).

2. Fewer deaths resulting from suicide and overdoses (e.g., methadone is regulated and therefore safer for opioid addicts, providing quality heroin to heroin-addicted individuals at appropriate doses is safer than street heroin or fentanyl at unknown doses).

3. Reduced crime rates (e.g., active heroin-addicted individuals experience extreme cravings, and many will steal to get a fix).

4. Enhanced safety for citizens (e.g., fewer impaired drivers on the road, fewer break-ins to cars and homes).

Mass Media Campaigns

A harm-reduction campaign funded by the liquor industry itself called "Friends don't let friends drive drunk" was intended to improve their public image and reduce drunk-driving casualties (Finn, 2012). The slogan has been ingrained in the minds of many Americans since 1983. Its effectiveness is difficult to measure. Although 2015 ended a 50-year decline for lives lost in traffic accidents, in 2014 and 2015, there was a 7.2% increase in fatal crashes. Of the 35,000 reported deaths from traffic accidents, about one third were due to drunk driving (Knight, 2016).

A popular large-scale U.S. media campaign referred to as "This is your brain on drugs" that showed an egg frying in a very hot pan was launched in 1987. Finn (2012) wrote that the message became material for comedy routines but that it did little to influence substance experimentation, use, and abuse. If anything, for youth who are thrill-seekers and impulsive, the campaign created more attraction than deterrence from wanting to experiment with drugs.

The more recent attempts to affect youth through media have focused on refusal skills and on empowering parents to become more engaged in the lives of their children (Finn, 2012). These messages may also be ineffective. When adolescents were asked whether they had seen the commercials, those who said they had reported little impact on their behavior. Conversely, there is evidence showing that the commercials were effective with parents (Finn, 2012)!

The expectations that children have about the effects of alcohol consumption predict the amount of alcohol they will consume later (Weinstein, Lisman, & Johnson, 2015). Weinstein et al. (2015) studied 183 Hispanic third-, fourth-, and fifth-grade students (50% girls) and found that alcohol expectancies could be modified. The researchers reported that their interventions were extremely brief and low-cost.

A web-based self-help intervention was found effective in reducing alcohol consumption. In the sample, 319 participants were low-risk users (LRUs), 298 were harmful/hazardous users (HHUs), and 312 scored in the suggestive range of being dependent (SDUs) on the AUDIT test. Although the program did suffer from low adherence (29% completed follow-up), it did reduce drinking in the HHU and SDU groups at 1-month follow-up. The authors emphasized the program's good cost-effectiveness (Monezi Andrade et al., 2016).

Newton, Deady, and Teesson (2014) recommended that prevention and early intervention should begin in the adolescent years. They noted that there are several evidence-based preventions and early intervention programs that have shown effectiveness in reducing substance use. Newton et al. went further in recommending that computers and the Internet be used to deliver evidence-based programs, suggesting as well that they have a better chance of reaching young people who are often reluctant to seek help for substance abuse. Ridout (2016) recommended the use of Facebook given that nearly all American college students use it.

Behavioral Addictions

Up to this point, the preventative efforts mentioned have focused on alcohol and other psychoactive drugs. But what about the behavioral addictions? What efforts are being made to help prevent them from developing? With work addiction, for example, there is research suggesting that an "overwork climate" fuels workaholism, but, besides that, there are few studies related to its prevention (Giannini & Loscalzo, 2016).

Werdell (2012) stated that food addiction prevention at the national level in the United States is almost nonexistent, whereas efforts are under way in Iceland. Research has shown that believing that products and/or behaviors are addictive leads to support for policies that focus on curbing consumption (Moran et al., 2016). Also, when the amount of junk food or unhealthy food available to children in schools is reduced, children do not react by eating more of these same foods outside school (Brownell & Gold, 2012).

Internet addiction prevention has become an important focus in South Korea (Cho, 2017). Cho (2017) reported that Taiwan had banned children under the age of two from using smartphones, tablets, and televisions. Parents allowing their children to use these devices face fines of up to $1500 U.S.! South Korean officials have become concerned due to several recent incidents: (a) a student in middle school killed his younger brother, mimicking an online game he had been playing, (b) a Korean man died while playing Internet games for 90 hours, (c) a Korean man jumped to his death after being expelled from an online game community, (d) another Korean man who was in his 20s was an online gamer who had his neck twisted to one side at a 70° angle, (e) a baby was choked to death while his parents played a game at an Internet café, and (f) still another Korean man died suddenly after playing a game for 10 consecutive days (Cho, 2017). There is now legislation in South Korea to have preventive Internet programs in all kindergartens, elementary through high schools, universities, and other public institutions (Cho, 2017). A program delivered in Bangkok, Thailand, has shown effectiveness in preventing gaming addiction among grade 4 and grade 5 students both immediately after the 8-week program and 3 months later (Apisitwasana, Perngparn, & Cottler, 2018).

Around the world, many jurisdictions have introduced Responsible Gambling (RG) programs with the intent of preventing gambling problems including addiction (Ladouceur, Shaffer, Blaszczynski, & Shaffer, 2017). Their synthesis of the empirical evidence revealed 29 articles that met at least one of their criteria. These studies revealed five primary responsible gambling strategies:

1. Self-exclusion. This is the practice whereby gamblers voluntarily banned themselves from gambling venues. These programs demonstrate some effectiveness. However, they have low utilization rates, and there is little evidence reporting long-term outcomes.

2. Using gambling behavior to develop algorithms. The idea behind algorithms is to identify potential problematic gamblers more effectively. Unfortunately, several of the currently offered algorithms are not based on empirical evidence or gambling behaviors themselves.

3. Limit setting. Limit setting involves gamblers presetting monetary and time limits before they begin gambling. Limit setting is effective for some individuals, although for others it can increase gambling problems.

4. Responsible gambling features in machines. In this approach, the gambling machine provides warning messages to gamblers with the intent of minimizing harm. These are "modestly effective" for reducing excessive gambling.

5. Employee training. In this approach, venue staff provides help to patrons experiencing problem gambling. These programs demonstrate partial effectiveness.

Ladouceur et al. (2017) cautioned, however, that the evaluation of most of these prevention programs has been a "haphazard process" (p. 232). Most have been implemented simply because they "seemed like good ideas" (p. 232) and not because they had demonstrated evidence-based evaluation.

Parental Strategies for Preventing Addiction

Baumrind and colleagues (Baumrind, 1991; Baumrind, Larzelere, & Owens, 2010) developed a theory of parenting styles based on interviews of primarily White, middle-class preschool children and their parents. Her theory identified four parenting styles: (a) authoritative (e.g., warm, sensitive, loving parents who make age-appropriate demands that are explained), (b) authoritarian (cold, rejecting parents who make coercive demands on their children), (c) permissive (warm, accepting, loving parents who are overindulgent and inattentive), and (d) uninvolved (e.g., emotionally detached from their children who provide little time or energy for childrearing). The authoritative parenting style was found to produce the best outcomes, resulting in children with high self-esteem, cooperativeness, self-control, and social maturity. In Asian cultures, however, Chen, Deater-Deckard, and Bell (2014) argued that an authoritarian parenting style does not result in the adverse outcomes associated with this parenting style in Canada.

Nonetheless, the authoritative parenting style produces positive results in children, and some research indicates that it is the least likely to result in addiction potential (Ahmadi et al., 2014; Stafstrom, 2014). A recent study has also shown that adolescent alcohol misuse is positively correlated with the parental provision of alcohol just as parents having favorable attitudes toward alcohol use and parental drinking are associated with teenage alcohol misuse (Yap, Cheong, Zaravinos-Tsakos, Lubman, & Jorm, 2017).

Parents play a crucial role in monitoring their children's activities (Wodarski, 2017). For example, they are in the best position to influence the computer experiences and habits of their children (Weigle & Reid, 2014). Family functioning is also important. Healthy family functioning is associated with less Internet addiction (Shi, Wang, & Zou, 2017).

Similarly, family therapy aimed at improving the affectionate relationship between adolescents and their parents reduces the likelihood of Internet addiction (Zhang, Brook, Leukefeld, & Brook, 2016). As another strategy for reducing Internet addiction, Kiraly, Nagygyorgy, Griffiths, and Demetrovics (2014) recommended that parents encourage their children to play together with real-life friends. This helps them develop real-life, real-time personal relationships.

Individual Strategies for Preventing Addiction

In addition to programs aimed at preventing addiction, there are some helpful ideas for individuals wanting to avoid addiction in their own lives. Although there is no guarantee, these ideas are worth considering:

1. Resolve past hurts and trauma with help from a counselor or psychologist. Early childhood trauma is associated with addictions. Presumably, the earlier one works through these hurts and traumas, the likelihood of addiction should diminish.
2. Seek counseling if impulsivity, poor self-control, or poor emotional regulation are issues. These are also associated with a higher likelihood of developing an addiction.
3. Surround yourself with supportive individuals. This may be especially true for those who are marginalized (e.g., LGBTQ individuals, non-White individuals).
4. Develop strong bonds with family, at school, at church, and with others who do not condone drug use. Similar to point 3, supportive individuals create a supportive community. If your parents are not supportive, finding a "parent surrogate" as a positive parental figure in your life is considered very helpful (Stevens, 2013, p. 252). Having positive connections to adults and elders is helpful for Alaskan native youth (Philip, Ford, Henry, Rasmus, & Allen, 2016).
5. Pick friends wisely. It will be harder to avoid using drugs if your friends use them regularly.
6. Delay use of legal drugs. Those who begin smoking or drinking early are more likely to develop addiction issues.
7. Monitor your use of legal drugs. Avoid drinking excessive quantities of alcohol, especially repeatedly, and if you smoke only allow yourself a few cigarettes a day.
8. Avoid the use of illegal drugs. Illegal drugs are illegal for a reason! Particularly avoid using nonprescribed opioids, nonprescribed stimulants (including nicotine products), and nonprescribed depressants. Each of these drug classes has high dependency potential.
9. Become informed regarding the consequences of drug use. Education is your weapon in avoiding or reducing drug use.
10. Participate in community anti-drug programs. In this way, you become part of the solution instead of the problem.
11. Learn effective refusal skills. The ability to refuse alcohol and other drugs is predictive of lower alcohol use among college students (Stevens, Littlefield, Blanchard, Talley, & Brown, 2016).
12. Avoid prescription opioid use wherever possible. This class of drugs is highly addictive and should be avoided wherever possible (Beauchamp, Winstanley, Ryan, & Lyons, 2014).

Some of these ideas were suggested at https://www.addiction.com/get-help/for-yourself/prevention/

PREVENTION PROGRAM SCENARIO

You have designed an indicated prevention program for teenagers, ages 13–17, of divorced families. Your goal is to reduce their likelihood of turning to alcohol and other drugs as they cope with the loss created by the divorce. You are aware that many adolescents feel shame and guilt when the marriage of their parents ends. Through negotiating with Child Welfare, you are now provided the names of children who meet your criteria and the parent who has primary legal and residential custody. You spent hours planning your program, and you believe it will make a difference. You find, however, that, when you phone the parents on your list, some of them hang up on you and others tell you that they are not interested.

1. What factors might explain why parents are so uninterested in your program?
2. What other strategies might you try to secure parental interest and consent?

Evaluation

Few people would argue against prevention efforts. Substance abuse is associated with many serious and costly consequences, including "criminal activity, traffic crashes, health problems, unintentional injuries, premature death, and lost earnings" (Popovici & French, 2013, p. 882). If we could prevent individuals from becoming dependent on substances, individual and societal impacts could be enormous.

Nonetheless, how can we ascertain if a prevention program is resulting in measurable outcomes? As Finn (2012) noted, outcome data is essential because it is not merely a question of whether a program works; instead, some programs have increased rather than decreased the target behaviors! In other words, some prevention efforts have resulted in increased use of illegal drugs. Some programs serve to normalize drug use, and others that have relied on scare tactics have increased the interest of thrill-seekers (Finn, 2012).

Deciding on the target behaviors and the goals of the program is also important. For example, if the target behavior is reducing the use of stimulants, is a program successful if it reduces stimulant use but results in more individuals smoking marijuana? Furthermore, if the goal is abstinence but the participants of a program continue using albeit in a less harmful way, is that program successful? Technically neither program is successful despite the unintended positive results.

Before we look further at program evaluation, however, we will begin first by looking at how counselors can evaluate their effectiveness and improve their work with clients. Second, methods for assessing client improvement will be considered.

Evaluating Your Effectiveness

Before considering your effectiveness as an addiction counselor, ensure that your client is receiving the appropriate level of care (Lopez-Goni, Fernandez-Montalvo, Arteaga, & Esarte, 2017). If a potential client needs to be hospitalized, for example, counseling efforts will not meet with much success. The American Society of Addiction Medicine (ASAM; 2018) criteria are required for use in over 30 states, and it has become the most widely used and comprehensive set of guidelines for placement. The ASAM criteria use six dimensions for service planning and treatment across services and levels of care. These dimensions include (a) acute intoxication and/or withdrawal potential, (b) biomedical conditions and complications, (c) emotional, behavioral, or cognitive conditions and complications, (d) readiness to change, (e) relapse, continued to use, or continued problem potential, and (f) recovery/living environment. There is a cost associated with the materials needed for the ASAM criteria. These can be purchased from https://www.asam.org/resources/the-asam-criteria.

It is also important that you have realistic expectations. Bricker (2015) noted that, in addiction treatment, only between 3% and 7% of the variance in client outcomes has to do with the counselor. Remember that most addictions are considered chronic, relapsing conditions, which means that if clients fail or relapse trying to achieve their goals, it may be more about the nature of their addiction than about your helping efforts. Nonetheless, it may be that you can improve and become a better addiction counselor.

Although you are receiving your training to become an addiction counselor, your skills are likely being evaluated at regular intervals. If you are using this book now as a resource, you have already finished your training. A problem with evaluating ourselves is that we may exaggerate the positives and thereby "look good" on a summation of our skills. On the other hand, getting feedback from our clients is not always accurate either (Jones & Markos, 1997).

A good idea is to periodically conduct a self-assessment of your attitudes and beliefs, knowledge, and skills. Lambie, Mullen, Swank, and Blount (2018) recently updated their Counseling Competencies Scale. This is a valid measure that is usually completed by an instructor/professor or work supervisor. Nonetheless, you could use this scale as a way to judge if you have work to do in any of the areas covered (a copy of the scale is available from http://webmedia.jcu.edu/counselingdepartment/files/2016/03/CCS-R-Evaluation.pdf). Another good scale is offered by the Council of Counseling Psychology Training Programs (n.d.; available from https://www.ccptp.org/assets/docs/copsy%20competencies%20final2.pdf) There are plenty of other scales to choose from if you desire. Tate, Bloom, Tassara, and Caperton (2014), for example, critiqued 41 instruments.

Another self-assessment worthy of mention is the Addiction Counseling Self-Efficacy Scale (ACSES; Murdock, Wendler & Nilsson, 2005). Factor analysis found that it measures self-efficacy in five areas: (a) specific addiction skills, (b) assessment, treatment planning, and referral skills, (c) comorbidity skills, (d) group counseling skills, and (e) basic counseling skills. The instrument has good reliability and validity (Murdock et al., 2005; Wendler, 2008).

It is also important to review your multicultural competencies. Gamst and Liang (2013) reviewed and critiqued 16 published multicultural competence instruments. When working with LGBTQ individuals, use inclusive language (Ross, Waehler, & Gray, 2013). Bidell and Whitman (2013) reviewed three scales that you can use to measure the extent to which you offer lesbian, gay, and bisexual affirmative counseling.

Another approach is to look at scales that measure the working alliance. The working alliance is foundational to successful addiction counseling (Shaw & Murray, 2014). Research suggests that, if the counselor and client have a positive alliance at the beginning of treatment, greater symptom change occurs (Marmarosh & Kivlighan, 2012). Although the Working Alliance Inventory is popular, it has psychometric problems (Doran, Safran, & Muran, 2016; Falkenstrom, Hatcher, Skjulsvik, Larsson, & Holmqvist, 2015). A six-item working alliance questionnaire (called the Session Alliance Inventory) is likely sufficient, and it can be administered repeatedly during counseling with a client (Falkenstrom et al., 2015; available from http://liu.diva-portal.org/smash/get/diva2:802104/FULLTEXT01.pdf). Two other brief measures described by Shaw and Murray (2014) are the Session Rating Scale (available from https://www.scribd.com/document/355449951/The-Session-Rating-Scale-pdf) and the Outcome Rating Scale (available from https://www.scottdmiller.com/wp-content/uploads/documents/OutcomeRatingScale-JBTv2n2.pdf), both of which can be used as well for measuring client outcomes (see next section called Evaluating Client Improvement).

For alliance ratings in group counseling, the Group Session Rating Scale (GSRS) can be used (Quirk, Miller, Duncan, & Owen, 2013; article about the GSRS available from http://www.scottdmiller.com/wp-content/uploads/2014/06/Group-SRS-Article.pdf). The Family Therapy Alliance Scale can be used for family counseling despite some problems with its construct validity (Johnson, Ketring, & Anderson, 2013).

Empathy is an important aspect of the working alliance, and, although it is often considered a nonspecific effect in addiction research, it varies substantially among counselors (Miller & Moyers, 2015). For example, research has found that the stronger the working alliance, the more motivated alcohol-dependent clients are to change their drinking pattern (Cook, Heather, & McCambridge, 2015).

Ensure that you are using empirically supported (i.e., evidence-based) treatments in your work with addicted individuals. The main types of treatment include cognitive-behavioral therapy, multidimensional family therapy, motivational enhancement therapy, relapse prevention therapy, and broad addiction-focused pharmacotherapy (Hartzler & Rabun, 2014).

Evaluating Client Improvement

Boswell, White, Sims, and Romans (2013) stated that, in one study, 29% of psychologists reported using an outcome assessment in their practice. One such measure is the Outcome Questionnaire-45.2 (OQ; Wells, Burlingame, Lambert, Hoag, & Hope, 1996). The OQ has good reliability (Wells et al., 1996), and a study found that the instrument's total score and the Symptom Distress subscale have strong validity support (Boswell et al., 2013). Weaker validity support was found for the Interpersonal Relations and Social Role subscales (Boswell et al., 2013). The OQ has also been used in a counseling center to provide support for those skeptical of whether counseling intervention makes a difference (Talley, & Clack, 2006). [A copy of the questionnaire itself is available from http://booksite.elsevier.com/9780123745170/Chapter%202/Chapter_2_Worksheet_2.4.pdf and scoring of it from http://www.projectechola.org/wp-content/uploads/2014/01/Outcome-Questionnaire-OQ-45.2-Quick-Guide-2.pdf]

Another measure of outcomes that do not rely on a standardized questionnaire but instead utilizes the client's perceptions of change is called "life space mapping" (Rodgers, 2006, p. 227). Rodgers (2006) presented preliminary results for his idea. It has the advantage of bringing the client into ownership for the change process (see article for details). Another flexible method is using client self-anchored scales to measure outcome, a solution-focused method developed by Franklin, Corcoran, Nowicki, and Streeter (1997; see article for details).

Deane, Kelly, Crowe, Lyons, and Cridland (2014) did telephone follow-up interviews with 700 clients (582 males, 118 females) 3 months after discharge from a residential drug and alcohol program. They boasted a 51% follow-up rate at the cost of $82 U.S. per completed interview. Of course, counselors themselves could do the interviews but preferably not with their own clients.

Another method of measuring outcomes is to use the scales for specific addictions that are listed in the section of Chapters 9 through 21 called Available Measures. Pick a measure that has demonstrated reliability and validity and use it at both the beginning and end of treatment.

For measuring outcomes when offering group counseling, Quirk, Miller, Duncan, and Owen (2012) created the four-item Group Session Rating Scale (request copy of this measure through Scott D. Miller's website http://www.scottdmiller.com/). The Eberly Center at Carnegie Mellon University offers several instruments for free that can be downloaded from its website, such as the Sample Group Work Self Evaluation and the Sample Self Evaluation Form together with various peer and group assessments (visit https://www.cmu.edu/teaching/designteach/teach/instructionalstrategies/groupprojects/tools/index.html).

For family counseling, one commonly used measure is the McMaster Family Assessment Device (Epstein, Baldwin, & Bishop, 1983). Each family member 12 years of age and older completes the 60-item scale. The instrument provides a measure of general functioning of the family and six subscales (i.e., problem-solving, communication, roles, affective responsiveness, affective involvement, and behavioral control) [The questions are available from http://chipts.ucla.edu/wp-content/uploads/downloads/2012/02/McMaster-FAD-Subscales.pdf and the scoring from http://dmhoma.pbworks.com/w/file/fetch/97996663/FAD%20Quick%20Guide%2007152015.pdf].

CLIENT IMPROVEMENT SCENARIO

You are a counselor in private practice, and your client's name is Frederick. Frederick has been addicted to using both alcohol and cocaine. Over the past 16 weeks of treatment, Frederick has successfully given up drinking and at other times given up cocaine. At no time has Frederick been able to remain abstinent from both drugs. Your measure of the working alliance suggests that Frederick believes that you are the right counselor for him.

1. To what extent would you believe you have been successful in counseling Frederick if he were to give up one drug indefinitely but remain on the other drug?
2. What strategies might you use to help Frederick abstain from both drugs?

Program Evaluation

Introduction

Program evaluation is defined as "a systematic study using research methods to collect and analyze data to assess how well a program is working and why" (United States Government Accountability Office [USGAO], 2012, p. 3). The USGAO (2012) document called *Designing Evaluations* is very useful if you are called upon to do an evaluation, and it can be downloaded at http://www.gao.gov/assets/590/588146.pdf. Evaluation is different from research. "Its primary purpose is to provide information to decision makers to help them make judgments about the effectiveness of a program and to improve it" (Thompson & Kegler, 2015, p. 338). Importantly, evaluation occurs within a political arena (Brandon & Sam, 2014). This means that stakeholders often have a vested interest in seeing a particular result. Several books have been written about program evaluation (see Amazon.com for a detailed listing), and anyone tasked with completing one would be well-advised to reference one or more of these texts.

Thompson and Kegler (2015) listed several reasons that we do evaluations (adapted and placed in question format):

1. Piloting program. Before we start using the program on a full-scale basis, does it work?
2. Suitable materials. Are the materials suitable for the people who will use them?
3. Quality control. Is the program being delivered the way it was designed?
4. Monitoring results. Is the program getting the desired results?
5. Early warning of problems. Are we getting any warning signs that could become serious if they are not addressed?
6. Unexpected benefits or problems. Is the program producing any unexpected benefits or problems?
7. Feedback for program managers. Can program managers improve the service?
8. Tracking progress. Is progress toward the program's goals being recorded?
9. Future programming. Will the evaluation data help us develop future programs?
10. Demonstrate program effectiveness. Is the program effective for the target population, and can these results be helpful to share with the public, to others who want to run similar programs, and to funders?

Several indirect benefits can result from evaluating a program as well (Thompson & Kegler, 2015):

1. Staff benefits. Staff hear from the people whom they are serving. They also hear the benefits of the program in participants' own words. Staff morale may improve when they are shown that their efforts make a difference or that improvements will be made to enhance effectiveness.
2. Participant benefits. Program participants know they have a voice in program delivery, which fosters a greater sense of inclusion and cooperation.
3. Advertising and marketing benefits. Media may promote the program if it demonstrates effectiveness.

The mission of the American Evaluation Association is the improvement of evaluation practices and methods, along with promoting evaluation as a profession, increasing its use, and supporting the generation of theory and knowledge regarding evaluation (Parsons et al., 2018). The *AEA's Ethical Guiding Principles* (Parsons et al., 2018) lists six principles, each of which has several subpoints. The five principles include (a) systematic inquiry, (b) competence, (c) integrity, (d) respect for people, and (e) common good and equity. An ethical evaluation should address all five principles.

As reported in the Prevention section of this chapter, several *prevention* programs targeted at addictions do make a substantial and measurable difference. Unfortunately, evaluations of bona fide *treatment interventions* in the addictions field have consistently reported either no or only small differences in outcome (Bergmark, 2015). Results will likely be poorer still if Schildhaus's (2015) suggestion is accepted. Schildhaus recommended that substance abuse treatment should be evaluated in a longitudinal, national study. In their editorial, DuPont, Compton, and McLellan (2015) urged that 5-year recovery should be the new standard for assessing the effectiveness of substance abuse treatment.

Evaluations conducted after a brief period following intervention may produce only transitory results. For example, a recent evaluation found that treatment benefit for heroin-addicted individuals was no longer evident after 12 months (Demaret et al., 2016).

Several types of evaluations can be conducted. Brandon and Sam (2014), for example, listed 25 different evaluation approaches and models. In a broad sense, there are summative and formative evaluations. Summative evaluations render a final judgment on certain aspects of a program's performance (e.g., were the goals or objectives met?). Formative evaluations, on the other hand, are designed to guide improvements to a program (e.g., how can we improve this program?). Concerning prevention evaluations, four types of evaluation are widely recognized: formative, process, outcome, and economic (Thompson & Kegler, 2015).

Formative evaluations are often conducted before a program is offered to ascertain whether it succeeds in accomplishing its goals. Process evaluations focus on the way a program is delivered contrasted with whether it achieves its goals. They often use both quantitative and qualitative methods to measure aspects of program delivery. Outcome evaluations are linked to the logic underlying the program, and these nearly always use an experimental or quasi-experimental design (e.g., does the program achieve its desired outcomes?). Finally, an economic evaluation looks at the costs and the benefits of a program (i.e., given the cost and the outcome, is the program worth continuing?) (Thompson & Kegler, 2015).

There are different methods for conducting an economic evaluation (e.g., cost analysis, threshold analysis, cost-effectiveness analysis, cost-utility analysis). These four methods are detailed in Thompson and Kegler (2015).

Gass, Foden, and Tucker (2017) described a fifth type of evaluation called a needs assessment. A needs assessment can answer questions related to the level of care that a client needs, the right program for a particular client, and how the desired outcome can be obtained. As Gass et al. expressed, a "needs assessment is intended to measure the gap between what is and what could be" (p. 429).

WHAT MIGHT YOUR EVALUATION PROGRAM LOOK LIKE?—PART I

Imagine you have gone on a diet that seems too good to be true. The diet requires that you restrict calories to 2500 per day, but, on weekends, you get to gorge yourself on both food and liquor—as much as you want (please note that this is a fictitious diet)! Besides weighing yourself regularly, what other outcomes are measurable? How long should you stay on the diet before you conclude that the diet is successful?

Teaching Program Evaluation

The next two sections review program evaluation for (a) prevention programs and (b) treatment programs. Before then, the work of Shannon and Cooper (2016) regarding teaching program evaluation will be highlighted. Shannon and Cooper began their chapter looking at Stevahn, King, Ghere, and Minnema's (2005) six competencies that students should learn regarding program evaluation (i.e., systematic inquiry, situational analysis, interpersonal competence, project management, professional practice, and reflective practice). Each is described as follows:

1. Systematic inquiry. This component refers to the technical aspects of program evaluation, including such skill sets as design, data analysis, analysis, and reporting. This requires that evaluators know how to pose questions, develop a plan to answer them, identify data sources, ascertain the validity and reliability of the data, gather the data, and then analyze it.
2. Situational analysis. This component refers to evaluators' needing to understand contextual components of the program and its readiness to be evaluated. This includes the needs of the program, strengths, and weaknesses, resources, and even political issues that can help or hinder the evaluation. It is important to include others in planning the evaluation, particularly the stakeholders (i.e., the people or group that is financing or most interested in the evaluation's results). This builds cooperation and "buy-in."
3. Interpersonal competence. Evaluators need to have good interpersonal skills both in speech and in writing with the key stakeholder(s). For example, they need to negotiate the boundaries and the budget for the evaluation.
4. Project management. The evaluator needs to both focus on the overall purpose of the evaluation and also supervise its project personnel and its budget. This involves developing written plans for what needs to occur and providing these plans to the appropriate people.
5. Professional practice. Evaluators need to work ethically and professionally, adhering to the American Evaluation Association's guidelines for evaluation noted earlier.
6. Reflective practice. Evaluators must think critically about themselves as practitioners and be open to learning more and improving their skills. For example, journaling, peer collaboration, and reflecting on completed evaluations are helpful.

Shannon and Cooper (2016) stressed that successful program evaluation requires a mix of interpersonal skills and knowledge of methodology. These skills can be developed through taking courses, working in the field, receiving mentorship, and engaging in reflective practice.

Prevention Evaluation

Unlike treatment programs, which may result in measurable short-term and long-term benefits, prevention programs might not result in changes for many years to come (Popovici & French, 2013). Additionally, given that some benefits may take a long time to emerge, evaluating a prevention program too soon may result in its termination prematurely (Popovici & French, 2013). Regardless, given the scarce public and private funds available for treatment and prevention, it is critical to know which cost-effective addiction interventions show evidence of reducing the long-term negative consequences associated with substance dependence and addictive behaviors (Popovici & French, 2013.

Thompson and Kegler (2015) wrote an excellent and highly recommended chapter regarding program evaluation for health promotion (i.e., prevention). Importantly, Thompson and Kegler stressed that evaluation should be included when a program is being designed, and then the evaluation should continue throughout the program. The program should be described, including such key elements as defining the target population and explaining the program's rationale, goals, and objectives; the components and activities that comprise the program; the logic underlying it; the resources required; and the stage of the program's development (i.e., planning, pilot, or implementation stage).

Treatment Evaluation

Nelson and Steele (2016) recommended a multifaceted approach to treatment evaluation. They surmised that research evidence is too narrowly defined and focused on treatment outcomes. Instead, they advanced four types of treatment evaluation as follows:

1. Outcome evaluation
   a. Efficacy. Does the treatment work when conditions are controlled (i.e., does it have internal validity)?
   b. Effectiveness. Does the treatment work in actual settings (i.e., does it have external validity)?
   c. System level. Does the treatment result in improvement in important systems?
   d. Mediators/moderators. In what ways and under what conditions does the treatment work?
2. Provider evaluation
   a. Perspective. Does the treatment appeal to providers?
   b. Retrospective. Does the treatment appeal to practitioners?
3. Consumer satisfaction
   a. Perspective. Does the treatment appeal to clients?
   b. Retrospective. Is the treatment satisfying to clients?
4. Economic evaluation
   a. Cost-effectiveness. Is the treatment as offered cost-effective?
   b. Cost offset. Does the treatment result in offsetting costs to other systems? (adapted from Nelson & Steele's, 2016, chart on p. 390)

Nelson and Steele further suggested an overarching question that they believe should guide treatment research: "Can a treatment be widely implemented with positive results?" (p. 391). The authors anticipated objections to their model. They believed that some would find it too ambitious and others would insist that outcome evaluation is sufficient.

Neale et al. (2014) used a Delphi method (i.e., a type of research that relies on the professional opinions of experts) with 10 addiction psychiatrists, nine senior residential staff, and six senior inpatient detoxification staff. The question asked was how addiction recovery should be measured. The authors' content analysis revealed that recovery ought to span 15 domains:

"substance use, tr[illegible]nt/support, psychological health, physical health, use o[illegible]tion/training/employment, income, housing, relat[illegible]nctioning, offending/anti-social behavior, w[illegible]reness, goals/aspirations, and spiritual[illegible]lson et al. recommended that [illegible] these 15 domains.

WHAT MIGHT Y[illegible] PROGRAM LO[illegible]

Regarding the 15 domains of Neale et al. (2014), [illegible]ed "drop-some ways that you could evaluate each domain? [illegible]eached, those conducted the evaluations yearly over the next 5 years, w[illegible]valuation study)?

Assessment

Overview

Chapters 9 through 21 each have a section called Diagnostic and Assessment Considerations. There you will find not only *DSM-5* criteria for those [illegible]ntly recognized in the DSM system but also severa[illegible]nts and screening instruments used for that particular addic[illegible]. Wherever these instruments are available online, links are provided. In several cases, clients can complete the instrument online and have it scored instantly, all at no cost. Given this feature of these stand-alone chapters, this section will look at assessment generally and provide several valuable links to instruments useful in addiction counseling practice.

Goodwin (2016) recommended that, from the first greeting, counselors adopt a deeply caring, compassionate, respectful, and accepting attitude toward clients. He also stressed to be careful when clients are using defense mechanisms, noting that these occur to protect people from overwhelming stress and anxiety. Helping clients reduce their defense mechanisms might become a goal of treatment but should not be addressed outright during the assessment. Goodwin also reminded counselors that substance use and substance use disorders (SUDs) are on a continuum, and using psychoactive drugs, whether legal or illicit, does not by itself predict or diagnose a SUD. The same applies to the other addictive behaviors described in this textbook. Furthermore, assessments are ongoing, and new information may override earlier hypotheses. Also, as clients receive treatment, new treatment goals may need to be developed over time (Goodwin, 2016). Lastly, Goodwin encouraged counselors to gather as much information as possible from referral sources, family and friends, interviews, assessment instruments, and lab results.

Del Boca, Darkes, and McRee (2016), Donovan (2013), Goodwin (2016), and Knott (2014) outlined the purpose and components regarding the assessment of addictive behaviors. These include the following:

- Creating a positive working alliance. This can be facilitated by using a motivational interviewing style.
- Ascertaining when working with minors if they can provide consent to treatment themselves and involving parents as desired or required.
- Treating any problem that requires urgent care.
- Gathering information from secondary sources where appropriate (e.g., parents, employer, friends, other counselors).
- Gathering information about clients. Take a thorough history and obtain detailed information about their substance use and/or addictive behaviors. This includes looking at the quantity and frequency of use and their pattern of use. If withdrawal symptoms are occurring, these need to be addressed.
- Ascertaining the *DSM-5* diagnosis and severity (if the particular addictive behavior is included in *DSM-5*).
- Deepening your understanding of clients' physical, emotional, cognitive, social, and contextual factors that trigger their addictive behavior. Also focus on problems and their severity within any or all areas.
- Identifying clients' assets and strengths.
- Determining clients' readiness to change.
- Determining clients' expectations of receiving help.
- Hooking the positive side of clients' ambivalence to change.
- Motivating clients to change their behavior.
- Providing feedback and a summary to clients.
- Integrating all information available into the most appropriate treatment and collaborating with clients regarding their choice.
- Monitoring clients' progress in making positive changes.
- Changing the treatment plan whenever needed.
- Ensuring that clients can afford sessions if you are in private practice.

Besides these components, also assess for suicide and homicide risk (a helpful section regarding suicide and homicide risk assessment was included in Chapter 6), overdose risk, any threats to dependent children, impact of substance use on children, polyaddictions, comorbidity, unsafe injecting practices, unsafe sexual practices, how the drug use is funded (Knott, 2014), and mental status (see Appendix D for an excellent example of a mental status examination). Also, assess for whether clients have a history of trauma, abuse, and violence; treatment history regarding mental health and addiction issues; cultural and diversity issues, strengths, and identities; language and speech problems; developmental issues; legal history and current status; spiritual views, issues, and available supports; coping skills; physical, sensory, or mobility challenges; relapse history; and diagnostic impressions (Goodwin, 2016).

Keep in mind that a substance-induced disorder can and does mimic nearly every other form of psychopathology (Margolis & Zweben, 2011). Cocaine withdrawal, for example, might produce an agitated depression, lengthy cocaine or other stimulant abuse can cause paranoia, individuals under the influence of hallucinogenic drugs might appear psychotic, chronic cannabis abusers might appear listless and lacking motivation for weeks or months following cessation of use, opioid-addicted individuals experience higher rates of depression compared with the general population, and those withdrawing from opioids might appear both depressed and anxious (Margolis & Zweben, 2011).

A counselor could conduct a theory-driven assessment, referring to Chapter 3. Best practice would dictate that you base your assessment on the biopsychosocial theory. An assessment intends to be inclusive of contributing and determining factors. Goodwin (2016) strongly encouraged practitioners to follow a holistic, biopsychosocial-spiritual model of addiction and argued that this "is necessary to formulate comprehensive and effective assessment and treatment plans" (p. 449).

Counselor assessment strategies include having clients complete tests, scales, inventories, and/or questionnaires (TSIQs). Some of these TSIQs need to be administered by a counselor or other mental health clinician. Mental health practitioners also rely heavily on interviews and history taking, which is sometimes accomplished in full or in part by using a history questionnaire.

If you are working for a substance abuse treatment center, the organization will likely have its own protocol for conducting the intake interview and history collection. If you are working independently, you might find Alderson's Personal Functioning Questionnaire (PFQ; the questionnaire, the manual, and the pie chart are available as free downloads from https://kevinalderson.ca/) helpful for this purpose. A time- and cost-savings measure is to email this to clients before you see them for the first session and either ask them to return it to you before you meet or have them bring it to the first session. The PFQ, which takes clients about 45 min to complete, collects information in 14 areas: background information, description of presenting problem(s), living arrangements and children, friendships, family of origin, spiritual beliefs, emotional health, drug use, physical health and medications, recreation and leisure activities, intimate romantic/sexual relationships, career choice, work and volunteer history, and ethnicity/diversity considerations. Clients also rate their functioning in most of these areas, providing the counselor a firsthand glimpse into areas that the client sees as problematic.

Another excellent history questionnaire is the Multimodal Life History Inventory, Third Edition (MLHI-3), by Clifford Lazarus (cost is about $40.00 for 20 inventories from researchpress.com). The first version of this instrument was the Multimodal Life History Questionnaire (MLHQ) by Clifford's late father, Arnold Lazarus (1989); an example of his original questionnaire can be found by visiting www.curelifeworks.com. The MLHI-3 and the MLHQ are based on Arnold Lazarus's multimodal approach to helping clients.

The most important guidelines for determining which TSIQs to use comes down to their reliability and validity (Del Boca et al., 2016). Reliability and validity are generally regarded as the two most important psychometric properties of an instrument. If a TSIQ does not report its psychometric properties, it likely means that these have not been determined. In the era of using evidence-based instruments, one is generally advised to avoid these TSIQs until (or if) their psychometric properties are published. Furthermore, some TSIQs produce biased results for diverse individuals (e.g., race/ethnicity, religion, LGBTQ) (Del Boca et al., 2016). The best way to ascertain this is to find out who made up the group on which the particular TSIQ was tested.

Many instruments have also been translated into several languages (Del Boca et al., 2016). The Addiction Severity Index, for example, has been translated into 17 languages, along with a computerized Spanish-language version (Del Boca et al., 2016).

Assessing alcohol and other SUDs (and their severity) is typically accomplished through individual verbal report or via written self-report measures (Del Boca et al., 2016). Interestingly, although one might suspect that addicted individuals would lie or minimize their behavioral excess on self-report measures, research indicates that most provide results with high validity (Rowe, Vittinghoff, Colfax, Coffin, & Santos, 2018; Secades-Villa & Fernandez-Hermida, 2003). Research has shown that TSIQs that include retrospective accounts regarding daily estimation of the quantity/frequency of addictive behaviors are both reliable and valid for 90 days to 6 months (and up to 12 months in one study) (Del Boca et al., 2016). Nonetheless, daily estimation measures in real time produce the most accurate results (Del Boca et al., 2016).

Mandatory or voluntary drug testing might be required in your work setting, and these include screening tests, confirmatory tests, urine testing, oral fluid testing, and hair testing (Knott, 2014). Knott (2014) provided the approximate amount of time that the following drugs can be detected in urine:

- Amphetamines including methamphetamine (2 days).
- Benzodiazepines (ultrashort-acting = 12 hours; intermediate-acting = 2–5 days; long-acting = 7 days or more).
- Buprenorphine and metabolites (8 days).
- Cocaine metabolite (2–3 days).
- Methadone (maintenance dosing; 7–9 days).
- Codeine, morphine, and heroin (heroin is detected in urine as metabolite morphine; 48 hours).
- Cannabinoids (single use = 3–4 days; moderate use [3 times a week] = 5–6 days; heavy use [daily] = 20 days; chronic heavy use [more than 3 times a day] = up to 45 days).

Instruments

First and foremost, arguably your best tool for assessing all mental disorders, including substances and addictive behaviors, is the *DSM-5* (APA, 2013). Purchase a copy and keep it nearby. The Screening, Brief Intervention, and Referral to Treatment (SBIRT) tool is excellent as well, published by the Substance Abuse and Mental Health Services Administration (SAMHSA; visit https://www.samhsa.gov/sbirt for details. Further details and a link to a free online SBIRT course can be found at https://www.integration.samhsa.gov/clinical-practice/sbirt). There is a free app for SBIRT (called SBIRT for Health Professionals) available for IOS devices at https://itunes.apple.com/us/app/sbirt-for-health-professionals/id1352895522?mt=8.

Samet, Waxman, Hatzenbuehler, and Hasin (2007) stated that, during the Clinical Trials Network of the National Institute on Drug Abuse, their preferred instruments were the Addiction Severity Index (ASI) and the Composite International Diagnostic Interview (CIDI). CIDI-5 is currently being developed and will, it is hoped, be available soon (see https://www.hcp.med.harvard.edu/wmhcidi/who-wmh-cidi-training/ for updates).

The ASI is a commonly used semistructured interview that addresses seven potential problem areas in substance-abusing patients. It takes about 1 hour with a skilled interviewer. The ASI is currently in its sixth version (ASI-6), and the ASI-MV (ASI-Multimedia Version) is the electronic version of it. The advantage of the ASI-MV is that the client administers it, and it can be completed in a counseling setting or remotely, whereas the paper-and-pencil versions require a trained interviewer to administer (see https://www.hazelden.org/web/public/asimv_main.page for details). Hazelden Publishing also markets the Behavioral Health Index-Multimedia Version (BHI-MV), which overviews client functioning in several key life areas. Hazelden can be contacted by calling 800-328-9000. Denis, Cacciola, and Alterman (2013) compared ASI-6 with ASI-5 and found ASI-6 to cover more comprehensive content in its scales. Note that ASI-5 is available for free (see http://adai.washington.edu/instruments/pdf/Addiction_Severity_Index_Baseline_Followup_4.pdf) as well as a complimentary treatment planning manual based on this index (http://jpwpkl.moe.gov.my/download/phocadownload/terkini/2014/sppk/ucd/BahanLDPCOMBATDAPS/asi%20manual.pdf).

There are many instruments available to counselors. For example, the Alcohol and Drug Abuse Institute at the University of Washington lists 1031 TSIQs (reference follows)! If you click the "more" button on the right of each TSIQ, it provides information regarding the instrument and where to get it.

1. Alcohol and Drug Abuse Institute, University of Washington. (n.d.). Screening and assessment instruments. Retrieved on April 16, 2019, from http://lib.adai.washington.edu/dbtw-wpd/exec/dbtwpub.dll?AC=QBE_QUERY&QY=find%20(Name%20/%20Acronym%20ct%20*)%20and%20(Status%20ct%20public)&XC=/dbtw-wpd/exec/dbtwpub.dll&BU=http%3A//lib.adai.washington.edu/instrumentsearch.htm&TN=instruments&SN=AUTO9271&SE=874&RN=0&MR=0&ES=1&CS=0&XP=&RF=Brief&EF=&DF=Full&RL=1&EL=1&DL=1&NP=3&ID=&MF=WPEngMsg.ini&MQ=&TI=0&DT=&ST=0&IR=14&NR=0&NB=0&SV=0&BG=0&FG=000000&QS=

2. SAMSHA-HRSA (n.d.; see reference following) contains many excellent resources. The first link under *Resources* is the *DSM-5 Online Assessment Measures*, produced by the American Psychiatric Association. Other resources include the Healthy Living Questionnaire, the Kessler 6 and Kessler 10, the Patient Stress Questionnaire, the Patient Satisfaction Survey, the M3 Checklist, and many more that are specific to different conditions including drug and alcohol use.

   SAMHSA-HRSA Center for Integrated Health Solutions. (n.d.). Screening tools. Retrieved on April 16, 2019, from https://www.integration.samhsa.gov/clinical-practice/screening-tools

3. NIDA (2018; see reference following) offers links to several useful screening tools. The group's website informs readers if each instrument is for screening just alcohol, just drugs, or both. They also provide information regarding whether the focus of each TSIQ is adults or adolescents, and whether it is self-administered or clinician administered.

   National Institute on Drug Abuse (NIDA; 2018, June). Screening tools and resources. Retrieved on April 16, 2019, from https://www.drugabuse.gov/nidamed-medical-health-professionals/screening-tools-resources

4. ASAM (n.d.; see reference following) also provides links to useful screening tools. They include AUDIT-C, CRAFFT Screening Tool, NIDA Modified ASSIST Drug Use Screening Tool, Online Screening Tool: Alcohol Screening, and Online Screening Tool: Drug Screening, and Online Assessment Measures: Cross-Cutting Symptom Measures.

   American Society of Addiction Medicine (ASAM). (n.d.). Screening and assessment tools. Retrieved on April 16, 2019, from https://www.asam.org/education/live-online-cme/fundamentals-program/additional-resources/screening-assessment-for-substance-use-disorders/screening-assessment-tools

5. Winters, K. C. (2004, August). Assessment of alcohol and other drug use behaviors among adolescents. Retrieved on April 16, 2019, from https://pubs.niaaa.nih.gov/publications/AssessingAlcohol/behaviors.htm

   This publication lists a good selection of instruments and interviews for working with adolescents. Winters also indicates whether there are norms and who comprises the normed group.

6. Healthyplace.com advertises itself as the "largest consumer mental health site on the net. We provide authoritative information and support to people with mental health concerns, along with their family members and other loved ones" (quoted from the website). Counselors should note that https://www.healthyplace.com/psychological-tests contains many tests that can be completed online covering both addictions and mental health issues.

7. Several drug-focused online quizzes are available from https://www.rehabs.com/assessments/

8. Adult Substance Abuse Subtle Screening Inventory – 4 (SASSI-4). https://sassi.com/

   Quoted from website:

   > Identifies high or low probability of substance use disorders and includes a prescription drug scale that identifies individuals likely to be abusing prescription medications. It also provides a measure of profile validity and clinical insight into the level of defensiveness and willingness to acknowledge experienced consequences of substance use disorder.

Most instruments are free, but the SASSI is not. Although the SASSI is a widely used instrument, Goodwin (2016) stated that it does *not* offer advantages over other instruments in screening for SUDs.

RESOURCES AND VIDEOS

Resources

The following list of Internet resources regarding *prevention* was first assembled by Fisher and Harrison (2013, p. 329):

1. SAMHSA Evidence-Based Practices Resource Center. https://www.samhsa.gov/ebp-resource-center
2. Center for the Application of Prevention Technologies. http://www.samhsa.gov/captus (they have an indirect link at https://recoverymonth.gov/organizations-programs/center-application-prevention-technologies-capt)Prevention principles .drugabuse.gov/pdf/prevention/RedBook.pdf
3. National Clearinghouse for Alcohol and Drug Information (NCADI). https://store.samhsa.gov/
4. Prevention specialist certification. internationalcredentialing.org/PSStandards.asp

Additional resources regarding *prevention* were listed by Smith and Luther (2013; these have been updated from source):

1. Government sites:
   a. Centers for Disease Control and Prevention (CDC): cdc.gov/
   b. National Education Association Health Information Network: http://www.nea.org/home/61155.htm
   c. National Institute on Alcohol Abuse and Alcoholism (NIAAA): niaaa.nih.gov/

   d. National Institute on Drug Abuse (NIDA): nida.nih.gov/
   e. National Institutes of Health (NIH): nih.gov/
   f. Substance Abuse and Mental Health Services Administration (SAMSHA), Department of Health and Human Services: samhsa.gov/
   g. U.S. Department of Health and Human Services (HHS): hhs.gov/
2. University-based sites:
   a. Higher Education Center for Alcohol and Drug Misuse Prevention and Recovery: https://hecaod.osu.edu/
   b. Center on Addiction: https://www.centeronaddiction.org/
3. Miscellaneous:
   a. American Society of Addiction Medicine (ASAM): https://www.asam.org/
   b. Drug Policy Alliance: drugpolicy.org/about
   c. Partnership for Drug-Free Kids: drugfree.org/
   d. Partnership for Responsible Drug Information: prdi.org/

Resources for *program evaluation* are available from each of the professional evaluation organizations. Visit their websites for details. Other helpful organizations are the Centers for Disease Control and Prevention (https://www.cdc.gov/eval/resources/index.htm), Evaluation Resource Centre (visit https://erc.undp.org/), and the UK's National Coordinating Centre for Public Engagement (visit https://www.publicengagement.ac.uk/do-engagement/evaluating-public-engagement/evaluation-resources).

Videos

To view these videos, search their titles on YouTube.

1. *Drug use prevention - school programming and protective factors | NCLEX-RN | Khan Academy.*
2. *Growing Up with Addiction and/or Mental Health Disorders - Prevention by Targeting Families.*
3. *Addiction Prevention - Prevent Addiction Early By Understanding How It Is Born.*
4. *CV-1407YTPart1* (12-Core Functions of Substance Abuse Counseling). Breining Institute.
5. *Program Evaluation Overview.* Stanford LEAP.
6. *Lecture 13: Program Evaluation.* Charlie Collins.

JOURNALS AND CONFERENCES

Journals

A few peer-reviewed journals focus on addiction prevention. They are included in the folowing list. Evaluation now has over 188 professional associations at the national and regional level worldwide (International Organization for Cooperation in Evaluation, 2018). Several of these associations have created journals and offered conferences. Eval Community (visit https://www.evalcommunity.com/), for example, lists approximately 30 journals that deal with evaluation research.

1. *Journal of Addiction & Prevention.* Quoted from website: "*Journal of Addiction & Prevention* is an online peer reviewed Open Access journal that encompasses all the habits that leads to addiction, such as tobacco, alcohol, narcotics, illicit drugs and behavioral addictions and focuses on latest and innovative research pertaining to preventive measures." Visit https://journals.indexcopernicus.com/search/details?id=32202
2. *Journal of Addiction and Preventive Medicine.* Quoted from website: "An international online, open access, peer reviewed journal that focuses on basic science, and clinical aspects of addiction. Additionally, it highlights the efforts of preventing addiction in the population at large and accepts articles related to that. The journal will accept manuscripts from clinicians such as physicians, psychologists, therapists, social workers in the field of Addiction Medicine as well as basic scientists." Visit https://www.elynsgroup.com/journal/journal-of-addiction-and-preventive-medicine
3. *Substance Abuse Treatment, Prevention, and Policy.* Quoted from website: "*Substance Abuse Treatment, Prevention, and Policy* is an open access, peer-reviewed journal that encompasses research concerning substance abuse, with a focus on policy issues." Visit https://substanceabusepolicy.biomedcentral.com/
4. *American Journal of Evaluation.* Quoted from website: "Each issue of the *American Journal of Evaluation (AJE)* explores decisions and challenges related to conceptualizing, designing and conducting evaluations. Four times/year it offers original, peer-reviewed, articles about the methods, theory, ethics, politics, and practice of evaluation." Visit http://aje.sagepub.com/
5. *Canadian Journal of Program Evaluation (CJPE).* Quoted from website: "Dedicated to the advancement of evaluation theory and practice." Visit https://evaluationcanada.ca/canadian-journal-program-evaluation

6. *Evaluation and Program Planning*. Quoted from website: "*Evaluation and Program Planning* is based on the principle that the techniques and methods of evaluation and planning transcend the boundaries of specific fields and that relevant contributions to these areas come from people representing many different positions, intellectual traditions, and interests." Visit http://www.journals.elsevier.com/evaluation-and-program-planning
7. *Evaluation: The International Journal of Theory, Research and Practice*. Quoted from website: "Over the last two decades, evaluation has become a major issue for academics, governmental and public organizations and businesses throughout the world. This has, however, resulted in a body of knowledge scattered across disciplines, professions and countries. To promote dialogue internationally and to build bridges within this expanding field, *Evaluation: The International Journal of Theory, Research and Practice* was launched in July 1995. Visit https://us.sagepub.com/en-us/nam/journal/evaluation

Conferences

Not all the following conferences are only on the topic of prevention. If you are interested in the prevention of a particular addiction, please see the section called Conferences in Chapters 9 through 21.

1. National Prevention Network. http://npnconference.org/
2. Substance Use Prevention Conference. https://actmissouri.org/events/annual-events/prevention-conference/
3. North Carolina Substance Misuse Prevention Conference. http://www.ncparentresourcecenter.org/ncprc-conference/
4. New Jersey Prevention Network Annual Addiction Conference. https://10times.com/new-jersey-prevention-network-annual-addiction
5. National Institute on Drug Abuse. https://www.drugabuse.gov/news-events/meetings-events/upcoming-meetings-events
6. American Society of Addiction Medicine. https://www.asam.org/

Below are a few of the organizations that host annual evaluation conferences:

1. American Evaluation Association. See website for details.
2. Canadian Evaluation Society. See website for details.
3. European Evaluation Society. See website for details.
4. UK Evaluation Society. See website for details.
5. Australian Evaluation Society. See website for details.

INDIVIDUAL EXERCISES

1. Meet with someone who has conducted an evaluation. As suggested by Shannon and Cooper (2016), evaluators are within college and university departments and in the local community. Also, faculty need to conduct evaluations for funders of their research.
2. Evaluate a class in which you are enrolled. Write down the strengths of the instructor and the course content on one half of the page and write the weaknesses or areas for improvement of the instructor or course content on the other half. Provide a global rating as well: Would you recommend this course to other students? Why or why not?
3. Consider advertising that you hear on the radio, see on the television, or read in a magazine that is either promoting (or dissuading) use of a legal drug (i.e., cigarettes, alcohol, prescription medication) or dissuading people from using illegal drugs. If you were to evaluate this media campaign, how would you ascertain its strengths and weaknesses? What would you want to measure? For how long would you conduct the evaluation study?

CLASSROOM EXERCISES

1. Shannon and Cooper (2016) suggested meeting and having discussions with evaluation stakeholders. They suggested it would not be difficult to find evaluators as they are within college and university departments, faculty research, and in the local community. University administrators would be included. An individual who

conducts evaluations could be invited to class to offer a brief presentation followed by questions from the students that they have developed in advance.

2. Assign students to groups of three or four. Each group either picks or is assigned a small program to evaluate. These could be chosen from programs at your college or university or other services on campus.

3. First, divide the class into two. Provide all the students with a published evaluation. Have students on one side focus on the strengths of the evaluation and students on the other side concentrate on its weaknesses. Either have students write the strengths and weaknesses on the board or have the two teams debate these in class.

CHAPTER SUMMARY

After 30 years of programming aimed at prevention, the most salient conclusion is that "no single strategy has consistently demonstrated a long-term impact" (McNeece & Madsen, 2012, p. 180). It is also important to keep in mind that, although chronic drug use has a negative impact on employment, casual drug use does not for most individuals who admit to using illicit drugs (McNeece & Madsen, 2012).

Prevention programs are effective in some cases, whereas other programs actually increase drug use. The Institute of Medicine and the National Institute on Drug abuse have adopted a classification of prevention programs that differ based on the intended audience. *Universal prevention* targets the general population, *selective intervention* focuses explicitly on at-risk populations, and *indicated prevention* is aimed at those experiencing early signs of substance abuse and related problem behaviors. Different cultures evince varying degrees of risk factors and protective factors, which either promote or diminish addictive behaviors, respectively.

Prevention programs are expensive, and they need to demonstrate effectiveness. This chapter also focused on evaluation. There are several other reasons that evaluations are conducted besides prevention. Some of these other reasons were embedded within the different types of evaluation included, such as counselor evaluation, client evaluation, prevention evaluation, program evaluation, and treatment evaluation. Evaluation can enrich the quality of our programs and our counseling practices.

The chapter then moved into an overview of client assessment. Chapters 9 through 21 each has a section called Diagnostic and Assessment Considerations. That section of each chapter includes *DSM-5* criteria for those addictions currently recognized in the DSM system but also several assessments and screening instruments used for that particular addiction. Assessment in this chapter was reviewed more generally. Several valuable links to instruments useful in addiction counseling practice were also provided.

REFERENCES

Ahmadi, V., Ahmadi, S., Dadfar, R., Nasrolahi, A., Abedini, S., & Azar-Abdar, T. (2014). The relationships between parenting styles and addiction potentiality among students. *Journal of Paramedical Sciences*, *5*(3), 2–6.

American Psychiatric Association (APA). (2013). *Diagnostic and statistical manual of mental disorders* (5th ed.). Washington, DC: Author.

American Society of Addiction Medicine (ASAM). (2018). *What is the ASAM criteria?* Retrieved on August 30, 2018, from https://www.asam.org/resources/the-asam-criteria/about

Antone, J., & Csiernik, R. (2017). The role of culture in prevention. In R. Csiernik & W. S. Rowe (Eds.), *Responding to the oppression of addiction: Canadian social work perspectives* (3rd ed., pp. 60–73). Toronto, ON: Canadian Scholars.

Apisitwasana, N., Perngparn, U., & Cottler, L. B. (2018). Effectiveness of school- and family-based interventions to prevent gaming addiction among grades 4–5 students in Bangkok, Thailand. *Psychology Research and Behavior Management*, *11*, 103–115.

Baumrind, D. (1991). The influence of parenting style on adolescent competence and substance use. *Journal of Early Adolescence*, *11*(1), 56–95.

Baumrind, D., Larzelere, R. E., & Owens, E. B. (2010). Effects of preschool parents' power assertive patterns and practices on adolescent development. *Parenting: Science and Practice*, *10*(3), 157–201.

Beauchamp, G. A., Winstanley, E. L., Ryan, S. A., & Lyons, M. S. (2014). Moving beyond misuse and diversion: The urgent need to consider the role of iatrogenic addiction in the current opioid epidemic. *American Journal of Public Health*, *104*(11), 2023–2029.

Bergmark, A. (2015). Where is the forest? *Addiction*, *110*(3), 416–417.

Bidell, M. P., & Whitman, J. S. (2013). A review of lesbian, gay, and bisexual affirmative counseling assessments. *Counseling Outcome Research and Evaluation*, *4*, 112–126.

Boswell, D. L., White, J., Sims, W. D., & Romans, J. S. C. (2013). Reliability and validity of the Outcome Questionnaire-45.2. *Psychological Reports*, *112*(3), 689–693.

Brandon, P. R., & Sam, A. L. A. (2014). Program evaluation. In B. S. McCrady & E. E. Epstein (Eds.), *Addictions: A comprehensive guidebook* (2nd ed., pp. 471–497). New York, NY: Oxford University Press.

Bricker, J. B. (2015). Climbing above the forest and the trees: Three future directions in addiction treatment research. *Addiction, 110*(3), 414–415.

Brownell, K. D., & Gold, M. S. (2012). Food and addiction: Scientific, social, legal, and legislative implications. In K. D. Brownell & M. S. Gold (Eds.), *Food and addiction: A comprehensive handbook* (pp. 439–446). New York, NY: Oxford University Press.

Centers for Disease Control and Prevention. (2018, May 4). *Tobacco industry marketing*. Retrieved on December 4, 2018, from https://www.cdc.gov/tobacco/data_statistics/fact_sheets/tobacco_industry/marketing/index.htm

Chen, N., Deater-Deckard, K., & Bell, M. A. (2014). The role of temperament by family environment interactions in child maladjustment. *Journal of Abnormal Child Psychology, 42*(8), 1251–1262.

Cho, C.-M. (2017). South Korea's efforts to prevent Internet addiction. In M. Israelashvili & J. L. Romano (Eds.), *The Cambridge handbook of international prevention science* (pp. 551–573). New York, NY: Cambridge University Press.

Cicero, T. J., Ellis, M. S., & Kasper, Z. A. (2017). Psychoactive substance use prior to the development of iatrogenic opioid abuse: A descriptive analysis of treatment-seeking opioid abusers. *Addictive Behaviors, 65*, 242–244.

Cook, S., Heather, N., & McCambridge, J. (2015). The role of the working alliance in treatment for alcohol problems. *Psychology of Addictive Behaviors, 29*(2), 371–381.

Csiernik, R., Rowe, W. S., & Watkin, J. (2017). Prevention as controversy: Harm reduction. In R. Csiernik & W. S. Rowe (Eds.), *Responding to the oppression of addiction: Canadian social work perspectives* (3rd ed., pp. 28–47). Toronto, ON: Canadian Scholars.

Deane, F. P., Kelly, P. J., Crowe, T. P., Lyons, G. C., & Cridland, E. K. (2014). The feasibility of telephone follow-up interviews for monitoring treatment outcomes of Australian residential drug and alcohol treatment programs. *Substance Abuse, 35*(1), 21–29.

Del Boca, F. K., Darkes, J., & McRee, B. (2016). Self-report assessments of psychoactive substance use and dependence. In K. J. Sher (Ed.), *The Oxford handbook of substance use and substance use disorders., Vol. 2* (pp. 430–465). New York, NY: Oxford University Press.

Demaret, I., Quertemont, E., Litran, G., Magoga, C., Deblire, C., Dubois, N., . . . Ansseau, M. (2016). Loss of treatment benefit when heroin-assisted treatment is stopped after 12 months. *Journal of Substance Abuse Treatment, 69*, 72–75.

Denis, C. M., Cacciola, J. S., & Alterman, A. I. (2013). Addiction Severity Index (ASI) summary scores: comparison of the Recent Status Scores of the ASI-6 and the Composite Scores of the ASI-5. *Journal of Substance Abuse Treatment, 45*(5), 444–450.

Donovan, D. M. (2013). Evidence-based assessment. In B. S. McCrady & E. E. Epstein (Eds.), *Addictions: A comprehensive guidebook* (2nd ed., pp. 311–351). New York, NY: Oxford University Press.

Doran, J. M., Safran, J. D., & Muran, J. C. (2016). The Alliance Negotiation Scale: A psychometric investigation. *Psychological Assessment, 28*, 885–897.

DuPont, R. L., Compton, W. M., & McLellan, A. (2015). Five-year recovery: A new standard for assessing effectiveness of substance use disorder treatment. *Journal of Substance Abuse Treatment, 58*, 1–5.

Elzerbi, C., Donoghue, K., & Drummond, C. (2015). A comparison of the efficacy of brief interventions to reduce hazardous and harmful alcohol consumption between European and non-European countries: A systematic review and meta-analysis of randomized controlled trials. *Addiction, 110*(7), 1082–1091.

Epstein, N. B., Baldwin, L. M., & Bishop, D. S. (1983). The McMaster Family Assessment Device. *Journal of Marital and Family Therapy, 9*(2), 171–180.

Falkenstrom, F., Hatcher, R. L., Skjulsvik, T., Larsson, M. H., & Holmqvist, R. (2015). Development and validation of a 6-item working alliance questionnaire for repeated administrations during psychotherapy. *Psychological Assessment, 27*, 169–183.

Federal Trade Commission. (2014, March). *Self-regulation in the alcohol industry: Report of the Federal Trade Commission.* Retrieved on December 4, 2018, from file:///C:/Users/alder/Desktop/140320alcoholreport.pdf

Finn, A. (2012). Substance abuse prevention programs for children, adolescents, and college students. In D. Capuzzi & M. D. Stauffer (Eds.), *Foundations of addictions counseling* (2nd ed., pp. 321–340). Upper Saddle River, NJ: Pearson Education.

Fisher, G. L., & Harrison, T. C. (2013). *Substance abuse: Information for school counselors, social workers, therapists, and counselors* (5th ed.). Upper Saddle River, NJ: Pearson Education.

Franklin, C., Corcoran, J., Nowicki, J., & Streeter, C. (1997). Using client self-anchored scales to measure outcomes in solution-focused therapy. *Journal of Systemic Therapies, 16*(3), 246–265.

Gamst, G. C., & Liang, C. T. H. (2013). A review and critique of multicultural competence measures: Toward a social justice-oriented health service delivery model. In F. A. Paniagua & A.-M. Yamada (Eds.), *Handbook of multicultural mental health: Assessment and treatment of diverse populations* (2nd ed., pp. 547–569). San Diego, CA: Elsevier Academic Press.

Gass, M., Foden, E. G., & Tucker, A. (2017). Program evaluation for health and human service programs: How to tell the right story successfully. In J. D. Christenson & A. N. Merritts (Eds.), *Family therapy with adolescents in residential treatment: Intervention and research* (pp. 425–441). Cham, Switzerland: Springer International.

Giannini, M., & Loscalzo, Y. (2016). Workaholism: Health risk and prevention in the organizations. In A. Di Fabio (Ed.), *Neuroticism: Characteristics, impact on job performance and health outcomes* (pp. 49–59). Hauppauge, NY: Nova Science.

Goodwin, L. R., Jr. (2016). Substance abuse assessment. In I. Marini & M. A. Stebnicki (Eds.), *The professional counselor's desk reference* (2nd ed., pp. 449–455). New York, NY: Springer.

Gordon R. S. (1983). An operational classification of disease prevention. *Public Health Reports, 98*, 107–109.

Hartzler, B., & Rabun, C. (2014). Training addiction professionals in empirically supported treatments: Perspectives from the treatment community. *Substance Abuse, 35*(1), 30–36.

Holder, H. D., Gruenewald, P. J., Ponicki, W. R., Treno, A. J., Grube, J. W., Saltz, R. F., . . . Roeper, P. (2000). Effective community-based interventions on high risk drinking and alcohol-related injuries. *Journal of the American Medical Association, 284*(18), 2341–2347.

Huston, C. (2015, February 4). *The 16 states that still allow smoking in bars and restaurants.* Retrieved on December 4, 2018, from https://www.marketwatch.com/story/the-16-states-that-still-allow-smoking-in-bars-and-restaurants-2015-02-03

Institute of Medicine. (1994). Reducing risks for mental disorders: Frontiers for preventive intervention research. In P. J. Mrazek & R. J. Haggerty (Eds.), *Committee on Prevention of Mental Disorders, Division of Biobehavorial Sciences and Mental Disorders.* Washington, DC: National Academy Press.

International Organization for Cooperation in Evaluation. (2018). *Home page.* Retrieved on December 13, 2018, from https://ioce.net/

Johnson, L. N., Ketring, S. A., & Anderson, S. R. (2013). Confirmatory factor analysis of the Family Therapy Alliance Scale: An evaluation of factor structure across parents and adolescents referred for at risk services. *Contemporary Family Therapy: An International Journal, 35,* 121–136.

Jones, W. P., & Markos, P. A. (1997). Client rating of counselor effectiveness: A call for caution. *Journal of Applied Rehabilitation Counseling, 28*(3), 23–28.

Kiraly, O., Nagygyorgy, K., Griffiths, M. D., & Demetrovics, Z. (2014). Problematic online gaming. In K. P. Rosenberg & L. Curtiss Feder (Eds.), *Behavioral addictions: Criteria, evidence, and treatment* (pp. 61–97). San Diego, CA: Academic Press.

Knight, F. (2016, October 11). Friends don't let friends drive drunk. *SW Helper.* Retrieved on December 6, 2018, from https://www.socialworkhelper.com/2016/10/11/friends-dont-let-friends-drive-drunk/

Knott, L. (2014, November 6). *Assessment of drug dependence.* Retrieved on April 16, 2019, from https://patient.info/doctor/assessment-of-drug-dependence

Kwon, J.-H. (2011). Toward the prevention of adolescent Internet addiction. In K. S. Young & C. Nabuco de Abreu (Eds.), *Internet addiction: A handbook and guide to evaluation and treatment* (pp. 223–243). Hoboken, NJ: John Wiley & Sons.

Lacsan, K., Arany, Z., & Farkas, A. (2017). The role of leisure in prevention and treatment of addiction. In Z. Benko, I. Modi, & K. Tarko (Eds.), *Leisure, health and well-being: A holistic approach* (pp. 115–120). New York, NY: Palgrave Macmillan.

Ladouceur, R., Shaffer, P., Blaszczynski, A., & Shaffer, H. J. (2017). Responsible gambling: A synthesis of the empirical evidence. *Addiction Research & Theory, 25,* 225–235.

Lambie, G. W., Mullen, P. R., Swank, J. M., & Blount, A. (2018). The Counseling Competencies Scale: Validation and refinement. *Measurement and Evaluation in Counseling and Development, 51*(1), 1–15.

Lazarus, A. A. (1989). *The practice of multimodal therapy: Systematic, comprehensive, and effective psychotherapy.* Baltimore, MD: Johns Hopkins University Press.

Lopez-Goni, J. J., Fernandez-Montalvo, J., Arteaga, A., & Esarte, S. (2017). Searching objective criteria for patient assignment in addiction treatment. *Journal of Substance Abuse Treatment, 76,* 28–35.

Margolis, R. D., & Zweben, J. E. (2011). *Treating patients with alcohol and other drug problems: An integrated approach* (2nd ed.). Washington, DC: American Psychological Association.

Marmarosh, C. L., & Kivlighan, D. M. Jr. (2012). Relationships among client and counselor agreement about the working alliance, session evaluations, and change in client symptoms using response surface analysis. *Journal of Counseling Psychology, 59,* 352–367.

McNeece, C. A., & Madsen, M. D. (2012). Preventing alcohol and drug problems. In C. A. McNeece & D. M. DiNitto (Eds.), *Chemical dependency: A systems approach* (4th ed., pp. 171–199). Upper Saddle River, NJ: Pearson Education.

Metzler, C. W., Eddy, J. M., & Lichtenstein, D. P. (2013). Prevention aimed at individuals. In B. S. McCrady & E. E. Epstein (Eds.), *Addictions: A comprehensive guidebook* (2nd ed., pp. 839–870). New York, NY: Oxford University Press.

Miller, W. R., & Moyers, T. B. (2015). The forest and the trees: Relational and specific factors in addiction treatment. *Addiction, 110*(3), 401–413.

Monezi Andrade, A. L., de Lacerda, R. B., Gomide, H. P., Ronzani, T. M., Andreoli Sartes, L. M., Martins, L. F., . . . Souza-Formigoni, M. L. O. (2016). Web-based self-help intervention reduces alcohol consumption in both heavy-drinking and dependent alcohol users: A pilot study. *Addictive Behaviors, 63,* 63–71.

Moran, A., Musicus, A., Soo, J., Gearhardt, A. N., Gollust, S. E., & Roberto, C. A. (2016). Believing that certain foods are addictive is associated with support for obesity-related public policies. *Preventive Medicine: An International Journal Devoted to Practice and Theory, 90,* 39–46.

Murdock, T. B., Wendler, A. M., & Nilsson, J. E. (2005). Addiction Counseling Self-Efficacy Scale (ACSES): Development and initial validation. *Journal of Substance Abuse Treatment, 29,* 55–64.

National Institute on Drug Abuse. (2003a, October). *Preventing drug use among children and adolescents (in brief): Chapter 4—Examples of research-based drug abuse prevention programs.* Retrieved on December 3, 2018, from https://www.drugabuse.gov/publications/preventing-drug-abuse-among-children-adolescents-in-brief/chapter-4-examples-research-based-drug-abuse-prevention-programs

National Institute on Drug Abuse. (2003b, October). *Preventing drug use among children and adolescents (in brief): Indicated programs.* Retrieved on December 5, 2018, from https://www.drugabuse.gov/publications/preventing-drug-abuse-among-children-adolescents/chapter-4-examples-research-based-drug-abuse-prevention-progr-2

National Institute on Drug Abuse. (2003c, October). *Preventing drug use among children and adolescents (in brief): Selective programs.* Retrieved on December 5, 2018, from https://www.drugabuse.gov/publications/preventing-drug-abuse-among-children-adolescents/chapter-4-examples-research-based-drug-abuse-prevention-progr-1

National Institute on Drug Abuse. (2003d, October). *Preventing drug use among children and adolescents (in brief): Universal programs.* Retrieved on December 5, 2018, from https://www.drugabuse.gov/publications/preventing-drug-abuse-among-children-adolescents/chapter-4-examples-research-based-drug-abuse-prevention-progr-0

National Institute on Drug Abuse. (2017, April). *Trends and statistics*. Retrieved on November 14, 2018, from https://www.drugabuse.gov/related-topics/trends-statistics

Neale, J., Finch, E., Marsden, J., Mitcheson, L., Rose, D., Strang, J., . . . Wykes, T. (2014). How should we measure addiction recovery? Analysis of service provider perspectives using online Delphi groups. *Drugs: Education, Prevention & Policy*, *21*(4), 310–323.

Nelson, T. D., & Steele, R. G. (2016). Beyond efficacy and effectiveness: A multifaceted approach to treatment evaluation. In A. E. Kazdin (Ed.), *Methodological issues and strategies in clinical research* (4th ed., pp. 389–401). Washington, DC: American Psychological Association.

Newton, N. C., Deady, M., & Teesson, M. (2014). Alcohol and substance use prevention and early intervention. In P. Byrne & A. Rosen (Eds.), *Early intervention in psychiatry: EI of nearly everything for better mental health* (pp 201–217). Hoboken, NJ: Wiley-Blackwell.

Parsons, B., Aponte-Solo, L., Bakken, L., Barela, E., Goodyear, L., Kelly, T., . . . Williams, V. (2018). *American Evaluation Association's ethical guiding principles*. Retrieved on November 13, 2018, from https://www.eval.org/p/cm/ld/fid=51

Philip, J., Ford, T., Henry, D., Rasmus, S., & Allen, J. (2016). Relationship of social network to protective factors in suicide and alcohol use disorder intervention for rural Yup'ik Alaska Native youth. *Psychosocial Intervention*, *25*, 45–54.

Polcin, D. L. (2014). Addiction science advocacy: Mobilizing political support to influence public policy. *International Journal of Drug Policy*, *25*(2), 329–331.

Popovici, I., & French, M. T. (2013). Economic evaluation of substance abuse interventions: Overview of recent research findings and policy implications. In B. S. McCrady & E. E. Epstein (Eds.), *Addictions: A comprehensive guidebook* (2nd ed., pp. 882–899). New York, NY: Oxford University Press.

Quirk, K., Miller, S., Duncan, B., & Owen, J. (2012). Group Session Rating Scale: Preliminary psychometrics in substance abuse group interventions. *Counselling and Psychotherapy Research*, 1–7 (no volume or issue indicated). Available from http://www.scottdmiller.com/wp-content/uploads/2014/06/Group-SRS-Article.pdf

Quirk, K., Miller, S., Duncan, B., & Owen, J. (2013). Group Session Rating Scale: Preliminary psychometrics in substance abuse group interventions. *Counselling & Psychotherapy Research*, *13*, 194–200.

Rastegar, D., & Fingerhood, M. (2016). *The American Society of Addiction Medicine handbook of addiction medicine*. New York, NY: Oxford University Press.

Ridout, B. (2016). Facebook, social media and its application to problem drinking among college students. *Current Opinion in Psychology*, *9*, 83–87.

Robertson, T. W., Yan, Z., & Rapoza, K. A. (2018). Is resilience a protective factor of Internet addiction? *Computers in Human Behavior*, *78*, 255–260.

Rodgers, B. (2006). Life space mapping: Preliminary results from the development of a new method for investigating counselling outcomes. *Counselling & Psychotherapy Research*, *6*, 227–232.

Ross, A. D., Waehler, C. A., & Gray, T. N. (2013). Heterosexual persons' perceptions regarding language use in counseling: Extending Dorland and Fischer (2001). *Counseling Psychologist*, *41*, 918–930.

Rowe, C., Vittinghoff, E., Colfax, G., Coffin, P. O., & Santos, G.-M. (2018). Correlates of validity of self-reported methamphetamine use among a sample of dependent adults. *Substance Use & Misuse*, *53*, 1742–1755.

Saltz, R. L., Paschall, M. J., McGaffigan, & Nygaard, P. M. (2010). Alcohol risk management on college settings: The Safer California Universities Randomized Trial. *American Journal of Preventive Medicine*, *39*, 491–499.

Samet, S., Waxman, R., Hatzenbuehler, M., & Hasin, D. S. (2007). Assessing addiction: Concepts and instruments. *Addiction Science & Clinical Practice*, *4*(1), 19–31.

Schildhaus, S. (2015). The evaluation of substance user treatment—A jubilee proposal for the 21st century. *Substance Use & Misuse*, *50*(8–9), 1055–1057.

Secades-Villa, R., & Fernandez-Hermida, J. R. (2003). The validity of self-reports in a follow-up study with drug addicts. *Addictive Behaviors*, *28*, 1175–1182.

Shannon, D. M., & Cooper, J. (2016). Teaching program evaluation. In M. C. Smith & N. DeFrates-Densch (Eds.), *Challenges and innovations in educational psychology teaching and learning* (pp. 425–437). Charlotte, NC: IAP Information Age.

Shaw, S. L., & Murray, K. W. (2014). Monitoring alliance and outcome with client feedback measures. *Journal of Mental Health Counseling*, *36*, 43–57.

Shi, X., Wang, J., & Zou, H. (2017). Family functioning and Internet addiction among Chinese adolescents: The mediating roles of self-esteem and loneliness. *Computers in Human Behavior*, *76*, 201–210.

Smith, R. L., & Luther, M. S. (2013). Prevention. In P. Stevens & R. L. Smith (Eds.), *Substance abuse counseling: Theory and practice* (5th ed., pp. 336–357). New York, NY: Pearson.

Stafstrom, M. (2014). Influence of parental alcohol-related attitudes, behavior and parenting styles on alcohol use in late and very late adolescence. *European Addiction Research*, *20*(5), 241–247.

Staras, S. A. S., Livingston, M. D., & Wagenaar, A. C. (2016). Maryland alcohol sales tax and sexually transmitted infections: A natural experiment. *American Journal of Preventive Medicine*, *50*, e73–e80.

Stautz, K., Frings, D., Albery, I. P., Moss, A. C., & Marteau, T. M. (2017). Impact of alcohol-promoting and alcohol-warning advertisements on alcohol consumption, affect, and implicit cognition in heavy-drinking young adults: A laboratory-based randomized controlled trial. *British Journal of Health Psychology*, *22*(1), 128–150.

Stevahn, L., King, J. A., Ghere, G., & Minnema, J. (2005). Establishing essential competencies for program evaluators. *American Journal of Evaluation*, *26*, 43–59.

Stevens, A. K., Littlefield, A. K., Blanchard, B. E., Talley, A. E., & Brown, J. L. (2016). Does drinking refusal self-efficacy mediate the impulsivity-problematic alcohol use relation? *Addictive Behaviors*, *53*, 181–186.

Stevens, P. W. (2013). Family treatment. In P. Stevens & R. L. Smith (Eds.), *Substance abuse counseling: Theory and practice* (5th ed., pp. 240–260). New York, NY: Pearson.

Talley, J. E., & Clack, R. J. (2006). Use of the Outcome Questionnaire 45.2 with a university population. *Journal of College Student Psychotherapy, 20*, 5–15.

Tanner-Smith, E. E., & Risser, M. D. (2016). A meta-analysis of brief alcohol interventions for adolescents and young adults: Variability in effects across alcohol measures. *American Journal of Drug and Alcohol Abuse, 42*(2), 140–151.

Tate, K. A., Bloom, M. L., Tassara, M. H., & Caperton, W. (2014). Counselor competence, performance assessment, and program evaluation: Using psychometric instruments. *Measurement and Evaluation in Counseling and Development, 47*(4), 291–306.

Texas Health and Human Services. (2016, November 1). *Universal, selective, and indicated prevention*. Retrieved on December 5, 2018, from https://www.dshs.texas.gov/sa/Prevention/classifications.shtm

Thompson, N. J., & Kegler, M. C. (2015). Program evaluation. In L. F. Salazar, R. A. Crosby, & R. J. DiClemente (Eds.), *Research methods in health promotion* (2nd ed., pp. 337–365). San Francisco, CA: Jossey-Bass.

Treno, A. J., Gruenewald, P. J., Lee, J. P., & Remer, L. G. (2007). The Sacramento Neighbourhood Alcohol Prevention Project: Outcomes from a community prevention trial. *Journal of Studies on Alcohol and Drugs, 68*(2), 197–207.

Treno, A. J., & Lee, J. P. (2013). Prevention aimed at the environment. In B. S. McCrady & E. E. Epstein (Eds.), *Addictions: A comprehensive guidebook* (2nd ed., pp. 871–881). New York, NY: Oxford University Press.

United States Government Accountability Office. (2012, January). *Designing evaluations*. Retrieved from http://www.gao.gov/assets/590/588146.pdf

Voas, R. B., Tippetts, A., Bergen, G., Grosz, M., & Marques, P. (2016). Mandating treatment based on interlock performance: Evidence for effectiveness. *Alcoholism: Clinical and Experimental Research, 40*(9), 1953–1960.

Voas, R. B., Tippetts, S. A., Johnson, M. B., Lange, J. E., & Baker, J. (2002). Operation Safe Crossing: Using science within a community intervention. *Addiction, 9*, 1214–1219.

Weigle, P., & Reid, D. (2014). Helping parents promote healthy and safe computer habits. *Adolescent Psychiatry, 4*(2), 92–97.

Weinstein, A., Lisman, S. A., & Johnson, M. D. (2015). Modifying alcohol expectancies of Hispanic children: Examining the effects of expectancy-targeted, developmentally congruous prevention videos. *Journal of Studies on Alcohol and Drugs, 76*(2), 237–246.

Wells, M., Burlingame, G., Lambert, M., Hoag, M., & Hope, C. (1996). Conceptualization and measurement of patient change during psychotherapy: Development of the Outcome Questionnaire and Youth Outcome Questionnaire. *Psychotherapy, 33*, 275–283.

Wendler, A. M. (2008). Validation of the Addiction Counseling Self-Efficacy Scale (ACSES). *Dissertation Abstracts International: Section B: The Sciences and Engineering, 68*(9-B), 6343.

Werch, C. E., & Owen, D. M. (2002). Iatrogenic effects of alcohol and drug prevention programs. *Journal of Studies on Alcohol, 63*(5), 581–590.

Werdell, P. (2012). From the front lines: A clinical approach to food and addiction. In K. D. Brownell & M. S. Gold (Eds.), *Food and addiction: A comprehensive handbook* (pp. 354–359). New York, NY: Oxford University Press.

Wodarski, J. S. (2017). Internet addiction: A growing threat to today's youth. *PsycCRITIQUES, 62*(50). No pagination specified.

Wood, E., Tyndall, M., Montaner, J., & Kerr, T. (2006). Summary of findings from the evaluation of a pilot medically supervised safer injecting facility. *Canadian Medical Association Journal, 175*(11), 1399–1404.

Yap, M. B. H., Cheong, T. W. K., Zaravinos-Tsakos, F., Lubman, D. I., & Jorm, A. F. (2017). Modifiable parenting factors associated with adolescent alcohol misuse: A systematic review and meta-analysis of longitudinal studies. *Addiction, 112*(7), 1142–1162.

Young, K. S. (2017). The evolution of Internet addiction. *Addictive Behaviors, 64*, 229–230.

Zhang, C., Brook, J. S., Leukefeld, C. G., & Brook, D. W. (2016). Longitudinal psychosocial factors related to symptoms of Internet addiction among adults in early midlife. *Addictive Behaviors, 62*, 65–72.

DESIGN

EVALUATE

PART II

Substance Addictions

9 Alcohol Addiction

iStock.com/vadimg

Learning Objectives

1. Learn about the history of alcohol use and alcohol use disorder (AUD)[1] in the United States.
2. Describe ways to assess and diagnose AUD, including the pathways toward developing AUD.
3. Define blood alcohol level, standard drink, alcohol addiction, and other essential terms.
4. Discriminate among low, moderate, and severe drinking and discern when moderation may be attainable by clients and when abstinence is the reasonable goal.
5. Learn about the empirically validated treatments for individuals with AUD and discover ways to counsel them.

[1]The term alcohol use disorder (AUD) will be used preferentially in this chapter as it is the name of the *DSM-5* diagnosis for this addiction.

CHALLENGING YOUR ASSUMPTIONS ABOUT THIS ADDICTION

1. How do you view individuals whom you see on the street that experience AUD? Articulate the judgments that you make of them.
2. How much empathy do you have toward individuals with AUD on a scale of 0 (i.e., no empathy) to 5 (i.e., absolute empathy)? What do you believe explains the rating you gave for empathy toward individuals with AUD?
3. What do you believe are the causes of AUD?
4. If you or a family member became addicted to alcohol, what strategy would you take for yourself or suggest to a family member in either overcoming or reducing the impact of alcohol dependence?
5. Many individuals with AUD refuse to attend Alcoholics Anonymous (AA) meetings because of their religious perspective and also perhaps because of the belief that they need to surrender control to a force outside themselves. Before reading this chapter, what is your view of AA? If you were struggling with alcohol dependence, how likely would you be to attend AA meetings regularly?

PERSONAL REFLECTIONS

A maniac was chopping down our back door. My sister had already called the police, and, shortly after that, three patrol cars arrived in front of our house and two in the back alley. Within minutes, all officers had their guns aimed at him. I was 15 years old, and my sister was 18. The maniac was our stepdad.

My mom met "Reggie" when I was 13. They fell in love, they married, and the rest is a nightmare from hell. Somehow unbeknown to my mom, Reggie was a skid-row individual with AUD. They only began living together following marriage, and, within a month, we knew the truth about him. He was Dr. Jekyll, and he was Mr. Hyde. One day, he would be sober, deeply apologetic, shaky, and without confidence or backbone. The next night, after an evening of hard drinks, he became the world's biggest a#&hole. As soon as he left the house to find a local pub, we all felt relief. When he returned a few hours later, I would shake in my bed until the fighting subsided sometime early the next morning.

On the night he chopped down our door, my mom had taken his house keys before he left to drink, unbeknown to him. But she did not lock the garage door where the ax was kept. That was the worst incident. To my knowledge, I was the last person to see him alive. A few years after their divorce, I needed a favor from him. He looked like hell. When I returned a couple of weeks later, he did not answer the door, and, a few days after that, I received the hysterical call from my mom.

And then there was my best friend at the time, "Barry." Barry and I started drinking together soon after I met him at age 19. Our drinking episodes were often stupid. We would get hammered more often than I care to admit. He eventually moved to a neighboring city, and, over time, he followed in his father's footsteps. AUD became his greatest vice, but he kept it together enough to work at a rather lucrative government job. Over time, employees began to complain about his erratic behavior and his inappropriate temper. They sent him 2000 miles away to an expensive and exclusive 28-day treatment. I suspected he would soon be in trouble when he called me the day after arriving home and told me that he had four double whiskeys and Coke in flight. After complaints at work erupted again, they fired him without further compassion or notice.

After losing his job, Barry went steadily downhill. One day after several months of unemployment, he drank all the liquor he had at home, and then drove to the store four blocks away to buy more. It was winter. He fell on ice leaving the store, knocked himself out, only to awaken minutes later to police hovering over him. The police charged him with a DUI, but that was nothing compared to what occurred 3 weeks later. He began having seizures, and his girlfriend thankfully got him to the hospital where a surgeon operated on his brain to release the internal hemorrhaging caused by his fall. I visited him a week or so later, and his words were gibberish. It seemed like he thought he was making sense, but his words were unintelligible. The surgery had damaged the speech center in his brain. Over time, his speech gradually improved. Within a few months, however, I had had enough of his friendship, which had become increasingly toxic and abusive. That was 2008.

How can people destroy their lives in such dramatic ways? How can alcohol get such an extreme grip on people that they cannot see the damage it is causing them and subsequently move in an entirely different direction? Why?

INSIDE AN ADDICTED PERSON'S MIND

Roberto, Age 42

My immediate family moved to Miami when I was 7 years old. From what I was told, it was not an easy escape from Cuba. Most of my relatives are still there, and I know not seeing them again was very hard on my parents. Perhaps that explains the way they treated me growing up. First off, my dad ignored me most of the time, but, when he did get involved, it was usually to discipline me for something I did that I thought was not a big deal. For example, I would stay at Jonathan house, and, if I returned home even an hour late, my mom would tell me that dad would take care of it later. I knew what taking care of it meant. It meant his big black belt across my buttocks several times, and he wouldn't stop until I began screaming. Well, I learned to start screaming horrifically earlier in my punishment to escape being beaten for longer durations.

For the most part, my mom ignored me, too. She often seemed anxious and depressed with little time to give to either my brother or me. When she did talk to me, it was usually yelling at me for something. It didn't seem like she knew how to speak at a normal level. I grew up thinking that I was worthless and unlovable. I only had Jonathan as my friend, and, by age 16, we were both drinking heavily. I remember laughing hysterically many times as we would talk about our lives and make up stories. At times, I felt more like crying, but dad taught me that guys don't cry. I got the belt more than once for thinking I could.

Jonathan eventually moved to somewhere in Colorado. We lost touch with each other. I was working in construction, and, every night after work, I would go with a few buddies to the nearby bar and get hammered. That led to more than one DUI charge. But it didn't matter because I didn't have anything to live for. I had become like my mom: anxious and depressed. Drinking helped immensely to numb those feelings, together with my feelings of unworthiness and self-loathing. Yes, I have gone through treatment centers, and, yes, I have abstained for periods up to 3 months. Life carries on, however, and my deep-rooted feelings of shame and guilt haunt me. Inevitably, once I feel I can't take it anymore, I succumb to closing down the bar most nights of the week. I will be honest this once: I crave alcohol, and I know it's what I need to get through the long days of nothingness.

I blame my parents for most of my problems. If they hadn't treated me so horribly, I'm sure I would not need to drink the way I do. Now, drinking and thinking about drinking is about the only thing that gives me pleasure. It's hard to swallow that, at my age, but I have no friends, and, even though my mom is still alive, I don't want anything to do with her. When I'm drunk is the only time I feel normal, and, when I'm sober, I cannot even stand to look in the mirror. The reflection I see there is despicable and disgusting. I did not turn out to be a nice person.

One Friday night changed my life forever. As I was driving home from the bar, I lost control and struck a telephone pole. As I was waking up, a police officer was banging on my window. As soon as I rolled it down, he told me to get out and blow on his breathalyzer. I remember he stood there shocked for a few moments, but I don't know what happened after that until I woke up the next morning in a cell. I found out I had blown 0.97, and this was the highest recording the officer had ever seen in someone who was still alive. I know I am still alive. But I wish I were dead.

Commentary

Roberto displays most of the symptoms of AUD, and he would be diagnosed as having a severe addiction. His drinking has become out of control. His symptoms include the following: (a) he has attempted to stay sober unsuccessfully, (b) he experiences strong cravings, (c) he spends a great deal of time drinking, (d) he is experiencing severe consequences because of his drinking, (e) he has a level of tolerance that would be lethal to most individuals, (f) he continues drinking and driving despite its dangerousness, and (g) he drinks despite how it has affected his relationships. Roberto has not developed recreational activities that do not include alcohol either. Given how high his blood alcohol concentration was when he blew into the breathalyzer (i.e., 0.97), withdrawal from alcohol would be life-threatening if it were not medically supervised.

Discussion

1. Do you know of anyone who you suspect has become dependent on alcohol? If "yes," which symptoms noted in the commentary apply to him or her?
2. Does this person have symptoms that are not listed in the commentary? If so, what are they?
3. If you were Roberto's counselor, how would you go about helping him?

COUNSELING SCENARIO

As you are reading, imagine that you are the client in this scenario. Note the areas in which the session could be improved on the part of the counselor.

Your name is Rosemary, a 30-year-old architect. Your employer sent you to a Betty Ford clinic for treatment of AUD. While there, the program pushed the idea that you should remain forever abstinent, but that never seemed like the right goal for you. It's not that you deny having a problem with alcohol; it's more that you don't see the connection between how it is affecting you at work and in other areas of your life. You would, however, call yourself a binge drinker. Your pattern is that you begin drinking on a Friday, and, once that begins, the entire weekend is spent sleeping and drinking. It is how you have come to deal with your loneliness. You have been out of the program for 3 weeks, and you've already started to relapse. Your employer smelled alcohol on your breath on Monday morning and has now sent you to see an addiction counselor in the community.

- Counselor: Good afternoon, Rosemary. Tell me exactly why you are drinking at this point after having gone through treatment.
- You: Ah, ahem, I'm not sure.
- Counselor: How many times have you used that excuse before? I was drunk so many times in the past and had so many blackouts that I know when someone is in denial right away. I could tell you stories that would make you beg for me to stop.
- You: I'm sure that won't be necessary. I can honestly say that I never have drunk alcohol the way that you must've in the past.
- Counselor: Do you really expect me to believe that?
- You: Absolutely. You don't even know me yet.
- Counselor: I know more about you than you realize. I have read the report I received from the Betty Ford clinic that you attended. It appears that you never did stop denying that you have a serious problem.
- You: I do not have a serious problem! I drink a lot during the weekend because I am lonely . . . that's all.
- Counselor: What are you prepared to do about your loneliness in that case?
- You: [sarcastically] Hook up every chance I get.
- Counselor: I do not think that you are taking my question seriously. If you don't have a problem with alcohol then why did your employer send you to me?
- You: My employer has had it out for me since day one. I'm sure he is a teetotaler.
- Counselor: I don't know your employer, but I can certainly tell you are not taking any of this seriously.
- You: I can't believe this. You haven't even got to know me, and you are already passing these judgments.
- Counselor: I'm not passing judgments on you, Rosemary. I'm trying to get you to see that you are still in denial.
- You: I am not in denial! I drink on the weekends. That's it. I've only missed 3 or 4 days from work, and I have worked there for nearly 8 months already.
- Counselor: Your employer tells me that you've missed more like seven or eight Mondays. You phone in sick, but he doesn't believe you.
- You: He is grossly exaggerating. I am not sure why I have to see you.
- Counselor: Rosemary, you know why. Just accept it. You are a full-blown alcoholic who is unwilling to take corrective action.
- You: Then there is no point in continuing to talk to you. You've already made up your mind about me, and I disagree. You don't know me and you never will.
- Counselor: Do you want to keep your job or don't you?
- You: Not if I have to put up with you. I would rather be unemployed!
- Counselor: So you want to play hardball, do ya?
- You: Todd, I really don't know what you are getting at. What is wrong with you? Why are you so angry?
- Counselor: What you are doing we call projection, Rosemary. You have kept so much bottled inside that it is now you who wants to punish the world and everyone in it.
- You: Thank you but I think I've had enough. I am leaving.
- Counselor: Okay. I will see you next Wednesday, same time and place.

From the Client's Perspective

1. What feelings with this interaction evoke in you?
2. What is missing for you in this dialogue?
3. What would you find more helpful from a counselor in this scenario?

From the Counselor's Perspective

1. What is interfering with developing a working alliance?
2. Going back to the Common Counseling Mistakes list in Chapter 6, which mistakes is the counselor making with Rosemary?
3. What personal issues do you believe Todd needs to work through if he is to become an effective counselor? Which defense mechanism(s) is Todd demonstrating in his dialogue with Rosemary?

Background Information

> *"So much wasted time"* (final words spoken before his death from AUD—David Cassidy, singer, actor).

The production of beer dates back approximately 20,000 years, and the fermentation of grape juice and wine is nearly as ancient (Guidot & Mehta, 2014). Interestingly, one of the first alcoholic drinks was fermented mare's milk in ancient Siberia. A version of this alcoholic beverage, known as kumis, is still drunk in some areas of Russia (Guidot & Mehta, 2014). Several religions (e.g., Islam and Mormonism) and societies (e.g., Saudi Arabia) have banned alcohol consumption indefinitely, whereas others have done so for a period, such as the Prohibition era in the United States between 1919 and 1933 (Guidot & Mehta, 2014). There is a biblical reference to Noah drinking wine and becoming drunk and a reference to Jesus consuming alcohol in moderation (Rastegar & Fingerhood, 2016).

In the United States, Dr. Benjamin Rush in about 1785 was the first to see the public health risks caused by excessive alcohol consumption and to discuss it as a medical condition (Blume, Rudisill, Hendricks, & Santoya, 2013). Magnus Huss, A Swedish physician, first referred to AUD as a disease in 1849.

The disease model that is practiced today is primarily due to the work of American E. Morton Jellinek (Blume et al., 2013). Jellinek's model continues to be embraced by AA, the National Council on Alcoholism, the National Institute on Alcohol Abuse and Alcoholism (NIAAA), and the American Medical Association (Milkman & Sunderwirth, 2010).

Political views on alcohol consumption have varied considerably over the years in the United States. Although the 1960s and early 1970s were considered drug-friendly, public concern about heavy alcohol and drug use increased toward the end of the 20th century. The drinking age had been lowered to 18 during the Vietnam War era but afterward increased again to age 21 (Ray, Courtney, & Guadalupe, 2013). Concern also grew regarding increased deaths from drunk driving, and groups such as Mothers Against Drunk Driving helped support stricter drunk-driving laws.

The most significant recent law passed in the United States regarding alcohol was the Comprehensive Alcohol Abuse and Alcoholism Prevention, Treatment, and Rehabilitation Act of 1970 (Pub. L. 91-616). This federal act focused on the prevention and treatment of AUD. It also gave rise to the NIAAA. NIAAA remains the largest funder of basic and applied alcohol research in the United States (MacKillop, Stojek, VanderBroek-Stice, & Owens, 2018).

According to the 2015 National Survey on Drug Use and Health, 138.3 million Americans aged 12 and older report that they actively consume alcohol, and 48.2% of this group reported that they had had at least one binge drinking episode within 30 days of taking the survey (Nehring, 2018). Furthermore, of those who become patients in the medical system, up to 40% experience problems with alcohol misuse (Nehring, 2018). There are more than 85,000 deaths each year due to alcohol in the United States (Nehring, 2018) and millions of deaths worldwide each year (Guidot & Mehta, 2014). Among the preventable causes of death, alcohol ranks in third place, trumped only by smoking and an unhealthy lifestyle of poor diet and physical inactivity (Heilig, 2015). Alcohol causes more deaths and disability than heroin, cocaine, and cannabis combined (Heilig, 2015).

Furthermore, approximately one third of all suicides and one quarter of all emergency room visits are alcohol-related (Lewis, 2015). The societal cost annually in the United States resulting from alcohol misuse is estimated at more than $249.0 billion (Morris, Winters, & Wagner, 2018). Today there is no refuting that excessive alcohol intake can have devastating effects on health and longevity.

There are many definitions of alcohol addiction (i.e., AUD), but one that incorporates its main features in few words was offered by Brooks and McHenry (2009): "Addiction involves a compulsive and excessive use of drugs and alcohol with subsequent negative consequences" (p. 113). The definition includes the compulsiveness that typifies addiction, the excessive use of the substance, and the adverse consequences that result. Morris et al. (2018) highlighted the progressive nature of the disorder, which over time replaces other life pleasures. Many definitions also refer to AUD as a "primary, chronic disease" (Rastegar & Fingerhood, 2016, pp. 60–61), denoting its harmful and all too commonly lethal trajectory. Furthermore, relapse is common among individuals with AUD and other substance-addicted individuals (Glantz, Moskalewicz, Caldas-de-Almeida, & Degenhardt, 2018).

Binge drinking is generally defined as heavy episodic drinking of at least five drinks in men and four drinks in women within a 2-hour period. Although other definitions exist, the 5+/ 4+ rule is most often used in alcohol research (Lewis, 2015). Despite this international convention, Pearson, Kirouac, and Witkiewitz (2016) argued that the 5+/ 4+ rule has not demonstrated unique predictive validity or clinical usefulness.

The NIAAA (2010) has a comparable definition for at-risk drinking. They defined at-risk drinking as follows:

1. For men: More than four drinks a day and not more than 14 drinks in a week.
2. For women: More than three drinks a day and not more than seven drinks in a week.

The kind of alcohol found in drinks is called ethyl alcohol or ethanol. It is mostly derived from plants, including fruits, grains, and cactus (Lewis, 2015). Alcohol is classified as a depressant (note that the other depressants are included in Chapter 13).

Alcohol metabolism begins with the enzyme called dehydrogenase, which breaks down alcohol to acetaldehyde. Acetaldehyde is further broken down into acetic acid before that metabolizes into carbon dioxide, water, and carbohydrates. Most of this metabolism occurs in the liver. Heavy drinking can lead to three conditions of the liver: (a) "fatty liver" resulting from fat accumulation around liver cells, (b) hepatitis resulting from inflammation of the liver, and/or (c) cirrhosis, which is a hardening of the liver (Lewis, 2015).

A *standard drink* refers to a beverage that contains 0.60 ounces of pure ethanol. Drinks that contain this amount include a 12-ounce can of beer, a 5-ounce glass of wine, or a drink with 1.5 ounces of 80-proof liquor. The alcohol concentration is measured in *proof.* The proof of a liquor is always twice the actual percentage of ethanol. For example, an 80-proof whiskey contains 40% alcohol. Similarly, 200 proof means pure ethanol (i.e., 100%) (Lewis, 2015).

The amount of alcohol in the blood is known as *blood alcohol level* (BAL) or *blood alcohol content* (BAC). BAL is measured in milligrams of alcohol per 100 liters of blood (mg/mL). The following effects typically occur at different BALs (Lewis, 2015):

1. 0.02: Feelings of warmth and relaxation.
2. 0.05–0.09: Increased talkativeness, increased happiness, and some impairment in motor skills and reaction time.
3. > 0.10: Slurred speech, unsteady gait, nausea, vomiting, and lowered inhibitions.
4. 0.30–0.40: Some individuals will experience severe stupor or coma.
5. > 0.40: The most likely outcome is death.

Individuals who have become addicted to alcohol, on the other hand, may not demonstrate any behavioral effects until their BAL has reached well over 0.10 (Lewis, 2015). An individual's reaction to consuming alcohol depends on several factors. Factors that reduce the impact of alcohol on a person include having a heavier weight and having tolerance. Factors that increase the impact of alcohol include gender (i.e., women are affected more than men), rapidity of consumption, and the amount of food in the stomach. Genetics may either increase or decrease the effect of alcohol on an individual (Rastegar & Fingerhood, 2016).

Withdrawal from higher doses may include tremors, seizures, and delirium tremens, and these symptoms may be life-threatening. Severe withdrawal is more likely to occur if an individual has elevated blood pressure and/or comorbid medical conditions. The most significant factor, however, is if the individual has a prior history of severe withdrawal (Rastegar & Fingerhood, 2016).

Not everyone who abuses alcohol or receives a diagnosis of an AUD at some point, however, necessarily needs to set abstinence as the goal. Based on extensive research, Miller and Munoz (2013) wrote the second edition of their book called *Controlling Your Drinking: Tools to Make Moderation Work for You*. Based on a database that included more than 8000 participants, Miller and Munoz reported that 15% of these individuals achieved stable moderation throughout the year (which meant staying under three drinks per day and averaging 10 standard drinks per week), another 23% achieved reasonably good moderation by reducing their drinking by two thirds or more (averaging about 14 drinks per week), 24% had been completely abstinent for at least a year, and 37% were still drinking.

Miller and Munoz (2013) stated that the most likely individuals to learn and maintain moderate drinking had certain qualities. These individuals

1. Were concerned about their drinking but alcohol had not yet caused major life disruption.
2. Recognized that they had problems with drinking, but they did not view themselves as individuals with AUD despite questioning this periodically.
3. Were less likely to have a family history of severe alcohol problems.
4. Had alcohol-related problems for less than 10 years.
5. Had never been physically addicted to alcohol. In other words, they could go for a week or two without consuming alcohol or taking tranquilizers, and they did not experience unpleasant physical symptoms of withdrawal.

More recently, Witkiewitz et al. (2017) analyzed data based on 3589 participants, which was integrated from three different sources. The individuals were receiving treatment for alcohol dependence. Regarding the sample, 73.0% were male, 82.0% were White, 41.7% were nonmarried, and the average age was 42.0. They identified seven patterns of drinking during treatment:

1. Persistent heavy drinking (18.7% sample).
2. Increasing heavy drinking (9.6%).
3. Heavy and low-risk drinking (6.7%).
4. Heavy drinking alternating with abstinence (7.9%).
5. Low-risk drinking (6.8%).
6. Increasing low-risk drinking (10.5%).
7. Abstinence (39.8%).

Witkiewitz et al. (2017) concluded

> Low-risk drinking is achievable for some individuals as they undergo treatment for alcohol dependence. Individuals with lower dependence severity, less baseline drinking, fewer negative mood symptoms and fewer heavy drinkers in their social networks have a higher probability of achieving low-risk drinking during treatment. (p. 2112)

In their sample, individuals in only two of the seven patterns of drinking appeared able to sustain a moderate drinking style: (a) those who were consistently low-risk drinkers during treatment and (b) those who were abstinent early in treatment who were at high probability of low-risk drinking during later weeks of treatment. In total, this amounted to 17% of their sample (Witkiewitz et al., 2017).

Many individuals who meet the criteria for an AUD never receive treatment because they report a desire to continue drinking (Mann, Aubin, & Witkiewitz, 2017). In a project called MATCH, DSM-IIIR criteria were used to ascertain individuals with AUD. For those people who were considered severely dependent (i.e., meaning they met more than six criteria out of nine), the likelihood of maintaining moderate drinking was lower than for those who drank moderately (defined as less than five standard drinks per occasion for men and less than four standard drinks per occasion for women; Mann et al., 2017). Together with the other research mentioned previously on reduced drinking, it appears that controlled drinking may be attainable for those who would be rated in *DSM-5* as having an AUD with low or moderate severity (Mann et al., 2017; Margolis & Zweben, 2011). In other words, the individuals who can achieve moderation would not be viewed as "hardcore" individuals with AUD by most people's definitions. Instead, they are in a lower-risk category throughout their pattern of drinking.

A common belief is that AUD is a disease that develops from excess consumption of alcohol and not from an innate quality of the individual (Gearhardt & Corbin, 2012). Nonetheless, the disease model of alcohol addiction has reduced stigma as it suggests that excessive alcohol intake is not a consequence emanating from lack of willpower or from an unwillingness to take responsibility for one's behavior (Gearhardt & Corbin, 2012).

Research suggests that there might be two types of individuals with AUD. A type I individual with AUD more likely develops alcohol problems later in life, whereas a type II individual with AUD develops AUD much sooner in life (late teens or early adulthood) and tends to be more violent (Brooks & McHenry, 2009).

Milkman and Sunderwirth (2010) described the stages of alcohol addiction according to Jellinek's research that was based on a questionnaire study of more than 2000 male individuals with AUD. Jellinek's stages are as follows:

1. Pre-alcoholic symptomatic phase. Individuals with AUD feel increasing tension about their drinking and drinking-related activities.
2. Prodromal phase. This phase begins with the onset of alcohol-related blackouts.
3. Crucial phase. During this stage, individuals experience a loss of control over their drinking. Even the taste of one drink seems to trigger full-blown drinking that continues until they feel too ill or too drunk to continue. The stage is also marked by increasing feelings of desperation and remorse and in some cases aggression.
4. Chronic phase. Prolonged periods of intoxication occur, often referred to as binges. Individuals with AUD often then drink with people who are "morally and intellectually inferior" (Milkman & Sunderwirth, 2010, p. 271) compared to their regular clique. Tolerance often diminishes in this phase, and fears and physical tremors that seem to come out of nowhere develop. Withdrawal is avoided by drinking continuously.

Timko, Moos, and Finney (2016) reviewed longitudinal research on the various courses of AUD and addiction. As the authors noted, many people will experiment with alcohol and other drugs and then quit. But for some, frequent use can lead to several different outcomes based on "onset, severity, and chronicity" (p. 54), and these are shaped by both personal and environmental influences. Seven long-term studies were based on community samples of men at follow-up periods ranging from 9 to 60 years. Remission rates varied from 27% to 69%. In a study of 420 middle-aged men in the Vietnam Era Twin Registry, four trajectories were noted in this sample as follows:

1. Severe chronic course (13% of the sample). Up to age 56, between 92% and 100% of these men were alcohol-addicted.
2. Severe nonchronic course (18%). These men were likely to have a diagnosis of alcohol dependence until age 41, after which the percentage declined to less than 10% to 20% between ages 51 and 56.
3. Young adult group (44%). Although these men were diagnosed as dependent at a young age, *none* received a diagnosis of alcohol dependence at age 42. Interestingly, however, nearly 10% had diagnoses later up to age 56.
4. Late-onset course (25%). The rate of alcohol dependence increased to age 41 in this group, after which it declined to about 30% by age 56.

These results were replicated in a later study of 323 non-twin Vietnam-era veterans (Timko et al., 2016). Because these samples were based on men only, it is unclear how transferable these findings are to women. Results from these and other studies led Timko et al. to conclude that AUDs often peak in late adolescence and then gradually decline into the mid-20s.

Regarding mostly men who have received treatment for AUDs, Finney and colleagues (as cited in Timko et al., 2016) summarized the results from 14 studies with follow-up periods of between 8 and 20 years. Remission rates were defined differently across studies, making the remission rates of between 21% and 83% difficult to interpret. Women were also underrepresented in these studies.

So, what happens when a person becomes addicted to alcohol? First, more alcohol is needed to achieve the desired pleasure. Over time, drinking becomes much less about attaining pleasure and more so about avoiding a "crappy" feeling. By this stage, experiencing ecstasy no longer occurs (Milkman & Sunderwirth, 2010).

The pleasure from drinking that once occurred invariably turns into pain in those who have become dependent (Maté, 2008). Addicted individuals do not always experience fallout from excessive drinking at first, but, over time, the consequences develop and expand in severity (Lewis, 2015). But the havoc doesn't end there. The people close to addicted individuals also experience consequences from their growing irrationality as well. The toll from alcohol addiction becomes severe as every life area becomes affected (e.g., personal, interpersonal, financial, occupational).

There are multiple pathways and causes of AUDs (King, Hasin, O'Connor, McNamara, & Cao, 2016; Krishnan, Sakharkar, Teppen, Berkel, & Pandey, 2014). Sagarkar and Sakharkar (2017) suggested that AUDs result from complex interactions of a person's genetics and environmental factors. The environmental factors included those at the societal level and personal levels (e.g., exposure to prenatal and postnatal stress, exposure to other drugs of abuse).

Cicchetti and Rogosch (2018) wrote that substance use disorders (SUDs), including AUD, are developmental disorders that typically emerge during adolescence or later in adulthood. They provided illustrations showing how child maltreatment contributes to problematic substance use during adolescence. A factor analysis focused on demographic, temperamental, and cognitive measures provided further support that early life adversity plays a prominent role in increasing the risk for SUDs and AUDs (Acheson, Vincent, Cohoon, & Lovallo, 2018). The types of adverse childhood experiences do not seem to matter much either, whether sexual abuse, physical abuse, or exposure to parental domestic violence (Fuller-Thomson, Roane, & Brennenstuhl, 2016).

Cicchetti and Rogosch (2018) argued that child maltreatment leads to the unsuccessful resolution of major developmental tasks with consequences that continue throughout the life span (i.e., childhood maltreatment leads to increased vulnerability). Children who are mistreated are more likely to externalize and internalize behavioral problems, including the development of AUD and other substance use and abuse in adolescence

(Cicchetti & Rogosch, 2018). Although traumatized children have an exaggerated reaction to uncertain threats, this trait continues in problematic drinkers when sober (Gorka et al., 2016). Higher levels of impulsivity and problems regulating emotions are also associated with childhood maltreatment (Wardell, Strang, & Hendershot, 2016). Whiteside and Lynam (as cited in Wardell et al., 2016) conducted a factor analysis on impulsivity measures and identified four components of impulsivity: (a) difficulty persevering and staying focused, (b) impaired ability to act without forethought, (c) sensation seeking for new and exciting experiences, and (d) negative urgency, which is acting hastily when feeling negative emotions. A fifth factor has been added more recently called positive urgency, which is acting rashly in response to positive emotions.

The most common and consistent predictor of alcohol problems is negative urgency (Wardell et al., 2016). Anthenien, Lembo, and Neighbors (2017) hypothesized that increased drinking occurs because of strong desires to increase positive feelings and diminish negative ones.

Genetic factors predicting AUD are present in at least half of those diagnosed with an AUD (Rastegar & Fingerhood, 2016). Psychiatric disorders such as antisocial personality disorder, affective disorders, and other SUDs may also contribute to the development of AUD (Rastegar & Fingerhood, 2016). An extensive and consistent literature has revealed that, the more parents drink, the more consumption occurs among their sons and daughters (Rossow, Keating, Felix, & McCambridge, 2016). Young adults who have a stronger drinking identity are more likely to abuse alcohol and subsequently experience drinking-related problems compared to those who do not strongly identify as drinkers (DiBello, Miller, Young, Neighbors, & Lindgren, 2018).

Kuntsche, Rossow, Engels, and Kuntsche (2016) argued that the age at first drink, a concept often considered in alcohol research and prevention, is not as important in understanding AUD. Instead, they stressed the importance of the progression that occurs from infrequent and lower-quantity drinking to more detrimental patterns of consumption.

Is light or moderate consumption of alcohol beneficial? There is little doubt that this will be up for furious debate over the ensuing months. Griswold, Fullman, Gakidou, and the GBD 2016 Alcohol Collaborators (2018) released a study that used 694 data sources of both individual and population-level alcohol consumption together with 592 prospective and retrospective studies on the risk of alcohol use. The data used was amalgamated from 1990 to 2016, and it encompassed 195 countries and territories. Risk estimates of Griswold et al. were based on a combined study population of 28 million individuals and 649,000 registered cases of respective outcomes. They concluded, "Our results show that the safest level of drinking is none" (Griswold et al., 2018, p. 12). In other words, the level of alcohol consumption that minimizes health risk is zero. Their findings contrast with those found in other studies. The amount of data used for this study, however, is like none other. Consequently, results noted in the next two paragraphs may soon be under heavy scrutiny.

Light to moderate amounts of alcohol have beneficial effects for some individuals, particularly concerning prevention of thrombosis of the heart (Gronbaek, 2009). Many studies have suggested that the benefit of reducing the risk of cardiovascular disease is in the range of 25%–30%, and two large American studies found that the protective effect is strongest among the elderly (Gronbaek, 2009). The benefits of alcohol have been described as following a J-shaped curve, meaning that up to one drink per day for women and up to two drinks per day for men can be beneficial, and, after that, the damaging effects of increased alcohol intake rise dramatically (Gronbaek, 2009). Low to moderate consumption can lower blood pressure and decrease the risk of diabetes. Most evidence suggests that the positive effects of drinking low to moderate amounts of wine or alcohol exceed the negative effects (Leighton Castro, Barriga, & Urquiaga, 1997). Moderate amounts of alcohol reduce the risk of kidney disease and possibly ischemic stroke (Rastegar & Fingerhood, 2016). Moderate drinking may also strengthen the immune system, thereby reducing the likelihood of catching a common cold (Barr, Helms, Grant, & Messaoudi, 2016).

Some alcohol intake does enhance emotional experiences and bonding with others (Sayette, Fairbairn, & Creswell, 2016). Consuming a moderate amount of alcohol after a mental stressor helps facilitate the recovery of the endocrine stress response by decreasing plasma ACTH and cortisol (Schrieks, Joosten, Klopping-Ketelaars, Witkamp, & Hendriks, 2016). In some families where there is AUD, alcohol helps the couple meld, avoid personal problems, and tolerate an otherwise dysfunctional marriage (Steinglass, as cited in Rosenberg, O'Connor, & Carnes, 2014).

The long-term effects of excessive alcohol consumption are covered later in the section called Physical Impacts (Long-Term Use). Here the short-term negative effects resulting from excessive drinking will be reviewed.

Alcohol is an interesting drug in that it first causes euphoria and disinhibition, qualities we often see with stimulants. At higher doses, however, it causes sedation as well as impairment in memory and coordination (Rastegar & Fingerhood, 2016). At still higher doses, overdose occurs, which is marked by drowsiness, cold and clammy skin, weak or rapid pulse, slurred speech, nausea, vomiting, and respiratory depression. If the dose is high enough, it may lead to sleep, coma, and death (Lewis, 2015; Rastegar & Fingerhood, 2016).

Some men become violent toward their partners or others following excessive drinking (Brem, Florimbio, Elmquist, Shorey, & Stuart, 2018; Subramani, Parrott, & Eckhardt, 2017). Others become increasingly suicidal. Sexual assaults are more likely to occur (Testa, Brown, & Wang, 2018; Wilhite, Mallard, & Fromme, 2018), and young women are more likely to engage in high-risk sexual activities such as not insisting that condoms be worn (Brown, Talley, Littlefield, & Gause, 2016).

Decision-making and other executive functions are affected, diminished working memory occurs, and discounting the negative consequences of excessive drinking increases in likelihood (Bo, Billieux, & Landro, 2016; Lechner, Day, Metrik, Leventhal, & Kahler, 2016; Spinola, Maisto, White, & Huddleson, 2017). For both perpetrators and victims, alcohol use is a risk factor for accidents of all kinds (Sethi et al., 2016; Storvoll, Moan, & Lund, 2016). In one study of 272 suicide attempters, every drink increased the risk of attempting suicide by 30% (Borges et al., 2017). Alcohol decreases inhibitions and increases impulsivity (Vera, Pilatti, Garimaldi, & Pautassi, 2018).

Experiencing hangovers is also a likely result of excessive drinking. Although many cures for hangovers have been proposed, none of them has sufficient evidence. Most recommended are simple analgesics (Rastegar & Fingerhood, 2016).

Approximately half of all Americans drink alcohol (Rastegar & Fingerhood, 2016). MacKillop et al. (2018) provided the prevalence rates for AUD symptoms from several large American studies. One of the largest of these studies was the NESARC. NESARC found that the lifetime prevalence for AUDs was just under 20%, and the 12-month prevalence rate was 8.5%. AUDs were most prevalent among men, Native Americans, White individuals, younger and unmarried adults, and those with lower income. An estimated 20.8 million Americans, ages 12 and older, have an SUD, with 15.7 million experiencing an AUD (Nehring, 2018). Approximately 8% of youth aged 12–20 engage in binge drinking (Morris, Winters, & Wagner, 2018). In both mental health settings and medical facilities, between 25% and 40% of clients are likely to have an AUD as an aspect of their presenting concerns, so counselors should always assess for overt or covert AUDs (McCrady, 2014; Nehring, 2018). In 2016, consumption of alcohol "was the leading risk factor globally" for ages 15–49 (Griswold et al., 2018, p. 1). For all age brackets combined, in 2018, it was the seventh leading risk factor worldwide (Griswold et al., 2018).

Diagnostic and Assessment Considerations

Chao and Ashraf (2016) suggested that the alcohol screening process can begin with the following question: "Do you sometimes drink beer, wine, or other alcoholic beverages?" (p. 44). If the client answers "No," screening can move on to other possible addictions. If the patient answers "Yes," an additional question could be "How many times in the past year have you had five (for men)/four (for women) or more drinks in 1 day?" (p. 44). Although the validity of self-reports regarding drug use is generally very good, those with severe mental illnesses (e.g., psychotic or bipolar disorders) can be especially inaccurate in providing self-report (Earleywine, 2016).

In *DSM-5*, the section that includes drugs is called Substance-Related and Addictive Disorders. *DSM-5* encompasses 10 separate classes of drugs.[2] The details of these are quite extensive, so the reader is referred to pages 481–585 of *DSM-5* (American Psychiatric Association [APA], 2013). SUDs are defined as "a cluster of cognitive, behavioral, and physiological symptoms indicating that the individual continues using the substance despite significant substance-related problems" (APA, 2013, p. 483).

Beresford, Wongngamnit, and Temple (2015) indicated that, in individuals with type I AUD (i.e., late-onset), it is typical that alcohol is the only drug used by the client. Conversely, in individuals with type II AUD (early-onset), polydrug dependence is more common.

Alcohol-related disorders are found on pages 490–503 of *DSM-5* (APA, 2013) and include AUD, alcohol intoxication, alcohol withdrawal, other alcohol-induced disorders, and unspecified alcohol-related disorder. As is true for other substance disorders contained in DSM, in contrast to DSM-4, a diagnosis distinguishing between *substance abuse* and *substance dependence* no longer occurs. Instead, a substance disorder is diagnosed by severity (i.e., by the number of diagnosable symptoms) as follows: (a) *mild*: 2 or 3, (b) *moderate*: 4 or 5, or (c) *severe*: 6 or more. *DSM-5* includes 11 listed criteria with two specifiers.

The overall diagnostic criteria for AUD is "A problematic pattern of alcohol use leading to clinically significant impairment or distress, as manifested by at least two of the following, occurring within a 12-month period" (APA, 2013, p. 490). The specific criteria include (a) loss of control over use, (b) continued desire or inability to reduce use, (c) much time is spent trying to obtain alcohol, use it, or recover from it, (d) cravings or a strong desire to use alcohol, (e) recurring use results in failure to fulfill obligations at work, school, or at home, (f) continuing use despite persistent or recurring problems socially and/or interpersonally, (g) social, occupational, or recreational activities are stopped or reduced because of use, (h) continuing use in situations where it is physically dangerous, (i) continuing use despite having a persistent or recurrent psychological or physical problem in which alcohol caused or exacerbated the condition, (j) tolerance, expressed as either a need for increasing amounts of alcohol or diminished effect from continuing use of the same amount of alcohol, and (k) withdrawal, expressed as the alcohol withdrawal diagnosis (begins on page 499) or alcohol or another related substance is taken to relieve or avoid symptoms of withdrawal. As noted earlier, there are two specifiers for this diagnosis. You can specify if the condition is an *early remission*, meaning between 3 months and 12 months, or in *sustained remission*, which requires 12 months or longer. You can also specify if the individual is *in a controlled environment*, meaning in a place where access to alcohol is difficult if not impossible. See Table 9.1 for DSM and ICD codes:

Slade et al. (2016) used DSM-IV and *DSM-5* definitions of AUD and compared these using 31,367 respondents to the World Health Organization's World Mental Health Survey Initiative. They found that the prevalence of *DSM-5* lifetime AUDs was a little lower than the prevalence using the DSM-IV definition. Interestingly, a large number of people were inconsistently identified across the two DSM classifications.

In the United Kingdom, Day and Jheeta (2016) stated that the UK Department of Health recommended that a diagnosis of dependence should be made only if an individual has an AUDIT score (this is a test that will be described in the section called Available Measures) of 20 or more and at least three of the following symptoms:

1. A strong desire or sense of compulsion to drink alcohol (an essential characteristic).
2. Difficulties in controlling drinking behavior in terms of onset, termination, or levels of consumption.
3. A physiological withdrawal state when drinking ceases or is reduced, evidenced by the characteristic alcohol withdrawal syndrome or use of a closely related substance with the intention of relieving or avoiding withdrawal symptoms, e.g., benzodiazepines (p. 112).
4. Evidence of tolerance, such that increased quantities of alcohol are required to achieve the effects initially produced by lesser amounts.
5. Progressive neglect of alternative pleasures or interests because of alcohol consumption or increased amounts of time necessary to obtain or drink alcohol or to recover from its effects.
6. Persisting with drinking alcohol despite clear evidence of overtly harmful consequences, such as liver damage, depressive mood, or impaired cognitive functioning (pp. 111–112).

[2]The 10 categories include alcohol; caffeine; cannabis; hallucinogens; inhalants; opioids; sedatives, hypnotics, and anxiolytics; stimulants; tobacco; and other (or unknown) substances.

TABLE 9.1 DSM and ICD Codes

DSM Code	Number of Symptoms Required	ICD-10	ICD-11
305.00	Mild: 2 or 3 symptoms	F10.10	Varies*
303.90	Moderate: 4 or 5 symptoms	F10.20	Varies*
303.90	Severe: 6 or more symptoms	F10.20	Varies*

*The alcohol codes in ICD-11 vary substantially as evident from the following (this is a partial list providing codes an addiction counselor will be most likely to use. The complete list that includes co-occurring medical conditions can be found at https://icd.who.int/ct11_2018/icd11_mms/en/release#/):

#	Specific Entity	Specific ICD-11 CODE
1	Alcohol dependence, unspecified (includes alcoholism)	6C40.2Z
2	Dementia due to use of alcohol	6D84.0
3	Alcohol-induced delirium	6C40.5
4	Alcohol-induced psychotic disorder, unspecified	6C40.6Z
5	Harmful pattern of use of alcohol, unspecified	6C40.1Z
6	Alcohol intoxication	6C40.3
7	Alcohol withdrawal, unspecified	6C40.4Z
8	Alcohol-induced psychotic disorder with hallucinations	6C40.60
9	Fetal alcohol syndrome	LD2F.00
10	Harmful effects of or exposure to noxious substances, chiefly nonmedicinal as to source, not elsewhere classified (includes not elsewhere classified)	NE61
11	Special screening examination for mental or behavioral disorders (includes screening for alcoholism)	QA0A.3
12	Alcohol rehabilitation	QB95.2
13	Family history of mental or behavioral disorder (includes alcoholism in family)	QC65
14	Nonalcoholic steatohepatitis	DB92.1
15	Other alcohol-induced disorders	6C40.7
	Alcohol-induced mood disorder	6C40.70
	Alcohol-induced anxiety disorder	6C40.71
16	Harmful pattern of use of alcohol, continuous	6C40.11
17	Alcohol withdrawal, uncomplicated	6C40.40
18	Alcohol withdrawal with seizures	6C40.42
19	Disorders due to use of alcohol, unspecified	6C40.Z
20	Intentional self-harm by exposure to or harmful effects of alcohol	PD00
21	Exposure to or harmful effects of undetermined intent of alcohol	PH50
22	Contact with health services for alcohol use counseling or surveillance	QA11
23	Personal history of mental or behavioral disorder (includes history of alcohol abuse)	QC46
24	Hazardous alcohol use	QE10
25	Alcohol-induced psychotic disorder with delusion	6C40.61

SUDs are often undetected or misdiagnosed, and this occurs most commonly when the client is "employed, married, white, insured, or female" (Margolis & Zweben, 2011, p. 59). Nehring (2018) suggested that a score of 2 or higher on the four-item CAGE (also found under Available Measures) questionnaire is indicative of problematic drinking. Lewis (2015) reminded the reader that evaluating an SUD is an ongoing process as new information constantly arises. The counselor should also ask about family history regarding alcohol and other SUDs in addition to personal history and family history regarding psychiatric disorders (Nehring, 2018). Some drugs such as cocaine may produce an agitated depression if the addicted individual stops using abruptly, and, for some, this may precipitate suicidality. Consequently, it is important to assess for suicidal thoughts, gestures, and previous attempts.

Margolis and Zweben (2011) recommended that clients be assessed regarding the degree to which they experience impaired functioning in work, family, peers, social/recreational activities, education, legal issues, physical health concerns, and psychological issues (note that these areas and others are contained in the Personal Functioning Questionnaire; the questionnaire, the manual, and the pie chart are available as free downloads from https://kevinalderson.ca/). Furthermore, it is important to ask questions about the types and amounts of drugs used and the frequency of use. Medical detoxification is based on both the types of drugs and the amount and frequency of use (Margolis & Zweben, 2011). The following can be used as a guide:

1. Drugs that often require medical detoxification. Withdrawal from alcohol and other depressants (e.g., barbiturates and benzodiazepines) can be fatal. The benzodiazepines are slow-acting drugs, and withdrawal almost always requires medical detoxification as seizures can occur even 2 weeks after stopping use.
2. Drugs that can be stopped abruptly. These include opioids (except when other medical conditions worsen with stress), cocaine, and crack. Nonetheless, stopping these drugs creates an intense craving and physical discomfort. Medically supervised residential care is still recommended (Margolis & Zweben, 2011).

Differential Diagnosis

DSM-5 includes a section on page 496 regarding differential diagnosis. The book indicates that the symptoms of AUD are similar to those seen in individuals addicted to sedatives, hypnotics, or anxiolytics. Furthermore, individuals with antisocial personality and preexisting conduct disorder also have AUD in most cases.

Wennberg, Bergman, and Berglund (2014) noted that alcohol problems are not a homogeneous syndrome. Their instrument, called the AVI-R2, is intended to help provide a differentiated diagnosis of alcohol problems.

Individuals who abuse alcohol often experience symptoms of anxiety and depression. Liappas, Paparrigopoulos, Tzavellas, and Christodoulou (2002) studied 28 individuals with AUD in Greece. They found that, following detoxification, all measures of psychopathology were substantially reduced. Consequently, it is important for counselors to distinguish between AUD and the psychological or psychiatric symptoms that it and other drugs may be creating within clients.

Comorbidity and Co-Addictions

Co-occurring disorders are the norm rather than the exception in individuals with an SUD including alcohol, and the relationship is bidirectional. Those with an SUD are likely to have a psychiatric disorder, and those with psychiatric disorders are likely to abuse substances (Margolis & Zweben, 2011). *DSM-5* indicated that individuals with bipolar disorders, schizophrenia, or antisocial personality disorder have a markedly increased rate of AUD. Several anxiety and depressive disorders are also related to AUDs. AUD is comorbid with nicotine addiction and addiction to various other drugs (Milkman & Sunderwirth, 2010; Verplaetse & McKee, 2017). Furthermore, AUDs co-occur with gambling and other behavioral addictions (Maté, 2008). Individuals with posttraumatic stress disorder (PTSD) are more likely to become dependent on alcohol (Dworkin, Wanklyn, Stasiewicz, & Coffey, 2018). Individuals with ADHD or borderline personality disorder are more likely to develop an AUD (Margolis & Zweben, 2011).

Interaction effects are also important to note with AUDs. For example, mixing alcohol with barbiturates has an interaction effect that is several times stronger than either drug used alone at the same dosage, and this can be lethal (Brooks & McHenry, 2009). Most past-year drinkers consume only alcohol. Those who use other drugs are more likely to be male, younger, never or previously married, with lower income and education (Saha et al., 2018).

Available Measures

Hagman (2017) created a 13-item questionnaire that has demonstrated reliability and validity. It is called the Brief 13-Item *DSM-5* Assessment (found in the Appendix of his article).

Connors, DiClemente, Velasquez, and Donovan (2013) suggested several websites where counselors can obtain many SUD questionnaires. Sites included the HABITS Lab at the University of Maryland, Baltimore County (https://habitslab.umbc.edu/); the Center on Alcoholism, Substance Abuse, and Addictions at the University of New Mexico (casaa.unm.edu); the Substance Use Screening and Assessment Instruments Database at the Alcohol and Drug Abuse Institute at the University of Washington (lib.adai.washington.edu/instruments); and the Healthy Lifestyles Guided Self-Change Program at Nova Southeastern Universities (NSU) Psychology Services Center (http://www.nova.edu/gsc/index.html). NIAAA also provides a free download of its publication called *Assessing Alcohol Problems: A Guide for Clinicians and Researchers* (2nd ed.; from https://pubs.niaaa.nih.gov/publications/AssessingAlcohol/index.htm).

National Institute on Drug Abuse (NIDA) provides several screening instruments, and they are available for free at https://www.drugabuse.gov/nidamed-medical-health-professionals/tool-resources-your-practice/additional-screening-resources

American Society of Addiction Medicine (ASAM) also provides several screening instruments. These are available at https://www.asam.org/education/live-online-cme/fundamentals-of-addiction-medicine/additional-resources/screening-assessment-for-substance-use-disorders/screening-assessment-tools

Chao and Ashraf (2016) reviewed several instruments including the CAGE, Alcohol Use Disorders Identification Test (AUDIT), and SMAST (Short Michigan Alcoholism Screening Test). They stated that the U.S. Preventive Services Task Force recommended that all clients who are 18 years or older be screened for AUD and that they recommended the use of the CAGE. If the CAGE score is 2 or higher, it should be followed by the AUDIT. The following are a few selected questionnaires (note that there are many available):

1. CAGE Questionnaire (Ewing, 1984). The CAGE comprises only four questions, and it is a popular screening instrument for alcohol use problems. The four questions are as follows:
   A. Have you ever felt a need to **C**ut down on your drinking? (C)
   B. Have people **A**nnoyed you by criticizing your drinking? (A)
   C. Have you ever felt bad or **G**uilty about your drinking? (G)
   D. Have you ever had a drink first thing in the morning to steady your nerves to get rid of a hangover (**E**ye-opener)? (E)

   A self-scoring version is available (unnecessary, however, as each "Yes" scores as 1 point) from https://patient.info/doctor/CAGE-Questionnaire and other sources.

2. TWEAK (Russell et al., 1994). Rastegar and Fingerhood (2016) suggested that the TWEAK questionnaire might be more useful for women than the CAGE questionnaire. TWEAK is also an acronym, and the questions are as follows:
   A. (**T** = Tolerance). How many drinks can you hold? OR How many drinks do you need to feel high?
   B. (**W** = Worried). Have close friends or relatives worried or complained about your drinking in the past year?
   C. (**E** = Eye-openers). Do you sometimes take a drink in the morning when you first get up?
   D. (**A** = Amnesia/blackouts). Has a friend or family member ever told you about things you said or did while you were drinking that you could not remember?
   E. (**K**[C] = Cut Down). Do you sometimes feel the need to cut down on your drinking?

   The test is scored on a 7-point scale. Questions 1 and 2 are scored either 1 or 2. For question 1, a tolerance-hold question scores 2 points if the respondent can hold 6 or more drinks. The tolerance-high question scores 2 points if three or more drinks are needed to feel high. For question 2, the respondent receives 2 points for a "yes" answer. A total score of 2 or higher indicates that clients are likely to be risk drinkers. A score of 3 or higher identifies harmful drinking or AUD (adapted from Rastegar & Fingerhood, 2016, p. 483).

3. CRAFFT. The CRAFFT can be used with children and teenagers under the age of 21. It is recommended by the American Academy of Pediatrics Committee on Substance Abuse for use with adolescents. Two or more positive items suggest the need for further assessment. Here are the six questions:
   A. Have you ever ridden in a CAR driven by someone (including yourself) who was "high" or had been using alcohol or drugs? (C)
   B. Do you ever use alcohol or drugs to RELAX, feel better about yourself, or fit in? (R)
   C. Do you ever use alcohol/drugs while you are by yourself, ALONE? (A)
   D. Do you ever FORGET things you did while using alcohol or drugs? (F)
   E. Do your family or FRIENDS ever tell you that you should cut down on your drinking or drug use? (F)
   F. Have you gotten into TROUBLE while you were using alcohol or drugs? (T)

4. Alcohol Use Disorders Identification Test (AUDIT). This is a 10-item paper-and-pencil test that was developed by the World Health Organization. Hagman (2016) found that it offered reasonable diagnostic proficiency when a score of greater than 8 and greater than 9 was used for females and males in college, respectively. A self-scoring version of the instrument is available from https://patient.info/doctor/alcohol-use-disorders-identification-test-audit.

5. Substance Abuse Subtle Screening Inventory (SASSI). According to its website (https://www.sassi.com/), the SASSI is a brief psychological questionnaire, available in both adult and adolescent versions, that can identify people with an SUD with a high degree of accuracy. There is a fee for this instrument. When I attended an addictions session at the American Counseling Association conference in 2017, several participants said that they used this questionnaire. Its reported empirically tested accuracy is between 93% and 94% (according to https://pubs.niaaa.nih.gov/publications/AssessingAlcohol/InstrumentPDFs/66_SASSI.pdf).

6. Alcohol Use Inventory (AUI; Horn, Wanberg, & Foster, 1986). The AUI is a 228-item multiple-choice questionnaire. It is easy to administer and score. Scores are compared to a clinical sample of people hospitalized for severe alcohol dependency.

7. Addiction Severity Index (ASI; McLellan, Luborsky, Woody, & O'Brien, 1980). The ASI is a commonly used semistructured interview that addresses seven potential problem areas in substance-abusing patients. It takes about 1 hour with a skilled interviewer. The ASI is currently in its sixth version (ASI-6), and the ASI-MV (ASI-Multimedia Version) is the electronic version of it. The advantage of the ASI-MV is that it is administered by the client, and it can be completed in a counseling setting or remotely, whereas the paper-and-pencil versions require a trained interviewer to administer (see https://www.hazelden.org/web/public/asimv_main.page for details). Hazelden Publishing also markets the Behavioral Health Index-Multimedia Version (BHI-MV), which overviews client functioning in several key life areas. Hazelden can be contacted by calling 800-328-9000. Denis, Cacciola, and Alterman (2013) compared ASI-6 with ASI-5 and found ASI-6 to cover more comprehensive content in its scales.

ASI-5 is available for free from http://adai.washington.edu/instruments/pdf/Addiction_Severity_Index_Baseline_Followup_4.pdf.

A free treatment planning manual based on this index is available from http://jpwpkl.moe.gov.my/download/phocadownload/terkini/2014/sppk/ucd/BahanLDPCOMBATDAPS/asi%20manual.pdf.

8. Michigan Alcoholism Screening Test (MAST; Selzer, 1971). The original test was 25 items. There are seven shorter versions available. The MAST is a commonly used self-report screening instrument and is ranked as the 41st most frequently used assessment instrument by professional counselors (Minnich, Erford, Bardhoshi, & Atalay, 2018). In their review of the instrument, Minnich et al. (2018) concluded that the MAST has good psychometric properties but cautioned that the cutoff score of 5 tends to overidentify men and underidentify women with AUDs. A revised, 22-item version is available with online scoring from both https://counsellingresource.com/quizzes/drug-testing/alcohol-mast/ and https://www.the-alcoholism-guide.org/michigan-alcoholism-screening-test.html.

9. Alcohol Dependence Scale (ADS). The ADS is a 25-item test that is widely used in both research and in practice. Although the printed instructions suggest using the ADS over the past 12-month period, one can alter the instructions to use it as an outcome measure at selected intervals following treatment. Studies have found the ADS to be both reliable and valid. The test is available from http://www.emcdda.europa.eu/attachements.cfm/att_4075_EN_tads.pdf. More information about the test is available from https://pubs.niaaa.nih.gov/publications/AssessingAlcohol/InstrumentPDFs/10_ADS.pdf.

HOW LIKELY IS YOUR CLIENT TO BE SUCCESSFUL AT ACHIEVING MODERATE DRINKING?

Most drinkers would prefer to learn to moderate their drinking instead of needing to become forever abstinent. In their book, *Controlling Your Drinking*, Miller and Munoz (2013) followed up drinkers over a period of up to 8 years, comparing those who had maintained moderate drinking with those who became abstinent. They used the MAST and the ADS as measurements. Here is what they found (these two tables can be used to determine the likelihood that a drinker can successfully achieve moderation):

MAST SCORES AND MODERATION

People who scored in this range on the MAST . . .	Showed these outcomes with regard to abstinence and moderation
Low 0–10	These people were the most likely to moderate their drinking with few or no problems. They were less likely to stop drinking altogether, although one in six did ultimately decide to quit.
Medium 11–18	People in this group were about equally likely to abstain or to attain moderate and problem-free drinking. Others in this group reduced their drinking substantially but continued to experience some problems.
High 19–28	This group was most likely to become completely abstinent. Only one in 12 maintained moderate and problem-free drinking. Most who overcame their drinking problems did so by stopping completely.
Very high 29 or higher	These people had the most difficulty. Everyone in this group who overcame their drinking problems did so by abstaining. In our studies, no one with a score this high has ever succeeded in maintaining problem-free moderation.

ADS SCORES AND MODERATION

People who scored in this range on the ADS . . .	Showed these outcomes with regard to abstinence and moderation
Low 0–14	These people were the most likely to moderate their drinking with few or no problems. They were less likely to stop drinking altogether, although one in 12 did ultimately decide to quit.

People who scored in this range on the ADS . . .	Showed these outcomes with regard to abstinence and moderation
Medium 15–20	People in this group were about equally likely to abstain or to attain moderate and problem-free drinking. Others reduced their drinking substantially but continued to experience some problems.
High 21–27	People in this group were about twice as likely to abstain as to maintain problem-free moderation. Only one in five maintained moderate and problem-free drinking.
Very high 28 or higher	Everyone in this group who overcame their drinking problems did so by abstaining. In our studies, no one with a score this high ever succeeded in maintaining problem-free moderation.

Source: From Miller, W. R., & Munoz, R. F. (2013). *Controlling your drinking, second edition: Tools to make moderation work for you* (2nd ed.). New York, NY: Guilford Press. Both charts used with permission.

Clinical Interview Questions

Edelman, Oldfield, and Tetrault (2018) noted that NIAAA recommended that practitioners screen for unhealthy alcohol use with just one question: "How many times in the past year have you had five or more drinks in a day (for men) or four or more drinks in a day (for women)?" (the NIAAA screening guide is available from https://pubs.niaaa.nih.gov/publications/Practitioner/PocketGuide/pocket.pdf). Asking the four questions of the CAGE for men or the TWEAK for women (see the previous section) is also a great starting place to assess for a possible AUD. The NIAAA (2003) recommended that counselors ask three, four, five, or six questions (each question adds a little more information) regarding drinking. Their question sets act as a flowchart. Please visit https://www.niaaa.nih.gov/research/guidelines-and-resources/recommended-alcohol-questions for details.

NIAAA (2011) recommended a two-question screening process to identify adolescents at risk for AUD. Their intervention and practitioner's guide is available at no cost (see reference at the end of the chapter). The question format changes somewhat depending on the age of the child. "Research indicates that the two age-specific screening questions (about friends' and patient's drinking) are powerful predictors of current and future alcohol problems in youth" (NIAAA, 2011, p. 8).

Brooks and McHenry (2009, beginning on p. 144) suggested that counselors should ask themselves the following questions to help ascertain important aspects of addiction:

1. Where is the addiction in the family?
2. Who is most affected by the addiction?
3. Is it really addiction?
4. In what phase is the drinking/drugging behavior?
5. What phase is the family in?
6. What phase of the life cycle is the individual with AUD in?
7. What does the family think about the addiction?
8. What solutions have the family already attempted?
9. What does the secrecy map look like?
10. What is the family history of addiction?
11. What patterns of over- and under-responsibility exist?
12. How is the power structure perceived in the family?

Generic Names and Street "Lingo"

Other names for alcohol include ethyl alcohol, ethanol, hard alcohol, liquor, spirits, intoxicants, adult beverage, booze, hooch, gut rot, rotgut, moonshine, the bottle, juice, sauce, liquid courage, hard stuff, brew, brewski, draft, suds, sixer, cold one, liquid bread, oats soda, tummy buster, 12-ounce curl, giggle juice, giggle water, vino, and redneck wine. Several other names are arguably less common.

Alcohol addiction is most commonly referred to as *alcoholism*. Other names for it include alcohol dependence and AUD. Throughout this chapter, AUD will be used in most instances because it is the diagnostic term used in *DSM-5*.

Neuroscience

Harris and Koob (2017) noted in their editorial that, over the past few years, a profound amount of research has occurred regarding AUD. Most notably, this is being evidenced in the integration of human research and neuroscience in the three areas of binging/intoxication, withdrawal and negative affect and preoccupation/anticipation.

Research suggests that between 48% and 66% of alcohol dependence is heritable (Mistral, 2016b). However, identifying the precise neurobiological mechanisms or the individual gene contributions underlying addictive disorders has remained unsuccessful (Mistral, 2016b; Sachs & Dodson, 2017). What is clear is that people do not directly inherit AUD (Maté, 2008).

Alcohol negatively affects nearly every human organ system, and its effects on the brain are profound (Merlo, 2012). Heilig (2015) stated that addiction is "a malfunction of some of the most fundamental brain circuits that make us tick" (p. 8). Substance-related deficits occur in frontal lobe functioning, which in turn create problems with impulse control, delay of gratification, memory, decision-making/reasoning, and planning. Together, these affect the ability to evaluate and cope with stressors rationally. Behavior is also impacted (Merlo, 2012).

Among the addictive drugs, alcohol is unique in that it does not bind with a high degree of affinity to any specific receptor or transporter (in contrast to drugs like opioids or stimulants). This explains why brain levels of alcohol need to be much higher than other addictive drugs to become psychoactive (Heilig & Spanagel, 2015).

Activation of the dopamine system occurs through all kinds of reinforcers in both animals and humans. In humans, for example, research has demonstrated that social attractiveness, sex, orgasm, and classical music in musicians can increase activity in the nucleus accumbens (Spanagel, Zink, & Sommer, 2013). Referring to alcohol, both the opioid and dopamine systems are affected, including the brain systems associated with dopamine release (e.g., ventral striatum, orbitofrontal cortex) (Gearhardt & Corbin, 2012).

Alcohol cannot activate dopamine transmission nearly to the same extent as cocaine or amphetamine. At the same time, alcohol-induced activation of the nucleus accumbens becomes lower as alcohol problems worsen. Unsurprisingly, individuals with AUD report that the high they used to receive from alcohol diminishes through the course of their addiction (Heilig, 2015).

Besides dopamine, alcohol affects the endorphin and the endocannabinoid systems (Heilig & Spanagel, 2015). The acute effects of alcohol result from its action on glutamatergic, GABAergic, and glycine-binding receptors in the brain. The effect of alcohol on these receptors creates central nervous system suppression. The rewarding properties of alcohol are believed to result from the release of endogenous opioids (Heilig & Spanagel, 2015).

The effect of alcohol varies among individuals. For example, genetic polymorphisms can lead to altered enzyme activity, which in turn leads to the slow elimination of acetaldehyde, which is toxic. About 10% of the Japanese population cannot tolerate alcohol, so, naturally, they are almost never diagnosed with alcohol addiction. The allele responsible for this is carried by around 50% of East Asian populations but is practically absent in White individuals (Spanagel et al., 2013).

AUD occurs because of complex interactions between an individual's genetic makeup and environmental interactions (Sagarkar & Sakharkar, 2017). As AUD develops, stress-related systems become dysregulated. Endocrine stress responses occur as the hypothalamus-pituitary-adrenocortical axis becomes involved. Several neurobiological systems become affected by alcohol (Heilig & Spanagel, 2015). Esel and Dinc (2017) concluded that the neurobiological changes that occur from occasional alcohol use to AUD result from the (a) downregulation of both the dopamine and gamma-aminobutyric acid systems, (2) upregulation of the glutamine system permanently, and (c) dysregulation of the stress systems (i.e., serotonin and corticotropin-releasing hormone). Norepinephrine has also been studied over the past few decades regarding its role in the development of AUD (Haass-Koffler, Swift, & Leggio, 2018).

Once AUD has developed, there is evidence that widespread morphological gray matter abnormalities occur, particularly in the prefrontal cortex (Gropper et al., 2016; Zhu et al., 2018). Alcohol dependence is also associated with "aberrant regional activities in multiple brain areas" (Tu, Wang, Liu, & Zheng, 2018, p. 847). Repetitive binge drinking might also produce long-lasting changes in neuroplasticity, which in turn contribute to the development of alcohol dependence (Loheswaran et al., 2016).

Physical Impacts (Long-Term Use)

"The clinical picture of alcohol is different for everyone, but there are consistent themes based on the pathophysiology of alcohol" (Johnson & Marzani-Nissen, 2012, p. 381). Many organ systems of the body may (but not necessarily) be affected by alcohol consumption. Some of the diseases that may result include anemia, gastritis, ulcers, and gastroesophageal reflux disease (GRD). Having a long history of GRD can lead to Barrett's esophagus, which is a well-known precursor lesion for esophageal cancer. Heavy drinking can also lead to esophageal tears, which can be life-threatening medical emergencies (Johnson & Marzani-Nissen, 2012).

AUD can also lead to pancreatitis, pancreatic cancer, and type II diabetes (in rare instances, type I diabetes). Head, neck, and liver cancers are associated with chronic and excessive alcohol use. Alcohol-related fatty liver disease and obesity are associated with advancement to cirrhosis. In the United States, approximately 33% of cases of cirrhosis are attributable to alcohol consumption. Both Alzheimer's or multi-infarct dementia can be caused or worsened by alcohol. Heavy drinking can lead to hypertension, cardiac arrhythmias, dilated cardiomyopathy, and stroke (Johnson & Marzani-Nissen, 2012; Rastegar & Fingerhood, 2016).

Alcohol suppresses the immune system, so heavy use of alcohol leads to increased likelihood of developing bacterial pneumonia, pulmonary tuberculosis, and HIV infection (Johnson & Marzani-Nissen, 2012; O'Halloran et al., 2016; Oldenburg et al., 2016). Alcoholic hepatitis (AH) is a major cause of hospitalization and mortality. Complications associated with AH have worsened in the United States, and drug therapy remains suboptimal (Nguyen, DeShazo, Thacker, Puri, & Sanyal, 2016).

Gout is associated with chronic excessive alcohol consumption (Johnson & Marzani-Nissen, 2012). Sleep problems are a common complaint of individuals with AUD (Chakravorty, Chaudhary, & Brower, 2016).

Brain damage can occur from long-term excessive consumption of alcohol (Lewis, 2015). Wernicke encephalopathy (WE) is caused by thiamine (vitamin B1) deficiency and is usually diagnosed by a cluster of three symptoms: gait ataxia, characteristic eye motions called *oculomotor abnormalities*, and global confusion. WE is not just found in individuals with AUD but also in those who are malnourished or are undergoing renal dialysis (Johnson & Marzani-Nissen, 2012). Korsakoff's syndrome (KS) is believed to be a residual disorder that develops in individuals who have WE. Individuals with KS experience "anterograde and retrograde amnesia, executive dysfunction, confabulation, apathy, as well as affective and social-cognitive impairments" (Arts, Walvoort, & Kessels, 2017, p. 2875). In their critical review, Arts et al. (2017) concluded that there is no convincing evidence that there is a progression from WE to KS, however. Nonetheless, those with WE tend to acquire KS (Johnson & Marzani-Nissen, 2012).

Women are at higher risk of developing some physical disorders from chronic excessive alcohol consumption. This includes liver disease, heart disease, muscle disease, brain damage, and mortality (Agabio, Campesi, Pisanu, Gessa, & Franconi, 2016).

Of all the drugs that are abused by women, alcohol is the most harmful to the fetus (Rastegar & Fingerhood, 2016). Pregnant women who drink might deliver babies who have fetal alcohol spectrum disorder, which includes fetal alcohol syndrome (Johnson & Marzani-Nissen, 2012). Several American medical groups (e.g., Centers for Disease Control and Prevention, U.S. Surgeon

General) have issued statements that no amount of alcohol can be safely consumed during pregnancy (Chao & Ashraf, 2016). Prenatal exposure to alcohol is the leading cause of intellectual disability in the United States (Chao & Ashraf, 2016).

Males with AUD are much more likely to experience permanent impotence compared with males who do not have AUD (O'Farrell, Kleinke, & Cutter, 1998). Men who drink are also more likely than women to develop atrial fibrillation (Rastegar & Fingerhood, 2016).

Besides the increased rate of the previous diseases that occur in individuals with chronic AUD, there is, of course, an increased likelihood of mortality from vehicular accidents, self-harm, and violence (Agardh et al., 2016; Rastegar & Fingerhood, 2016). Of those between ages 15 and 24, 46% of deaths are caused by alcohol-related accidents (Milkman & Sunderwirth, 2010). Overall, alcohol causes a higher death rate than all illegal drugs combined in the United States (Milkman & Sunderwirth, 2010).

Withdrawal symptoms from any drug, including alcohol, tend to be a mirror image of the acute effects caused by that drug. A hangover, for example, often results in anxiety, shakiness, insomnia, and other symptoms caused by the nervous system re-creating homeostasis following consumption of a depressant (Heilig, 2015).

Withdrawal from alcohol *dependence*, however, is a whole different matter and needs to be medically monitored. Chao and Ashraf (2016) included directives on how to recognize withdrawal. They wrote that alcohol withdrawal begins 6–48 hours after the last drink, generally peaking after 24 hours. Withdrawal symptoms include tremulousness, profuse sweating, insomnia, increased blood pressure and heart rate, nausea/vomiting, loss of appetite, headache, anxiety, and irritability. Chao and Ashraf suggested using the Clinical Institute Withdrawal Assessment for Alcohol Scale, Revised (CIWA-Ar; Sullivan, Sykora, Schneiderman, Naranjo, & Sellers, 1989). The scale is available for free and scored online at https://www.merckmanuals.com/medical-calculators/CIWA.htm.

Seizures occur in about 3% of those who are physically dependent on alcohol, occurring 12–48 hours following the last drink. Delirium tremens (DTs) occur in about 5% of physically dependent individuals, occurring within 48–72 hours after the last drink (Chao & Ashraf, 2016). DTs are characterized by delirium, tremors, autonomic instability (e.g., fever, tachycardia, high blood pressure), agitation or stupor, and tactile and/or visual hallucinations. Without treatment, DTs incur about a 20% mortality rate (Chao & Ashraf, 2016). The treatment of choice for DTs are benzodiazepines administered at very high doses to achieve sedation (Rastegar & Fingerhood, 2016).

The HAMS Harm Reduction Network (2015) estimated the likelihood of an individual with AUD going through life-threatening withdrawal. They wrote that an individual will not go through withdrawal if they have never drunk for 2 days in a row. They estimated that a woman of average weight having six standard drinks a day every day for a month would have a 50-50 chance of experiencing minor withdrawal that will not likely be life-threatening (the equivalent for men of average weight will be eight standard drinks a day for a month). If the same woman had been drinking 11 standard drinks a day for a month, the risk increases to 50-50 for going through major life-threatening withdrawal (the equivalent for men of average weight will be 13 standard drinks a day for a month). There remains little chance of withdrawal for anyone who has been drinking less than 3 days in a row. Although the chart available at http://hams.cc/odds/ is a helpful indicator, the author makes clear that these are ballpark guesstimates as the type of experiments needed to test this empirically would not pass ethics review boards.

Mental, Emotional, and Spiritual Impacts

One of the most important traits linked to alcohol-related problems/dependence is negative urgency, which is the impulsive risk-taking that occurs during times of experiencing extremely negative emotional states (VanderVeen et al., 2016). Alcohol use itself is associated with increases in impulsivity (Trull, Wycoff, Lane, Carpenter, & Brown, 2016). A vicious cycle is further perpetuated by the fact that alcohol can create negative emotional states, thus leading to further alcohol consumption.

As Milkman and Sunderwirth (2010) explained, beneath the surface of an individual with chronic AUD who might appear to be "happy-go-lucky" is a person who suffers from deep feelings of worthlessness and despair. Maté (2008) noted that individuals with all addictions (substances and behavioral) experience cravings and shame. Drinking lowers inhibitions, which means that the perception of what constitutes appropriate behavior is affected. Inappropriate behaviors (verbal and physical) engaged in while intoxicated can lead to further shame, guilt, and worry.

When individuals with AUD are intoxicated, they may switch between bouts of crying and hysteria to anger, followed by verbal or physical abuse. Their moods are highly erratic and often unpredictable. When they try to stop drinking, they feel anxious and depressed. Alcohol can exacerbate existing problems with depression, irritability, and anxiety/uncontrollable worry (Pape & Norstrom, 2016). Alcohol problems are also associated with suicidal ideation, and this link has been recently replicated in Alaskan undergraduates (DeCou & Skewes, 2016).

Low sodium levels in blood plasma is a common electrolyte disturbance that occurs in individuals with AUD. Michal et al. (2016) found that individuals with AUD who have the lowest concentration of sodium in their blood also experienced the worst mental health, impulsivity, and neuroticism compared to those with less-severe electrolyte imbalance.

Following withdrawal from alcohol, negative affects often continue for several weeks. Fatigue and tension often persist for up to 5 weeks, anxiety up to 9 months, and, in approximately 20%–25% of individuals with AUD, anxiety and depression continue for up to 2 years postwithdrawal (Mason & Higley, 2012).

Nakash, Nagar, Barker, and Lotan (2016) conducted a study on 110 young men who identified as either Orthodox or secular Jews. The Orthodox participants drank less alcohol and reported fewer alcohol cravings compared to the secular group. They also found that religion provided a sense of meaning, which the authors concluded was a protective factor against alcohol craving. Furthermore, a factor associated with a religious lifestyle (i.e., low exposure to mass media) was also concluded to serve as a protective factor for alcohol use and craving.

Ransome and Gilman (2016) analyzed data from Wave 2 of the NESARC (N = 26,784) and concluded that attending religious services, religiosity, and spirituality acted as protective factors against developing AUDs. Chartier et al. (2016) arrived at similar conclusions in their study of African American, European American, and Hispanic American adults (N = 7716; 53% female). Religious involvement was negatively associated with the number of lifetime alcohol addiction symptoms and the maximum number of drinks consumed.

Psychosocial Impacts (Relationships, Career/Work, Legal, Financial)

"Alcoholism is a chronic disease that negatively affects family relationships" (de Oliveira Mangueira & de Oliveira Lopes, 2016, p. 2401). For example, rates of separation and divorce are up to seven times higher than the general population. Spousal violence occurs at a higher rate for both men and women with AUDs. The children and spouses of individuals with AUD are more likely to experience emotional and behavioral problems (McCrady, 2014). The individual with AUD in the family is often disrespected and seen as untrustworthy, unreliable, and unworthy. Family members may be forced to "tiptoe" around the house, afraid of unintentionally provoking the individual with AUD.

Some individuals with AUD will drink when they're alone or in secret. This may include hiding alcohol in unusual places with the hope that others will not find their stash. The individual with AUD may also begin losing interest in other activities and either become socially isolated or begin to pull back from others who do not drink. Either way, AUD creates substantial social consequences.

AUDs can impact many areas of peoples' lives such as their socioeconomic status and employment (Nehring, 2018). Besides the cost to the individuals with AUD themselves, the cost to society is substantial in areas, including "violence, criminality, accidents, workplace, education, early exposure, social benefits, early retirement, and mortality" (Moraes & Becker, 2017, p. 393).

Individuals with AUD may experience problems with the legal system due to driving under the influence (DUI), involvement with the child welfare system, drug-related charges, and alcohol-related offenses such as assault (McCrady, 2014). Voas, Tippetts, Bergen, Grosz, and Marques (2016) looked at that those DUI offenders who had ignition interlock devices (i.e., a breath alcohol ignition device that acts as a breathalyzer inside an individual's vehicle) installed in their vehicles. If offenders attempted to drive their vehicle while intoxicated on three occasions, they were required to enter treatment. Voas et al. concluded that the program was effective as it resulted in one third lower DUI recidivism following the mandatory treatment program.

The children of individuals with AUD (CoAs) are also affected. The published literature regarding CoAs is voluminous: Keller, Gilbert, Haak, and Bi (2017) mentioned that there are thousands of studies on this topic. The most studied outcome for CoAs is their substantially increased risk for developing drinking problems themselves with a recent meta-analysis suggesting a small to moderate relationship. CoAs are at higher risk of developing problems with general drug abuse and dependence. They are more likely to experience externalizing problems, ADHD, oppositional defiant disorder, conduct disorder, and antisocial behavior. They also experience a higher incidence of internalizing symptoms such as low self-esteem, loneliness, behavioral inhibition, feelings of shame and guilt, PTSD, depression, suicidality, and numerous other anxiety disorders (Keller et al., 2017). Approximately one in four children in the United States has grown up in a family dealing with AUD or dependence (Brooks & McHenry, 2009).

Working With Diverse Populations

Sex Differences

> *"Substance use and abuse [is] 'almost inevitable' for women and girls coping with abusive experiences"* (Milkman & Sunderwirth, 2010, p. 106).

In the book, *Lady Lushes*, McClellan (2017), a medical historian, used several sources to demonstrate the belief that using alcohol was antithetical to having an idealized feminine role, thereby bringing substantial stigma to females with AUD from the late 19th through the 20th century. Despite this stigma, women also develop AUDs (Anthenelli et al., 2018).

Anthenelli et al. (2018) examined some of the neuroscience underlying these differences. They found differences between women and men in their serotonergic and peripheral mechanisms that mediate stressor-specific endocrine responses, regardless of alcohol dependence history. Salvatore, Cho, and Dick (2017) found in their review of evidence that, although there are substantial sex differences for many alcohol outcomes, most evidence suggests that the source and extent of genetic influences on both alcohol consumption and AUDs are the same across sexes.

Windle (2016) found that 8th-grade females reported more alcohol use and AUDs compared to boys in the past 30 days and past year. Although alcohol use by the sexes converged by 10th grade, more males by 12th grade reported binge drinking in the past 2 weeks and being drunk in the past year compared with females.

The gap between the sexes has been narrowing in recent decades regarding the prevalence of AUDs, especially among adolescents (Agabio et al., 2016). Overall, analyses of 16 surveys from 10 countries found that males and females are similar in their likelihood of being a current drinker (Wilsnack, Vogeltanz, Wilsnack, & Harris, 2000). Although women are more likely to drink alcohol because of stress and negative emotions, men are more likely to drink to enhance positive emotions (Agabio et al., 2016).

Erol and Karpyak (2015) reviewed the research found in several databases and concluded that more women than men are lifetime abstainers, they drink less, and they are less likely to engage in problem drinking or develop alcohol-related disorders. For women who drink excessively, however, they are more likely to develop medical problems compared with men. In a study of emergency room data from 18 countries ($N = 14{,}026$), injuries attributable to alcohol were higher for males than females, as were injuries resulting from violence (Cherpitel et al., 2015). Women, on average, constitute about 30% of admissions into treatment for a substance abuse disorder (Grella, 2013). A cohort of 850 outpatients (19% women) was followed up prospectively 20 years later (Bravo, Gual, Lligona, & Colom, 2013). Bravo et al. (2013) found that the women did better while under treatment and achieved better long-term drinking outcomes as well.

The consistent sex differences that have been found include the following:

1. Males report drinking more frequently and in larger amounts.
2. Males have higher rates of heavy episodic drinking.

3. Males are more likely to develop behavioral problems in consequence of drinking.
4. Females tend to eliminate alcohol faster than males, although, because of having lower antidiuretic hormone levels, they initially have higher blood alcohol concentration.
5. Women are at higher risk than men for adverse medical and psychosocial consequences of substance use.
6. Women are more likely than men to have a primary mental health disorder that precedes the development of an SUD.
7. According to *DSM-5*, the 12-month prevalence of AUD in males is 17.6% and 10.4% for females.
8. Males have higher mortality from alcohol compared with females. Worldwide, 7.6% of male deaths and 4.0% of female deaths were due to alcohol in 2012 (Brady & Maria, 2015; Nehring, 2018; Nolen-Hoeksema, 2013; Salvatore et al., 2017).

In interviews with 189 individuals seeking alcohol detoxification (27% female), Stein et al. (2016) found that men were significantly more concerned than women about money, drug use, transmissible diseases, and physical illness. Krentzman (2017) conducted a study with 92 men and 65 women who entered abstinence-based treatment for drinking. She found that women scored higher for forgiveness of others but lower than men for negative religious coping (i.e., having an insecure relationship with a higher power and believing that higher power to be punishing).

Adolescents and Youth

Alcohol-related accidents constitute 46% of young adult deaths between ages 15 and 24 (Milkman & Sunderwirth, 2010). Although alcohol use among adolescents in the United States peaked in 1979, it has declined since then but remains the most used substance among teenagers (Morris et al., 2018). Furthermore, in their study of 24,445 youth (ages 12–20), Richter, Pugh, Peters, Vaughan, and Foster (2016) found that, on all measures of potentially risky drinking (PRD), underage drinkers exceeded the rates of PRD found in adults.

Rates of AUDs peak in late adolescence and decrease substantially into the mid-20s. Nonetheless, using data from the British Cohort Study (N = 6515), Percy and McKay (2015) found that alcohol consumption patterns established at age 16 remained consistent at least to age 26. Copeland et al. (2012) used prospective data on 1420 children who were followed into late adolescence and young adulthood. The researchers concluded that it was symptoms of alcohol abuse and not dependence that best predicted long-term continuance of alcohol problems. Research has also shown that self-reports of the amount of drug use, including alcohol, by adolescents are valid except in settings where it is not in their best interest to disclose (e.g., juvenile justice system; Margolis & Zweben, 2011).

Liang and Chikritzhs (2015) used data from Wave I, Wave III, and Wave IV of the National Longitudinal Study of Adolescent Health in the United States and looked at the age when young people started drinking and the likelihood that they would be a heavy alcohol user in adulthood. Their sample included 2316 participants who were first tested in grade 7 (age 11 or 12), again in grade 12 (age 17 or 18), and again at the average age of 29. They found that, the younger the participants used alcohol (under age 18), the higher the risk of heavy alcohol use in adulthood. Regarding these findings, they recommended abstinence from alcohol until the age of 18 years as a strategy for reducing the risk of alcohol problems in adulthood. The researchers did not, however, factor in the influence of parental supervision of light drinking during childhood/adolescence.

Neurologically, adolescence is a period where critical structural and functional developments occur in the brain (Elofson, Gongvatana, & Carey, 2013; Silveri, 2012). Epigenetic factors exert an influence in linking the expression of genes with stress and external experiences during brain development (Guerrini, Quadri, & Thomson, 2014). In her review, Silveri (2012) concluded that adolescents' brains are vulnerable to the effects of alcohol. Heavy alcohol use in adolescence is associated with several deficits that may persist. Kaarre et al. (2018) found evidence that long-term alcohol use in adolescence, even when not meeting diagnostic criteria for an AUD, is related to changes in connectivity and cortical excitability. Other research found that gray matter volume was significantly smaller in several brain regions among a sample of 35 drinking young adults, ages 22–38, when compared to 27 control subjects (Heikkinen et al., 2017).

Grigsby, Forster, Unger, and Sussman (2016) reviewed 52 studies published between 1990 and 2015 to determine risk and protective factors of having negative consequences from alcohol among adolescents. They found that negative consequences were related to the following:

1. Intrapersonal factors (e.g., personality traits, depression, drinking motives).
2. Interpersonal factors (e.g., exposure to violence, usage by parents and peers).
3. Attitudinal factors (e.g., exposure to media advertising alcohol, religiosity).

Grigsby et al. concluded that all of these were risk factors for developing negative consequences from drinking, and they concluded that more research was needed regarding protective factors. Another study found that spending time with antisocial peers and siblings predicted a higher likelihood of heavy drinking and harm from alcohol for 13-year-olds (N = 1833) in Victoria, Australia (Kim et al., 2017). Treloar and Miranda (2017) studied frequent heavy drinkers aged 15–24 years (44 males, 42 females) and found that the degree to which youth report greater reductions in craving and tension while drinking relative to times when not drinking is linked with the severity of AUD (i.e., less craving and tension when drinking equals greater alcohol problems).

Poor sleep quality and psychiatric symptoms among college students are associated with heavy drinking patterns (Miller et al., 2017). Stressors during adolescence increase the risk for problematic alcohol use (Casement, Shaw, Sitnick, Musselman, & Forbes, 2015). Having an anxiety disorder is associated with developing alcohol problems in adolescence (Wolitzky-Taylor et al., 2015).

A prospective birth cohort study suggested that "problematic alcohol use in adolescence [age 16] predicts vulnerability to hypomanic or manic symptoms [at age 23]" (Fasteau, Mackay, Smith, & Meyer, 2017, p. 232).

Lee, Chassin, and Villalta (2013) used data from a longitudinal study of familial AUD to look at how some adolescent drinkers "mature out" of drinking in adulthood. Their analyses classified participants during late adolescence (ages 17–22), young adulthood (ages 23–28), and again in adulthood (ages 29–40). The researchers found that maturing out was most common among initial high-risk drinkers, but they did not typically become abstainers; instead, most became moderate-risk drinkers.

It is often believed that participation in sports will reduce the use of substances, including alcohol, consumed by adolescents. Veliz, Boyd, and McCabe (2015) used a large national sample of 8th- and 10th-grade students (N = 21,049) and found that adolescents who participated in high-contact sports (i.e., football, wrestling, hockey, and lacrosse) had a higher likelihood of using substances during the past 30 days and beginning substance use at earlier ages. Furthermore, adolescents who participated in noncontact sports (i.e., cross-country, gymnastics, swimming, tennis, track, and volleyball) had a lower probability of smoking cigarettes and marijuana during the past 30 days.

Race and Ethnicity

Caetano et al. (2015) analyzed data from the 2003–2011 National Violent Death Reporting System, which included 59,384 persons across U.S. ethnic groups who had committed suicide. The researchers found that the strongest determinant before suicide among *all* ethnic groups was the presence of an alcohol problem.

Luczak, Liang, and Wall (2017) compared 604 Chinese, Korean, and White American college students regarding whether ethnicity and the ALDH2*2 variant allele moderated AUDs. The researchers found that Chinese and Koreans with the ALDH2*2 allele were at lower risk for AUD symptoms. Asian Americans have a low prevalence rate of SUDs and AUD resulting from several biological, genetic, and environmental influences, some of which are related to the way in which they metabolize alcohol (Matsushita & Higuchi, 2017; Yalisove, 2010).

Bhala et al. (2016) assessed liver- and alcohol-related hospitalizations and deaths in Scotland between 2001 and 2010 using self-reported measures of ethnicity. The White Scottish population was the standard reference population. For all liver diseases, the Chinese had approximately 50% higher risks for men and women, as did other South Asian men and Pakistani women. African-origin men, White British men and women, and other White women had lower risks for liver diseases. For alcohol-related deaths, White Irish men and mixed-background women had an almost twofold higher risk, whereas Pakistani and Chinese men and women had a lower risk.

Native Americans experience high rates of SUDs and multi-SUD (Enoch & Albaugh, 2017; Gilder, Stouffer, Lau, & Ehlers, 2016), including twice the expected rate of AUD compared to White individuals (Yalisove, 2010). They are also seven times more likely to die from AUD compared to the average American (Yalisove, 2010). PTSD and AUD are overrepresented in American Indians and Alaskan Natives (AIAN; Emerson, Moore, & Caetano, 2017). Emerson et al. (2107) found that AIAN exposed to PTSD were more likely to experience AUD than non-Hispanic Whites and the general U.S. population. Nehring (2018) noted that Native Americans eliminate alcohol more quickly compared with European Americans.

White college students are more likely to drink at a higher frequency and quantity than Black students (Wade & Peralta, 2017). Wade and Peralta (2017) found that African American students were more likely to abstain and less likely to engage in heavy episodic drinking than their White counterparts.

American adults who report greater public religiosity are at lower risk for AUD. This may be particularly important for non-Hispanic Blacks, whereas intrinsic religiosity may be especially important for non-Hispanic Whites (Meyers, Brown, Grant, & Hasin, 2017). Non-Hispanic Blacks have lower-than-expected AUD risk compared with non-Hispanic Whites, despite experiencing greater stress, stressors, and socioeconomic disadvantage. Ransome and Gilman (2016) used data from Wave 2 of the NESARC (N= 26,784) and concluded that the difference between Black and White individuals is mostly the result of attending religious services, subjective religiosity, and spirituality.

Zapolski, Pedersen, McCarthy, and Smith (2014) noted the paradox that, although African Americans report later initiation of drinking and lower rates of use at almost all age levels compared to Whites, they have higher levels of alcohol problems compared to European Americans. Zapolski et al. suggested that the lower rates might be because African American culture has norms against heavy drinking and intoxication. African Americans are also more likely to experience legal difficulties from drinking compared to European Americans, and this may lead to reduced consumption. Nonetheless, low-income African American men appear to be at the highest risk for AUD and related problems.

Notwithstanding the previous report, Williams et al. (2016) stated that AUDs have worse consequences for racial/ethnic minority groups compared with Whites. In their study of veteran patients, Williams et al. found that the prevalence of AUDs was highest among Black men and women and lowest among White men and Hispanic women. Furthermore, employment disadvantages have a worse effect on minority groups regarding heavy drinking compared to Whites (Lo & Cheng, 2015).

Kerr and Greenfield (2015) analyzed data from 8553 respondents who drank alcohol and drove a car in the past year. In comparison to White drinkers, Black and Hispanic drinkers reported a higher number of standard drinks before perceiving that they were impaired. The researchers concluded that this might suggest that Black and Hispanic drinkers are more likely to underestimate reporting of impaired driving. Potentially, their findings also suggest that they may drive under a higher severity of impairment.

Levy, Catana, Durbin-Johnson, Halsted, and Medici (2015) reviewed the charts of 791 patients with alcoholic liver disease who were admitted or followed as outpatients at the University of California Davis Medical Center between 2002 and 2010. After controlling for several variables, they found that Hispanic patients presented 4–10 years earlier than White patients. The proportion of individuals presenting with severe alcoholic hepatitis was similar in Hispanic and White patients but lower in African American patients.

Nonpsychiatric Disabilities

Most research has found that disabled individuals have a higher prevalence of an SUD than University of California Davis Medical Center people without disabilities (Glazier & Kling, 2013). Glazier and King (2013) examined 9 years (i.e., 2002–2010) of nationally representative data from the National Survey on Drug Use and Health. They compared 316,746 individuals without disabilities to 20,904 people with disabilities and found that alcohol abuse (as defined by binge drinking, i.e., five or more drinks at one sitting) was lower for the disabled sample.

Alternatively, people with mild to borderline intellectual disabilities (i.e., IQ scores between 50 and 85) have a higher likelihood of developing AUD compared to individuals without intellectual disabilities (van Duijvenbode, Didden, Korzilius, Trentelman, & Engels, 2013). Those who have experienced traumatic head injuries or spinal cord injuries often experience higher rates of having an SUD than those with intellectual disabilities (Weiss, 2017). It has also been found that prisoners with intellectual disability are also more likely to have abused alcohol and other substances. In a study of 33 sentenced prisoners, McGillivray and Newton (2016) found that most reported a state of intoxication when committing their offense.

Mothers who drink during their pregnancy may bear children who experience fetal alcohol spectrum disorders (FASDs). Domeij et al. (2018) reviewed the results from 18 qualitative studies of individuals with FASD and found that these individuals experience a variety of disabilities "ranging from somatic problems, high pain tolerance, destructive behavior, hyperactivity, and aggressiveness, to social problems with friendship, school attendance, and maintenance of steady employment. . . . [They also] feel different from others" (p. 741). Individuals with FASD must learn to cope with a myriad of medical, cognitive, behavioral, and social deficits throughout their lives (Wilhoit, Scott, & Simecka, 2017).

Lesbian, Gay, Bisexual, and Transgender (LGBT)

Compared with their heterosexual counterparts, lesbian, gay, and bisexual (LGB) individuals are more likely to use and abuse alcohol (Allen & Mowbray, 2016). Allen and Mowbray (2016) used data from the National Epidemiologic Survey on Alcohol-Related Conditions. Their sample consisted of individuals who had disclosed an AUD at some point in their lifetime (N = 10,874 heterosexual, 182 gay or lesbian, and 126 bisexual individuals). Allen and Mowbray found that LGB individuals reported higher rates for AUD severity than the heterosexual individuals in the sample.

LGB individuals in a Canadian study reported that their lives were more stressful, they felt fewer links to a supportive community, and they experienced higher odds of having adverse mental health outcomes compared to the heterosexual respondents (N = 222,548; Pakula, Carpiano, Ratner, & Shoveller, 2016). Youth who experience same-sex attraction report higher prevalence of substance use (Bowring, Vella, Degenhardt, Hellard, & Lim, 2015). Bowring et al. (2015) noted that several studies have found that sexual identity, sexual behavior, and sexual attraction do not always correspond, especially with young people. Consequently, researchers should not assume that these aspects of sexuality are consistent within individuals.

In another study, it was found that discrimination based on sexual orientation was associated with AUDs, especially among bisexuals, Hispanics, and less-educated sexual minority adults (Slater, Godette, Huang, Ruan, & Kerridge, 2017). In most studies, the highest rates of substance use are found among bisexual individuals (Parnes, Rahm-Knigge, & Conner, 2017).

Transgender individuals also experience a high prevalence of hazardous drinking. A review of 44 studies found, however, that the estimates varied widely across studies. Many of the studies were found to be methodologically weak, and few attempts were made to separate sex and gender (Gilbert, Pass, Keuroghlian, Greenfield, & Reisner, 2018).

War Veterans

Combat has always had negative effects on enlisted personnel, but it remains uncertain if these sequelae have varied historically. For example, Frueh and Smith (2012) estimated the rates of suicide, AUD, and probable psychiatric illness within Union Forces during the U.S. Civil War. Suicide rates ranged from 8.74 to 14.54 per 100,000 during the war and then surged to 30.4 the year following the war. The rate for African Americans ranged from 17.7 in the first year that they entered the war (1863) to 0 in their second year, followed by 1.8 in the year following the war. Back then, rates for chronic AUD were extremely low (< 1.0%) by today's standards.

McNally (2012) commented on the research by Frueh and Smith (2012), and, interestingly, very low rates of mental disorders were found, and there was no reported syndrome comparable to what we now call PTSD. McNally offered two reasons for this. First, the proportion of soldiers who served in combat roles was 90% during the Civil War, whereas it was 30% during World War II and 15% during the Vietnam War. Second, the death rate during the Civil War from combat and disease was very high (higher than in World War II and the Vietnam War). The explanation that McNally offered was that, during the Civil War, military doctors were very reluctant to call a soldier psychologically unfit for duty. Consequently, what might have been called malingering may have been a true psychiatric illness. The other possibility was that the doctors were treating soldiers facing severe physical injuries and they may have failed to record mental disorders.

What **is** clear today is that American military personnel and veterans have a higher likelihood of abusing alcohol in general than Americans who have not served (Allen, Crawford, & Kudler, 2016; Walker et al., 2017). Veterans of the wars in Afghanistan and Iraq are more likely to drink excessively and to meet criteria for PTSD and major depressive disorder (Cadigan, Klanecky, & Martens, 2017). Herrold, Pape, Li, and Jordan (2017) referred to probable AUD as "endemic" among veterans returning from Iraq and Afghanistan (p. e1712).

Those who have developed PTSD are at a much higher probability of developing an AUD than those who have never enlisted (Cucciare, Weingardt, Valencia-Garcia, & Ghaus, 2015). Furthermore, those personnel who have experienced the highest combat exposure have significantly higher rates of heavy and binge drinking compared to those with lower exposure (Bray, Brown, & Williams, 2013).

Experiencing both alcohol dependence and PTSD results in a worse prognosis than if only one or the other were present (Ralevski et al., 2016). Veterans may drink to cope while at the same time they often avoid seeking help for alcohol-related problems due to the perceived stigma (Miller, Pedersen, & Marshall, 2017). Nonetheless, most veterans receiving their healthcare from the Veterans Health Administration who drink excessively report that they have been advised to reduce or abstain from drinking (Farmer, Stahlman, & Hepner, 2017). Work stress has also been suggested as leading to poor sleep quality and alcohol-related problems among U.S. Navy members during deployment (Bravo, Kelley, & Hollis, 2016).

Based on an online study of 702 women veterans (36% lesbian/bisexual), prevalence and severity of AUD were higher among the sexual minority sample compared with their heterosexual counterparts (Lehavot, Williams, Millard, Bradley, & Simpson, 2016). In a study of 1065 veterans who had become HIV-positive from having had sex with men, more than 10% reported engaging in consistent and long-term AUD (Marshall et al., 2015).

Williams et al. (2016) studied racial/ethnic differences in patients from the U.S. Veterans Health Administration. Their sample consisted of 810,902 (17.4%) African Americans, 302,331 (6.5%) Hispanics, and 3,553,170 (76.1%) White patients. The overall prevalence of AUDs was 6.5%. Furthermore, the prevalence was 9.8% among African Americans, 7.1% among Hispanics, and 5.7% among White patients. Although you might recall reading earlier that the prevalence of AUD is lower in African Americans compared to the general American adult population, this study suggests that, in veterans today, it is highest in African Americans, followed by Hispanics in second place and Whites in third place.

Fuehrlein et al. (2016) analyzed data from the National Health and Resilience in Veterans Study. This nationally representative American sample included 3157 veterans aged 21 and older. The researchers found that more than 40% of U.S. military veterans have experienced a lifetime history of AUD. Many have also experienced other psychiatric disorders together with elevated rates of suicidal ideation and attempts.

In countries faced with armed conflict, it is not just military personnel and veterans who are affected, of course. Civilians living in war-torn countries face considerable risk of developing an AUD. To date, "the humanitarian response and research on this issue are inadequate" (Roberts & Ezard, 2015, p. 889).

Medications and Other Relevant Physical Interventions

Holt and Tobin (2018) provided a review of the pharmacotherapy for AUD, and this section is mostly drawn from their work. Despite the destructiveness caused by AUD, most individuals with AUD do not seek treatment. In 2015, only 8.2% of individuals with AUD over the age of 12 received treatment of any kind for their addiction. For example, in 2012, of all privately insured individuals with AUD in the United States, only 3% received pharmaceuticals for AUD. Holt and Tobin cautioned that most studies had focused predominantly on male patients and consequently may not be as generalizable to women.

A sample of 475 physician-completed surveys focused on their use of pharmacotherapy for AUD. The study focused on family medicine physicians and psychiatrists. Although most of the physicians had used medications to treat AUDs (74.7%), the family physicians who prescribed FDA-approved medications reported their limited success in actual treatment (Ponce Martinez, Vakkalanka, & Ait-Daoud, 2016).

Medications Approved by the Food and Drug Administration (FDA)

Three medications have been approved to date. The FDA has approved no additional medications since 2004 (Campbell, Lawrence, & Perry, 2018).

Disulfiram.

This medication is commonly called Antabuse, and the FDA first approved it in 1948. Individuals who take this medication daily will have an extremely unpleasant reaction if they begin drinking alcohol. Because it is a deterrent medication, the individual taking it needs to be sufficiently motivated. Disulfiram works as an acetaldehyde dehydrogenase inhibitor. As acetaldehyde accumulates in the body, it creates the disulfiram reaction: flushing, headache, nausea, vomiting, lightheadedness, and excessive perspiring. In some cases, it will lead to substantial changes in blood pressure, which can be life-threatening. When taken consistently, disulfiram is of substantial benefit in fostering abstinence.

Acamprosate.

The precise action of how this drug works is still uncertain. The FDA approved it in 2004. It is shown to be effective in maintaining abstinence and in reducing heavy drinking days. It can also be used by individuals experiencing moderate liver disease.

Naltrexone.

Naltrexone is a potent opioid antagonist. It is thought to work by blocking the endorphin pathway, thereby making drinking alcohol less pleasurable. The oral version of naltrexone was approved in 1995, and it is safe for drinkers with advanced liver disease but contraindicated in those taking opioids. The FDA approved an extended-release injectable version of the drug in 2006.

Medications *Not* Approved by the FDA (Off-Label Use)

Topiramate.

This anticonvulsant has been studied for over 15 years with those who are alcohol-dependent. A meta-analysis noted by Holt and Tobin (2018) found that it created a small to moderate effect size when compared to placebo in promoting abstinence and in reducing heavy drinking days.

Gabapentin.

Gabapentin is another anticonvulsant that has shown promising results. Studies have shown that it promotes abstinence and reduces heavy drinking days. The evidence is also building that it may be useful in outpatient management of alcohol withdrawal syndrome.

Varenicline (also known as "Chantix" and "Champix").

Recent evidence has suggested that varenicline is helpful in reducing cravings for both alcohol and nicotine. This drug is known as a nicotine receptor partial agonist and has been used primarily in the treatment of tobacco use disorder.

Medications Not Approved by the FDA (Off-Label Use) With Little Evidence of Efficacy

These medications currently only have weak evidence supporting their effectiveness with AUD. They include zonisamide, pregabalin, ondansetron, and baclofen. The opioid antagonist nalmefene has been approved for the treatment of AUD, but it is not currently available in the United States. Several meta-analyses support nalmefene's efficacy in lowering alcohol consumption (Mann et al., 2016). An indirect meta-analysis found that nalmefene was more effective than naltrexone for reducing alcohol consumption (Soyka, Friede, & Schnitker, 2016).

Psilocybin ("Magic Mushrooms")

Bogenschutz and Forcehimes (2017) reported that they were conducting a trial of psilocybin-assisted treatment for AUD. Their program involved two therapists and consisted of 19 sessions with high-dose psilocybin administered before three of the sessions. The manualized behavioral treatments were referred to as Motivational Enhancement and Taking Action. The results of this study have not yet been published.

Nonpharmaceutical Treatments

Transcranial magnetic stimulation (TMS) is a noninvasive technique that is currently FDA-approved for clients who have found little benefit from antidepressant medications. Electromagnetic induction is targeted at some regions of the brain. With individuals with AUD, some success at reducing cravings has been attained with TMS that has targeted the prefrontal cortex (Campbell et al., 2018). Transcranial direct current stimulation is another noninvasive technique where mild-to-direct current is applied to the brain area of interest for several minutes. With individuals with AUD, the brain region targeted has again been the prefrontal cortex. An invasive procedure has been tried called deep brain stimulation. This requires implanting electrodes into targeted brain regions. The technique has support for some participants who reported that alcohol cravings were reduced for up to 8 years (Campbell et al., 2018).

Specific Counseling Considerations

ROLEPLAY SCENARIOS

Roleplay in dyads with one of you acting as the counselor and the other as the counselee. If roleplay is not possible, work individually in writing out a list of your suggestions.

Roleplay #1

Abey, age 20, belongs to the Omaha tribe. She tells you that she grew up on a reservation but left to begin college. Now in her second year, Abey is studying to become a counselor. According to Abey, socializing with other American Indians has not been good for her. They drink every night, and it gets worse on weekends. Although Abey doesn't believe that she has a drinking problem, she is concerned because of the amount of alcohol that she is consuming.

Roleplay #2

Roy is a 58-year-old unemployed bartender who has just received his third DUI. The court has mandated him to see you. You find Roy to be obstinate and difficult. He tells you more than once to mind your own business in a derogatory fashion, and you feel offended by his language. Nonetheless, you keep this to yourself in hopes that you can develop a working alliance with him. After two sessions, it appears that he is trusting you as he tells you that, on average, he drinks more than 12 drinks a day. This pattern has persisted for 20 years. He is concerned that he won't be able to stop drinking, and he also wonders how bad withdrawal will be if he tries to quit "cold turkey."

Goals and Goal Setting

American Society of Addiction Medicine (ASAM; 2018) criteria are required for use in over 30 states, and it has become the most widely used and comprehensive set of guidelines for placement. ASAM criteria use six dimensions for service planning and treatment across services and levels of care: (a) acute intoxication and/or withdrawal potential, (b) biomedical conditions and complications, (c) emotional, behavioral, or cognitive conditions and complications, (d) readiness to change, (e) relapse, continued

HOW WOULD AN ADDICTION COUNSELOR HELP THIS PERSON??

You are working as a professional counselor. Becky, age 24, comes to see you alone at first because of several problems she is experiencing. She tells you that she struggles with fully accepting herself as a lesbian woman, even though she has always had strong sexual attractions for women and experiences little to no attraction for men. As you collect her history, you find out that she was raised within a strict Mormon family. Her mother and father have disowned her and have told her she is not welcome back at home unless she renounces her lesbian identity and her partner, Sara, whom she has been involved with for the past 4 years. Becky and Sara have lived together now for about 18 months.

Note: Remember to view clients within their environmental contexts, keeping in mind societal, parental/familial, cultural/spiritual, and peer influences. Specifically, become aware of the impact that the following influences have and continue to have in your clients' lives: race, language, religion and spirituality, gender, familial migration history, sexual/affectional orientation, age and cohort, physical and mental capacities, socioeconomic situation and history, education, and history of traumatic experience.

1. What defines this person's environment, past and present?
2. Who is this person sitting in front of me, taking into account environmental and personal characteristics?
3. What defines the problem that he or she is presenting in their multicultural milieu?

to use, or continued problem potential, and (f) recovery/living environment. There is a cost associated with the materials needed for the ASAM criteria. These can be purchased from https://www.asam.org/resources/the-asam-criteria.

Based on the six dimensions of multidimensional assessment, treatment decision-making and goal setting are based on five broad levels of care (i.e., numbered 0.5, 1, 2, 3, 4). These numbered levels are as follows:

0.5 = Early intervention.

1 = Outpatient services.

2 = Intensive outpatient/partial hospitalization services.

3 = Residential/inpatient services.

4 = Medically managed intensive inpatient services.

These broad levels are further broken down into sublevels (e.g., 2.1, 2.5, 3.3). For details, visit ASAM's website at https://www.asam.org/resources/the-asam-criteria/about. Based on several studies, Miller (2016) concluded that the ASAM criteria have failed at matching clients to levels of treatment intensity. Instead, he advocates that individuals should "make informed choices from a menu of evidence-based options" (p. 94).

Clients have their own goals, and, as counselors, it is our job to work collaboratively with them. Controlled drinking is attainable by some who are low to moderate in their severity of drinking (see the section earlier called Background Information for details). Kadden and Skerker (1999) noted that some clients would want to achieve controlled drinking even when abstinence is recommended. Kadden and Skerker suggested an approach for dealing with this request. The counselor and client can agree that the client will consume only a certain amount of alcohol daily (e.g., two or three drinks) without exception for weeks. Many alcohol-addicted individuals are unable to meet such an expectation. The intent is that this feedback of being unable to manage controlled drinking will help the client realize that abstinence is the only viable goal. Hodgins, Leigh, Milne, and Gerrish (1997) offered individuals with AUD seeking treatment the choice of either abstinence or reduced drinking. Half of the participants initially chose reduced drinking, but, after 4 weeks, two thirds chose abstinence.

What cutoff regarding the number of drinks is associated with the likelihood of successfully attaining controlled drinking? Sanchez-Craig, Wilkinson, and Davila (1995) investigated this and found that, for men, those who could manage consuming no more than four drinks per day and 16 drinks per week (for women, three drinks per day and 12 drinks per week maximum) were more likely to succeed at continuing controlled drinking. Those who exceeded these amounts continued to experience social problems related to excessive drinking.

Other goals that clients may bring to counseling fall under the category of harm reduction. Examples include the following:

1. Reduce cravings for alcohol (Holt & Tobin, 2018).
2. Lower the quantity of alcohol consumed (Holt & Tobin, 2018; e.g., only purchase two minibottles, leave credit cards at home, and take just $10 to the bar).

3. Lower the number of heavy drinking days (Holt & Tobin, 2018).
4. Reduce the number of visits to the emergency room with fewer hospitalizations (Holt & Tobin, 2018).
5. Practice safer sex when drinking.
6. Avoid DUIs by having a designated driver or taking a taxi/Uber home.
7. Use alternative substances considered less harmful such as coffee or marijuana (Earleywine, 2016).
8. Attend fewer bars and nightclubs (Nordfjaern, Bretteville-Jensen, Edland-Gryt, & Gripenberg, 2016).

An eye-opening example of harm reduction was offered by Earleywine (2016). A person attending AA who was teased about his excessive coffee and cigarette use retorted, "Coffee and cigarettes never made me wake up broke and naked" (p. 38).

Stages of Change Strategies

The processes of change mentioned are based on those outlined by Connors, DiClemente, Velasquez, and Donovan (2013) and Prochaska, Norcross, and DiClemente (1994). The definitions for the various processes can be found in Chapter 6. Besides these processes, other strategies are included that have separate citations.

The University of Rhode Island Change Assessment Scale (URICA) is a helpful scale in determining where a client is currently regarding the stages of change model. There are 24-, 28-, and 32-item versions of the scale.

A 24-item version is published for alcohol or drug problems. The scale, however, is generic and can be easily adapted for use with other addictions. It is available with norms as a free download from https://www.guilford.com/add/miller11_old/urica.pdf.

Specific precontemplation strategies.

Please visit the section called Relevant Mutual Support Groups, Websites, and Videos for free or low-cost information and resources that may help someone move out of precontemplation.

Watching movies focused on AUD may help some individuals in the precontemplation phase begin considering change. A few good choices are

1. *Smashed* (2012).
2. *Days of Wine and Roses* (1962).
3. *Leaving Las Vegas* (1995).
4. *Barfly* (1987).
5. *The Spectacular Now* (2013) (likely best suited for adolescents).

Some individuals who have developed an AUD can be encouraged to read a book that speaks to their dependency. A few good choices are

1. *Alcohol Explained* (by William Porter, 2015). This book is described as "the definitive, ground-breaking guide to alcohol and alcoholism" on the Amazon.com website. It provides a layperson's explanation of how AUD develops and how to overcome it. The author himself had earlier suffered from AUD.
2. *Beyond Recovery: A Journey of Grace, Love, and Forgiveness* (by Shawn Langwell, 2016). The author provides a "front row seat to what it looks like to hit bottom" as quoted on the Amazon.com website. Shawn describes his downward spiral into AUD.
3. *The Big Book of Alcoholics Anonymous* (by Bob Smith and Bill Wilson, 2013, paperback edition). This is the original 1939 basic text that is used in AA meetings worldwide. The book describes how to recover from AUD and is written by the founders of AA: "Bill W." and "Dr. Bob" as they are known.
4. *SMART Recovery* (by William Abbot, Jim Braastad, John Frahm, Randy Lindel, Richard Phillips, Henry Steniberger, and Rosemary Hardin, 2013, 3rd edition workbook). The handbook is written in a simple, straightforward manner. It includes many exercises, techniques, and strategies to help individuals who are addicted using the Self-Management Addiction Recovery Program (SMART).
5. *Rational Recovery: The New Cure for Substance Addiction* (by Jack Trimpey, 1996, paperback edition). In this book, the founder of Rational Recovery explains his approach.
6. *Controlling Your Drinking: Tools to Make Moderation Work for You* (by William R. Miller and Ricardo F. Munoz, 2013, 2nd edition). This book is written by distinguished clinician-researchers who have spent more than 40 years studying moderation.

The Substance Abuse and Mental Health Services Administration (SAMHSA; 1999–2012) offered suggestions that may help clients move from the precontemplation stage. They suggested that clients need information that shows them the connection between their use of substances and their problems. A brief intervention, for example, might involve educating the person about the adverse consequences of developing an SUD. Motivational efforts include establishing rapport, asking permission, and building trust. The intent is to help the client develop awareness of how substance use is creating difficulties.

Some strategies are as follows:

1. Help clients look at the meaning behind events that led to them seeking treatment.
2. Have clients talk about their perception of their problem.
3. Provide clients feedback regarding the results of the assessment.
4. Encourage clients to look at the pros and cons of substance use.
5. Explore the discrepancies between the client's perception of the problem and the perception of others.
6. If possible, agree on the direction or the next step for clients to take after leaving the session.

7. Tell clients that you are concerned and that your door is open for further discussion/exploration at another time.
8. Commend clients for attending the session.

Specific contemplation strategies.

For some addicted individuals, the contemplation stage lasts for many years. They may move forward to the preparation stage or revert to the precontemplation stage. Consequently, it is important to use nonconfrontational methods during the contemplation stage.

During this stage, SAMHSA (1999–2012) recommended that clients explore their feelings of ambivalence and the conflicts between their values and their SUD. Some of the motivational techniques here include the following:

1. Help clients realize that their ambivalence is normal.
2. Assist clients in deciding on change by weighing the pros and cons of their SUD; helping them move from extrinsic to intrinsic reasons to quit or reduce use; clarifying their values concerning change; and emphasizing their free choice, self-efficacy, and responsibility for making change.
3. Focus again on feedback from previous assessments.
4. Encourage clients to make statements regarding their intent and commitment to change.
5. Help clients talk about their self-efficacy and their expectations regarding counseling.
6. Provide a summary of self-motivational statements to clients.
7. Display curiosity about clients, which helps strengthen the working alliance. This might also help them feel comfortable talking about other problems.
8. When clients make a negative statement, put a positive spin on it.

Although it is important to acknowledge the extrinsic reasons for pushing clients to change, the goal is to help them find internal reasons that change is important. A good question to ask in this stage is, "If you were to make a change, what would it be or what would it look like?" The idea of trying abstinence for a specified period could also be raised as a possibility with the client.

Some individuals with AUD in this stage would benefit from attending a mutual support group (MSG). This could include attending AA, SMART Recovery, or Rational Recovery.

Specific preparation strategies.

Clients have reached the preparation stage once they decide that change is important to them. An important aspect of this stage is planning steps toward recovery. Strengthening their commitment toward this goal is important. A list of the options for treatment might be handed to the client and then each option could be discussed with the goal of deciding collaboratively on the best choice.

SAMHSA (1999–2012) recommended the following motivational strategies during the preparation stage:

1. Help clients clarify their own goals and strategies for making the change.
2. Offer clients the list of options for treatment.
3. Provide clients with expertise and advice after first asking their permission.
4. Work at creating a change or treatment plan with details regarding implementation.
5. Lower barriers to change as much as possible.
6. Assist the client in soliciting social support for the change.
7. Discuss treatment expectations and expectancies and the clients' responsibilities in the process.
8. Dialogue with clients what has worked for them in the past or for others whom they know.
9. Problem solve with the client regarding finances, childcare, transportation to work, and other potential barriers.
10. Encourage clients to tell significant others about the plan to change.

Skills training should also occur during this stage. For example, if clients are unable to avoid others who are continuing to drink, they need to learn and practice assertion skills repetitively. Clients need to have a plan for dealing with their high-risk situations, which differ somewhat from person to person. For example, if they always drive home from work and pass their favorite liquor store, they should change their route to get home. Other ideas to implement *before* their chosen quit day (i.e., preparation strategies) can be found in Appendix B.

Specific action strategies.

While drinkers try out their new behaviors, none of these is stable yet. Continuing to practice skills begun in the preparation stage is important. It is during the action stage that clients take steps to accomplish their goal. The following are a few examples:

1. Enter a treatment program as previously decided in the preparation stage.
2. Begin to moderate drinking, implementing strategies for doing so as decided in the preparation stage.
3. Begin abstinence from alcohol, implementing strategies for doing so as decided in the preparation stage.
4. Implement relapse prevention strategies that were decided in the preparation stage.

As clients implement their action stage, it is important that they remain willing to revise their action plans as they proceed. For example, clients may need to implement more strategies to moderate drinking or maintain abstinence that were not considered initially or possibly even thought of initially. Provide clients help in executing their action plans and help them practice the skills needed to maintain moderate drinking or abstinence.

Some of the SAMHSA (1999–2012) recommended motivational strategies during the action stage include the following:

1. Maintain a strong working alliance and reinforce the criticalness of remaining in recovery.
2. Help clients appreciate that change happens in small steps. If they are unsuccessful, help them explore the reasons and either alter the strategies or change the goal.

3. Acknowledge clients' hesitance and difficulties during the early stages of change.

4. If not accomplished during the preparation stage, help clients identify their high-risk situations and develop strategies for dealing with them.

5. Guide clients in helping them find new activities that help them feel positive.

6. Assist the client in ascertaining whether they have healthy family and social support.

Evidence-based therapies are consistent in recommending that treatment for AUD should be based on cognitive-behavioral therapy (CBT), motivational interviewing (MI) or motivational enhancement therapy (MET), 12-step support or other MSGs, and contingency management (Campbell et al., 2018). Given that the effect size reported in most of the meta-analyses regarding treatment for AUD is small, one can conclude that psychosocial interventions alone are insufficient (Campbell et al., 2018). This is also true regarding meta-analysis of interventions for adolescents and young adults (Tanner-Smith & Risser, 2016). The latest Cochrane review suggested that brief therapies have a modest effect at best (Kaner et al., 2018), and this includes brief interventions used in emergency rooms (Schmidt et al., 2016). Kaner et al. (2018) also concluded that longer durations of counseling likely have little additional effect.

A recent meta-analysis based on 48 studies and encompassing 8984 participants focused on answering the question of whether the duration of therapy matters regarding AUD (Schmidt, Bojesen, Nielsen, & Andersen, 2018). The researchers found that the number of planned weeks, the duration of sessions, the frequency of sessions per week, and the actual number of attended sessions were associated with long-term alcohol use outcomes. This meta-analysis provides further support to the modest gains realized by alcohol treatment programs.

Morrison, Lin, and Gersh (2018) suggested that treatment of AUD should be supplemented with pharmacotherapy and other treatments. Morrison et al., for example, suggested integrative treatments. These may include acupuncture, yoga, exercise, mindfulness, hypnosis, biofeedback, neurofeedback, music and art therapy, and herbal therapies. A book by Mistral (2016a) focused on integrated approaches with drug and alcohol problems.

As impulsivity and distress tolerance are key features in the development and maintenance of SUDs, Greenberg, Martindale, Fils-Aime, and Dolan (2016) suggested that treatments should focus on emphasizing distress tolerance skills, particularly the appraisal of aversive emotions. Eye movement desensitization and reprocessing (EMDR), which is a psychotherapy treatment involving eight phases (see http://www.emdr.com/what-is-emdr/ for details) that was originally designed to treat traumatic memories, has been suggested following the initial phase of treatment (Marich, 2017), and so has transcendental meditation (Gryczynski et al., 2018). Klostermann (2016) stated that marital and family approaches are also efficacious regarding prevention and treatment of SUDs. Although interest is strong in the family therapy field for working with AUDs, there are few models for working with whole families (McCrady, 2014).

Couples counseling can be helpful for individuals with AUD who are in a primary relationship (MacKillop et al., 2018; McCrady & Epstein, 2015). Couples counseling should focus on clients and their partners' communication skills, rebuilding trust, and working through negative feelings like guilt, resentment, and anger (Merlo, 2012). Individuals with AUD are also encouraged to change their social support to those who are nondrinkers (Milkman & Sunderwirth, 2010), and research has demonstrated the benefit of creating an abstinent social support network (Litt, Kadden, Tennen, & Kabela-Cormier, 2016).

Fowler, Holt, and Joshi (2016) conducted a systematic review of technology-based interventions for adult drinkers. Eight studies met their inclusion criteria. Despite the interventions varying in design, most of the studies found that positive effects resulted from the mobile technology-based interventions. Campbell et al. (2018) concluded that, whereas computer-based and app-based programs have demonstrated many benefits and are cost-effective, it remains questionable whether they are efficacious as interventions. Social networking sites have also shown promise in reducing alcohol intake during festive occasions (Flaudias et al., 2015).

As noted by Rastegar and Fingerhood (2016), clients often experience a "honeymoon period" where they come to believe that their drinking problem is behind them and that continuing sessions is no longer necessary. During these honeymoon periods, clients are at the highest risk of relapse. Clients need ongoing support during the early stages of their treatment. Individuals with severe AUD will often benefit the most from an intensive, specialized program that occurs over a more extended period (Merlo, 2012).

Gearhardt and Corbin (2012) reported that consuming sugar has been helpful to some individuals with AUD in recovery. They stated that about one fourth of males with AUD report that consumption of high-sugar foods helps them refrain from drinking.

McCrady (2014) wrote an excellent step-by-step guide for treating people with AUD (her chapter is recommended reading). Her approach takes into consideration seven areas: (a) severity of the problem, (b) other life problems besides addiction, (c) client expectations, (d) the working alliance and the client's motivation, (e) variables that maintain the current drinking pattern, (f) the client's social support systems, and (g) maintaining change. Regarding severity, McCrady stated that a brief motivational intervention (BMI) may be sufficient for those at the mild end but more intensive interventions will be required for those who are moderate or severe in their AUD. Clients have expectations, and it is important to discuss these and provide honest feedback. For clients who are more severe in their addiction, McCrady tells them that about 25% of clients maintain abstinence for at least 1 year after treatment, whereas another 10% will use alcohol moderately. Furthermore, most clients following treatment will reduce the amount they drink by about 87%, and alcohol-related problems will diminish by about 60% (based on research by Miller et al., as cited in McCrady, 2014).

Brief interventions have also been developed for clients with AUD. DiClemente, Bellino, and Neavins (1999) noted that there are three motivational treatment approaches available to counselors: (a) BMI, (b) MI, and (c) MET. BMI involves an intervention of between one and four sessions (with each session lasting from 10 to 60 min) that relies on direct advice and information on the adverse consequences that result from abusing alcohol. The approach is generally regarded as more relevant for problem drinkers than for those who are dependent. The goal is often reduced drinking and not abstinence.

MI is often used with less-motivated clients (DiClemente, Bellino, & Neavins, 1999), and it is described in Chapter 6 with an example provided later in this chapter. MET was initially developed for Project MATCH, which was an 8-year national and multisite trial that began in 1989. MET comprises four treatment sessions over 12 weeks. It combines MI techniques but in a briefer, less-intensive format. Preceding MET is an extensive assessment. In session 1, the counselor provides individualized feedback to clients regarding their drinking pattern. In session 2, the counselor uses MI techniques to help increase clients' commitment to change. During sessions 3 and 4, the counselor reviews client progress and further explores the remaining ambivalent feelings that clients may still possess regarding change. Other ideas to implement *beginning* their chosen quit day (i.e., action strategies) can be found in Appendix B.

Specific maintenance strategies and relapse prevention.

Note: Maintenance strategies and relapse prevention are also, for many, partly facilitated by regular attendance at relevant MSGs. A list of such MSGs and helpful websites is found in an upcoming section entitled Relevant Mutual Support Groups, Websites, and Videos.

In the maintenance stage, addicted individuals establish and practice new behaviors long term. Clients need help in this stage with relapse prevention. Celebrating clients' success and reassuring them maintains a positive working alliance. Present actions may need to be evaluated and long-term goals redefined.

SAMHSA (1999–2012) recommended several motivational strategies:

1. Help clients explore and try out alternative activities.
2. Affirm clients' resolve and self-efficacy beliefs.
3. Practice new coping strategies with clients to ensure that they know how to use these appropriately.
4. Maintain ways of continuing as a support to clients (e.g., book sessions periodically, follow-up phone calls at regular intervals, assuring clients that you are there for them).
5. Normalize relapse. It is estimated that between 45% and 75% of individuals with AUD who have received treatment will relapse within 3 years (Hauser, Wilden, Batra, & Rodd, 2017), and most relapse occurs within 90 days of abstinence (Brooks & McHenry, 2009). Develop a lapse and relapse plan with clients so they know what to do should this occur.

The book called *Living Sober* by AA (available through Amazon.com) includes the famous HALT formula for helping to avoid relapse. HALT is an acronym that consists of four reasons that individuals with AUD often relapse. Individuals with AUD should avoid staying **H**ungry, **A**ngry, **L**onely, or **T**ired.

In their sample of 171 participants, Mo and Deane (2016) found that their most consistent finding was that craving predicted relapse, whereas change in negative affect predicted the severity of alcohol problems. It is critical that clients learn that lapses or relapses should be viewed as learning opportunities. They provide clients with feedback that allows them to "tweak" their maintenance program, whether through developing or practicing coping skills or finding new ways to deal with high-risk situations.

Relapse often follows a predictable sequence. Rastegar and Fingerhood (2016) stated that the following often occurs: (a) denial becomes reactivated, (b) the addicted individual progressively isolates, becomes defensive, and builds a crisis to justify the progression of symptoms (e.g., depressed mood, loss of control over behavior), and (c) relapse back to drinking.

Pekala (2017) reviewed hypnosis within the addictions field. He concluded that suggestions for increasing self-esteem, serenity, and decreasing anger and impulsivity provided an adjunctive method for helping clients deal better with their drug and alcohol problems and maintain abstinence. Individuals with a history of impulsivity who have gone through many previous detoxifications for alcohol dependence are the highest relapse risk (Czapla et al., 2016).

Engel et al. (2016) conducted a follow-up study 5 months after individuals with AUD had gone through detoxification. Using an instrument called the SCL-90-R, they determined that high levels of psychological distress substantially increases the risk of relapse. Interventions aimed at teaching clients soon after detox to reduce their experience of psychological distress are warranted. Other ideas for relapse prevention can be found in Appendix C.

Motivational Interviewing

Becker, Jones, Hernandez, Graves, and Spirito (2016) studied 97 adolescent drinkers who presented to emergency rooms. These adolescents completed a 3-month assessment. The authors concluded that motivation-enhancing treatments worked best if the teenagers were under 16 years of age. Older teenagers demonstrated substantially worse drinking outcomes than younger teenagers regardless of whether they received motivation-enhancing treatments.

There is research indicating that MI is not always effective (Bertholet, Palfai, Gaume, Daeppen, & Saitz, 2014). Overall, however, MI has been used successfully to one extent or another with several populations of adult drinkers. Some examples include patients who are low functioning intellectually (Borsari, Apodaca, Yurasek, & Monti, 2017), depressed individuals (Satre, Delucchi, Lichtmacher, Sterling, & Weisner, 2013), pregnant women (Rendall-Mkosi et al., 2013), incarcerated drinkers (Owens & McCrady, 2016), soldiers (Walker et al., 2017), HIV+ individuals (Myers et al., 2017), and drinkers 60 years of age and older (Andersen et al., 2015).

MI has also been used successfully with young adults. Examples here include American Indian and Alaska Native youth (Dickerson, Brown, Johnson, Schweigman, & D'Amico, 2016), homeless young adults (Tucker, D'Amico, Ewing, Miles, & Pedersen, 2017), and socially anxious college drinkers (Hu, 2016). A Cochrane review concluded that MI produced modest yet beneficial effects with young adults (Grant, Pedersen, Osilla, Kulesza, & D'Amico, 2016).

Furthermore, clients experience MI positively. They appreciate its nonconfrontational approach, affirmation, the development of discrepancies between beliefs and behavior, and the positive working alliance (Jones, Latchford, & Tober, 2016).

The telephone has been successfully used to provide motivational interventions aimed at reducing drinking among college students (Borsari et al., 2014). Videoconferencing has also been used successfully to deliver a BMI to reduce heavy drinking among patients in emergency department settings (Celio et al., 2017).

Here is an example of how MI could be used to help an addicted individual decide that counseling might be the best first step to take in recovery. (Pertaining to Chapter 6's description of MI, the following is an example of the process called *focusing*. It also includes creating a discrepancy. This example represents the third session.)

Counselor: Hi, David. It's good to see you again.

Client: Likewise. It's been a tough couple of weeks.

Counselor: What has been happening, David?

Client: Well, I was successful in reducing my drinking for about 10 of the past 14 days, but I got absolutely drunk on 3 or 4 other days. I feel terribly hung over today, in fact.

Counselor: I understand how challenging this is. I do need to clarify something, however. In our first two sessions, you told me that you know that you need to stop drinking altogether because of the medical problems heavy drinking has already created for you. If your goal is to reduce drinking, I simply need to be on the same page with you.

Client: You're right in pointing that out, and I guess I'm thinking I might've changed my goal without telling you.

Counselor: You are certainly entitled to change your goal. To what extent do you think a goal of reduced drinking is realistic for you?

Client: Ah, what do you mean?

Counselor: I recall you telling me that you have tried to reduce your drinking for the past 10 or more years, and you have never been successful in achieving this for more than 2 weeks.

Client: Right, I did tell you that. And, honestly, I cannot disagree with you. I just don't think I can stop altogether right now. My wife is hounding me like never before, and I have two teenage daughters who are driving me mad.

Counselor: It sounds like the stresses in your life are affecting your decision-making.

Client: I know what you're saying. I just can't imagine living without alcohol in my life.

Counselor: I know how challenging it can be when you have stresses at home. Let me work with you on the goal that makes the most sense to you right now.

Client: I know the goal that makes the most sense is complete abstinence. I know that without any doubt. I just don't think I can succeed.

Counselor: You're saying that you know what the best choice is but you don't have much confidence in succeeding at it. Yet, every time I see you, I witness your strength of character. You also have a bachelor's degree in business administration. How do you make sense of the discipline and tenacity that you have demonstrated in several areas of your life and the part of you that doesn't feel capable of remaining abstinent?

Client: I need to think about that. I am successful in business, and I do have a good home life for the most part.

Counselor: You have demonstrated success in both business and in your relationships with important family members. You have shown time and time again that you can succeed at what matters to you.

Client: Thank you for believing in me. I don't know why I lose touch with my strengths. I clearly want to choose abstinence, and I need your help more than ever to do it.

Insight-Oriented Interventions

Early psychoanalytic theory stressed pleasurable and aggressive drives to explain the appeal of alcohol and drugs. Freud, for example, focused heavily on libidinal drives such as oral and erotic impulses. A contemporary perspective focuses greater emphasis on intolerable pain and/or confusing emotions that drive addiction (Khantzian, 2003). According to Khantzian (2003), over the past 30 years, the psychodynamic approach has focused on four considerations:

1. Addictions represent a special adaptation to a range of human problems.
2. It is motivated by an attempt to self-medicate against unbearable painful emotions.
3. The overarching problem is an inability to self-regulate.
4. The disorder is driven by a disordered personality that predisposes and keeps individuals engaged in addictive behaviors.

Sweet (2012) focused on how alcohol and drugs can reduce or help avoid feelings of intense anxiety and, in turn, create "manic grandiosity" (p. 116). Addiction occurs in response to a fragile and fragmented self, deluged with problems together with a primitive superego. Self-reproach and recrimination are pronounced, and, in some cases, violent aggression occurs, more typically leading to self-harm and sometimes suicide. Addiction results from disordered attachments and the foreclosure of symbolization. The internal object relations of an addicted individual were damaged in childhood. Object relations refers to the attachments that people form with significant others, generally beginning with their attachment toward parents.

Spiritual Interventions

Spirituality has been linked with having a sense of meaning and purpose in life, and it does not require believing in a higher power. Nonetheless, research has found that religious people consume less alcohol and have fewer problems related to alcohol (Lucchetti, Koenig, Pinsky, Laranjeira, & Vallada, 2014; Meyers et al., 2017). Greater religiousness appears to act as a form of positive coping (Jankowski, Meca, Lui, & Zamboanga, 2018). Some Hispanic Roman Catholic Priests practice juramento with individuals who need to abstain from alcohol. *Juramentos* are pledges that people make to abstain from alcohol use. Most of the priests surveyed in Cuadrado's (2014) study reported that juramentos were effective.

Chaplains in the military and Veterans Affairs also play a positive role in the treatment of alcohol dependence (Allen, Nieuwsma, & Meador, 2014).

Participants who attended a residential 12-step treatment program demonstrated increased spirituality upon completion (Ranes, Johnson, Nelson, & Slaymaker, 2017). Hodge and Lietz (2014) wrote about how spiritual beliefs and practices can be incorporated into CBT.

Johnson and Kristeller (2013) recommended that counselors discuss how their clients' faith traditions might help ascertain the type of help that should be provided, including attendance in mutual help groups. Indigenous individuals may also find support through attending the Native American Church (Prue, 2013).

Krentzman, Webb, Jester, and Harris (2018) conducted a 30-month longitudinal study of 364 individuals with alcohol dependence. They focused on the degree to which participants forgave themselves and others, taking measures every 6 months. Krentzman et al. found that, over the 30 months, participants experienced an increase in forgiveness for themselves but particularly an increase in the forgiveness of others. The authors provided ideas for facilitating forgiveness in alcohol treatment.

Cognitive-Behavioral Therapy

CBT can be facilitated using the triple column technique. It can be used both by counselors in their work with clients and by clients alone. The full instructions for using the technique are found in Chapter 6. The following are some of the cognitions that can be problematic for clients with alcohol addiction.

Automatic Thought or Belief	Questioning it	Healthier Thought or Belief
I cannot live without alcohol. Life without it is unbearable.		The basic needs in life do not include alcohol. Drinking is bad for me, and I must change this pattern. I can learn to live without alcohol and find meaning and purpose in life.
Everyone I know drinks. I cannot manage without having friends.		Over time, I will learn to say no to alcohol. Until that time, I can make some new friends who are abstinent from alcohol.
I cannot resist entering a store that sells liquor. There is no way I can avoid alcohol.		I will learn coping strategies to avoid purchasing alcohol.
I am filled with shame, guilt, and doubt when I am not drinking.		When I become abstinent from alcohol, I can get help to overcome these feelings.
Life is boring and unsatisfying. Without alcohol, I never feel euphoric. Instead, I am depressed and wish I were dead.		Life has only become boring and unsatisfying because of poor choices. I need to find activities that are meaningful and fulfilling. I will take full responsibility for improving my life.

Regardless of which interventions counselors use, the working alliance (the relationship that develops between the counselor and client) remains sacrosanct. This is also true in CBT (Maisto et al., 2015). Maisto et al. (2015) recommended that future research look at the changes that occur in the working alliance throughout treatment for AUD to see how this affects outcomes over time.

Behavioral approaches and CBT have been extensively studied regarding their usefulness in working with clients who have AUD. Croxford, Notley, Maskrey, Holland, and Kouimtsidis (2015) stated that there is a consensus that detoxification from alcohol dependency should be planned. They offered a 6-week CBT group intervention and then evaluated it. Croxford et al. concluded that the intervention was well accepted and that it adequately prepared participants for detoxification.

Budney, Brown, and Stanger (2013) focused on behavioral approaches to SUDs. They acknowledged that the distinction between behavioral approaches and CBT approaches is somewhat arbitrary. In their chapter, they focused on cue exposure training, aversion therapy, the community reinforcement approach, and contingency management. These approaches are explained in Chapter 6.

Harrell, Pedrelli, Lejuez, and MacPherson (2014) wrote about some of the established CBT interventions for an AUD. Social learning theory (SLT) has had a significant influence on CBT-based approaches (see Chapter 3 for a closer look at SLT). This theory hypothesizes that alcohol use begins because of socialization and continues because of operant conditioning while being maintained by environmental influences and cognitive factors. CBT interventions based on SLT are targeted at improving coping skills, increasing self-efficacy, looking at expectancies for the effects of alcohol use, and learning to manage cravings and triggers associated with alcohol cues.

Harrell et al. (2014) also looked at the relapse prevention model and CBT interventions based on it. An important cognitive strategy is for clients not to see lapses and relapses as treatment failures but instead as part of their recovery from an AUD. The intent behind relapse prevention is focused on helping clients develop coping strategies to prevent a slip or lapse from turning into a full-blown relapse. Some strategies used include skills training, cognitive restructuring, and lifestyle balance.

Regarding treatment approaches, Harrell et al. (2014) looked at functional analysis (considering the environmental factors maintaining a behavior including antecedents and consequences), coping and social skills training, cue exposure, behavioral couples therapy, and behavioral self-control training. Meta-analyses have shown that social skills training, behavioral contracting, and behavioral marital therapy have the strongest support (Burdenski, 2012; Harrell et al., 2014). Behavioral couples therapy has the most research support for helping couples deal with the difficulties of recovery (Burdenski, 2012).

Other approaches used in CBT include problem-solving, understanding patterns of substance use, and identifying and changing cognitive distortions (Mastroleo & Monti, 2013). Mastroleo and Monti (2013) outlined that coping skills usually concern four major themes: (a) interpersonal skills for creating stronger bonds with others, (b) cognitive and emotional coping strategies for mood regulation, (c) coping skills for enhancing daily living and for dealing with stressful life events, and (d) coping in environments where substance use cues occur.

Rational emotive behavior therapy, which is one approach to CBT, can be used with addictions. For example, Albert Ellis's ABC approach is used in Self-Management and Recovery Training (SMART) recovery programs (Gerstein & Ellis, 2014).

CBT has proven helpful with many problems faced by alcohol-dependent individuals. CBT has been used successfully to help participants cope with or moderate cue-induced craving using cognitive strategies (Naqvi et al., 2015). CBT has been effective in reducing intimate partner violence perpetrated by both men with AUDs (Satyanarayana et al., 2016) and women with AUDs (Wupperman et al., 2012). Women receiving a specific approach designed for them (i.e., female-specific CBT) reported satisfaction with the program and substantial reductions in drinking (Epstein et al., 2018). CBT programs have successfully helped alcohol-addicted individuals to improve their sleep (Brower, 2015; Kaplan, McQuaid, Batki, & Rosenlicht, 2014; Zhabenko et al., 2016). CBT has also been found helpful to some extent with individuals who experience both chronic depression and alcohol dependence (Penberthy et al., 2014; Riper et al., 2014).

Nyamathi et al. (2017) compared a program of dialectical behavior therapy (DBT) with a program based on health promotion (HP). They found that the DBT program was more effective than the HP program in maintaining drug and alcohol abstinence at the 6-month follow-up.

The United Nations Office on Drugs and Crime (2007) created a leaders' guide for cognitive behavioral and relapse strategies. It contains several good ideas (please see reference list for website).

Following an outpatient group CBT program, Rose, Skelly, Badger, Naylor, and Helzer (2012) offered an automated telephone program focused on self-monitoring, skills practice, and feedback. They offered the telephone program for 90 days, and, at the end of it, participants ($N = 21$) reported that it increased their self-awareness, and they particularly found the therapist feedback component helpful.

Web-based interventions have also become increasingly popular. Kiluk et al. (2016) compared a computer-based delivery of CBT for individuals with AUD with those receiving their standard CBT treatment. The authors concluded that their preliminary trial showed that their computer-based program appears to be safe, feasible, and efficacious.

Wiers et al. (2015) tested an online program focused on helping individuals with AUD change their cognitive biases. Although 615 participants were initially screened into the study, 314 initiated training, but only 136 completed the pretest, four sessions of computerized training, and a posttest. Despite this high attrition, the authors concluded that online interventions are helpful in reducing drinking.

Johansson et al. (2017) created a web-based CBT program with eight modules delivered over 10 weeks. The program was offered to 4165 potential participants who scored in the hazardous use category or higher on the Alcohol Use Disorders Identification Test (AUDIT). At follow-up, 1043 participants had fully engaged in the program, and these individuals were ranked as having lower AUD severity.

Mellentin, Nielsen, Nielsen, Yu, and Stenager (2016) created a cue exposure treatment as a smartphone application. The app is intended as aftercare for individuals with AUD following attendance at group sessions. This study is under way but has not yet released results. A similar study focused on modifying attentional bias with both alcohol- and cannabis-dependent individuals is similarly under way (Heitmann et al., 2017).

RELEVANT MUTUAL SUPPORT GROUPS, WEBSITES, AND VIDEOS

Mutual Support Groups

For the Addicted Individual

1. SMART Recovery—Self -Management and Recovery training. http://www.smartrecovery.org/

   Quoted from website:

   SMART Recovery is the leading self-empowering addiction recovery support group. Our participants learn tools for addiction recovery based on the latest scientific research and participate in a worldwide community which includes free, self-empowering, science-based mutual help groups.

   SMART Recovery, a nonprofit corporation, was originally named the Rational Recovery Self-Help Network and was affiliated with Rational Recovery Systems, a for-profit corporation owned by Jack Trimpey. In 1994, the nonprofit changed its name to SMART Recovery and ended all affiliation with Trimpey. This change occurred because of disagreements between Trimpey and the nonprofit's board of directors about the program of recovery to be offered in the self-help groups.

2. Rational Recovery. https://rational.org

   Quoted from website:

   The combined mission of Rational Recovery Systems, Inc., is (1) to disseminate information on independent recovery from addiction through planned, permanent abstinence, (2) to make self-recovery a viable option to all addicted people everywhere, and (3) to make informed consent to addiction treatment and recovery group participation available to all addicted people.

3. LifeRing Secular Recovery. https://lifering.org/

   Quoted from website:

   LifeRing Secular Recovery is an abstinence-based, worldwide network of individuals seeking to live in recovery from addiction to alcohol or other non-medically indicated drugs. In LifeRing, we offer each other peer-to-peer support in ways that encourage personal growth and continued learning through personal empowerment. Our approach is based on developing, refining, and sharing our own personal strategies for continued abstinence and crafting a rewarding life in recovery. In short, we are sober, secular, and self-directed.

4. Secular Organizations for Sobriety. http://www.sossobriety.org/

   Quoted from website:

   Secular Organizations for Sobriety (SOS) is a nonprofit network of autonomous, non-professional local groups, dedicated solely to helping individuals achieve and maintain sobriety/abstinence from alcohol and drug addiction, food addiction and more. Watch the award-winning short documentary about SOS! "No God at the Bottom of a Glass" is an award-winning short documentary produced by Sarah Barker of Creative Media Hub. The film tells the story of Secular Organizations for Sobriety (SOS), the brainchild of founder, James Christopher.

5. Women for Sobriety. https://womenforsobriety.org/

   Quoted from website:

   Women for Sobriety (WFS) is an organization whose purpose is to help all women find their individual path to recovery through discovery of self, gained by sharing experiences, hopes and encouragement with other women in similar circumstances. We are an abstinence-based self-help program for women facing issues of alcohol or drug addiction. Our "New Life" Program acknowledges the very special needs women have in recovery – the need to nurture feelings of self-value and self-worth and the desire to discard feelings of guilt, shame, and humiliation.

6. Alcoholics Anonymous. https://www.aa.org/

   Quoted from website:

   Alcoholics Anonymous is an international fellowship of men and women who have had a drinking problem. It is nonprofessional, self-supporting, multiracial, apolitical, and available almost everywhere.

7. Dual Recovery Anonymous. http://www.draonline.org/

   Quoted from website:

   Dual Recovery Anonymous™ is a Fellowship of men & women who meet to support each other in our common recovery from two No-Fault illnesses: an emotional or psychiatric illness and chemical dependency.

8. Addiction.com. https://www.addiction.com/get-help/for-yourself/treatment/self-help-support-groups/

   Quoted from website:

   Like most any other problem in life, it can help a lot to talk to people who know exactly what you're dealing with because they've been there, too.

For the Partner and/or Family

These groups are intended to help family members refrain from behaviors that may trigger the addict. They also target underlying maladaptive thoughts and behaviors of the co-addict. Lastly, they focus on facilitating spiritual growth.

1. Al-Anon/Alateen. https://al-anon.org/

   Quoted from website:

   Al-Anon and Alateen members are people just like you and me–people who have been affected by someone else's drinking. They are parents, children, spouses, partners, brothers, sisters, other family members, friends, employers, employees, and coworkers of alcoholics.

2. Adult Children of Alcoholics. http://www.adultchildren.org/

   Quoted from website:

   The program is Adult Children of Alcoholics. The term "adult child" is used to describe adults who grew up in alcoholic or dysfunctional homes and who exhibit identifiable traits that reveal past abuse or neglect.

3. Codependents Anonymous (CODA). http://www.codependents.org/. This site takes you to their subscription page for individuals to receive their emails.

4. Recovering Couples Anonymous (RCA). http://www.recovering-couples.org/

   Quoted from website:

   Ours is a fellowship of recovering couples. We suffer from many addictions and dysfunctions, and we share our experience, strength, and hope with each other that we may solve our common problems and help other recovering couples restore their relationships. The only requirement for membership is the desire to remain committed to each other and to develop new intimacy.

Websites

1. http://www.aabigbook.com/ has online access to the Big Book, AA, Cocaine A, Cyrstal Meth A, Recovery Organizations, Debtors A, Gamblers A, Marijuana A, Narcotics A, Overeaters A, Sexaholics A.
2. http://www.alcoholscreening.org/Home.aspx has alcohol screening.
3. http://www.alcoholhelpcenter.net/ has alcohol screening and resources.
4. http://www.downyourdrink.org.uk/ is an alcohol self-help site.
5. http://www.drinkerscheckup.com/ has alcohol screening.
6. http://www.thecounselors.com/ offers online counseling.
7. https://thrivehealth.org.au/university-of-queensland-health-service/survey.php is an alcohol site mainly for students.
8. National Institute on Alcohol Abuse and Alcoholism. https://www.niaaa.nih.gov/
9. National Institute on Drug Abuse. https://www.drugabuse.gov/drugs-abuse/alcohol
10. Help Guide.org. https://www.helpguide.org/articles/addictions/alcoholism-and-alcohol-abuse.htm
11. Addictions and Recovery.org. https://addictionsandrecovery.org/alcohol.htm

Videos

To view these videos, search their titles on YouTube.

1. *The Truth About Alcohol - BBC Documentary.*
2. *HBO Documentary: Risky Drinking* (2015).
3. *Addiction and Recovery: A How to Guide | Shawn Kingsbury | TEDxUIdaho.*
4. *Wasted: Beating Alcohol Addiction Through Evidence-Based Treatment.*
5. *Alcohol Will Kill You . . . The Documentary You Must See!*

RELEVANT PHONE APPS

Generic Addiction Apps

Note: Generic apps are described in Chapter 6.

This list is not exhaustive. New apps are continually being developed. Do an Internet search to find out the latest apps available. Most are for specific addictions, but some, such as these four, are generic.

1. I Am Sober. https://play.google.com/store/apps/details?id=com.thehungrywasp.iamsober
2. Sober Time. https://play.google.com/store/apps/details?id=com.sociosoft.sobertime
3. Pocket Rehab: Get Sober & Addiction Recovery. https://play.google.com/store/apps/details?id=com.getpocketrehab.app
4. Loop Habit Tracker. https://play.google.com/store/apps/details?id=org.isoron.uhabits

Specialized Apps

1. 12 Steps AA Companion. This app is available for both IOS and Android systems. It follows the 12-step program of AA. There is a small fee for this app.
2. Stop Drinking with Andrew Johnson. This app may help individuals with AUD who have cravings. The app provides positive messages, tools for relaxing, and even hypnotherapy. There is a small fee for this app.
3. Twenty-Four Hours a Day. This app is available for both IOS and Android systems. Designed by the Hazelden Betty Ford Foundation. Hazelden is world renowned, and this is an excellent app. There is a small fee for this app.
4. SoberToolPro. This app is available for both IOS and Android systems. There is a small fee for this app.

   Quoted from website:

   This App has also been useful for treatment centers, alcoholism and addiction counselors, psychiatrists, and 12 Step Sponsors for the alcoholic or addicted individual who need a resource for finding answers to common issues experienced by the alcoholic and addict.
5. Addiction-Comprehensive Health Enhancement Support System (A-CHESS). https://www.chess.health/

   Quoted from website:

   Providers and payers use the A-CHESS Platform to improve the recovery outcomes of their patients and members through evidence-based technology that offers a continuous connection between patients and their peers and care team, builds social relatedness, enhances coping competence, and develops their motivations.

6. https://www.moderatedrinking.com/home/default_home.aspx?p=register_login NOTE: THIS IS A WEB APP. There is a moderate monthly or annual fee for this app. Quoted from website:

   This web app is for people who want to change their drinking by moderating or cutting back. Its effectiveness has been demonstrated in a randomized clinical trial funded by NIH/NIAAA. It is also listed on SAMHSA's National Register of Evidence-based Programs and Practices.

7. Ray's Night Out. This app is available for both IOS and Android systems, and there is no cost.

   Quoted from website:

   Ray's Night Out is an app designed to help young people learn safe drinking strategies and important facts about alcohol. Users of 'Ray's Night Out' take Ray the panda for a night out, buying drinks and food, dancing and playing bar trivia. Users collect good vibe points to unlock rewards and take selfies with Ray while taking care that he doesn't cross his 'stupid line' for drinking – the point where a good night out turns bad. . . . The app is targeted to young people aged 15 to 25. However, it is also a great resource for clinicians, teachers, practitioners, and parents to help guide young people's understanding of alcohol use and its limits.

8. A-Chess. http://techwonderz.com/best-addiction-recovery-apps-2018/

   Quoted from website:

   This is a brand new mobile app that has been developed by researchers. In fact, A-CHESS was highly recommended by a scientist named Kathleen Boyle who has described it as the most effective alternate innovation in the technology field because it provides extensive support in the recovery of alcoholics. This helps [prevent] relapse after leaving the recovery program. The main feature of this app is that if the alcoholic is near a liquor store or at some place where alcohol is consumed, it will take the location and other details and warns if there is a possibility of danger. So if you [are] found at such a place, the phone will [. . .] instant FaceTime with a counselor. There are some additional features such as it offers relaxation strategies and motivational thoughts and assess the risk of a relapse. [sic]

JOURNALS AND CONFERENCES

Journals

There are innumerable journals that publish articles about alcohol addiction. The following is, therefore, an incomplete list of 19 journals that publish in the addictions field. Please visit their websites for further details.

1. *Addiction*. https://onlinelibrary.wiley.com/journal/13600443

   Quoted from website:

   Addiction is the official journal of the Society for the Study of Addiction, and has been in publication since 1884. The journal publishes peer-reviewed research reports on pharmacological and behavioural addictions, bringing together research conducted within many different disciplines.

2. *Alcohol Research & Health* (ARH). ARH is the official journal of the National Institute on Alcohol Abuse and Alcoholism. https://pubs.niaaa.nih.gov/publications/arh341/toc34_1.htm

3. *Psychology of Addictive Behaviors*. A journal of the American Psychological Association. http://www.apa.org/pubs/journals/adb/index.aspx

4. *Alcoholism: Clinical and Experimental Research*. https://onlinelibrary.wiley.com/journal/15300277

5. *American Journal on Addictions*. https://onlinelibrary.wiley.com/journal/15210391

   Quoted from website:

   As the official journal of the American Academy of Addiction Psychiatry, *The American Journal of Addictions* provides a forum for the dissemination of information in the extensive field of addiction, including topics ranging from codependence to genetics, epidemiology to dual diagnostics, etiology to neuroscience, and much more.

6. *American Journal of Drug and Alcohol Abuse*. https://www.tandfonline.com/toc/iada20/current

7. *Addiction Research & Theory*. https://www.tandfonline.com/loi/iart20

8. *Addictive Behaviors*. https://www.journals.elsevier.com/addictive-behaviors/

9. *Journal of Addiction Medicine*. https://journals.lww.com/journaladdictionmedicine/pages/default.aspx

10. *Substance Use & Misuse*. https://www.tandfonline.com/loi/isum20
11. *Journal of Substance Use*. https://www.tandfonline.com/loi/ijsu20
12. *Journal of Substance Abuse Treatment*. https://www.journals.elsevier.com/journal-of-substance-abuse-treatment/
13. *Addictive Disorders & Their Treatment*. https://journals.lww.com/addictiondisorders/pages/default.aspx
14. *Alcohol and Alcoholism*. https://academic.oup.com/alcalc/
15. *Alcohol*. https://www.journals.elsevier.com/alcohol/
16. *Alcoholism Treatment Quarterly*. https://www.tandfonline.com/toc/watq20/current
17. *Drug and Alcohol Dependence*. https://www.journals.elsevier.com/drug-and-alcohol-dependence/
18. *Drug and Alcohol Review*. https://onlinelibrary.wiley.com/journal/14653362
19. *International Journal of Mental Health and Addiction*. https://www.springer.com/public+health/journal/11469

Conferences

1. American Society of Addictive Medicine hosts an annual conference. Details can be found at https://www.asam.org/education/live-online-cme/the-asam-annual-conference
2. Substance Abuse and Mental Health Services Administration lists several conferences. Details can be found at https://www.samhsa.gov/
3. National Institute on Drug Abuse lists several conferences. Details can be found at https://www.drugabuse.gov/news-events/meetings-events
4. National Institute on Alcohol Abuse and Alcoholism (NIAAA). Details of meetings and conference can be found at https://www.niaaa.nih.gov/
5. National Conference on Alcohol & Addiction Disorders. This conference used to be known as the National Addiction Conference. They provided notice of the name change on March 8, 2018. Please type the name of the conference into Google for the latest conference details.
6. International Society of Addiction Medicine (ISAM). See http://www.isamweb.org/annual-meetings/ for details.
7. National Association for Alcoholism and Drug Abuse Counselors (NAADAC). This is the Association for Addiction Professionals. Details of their annual conference can be found at https://www.naadac.org/annualconference
8. Canadian Society of Addiction Medicine. Details of their annual conference can be found at https://www.csam-smca.org/

A couple of additional conferences worth checking out are as follows (check their websites for details):

9. International Conference on Addictive Disorders and Alcoholism.
10. International Conference on Addiction Research & Therapy.

INDIVIDUAL EXERCISES

1. Attend a bar on a busy night (likely Friday or Saturday is best). Do one of the following:
   - If you are with friends, decide that you will either remain abstinent and be the designated driver or, if you choose to drink, drink only a small amount. Pay attention to your friends who drink more. What characterizes the change in their behavior as they consume increasing amounts of alcohol? What do you like about their behavior and what do you dislike?
   - If you go by yourself, sit somewhere close to people who are drinking excessively. Without appearing obvious, take notice of their behavior. What characterizes people who drink heavily? What signs inform you that this person(s) has had too much to drink?
2. Attend an AA meeting. You will need to check on the web for meetings that are scheduled in your area. Be sure to pick one that is an open meeting, which means that anyone can attend. Take note of the adverse consequences that alcohol has created for members who speak at the meeting.
3. Skim or read *The Big Book*. What most stands out for you in the way this book is written? Which parts of the 12 steps do you agree with and which parts strike you the wrong way? Ask yourself why you have this reaction.

CLASSROOM EXERCISES

1. Prohibition occurred in the United States between 1920 and 1933. During that time, there was a nationwide ban on alcohol production, importation, transportation, and sale. Have the class split into two for debate. One side of the class takes the position that prohibition should be re-enacted, and the other half of the class takes the perspective that the drinking age should be lowered to 18 as it is in some Canadian provinces.

2. Have your students split into two groups based on whether they have ever gotten drunk or intoxicated. Create groups of four ensuring that at least one student who has ever gotten drunk or intoxicated is in each group. Have the student(s) who has consumed alcohol excessively in each group tell the others about the pros and cons of his/her/their experience. Furthermore, what advice would this student(s) provide the other students in her/his/their group regarding consumption of alcohol?

3. Invite a speaker from SMART Recovery, Rational Recovery, or AA to attend your class and share their experience with excessive drinking. At a class before the speaker is scheduled, ensure that the students have questions that they would want to ask the speaker.

CHAPTER SUMMARY

Alcohol use has a long history dating back approximately 20,000 years, but its consequences today are staggering. There are more than 85,000 deaths each year due to alcohol in the United States. The societal cost annually to the United States is estimated at more than $249.0 billion. *Addiction* involves a compulsive and excessive use of drugs and alcohol with subsequent negative consequences. Binge drinking is defined as more than four drinks a day and not more than 14 drinks in a week for men, and more than three drinks a day and not more than seven drinks in a week for women. Relapse is common for those who become dependent on alcohol. Although most individuals with AUD would prefer to learn how to moderate their drinking, it is unlikely that most can do so who have become severely dependent on alcohol. The course of AUD does vary, however, from person to person.

An important cause of AUD and drug addiction is child maltreatment. Others, however, may have a strong genetic predisposition to developing an AUD. Still others may become dependent because of what they initially perceive to be the positive effects of drinking such as becoming less inhibited, less stressed or depressed, and more sociable. Over time, however, those who become dependent begin to experience adverse consequences in several areas of their lives.

The beneficial effects of light to moderate drinking remain controversial. Recent global research has suggested that there is not a safe amount of alcohol that can be consumed regularly.

Therapies for alcohol addiction include three medications that have been approved by the FDA. These include disulfiram, acamprosate, and naltrexone. Counseling approaches have mostly focused on behavioral methods, CBT, MI, and contingency management. Couples counseling, group counseling, and in some cases family counseling have been recommended. Some have suggested integrative treatment that also includes acupuncture, yoga, exercise, mindfulness, hypnosis, biofeedback, neurofeedback, music and art therapy, and herbal therapies.

REFERENCES

Acheson, A., Vincent, A. S., Cohoon, A. J., & Lovallo, W. R. (2018). Defining the phenotype of young adults with family histories of alcohol and other substance use disorders: Studies from the family health patterns project. *Addictive Behaviors, 77*, 247–254.

Agabio, R., Campesi, I., Pisanu, C., Gessa, G. L., & Franconi, F. (2016). Sex differences in substance use disorders: Focus on side effects. *Addiction Biology, 21*(5), 1030–1042.

Agardh, E. E., Danielsson, A.-K., Ramstedt, M., Ledgaard Holm, A., Diderichsen, F., Juel, K., . . . Allebeck, P. (2016). Alcohol-attributed disease burden in four Nordic countries: A comparison using the global burden of disease, injuries and risk factors 2013 study. *Addiction, 111*(10), 1806–1813.

Allen, J. L., & Mowbray, O. (2016). Sexual orientation, treatment utilization, and barriers for alcohol related problems: Findings from a nationally representative sample. *Drug and Alcohol Dependence, 161*, 323–330.

Allen, J. P., Crawford, E. F., & Kudler, H. (2016). Nature and treatment of comorbid alcohol problems and post-traumatic stress disorder among American military personnel and veterans. *Alcohol Research: Current Reviews, 38*(1), 133–140.

Allen, J. P., Nieuwsma, J. A., & Meador, K G. (2014). The role of military and Veterans Affairs chaplains in the treatment of alcohol problems. *Pastoral Psychology, 63*, 1–11.

American Psychiatric Association (APA). (2013). *Diagnostic and statistical manual of mental disorders* (5th ed.). Washington, DC: Author.

American Society of Addiction Medicine (ASAM). (2018). *What is the ASAM criteria?* Retrieved on August 30, 2018, from https://www.asam.org/resources/the-asam-criteria/about

Andersen, K., Bogenschutz, M. P., Buhringer, G., Behrendt, S., Bilberg, R., Braun, B., . . . Nielsen, A. S. (2015). Outpatient treatment of alcohol use disorders among subjects 60+ years:

Design of a randomized clinical trial conducted in three countries (Elderly Study). *BMC Psychiatry, 15*, 1–11.

Anthenelli, R. M., Heffner, J. L., Blom, T. J., Daniel, B. E., McKenna, B. S., & Wand, G. S. (2018). Sex differences in the ACTH and cortisol response to pharmacological probes are stressor-specific and occur regardless of alcohol dependence history. *Psychoneuroendocrinology, 94*, 72–82.

Anthenien, A. M., Lembo, J., & Neighbors, C. (2017). Drinking motives and alcohol outcome expectancies as mediators of the association between negative urgency and alcohol consumption. *Addictive Behaviors, 66*, 101–107.

Arts, N. J. M., Walvoort, S. J. W., & Kessels, R. P. C. (2017). Korsakoff's syndrome: A critical review. *Neuropsychiatric Disease and Treatment, 13*, 2875–2890.

Barr, T., Helms, C., Grant, K., & Messaoudi, I. (2016). Opposing effects of alcohol on the immune system. *Progress in Neuro-Psychopharmacology & Biological Psychiatry, 65*, 242–251.

Becker, S. J., Jones, R. N., Hernandez, L., Graves, H. R., & Spirito, A. (2016). Moderators of brief motivation-enhancing treatments for alcohol-positive adolescents presenting to the emergency department. *Journal of Substance Abuse Treatment, 69*, 28–34.

Beresford, T. P., Wongngamnit, N., & Temple, B. A. (2015). Alcoholism: Diagnosis and natural history in the context of medical disease. In J. Neuberger & A. DiMartini (Eds.), *Alcohol abuse and liver disease* (pp. 23–34). New York, NY: Wiley-Blackwell.

Bertholet, N., Palfai, T., Gaume, J., Daeppen, J.-B., & Saitz, R. (2014). Do brief alcohol motivational interventions work like we think they do? *Alcoholism: Clinical and Experimental Research, 38*, 853–859.

Bhala, N., Cezard, G., Ward, H. J. T., Bansal, N., Bhopal, R., & Scottish Health and Ethnicity Linkage Study (SHELS) Collaboration, Scotland. (2016). Ethnic variations in liver- and alcohol-related disease hospitalisations and mortality: The Scottish health and ethnicity linkage study. *Alcohol and Alcoholism, 51*, 593–601.

Blume, A. W., Rudisill, D. M., Hendricks, S., & Santoya, N. (2013). Disease model. In P. M. Miller, S. A. Ball, M. E. Bates, A. W. Blume, K. M. Kampman, D. J. Kavanagh, M. E. Larimer, N. M. Petry, & P. De Witte (Eds.), *Principles of addiction: Comprehensive addictive behaviors and disorders, Vol 1* (pp. 71–76). San Diego, CA: Elsevier Academic Press.

Bo, R., Billieux, J., & Landro, N. I. (2016). Binge drinking is characterized by decisions favoring positive and discounting negative consequences. *Addiction Research & Theory, 24*(6), 499–506.

Bogenschutz, M. P., & Forcehimes, A. A. (2017). Development of a psychotherapeutic model for psilocybin-assisted treatment of alcoholism. *Journal of Humanistic Psychology, 57*, 389–414.

Borges, G., Cherpitel, C. J., Orozco, R., Ye, Y., Monteiro, M., Hao, W., & Benegal, V. (2017). A dose-response estimate for acute alcohol use and risk of suicide attempt. *Addiction Biology, 22*(6), 1554–1561.

Borsari, B., Apodaca, T. R., Yurasek, A., & Monti, P. M. (2017). Does mental status impact therapist and patient communication in emergency department brief interventions addressing alcohol use? *Journal of Substance Abuse Treatment, 73*, 1–8.

Borsari, B., Short, E. E., Mastroleo, N. R., Hustad, J. T.P., Tevyaw, T. O., Barnett, N. P., . . . Monti, P. M. (2014). Phone-delivered brief motivational interventions for mandated college students delivered during the summer months. *Journal of Substance Abuse Treatment, 46*, 592–596.

Bowring, A. L., Vella, A. M., Degenhardt, L., Hellard, M., & Lim, M. S. C. (2015). Sexual identity, same-sex partners and risk behaviour among a community-based sample of young people in Australia. *International Journal of Drug Policy, 26*, 153–161.

Brady, K. T., & Maria, M. M.-S. (2015). Women and addiction. In M. Galanter, H. D. Kleber, & K. T. Brady (Eds.), *The American Psychiatric Publishing textbook of substance abuse treatment* (5th ed., pp. 597–606). Arlington, VA: American Psychiatric Publishing.

Bravo, A. J., Kelley, M. L., & Hollis, B. F. (2016). Social support, depressive symptoms, and hazardous alcohol use among navy members: An examination of social support as a protective factor across deployment. *Journal of Social and Clinical Psychology, 35*(8), 693–704.

Bravo, F., Gual, A., Lligona, A., & Colom, J. (2013). Gender differences in the long-term outcome of alcohol dependence treatments: An analysis of twenty-year prospective follow up. *Drug and Alcohol Review, 32*, 381–388.

Bray, R. M., Brown, J. M., & Williams, J. (2013). Trends in binge and heavy drinking, alcohol-related problems, and combat exposure in the U.S. military. *Substance Use & Misuse, 48*, 799–810.

Brem, M. J., Florimbio, A. R., Elmquist, J., Shorey, R. C., & Stuart, G. L. (2018). Antisocial traits, distress tolerance, and alcohol problems as predictors of intimate partner violence in men arrested for domestic violence. *Psychology of Violence, 8*(1), 132–139.

Brooks, F., & McHenry, B. (2009). *A contemporary approach to substance abuse and addiction counseling: A counselor's guide to application and understanding*. Alexandria, VA: American Counseling Association.

Brower, K. J. (2015). Assessment and treatment of insomnia in adult patients with alcohol use disorders. *Alcohol, 49*, 417–427.

Brown, J. L., Talley, A. E., Littlefield, A. K., & Gause, N. K. (2016). Young women's alcohol expectancies for sexual risk-taking mediate the link between sexual enhancement motives and condomless sex when drinking. *Journal of Behavioral Medicine, 39*(5), 925–930.

Budney, A. J., Brown, P. C., & Stanger, C. (2013). Behavioral treatments. In B. S. McCrady & E. E. Epstein (Eds.), *Addictions: A comprehensive guidebook* (2nd ed., pp. 411–433). New York, NY: Oxford University Press.

Burdenski, T. K., Jr. (2012). Recovering from substance misuse. In P. A. Robey, R. E. Wubbolding, & J. Carlson (Eds.), *Contemporary issues in couples counseling: A choice theory and reality therapy approach* (pp. 59–77). New York, NY: Routledge/Taylor & Francis.

Cadigan, J. M., Klanecky, A. K., & Martens, M. P. (2017). An examination of alcohol risk profiles and co-occurring mental health symptoms among OEF/OIF veterans. *Addictive Behaviors, 70*, 54–60.

Caetano, R., Kaplan, M. S., Huguet, N., Conner, K., McFarland, B. H., Giesbrecht, N., & Nolte, K. B. (2015). Precipitating circumstances of suicide and alcohol intoxication among U.S. ethnic groups. *Alcoholism: Clinical and Experimental Research, 39*, 1510–1517.

Campbell, E. J., Lawrence, A. J., & Perry, C. J. (2018). New steps for treating alcohol use disorder. *Psychopharmacology, 235*, 1759–1773.

Casement, M. D., Shaw, D. S., Sitnick, S. L., Musselman, S. C., & Forbes, E. E. (2015). Life stress in adolescence predicts early adult reward-related brain function and alcohol dependence. *Social Cognitive and Affective Neuroscience, 10*, 416–423.

Celio, M. A., Mastroleo, N. R., DiGuiseppi, G., Barnett, N. P., Colby, S. M., Kahler, C. W., . . . Monti, P. M. (2017). Using video conferencing to deliver a brief motivational intervention for alcohol and sex risk to emergency department patients: A proof-of-concept pilot study. *Addiction Research & Theory*, *25*, 318–325.

Chakravorty, S., Chaudhary, N. S., & Brower, K. J. (2016). Alcohol dependence and its relationship with insomnia and other sleep disorders. *Alcoholism: Clinical and Experimental Research*, *40*(11), 2271–2282.

Chao, F., & Ashraf, N. (2016). Alcohol. In P. Levounis, E. Zerbo, & R. Aggarwal (Eds.), *Pocket guide to addiction assessment and treatment* (pp. 39–63). Arlington, VA: American Psychiatric Association.

Chartier, K. G., Dick, D. M., Almasy, L., Chan, G., Aliev, F., Schuckit, M. A., . . . Hesselbrock, V. M. (2016). Interactions between alcohol metabolism genes and religious involvement in association with maximum drinks and alcohol dependence symptoms. *Journal of Studies on Alcohol and Drugs*, *77*, 393–404.

Cherpitel, C. J., Ye, Y., Bond, J., Borges, G., Monteiro, M., Chou, P., & Hao, W. (2015). Alcohol attributable fraction for injury morbidity from the dose-response relationship of acute alcohol consumption: Emergency department data from 18 countries. *Addiction*, *110*, 1724–1732.

Cicchetti, D., & Rogosch, F. A. (2018). A developmental psychopathology perspective on substance use: Illustrations from the research on child maltreatment. In H. E. Fitzgerald & L. Puttler (Eds.), *Alcohol use disorders: A developmental science approach to etiology* (pp. 17–29). New York, NY: Oxford University Press.

Connors, G. J., DiClemente, C. C., Velasquez, M. M., & Donovan, D. M. (2013). *Substance abuse treatment and the stages of change: Selecting and planning interventions* (2nd ed.). New York, NY: Guilford Press.

Copeland, W. E., Angold, A., Shanahan, L., Dreyfuss, J., Dlamini, I., & Costello, E. J. (2012). Predicting persistent alcohol problems: A prospective analysis from the Great Smoky Mountain Study. *Psychological Medicine*, *42*, 1925–1935.

Croxford, A., Notley, C. J., Maskrey, V., Holland, R., & Kouimtsidis, C. (2015). An exploratory qualitative study seeking participant views evaluating group cognitive behavioral therapy preparation for alcohol detoxification. *Journal of Substance Use*, *20*, 61–68.

Cuadrado, M. (2014). Hispanic use of juramentos and Roman Catholic priests as auxiliaries to abstaining from alcohol use/misuse. *Mental Health, Religion & Culture*, *17*(10), 1015–1022.

Cucciare, M. A., Weingardt, K. R., Valencia-Garcia, D., & Ghaus, S. (2015). Post-traumatic stress disorder and illicit drug use in veterans presenting to primary care with alcohol misuse. *Addiction Research & Theory*, *23*, 287–293.

Czapla, M., Simon, J. J., Richter, B., Kluge, M., Friederich, H.-C., Herpertz, S., . . . Loeber, S. (2016). The impact of cognitive impairment and impulsivity on relapse of alcohol-dependent patients: Implications for psychotherapeutic treatment. *Addiction Biology*, *21*(4), 873–884.

Day, E., & Jheeta, M. (2016). Management of alcohol use disorders in the UK. In W. Mistral (Ed.), *Integrated approaches to drug and alcohol problems: Action on addiction* (pp. 109–125). New York, NY: Routledge.

DeCou, C. R., & Skewes, M. C. (2016). Symptoms of alcohol dependence predict suicide ideation among Alaskan undergraduates. *Crisis: The Journal of Crisis Intervention and Suicide Prevention*, *37*(3), 232–235.

Denis, C. M., Cacciola, J. S., & Alterman, A. I. (2013). Addiction Severity Index (ASI) summary scores: comparison of the Recent Status Scores of the ASI-6 and the Composite Scores of the ASI-5. *Journal of Substance Abuse Treatment*, *45*(5), 444–450.

de Oliveira Mangueira, S., & de Oliveira Lopes, M. V. (2016). Clinical validation of the nursing diagnosis of dysfunctional family processes related to alcoholism. *Journal of Advanced Nursing*, *72*(10), 2401–2412.

DiBello, A. M., Miller, M. B., Young, C. M., Neighbors, C., & Lindgren, K. P. (2018). Explicit drinking identity and alcohol problems: The mediating role of drinking to cope. *Addictive Behaviors*, *76*, 88–94.

Dickerson, D. L., Brown, R. A., Johnson, C. L., Schweigman, K., & D'Amico, E. J. (2016). Integrating motivational interviewing and traditional practices to address alcohol and drug use among urban American Indian/Alaska Native youth. *Journal of Substance Abuse Treatment*, *65*, 26–35.

DiClemente, C. C., Bellino, L. E., & Neavins, T. M. (1999). Motivation for change and alcoholism treatment. *Alcohol Research & Health*, *23*(2), 86–92.

Domeij, H., Fahlstrom, G., Bertilsson, G., Hultcrantz, M., Munthe-Kaas, H., Gordh, C. N., & Helgesson, G. (2018). Experiences of living with fetal alcohol spectrum disorders: A systematic review and synthesis of qualitative data. *Developmental Medicine & Child Neurology*, *60*(8), 741–752.

Dworkin, E. R., Wanklyn, S., Stasiewicz, P. R., & Coffey, S. F. (2018). PTSD symptom presentation among people with alcohol and drug use disorders: Comparisons by substance of abuse. *Addictive Behaviors*, *76*, 188–194.

Earleywine, M. (2016). *Substance use problems* (2nd ed.). Ashland, OH: Hogrefe.

Edelman, E. J., Oldfield, B. J., & Tetrault, J. M. (2018). Office-based addiction treatment in primary care: Approaches that work. *Medical Clinics of North America*, *102*, 635–652.

Elofson, J., Gongvatana, W., & Carey, K. B. (2013). Alcohol use and cerebral white matter compromise in adolescence. *Addictive Behaviors*, *38*, 2295–2305.

Emerson, M. A., Moore, R. S., & Caetano, R. (2017). Association between lifetime posttraumatic stress disorder and past year alcohol use disorder among American Indians/Alaska Natives and non-Hispanic Whites. *Alcoholism: Clinical and Experimental Research*, *41*, 576–584.

Engel, K., Schaefer, M., Stickel, A., Binder, H., Heinz, A., & Richter, C. (2016). The role of psychological distress in relapse prevention of alcohol addiction. Can high scores on the SCL-90-R predict alcohol relapse? *Alcohol and Alcoholism*, *51*(1), 27–31.

Enoch, M.-A., & Albaugh, B. J. (2017). Review: Genetic and environmental risk factors for alcohol use disorders in American Indians and Alaskan Natives. *American Journal on Addictions*, *26*(5), 461–468.

Epstein, E. E., McCrady, B. S., Hallgren, K. A., Cook, S., Jensen, N. K., & Hildebrandt, T. (2018). A randomized trial of female-specific cognitive behavior therapy for alcohol dependent women. *Psychology of Addictive Behaviors*, *32*, 1–15.

Erol, A., & Karpyak, V. M. (2015). Sex and gender-related differences in alcohol use and its consequences: Contemporary knowledge and future research considerations. *Drug and Alcohol Dependence*, *156*, 1–13.

Esel, E., & Dinc, K. (2017). Neurobiology of alcohol dependence and implications on treatment. *Turk Psikiyatri Dergisi*, *28*(1), 1–10.

Ewing, J. A. (1984). Detecting alcoholism: The CAGE Questionnaire. *JAMA, 252*(140), 1905–1907.

Farmer, C. M., Stahlman, S., & Hepner, K. A. (2017). "You should drink less": Frequency and predictors of discussions between providers and patients about reducing alcohol use. *Substance Use & Misuse, 52*(2), 139–144.

Fasteau, M., Mackay, D., Smith, D. J., & Meyer, T. D. (2017). Is adolescent alcohol use associated with self-reported hypomanic symptoms in adulthood? – Findings from a prospective birth cohort. *Psychiatry Research, 255*, 232–237.

Flaudias, V., de Chazeron, I., Zerhouni, O., Boudesseul, J., Begue, L., Bouthier, R., . . . Brousse, G. (2015). Preventing alcohol abuse through social networking sites: A first assessment of a two-year ecological approach. *Journal of Medical Internet Research, 17*(12), 1–9.

Fowler, L. A., Holt, S. L., & Joshi, D. (2016). Mobile technology-based interventions for adult users of alcohol: A systematic review of the literature. *Addictive Behaviors, 62*, 25–34.

Frueh, B. C., & Smith, J. A. (2012). Suicide, alcoholism, and psychiatric illness among union forces during the U.S. Civil War. *Journal of Anxiety Disorders, 26*, 769–775.

Fuehrlein, B. S., Mota, N., Arias, A. J., Trevisan, L. A., Kachadourian, L. K., Krystal, J. H., . . . Pietrzak, R. H. (2016). The burden of alcohol use disorders in US military veterans: Results from the National Health and Resilience in Veterans Study. *Addiction, 111*, 1786–1794.

Fuller-Thomson, E., Roane, J. L., & Brennenstuhl, S. (2016). Three types of adverse childhood experiences, and alcohol and drug dependence among adults: An investigation using population-based data. *Substance Use & Misuse, 51*(11), 1451–1461.

Gearhardt, A. N., & Corbin, W. R. (2012). Interactions between alcohol consumption, eating, and weight. In K. D. Brownell & M. S. Gold (Eds.), *Food and addiction: A comprehensive handbook* (pp. 249–253). New York, NY: Oxford University Press.

Gerstein, J., & Ellis, A. (2014). Denial. In J. Carlson & W. Knaus (Eds.), *Albert Ellis revisited* (pp. 253–266). New York, NY: Routledge/Taylor & Francis.

Gilbert, P. A., Pass, L. E., Keuroghlian, A. S., Greenfield, T. K., & Reisner, S. L. (2018). Alcohol research with transgender populations: A systematic review and recommendations to strengthen future studies. *Drug and Alcohol Dependence, 186*, 138–146.

Gilder, D. A., Stouffer, G. M., Lau, P., & Ehlers, C. L. (2016). Clinical characteristics of alcohol combined with other substance use disorders in an American Indian community sample. *Drug and Alcohol Dependence, 161*, 222–229.

Glantz, M. D., Moskalewicz, J., Caldas-de-Almeida, J. M., & Degenhardt, L. (2018). Alcohol-use disorders. In K. M. Scott, P. de Jonge, D. J. Stein, & R. C. Kessler (Eds.), *Mental disorders around the world: Facts and figures from the WHO World Mental Health Surveys* (pp. 223–242). New York, NY: Cambridge University Press.

Glazier, R. E., & Kling, R. N. (2013). Recent trends in substance abuse among persons with disabilities compared to that of persons without disabilities. *Disability and Health Journal, 6*, 107–115.

Gorka, S., Hee, D., Lieberman, L., Mittal, V., Phan, K., & Shankman, S. (2016). Reactivity to uncertain threat as a familial vulnerability factor for alcohol use disorder. *Psychological Medicine, 46*(16), 3349–3358.

Grant, S., Pedersen, E. R., Osilla, K. C., Kulesza, M., & D'Amico, E. J. (2016). Reviewing and interpreting the effects of brief alcohol interventions: Comment on a Cochrane review about motivational interviewing for young adults. *Addiction, 111*(9), 1521–1527.

Greenberg, L. P., Martindale, S. L., Fils-Aime, L. R., & Dolan, S. L. (2016). Distress tolerance and impulsivity are associated with drug and alcohol use consequences in an online community sample. *Journal of Cognitive Psychotherapy, 30*(1), 50–59.

Grella, C. (2013). Gender-specific treatments for substance use disorders. In P. M. Miller, S. A. Ball, M. E. Bates, A. W. Blume, K. M. Kampman, D. J. Kavanagh, M. E. Larimer, N. M. Petry, & P. De Witte (Eds.), *Comprehensive addictive behaviors and disorders, Vol. 3: Interventions for addiction* (pp. 177–185). San Diego, CA: Elsevier Academic Press.

Grigsby, T. J., Forster, M., Unger, J. B., & Sussman, S. (2016). Predictors of alcohol-related negative consequences in adolescents: A systematic review of the literature and implications for future research. *Journal of Adolescence, 48*, 18–35.

Griswold, M. G., Fullman, N., Gakidou, E., & the GBD 2016 Alcohol Collaborators. (2018, August 23). Alcohol use and burden for 195 countries and territories, 1990–2016: A systematic analysis for the Global Burden of Disease Study 2016. *Lancet* [pp. 1–21; published online at http://dx.doi.org/10.1016/S0140-6736(18)31310-2].

Gronbaek, M. (2009). The positive and negative health effects of alcohol- and the public health implications. *Journal of Internal Medicine, 265*, 407–420.

Gropper, S., Spengler, S., Stuke, H., Gawron, C. K., Parnack, J., Gutwinski, S., . . . Bermpohl, F. (2016). Behavioral impulsivity mediates the relationship between decreased frontal gray matter volume and harmful alcohol drinking: A voxel-based morphometry study. *Journal of Psychiatric Research, 83*, 16–23.

Gryczynski, J., Schwartz, R. P., Fishman, M. J., Nordeck, C. D., Grant, J., Nidich, S., . . . O'Grady, K. E. (2018). Integration of transcendental meditation (TM) into alcohol use disorder (AUD) treatment. *Journal of Substance Abuse Treatment, 87*, 23–30.

Guerrini, I., Quadri, G., & Thomson, A. D. (2014). Genetic and environmental interplay in risky drinking in adolescents: A literature review. *Alcohol and Alcoholism, 49*, 138–142.

Guidot, D. M., & Mehta, A. J. (2014). A brief history of alcohol use and abuse in human history. In D. M. Guidot & A. J. Mehta (Eds.), *Alcohol use disorders and the lung: A clinical and pathophysiological approach* (pp. 3–6). Totowa, NJ: Humana Press,

Haass-Koffler, C. L., Swift, R. M., & Leggio, L. (2018). Noradrenergic targets for the treatment of alcohol use disorder. *Psychopharmacology, 235*, 1625–1634.

Hagman, B. T. (2016). Performance of the AUDIT in detecting *DSM-5* alcohol use disorders in college students. *Substance Use & Misuse, 51*(11), 1521–1528.

Hagman, B. T. (2017). Development and psychometric analysis of the Brief *DSM-5* Alcohol Use Disorder Diagnostic Assessment: Towards effective diagnosis in college students. *Psychology of Addictive Behaviors, 31*(7), 797–806.

HAMS Harm Reduction Network. (2015). *Harm reduction for alcohol: The odds of going through alcohol withdrawal.* Retrieved on August 19, 2018, from http://hams.cc/odds/

Harrell, N. O., Pedrelli, P., Lejuez, C. W., & MacPherson, L. (2014). Alcohol problems. In S. G. Hofmann, D. J. A. Dozois, W. Rief, & J. A. Smits (Eds.), *The Wiley handbook of cognitive behavioral therapy, Vols. 1–3* (pp. 1315–1337). New York, NY: Wiley-Blackwell.

Harris, R. A., & Koob, G. F. (2017). The future is now: A 2020 view of alcoholism research. *Neuropharmacology, 122*, 1–2.

Hauser, S. R., Wilden, J. A., Batra, V., & Rodd, Z. A. (2017). Deep brain stimulation: A possible therapeutic technique for treating refractory alcohol and drug addiction behaviors. In R. R. Watson & S. Zibadi (Eds.), *Addictive substances and neurological disease: Alcohol, tobacco, caffeine, and drugs of abuse in everyday lifestyles* (pp. 239–248). San Diego, CA: Elsevier Academic Press.

Heikkinen, N., Niskanen, E., Kononen, M., Tolmunen, T., Kekkonen, V., Kivimaki, P., . . . Vanninen, R. (2017). Alcohol consumption during adolescence is associated with reduced grey matter volumes. *Addiction, 112*, 604–613.

Heilig, M. (2015). *The thirteenth step: Addiction in the age of brain science*. New York, NY: Columbia University Press.

Heilig, M., & Spanagel, R. (2015). Neurobiology of alcohol use disorder. In M. Galanter, H. D. Kleber, & K. T. Brady (Eds.), *The American Psychiatric Publishing textbook of substance abuse treatment* (5th ed., pp. 145–157). Arlington, VA: American Psychiatric

Heitmann, J., van Hemel-Ruiter, M. E., Vermeulen, K. M., Ostafin, B. D., MacLeod, C., Wiers, R. W., . . . de Jong, P. J. (2017). Internet-based attentional bias modification training as add-on to regular treatment in alcohol and cannabis dependent outpatients: A study protocol of a randomized control trial. *BMC Psychiatry, 17*, 1–13.

Herrold, A. A., Pape, T. L.-B., Li, X., & Jordan, N. (2017). Association between alcohol craving and health-related quality of life among veterans with co-occurring conditions. *Military Medicine, 182*, e1712–e1717.

Hodge, D. R., & Lietz, C. A. (2014). Using spiritually modified cognitive-behavioral therapy in substance dependence treatment: Therapists' and clients' perceptions of the presumed benefits and limitations. *Health & Social Work, 39*, 200–210.

Hodgins, D. C., Leigh, G., Milne, R., & Gerrish, R. (1997). Drinking goal selection in behavioral self-management treatment of chronic alcoholics. *Addictive Behaviors, 22*(2), 247–255.

Holt, S. R., & Tobin, D. G. (2018). Pharmacotherapy for alcohol use disorder. *Medical Clinics of North America, 102*, 653–666.

Horn, J. L., Wanberg, K. W., & Foster, F. M. (1986). *The Alcohol Use Inventory (AUI)*. Minneapolis, MN: National Computer Systems.

Hu, J. (2016). Effects of a social anxiety and motivational interviewing treatment on socially anxious college drinkers. *Dissertation Abstracts International: Section B: The Sciences and Engineering*, 77(3-B(E)). No pagination specified.

Jankowski, P. J., Meca, A., Lui, P. P., & Zamboanga, B. L. (2018). Religiousness and acculturation as moderators of the association linking acculturative stress to levels of hazardous alcohol use in college students. *Psychology of Religion and Spirituality*. No pagination specified.

Johansson, M., Sinadinovic, K., Hammarberg, A., Sundstrom, C., Hermansson, U., Andreasson, S., & Berman, A. (2017). Web-based self-help for problematic alcohol use: A large naturalistic study. *International Journal of Behavioral Medicine, 24*, 749–759.

Johnson, B. A., & Marzani-Nissen, G. (2012). Alcohol: Clinical aspects. In B. A. Johnson (Ed.), *Addiction medicine: Science and practice* (vols. 1 and 2; pp. 381–395). New York, NY: Springer Science + Business Media.

Johnson, T. J., & Kristeller, J. L. (2013). Spirituality and addiction. In P. M. Miller, S. A. Ball, M. E. Bates, A. W. Blume, K. M. Kampman, D. J. Kavanagh, M. E. Larimer, N. M. Petry, & P. De Witte (Eds.), *Principles of addiction: Comprehensive addictive behaviors and disorders, Vol 1* (pp. 283–291). San Diego, CA: Elsevier Academic Press.

Jones, S. A., Latchford, G., & Tober, G. (2016). Client experiences of motivational interviewing: An interpersonal process recall study. *Psychology and Psychotherapy: Theory, Research and Practice, 89*(1), 97–114.

Kaarre, O., Kallioniemi, E., Kononen, M., Tolmunen, T., Kekkonen, V., Kivimaki, P., . . . Maata, S. (2018). Heavy alcohol use in adolescence is associated with altered cortical activity: A combined TMS-EEG study. *Addiction Biology, 23*, 268–280.

Kadden, R. M., & Skerker, P. M. (1999). Treatment decision-making and goal setting. In B. S. McCrady & E. E. Epstein (Eds.), *Addictions: A comprehensive guidebook* (pp. 216–231). New York, NY: Oxford University Press.

Kaner, E. F., Beyer, F. R., Muirhead, C., Campbell, F., Pienaar, E. D., Bertholet, N., . . . Burnand, B. (2018). Effectiveness of brief alcohol interventions in primary care populations. *Cochrane Database of Systematic Reviews, 2*, CD004148

Kaplan, K. A., McQuaid, J., Batki, S. L., & Rosenlicht, N. (2014). Behavioral treatment of insomnia in early recovery. *Journal of Addiction Medicine, 8*, 395–398.

Keller, P. S., Gilbert, L. R., Haak, E. A., & Bi, S. (2017). Parental alcoholism. In D. Morley, X. Li, & C. Jenkinson (Eds.), *Children and young people's response to parental illness: A handbook of assessment and practice* (pp. 82–105). New York, NY: Routledge/Taylor & Francis.

Kerr, W. C., & Greenfield, T. K. (2015). Racial/ethnic disparities in the self-reported number of drinks in 2 hours before driving becomes impaired. *American Journal of Public Health, 105*, 1409–1414.

Khantzian, E. J. (2003). Understanding addictive vulnerability: An evolving psychodynamic perspective. *Neuropsychoanalysis, 5*(1), 53–56.

Kiluk, B. D., Devore, K. A., Buck, M. B., Nich, C., Frankforter, T. L., LaPaglia, D. M., . . . Carroll, K. M. (2016). Randomized trial of computerized cognitive behavioral therapy for alcohol use disorders: Efficacy as a virtual stand-alone and treatment add-on compared with standard outpatient treatment. *Alcoholism: Clinical and Experimental Research, 40*, 1991–2000.

Kim, M. J., Mason, W. A., Herrenkohl, T. I., Catalano, R. F., Toumbourou, J. W., & Hemphill, S. A. (2017). Influence of early onset of alcohol use on the development of adolescent alcohol problems: A longitudinal binational study. *Prevention Science, 18*, 1–11.

King, A. C., Hasin, D., O'Connor, S. J., McNamara, P. J., & Cao, D. (2016). A prospective 5-year re-examination of alcohol response in heavy drinkers progressing in alcohol use disorder. *Biological Psychiatry, 79*(6), 489–498.

Klostermann, K. (2016). Marital and family approaches. In K. J. Sher (Ed.), *The Oxford handbook of substance use and substance use disorders, Vol. 2* (pp. 567–581). New York, NY: Oxford University Press.

Krentzman, A. R. (2017). Longitudinal differences in spirituality and religiousness between men and women in treatment for alcohol use disorders. *Psychology of Religion and Spirituality, 9*, S11–S21.

Krentzman, A. R., Webb, J. R., Jester, J. M., & Harris, J. I. (2018). Longitudinal relationship between forgiveness of self and forgiveness of others among individuals with alcohol use disorders. *Psychology of Religion and Spirituality, 10*, 128–137.

Krishnan, H. R., Sakharkar, A. J., Teppen, T. L., Berkel, T. D. M., & Pandey, S. C. (2014). The epigenetic landscape of alcoholism. *International Review of Neurobiology, 115*, 75–116.

Kuntsche, E., Rossow, I., Engels, R., & Kuntsche, S. (2016). Is 'age at first drink' a useful concept in alcohol research and prevention? We doubt that. *Addiction, 111*(6), 957–965.

Lechner, W. V., Day, A. M., Metrik, J., Leventhal, A. M., & Kahler, C. W. (2016). Effects of alcohol-induced working memory decline on alcohol consumption and adverse consequences of use. *Psychopharmacology, 233*(1), 83–88.

Lee, M. R., Chassin, L., & Villalta, I. K. (2013). Maturing out of alcohol involvement: Transitions in latent drinking statuses from late adolescence to adulthood. *Development and Psychopathology, 25*, 1137–1153.

Lehavot, K., Williams, E. C., Millard, S. P., Bradley, K. A., & Simpson, T. L. (2016). Association of alcohol misuse with sexual identity and sexual behavior in women veterans. *Substance Use & Misuse, 51*, 216–229.

Leighton, F., Castro, C., Barriga, C., & Urquiaga, E. I. (1997). [Wine and health. Epidemiological studies and possible mechanisms of the protective effects]. *Revista Medica de Chile, 125*(4), 483–491.

Levy, R. E., Catana, A. M., Durbin-Johnson, B., Halsted, C. H., & Medici, V. (2015). Ethnic differences in presentation and severity of alcoholic liver disease. *Alcoholism: Clinical and Experimental Research, 39*, 566–574.

Lewis, T. F. (2015). Alcohol addiction. In R. L. Smith (Ed.), *Treatment strategies for substance and process addictions* (pp. 33–55). Alexandria, VA: American Counseling Association.

Liang, W., & Chikritzhs, T. (2015). Age at first use of alcohol predicts the risk of heavy alcohol use in early adulthood: A longitudinal study in the United States. *International Journal of Drug Policy, 26*, 131–134.

Liappas, J., Paparrigopoulos, T., Tzavellas, E., & Christodoulou, G. (2002). Impact of alcohol detoxification on anxiety and depressive symptoms. *Drug and Alcohol Dependence, 68*, 215–220.

Litt, M. D., Kadden, R. M., Tennen, H., & Kabela-Cormier, E. (2016). Network Support II: Randomized controlled trial of Network Support treatment and cognitive behavioral therapy for alcohol use disorder. *Drug and Alcohol Dependence, 165*, 203–212.

Lo, C. C., & Cheng, T. C. (2015). Race, employment disadvantages, and heavy drinking: A multilevel model. *Journal of Psychoactive Drugs, 47*, 221–229.

Loheswaran, G., Barr, M. S., Rajji, T. K., Blumberger, D. M., Le Foll, B., & Daskalakis, Z. J. (2016). Alcohol intoxication by binge drinking impairs neuroplasticity. *Brain Stimulation, 9*(1), 27–32.

Lucchetti, G., Koenig, H. G., Pinsky, I., Laranjeira, R., & Vallada, H. (2014). Religious beliefs and alcohol control policies: A Brazilian nationwide study. *Revista Brasileira de Psiquiatria, 36*, 4–10.

Luczak, S. E., Liang, T., & Wall, T. L. (2017). Age of drinking initiation as a risk factor for alcohol use disorder symptoms is moderated by ALDH2*2 and ethnicity. *Alcoholism: Clinical and Experimental Research, 41*, 1738–1744.

MacKillop, J., Stojek, M., VanderBroek-Stice, L., & Owens, M. M. (2018). Evidence-based treatment for alcohol use disorders: A review through the lens of the theory x efficacy matrix. In D. David, S. J. Lynn, & G. H. Montgomery (Eds.), *Evidence-based psychotherapy: The state of the science and practice* (pp. 219–252). New York, NY: Wiley-Blackwell.

Maisto, S. A., Roos, C. R., O'Sickey, A. J., Kirouac, M., Connors, G. J., Tonigan, J. S., & Witkiewitz, K. (2015). The indirect effect of the therapeutic alliance and alcohol abstinence self-efficacy on alcohol use and alcohol-related problems in Project MATCH. *Alcoholism: Clinical and Experimental Research, 39*, 504–513.

Mann, K., Aubin, H.-J., & Witkiewitz, K. (2017). Reduced drinking in alcohol dependence treatment, what is the evidence? *European Addiction Research, 23*, 219–230.

Mann, K., Torup, L., Sorensen, P., Gual, A., Swift, R., Walker, B., & van den Brink, W. (2016). Nalmefene for the management of alcohol dependence: Review on its pharmacology, mechanism of action and meta-analysis on its clinical efficacy. *European Neuropsychopharmacology, 26*(12), 1941–1949.

Margolis, R. D., & Zweben, J. E. (2011). *Treating patients with alcohol and other drug problems: An integrated approach* (2nd ed.). Washington, DC: American Psychological Association.

Marich, J. (2017). EMDR therapy and the recovery community: Relational imperatives in treating addiction. In M. Nickerson (Ed.), *Cultural competence and healing culturally based trauma with EMDR therapy: Innovative strategies and protocols* (pp. 279–293). New York, NY: Springer.

Marshall, B. D. L., Operario, D., Bryant, K. J., Cook, R. L., Edelman, E. J., Gaither, J. R., . . . Fiellin, D. A. (2015). Drinking trajectories among HIV-infected men who have sex with men: A cohort study of United States veterans. *Drug and Alcohol Dependence, 148*, 69–76.

Mason, B. J., & Higley, A. E. (2012). Human laboratory models of addiction. In K. D. Brownell & M. S. Gold (Eds.), *Food and addiction: A comprehensive handbook* (pp. 14–19). New York, NY: Oxford University Press.

Mastroleo, N. R., & Monti, P. M. (2013). Cognitive-behavioral treatment for addictions. In B. S. McCrady & E. E. Epstein (Eds.), *Addictions: A comprehensive guidebook* (2nd ed., pp. 391–410). New York, NY: Oxford University Press.

Maté, G. (2008). *In the realm of hungry ghosts: Close encounters with addiction*. Toronto, ON: Vintage Books.

Matsushita, S., & Higuchi, S. (2017). Review: Use of Asian samples in genetic research of alcohol use disorders: genetic variation of alcohol metabolizing enzymes and the effects of acetaldehyde. *American Journal on Addictions, 26*(5), 469–476.

McClellan, M. L. (2017). *Lady lushes: Gender, alcoholism, and medicine in modern America*. Piscataway, NJ: Rutgers University Press.

McCrady, B. S. (2014). Alcohol use disorders. In D. H. Barlow (Ed.), *Clinical handbook of psychological disorders: A step-by-step treatment manual* (5th ed., pp. 533–587). New York, NY: Guilford Press.

McCrady, B. S., & Epstein, E. E. (2015). Couple therapy and alcohol problems. In A. S. Gurman, J. L. Lebow, & D. K. Snyder (Eds.), *Clinical handbook of couple therapy* (5th ed., pp. 555–584). New York, NY: Guilford Press.

McGillivray, J. A., & Newton, D. C. (2016). Self-reported substance use and intervention experience of prisoners with intellectual disability. *Journal of Intellectual and Developmental Disability, 41*(2), 166–176.

McLellan, A. T., Luborsky, L., Woody, G. E., & O'Brien, C. P. (1980). An improved diagnostic instrument for substance abuse patients: The Addiction Severity Index. *Journal of Nervous & Mental Diseases, 168*, 26–33.

McNally, R. J. (2012). Psychiatric disorder and suicide in the military, then and now: Commentary on Frueh and Smith. *Journal of Anxiety Disorders, 26*, 776–778.

Mellentin, A. I., Nielsen, B., Nielsen, A. S., Yu, F., & Stenager, E. (2016). A randomized controlled study of exposure therapy as aftercare for alcohol use disorder: Study protocol. *BMC Psychiatry, 16*(112), 1–8.

Merlo, L. J. (2012). Psychological treatments for substance use disorders. In K. D. Brownell & M. S. Gold (Eds.), *Food and addiction: A comprehensive handbook* (pp. 285–289). New York, NY: Oxford University Press.

Meyers, J. L., Brown, Q., Grant, B. F., & Hasin, D. (2017). Religiosity, race/ethnicity, and alcohol use behaviors in the United States. *Psychological Medicine, 47*, 103–114.

Michal, O., Magdalena, M.-Z., Halina, M., Magdalena, B.-Z., Tadeusz, N., Elzbieta, M., & Marcin, W. (2016). Hyponatremia effect in patients with alcohol dependence on their physical and mental health status. *Alcohol, 57*, 49–53.

Milkman, H. B., & Sunderwirth, S. G. (2010). *Craving for ecstasy and natural highs: A positive approach to mood alteration*. Thousand Oaks, CA: SAGE.

Miller, M. B., Van Reen, E., Barker, D. H., Roane, B. M., Borsari, B., McGeary, J. E., . . . Carskadon, M. A. (2017). The impact of sleep and psychiatric symptoms on alcohol consequences among young adults. *Addictive Behaviors, 66*, 138–144.

Miller, S. M., Pedersen, E. R., & Marshall, G. N. (2017). Combat experience and problem drinking in veterans: Exploring the roles of PTSD, coping motives, and perceived stigma. *Addictive Behaviors, 66*, 90–95.

Miller, W. R. (2016). Sacred cows and greener pastures: Reflections from 40 years in addiction research. *Alcoholism Treatment Quarterly, 34*(1), 92–115.

Miller, W. R., & Munoz, R. F. (2013). *Controlling your drinking, second edition: Tools to make moderation work for you* (2nd ed.). New York, NY Guilford Press.

Minnich, A., Erford, B. T., Bardhoshi, G., & Atalay, Z. (2018). Systematic review of the Michigan Alcoholism Screening Test. *Journal of Counseling & Development, 96*, 335–344.

Mistral, W. (Ed.) (2016a). *Integrated approaches to drug and alcohol problems: Action on addiction*. New York, NY: Routledge.

Mistral, W. (2016b). From substance use to addiction. In W. Mistral (Ed.), *Integrated approaches to drug and alcohol problems: Action on addiction* (pp. 3–15). New York, NY: Routledge.

Mo, C., & Deane, F. P. (2016). Reductions in craving and negative affect predict 3-month post-discharge alcohol use following residential treatment. *International Journal of Mental Health and Addiction, 14*(5), 761–774.

Moraes, E., & Becker, P. (2017). Indirect costs and the burden of alcohol- and drug-related problems. In D. Razzouk (Ed.), *Mental health economics: The costs and benefits of psychiatric care* (pp. 393–400). Cham, Switzerland: Springer International.

Morris, S. L., Winters, K. C., & Wagner, E. F. (2018). F10.2 Alcohol dependence. In J. B. Schaffer & E. Rodolfa (Eds.), *An ICD-10-CM casebook and workbook for students: Psychological and behavioral conditions* (pp. 31–43). Washington, DC: American Psychological Association.

Morrison, M. F., Lin, K., & Gersh, S. (2018). Addictions: Evidence for integrative treatment. In D. A. Monti & A. B. Newberg (Eds.), *Integrative psychiatry and brain health* (2nd ed., pp. 1–22). New York, NY: Oxford University Press.

Myers, B., Sorsdahl, K., Morojele, N. K., Kekwaletswe, C., Shuper, P. A., & Parry, C. D. H. (2017). "In this thing I have everything I need": Perceived acceptability of a brief alcohol-focused intervention for people living with HIV. *AIDS Care, 29*(2), 209–213.

Nakash, O., Nagar, M., Barker, Y., & Lotan, D. (2016). The association between religiosity and alcohol use: The mediating role of meaning in life and media exposure. *Mental Health, Religion & Culture, 19*(6), 574–586.

Naqvi, N. H., Ochsner, K. N., Kober, H., Kuerbis, A., Feng, T., Wall, M., & Morgenstern, J. (2015). Cognitive regulation of craving in alcohol-dependent and social drinkers. *Alcoholism: Clinical and Experimental Research, 39*, 343–349.

National Institute on Alcohol Abuse and Alcoholism (NIAAA). (2003). Recommended alcohol question. Retrieved on August 15, 2018, from https://www.niaaa.nih.gov/research/guidelines-and-resources/recommended-alcohol-questions

National Institute on Alcohol Abuse and Alcoholism (NIAAA). (2010). *Alcohol use and alcohol use disorders in the United States: A 3-year follow-up: main findings from the 2004–2005 Wave 2 National Epidemiologic Survey on Alcohol and Related Conditions (NESARC)*. Bethesda, MD: National Institutes of Health. Available at http://pubs.niaaa.nih.gov/publications/NESARC_DRM2/NESARC2DRM.pdf

National Institute on Alcohol Abuse and Alcoholism (NIAAA). (2011). *Alcohol screening and brief intervention for youth: A practitioner's guide. NIH Publication No. 11-7805*. Rockville, MD: NIAAA, DHHS, and AAP. Retrieved on August 15, 2018, from https://pubs.niaaa.nih.gov/publications/Practitioner/YouthGuide/YouthGuide.pdf

National Institute on Alcohol Abuse and Alcoholism (NIAAA). (2017, June). *Alcohol facts and statistics*. Retrieved from https://www.niaaa.nih.gov/alcohol-health/overview-alcohol-consumption/alcohol-facts-and-statistics

Nehring, S. (2018). *Alcohol use disorder*. Retrieved on September 11, 2018, from http://knowledge.statpearls.com/chapter/surgery-thoracic/17343/

Nguyen, T. A., DeShazo, J. P., Thacker, L. R., Puri, P., & Sanyal, A. J. (2016). The worsening profile of alcoholic hepatitis in the United States. *Alcoholism: Clinical and Experimental Research, 40*(6), 1295–1303.

Nolen-Hoeksema, S. (2013). Gender differences. In P. M. Miller, S. A. Ball, M. E. Bates, A. W. Blume, K. M. Kampman, D. J. Kavanagh, M. E. Larimer, N. M. Petry, & P. De Witte (Eds.), *Principles of addiction: Comprehensive addictive behaviors and disorders, Vol 1* (pp. 141–147). San Diego, CA: Elsevier Academic Press.

Nordfjaern, T., Bretteville-Jensen, A. L., Edland-Gryt, M., & Gripenberg, J. (2016). Risky substance use among young adults in the nightlife arena: An underused setting for risk-reducing interventions? *Scandinavian Journal of Public Health, 44*(7), 638–645.

Nyamathi, A. M., Shin, S. S., Smeltzer, J., Salem, B. E., Yadav, K., Ekstrand, M. L., . . . Faucette, M. (2017). Achieving drug and alcohol abstinence among recently incarcerated homeless women: A randomized controlled trial comparing dialectical behavioral therapy-case management with a health promotion program. *Nursing Research, 66*, 432–441.

O'Farrell, T. J., Kleinke, C. L., & Cutter, H. S. G. (1998). Sexual adjustment of male alcoholics: Changes from before to after receiving alcoholism counseling with and without marital therapy. *Addictive Behaviors, 23*, 419–425.

O'Halloran, E. B., Curtis, B. J., Afshar, M., Chen, M. M., Kovacs, E. J., & Burnham, E. L. (2016). Alveolar macrophage inflammatory mediator expression is elevated in the setting of alcohol use disorders. *Alcohol, 50*, 43–50.

Oldenburg, C. E., Mitty, J. A., Biello, K. B., Closson, E. F., Safren, S. A., Mayer, K. H., & Mimiaga, M. J. (2016). Differences in attitudes about HIV pre-exposure prophylaxis use among stimulant versus alcohol using men who have sex with men. *AIDS and Behavior, 20*(7), 1451–1460.

Owens, M. D., & McCrady, B. S. (2016). A pilot study of a brief motivational intervention for incarcerated drinkers. *Journal of Substance Abuse Treatment, 68*, 1–10.

Pakula, B., Carpiano, R. M., Ratner, P. A., & Shoveller, J. A. (2016). Life stress as a mediator and community belonging as a moderator of mood and anxiety disorders and co-occurring disorders with heavy drinking of gay, lesbian, bisexual, and heterosexual Canadians. *Social Psychiatry and Psychiatric Epidemiology, 51*, 1181–1192.

Pape, H., & Norstrom, T. (2016). Associations between emotional distress and heavy drinking among young people: A longitudinal study. *Drug and Alcohol Review, 35*(2), 170–176.

Parnes, J. E., Rahm-Knigge, R. L., & Conner, B. T. (2017). The curvilinear effects of sexual orientation on young adult substance use. *Addictive Behaviors, 66*, 108–113.

Pearson, M. R., Kirouac, M., & Witkiewitz, K. (2016). Questioning the validity of the 4+/5+ binge or heavy drinking criterion in college and clinical populations. *Addiction, 111*(10), 1720–1726.

Pekala, R. J. (2017). Addictions and relapse prevention. In G. R. Elkins (Ed.), *Handbook of medical and psychological hypnosis: Foundations, applications, and professional issues* (pp. 443–451). New York, NY: Springer.

Penberthy, J. K., Gioia, C. J., Konig, A., Martin, A. M., Cockrell, S. A., & Meshberg-Cohen, S. (2014). Co-occurring chronic depression and alcohol dependence: A novel treatment approach. *Addictive Disorders & Their Treatment, 13*, 54–67.

Percy, A., & McKay, M. (2015). The stability of alcohol consumption between age 16 and 26: Evidence from a National Birth Cohort Study. *Journal of Adolescence, 44*, 57–69.

Ponce Martinez, C., Vakkalanka, P., & Ait-Daoud, N. (2016). Pharmacotherapy for alcohol use disorders: Physicians' perceptions and practices. *Frontiers in Psychiatry, 7*, 1–6.

Prochaska, J. O., Norcross, J. C., & DiClemente, C. C. (1994). *Changing for good*. New York, NY: Avon Books.

Prue, B. (2013). Indigenous supports for recovery from alcoholism and drug abuse: The native American church. *Journal of Ethnic & Cultural Diversity in Social Work: Innovation in Theory, Research & Practice, 22*, 271–287.

Ralevski, E., Southwick, S., Jackson, E., Jane, J. S., Russo, M., & Petrakis, I. (2016). Trauma- and stress-induced response in veterans with alcohol dependence and comorbid post-traumatic stress disorder. *Alcoholism: Clinical and Experimental Research, 40*, 1752–1760.

Ranes, B., Johnson, R., Nelson, L., & Slaymaker, V. (2017). The role of spirituality in treatment outcomes following a residential 12-Step program. *Alcoholism Treatment Quarterly, 35*, 16–33.

Ransome, Y., & Gilman, S. E. (2016). The role of religious involvement in Black-White differences in alcohol use disorders. *Journal of Studies on Alcohol and Drugs, 77*, 792–801.

Rastegar, D., & Fingerhood, M. (2016). *The American Society of Addiction Medicine handbook of addiction medicine*. New York, NY: Oxford University Press.

Ray, L. A., Courtney, K. E., & Guadalupe, A. B. (2013). Alcohol use disorders. In W. E. Craighead, D. J. Miklowitz, & L. W. Craighead (Eds.), *Psychopathology: History, diagnosis, and empirical foundations* (2nd ed., pp. 550–582). Hoboken, NJ: John Wiley & Sons.

Rendall-Mkosi, K., Morojele, N., London, L., Moodley, S., Singh, C., & Girdler-Brown, B. (2013). A randomized controlled trial of motivational interviewing to prevent risk for an alcohol-exposed pregnancy in the Western Cape, South Africa. *Addiction, 108*, 725–732.

Richter, L., Pugh, B. S., Peters, E. A., Vaughan, R. D., & Foster, S. E. (2016). Underage drinking: Prevalence and correlates of risky drinking measures among youth aged 12-20. *American Journal of Drug and Alcohol Abuse, 42*, 385–394.

Riper, H., Andersson, G., Hunter, S. B., de Wit, J., Berking, M., & Cuijpers, P. (2014). Treatment of comorbid alcohol use disorders and depression with cognitive-behavioural therapy and motivational interviewing: A meta-analysis. *Addiction, 109*, 394–406.

Roberts, B., & Ezard, N. (2015). Why are we not doing more for alcohol use disorder among conflict-affected populations? *Addiction, 110*, 889–890.

Rose, G. L., Skelly, J. M., Badger, G. J., Naylor, M. R., & Helzer, J. E. (2012). Interactive voice response for relapse prevention following cognitive-behavioral therapy for alcohol use disorders: A pilot study. *Psychological Services, 9*, 174–184.

Rosenberg, K. P., O'Connor, S., & Carnes, P. (2014). Sex addiction: An overview. In K. P. Rosenberg & L. Curtiss Feder (Eds.), *Behavioral addictions: Criteria, evidence, and treatment* (pp. 215–236). San Diego, CA: Elsevier Academic Press.

Rossow, I., Keating, P., Felix, L., & McCambridge, J. (2016). Does parental drinking influence children's drinking? A systematic review of prospective cohort studies. *Addiction, 111*(2), 204–217.

Russell, M., Martier, S. S., Sokol, R. J., Mudar, P., Bottoms, S., Jacobson, S., & Jacobson, J. (1994). Screening for pregnancy risk-drinking. *Alcoholism: Clinical and Experimental Research, 18*(5), 1156–1161.

Sachs, B. D., & Dodson, K. (2017). Serotonin deficiency and alcohol use disorders. In R. R. Watson & S. Zibadi (Eds.), *Addictive substances and neurological disease: Alcohol, tobacco, caffeine, and drugs of abuse in everyday lifestyles* (pp. 181–189). San Diego, CA: Elsevier Academic Press.

Sagarkar, S., & Sakharkar, A. (2017). Epigenetics and alcohol use disorders. In D. H. Yasui, J. Peedicayil, & D. R. Grayson (Eds.), *Neuropsychiatric disorders and epigenetics* (pp. 361–397). San Diego, CA: Elsevier Academic Press.

Saha, T. D., Grant, B. F., Chou, S. P., Kerridge, B. T., Pickering, R. P., & Ruan, W. J. (2018). Concurrent use of alcohol with other drugs and *DSM-5* alcohol use disorder comorbid with other drug use disorders: Sociodemographic characteristics, severity, and psychopathology. *Drug and Alcohol Dependence, 187*, 261–269.

Salvatore, J. E., Cho, S.-B., & Dick, D. M. (2017). Genes, environments, and sex differences in alcohol research. *Journal of Studies on Alcohol and Drugs, 78*, 494–501.

Sanchez-Craig, M., Wilkinson, A., & Davila, R. (1995). Empirically based guidelines for moderate drinking: 1-year results from three studies with problem drinkers. *American Journal of Public Health, 85*(6), 823–828.

Satre, D. D., Delucchi, K., Lichtmacher, J., Sterling, S. A., & Weisner, C. (2013). Motivational interviewing to reduce hazardous drinking and drug use among depression patients. *Journal of Substance Abuse Treatment, 44*, 323–329.

Satyanarayana, V. A., Nattala, P., Selvam, S., Pradeep, J., Hebbani, S., Hegde, S., & Srinivasan, K. (2016). Integrated cognitive behavioral intervention reduces intimate partner violence among alcohol dependent men, and improves mental health outcomes in their spouses: A clinic based randomized controlled trial from South India. *Journal of Substance Abuse Treatment, 64*, 29–34.

Sayette, M. A., Fairbairn, C. E., & Creswell, K. G. (2016). Alcohol and emotion: The importance of social context. In C. E. Kopetz & C. W. Lejuez (Eds.), *Addictions: A social psychological perspective* (pp. 98–119). New York, NY: Routledge/Taylor & Francis.

Schmidt, C. S., Schulte, B., Seo, H.-N., Kuhn, S., O'Donnell, A., Kriston, L., . . . Reimer, J. (2016). Meta-analysis on the effectiveness of alcohol screening with brief interventions for patients in emergency care settings. *Addiction, 111*(5), 783–794.

Schmidt, L. K., Bojesen, A. B., Nielsen, A. S., & Andersen, K. (2018). Duration of therapy – does it matter?: A systematic review and meta-regression of the duration of psychosocial treatments for alcohol use disorder. *Journal of Substance Abuse Treatment, 84*, 57–67.

Schrieks, I., Joosten, M., Klopping-Ketelaars, W., Witkamp, R., & Hendriks, H. (2016). Moderate alcohol consumption after a mental stressor attenuates the endocrine stress response. *Alcohol, 57*, 29–34.

Selzer, M. L. (1971). The Michigan Alcoholism Screening Test: The quest for a new diagnostic instrument. *American Journal of Psychiatry, 127*(12), 1653–1658.

Sethi, M., Heyer, J. H., Wall, S., DiMaggio, C., Shinseki, M., Slaughter, D., & Frangos, S. G. (2016). Alcohol use by urban bicyclists is associated with more severe injury, greater hospital resource use, and higher mortality. *Alcohol, 53*, 1–7.

Silveri, M. M. (2012). Adolescent brain development and underage drinking in the United States: Identifying risks of alcohol use in college populations. *Harvard Review of Psychiatry, 20*, 189–200.

Slade, T., Chiu, W.-T., Glantz, M., Kessler, R. C., Lago, L., Sampson, N., . . . Degenhardt, L. (2016). A cross-national examination of differences in classification of lifetime alcohol use disorder between DSM-IV and *DSM-5*: Findings from the World Mental Health Survey. *Alcoholism: Clinical and Experimental Research, 40*(8), 1728–1736.

Slater, M. E., Godette, D., Huang, B., Ruan, W. J., & Kerridge, B. T. (2017). Sexual orientation-based discrimination, excessive alcohol use, and substance use disorders among sexual minority adults. *LGBT Health, 4*, 337–344.

Soyka, M., Friede, M., & Schnitker, J. (2016). Comparing nalmefene and naltrexone in alcohol dependence: Are there any differences? Results from an indirect meta-analysis. *Pharmacopsychiatry, 49*, 66–75.

Spanagel, R., Zink, M., & Sommer, W. H. (2013). Neurobiology of alcohol addiction. In D. W. Pfaff (Ed.), *Neuroscience in the 21st century* (pp. 2745–2773). New York, NY: Springer.

Spinola, S., Maisto, S. A., White, C. N., & Huddleson, T. (2017). Effects of acute alcohol intoxication on executive functions controlling self-regulated behavior. *Alcohol, 61*, 1–8.

Stein, M. D., Risi, M. M., Flori, J. N., Conti, M. T., Anderson, B. J., & Bailey, G. L. (2016). Gender differences in the life concerns of persons seeking alcohol detoxification. *Journal of Substance Abuse Treatment, 63*, 34–38.

Storvoll, E. E., Moan, I. S., & Lund, I. O. (2016). Negative consequences of other people's drinking: Prevalence, perpetrators and locations. *Drug and Alcohol Review, 35*(6), 755–762.

Subramani, O. S., Parrott, D. J., & Eckhardt, C. I. (2017). Problematic drinking mediates the association between urgency and intimate partner aggression during acute intoxication. *Alcoholism: Clinical and Experimental Research, 41*, 1602–1611.

Substance Abuse and Mental Health Services Administration (SAMHSA). (1999–2012). *Enhancing motivation for change in substance abuse treatment, treatment improvement protocol (TIP), Series 35, Chapter 4.* Rockville, MD: Author. Retrieved on August 31, 2018, from https://store.samhsa.gov/shin/content/SMA13-4212/SMA13-4212.pdf

Sullivan, J. T., Sykora, K., Schneiderman, J.., Naranjo, C. A., & Sellers, E. M. (1989). Assessment of alcohol withdrawal: The revised Clinical Institute Withdrawal Assessment for Alcohol Scale (CIWA-Ar). *British Journal of Addiction, 84*, 1353–1357.

Sweet, A. D. (2012). Internal objects and self-destructive behaviours: A clinical case highlighting dissociation, splitting and the role of the primitive super-ego in the addictions. *Scandinavian Psychoanalytic Review, 35*, 116–126.

Tanner-Smith, E. E., & Risser, M. D. (2016). A meta-analysis of brief alcohol interventions for adolescents and young adults: Variability in effects across alcohol measures. *American Journal of Drug and Alcohol Abuse, 42*(2), 140–151.

Testa, M., Brown, W. C., & Wang, W. (2018). Do men use more sexually aggressive tactics when intoxicated? A within-person examination of naturally occurring episodes of sex. *Psychology of Violence*. No pagination specified.

Timko, C., Moos, R. H., & Finney, J. W. (2016). The course of substance use disorders: Trajectories, endpoints, and predictors. In E. J. Bromet (Ed.), *Long-term outcomes in psychopathology research: Rethinking the scientific agenda* (pp. 53–76). New York, NY: Oxford University Press.

Treloar, H., & Miranda, R., Jr. (2017). Craving and acute effects of alcohol in youths' daily lives: Associations with alcohol use disorder severity. *Experimental and Clinical Psychopharmacology, 25*, 303–313.

Trull, T. J., Wycoff, A. M., Lane, S. P., Carpenter, R. W., & Brown, W. C. (2016). Cannabis and alcohol use, affect and impulsivity in psychiatric out-patients' daily lives. *Addiction, 111*(11), 2052–2059.

Tu, X., Wang, J., Liu, X., & Zheng, J. (2018). Aberrant regional brain activities in alcohol dependence: A functional magnetic resonance imaging study. *Neuropsychiatric Disease and Treatment, 14*, 847–853.

Tucker, J. S., D'Amico, E. J., Ewing, B. A., Miles, J. N. V., & Pedersen, E. R. (2017). A group-based motivational interviewing brief intervention to reduce substance use and sexual risk behavior among homeless young adults. *Journal of Substance Abuse Treatment, 76*, 20–27.

United Nations Office on Drugs and Crime. (2007, September). *Leader's guide: Cognitive behavioural & relapse strategies.* Retrieved on February 9, 2018, from http://www.unodc.org/ddt-training/treatment/VOLUME%20B/Volume%20B%20-%20Module%203/1.Leaders%20Guide/Presentation%20-%20VolB_M3.pdf

van Duijvenbode, N., Didden, R., Korzilius, H. P. L. M., Trentelman, M., & Engels, R. C. M. E. (2013). Executive control in long-term abstinent alcoholics with mild to borderline intellectual disability: The relationship with IQ and severity of alcohol use-related problems. *Research in Developmental Disabilities, 34*, 3583–3595.

VanderVeen, J., Plawecki, M. H., Millward, J. B., Hays, J., Kareken, D. A., O'Connor, S., & Cyders, M. A. (2016). Negative urgency, mood induction, and alcohol seeking behaviors. *Drug and Alcohol Dependence*, *165*, 151–158.

Veliz, P. T., Boyd, C. J., & McCabe, S. E. (2015). Competitive sport involvement and substance use among adolescents: A nationwide study. *Substance Use & Misuse*, *50*, 156–165.

Vera, B. D. V., Pilatti, A., Garimaldi, J., & Pautassi, R. M. (2018). Acute effects of alcohol intoxication on decision making and impulsivity in at-risk gamblers with or without problematic drinking. *Psychology & Neuroscience*. No pagination specified.

Verplaetse, T. L., & McKee, S. A. (2017). An overview of alcohol and tobacco/nicotine interactions in the human laboratory. *American Journal of Drug and Alcohol Abuse*, *43*(2), 186–196.

Voas, R. B., Tippetts, A., Bergen, G., Grosz, M., & Marques, P. (2016). Mandating treatment based on interlock performance: Evidence for effectiveness. *Alcoholism: Clinical and Experimental Research*, *40*(9), 1953–1960.

Wade, J., & Peralta, R. L. (2017). Perceived racial discrimination, heavy episodic drinking, and alcohol abstinence among African American and White college students. *Journal of Ethnicity in Substance Abuse*, *16*, 165–180.

Walker, D. D., Walton, T. O., Neighbors, C., Kaysen, D., Mbilinyi, L., Darnell, J., . . . Roffman, R. A. (2017). Randomized trial of motivational interviewing plus feedback for soldiers with untreated alcohol abuse. *Journal of Consulting and Clinical Psychology*, *85*, 99–110.

Wardell, J. D., Strang, N. M., & Hendershot, C. S. (2016). Negative urgency mediates the relationship between childhood maltreatment and problems with alcohol and cannabis in late adolescence. *Addictive Behaviors*, *56*, 1–7.

Weiss, T. C. (2017, November 24). Addiction and substance abuse among persons with disabilities. *Disabled World*. Retrieved on August 27, 2018, from https://www.disabled-world.com/medical/pharmaceutical/addiction/serious.php

Wennberg, P., Bergman, H., & Berglund, M. (2014). The AVI-R2: An inventory for a differentiated diagnosis of alcohol problems. *Nordic Journal of Psychiatry*, *68*, 266–269.

Wiers, R. W., Houben, K., Fadardi, J. S., van Beek, P., Rhemtulla, M., & Cox, W. (2015). Alcohol cognitive bias modification training for problem drinkers over the web. *Addictive Behaviors*, *40*, 21–26.

Wilhite, E. R., Mallard, T., & Fromme, K. (2018). A longitudinal event-level investigation of alcohol intoxication, alcohol-related blackouts, childhood sexual abuse, and sexual victimization among college students. *Psychology of Addictive Behaviors*, *32*, 289–300.

Wilhoit, L. F., Scott, D. A., & Simecka, B. A. (2017). Fetal alcohol spectrum disorders: Characteristics, complications, and treatment. *Community Mental Health Journal*, *53*(6), 711–718.

Williams, E. C., Gupta, S., Rubinsky, A. D., Jones-Webb, R., Bensley, K. M., Young, J. P., . . . Harris, A. H. (2016). Racial/ethnic differences in the prevalence of clinically recognized alcohol use disorders among patients from the U.S. Veterans Health Administration. *Alcoholism: Clinical and Experimental Research*, *40*(2), 359–366.

Wilsnack, R. W., Vogeltanz, N. D., Wilsnack, S. C., & Harris, T. R. (2000). Gender differences in alcohol consumption and adverse drinking consequences: Cross-cultural patterns. *Addiction*, *95*, 251–265.

Windle, M. (2016). Drinking over the lifespan: Focus on early adolescents and youth. Alcohol Research: *Current Reviews*, *38*, 95–101.

Witkiewitz, K., Pearson, M. R., Hallgren, K. A., Maisto, S. A., Roos, C. R., Kirouac, M., . . . Heather, N. (2017). Who achieves low risk drinking during alcohol treatment? An analysis of patients in three alcohol clinical trials. *Addiction*, *112*(12), 2112–2121.

Wolitzky-Taylor, K., Guillot, C. R., Pang, R. D., Kirkpatrick, M. G., Zvolensky, M. J., Buckner, J. D., & Leventhal, A. M. (2015). Examination of anxiety sensitivity and distress tolerance as transdiagnostic mechanisms linking multiple anxiety pathologies to alcohol use problems in adolescents. *Alcoholism: Clinical and Experimental Research*, *39*, 532–539.

Wupperman, P., Marlatt, G. A., Cunningham, A., Bowen, S., Berking, M., Mulvihill-Rivera, N., & Easton, C. (2012). Mindfulness and modification therapy for behavioral dysregulation: Results from a pilot study targeting alcohol use and aggression in women. *Journal of Clinical Psychology*, *68*, 50–66.

Yalisove, D. (2010). *Developing clinical skills for substance abuse counseling*. Alexandria, VA: American Counseling Association.

Zapolski, T. C. B., Pedersen, S. L., McCarthy, D. M., & Smith, G. T. (2014). Less drinking, yet more problems: Understanding African American drinking and related problems. *Psychological Bulletin*, *140*, 188–223.

Zhabenko, O., Zhabenko, N., Conroy, D. A., Chaban, O., Oliinyk, A., Frankova, I., . . . Zucker, R. A. (2016). An open uncontrolled pilot trial of online cognitive-behavioral therapy for insomnia for Ukrainian alcohol-dependent patients. In A. L. M. Andrade & D. De Micheli (Eds.), *Innovations in the treatment of substance addiction* (pp. 165–181). Cham, Switzerland: Springer International.

Zhu, J., Wang, Y., Wang, H., Cheng, W., Li, Z., Qian, Y., . . . Yu, Y. (2018). Abnormal gray matter asymmetry in alcohol dependence. *NeuroReport: For Rapid Communication of Neuroscience Research*, *29*, 753–759.

10 Cannabis Addiction

iStock.com/vcabezonic

Learning Objectives

1. Learn about the difference between THC and CBD and how each affects the body separately and together.
2. Become aware of how legalization may affect usage levels.
3. Become familiar with the many effects that cannabis has on individuals.
4. Become informed about the diagnostic criteria for cannabis use disorder.
5. Discover the two most effective methods for treating cannabis addicts.

CHALLENGING YOUR ASSUMPTIONS ABOUT THIS ADDICTION

1. What is your current attitude regarding cannabis use? To what extent does your opinion change, if any, regarding those who use regularly and heavily?
2. If you have (or anticipate having) children, how would you feel if your child began smoking pot almost every day? What if she or he began smoking heavily? What actions would you take, if any?
3. If you came home and found your significant other and a few friends so stoned together that they could hardly speak or function, what reaction would you have? What would you say, and what would you do?
4. Do you support the legalization of cannabis and, if so, under what conditions? If not, on what basis do you believe legalization is contraindicated?
5. If you were (or are) ill and discovered that cannabis might relieve some of your symptoms, what would you want to know before deciding for or against its use?

PERSONAL REFLECTIONS

When I was using, I always asked for the strongest pot . . . so do the other addicted cannabis users I know. People are more likely to become addicted to cannabis if the product they are using has high THC content.

Still, to this day, every time I smell the burning bud as I am out and about, I inhale deeply, sweetly remembering the many times I was high and had amazingly wonderful experiences. We call this *euphoric recall*. Deception, minimization, and denial were our secret friends. It is a tendency of people with addictive disorders to remember their use by focusing only on the positive memories associated with it. Somehow the multitude of negative experiences and negative consequences seem to disappear when one reminisces about the "good ole times." Forgetting easily how emotionally unavailable and numb I had become, how insensitive to others I had become, how impulsive and irrational at times I had become: and how inhuman I was becoming at some deep level.

You read about some of *my* struggles with cannabis back in the Preface. I shared as much as I felt comfortable but hid so much pain associated with 42 years of use, sometimes intermittent and sometimes continuous. But now my eyes are open as I watch the sequence occur in other addicts. My ears are open, too, as I hear their gasping coughs as if their last breath had just been exhaled.

I don't have to look far past my nose. A very close family member is also a cannabis addict, and we both quit at about the same time in October 2014. We hadn't planned to quit together but somehow serendipitously ended up in the same psychological place at the same time. And then there is one of my closest young friends who began smoking up since he was in his early teens. He lived in my basement for several months at one point, and I remember so many times wanting to have deep philosophical talks with him but realizing that he was psychically unavailable morning, noon, and night. At that point in my life, I felt deeply alone and having another person with cannabis use disorder in the house who was using as constantly as he could did not ease any of my sunken and defeated feelings.

There is growing irritability that develops in addicted cannabis users over time. This occurs even with cannabis, the drug that so many use to relax and feel gentler inside. Often forgetful and sometimes rude without intention, I eventually had to ask my friend to move out. At the time, I doubt he was aware of any of that.

You see, cannabis affects our episodic memory. There are people I met in the past that, when I see them today, I have no idea who they are even though they remember me. They have that look of knowing in their eyes, while I stare blindly inside myself and pretend that I know them. And some of them seem to know me quite well. It is a most disarming feeling. It happened to me again this past Saturday night. There are movies I watched when I was using that I could not tell you a thing about. If I were to watch the film again, a few memories would return to me like a flashback following an LSD trip. Thank God, I have found myself.

Background Information

Cannabis refers to all preparations (e.g., marijuana, hashish, hash oil) derived from the flowering tops, stems, leaves, and seeds of hemp plants (e.g., *Cannabis sativa, Cannabis indica, Cannabis americana*). Cannabis is most often used as a mild hallucinogenic resulting from its psychoactive ingredient, delta-9-tetrahydrocannabinol (THC), and/or for its controversial medical properties that include the substance called cannabinol (CBD). Cannabis is classified as a hallucinogen because it alters perceptions at lower doses and produces hallucinations at higher doses (Csiernik, 2016). *Cannabis sativa* contains at least 144 compounds called *cannabinoids* and more than 1100 other compounds, including terpenoids and flavonoids (Englund, Freeman, Murray, & McGuire, 2017). Cannabis also contains caryophyllene oxide, which is the substance trained dogs scent for when detecting hidden marijuana (Salhab, 2017). Cannabis can be smoked, liquified, and swallowed, often baked into cookies, brownies, or cakes. Cannabis oil typically has the highest THC content, but even marijuana's potency has increased significantly since the advent of hydroponics (Csiernik, 2016).

Cannabis has a long history, with accounts of it being used medicinally since at least 2700 BC (Miller & Oberbarnschiedt, 2017). The earliest recorded reference to marijuana use dates back 12,000 years ago in China (Ouzir & Errami, 2016). It was first brought to the west between 1845 and 1919 by East Indian emigrants who moved to Trinidad to work on sugarcane plantations (Maharajh, Ali, & Maharaj, 2014). The emigrants used it for both its perceived medicinal properties and to help them adjust to the new hostile environment they found themselves in. Until 1950, it remained a legal drug in the Caribbean that could be purchased in shops and parlors. But, over time, people's perceptions of it changed. Cannabis became criminalized in most countries following the Single Convention on Narcotic Drugs in 1961, an international treaty intended to halt the production and distribution of many psychoactive drugs except for purposes of research and medical treatment (Englund et al., 2017). The Single Convention had "incorrectly labelled cannabis as a narcotic and thus purposefully shaped international drug policy regarding this drug for over half a century" (Csiernik, 2016, p. 335).

Today, marijuana is the most prevalent illicit drug around the world (Earleywine, 2016). But so are the problems associated with its use as the potency of cannabis sold on both the legal and illegal market increases (Englund et al., 2017). Although cannabis is controlled under Schedule I of the Comprehensive Drug Abuse Prevention and Control Act of 1970 in the United States, several states have already legalized for recreational use, and many others have legalized for medicinal purposes.

Although there are several countries where possession of cannabis is legal to one extent or another, currently the only country that has legalized possession, selling, cultivation, and transport is Uruguay. Uruguay legalized cannabis in December 2013. Research conducted about 1–1.5 years later revealed that the lifetime prevalence of using marijuana had quadrupled in that country from 2001 to 2014. In a subsample of 294 users (58% men, 41.2% women), 45% consumed pot 5 or more days a week (Boidi, Cruz, & Queirolo, 2015). Boidi et al. (2015) concluded that their preliminary data indicated

> Marijuana consumption is higher among young adults, which also poses a challenge related to control and regulation. Data indicate that among regular consumers, the frequency of consumption has significantly increased. It is reasonable to assume, thus, that risk behaviors have also increased with the frequency of consumption. (p. 9)

The medicalization and legalization of cannabis products remain highly controversial. The benefits of legalization are several, including the information that will be gleaned by studying an increased number of users at varying dose levels of THC. This may lead to cannabis use guidelines, including the most beneficial ratio of THC to CBD[1] (Englund et al., 2017). Miron (as cited by Balkin, 2015) estimated that, in 2010, the United States spent about $13.7 billion on cannabis criminalization procedures. If legalized, these monies could be spent in other ways. Furthermore, when cannabis and other drugs are acquired illegally, they do not come with a guarantee of purity. The slang term *dusting*, for example, refers to adding PCP, heroin, fentanyl, or other drugs to marijuana to increase its potency.

On the other hand, many concerns have been raised regarding the medical and recreational use of cannabis. The effect of both legal and illegal psychoactive drugs is influenced not only by their psychopharmacological effects but also by their social acceptability and their accessibility (Atkinson, 2016). Legalizing a drug increases acceptability and accessibility while simultaneously increasing consumption levels. When alcohol sales on Sundays occurred in the United States, for example (thereby increasing accessibility), overall consumption increased (Yoruk, 2014). A legalized market would decrease people's perceptions of the risks associated with use and would likely lead to an increase in problems with youth (Earleywine, 2016). In their review, Firmin, Pugh, Sohn, Voss, and Cltuang (2016) concluded that legalized marijuana would have a negative effect on the American people. They point out that, once legalized, "it is highly unlikely to be reversed" (p. 24). Arguable negative impacts have also been expressed regarding upcoming legalization in Canada with a suggestion that decriminalization ought to occur—and not legalization—until we know more about cannabis (Kalant, 2016).

Miller and Oberbarnschiedt (2017) released a disconcerting report regarding medical marijuana (MM). They wrote that it "does not meet the legal definition of drug as defined by the U.S. Food and Drug Administration (FDA) in the US" (Miller & Oberbarnschiedt, 2017, p. 335). For a drug to be considered safe by the FDA, it must undergo 12 stages of drug testing: MM has *not* been subjected to any of these stages. Furthermore, MM is not available in pharmacies, does not proceed through the typical prescribing route, and may be grown by care providers who receive no supervision or regulation (Miller & Oberbarnschiedt, 2017). Studies that have claimed medicinal properties were performed on cannabinoids, not on smoked marijuana and THC. Marijuana is also associated with the use of other drugs (Miller & Oberbarnschiedt, 2017).

Miller and Oberbarnschiedt (2017) wrote that the addiction potential for marijuana is comparable to that of alcohol and nicotine, and they predict legalization will lead to an increase in cannabis addiction levels. Lastly, Csiernik (2016. p. 164) stated that the long-term effects of hallucinogens are "purely psychological" with only one exception: cannabis. Cannabis is known to have negative effects on one's long-term physical health as well.

---

[1]The interaction of these will be discussed later.

Although the percentage of CBD in street cannabis has been decreasing (Morgan, Freeman, Schafer, & Curran, 2010), the percentage of THC in it has increased dramatically. In the United States it was about 4% in 1995 and is now on average about 12%, whereas, in Europe and Australia, 15% THC is more common with about 0.1% CBD (Curran et al., 2016). Some hashish has been found with 60% THC, and new extraction methods have produced hash oil with upwards of 75% THC (Englund et al., 2017).

In the United States, the National Institute of Drug Abuse provides researchers with cannabis containing less than 4% THC (Curran et al., 2016). Given the substantially increased potency of street cannabis today, the generalizability of results from earlier longitudinal studies and even most current experimental studies is limited (Curran et al., 2016). This is critical as we know that cannabis with higher concentrations of THC is more harmful regarding its risks (e.g., addiction, psychosis, cognitive impairment) (Englund et al., 2017). Cannabis consumed with tobacco increases its addictive potential (Englund et al., 2017).

Most research has focused on THC and CBD. These two substances seem to have opposite effects on the brain and behavior. For example, although THC can create psychotic symptoms, anxiety, and impaired learning, CBD can reduce psychotic symptoms and anxiety; it can also enhance learning. When combined, CBD can offset many of the harmful effects of THC (Curran et al., 2016). However, it is currently unknown what the ideal percentage of THC to CBD is in a cannabis product (Englund et al., 2017). These experiments are more likely to occur following increased legalization of cannabis throughout many parts of the world.

Users of cannabis seek out its pleasurable qualities, which may include euphoria, enhanced sociability, an increased pleasure of food, and increased enjoyment of sexual experiences while under its influence (Salhab, 2017). A person who is "high" usually presents as euphoric, sedated, impaired in judgment, and displaying inappropriate affect or grandiosity (Balkin, 2015). The "stoned" experience is variable, however, and other indicators of a high person might be a tendency to eat and giggle lots (Curran et al., 2016). High individuals might report a heightened appreciation for music and color (Curran et al., 2016).

Smoking cannabis with a water pipe is considered the most efficient way to produce its effects (Salhab, 2017). Inhaled or smoked THC appears in the blood between 3 and 10 min with effects that may last for several hours, whereas orally ingested THC appears in the blood between 30 and 60 min and effects continue for 4–6 hours (Salhab, 2017).

Recent research suggests that there are three distinguishable pathways of cannabis use (in 14- to 30-year-olds) that begins in early adolescence: (a) continuous increasing risk, (b) increased risk followed by decreasing risk (i.e., maturing out risk), and (c) continuing low risk (Kosty, Seeley, Farmer, Stevens, & Lewinsohn, 2017). DeRamus (2011) suggested that there are three motivators for pot smokers: (a) stress release, (b) social purposes, and (c) psychological reasons. DeRamus concluded that stress is the most common reason that people smoke marijuana. He added that, whereas smoking pot appears to offer an escape from negative emotions, the reality is that 80% of what people call stress is self-created. Those who smoke for social reasons do so because pot helps them become less inhibited around others. Psychological smokers are motivated to smoke marijuana because they are experiencing diagnosable psychiatric disorders (e.g., depression, schizophrenia, or another psychosis).

Individuals use marijuana for different reasons, and sometimes for a multitude of reasons (Zvolensky, Bonn-Miller, Leyro, Johnson, & Bernstein, 2011). Substance use may result from individuals wanting to increase their positive affect (Trull, Wycoff, Lane, Carpenter, & Brown, 2016). Furthermore, more-impulsive individuals experience greater stress reduction from using substances compared to those who are less impulsive, increasing the likelihood that they will repeatedly use (Trull et al., 2016). In one study, some factors that predict that a person will become dependent over a 3-year period included living alone, having major financial problems, and experiencing lessening ability to control usage (Atkinson, 2016). Critical life events (e.g., parental separation, early parental death) in addition to mental and social conflicts are also related to cannabis addiction (Schlossarek, Kempkensteffen, Reimer, & Verthein, 2016). Protective factors that reduce the likelihood of young people using cannabis include religiosity, warmth, and parental monitoring (Sharma, 2009).

We also know that an important risk factor for all addictions, including cannabis, is childhood maltreatment (Wardell, Strang, & Hendershot, 2016). Childhood maltreatment includes emotional, physical, and sexual abuse and emotional and physical neglect. Wardell et al. (2016) concluded that maltreatment is correlated with high levels of impulsivity and emotional dysregulation. Whiteside and Lynam (2001) had earlier conducted a factor analysis that identified four factors regarding impulsivity: (a) displaying a lack of perseverance, (b) acting without forethought, (c) sensation-seeking, and (d) acting carelessly when experiencing negative emotions. Wardell et al. concluded that list item "d" (i.e., acting carelessly) was most associated with later problems with cannabis and alcohol.

Cannabis users are 2.87 times more likely to experience cannabis dependency if they had been unemployed for at least 3 months compared to those who were consistently employed (Boden, Lee, Horwood, Grest, & McLeod, 2017). From a neuroscience perspective, one study found that those carrying a gene variant that "favors hyperactivity of the endocannabinoid (eCB) system were significantly less likely to become cannabis dependent" (Kosten, Newton, De La Garza, & Haile, 2014, p. 764). Another study concluded that alcohol and other drug use disorders are "individually heritable" (Wetherill et al., 2015, p. 617). Consequently, genetic predisposition may be a causative factor in cannabis addiction as well.

Currently, the greatest concern involves synthetic cannabinoids (called *spice drugs*), which are herbs sprayed or soaked with THC-like chemicals made in laboratories. The list of these chemicals continues to grow, and, although most are now illegal in the United States, new variations continue to be produced (for a growing list of these see https://en.wikipedia.org/wiki/Synthetic_cannabinoids).

Spice drugs have caused some severe adverse reactions, including death (Englund et al., 2017). Consequently, they are the widest class of new drugs that are being monitored by the European Monitoring Centre on Drugs and Drug Abuse (Pintori, Loi, & Mereu, 2017). Spice drugs do not contain any CBD, thereby having no substance that helps offset their negative effects. They induce a faster effect than cannabis products, and they are associated with more severe psychosis. At higher doses, they create unpleasant arousal, anxiety, agitation, auditory and visual delusions, hallucinations, agitation, aggressiveness, intense paranoia, and possibly coma and stroke (Pintori et al., 2017). Recently, the Centers for Disease Control and Prevention and several health departments investigated cases of severe bleeding among individuals in the United States who had used synthetic cannabinoids (American Association of Poison Control Centers, 2018).

Before I review what is harmful about cannabis, I will look at the ways it can be beneficial. Public health messages to the public have been distorted by the fact that researchers have studied the negative effects more thoroughly than the positive ones (Curran et al., 2016). In ancient times, *Cannabis sativa* was used by the Chinese for its psychoactive effects. It was once used in India to relieve pain and create tranquillity, in addition to its hypnotic, anti-inflammatory, and anticonvulsant properties (Salhab, 2017). Most users today subjectively rate the benefits as outweighing the risks (Curran et al., 2016). Some report a belief that they have "arrived at a transcendent insight" (Atkinson, 2016, p. 14).

Positive effects noted have included "enhanced divergent thinking" and creativity (Curran et al., 2016, p. 302) following both oral and smoked administrations at smaller doses (and decreased divergent thinking and creativity at higher does; Atkinson, 2016). Cannabis creates euphoria, relaxation in some, a substantial sense of calmness, and decreased psychomotor activity (Atkinson, 2016). Users may experience focused attention on internal sensations within the body (Atkinson, 2016). Social anxiety is reduced, thereby enhancing some users' ability to become friendlier. Boring tasks can feel less boring. Some researchers have found that it can decrease hostility, anxiety, and sadness (Trull et al., 2016).

Due to activation of the mesolimbic dopamine system, users may pay more attention to one particular thing, despite possible impairment of their executive functioning (Atkinson, 2016). Light users might not experience functional impairments or any problematic outcomes (Asbridge, Duff, Marsh, & Erickson, 2014).

Although cannabis remains illegal in most countries, there are several where physicians can prescribe cannabis products for medicinal purposes. Cannabis products can improve the symptoms of some diseases (e.g., lessening eye pressure, involuntary movements, and perception of pain). It can increase appetite, help prevent weight loss, and perhaps improve pain tolerance (Zvolensky et al., 2011). Although cannabinoids can diminish nausea in those receiving chemotherapy or radiation therapy (Zvolensky et al., 2011), chronic users may develop severe or excessive vomiting (Rastegar & Fingerhood, 2016). Cannabis has also been used to treat migraines and some types of seizures, epilepsy, and muscle spasms (Csiernik, 2016). Cannabis can sometimes reduce symptoms of gastrointestinal disorders, depression, anxiety, tension, multiple sclerosis, arthritis, sleep problems, cancer, and other severe illnesses (Csiernik, 2016).

CBD has been shown to reduce the symptoms of cannabis withdrawal with a ratio of CBD to THC of 1:1 (Englund et al., 2017). CBD has also been used to treat acute schizophrenia (Salhab, 2017). Some research suggests that CBD might reduce the likelihood of relapse in individuals with opioid use disorders (OUDs) (Hurd, Michaelides, Miller, & Jutras-Aswad, 2014). Lastly, self-reports suggest that, thanks to medicinal marijuana, some users have stopped using "hard" drugs (Earleywine, 2016).

Cochrane reviews are considered the "gold standard" in the medical profession. A recent Cochrane review concluded that cannabis products might have benefits for chronic neuropathic pain that outweighs its potential harms (Mucke, Phillips, Radbruch, Petzke, & Hauser, 2018). This conclusion was also made in a recent meta-analysis (Aviram & Samuelly-Leichtag, 2017).

Individuals who have comorbid attention deficit hyperactivity disorder and cocaine dependence who use cannabis are more likely to continue seeking help for their cocaine addiction compared to those who do not use cannabis (Aharonovich et al., 2006). There is also a growing body of research that suggests that cannabis may be successfully used as a substitute by some individuals with sOUDs (Lucas, 2017). However, a recent study of 34,653 adults who were interviewed at wave 1 (2001–2002) who had either moderate-to-severe pain or were using opioids for nonmedical reasons were interviewed again at wave 2 (2004–2005). Those who used cannabis were more likely to develop nonmedical prescription opioid use and OUD at wave 2 (Olfson, Wall, Liu, & Blanco, 2018). In other words, cannabis acted more often as a gateway drug to opioid problems than as a resolution to it.

Although cannabis products are effective in reducing neuropathic pain and sleep disturbance in individuals with multiple sclerosis (MS) (Rog, Nurmikko, Friede, & Young, 2005), they do not have a significant effect on reducing MS-associated tremors (Fox, Bain, Glickman, Carroll, & Zajicek, 2004). However, there is also a neurological caution in using cannabis: "some neurological disorders or symptoms (e.g. multiple sclerosis, seizures, epilepsy, headache) may be caused or exacerbated by the same treatment supposed to cure them" (Solimini, Rotolo, Pichini, & Pacifici, 2017, p. 527).

Another Cochrane review concluded that evidence to date is inconclusive regarding whether CBD has an antipsychotic effect (McLoughlin et al., 2014). Furthermore, the evidence that cannabis is effective in reducing anxiety is "surprisingly not well-documented" (Turna, Patterson, & Van Ameringen, 2017, p. 1006).

Now I will focus on the negative acute (short-term) effects of using cannabis. In later sections of the chapter dealing with *impacts*, the long-term effects, particularly resulting from heavy frequency and potency, will be reviewed.

Although cannabis does not appear to create psychological impairment in most users, it does pose a distinct risk for a small percentage of individuals (Csiernik, 2016). Most people do not experience any discernible problems from using cannabis, at least not that they observe (Sparks, 2016). When problems do develop, many users will dismiss the possibility that cannabis is the source of their difficulties (Sparks, 2016). This is common with substance abusers and with those who become addicted. The dramatic changes that occur from addiction to "harder" drugs are usually not present with cannabis use, and those that do develop may not emerge for years. The changes that may unfold from cannabis use are often subtle and insidious (Schwartz, 2013). THC is extremely fat-soluble, meaning that it stores in the body's fatty tissues, including the brain (Marijuana, 2016). THC can be detected in a user's body for up to a month. Similarly, poorer cognitive performance following abstinence from cannabis can persist for up to 28 days (Hart & Shytle, 2011). Consequently, one can be under the influence of the drug and not realize it. For example, the subtle changes in personality—such as increased impulsivity, decreased inhibitions (Pintori et al., 2017), reduced emotional control, and increased risk-taking (Trull et al., 2016)—may go unnoticed.

Working memory and episodic memory are impaired from cannabis use, and this, in turn, impairs the encoding of new memories. Consequently, some memories and experiences cannot later be retrieved (Curran et al., 2016). Working memory impairment is most evident in tasks requiring mental processing such as performing mental arithmetic, for example, and not so much in rote memory tasks over a short period (e.g., remembering an address) (Curran et al., 2016). Distortion of time may occur such that time intervals are not estimated accurately, and activities are done more slowly than normal (Atkinson, 2016). Decreased psychomotor activity occurs, some to the degree of becoming cataleptic (Atkinson, 2016).

Although cannabis usually induces relaxation in users, it also creates panic attacks and anxiety in some individuals under certain conditions (Zvolensky et al., 2011). Decreased motivation is common for those who are high on cannabis, and the diminutive effect of cannabis on motivation may be higher compared with other abused drugs (Atkinson, 2016). Prolonged motivational deficits caused by long-term cannabis use is referred to as the *amotivational syndrome*. The syndrome often creates a feeling of boredom at work and the diminished capacity to take initiative exacerbates the boredom (Margolis & Zweben, 2011). Frequent cannabis users in the Netherlands ($M = 39$ times and 51 times in two cities over 3 months) experienced "increased dissociation and psychedelic state, as well as fatigue, confusion, depression and anxiety, and decreased arousal, positive mood, vigor, friendliness, and elation" (van Wel et al., 2015, p. 324).

Smoking even small amounts of cannabis is harmful to the lungs. Smoking a single joint, for example, reduces breathing capacity to a similar degree as smoking five cigarettes (Csiernik, 2016). Compared with tobacco smoke, cannabis smoke creates greater fine damage to the lungs, which is what makes it more difficult to utilize oxygen efficiently (Csiernik, 2016). Cannabis use may also have cardiovascular effects. Marijuana use, for example, raises the heart rate by 20%–100% after about 20 min (Balkin, 2015), and, in some cases, heart attacks or fatal strokes result (Csiernik, 2016; Salhab, 2017; Wolff, Rouyer, & Geny, 2014).

The likelihood of having a serious motor vehicle accident almost doubles when one is high on cannabis (Rastegar & Fingerhood, 2016). Although alcohol intoxication is the leading cause of driving impairment resulting in accidents in youth between ages 18 and 30, cannabis follows in second place (Csiernik, 2016).

Regarding prevalence, cannabis is one of the most *abused* substances in the world. In the United States and globally, it *is* the most commonly used illicit drug (Atkinson, 2016; Salhab, 2017).

About 48% of Americans have tried cannabis, whereas 6.5% of high school seniors admit to using it *daily* (Salhab, 2017). It is currently estimated that 9% of users will become addicted, but perhaps as high as 17% for those who begin in their teens (Hart & Shytle, 2011; Salhab, 2017). Teens, on average, will become addicted within the first 5 years of use. By contrast, alcohol dependence does not develop, on average, until 10 years of use (Atkinson, 2016). Most who become addicted to cannabis do so before age 25, likely a result of the earlier age of onset for the use of this drug compared to other drugs, including alcohol (Atkinson, 2016). Up to 50% of daily users are at risk of dependency (Salhab, 2017; Sparks, 2016). Treatment admissions for cannabis use disorder (CUD) in the United States have doubled over the past 10–15 years and now constitute the greatest overall percentage of total treatment admissions compared with all other illegal drugs (Kosten et al., 2014). Cannabis also accounts for the greatest number of admissions in Europe compared with other drugs (Curran et al., 2016).

Diagnostic and Assessment Considerations

Cannabis-related disorders are found on pages 509–519 of *DSM-5* (APA, 2013) and include CUD, cannabis intoxication, cannabis withdrawal, other cannabis-induced disorders, and unspecified cannabis-related disorder. As is true for other substance disorders contained in *DSM-5*, in contrast to DSM-IV, a diagnosis distinguishing between *substance abuse* and *substance dependence* no longer occurs. Instead, a substance disorder is diagnosed by *severity* (i.e., by the number of diagnosable symptoms) as follows: (a) *mild*: 2 to 3, (b) *moderate*: 4 to 5, or (c) *severe*: 6 or more. *DSM-5* includes 11 listed criteria with two specifiers.

The overall diagnostic criteria for CUD is "A problematic pattern of cannabis use leading to clinically significant impairment or distress, as manifested by at least two of the following, occurring within a 12-month period" (APA, 2013, p. 509). The specific criteria include (a) loss of control over use, (b) continued desire or inability to reduce use, (c) much time is spent trying to obtain cannabis, use it, or recover from it, (d) cravings or a strong desire to use cannabis, (e) recurring use results in failure to fulfill obligations at work, school, or at home, (f) continuing use despite persistent or recurring problems socially and/or interpersonally, (g) social, occupational, or recreational activities are stopped or reduced because of use, (h) continuing use in situations where it is physically dangerous, (i) continuing use despite having a persistent or recurrent psychological or physical problem in which cannabis caused or exasperated the condition, (j) tolerance, expressed as either a need for increasing amounts of cannabis or diminished effect from continuing use of the same amount of cannabis, and (k) withdrawal, expressed as the cannabis withdrawal diagnosis (begins on page 517) or cannabis or another related substance is taken to relieve or avoid symptoms of withdrawal. As noted earlier, there are two specifiers for this diagnosis. You can specify if the condition is an *early remission*, meaning, between 3 months and 12 months, or in *sustained remission*, which requires 12 months or longer. You can also specify if the individual is *in a controlled environment*, meaning, in a place where access to cannabis is difficult if not impossible. See Table 10.1 for DSM and ICD codes.

TABLE 10.1 DSM and ICD Codes

DSM Code	Number of Symptoms Required	ICD-10	ICD-11
305.20	Mild: 2 or 3 symptoms	F12.10	6C41*
304.30	Moderate: 4 or 5 symptoms	F12.20	6C41
304.30	Severe: 6 or more symptoms	F12.20	6C41

*The cannabis codes in ICD-11 mostly begin with 6C41 but are then further distinguished by presence of the entities on the following page.

#	Specific Entity	Specific ICD-11 Code
1	Cannabis-induced delirium	6C41.5
2	Cannabis dependence, unspecified	6C41.2Z
3	Cannabis intoxication	6C41.3
4	Cannabis withdrawal	6C41.4
5	Harmful effects of drugs, medicaments, or biological substances, not elsewhere classified (includes cannabis poisoning)	NE60
6	Cannabis-induced psychotic disorder	6C41.6
7	Other cannabis-induced disorders Cannabis-induced mood disorder Cannabis-induced anxiety disorder	6C41.7 6C41.70 6C41.71
8	Disorders due to use of cannabis, unspecified	6C41.Z
9	Intentional self-harm by exposure to or harmful effects of cannabinoids or hallucinogens (includes intentional overdose of cannabis)	PC 93
10	Hazardous use of cannabis	QE11.1
11	Harmful pattern of use of cannabis, unspecified	6C41.1Z
12	Cannabis dependence, current use	6C41.20
13	Other specified disorders due to use of cannabis	6C41.Y
14	Unintentional exposure to or harmful effects of cannabinoids or hallucinogens (includes harmful effect of natural cannabis)	PB23
15	Single episode of harmful use of cannabis	6C41.0
16	Harmful pattern of use of cannabis, episodic	6C41.10
17	Harmful pattern of use of cannabis, continuous	6C41.11
18	Cannabis dependence, early full remission	6C41.21
19	Cannabis dependence, sustained partial remission	6C41.22
20	Cannabis dependence, sustained full remission	6C41.23
21	Assault by exposure to or harmful effects of cannabinoids or hallucinogens (includes assault by exposure to or harmful effects of cannabis)	PE83
22	Exposure to or harmful effects of undetermined intent of cannabinoids or hallucinogens (includes harmful effects of or exposure to cannabis, undetermined intent)	PH43

Differential Diagnosis

As *DSM-5* makes clear, it can be difficult to distinguish problematic use from nonproblematic use of cannabis. If social, behavioral, or psychological problems are evident, causation is difficult to ascertain, particularly if involvement with other drugs is occurring. This is especially so when others are referring an individual for treatment. Anxiety symptoms caused by cannabis might be misclassified or misdiagnosed as anxiety created by a primary mental disorder, and vice versa. This is also true with symptoms that might appear as "panic disorder, major depressive disorder, delusional disorder, bipolar disorder, or schizophrenia, paranoid type" (APA, 2013, p. 515). Chronic use of cannabis can also create an amotivational syndrome that could be misdiagnosed as dysthymia.

Comorbidity and Co-Addictions

Nearly 75% of cannabis users also smoke tobacco; an estimated 7 million Americans smoke both (Kosten et al., 2014). As noted earlier, cannabis use can precipitate psychosis in those predisposed to it (Hart & Shytle, 2011). Nonetheless, it is important to determine whether cannabis induced the psychosis or whether the psychotic disorder is primary (i.e., preceded the cannabis use) as treatments for each are different (Aggarwal, Banerjee, Singh, Mattoo, & Basu, 2012).

Although people entering treatment will often mention alcohol and harder drug use, they often will mention cannabis and nicotine use as an afterthought with little awareness of how these drugs may be hurting their health (Sparks, 2016). Cannabis use is comorbid with other substance use disorders (SUDs) (APA, 2013).

Cannabis users with a psychiatric disorder are more likely to develop CUD (Atkinson, 2016). Research has shown that people are more at risk for cannabis use and addiction if they (a) experience social anxiety disorder (Buckner et al., 2008), (b) have a family history of use, (c) began using early, (d) experience posttraumatic stress disorder, (e) experience certain personality disorders (antisocial, dependent, histrionic; Csiernik, 2016), and/or (f) have an externalizing disorder (e.g., attention deficit disorder, attention deficit hyperactivity disorder, conduct disorder, oppositional defiant disorder) (Atkinson, 2016; Maté, 2008). Those with mood disorders (including bipolar disorder) and anxiety disorders are more likely to use cannabis and other substances (Atkinson, 2016; Curran et al., 2016). A preexisting depressive or anxiety disorder also increases the likelihood of cannabis addiction (Curran et al., 2016).

Available Measures

Balkin (2015) stated that CUD could be assessed via a clinical interview in addition to specialized instruments. Counselors have several instruments at their disposal. Here is a list of the most common (not listed in any specific order):

Specific Measures

1. Marijuana Motives Measure. This instrument was factor analyzed, and it measures enhancement, conformity, expansion, coping, and social motives for use. The measure is described by Simons, Correia, and Carey (2000) and Simons, Correia, Carey, and Borsari (1998).
2. Cannabis Use Problems Identification Test (CUPIT; Bashford, Flett, & Copeland, 2010). A 16-question inventory covering the past 12 months of use. Useful for initial screening and deciding on treatment issues. Available from http://www.massey.ac.nz/massey/learning/departments/school-of-psychology/research/cupit/clinicians/clinicians_home.cfm
3. Adult Cannabis Problems Questionnaire (Copeland, Gilmore, Gates, & Swift, 2005). A 21-item inventory focused on the past 3 months. Available from https://drugsinmind.net/13.cannabis/_index.files/cannabis-problems-questionnaire.pdf

   There is also an adolescent version. Available from https://drugsinmind.net/13.cannabis/_index.files/adolescent-cannabis-problems-questionnaire.pdf
4. Cannabis Use Disorders Identification Test-Revised (CUDIT-R; Adamson et al., 2010). As a brief eight-item assessment tool, the CUDIT-R provides a simple and reliable measure of the severity of problematic cannabis use. This article extends the utility of the CUDIT-R by demonstrating its sensitivity to change in a treatment sample, with definitions of reliable and clinically significant change applicable to research and clinical settings. Available from https://bpac.org.nz/BPJ/2010/June/docs/addiction_CUDIT-R.pdf
5. Marijuana Craving Questionnaire (MCQ; Heishman, Singleton, & Ligouri, 2001). Available from https://osf.io/v8y34/
6. Cannabis Abuse Screening Test (CAST; Legleye, Karila, Beck, & Reynaud, 2007; Legleye, Kraus, Piontek, Phan, & Jouanne, 2012).
7. Reasons for Quitting Questionnaire. DeRamus (2011) wrote that this questionnaire "is based on earlier work with tobacco cessation and has been modified based on initial results with people who use marijuana and seek treatment" (p. 30).

   Questionnaire available from https://www.drugtimes.org/marijuana-dependence/reasons-for-quitting-questionnaire.html

General Measures

1. Alcohol, Smoking and Substance Involvement Screening Test (ASSIST; WHO ASSIST Working Group, 2002). This questionnaire is used via face-to-face interaction with a client. It includes only seven questions, of which six are scored. This brief measure shows a good ability to discriminate among use, abuse, and dependence (Asbridge et al., 2014). Available from http://apps.who.int/iris/bitstream/10665/44320/1/9789241599382_eng.pdf
2. Severity of Dependence Scale (SDS; Gossop et al., 1995). Measures cannabis as well as other substances. A five-question screening tool looking at use over the past 3 months. Better used for longitudinal follow-up than for individual use. Available from http://www.emcdda.europa.eu/attachements.cfm/att_7364_EN_english_sds.pdf
3. Substance Abuse Subtle Screening Inventory–3 (SASSI-3; Miller & Lazowski, 1999). This one is not specific to cannabis but instead looks at dependency versus use of substances.
4. Car, Relax, Alone, Forget, Friends, Trouble Inventory. "The CRAFFT is a behavioral health screening tool for use with children under the age of 21 and is recommended by the American Academy of Pediatrics' Committee on Substance Abuse for use with adolescents" (para. 1). The CRAFFT and instructions for use are available from https://www.integration.samhsa.gov/clinical-practice/sbirt/adolescent_screening,_brieft_intervention_and_referral_to_treatment_for_alcohol.pdf
5. Self-Efficacy Questionnaire. Deramus (2011) noted that this questionnaire is extracted from the *Brief Counseling for Marijuana Dependence Manual* (available for free from https://www.integration.samhsa.gov/clinical-practice/sbirt/Brief_Counseling_for_Marijuana_Dependence.pdf)
6. Structured Clinical Interview for *DSM-5* (SCID-5). A general interview for diagnosis purposes (available from https://www.amazon.com/Structured-Clinical-Interview-Disorders-Scid-5-cv/dp/1585624616/ref=sr_1_1?ie=UTF8&qid=1513038044&sr=8-1&keywords=structured+clinical+interview+for+dsm-5). *Note*: There is a cost for this measure.

Clinical Interview Questions

The various questionnaires and inventories mentioned in the previous section together contain a long list of questions that can be asked in an interview. The Structured Clinical Interview for *DSM-5* can be used, but remember there is a cost to using this instrument. Marijuana Anonymous World Services (2017) provides a list of 12 questions that can be asked. The word *marijuana* in this list can be substituted for *cannabis* to be more inclusive.

The following questions may help you determine whether marijuana is a problem in your life:

1. Has smoking pot stopped being fun?
2. Do you ever get high alone?
3. Is it hard for you to imagine a life without marijuana?
4. Do you find that your friends are determined by your marijuana use?
5. Do you use marijuana to avoid dealing with your problems?
6. Do you smoke pot to cope with your feelings?
7. Does your marijuana use let you live in a privately defined world?
8. Have you ever failed to keep promises you made about cutting down or controlling your use of marijuana?
9. Has your use of marijuana caused problems with memory, concentration, or motivation?
10. When your stash is nearly empty, do you feel anxious or worried about how to get more?
11. Do you plan your life around your marijuana use?
12. Have friends or relatives ever complained that your using is damaging your relationship with them?

If you answered yes to any of the above questions, you may have a problem with marijuana. (Marijuana Anonymous World Services, 2017, para. 1)

Generic Names and Street "Lingo"

Csiernik (2016) listed many of the names that denote cannabis and/or marijuana (also spelled marihuana by some), including "A-bomb (mixed with heroin or opium), Acapulco gold, Acapulco red, ace, bazooka (mixed with cocaine), BC Bud, bhang, blunt, boom, B.T., chronic, Columbian, doobie, dope, gangster, ganja, grass, hemp, herb, home grown, jay, kiff, Mary Jane, Maui Wowie, Northern lights, pot, purple haze, ragweed, reefer, sinse, skunk, smoke, spliff, tea, Thai stick, weed" (p. 180). Two other words mentioned by Curran et al. (2016) are charas and resin. Hash, hashish, and hash oil are other terms.

Dabs is a term that has appeared in recent years.

> Dabs are concentrated doses of cannabis that are made by extracting THC and other cannabinoids using a solvent like butane or carbon dioxide, resulting in sticky oils also commonly referred to as wax, shatter, budder, and butane hash oil (BHO). They're heated on a hot surface, usually a nail, and then inhaled through a dab rig. (Leafly, 2017, para. 1)

Smoking dabs requires the concentrate noted previously, a small pick, a special bong, and a blowtorch. Given that a blowtorch is required to both make dabs and to smoke it, many novices have accidentally exploded their kitchens and basements (Watson Seupel, 2014).

Another term with a simple history is *420*. The term was coined by then-17-year-old Brad Bann on a Saturday in October 1970. Brad was known as the Bebe, and his teenage clique was called the Bebes. On a Saturday in October 1970, he and the Bebes were hanging out in a bedroom when Brad noticed the time and said, "It's 4:20, time for bong loads." 420 soon became code in their neighborhood for pot. Another group, which Brad called the *Waldos*, made the term 420 famous across the United States (Griffin, 2012). Today April 20 (i.e., 420) has become known as *National Weed Day* by cannabis users.

Neuroscience

Not surprisingly, cannabis' reward system involves the mesolimbic dopamine system, as is true of other abused substances (Atkinson, 2016). When cannabis chemicals enter the body, they bind to two kinds of receptors known as cannabinoid receptor 1 and cannabinoid receptor 2 (CB-1 and CB-2; Hart & Shytle, 2011). Because they are more prevalent than opioid receptors, it is believed that they affect more regions of the brain. CB-2 receptors are mostly located in the immune cells. Consequently, researchers speculate that cannabinoids may modulate the immune system in some capacity (Hart & Shytle, 2011).

CB-1 receptors are found mostly in the central nervous system, and they are related to the functioning and development of the brain (Balkin, 2015). CB-1 receptors are found in the basal ganglia (which includes the caudate nucleus), putamen, globus pallidus, cerebellum, hippocampus, cerebral cortex, and the nucleus accumbens. This suggests that cannabis modulates a range of behaviors (Hart & Shytle, 2011). Current research indicates that synthetic cannabinoids mostly affect CB-1 receptors (Pintori et al., 2017).

Although the neurotransmitter serotonin is most closely aligned with hallucinogen use, cannabis is instead identified with the fatty acid neurotransmitter called anandamide. This is speculated to explain why cannabis works differently from other hallucinogens (Csiernik, 2016). When an individual smokes marijuana, THC travels quickly to the brain and bonds with receptors and anandamines, both of which are prevalent in the limbic system (Csiernik, 2016). Although most PET studies have found that THC can increase dopamine in the striatum, this occurs to a much lesser degree compared with other recreational drugs (Curran et al., 2016). There is currently weak support for implicating dopamine in cannabis addiction (Curran et al., 2016). Nonetheless, in cannabis addicts, "cortical control of the mesolimbic circuitry malfunctions and this leads to an overvaluing of drug related reinforcers and an undervaluing of natural reinforcers" (Atkinson, 2016, p. 28). Furthermore, there is evidence that marijuana might decrease neural response in the nucleus accumbens, which in turn may increase the risk of further drug use and addiction (Martz et al., 2016). Some research suggests that the genetic risk for cannabis addiction may link to genes like ELTD1 on chromosome 1, GABRA2 on chromosome 4, and CNRI on chromosome 6 (Agrawal et al., 2008).

Physical Impacts (Long-Term Use)

There are several unhealthy consequences to using cannabis products regularly and frequently over a prolonged period. Because the potency (percentage of THC) in cannabis is variable over both time and across regions, it is impossible currently to accurately predict what potency (combined with what percentage of CBD) will lead to health consequences and addiction, and over what duration of time, compared to which will not cause negative consequences (Asbridge et al., 2014). Pearson (2019) meta-analyzed 19 studies that examined the relationship between cannabis use and negative consequences. He found that cannabis use "had a medium-sized association with consequences" (from abstract). Due to the heterogeneity of the studies, however, Pearson was unable to isolate these negative impacts. He concluded that additional studies need to be conducted with additional indicators.

Abusing smoked cannabis long term is as bad or worse for one's lungs compared with cigarette smoking. The carcinogens and the tars increase the likelihood for not only lung cancer but also for neck and head cancers (Milkman & Sunderwirth, 2010). One of the problems with cannabis is that it burns 16 times hotter than tobacco (Smith, 2013). Compared to tobacco, cannabis smoke also produces twice as many mutagens, which are substances that create permanent changes in genetic material (Smith, 2013).

Marijuana smoke contains at least 50% more carcinogens than tobacco products. Cannabis smokers also absorb approximately four times more tar into their lungs and experience about an 8% greater risk of developing lung cancer than those who don't smoke (Balkin, 2015). Like tobacco smokers, those who smoke cannabis experience similar degrees of pulmonary problems (Hart & Shytle, 2011). These include reduced lung capacity, chronic cough, increased mucus in the lungs (Balkin, 2015), and wheezing (Zvolensky et al., 2011). Other severe respiratory diseases can occur, too, the most frequent of which is chronic bronchitis (Zvolensky et al., 2011). About 74% of those who smoke cannabis also smoke tobacco (Kosten et al., 2014), and there is evidence that smoking tobacco increased the potential for cannabis addiction (Englund et al., 2017).

Birth defects are likelier in children born to mothers who have abused cannabis (Salhab, 2017), resulting in neurophysiological and behavioral disorders (Atkinson, 2016). When a fetus is exposed to cannabis, it becomes at increased risk of placental abruptions, premature births, and lower birth weight (Rastegar & Fingerhood, 2016).

Long-term studies have shown that cannabis abuse creates cognitive deficits, including delayed processing speed, judgment, reduced problem-solving ability, decreased attentional capability, poorer working memory, learning difficulties, and reduced impulse control (Atkinson, 2016; Balkin, 2015). It remains unclear whether cognitive functions ever return completely to preuse levels following long-term abstinence, however (Balkin, 2015). A longitudinal study found that users who began abusing cannabis in adolescence experienced neuropsychological deficits that did not restore following cessation (Rastegar & Fingerhood, 2016). The cognitive impairments are known to exist for months and even years after quitting cannabis (Zvolensky et al., 2011). Long-term users experience difficulties with executive functioning such as the ability to solve problems, make decisions, and think abstractly (Csiernik, 2016). Cannabis affects "our most valued human faculties – the abilities to test reality, reason, control our impulses, set priorities, relate to others, and reach our goals" (Atkinson, 2016, p. 11).

Although regular users of cannabis experience poorer academic performance, it is unclear if factors other than cannabis use are to blame (Englund et al., 2017). Cannabis can create an overfocus on insignificant things, and impaired judgment can make it difficult to refocus on other matters (Atkinson, 2016). As noted earlier, regarding cognitive effects, CBD can reverse some of the negative impacts of THC (Englund et al., 2017). Although longitudinal studies have revealed a reduction in IQ scores in heavy cannabis users (Atkinson, 2016), the studies upon which this finding is based are confounded with small numbers of participants (Englund et al., 2017). Other longitudinal studies have suggested that reduced IQ scores may be due to other factors (Englund et al., 2017).

Regular users also experience decreased energy, immune system deficiencies, increased likelihood of having endocrine problems, decreased sperm production, inhibited ovulation, and decreased fertility (Csiernik, 2016).

Over time, the brain becomes increasingly unresponsive to the effect of naturally occurring reinforcers such as employment, cannabis's, and social aspects of life (Atkinson, 2016). Deficits in psychosocial functioning are postulated to occur because of cannabis's effect on cognition and motivation (Atkinson, 2016). One's ability to experience pleasure can be affected by long-term use of cannabis (Balkin, 2015). Physical coordination can also be affected (Balkin, 2015; Pintori et al., 2017). One of the signs that someone may be misusing marijuana includes animated behavior and talking loudly (Smith, 2013). Poor academic and work performance are also correlated with regular cannabis use (Kosten et al., 2014).

High-potency cannabis use and the onset of mental illness, particularly schizophrenia, are strongly correlated as well (Hamilton, 2017; Kosten et al., 2014). This is currently an area of deep controversy. The question is whether the relationship is only correlational or if it is also causal. In other words, which comes first: Does cannabis use *cause* psychosis, or does psychosis lead one to want to use cannabis? (Zvolensky et al., 2011). Most people who use cannabis do not develop psychotic disorders, and many psychotic individuals have never used cannabis (Curran et al., 2016). We know that cannabis can catalyze a psychotic reaction for those predisposed to it (Hart & Shytle, 2011; Rastegar & Fingerhood, 2016), and we also know that individuals living with schizophrenia are likelier to relapse if they use cannabis (Englund et al., 2017). Furthermore, interventions targeted at helping psychotic individuals refrain from cannabis use have been unsuccessful (Englund et al., 2017). We also know that, the earlier one uses it, the earlier the psychotic disorder manifests in those predisposed, and that effect has been most pronounced in women compared with men (Agabio, Campesi, Pisanu, Gessa, & Franconi, 2016). Nonetheless, the type of cannabis used might make a difference as well. Self-reported use of hash, even when used daily, is not associated with an increased risk of psychosis, whereas self-reported daily use of "skunk weed" and "negligible amounts of cannabidiol (CBD) is associated with a fivefold greater chance of having schizophrenia" (Curran et al., 2016). A major concern and ongoing controversy relate to the impact that cannabis use has on the brain's development during adolescence. Chronic users who begin using cannabis in adolescence may experience changes to the structure and functions of their brains (e.g., smaller volume of cortical gray matter and reduced activation in prefrontal brain regions), thus creating indefinite learning and memory problems (Balkin, 2015; Kosten et al., 2014; Trull et al., 2016). A particular concern is expressed in the literature for those using cannabis regularly before the age of 17 (Kosten et al., 2014). For example, research has demonstrated that decreased processing speed and impaired executive function remain for at least 3 years following cannabis cessation in younger users (Meruelo, Castro, Cota, & Tapert, 2017). Other findings conclude that cannabis has a harmful effect on prospective memory in young adults, yet many may remain unaware of this impact (Bartholomew, Holroyd, & Heffernan, 2010).

Is cannabis a "gateway drug" to use of harder drugs? Research does support the idea that some cannabis users segue into harder drugs, particularly heavy users and those who begin using in adolescence (Curran et al., 2016; Holley, 2009). As in the research concerning psychosis, causality is undetermined. Those who have a dealer for cannabis usually have access to harder drugs so that access may be the determining factor.

The "reverse gateway" is also possible, meaning that cannabis users may segue into using tobacco products (Curran et al., 2016). Beyond the gateway theory, regular use of cannabis is strongly correlated with cannabis dependence (Kosten et al., 2014). Daily use of high-potency cannabis is most strongly correlated with addiction (Balkin, 2015; Englund et al., 2017).

Dependency on cannabis develops within 5 years for about 50% of cannabis users (Atkinson, 2016). For those who become addicted, most have used almost every day for 10 years or more, and on average have tried to quit six times (Sparks, 2016). Half of individuals with CUD who decide to stop using will reinitiate use within 2 weeks, and, of the other half, about half will relapse within a year (Balkin, 2015). "In fact, more people fail at abstaining from smoking marijuana than any other illegal drug *combined*" (DeRamus, 2011, p. 11).

Withdrawal begins occurring 4–8 hours after abrupt termination and typically lasts 3–4 weeks (Csiernik, 2016). Cognitive impairments for adults who stop using cannabis cease after 4–6 weeks (Curran et al., 2016). The cannabis withdrawal syndrome affects about 50% of daily users (Curran et al., 2016). Withdrawal symptoms may include insomnia and sleep disturbances with vivid dreaming, decreased appetite, aches and pains, headache, fever, anxiety, shakiness, sweating, dysphoria, anger, irritability, drug craving, and aggressive behavior in some cases (Atkinson, 2016; Csiernik, 2016; Hart & Shytle, 2011; Rastegar & Fingerhood, 2016). Additional withdrawal symptoms include a general "blah" feeling and "inner unrest" (Hanson, 2009, p. 111). The most typical symptom of quitting cannabis is having difficulty sleeping (Sparks, 2016). The worse the withdrawal effects experienced by an individual, the greater the likelihood of relapse (Atkinson, 2016). Withdrawal effects from synthetic cannabinoids may include anxiety, irritability, diarrhea, insomnia, tremor, profuse sweating, and tachycardia (Pintori et al., 2017).

Mental, Emotional, and Spiritual Impacts

Most of the mental effects, which are largely physical manifestations resulting from the frequent use of cannabis, were covered in the previous section about physical effects. One potentially positive effect noted in recent research is that chronic cannabis use blunts one's reaction to stress, and there is speculation as to whether this may reduce one's vulnerability to stress or reduce stress-related disorders (Cuttler et al., 2017). At the same time, regular marijuana use can increase one's reactivity to stress and irritability (Volkow et al., 2014).

Chronic use of cannabis is associated with hostility and anxiety disorders (Curran et al., 2016; Trull et al., 2016). Although there are statistical correlations between cannabis use and depression (Curran et al., 2016), the strength of these associations is somewhat weak (Zvolensky et al., 2011). Cannabis can create apathy and emotional lability (particularly flat affect) together with an inability to control emotions and behavior (Csiernik, 2016).

A PsycINFO search reveals the dearth of peer-reviewed journal articles and books when "cannabis" and "spirituality" are used as search terms: One of each were found. A two-volume book, edited by Ellens (2014), reviews how ayahuasca, cannabis, LSD, peyote, and psilocybin have been used historically and in several religions to achieve altered states. A recent edited book by Gray (2016) "explores the use of marijuana in a wide range of spiritual practices, including meditation, yoga, chanting, visualization, shamanism, group ceremonies, work with other entheogens, and as a creative aid" (book description on the Amazon website).

Dr. Sona Patel (2017), in her website, wrote about the role that marijuana and spirituality have played in our cultural history. She reported that marijuana and cannabis had been used in religious ceremonies for either hundreds or thousands of years. Patel provided information about the use of cannabis for medical and religious reasons in ancient India, Africa, China, Central Asia, Europe, and the Middle East. Currently, cannabis is also used in religious ceremonies in India, Jamaica, and in other parts of South and North America.

The only peer-reviewed published empirical study on PsycINFO is by Baker, Sellman, and Horn (2007). They stated that they conducted the first study, and arguably the only published study, to look at the spiritual experiences, beliefs, and practices of New Zealanders entering substance abuse treatment. Of the 90 admittees included in their research, 93%, 63%, and 34% were alcohol, cannabis, or other drug dependent, respectively. Consequently, there was an overlap of addictions in the sample. Most participants stated that they were spiritual but not religious, and most reported having a life-altering or religious experience before admission. Older individuals were most likely to be affiliated with a religion and to be affiliated with 12-step meetings.

Although a website includes the statement that cannabis can help people "awaken from illusion and get 'real'" (*Cannabis and spirituality*, n.d.), this seems hardly likely for someone who has become addicted. As written in Chapter 1, addicted individuals become selfish, self-centered individuals over time as their drug or behavior becomes the most important "god" to them. Furthermore, anecdotally at least, daily and chronic use of cannabis may affect one's ability to be fully present and emotionally available to a partner or a loved one.

Psychosocial Impacts (Relationships, Career/Work, Legal, Financial)

The greatest negative psychosocial impacts reportedly occur with adolescent heavy cannabis users, which includes a gateway effect into the use of harder drugs, quitting school early, cognitive impairments, increased risk for psychosis, and increased risk for addiction and suicide attempts (Hall, 2015; Silins et al., 2014). When asked about substances that have caused adverse consequences, a study of 7437 American high school students found that, compared to alcohol, cannabis users found they experienced less energy and interest, diminished school or work performance, and reported more relationship problems with teachers or supervisors (Palamar et al., 2014). In a sample of 110 Swiss adolescents (aged 12–19), cannabis dependence was associated with dysfunctional coping strategies and disrupted peer relationships (Cascone, Zimmermann, Auckenthaler, & Robert-Tissot, 2011). Frequent use of marijuana doubles a teenager's risk of experiencing anxiety and/or depression, and, in turn, depressed adolescents are at least twice as likely to become addicted to cannabis (DeRamus, 2011).

For some at least, marijuana use interferes with workplace productivity (Zvolensky et al., 2011). A 39-year longitudinal study from Sweden (Danielsson, Agardh, Hemmingsson, Allebeck, & Falkstedt, 2014) found that, in their country, those who began using cannabis heavily since adolescence were 30% more likely to be on a disability pension (available to those between ages 16 and 65 compared to those who had not used cannabis more than 50 times in total. Finally, risky sexual behavior is also associated with cannabis use (Agrawal et al., 2016).

Working With Diverse Populations

Sex Differences

Many sex differences have been found in research focused on SUDs, although few differences have been found with cannabis use (Agabio et al., 2016). Males are more likely to use cannabis than females (although the gap is lessening), and they are more likely to abuse and become addicted (Tartaglia, Miglietta, & Gattino, 2017). When women become addicted to cannabis, they also seek treatment at younger ages compared to men (Agabio et al., 2016).

Cannabis is the most frequently used illicit drug by pregnant women (Morris, 2015). Women who began using as teenagers are more likely to report engaging in repeated unprotected sex than nonusers and those who began using cannabis after their teenage years (Agrawal et al., 2016). Nonaddicted women who begin using at younger ages also predicts poorer memory, a finding not found in nonaddicted men (Curran et al., 2016). There is also a neurological difference in that women users have a larger right amygdala compared to female controls, whereas men users have a smaller prefrontal cortex compared to male controls (Agabio et al., 2016).

Adolescents and Youth

Adolescence is a vulnerable time for developing an SUD (Winters & Lee, 2008), and it is also a time when the brain may be more vulnerable to the effect of drugs (Curran et al., 2016). About 17% of adolescent cannabis users will develop CUD by age 24, and half of these teenagers will be dependent within 5 years of beginning use (Atkinson, 2016). By contrast, Atkinson (2016) stated that the median age for becoming an alcoholic is double this (i.e., within about 10 years).

Although cannabis use has been decreasing among adolescents over the past few years (Keyes, Wall, Feng, Cerda, & Hasin, 2017), it remains common in youth, and it is associated with inattentiveness, increased levels of depression, and suicide risk (Osuch, Vingilis, Ross, Forster, & Summerhurst, 2013). In many American inner-city schools, marijuana has become a more popular drug than alcohol, with some beginning use as early as age 12 (Maharajh et al., 2014). Depressive symptoms are more common when cannabis is used early and used continuously (Andrade & de Lima Argimon, 2008). Teenagers and young adults who are frequent users of marijuana are also more likely to experience increases in negative affect (Ross et al., 2018). Greater use of alcohol and marijuana is associated with worse academic performance in high school for all youth, especially for non-White youth (D'Amico et al., 2016).

A sample of 2120 adolescents (940 cannabis users, 1180 non-users) in the Netherlands found that cannabis use at age 16 predicted psychosis 3 years later, and a reverse relationship was also found (i.e., psychosis vulnerability at age 13 predicted cannabis use 3 years later; Griffith-Lendering et al., 2013). Furthermore, those who begin using at earlier ages continue to show decreased processing speed and diminished executive functioning 3 years later (Meruelo et al., 2017).

But it is not just early use that produces long-standing deficits. Beginning cannabis use later in adolescence or early adulthood is associated with several adverse outcomes later, including "poor educational outcome, lower income, greater dependency on social assistance, unemployment, and lower relationship and life satisfaction" (Csiernik, 2016, p. 184). Because their mesolimbic systems respond especially well to reward and their prefrontal cortexes are not fully developed, adolescents are at high risk of impulsive decision-making (Atkinson, 2016). Furthermore, it is speculated that the damage to an adolescent's IQ caused by regular and heavy cannabis use is permanently lowered by 5–8 IQ points (similar to those exposed to high levels of lead; Atkinson, 2016).[2] Cannabis use in adolescence negatively affects episodic memory (Duperrouzel et al., 2019).

Dorard et al. (2017) found that, with 120 youth ages 14–25 (mean age = 17.9 years; 95 males, 25 females) who were receiving treatment as outpatients for cannabis dependence, 35% were alexithymic with the analysis, showing that their greatest difficulty was in describing feelings together with high trait anxiety (Dorard et al., 2017). Adolescent cannabis users are more likely to have a higher body mass index than nonusers, and this is not explained by other factors such as depression, race, ethnicity, IQ, nicotine use, or alcohol use (Ross, Graziano, Pacheco-Colon, Coxe, & Gonzalez, 2016).

High school students who score high on trait impulsivity and have a history of behavioral addictions are more likely to use tobacco, alcohol, or marijuana (Chuang et al., 2017). A large-scale study (N = 6496) found that use of these three substances is also associated with the use of prescription opioids in 18- to 25-year-old men. Marijuana use was only associated with subsequent abuse of prescription opioids in young women (Fiellin, Tetrault, Becker, Fiellin, & Hoff, 2013). *Mulling* (i.e., adding tobacco to joints) is a common practice among young cannabis users and should be considered when working with adolescents (Belanger, Akre, Kuntsche, Gmel, & Suris, 2011).

Withdrawal symptoms are also common with adolescents receiving outpatient treatment. Of 90 adolescents in one clinic who reported cannabis as their drug of choice, 40% experienced withdrawal symptoms (Greene & Kelly, 2014).

Race and Ethnicity

The population of racial and ethnic groups is growing faster in the United States compared to Whites (Wu, Zhu, & Swartz, 2016).

[2]For more information concerning the neuroscience regarding cannabis' effects on adolescents, see Meruelo et al. (2017).

Research has found that adolescents who are immigrants or born to immigrants are at increased risk of substance use (Chedebois et al., 2009). Black-White youth are less likely to use substances compared to either Black or White youth (Goings, Butler-Bente, McGovern, & Howard, 2016). Several studies have found that Hispanic adolescents report greater usage of most major drugs compared to non-Hispanic White and African American teenagers (Cardoso, Goldbach, Cervantes, & Swank, 2016; Suerken et al., 2014; Unger, Schwartz, Huh, Soto, & Baezconde-Garbanati, 2014). The reasons for this finding include discrimination, immigration, community violence, and poverty (Cardoso et al., 2016). Recent research has suggested a moderating variable: The parent-adolescent relationship between Hispanic youth has a greater impact on alcohol and marijuana use compared with non-Hispanic White youth (Moreno, Janssen, Cox, Colby, & Jackson, 2017).

African American youth (ages 12–18) are most likely to use marijuana and alcohol concurrently, followed next by White youth, whereas other racial and ethnic minority teenagers are most likely to only use marijuana (Banks, Rowe, Mpofu, & Zapolski, 2017). When looking at cannabis use only, research has found that non-White individuals are most likely to become regular users of cannabis compared to Whites (Pacek, Mauro, & Martins, 2015; Wu et al., 2016). A study of past 30-day prevalence between 1999 and 2012 found that cannabis use was lowest among Asians and highest among Native Americans (Johnson et al., 2015). Native Americans are also likely to begin using substances earlier than other youth (Stanley & Swaim, 2015).

Early use and regular use has been found to lead to greater suicidality among Mexican adolescents. In a study of 1071 adolescents in Mexico, those who used cannabis from an early age (before age 15) and those who used heavily for the past 12 months were more likely to think about and attempt suicide compared to noncannabis users (Borges, Benjet, Orozco, Medina-Mora, & Menendez, 2017).

Nonpsychiatric Disabilities

As noted previously, cannabis products have been found useful in treating or ameliorating some medical disorders. Both adults (Glazier & Kling, 2013) and youth (Maharajh et al., 2014) with disabilities report higher levels of cannabis use than those who are not disabled. Adolescents who live in residential care facilities and those with behavioral problems are also more at risk of SUDs, found in one study to result from deviant peer affiliations (Kepper, van den Eijnden, Monshouwer, & Vollebergh, 2014).

Another study found that youth with mobility issues, learning problems, and emotional disabilities were more likely to use marijuana. What distinguished them from other peers was greater exposure to risk factors concomitant with fewer protective factors (Blum, Kelly, & Ireland, 2001).

Lesbian, Gay, Bisexual, and Transgender (LGBT)

It has long been established that LGBT adolescents and adults use substances more than those who do not define as LGBT (Gonzalez, Gallego, & Bockting, 2017; Lowry, Johns, Robin, & Kann, 2017; Mereish, Goldbach, Burgess, & DiBello, 2017). The reasons for this increased use are related to psychosocial stress caused by discrimination, harassment, victimization, prejudice, and internalized homophobia (Goldbach, Schrager, Dunlap, & Holloway, 2015; Gonzalez et al., 2017; Lowry et al., 2017).

Regarding cannabis specifically, lesbian, gay, and bisexual adolescents use marijuana more than heterosexual teenagers (Goldbach et al., 2015). Sexual minority women are more likely to use cannabis than heterosexual women, which has been explained due to higher levels of exposure to trauma and posttraumatic disorder (Dworkin, Kaysen, Bedard-Gilligan, Rhew, & Lee, 2017). Cannabis use among bisexual women in a Canadian study was five times higher than Canadian women in general (Robinson, Sanches, & MacLeod, 2016). Bisexual men are also much more likely to use marijuana than gay and heterosexual men (Parnes, Rahm-Knigge, & Conner, 2017). Transgender men report significantly higher rates of cannabis use than transgender women (Gonzalez et al., 2017).

War Veterans

Recent research has found that past-year cannabis use among American veterans is about 9%; older and female veterans had lower rates compared to males (Davis, Lin, Ilgen, & Bohnert, 2018). Overall their past-year usage rates compare to that of the U.S. general population. However, the rate of those who used MM over the past year was more than double that of the general population (Davis et al., 2018). Reasons for medical use of cannabis include sleep-related issues and pain management (Davis et al., 2018). The adolescent children of veterans are more likely to use cannabis compared to nonveteran teenage children (Lipari et al., 2017).

Cannabis use is substantially associated with mental health problems in veterans, including suicidality (Kimbrel et al., 2017). Veterans experiencing major depressive disorder (Metrik et al., 2016) and/or posttraumatic stress disorder (PTSD) also remain at high risk of developing CUD (Gentes et al., 2016; Metrik et al., 2016). For veterans in residential care, those who continue using cannabis are likely to experience less respite from PTSD symptoms compared to nonusers (Bonn-Miller, Boden, Vujanovic, & Drescher, 2013). A study based on 341 veterans with PTSD found that the diagnosis itself was significantly associated with greater use of marijuana and depressants as compared to the use of cocaine and amphetamines (Calhoun et al., 2000).

Medications and Other Relevant Physical Interventions

Before looking at the medications that can be used to help with CUD and/or withdrawal, it is important to note that cannabis has been used in a harm reduction approach as a safer alternative for those using drugs that cause greater sequelae, including alcohol (Maharajh et al., 2014). Subbaraman (2014), however, suggested that recommending this for alcohol substitution is premature given what we currently know. Some MM users have been able to replace prescription medications with cannabis products (Lucas & Walsh, 2017). Inpatient hospitalization for CUDs remains rare although somewhat more common with adolescents who may be admitted for 1–2 weeks (Balkin, 2015).

One common antidepressant that has been found to worsen the symptoms of cannabis withdrawal is bupropion (Wellbutrin) (Hart & Shytle, 2011). The FDA has not yet approved any medication for CUD (National Institute on Drug Abuse, 2017; Sparks, 2016). Because sleep problems are common in cannabis withdrawal, sleep aids are sometimes prescribed such as Ambien (Zolpidem), buspirone (BuSpar), and gabapentin (Horizant, Neurontin). If sleep improves, these medications may indirectly improve executive functioning. Also being studied currently are the nutritional supplement N-acetylcysteine and chemicals called FAAH inhibitors. Other substances that will soon be studied are called allosteric modulators. These modulators may inhibit THC's rewarding effects (National Institute on Drug Abuse, 2017).

Other drugs that have some empirical support for helping cannabis withdrawal include fluoxetine, nefazodone (Sparks, 2016), Sativex, dronabinol (Marinol), nabilone (Cesamet), dexanabinol (Salhab, 2017), rimonabant, lithium (Elkashef & Montoya, 2012), nefazodone, naltrexone, and divalproex (Hart & Shytle, 2011). Perhaps most surprising is that orally administered THC has been used to decrease the physiological and subjective effects of cannabis withdrawal (Hart & Shytle, 2011).

DeRamus (2011) recommended taking omega-3 fatty acids, although the source of this information appears to be anecdotal. For psychotic adolescents who use cannabis, a recent study found that clozapine reduced cannabis use compared to those with no medication (Tang, Ansarian, & Courtney, 2017). D'Souza et al. (2019) found evidence that a fatty acid (i.e., amide hydrolase inhibitor, PF-04457845) reduced cannabis withdrawal symptoms in men. Bhardwaj et al. (2018) reported that "the cannabis extract nabiximols (Sativex) effectively suppreses [*sic*] withdrawal symptoms and cravings in treatment resistant cannabis dependent individuals" (p. 1).

INSIDE AN ADDICTED PERSON'S MIND

Rock, Age 19

As you might have guessed, I was not born with the name Rock. When I was really high one night, I began focusing on the character of Dwayne Johnson in the 2017 movie *Baywatch*. I knew as I watched that I wanted to be like him, so the next day I legally changed my name. Perhaps that sounds impulsive, but it completely made sense when I did it.

My parents were furious, but they live in Chicago, and I'm in Las Vegas. They took offense that I changed my name from Bert, which was my grandfather's name. I don't care. I had lots of conflicts with them growing up. They didn't understand my stoner friends. They thought I was going to hell because of these guys. Well, I didn't go to hell; instead, I went to Vegas. I love the bright lights, the sounds, because everything comes alive after I smoke a few joints. Truthfully, I smoke up all the time, even during breaks at work. The high is all I look forward to most days.

I love to walk around shirtless everywhere, and, even though I get a lot of disapproving looks, I don't give a shit. I'm young, cute, and most chicks think I'm hot. The other day a good-looking babe came up to me with that look of knowing. She was pissed when I looked distant and acted unfamiliar. She raged at me, screaming, "I CAN'T BELIEVE I EVER SLEPT WITH YOU!" It didn't phase me I thought: I was too stoned to care. Today, like yesterday, was about me and only me.

Despite my nonchalance, however, I couldn't get her off my mind. Why couldn't I remember her? Am I sleeping too much or not eating properly? Is pot affecting my memory? Is my job at Jack in the Box causing me too much stress? I think more about that, going into the many burgers I cook every day for ungrateful customers, the attitude I get from my boss who says I always seem stoned and to smarten up or I will get fired. This job is getting to me! The stress is overwhelming; I don't know why I put up with this crap. Focus, my only focus is on my stress, my job, my finances, my memory, my . . . **SHEBANG!**

I wake up days later, a coma I was told, by a nurse standing over me. I had walked off a curb without looking first. My legs are in casts, elevated from the bed. One arm is also in a cast. She speaks up and says, "You're lucky, Rock. Dr. Gilbertson said you will recover fully. How do you feel?"

I don't answer immediately. Everything seems weird; I feel waves of warmth in my body, I feel weightless, I feel euphoric and itchy at the same time. I reply, "I need a joint . . . I need a joint right now." The nurse chuckles, "It's just the morphine. Often people say odd things when they are on it." My anger goes to 10 immediately,

(Continued)

(Continued)

and I yell at the top of my lungs, "I'M NOT PHUCKING KIDDING!!! BRING ME MY POT!!!" The nurse immediately changes her attitude, tells me such language will not be tolerated and walks away. I lie there, becoming increasingly irritable. How dare she act that way!

Commentary

At age 19, Rock's use of cannabis is already problematic, and he can already be diagnosed as having CUD (American Psychiatric Association [APA], 2013). Whether his use can be classified as an addiction remains unclear, however. What we do know from Rock's presentation is that he has become a regular heavy user, and he experiences the following symptoms: (a) episodic memory deficits, (b) concentration difficulties, (c) loss of peripheral awareness (i.e., overfocus on a current thought), (d) relationship issues with family, (e) employment problems, (f) reduced inhibitions, and (g) quick temper/irritability.

Discussion

1. Do you know of anyone who you suspect has become dependent on cannabis? If "yes," which symptoms noted in the commentary apply to him or her?
2. Does this person have symptoms that are not listed in the commentary? If so, what are they?
3. If you were Rock's counselor, how would you go about helping him?

Specific Counseling Considerations

ROLEPLAY SCENARIOS

Roleplay in dyads with one of you acting as the counselor and the other as the counselee. If roleplay is not possible, work individually in writing out a list of your suggestions.

Roleplay #1

Pedro, a 15-year-old Hispanic adolescent, born and raised in Miami, is brought to you by his parents, José and Georgina. They are deeply concerned about Pedro's constant use of marijuana. According to José, Pedro is always high: morning, noon, and night. Pedro hangs out with a gang of Hispanic youth, all of whom spend their time together getting high and partying until late hours. Georgina recently found a large stash of marijuana in Pedro's bedroom and now believes that he is dealing. Pedro has also missed a great deal of school, and, in all endeavors, he is reportedly unmotivated and apathetic. He is now meeting with you alone, and it becomes immediately apparent that he is not interested in talking about his pot use or his life with you.

Roleplay #2

Christina, age 37, is a single White woman who has come to you because she has recently lost her job as a legal secretary. After 8 years at the law firm, she feels resentful and harbors deep animosity and resentment toward her employer. When asked about what led to her dismissal, Christina shows you a letter from the firm outlining their reasons. It appears Christina was fired for unprofessional conduct, as outlined in the following areas:

1. She had become slow and inefficient in her work.
2. She often seemed distracted.
3. She had become impatient and short-tempered with clients.
4. She had become forgetful and was missing deadlines, placing lawyers in an awkward position when meeting with clients.

During your assessment, you find out that Christina has been struggling in several areas of her life. She blames these difficulties on her father's death a few months earlier, but, through careful probing, you discover that her problems began closer to a year ago when she started smoking hash most nights with her roommate. When you bring this to Christina's attention, she becomes immediately snarky with you and demeaning, saying that you have no idea about how helpful smoking hash has been to her, particularly in dealing with her father's death.

HOW WOULD AN ADDICTION COUNSELOR HELP THIS PERSON?

You are working as a professional counselor. Danny is a 35-year-old African American man who has worked at a bank since graduating from college 11 years ago. Danny tells you that he had become a "raging" alcoholic during college and continued until his parents helped get him admitted to a treatment center 4 years ago. He still attends the odd AA meeting but increasingly finds that he doesn't relate well to the others there. More than one other member has suggested that Danny look at his use of high-potency marijuana as they believe he has simply transferred his addiction from alcohol to cannabis. Danny is annoyed with these comments, which he interprets as all-out accusations. As you discover, Danny has used cannabis products since he was 14 years old, and he does not see any problem with continuing to use. You notice he coughs every few minutes, and you detect a wheezing sound as he breathes.

Danny tells you that his boss sent him to you after two customers recently complained that he smells like pot when they are at the counter. He reassures you that he has never smoked pot at work, but he does smoke up almost continuously from when he gets home from work until he retires to bed. "Pot helps me relax and then fall asleep," Danny states. Without pot, Danny believes he would strongly desire to begin drinking again. When questioned, you find out that he indeed had a relapse with alcohol after he tried quitting cannabis 2 years ago. Back then, the relapse lasted 2 weeks, and he only regained control after he began smoking cannabis again.

Remember to view clients within their environmental contexts, keeping in mind societal, parental/familial, cultural/spiritual, and peer influences. Specifically, become aware of the impact that the following influences have and continue to have in your clients' lives: race, language, religion and spirituality, gender, familial migration history, sexual/affectional orientation, age and cohort, physical and mental capacities, socioeconomic situation and history, education, and history of traumatic experience.

1. What defines this person's environment, past and present?
2. Who is this person sitting in front of me, taking into account environmental and personal characteristics?
3. What defines the problem that he or she is presenting within their multicultural milieu?

Goals and Goal Setting

Understanding one's reasons for using cannabis together with the degree of addiction will help the counselor and client decide collaboratively what an appropriate goal looks like. Some heavy cannabis users can reduce their use with little to no difficulty. Many regular users of cannabis do want to quit. In 1998, 35% of admissions in U.S. public treatment facilities were for marijuana problems (Zvolensky et al., 2011). The most frequently mentioned reason provided of adults who want to quit is worry regarding one's physical and psychological health (Zvolensky et al., 2011).

As Dahl (2015) noted, some individuals incorporate cannabis use into their identity. A cannabis identity may represent a desired representation as an unrestrained, independent, and free-thinking individual. A cannabis addict, however, has an identity that is likely in need of repair (Dahl, 2015). This may follow an inability to cut down usage together with resultant negative consequences.

If a harm reduction approach is taken, risks are reduced if

1. Delaying usage until early adulthood.
2. Using safer forms of inhalation (e.g., vaporizers).
3. Using less potent varieties of marijuana.
4. Avoid driving after use for 3–4 hours.
5. Abstaining altogether if at higher risk of problems (e.g., family history of psychosis, cardiovascular problems, being pregnant) (Crépault, 2014).

Stages of Change Strategies

The processes of change mentioned are based on those outlined by Connors, DiClemente, Velasquez, and Donovan (2013) and Prochaska, Norcross, and DiClemente (1994). The definitions for the various processes can be found in Chapter 6. Besides these processes, other strategies are included that have separate citations.

The University of Rhode Island Change Assessment Scale (URICA) is a helpful scale for determining where the client is currently at regarding the stages of change model. There are 24-, 28-, and 32-item versions of the scale.

A 24-item version is published for alcohol or drug problems. The scale, however, is generic and can be easily adapted for use with other addictions. It is available with norms as a free download from https://www.guilford.com/add/miller11_old/urica.pdf.

Specific precontemplation strategies.

Please visit the section of this chapter called Relevant Mutual Support Groups, Websites, and Videos for free or low-cost information and resources that may help someone move out of precontemplation.

Given the continuing legalization of cannabis throughout the United States and other countries, convincing regular heavy users that they have become "addicted" is arguably a challenging task. One book that is an easy read and provides in layperson's terms a personal and professional look at cannabis addiction is by Tony DeRamus (2011; see reference list) called the *Secret Addiction*. Free information is also available from his website at http://www.secretaddiction.org/.

There are many documentaries, videos, and movies about cannabis. A note of caution, however: Many of these resources are as political as they are educational, espousing the medical benefits of cannabis more than looking at the harmful consequences, or otherwise promoting its use. Here are a few that provide a more balanced perspective:

1. The Best Marijuana Documentary (approx. 1 hr. 44 min.). Available from https://www.youtube.com/watch?v=MESZh-_uyUQ
2. Negative Effects of Cannabis Documentary (approx. 35 min). Available from https://www.youtube.com/watch?v=uhRoIUaiZbs
3. Full CNN Documentary Weed Parts 1–3 (2013–2015; approx. 2 hrs. 9 min.). Available from https://www.youtube.com/watch?v=PRLYV0_6zY8
4. Marijuana Documentary, HD Documentaries 2017 (approx. 45 min). Available from https://www.youtube.com/watch?v=96vWCn2O7i4
5. In Pot We Trust (approx. 1 hr. 27 min.). Available from https://www.youtube.com/watch?v=Gps3-ySZ-zY

Specific contemplation strategies.

As is true for every addiction, motivational interviewing (MI) (as exemplified later in this chapter) is an effective method for helping bring clients to the next stage. As feeling ambivalent is a marked emotion for most unrecovered addicts, the following method may be helpful in beginning a dialogue about harm reduction or abstaining. This method is adapted from Hill (2014).

Decision-making chart.

1. In the second column, list the benefits and drawbacks associated with the use of your substance.
2. In the third column, give each benefit a score of 1 to 10, based on how much that benefit means to you. Do not give any two benefits the same weighting. Also do this for the drawbacks using scores of −1 to −10, based on how negative these consequences are to you. Again, do not give two drawbacks the same weighting.
3. In the fourth column, first decide what percent of reduction you would need to attain to return your use to a healthy or at least nondetrimental level. Rewrite your score for how much it would change if you reduced your use to that level. You can use a zero if you believe the benefit or drawback will be at that level.
4. In the fifth column, write down how each score would change if you abstained from the substance.

Ask in session or have clients ask themselves the following questions:

1. Is reducing use an option for you? What evidence do you have that this is a viable option? What evidence do you have that this is *not* a viable option for you? What specific steps would you need to take to reduce your use to the specified level?
2. Is abstaining a better or needed choice for you? What evidence do you have for or against choosing this option?
3. How do these results fit for you? What was surprising? Which choice makes the most sense to you?

Specific preparation strategies.

As DeRamus (2011) pointed out, sometimes the obvious needs to be stated with addicts. If one is keeping weed or paraphernalia in the house, one is likely not serious about quitting. In the preparation stage, everything related to cannabis needs to be eliminated permanently. If the dealer's number is not memorized, clients should delete this number and tell others who know it not to remind them of the number under any circumstances. The client should ask cannabis-using significant others to avoid indulging while in one's presence and to not offer or provide cannabis to the client under any circumstance. It might be easier to simply avoid having contact with some individuals who are strong triggers for using for a period of time. On the other hand, clients may have ignored or shunned people in their lives during their cannabis using periods (DeRamus, 2011), so now is a good time for them to reconnect to these people and let them know of the impending change.

Many users falsely believe that cannabis makes them more creative and funnier: That is simply not true (DeRamus, 2011). Users should remind themselves that much of their cannabis use created illusory benefits. Although music and meals might have seemed enhanced in some way, the memory of these experiences is fainter or nonexistent a few days or even hours later.

This is a helpful time for clients to begin attending a mutual support group such as Narcotics Anonymous or, if available in one's city, Marijuana Anonymous meetings. Continuing to learn about cannabis addiction is also recommended during this stage. Other ideas for *before* their chosen quit day (i.e., preparation strategies) can be found in Appendix B.

Specific action strategies.

Balkin (2015) stated that there are two primary methods that appear most helpful in treating CUDs. First, there is motivational enhancement therapy (MET; manual written by Miller, Zweben,

Example of Decision-Making Chart				
#	Value	Continue Using at Current Level	Reduce Use by 90%	Completely Abstain
BENEFITS				
1	Relaxation	8	2	0
2	Escapism	6	2	0
3	More talkative	3	2	0
4	Mood improvement/ euphoria	10	2	0
5	Enjoy with friends	2	1	0
Total		29	9	0
DRAWBACKS				
6	Motivation problems	–8	–1	0
7	Memory deficits	-2	0	0
8	Pressure from spouse	–10	-3	0
9	Irritability	-6	0	0
10	Increased impulsiveness	-9	0	0
11	Emotional availability	-7	–1	0
Total		-42	-5	0
GRAND TOTAL		**–13**	**4**	**0**

DiClemente, & Rychtarik, 1999, available at no cost at https://pubs.niaaa.nih.gov/publications/ProjectMatch/match02.pdf). MET is a manualized two- to five-session method of providing MI. Second, Balkin included cognitive-behavioral therapy (CBT) as helpful. A systematic review found that CBT may be superior to MI, but results were inconclusive (Chatters et al., 2016).

Many individuals with CUDs find ways to quit on their own without outside help (Feingold, Fox, Rehm, & Lev-Ran, 2015), but clearly this is not attainable by all. While providing promising outcomes, Balkin (2015) cautioned counselors that 50% of individuals who begin treatment for cannabis relapse within 2 weeks, and half of the half who are successful short term would relapse within a year. In total, only 10%–30% who begin treatment will be still abstaining after 12 months. Finally, Balkin recommended that using the previous two approaches together with a 12-step program may be most effective and efficient (a 12-step facilitation manual written by Nowinski, Baker, & Carroll, 1999, is also available at no cost from https://pubs.niaaa.nih.gov/publications/ProjectMatch/match01.pdf).

Walther, Gantner, Heinz, and Majic (2016) concluded from the literature that systemic multidimensional family therapy was beneficial for heavy-use younger teenagers who also have comorbid psychiatric conditions. Wittenauer, Ascher, Briggie, Kreiter, and Chavez (2015) suggested, with caution due to limited evidence, that mindfulness and yoga may have value in helping adolescents stop using cannabis.

Providing vouchers for abstinence (a contingency management technique) proved helpful for adult cannabis users who quit over both the short term and during follow-up, particularly when used in combination with CBT (Chatters et al., 2016). A thorough review of the literature in both English and German languages found that what most stood out regarding determinants of cannabis dependence was a wide range of comorbid mental disorders (Schlossarek et al., 2016), suggesting that comorbid conditions will need to be treated concurrently with cannabis dependence for many addicts. In one study, a four-session treatment protocol for cannabis users was more effective when the program was offered over 3 months instead of 1 month (Jungerman, Andreoni, & Laranjeira, 2007).

When individuals quit using cannabis, they become less likely to use other substances. They are also more likely to have relied on positive social influences and to have made use of mutual support groups (Hodgins, Kim, & Stea, 2017).

DeRamus (2011) cautioned that nearly everyone who stops using cannabis continues thinking about it. He tells those who decide to quit that thinking about use is not a problem, so long as the user does not act on these desires. DeRamus also offered many suggestions to cannabis users who are quitting in the areas of actions, thoughts, lifestyle, social interactions and environment, and suggestions for high-risk situations (pp. 124–127). These are summarized in the following (mostly quoted):

Actions.

1. Avoid or escape from situations that make you want to smoke marijuana.
2. Delay decisions to give in to temptation.
3. Change your physical position (e.g., don't stay in the same place; stand, stretch, walk around).
4. Carry things to put in your mouth.
5. Carry objects to fiddle with.
6. Have a distracting activity available.

Thoughts.

1. Self-talk (e.g., remind yourself of your reasons for quitting).
2. Imagery and visualization (e.g., imagine the health benefits of having quit smoking marijuana).
3. Thought-stopping.
4. Distraction.

Lifestyle.

1. Exercise or take a brisk daily walk.
2. Practice relaxation or meditation techniques regularly.
3. Pray lots.
4. Take up a hobby or restart an old hobby you used to enjoy.
5. Drink less coffee, switch to decaf, drink herbal teas.
6. Engage in an enjoyable activity several times a week.
7. Change routines associated with smoking marijuana.

Social interactions and environment.

1. Remove smoking paraphernalia.
2. Go to places where it's difficult to get high.
3. Spend time with friends who don't smoke.
4. Learn to be appropriately assertive.

Specific suggestions for some common high-risk situations.

1. Tension relief and negative emotions. Develop relaxation techniques, exercise, write down your feelings, or talk to a friend or counselor.
2. Anger, frustration, and interpersonal conflict. Learn to handle situations directly.
3. Fatigue and low energy. Do muscle relaxation, take a brisk walk, etc.
4. Insomnia. Don't fight it. Instead, get up and do something constructive.
5. Timeout. Take breaks from what you are doing to help avoid fatigue.
6. Self-image. Create a new image (e.g., get a haircut, buy different clothes).
7. Social pressure. Remember your commitment not to use cannabis. Walk away from users if necessary.
8. Situations involving alcohol. Be especially careful if you decide to keep drinking after quitting cannabis.
9. Cravings and urges. Break the chain of responding to them. In other words, don't give in.

When tempted to use again, DeRamus (2011) suggested creating a *love list*, which is a list of things the cannabis user loves about not using any more. Some examples that DeRamus offered (pp. 153–154) include the following:

Example of a love list.

- I love not having the munchies.
- I love being a better parent.
- I love not having the secret from people who don't smoke.
- I love saving money for other things that are important to me.
- I love remembering.
- I love keeping my word to friends and family.
- I love breathing easier; each breath makes my lungs cleaner.
- I love speaking in sentences without forgetting what I was saying.
- I love having time to think and ponder about humans and our souls.
- I love feeling better about myself.
- I love being free.
- I love that I LOVE being free.

Other ideas for *beginning* their chosen quit day (i.e., action strategies) can be found in Appendix B.

Specific maintenance strategies and relapse prevention.

Note: Maintenance strategies and relapse prevention is also, for many, partly facilitated by regular attendance at relevant mutual support groups. A list of such mutual support groups and helpful websites is found in an upcoming section entitled Relevant Mutual Support Groups, Websites, and Videos.

Given the high relapse rates for cannabis users and those who become addicted (Balkin, 2015), maintenance strategies and relapse prevention are important. DeRamus (2011) stressed that the user must not let ANYTHING become a reason to use again. He suggested that in helping to prevent relapse, users should avoid 15 things (most of which are emotions). His list (pp. 199–201) includes exhaustion, dishonesty, impatience, argumentativeness, depression, frustration, self-pity, cockiness, complacency, expecting too much from others, letting up on disciplines, wanting too much, forgetting gratitude, it can't happen to me, and omnipotence. Given that tiredness and negative emotions occur in all of us under the right circumstances, a better strategy than avoidance is likely to learn how to manage and cope when these occur. Learning emotional regulation might be advisable as well (Kabat-Zinn, 2013).

The counselor should help the client anticipate likely problems that may occur following a quit attempt and learn to anticipate and cope with high-risk situations. Cravings can be monitored and recognized early so that skills and coping strategies can be implemented (Sparks, 2016). Sleep deprivation can lead to relapse and, given that sleep difficulties are a common withdrawal symptom, medications and behavioral methods for sleep should be considered (Ara, Jacobs, Bhat, & McCall, 2016). Other ideas for relapse prevention can be found in Appendix C.

Motivational Interviewing

As stated earlier, MET, (manual written by Miller et al., 1999, available at no cost at https://pubs.niaaa.nih.gov/publications/ProjectMatch/match02.pdf) has demonstrated effectiveness. It is entrenched in the transtheoretical model. W. R. Miller (as cited in Balkin, 2015) outlined five essential principles of MET: (a) display empathy, (b) create discrepancies, (c) avoid arguments, (d) allow resistance to occur, and (e) support the client's self-efficacy. Labeling the client is also avoided. It is a positive sign when clients present an increase in both positive self-statements and desire to change. MET is most efficacious when combined with other methods such as CBT (Balkin, 2015).

Here is a sample transcript of what the end of session 2 might look like in MET. Session 3 is not scheduled until week 6, and session 4 is scheduled at week 12. (Pertaining to Chapter 7's description of MI, the following is an example of the process called *focusing*.)

Client: You have certainly helped me see how cannabis has been hurting me for the past 10 years. I'm not sure if I am an addict, however, and I wonder if I can just cut back my use.

Counselor: Robert, we are nearing the end of our session. Let me take a few minutes to summarize our discussion before we book our next session for a month from now. Last session you told me that you are concerned that you might be addicted to cannabis because you have struggled with cutting down your use for the past 6 months. As you might recall, I mentioned that, in my approach, I avoid labels, as these are sometimes not helpful for people. Regardless, you have described both today and last session that you have lost your motivation for all kinds of fun activities that you used to engage in. You have on numerous occasions found yourself being forgetful of important tasks such as locking the front door when you leave home and leaving a reefer burning in various places around your home. Despite your many attempts to cut down on your cannabis use, you believe that cutting back might still be possible for you. Is that an accurate recap?

Client: Yes, you certainly have put that together nicely. Do you think I should abstain at this point?

Counselor: You still believe that I could answer that for you.

Client: I guess I just want your opinion.

Counselor: I suspect that you believe my opinion might sway your decision. How might that actually do a disservice to you, Robert?

Client: Well, I guess I could blame you if I was not successful in quitting.

Counselor: That strikes me as a possibility. Would you book your next appointment with the receptionist before you leave?

Client: I will. Thank you, Dr. Michaels. I appreciate your believing in me.

Insight-Oriented Interventions

There is a scarcity of psychoanalytic research concerning cannabis smokers. The little research that exists focuses on substance abuse in general (Hachet, 2005, 2006). Reasons for this include (a) addiction specialists minimize the importance of cannabis abuse, (b) the area lacks political interest, (c) psychodynamics are overridden by legislative concerns, and (d) most psychoanalysts pay little attention to patients using cannabis (Hachet, 2005, 2006).

One study advanced the use of an insight-adherence-abstinence model in helping young psychotic individuals, many of whom presented with cannabis abuse (Miller, Mccormack, & Sevy, 2008). Insight-oriented approaches may have many applications with addicted cannabis users given the high psychiatric comorbidity in this population. Currently, however, research is lacking.

Spiritual Interventions

The ritualistic use of cannabis was a significant role in a number of well-known religions in the ancient world, including Hinduism, Taoism, Judaism, Christianity, and Buddhism (Bennett, 2014). Although religions can certainly promote drug use for ceremonial purposes, having spiritual beliefs has a strong effect on reducing drug involvement when use is deemed unacceptable. Several studies have shown a strong correlation between religiosity and lower rates of cannabis use in adolescents (Chu, 2007; Nguyen, 2017; Varma, Moore, Cataldi, Estoup, & Stewart, 2017). Nguyen (2017) computed statistics based on 12,984 adolescents from the 2013 National Survey on Drug Use and Health data. Nguyen found that religious girls use both alcohol and marijuana less than do religious boys. Religion also played a role in reducing use among African American youth but not in Asian American youth. Another study found that young Latino adults were less likely to use substances if they practiced religion publicly (Escobar & Vaughan, 2014). Although there remains a dearth of studies espousing the benefit of spiritual interventions, it would appear from correlational research that such may be helpful for at least religiously oriented cannabis users.

Cognitive-Behavioral Therapy

CBT can be facilitated using the triple column technique. It can be used both by counselors in their work with clients and by clients alone. The full instructions for using the technique are found in Chapter 6. The following are some of the cognitions that can be problematic for clients with this addiction (these are based on the five maladaptive schemas found by Grebot, Dardard, & Briet, 2016).

In a French study of maladaptive schemas in 199 undergraduate students, participants were divided into four groups: cannabis-dependent users (N = 24), cannabis abusers (N = 40),

Automatic Thought or Belief	Questioning It	Healthier Thought or Belief
I feel emotionally deprived and lacking.		Once I am clean, I will become more emotionally available. I can create deeper relationships with others.
Too many important people have abandoned me in my life.		I can focus my attention on close friends and/or an intimate partner. If I do get rejected, I will survive and work on becoming a stronger person.
I have a hard time trusting other people.		I will give significant others the benefit of the doubt. People will prove their trustworthiness to me over time, and vice versa.
I am impulsive and struggle with controlling my actions.		Once I am clean, I will become less impulsive. I will regain control over my behavior.
I feel powerless in life; other people seem to have more control over their life circumstances.		Once I am clean, I will find it easier to set goals and stick to them. I will embrace my personal power.

cannabis nonproblematic users ($N = 52$), and healthy control subjects ($N = 83$). Compared to the other three groups, cannabis-dependent users had significantly higher scores in the overall number of maladaptive schemas. These schemas were particularly notable in five areas: emotional deprivation, abandonment, mistrust/abuse, insufficient self-control, and subjugation. They were also more likely to use two "immature" psychological defense mechanisms (i.e., autistic fantasy, projection) (Grebot, Dardard, & Briet, 2016).

CBT allows counselors to not only help clients change their thoughts but it is also helpful in teaching social skills (Balkin, 2015). It will be important to teach *cannabis refusal skills*, which are skills needed to refuse cannabis when offered. The skill set includes both verbal and nonverbal communication: learning to say "NO" and meaning it, in other words. Part of this teaching is helping clients to refuse pot and not feel guilty about doing so. Roleplaying is helpful in teaching refusal skills. Another important set is to help clients identify high-risk situations and ways to deal with these assertively, teach coping strategies for dealing with urges, encourage social support, and manage feelings in a healthy manner (Balkin, 2015). Monitoring cravings, moods, and behaviors is also important in CBT (Sparks, 2016). The intent is to teach the client enhanced self-control and problem-solving strategies (Sparks, 2016).

RELEVANT MUTUAL SUPPORT GROUPS, WEBSITES, AND VIDEOS

Mutual Support Groups

For the Addicted Individual

1. Marijuana Anonymous (MA). https://www.marijuana-anonymous.org/

   Quoted from website:

   Marijuana Anonymous is a fellowship of people who share our experience, strength, and hope with each other that we may solve our common problem and help others to recover from marijuana addiction. The only requirement for membership is a desire to stop using marijuana. There are no dues or fees for membership. We are self-supporting through our own contributions. MA is not affiliated with any religious or secular institution or organization and has no opinion on any outside controversies or causes. Our primary purpose is to stay free of marijuana and to help the marijuana addict who still suffers achieve the same freedom. We can do this by practicing our suggested Twelve Steps of recovery and by being guided as a group by our Twelve Traditions. Marijuana Anonymous uses the basic 12 Steps of Recovery founded by Alcoholics Anonymous, because it has been proven that the 12 Step Recovery program works!

2. SMART Recovery—Self -Management and Recovery training. http://www.smartrecovery.org/

   Quoted from website:

   SMART Recovery is the leading self-empowering addiction recovery support group. Our participants learn tools for addiction recovery based on the latest scientific research and participate in a world-wide community which includes free, self-empowering, science-based mutual help groups.

For the Partner and/or Family

These groups are intended to help family members refrain from behaviors that may trigger the addict. They also target underlying maladaptive thoughts and behaviors of the co-addict. Lastly, they focus on facilitating spiritual growth.

Marijuana Anonymous (MA). https://www.marijuana-anonymous.org/

Quoted from website:

As the addict approaches their bottom and their disease worsens, family members and friends have a tendency to enable the addict, allowing them to postpone the ultimate repercussions of their using. Understandably, loved ones try to ease the suffering the addict may be feeling because of loyalty, love, caring, and a sense of responsibility. Family and friends may give money (which likely goes to buying more marijuana), buy food, pay rent and bills, bail them out of jail, etc. By trying to save the addict from him or herself, you are doing both yourself and the addict a disservice.

Websites

1. Learn About Marijuana. http://learnaboutmarijuanawa.org/index.htm
2. Marijuana Addiction Today. https://www.psychologytoday.com/blog/our-empathic-nature/201205/marijuana-addiction-today
3. 10 Common Marijuana Addiction Symptoms. https://www.addictions.com/marijuana/10-common-marijuana-addiction-symptoms/
4. Addictions and Recovery.org. https://www.addictionsandrecovery.org/
5. Many great resources are available from https://cannabissupport.com.au/shop/clinicians/

Videos

To view these videos, search their titles on YouTube.

1. *Dr. Gabor Maté - Cannabis and Addiction.*
2. *Marijuana: A Second Class Addiction.* David Goldenkranz.
3. *Is marijuana addiction serious or real? Why I quit marijuana and the weed withdrawal symptoms.* Cg Kid.
4. *Why Quitting Marijuana Is Difficult for Some People (psychological addiction).* Tristan Weatherburn.
5. *The Truth About Smoking Cannabis | BBC Documentary.*

RELEVANT PHONE APPS

Generic Addiction Apps

Note: Generic apps are described in Chapter 6.

This list is not exhaustive. New apps are continually being developed. Do an Internet search to find out the latest apps available. Most are for specific addictions, but some, such as these four, are generic.

1. I Am Sober. https://play.google.com/store/apps/details?id=com.thehungrywasp.iamsober
2. Sober Time. https://play.google.com/store/apps/details?id=com.sociosoft.sobertime
3. Pocket Rehab: Get Sober & Addiction Recovery. https://play.google.com/store/apps/details?id=com.getpocketrehab.app
4. Loop Habit Tracker. https://play.google.com/store/apps/details?id=org.isoron.uhabits

Specialized Apps

1. Marijuana Anonymous.

   https://play.google.com/store/apps/details?id=org.marijuana_anonymous.MA_Mobile&hl=en_US

   Quoted from website:

   This is the official 12 Step recovery app of Marijuana Anonymous. Anyone with a desire to stop using marijuana will benefit from the useful tools and resources included. If you encounter problems with this app, please contact us so we may work with you to get the app running. We're here to help.

   This app contains a lot of information on the addiction including: (a) general information on what marijuana addiction looks like, (b) what Marijuana Anonymous can do to help in one's recovery, (c) what to expect in an online meeting, (d) a discussion of the 12 Step Program, (e) a chat line for member support, and (f) a sobriety date counter and more. It's a very useful app and easy to use.

2. Quit Cannabis.

   For android: https://play.google.com/store/apps/details?id=com.applikey.quitcannabis

   For iphone: https://itunes.apple.com/us/app/quit-cannabis/id1050636063?mt=8

   Quoted from website:

   Quit Cannabis is an app that contains much more than the simple title can reflect. It is motivating program that will encourage you to quit smoking cannabis and tobacco, and continue moving in the right direction.

   Features:

   Health – shows what happens to your body without cannabis and tobacco

Statistics – shows time since quit

- shows life gained
- shows money saved from weed and cigarettes
- shows avoided joints, cigarettes and tar

Motivation – informative articles with useful methods and techniques to help you quit your habit

Motivator Alarm – notifies you at your desired time with the daily motivational quote.

When beginning this app, the user is queried about their cannabis (or other substance) use. The app calculates how much time has elapsed since you began using the substance as well as the health benefits of quitting, money saved, and life gained. It does not require you to keep a daily log of your substance usage or adjust health benefits accordingly. It includes some motivational articles. It does not provide the opportunity to chat about your progress and hurdles with other people experiencing the same addiction.

3. Dependn' – Quit weed, tobacco and alcohol

   https://itunes.apple.com/us/app/dependn-quit-weed-tobacco-alcohol-stop-drinking-smoking/id1093903062?mt=8

   Quoted from website:

   Dependn' is the only iPhone app which has been created by and for doctors and patients. Start monitoring your addictions now, and track your progress! The app can be used for any form of addiction (alcohol, tobacco, cannabis, antidepressants, sex, video games, etc).

   Dependn' is a very basic app used to track your substance use and show progress being made in overcoming your addiction. Data can be exported if you choose to do so. The drawback with this app is that it does not provide any background information on the addiction or possible strategies one could use.

JOURNALS AND CONFERENCES

Journals

1. *Cannabis and Cannabinoid Research.* This new journal is "a peer-reviewed journal entirely dedicated to the scientific, medical, and psychosocial exploration of clinical cannabis, cannabinoids, and the endocannabinoid system" (Piomelli, 2016, p. 1). Visit http://www.liebertpub.com/overview/cannabis-and-cannabinoid-research/633/
2. *IACM-Bulletin.* Published by the International Association for Cannabis as Medicine (IACM). Quoted from website: "The IACM-Bulletin is a FREE bi-weekly e-mail newsletter, covering news topics on all aspects of Cannabis as medicine." Visit http://www.cannabis-med.org/english/bulletin/iacm.php
3. *Cannabinoids.* Published by the International Association for Cannabis as Medicine (IACM). Quoted from website: "CANNABINOIDS is a peer-reviewed online journal of the [IACM. It] intends to become an important source of information on medical and scientific aspects of cannabis and the cannabinoids in the web and to inform the readers up to date on issues under discussion." Visit http://www.cannabis-med.org/index.php?tpl=cannabinoidslist&lng=en
4. *International Journal of Medical Cannabinoids.* This journal looks at current research in basic science and the clinical use of cannabinoids. Quoted from website: It "is a peer-reviewed, professional journal that addresses all aspects of the safe use and management of cannabinoids in medical practice. The Journal provides guidance to physicians and healthcare professionals on how to safely prescribe and responsibly manage this emerging therapeutic class." Visit http://www.wmpllc.org/ojs-2.4.2/index.php/IJMC/index
5. *Journal of Cannabis Therapeutics.* This journal was only published between 2001 and 2004. It contained high-quality research looking at the experimental and clinical use of cannabis.

Conferences

Several conferences have recently become popular regarding cannabis. Below are just a few possibilities to consider attending.

1. *World Medical Cannabis Conference and Expo.* Check website for current details.
2. *Emerald Conference.* Quoted from website: "The Emerald Conference is the most technical and comprehensive science conference in the cannabis industry. [It] is devoted to the free exchange of ideas and fresh insights on topics like cannabis analytical testing, inter-lab comparisons, extraction, and industry best practices. Whether you are a clinician, testing lab owner, cultivator, extractor & producer professional, policy maker, dispensary operator, or an analytical chemist, the Emerald Conference will educate and illuminate with an atmosphere of collaboration and partnership." Visit https://www.theemeraldconference.com/
3. *Institute of Cannabis Research.* Check website for current details.
4. *International Cannabinoid Research Society.* Visit http://www.icrs.co/
5. *The Semi-Annual Crypto Cannabis Conference.* For details visit https://www.cryptocannabisconference.com/

COUNSELING SCENARIO

As you are reading, imagine that you are the client in this scenario. Note the areas in which the session could be improved on the part of the counselor.

Your name is Christina, a 28-year-old Pacific Islander working as a waitress at Denny's restaurant. You are finding it difficult to stay motivated toward your goal of returning to school to become a dentist. Since high school, you have partied more than any of your friends, and, although most of them have gone on to college and university, you have worked at minimum wage jobs. You are tired of how poor you are all the time, so you go to a counselor at a free counseling agency. You decide you will begin by disclosing your daily use of hashish.

- You: I am beginning to wonder if my use of hashish is interfering with my motivation to become a dentist. I just can't seem to get going on my dreams.
- Counselor: Well, Christina, I can tell you that hashish is not your problem at all. I have been smoking weed for more than 25 years. The only issue I've ever had with it is that some mornings I feel a bit groggy, but this wears off after I get moving. If you're unmotivated, I think you best appraise your "dream" and adjust it: Make it more realistic for yourself.
- You: But I got good marks in high school. I know I have the brains to do dentistry.
- Counselor: Doesn't matter. You don't have the necessary discipline.
- You: I thought my daily ingestion of hashish might have something to do with my lack of motivation. Do you honestly not think this could be interfering?
- Counselor: Let me ask you something that will help answer your question: Are you usually so high that you hallucinate and see stuff that just isn't there? It's happened to me a few times, but I just blame that on the quality of pot I get from my dealer sometimes.
- You: I can't say I've ever hallucinated from hash at all!
- Counselor: I didn't think so. That's why I know you should stop blaming cannabis for your lack of drive, motivation, and desire to become a dentist. It is time you take full responsibility for your inaction.
- You: This is *not* what I expected to hear from you!
- Counselor: I know. A lot of young people, like yourself, want to blame everything that's bad on either their parents or their substance use. Heck, even on mushrooms you can get through school if you want to! I used it nearly every weekend for 3 years of graduate training, and, if anything, it helped me feel passionate about becoming a counselor.
- You: Hum, I guess I have been doing that. Thank you for your time.
- Counselor: No problem. Next time we meet, let's begin some career counseling. Perhaps a career like becoming a dental assistant would be more suitable for you.
- You: Really? That is what you think I would be well suited for? I don't think you know me at all!

From the Client's Perspective

1. How would you feel if your counselor minimized the impact of your drug use? What would you feel if a counselor unilaterally decided to downsize your career aspirations?
2. What is missing for you in this dialogue?
3. What would you find more helpful from a counselor in this scenario?

From the Counselor's Perspective

1. What is interfering with developing a working alliance?
2. Going back to the Common Counseling Mistakes list in Chapter 6, which mistakes is the counselor making with Christina?
3. When is it appropriate, if ever, for a counselor to unilaterally decide on the treatment goals for a client?
4. What strategies should counselors use when a client's problem mimics their unresolved issues?

INDIVIDUAL EXERCISES

1. Spend time thinking about people you know who use cannabis. What qualities do you ascribe to cannabis users? Does everyone you know who uses cannabis have these qualities?

2. Do you know anyone who uses cannabis heavily and regularly? If so, spend some time talking to this person about their use. What motivates him or her to continue using? What concerns does she or he have about quitting?

3. Watch the movie *Up in Smoke* (1978), starring Tommy Chong and Cheech Marin. In what ways does the movie accurately portray marijuana smokers? In what ways is it not accurate?

CLASSROOM EXERCISES

1. Have the class split into two based on each student's honest opinion: those who believe that cannabis is a harmful drug that should be carefully regulated on one side and those who believe that cannabis should be fully legalized or decriminalized with little to no government intervention on the other. At the end of the debate, have a member of each team write the key points on the board supporting that team's perspective.

2. Divide the class into four or more groups. Each group is given the task of finding either a brief video exalting the effects of cannabis or a brief video that rebukes it. Show the videos in class or assign watching them as homework. Then discuss the content of these videos.

3. Invite one or more speakers to your class who belong to one of the cannabis advocacy groups, such as the National Cannabis Industry Association, the Drug Policy Alliance, Americans for Safe Access, Marijuana Policy Project, or the Multidisciplinary Association for Psychedelic Studies. Have students prepare in advance some questions for the speakers.

CHAPTER SUMMARY

Although DSM does not use the term cannabis addiction, it does contain a diagnosis for problematic cannabis use called CUD. Studies suggest, however, that a percentage of users do become dependent on cannabis. Cannabis becomes increasingly important to addicts, it changes their mood to help them cope, they require increasing amounts of the substance, if they stop they experience withdrawal symptoms, excessive use and its sequelae create conflicts with significant others, and relapse is exceedingly common for those trying to quit.

Cannabis has an insidious effect on regular heavy users, so much so that changes (e.g., increased impulsivity, lowered inhibitions, memory deficits, diminished problem-solving abilities and goal-setting capability, difficulty remembering the best word choice in a conversation, decreased motivation) are often not acknowledged or dismissed as negligible (i.e., denial of consequences). As is true for other addicts, responsibility for the problem and its consequences is often projected onto others.

The best treatments for cannabis addiction include CBT and MET, which is a variant of MI. There is currently no approved medication to assist with either withdrawal from cannabis or to reduce urges/cravings.

REFERENCES

Adamson, S. J., Kay-Lambkin, F. J., Baker, A. L., Lewin, T. J., Thornton, L., Kelly, B. J., & Sellman, J. D. (2010). An improved brief measure of cannabis misuse: The Cannabis Use Disorders Identification Test-Revised (CUDIT-R). *Drug and Alcohol Dependence, 110*, 137–143.

Agabio, R., Campesi, I., Pisanu, C., Gessa, G. L., & Franconi, F. (2016). Sex differences in substance use disorders: Focus on side effects. *Addiction Biology, 21*(5), 1030–1042.

Aggarwal, M., Banerjee, A., Singh, S. M., Mattoo, S. K., & Basu, D. (2012). Substance-induced psychotic disorders: 13-year data from a de-addiction centre and their clinical implications. *Asian Journal of Psychiatry, 5*(3), 220–224.

Agrawal, A., Few, L., Nelson, E. C., Deutsch, A., Grant, J. D., Bucholz, K. K., . . . Lynskey, M. T. (2016). Adolescent cannabis use and repeated voluntary unprotected sex in women. *Addiction, 111*(11), 2012–2020.

Agrawal, A., Pergadia, M. L., Saccone, S. F., Lynskey, M. T., Wang, J. C., Martin, N. G., . . . Madden, P. A. F. (2008). An autosomal linkage scan for cannabis use disorders in the nicotine addiction genetics project. *Archives of General Psychiatry, 65*(6), 713–722.

Aharonovich, E., Garawi, F., Bisaga, A., Brooks, D., Raby, W. N., Rubin, E., . . . Levin, F. R. (2006). Concurrent cannabis use during treatment for comorbid ADHD and cocaine dependence: effects on outcome. *American Journal of Drug & Alcohol Abuse, 32*(4), 629–635.

American Association of Poison Control Centers. (2018). *Synthetic cannabinoids*. Retrieved on June 20, 2018, from http://www.aapcc.org/alerts/synthetic-cannabinoids/

American Psychiatric Association (APA). (2013). *Diagnostic and statistical manual of mental disorders* (5th ed.). Washington, DC: Author.

Andrade, T. M. R., & de Lima Argimon, I. I. (2008). Depressive symptoms in young cannabis users. *Sintomas depressivos e uso de cannabis em adolescentes, 13*(3), 567–573.

Ara, A., Jacobs, W., Bhat, I. A., & McCall, W. V. (2016). Sleep disturbances and substance use disorders: A bi-directional relationship. *Psychiatric Annals, 46*(7), 408–412.

Asbridge, M., Duff, C., Marsh, D. C., & Erickson, P. G. (2014). Problems with the identification of 'problematic' cannabis use: Examining the issues of frequency, quantity, and drug use environment. *European Addiction Research, 20*(5), 254–267.

Atkinson, D. L. (2016). Marijuana's effects on the mind: Intoxication, effects on cognition and motivation, and addiction. In *Marijuana and mental health* (pp. 11–37). Arlington, VA: American Psychiatric.

Aviram, J., & Samuelly-Leichtag, G. (2017). Efficacy of cannabis-based medicines for pain management: A systematic review and meta-analysis of randomized controlled trials. *Pain Physician, 20*(6), E755–E796.

Baker, M. P., Sellman, J. D., & Horn, J. (2007). The spiritual characteristics of New Zealanders entering treatment for alcohol/other drug dependence. *Alcoholism Treatment Quarterly, 24*(4), 137–155.

Balkin, R. S. (2015). Marijuana addiction. In R. L. Smith (Ed.), *Treatment strategies for substance abuse and process addictions* (pp. 75–90) [Kindle version]. Retrieved from Amazon.ca.

Banks, D. E., Rowe, A. T., Mpofu, P., & Zapolski, T. C. B. (2017). Trends in typologies of concurrent alcohol, marijuana, and cigarette use among US adolescents: An ecological examination by sex and race/ethnicity. *Drug and Alcohol Dependence, 179*, 71–77.

Bartholomew, J., Holroyd, S., & Heffernan, T. M. (2010). Does cannabis use affect prospective memory in young adults? *Journal of Psychopharmacology, 24*(2), 241–246.

Bashford, J., Flett, R., & Copeland, J. (2010). The Cannabis Use Problems Identification Test (CUPIT): Development, reliability, concurrent and predictive validity among adolescents and adults. *Addiction, 105*(4), 615–625.

Belanger, R. E., Akre, C., Kuntsche, E., Gmel, G., & Suris, J.-C. (2011). Adding tobacco to cannabis—Its frequency and likely implications. *Nicotine & Tobacco Research, 13*(8), 746–750.

Bennett, C. (2014). The magic and ceremonial use of cannabis in the ancient world. In E. J. Harold (Ed.), *Seeking the sacred with psychoactive substances: Chemical paths to spirituality and to God* (Vols. 1–2, pp. 23–55). Santa Barbara, CA: Praeger/ABC-CLIO.

Bhardwaj, A. K., Allsop, D. J., Copeland, J., McGregor, I. S., Dunlop, A., Shanahan, M., . . . Lintzeris, N. (2018). Randomised Controlled Trial (RCT) of cannabinoid replacement therapy (Nabiximols) for the management of treatment-resistant cannabis dependent patients: A study protocol. *BMC Psychiatry, 18*, 1–14.

Blum, R. W., Kelly, A., & Ireland, M. (2001). Health-risk behaviors and protective factors among adolescents with mobility impairments and learning and emotional disabilities. *Journal of Adolescent Health, 28*, 481–490.

Boden, J. M., Lee, J. O., Horwood, L., Grest, C. V., & McLeod, G. F. (2017). Modelling possible causality in the associations between unemployment, cannabis use, and alcohol misuse. *Social Science & Medicine, 175*, 127–134.

Boidi, M., Cruz, J. M., & Queirolo, R. (2015). Marijuana legalization in Uruguay and beyond: Executive summary. Washington, DC: Woodrow Wilson International Center for Scholars. Retrieved on December 20, 2017, from https://www.wilsoncenter.org/sites/default/files/Marijuana%20Legalization%20in%20Uruguay%20and%20Beyond_brief%20report_v3%20%282%29.pdf

Bonn-Miller, M. O., Boden, M. T., Vujanovic, A. A., & Drescher, K. D. (2013). Prospective investigation of the impact of cannabis use disorders on posttraumatic stress disorder symptoms among veterans in residential treatment. *Psychological Trauma: Theory, Research, Practice, and Policy, 5*, 193–200.

Borges, G., Benjet, C., Orozco, R., Medina-Mora, M.-E., & Menendez, D. (2017). Alcohol, cannabis and other drugs and subsequent suicide ideation and attempt among young Mexicans. *Journal of Psychiatric Research, 91*, 74–82.

Buckner, J. D., Schmidt, N. B., Lang, A. R., Small, J. W., Schlauch, R. C., & Lewinsohn, P. M. (2008). Specificity of social anxiety disorder as a risk factor for alcohol and cannabis dependence. *Journal of Psychiatric Research, 42*(3), 230–239.

Calhoun, P. S., Sampson, W. S., Bosworth, H. B., Feldman, M. E., Kirby, A. C., Hertzberg, M. A., . . . Beckham, J. C. (2000). Drug use and validity of substance use self-reports in veterans seeking help for posttraumatic stress disorder. *Journal of Consulting and Clinical Psychology, 68*, 923–927.

Cannabis and spirituality. (n.d.). Retrieved on December 13, 2017, from http://www.cannabisandspirituality.com/

Cardoso, J. B., Goldbach, J. T., Cervantes, R. C., & Swank, P. (2016). Stress and multiple substance use behaviors among Hispanic adolescents. *Prevention Science, 17*(2), 208–217.

Cascone, P., Zimmermann, G., Auckenthaler, B., & Robert-Tissot, C. (2011). Cannabis dependence in Swiss adolescents: Exploration of the role of anxiety, coping styles, and psychosocial difficulties. *Swiss Journal of Psychology, 70*(3), 129–139.

Chatters, R., Cooper, K., Day, E., Knight, M., Lagundoye, O., Wong, R., & Kaltenthaler, E. (2016). Psychological and psychosocial interventions for cannabis cessation in adults: A systematic review. *Addiction Research & Theory, 24*(2), 93–110.

Chedebois, L., Regner, I., van Leeuwen, N., Chauchard, E., Sejourne, N., Rodgers, R., & Chabrol, H. (2009). Relative contributions of acculturation and psychopathological factors to cannabis use among adolescents from migrant parents. *Addictive Behaviors, 34*, 1023–1028.

Chu, D. C. (2007). Religiosity and desistance from drug use. *Criminal Justice and Behavior, 34*, 661–679.

Chuang, C.-W. I., Sussman, S., Stone, M. D., Pang, R. D., Chou, C.-P., Leventhal, A. M., & Kirkpatrick, M. G. (2017). Impulsivity and history of behavioral addictions are associated with drug use in adolescents. *Addictive Behaviors, 74*, 41–47.

Connors, G. J., DiClemente, C. C., Velasquez, M. M., & Donovan, D. M. (2013). *Substance abuse treatment and the stages of change: Selecting and planning interventions* (2nd ed.). New York, NY: Guilford Press.

Copeland, J., Gilmore, S., Gates, P., & Swift, W. (2005). The Cannabis Problems Questionnaire: Factor, structure, reliability and validity. *Drug and Alcohol Dependence, 80*, 313–319.

Crépault, J. F. (2014, October). *Cannabis policy framework*. Toronto, ON: Centre for Addiction and Mental Health. Retrieved on November 22, 2017, from https://www.camh.ca/en/hospital/about_camh/influencing_public_policy/documents/camhcannabispolicyframework.pdf

Csiernik, R. (2016). *Substance use and abuse: Everything matters* (2nd ed.). Toronto, ON: Canadian Scholars Press.

Curran, H., Freeman, T. P., Mokrysz, C., Lewis, D. A., Morgan, C. J., & Parsons, L. H. (2016). Keep off the grass? Cannabis, cognition and addiction. *Nature Reviews Neuroscience, 17*(5), 293–306.

Cuttler, C., Spradlin, A., Nusbaum, A. T., Whitney, P., Hinson, J. M., & McLaughlin, R. J. (2017). Blunted stress reactivity in chronic cannabis users. *Psychopharmacology, 234*(15), 2299–2309.

Dahl, S. L. (2015). Remaining a user while cutting down: The relationship between cannabis use and identity. *Drugs: Education, Prevention & Policy, 22*(3), 175–184.

D'Amico, E. J., Tucker, J. S., Miles, J. N. V., Ewing, B. A., Shih, R. A., & Pedersen, E. R. (2016). Alcohol and marijuana use trajectories in a diverse longitudinal sample of adolescents: Examining use patterns from age 11 to 17 years. *Addiction, 111*(10), 1825–1835.

Danielsson, A.-K., Agardh, E., Hemmingsson, T., Allebeck, P., & Falkstedt, D. (2014). Cannabis use in adolescence and risk of future disability pension: A 39-year longitudinal cohort study. *Drug and Alcohol Dependence, 143*, 239–243.

Davis, A. K., Lin, L. A., Ilgen, M. A., & Bohnert, K. M. (2018). Recent cannabis use among Veterans in the United States: Results from a national sample. *Addictive Behaviors, 76*, 223–228.

Deerwester, J. (2017, March 21). Woody Harrelson swears off marijuana after 30 years. *USA Today*. Retrieved on November 29, 2017, from https://www.usatoday.com/story/life/people/2017/03/21/woody-harrelson-swears-off-marijuana-after-30-years/99440670/

DeRamus, T. (2011). *The secret addiction: Overcoming your marijuana dependency*. Montgomery, TX: SMA International.

Dorard, G., Bungener, C., Phan, O., Edel, Y., Corcos, M., & Berthoz, S. (2017). Is alexithymia related to cannabis use disorder? Results from a case-control study in outpatient adolescent cannabis abusers. *Journal of Psychosomatic Research, 95*, 74–80.

D'Souza, D. C., Cortes-Briones, J., Creatura, G., Bluez, G., Thurnauer, H., Deaso, E., . . . Skosnik, P. D. (2019). Efficacy and safety of a fatty acid amide hydrolase inhibitor (PF-04457845) in the treatment of cannabis withdrawal and dependence in men: A double-blind, placebo-controlled, parallel group, phase 2a single-site randomised controlled trial. *Lancet Psychiatry, 6*(1), 35–45.

Duperrouzel, J. C., Hawes, S. W., Lopez-Quintero, C., Pacheco-Colon, I., Coxe, S., Hayes, T., & Gonzalez, R. (2019). Adolescent cannabis use and its associations with decision-making and episodic memory: Preliminary results from a longitudinal study. *Neuropsychology*. Advance online publication. http://dx.doi.org/10.1037/neu0000538

Dworkin, E. R., Kaysen, D., Bedard-Gilligan, M., Rhew, I. C., & Lee, C. M. (2017). Daily-level associations between PTSD and cannabis use among young sexual minority women. *Addictive Behaviors, 74*, 118–121.

Earleywine, M. (2016). *Substance use problems* (2nd ed.). Ashland, OH: Hogrefe.

Elkashef, A., & Montoya, I. (2012). Pharmacotherapy of addiction. In J. C. Verster, K. Brady, M. Galanter, & P. Conrod (Eds.), *Drug abuse and addiction in medical illness: Causes, consequences and treatment* (pp. 107–119). New York, NY: Springer Science + Business Media.

Ellens, J. H. (Ed.) (2014). *Seeking the sacred with psychoactive substances—Chemical paths to spirituality and to God: History and practices; Insights, arguments, and controversies* (Vols. 1–2). Santa Barbara, CA: Praeger/ABC-CLIO.

Englund, A., Freeman, T. P., Murray, R. M., & McGuire, P. (2017). Can we make cannabis safer? *Lancet Psychiatry, 4*(8), 643–648.

Escobar, O. S., & Vaughan, E. L. (2014). Public religiosity, religious importance, and substance use among Latino emerging adults. *Substance Use & Misuse, 49*, 1317–1325.

Feingold, D., Fox, J., Rehm, J., & Lev-Ran, S. (2015). Natural outcome of cannabis use disorder: A 3-year longitudinal follow-up. *Addiction, 110*, 1963–1974.

Fiellin, L. E., Tetrault, J. M., Becker, W. C., Fiellin, D. A., & Hoff, R. A. (2013). Previous use of alcohol, cigarettes, and marijuana and subsequent abuse of prescription opioids in young adults. *Journal of Adolescent Health, 52*(2), 158–163.

Firmin, M. W., Pugh, K. C., Sohn, V. A., Voss, A. T., & Cltuang, Y.-R. (2016). Potential implications of legalized marijuana. *Psychology and Education: An Interdisciplinary Journal, 53*(3–4), 24–35.

Fox, P., Bain, P. G., Glickman, S., Carroll, C., & Zajicek, J. (2004). The effect of cannabis on tremor in patients with multiple sclerosis. *Neurology, 62*(7), 1105–1109.

Gentes, E. L., Schry, A. R., Hicks, T. A., Clancy, C. P., Collie, C. F., Kirby, A. C., . . . Calhoun, P. S. (2016). Prevalence and correlates of cannabis use in an outpatient VA posttraumatic stress disorder clinic. *Psychology of Addictive Behaviors, 30*, 415–421.

Glazier, R. E., & Kling, R. N. (2013). Recent trends in substance abuse among persons with disabilities compared to that of persons without disabilities. *Disability and Health Journal, 6*, 107–115.

Goings, T. C., Butler-Bente, E., McGovern, T., & Howard, M. O. (2016). Prevalence and correlates of substance use in Black, White, and biracial Black-White adolescents: Evidence for a biracial intermediate phenomena. *American Journal of Orthopsychiatry, 86*, 527–539.

Goldbach, J. T., Schrager, S. M., Dunlap, S. L., & Holloway, I. W. (2015). The application of minority stress theory to marijuana use among sexual minority adolescents. *Substance Use & Misuse, 50*, 366–375.

Gonzalez, C. A., Gallego, J. D., & Bockting, W. O. (2017). Demographic characteristics, components of sexuality and gender, and minority stress and their associations to excessive alcohol, cannabis, and illicit (noncannabis) drug use among a large sample of transgender people in the United States. *Journal of Primary Prevention, 38*, 419–445.

Gossop, M., Darke, S., Griffiths, P., Hando, J., Powis, B., Hall, W., & Strang, J. (1995). The Severity of Dependence Scale (SDS): Psychometric properties of the SDS in English and Australian samples of heroin, cocaine and amphetamine users. *Addiction, 90*, 607–614.

Gray, S. (Ed.) (2016). *An explorer's guide to an ancient plant spirit ally*. South Paris, ME: Park Street Press.

Grebot, E., Dardard, J., & Briet, G. (2016). Schémas précoces inadaptés, croyances addictives et styles défensifs chez des étudiants consommateurs de cannabis. [Early maladaptive schemas, addictive beliefs and defensive styles among student cannabis users]. *Annales medico-psychologiques, 174*(2), 93–99.

Greene, M., & Kelly, J. F. (2014). The prevalence of cannabis withdrawal and its influence on adolescents' treatment response and outcomes: A 12-month prospective investigation. *Journal of Addiction Medicine*, *8*(5), 359–367.

Griffin, R. (2012, October 15). The true origin of 420: Setting the record straight. *420 Magazine*. Retrieved from https://www.420magazine.com/2012/10/the-true-origin-of-420-setting-the-record-straight/

Griffith-Lendering, M. F. H., Wigman, J. T. W., van Leeuwen, A. P., Huijbregts, S. C. J., Huizink, A. C., Ormel, J., . . . Vollebergh, W. A. M. (2013). Cannabis use and vulnerability for psychosis in early adolescence—A TRAILS study. *Addiction*, *108*(4), 733–740.

Hachet, M. P. (2005). Are psychoanalysts interested in cannabis smokers? *Alcoologie et Addictologie*, *27*(2), 131–139.

Hachet, P. (2006). Follow up of cannabis users by psychoanalysts. *Annales Medico-Psychologiques*, *164*, 225–229.

Hall, W. (2015). What has research over the past two decades revealed about the adverse health effects of recreational cannabis use? *Addiction*, *110*(1), 19–35.

Hamilton, I. (2017). Cannabis, psychosis and schizophrenia: Unravelling a complex interaction. *Addiction*, *112*(9), 1653–1657.

Hanson, D. (2009). Marijuana withdrawal: A survey of symptoms. *The Praeger International Collection on Addictions, Vol 2: Psychobiological Profiles*, 111–124.

Hart, C. L., & Shytle, R. D. (2011). Potential pharmacotherapies for cannabis dependence. In B. A. Johnson (Ed.), *Addiction Medicine: Science and Practice* (Vol. 1, pp. 1063–1082). New York, NY: Springer.

Heishman, S. J., Singleton, E. G., & Ligouri, A. (2001). Marijuana Craving Questionnaire: Development and initial validation of a self-report instrument. *Addiction*, *96*, 1023–1034.

Hill, C. E. (2014). *Helping skills: Facilitating exploration, insight, and action* (4th ed.). Washington, DC: American Psychological Association.

Hodgins, D. C., Kim, H. S., & Stea, J. N. (2017). Increase and decrease of other substance use during recovery from cannabis use disorders. *Psychology of Addictive Behaviors*, *31*(6), 727–734.

Holley, M. F. (2009). Marijuana interaction with methamphetamine addiction. *The Praeger International Collection on Addictions, Vol 2: Psychobiological Profiles*, 125–140.

Hurd, Y. L., Michaelides, M., Miller, M. L., & Jutras-Aswad, D. (2014). Trajectory of adolescent cannabis use on addiction vulnerability. *Neuropharmacology, 76*(Part B), 416–424.

Johnson, R. M., Fairman, B., Gilreath, T., Xuan, Z., Rothman, E. F., Parnham, T., & Furr-Holden, C. D. M. (2015). Past 15-year trends in adolescent marijuana use: Differences by race/ethnicity and sex. *Drug and Alcohol Dependence*, *155*, 8–15.

Jungerman, F. S., Andreoni, S., & Laranjeira, R. (2007). Short term impact of same intensity but different duration interventions for cannabis users. *Drug and Alcohol Dependence*, *90*, 120–127.

Kabat-Zinn, J. (2013). *Full catastrophe living: Using the wisdom of your body and mind to face stress, pain, and illness* (Rev. ed.). New York, NY: Bantam.

Kalant, H. (2016). A critique of cannabis legalization proposals in Canada. *International Journal of Drug Policy*, *34*, 5–10.

Kepper, A., van den Eijnden, R., Monshouwer, K., & Vollebergh, W. (2014). Understanding the elevated risk of substance use by adolescents in special education and residential youth care: The role of individual, family and peer factors. *European Child & Adolescent Psychiatry*, *23*, 461–472.

Keyes, K. M., Wall, M., Feng, T., Cerda, M., & Hasin, D. S. (2017). Race/ethnicity and marijuana use in the United States: Diminishing differences in the prevalence of use, 2006–2015. *Drug and Alcohol Dependence*, *179*, 379–386.

Kimbrel, N. A., Newins, A. R., Dedert, E. A., Van Voorhees, E. E., Elbogen, E. B., Naylor, J. C., . . . Calhoun, P. S. (2017). Cannabis use disorder and suicide attempts in Iraq/Afghanistan-era veterans. *Journal of Psychiatric Research*, *89*, 1–5. doi:10.1016/j.jpsychires.2017.01.002

Kosten, T. R., Newton, T. F., De La Garza, R., II, & Haile, C. N. (2014). Substance-related and addictive disorders. *The American Psychiatric Publishing textbook of psychiatry* (6th ed., pp. 735–813). Arlington, VA: American Psychiatric Publishing.

Kosty, D. B., Seeley, J. R., Farmer, R. F., Stevens, J. J., & Lewinsohn, P. M. (2017). Trajectories of cannabis use disorder: Risk factors, clinical characteristics and outcomes. *Addiction*, *112*(2), 279–287.

Leafly. (2017). *Dabbing 101: What are dabs and how are they made?* Retrieved from https://www.leafly.com/news/cannabis-101/is-dabbing-good-or-bad-or-both

Legleye, S., Karila, L., Beck, F., & Reynaud, M. (2007). Validation of the CAST, a general population Cannabis Abuse Screening Test. *Journal of Substance Use*, *12*(4), 233–242.

Legleye, S., Kraus, L., Piontek, D., Phan, O., & Jouanne, C. (2012). Validation of the Cannabis Abuse Screening Test in a sample of cannabis inpatients. *European Addiction Research*, *18*, 193–200.

Lipari, R., Palen, L.-A., Ashley, O. S., Penne, M., Kan, M., & Pemberton, M. (2017). Examination of veteran fathers' parenting and their adolescent children's substance use in the United States. *Substance Use & Misuse*, *52*, 698–708.

Lowry, R., Johns, M. M., Robin, L. E., & Kann, L. K. (2017). Social stress and substance use disparities by sexual orientation among high school students. *American Journal of Preventive Medicine*, *53*, 547–558.

Lucas, P. (2017). Rationale for cannabis-based interventions in the opioid overdose crisis. *Harm Reduction Journal*, *14*(1), 58.

Lucas, P., & Walsh, Z. (2017). Medical cannabis access, use, and substitution for prescription opioids and other substances: A survey of authorized medical cannabis patients. *International Journal of Drug Policy*, *42*, 30–35.

Maharajh, H. D., Ali, J. K., & Maharaj, M. (2014). Transitional drug use: Switching from alcohol disability to marijuana creativity. In *Public health concern: Smoking, alcohol and substance use* (pp. 137–147). Hauppauge, NY: Nova Biomedical Books.

Margolis, R. D., & Zweben, J. E. (2011). *Treating patients with alcohol and other drug problems: An integrated approach* (2nd ed.). Washington, DC: American Psychological Association.

Marijuana. (2016). *Health Horns University Health Services*. Retrieved on December 5, 2017, from https://www.healthyhorns.utexas.edu/marijuana.html

Marijuana Anonymous World Services. (2017). *The twelve questions of Marijuana Anonymous*. Retrieved from https://www.marijuana-anonymous.org/how-it-works/the-twelve-questions

Martz, M. E., Trucco, E. M., Cope, L. M., Hardee, J. E., Jester, J. M., Zucker, R. A., & Heitzeg, M. M. (2016). Association of marijuana use with blunted nucleus accumbens response to reward anticipation. *JAMA Psychiatry*, *73*(8), 838–844.

Maté, G. (2008). *In the realm of hungry ghosts: Close encounters with addiction*. Toronto, ON: Vintage Books.

McLoughlin, B. C., Pushpa-Rajah, J. A., Gillies, D., Rathbone, J., Variend, H., Kalakouti, E., & Kyprianou, K. (2014). Cannabis and schizophrenia. *Cochrane Database of Systematic Reviews*, CD004837.

Mereish, E. H., Goldbach, J. T., Burgess, C., & DiBello, A. M. (2017). Sexual orientation, minority stress, social norms, and substance use among racially diverse adolescents. *Drug and Alcohol Dependence, 178*, 49–56.

Meruelo, A. D., Castro, N., Cota, C. I., & Tapert, S. F. (2017). Cannabis and alcohol use, and the developing brain. *Behavioural Brain Research, 325*(Part A), 44–50.

Metrik, J., Jackson, K., Bassett, S. S., Zvolensky, M. J., Seal, K., & Borsari, B. (2016). The mediating roles of coping, sleep, and anxiety motives in cannabis use and problems among returning veterans with PTSD and MDD. *Psychology of Addictive Behaviors, 30*, 743–754.

Milkman, H. B., & Sunderwirth, S. G. (2010). *Craving for ecstasy and natural highs: A positive approach to mood alteration*. Thousand Oaks, CA: SAGE.

Miller, F. G., & Lazowski, L. E. (1999). *The Substance Abuse Subtle Screening Inventory-3 (SASSI-3) manual*. Springville, IN: SASSI Institute.

Miller, N. S., & Oberbarnschiedt, T. (2017). Current medical and legal status for smoked "medical marijuana" and addiction. *Psychiatric Annals, 47*(6), 335–340.

Miller, R., Mccormack, J., & Sevy, S. (2008). An integrated treatment program for first-episode schizophrenia. In J. F. M. Gleeson, E. Killackey, & H. Krstev (Eds.), *Psychotherapies for the psychoses: Theoretical, cultural and clinical integration* (pp. 151–166). New York, NY: Routledge/Taylor & Francis.

Miller, W. R., Zweben, A., DiClemente, C. C., & Rychtarik, R. G. (1999). *Motivational Enhancement Therapy Manual: A clinical research guide for therapists treating individuals with alcohol abuse and dependence*. Rockville, MD: U.S. Department of Health and Human Services.

Moreno, O., Janssen, T., Cox, M. J., Colby, S., & Jackson, K. M. (2017). Parent-adolescent relationships in Hispanic versus Caucasian families: Associations with alcohol and marijuana use onset. *Addictive Behaviors, 74*, 74–81.

Morgan, C. J. A., Freeman, T. P., Schafer, G. L., & Curran, H. V. (2010). Cannabidiol attenuates the appetitive effects of DELTA9-tetrahydrocannabinol in humans smoking their chosen cannabis. *Neuropsychopharmacology, 35*(9), 1879–1885.

Morris, C. V. (2015). Enduring neurobiological implications of prenatal exposure to cannabis. *Dissertation Abstracts International: Section B: The Sciences and Engineering, 76*(3-B(E)). No pagination specified.

Mucke, M., Phillips, T., Radbruch, L., Petzke, F., & Hauser, W. (2018). Cannabis-based medicines for chronic neuropathic pain in adults. *Cochrane Database of Systematic Reviews, 3*, CD012182.

National Institute on Drug Abuse. (2017, December). *Available treatments for marijuana use disorders*. Retrieved on January 5, 2018, from https://www.drugabuse.gov/publications/research-reports/marijuana/available-treatments-marijuana-use-disorders

Nguyen, N. N. (2017). Factors influencing adolescent alcohol and marijuana use: The role of religiosity, school-based prevention programs, parental influence, and peer influence. *Dissertation Abstracts International Section A: Humanities and Social Sciences, 77*(8-A(E)). No pagination specified.

Nowinski, J., Baker, S., & Carroll, K. (1999). *Twelve Step Facilitation Therapy Manual: A clinical research guide for therapists treating individuals with alcohol abuse and dependence*. Rockville, MD: U.S. Department of Health and Human Services.

Olfson, M., Wall, M. M., Liu, S.-M., & Blanco, C. (2018). Cannabis use and risk of prescription opioid use disorder in the United States. *American Journal of Psychiatry, 175*(1), 47–53.

Osuch, E., Vingilis, E., Ross, E., Forster, C., & Summerhurst, C. (2013). Cannabis use, addiction risk and functional impairment in youth seeking treatment for primary mood or anxiety concerns. *Special Issue: Education of health professionals about adolescent psychiatry, 25*(3), 309–314.

Ouzir, M., & Errami, M. (2016). Etiological theories of addiction: A comprehensive update on neurobiological, genetic and behavioural vulnerability. *Pharmacology, Biochemistry and Behavior, 148*, 59–68.

Pacek, L. R., Mauro, P. M., & Martins, S. S. (2015). Perceived risk of regular cannabis use in the United States from 2002 to 2012: Differences by sex, age, and race/ethnicity. *Drug and Alcohol Dependence, 149*, 232–244.

Palamar, J. J., Fenstermaker, M., Kamboukos, D., Ompad, D. C., Cleland, C. M., & Weitzman, M. (2014). Adverse psychosocial outcomes associated with drug use among US high school seniors: A comparison of alcohol and marijuana. *American Journal of Drug and Alcohol Abuse, 40*(6), 438–446.

Parnes, J. E., Rahm-Knigge, R. L., & Conner, B. T. (2017). The curvilinear effects of sexual orientation on young adult substance use. *Addictive Behaviors, 66*, 108–113.

Patel, S. (2017). *Marijuana and spirituality*. Retrieved on December 12, 2017, from http://www.doc420.com/marijuana-and-spirituality/

Pearson, M. R. (2019, March 7). A meta-analytic investigation of the associations between cannabis use and cannabis-related negative consequences. *Psychology of Addictive Behaviors, 33*(3), 190–196. Advance online publication.

Pintori, N., Loi, B., & Mereu, M. (2017). Synthetic cannabinoids: The hidden side of spice drugs. *Behavioural Pharmacology, 28*(6), 409–419.

Piomelli, D. (2016). Introduction to *Cannabis and Cannabinoid Research*. *Cannabis and Cannabinoid Research 1*(1), 1–2.

Prochaska, J. O., Norcross, J. C., & DiClemente, C. C. (1994). *Changing for good*. New York, NY: Avon Books.

Rastegar, D., & Fingerhood, M. (2016). *The American Society of Addiction Medicine handbook of addiction medicine*. New York, NY: Oxford University Press.

Robinson, M., Sanches, M., & MacLeod, M. A. (2016). Prevalence and mental health correlates of illegal cannabis use among bisexual women. *Journal of Bisexuality, 16*, 181–202.

Rog, D. J., Nurmikko, T. J., Friede, T., & Young, C. A. (2005). Randomized, controlled trial of cannabis-based medicine in central pain in multiple sclerosis. *Neurology, 65*(6), 812–819.

Ross, C. S., Brooks, D. R., Aschengrau, A., Siegel, M. B., Weinberg, J., & Shrier, L. A. (2018). Positive and negative affect following marijuana use in naturalistic settings: An ecological momentary assessment study. *Addictive Behaviors, 76*, 61–67.

Ross, J., Graziano, P., Pacheco-Colon, I., Coxe, S., & Gonzalez, R. (2016). Decision-making does not moderate the association between cannabis use and body mass index among adolescent cannabis users. *Journal of the International Neuropsychological Society, 22*(9), 944–949.

Salhab, A. (2017). Embattled cannabis: Pharmacological, medical, recreational, and adverse effects aspects. *Journal of Substance Use, 22*(2), 236–239.

Schlossarek, S., Kempkensteffen, J., Reimer, J., & Verthein, U. (2016). Psychosocial determinants of cannabis dependence: A systematic review of the literature. *European Addiction Research, 22*(3), 131–144.

Schwartz, A. (2013, July 23). M Is for marijuana: A is for addict. *The Fix*. Retrieved on December 5, 2017, from https://www.thefix.com/content/Marijuana-Anonymous2089

Sharma, M. (2009). Determinants of marijuana use, abuse and dependence: Editorial. *Journal of Alcohol and Drug Education*, *53*(1), 3–6.

Silins, E., Horwood, L. J., Patton, G. C., Fergusson, D. M., Olsson, C. A., Hutchinson, D. M., . . . Mattick, R. P. (2014). Young adult sequelae of adolescent cannabis use: An integrative analysis. *Lancet Psychiatry*, *1*(4), 286–293.

Simons, J., Correia, C. J., & Carey, K. B. (2000). A comparison of motives for marijuana and alcohol use among experienced users. *Addictive Behaviors*, *25*(1), 153–160.

Simons, J., Correia, C. J., Carey, K. B., & Borsari, B. E. (1998). Validating a five-factor marijuana motives measure: Relations with use, problems, and alcohol motives. *Journal of Counseling Psychology*, *45*(3), 265–273.

Smith, R. L. (2013). The major substances of abuse and the body. In P. Stevens & R. L. Smith (Eds.), *Substance abuse counseling: Theory and practice* (5th ed., pp. 51–97). New York, NY: Pearson.

Solimini, R., Rotolo, M. C., Pichini, S., & Pacifici, R. (2017). Neurological disorders in medical use of cannabis: An update. *CNS & Neurological Disorders Drug Targets*, *16*(5), 527–533.

Sparks, G. M. (2016). Treatment of marijuana addiction: Clinical assessment and psychosocial and pharmacological interventions. In M. T. Compton (Ed.), *Marijuana and mental health* (pp. 171–198). Arlington, VA: American Psychiatric Association.

Stanley, L. R., & Swaim, R. C. (2015). Initiation of alcohol, marijuana, and inhalant use by American-Indian and white youth living on or near reservations. *Drug and Alcohol Dependence*, *155*, 90–96.

Subbaraman, M. S. (2014). Can cannabis be considered a substitute medication for alcohol? *Alcohol and Alcoholism*, *49*(3), 292–298.

Suerken, C. K., Reboussin, B. A., Sutfin, E. L., Wagoner, K. G., Spangler, J., & Wolfson, M. (2014). Prevalence of marijuana use at college entry and risk factors for initiation during freshman year. *Addictive Behaviors*, *39*, 302–307.

Tang, S. M., Ansarian, A., & Courtney, D. B. (2017). Clozapine treatment and cannabis use in adolescents with psychotic disorders—A retrospective cohort chart review. *Journal of the Canadian Academy of Child and Adolescent Psychiatry/Journal de l'Académie canadienne de psychiatrie de l'enfant et de l'adolescent*, *26*(1), 51–58.

Tartaglia, S., Miglietta, A., & Gattino, S. (2017). Life satisfaction and cannabis use: A study on young adults. *Journal of Happiness Studies*, *18*, 709–718.

Trull, T. J., Wycoff, A. M., Lane, S. P., Carpenter, R. W., & Brown, W. C. (2016). Cannabis and alcohol use, affect and impulsivity in psychiatric out-patients' daily lives. *Addiction*, *111*(11), 2052–2059.

Turna, J., Patterson, B., & Van Ameringen, M. (2017). Is cannabis treatment for anxiety, mood, and related disorders ready for prime time? *Depression & Anxiety*, *34*(11), 1006–1017.

Unger, J. B., Schwartz, S. J., Huh, J., Soto, D. W., & Baezconde-Garbanati, L. (2014). Acculturation and perceived discrimination: Predictors of substance use trajectories from adolescence to emerging adulthood among Hispanics. *Addictive Behaviors*, *39*, 1293–1296.

van Wel, J., Spronk, D., Kuypers, K., Theunissen, E., Toennes, S., Verkes, R., & Ramaekers, J. (2015). Psychedelic symptoms of cannabis and cocaine use as a function of trait impulsivity. *Journal of Psychopharmacology*, *29*(3), 324–334.

Varma, M., Moore, L. S., Cataldi, J., Estoup, A. C., & Stewart, D. G. (2017). Religiosity and adolescent marijuana use. *Mental Health, Religion & Culture*, *20*, 229–238.

Volkow, N. D., Wang, G.-J., Telang, F., Fowler, J. S., Alexoff, D., Logan, J., . . . Tomasi, D. (2014). Decreased dopamine brain reactivity in marijuana abusers is associated with negative emotionality and addiction severity. *PNAS Proceedings of the National Academy of Sciences of the United States of America*, *111*(30), E3149–E3156.

Walther, L., Gantner, A., Heinz, A., & Majic, T. (2016). Evidence-based treatment options in cannabis dependency. *Deutsches Arzteblatt International*, *113*(39), 653–659.

Wardell, J. D., Strang, N. M., & Hendershot, C. S. (2016). Negative urgency mediates the relationship between childhood maltreatment and problems with alcohol and cannabis in late adolescence. *Addictive Behaviors*, *56*, 1–7.

Watson Seupel, C. (2014, February 26). Dabs—marijuana's explosive secret. *CNBC News*. Retrieved from https://www.cnbc.com/2014/02/26/dabsmarijuanas-explosive-secret.html

Wetherill, L., Agrawal, A., Kapoor, M., Bertelsen, S., Bierut, L. J., Brooks, A., . . . Foroud, T. (2015). Association of substance dependence phenotypes in the COGA sample. *Addiction Biology*, *20*(3), 617–627.

Whiteside, S. P., & Lynam, D. R. (2001). The Five Factor Model and impulsivity: Using a structural model of personality to understand impulsivity. *Personality and Individual Differences*, *30*, 669–689.

WHO ASSIST Working Group. (2002). The Alcohol, Smoking and Substance Involvement Screening Test (ASSIST): Development, reliability and feasibility. *Addiction*, *97*, 1183–1194.

Winters, K. C., & Lee, C.-Y. S. (2008). Likelihood of developing an alcohol and cannabis use disorder during youth: Association with recent use and age. *Drug and Alcohol Dependence*, *92*(1–3), 239–247.

Wittenauer, J., Ascher, M., Briggie, A., Kreiter, A., & Chavez, J. (2015). The role of complementary and alternative medicine in adolescent substance use disorders. *Adolescent Psychiatry*, *5*(2), 96–104.

Wolff, V., Rouyer, O., & Geny, B. (2014). "Adverse health effects of marijuana use": Comment. *New England Journal of Medicine*, *371*(9), 878.

Wu, L.-T., Zhu, H., & Swartz, M. S. (2016). Trends in cannabis use disorders among racial/ethnic population groups in the United States. *Drug and Alcohol Dependence*, *165*, 181–190.

Yoruk, B. K. (2014). Legalization of Sunday alcohol sales and alcohol consumption in the United States. *Addiction*, *109*(1), 55–61.

Zvolensky, M. J., Bonn-Miller, M. O., Leyro, T. M., Johnson, K. A., & Bernstein, A. (2011). Marijuana: An overview of the empirical literature. In B. Johnson (Ed.), *Addiction medicine* (pp. 445–461). New York, NY: Springer.

11 Opioid Addiction

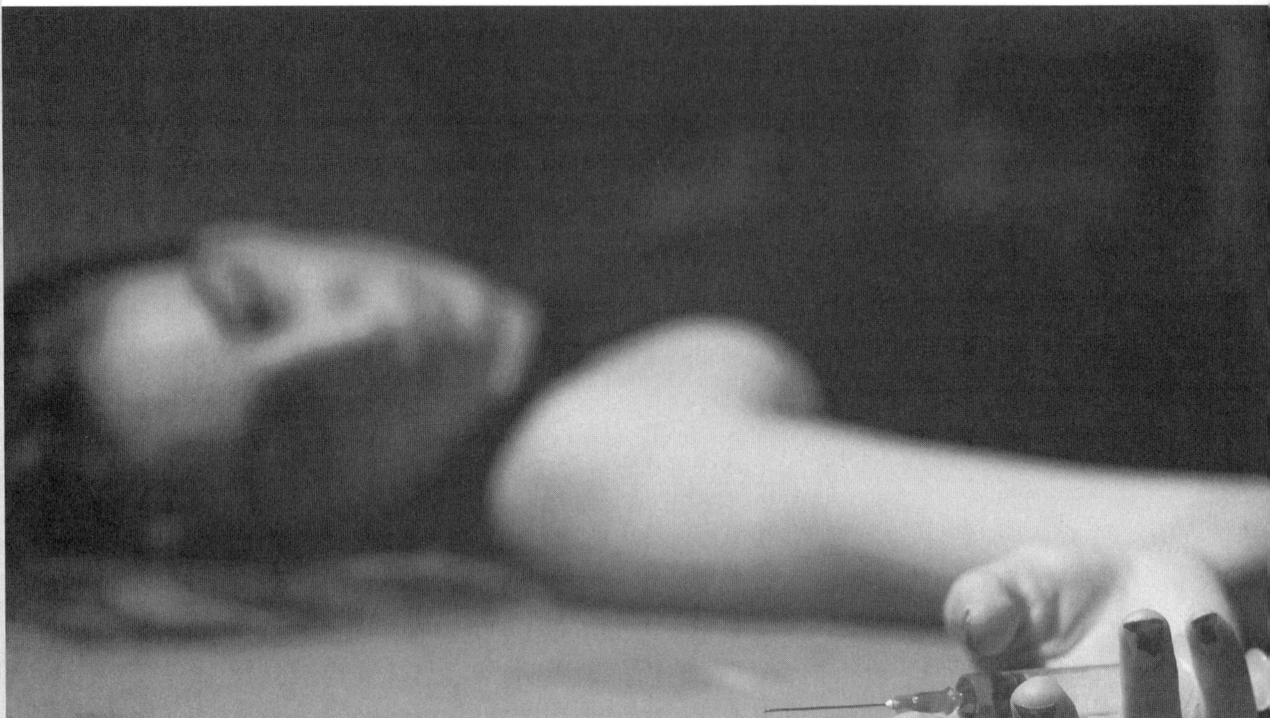

iStock.com/VladimirFLoyd

Learning Objectives

1. Learn about the three types of opioids.
2. Describe the effect that opioids have on people.
3. Understand the causes of opioid addiction.
4. Learn how to diagnose opioid use disorder.
5. Discover effective strategies for treating opioid addicts.

CHALLENGING YOUR ASSUMPTIONS ABOUT THIS ADDICTION

1. For whom would you feel greater empathy and sympathy, an individual in chronic pain who became addicted to opioids for pain relief or an individual who began using heroin recreationally and who then became addicted to it? You likely have an immediate gut reaction to these two types of addicts. Now question your gut reaction. Given that addiction occurs in every stratum of society and among people at every socioeconomic level, on what basis would you distinguish between these two individuals who became addicted unintentionally and against their better judgment?
2. Spend time at home in a visualization exercise. Think about a friend or family member and imagine that he or she has become a heroin addict. What efforts would you make to try and help this individual? What if nothing you tried worked: At what point would you stop trying? How would you feel at the point in which you need to surrender and stop offering support?
3. Before reading this chapter, if you knew you were going to become addicted to heroin, what steps would you take to help prevent this occurrence? If you then became a heroin addict, what steps would you take to get through it?
4. If none of the steps you took in the previous question were sufficient to overcome your heroin addiction, how likely would you be to move to a faraway city, leaving your friends and family behind so that you could start a new life? What would be the emotional impact of moving, knowing that it is your last hope for leading an abstinent life from heroin?
5. Should the United States decriminalize all drugs? This would allow physicians to prescribe drugs like heroin to heroin addicts, which in turn would help prevent heroin deaths and reduce crime in two ways: (a) heroin-addicted individuals themselves would be less likely to commit crimes, and (b) it would reduce the illegal drug trade. Discuss your view with a friend or family member.

PERSONAL REFLECTIONS

A close family member has needed to take prescription opioids such as Percocet and OxyContin (both brand names for the opioid called oxycodone) for several years due to severe back pain. Given the duration and dosage of use, she is likely addicted. One of the unfortunate consequences of taking opioids long term is that tolerance develops, at which point the drugs become increasingly ineffective for managing pain. Now her pain is unbearable following four surgeries, but her doctor is saying that there is nothing further that can be done. Where does she turn?

I know that some people also begin opioids initially for recreational use or to manage psychological pain. Opioids are used to numb more than just the body. Throughout my career, I have worked with only a handful of opioid addicts. The addicted individuals I have seen are maintained on either methadone or Suboxone (which is a combination of buprenorphine and naloxone). Why do these individuals appear incapable of becoming abstinent from opioids completely?

In writing this chapter, I am as curious as you are to get the full scoop on this class of drugs that have created a crisis throughout the United States and many other countries in the world. I asked myself, "Why don't they just stop using after they experience severe adverse consequences?" "Why are people dying, especially from fentanyl use?" "Why would drug dealers risk killing their customers by giving them fentanyl instead of heroin?"

Background Information

Opioids are an inclusive term that refers to natural, synthetic, or semisynthetic drugs (Csiernik, 2016). They are also referred to as narcotics, opiates (opium derivatives), narcotic analgesics, and opioid analgesics. These include opium, codeine, morphine, heroin, oxycodone, fentanyl, carfentanil, and methadone, among others. They can be smoked, taken orally or across a mucous membrane, or injected intravenously.

Natural opioids are derived from the Asian poppy, *Papaver somniferum* (Csiernik, 2016). Opioids are commonly used as painkillers or anesthetics. They do not eliminate pain but rather disguise it. They mask the emotional reaction to pain while simultaneously producing euphoria. Opioids can also be called depressants because they slow down the functioning of the central nervous system (Csiernik, 2016).

Opioids share the spotlight with benzodiazepines as the most commonly misused controlled drugs (Rastegar & Fingerhood, 2016). An estimated 26 to 36 million individuals abuse opioids worldwide (Truong, Moukaddam, Toledo, & Onigu-Otite, 2017). The problem remains worse in the United States, where the opioid use epidemic continues raging. There are more than 2 million

Americans who suffer from prescription opioid abuse, and the number of overdose deaths from prescription opioids in the United States has quadrupled since 1999 (Truong et al., 2017). Ruhm (2017) even argued that opioid and heroin mortality rates might be 24% and 22% greater than reported rates. No longer primarily an urban problem, opioid and heroin dependence has become a significant issue across the country (Meyer & Phillips, 2015).

Opium may have been used as early as 2100 BC by the Sumerians (Norn, Kruse, & Kruse, 2005). It spread to India and China due to the Arab trade in the 8th century AD and to Europe between the 10th and 13th centuries AD (Brownstein, 1993). Opium addiction has been documented ever since the 16th century in countries such as Turkey, Egypt, Germany, England, and especially China, where opium became the new tobacco. In 1803, morphine was discovered, and it began to be used decades later as an anesthetic during surgery (Csiernik, 2016). In 1874, heroin was synthesized in England from morphine with the hopes of it being free from abuse liability (Brownstein, 1993). It was not marketed until 1898, however, by the Bayer company in Germany (Csiernik, 2016).

The creation of new opioids did not stop there: methadone was created in 1946 and fentanyl followed in 1959. Methadone maintenance treatment (MMT) emerged in the late 1960s and early 1970s in reaction to the heroin wave and has been validated numerous times (Courtwright, 2015).

Today's current opioid epidemic consists primarily of prescription drugs, heroin, and fentanyl. In 2014, 18,893 lethal overdoses in the United States were related to prescription opioids and 10,574 due to heroin (Chopra & Marasa, 2017). Fentanyl-contaminated heroin (FCH) is also becoming widespread in the United States; 11% of the 199 nonmedical-prescription opioid users in one study reported known or suspected FCH exposure in the past 6 months (Macmadu, Carroll, Hadland, Green, & Marshall, 2017). Users are also rarely able to identify when fentanyl is in their drugs (Carroll, Marshall, Rich, & Green, 2017).

Whereas violence accompanied the heroin wave of the 1970s, the current opioid epidemic has not seen an increase in crime rates (Szalavitz & Rigg, 2017). The demographics of users are now shifting toward White individuals, people living in rural areas, younger populations, and females (Meiman, Tomasallo, & Paulozzi, 2015; Salani, Zdanowicz, & Joseph, 2016).

Opioids are drugs that bind particularly on the opioid receptors and produce morphine-like effects. Opioids can be categorized into three groups: (a) natural opioids derived directly from opium or dried poppy juice (i.e., codeine, morphine, opium), (b) semisynthetic opioids, which are potent, chemically modified versions of natural opioids (i.e., heroin, hydromorphone, oxycodone), and (c) synthetic opioids, which mimic the effects of natural opioids but are not structurally similar (i.e., fentanyl, hydrocodone, methadone) (Csiernik, 2016).

Opioids are known for producing euphoria; however, they can have different effects depending on the individual. Although they produce euphoria among those who become/are addicted, opioids primarily induce sedation among those who are not addicted (Rastegar & Fingerhood, 2016). They may also sicken some individuals (Earleywine, 2016); opium itself has an unpleasant smell and bitter taste that frequently produces nausea when consumed. Heroin is the most highly addictive opioid, followed by morphine (Csiernik, 2016).

Opioid addiction is a chronic disorder that involves frequent relapses. It results in a lower quality of life regarding physical health, psychological health, and social relationships (Patra, Sarkar, Basu, & Mattoo, 2016). The mortality rate of opioid-addicted individuals is about 6 to 20 times greater than that of the general population (Hser, Evans, Grella, Ling, & Anglin, 2015). Stable abstinence from opioid use is less than 30% after 10–30 years, and many abstinent addicted individuals will use alcohol or other drugs instead (Hser et al., 2015). Five years of abstinence, however, will substantially increase the likelihood of future abstinence.

Prescription opioids (i.e., painkillers) were the most common new drug of abuse among first-time drug users aged 12 and older in 2005 and 2006, replacing marijuana (Renner & Suzuki, 2011). New users tend to be White, employed, and educated. Among nonmedical users, usage varies from infrequent use (once or twice per year) to daily (Compton, Jones, & Baldwin, 2016). There are currently estimated to be roughly 100 million Americans who live with some form and level of chronic pain, which constitutes more people than are affected by diabetes, heart disease, and cancer combined (Winerman, 2018).

Prescription opioid-addicted individuals can be divided into two subgroups (Compton & Weaver, 2015): those who use prescription opioids as a primary drug of abuse and those who develop addiction from prescription painkillers. For the former, prescription opioids may be used as club drugs as they are perceived to enhance the sensory experience at dance parties (Weaver, Delos Reyes, & Schnoll, 2014). For the latter, Cicero, Ellis, and Kasper (2017) found that nearly half of patients in drug treatment programs for opioid abuse were first exposed to opioids through a prescription to treat pain. Of these pain patients, 94.6% of them had already been exposed to another psychoactive substance, especially alcohol, nicotine and/or tobacco, marijuana, and illicit stimulants.

Many scholars have studied the apparent transition of nonmedical prescription opioid users to heroin (Clements, Lopez, Rachakonda, Sedky, & Pumariega, 2016). For U.S. veterans who never reported illicit opioid use before, "New-onset non-medical use of prescription opioids (NMUPO) is a strong risk factor for heroin initiation" (Banerjee et al., 2016, p. 2021). Martins, Segura, et al. (2017) found that young adults who use prescription opioids nonmedically are nine times more likely to use heroin than other young adults. The literature also supports a strong correlation between a decrease in the numbers of opioid prescriptions given and an increase in heroin use (Clements et al., 2016). In Kentucky, for example, policies aimed at restricting prescription painkillers made heroin more available and cheap (Perkins & Shannon, 2016). Cicero, Ellis, and Harney (2015) also found that accessibility and cost were the primary reasons that individuals switched from prescription opioids to heroin.

On the other hand, Compton et al. (2016) argued that a causal link between decreasing opioid prescriptions and increased heroin use is unlikely. According to their research, the transition from nonmedical prescription use to heroin occurs at a low rate, and it is rare for nonmedical users of prescription opioids also to use heroin. They suggested that the transition happens primarily among those with heavy and frequent nonmedical use and those with prescription opioid addictions.

Individuals who use both heroin and prescription opioids are likely to be young, White males in poor health (physical and mental) who misuse other prescription medications and began misuse as adolescents (Rigg & Monnat, 2015). Those who use only heroin are more likely to be older, at a socioeconomic disadvantage, disconnected from social institutions, and involved in crime and have easy access to heroin. Finally, those who use only prescription painkillers appear to be the most stable of the three subgroups

(Rigg & Monnat, 2015). However, little research has been done to differentiate between heroin and prescription opioid users (Karakula et al., 2016).

As previously mentioned, heroin is the most addictive of the opioids. Studies suggest that around 50% of people will become addicted to the controlled use of heroin (Imperio, 2016). Compared to other drug users, heroin users tend to be younger, not married, and less involved in the criminal justice system (Perkins & Shannon, 2016). However, they tend to use other substances and engage in high-risk substance-using behaviors (such as injecting) more than other drug users. People at the highest risk for heroin use tend to be male, have a high school diploma or less, earn less than $20,000 per year, participate in government assistance, and report the use of alcohol, cigarettes, or marijuana before the age of 21 (Burbage, 2018).

Unlike marijuana, methamphetamine, and cocaine, heroin use often increases with age (Earleywine, 2016). Darke, Torok and Ross (2017) found five development trajectories that lead to heroin use: (a) social disadvantage, (b) parental drug use/psychopathology, (c) childhood abuse and neglect, (d) early-onset psychopathology and antisocial behaviors, and (e) a developmental sequence of drug onsets. Pani et al. (2016) found a five-factor aggregation of psychological symptoms in heroin users: "worthlessness and being trapped," "somatic symptoms," "sensitivity-psychoticism," "panic-anxiety," and "violence-suicide." Milkman and Frosch (as cited in Milkman & Sunderwirth, 2010) noted that heroin users tend to struggle with low self-esteem.

Heroin use is a high-risk activity: It can increase one's risk of dying prematurely by three to four times (Lopez-Quintero et al., 2015). Young adults (under age 30) addicted to heroin are more likely to reuse and share syringes, use powder cocaine, and have been addicted to prescription opioids before heroin use than heroin-addicted individuals above 30 years of age (Cedarbaum & Banta-Green, 2016). In a study by Linas et al. (2015), heroin-addicted individuals were more likely to engage in illicit drug use if they were with someone who was using drugs, in an abandoned space, or wandering.

Like other addictions, opioid addiction can be caused by a desire to escape the pain. Heroin, for example, can ease both physical and psychological pain (Maté, 2008). Addiction can also result from comorbid mental disorders, spiritual deprivation, isolation, or child abuse or neglect (Hser et al., 2015; Maté, 2008). Schwaninger et al. (2017) found that 93% of heroin-addicted patients reported childhood abuse and neglect. Similarly, around three quarters of adult intravenous opioid users in the North American Opiate Medication Initiative study experienced childhood abuse or neglect (Krausz et al., 2014). Those who reported childhood maltreatment also had more severe reported symptoms of posttraumatic stress, anxiety, and paranoia than those who did not.

Examples of childhood trauma that could influence later drug use include persistent violence, sexual abuse, neglect, traumatic bereavements, and adult alcohol use (Hammersley et al., 2016). Adoptees and individuals who experienced a parental suicide attempt as children are also more likely to have an opioid use disorder (OUD) during their lifetime (O'Brien, Salas-Wright, Vaughn, & LeCloux, 2015; Yoon, Westermeyer, Warwick, & Kuskowski, 2012).

Families characterized by lack of understanding, conflict, rejection, and nonacceptance increase the risk of addiction (Mirkovic-Hajdukov, Spahic, Softic, Becirovic, & Simic, 2017). On the other hand, supportive families and friends, education, leisure activities, employment, and financial resources decrease the likelihood of addiction (Earleywine, 2016; Hser et al., 2015).

Opioid abusers may have a particular personality profile. Raketic et al. (2017) used the Revised NEO Personality Inventory to find that women with opioid addiction scored higher on neuroticism and extraversion and lower on agreeableness and conscientiousness than both alcohol-addicted and control groups. According to Khantzian (as cited in Milkman & Sunderwirth, 2010), opioid users may be drawn to narcotics rather than other drugs because of their anti-aggression and antirage capabilities; addicts' life histories are replete with periods of uncontrolled anger and violent episodes before drug use.

Opioid dependence is moderately heritable (Nelson et al., 2016). Research has shown that opioid addiction is associated with short-term reward-chasing behavior (Myers et al., 2016), emotion regulation impairments, and low mindfulness (Wilson et al., 2017). However, it is unclear whether these associations are causes or effects of addiction.

Concerning prescription opioids, the research of Cicero et al. (2017) suggested that almost 95% of pain patients who become addicted to painkillers have already experienced other psychoactive substances. Huffman et al. (2015) found that having nonopioid substance use disorders (SUDs) (along with high opioid doses) increases the odds of opioid addiction by 28 times. Lin et al. (2015) also found that, among patients in residential addiction treatment with comorbid pain, opioid addiction was associated with being younger, White, female, having a lower pain acceptance, and using cocaine. Prescription opioid addiction, therefore, appears to occur alongside other SUDs.

Prescription opioid misuse can lead to heroin dependency (Miller, Miller, & Barnes, 2016). Also, the age of initial heroin use is a strong predictor of future regular use (Woodcock, Lundahl, Stoltman, & Greenwald, 2015). If users inject the first time, then they have a higher chance of transitioning to daily use faster than if they had not injected (Hines et al., 2017).

Opioids have their legitimate place in medical practice. Although they are primarily used for pain relief and anesthesia, they can also suppress diarrhea, act as a replacement drug for heroin-addicted individuals (e.g., methadone), and suppress a cough. Furthermore, most individuals taking opioids for noncancerous, chronic pain do not become opioid addicts. This was demonstrated in a meta-analysis that comprised a sample of over 6000 people (Furlan, Sandoval, Mailis-Gagnon, & Tunks, 2006).

The most potent opioids like carfentanil (also spelled carfentanyl) are approved only within a veterinary practice. Drugs like carfentanil and a more recent compound sold on the street known as W-18 are claimed to be 100 times more potent than fentanyl. These two drugs are resulting in an increased number of opioid deaths (Sheikh, 2016).

The acute effects of opioids include analgesia, respiratory depression, miosis (i.e., excessive contraction of the pupil), and euphoria (Rastegar & Fingerhood, 2016). Overdoses are characterized by respiratory depression and lack of consciousness. If overdose is caught early enough, naloxone, which is an opioid antagonist, can prevent death. Interestingly, aside from the risk of overdose, few long-term complications occur with chronic opioid use. Most of the complications experienced by heroin-addicted individuals are due to the use of needles (Rastegar & Fingerhood, 2016).

The rates of both opiate and heroin addiction (along with consequent overdoses) have skyrocketed in America over the past decade (Littrell, 2017). The estimated number of Americans who are dependent on or abuse opioids is more than 2 million (Rastegar & Fingerhood, 2016). With overall relapse rates for SUDs being as high as 91% (Chopra & Marasa, 2017), relapse rates for opioids fall anywhere from 80% to above 90% (Maté, 2008). Even with hospital treatment, over 70% of opioid-addicted individuals eventually relapse.

In 2011, the Drug Abuse Warning Network (DAWN) reported that there were an estimated 1.4 million emergency department visits caused by misuse or abuse of prescription drugs, which was higher than the rates for illicit drugs combined (Rastegar & Fingerhood, 2016). Voon, Karamouzian, and Kerr (2017) conducted two meta-analyses and found that between 48% and 60% of individuals who use prescription opioids nonmedically have chronic noncancer pain. According to another literature review done by Vowles et al. (2015), rates of opioid misuse among individuals with chronic pain are between 21% and 29% (Vowles et al., 2015), whereas rates of addiction are between 8% and 12%. Around one third of long-stay residents are prescribed opioids, and around 15% are prescribed opioids long term (Hunnicutt et al., 2018). In one Canadian study, self-reported nonmedical prescription opioid use (NMPOU) prevalence rates were 15.5% in students and 5.9% in adults (Fischer et al., 2013).

Heroin use and addiction increased significantly between the years 2001–2002 and 2012–2013, particularly among White individuals (Martins, Sarvet, et al., 2017). The 2013 National Survey on Drug Use and Health reported that around 4.8 million Americans used heroin at some point in their lives, which is 1.8% of all people aged 12 or older in the country; 681,000 had used heroin in the past year; and 289,000 had used in the past month (Rastegar & Fingerhood, 2016). The estimated number of Americans with heroin dependence or abuse was 517,000, which is more than twice what it was in 2002 (Rastegar & Fingerhood, 2016).

Palamar, Shearston, Dawson, Mateu-Gelabert, and Ompad (2016) conducted a study of high school seniors and found that about one eighth of them reported lifetime nonmedical opioid use, with 1.2% reporting lifetime heroin use. Over three quarters of the heroin users also used nonmedical opioids. Another study found that 18.4% of young adult respondents had used heroin at some time in their lives, and 7.3% had used in the past year (Rastegar & Fingerhood, 2016). Among injection heroin users in San Francisco, 40% reported having at least one overdose in their lifetime, and 33% reported having two or more (Rastegar & Fingerhood, 2016).

Among a nationally representative sample of the U.S. population, 7.6% of men and 8.2% of women with NMPOU ever received treatment (Kerridge et al., 2015). In another study of NESARC respondents with prescription drug use disorders, the lifetime probability of seeking treatment was 42%, and the median delay until first treatment was 3.83 years (Blanco et al., 2013).

It is often difficult for providers-in-training to understand the experiences of someone with an addiction. The following passage, a composite adapted from individual stories found online, is intended to provide an "insider's" perspective on heroin (or other opioid) use. The effects from drugs are subjective; this portrayal is not indicative of every experience with the drug. The composite was adapted from

- https://www.huffingtonpost.com/entry/what-it-feels-like-to-be-an-opioid-addict_us_596fbfd0e4b0aa14ea76d8c4,
- https://www.crossroadstreatmentcenters.com/blog/2017/what-s-it-like-to-be-addicted-to-opiates/,
- https://www.verywellmind.com/what-is-it-like-to-be-addicted-to-heroin-67379,
- https://www.buzzfeed.com/lukelewis/700-words-that-explain-exactly-what-it-feels-like-to-do-hero, and
- https://www.quora.com/How-does-it-feel-to-be-high-on-heroin

Getting High on Heroin and Other Opioids

"What does it feel like to do heroin?" First, by contrast, "uppers" create the most obvious euphoria. For example, if you take Adderall/coke/meth/speed/MDMA, you will get this shining-bright euphoria, self-confidence, energy, and other drug-specific feelings (for meth, you feel as if you are king and, for MDMA, you feel as if you love everyone). However, you owe these drugs back what they delivered to you. After a meth binge, or lots of MDMA use, or staying up all night on coke, you will feel like shit. To an extent, this aspect resembles an alcoholic hangover.

On the other hand, for many people who experiment with heroin, they are underwhelmed (not including IV usage, but most experimenters rarely inject the first time). They just feel good, chill, happy, but they feel as if this spooky drug "heroin" hasn't delivered. They are just mellow. "It has all been a lie," they think. It doesn't make you do stupid shit or stay up all day and hallucinate like amphetamines or coke. It doesn't empty your serotonin like MDMA or give you a hangover like alcohol. People tend just to think "oh, what a lovely drug." The next day they wake up, and everything is normal. No headache or shitty feeling, just a slight afterglow. But heroin sneaks up on you; the "perfect" drug eventually becomes needed by your body, and the dread that follows not having more is a horrible feeling.

Heroin just feels very nice. You just want to lie there and enjoy it. Everything that bothers you is gone, and you feel so happy at the moment, and you don't want it to end. You will *not* notice a psychedelic effect but, instead, just sedation, relaxation, and pure euphoria/bliss. Everything is blissful and beautiful psychologically. You love everything. It is sensual. All your nerves are on fire, and just having someone run their fingers along your skin feels delicious. It isn't sexual really. I think it is merely that the intensity of the experience lends itself to being described that way. It is difficult to orgasm while high on heroin.

Anyone who wants to try heroin, and isn't already wrapped up in the lifestyle, is full of pain. They feel as if they are different from everyone else to the extent that they want to try something that they know will ruin their lives yet don't care. If you or anyone else feel this pain, I will tell you heroin will not make it go away. I promise. Soon enough, all the feelings you feel now, you will feel again—amplified by the fact that this time you really are different, and you now have no one who cares about you, and you now have more fears than before. Heroin was never my problem. I was. Heroin was what I used to fix me, and it didn't work. It never does. If you're wondering how to make your mind shut up and how to numb those pesky feelings, then I have to state a cliché: "Work on them. Talk to others who feel the same or have been through the same." Anyone who tries heroin will end up doing what I just described if they don't die first.

The insidious part is how the drug can hook you. Heroin makes you feel that your problems have disappeared, but, when you come down, they're still there waiting for you. What was once a pleasant drift down on a hang glider becomes a terrifying plane crash. All of this is to say heroin feels ridiculously great, and that's precisely what's wrong with it. One of its most significant effects is the feeling of carelessness, but "responsibly" using heroin requires an extreme degree of carefulness that many people couldn't achieve even if sober. I don't recommend trying it, especially not injecting it. It's seriously addictive for a reason. It's because it is the best feeling ever . . . while it lasts. It's the perfect drug for many, but just too perfect. Anything that's too good to be true usually is. Even if you use it often enough for a few weeks, the downward spiral of heroin addiction takes hold. It's the hardest drug to come off, and the easiest to get addicted to.

I can easily say I've blown over $600,000, maybe more, trying to score heroin. I have also experienced the daily struggle of wanting and needing to use because my body is going into withdrawal. If you begin using, you will need to find a doctor who will prescribe you suboxone or methadone to kill the pain of the horrific withdrawals. Also, the boredom, pain, suffering, and depression that come along with the aftermath is just indescribable. I wouldn't wish this upon my worst enemy. NOBODY will understand what "hanging" from heroin feels like unless you've physically been through it. They will tell you to "tough it out" or you'll get through one day without it . . . you'll be fine, they say. It's an absolute nightmare beyond nightmares.

I've been clean for quite a while now, and I hope I never relapse. I thought I could never become addicted, but I succumbed before I ever knew it. Heroin took over my entire person. I no longer cared about my daughter, my family, my job, or myself. When I quit using and got back to "myself," I appreciated those things 100 times more. Waking up in the morning and not feeling sick or having the need to get high was a huge blessing itself. These are things I can no longer take for granted.

Humanity may *seem* beautiful. On a crowded bus, I just felt love and peace. Heroin is a wonder drug. Heroin is better than everything else. Heroin makes me who I wish I were. Heroin makes life worth living. Heroin is better than everything else. Heroin builds up a tolerance fast. Heroin starts to cost more money. I need heroin to feel normal. I don't love anymore. Now I'm sick. I can't afford the heroin that I need. How did $10 used to get me high? Now I need $100.

For the next 20 plus years, I lived the life of opioid addiction. Becoming homeless, I lived on the streets, slept on the ground, and in homeless shelters. The last time I used an opioid was in 2014. What is the craving like for an opioid? Imagine you haven't eaten for 3 or 4 days. You are starving. Can you feel it? What it's like to be really starving? What would you be thinking about? You would be thinking about food. You would be needing, craving food. Now, let's go further. Let's say that food is restricted because of famine or government control. All that exists is a black market for food, but the food remains scarce and expensive. What would you do if you were starving? Would you break the law? Would you steal to eat and to live?

This craving for food is measured in days, but the craving for opioids is measured in hours. Four to 5 hours after your last use you begin to "starve." And you crave. Everything but your need for these opioids falls away. You begin to focus solely on what you need to do to survive. You don't have a choice. You really don't. The word "desperate" describes you and every fiber of your being. Without the drug, you will believe you're dying. The desperation leads you to do things that you know are wrong. For example, if you became desperate for water (e.g., stranded in the desert for days), you would drink out of a dirty toilet to survive. You do these things knowing that it is not *who* you are. In the middle of this addiction, you cannot understand why you are hurting the people you love. Consequently, you cannot explain it to others. It can rip a family apart.

Opioid addiction often results from feeling psychological or physical pain. For individuals who must rely on pain medication to merely get out of bed or walk across the room, opioid medication is both a lifesaver and a shackle. If sufficient tolerance develops and the pain medication stops working, they might find themselves bedridden and unable to move without agony if they don't see another solution that works.

[Another user is trying to stop using heroin.] Well, I have tried for many years now. I have been to prison 15 times, and, each time I come out, clean, I still use again. Why? I feel nothing I have ever experienced compares in the slightest, nothing in my life feels like it is worth giving up heroin; there is no sense of hope at the end of the tunnel. It's just too difficult to stop. Imagine feeling good about yourself, but, when you wake up, everything has changed, life is shit again until you have a bag of gear [heroin]. Even when taking medication like methadone or Subutex, all you can think about is how to get your hands on more money to "score"—even though you don't need it, you don't feel ill, you just want heroin. Life is empty without heroin; there is nothing that acts as a suitable replacement, nothing to make you look forward. You look at yourself in the mirror and realize how skinny and ugly you are. The road to making it right seems overwhelming. You just think to yourself, "screw it," and carry on taking more drugs.

I have lost everything due to this shit, or my lack of restraint. I'm not allowed to see my 4-year-old son. My family can't even look at me anymore. I walk with my head down all the time; my life feels worthless without the pursuit of money for drugs by stealing. I wake up every day and think I don't want this life anymore: scoring, and then stealing to score more. I look at the Subutex—it is meant to help you change and stop using, yet all I want is a hit of "gear." I don't inject it, just smoke it. I am here about to take two 8-mg tablets of Subutex and all I can think is, "Why should I take them?" Once I do, I cannot do heroin for at least 16 hours because Subutex blocks the effects of the gear. Heroin provides you a feeling of everything is okay, nothing is that bad, and everything can wait until tomorrow. Without it, life is shit.

Fentanyl is very much stronger milligram for milligram, but, despite being stronger, it lacks a certain enjoyable feeling that most other opiates have. And it doesn't last long, so, if many other addicted people or I could choose an opiate to fix up with, I would pick uncut heroin or morphine any day to shoot up over fentanyl. It is very easy to overdose on fentanyl, and the withdrawals also start faster and are often worse. However, douchebags continue to make and sell it.

Diagnostic and Assessment Considerations

Opioid-related disorders are found on pages 540–550 of *DSM-5* (APA, 2013) and include OUD, opioid intoxication, opioid withdrawal, other opioid-induced disorders, and unspecified opioid-related disorder. As is true for other substance disorders contained in *DSM-5*, in contrast to DSM-IV, a diagnosis distinguishing between *substance abuse* and *substance dependence* no longer occurs. Instead, a substance disorder is diagnosed by severity (i.e., by the number of diagnosable symptoms) as follows: (a) *mild*: 2 to 3, (b) *moderate*: 4 to 5, or (c) *severe*: 6 or more. *DSM-5* includes 11 listed criteria with two specifiers.

The overall diagnostic criteria for OUD is "a problematic pattern of opioid use leading to clinically significant impairment or distress, as manifested by at least two of the following, occurring within a 12-month period" (APA, 2013, p. 541). The specific criteria include (a) loss of control over use, (b) continued desire or inability to reduce use, (c) much time is spent trying to obtain opioids, use it, or recover from it, (d) cravings or a strong desire to use opioids, (e) recurring use results in failure to fulfill obligations at work, school, or at home, (f) continuing use despite persistent or recurring problems socially and/or interpersonally, (g) social, occupational, or recreational activities are stopped or reduced because of use, (h) continuing use in situations where it is physically dangerous, (i) continuing use despite having a persistent or recurrent psychological or physical problem in which opioids caused or exasperated the condition, (j) tolerance, expressed as either a need for increasing amounts of opioids or diminished effect from continuing use of the same amount of opioids, and (k) withdrawal, expressed as the opioid withdrawal diagnosis (begins on page 547) or opioid or another related substance is taken to relieve or avoid symptoms of withdrawal.

As noted earlier, there are two specifiers for this diagnosis. You can specify if the condition is an early remission, meaning between 3 months and 12 months, or in sustained remission, which requires 12 months or longer. You can also specify if the individual is on maintenance therapy such as methadone or buprenorphine. See Table 11.1 for DSM and ICD codes.

Rastegar and Fingerhood (2016) wrote that the diagnosis of SUDs was based on having at least two of 11 criteria that can be divided into four groups or clusters. These are summarized as follows:

Group I: impaired control

1. Substance use in larger amounts or over a longer period than was originally intended.
2. Persistent desire to cut down on use or multiple unsuccessful attempts at cutting down or stopping use.
3. A great deal of time spent using a substance or recovering from its effects.
4. Intense desire to use or craving for the substance.

Group II: social impairment

5. Substance use resulting in failure to fulfill obligations at work, school, or home.
6. Substance use causing or exacerbating interpersonal problems.
7. Important social, occupational, or recreational activities given up or reduced due to substance use.

Group III: risky use

8. Recurrent use of a substance in physically hazardous situations.
9. Continued use despite negative physical or psychological consequences.

Group IV: pharmacological dependence

10. Tolerance to the effects of the substance.
11. Withdrawal symptoms with cessation of the substance. (pp. 7–8)

In the World Health Organization;s *International Classification of Diseases, Version 10* (ICD-10), "mental and behavioral disorders" begin with the letter F, whereas those due to "psychoactive substance use" begin with F10–F19. Then each drug is further categorized according to the person's involvement with it as follows: acute intoxication (F1x.0), harmful use (F1x.1), or dependence syndrome (F1x.2) (Rastegar & Fingerhood, 2016).

Diagnosis and assessment may require drug testing, which should be done openly to avoid undermining the client's trust (Rastegar & Fingerhood, 2016). Urine testing is the most frequently

TABLE 11.1 DSM and ICD Codes

DSM Code	Number of Symptoms Required	ICD-10	ICD-11
305.50	Mild: 2 or 3 symptoms	F11.10	6C43*
304.00	Moderate: 4 or 5 symptoms	F11.20	6C43*
304.00	Severe: 6 or more symptoms	F11.20	6C43*

*The opioid codes in ICD-11 mostly begin with 6C43 but are then further distinguished by the presence of the following (this is a partial list providing codes an addiction counselor will be most likely to use. There are specific codes for the different drugs in the opioid class such as heroin. The complete list of codes for specific opioid drugs and co-occurring medical conditions can be found at https://icd.who.int/ct11_2018/icd11_mms/en/release#/):

#	Specific Entity	Specific ICD-11 Code
1	Opioid-induced delirium	6C43.5
2	Harmful pattern of use of opioids, unspecified	6C43.1Z
3	Opioid dependence, unspecified	6C43.2Z
4	*Cannabis* intoxication	6C43.3
5	Opioid withdrawal	6C43.4
6	Opioid-induced psychotic disorder	6C43.6
7	Other opioid-induced disorders	6C43.7
	Opioid-induced mood disorder	6C43.70
	Opioid-induced anxiety disorder	6C43.71
8	Disorders due to use of opioids, unspecified	6C43.Z
9	Hazardous use of opioids	QE11.0
10	Opioid dependence, current use	6C43.20
11	Other specified disorders due to use of opioids	6C43.Y
12	Single episode of harmful use of opioids	6C43.0
13	Harmful pattern of use of opioids, episodic	6C43.10
14	Harmful pattern of use of opioids, continuous	6C43.11
15	Opioid dependence, early full remission	6C43.21
16	Opioid dependence, sustained partial remission	6C43.22
17	Opioid dependence, sustained full remission	6C43.23
18	Harmful effects of drugs, medicaments, or biological substances, not elsewhere classified (includes harmful effects of opioids or related analgesics)	NE60
19	Unintentional exposure to or harmful effects of opioids or related analgesics	PB20
20	Intentional self-harm by exposure to or harmful effects of opioids or related analgesics	PC90
21	Intentional self-harm by exposure to or harmful effects of psychostimulants (includes intentional overdose of opioid receptor antagonists)	PC92
22	Unintentional exposure to or harmful effects of psychostimulants (includes unintentional exposure to or harmful effects of opioid receptor antagonists)	PB22
23	Assault by exposure to or harmful effects of opioids or related analgesics	PE80
24	Assault by exposure to or harmful effects of psychostimulants (includes assault by exposure to or harmful effects of opioid receptor antagonists)	PE82
25	Intentional self-harm by exposure to or harmful effects of analgesics, antipyretics, or nonsteroidal anti-inflammatory drugs (includes intentional self-poisoning by and exposure to nonopioid analgesics, antipyretics, and antirheumatics)	PC94
26	Exposure to or harmful effects of undetermined intent of opioids or related analgesics	PH40
27	Family history of mental or behavioral disorder (includes family history of conditions classifiable as mental or behavioral disorders due to use of opioids)	QC65
28	Exposure to or harmful effects of undetermined intent of psychostimulants (includes harmful effects of or exposure to noxious substances, drugs, medicaments or biological substances, psychostimulants, opioid receptor antagonists, undetermined intent)	PH42
29	Drugs, medicaments, or biological substances associated with injury or harm in therapeutic use (includes drugs, medicaments, or biological substances associated with injury or harm in therapeutic use, analgesics, antipyretics or anti-inflammatory drugs, opioids or related analgesics)	PL00

used method to detect recent drug use. When a thorough and honest assessment of drug use is not undertaken, misdiagnoses are "alarmingly common" (Earleywine, 2016, p. 14). The American Society of Addiction Medicine (ASAM; Rastegar & Fingerhood, 2016) looks AT six criteria to assess patients' drug involvement:

1. Acute intoxication and/or withdrawal potential.
2. Biomedical conditions and complications.
3. Emotional, behavioral, or cognitive conditions and complications.
4. Readiness to change.
5. Relapse, continued use, or continued problem potential.
6. Recovery/living environment. (p. 37)

Following diagnosis and assessment, ASAM (Rastegar & Fingerhood, 2016) determines the required treatment for patients. Their four choices include the following: (a) outpatient treatment, (b) intensive outpatient treatment or partial hospitalization, (c) residential treatment, or (d) intensive inpatient treatment.

Differential Diagnosis

DSM-5 noted that individuals with OUD often develop opioid-induced disorders. These induced disorders might resemble primary mental disorders such as depression and persistent depressive disorder (i.e., dysthymia). Nonetheless, compared to other drugs of abuse, opioids are likely to produce fewer symptoms of mental disturbance.

Opioid intoxication needs to be distinguished from that caused by alcohol or other depressants (including sedative-hypnotics; see Chapter 13 for a close look at depressants). *DSM-5* also noted that opioid withdrawal is marked by anxiety and restlessness, and this is also seen with those withdrawing from depressants (including sedative-hypnotics). Additionally, opioid withdrawal results in rhinorrhea (i.e., the nasal cavity fills with substantial amounts of mucus) and lacrimation (i.e., the flow of tears), which are *not* seen when withdrawing from sedatives.

The best ways to distinguish intoxication/withdrawal is that those intoxicated on or withdrawing from opioids will have pupil constriction and will respond to naloxone, whereas those intoxicated with alcohol or other depressants will *not* show these indicators. Note, however, that dilated pupils are also observed in hallucinogen intoxication and stimulant intoxication. Consequently, it is important to look for other signs or symptoms of withdrawal from opioids: nausea, vomiting, diarrhea, abdominal cramps, rhinorrhea, or lacrimation.

Comorbidity and Co-Addictions

According to *DSM-5*, the medical conditions that most often co-occur with OUD are viral infections (e.g., HIV, hepatitis C virus) and bacterial infections. This is especially true of those opioid users who inject. Opioid users are at risk for developing mild to moderate depression (i.e., dysthymia and in some cases major depressive disorder).

Polysubstance use is common among addicted individuals and is likely involved in most opioid overdose deaths (Dupont, 2018). Heroin and NMPOU are often comorbid (Salani et al., 2016). Opioid users also often use tobacco, with possible comorbid rates of 95% (Saxon & McCance-Katz, 2016); nonmedical benzodiazepines, 93% (Mateu-Gelabert et al., 2017); cannabis, 46.5% (Fuster et al., 2017); and cocaine, 30–60% (Stauffer et al., 2016). Hepatitis C virus is another risk factor for individuals who inject drugs; one study found that 34% of opioid-dependent patients in medication-assisted therapy (MAT) had chronic infection (Schulte et al., 2015).

NMPOU is commonly comorbid with chronic pain, depression, and anxiety disorders (Brady, McCauley, & Back, 2016; Wilson et al., 2018). It is also associated with posttraumatic stress disorder (PTSD), especially among women (Hassan, Foll, Imtiaz, & Rehm, 2017; Smith, Smith, Cercone, McKee, & Homish, 2016); borderline, schizotypal and antisocial personality disorders (Kerridge et al., 2015); mood disorders (Martins et al., 2012); and attachment avoidance (Andersen, 2012). Obsessive-compulsive disorder (OCD) has been found to be commonly comorbid among opioid-dependent women with a history of childhood sexual abuse (Peles et al., 2014). Heroin users are likely to have comorbid attention deficit hyperactivity disorder (ADHD; Liao et al., 2017), and binge eating disorder and food addiction have been shown to be more prevalent among male patients with heroin use disorder than in controls (Canan, Karaca, Sogucak, Gecici, & Kuloglu, 2017). Lastly, around 20% of methadone maintenance patients aged 50 or older identify as pathological gamblers (Engel & Rosen, 2015).

Available Measures

There are several measures available that can be used for assessing substance abuse. The National Institute on Drug Abuse (2018) provides a link to many evidence-based screening tools and resource materials. Because they update this list periodically, the link may change over time. Counselors are advised to search in Google for "Chart of Evidence-Based Screening Tools for Adults and Adolescents." The Network of Alcohol and Other Drugs Agencies (Deady, 2009) created a 225-page document that reviewed assessment and outcome measures for drug and alcohol settings that contains many useful assessment instruments. The document is available for free on the Internet (see the reference list for details). Following is a list of a few available measures, some of which are contained in the webpages alluded to previously (note that the first 13 measures are also included in Chapter 13):

1. Alcohol, Smoking and Substance Involvement Screening Test (ASSIST; WHO ASSIST Working Group, 2002). This questionnaire is used via face-to-face interaction with a client. It includes only seven questions, of which six are scored. This brief measure shows a good ability to discriminate among use, abuse, and dependence (Asbridge, Duff, Marsh, & Erickson, 2014). Available from http://apps.who.int/iris/bitstream/10665/44320/1/9789241599382_eng.pdf
2. Severity of Dependence Scale (SDS; Gossop et al., 1995). Measures several substances. A five-question screening tool looks at use over the past 3 months. Better used for longitudinal follow-up in quantitative studies than for individual use with clients. Available from http://www.emcdda.europa.eu/attachements.cfm/att_7364_EN_english_sds.pdf

3. Car, Relax, Alone, Forget, Friends, Trouble Inventory. "The CRAFFT is a behavioral health screening tool for use with children under the age of 21 and is recommended by the American Academy of Pediatrics' Committee on Substance Abuse for use with adolescents" (p. 4, https://s21151.pcdn.co/wp-content/uploads/2016/11/LSC-Crafft-Screening-Tool-Kit-2017.pdf). The CRAFT and instructions for use are available from https://www.integration.samhsa.gov/clinical-practice/sbirt/adolescent_screening,_brieft_intervention_and_referral_to_treatment_for_alcohol.pdf.

4. Timeline Followback Method Assessment (TLFB). Earleywine (2016) wrote that this is an informative assessment of drug use that has proven itself to be reliable and valid over long periods in many studies. This assessment can be administered by an interviewer, self-administered, or administered by a computer. The timeline of use is within the last 7 days to 2 years before the interview date. The TLFB can be downloaded from https://cde.drugabuse.gov/instrument/d89c8e23-16e5-625a-e040-bb89ad43465d

5. Inventory of Drug Use Consequences (InDUC-2L). This is a self-report questionnaire focused on the adverse consequences of drug use across several domains. It can be useful to have clients complete this to be later reviewed and discussed as part of the assessment process (Earleywine, 2016). This questionnaire and several other worthwhile assessment tools are available at no cost to counselors from the Center on Alcoholism, Substance Abuse, and Addictions (CASAA) located in New Mexico at http://casaa.unm.edu/Instruments

6. Brief Situational Confidence Questionnaire (BSCQ). In this questionnaire, clients report their confidence and sense of self-efficacy in their ability to resist alcohol and/or drug use. It is available from Nova Southeastern University at http://www.nova.edu/gsc/forms/appendix_d_brief_situational_confidence_questionnaire.pdf

7. Readiness Ruler (Rollnick, Miller, & Butler, as cited in Earleywine, 2016). The Readiness Ruler allows clients to rate their readiness to change along a continuum. A version of this that includes a description of the stages of change model is available from Zimmerman, Olsen, and Bosworth (2000) and can be accessed from https://www.aafp.org/afp/2000/0301/p1409.html

8. Drug Abuse Screening Test (DAST). There is a 20-item DAST-20 available for adults and a separate one for adolescents. There is also a DAST-10 that includes only 10 items.

   Harvey Skinner from York University created the DAST. A limitation of the questionnaire is that the content is obvious and clients can easily fake their results on it. The three versions of the questionnaire can be found at http://www.emcdda.europa.eu/attachements.cfm/att_61480_EN_DAST%202008.pdf

9. APA's online assessment measures. The American Psychiatric Association offers several questionnaires at no cost that can help mental health practitioners with their assessments (go to https://www.psychiatry.org/psychiatrists/practice/dsm/educational-resources/assessment-measures#Disorder). See the *DSM-5* Self-Rated Level 1 Cross-Cutting Symptom Measures (adult, ages 6–17, or ages 11–17) to get a general diagnostic picture of an individual or the specific measure for substance use in each age category. Quoted from the webpage:

   The APA is offering several "emerging measures" in Section III of *DSM–5*. These patient assessment measures were developed to be administered at the initial patient interview and to monitor treatment progress, thus serving to advance the use of initial symptomatic status and patient-reported outcome (PRO) information, as well as the use of "anchored" severity assessment instruments. Instructions, scoring information, and interpretation guidelines are included. Clinicians and researchers may provide APA with feedback on the instruments' usefulness in characterizing patient status and improving patient care (para. 1).

   About the Measures

   These measures should be used to enhance clinical decision-making and not as the sole basis for making a clinical diagnosis. Further information on these measures can be found in *DSM–5*. (p. 1)

10. American Society of Addiction Medicine (ASAM) criteria. ASAM created its criteria from a collaboration that began in the 1980s. The society reports that it is the most widely used and comprehensive set for clients with addiction issues. The criteria are required in over 30 states. The ASAM criteria use six dimensions for service planning and treatment across services and levels of care. These dimensions include (a) acute intoxication and/or withdrawal potential, (b) biomedical conditions and complications, (c) emotional, behavioral, or cognitive conditions and complications, (d) readiness to change, (e) relapse, continued to use, or continued problem potential, and (f) recovery/living environment. There is a cost associated with the materials needed for the ASAM criteria. These can be purchased from https://www.asam.org/resources/the-asam-criteria. Based on several studies, Miller (2016) concluded that the ASAM criteria have failed at matching clients to levels of treatment intensity. Instead, he advocates that individuals should "make informed choices from a menu of evidence-based options" (p. 94).

11. Substance Abuse Subtle Screening Inventory (SASSI). According to the website (https://www.sassi.com/), the SASSI is a brief psychological questionnaire, available in both adult and adolescent versions, that can identify people with an SUD with a high degree of accuracy. There is a fee for this instrument. When I attended an addictions session at the American Counseling Association conference in 2017, several participants said that they used this questionnaire. Its reported empirically tested accuracy is between 93% and 94% (according to https://pubs.niaaa.nih.gov/publications/AssessingAlcohol/InstrumentPDFs/66_SASSI.pdf).

12. Structured Clinical Interview for *DSM-5* (SCID-5). A general interview for diagnosis purposes (available from https://www.amazon.com/Structured-Clinical-Interview-Disorders-Scid-5-cv/dp/1585624616/ref=sr_1_1?ie=UTF8&qid=1513038044&sr=8-1&keywords=structured+clinical+interview+for+dsm-5). There is a cost for this measure.
13. Addiction Severity Index, Version 6 (ASI-6). The ASI is one of the most widely used clinical assessment instruments for individuals with SUDs. It was revised to version 6 in 2006 (McLellan, Cacciola, Alterman, Rikoon, & Carise, 2006), and it has acceptable scalability, reliability, and concurrent validity (Cacciola, Alterman, Habing, & McLellan, 2011; Thylstrup, Bloomfield, & Hesse, 2018). The ASI is administered as a semistructured interview addressing seven problem areas in substance-abusing clients (i.e., medical status, employment and support, drug use, alcohol use, legal status, family/social status, and psychiatric status). It takes a skilled interviewer approximately 1 hour to complete. A modified version (i.e., mASI) is now available that assesses all SUDs and gambling disorders (Denis et al., 2016).
14. Prescription Drug Use Questionnaire (PDUQ). The PDUQ has 42 items and can assist counselors in screening for SUDs with patients prescribed opioids for chronic pain (see https://www.ncbi.nlm.nih.gov/pmc/articles/PMC2630195/). There is also a 31-item version that clients can complete (see https://www.jpsmjournal.com/article/S0885-3924(08)00202-9/pdf).
15. Screener and Opioid Assessment for Patients with Pain (SOAPP). This 14-item self-report measure helps counselors decide how much a client on long-term opioid treatment should be monitored. The measure is available for free along with the administration and scoring instructions from http://www.nhms.org/sites/default/files/Pdfs/SOAPP-14.pdf. The revised SOAP-R is a 24-item questionnaire (details at https://www.ncbi.nlm.nih.gov/pmc/articles/PMC2359825/).
16. Other questionnaires that measure misuse in those prescribed opioids for chronic pain include the (a) Current Opioid Misuse Measure (COMM), a 17-item questionnaire (available from https://www.opioidprescribing.com/documents/09-comm-inflexxion.pdf); (b) the 20-item Addiction Behaviors Checklist (ABC; details at https://www.jpsmjournal.com/article/S0885-3924(06)00441-6/fulltext); and (c) the eight-item Prescription Opioid Misuse Index (POMI; details at http://www.wehavins.com/wp-content/uploads/2017/12/POMI-test-article-probably-the-best-1.pdf).

Clinical Interview Questions

Note that these same questions are also suggested in Chapter 13, albeit modified to be specific to opioid use. The modified CAGE (remember the original CAGE is a four-item test used to assess alcohol problems) can be asked as questions to help assess drug addiction:

1. Have you ever thought you should Cut down on your opioid use?
2. Have you ever felt Annoyed when people have commented on your opioid use?
3. Have you ever felt Guilty or badly about your opioid use?
4. Have you ever used opioids to Ease withdrawal symptoms or to avoid feeling low after using? (Melemis, 2018, para. 3)

Johns Hopkins University developed a self-test to identify alcohol use disorder, which was adapted to include drugs as well as alcohol. The questions include

1. Do you lose time from work due to opioid use?
2. Is opioid use making your home life unhappy?
3. Do you use opioids because you are shy with other people?
4. Is opioid use affecting your reputation?
5. Have you ever felt remorse after using opioids?
6. Have you gotten into financial difficulties as a result of your opioid use?
7. Do you turn to lower companions and an inferior environment when using opioids?
8. Does your opioid use make you careless of your family's welfare?
9. Has your ambition decreased since using opioids?
10. Do you crave opioids at a definite time daily?
11. Do you want opioids the next morning?
12. Does your opioid use cause you to have difficulties in sleeping?
13. Has your efficiency decreased since using opioids?
14. Is your opioid use jeopardizing your job or business?
15. Do you use opioids to escape from worries or troubles?
16. Do you use opioids alone?
17. Have you ever had a complete loss of memory?
18. Has your physician ever treated you for opioid use?
19. Do you use opioids to build your self-confidence?
20. Have you ever been in a hospital or institution on account of opioid use? (AddictScience.com, n.d., p. 1)

Below are a few common questions that can be asked:

1. Do you feel you must consume opioids to get through your day?
2. Have you ever sought medical attention because of your opioid use?

3. Has your performance at school, work, or home been affected by your opioid consumption?
4. Do you constantly think about the next time you will use opioids?
5. Has your opioid use interfered or caused problems with your personal relationships?
6. Have you suffered from memory loss after using opioids?
7. Do you experience withdrawal symptoms after not consuming opioids for an extended period?
8. Do you go to extensive lengths to obtain opioids?
9. Do you remain intoxicated for several days at a time?
10. Do you say or do things while high that you later regret when not high? (adapted from Laplante, 2018, p. 1)

Generic Names and Street "Lingo"

Common names for opioids, including narcotics, opiates (opium derivatives), narcotic analgesics, and opioid analgesics (Csiernik, 2016). The most abused opioids have their slang terms as well:

1. Opium: A-bomb (when mixed with cannabis), aunti, Aunti Emma, big O, black pill, Chinese molasses, Chinese tobacco, dreams, dream stick, God's medicine, joy plant, midnight oil, and O.
2. Heroin: Aunt Hazel, bag of gear, Bart Simpson, big H, big Harry, black tar, blue velvet, bobby brown, brown crystal, dust, H, hardball (mixed with cocaine), horse, junk, Mexican Mud, nickel deck, red chicken, scag, smack, speedball (mixed with cocaine), spider.
3. Morphine: dreamer, first line, God's drug, M, Miss Emma, monkey, Mr. Blue, mud, Murphy, and white stuff.
4. Codeine: AC/DC, Captain Cody, Cody, coties, dreamer, fours, nods, schoolboy, sizzurp (a mixture of codeine, antihistamines, Sprite, and dissolved Jolly Rancher candy), and syrup.
5. Fentanyl: Apache, China girl, Chinatown, dance fever, friend, goodfella, great bear, jackpot, king ivory, murder 8, Tango and Cash, and TNT (Csiernik, 2016).

Neuroscience

Opioid addiction has been conclusively linked to neither the dopaminergic system nor any opioid receptor (Hancock et al., 2015; Thiruchselvam, Malik, & Le Foll, 2017). However, it is likely that the endogenous opioid system plays a leading role. This system consists of the mu, kappa, and delta opioid receptors along with endorphins, the brain's "natural narcotics" (Maté, 2008; Reed, Butelman, & Kreek, 2017). Opioids mimic endorphins by acting on opioid receptors that trigger dopamine discharge (Maté, 2008; Rastegar & Fingerhood, 2016). When used long-term, opioids cause a relative endorphin deficiency, which contributes to users' craving for more (Reed et al., 2017).

Opioids permanently change brain biochemistry and may also affect cell development and structure (Csiernik, 2016). One study of opioid-addicted individuals demonstrated that healthy controls outperformed the addicted group in an acquired equivalence task as memory load grew (Myers et al., 2017). The authors suggested that opioid users may have basal ganglia dysfunction, which would impact their learning and memory. Also, drug addiction, in general, has been linked to dysfunctions in the orbitofrontal cortex, which makes drug users more prone to maladaptive decisions (Maté, 2008).

Opioid-addicted individuals have lower striatal dopamine transporter (DAT) levels than healthy controls, which may be linked to novelty-seeking behavior and cognitive flexibility (Liang et al., 2017). One study found heroin-addicted individuals to have about 15% lower DAT levels in the striatum than in healthy controls (Xu et al., 2017), and the decreased levels persist even after abstinence (Yuan et al., 2017). Chronic heroin abuse results in impairments in brain activity, particularly in attentional processing, brain response inhibition, cortical plasticity, and the nucleus accumbens function network, the latter of which remains even after 3 years of abstinence (Motlagh et al., 2016; Zou et al., 2015).

Genes that may factor into opioid and heroin addictions are ZNF804A, which has been linked to decision-making and gray matter volume in heroin-dependent individuals (Sun et al., 2016), and OPRD1 (Sharafshah et al., 2017). Opioid addiction is associated with decreased levels of neuropeptide Y as well as alpha-5 receptor levels in the nucleus accumbens (Goncalves, Martins, Baptista, Ambrosio, & Silva, 2016; Lingford-Hughes et al., 2016). Lastly, a longer duration of heroin dependence is associated with increased levels of various humoral immunologic indicators such as IgA, IgG, IgM, and complement component 3 (Simonovska et al., 2016).

Physical Impacts (Long-Term Use)

Opioids have both a high physical and psychological dependence liability (Csiernik, 2016), and long-term abstinence is uncommon (Rastegar & Fingerhood, 2016). Using opioids regularly and for an extended period will cause physical dependence in the user, including tolerance to the drugs' effects—except for constipation and miosis (i.e., constricted pupils)—and withdrawal symptoms when the drug is discontinued (Rastegar & Fingerhood, 2016). Tolerance develops within days of continued use but not when administered intermittently (Csiernik, 2016).

Csiernik (2016) described opioid withdrawal as follows:

> Withdrawal from opioids, which may begin as early as a few hours after the last administration, produces uneasiness, chills, nausea and vomiting, stomach cramps and diarrhea, insomnia, fever, irritability, restlessness, excessive sweating, and crawling skin sensations known as paresthesia. (pp. 127–128)

The pain of opioid withdrawal, and especially heroin withdrawal, can be as severe as that experienced by people with bone cancer. Symptoms peak after 2–5 days and then gradually diminish over 7–10 days (Csiernik, 2016). In comparison to other drug addictions, opioid withdrawal is rarely life-threatening (Milkman & Sunderwirth, 2010).

The most severe complication of opioid use is overdose (Rastegar & Fingerhood, 2016). Opioid overdose is characterized by depressed levels of consciousness, decreased respiration, and constricted pupils. One study of San Francisco heroin users found that 40% had at least one overdose in the past, whereas 68% of an Australian cohort of heroin users experienced at least one overdose (Rastegar & Fingerhood, 2016). Another study of 615 heroin users in Australia found that 52.8% of deaths were caused by overdose (Darke et al., 2016). Alarmingly, many heroin users who died of an overdose in America from 2010 to 2014 had administered an amount that would not have been expected to be fatal for those drug-experienced individuals (Siegel, 2016).

For injection users, HIV was a significant cause of mortality until 1996, when hepatitis C took its place (Rastegar & Fingerhood, 2016). Endocarditis, or inflammation of the heart's inner lining, is another serious complication of injection drug use. One study estimated the incidence rate to be seven cases per 1000 person-years (Rastegar & Fingerhood, 2016).

Infants of mothers who used opioids during pregnancy may be born opioid-dependent and experience withdrawal at birth (Rastegar & Fingerhood, 2016). One study of 131 mother–infant pairs found the prevalence of neonatal abstinence syndrome to be 8.7%, primarily from illicit opioids and/or methadone (McQueen, Murphy-Oikonen, & Desaulniers, 2015). Some studies suggest that children born to mothers with opioid addiction suffer from long-term cognitive development impairment, although it is not certain how opioids affect the developing infant brain (Peltz & Anand, 2015). Although opioids do not appear to cause congenital disabilities, methadone may cause lower birth weight and smaller head circumference (Rastegar & Fingerhood, 2016).

As mentioned previously, chronic opioid use causes cognitive deficits including poor cognitive flexibility, diminished impulse control, and impaired information processing (Liang et al., 2017; Wang, Kydd, & Russell, 2015). Opioid-addicted individuals tend to "chase rewards" more than controls, meaning they are less likely to repeat prior successful responses when expectancies are violated (Myers et al., 2016). Heroin users are particularly biased toward immediate gratification and have a reduced sensitivity to the optimality of a decision (Scherbaum, Haber, Morley, Underhill, & Moustafa, 2018). They also demonstrate increased impulsivity (Jones, Vadhan, Luba, & Comer, 2016).

Opioid users' decision-making deficits seem to persist at least 1.5 years after cessation of use (Biernacki, McLennan, Terrett, Labuschagne, & Rendell, 2016). Their selective deficit in learning from punishment may contribute to their pursuit of drug use even at the cost of adverse consequences (Myers et al., 2017). Sleep disturbances also persist after abstinence (Ara, Jacobs, Bhat, & McCall, 2016) and may in turn increase cravings for the drug (Lydon-Staley et al., 2017).

Other long-term effects of heroin and other opioids include pulmonary complications, constipation, menstrual irregularities in women, and reduction in reproductive hormone levels in both men and women (Csiernik, 2016). Ironically, long-term opioid misuse may cause hyperalgesia, or increased sensitivity to pain (Wachholtz, Foster, & Cheatle, 2015). It can also increase the risk of depression recurrence (Scherrer et al., 2016) as well as the risk of suicide (Ilgen et al., 2016).

Mental, Emotional, and Spiritual Impacts

One positive aspect of opioids is their powerful mood-enhancing and anxiety-relieving effects, although these decrease with tolerance (Csiernik, 2016). A study of 60 individuals entering substance abuse treatment facilities found that heroin users were more satisfied with living arrangements and had less previous criminal justice involvement than other users (Perkins & Shannon, 2016). In patients with chronic pain, opioids can also have a positive effect on quality of life. One study showed that extended-release hydrocodone improved the patients' general activities, walking, work/daily living, relationships, and enjoyment of life (Hale, Zimmerman, Ma, & Malamut, 2017).

Instead of inducing criminal activity, opioids tend to calm people down (Maté, 2008). However, addicted individuals may become irritable and more likely to act violently during withdrawal, possibly due to higher plasma oxytocin levels (Nikolaou, Kapoukranidou, Ndungu, Floros, & Kovatsi, 2017). In one study of abstinent heroin-dependent patients, oxytocin was linked to aggression (Gerra et al., 2017). The authors of the study suggest that oxytocin promotes defensive and antisocial behaviors when social cues are interpreted as "unsafe." Aggression toward others is also associated with bipolar spectrum disorder in heroin-addicted patients, whereas self-harm is linked to a dual diagnosis of chronic psychosis (Maremmani et al., 2018).

In general, substance users demonstrate elevated rates of alexithymia, or a diminished capacity to identify and/or express their own emotions (Earleywine, 2016). Opioid-addicted individuals also show signs of deficits in emotional and cognitive empathy: they have higher personal distress scores than controls (Stange et al., 2017) and have low empathic concern for others (Tomei, Besson, Reber, Rougemont-Bucking, & Grivel, 2017).

Addiction can have a devastating impact on an addict's spirituality (Stoddart, 2013). Addiction can paralyze a person's moral compass. When addicted individuals have no money and they desperately need drugs, they may participate in immoral and illegal acts. Getting the "fix" is all that matters. Even when addicted individuals quit using, repairing spirituality takes time. The "habit" of immorality is a habit that needs to be broken. Compared to nonaddicts, heroin-addicted individuals are more likely to have experienced family separations and lack "a clearly defined purpose in life" (Coleman, Kaplan, & Downing, 1986, p. 5).

Psychosocial Impacts (Relationships, Career/Work, Legal, Financial)

Drug addiction affects nearly every area of an addict's life. A substantial impact occurs within the families of heroin addicts. As the addiction worsens, relationships are strained and often fail. Heroin alters a person's sense of self and reduces their empathy toward others. People with a history of drug abuse generally face stigmatization from the public, which in turn leads to poorer social functioning (Lang & Rosenberg, 2017; von Hippel et al., 2017).

Although the influence of family factors on the development and/or on the maintenance of heroin addiction remains unclear, research suggests that negative family factors are important throughout heroin addiction (Pomini et al., 2014; Xu, Zhang, Lu, Chen, & Zhao, 2009). Research comparing 70 alcoholics and heroin-addicted individuals with 127 participants in a control group found that narcotic-addicted individuals more commonly reported maternal and paternal overprotection. Furthermore, the narcotic-addicted individuals had more disturbed parenting than the alcoholic group, particularly with their fathers (Bernardi, Jones,

& Tennant, 1989). Another study found that adolescent heroin-addicted individuals displayed more hostility toward their fathers (Jiloha, Agnihotri, & Munjal, 1988).

Over time, the addicted individual typically loses the support of family and friends. Simultaneously, their new friends are often users themselves, thus leading to further entrenchment in the addictive lifestyle. Having support is important to recovery. In one study of 159 participants, addicted individuals maintained on methadone reported that having at least one good friend and a structured daily activity had a positive impact on their quality of life (De Maeyer et al., 2011).

The financial burden caused by heroin addiction is enormous while the addiction itself makes it hard to sustain employment. Consequently, heroin addiction might leave a person homeless and destitute. Most addicted individuals will need to steal to afford their supply. Legal consequences often follow. Because of its exceptionally high dependence potential, heroin, unlike most other drugs, is illegal globally (Csiernik, 2016).

Working With Diverse Populations

Sex Differences

Females are generally more vulnerable to developing drug addictions than men due to higher responsiveness (Fattore, Melis, Fadda, & Fratta, 2014). For example, females with comorbid pain appear to be more susceptible to opioid misuse than their male counterparts because of a lower tolerance for pain (Lin et al., 2015). Women are also more likely than men to report NMPOU along with major depressive episodes, whereas men are more likely to report NMPOU alone (Fink et al., 2015). Also, women experience more of the side effects of heroin than men do (Agabio, Campesi, Pisanu, Gessa, & Franconi, 2016). However, testosterone levels are suppressed in male regular opioid users, whereas they are not affected in females (Bawor et al., 2015).

Although women are more likely to misuse prescription opioids (Hemsing, Greaves, Poole, & Schmidt, 2016), men are more likely to use heroin. One study in Italy found that female heroin users often have psychiatric comorbidity, including depression, self-injury, and suicide attempts (Vigna-Taglianti et al., 2016). The authors also found that females were more likely to be unemployed, better educated, and live with their partner and children than were men. These findings are echoed by another study done in China (Zhou, Li, Wei, Li, & Zhuang, 2017).

Opioid use during pregnancy can cause complications, neonatal withdrawal symptoms, and the sudden death of the infant (Ashraf, Ashraf, Asif, & Basri, 2016). One study of mothers undergoing MMT found that around half had reported ever thinking about suicide and around one fourth had reported past-year ideation (Sarid, Isralowitz, Yehudai, & Reznik, 2016). Also, mothers with an SUD are twice as likely to lose custody of their children (Chopra & Marasa, 2017).

Adolescents and Youth

According to SAMHSA (as cited in Russell, Trudeau & Leland, 2015), fewer than 9% of 12- to 17-year-olds in need receive substance abuse recovery services or other mental health services. Indeed, specific barriers limit the amount of treatment that adolescent addicted individuals can receive, including provider knowledge deficits, limitations in legislation governing opioids, and a lack of evidence supporting treatments options (Rastegar & Fingerhood, 2016; Wenner & Gigli, 2016). A significant percentage of American adolescents experiment with drugs; in particular, around 15%–20% of American adolescents have misused prescription opioids (Hsiao & Walker, 2016; Rajan, Ruggles, Guarino, & Mateu-Gelabert, 2018). Alarmingly, one study of the Nationwide Emergency Department Sample from 2006–2012 showed that most prescription opioid poisonings by adolescents aged 15–17 years were intentional (Tadros, Layman, Davis, Bozeman, & Davidov, 2016).

Psychiatric illnesses tend to precede the onset of any SUD, including opioid abuse (Rastegar & Fingerhood, 2016). NMPOU in adolescents is associated with depressive symptoms as well as nonmedical sedative and stimulant misuse (Edlund et al., 2015; Lin, Walton, Bonar, & Blow, 2016). In one study done in Ohio, the number of opioid prescriptions filled by adults was significantly associated with the number of adolescents seeking treatment for opioid misuse, suggesting that adolescents obtain the prescriptions from the adults in their lives (McKnight et al., 2017).

Adolescents with OUD often use cannabis as well (Zaman, Malowney, Knight, & Boyd, 2015). In a small group of adolescents recovering from opioid addiction at Massachusetts Recovery High Schools, Vosburg et al. (2016) found that 58% of prescription opioid abusers became addicted to them, and many initiated prescription-opioid abuse while under the influence of marijuana.

Youth who begin polysubstance use often attribute the escalation from single substances to peer influence over several years (Russell et al., 2015). Using alcohol, cigarettes, or marijuana (which are generally viewed as less-harmful substances) before the age of 21 increases the risk of using heroin and prescription opioids (Burbage, 2018; Harris, 2016). Austic, McCabe, Stoddard, Ngo, and Boyd (2015) found that 16 years of age is the peak age for starting to use prescription opioids, stimulants, sedatives, and anxiolytics (both medically and nonmedically). Similarly, Parker (2017) found that the peak risk for transitioning from NMPOU initiation to opioid dependence within 12 months is when adolescents are 14–15 years of age.

Other risk factors for opioid misuse among adolescents include sexual orientation, abuse and neglect, gender, and race/ethnicity. Concerning sexual orientation, one study of Chinese adolescents found that sexual minorities and unsure adolescents were at a higher risk of NMPOU (Li et al., 2018). Another study of Chinese senior high school students found that physical, emotional, and sexual abuse or neglect were positively correlated with NMPOU (Lei et al., 2018). In the United States, males with poor school grades (D or F) and females who frequently argued with their parents were about three times more likely than other males and females to have prescription OUD (Prince, 2015).

In comparison to primarily marijuana or alcohol users, adolescent opioid users are more likely to be Caucasian, older, female, and not attending school (Godley et al., 2017; Vaughn, Nelson, Salas-Wright, Qian, & Schootman, 2016). At the same time, NMPOU rates among Caucasian youth have been declining, whereas rates among Hispanic, Black, and other youth of color have persisted or increased (Rajan et al., 2018). Hispanics appear to be nearly twice as likely as Caucasian youth to have NMPOU disorder rather than alcohol or marijuana use disorders (Prince, 2015). Another study found that Black adolescents have the highest prevalence rate of NMPOU compared to other ethnicities (Ford & Rigg, 2015).

Adolescents reporting NMPOU have higher odds of heroin use than those reporting no NMPOU (Yantsides, Tracy, & Skeer, 2017). Heroin use in adolescence is also associated with being male, carrying a weapon in the past 30 days, a history of sexual intercourse, dating violence victimization, and reporting other drug use. Those who initiate NMPOU at ages 10–12 years have the highest risk of transitioning to heroin use (Cerda, Santaella, Marshall, Kim, & Martins, 2015).

Although NMPOU during adolescence is a strong predictor of continued use at age 35, using prescription opioids strictly for medical reasons is not (McCabe, Veliz, & Schulenberg, 2016). Still, half a million children in the United States are affected by chronic postsurgical pain every year, which is a significant risk factor for opioid initiation (Chidambaran et al., 2017). Of a study of 144 adolescents undergoing spine fusion surgery, Chidambaran et al. (2017) found that 41.8% were affected by persistent pain a year after the surgery. In another study, 12.5% of adolescents surveyed at a Level I trauma center were using prescription opioids a full year after their injury hospitalization (Whiteside et al., 2016). Sustained opioid use was linked to preinjury marijuana use.

Although past research suggested that sports participation could predict adolescent illicit opioid use, recent research has contradicted this theory. Schaefer and Petkovsek (2017) found that social learning and low self-control are better predictors of NMPOU than participation in sports. In their study of 12th-graders, Veliz, Boyd, and McCabe (2017) found no differences in NMPOU and/or heroin use among competitive sports participants and nonparticipants. Another study found that, between 1997 and 2014, adolescents who engaged in sports and exercise had lower self-reports of lifetime NMPOU and heroin use compared with those who did not participate in sports or exercise (Veliz, Boyd, & McCabe, 2016). Thus, it appears that sports and exercise act as a buffer to NMPOU.

Race and Ethnicity

U.S.-born individuals in 2013 were substantially more likely than immigrants to be diagnosed with an SUD (Salas-Wright, Vaughh, Clark Goings, Cordova, & Schwartz, 2018). Data from the National Epidemiologic Survey of Alcohol and Related Conditions-III (NESARC-III) suggested that SUD prevalence rates were higher for White participants at younger ages and Black participants at older ages (Vasilenko, Evans-Polce, & Lanza, 2017). From 2004 to 2011, emergency department visits related to nonmedical use of opioid and benzodiazepine prescriptions increased significantly for all three major ethnicities: non-Hispanic Whites, Hispanics, and Blacks (Jones & McAninch, 2015). Overdose deaths increased for all three ethnicities as well. From 2002 to 2015, deaths attributable to synthetic opioids other than methadone increased especially for Black individuals, whereas deaths due to heroin increased especially for non-Hispanic Whites (Kandel, Hu, Griesler, & Wall, 2017).

The heroin epidemic is most associated with White ethnicity. Among NMPO users from 2008 to 2011, the odds of heroin use increased especially among non-Hispanic Whites and Hispanics (Martins, Santaella-Tenorio, Marshall, Maldonado, & Cerda, 2015). Injection abuse (prescription opioid or heroin) is associated with being non-Hispanic White or non-Hispanic other (Jones, Christensen, & Gladden, 2017; Lake et al., 2016). Among females reporting NMPOU in the past 30 days in the National Survey of Drug Use and Health conducted between 2005 and 2014, polysubstance use was highest in non-Hispanic White women and women with lower educational attainment (Jarlenski et al., 2017).

Non-Hispanic White youth reported consistently higher levels of NMPOU than Hispanic and Black youth on the National Survey on Drug Use and Health from 2004 to 2013 (Vaughn et al., 2016). This is contradicted by another study by Ford and Rigg (2015), which concluded that Black youth had the highest prevalence rate of prescription opioid misuse in 2012. Another study found that NMPOU in 2015 persisted or increased among Hispanic, Black, and "other" youth but declined among White youth (Rajan et al., 2018).

An increasing amount of research indicates that racial and ethnic minority groups receive inadequate pain treatment as compared to that obtained by White individuals (Jimenez, 2015). For example, Hispanic ethnicity is associated with premature discharge at 6 months from MMT (Proctor et al., 2015). One study of office-based opioid treatment patients found that Black and Hispanic ethnicity were associated with lower odds of retention in the program after 1 year (Weinstein et al., 2017). This difference in treatment could be due to ethnic bias: In an online virtual-patient study done by Hollingshead (2017), 97 medical students did not report significant explicit ethnic bias but demonstrated implicit preferences for non-Hispanic White patients as compared to Hispanic patients. Approximately one third of the participants made significantly different chronic pain management decisions for both ethnic groups.

White individuals likely have better access to opioids than do those of other ethnicities. For example, one study of nontraumatic dental-related emergency room visits in the United States found that more opioids were prescribed to non-Hispanic Whites than to those of other ethnicities (Okunseri, Dionne, Gordon, Okunseri, & Szabo, 2015). In Vancouver, Canada, Caucasian ethnicity (along with a daily injection of heroin) was associated with decreased time to MMT initiation (Bach et al., 2015). Lastly, one study found that White, educated patients were best able to use office-based buprenorphine treatment, whereas Black or Latino/a low-income patients experienced the treatment as isolating (Hatcher, Mendoza, & Hansen, 2018).

As evident from the preceding paragraph, there has been little research in the United States focused on opioid addiction in Asian or Native American populations. Most studies focus on Hispanic, non-Hispanic White, and Black individuals.

Nonpsychiatric Disabilities

In general, drug use disorders as defined by the *DSM-5* are associated with significant disability (Grant et al., 2016). Opioids are especially linked to physical disabilities due to their painkilling effects. The estimated disability-adjusted life years lost globally to opioid dependence were 9.2 million in 2010 alone, with North America being the region with the highest rate (Degenhardt et al., 2014).

Opioid use is common among disabled Medicare beneficiaries under the age of 65 (Morden et al., 2014). NMPOU is associated with DSM-IV Axis I and II mental disorders and physical conditions such as arteriosclerosis, cardiovascular disease, and arthritis (Katz, El-Gabalaway, Keyes, Martins, & Sareen, 2013). Having early opioid prescriptions for injury hospitalizations is associated with work disability 6 months after the injury (Berecki-Gisolf, Collie, & McClure, 2013). Also, chronic pain patients who experience moderate to extreme pain, or who are high pain catastrophizers, report greater opioid misuse than those who do/are not (Blanco et al., 2016; Lazaridou et al., 2017).

Lesbian, Gay, Bisexual, and Transgender (LGBT)

Most of the available research focuses on heterosexual sex and HIV risk among heroin addicts. That said, there is a body of evidence suggesting that sexual minorities have an unusually high prevalence among substance users (Wallace & Santacruz, 2017). For example, in one study of 128 Black inpatient opiate users, the self-reported rate of same-sex behavior was 10% (Craig, 1987), which is well over the rate in the general population. Sexual minority youth in the United States are more likely to report misuse of prescription opioids and tranquilizers than heterosexual youth (Kecojevic et al., 2012). Also, opioids (primarily heroin) may be used at "circuit parties," which are mainly gay-oriented (Ross & Williams, 2001).

Drug use by injection is often reported by gay and bisexual men in Australia (Lea et al., 2013). Men who have sex with men are especially vulnerable to HIV infection through injection drug use (Johnston et al., 2010).

In Philadelphia, Kecojevic, Corliss, and Lankenau (2015) studied 191 young men who have sex with men and found that those who used opioids did so to facilitate sex with other men by making receptive anal sex less painful. Another motive for using opioids was to cope better with depression, stress management, or everyday hardships.

A study in San Francisco found that a higher percentage of men who have sex with men (24.0%) via injection were HIV-positive as compared to heterosexual males (3.7%) and females (13.0%). Although the heterosexual males and females primarily injected heroin, the men who have sex with men injected mainly methamphetamine (Jin, Huriaux, Loughran, Packer, & Raymond, 2014). Another study in San Francisco found that young injection drug users often experience at least one overdose (48% in their sample; Ochoa, Hahn, Seal, & Moss, 2001).

War Veterans

Veterans experience a high incidence of chronic pain and treatment over extended periods with opioids (Vanderlip et al., 2014). In 2010, 26.4% of active duty service members received at least one prescription for opioids (Jeffery, May, Luckey, Balison, & Klette, 2014). In one cohort study of veterans of Operations Enduring Freedom/Iraqi Freedom/New Dawn, 8.3% received one or more opioid prescriptions (Bastian et al., 2017). Opioid use among Iraq and Afghanistan veterans is generally lower than that of other veterans (Hudson, 2016), yet many of them have still experienced opioid-related overdoses (Bennett, Elliott, Golub, Wolfson-Stofko, & Guarino, 2017). Heroin use may pose a lower risk on the field: Veterans serving in Vietnam had high rates of heroin use (34%) and heroin dependence (20%), but only 1% became re-addicted in the first year after their return to the United States (Hall & Weier, 2017).

Veterans are often given overlapping prescriptions that pose a safety risk. In 2012, 328,398 veterans filled at least 10 opioid prescriptions, and 77% of them also received psychotropic drugs (Barry, Sofuoglu, Kerns, Wiechers, & Rosenheck, 2015). Among VA buprenorphine recipients in 2012, 26% received an overlapping opioid prescription from Medicare Part D (Gellad et al., 2017). Lastly, 10% of pregnant veterans between 2001 and 2010 received Veterans Health Administration (VHA) prescription opioids during their pregnancy window due to psychiatric diagnoses, back problems, or other nontraumatic joint disorders (Kroll-Desrosiers et al., 2016).

OUD—especially NMPOU—among veterans is associated with mental health diagnoses, especially PTSD (Seal et al., 2012), increased risk of suicide (Bohnert, Ilgen, Louzon, McCarthy, & Katz, 2017), increased risk of heroin initiation (Banerjee et al., 2016), and other reintegration problems such as drug and alcohol use disorders, traumatic brain injury, unemployment, and homelessness (Golub & Bennett, 2013). Veterans who receive high numbers (>20) of opioid prescriptions during the year are likely to be diagnosed with metastatic cancer, other medical illnesses, and various forms of pain, drug abuse, alcohol abuse, mood disorders, and anxiety (Petrakis, Sofuoglu, & Rosenheck, 2015).

Research suggests that veterans tend to underestimate their risk for opioid overdose (Wilder et al., 2016), and they may be uninformed about treatment options such as naloxone (Tiffany, Wilder, Miller, & Winhusen, 2016). Only 8% of VHA patients with alcohol or opioid dependence received detoxification in the fiscal year 2013 (Timko, Gupta, Schultz, & Harris, 2016). The odds of receiving pharmacotherapy for OUD are even lower for prison-involved veterans (Finlay et al., 2016).

Medications and Other Relevant Physical Interventions

The American government's response to the opioid crisis has been to expand the availability of opioid maintenance treatment (OMT) (Littrell, 2017). Buprenorphine products (namely a buprenorphine and naloxone combination) and methadone are the primary forms of MAT authorized for opioids addiction in the United States (McElrath, 2018). Although it has been believed that adding naloxone to buprenorphine helps to decrease its abuse potential (Chang & Chen, 2018), a study of 3455 opioid-addicted individuals in Western Australia between 2001 and 2010 did *not* support the contention that adding naloxone improves the safety profile of buprenorphine (Kelty, Cumming, Troeung, & Hulse, 2018).

Methadone is a synthetic narcotic that binds with opioid receptors in the brain, thereby blocking heroin molecules to the same binding sites (Maté, 2008). Methadone is a full agonist (Rastegar & Fingerhood, 2016). When taken orally, however, it does not create a "high" in chronic opioid users (Earleywine, 2016; Maté, 2008). Naltrexone is an opioid antagonist, meaning that it blocks the effect of opioids (Rastegar & Fingerhood, 2016). Naloxone is also an opioid antagonist, and it can prevent fatal outcomes when administered promptly (McDonald, Campbell, & Strang, 2017). Naloxone begins working within 30 seconds of injection, whereas naltrexone has a much longer duration of action (Csiernik, 2016). Buprenorphine is a medication that has both partial agonist and antagonistic properties (Earleywine, 2016).

INSIDE AN ADDICTED PERSON'S MIND

Brandon, Age 37

People look at me as though I've always been this way, and that bothers me. Most turn away to avoid eye contact. I believe it keeps them in denial from knowing that people are struggling this much in life. You see, even though I'm lying with my sleeping bag and other worldly possessions in the entrance of another nameless store, I *have* a name, and it is Brandon. No one stops even to ask my name. Just another heroin addict, they think, as they gleefully walk by pretending that we live in different universes of existence.

Like I implied, I wasn't always this way. I started likely the same as you with dreams and aspirations and hopes for an unpredictable future. I've always seen myself as a bit of an intellectual. I try to make sense of why people treat each other the way that they do. Please don't ask me about my family of origin because I *am* going to tell you if you stop ever to listen. My dad was a construction worker who hit the bottle hard every night while my mother went out to her "night job" to make extra money to pay for our family of six. I have no contact with my three siblings. They have no idea what happened to me, and I have no idea about them either. My dad was physically and emotionally abusive, but I suppose, if I had children, I would likely end up following in his footsteps. I thought about that lots of times. The idea bothers me a great deal.

The hardest part of coming out of a heroin binge is facing the stark reality in front of you. There you are, possibly alone, possibly with one or more others, but, regardless, you still wake up alone. If I had a mirror, my reflection alone would make me want to inject again. There is nothing happy in my face. The only happiness shoots in my veins as often as I can get my hands on the next fix.

Remember, I see the way that you look at me. You think I am a pathetic excuse for a human being. Do you think that I have not tried? I was on methadone for 3 years, and that was the hardest 3 years of my life. It wasn't just the side effects from the methadone, but it was like the k. d. lang song, "Constant Craving," repeatedly playing in my head. All I could think about every time I got my methadone was that this would prevent me from shooting the dream [heroin]. You see, a heroin-addicted individual never gets tired of dreaming; it's reality that sucks. I cannot imagine that you could understand how the craving drives an addicted individual to be like a maniac at times. I mean, at least until the craving is satisfied. Then harps play, and sweet bliss takes over for the next few hours. But the harps always stop playing.

Methadone was helpful in one way: it showed me how truly pathetic and worthless I really am. I tried working a job, but any little criticism was like a bomb dropping on me, reminding me of how my dad would scream while beating me senseless at the same time. I became dysfunctional, and I would get fired from jobs because you are not allowed to shut down completely, frozen like a child knowing abuse will follow the minor criticism. My last job was at McDonald's, and my boss yelled at me because I wasn't getting the burgers out fast enough. I froze in front of him. He didn't ask why; he just said "you are done here."

I can no longer see a future. A slow suicide seems like the only option. But every time I get high, I think that maybe, someday, in the middle of my euphoria will be a God who drops down from the heavens to save me. I keep waiting.

Commentary

Brandon demonstrates a phenomenon in psychology called the "double bind." A *double bind* occurs when a person is faced with two demands that are irreconcilable, or where a choice needs to be made between two undesirable actions. When Brandon stopped using and began taking methadone, he needed to face a reality that only reminded him of how shell-shocked he had become since childhood. Furthermore, his cravings continued unabated. When Brandon injected heroin, while knowing that he was on a collision course, he at least felt some degree of euphoria while he waited for magical salvation.

Brandon meets the criteria in *DSM-5* of having an OUD. He experiences a loss of control over the use of heroin, he cannot reduce its use, he craves it, he is unable to fulfill obligations at work, and when he stops using he needs another opioid (i.e., methadone) to avoid withdrawal. In his portrayal, the remaining criteria for OUD were not indicated but could be readily ascertained in a counseling session.

Discussion

1. Do you know of anyone who you suspect has become dependent on opioids? If "yes," which symptoms noted in the commentary apply to him or her?
2. Does this person have symptoms that are not listed in the commentary? If so, what are they?
3. If you were Brandon's counselor, how would you go about helping him?

Injectable extended-release naltrexone and low-dose oral naltrexone are approved to prevent relapse in opioid-addicted individuals (Bisaga et al., 2018). A nonopioid drug that was approved by the U.S. Food and Drug Administration (FDA) in 2018 for adults experiencing opioid withdrawal is lofexidine, a medication that was historically used to treat high blood pressure (FDA News Release, 2018).

Huhn and Dunn (2017) stated that buprenorphine is underutilized because not all physicians have a waiver to prescribe it, or those who have the waiver do not prescribe it to capacity. McDonald et al. (2017) stated that, although take-home naloxone (THN) occurs in many jurisdictions, the rising death toll of opioid overdose shows that the current THN coverage is insufficient.

Unfortunately, dropout is a core problem for OMT (Muller, Bjornestad, & Clausen, 2018). Furthermore, there is evidence that adherence to buprenorphine is negatively affected by those experiencing psychiatric comorbidity (Litz & Leslie, 2017). Jarvis et al. (2017) found that, in their study of 140 unemployed heroin-addicted individuals between 2006 and 2010, providing incentives for naltrexone adherence increased opiate abstinence.

In Norway, there has been vocal resistance from opioid-addicted individuals to their newest medication, buprenorphine-naloxone (BNX), due to side effects (Muller et al., 2018). Muller et al. (2018) surveyed more than 1000 individuals receiving OMT. Buprenorphine monopreparate (BUP) and methadone (MET) were compared. Overall, patients reported satisfaction with OMT despite the drugs having widely prevalent side effects. The most side effect burden was reported for MET, and BNX had the lightest. At the same time, BNX users were more dissatisfied with their medication (Muller et al., 2018).

Ibogaine, a natural hallucinogen found in the roots of an African rainforest shrub, has received some good reviews regarding its ability to reduce withdrawal symptoms and eliminate the desire for opioids (Brown & Alper, 2018; Noller, Frampton, &Yazar-Klosinski, 2018). The drug, however, is not entirely safe, and some deaths have been reported (Schep, Slaughter, Galea, & Newcombe, 2016) as well as mania in some individuals who do not have a prior history of bipolar disorder (Marta, Ryan, Kopelowicz, & Koek, 2015).

Abruptly withdrawing from methadone is worse than heroin withdrawal (Tarman & Werdell, 2014). The side effects from taking methadone include weight gain, constipation, numbness in the extremities, sedation, dental issues due to decreased salivation, and even hallucinations for some individuals (Csiernik, 2016). A controversial treatment for heroin addiction is the administration of pharmaceutical quality heroin that is injected in specialized medical clinics that are safe and clean. This is known as *heroin-assisted treatment*, or HAT (Csiernik, 2016).

Specific Counseling Considerations

ROLEPLAY SCENARIOS

Roleplay in dyads with one of you acting as the counselor and the other as the counselee. If roleplay is not possible, work individually in writing out a list of your suggestions.

Roleplay #1

Hanna, age 46, came to see you because she has been using OxyContin for the past 2 years due to the pain she reportedly experiences from an injury at work. She has remained unable to work ever since and is now seeing you because she wants you to write a letter so that she can continue to receive disability benefits. After Hanna signed a release form so you can talk to her employer, you find out that a ladder had fallen on her and, while it struck her in the lower back region, the ladder only weighed about 30 pounds, and it seemed unlikely that it would result in a substantial back injury. Nonetheless, Hannah has complained of severe pain ever since the accident.

Roleplay #2

Chuck, age 28, came to see you because he is currently unable to work in the United States. Chuck is originally from Canada, but, after marrying Margarita, who was born in Los Angeles, he moved there to be with her 5 months ago. He has been waiting ever since to get a green card. Chuck tells you that he has been addicted to heroin since he was 18 years old. Margarita is aware of his addiction, but, when she met him, Chuck had been clean for a few months. She believed that his abstinence would be permanent, and she still thinks this today. Chuck tells you, however, that he has been stealing for the past 3 months to support his heroin addiction. He feels terrible about this and does not know whether he should tell Margarita or keep this to himself.

Goals and Goal Setting

A common goal for opioid-addicted individuals is harm reduction. That might include cutting down on the use of opioids or through using a related drug that is legal. One approach that has been tried with success for some individuals is substituting medical marijuana for opioid use (Walsh et al., 2017). A substantial amount of literature has demonstrated the clinical effectiveness of MAT (American Society of Addiction Medicine [ASAM], n.d.). Despite this knowledge and the worsening epidemic, MAT is significantly underutilized (ASAM, n.d.). There are an estimated 2.5 million individuals who need treatment for OUD. According to the Blue Cross Blue Shield Association, the number of members diagnosed with opioid addiction surged 493%, whereas the percentage of members using MAT only rose by 65% (ASAM, n.d.). ASAM (n.d.) concluded that the rate of diagnoses has increased

HOW WOULD AN ADDICTION COUNSELOR HELP THIS PERSON?

You are working as a professional counselor. Giles and Moira have come to see you to find out how they can help their addicted daughter, Jessica, who is 21 years old. Giles begins the conversation by telling you that he has been taking extended-release morphine capsules for the past 10 months due to severe cancer pain. He tells you that the side effects have included frequent grogginess and feeling "spacey." With guilt in his voice, he says, "I had no idea that Jessica was stealing these from me. My doctor would give me 100 pills at a time, and I could take up to 10 a day. I did not count how many I was taking." As the conversation proceeds, you discover that Jessica is now hanging out with a small group of male and female heroin-addicted individuals in their thirties. She is away from home most of the time, only returning to crash after a few days. Moira tells you that she has started to steal cash and jewelry from her. They want to know how they can help their daughter.

Remember to view clients within their environmental contexts, keeping in mind societal, parental/familial, cultural/spiritual, and peer influences. Specifically, become aware of the impact that the following influences have and continue to have in your clients' lives: race, language, religion and spirituality, gender, familial migration history, sexual/affectional orientation, age and cohort, physical and mental capacities, socioeconomic situation and history, education, and history of traumatic experience.

1. What defines this person's environment, past and present?
2. Who is this person sitting in front of me, taking into account environmental and personal characteristics?
3. What defines the problem that he or she is presenting within their multicultural milieu?

eightfold compared to the rate of those using MAT. ASAM stated there are three reasons for this underutilization: (a) many people have insufficient or limited insurance coverage, (b) there are not enough physicians qualified to prescribe MAT, and (c) access to addiction specialists is limited. Some individuals may need the additional support provided by an inpatient or outpatient rehabilitation program.

Other methods of harm reduction that have been suggested include the provision of quality heroin to addicted individuals (Rastegar & Fingerhood, 2016) and providing heroin-addicted individuals with foil to encourage them to smoke heroin instead of injecting it (Earleywine, 2016). Given that injection drug use is a major factor in HIV transmission, Ompad et al. (2017) recommended that addicted individuals be provided more syringes and condoms.

As addiction is on a continuum and each person is unique, some individuals may have abstinence from both opioids and MAT as their short-term or long-term goal. Here are a few goals in that category (adapted from Johnson, 2017):

1. Quitting "cold turkey" from all opioids. This might be the most common method for those addicted to prescription painkillers. Quitting opioids all at once will bring on a quick and potentially intense withdrawal. Nonetheless, the withdrawal will not be life-threatening, and successfully getting through it may create additional motivation to remain clean.
2. Tapering off opioids slowly. This could be attempted by tapering off from the drug of choice or by using MAT initially and then tapering off from the opioid substitute.
3. Ibogaine opioid detox. The drug binds to the same receptors as opioids, and a single administration can reduce withdrawal symptoms by 80%–90%. Ibogaine is nonaddictive. Some clinics specialize in this treatment (e.g., https://clearskyibogaine.com/). For some individuals, ibogaine also eliminates the desire for opioids (Brown & Alper, 2018; Noller et al., 2018). The drug is not without its downfalls, as some deaths have been reported (Schep et al., 2016), as well as mania in some individuals who do not have a prior history of bipolar disorder (Marta et al., 2015).
4. Waismann opioid detoxification therapy. Individuals receiving this method are put to sleep under light anesthesia and given a drug to eliminate all opioids from the body quickly. This results in a painless withdrawal. The method is costly (e.g., $18,000 or more, which includes a 5- to 7-day inpatient program and 24-hour monitoring). The program is not covered by insurance.
5. Vivitrol (i.e., naltrexone). Individuals can receive a shot of Vivitrol once a month. Vivitrol blocks opioid receptors in the brain.

6. Committing to opioid abstinence no matter what is required. Although this goal might not be attainable for many or most opioid addicts, there is no question that some individuals do whatever is needed to remain clean. Some people may develop *metanoia*, which is a substantial change in the way one thinks and/or lives, often resulting from a spiritual conversion. Merriam-Webster (https://www.merriam-webster.com/dictionary/metanoia) defines metanoia as "a transformative change of heart."

Stages of Change Strategies

The processes of change mentioned are based on those outlined by Connors, DiClemente, Velasquez, and Donovan (2013) and Prochaska, Norcross, and DiClemente (1994). The definitions for the various processes can be found in Chapter 6. Besides these processes, other strategies are included that have separate citations.

The University of Rhode Island Change Assessment Scale (URICA) is a helpful scale for determining where the client is currently at regarding the stages of change model. There are 24-, 28-, and 32-item versions of the scale.

A 24-item version is published for alcohol or drug problems. The scale, however, is generic and can be easily adapted for use with other addictions. It is available with norms as a free download from https://www.guilford.com/add/miller11_old/urica.pdf.

Specific precontemplation strategies.

Opioid-addicted individuals may be triggered to break out of denial through watching movies that accurately depict addiction. Here are a few good choices:

1. *Rush* (1991) is the story of a woman forced to inject drugs in front of a drug dealer and becomes addicted to drugs to avoid breaking her cover.
2. *Drugstore Cowboy* (1989) follows a group of drug-addicted individuals traveling across the U.S. Pacific Northwest in 1971, supporting their addiction by robbing pharmacies and hospitals.
3. *Trainspotting* (1996) is about heroin addiction with one actor who endures withdrawal in a cheap hotel room.
4. *The Wolf of Wall Street* (2013) provides a realistic look at drug addiction, the side effects, and the comedown from the drugs.
5. *Last Days* (2005) was inspired by the final days of Nirvana's lead singer, Kurt Cobain.
6. *Ben: Diary of a Heroin Addict* (2008) is a documentary available from YouTube (https://www.youtube.com/watch?v=7thZbHTvZIQ).
7. *Midnight Cowboy* (1969) was an early movie that portrayed heroin addiction in a gritty manner.

Alternatively, reading books may prove helpful to some. Here are a few good choices:

1. *Dark Paradise: A History of Opiate Addiction in America* (by David Courtwright, 2001).

   Quoted from Amazon.com website:

   In a newly enlarged edition of this eye-opening book, David T. Courtwright offers an original interpretation of a puzzling chapter in American social and medical history: the dramatic change in the pattern of opiate addiction—from respectable upper-class matrons to lower-class urban males, often with a criminal record. Challenging the prevailing view that the shift resulted from harsh new laws, Courtwright shows that the crucial role was played by the medical rather than the legal profession.

2. *American Fix: Inside the Opioid Addiction Crisis—and How to End It* (by Ryan Hampton, 2020).

   Quoted from Amazon.com website:

   Nearly every American knows someone who has been affected by the opioid crisis. Addiction is a trans-partisan issue that impacts individuals from every walk of life. Millions of Americans, tired of watching their loved ones die while politicians ignore this issue. Where is the solution? Where is the hope? Where's the outrage?

3. *The Big Fix: Hope After Heroin* (by Tracey Mitchell, 2017).

   Quoted from Amazon.com website:

   After surviving nearly a decade of heroin abuse and hard living on the streets of San Francisco's Tenderloin District, Tracey Helton Mitchell decided to get clean for good. With raw honesty and a poignant perspective on life that only comes from starting at rock bottom, *The Big Fix* tells her story of transformation from homeless heroin addict to stable mother of three—and the hard work and hard lessons that got her there. Rather than dwelling on the pain of addiction, Tracey focuses on her journey of recovery and rebuilding her life, while exposing the failings of the American rehab system and laying out a path for change. Starting with the first step in her recovery, Tracey re-learns how to interact with men, build new friendships, handle money, and rekindle her relationship with her mother, all while staying sober, sharp, and dedicated to her future.

4. *The Heroin Diaries: The Year in the Life of a Shattered Rock Star* (by Nikki Sixx, 2007).

   Quoted from Amazon.com website:

   The notorious co-founder of the legendary rock band Mötley Crüe presents a candid and harrowing account of his descent into the hell of drug addiction, describing the impact of heroin on his life and the band.

5. *Junkbox Diaries: A Day in the Life of a Heroin Addict* (by Herbert Stepherson, 2017).

   Quoted from Amazon.com website:

   What is a junkbox? A person who is just so all consumed by addiction and drugs that they do not care about what goes into their body. They don't shower, they barely eat, and the only sleep they get is a result from a high dose shot of some "high quality" heroin. Since 2002, he [Herb Stepherson] has been involved in the fight for his life. He has been battling the nightmares of addiction for the past fourteen years. His first drug use was at fifteen, which was alcohol and from there quickly progressed to prescription pain medication and ultimately cocaine and heroin. Heroin and cocaine took him to the absolute edges of humanity. He ended up homeless, eating food out of dumpsters, and strung out in some of the roughest neighborhoods in Chicago, in the dead of winter. The winter months are brutal in the Midwest. Herb slept in abandon [*sic*] buildings, airport terminals, and under bridges clinging to two basic needs: more heroin and to be numbed from the wreckage that this drug was creating in his life. All the while trying his best to keep hope alive that maybe one day he would finally be able to conquer this demon of addiction and recover.

6. *Smack* (by Melvin Burgess, 1999).
   Quoted from Amazon.com website:
   Gemma: "My parents are incompetent. They haven't got a clue . . ."
   Tar: "I know it sounds stupid, but it was like the flowers had come out for Gemma . . ." Lily: "They did everything they could to pin me down . . . my mum, my dad, school . . ." Rob: "We stood for a while breathing big long breaths of air. It was cold and pure . . . You could feel it inside you, doing you good."
   How do these teens come to run away from home? To be users? Addicts? As their stories intertwine and build, SMACK never lets up the pace. It is a book about people, families—real and those constructed by young people with no one to turn to but each other. SMACK is a book about a drug and the hold it can have. Written directly for its audience of young people and unflinching in its honesty, SMACK is the teen book of the year.

Remember that people in this stage do not view their behavior as a problem. That may result from either denial or from not having experienced any severe consequences yet. They might say that they are only experiencing *positive* consequences from their substance use behavior. Most often they are not wanting to hear about negative consequences or be given advice on quitting their addiction.

Counselors can assist addicted individuals in the precontemplation stage as outlined in Chapter 6. Some of the strategies suggested include the following (these are adapted from materials originally provided at https://integratedrecovery.org/):

1. Create rapport with the client and build trust.
2. Ask permission of the client to address the topic of change.
3. Agree on the direction that counseling will take.
4. Listen to the client's perception of her or his drug use.
5. Pay attention to the aspects of substance use the client enjoys.
6. Try to create doubt and evoke concern in the client about their substance use.
7. If others are present for the session, look at the discrepancies between the client's perception and the others' perception of the substance use.
8. Express empathy and keep the door open.

Specific contemplation strategies.

Clients in the contemplation stage are typically ambivalent about change, but at least they know they have a problem and they are considering the possibility of stopping or cutting back soon. This is an ideal time to provide relevant information, help them re-evaluate their substance use behavior, and talk about treatment options for if or when they want to make a change. Many people stay in the contemplation stage for months or years.

Counselors can help addicted individuals create a cost-benefit analysis by assisting them in considering the pros and cons of their behavior. One can help clients think about their previous attempts to stop using opioids and the factors that led to relapse. Counselors can also teach their clients different ways to control or quit their addictive behavior. Although some clients will move forward to the preparation stage, some will move back to precontemplation.

Specific preparation strategies.

In the preparation stage, the client has moved toward planning and preparing to begin a change process. A thorough and well-considered plan is important to success. Although the following is not an exhaustive list, it provides some questions that should be answered during preparation:

1. The WHAT of making the change. Is the intention to cut down, reduce harm, or quit altogether?
2. The HOW of making the change.
   A. If the goal is to reduce opioid use, how much should it be reduced so that one knows the goal has been reached?
   B. Obtain the necessary resources. If the goal is to substitute a legal drug, which drug will it be?
   C. Get rid of triggers. What are the triggers and/or high-risk situations that lead to use and/or cravings?
   D. Develop a strategy for coping with triggers and/or high-risk situations. Will the addicted individual need to avoid having contact with friends who are still using? How will he or she avoid contacting one or more drug dealers?
   E. Have support in place. Whom can the addicted person turn to for emotional and social support?
   F. Attend a mutual support group. Which is the most appropriate group to attend regularly?
3. The WHERE of making the change.
   A. Treatment modality. Will the addicted individual need inpatient or outpatient treatment?
   B. Possible relocation. Will the addicted individual need to find a clean, safe place to begin a new life?

Other ideas for *before* their chosen quit day (i.e., preparation strategies) can be found in Appendix B.

Specific action strategies.

There are many action strategies available for drug addictions, each with varying degrees of efficacy and effectiveness. For many opioid addicts, the action stage begins in a detox or treatment facility. According to the plans made during the preparation stage, the action stage may occur in small, gradual steps or may consist of a complete life change.

Rastegar and Fingerhood (2016) summarized treatment choices for an opioid-dependent person. These can be roughly categorized as (a) detoxification, which is medically supervised and generally followed by psychosocial treatment, (b) psychosocial treatment, and (c) MAT, which usually includes either an opioid agonist (i.e., methadone or buprenorphine) or an opioid antagonist (i.e., naltrexone). Drug courts are another approach whereby an addicted individual charged with an offense can participate in substance use treatment instead of incarceration. The approach is generally to connect participants with extended-release naltrexone. Extended-release naltrexone is expensive, and its effectiveness at reducing recidivism when required by a drug court remains unknown (Robertson & Swartz, 2018).

The psychosocial treatments available include brief interventions, mutual support groups, drug counseling, behavioral and cognitive-behavioral counseling, analytic counseling, and residential treatment (Rastegar & Fingerhood, 2016). Although Dugosh et al. (2016) recently surmised that psychosocial interventions added to the treatment effectiveness of MAT for opioid addicts, Schwartz (2016) concluded that their results were flawed. Dugosh et al. focused on 27 studies, nine of which were incorrectly reviewed or had substantial methodological limitations. Another nine focused on contingency management and methadone treatment conducted in China, and these findings might not be generalizable to the United States. Schwartz also critiqued the remaining nine studies as inadequate. Schwartz wrote that studies conducted by him and his colleagues found no difference in opioid use between those individuals provided methadone with or without counseling. Petry (2013) had made similar comments earlier regarding results from a different study. Petry concluded that psychosocial interventions did not improve outcomes relative to MAT.

Although clinical guidelines around the world suggest psychosocial treatments as a recommended strategy, meta-analytic studies have *not* shown any benefit for manual-based treatments beyond "routine counseling" (Day & Mitcheson, 2017, p. 1329). Day and Mitcheson (2017) concluded nonetheless that psychosocial interventions could be interpreted in both a positive and negative fashion. Consequently, current evidence suggests that, whereas counselors can create a positive working alliance and play a supportive role in working with opioid addicts, counselors should remain skeptical regarding the added benefit they provide opioid-dependent clients.

About one fifth of counselors in a sample of 725 admitted that they did not know enough about the effectiveness of either buprenorphine or methadone in helping opioid-addicted individuals (Aletraris, Edmond, Paino, Fields, & Roman, 2016). Aletraris et al. (2016) recommended that physicians, counselors, and clients need to be informed of that which has proven effective in helping addicted individuals remain abstinent from opioid use.

Keeping opioid-addicted individuals attending psychosocial treatment is also problematic. McHugh et al. (2013) noted several studies, including their own, that found that younger clients are at the highest risk of early treatment dropout. Brigham et al. (2014) found that Community Reinforcement and Family Training for Treatment Retention (CRAFT-T) improved the outcomes for patients completing opioid detoxification but also noted that their results are preliminary and need further confirmation. Schacht, Brooner, King, Kidorf, and Peirce (2017) found that, with their 58 participants who experienced both PTSD and OUD, monetary incentives were needed to increase attendance. These authors stated that incentives are well supported in the research to improve adherence to substance use treatment goals. A study by Saunders et al. (2015) found that, for clients with PTSD and co-occurring OUDs, MAT combined with integrated cognitive-behavioral therapy (CBT) resulted in the greatest improvements in substance use.

Acceptance and commitment therapy has been used in a pilot study with opioid-addicted patients with chronic pain (Smallwood, Potter, & Robin, 2016). Saedy et al. (2018) recently found that short-term individual acceptance and commitment therapy reduced craving beliefs in opioid-dependent patients receiving methadone maintenance, and this effect remained 12 weeks after completion. Mindfulness approaches have also been helpful in teaching opioid-addicted individuals to better regulate their emotions (Lee, Lin, Wang, & Yen, 2016) and for pain reduction in chronic pain patients who received opioids (Garland et al., 2017).

Therapeutic communities became prominent in the United States during the heroin crisis of the 1960s, and they were then recognized as the most effective intervention (Mullen & Arbiter, 2017). The year 2018 marked the 60th anniversary of the formation of therapeutic communities in the United States. Today's therapeutic communities have evolved, and today they are more focused on conventional medical and clinical interventions. Therapeutic communities were group-based approaches to drug addiction that were usually residential where clients and counselors lived together. Today they are increasingly day programs.

Garrido-Fernandez, Marcos-Sierra, Lopez-Jimenez, and de Alda (2017) compared multifamily therapy with a reflecting team (MFTRT) to a standard treatment group following an MMT program. The MFTRT group showed more improvement with reduced addiction severity in several of the areas evaluated, including improvement in employment and social support.

Several studies have looked at group counseling approaches for adult opioid-addicted individuals (Fogger & Lehmann, 2017; Shigakova, 2016), addicted individuals receiving methadone (Barry et al., 2014), and adolescent opioid-addicted individuals (Pugatch, Knight, McGuiness, Sherritt, & Levy, 2014). The effectiveness of groups remains uncertain, but they do tend to increase adherence to treatment protocols.

Morrison, Lin, and Gersh (2018) argued that an integrated approach is often preferable. Studies using integrative treatments have focused on cigarette smoking, alcohol, and opiate use disorders. Recall from Chapter 6 that the integrative approach mixes mainstream therapies (i.e., psychological and pharmacological) with complementary and alternative therapies. For example, female heroin-addicted individuals have found group music therapy helpful in changing their moods, energy level, sense of self, and level of enjoyment (Gardstrom, Klemm, & Murphy, 2017); various types of acupuncture have proven helpful with recovery (Baker & Chang, 2016; Liang, Lin, Zhang, Ungvari, & Tang, 2016; Wu, Leung, & Yew, 2016); hypnosis may assist in pain management (Bubenzer & Huang, 2014); and cue-exposure therapy combined with biofeedback therapy has shown effectiveness in reducing cravings in heroin addicts. Other ideas for *beginning* their chosen quit day (i.e., action strategies) can be found in Appendix B.

Specific maintenance strategies and relapse prevention.

Note: Maintenance strategies and relapse prevention are also, for many, partly facilitated by regular attendance at relevant self-help groups. A list of such self-help groups and helpful websites is found in an upcoming section entitled Relevant Mutual Support Groups, Websites, and Videos.

The focus of this stage is to continue the progress that began in the action stage. For most opioid addicts, this will involve remaining abstinent while continuing to take their MAT. If a lapse or relapse occurs, the addicted individual needs to have a plan for harm reduction during this period (e.g., wear a condom during sex, do not share needles, do not operate machinery or a vehicle) and a plan to become abstinent again. The lapse or relapse needs to be viewed as a learning opportunity by both the counselor and the addict. Lapse and relapse are the rule rather than the exception. Most addicted individuals will need to recycle through the stages more than once, and some will never maintain indefinite abstinence.

Often addicted individuals become complacent once the focus on reaching the goal is no longer as meaningful or important, and they may come to believe that a small lapse is allowable. This is why it is critical that addicted individuals learn new ways of coping with stress during the action stage and that they practice these to the point of overlearning so that they become automatic.

Unnithan, Gossop, and Strang (1992) looked at relapse among 42 opiate-addicted individuals who had received outpatient detoxification treatment in London, England. The questionnaires revealed that interpersonal factors and drug-related cues were most associated with the lapse to opiate use. Most common high-risk situations include regularly meeting other drug users and being offered drugs together with persistent negative moods. Other ideas for relapse prevention can be found in Appendix C.

Motivational Interviewing

Motivational interviewing (MI) is often used together with CBT. Consequently, when researchers report effectiveness, the two approaches are often confounded.

Chang, Compton, Almeter, and Fox (2015) used MI over 4 weeks with older adults experiencing chronic pain regarding prescription opioid adherence. At post-test and 1-month follow-up, the participants were found to be less likely to misuse prescription opioids, and they decreased their substance use, increased their self-efficacy, increased their motivation to change, and decreased depression scores. There was no control group in the study.

Secades-Villa, Fernande-Hermida, and Arnaez-Montaraz (2004) randomly assigned 40 heroin users to either an MI group or a control condition. The MI group experienced higher retention rates (i.e., 50%) in the outpatient program than the control group (20%). The authors viewed their study as a pilot project. Beckerleg (2001) used MI with 20 heroin users in Kenya. She concluded that MI was acceptable to the participants and found to be useful by them.

MI is useful as well for establishing a strong working alliance. Here is an example of how MI could be used to help an opioid-addicted individual decide to make a change. (Pertaining to Chapter 6's description of MI, the following is an example of the process called *evoking*. Carl is the client, age 45, and this is the second part of their first session.)

Client: I honestly don't know if I can do anything about this, Joyce. I have been addicted to heroin for 20 years.

Counselor: What has this 20 years been like for you, Carl?

Client: My God, it has been a living nightmare. I have been on the street most of these years, you know. I have slept in every free drop-in center and often in the outdoors, been robbed several times, and overdosed on fentanyl twice.

Counselor: You really have gone through a horrific experience with your addiction. I cannot imagine how you must feel having survived so much already.

Client: I fear this is only the beginning of my suffering, Joyce. It just makes me sick to think about my addiction.

Counselor: I certainly hear in your words how tired you are dealing with heroin in your life and the overdoses.

Client: You have that right. Some days I do not think I can go on much longer.

Counselor: Heroin has even left you thinking that your life may soon end. I keep hearing the pain in your voice and your stories, Carl. But I also hear hope.

Client: Really? You hear hope in my voice?

Counselor: Yes, I do. You are so tired of this nightmare, and you know you have to do something before it is too late.

Client: I know you are right, Joyce. I don't think I have what it takes to become clean.

Counselor: I understand your fear of facing this right now, and I don't want to push you faster than what feels right for you.

Client: But I do want to face this! I cannot go on this way!

Counselor: I know. I know you are ready to take some small steps at least right now. If you let me, I would be more than pleased to help you begin planning a way to live the life that you so much crave to live.

Client: If you can do this for me, I will be forever grateful.

Counselor: In that case, let's get started.

Insight-Oriented Interventions

In her dissertation, Plummer (2013) concluded that there are many psychodynamic conflicts in the life of heroin injectors.

She mainly focused on relational trauma both in the past and in the present regarding the substantial role they play in the lives of heroin users.

Rob Hale, a psychiatrist as well as a psychoanalyst, described his 13 years as a consultant to the staff at a drug-dependency unit (Hale, 2013). Hale noted another chapter author who described what it is like for many who work in the field of addictions: "[it is difficult to witness] the pain of seeing attractive, intelligent young people who have reduced themselves to skin and bone" (from abstract). He used a theory by Classer to facilitate understanding of the addicts' terror of relationships. Hale likened addicts' need for their drugs to that of perverse individuals' need for perversion. A drug-dependency unit was compared to how mothers help their infants cope with overwhelming feelings. The feelings are projected onto the mother, who processes them in her mind and returns the projection to the baby in a more accessible form.

Lesourne (1995) advanced the notion that addicted individuals have a double personality. One personality is conforming and law-abiding, and the other is rebellious and intent on immediate, unrestrained, and regressive gratification. Narayan (1994) used a Hindi version of the Motivation Analysis Test and found that heroin-addicted individuals had more conflicts in sentiments related to self-concept and sweetheart-spouse. He also saw more conflicts regarding fear. Isralowitz, Telias, and Abu-Saad (1994) found that heroin-addicted individuals in Israel receiving community treatment had a more liberal attitude toward illegal drug use and were more risk-taking, rebellious, and desirous of self-gratification compared to imprisoned addicted individuals and the nondrug-using control group.

Blatt, McDonald, Sugarman, and Wilber (1984) offered their psychodynamic theory of opiate addiction. They suggested that opiate-addicted individuals are dealing with intense depression and that most are severely neurotic or character-disordered. Blatt et al. further indicated that opiate-addicted individuals have a tough time managing painful, dysphoric affects, especially depression, anger, and anxiety. They added guilt, shame, and profound feelings of self-criticism and worthlessness together with feelings of deprivation, neglect, and a lack of love and affection. Rather than deal with these emotions, the authors hypothesized that addicted individuals prefer to withdraw from the pain and stress of interpersonal relationships; instead, they experience self-induced grandiosity and omnipotent feelings of bliss through their use of opiates. Blatt et al. concluded that research was needed to confirm their formulations. Earlier, Corman and Khantzian (1976), using the psychodynamic approach, suggested that opioid-addicted individuals experience disorganized rage, anxiety, and depression. In their case study, they hypothesized that the patient had low self-esteem and was narcissistic and dependent. The patient had earlier experienced emotional deprivation.

White (1999), using a transactional analysis perspective, viewed heroin use as a passive behavior that allows users to incapacitate and feel like they are establishing a transactional symbiosis and attachment with the drug. White went on to postulate that, if this is true, it might lend itself to a transferential treatment modality, which was hypothesized to weaken the attraction to heroin.

More recently, Johnson and Mosri (2016) have offered a neuropsychoanalytic approach. These authors have used neuroscience to advance psychoanalytic theory. Furthermore, they have suggested that neuroscience should become the basic science underlying psychoanalysis, which they believe will improve its status in the scientific community.

Spiritual Interventions

In a qualitative study, Melin, Eklund, and Lindgren (2017) interviewed 13 individuals living with opioid dependence. The participants described living with opioid addiction as a constant struggle in a life without dignity and filled with chaos, alienation, and pain. They noted that the drug filled a spiritual emptiness. This suggests that a spiritual intervention may be beneficial for at least some opioid addicts. In a study comprising 40 heroin addicts, 40 psychiatric outpatients, and 31 college students, the heroin-addicted individuals were the least likely to have a clearly defined purpose in life (Coleman et al., 1986).

Best, Ghufran, Day, Ray, and Loaring (2008) surveyed 107 former problematic heroin users who had remained abstinent for an average of 10 years. How did they become abstinent? The most commonly expressed reason was that they were tired of the lifestyle followed by reasons about their psychological health. When asked how they sustained abstinence, clients reported that it was through social network factors (moving away from drug-using friends, support from nonusing friends), practical factors like accommodation and employment, as well as religious or spiritual factors. Other research supports the idea that spiritual and religious experiences assist in substance abuse recovery (Heinz, Epstein, & Preston, 2007).

Some view mindfulness-based interventions (MBIs) as a spiritual practice. Majeed, Ali, and Sudak (2018) noted that there is evidence suggesting that MBIs such as meditation, yoga, and stress reduction help individuals in pain. MBIs alter their perception of pain while also increasing mobility and improving functioning and well-being. In focus groups of inner-city HIV-positive, opioid-addicted individuals who were asked for their views of spirituality, Arnold, Avants, Margolin, and Marcotte (2002) found that two dominant themes emerged: (a) spirituality was a source of strength and protection of self and (b) spirituality acted as a source of altruism and protection of others.

Haozous and Knobf (2013) interviewed 13 southwest American Indians experiencing cancer pain and 11 healthcare providers, caregivers, and community members. The authors concluded that American Indian patients see pain in a multidimensional way. The American Indians interviewed found it essential that they participate in spiritual and cultural activities as part of their pain management treatment.

A pilot study found that a mosque-based methadone maintenance program was a helpful alternative for Muslim individuals facing addiction issues (Rashid et al., 2014). Another study found that positive religious coping can help opioid-addicted individuals refrain from relapsing, whereas negative religious coping acted as a barrier (Puffer, Skalski, & Meade, 2012). In a study of 380 homeless individuals in Canada, those who attended religious ceremonies at least weekly (i.e., the frequent attendees) were compared to those who attended less frequently. Frequent attendees had lower rates of alcohol, cocaine, and opioid use than infrequent attendees.

Cloutier-Gill, Wood, Millar, Ferris, and Eugenia Socias (2016) provided a case report of a 37-year-old female with severe OUD for the past 19 years. After 4 days of ibogaine treatment, she remained abstinent after an ongoing 18-month period. Cloutier-Gill et al. hypothesized that ibogaine may bring about a transformative or spiritual experience. Other studies have supported the notion that ibogaine is associated with long-term abstinence (as cited in Cloutier-Gill et al., 2016). The drug, however, is not entirely safe, and some deaths have been reported (Schep et al., 2016) as well as mania in some individuals who do not have a prior history of bipolar disorder (Marta et al., 2015). The drug is not approved by the FDA.

Cognitive-Behavioral Therapy

CBT can be facilitated using the triple column technique. It can be used both by counselors in their work with clients and by clients alone. The full instructions for using the technique are found in Chapter 6. The following are some of the cognitions that can be problematic for clients with this addiction.

Automatic Thought or Belief	Questioning It	Healthier Thought or Belief
I cannot imagine living without heroin.		Begin to imagine that you can live without heroin. You may require medication-assisted therapy, and, if you choose, you can be weaned off that as well.
My physical pain is unmanageable without prescription opioids.		There are other methods of reducing pain besides opioids. Examples include mindfulness, stress reduction, yoga, and hypnosis.
I am a worthless human being.		Everyone has worth, including me. I need to take back my dignity.
I cannot stand the side effects of taking methadone.		I know that the side effects are still better than the alternative of living my life as an active heroin addict.
My opioid use is going to kill me, and there is nothing I can do about it.		Opioids might kill me if I don't do something about my addiction. I am the one who gets to decide what goes into my body and what does not. It is time to get help.

As noted in the section earlier about the action stage of the transtheoretical model of change, CBT also receives mixed reviews regarding its efficacy in helping opioid addicts. Some studies suggest it is helpful in improving quality of life (Zhuang, An, & Zhao, 2014) and increasing compliance regarding treatment efforts (Willner-Reid et al., 2016), whereas other studies indicate it adds little to reducing relapse rates (Otto et al., 2014; Tavakolian & Abolghasemi, 2016). Similarly, in a review regarding how helpful behavioral interventions are in buprenorphine maintenance treatment, four studies found that a behavioral intervention added no benefit beyond medical management, whereas another four studies revealed some benefit, particularly contingency management (Carroll & Weiss, 2017). A systematic review and meta-analysis of contingency management interventions for the treatment of opioid addiction concluded that contingency management is efficacious for treating drug use (Ainscough, McNeill, Strang, Calder, & Brose, 2017).

Petry (2012) arrived at the same conclusion and stated that there is now a vast empirical literature demonstrating the beneficial effects of contingency management. She noted that there are three fundamental principles of contingency management:

1. Monitoring. The behavior targeted for change is frequently monitored.
2. Immediate reinforcers. Immediate positive reinforcers that are tangible need to be provided each time the behavior occurs.
3. Withholding reinforcers when needed. During times when the behavior does not occur, positive reinforcers are withheld.

Early maladaptive schemas also appear amenable to change through CBT (Shorey, Stuart, Anderson, & Strong, 2013). CBT offered in a group has also proven helpful in teaching coping skills and increasing self-efficacy in opioid-dependent clients. A reduction of drug use was also found in the CBT group at both 6 and 12 months follow-up in this study (Kouimtsidis, Reynolds, Coulton, & Drummond, 2012).

An Internet-based community reinforcement approach plus contingency management reportedly increased abstinence among 170 opioid-dependent adults (Christensen et al., 2014). In another study, an automated computer-based intervention based on CBT was used to deliver real-time assistance by phone for opioid-addicted individuals in methadone maintenance and was overall found to increase patient engagement and continued use of methadone (Moore et al., 2017). Similarly, Kim, Marsch, Acosta, Guarino, and Aponte-Melendez (2016) found that adding technology-delivered behavior therapy was more effective regarding opioid abstinence than MMT alone.

Behavioral couples therapy (BCT) was compared to 12-step-oriented individually based treatment (IBT) for drug-abusing women (74% opioid). The group receiving BCT plus IBT reported the most improved relationship satisfaction and prevention of relationship breakup. Both the BCT plus IBT and the IBT group alone reported fewer substance-related problems at the end of treatment (O'Farrell, Schumm, Murphy, & Muchowski, 2017).

RELEVANT MUTUAL SUPPORT GROUPS, WEBSITES, AND VIDEOS

Mutual Support Groups

For the Addicted Individual

1. Narcotics Anonymous. https://na.org/

   Quoted from website:

   Narcotics Anonymous is a global, community-based organization with a multilingual and multicultural membership. NA was founded in 1953, and our membership growth was minimal during our initial twenty years as an organization. Since the publication of our Basic Text in 1983, the number of members and meetings has increased dramatically. Today, NA members hold nearly 67,000 meetings weekly in 139 countries. We offer recovery from the effects of addiction through working a twelve-step program, including regular attendance at group meetings. The group atmosphere provides help from peers and offers an ongoing support network for addicted individuals who wish to pursue and maintain a drug-free lifestyle. Our name, Narcotics Anonymous, is not meant to imply a focus on any particular drug; NA's approach makes no distinction between drugs, including alcohol. Membership is free, and we have no affiliation with any organizations outside of NA, including governments, religions, law enforcement groups, or medical and psychiatric associations. Through all of our service efforts and our cooperation with others seeking to help addicts, we strive to reach a day when every addict in the world has an opportunity to experience our message of recovery in their own language and culture.

2. Smart Recovery—Self-Management and Recovery Training. https://www.smartrecovery.org/

   Quoted from website:

   SMART Recovery is the leading self-empowering addiction recovery support group. Our participants learn tools for addiction recovery based on the latest scientific research and participate in a world-wide community which includes free, self-empowering, science-based mutual help groups.

   SMART Recovery, a non-profit corporation, was originally named the Rational Recovery Self-Help Network, and was affiliated with Rational Recovery Systems, a for-profit corporation owned by Jack Trimpey. In 1994, the non-profit changed its name to SMART Recovery, and ended all affiliation with Trimpey. This change occurred because of disagreements between Trimpey and the non-profit's board of directors about the program of recovery to be offered in the self-help groups.

3. Rational Recovery. https://rational.org

   Quoted from website:

   The combined mission of Rational Recovery Systems, Inc., is (1) to disseminate information on independent recovery from addiction through planned, permanent abstinence, (2) to make self-recovery a viable option to all addicted people everywhere, and (3) to make informed consent to addiction treatment and recovery group participation available to all addicted people.

4. Opiates Anonymous World Services. http://www.opa12.org/home.html

   Quoted from website:

   Our Mission Statement: Opiates Anonymous World Service's purpose is to serve Opiates Anonymous service structures and members in their efforts to carry the message to the addict who still suffers. It is our belief that every addict should have an opportunity to hear our message of hope. As the result of our experience with the original twelve-step program as outlined in the book Alcoholics Anonymous, we no longer suffer. We have recovered from a hopeless state of mind, body and spirit.

For the Partner and/or Family

1. Smart Recovery—Self-Management and Recovery Training. https://www.smartrecovery.org/ (see previous description under For the Addicted Individual).

2. Nar-Anon. https://www.nar-anon.org/

   Quoted from website:

   The Nar-Anon Family Groups is primarily for those who know or have known a feeling of desperation concerning the addiction problem of someone very near to you. We have traveled that unhappy road too, and found the answer with serenity and peace of mind. When you come into the family group, you are no longer alone, but among true friends who understand your problem as few others could. We respect your confidence and anonymity as we know you will respect ours. We hope to give you the assurance that no situation is too difficult, and no unhappiness is too great to be overcome.

Websites

1. Opioids: Addiction, Withdrawal and Recovery. https://www.addictionsandrecovery.org/opioid-opiate-recovery.htm
2. Understanding Drug Use and Addiction. https://www.drugabuse.gov/publications/drugfacts/understanding-drug-use-addiction
3. Foundation for a Drug-Free World. https://www.drugfreeworld.org/about-us/about-the-foundation.html

4. U.S. Department of Health and Human Services. https://www.hhs.gov/opioids/about-the-epidemic/index.html
5. U.S. Food & Drug Administration. https://www.fda.gov/drugs/information-drug-class/opioid-medications

Videos

To view these videos, search their titles on YouTube.

1. *Opioid Addiction Is Treatable. Why Aren't We Doing It? | Sharon Levy | TEDxBeaconStreet.*
2. *The heroin denial epidemic | Tim Ryan | TEDxNaperville.*
3. *Opioids Epidemic in America Opioid Addiction Explained Documentary 2018.*
4. *Addicted: The Opioid Epidemic.*
5. *The Science of Opioids.*

RELEVANT PHONE APPS

Generic Addiction Apps

Note: Generic apps are described in Chapter 6.

This list is not exhaustive. New apps are continually being developed. Do an Internet search to find out the latest apps available. Most are for specific addictions, but some, such as these four, are generic.

1. I Am Sober. https://play.google.com/store/apps/details?id=com.thehungrywasp.iamsober
2. Sober Time. https://play.google.com/store/apps/details?id=com.sociosoft.sobertime
3. Pocket Rehab: Get Sober & Addiction Recovery. https://play.google.com/store/apps/details?id=com.getpocketrehab.app
4. Loop Habit Tracker. https://play.google.com/store/apps/details?id=org.isoron.uhabits

Specialized Apps

Due to the opioid crisis, several apps are currently in development. These two apps are only suggestive of what will soon be available:

1. NA Meeting Search 3.6.1. For smartphones, visit https://play.google.com/store/apps/details?id=org.na.naapp&hl=en_US. For IOS, visit https://apps.apple.com/us/app/na-meeting-search/id627643748

   Quoted from website: "This is the only recovery app based on the narcotics anonymous basic text book that you will ever need to maintain your daily reprieve. It is a perfect companion app for your 12 step program."

2. Opioid Calculator. (Smartphone and IOS) https://play.google.com/store/apps/details?id=au.edu.anzca.opioidcalculatorapp&hl=en_US

   or https://itunes.apple.com/us/app/opioid-calculator/id1039219870

   Quoted from website:

   This Opioid Calculator Application is a tool for the calculation of total oral Morphine Equivalent Daily Dose (oMEDD). A particular design feature of the app is that it simplifies the calculation of oMEDD in cases where combinations of opioids are used. It is designed to provide easy accessibility and consistency to facilitate research, improve education and fill a void in availability of reference conversion data in clinical practice. This opioid calculator is produced by the Faculty of Pain Medicine of the Australian and New Zealand College of Anaesthetists (FPM ANZCA) which is the peak body responsible for the education, training, continuing professional development and maintenance of standards of clinical practice for specialist pain medicine physicians in Australia and New Zealand.

JOURNALS AND CONFERENCES

Journals

There are innumerable journals that publish articles about opioid addictions. The following is, therefore, an incomplete list of 10 journals. Several are about pain, which is often treated with opioid medications. Please visit their websites for further details.

1. *Drug and Alcohol Dependence.* https://www.journals.elsevier.com/drug-and-alcohol-dependence/
2. *American Journal on Addictions.* https://onlinelibrary.wiley.com/journal/15210391

3. *American Journal of Drug and Alcohol Abuse*. https://www.tandfonline.com/loi/iada20
4. *Addiction*. https://onlinelibrary.wiley.com/journal/13600443
5. *Journal of Pain & Palliative Care Pharmacotherapy*. https://www.tandfonline.com/toc/ippc20/current
6. *Journal of Pain and Symptom Management*. https://www.journals.elsevier.com/journal-of-pain-and-symptom-management/
7. *Journal of Pain*. https://www.journals.elsevier.com/the-journal-of-pain/
8. *Pain*. https://journals.lww.com/pain/pages/default.aspx
9. *Pain Medicine*. https://academic.oup.com/pain medicine
10. *Pain Research & Management*. https://www.hindawi.com/journals/prm/

Conferences

You will likely find a growing number of conferences directed at opioid addiction given the raging crisis in the United States. Some of these will be at the local or state level. For example, in 2018, there was an Opioid and Heroin Mississippi Drug Summit that was aimed at informing the community about the growing epidemic in the state of Mississippi.

1. National Drug Abuse and Heroin Summit. Its website touts this as the largest annual conference addressing the opioid crisis. Do a Google search for its upcoming conference.
2. Annual Summit on Opioids, Heroin and Drug Abuse. Do a Google search for its upcoming conference.
3. Annual National Opioid Crisis Management Congress. Details at https://brinetwork.com/4th-annual-national-opioid-crisis-management-congress/
4. Annual Summit on Opioids Drugs. Details at https://eventegg.com/opioids-conference/

COUNSELING SCENARIO

As you are reading, imagine that you are the client in this scenario. Note the areas in which the session could be improved on the part of the counselor.

Your name is Tiffany, a 19-year-old who started using cannabis when you were 12 and, after trying several other drugs, you have been injecting heroin for the past 3 years. You dropped out of school when your heroin use began as you could no longer get to classes on time. Your family has rejected you because of your heroin use, and you are living on the street. Out of necessity, you became a sex worker soon after turning 17. Recently, after breaking into a few houses with other addicted individuals to steal cash and jewelry, one night you got caught. You were sent to a drug court, and you chose to receive medical-assisted treatment and meet with an addiction counselor. This is your second session.

- You: Not you again! I asked last session to be transferred to someone else.
- Counselor: I am sorry that you were not reassigned, Tiffany. After I discussed your request with the team, they decided that I was best suited to work with you.
- You: I doubt that very much. I bet you didn't even try.
- Counselor: I did make the request, but you are correct—I believe I am best suited to help you.
- You: Just how do you think you're going to help me? Last session you said, and I quote, "You probably enjoy tramping around downtown." There must be a female counselor that I could see instead of you.
- Counselor: Sorry, Tiffany. That is not the way it works at our agency. You are required to see me for the next 6 months on a weekly basis. You had better get used to it.
- You: I doubt if I ever will!
- Counselor: Let's move on. How are you doing on the methadone?
- You: It makes me sick just like you!
- Counselor: Listen, I am sorry if we got off on the wrong foot. I apologize for what I said last week.
- You: I still don't like this, but I guess I have no choice.
- Counselor: How are you paying for your expenses?

(Continued)

(Continued)

- You: If you stand up I'll show you!
- Counselor: Tiffany, I understand why you are upset. It is an important question that I have to ask all of my clients.
- You: My parents let me move back in with them now that I am getting help and taking methadone. I have started working part-time at a nearby drugstore.
- Counselor: I won't say what I think about that choice for you.
- You: Good! I didn't ask you what you think.
- Counselor: You have a lot of anger inside you. Perhaps we should work again today on anger management like we did last week. How did you make out with your homework?
- You: What homework? I don't do homework! I quit school, remember?
- Counselor: I asked you to try taking deep breaths when you notice that you are getting upset. You told me last week that your family really knows how to push your buttons and trigger you.
- You: They are always triggering me. They are everything to do with why it turned out this way, you know. Not that you ever asked me about that, but do you honestly think I became a heroin addict just because it is fun? There is nothing fun about my life.
- Counselor: Let's focus right now on your anger. There has been anger in your voice since you sat down here today.
- You: What do you expect after the way you talked to me last session?
- Counselor: I already apologized for that. How is it serving you to keep bringing up the past?
- You: Why do you keep doing this to me, Aaron?
- Counselor: Doing what?
- You: You are always pushing me into a corner! I have a past, and my past has destroyed my life.
- Counselor: Can you not accept some responsibility for how you turned out and the choices that you have made?
- You: I AM LEAVING! I HAVE HAD IT WITH YOU! [storms out of Aaron's office].

[Later in supervision:

- Supervisor: How did it go today with Tiffany?
- Aaron: She is filled with anger and will not accept any responsibility for her life.
- Supervisor: I see. How do you think you should proceed with counseling her?
- Aaron: I need to take a "tough love" approach. She needs to know that I will call her out on her rationalizations and projections.]

From the Client's Perspective

1. How would you feel if you were referred to as a "tramp" in the first session?
2. What is missing for you in this dialogue?
3. What would you find more helpful from a counselor in this scenario?

From the Counselor's Perspective

1. What is interfering with developing a working alliance?
2. Going back to the Common Counseling Mistakes list in Chapter 6, which mistakes is the counselor making with Tiffany?
3. What do you think of taking a "tough love" approach to counseling a young opioid addict? What advantages and disadvantages do you see with calling people out when they do not take sufficient responsibility for either their lives or the change process?

INDIVIDUAL EXERCISES

1. Find out from your local addiction agency if you may observe a group for opioid addicts. If this is not possible, find out when they have an open night at a local Narcotics Anonymous meeting and attend it instead. What characterizes the stories that you hear? Where do you see these individuals expressing hope for a better future?
2. Talk to someone you know that needs to take opioid medication for either severe acute or chronic pain. What

side effects do they experience? What do they do to help manage the side effects?

3. With a friend or family member, watch one of the Hollywood movies about heroin addiction suggested earlier (i.e., in the section called Specific Precontemplation Strategies). What struck you as an accurate portrayal, and what aspects (if any) seemed exaggerated for effect? Discuss what both of you learned from the movie about heroin addiction.

CLASSROOM EXERCISES

1. Show one of the videos in class from the section called Relevant Mutual Support Groups and Websites. Following the viewing, lead a discussion about the video or have students break into groups of four to discuss it. What did students learn from watching the video that they did not already know? Which parts did they already know?
2. Invite a speaker from Narcotics Anonymous to talk to your class. Ensure that students have prepared a list of questions for the speaker well in advance and have the students decide which questions they will ask.
3. The following is a common demonstration of suggestion. Place three chairs at the front of your class. Let the class know that you are going to try a simple experiment to ascertain if some degree of analgesia can be created in a volunteer's hand. Tell them that this is not going to hurt, but instead it will involve having another student in the class apply equal pressure to both palms with the sharp side of a typical house or vehicle key (either use your key or borrow one from a student). Now invite the volunteer to step forward and take a seat at the front of the class. Now ask for a second volunteer to come forward who will be the one to administer pressure on the palms of both hands. Once the volunteer takes their seat, sit down yourself in the third chair and ask the first volunteer to close their eyes. Tell the volunteer that the right hand is becoming numb. Continue suggesting numbness of the right hand (e.g., "Your right hand is getting number [pronounced 'nummer'] and number and number, you are losing feeling in your right hand, it is getting paralyzed and anesthetized") and ask the volunteer to raise a finger in the right hand when he or she feels a degree of numbness has developed. Then have the second volunteer apply equal pressure to first the left hand using the key and then the right hand. Ask the first volunteer if he or she felt a difference. As a precaution, ask the first volunteer at the end of the demonstration to once again close their eyes and say two times, "Both hands have become completely normal in every respect." Following the demonstration, lead a discussion regarding alternative ways of managing or lowering pain through suggestion, mindfulness, or yoga instead of through opioid medications. What are the possible strengths of this approach and what are the weaknesses?

CHAPTER SUMMARY

The United States and many parts of the world are experiencing an epidemic crisis due to opioid addiction. The death caused by opioid use for thousands of individuals is often due to unsuspecting addicted individuals receiving potent drugs like fentanyl, carfentanil, or W-18 instead of the opioids for which they have developed tolerance. Opioids are an inclusive term that refers to natural, synthetic, or semisynthetic drugs that mask the emotional reaction to pain while simultaneously producing euphoria. In a three-drug classification system (e.g., stimulants, depressants, hallucinogens), opioids can be referred to as depressants because they slow down the central nervous system.

Opioid addiction is a chronic disorder that involves frequent relapses. It results in a lower quality of life regarding physical health, psychological health, and social relationships. The mortality rate of opioid-addicted individuals is about 6 to 20 times greater than that of the general population. Like other addictions, opioid addiction can be caused by a desire to escape physical and/or psychological pain.

The most effective approach to treating opioid addiction is through MAT. In the United States, this is mostly buprenorphine products (namely a buprenorphine and naloxone combination) and methadone. Although methadone is a synthetic narcotic and a full agonist, both naltrexone and naloxone are opioid antagonists. Buprenorphine is a medication that has both partial agonist and antagonistic properties. Opioid-addicted individuals frequently drop out from receiving MAT. Some studies have shown that CBT has reduced dropout rates.

Overall, counseling approaches have had equivocal results with opioid addicts: some people are helped through various forms of counseling, whereas others receive little benefit. Consequently, the main thrust of treatment has focused on MAT. The psychological approach that has offered the greatest help to opioid-addicted individuals is contingency management. Some research suggests that early maladaptive schemas appear amenable to change through CBT, and group CBT is helpful in teaching coping skills and increasing self-efficacy.

REFERENCES

AddictScience.com. (n.d.). *20-Question Addiction Questionnaire*. Retrieved on June 29, 2018, from http://www.addictscience.com/20-question-addiction-questionnaire/

Agabio, R., Campesi, I., Pisanu, C., Gessa, G. L., & Franconi, F. (2016). Sex differences in substance use disorders: Focus on side effects. *Addiction Biology*, *21*(5), 1030–1042.

Ainscough, T. S., McNeill, A., Strang, J., Calder, R., & Brose, L. S. (2017). Contingency management interventions for non-prescribed drug use during treatment for opiate addiction: A systematic review and meta-analysis. *Drug and Alcohol Dependence*, *178*, 318–339.

Aletraris, L., Edmond, M. B., Paino, M., Fields, D., & Roman, P. M. (2016). Counselor training and attitudes toward pharmacotherapies for opioid use disorder. *Substance Abuse*, *37*, 47–53.

American Psychiatric Association (APA). (2013). *Diagnostic and statistical manual of mental disorders* (5th ed.). Washington, DC: Author.

American Society of Addiction Medicine (ASAM). (n.d.). *Patient-centered opioid addiction treatment (P-COAT)*. Retrieved on October 8, 2018, from https://www.asam.org/docs/default-source/advocacy/pcoat-brief-final.pdf?sfvrsn=507041c2_2

Andersen, T. E. (2012). Does attachment insecurity affect the outcomes of a multidisciplinary pain management program? The association between attachment insecurity, pain, disability, distress, and the use of opioids. *Social Science & Medicine*, *74*(9), 1461–1468.

Ara, A., Jacobs, W., Bhat, I. A., & McCall, W. V. (2016). Sleep disturbances and substance use disorders: A bi-directional relationship. *Psychiatric Annals*, *46*, 408–412.

Arnold, R. M., Avants, S. K., Margolin, A., & Marcotte, D. (2002). Patient attitudes concerning the inclusion of spirituality into addiction treatment. *Journal of Substance Abuse Treatment*, *23*, 319–326.

Asbridge, M., Duff, C., Marsh, D. C., & Erickson, P. G. (2014). Problems with the identification of 'problematic' cannabis use: Examining the issues of frequency, quantity, and drug use environment. *European Addiction Research*, *20*(5), 254–267.

Ashraf, I., Ashraf, S., Asif, J. A., & Basri, R. (2016). Metabolic effects of opiate use during pregnancy: A reappraisal. *International Medical Journal*, *23*(5), 481–484.

Austic, E., McCabe, S. E., Stoddard, S. A., Ngo, Q. E., & Boyd, C. (2015). Age and cohort patterns of medical and nonmedical use of controlled medication among adolescents. *Journal of Addiction Medicine*, *9*, 376–382.

Bach, P., Milloy, M.-J., Nguyen, P., Koehn, J., Guillemi, S., Kerr, T., & Wood, E. (2015). Gender differences in access to methadone maintenance therapy in a Canadian setting. *Drug and Alcohol Review*, *34*, 503–507.

Baker, T. E., & Chang, G. (2016). The use of auricular acupuncture in opioid use disorder: A systematic literature review. *American Journal on Addictions*, *25*, 592–602.

Banerjee, G., Edelman, E., Barry, D. T., Becker, W. C., Cerda, M., Crystal, S., . . . Marshall, B. D. (2016). Non-medical use of prescription opioids is associated with heroin initiation among US veterans: A prospective cohort study. *Addiction*, *111*(11), 2021–2031.

Barry, D. T., Savant, J. D., Beitel, M., Cutter, C. J., Schottenfeld, R. S., Kerns, R. D., . . . Carroll, K. M. (2014). The feasibility and acceptability of groups for pain management in methadone maintenance treatment. *Journal of Addiction Medicine*, *8*, 338–344.

Barry, D. T., Sofuoglu, M., Kerns, R. D., Wiechers, I. R., & Rosenheck, R. A. (2015). Prevalence and correlates of co-prescribing psychotropic medications with long-term opioid use nationally in the Veterans Health Administration. *Psychiatry Research*, *227*(2–3), 324–332.

Bastian, L. A., Driscoll, M. A., Heapy, A. A., Becker, W. C., Goulet, J. L., Kerns, R. D., . . . Haskell, S. G. (2017). Cigarette smoking status and receipt of an opioid prescription among veterans of recent wars. *Pain Medicine*, *18*(6), 1089–1097.

Bawor, M., Bami, H., Dennis, B. B., Plater, C., Worster, A., Varenbut, M., . . . Samaan, Z. (2015). Testosterone suppression in opioid users: A systematic review and meta-analysis. *Drug and Alcohol Dependence*, *149*, 1–9.

Beckerleg, S. (2001). Counselling Kenyan heroin users: Cross-cultural motivation? *Health Education*, *101*, 69–73.

Bennett, A. S., Elliott, L., Golub, A., Wolfson-Stofko, B., & Guarino, H. (2017). Opioid-involved overdose among male Afghanistan/Iraq-era U.S. Military veterans: A multidimensional perspective. *Substance Use & Misuse*, *52*(13), 1701–1711.

Berecki-Gisolf, J., Collie, A., & McClure, R. (2013). Work disability after road traffic injury in a mixed population with and without hospitalisation. *Accident Analysis and Prevention*, *51*, 129–134.

Bernardi, E., Jones, M., & Tennant, C. (1989). Quality of parenting in alcoholics and narcotic addicts. *British Journal of Psychiatry*, *154*, 677–682.

Best, D. W., Ghufran, S., Day, E., Ray, R., & Loaring, J. (2008). Breaking the habit: A retrospective analysis of desistance factors among formerly problematic heroin users. *Drug and Alcohol Review*, *27*, 619–624.

Biernacki, K., McLennan, S. N., Terrett, G., Labuschagne, I., & Rendell, P. G. (2016). Decision-making ability in current and past users of opiates: A meta-analysis. *Neuroscience and Biobehavioral Reviews*, *71*, 342–351.

Bisaga, A., Mannelli, P., Yu, M., Nangia, N., Graham, C. E., Tompkins, D. A., . . . Sullivan, M. A. (2018). Outpatient transition to extended-release injectable naltrexone for patients with opioid use disorder: A phase 3 randomized trial. *Drug and Alcohol Dependence*, *187*, 171–178.

Blanco, C., Iza, M., Schwartz, R. P., Rafful, C., Wang, S., & Olfson, M. (2013). Probability and predictors of treatment-seeking for prescription opioid use disorders: A national study. *Drug and Alcohol Dependence*, *131*(1–2), 143–148.

Blanco, C., Wall, M. M., Okuda, M., Wang, S., Iza, M., & Olfson, M. (2016). Pain as a predictor of opioid use disorder in a nationally representative sample. *American Journal of Psychiatry*, *173*, 1189–1195.

Blatt, S. J., McDonald, C., Sugarman, A., & Wilber, C. (1984). Psychodynamic theories of opiate addiction: New directions for research. *Clinical Psychology Review*, *4*, 159–189.

Bohnert, K. M., Ilgen, M. A., Louzon, S., McCarthy, J. F., & Katz, I. R. (2017). Substance use disorders and the risk of suicide mortality among men and women in the US Veterans Health Administration. *Addiction*, *112*(7), 1193–1201.

Brady, K. T., McCauley, J. L., & Back, S. E. (2016). Prescription opioid misuse, abuse, and treatment in the United States: An update. *American Journal of Psychiatry*, *173*(1), 18–26.

Brigham, G. S., Slesnick, N., Winhusen, T. M., Lewis, D. F., Guo, X., & Somoza, E. (2014). A randomized pilot clinical trial to evaluate the efficacy of Community Reinforcement and Family Training for Treatment Retention (CRAFT-T) for improving outcomes for patients completing opioid detoxification. *Drug and Alcohol Dependence*, *138*, 240–243.

Brown, T. K., & Alper, K. (2018). Treatment of opioid use disorder with ibogaine: Detoxification and drug use outcomes. *American Journal of Drug & Alcohol Abuse*, *44*, 24–36.

Brownstein, M. J. (1993). A brief history of opiates, opioid peptides, and opioid receptors. *Proceedings of the National Academy of Sciences of the United States of America*, *90*, 5391–5393.

Bubenzer, T., & Huang, H. (2014). Posthypnotic use of olfactory stimulus for pain management. *International Journal of Clinical and Experimental Hypnosis*, *62*, 188–194.

Burbage, M. L. (2018). Lifetime heroin use among Americans: An exploration of social determinants. *Dissertation Abstracts International Section A: Humanities and Social Sciences*, *78*(11-A(E)). No pagination specified.

Cacciola, J. S., Alterman, A. I., Habing, B., & McLellan, A. T. (2011). Recent status scores for version 6 of the Addiction Severity Index (ASI-6). *Addiction*, *106*, 1588–1602.

Canan, F., Karaca, S., Sogucak, S., Gecici, O., & Kuloglu, M. (2017). Eating disorders and food addiction in men with heroin use disorder: A controlled study. *Eating and Weight Disorders*, *22*(2), 249–257.

Carroll, J. J., Marshall, B. D. L., Rich, J. D., & Green, T. C. (2017). Exposure to fentanyl-contaminated heroin and overdose risk among illicit opioid users in Rhode Island: A mixed methods study. *International Journal of Drug Policy*, *46*, 136–145.

Carroll, K. M., & Weiss, R. D. (2017). The role of behavioral interventions in buprenorphine maintenance treatment: A review. *American Journal of Psychiatry*, *174*, 738–747.

Cedarbaum, E. R., & Banta-Green, C. J. (2016). Health behaviors of young adult heroin injectors in the Seattle area. *Drug and Alcohol Dependence*, *158*, 102–109.

Cerda, M., Santaella, J., Marshall, B. D. L., Kim, J. H., & Martins, S. S. (2015). Nonmedical prescription opioid use in childhood and early adolescence predicts transitions to heroin use in young adulthood: A national study. *Journal of Pediatrics*, *167*(3), 605–612.

Chang, H.-M., & Chen, L.-Y. (2018). Management of chronic pain and opioid dependence with buprenorphine/naloxone. *Psychiatry and Clinical Neurosciences*, *72*, 454.

Chang, Y.-P., Compton, P., Almeter, P., & Fox, C. H. (2015). The effect of motivational interviewing on prescription opioid adherence among older adults with chronic pain. *Perspectives in Psychiatric Care*, *51*, 211–219.

Chidambaran, V., Ding, L., Moore, D. L., Spruance, K., Cudilo, E. M., Pilipenko, V., . . . Sadhasivam, S. (2017). Predicting the pain continuum after adolescent idiopathic scoliosis surgery: A prospective cohort study. *European Journal of Pain*, *21*, 1252–1265.

Chopra, N., & Marasa, L. H. (2017). The opioid epidemic: Challenges of sustained remission. *International Journal of Psychiatry in Medicine*, *52*(2), 196–201.

Christensen, D. R., Landes, R. D., Jackson, L., Marsch, L. A., Mancino, M. J., Chopra, M. P., & Bickel, W. K. (2014). Adding an Internet-delivered treatment to an efficacious treatment package for opioid dependence. *Journal of Consulting and Clinical Psychology*, *82*, 964–972.

Cicero, T. J., Ellis, M. S., & Harney, J. (2015). Shifting patterns of prescription opioid and heroin abuse in the United States. *New England Journal of Medicine*, *373*(18), 1789–1790.

Cicero, T. J., Ellis, M. S., & Kasper, Z. A. (2017). Psychoactive substance use prior to the development of iatrogenic opioid abuse: A descriptive analysis of treatment-seeking opioid abusers. *Addictive Behaviors*, *65*, 242–244.

Cicero, T. J., Ellis, M. S., Surratt, H. L., & Kurtz, S. P. (2014). The changing face of heroin use in the United States: A retrospective analysis of the past 50 years. *JAMA Psychiatry*, *71*(7), 821–826.

Clements, D., Lopez, J. C., Rachakonda, S., Sedky, K., & Pumariega, A. (2016). Physical pain, opiate prescription medications, and heroin addiction: A case series. *Addictive Disorders & Their Treatment*, *15*(4), 175–182.

Cloutier-Gill, L., Wood, E., Millar, T., Ferris, C., & Eugenia Socias, M. (2016). Remission of severe opioid use disorder with ibogaine: A Case Report. *Journal of Psychoactive Drugs*, *48*, 214–217.

Coleman, S. B., Kaplan, J. D., & Downing, R. W. (1986). Life cycle and loss: The spiritual vacuum of heroin addiction. *Family Process*, *25*(1), 5–23.

Compton, P., & Weaver, M. F. (2015). Responsible opioid use. *Journal of Pain & Palliative Care Pharmacotherapy*, *29*(2), 166–168.

Compton, W. M., Jones, C. M., & Baldwin, G. T. (2016). Relationship between nonmedical prescription-opioid use and heroin use. *New England Journal of Medicine*, *374*(2), 154–163.

Connors, G. J., DiClemente, C. C., Velasquez, M. M., & Donovan, D. M. (2013). *Substance abuse treatment and the stages of change: Selecting and planning interventions* (2nd ed.). New York, NY: Guilford Press.

Corman, A. G., & Khantzian, E. J. (1976). Psychiatric care of a methadone patient. *Psychiatric Annals*, *6*(4), 158–164.

Courtwright, D. T. (2015). Preventing and treating narcotic addiction—A century of federal drug control. *New England Journal of Medicine*, *373*(22), 2095–2097.

Craig, R. J. (1987). MMPI-derived prevalence estimates of homosexuality among drug-dependent patients. *International Journal of the Addictions*, *22*, 1139–1145.

Csiernik, R. (2016). *Substance use and abuse: Everything matters* (2nd ed.). Toronto, ON: Canadian Scholars Press.

Darke, S., Marel, C., Mills, K. L., Ross, J., Slade, T., & Tessson, M. (2016). Years of potential life lost amongst heroin users in the Australian Treatment Outcome Study cohort, 2001–2015. *Drug and Alcohol Dependence*, *162*, 206–210.

Darke, S., Torok, M., & Ross, J. (2017). Developmental trajectories to heroin dependence: Theoretical and clinical issues. *Journal of Applied Social Psychology*, *47*(3), 165–171.

Day, E., & Mitcheson, L. (2017). Psychosocial interventions in opiate substitution treatment services: Does the evidence provide a case for optimism or nihilism? *Addiction*, *112*, 1329–1336.

Deady, M. (2009). Review of screening, assessment and outcome measures for drug and alcohol settings. *Network of Alcohol and Other Drugs Agencies*. Retrieved on June 28, 2018, from http://www.drugsandalcohol.ie/18266/1/NADA_A_Review_of_Screening%2C_Assessment_and_Outcome_Measures_for_Drug_and_Alcohol_Settings.pdf

Degenhardt, L., Charlson, F., Mathers, B., Hall, W. D., Flaxman, A. D., Johns, N., & Vos, T. (2014). The global epidemiology and burden of opioid dependence: Results from the global burden of disease 2010 study. *Addiction*, *109*, 1320–1333.

De Maeyer, J., Vanderplasschen, W., Lammertyn, J., van Nieuwenhuizen, C., Sabbe, B., & Broekaert, E. (2011). Current quality of life and its determinants among opiate-dependent individuals five years after starting methadone treatment. *Quality of Life Research: An International Journal of Quality of Life Aspects of Treatment, Care & Rehabilitation*, *20*(1), 139–150.

Denis, C., Fatseas, M., Beltran, V., Serre, F., Alexandre, J.-M., Debrabant, R., . . . Auriacombe, M. (2016). Usefulness and validity of the modified Addiction Severity Index: A focus on alcohol, drugs, tobacco, and gambling. *Substance Abuse*, *37*(1), 168–175.

Dugosh, K., Abraham, A., Seymour, B., McLoyd, K., Chalk, M., & Festinger, D. (2016). A systematic review on the use of psychosocial interventions in conjunction with medications for the treatment of opioid addiction. *Journal of Addiction Medicine*, *10*(2), 93–103.

DuPont, R. L. (2018). The opioid epidemic is an historic opportunity to improve both prevention and treatment. *Brain Research Bulletin*, *138*, 112–114.

Earleywine, M. (2016). *Substance use problems* (2nd ed.). Ashland, OH: Hogrefe.

Edlund, M. J., Forman-Hoffman, V. L., Winder, C. R., Heller, D. C., Kroutil, L. A., Lipari, R. N., & Colpe, L. J. (2015). Opioid abuse and depression in adolescents: Results from the National Survey on Drug Use and Health. *Drug and Alcohol Dependence*, *152*, 131–138.

Engel, R. J., & Rosen, D. (2015). Pathological gambling and treatment outcomes for adults age 50 or older in methadone maintenance treatment. *Journal of Gerontological Social Work*, *58*(3), 306–314.

Fattore, L., Melis, M., Fadda, P., & Fratta, W. (2014). Sex differences in addictive disorders. *Frontiers in Neuroendocrinology*, *35*(3), 272–284.

FDA News Release. (2018, May 16). *FDA approves the first non-opioid treatment for management of opioid withdrawal symptoms in adults.* Retrieved on October 6, 2018, from. Https://www.fda.gov/NewsEvents/Newsroom/PressAnnouncements/ucm607884.htm

Fink, D. S., Hu, R., Cerda, M., Keyes, K. M., Marshall, B. D. L., Galea, S., & Martins, S. S. (2015). Patterns of major depression and nonmedical use of prescription opioids in the United States. *Drug and Alcohol Dependence*, *153*, 258–264.

Finlay, A. K., Harris, A. H. S., Rosenthal, J., Blue-Howells, J., Clark, S., McGuire, J., . . . Binswanger, I. (2016). Receipt of pharmacotherapy for opioid use disorder by justice-involved U.S. Veterans Health Administration patients. *Drug and Alcohol Dependence*, *160*, 222–226.

Fischer, B., Ialomiteanu, A., Boak, A., Adlaf, E., Rehm, J., & Mann, R. E. (2013). Prevalence and key covariates of non-medical prescription opioid use among the general secondary student and adult populations in Ontario, Canada. *Drug and Alcohol Review*, *32*(3), 276–287.

Fogger, S. A., & Lehmann, K. (2017). Recovery beyond buprenorphine: Nurse-led group therapy. *Journal of Addictions Nursing*, *28*, 152–156.

Ford, J. A., & Rigg, K. K. (2015). Racial/ethnic differences in factors that place adolescents at risk for prescription opioid misuse. *Prevention Science*, *16*, 633–641.

Furlan, A. D., Sandoval, J. A., Mailis-Gagnon, A., & Tunks (2006). Opioids for chronic noncancer pain: A meta-analysis of effectiveness and side effects. *CMAJ*, *174*(11), 1589–1594.

Fuster, D., Sanvisens, A., Bolao, F., Zuluaga, P., Rivas, I., Farre, M., . . . Muga, R. (2017). Cannabis as secondary drug is not associated with a greater risk of death in patients with opiate, cocaine, or alcohol dependence. *Journal of Addiction Medicine*, *11*(1), 34–39.

Gardstrom, S. C., Klemm, A., & Murphy, K. M. (2017). Women's perceptions of the usefulness of group music therapy in addictions recovery. *Nordic Journal of Music Therapy*, *26*, 338–358.

Garland, E. L., Bryan, C. J., Finan, P. H., Thomas, E. A., Priddy, S. E., Riquino, M. R., & Howard, M. O. (2017). Pain, hedonic regulation, and opioid misuse: Modulation of momentary experience by Mindfulness-Oriented Recovery Enhancement in opioid-treated chronic pain patients. *Drug and Alcohol Dependence*, *173*, S65–S72.

Garrido-Fernandez, M., Marcos-Sierra, J. A., Lopez-Jimenez, A., & de Alda, I. O. (2017). Multi-family therapy with a reflecting team: A preliminary study on efficacy among opiate addicts in methadone maintenance treatment. *Journal of Marital and Family Therapy*, *43*, 338–351.

Gellad, W. F., Zhao, X., Thorpe, C. T., Thorpe, J. M., Sileanu, F. E., Cashy, J. P., . . . Good, C. B. (2017). Overlapping buprenorphine, opioid, and benzodiazepine prescriptions among veterans dually enrolled in Department of Veterans Affairs and Medicare Part D. *Substance Abuse*, *38*, 22–25.

Gerra, L. M., Gerra, G., Mercolini, L., Manfredini, M., Somaini, L., Pieri, C. M., . . . Marchesi, C. (2017). Increased oxytocin levels among abstinent heroin addicts: Association with aggressiveness, psychiatric symptoms and perceived childhood neglect. *Progress in Neuro-Psychopharmacology & Biological Psychiatry*, *75*, 70–76.

Godley, M. D., Passetti, L. L., Subramaniam, G. A., Funk, R. R., Smith, J. E., & Meyers, R. J. (2017). Adolescent Community Reinforcement Approach implementation and treatment outcomes for youth with opioid problem use. *Drug and Alcohol Dependence*, *174*, 9–16.

Golub, A., & Bennett, A. S. (2013). Prescription opioid initiation, correlates, and consequences among a sample of OEF/OIF military personnel. *Substance Use & Misuse*, *48*(10), 811–820.

Goncalves, J., Martins, J., Baptista, S., Ambrosio, A. F., & Silva, A. P. (2016). Effects of drugs of abuse on the central neuropeptide Y system. *Addiction Biology*, *21*, 755–765.

Gossop, M., Darke, S., Griffiths, P., Hando, J., Powis, B., Hall, W., & Strang, J. (1995). The severity of dependence scale (SDS): Psychometric properties of the SDS in English and Australian samples of heroin, cocaine and amphetamine users. *Addiction*, *90*, 607–614.

Grant, B. F., Saha, T. D., Ruan, W. J., Goldstein, R. B., Chou, S. P., Jung, J., . . . Hasin, D. S. (2016). Epidemiology of *DSM-5* drug use disorder: Results from the National Epidemiologic Survey on Alcohol and Related Conditions—III. *JAMA Psychiatry*, *73*, 39–45.

Hale, M. E., Zimmerman, T. R., Jr., Ma, Y., & Malamut, R. (2017). Evaluation of quality of life, functioning, disability, and work/school productivity following treatment with an extended-release hydrocodone tablet formulated with abuse-deterrence technology: A 12-month open-label study in patients with chronic pain. *Pain Practice*, *17*, 229–238.

Hale, R. (2013). In search of a reliable container: Staff supervision at a drug dependency unit. In M. Bower, R. Hale, & H. Wood (Eds.), *Addictive states of mind* (pp. 199–210). London, England: Karnac Books.

Hall, W., & Weier, M. (2017). Lee Robins' studies of heroin use among US Vietnam veterans. *Addiction, 112*, 176–180.

Hammersley, R., Dalgarno, P., McCollum, S., Reid, M., Strike, Y., Smith, A., . . . Liddell, D. (2016). Trauma in the childhood stories of people who have injected drugs. *Addiction Research & Theory, 24*(2), 135–151.

Hancock, D. B., Levy, J. L., Gaddis, N. C., Glasheen, C., Saccone, N. L., Page, G. P., . . . Johnson, E. O. (2015). Cis-expression quantitative trait loci mapping reveals replicable associations with heroin addiction in OPRM1. *Biological Psychiatry, 78*(7), 474–484.

Haozous, E. A., & Knobf, M. T. (2013). "All my tears were gone": Suffering and cancer pain in southwest American Indians. *Journal of Pain and Symptom Management, 45*, 1050–1060.

Harris, B. R. (2016). Talking about screening, brief intervention, and referral to treatment for adolescents: An upstream intervention to address the heroin and prescription opioid epidemic. *Preventive Medicine: An International Journal Devoted to Practice and Theory, 91*, 397–399.

Hassan, A. N., Foll, B. L., Imtiaz, S., & Rehm, J. (2017). The effect of post-traumatic stress disorder on the risk of developing prescription opioid use disorder: Results from the National Epidemiologic Survey on Alcohol and Related Conditions III. *Drug and Alcohol Dependence, 179*, 260–266.

Hatcher, A. E., Mendoza, S., & Hansen, H. (2018). At the expense of a life: Race, class, and the meaning of buprenorphine in pharmaceuticalized "care." *Substance Use & Misuse, 53*, 301–310.

Heinz, A., Epstein, D. H., & Preston, K. L. (2007). Spiritual/religious experiences and in-treatment outcome in an inner-city program for heroin and cocaine dependence. *Journal of Psychoactive Drugs, 39*, 41–49.

Hemsing, N., Greaves, L., Poole, N., & Schmidt, R. (2016). Misuse of prescription opioid medication among women: A scoping review. *Pain Research & Management, Article ID 1754195*, 1–8.

Hines, L. A., Lynskey, M., Morley, K. I., Griffiths, P., Gossop, M., Powis, B., & Strang, J. (2017). The relationship between initial route of heroin administration and speed of transition to daily heroin use. *Drug and Alcohol Review, 36*(5), 633–638.

Hollingshead, N. A. (2017). Examining the influence of Hispanic ethnicity and ethnic bias on medical students' pain decisions. *Dissertation Abstracts International: Section B: The Sciences and Engineering, 78*(3-B(E)). No pagination specified.

Hser, Y.-I., Evans, E., Grella, C., Ling, W., & Anglin, D. (2015). Long-term course of opioid addiction. *Harvard Review of Psychiatry, 23*(2), 76–89.

Hsiao, R. C.-J., & Walker, L. R. (2016). Understanding adolescent substance use disorders in the era of marijuana legalization, opioid epidemic, and social media. *Child and Adolescent Psychiatric Clinics of North America, 25*, xiii–xiv.

Hudson, T. J. (2016). National analysis of opioid use among OEF/OIF/OND veterans with traumatic brain injury in the Veterans Healthcare System. *Dissertation Abstracts International Section A: Humanities and Social Sciences, 76*(9-A(E)). No pagination specified.

Huffman, K. L., Shella, E. R., Sweis, G., Griffith, S. D., Scheman, J., & Covington, E. C. (2015). Nonopioid substance use disorders and opioid dose predict therapeutic opioid addiction. *Journal of Pain, 16*(2), 126–134.

Huhn, A. S., & Dunn, K. E. (2017). Why aren't physicians prescribing more buprenorphine? *Journal of Substance Abuse Treatment, 78*, 1–7.

Hunnicutt, J. N., Chrysanthopoulou, S. A., Ulbricht, C. M., Hume, A. L., Tjia, J., & Lapane, K. L. (2018). Prevalence of long-term opioid use in long-stay nursing home residents. *Journal of the American Geriatrics Society, 66*(1), 48–55.

Ilgen, M. A., Bohnert, A. S. B., Ganoczy, D., Bair, M. J., McCarthy, J. F., & Blow, F. C. (2016). Opioid dose and risk of suicide. *Pain, 157*(5), 1079–1084.

Imperio, C. G. (2016). From behavior to epeigenetics: Individual differences in heroin addiction. *Dissertation Abstracts International: Section B: The Sciences and Engineering, 77*(3-B(E)). No pagination specified.

Isralowitz, R. E., Telias, D., & Abu-Saad, I. (1994). Psychological characteristics of heroin addicts in Israel: A status model comparison. *Journal of Social Psychology, 134*, 399–401.

Jarlenski, M., Barry, C. L., Gollust, S., Graves, A. J., Kennedy-Hendricks, A., & Kozhimannil, K. (2017). Polysubstance use among US women of reproductive age who use opioids for nonmedical reasons. *American Journal of Public Health, 107*(8), 1308–1310.

Jarvis, B. P., Holtyn, A. F., DeFulio, A., Dunn, K. E., Everly, J. J., Leoutsakos, J.-M. S., . . . Silverman, K. (2017). Effects of incentives for naltrexone adherence on opiate abstinence in heroin-dependent adults. *Addiction, 112*, 830–837.

Jeffery, D. D., May, L., Luckey, B., Balison, B. M., & Klette, K. L. (2014). Use and abuse of prescribed opioids, central nervous system depressants, and stimulants among U.S. active duty military personnel in FY 2010. *Military Medicine, 179*(10), 1141–1148.

Jiloha, R. C., Agnihotri, B. R., & Munjal, G. C. (1988). Adolescent heroin: Addicts and their families. *Journal of Personality and Clinical Studies, 4*(2), 201–203.

Jimenez, S. C. (2015). Using the millon behavioral medicine diagnostic (MBMD) to predict outcomes of spinal cord stimulation for the treatment of chronic nonmalignant pain for patients who identify as white. *Dissertation Abstracts International: Section B: The Sciences and Engineering, 76*(5-B(E)). No pagination specified.

Jin, H., Huriaux, E., Loughran, E., Packer, T., & Raymond, H. F. (2014). Differences in HIV risk behaviors among people who inject drugs by gender and sexual orientation, San Francisco, 2012. *Drug and Alcohol Dependence, 145*, 180–184.

Johnson, B., & Mosri, D. F. (2016). The neuropsychoanalytic approach: Using neuroscience as the basic science of psychoanalysis. *Frontiers in Psychology, 7*, 1–12.

Johnson, R. (2017, July 30). *10 ways to quit opioids, heroin, & get off prescription painkillers.* Retrieved on October 8, 2018, from https://opiate-freedom-center.com/8-ways-to-opioid-detox-success/

Johnston, L. G., Holman, A., Dahoma, M., Miller, L. A., Kim, E., Mussa, M., . . . Sabin, K. (2010). HIV risk and the overlap of injecting drug use and high-risk sexual behaviours among men who have sex with men in Zanzibar (Unguja), Tanzania. *International Journal of Drug Policy, 21*, 485–492.

Jones, C. M., Christensen, A., & Gladden, R. M. (2017). Increases in prescription opioid injection abuse among treatment admissions in the United States, 2004–2013. *Drug and Alcohol Dependence, 176*, 89–95.

Jones, C. M., & McAninch, J. K. (2015). Emergency department visits and overdose deaths from combined use of opioids and benzodiazepines. *American Journal of Preventive Medicine, 49*, 493–501.

Jones, J. D., Vadhan, N. P., Luba, R. R., & Comer, S. D. (2016). The effects of heroin administration and drug cues on impulsivity. *Journal of Clinical and Experimental Neuropsychology, 38*(6), 709–720.

Kandel, D. B., Hu, M.-C., Griesler, P., & Wall, M. (2017). Increases from 2002 to 2015 in prescription opioid overdose deaths in combination with other substances. *Drug and Alcohol Dependence, 178*, 501–511.

Karakula, S. L., Weiss, R. D., Griffin, M. L., Borges, A. M., Bailey, A. J., & McHugh, R. (2016). Delay discounting in opioid use disorder: Differences between heroin and prescription opioid users. *Drug and Alcohol Dependence, 169*, 68–72.

Katz, C., El-Gabalawy, R., Keyes, K. M., Martins, S. S., & Sareen, J. (2013). Risk factors for incident nonmedical prescription opioid use and abuse and dependence: Results from a longitudinal nationally representative sample. *Drug and Alcohol Dependence, 132*, 107–113.

Kecojevic, A., Corliss, H. L., & Lankenau, S. E. (2015). Motivations for prescription drug misuse among young men who have sex with men (YMSM) in Philadelphia. *International Journal of Drug Policy, 26*, 764–771.

Kecojevic, A., Wong, C. F., Schrager, S. M., Silva, K., Bloom, J. J., Iverson, E., & Lankenau, S. E. (2012). Initiation into prescription drug misuse: Differences between lesbian, gay, bisexual, transgender (LGBT) and heterosexual high-risk young adults in Los Angeles and New York. *Addictive Behaviors, 37*, 1289–1293.

Kelty, E., Cumming, C., Troeung, L., & Hulse, G. (2018). Buprenorphine alone or with naloxone: Which is safer? *Journal of Psychopharmacology, 32*, 344–352.

Kerridge, B. T., Saha, T. D., Chou, S. P., Zhang, H., Jung, J., Ruan, W. J., . . . Hasin, D. S. (2015). Gender and nonmedical prescription opioid use and *DSM-5* nonmedical prescription opioid use disorder: Results from the National Epidemiologic Survey on Alcohol and Related Conditions—III. *Drug and Alcohol Dependence, 156*, 47–56.

Kim, S. J., Marsch, L. A., Acosta, M. C., Guarino, H., & Aponte-Melendez, Y. (2016). Can persons with a history of multiple addiction treatment episodes benefit from technology delivered behavior therapy? A moderating role of treatment history at baseline. *Addictive Behaviors, 54*, 18–23.

Kouimtsidis, C., Reynolds, M., Coulton, S., & Drummond, C. (2012). How does cognitive behaviour therapy work with opioid-dependent clients? Results of the UKCBTMM Study. *Drugs: Education, Prevention & Policy, 19*, 253–258.

Krausz, M. R., Saddichha, S., Strehlau, V., Taplin, C., Li, K., Al-desouki, M., & Schuetz, C. (2014). Is exposure to childhood maltreatment associated with adult psychological distress among adult intravenous drug user? *Mental Health and Substance Use, 7*(3), 207–216.

Kroll-Desrosiers, A. R., Skanderson, M., Bastian, L. A., Brandt, C. A., Haskell, S., Kerns, R. D., & Mattocks, K. M. (2016). Receipt of prescription opioids in a national sample of pregnant veterans receiving Veterans Health Administration care. *Women's Health Issues, 26*(2), 240–246.

Lake, S., Kerr, T., Buxton, J., Guillemi, S., Parashar, S., Montaner, J., . . . Milloy, M.-J. (2016). Prescription opioid injection among HIV-positive people who inject drugs in a Canadian setting. *AIDS and Behavior, 20*, 2941–2949.

Lang, B., & Rosenberg, H. (2017). Public perceptions of behavioral and substance addictions. *Psychology of Addictive Behaviors, 31*(1), 79–84.

Laplante, C. (2018). What are drug addiction assessments for? *Project Know*. Retrieved on June 29, 2018, from https://www.projectknow.com/research/assessment/

Lazaridou, A., Franceschelli, O., Buliteanu, A., Cornelius, M., Edwards, R. R., & Jamison, R. N. (2017). Influence of catastrophizing on pain intensity, disability, side effects, and opioid misuse among pain patients in primary care. *Journal of Applied Biobehavioral Research, 22*, 1–13.

Lea, T., Mao, L., Bath, N., Prestage, G., Zablotska, I., de Wit, J., & Holt, M. (2013). Injecting drug use among gay and bisexual men in Sydney: Prevalence and associations with sexual risk practices and HIV and hepatitis C infection. *AIDS and Behavior, 17*, 1344–1351.

Lee, K.-H., Lin, H.-C., Wang, P.-W., & Yen, C.-F. (2016). An integrated model of depression, compulsion, and mindfulness among heroin abusers in Taiwan. *American Journal on Addictions, 25*(3), 227–232.

Lei, Y., Xi, C., Li, P., Luo, M., Wang, W., Pan, S., . . . Lu, C. (2018). Association between childhood maltreatment and non-medical prescription opioid use among Chinese senior high school students: The moderating role of gender. *Journal of Affective Disorders, 235*, 421–427.

Lesourne, O. (1995). Addictive behaviors and splitting of the ego. *Topique: Revue Freudienne, 25*(56), 151–166.

Li, P., Huang, Y., Guo, L., Wang, W., Xi, C., Lei, Y., . . . Lu, C. (2018). Sexual attraction and the nonmedical use of opioids and sedative drugs among Chinese adolescents. *Drug and Alcohol Dependence, 183*, 169–175.

Liang, C.-S., Ho, P.-S., Yen, C.-H., Chen, C. Y., Kuo, S.-C., Huang, C.-C., . . . Huang, S.-Y. (2017). The relationship between the striatal dopamine transporter and novelty seeking and cognitive flexibility in opioid dependence. *Progress in Neuro-Psychopharmacology & Biological Psychiatry, 74*, 36–42.

Liang, H.-J., Lin, Y., Zhang, C., Ungvari, G. S., & Tang, W.-K. (2016). Drug addiction: A global challenge. *East Asian Archives of Psychiatry, 26*(2), 43–44.

Liao, Y.-T., Chen, C.-Y., Ng, M.-H., Huang, K.-Y., Shao, W.-C., Lin, T.-Y., . . . Gossop, M. (2017). Depression and severity of substance dependence among heroin dependent patients with ADHD symptoms. *American Journal on Addictions, 26*(1), 26–33.

Lin, L. (A.), Bohnert, A. S. B., Price, A. M., Jannausch, M., Bonar, E. E., & Ilgen, M. A. (2015). Pain acceptance and opiate use disorders in addiction treatment patients with comorbid pain. *Drug and Alcohol Dependence, 157*, 136–142.

Lin, L. A., Walton, M. A., Bonar, E. E., & Blow, F. C. (2016). Trajectories of nonmedical use of prescription opioids among adolescents in primary care. *Addiction Research & Theory, 24*, 514–520.

Linas, B. S., Latkin, C., Westergaard, R. P., Chang, L. W., Bollinger, R. C., Genz, A., & Kirk, G. D. (2015). Capturing illicit drug use where and when it happens: An ecological momentary assessment of the social, physical and activity environment of using versus craving illicit drugs. *Addiction, 110*(2), 315–325.

Lingford-Hughes, A., Myers, J., Watson, B., Reid, A. G., Kalk, N., Feeney, A., . . . Nutt, D. J. (2016). Using. *NeuroImage, 132*, 1–7.

Littrell, J. (2017). Expanding access to Medication Assisted Treatment: The U.S. government's response to the current heroin epidemic. *Social Work in Mental Health, 15*(2), 209–229.

Litz, M., & Leslie, D. (2017). The impact of mental health comorbidities on adherence to buprenorphine: A claims based analysis. *American Journal on Addictions, 26*, 859–863.

Lopez-Quintero, C., Roth, K. B., Eaton, W. W., Wu, L.-T., Cottler, L. B., Bruce, M., & Anthony, J. C. (2015). Mortality among heroin users and users of other internationally regulated drugs: A 27-year follow-up of users in the Epidemiologic Catchment Area Program household samples. *Drug and Alcohol Dependence, 156*, 104–111.

Lydon-Staley, D. M., Cleveland, H., Huhn, A. S., Cleveland, M. J., Harris, J., Stankoski, D., . . . Bunce, S. C. (2017). Daily sleep quality affects drug craving, partially through indirect associations with positive affect, in patients in treatment for nonmedical use of prescription drugs. *Addictive Behaviors, 65*, 275–282.

Macmadu, A., Carroll, J. J., Hadland, S. E., Green, T. C., & Marshall, B. D. L. (2017). Prevalence and correlates of fentanyl-contaminated heroin exposure among young adults who use prescription opioids non-medically. *Addictive Behaviors, 68*, 35–38.

Majeed, M. H., Ali, A. A., & Sudak, D. M. (2018). Mindfulness-based interventions for chronic pain: Evidence and applications. *Asian Journal of Psychiatry, 32*, 79–83.

Maremmani, A. G. I., Gazzarrini, D., Fiorin, A., Cingano, V., Bellio, G., Perugi, G., & Maremmani, I. (2018). Psychopathology of addiction: Can the SCL90-based five-dimensional structure differentiate heroin use disorder from a non-substance-related addictive disorder such as gambling disorder? *Annals of General Psychiatry, 17*, 1–9.

Marta, C. J., Ryan, W. C., Kopelowicz, A., & Koek, R. J. (2015). Mania following use of ibogaine: A case series. *American Journal on Addictions, 24*, 203–205.

Martins, S. S., Fenton, M. C., Keyes, K. M., Blanco, C., Zhu, H., & Storr, C. L. (2012). Mood and anxiety disorders and their association with non-medical prescription opioid use and prescription opioid-use disorder: Longitudinal evidence from the National Epidemiologic Study on Alcohol and Related Conditions. *Psychological Medicine, 42*(6), 1261–1272.

Martins, S. S., Santaella-Tenorio, J., Marshall, B. D. L., Maldonado, A., & Cerda, M. (2015). Racial/ethnic differences in trends in heroin use and heroin-related risk behaviors among nonmedical prescription opioid users. *Drug and Alcohol Dependence, 151*, 278–283.

Martins, S. S., Sarvet, A., Santaella-Tenorio, J., Saha, T., Grant, B. F., & Hasin, D. S. (2017). Changes in US lifetime heroin use and heroin use disorder: Prevalence from the 2001–2002 to 2012–2013 National Epidemiologic Survey on Alcohol and Related Conditions. *JAMA Psychiatry, 74*(5), 445–455.

Martins, S. S., Segura, L. E., Santaella-Tenorio, J., Perlmutter, A., Fenton, M. C., Cerda, M., . . . Hasin, D. S. (2017). Prescription opioid use disorder and heroin use among 12–34 year-olds in the United States from 2002 to 2014. *Addictive Behaviors, 65*, 236–241.

Maté, G. (2008). *In the realm of hungry ghosts: Close encounters with addiction*. Toronto, ON: Vintage Books.

Mateu-Gelabert, P., Jessell, L., Goodbody, E., Kim, D., Gile, K., . . . Guarino, H. (2017). High enhancer, downer, withdrawal helper: Multifunctional nonmedical benzodiazepine use among young adult opioid users in New York City. *International Journal of Drug Policy, 46*, 17–27.

McCabe, S. E., Veliz, P., & Schulenberg, J. E. (2016). Adolescent context of exposure to prescription opioids and substance use disorder symptoms at age 35: A national longitudinal study. *Pain, 157*, 2173–2178.

McDonald, R., Campbell, N. D., & Strang, J. (2017). Twenty years of take-home naloxone for the prevention of overdose deaths from heroin and other opioids—Conception and maturation. *Drug and Alcohol Dependence, 178*, 176–187.

McElrath, K. (2018). Medication-assisted treatment for opioid addiction in the United States: Critique and commentary. *Substance Use & Misuse, 53*, 334–343.

McHugh, R. K., Murray, H. W., Hearon, B. A., Pratt, E. M., Pollack, M. H., Safren, S. A., & Otto, M. W. (2013). Predictors of dropout from psychosocial treatment in opioid-dependent outpatients. *American Journal on Addictions, 22*, 18–22.

McKnight, E. R., Bonny, A. E., Lange, H. L. H., Kline, D. M., Abdel-Rasoul, M., Gay, J. R., & Matson, S. C. (2017). Statewide opioid prescriptions and the prevalence of adolescent opioid misuse in Ohio. *American Journal of Drug and Alcohol Abuse, 43*, 299–305.

McLellan, A. T., Cacciola, J. C., Alterman, A. I., Rikoon, S. H., & Carise, D. (2006). The Addiction Severity Index at 25: Origins, contributions and transitions. *American Journal on Addictions, 15*(2), 113–124.

McQueen, K. A., Murphy-Oikonen, J., & Desaulniers, L. (2015). Maternal substance use and Neonatal Abstinence Syndrome: A descriptive study. *Maternal and Child Health Journal, 19*, 1756–1765.

Meiman, J., Tomasallo, C., & Paulozzi, L. (2015). Trends and characteristics of heroin overdoses in Wisconsin, 2003–2012. *Drug and Alcohol Dependence, 152*, 177–184.

Melemis, S. M. (2018, June 12). Substance abuse quiz: Are you addicted to drugs or alcohol? *Addiction and Recovery*. Retrieved on June 29, 2018, from https://www.addictionsandrecovery.org/addiction-self-test.htm

Melin, Y., Eklund, M., & Lindgren, B.-M. (2017). Experiences of living with opioid dependence: An interview study among individuals participating in medication-assisted treatment. *Issues in Mental Health Nursing, 38*, 9–17.

Meyer, M., & Phillips, J. (2015). Caring for pregnant opioid abusers in Vermont: A potential model for non-urban areas. *Preventive Medicine, 80*, 18–22.

Milkman, H. B., & Sunderwirth, S. G. (2010). *Craving for ecstasy and natural highs: A positive approach to mood alteration*. Thousand Oaks, CA: SAGE.

Miller, H. V., Miller, J. M., & Barnes, J. C. (2016). Reentry programming for opioid and opiate involved female offenders: Findings from a mixed methods evaluation. *Journal of Criminal Justice, 46*, 129–136.

Miller, W. R. (2016). Sacred cows and greener pastures: Reflections from 40 years in addiction research. *Alcoholism Treatment Quarterly, 34*(1), 92–115.

Mirkovic-Hajdukov, M., Efendic Spahic, T., Softic, R., Becirovic, E., & Simic, J. (2017). Family atmosphere and relationships as predictors of heroin addiction. *Psychiatria Danubina, 29*(Suppl 2), 129–133.

Moore, B. A., Buono, F. D., Printz, D. M. B., Lloyd, D. P., Fiellin, D. A., Cutter, C. J., . . . Barry, D. T. (2017). Customized recommendations and reminder text messages for automated, computer-based treatment during methadone. *Experimental and Clinical Psychopharmacology, 25*, 485–495.

Morden, N. E., Munson, J. C., Colla, C. H., Skinner, J. S., Bynum, J. P. W., Zhou, W., & Meara, E. (2014). Prescription opioid use among disabled Medicare beneficiaries: Intensity, trends, and regional variation. *Medical Care, 52*, 852–859.

Morrison, M. F., Lin, K., & Gersh, S. (2018). Addictions: Evidence for integrative treatment. In D. A. Monti & A. B. Newberg (Eds.), *Integrative psychiatry and brain health* (2nd ed., pp. 1–22). New York, NY: Oxford University Press.

Motlagh, F., Ibrahim, F., Menke, J., Rashid, R., Seghatoleslam, T., & Habil, H. (2016). Neuroelectrophysiological approaches in heroin addiction research: A review of literatures. *Journal of Neuroscience Research*, *94*(4), 297–309.

Mullen, R., & Arbiter, N. (2017). The US therapeutic community 2017. *Therapeutic Communities*, *38*, 206.

Muller, A. E., Bjornestad, R., & Clausen, T. (2018). Dissatisfaction with opioid maintenance treatment partly explains reported side effects of medications. *Drug and Alcohol Dependence*, *187*, 22–28.

Myers, C. E., Rego, J., Haber, P., Morley, K., Beck, K. D., Hogarth, L., & Moustafa, A. A. (2017). Learning and generalization from reward and punishment in opioid addiction. *Behavioural Brain Research*, *317*, 122–131.

Myers, C. E., Sheynin, J., Balsdon, T., Luzardo, A., Beck, K. D., Hogarth, L., . . . Moustafa, A. A. (2016). Probabilistic reward- and punishment-based learning in opioid addiction: Experimental and computational data. *Behavioural Brain Research*, *296*, 240–248.

Narayan, R. (1994). Psychodynamic motivational patterns in heroin addicts. *Pharmacopsychoecologia*, *7*(1), 13–16.

National Institute on Drug Abuse (NIDA). (2018). *Chart of evidence-based screening tools for adults and adolescents*. Retrieved on June 28, 2018, from https://www.drugabuse.gov/nidamed-medical-health-professionals/tool-resources-your-practice/screening-assessment-drug-testing-resources/chart-evidence-based-screening-tools-adults

Nelson, E. C., Agrawal, A., Heath, A. C., Bogdan, R., Sherva, R., Zhang, B., . . . Montgomery, G. W. (2016). Evidence of CNIH3 involvement in opioid dependence. *Molecular Psychiatry*, *21*(5), 608–614.

Nikolaou, K., Kapoukranidou, D., Ndungu, S., Floros, G., & Kovatsi, L. (2017). Severity of withdrawal symptoms, plasma oxytocin levels, and treatment outcome in heroin users undergoing acute withdrawal. *Journal of Psychoactive Drugs*, *49*(3), 233–241.

Noller, G. E., Frampton, C. M., & Yazar-Klosinski, B. (2018). Ibogaine treatment outcomes for opioid dependence from a twelve-month follow-up observational study. *American Journal of Drug & Alcohol Abuse*, *44*, 37–46.

Norn, S., Kruse, P. R., & Kruse, E. (2005). History of opium poppy and morphine. *Dansk Medicinhistorisk Arbog*, *33*, 171–184.

O'Brien, K. H. M., Salas-Wright, C. P., Vaughn, M. G., & LeCloux, M. (2015). Childhood exposure to a parental suicide attempt and risk for substance use disorders. *Addictive Behaviors*, *46*, 70–76.

Ochoa, K. C., Hahn, J. A., Seal, K. H., & Moss, A. R. (2001). Overdosing among young injection drug users in San Francisco. *Addictive Behaviors*, *26*, 453–460.

O'Farrell, T. J., Schumm, J. A., Murphy, M. M., & Muchowski, P. M. (2017). A randomized clinical trial of behavioral couples therapy versus individually-based treatment for drug-abusing women. *Journal of Consulting and Clinical Psychology*, *85*, 309–322.

Okunseri, C., Dionne, R. A., Gordon, S. M., Okunseri, E., & Szabo, A. (2015). Prescription of opioid analgesics for nontraumatic dental conditions in emergency departments. *Drug and Alcohol Dependence*, *156*, 261–266.

Ompad, D. C., Wang, J., Dumchev, K., Barska, J., Samko, M., Zeziulin, O., . . . DeHovitz, J. (2017). Patterns of harm reduction service utilization and HIV incidence among people who inject drugs in Ukraine: A two-part latent profile analysis. *International Journal of Drug Policy*, *43*, 7–15.

Otto, M. W., Hearon, B. A., McHugh, R. K., Calkins, A. W., Pratt, E., Murray, H. W., . . . Pollack, M. H. (2014). A randomized, controlled trial of the efficacy of an interoceptive exposure-based CBT for treatment-refractory outpatients with opioid dependence. *Journal of Psychoactive Drugs*, *46*, 402–411.

Palamar, J. J., Shearston, J. A., Dawson, E. W., Mateu-Gelabert, P., & Ompad, D. C. (2016). Nonmedical opioid use and heroin use in a nationally representative sample of US high school seniors. *Drug and Alcohol Dependence*, *158*, 132–138.

Pani, P. P., Maremmani, A. G., Trogu, E., Vigna-Taglianti, F., Mathis, F., Diecidue, R., . . . Maremmani, I. (2016). Psychic structure of opioid addiction: Impact of lifetime psychiatric problems on SCL-90-based psychopathologic dimensions in heroin-dependent patients. *Addictive Disorders & Their Treatment*, *15*(1), 6–16.

Parker, M. A. (2017). Extra-medical prescription pain reliever use, dependence, and persistence among adolescents. *Dissertation Abstracts International: Section B: The Sciences and Engineering*, *77*(10-B(E)). No pagination specified.

Patra, B. N., Sarkar, S., Basu, D., & Mattoo, S. K. (2016). Quality of life of opioid- and alcohol-dependent treatment seeking men in North India. *Journal of Substance Use*, *21*(3), 317–322.

Peles, E., Adelson, M., Seligman, Z., Bloch, M., Potik, D., & Schreiber, S. (2014). Psychiatric comorbidity differences between women with history of childhood sexual abuse who are methadone-maintained former opiate addicts and non-addicts. *Psychiatry Research*, *219*(1), 191–197.

Peltz, G., & Anand, K. J. S. (2015). Long-acting opioids for treating neonatal abstinence syndrome: A high price for a short stay? *JAMA: Journal of the American Medical Association*, *314*, 2023–2024.

Perkins, E., & Shannon, L. (2016). Understanding differences between heroin and other drug users among individuals entering treatment. *Journal of Social Work Practice in the Addictions*, *16*(3), 306–320.

Petrakis, I. L., Sofuoglu, M., & Rosenheck, R. (2015). VA patients with high numbers of opioid prescriptions: A national study of sociodemographic and diagnostic characteristics, health service, and psychotropic medication use. *Addictive Disorders & Their Treatment*, *14*(4), 167–175.

Petry, N. M. (2012). *Contingency management for substance abuse treatment: A guide to implementing evidence-based practice*. New York, NY: Routledge/Taylor & Francis Group.

Petry, N. M. (2013). Commentary on Ling et al. (2013): Is there a role for psychotherapy in the treatment of opioid dependence? *Addiction*, *108*, 1799–1800.

Plummer, J. (2013). In the arms of addiction: A qualitative study on heroin injectors' relationship to the needle. *Dissertation Abstracts International: Section B: The Sciences and Engineering*, *73*(10-B(E)). No pagination specified.

Pomini, V., Gournellis, R., Kokkevi, A., Tomaras, V., Papadimitriou, G., & Liappas, J. (2014). Rejection attitudes, poor parental bonding, and stressful life events in heroin addicts' families. *Substance Use & Misuse*, *49*(14), 1867–1877.

Prince, J. D. (2015). Opioid analgesic use disorders among adolescents in the United States. *Journal of Child & Adolescent Substance Abuse*, *24*, 28–36.

Prochaska, J. O., Norcross, J. C., & DiClemente, C. C. (1994). *Changing for good*. New York, NY: Avon Books.

Proctor, S. L., Copeland, A. L., Kopak, A. M., Hoffmann, N. G., Herschman, P. L., & Polukhina, N. (2015). Predictors of patient retention in methadone maintenance treatment. *Psychology of Addictive Behaviors, 29*, 906–917.

Puffer, E. S., Skalski, L. M., & Meade, C. S. (2012). Changes in religious coping and relapse to drug use among opioid-dependent patients following inpatient detoxification. *Journal of Religion and Health, 51*, 1226–1238

Pugatch, M., Knight, J. R., McGuiness, P., Sherritt, L., & Levy, S. (2014). A group therapy program for opioid-dependent adolescents and their parents. *Substance Abuse, 35*, 435–441.

Rajan, S., Ruggles, K. V., Guarino, H., & Mateu-Gelabert, P. (2018). Heroin use and drug injection among youth also misusing prescription drugs. *American Journal of Health Behavior, 42*, 144–155.

Raketic, D., Barisic, J. V., Svetozarevic, S. M., Gazibara, T., Tepavcevic, D. K., & Milovanovic, S. D. (2017). Five-factor model personality profiles: The differences between alcohol and opiate addiction among females. *Psychiatria Danubina, 29*(1), 74–80.

Rashid, R. A., Kamali, K., Habil, M. H., Shaharom, M. H., Seghatoleslam, T., & Looyeh, M. Y. (2014). A mosque-based methadone maintenance treatment strategy: Implementation and pilot results. *International Journal of Drug Policy, 25*, 1071–1075.

Rastegar, D., & Fingerhood, M. (2016). *The American Society of Addiction Medicine handbook of addiction medicine*. New York, NY: Oxford University Press.

Reed, B., Butelman, E. R., & Kreek, M. J. (2017). Endogenous opioid system in addiction and addiction-related behaviors. *Current Opinion in Behavioral Sciences, 13*, 196–202.

Renner, J. A., & Suzuki, J. (2011). Opiates and prescription drugs. In B. A. Johnson (Ed.), *Addiction medicine: Science and practice* (pp. 463–493). New York, NY: Springer.

Rigg, K. K., & Monnat, S. M. (2015). Comparing characteristics of prescription painkiller misusers and heroin users in the United States. *Addictive Behaviors, 51*, 106–112.

Robertson, A. G., & Swartz, M. S. (2018). Extended-release naltrexone and drug treatment courts: Policy and evidence for implementing an evidence-based treatment. *Journal of Substance Abuse Treatment, 85*, 101–104.

Ross, M. W., & Williams, M. L. (2001). Sexual behavior and illicit drug use. *Annual Review of Sex Research, 12*, 290–310.

Ruhm, C. J. (2017). Geographic variation in opioid and heroin involved drug poisoning mortality rates. *American Journal of Preventive Medicine, 53*(6), 745–753.

Russell, B. S., Trudeau, J. J., & Leland, A. J. (2015). Social influence on adolescent polysubstance use: The escalation to opioid use. *Substance Use & Misuse, 50*, 1325–1331.

Saedy, M., Ardani, A. R., Kooshki, S., Firouzabadi, M. J., Emamipour, S., Mahboub, L. D., & Mojahedi, M. (2018). Effectiveness of acceptance-commitment therapy on craving beliefs in patients on methadone maintenance therapy: A pilot study. *Journal of Rational-Emotive & Cognitive-Behavior Therapy, 36*, 288–302.

Salani, D. A., Zdanowicz, M., & Joseph, L. (2016). Heroin use. *Journal of Psychosocial Nursing and Mental Health Services, 54*(6), 31–37.

Salas-Wright, C. P., Vaughn, M. G., Clark Goings, T. T., Cordova, D., & Schwartz, S. J. (2018). Substance use disorders among immigrants in the United States: A research update. *Addictive Behaviors, 76*, 169–173.

Sarid, O., Isralowitz, R., Yehudai, M., & Reznik, A. (2016). Suicidal ideation among heroin-abusing mothers in methadone maintenance treatment. *Crisis: The Journal of Crisis Intervention and Suicide Prevention, 37*(6), 461–464.

Saunders, E. C., McGovern, M. P., Lambert-Harris, C., Meier, A., McLeman, B., & Xie, H. (2015). The impact of addiction medications on treatment outcomes for persons with co-occurring PTSD and opioid use disorders. *American Journal on Addictions, 24*, 722–731.

Saxon, A. J., & McCance-Katz, E. F. (2016). Some additional considerations regarding the American Society of Addiction Medicine National Practice Guideline for the use of medications in the treatment of addiction involving opioid use. *Journal of Addiction Medicine, 10*(3), 140–142.

Schacht, R. L., Brooner, R. K., King, V. L., Kidorf, M. S., & Peirce, J. M. (2017). Incentivizing attendance to prolonged exposure for PTSD with opioid use disorder patients: A randomized controlled trial. *Journal of Consulting and Clinical Psychology, 85*, 689–701.

Schaefer, B. P., & Petkovsek, M. A. (2017). Adolescent use of opioids and stimulants: Testing the influence of peers, self-control, and sports participation. *Criminal Justice Studies: A Critical Journal of Crime, Law & Society, 30*, 365–380.

Schep, L. J., Slaughter, R. J., Galea, S., & Newcombe, D. (2016). Ibogaine for treating drug dependence. What is a safe dose? *Drug & Alcohol Dependence, 166*, 1–5.

Scherbaum, S., Haber, P., Morley, K., Underhill, D., & Moustafa, A. A. (2018). Biased and less sensitive: A gamified approach to delay discounting in heroin addiction. *Journal of Clinical and Experimental Neuropsychology, 40*, 139–150.

Scherrer, J. F., Salas, J., Copeland, L. A., Stock, E. M., Schneider, F. D., Sullivan, M., . . . Lustman, P. J. (2016). Increased risk of depression recurrence after initiation of prescription opioids in noncancer pain patients. *Journal of Pain, 17*(4), 473–482.

Schulte, M., Hser, Y., Saxon, A., Evans, E., Li, L., Huang, D., . . . Ling, W. (2015). Risk factors associated with HCV among opioid-dependent patients in a multisite study. *Journal of Community Health, 40*(5), 940–947.

Schwaninger, P. V., Mueller, S. E., Dittmann, R., Poespodihardjo, R., Vogel, M., Wiesbeck, G. A., . . . Petitjean, S. A. (2017). Patients with non-substance-related disorders report a similar profile of childhood trauma experiences compared to heroin-dependent patients. *American Journal on Addictions, 26*(3), 215–220.

Schwartz, R. P. (2016). When added to opioid agonist treatment, psychosocial interventions do not further reduce the use of illicit opioids: A comment on Dugosh et al. *Journal of Addiction Medicine, 10*(4), 283–285.

Seal, K. H., Shi, Y., Cohen, G., Cohen, B. E., Maguen, S., Krebs, E. E., & Neylan, T. C. (2012). Association of mental health disorders with prescription opioids and high-risk opioid use in US veterans of Iraq and Afghanistan. *JAMA: Journal of the American Medical Association, 307*(9), 940–947.

Secades-Villa, R., Fernande-Hermida, J. R., & Arnaez-Montaraz, C. (2004). Motivational interviewing and treatment retention among drug user patients: A pilot study. *Substance Use & Misuse, 39*, 1369–1378.

Sharafshah, A., Fazel, H., Albonaim, A., Omarmeli, V., Rezaei, S., Mirzajani, E., . . . Keshavarz, P. (2017). Association of OPRD1 gene variants with opioid dependence in addicted male individuals undergoing methadone treatment in the north of Iran. *Journal of Psychoactive Drugs, 49*, 242–251.

Sheikh, N. (2016, August 9). *Deadly carfentanil: 100 times stronger than fentanyl.* Retrieved on October 2, 2018, from https://sobernation.com/deadly-carfentanil/

Shigakova, F. A. (2016). Group psychotherapy in rehabilitation of female opium addicts in Uzbekistan. *International Journal of Group Psychotherapy, 66*(1), 120–131.

Shorey, R. C., Stuart, G. L., Anderson, S., & Strong, D. R. (2013). Changes in early maladaptive schemas after residential treatment for substance use. *Journal of Clinical Psychology, 69*, 912–922.

Siegel, S. (2016). The heroin overdose mystery. *Current Directions in Psychological Science, 25*(6), 375–379.

Simonovska, N., Zafirova-Ivanovska, B., Babulovska, A., Pereska, Z., Jurukov, I., & Trenchevska-Siljanovska, L. (2016). Influence of duration of heroin dependence on humoral immunologic indicators. *Journal of Addiction Medicine, 10*(6), 448–452.

Smallwood, R. F., Potter, J. S., & Robin, D. A. (2016). Neurophysiological mechanisms in acceptance and commitment therapy in opioid-addicted patients with chronic pain. *Psychiatry Research: Neuroimaging, 250*, 12–14.

Smith, K. Z., Smith, P. H., Cercone, S. A., McKee, S. A., & Homish, G. G. (2016). Past year non-medical opioid use and abuse and PTSD diagnosis: Interactions with sex and associations with symptom clusters. *Addictive Behaviors, 58*, 167–174.

Stange, K., Kruger, M., Janke, E., Lichtinghagen, R., Bleich, S., Hillemacher, T., & Heberlein, A. (2017). Positive association of personal distress with testosterone in opiate-addicted patients. *Journal of Addictive Diseases, 36*, 167–174.

Stauffer, C. S., Musinipally, V., Suen, A., Lynch, K. L., Shapiro, B., & Woolley, J. D. (2016). A two-week pilot study of intranasal oxytocin for cocaine-dependent individuals receiving methadone maintenance treatment for opioid use disorder. *Addiction Research & Theory, 24*(6), 490–498.

Stoddart, T. (2013, May 8). *Addiction: A disease of spirituality.* Retrieved on October 4, 2018, from https://sobernation.com/addiction-a-disease-of-spirituality/

Sun, Y., Zhao, L.-Y., Wang, G.-B., Yue, W.-H., He, Y., Shu, N., . . . Shi, J. (2016). ZNF804A variants confer risk for heroin addiction and affect decision making and gray matter volume in heroin abusers. *Addiction Biology, 21*(3), 657–666.

Szalavitz, M., & Rigg, K. K. (2017). The curious (dis)connection between the opioid epidemic and crime. *Substance Use & Misuse, 52*(14), 1927–1931.

Tadros, A., Layman, S. M., Davis, S. M., Bozeman, R., & Davidov, D. M. (2016). Emergency department visits by pediatric patients for poisoning by prescription opioids. *American Journal of Drug and Alcohol Abuse, 42*, 550–555.

Tarman, V., & Werdell, P. (2014). *Food junkies: The truth about food addiction.* Toronto, ON: Dundurn.

Tavakolian, E., & Abolghasemi, A. (2016). Effects of cognitive restructuring training on neurocognitive functions in opioid addicts. *Archives of Psychiatry and Psychotherapy, 18*(1), 14–21.

Thiruchselvam, T., Malik, S., & Le Foll, B. (2017). A review of positron emission tomography studies exploring the dopaminergic system in substance use with a focus on tobacco as a co-variate. *American Journal of Drug and Alcohol Abuse, 43*, 197–214.

Thylstrup, B., Bloomfield, K., & Hesse, M. (2018). Incremental predictive validity of the Addiction Severity Index psychiatric composite score in a consecutive cohort of patients in residential treatment for drug use disorders. *Addictive Behaviors, 76*, 201–207.

Tiffany, E., Wilder, C. M., Miller, S. C., & Winhusen, T. (2016). Knowledge of and interest in opioid overdose education and naloxone distribution among US veterans on chronic opioids for addiction or pain. *Drugs: Education, Prevention & Policy, 23*, 322–327.

Timko, C., Gupta, S., Schultz, N., & Harris, A. H. S. (2016). Veterans' service utilization patterns after alcohol and opioid detoxification in VHA care. *Psychiatric Services, 67*(4), 460–464.

Tomei, A., Besson, J., Reber, N., Rougemont-Bucking, A., & Grivel, J. (2017). Personal distress and empathic concern in methadone-maintained patients. *Journal of Substance Use, 22*, 37–41.

Truong, A., Moukaddam, N., Toledo, A., & Onigu-Otite, E. (2017). Addictive disorders in adolescents. *Psychiatric Clinics of North America, 40*(3), 475–486.

Unnithan, S., Gossop, M., & Strang, J. (1992). Factors associated with relapse among opiate addicts in an out-patient detoxification programme. *British Journal of Psychiatry, 161*, 654–657.

Vanderlip, E. R., Sullivan, M. D., Edlund, M. J., Martin, B. C., Fortney, J., Austen, M., . . . Hudson, T. (2014). National study of discontinuation of long-term opioid therapy among veterans. *Pain, 155*(12), 2673–2679.

Vasilenko, S. A., Evans-Polce, R. J., & Lanza, S. T. (2017). Age trends in rates of substance use disorders across ages 18–90: Differences by gender and race/ethnicity. *Drug and Alcohol Dependence, 180*, 260–264.

Vaughn, M. G., Nelson, E. J., Salas-Wright, C. P., Qian, Z., & Schootman, M. (2016). Racial and ethnic trends and correlates of non-medical use of prescription opioids among adolescents in the United States 2004–2013. *Journal of Psychiatric Research, 73*, 17–24.

Veliz, P., Boyd, C. J., & McCabe, S. E. (2016). Nonmedical prescription opioid and heroin use among adolescents who engage in sports and exercise. *Pediatrics, 138*(2), 1–11.

Veliz, P., Boyd, C. J., & McCabe, S. E. (2017). Nonmedical use of prescription opioids and heroin use among adolescents involved in competitive sports. *Journal of Adolescent Health, 60*, 346–349.

Vigna-Taglianti, F. D., Burroni, P., Mathis, F., Versino, E., Beccaria, F., Rotelli, M., . . . Bargagli, A. M. (2016). Gender differences in heroin addiction and treatment: Results from the VEdeTTE cohort. *Substance Use & Misuse, 51*(3), 295–309.

von Hippel, C., Henry, J. D., Terrett, G., Mercuri, K., McAlear, K., & Rendell, P. G. (2017). Stereotype threat and social function in opioid substitution therapy patients. *British Journal of Clinical Psychology, 56*, 160–171.

Voon, P., Karamouzian, M., & Kerr, T. (2017). Chronic pain and opioid misuse: A review of reviews. *Substance Abuse Treatment, Prevention, and Policy, 12*, 1–9.

Vosburg, S. K., Eaton, T. A., Sokolowska, M., Osgood, E. D., Ashworth, J. B., Trudeau, J. J., . . . Katz, N. P. (2016). Prescription opioid abuse, prescription opioid addiction, and heroin abuse among adolescents in a recovery high school: A pilot study. *Journal of Child & Adolescent Substance Abuse, 25*, 105–112.

Vowles, K. E., McEntee, M. L., Julnes, P. S., Frohe, T., Ney, J. P., & van der Goes, D. N. (2015). Rates of opioid misuse, abuse, and addiction in chronic pain: A systematic review and data synthesis. *Pain, 156*(4), 569–576.

Wachholtz, A., Foster, S., & Cheatle, M. (2015). Psychophysiology of pain and opioid use: Implications for managing pain in patients with an opioid use disorder. *Drug and Alcohol Dependence, 146*, 1–6.

Wallace, B. C., & Santacruz, E. (2017). Addictions and substance abuse in the LGBT community: New approaches. In R. Ruth & E. Santacruz (Eds.), *LGBT psychology and mental health: Emerging research and advances* (pp. 153–175). Santa Barbara, CA: Praeger/ABC-CLIO.

Walsh, Z., Gonzalez, R., Crosby, K., Thiessen, M. S., Carroll, C., & Bonn-Miller, M. O. (2017). Medical cannabis and mental health: A guided systematic review. *Clinical Psychology Review, 51*, 15–29.

Wang, G. Y., Kydd, R., & Russell, B. R. (2015). Auditory event-related potentials in methadone substituted opiate users. *Journal of Psychopharmacology, 29*, 983–995.

Weaver, M., Delos Reyes, C., & Schnoll, S. (2014). Club drug addiction. In G. O. Gabbard (Ed.), *Gabbard's treatments of psychiatric disorders* (5th ed., pp. 851–858). Arlington, VA: American Psychiatric.

Weinstein, Z. M., Cheng, D. M., Quinn, E., Hui, D., Kim, H., Gryczynski, G., & Samet, J. H. (2017). Psychoactive medications and disengagement from office based opioid treatment (obot) with buprenorphine. *Drug and Alcohol Dependence, 170*, 9–16.

Wenner, A., & Gigli, K. H. (2016). Opioid addiction in adolescents: A background and policy brief. *Journal of Pediatric Health Care, 30*(6), 606–609.

White, T. (1999). Heroin use as a passive behavior. *Transactional Analysis Journal, 29*, 273–277.

Whiteside, L. K., Russo, J., Wang, J., Ranney, M. L., Neam, V., & Zatzick, D. F. (2016). Predictors of sustained prescription opioid use after admission for trauma in adolescents. *Journal of Adolescent Health, 58*, 92–97.

WHO ASSIST Working Group. (2002). The Alcohol, Smoking and Substance Involvement Screening Test (ASSIST): Development, reliability and feasibility. *Addiction, 97*(9), 1183–1194.

Wilder, C. M., Miller, S. C., Tiffany, E., Winhusen, T., Winstanley, E. L., & Stein, M. D. (2016). Risk factors for opioid overdose and awareness of overdose risk among veterans prescribed chronic opioids for addiction or pain. *Journal of Addictive Diseases, 35*, 42–51.

Willner-Reid, J., Whitaker, D., Epstein, D. H., Phillips, K. A., Pulaski, A. R., Preston, K. L., & Willner, P. (2016). Cognitive-behavioural therapy for heroin and cocaine use: Ecological momentary assessment of homework simplification and compliance. *Psychology and Psychotherapy: Theory, Research and Practice, 89*, 276–293.

Wilson, J. D., Vo, H., Matson, P., Adger, H., Barnett, G., & Fishman, M. (2017). Trait mindfulness and progression to injection use in youth with opioid addiction. *Substance Use & Misuse, 52*(11), 1486–1493.

Wilson, M., Gogulski, H. Y., Cuttler, C., Bigand, T. L., Oluwoye, O., Barbosa-Leiker, C., & Roberts, M. A. (2018). Cannabis use moderates the relationship between pain and negative affect in adults with opioid use disorder. *Addictive Behaviors, 77*, 225–231.

Winerman, L. (2018, November). The rise of non-drug pain treatment. *Monitor on Psychology 2019 Trends Report* (pp. 46–49). Washington DC: American Psychological Association.

Woodcock, E. A., Lundahl, L. H., Stoltman, J. J. K., & Greenwald, M. K. (2015). Progression to regular heroin use: Examination of patterns, predictors, and consequences. *Addictive Behaviors, 45*, 287–293.

Wu, S. L. Y., Leung, A. W. N., & Yew, D. T. W. (2016). Acupuncture for detoxification in treatment of opioid addiction. *East Asian Archives of Psychiatry, 26*(2), 70–76.

Xu, H., Zhang, C., Lu, G.-h., Chen, H.-h., & Zhao, M. (2009). A study of family function in family members of heroin addicts in voluntary detoxification. *Chinese Journal of Clinical Psychology, 17*(5), 647–648.

Xu, S., Liu, Y., Li, Y., Deng, Y., Yuan, J., Lv, R., . . . Liu, X. (2017). Availability of dopamine transporters in heroin-dependent subjects: A 18F-FECNT PET imaging study. *Psychiatry Research: Neuroimaging, 263*, 121–126.

Yantsides, K. E., Tracy, M. R., & Skeer, M. (2017). Non-medical use of prescription drugs and its association with heroin use among high school students. *Journal of Substance Use, 22*, 102–107.

Yoon, G., Westermeyer, J., Warwick, M., & Kuskowski, M. A. (2012). Substance use disorders and adoption: Findings from a national sample. *PLoS ONE, 7*(11), 1–6.

Yuan, J., Liu, X. D., Han, M., Lv, R. B., Wang, Y. K., Zhang, G. M., & Li, Y. (2017). Comparison of striatal dopamine transporter levels in chronic heroin-dependent and methamphetamine-dependent subjects. *Addiction Biology, 22*, 229–234.

Zaman, T., Malowney, M., Knight, J., & Boyd, J. W. (2015). Co-occurrence of substance-related and other mental health disorders among adolescent cannabis users. *Journal of Addiction Medicine, 9*, 317–321.

Zhou, K., Li, H., Wei, X., Li, X., & Zhuang, G. (2017). Medication adherence in patients undergoing methadone maintenance treatment in Xi'an, China. *Journal of Addiction Medicine, 11*, 28–33.

Zhuang, S.-M., An, S.-H., & Zhao, Y. (2014). Effect of cognitive behavioural interventions on the quality of life in Chinese heroin-dependent individuals in detoxification: A randomised controlled trial. *Journal of Clinical Nursing, 23*, 1239–1248.

Zimmerman, G. L., Olsen, C. G., & Bosworth, M. F. (2000). A 'stages of change' approach to helping patients change behavior. *American Family Physician, 61*(5), 1409–1416.

Zou, F., Wu, X., Zhai, T., Lei, Y., Shao, Y., Jin, X., . . . Yang, Z. (2015). Abnormal resting-state functional connectivity of the nucleus accumbens in multi-year abstinent heroin addicts. *Journal of Neuroscience Research, 93*, 1693–1702.

12 Nicotine Addiction

iStock.com/M

Learning Objectives

1. Become aware of the extent of the most preventable cause of disease and death both in the United States and worldwide.
2. Learn about the physical effects and health consequences that result from smoking.
3. Become familiar with the *DSM-5* and ICD-11 codes for nicotine-related disorders.
4. Summarize the best medical smoking cessation methods.
5. Discover the best ways to counsel nicotine addicts.

"Lung cancer claimed your lives,

But it never claimed your spirits"

(Kevin Alderson, January 12, 2011)

CHALLENGING YOUR ASSUMPTIONS ABOUT THIS ADDICTION

1. If you are a smoker, ask yourself the following questions: "To what extent do you like, or *not* like, the relationship you have with smoking? If you do not like this relationship, what will you do to begin 'breaking off' with smoking?" If you do *not* smoke, ask yourself the following questions: "What keeps you from smoking? To what extent do you project your reasons onto those who *do* smoke, thereby 'judging them' harder than you think is desirable for a counselor?"
2. If you had (or have) a son or daughter, what preventable steps would you take to reduce the likelihood that he or she will begin smoking? At what age would you start taking these steps?
3. What are your views concerning smoking in closed public spaces? Should venues that do not usually permit smoking allow it on regularly scheduled dates (e.g., every Thursday) to promote their business and/or lessen the stigma from smoking? Why or why not?
4. Smoking and chewing tobacco cause cancer and are also extremely addicting, yet tobacco companies continue advertising and selling tobacco products worldwide. There are also those who believe that individuals should have the right to use products (in some cases even powerful psychoactive drugs), even if they are harmful to health. What do you believe should be done to minimize the negative impact of tobacco products in the United States, if anything?
5. What is your opinion regarding electronic cigarettes (e-cigarettes) when used by adults? What is your opinion regarding e-cigarettes when used by nonsmoking adolescents for the stimulation provided by nicotine? Does your opinion change if adolescents who also smoke cigarettes use the e-cigarettes? Why or why not?

PERSONAL REFLECTIONS

"A Chilling Forever"

A Forever
I remember you as a kind gentle soul,
A man who brought smiles when he said hello,
But what you didn't tell me,
And maybe just as well,
That when you said goodbye,
You meant it would be forever.
To my late father, George Frederick Alderson

A Chilling
I remember seeing you outside on the coldest days,
Huddled in a corner,
Standing alone.
Smoking desperately to breathe,
And breathing desperately to smoke,
Until you could breathe no more.
To my friend, Dolores Clarkson

A Chilling Forever
Lung cancer claimed your lives,
But it never claimed your spirits.
Dr. Kevin George Alderson,
January 12, 2011

Late one morning in September 1966, I remember saying goodbye to my father while he was being taken out from our home on a stretcher. He said, "Goodbye, son." No one could ever tell me exactly how much he smoked, but one brother-in-law thought it was around three packs a day. The day before my 10th birthday, we received the fatal call from the hospital.

For 10 consecutive years (i.e., 1982–1992), I worked with one smoker after another using hypnotherapy and behavioral techniques. No one has to tell me about the horrors of smoking. Most days, I just wish I had my dad back.

Background Information

The Bill and Melinda Gates Foundation provides substantial funding for the Global Burden of Disease Study (GBDS), which is an international collaboration from researchers in 127 countries. Reitsma et al. (2017) analyzed GBDS data from 195 countries and territories between 1990 and 2015 to look at the smoking prevalence and attributable disease burden. Worldwide, smoking prevalence is 25% among males and 5.4% among females. The decrease in the prevalence of tobacco consumption between 1990 and 2015 is an encouraging 28.4% reduction among males and 34.4% reduction among females. Nonetheless, smoking resulted in 11.5% of all global deaths in 2015 (6.4 million people), with 52.2% of these deaths occurring in four countries (i.e., China, India, the

United States, and Russia). Unquestionably, smoking is "a global health disaster" (Manning, 2017, para. 6).

Nicotine is a powerful drug. Referring to an overwhelming amount of data, Mayer (2014) concluded that "more than 0.5 g of oral nicotine is required to kill an adult" (p. 7). An amount of 0.5 grams equals 0.02 ounces, which is equivalent to about 10 drops. Consequently, despite a common myth that one drop of pure nicotine placed on the tongue is lethal, the correct amount is 10 drops or more. Although the lethality of pure nicotine does not compare to the lethality of pure cyanide, for example, which only requires 50–200 mg (0.002–0.007 ounces; about 10 times the potency of nicotine) to cause death (Gracia & Shepherd, 2014), 10 drops is a minuscule amount for a drug intended to provide pleasure in contrast to death!

Nicotine is also unique in that it has biphasic properties (i.e., biphasic means having two phases). Nicotine might be the only drug in common use that can act as both a stimulant and a depressant, at times stimulating brain activity and at other times suppressing it (Ashton, Millman, Telford, & Thompson, 1973; Benowitz, Porchet, & Peyton, 1989; Nagaya, Takahashib, Yoshidab, & Yokoyamab, 1992; Netter, Muller, & Kamradik, 1994). For example, smokers often find that their first cigarette of the day helps get them going (stimulating effect) yet later find that it relaxes them (depressant effect). Smokers take shallower inhalations to create a stimulating effect; they inhale deeply to produce a more relaxing effect. Coincidentally, deep breathing without smoking also creates relaxation (Alderson, 2011). Additionally, "light smoking may stimulate the peripheral sympathetic nervous system, whereas heavy smoking may depress the system" (Nagaya et al., 1992, p. 327). Lastly, smokers' moods and environments play a role in how they experience nicotine's effects (Perkins et al., 1994).

As almost any smoker will tell you, smoking is not easy to stop. Like other addictive disorders, nicotine addiction is a chronic, relapsing condition. Chaiton et al. (2016) set about to establish the average number of times it takes for a smoker to quit permanently. Previous estimates have relied on lifetime recall in cross-sectional samples of successful quitters only. Chaiton et al. used data from 1277 participants from the Ontario Tobacco Survey, a longitudinal survey that followed smokers every 6 months for up to 3 years beginning in 2005. The analysis revealed that it often takes smokers up to 30 or more quit attempts before they are finally successful.

Smoking ***is*** the leading preventable cause of premature death and preventable disease worldwide (West, 2017). In the United States alone, where tobacco is the most common substance of abuse, smoking results in a loss of 5.1 million years of potential life and $96.8 billion in productivity each year (Carey & Wilkinson, 2016; Rastegar & Fingerhood, 2016). That is a financial loss greater than that of all other legal and illegal drugs combined (Milkman & Sunderwirth, 2010).

Nicotine is the chemical found in tobacco plants that causes addiction. Tobacco can be snuffed, chewed, or dipped, but it is often smoked in cigarette form. As the opening photo of this chapter depicted, nicotine can also be inhaled today using a vaping device (i.e., e-cigarette). The use of vaping products by youth has increased significantly, leading the U.S. Food and Drug Administration (FDA; 2018) to introduce new measures aimed at restricting their access.

After inhalation, nicotine reaches the brain within 8–20 seconds. It stimulates the release of adrenaline into the bloodstream, which may act as a sedative, depending on the individual's nervous system (Felman, 2018).

Nicotine by itself is not excessively harmful; however, as a key ingredient of tobacco and cigarettes, it is commonly coupled with toxic chemicals such as tar, carbon monoxide, arsenic, ammonia, methanol, and butane (Irish Cancer Society, n.d.). Each time individuals smoke, they ingest carcinogens, teratogens, and atherogens, all of which are dangerous substances that can cause long-term disease (Batra et al., 2016).

Tobacco originates from two Andean plants, *Nicotiana tabacum* and *Nicotiana rustica*, which have been cultivated in South America since 5000–3000 BC (Musk & De Klerk, 2003). Like many other psychoactive substances, tobacco (and therefore nicotine) was reportedly used by Indigenous peoples in Australia, North America, and South America thousands of years ago (Ouzir & Errami, 2016). These individuals chewed, ate, and drank tobacco as well as used it in rituals and medicines such as eye drops, analgesics, antiseptics, and insecticides.

The earliest tobacco-related artifacts ever found were snuffing instruments, suggesting that snuffing was the precursor to smoking (Musk & De Klerk, 2003). By the time Columbus's crew was introduced to tobacco after reaching Cuba in 1492, pipes had become the most popular form of tobacco smoking. Early explorers brought tobacco and its seeds back to Europe, and smoking grew into an activity of the affluent and rich. King James I of England famously described smoking as "a custom loathsome to the eye, hateful to the nose, harmful to the brain, [and] dangerous to the lungs" (as cited in Musk & De Klerk, 2003, p. 287).

The first manufactured cigarettes were marketed in England in the 1850s (Musk & De Klerk, 2003). They were convenient even to soldiers in the trenches of World War I, making them more popular than other smoking instruments. Henceforth, smoking steadily grew across the globe until medical practitioners noticed a rising trend in lung cancer in the 1920s and 1930s. Then, in the 1950s, studies began linking lung cancer to smoking, and dopamine's role in nicotine addiction garnered attention (Dumont, Maex, & Gutkin, 2018; Musk & De Klerk, 2003).

For decades, the tobacco industry denied what science was proving about the harmful effects of smoking. However, in the 1990s, internal documents from the tobacco industry reached the public (Lee, Gilmore, & Collin, 2004). It became apparent that the industry was fully aware of nicotine addiction, was overtly targeting specific populations, and was involved in covert operations to stymie global tobacco control efforts.

Smoking is now proven to cause a myriad of diseases and adverse health effects such as various cancers, chronic obstructive pulmonary disease (COPD), premature skin aging, impaired fertility, cataracts, and many more. Its social acceptability has decreased over the years due to countermarketing, leading to a lowered smoking prevalence (Gearhardt & Corbin, 2012). However, despite its dangerous effects, tobacco is still readily available to much of the adult population. Musk and De Klerk (2003) compared tobacco to asbestos, both of which have been used since ancient times and have been proven to cause serious disease. However, where asbestos is now strictly regulated and virtually eliminated, tobacco remains readily available.

Nowadays, one can find tobacco in various forms, including cigarettes, cigars, chewing tobacco, e-cigarettes, hookah, water pipes, and roll-your-own cigarettes (Donaldson, Hoffman, Zandberg, & Blake, 2017). Still, the most prevalent form of use is the commercially produced cigarette (Brennan, Levesque, & Riley, 2016).

Nicotine addiction is an addiction to nicotine. It "occurs when smokers come to rely on smoking to modulate mood and arousal, relieve withdrawal symptoms, or both. Light or occasional smokers smoke mainly for positive reinforcement in specific situations" (Benowitz, 2010, p. 2301).

West (2017) suggested that smoking is maintained by the positive and negative reinforcements of nicotine, its affordability and palatability, and the distance and uncertainty of its adverse health consequences. By itself, nicotine has poor reinforcing effects; however, tobacco products are designed to optimize the delivery of nicotine to central nervous system receptors and also promote conditioned learning through sensory cues (Alpert, Agaku, & Connolly, 2016).

The sensory aspect of smoke inhalation is rewarding in itself due to a behavioral conditioning process (Patterson, Schnoll, & Lerman, 2011). Denicotinized cigarettes, for example, still result in smoking satisfaction and craving reduction. Similarly, researchers have proposed that "anticipated pleasure or satisfaction, the need to alleviate a nicotine-induced drive state and a stimulus-driven impulse" all play important roles in tobacco smoking (Wehbe, Ubhi, & West, 2018, p. 135). That being said, Wehbe et al. (2018) found in their study of 566 smokers attending treatment that almost half reported automatic urges to be dominant, whereas a substantial proportion of them did not anticipate pleasure or relief.

Another reason that smokers may continue to use cigarettes is to lose weight or control their weight (Morean & Wedel, 2017). Many people will resume smoking if they gain a modest amount of weight after quitting (Evatt & Griffiths, 2012). In fact, smoking cessation is often accompanied by food cravings and a weight gain of around 3–5 kilograms (6.6–11 pounds) because metabolism slows down (Blumenthal & Gold, 2012).

Besides the positive reinforcements, smokers also smoke to reduce negative emotions (e.g., stress, depression) or cope with emotional distress (Bold, 2017; Nellum, 2018; Park, Luberto, O'Cleirigh, Peres, & Wilner, 2017; Serre, Fatseas, Denis, Swendsen, & Auriacombe, 2018). Stress can be caused by various factors, one of which is attachment anxiety. In one study by Le (2018), attachment anxiety was shown to mediate between childhood adversity and current smoking statistically. Social anxiety is also linked to a high prevalence of smoking and failure to quit (Watson, Heffner, McClure, Mull, & Bricker, 2017). Smokers with moderate to high levels of social anxiety pose more risk factors, particularly mental health symptoms, than smokers with low social anxiety. Also, self-perceived physical ill health in children and adolescents is linked to tobacco, alcohol, and cannabis use (Kirkcaldya, Siefenb, Surallb, & Bischoff, 2004).

Smokers may also take up the habit to diminish pain. Moderate pain interference (i.e., the impact of pain in one's life) is associated with nicotine dependence, and high pain may predict the development of nicotine dependence especially among males (McDermott, Joyner, Hakes, Okey, & Cougle, 2018). One study of 60 daily smokers who were exposed to the World Trade Center disaster found that participants with relatively greater respiratory symptoms and high anxiety sensitivity relapsed earlier following cessation treatment (Zvolensky et al., 2017).

Nicotine dependence consists of biological, behavioral, and cognitive components (Karam-Hage, Minnix, & Cinciripini, 2012). Not surprisingly, genetic factors contribute to both nicotine and alcohol addiction (Tyndale, 2003). Evidence suggests that DRD2 and ANKK1 genes are mainly associated with these addictions (Ma, Yuan, Jiang, Cui, & Li, 2015). Decreased nicotine metabolism (encoded by cytochrome CYP2A6) among European American young adults also increases the risk of nicotine dependence (Olfson et al., 2018).

The majority of smokers begin smoking before they are 18 years old (Blumenthal & Gold, 2012). Over four fifths of adults who ever smoked daily experimented with cigarettes when they were children or adolescents, and more than one half of adolescents who experiment with smoking will become adult smokers (Carey & Wilkinson, 2016).

Nicotine exposure during adolescence preconditions a person toward subsequent substance use (Cross, Lotfipour, & Leslie, 2017). Young people may start smoking due to personal risk factors and/or family or school environments—that is, smoking may be seen as a potential bonding activity with parents or with friends (Morojele, Brook, & Brook, 2016). Sensation seeking may also contribute to smoking as it is considered a risky behavior (Schiff, 2018).

Among current smokers, a smoking environment increases the urge to smoke and promotes smoking behavior, making it harder to quit (Stevenson et al., 2017). Similarly, secondhand smoke exposure is associated with higher odds of initiating smoking and a higher risk for ischemic heart disease among nonsmokers (Braverman Bronstein, Lomelin Gascón, Eugenio-González, & Barrientos-Gutierrez, 2018; Okoli et al., 2016; Rostron, 2013). Having two smoking parents (as compared to zero or one) is associated with higher rates of nicotine dependence in adulthood (Kardia, Pomerleau, Rozek, & Marks, 2003). These rates are even higher regarding prenatal smoking exposure, which is also linked to general adolescent drug experimentation and higher offspring BMI in adulthood (Hill, Shen, Wellman, Rickin, & Lowers, 2005; Lotfipour et al., 2014). If a mother quits smoking during the first trimester of pregnancy, however, it may decrease the odds of her children developing smoking habits in the future (Niemela et al., 2017).

Early life exposure to nicotine (which is a developmental neurotoxin) has been linked to decreased intellectual ability, conduct disorders, and hyperactivity-impulsivity behaviors (Lauterstein, 2017). Likewise, lower cognitive ability in childhood has been linked to a higher likelihood of taking up smoking and a lower likelihood of quitting in adulthood (Daly & Egan, 2017).

The way that cigarettes are packaged is meant to—and indeed does—influence consumers' perception, regardless of the tobacco blend, flavoring, or additives (Lempert & Glantz, 2017). For example, red and darker colors are perceived as fuller flavored and stronger, whereas white and lighter colors are seen to be lighter and less harmful.

Tobacco users often underestimate the harm of the products they use when compared to people who have never smoked (Bernat, Ferrer, Margolis, & Blake, 2017). For example, cigarettes (versus other nicotine products such as cigars and pipes) cause the most harm to users worldwide, yet users tend to view them as less addictive than do nonusers (Cooper, Loukas, Harrell, & Perry, 2017; Nutt et al., 2014). The same also applies to e-cigarette smokers. Although limited short-term studies suggest that e-cigarettes may be less harmful than traditional cigarettes, they have not been shown to be an effective smoking cessation method as marketed by the industry (Nowak, Jorres, & Ruther, 2014; Zborovskaya, 2017).

Water pipe tobacco smoking (whereby tobacco smoke is passed through water before inhalation) is also perceived as less harmful than traditional smoking (Aboaziza & Eissenberg, 2015). Still, it is associated with nicotine dependence, disability, disease, and death. In fact, all combustible forms of nicotine are much more harmful than noncombustible forms (Nutt et al., 2014).

Results from Tverdal and Bjartveit's (2011) study of 16,932 Norwegian men, aged 20–49, also indicated that there was no difference regarding survival between cigarette smokers and pipe smokers, despite the substantially less nicotine found in pipe smoke. Tverdal and Bjartveit concluded that pipe smoking is not safer than cigarette smoking.

Compared to smokers who use only one type of tobacco product, multiple product users tend to smoke more per day. They also make more attempts to quit and report greater exposure to both advertising and countermarketing for tobacco compared with those who smoke only one tobacco product (Guydish, Tajima, et al., 2016). Interestingly, smokers prefer to feel responsible for their choice, opting for agency and self-efficacy over addiction (Morphett, Carter, Hall, & Gartner, 2016, 2017). In an interview study with 29 Australian smokers, most participants did not relate to tobacco dependence being described as a "chronic brain disease" and did not want to adopt a "sick role" (Morphett, Carter, Hall, & Gartner, 2017).

Many smokers are motivated to quit by feelings of stigmatization and exposure to information about adverse health effects (Donaldson, Hoffman, Zandberg, & Blake, 2017; O'Connor, Rees, Rivard, Hatsukami, & Cummings, 2017). However, Waters et al. (2016) found in their study of 333 university smokers that a belief in the inevitability of addiction after starting smoking was inversely associated with quit intentions. Therefore, they suggest that health practitioners be wary of emphasizing the addictiveness of nicotine to smokers.

Are there any positive effects attributable to ingesting nicotine? Tobacco smoking suppresses an individual's appetite, thus allowing many smokers to lose weight (White & O'Malley, 2012). It also heightens positive affect and decreases negative affect. Particularly among individuals with psychiatric conditions such as attention deficit/hyperactivity disorder (ADHD) and schizophrenia, nicotine (even during tobacco abstinence) can improve cognitive and emotional processing (Besson & Forget, 2016).

What adverse effects occur, if any, from being a light smoker? Formagini, Gomide, Perales, and Colugnati (2017) used data from the 2013 Brazilian National Health Research survey (N = 48,282) and compared light smokers (LS; ≤10 cigarettes per day) and nondaily smokers (NDS) with moderate/heavier smokers (MHS). In their large sample, 12.4% smoked manufactured cigarettes. Among the smokers, 12.8% were NDS, 47.4% were LS, and 39.8% were MHS. Compared to nonsmokers, LS had higher odds of experiencing poorer self-rated health, including depression and lung diseases. Nondaily smoking was also associated with lung disease.

Korhonen, Broms, Levalahti, Koskenvuo, and Kaprio (2009) used longitudinal data in Finland to ascertain if intermittent smoking is associated with health risk (questionnaires from 1975 and 1981 were used as data points to compare with lung cancer incidence between 1982 and 2004). Their sample consisted of 21,340 persons who indicated that they were smokers. Of this group, 641 (3%) were occasional cigarette smokers. Korhonen et al. did not find any evidence of elevated risk of lung cancer among occasional smokers.

Nicotine addiction is the most prevalent addiction worldwide (Beresford, Wongngamnit, & Temple, 2015). Smoking rates are decreasing in countries such as the United States but are on the rise in developing nations as they become more affluent (Heilig, 2015; Patterson et al., 2011). In the United States, more than one third of smokers try to quit each year; less than 10% succeed (Milkman & Sunderwirth, 2010).

The prevalence of smoking among American adults was about 25% a decade ago and is currently hovering around 15% (Prasad, Kaisar, & Cucullo, 2017). Although cigarette smoking has dramatically decreased, other tobacco products such as e-cigarettes have gained more ground (O'Gara, Sharma, Boyle, & Taylor, 2017). The overall prevalence of nicotine dependence has, therefore, remained steady from 1964 to 2002, even increasing among some groups (Glasser, 2010; Goodwin, Keyes, & Hasin, 2009). Thankfully, secondhand smoke is on the decline; levels of exposure diminished from 53% to 16.7% between 2005 and 2010 (Rostron, 2013).

Tobacco use is most prevalent among young adults aged 18–25 (37%) and the male gender (31% versus 20% for females; Rastegar & Fingerhood, 2016). Men have a higher prevalence of tobacco use than do women in all ethnic groups in the United States (Milkman & Sunderwirth, 2010). Indigenous peoples, particularly the Northern Plains American Indians, tend to have a high prevalence rate due to using tobacco in traditional ceremonies (Tanner et al., 2018).

Nearly half of the cigarettes smoked in America are done so by individuals with psychiatric and/or substance use disorders (SUDs; Anthenelli, 2014). The overall smoking rate among individuals with psychiatric disorders is about 41% (Park, Luberto, O'Cleirigh, Perez, & Wilner, 2017). Populations for which smoking is more prevalent include individuals with serious psychological distress (Kulik & Glantz, 2017), a separate drug use disorder, an alcohol disorder, major depressive disorder, or socioeconomic disadvantages (Secades-Villa et al., 2013). For instance, opioid-dependent individuals may have a smoking prevalence as high as 95% (Chun, Haug, Guydish, Sorensen, & Delucchi, 2009), and the prevalence among individuals with schizophrenia is estimated to be between 64% and 79% (Cather, Pachas, Cieslak, & Evins, 2017). Meta-analyses estimate the prevalence of smoking among individuals with binge eating disorder to be about 47% and individuals with bulimia nervosa to be about 39% (Solmi et al., 2016).

Youth smoking accounts for about half of all new cigarette smokers (Rastegar & Fingerhood, 2016). Around 3000–4000 American children and youth begin smoking each day, of which about 1000 will become active smokers (Eguae, 2018; Maharaj & Ternullo, 2001).

In 2007, an estimated 22% of 12th-grade students were current smokers (Johnston et al., as cited in Milkman & Sunderwirth, 2010). A more recent study estimated smoking rates for middle/high school students to be 7.9% for e-cigarettes, 9.3% for marijuana, and 6.6% for dual use (Dai & Hao, 2017). For university students, the rates are higher; 19.2% of respondents in the southeastern United States used marijuana and 16.4% used hookah (Berg et al., 2015). The least commonly used smoking products were smokeless tobacco products (2.6%) and e-cigarettes (4.5%). Likewise, a Canadian study of young adults found the prevalence of cigarette use to be 36.3%: 10.1% for cigarettes only and 26.2% for polytobacco use (Bombard, Pederson, Koval, & O'Hegarty, 2009).

The majority of youth smokers appears to use mentholated cigarettes. Approximately one fourth of all cigarettes sold in the

United States in 2010 were mentholated (Okuyemi, Lawrence, Hammons, & Alexander, 2010). In a study of teenage smokers applying to a cessation study, menthol smokers accounted for 93% of respondents (Moolchan, 2004). This percentage is much higher than that of adult smokers in substance abuse treatment, of which about half use menthol cigarettes (Gubner, Williams, Pagano, Campbell, & Guydish, 2018). Also, an estimated 80% of African American young smokers use mentholated cigarettes (Okuyemi, Lawrence, Hammons, & Alexander, 2010).

Smokeless tobacco products (STPs) are not as prevalent as cigarettes and were used by 2.7% of U.S. adults in 2016 (Jones et al., 2017). STP use is more common among males and adults with lower education (Jones et al., 2017). Electronic nicotine delivery systems (ENDSs) were used by 5.4% of adults interviewed in the Nation Epidemiological Survey on Alcohol and Related Conditions-III and were virtually always concurrent with cigarette use (Chou et al., 2017).

Diagnostic and Assessment Considerations

Tobacco-related disorders are found on pages 571–577 of *DSM-5* (APA, 2013) and include tobacco use disorder (TUD), tobacco withdrawal, other tobacco-induced disorders, and unspecified tobacco-related disorder. As is true for other substance disorders contained in *DSM-5*, in contrast to DSM-IV, a diagnosis distinguishing between *substance abuse* and *substance dependence* no longer occurs. Instead, a substance disorder is diagnosed by *severity* (i.e., by the number of diagnosable symptoms) as follows: (a) *mild*: 2 to 3, (b) *moderate*: 4 to 5, or (c) *severe*: 6 or more. *DSM-5* includes 11 listed criteria with two specifiers.

The overall diagnostic criteria for TUD is "a problematic pattern of tobacco use leading to clinically significant impairment or distress, as manifested by at least two of the following, occurring within a 12-month period" (APA, 2013, p. 571). The specific criteria include (a) loss of control over use, (b) continued desire or inability to reduce use, (c) much time is spent trying to obtain tobacco or use it, (d) cravings or a strong desire to use tobacco, (e) recurring use results in failure to fulfill obligations at work, school, or at home, (f) continuing use despite persistent or recurring problems socially and/or interpersonally, (g) social, occupational, or recreational activities are stopped or reduced because of use, (h) continuing use in situations where it is physically dangerous such as smoking in bed, (i) continuing use despite having a persistent or recurrent psychological or physical problem in which tobacco caused or exasperated the condition, (j) tolerance, expressed as either a need for increasing amounts of tobacco or diminished effect from continuing use of the same amount of tobacco, and (k) withdrawal, expressed as the tobacco withdrawal diagnosis (begins on page 517) or tobacco or another related substance such as nicotine is taken to relieve or avoid symptoms of withdrawal. There are two specifiers for this diagnosis. You can specify if the condition is an *early remission*, meaning between 3 months and 12 months, or in *sustained remission*, which requires 12 months or longer. You can specify if the client is *on maintenance therapy* such as nicotine replacement medication. You can also specify if the individual is *in a controlled environment*, meaning in a place where access to tobacco is difficult if not impossible. See Table 12.1 for DSM and ICD codes:

DiFranza (2014) took exception to the *DSM-5* regarding nicotine addiction because it treats the disorder as a continuous rather than a dichotomous measure. In doing so, DiFranza argued that three diagnostic thresholds are ignored or minimized: (a) withdrawal only occurs in daily smokers, (b) social and/or occupational impairments, and (c) that these three criteria are clustered within a 12-month duration. Furthermore, given that scientific standards of proof have not established the validity of the *DSM-5* criteria for tobacco addiction, DiFranza recommended that the criteria should be viewed as "working hypotheses" (p. 1529).

Differential Diagnosis

DSM-5 does not provide information concerning a differential diagnosis for TUD; however, it mentions "associated features" (APA, 2013, p. 573) that include smoking within 30 min after awakening, smoking daily, increasing the amount smoked daily, and waking during the night to smoke. Regarding tobacco withdrawal, however, one needs to distinguish it from withdrawal due to other substances (i.e., depressants, stimulants, opioids, and caffeine) and other mental disorders such as anxiety, mood disorders, and sleep disorders. If the symptoms are reduced with nicotine replacement medications, the diagnosis of tobacco withdrawal is confirmed.

Comorbidity and Co-Addictions

Considered a gateway drug, nicotine is often accompanied by other drugs or substances (Richter, Pugh, Smith, & Ball, 2017). In fact, an estimated four fifths of individuals in addiction treatment are smokers (Guydish, Passalacqua, et al., 2016). Nicotine has a shared genetic liability with substances such as alcohol and cannabis as well as conduct disorder (Grant et al., 2015). Due to its destressing nature, it is also prevalent among individuals with psychiatric disorders and/or behavioral addictions such as sex addiction and pathological gambling (Anthenelli, 2014; Maté, 2008).

It should be noted that tobacco use, when occurring in conjunction with psychiatric and/or substance use disorders, is rarely treated because of concerns that nicotine withdrawal may compromise recovery (Das, Hickman, & Prochaska, 2017; Gass, Morris, Winters, VanderVeen, & Chermack, 2018). However, tobacco treatment has not been shown to impact recovery adversely (Rohsenow, Martin, Tidey, Colby, and Monti (2017).

Many smokers smoke to regulate their negative emotions or cope with emotional distress, both of which are prevalent in people with mental illness (Park, Luberto, O'Cleirigh, Perez, & Wilner, 2017). Sadly, people with severe psychiatric disorders have high mortality rates influenced mainly by smoking. Cancer, heart disease, and cerebrovascular and respiratory disease—their major causes of death—are all smoking-related (Anthenelli, 2014).

Smoking is most associated with schizophrenia, schizoaffective disorder, and bipolar disorder (Anthenelli, 2014; Muller & de Haan, 2017). High rates can also be found in people with major depressive disorder, generalized anxiety, posttraumatic stress disorder (PTSD), panic disorder, and social phobia (Anthenelli, 2014). Also, lifetime trauma exposure is linked to general substance use beyond what can be explained by PTSD and depression (Waldrop & Cohen, 2014).

TABLE 12.1 DSM and ICD Codes

DSM Code	Number of Symptoms Required	ICD-10	ICD-11
305.1	Mild: 2 or 3 symptoms	Z72.0	6C4A*
305.1	Moderate: 4 or 5 symptoms	F17.200	6C4A
305.1	Severe: 6 or more symptoms	F17.200	6C4A

*ICD-11 has codes for both nicotine use and tobacco abuse. The tobacco codes in ICD-11 mostly begin with QA, QB, QC, QD, or QE and the nicotine codes in ICD-11 mostly begin with 6C4A. Here are a few examples from ICD-11:

#	SPECIFIC ENTITY	Specific ICD-11 Code
1	Harmful pattern of use of *nicotine*, unspecified	6C4A.1Z
2	*Nicotine* dependence, unspecified	6C4A.2Z
3	*Nicotine* intoxication	6C4A.3
4	*Tobacco* rehabilitation	QB95.8
5	*Tobacco* use	QE13
6	*Nicotine* withdrawal	6C4A.4
7	Contact with health services for *tobacco* use counseling	QA13
8	Disorders due to use of *nicotine*, unspecified	6C4A.Z
9	Fetus and newborn affected by maternal use of *tobacco*	KA06.1
10	Problems associated with exposure to *tobacco* smoke	QD70.5
11	Harmful pattern of use of *cannabis*, unspecified	6C41.1Z
12	*Nicotine* dependence, current use	6C4A.20
13	Other specified disorders due to use of *nicotine*	6C4A.Y
14	Single episode of harmful use of *nicotine*	6C4A.0
15	Harmful pattern of use of *nicotine*, episodic	6C4A.10
16	Harmful pattern of use of *nicotine*, continuous	6C4A.11
17	*Nicotine* dependence, early full remission	6C4A.21
18	*Nicotine* dependence, sustained partial remission	6C4A.22
19	*Nicotine* dependence, sustained full remission	6C4A.23

Regarding major depressive disorder, research has found that depressive symptoms can cause a person to initiate smoking, and vice versa (Needham, 2007; Patterson et al., 2011). Smokers with major depression are more likely to have higher levels of nicotine dependence and relapse compared to smokers without depressive symptoms (Margolis & Zweben, 2011), probably because of heightened negative emotions during quit attempts (Patterson et al., 2011).

Individuals with ADHD are generally more likely to develop an addiction, including nicotine addiction (Ohlmeier et al., 2013). They tend to start smoking earlier and have a harder time quitting compared to their peers (Bidwell, Balestrieri, Colby, Knopik, & Tidey, 2018). However, nicotine has the benefit of improving attention, ability to concentrate, and control of impulses in this population, so it is likely used as a form of "self-medication" (Ohlmeier et al., 2013). Indeed, during a period of abstinence, ADHD smokers experience more impatience, restlessness, and difficulty concentrating than other smokers (Bidwell et al., 2018). ADHD smokers also respond more strongly to sensorimotor aspects of smoking, which may be used to relieve withdrawal.

The relationship between eating disorders and tobacco smoking remains unclear; however, Solmi et al. (2016) found in their meta-analyses that people with bulimia nervosa (BN) and binge eating disorder (BED) were significantly more likely to smoke than were healthy controls, whereas people with anorexia (AN) were not. This could be related to theories that both nicotine and highly palatable foods engage the reward system of the brain (Criscitelli & Avena, 2016).

The substance most commonly used concurrently with tobacco is alcohol; approximately 70%–80% of individuals with alcohol use disorder are also smokers (Diehl & Scherbaum, 2008; Giorgi et al., 2017; Maté, 2008), and these concurrent users are found more frequently in socioeconomically disadvantaged groups (Twyman et al., 2016). Smokers with alcohol problems, unfortunately, have less favorable outcomes in smoking cessation programs than smokers who are not problem drinkers (Sells, Waters, & MacLean, 2017). They also have a higher risk of developing serious diseases such as cancer and cardiovascular disease (Giorgi et al., 2017). Sells et al. (2017) found that smokers who were high-risk drinkers had stronger abstinence-induced cravings and attentional biases toward smoking cues compared with those who were low-risk drinkers. Additionally, inattention and hyperactivity/impulsivity levels below the ADHD threshold are dually associated with nicotine and alcohol dependence (Heffner, Johnson, Blom, & Anthenelli, 2010). Very high rates of smoking have also been found among opiate users and opiate-replacement therapy users (Guydish, Passalacqua, et al., 2016).

In terms of behavioral addictions, smoking is one of the most prevalent disorders co-occurring with disordered gambling (Boothby, Kim, Romanow, Hodgins, & McGrath, 2017). It is associated with more severe or extensive gambling in adults, and a recent study of youth gamblers found that smoking in both low- and high-risk gamblers was linked to more extensive gambling (Weinberger et al., 2015).

High rates of smoking are also found among people with human immune deficiency disease (Ogbonna, 2018). Lastly, cigarette smoking is associated to some extent with coffee consumption (Ware et al., 2017).

Available Measures

Following is a list of a few available measures for nicotine addiction:

1. Fagerstrom Test for Nicotine Dependence (FTND; Heatherton, Kozlowski, Frecker, & Fagerstrom, 1991). This is the second version of an earlier test called the Fagerstrom Tolerance Test. The National Institute on Drug Abuse referred to this six-item test as a "standard instrument for assessing the intensity of physical addiction to nicotine" (https://cde.drugabuse.gov/instrument/d7c0b0f5-b865-e4de-e040-bb89ad43202b, para. 1). The test is available and scored online from https://www.thecalculator.co/health/Fagerstrom-Test-For-Nicotine-Addiction-1037.html and an online version that also scores the test from https://www.thecalculator.co/health/Fagerstrom-Test-For-Nicotine-Addiction-1037.html.
2. Smoking Consequences Questionnaire (SCQ; Brandon & Baker, 1991). A commonly used measure is the 50-item self-report SCQ. Garey et al. (2018) reported that the original measure had poor psychometric properties. The researchers found, however, that a shorter version with 35 items had excellent construct validity and reliability. The five factors were named (a) immediate negative consequences, (b) long-term negative consequences, (c) sensory satisfaction, (d) negative affect reduction, and (e) appetite-weight control.
3. Hooked on Nicotine Checklist (HONC; DiFranza et al., 2002). The HONC is a 10-item instrument used with adolescents, ages 12–15. The checklist has good validity and reliability. Visit https://cancercontrol.cancer.gov/brp/tcrb/guide-measures/honc.html and download a copy of it.
4. Smoking Cessation Self-Efficacy Questionnaire (SEQ-12; Clyde, Pipe, Els, Reid, & Tulloch, 2017). This 12-item questionnaire has good initial validity "for evaluating overall cessation self-efficacy, regardless of psychiatric status" (Clyde et al., 2017, p. 162).
5. Barriers to Cessation Scale (BCS; Macnee & Talsma, 1995). The BCS contains 19 items. Garey et al. (2017) studied its psychometric properties and found the instrument to have good reliability and to effectively measure perceived barriers to cessation across several domains.
6. Cessation Fatigue Scale (CFS; Mathew, Heckman, Meier, & Carpenter, 2017). This 17-item scale measures the fatigue that can occur with smokers who have tried to quit smoking any number of times. The scale has good construct validity for measuring and evaluating a client's sense of self-efficacy to quit smoking.
7. Alcohol, Smoking and Substance Involvement Screening Test (ASSIST; WHO ASSIST Working Group, 2010; manual available from https://www.who.int/substance_abuse/publications/assist/en/). This questionnaire is used via face-to-face interaction with a client. It includes only seven questions, of which six are scored. This brief measure shows a good ability to discriminate among use, abuse, and dependence (Asbridge, Duff, Marsh, & Erickson, 2014). Available from http://apps.who.int/iris/bitstream/10665/44320/1/9789241599382_eng.pdf.

Clinical Interview Questions

Instead of asking questions, counselors could ask clients to complete the Tobacco Use Questionnaire, which is used by Hamilton Public Health Services. It is a useful form for collecting information from clients regarding their tobacco use. Available at http://youcanmakeithappen.ca/wp-content/uploads/Appendix-B3-Tobacco-Use-Questionnaire.pdf.

The Global Adult Tobacco Survey Collaborative Group (2011) created a list of tobacco questions that may be used in surveys and that may also be helpful for use with clients. See their free 50-page PDF at https://www.who.int/tobacco/surveillance/en_tfi_tqs.pdf

Damian O'Hara, a former chain smoker, wrote a blog as part of Allen Carr's Easy Way to Stop Smoking website (see http://allencarrseasywaytostopsmoking.blogspot.com/2008/02/eight-questions-every-smoker-should-ask.html). He suggested that smokers ask themselves eight questions (quoted from the website):

1. When did you decide to become a smoker for life?
2. If smoking is so great, why does everyone want to quit?

3. Have you ever met a smoker who would encourage their kids to start smoking?
4. If smoking relieves stress, why aren't smokers less stressed than nonsmokers?
5. If physical withdrawal from nicotine is so bad, then why can chain smokers sleep through the night?
6. What is the true cost of smoking?
7. Why doesn't it take your willpower not to take cyanide?
8. If smoking helps to control weight, why do we see so many overweight smokers?

Generic Names and Street "Lingo"

Tobacco smoking, hookah smoking, smokeless tobacco (i.e., chewing tobacco), e-cigarettes, and cigarettes go by various slang names. Hookah smoking is sometimes called narghile, argileh, shisha, hubble-bubble, or goza (MedicineNet, n.d.). Smokeless tobacco is also called snuff, chew, wad, and dip (NIDA, n.d.). Other names for it include spit tobacco, snus, and snuff (MedicineNet, n.d.). E-cigarettes are sometimes referred to as vapes, vape pipes, or E-cigs (New Health Advisor, 2019).

Cigarettes are called smokes, cancer sticks, and coffin nails (National Institute on Drug Abuse, n.d.). Cigarettes are also referred to as cigs or butts (MedicineNet, n.d.). A much longer list of alternate names for cigarettes can be found at http://dare.wisc.edu/survey-results/1965-1970/tobacco-liquor/dd6b.

Neuroscience

Nicotine is a stimulant in the central nervous system (Bedendo, Andrade, & Noto, 2016). Nicotine plays a central role in addiction to tobacco, and, among the available tobacco products, cigarettes are the most addictive (Attwood et al., 2013). After nicotine enters the lungs, it is sent quickly to the brain, where it attaches to nicotinic acetylcholine receptors (NARs; Attwood et al., 2013, p. 768). These receptors, located in different parts of the brain, create different effects, but the one of particular importance is in the ventral tegmental area (VTA; see Chapter 4 for a review and Dumont et al., 2018). Once nicotine attaches to the NARs in the VTA, some of the neuronal activation is sent to the nucleus accumbens (NA) in the forebrain. In turn, the NA releases dopamine. These responses are automatic, and, parallel to other substances and addictive behaviors, the dopamine release creates cravings for additional nicotine once dopamine levels subside (Attwood et al., 2013). There is research evidence that chronic tobacco smoking can lead to "persistent deficits in dopamine function" (Cosgrove, 2016, p. 174).

Nicotine also leads to the release of several other neurotransmitters, including glutamate (Castillo-Rolón, Arenas-López, Mihailescu, Hernandez-Gonzalez, & Hernández-López, 2018). Glutamate is an excitatory neurotransmitter, which causes an additional release of dopamine (Schulte et al., 2017). GABA, however, lowers the dopamine release temporarily, resulting in an initial calming effect. However, within minutes, nicotine again exerts its influence by inhibiting the release of GABA (Milkman & Sunderwirth, 2010). The result is higher dopamine levels in the NA. Additionally, there is an unknown substance in cigarette smoke that prevents monoamine oxidase (MAO) from breaking down dopamine. So, as Milkman and Sunderwirth (2010) explained, "smoking is a triple-sided sword" (p. 89). That is, one "sword" directly increases dopamine levels, one blocks the dopamine inhibitor, and yet another inhibits the destruction of dopamine (i.e., MAO). The result of these three actions makes nicotine one of the most addicting of all drugs in society, including those that are legal and illegal (Milkman & Sunderwirth, 2010).

Physical Impacts (Long-Term Use)

Chronic smoking causes a variety of health problems that reduce one's quality of life (Bloom et al., 2017). Inhaling tobacco smoke causes blood vessels to tighten, thereby increasing blood pressure and the risk for blood clots (Pietrangelo & Cherney, 2017). This reduced blood flow contributes to wrinkly and dry skin, hair loss and balding, erectile dysfunction in men, early menopause in women, and infertility in both sexes. During pregnancy, smoking can cause miscarriage and/or long-term effects in the child such as asthma, growth problems, or sudden infant death syndrome (Pietrangelo & Cherney, 2017).

Smokeless tobacco causes mouth cancer, gum disease, and tooth loss (Christen & McDonald, 1987), and it stains teeth as well as fingers when handled (Pietrangelo & Cherney, 2017). Smoking tobacco damages airways, often leading to persistent coughing and reduced immune system functioning. Hence, smokers are at higher risk for infections and disease (Pietrangelo & Cherney, 2017).

As previously mentioned, smoking—and inhaling secondhand smoke—is associated with such diseases as cardiovascular disease, respiratory illness, COPD, cognitive impairment, multiple sclerosis, and cancer (Rastegar & Fingerhood, 2016). Two studies have shown the likelihood of smokers developing COPD to be approximately 25%–50% (Rastegar & Fingerhood, 2016). Likewise, smokers are 30%–40% more likely to develop type 2 diabetes compared to nonsmokers (Centers for Disease Control and Prevention, 2018b). Nicotine addiction is linked to primary glutamatergic dysfunction, which may factor into the high relapse rate of smokers (Akkus et al., 2016).

Smokers die an average of 10 years earlier than nonsmokers (Prasad, Kaisar, & Cucullo, 2017). Smoking at higher intensities and longer durations increases the risk of an aneurysm rupture, a threat that does not decrease after short-term cessation (Buis & Batjer, 2017). Although the leading cause of death attributable to smoking is coronary heart disease, lung cancer is also a major concern. Thirty years after quitting, former smokers still have a higher risk of developing lung cancer than never-smokers, with users of unfiltered high-tar cigarettes having the highest risk (Raster & Fingerhood, 2016). Tobacco smokers also have a long-lasting susceptibility toward subsequent substance use due to physical changes in their bodily systems (Cross, Lotfipour, & Leslie, 2017).

Smokers, especially female smokers, appear to have a lower pain threshold than nonsmokers (Bagot, Wu, Cavallo, & Krishnan-Sarin, 2017). This lower pain threshold continues for at least 42 hours after abstinence. As well, smoking is associated with abdominal pain, discomfort, and gastrointestinal disorders (Zvolensky et al., 2017). Visceral sensitivity and anxiety appear to increase the odds of relapse.

People who smoke tend to weigh less than nonsmokers because of tobacco's appetite-suppressant effects (Evatt & Griffiths, 2012). Because smoking dulls sensory perceptions, food tastes and smells better after cessation (White & O'Malley, 2012). This increased appetite after cessation may persist for 6 months or longer, usually leading to a gain of about 6.5 pounds (Rastegar & Fingerhood, 2016). However, other estimates approximate a weight gain of 10–12 pounds due to compulsive overeating and lowered metabolism after cessation (Tarman & Werdell, 2014). Weight gain often leads smokers to relapse.

Compared to other drugs, nicotine withdrawal is less severe and causes fewer physical symptoms (Gearhardt & Corbin, 2012). These symptoms include craving, irritability, increased caloric intake, disturbed sleep patterns, and possible temporary congestion and respiratory discomfort (Christen & McDonald, 1987; Zvolensky et al., 2017). One study conducted among 353 adolescent new-smokers found that tolerance and impaired control preceded withdrawal, whereas impaired control preceded attempts to quit (Kandel, Hu, & Yamaguchi, 2009). Research has also shown that anxiety and having an attenuated stress response are linked to stronger withdrawal symptoms, thus leading to relapse (Bakhshaie et al., 2018; Zvolensky et al., 2017).

Mental, Emotional, and Spiritual Impacts

TUD is associated with psychiatric disorders (Malone, Harrison, & Daker-White, 2018). Researchers also know that sleep problems are common among smokers compared with nonsmokers (Branstetter, Horton, Mercincavage, & Buxton, 2016).

Ward, Kedia, Webb, and Relyea (2012) studied all Tennessee residents who received federal block grant funding between July and December 2004. They analyzed the data for 855 clients who were current cigarette smokers. Ward et al. found that nicotine dependence was associated with poorer self-rated overall health and past-month depression compared to nonsmokers. Major depression is frequently associated with smoking, but a causal link has not yet been found (Patten et al., 2017). Similarly, lower levels of happiness are linked to smoking (Churchill & Farrell, 2017; Foulds & Lubman, 2017). Anxiety, distress, and other negative affective states are correlated with smoking (Lyvers, Carlopio, Bothma, & Edwards, 2014).

Lyvers et al. (2014) compared 61 current smokers who had smoked daily for at least 1 year, 36 ex-smokers who had not smoked a cigarette for at least 1 year, and 86 never-smokers. The results supported their hypothesis that long-term abstinent ex-smokers and never-smokers did not significantly differ on measures of mood, mood regulation, and executive functioning. The current smokers, on the other hand, were significantly worse in functioning on all measures compared to the other two groups. Lyvers et al. concluded that their results regarding smoking are consistent with other findings regarding drug addictions that long-term abstinence results in improvement in moods and cognitive functioning.

McKenzie, Olsson, Jorm, Romaniuk, and Patton (2010) studied a cohort of 1943 adolescents in Victoria, Australia, over 10 years. The researchers concluded that adolescent smokers who had depression and anxiety symptoms as teenagers were at higher risk for nicotine dependence in young adulthood.

Although the relationship between nicotine addiction and spirituality has not been systematically explored, Hodge, Andereck, and Montoya (2007) found in their predominantly Hispanic sample ($N = 249$) that the participants who adhered to a spiritual and religious lifestyle were least likely to smoke (or consume alcohol or gamble). The other two reference groups were participants who defined as neither spiritual nor religious and those who were spiritual but not religious. This provides some evidence that religion, more than spirituality alone, may act as a protective factor, at least within a Hispanic community.

Psychosocial Impacts (Relationships, Career/Work, Legal, Financial)

One of the most disturbing aspects regarding *relationships* (in a broad sense) is the tobacco industry's intentional efforts to conceal the health consequences of its products (Hebert, 2005). Entrepreneurs generally recommend that honesty and integrity are hallmarks of great leadership and business ethics (Jacobs, 2004).

Recent research has found that heavier smokers and those trying to quit are more susceptible to the effect of advertising (Guydish, Tajima, et al., 2016). Adolescence is also a time of heightened suggestibility (Alderson, 2004), but a stronger influence than media are their relationships. The most important determinant of adolescents who take up smoking is that their friends and partners are smokers (Garcia-Rodriguez et al., 2011). Other relational factors that lead to smoking is if parents smoke, if there is low parental support for remaining a nonsmoker, and if prosmoking attitudes are prevalent in the household (West, 2017).

Relationships also play a substantial role in adults regarding smoking cessation. In their study of 238 tobacco-using couples (aged 18–45), Foulstone, Kelly, and Kifle (2017) found that both males and females were more likely to quit smoking if they had positive relationships with their opposite-sex partners. Additionally, males were more likely to quit if their female partners had stopped smoking. In a study of 63 Chinese participants in California, many experienced conflicts in their homes because of smoking, and participants realized the benefits of quitting to re-instill family harmony and to have a positive effect on children's health (Saw et al., 2017).

Smoking may have consequences for some individuals in their work settings. A study by Borland, Cappiello, and Owen (1997) found that, in their sample of 794 smokers working in medium-sized companies, 39% reported that they left work to smoke one or more times per day during nonbreak periods. Employment consequences might also result if an employee experiences increased irritability when unable to smoke a regularly needed cigarette.

Two of the most cogent reasons that smokers want to quit are financial and wanting a better quality of life (Aguiar et al., 2011). Quality of life is partly dependent on one's relationships with others, whereas the financial savings from quitting smoking are indisputable. On average, out-of-pocket costs for smokers across the United States purchasing tobacco products range from a lifetime low of $87,304 ($1712 yearly) in Georgia to a lifetime high of $187,267 ($3672 annually) in Connecticut (McCann, 2019). If you are helping clients to quit smoking, providing these statistics might be helpful for them in weighing the pros and cons of this expense combined with the fact that smoking remains the most preventable cause of disease in the world. Even the lower amount of $1700 would provide an all-inclusive vacation for two to a sun destination annually!

Working With Diverse Populations

Sex Differences

A few sex differences exist between male and female smokers, particularly in terms of risk and treatment. Among men with genetic dispositions toward strong nicotine cravings, being married and having positive social integration appear to reduce their risk of nicotine dependence when stressed (Perry, 2016). Interestingly, the same positive effects were not found among women.

Although fewer women smoke than men, the quit ratio for women is slightly lower (Patterson et al., 2011). This may be because women are more strongly affected by negative emotions, which smoking helps to reduce. For example, depression and smoking are more closely associated among women than men (Husky, Mazure, Paliwal, & McKee, 2008). Likewise, among women only, a history of childhood adversity appears to give stressful life events more power over their ability to stop smoking (Smith et al., 2016). Especially among low-income women with young children, neighborhood crime appears to contribute to smoking relapse (Nellum, 2018). These studies suggest that women may continue smoking more than men do to cope with negative emotions.

For female smokers, the risks for coronary heart disease, lung disease, and general health problems are higher than for male smokers (Agabio, Campesi, Pisanu, Gessa, & Franconi, 2016). Females also appear to be more vulnerable to the side effects of treatment medications than men. Also, nicotine reduces circulating estrogen levels in women, contributing to the risk for early menopause and cerebrovascular disease (Raval et al., 2011).

Maternal smoking poses risks for both the mother and child, including adverse birth outcomes (Nellum, 2018). Many women quit smoking during pregnancy only to pick up the habit again 6 months after delivery (Logan, Rothenbacher, & Genuneit, 2017). Most women who smoke during pregnancy do not seek treatment, but up to a fourth of them use complementary and alternative medicine treatments such as mindfulness, yoga, and acupuncture (Loree, Ondersma, & Grekin, 2017). Research suggests that promoting breastfeeding alongside smoking cessation may motivate mothers to continue abstaining (Logan, Rothenbacher, & Genuneit, 2017).

One study of long-term abstinence in smokers who attended a smoking cessation clinic found no significant differences between men and women (Marqueta, Nerin, Gargallo, & Beaumonte, 2017). However, there were slight differences in treatment approaches for both sexes.

Women metabolize nicotine significantly faster than men, meaning they may require higher doses during nicotine replacement therapy (Patterson et al., 2011). Varenicline (trade names for this medication are *Chantix* and *Champix*) may be a better choice for women rather than nicotine replacement therapy (Glatard et al., 2017). However, transdermal nicotine patches appear to be just as effective for men as varenicline or sustained-release bupropion (trade names for this drug are *Wellbutrin* and *Zyban*) (Smith et al., 2017; Smith, Zhang, Weinberger, Mazure, & McKee, 2017).

Menstruation influences quit success, and more women will find success if they attempt to quit during the follicular phase of their cycle (Patterson et al., 2011). That being said, another study found that, on the first and third days of abstinence, craving increased during the follicular phase but decreased during the luteal phase (Carlson, Allen, Allen, & al-Absi, 2017).

Women using hormonal contraceptives appear to have significantly greater withdrawal than other women and men before quitting, during quitting, and 1 week after stopping smoking (Allen, Carlson, Eberly, Hatsukami, & Piper, 2018). However, they may also have higher odds of short-term abstinence compared to their male counterparts.

Adolescents and Youth

As previously mentioned, most smokers begin the habit before they are 18 years of age (Blumenthal & Gold, 2012; O'Brien, 2007). Over 20% of youth use tobacco products, with noncigarette tobacco product use becoming increasingly common (Harrell, Naqvi, Plunk, Ji, & Martins, 2017). In one study of Spanish adolescent smokers, most of them reported that they smoked because it relaxed them (Borderias, Duarte, Escario, & Molina, 2015). Another study of 165 adolescent smokers estimated the average amount smoked per day to be three cigarettes (Rubinstein, Rait, & Prochaska, 2014).

Despite being more likely to quit than older adults, young adults seek less treatment and advice from health care providers (Gorman, 2018). This is problematic because nicotine has various adverse effects on youth such as decreased brain development (Pepper, Farrelly, & Watson, 2018), a higher risk of severe nicotine dependence later in life (Hu, Griesler, Wall, & Kandel, 2014), and a long-lasting vulnerability to substance use during adulthood (Cross, Lotfipour, & Leslie, 2017; Richter, Pugh, Smith, & Ball, 2017). Indeed, nearly all urban adolescent participants of one study reported using an average of two substances in addition to cigarettes (McKelvey, Ramo, Delucchi, & Rubinstein, 2017). Mirroring the adult population, smoking in adolescence is associated with clinical depression (McKelvey, Ramo, Delucchi, & Rubinstein, 2017; Patterson et al., 2011), impulsivity and behavioral addictions (Weckler et al., 2017), alcohol use disorder (Grucza & Bierut, 2006), and—particularly among heavy smokers—"harder drug" addictions such as cocaine and opiate addiction (Fortuna, Porche, Alam, Douglass, & Kim, 2012).

McKelvey and Halpern-Felsher's (2017) study of Californian adolescents found that adolescents in 2015 perceived smoking to be a higher-risk activity compared to adolescents in 2001, and 94% reported that they were very unlikely to smoke. However, already-smokers tend to believe that their smoking behavior isn't urgent enough for professional help (Balch et al., 2004). They may be ignorant of cessation programs (Balch et al., 2004), or they may also not truly understand what addiction is or that it can lead to difficulty quitting (Roditis, Lee, & Halpern-Felsher, 2016). Adolescent smokers, therefore, seem optimistic and tend to exempt themselves when talking about addiction, mortality, and tobacco-related diseases (Mantler, 2013).

Unfortunately, youth often hold misconceptions about the dangers of smoking. For instance, some urban youth will remove the paper liner of a small cigar (an activity called "freaking") because they believe that the paper liner is what leads to addiction and cancer (Fabian, Canlas, Potts, & Pickworth, 2012). As another example, one fifth of a Californian high school sample believed e-cigarette smoke was just water, and another one fifth thought e-cigarettes weren't a tobacco product (Gorukanti, Delucchi, Ling, Fisher-Travis, & Halpern-Felsher, 2017).

In regard to e-cigarettes, youth and young adults are often targeted by television ads, which increase their intention to use

(Stroup & Branstetter, 2018). Smokers who switch from traditional to e-cigarettes are more likely to be young adults, living in the South or West of the United States, individuals with higher education, and romantically involved with a partner (Park et al., 2017). A study of American adolescent e-cigarette users from 2011 to 2015 (in grades 6–12) found that past-month e-cigarette use was associated with past-month use of other tobacco products but not with cigarette quit attempts or contemplation (Chaffee, Couch, & Gansky, 2017). This suggests that adolescents are not using e-cigarettes to quit smoking but as a supplement instead. Interestingly, sports participation appears to reduce youth's likelihood of smoking traditional cigarettes but not e-cigarettes (Veliz, McCabe, McCabe, & Boyd, 2017).

Menthol as an additive to cigarettes is considered a contributing factor to the appeal that smoking has for youth (Eguae, 2018). Menthol has a minty flavor, masking the taste of tobacco, and provides a cooling sensation that reduces throat irritation (Healton, Beck, Cartwright, & Vallone, 2010). It is particularly popular among African American girls (Moolchan, 2004), with an estimated 80% of African American young smokers using mentholated cigarettes (Okuyemi, Lawrence, Hammons, & Alexander, 2010).

Menthol has been shown to increase smoking urgency, leading youth to have their first cigarette earlier in the day compared to nonmenthol smokers (Collins & Moolchan, 2006). This could be because menthol inhibits nicotine metabolism (Hammons, 2010). Research has also indicated that menthol may make cigarettes more addictive (Fu et al., 2008). That being said, any flavoring seems to make smoking more appealing to youth because they enjoy having a variety of tastes (Huang et al., 2017).

Certain countries have implemented policy changes to decrease smoking in this vulnerable population. During the FDA's 2009 ban on flavored cigarettes, youth were less likely to smoke and more likely to smoke less (Courtemanche, Palmer, & Pesko, 2017). Some substitution did appear to happen with increases in menthol cigarettes, cigars, and pipes, but overall smoking decreased by 6%. Likewise, Australia's 2012 implementation of plain packaging for all tobacco products led to a rise in support for plain packaging among youth, regardless of whether they were never-smokers, experimenters/ex-smokers, or current smokers (Dunlop, Perez, Dessaix, & Currow, 2017). In 2014, the United States launched the adolescent tobacco prevention mass media campaign called truth®, hoping to create "the generation that ends smoking" (Hair et al., 2017, p. 568). The effectiveness of this campaign is currently uncertain.

Race and Ethnicity

Various researchers have demonstrated that providing culturally sensitive treatment programs increases the chances of smoking cessation in ethnic groups (Hooper, Antoni, Okuyemi, Dietz, & Resnicow, 2017; Kim, 2017; Rollins, 2017). Nonetheless, knowledge about group differences regarding tobacco use needs to occur before this can be done on a broad scale (Moolchan et al., 2007). For example, early onset of tobacco use is typically associated with more severe risk factors; however, African Americans tend to have a later age of tobacco use onset but have greater health consequences. This difference would ideally factor into the treatment that African Americans receive.

Compared to Caucasian smokers, African Americans smoke about 35% fewer cigarettes, prefer mentholated and high-nicotine cigarettes, and have slower nicotine metabolisms (Patterson et al., 2011). Despite smoking less, African Americans are more likely to develop harmful health-related illnesses associated with smoking compared with any other ethnic group. Possible causes are lower medication adherence, lower access to healthcare, and higher rates of health factors such as diabetes and high blood pressure in this population (Jones, 2018).

Likewise, African Americans are more motivated to quit than Caucasians but are less likely to achieve total abstinence. This could be due to two reasons: (a) genetic factors, as research has found genes that influence the time to the first cigarette of the day in different ethnicities or (b) the way that African Americans smoke, as they tend to inhale more deeply than Caucasian smokers (Patterson et al., 2011). Cessation goals could also influence quit success: One study of smokers living with HIV found that African Americans were more likely to quit if they had a goal other than complete abstinence, whereas Caucasian smokers were more likely to stop if their goal was total abstinence (Valera et al., 2017). Interestingly, Caucasian smokers report withdrawal symptoms more commonly than Hispanic or African American smokers, which may impact their cessation attempts as well (Weinberger, Platt, Smith, & Goodwin, 2017).

Native Americans use smokeless tobacco in many cultural rituals. Because of this, they are disproportionately affected by tobacco-related diseases (Rollins et al., 2017). Northern Plains Native Americans appear to have a higher prevalence of smoking than Southwest tribes (Tanner et al., 2018). Both populations demonstrate risk for tobacco-related diseases from high cotinine[1] levels among nonsmokers as well, suggesting secondhand smoke exposure. Also, at least in Australia and Alaska, Indigenous women are more likely than non-Indigenous women to use tobacco during pregnancy (Koller et al., 2017; Tzelepis et al., 2017). Pregnant mothers may be motivated to quit smoking by being tested for cotinine and learning about fetal exposure to carcinogens (Koller et al., 2017).

Sreeramareddy, Pradhan, Mir, and Sin (2014) analyzed data from nine South and Southeast Asian countries (i.e., India, Pakistan, Nepal, Bangladesh, Maldives, Philippines, Cambodia, Indonesia, and Timor Leste) to look at prevalence and social aspects of smoking and smokeless tobacco (SLT) use. Smoking prevalence among women was very low in all nine countries (range: 4.02%–9.8%). Smoking prevalence among men was very high in Indonesia (72.3%), Timor Leste (69.5%), Bangladesh (60.0%), and Maldives (47.3%). SLT was common in India (36.7%), Nepal (34.8%), and Bangladesh (21.4%).

Choi, Rankin, Stewart, and Oka (2008) conducted a meta-analysis of smoking behavior among Asian Americans. They similarly found high prevalence rates of cigarette smoking (range: 26%–70%). Choi et al. concluded that "acculturation may have a protective effect on smoking behavior in Asian men and a harmful effect in Asian women and adolescents" (p. 67). Acculturated men were 53% less likely to smoke compared with nonacculturated or "traditional" men. Acculturated women, on the other hand, were five times more likely to smoke compared with nonacculturated or "traditional" women. Similarly, acculturated adolescents were twice as likely to smoke compared with traditional adolescents. Korean Americans have the highest smoking rate among Asian Americans (Kim, 2017).

[1] *Cotinine* is the primary metabolite of nicotine, and it is used as a biomarker for exposure to tobacco smoke.

Nonpsychiatric Disabilities

Lodge (2016) wrote that there is scant research evidence regarding smoking among individuals with intellectual disabilities. The studies that are available provide equivocal results. Some studies cited by Lodge indicated a lower smoking prevalence compared to that of the general population, an Australian study reported a higher smoking prevalence (36%) with people with mild intellectual disability, and another study found that smoking prevalence with intellectually challenged individuals is similar to that of the general population.

The Centers for Disease Control and Prevention (CDC; 2018a) stated that "the percentage of adults who smoke cigarettes is higher among people with disabilities [25.4%] than people without disabilities [17.3%]" (para. 3). Individuals with mobility impairments also have higher smoking rates compared to the general population (Borrelli, Busch, & Trotter, 2013).

In a study of 106 individuals with epilepsy compared to a control group ($N = 96$), no differences were found in smoking prevalence rates (Yeni, Tumay, Tonguc, Azaroglu, & Bozok, 2015). Given the small sample size, however, these findings should be viewed with caution until they are replicated with a larger sample.

Lesbian, Gay, Bisexual, and Transgender (LGBT)

Minimal research has been published concerning smoking and the LGBTQ community. What is known is that smoking has a much higher prevalence among LGBTQ individuals—whether they be youth, young adults, or adults—compared to their heterosexual and cisgender counterparts (Baskerville, Shuh, Wong-Francq, Dash, & Abramowicz, 2017; Matthews, Cesario, Ruiz, Ross, & King, 2017). Baskerville et al. (2017) provided estimates of daily smoking prevalence with LGBTQ adults between 33% and 45%, compared with 18.9% for non-LGBTQ adults. Rates for LGBTQ youth and young adults might be double the rate for non-LGBTQ youth and young adults (Baskerville et al., 2017). Several reasons for this disparity were offered by Baskerville et al. in their review of the literature, including minority stress, victimization, harassment, and other possible factors.

War Veterans

Because individuals with PTSD and other mental disorders have high rates of smoking and low quit rates, it is not surprising that these rates carry over to veterans as well. Nicotine shares the spotlight with alcohol as the most common substances of abuse among veterans (Moore, 2012). Approximately 22.7 million American veterans and their family members are in danger of tobacco-related health problems (Ogbonna, 2018).

During the Gulf War (1990–1991), troops were directly targeted by tobacco companies with free cigarettes, branded items, ways to communicate with family, and "welcome home" events (Smith & Malone, 2009). Authorities often perceived the companies as benefactors and enabled them despite military tobacco control efforts beginning in 1986.

Among veterans participating in a smoking cessation treatment study, three factors were found by Travaglini, Li, Brown, and Bennett (2017) to predict greater treatment engagement: (a) those who had never been married, (b) previous attendance in a smoking cessation group, and (c) more severe symptoms as measured by the Brief Psychiatric Rating Scale. Interestingly, the study by Scherrer et al. (2008) of 6099 members of the Vietnam Era Twin Registry found that combat exposure was associated with lifetime nicotine dependence only through genetic/environmental factors related to PTSD.

The Veterans Health Administration (VHA) requires specialty care settings to screen for tobacco use and offer smoking cessation treatment (Gifford, Tavakoli, Wisdom, & Hamlett-Berry, 2015). However, there are still critical gaps in the provision of smoking cessation treatment in these settings. One study of 137 veterans enrolled in an SUD treatment program as well as a tobacco cessation education program found that only 14.4% of 1-month follow-up respondents reported abstinence from tobacco (Vest et al., 2014). Vander Weg et al. (2017) studied 898 adult veteran smokers attending four VHA programs for tobacco addiction and found similarly disappointing results. Vander Weg et al. recommended that VHA programs need to alter clinician behavior and enhance postdischarge follow-up. Another potential treatment option is home telehealth and motivational interviewing (MI), which veterans appear open to trying (Peterson, Battaglia, Fehling, Williams, & Lambert-Kerzner, 2017).

Veterans living with HIV (PLHIV) have a high rate of smoking. Using data from a national random sample of veterans, smoking prevalence was estimated from self-report of both smoking status and HIV. Results revealed that 42% of PLHIV smoked daily, compared to 18% of veterans without HIV and 30% of nonveterans living with HIV (Wilson, Pacek, Dennis, Bastian, Beckham, & Calhoun, 2017).

Medications and Other Relevant Physical Interventions

Studies conducted over the past 25 years have found that several medications are helpful for smokers who want to quit. These include varenicline, bupropion sustained-release (SR), and nicotine-replacement treatments (NRTs; Greenfield & Weiss, 2017). There is also some evidence that transcranial direct current brain stimulation helps smokers resist smoking (Falcone et al., 2016).

Varenicline was approved in 2006 by the FDA (Anthenelli, 2014). This designer drug was created explicitly for smoking cessation. It has been found in studies to be more effective than bupropion (Anthenelli, 2014). However, varenicline has not demonstrated greater effectiveness than NRT (Rastegar & Fingerhood, 2016). Varenicline does not substantially reduce postcessation weight gain (White & O'Malley, 2012). It does, however, reduce craving and withdrawal, and it lowers the satisfaction from having a "slip," thereby reducing the likelihood of relapse (Patterson et al., 2011). The most common side effects of varenicline include nausea and sleep disorders (Rastegar & Fingerhood, 2016).

Bupropion, which is an antidepressant medication, was approved as a smoking aid in 1997 (Anthenelli, 2014). Bupropion has also been used with the nicotine patch (Anthenelli, 2014). In contrast to varenicline and NRT, bupropion consistently reduces postcessation weight gain (White & O'Malley, 2012). Interestingly, bupropion is sometimes abused for its stimulating effects, and the

INSIDE AN ADDICTED PERSON'S MIND

Bernadette, Age 79

You would think I would have quit by now. Like so many of my peers, smoking was the thing to do back in the 1950s. Some of you might remember the television series *Happy Days*. Well, those *were* the days! The boys were tough, and the girls were gentle; at least that's the way I saw it. But, if you wanted to be cool, you smoked. Your parents smoked, your teachers smoked, actors and actresses smoked on black-and-white television, and it seemed that everyone smoked everywhere. I especially remember bingo halls when I was a youngster. The entire family would head off to the bingo hall, and we would play bingo with smoke billowing from nearly everyone who was anyone.

I wanted to be someone, so I started smoking at age 13. I remember the brand was Camels. An ad from back in the 1950s told me that doctors smoked it more than any other brand; check it out yourself if you doubt me. In fact, doctors recommended that you smoke! That first cigarette nearly done me in! I was dizzy, felt nauseous, and I just wanted to be by myself. My friends, however, saw this as some kind of hazing and they just laughed while we hung out near the Mississippi River.

The White kids left us alone, you know. There is no question that these were difficult times if you were colored folk. I guess my family was darker than most, and that didn't help any. It seemed that smoking was the one thing that made me popular with other girls and with the boys. Don't think for a moment that the kids of my age didn't have interest in those boys in the leather jackets and white tee shirts. But, unless you wanted to be known as a hussy, or, even worse, a harlot (look it up if you don't know what it means), you did not play around with boys seriously until you got married.

Back to smoking. It wasn't long until I was smoking a pack a day, but my habit grew throughout my 20s until I was smoking two packs a day. Yes, I tried to quit several times but not until I was in my 40s. By then, they were telling us that smoking causes lung cancer. Several people I knew died of it, and most of them smoked as I recall. I kept trying and trying to quit, but something kept bringing me right back. Well, let me be honest. Ever saw a fiddle shake because the fiddler plays it too hard? That was me! I became so shaky, jittery—and depressed—that I had to light up another.

They tell me it will age you, but heck, I have aged because I am old! Seriously, though, I do look like a stale old muffin most of the time, but what do you expect at my age? I am no prima donna, that's for sure. I do wonder if these cigarettes are going to be the end of me. I cough all the time and been spitting up a lot of bad stuff. I live alone and not sure there is much point to quitting now. Suppose I lived longer than I would have reckoned anyway.

Commentary

Bernadette has smoked for most of her life, and, at two packs a day, she is hooked. As you read earlier, she fits most of the criteria for *severe* TUD as defined in *DSM-5* (APA, 2013): (a) she has lost control over her use, (b) she is unable to reduce use of tobacco, (c) she spends a fair amount of time smoking given her two packs a day, (d) she craves smoking if she tries to quit, (e) she continues use despite its health consequences, and (f) she experiences withdrawal symptoms whenever she quits smoking.

Discussion

1. You likely know people who still smoke, perhaps family, friends, or acquaintances. Which symptoms noted in the commentary apply to him, her, or them?
2. Does this person(s) have symptoms that are not listed in the commentary? If so, what are they?
3. If you were Bernadette's counselor, how would you go about helping her?
4. If Bernadette were already near death from old age, do you believe it would still make sense for her to quit smoking, or would it better that she continue smoking until her death? Why or why not?

intensity of the impact depends on whether the medication is inhaled nasally or administered intravenously (Baribeau & Araki, 2013). Baribeau and Araki (2013) recommended that physicians be careful when prescribing bupropion to unfamiliar patients.

Anthenelli (2014) stated that nicotine patches have the advantage of a slower, longer-acting release compared with the fast-acting release that quickly dissipates with nicotine gum, lozenges, and inhalers. Consequently, the two (i.e., the patch and another NRT) are often used concurrently. None of the NRTs have demonstrated greater effectiveness over other varieties of NRT, except higher-dose nicotine gum (i.e., 4 mg) appears to be more helpful for highly dependent smokers (Rastegar & Fingerhood, 2016). NRT increases smoking cessation rates by about 60% (Rastegar & Fingerhood, 2016). Although NRT is effective at helping people quit smoking, it does not reduce hunger or weight gain appreciably (White & O'Malley, 2012).

Nortriptyline, another antidepressant, has been shown to be helpful for individuals without psychiatric disorders but also for smokers with histories of major depression. An antihypertensive drug called clonidine has some effect as a smoking cessation aid as well. However, both nortriptyline and clonidine create dry mouth, sedation, and dizziness in some individuals (Anthenelli, 2014).

Medical researchers will continue looking for additional drugs to help individuals stop smoking and to keep trying variations of existing ones. Rose and Behm (2017), for example, found varenicline used in combination with bupropion was helpful for highly dependent smokers, and Hurt et al. (2017) found varenicline combined with lorcaserin (trade name is *Belviq*, a weight loss drug) helpful in weight reduction with overweight and obese smokers.

Although the previously described medications are effective for many smokers, Littlewood et al. (2017) stated that, whereas pharmacotherapy may seem like the "silver bullet" (p. 3417), its efficacy is influenced by psychological factors. Smokers will quit when they are ready, and they will not regardless of how much medication you provide them. Allen Carr (1999) reminded us of that in his popular book entitled *Easy Way to Stop Smoking* (his third edition is available for free download from http://prdupl02.ynet.co.il/ForumFiles_2/15119301.pdf).

Specific Counseling Considerations

ROLEPLAY SCENARIOS

Roleplay in dyads with one of you acting as the counselor and the other as the counselee. If roleplay is not possible, work individually in writing out a list of your suggestions.

Roleplay #1

Bitan, age 26, migrated from Bangladesh 3 years ago. Since arriving in Albuquerque, he met Lucy, a fun-loving, attractive Caucasian 22-year-old. They are now thinking about getting married. Lucy, however, wants Bitan to quit smoking before she agrees to marry him. The two of them come to your office together, and Bitan tells you that he has smoked since he was 10. All the men in his family smoke, and he sees it as an important way of demonstrating his masculinity. You soon realize the only reason Bitan wants to quit smoking is because of Lucy's ultimatum. *Note*: you could roleplay this with just having either Bitan or Lucy as your client.

Roleplay #2

Darlene is 33 years old, and she works for a small printing company. Darlene was not concerned about her smoking until the company brought in a no-smoking policy. The bosses told her that, if she continues smoking on site, she had best look for another job elsewhere. Darlene did not want to stop smoking, at least not right now. She feels pressured to quit because of the new company policy. Because she learned her skills on the job, she is concerned she would be unable to find another job in the printing business quickly. She has come to see you for help in quitting smoking, but it's very evident that she is ambivalent and is harboring anger toward her boss over this shift in policy.

Goals and Goal Setting

One of two goals is likely to be the focus of intervention: abstinence or harm reduction. Given that goal-setting is a collaboration between the counselor and the client, it is essential that clients be provided with the best information available in helping them make a decision regarding their tobacco and/or nicotine use.

Harm reduction.

Regarding harm reduction, Stead and Lancaster's (2007) review is found in the Cochrane Database, which is known as the gold standard for clinical trials, particularly in the medical profession. Stead and Lancaster reviewed 16 trials of interventions targeted at helping smokers reduce harm. In nine of the trials, NRT helped 50% of the participants reduce the amount that they smoked. However, few were able to sustain a reduction of 50% or higher successfully. Nonetheless, NRT significantly increased the odds of quitting. Stead and Lancaster concluded that "there is insufficient evidence about long-term benefit to support the use of interventions intended to help smokers reduce but not quit smoked tobacco use" (p. 2). The authors did not find any trials that reported the long-term effects on health of reducing use. Consequently, it

HOW WOULD AN ADDICTION COUNSELOR HELP THIS PERSON?

You are working as a professional counselor. Lance, age 42, just retired from the military after 20 years of service. He tells you that these were gratifying years, and he is retired on a full pension that now provides him 50% of his final salary. He witnessed terrible catastrophes in Afghanistan a few years ago, and Lance tells you that he has never been the same since. He said that, unlike many of his comrades, he does not feel that he is experiencing PTSD. However, both his drinking and his tobacco use have escalated substantially to the point where he doesn't think that he can quit either without help. That is why he sees you. Through the next 2 months of working with him, you find that, when Lance stops drinking, he smokes an extra pack of cigarettes a day. The converse is also true: when Lance stops smoking, he drinks an extra micky of Jack Daniel's a day. Lance is nearly ready to give up, but he hangs in there because he believes you can help him.

Remember to view clients within their environmental contexts, keeping in mind societal, parental/familial, cultural/spiritual, and peer influences. Specifically, become aware of the impact that the following influences have and continue to have in your clients' lives: race, language, religion and spirituality, gender, familial migration history, sexual/affectional orientation, age and cohort, physical and mental capacities, socioeconomic situation and history, education, and history of traumatic experience.

1. What defines this person's environment, past and present?
2. Who is this person sitting in front of me, taking into account environmental and personal characteristics?
3. What defines the problem that he or she is presenting within their multicultural milieu?

remains uncertain how much health benefit will result from reducing the use of tobacco products. Furthermore, Beard et al. (2013) found that, when smokers reported that they were reducing their cigarette consumption, they only smoked one or two fewer cigarettes per day on average.

Abstinence.

Anesi, Halpern, Harhay, Volpp, and Saulsgiver (2017) conducted a secondary analysis for individuals who had selected a smoking quit date between 0 and 90 days following enrollment in a cessation program. In total, 1848 individuals provided a quit date. Analysis by Anesi et al. revealed that the probabilities of remaining abstinent at 6 months if participants selected quit dates in weeks 1, 5, 10, and 13 were 39.6%, 22.6%, 10.9%, and 4.3%, respectively. Their study provides support in suggesting to individuals quitting smoking that they should decide to quit within 1 week of beginning a smoking cessation program.

A 2012 Cochrane review found that smokers can either quit abruptly or gradually reduce their smoking until they stop altogether. Both approaches have comparable quit rates (Rastegar & Fingerhood, 2016).

In a study of 340 smokers receiving cessation help and substance abuse treatment concurrently, Rohsenow et al. (2017) did not find that smoking treatment harmed SUD treatment. The takeaway from this study is that addiction counselors should have no reluctance to treating nicotine addiction at the same time as other addictions.

Stages of Change Strategies

The processes of change mentioned are based on those outlined by Connors, DiClemente, Velasquez, and Donovan (2013) and Prochaska, Norcross, and DiClemente (1994). The definitions for the various processes can be found in Chapter 6. Besides these processes, other strategies are included that have separate citations.

The University of Rhode Island Change Assessment Scale (URICA) is a helpful scale for determining where the client is currently regarding the stages of change model. There are 24-, 28-, and 32-item versions of the scale.

A 24-item version is published for alcohol or drug problems. The scale, however, is generic and can be easily adapted for use with other addictions. It is available with norms as a free download from https://www.guilford.com/add/miller11_old/urica.pdf.

Specific precontemplation strategies.

Please visit the section of this chapter called Relevant Mutual Support Groups, Websites, and Videos for free or low-cost information and resources that may help someone move out of precontemplation.

Even if your client sees you for a different reason, Gary Tedeschi (as cited in Bray, 2016) recommended that counselors use the "five A's" (para. 21) to open up discussion regarding smoking with clients. The five A's include the following:

- Ask each client about their tobacco use.
- Advise all tobacco users to quit.
- Assess whether the client is ready to quit.
- Assist the client with a quit plan.
- Arrange follow-up contact to mitigate relapse. (para. 21)

Also, since 2011, smokers can receive cessation counseling through Medicare, which will cover two attempts per year with each including up to four sessions (see http://tobacco-cessation.org/whatworkstoquit/counsel.html). Every state in the United States and province/territory in Canada also has a Tobacco Quit Line (details at http://map.naquitline.org/).

From the beginning, the transtheoretical stages of change model was based on studies examining individuals who attempted successfully and unsuccessfully to quit smoking. Since then, Cochrane reviews have not found evidence that smoking cessation programs based on stages are any more effective than programs that are non-stage-based. In reviewing Cochrane evidence, Young and Skorga (2011) concluded that there was no reason for public health nurses to design stage-based cessation programs for patients. Her review, although not explicitly stated, was likely based on the Cochrane review by Cahill, Lancaster, and Green (2010). Herzog (2008) surmised that the evidence does not indicate that the stages of change are qualitatively distinct categories.

Cahill et al. (2010) concluded that there is no reason to restrict quitting advice and encouragement to only those individuals in the preparation and action stages. Quitting advice and encouragement are helpful at every stage of quitting smoking.

Evidence for the transtheoretical model in helping adolescents stop smoking is stronger. Robinson (2012) conducted an integrative review of smoking cessation in adolescents using the transtheoretical model and found that stage-based interventions promoted smoking cessation in adolescents. Rios, Herval, Ferreira, and Freire (2019) performed a systematic review and meta-analysis on 11 studies with a total of 6469 adolescents from five middle- to high-income countries. Rios et al. found that 41% of the smokers were at the precontemplation stage. They concluded that the group displayed more unfavorable smoking-related behaviors and characteristics than adolescents in later stages. Consequently, the authors suggested that smoking cessation interventions targeting adolescents should pay particular attention to precontemplators.

Books that may be offered to individuals in the precontemplation stage include the following:

1. Allen Carr's (1999) book entitled *Easy Way to Stop Smoking* was mentioned earlier in the chapter (his third edition is available for free download from http://prdupl02.ynet.co.il/ForumFiles_2/15119301.pdf). Although the notion advanced by Carr is simplistic (i.e., anyone can quit if they are determined), it is a good read.
2. Dr. Dee Burton's book, *21 Days to Stop Smoking*, published in 2014 is highly rated.
3. Janet Urban's book, *Smoking Cessation: A Review of the Literature*, published in 2015, is a good choice for someone who still needs to be convinced of the importance of quitting.
4. There is also a *Quitting Smoking for Dummies* book, written by Dr. David Brizer, that was published in 2003.

WhyQuit.com has links to two brief videos and much information about smoking and nicotine (visit https://whyquit.com/whyquit/LinksMovies.html). Smoking in the movies, according to Woolston (2019), is on the increase, including shows aimed at children such as *101 Dalmatians, The Nutty Professor*, and *Honey, I Shrunk the Kids*. Tynan, Polansky, Titus, Atayeva, and Glantz (2017) agreed that an increase has occurred in top-grossing movies in the United States between 2010 and 2016. The authors contrasted this with the trend toward less smoking in movies that were produced between 2005 and 2010. Tynan et al. also noted that "the Surgeon General has concluded that there is a causal relationship between depictions of smoking in the movies and the initiation of smoking among young persons" (para. 1).

Other strategies that can be used during the precontemplation phase are covered in other chapters. These ideas include building rapport and trust, creating doubt and evoking concern, offering factual information, helping clients examine discrepancies, and expressing concern.

Specific contemplation strategies.

Shake (2017), in her dissertation research, explored the emotions that smokers experienced during the contemplation stage of smoking cessation. Her qualitative study included seven participants between the ages of 43 and 79 in Corpus Christi, Texas. Her investigation revealed eight emotions during cessation: fear of developing a smoking-related disease, fear of not being successful in quitting, fear of losing family relationships and other connections, feeling entrapped, anxiety about finding alternative activities to smoking, experiencing inner conflict, feeling a sense of freedom, and a determination to quit.

Counselors can help clients in the contemplation stage to look at a decisional balance regarding a potential decision to quit (i.e., weighing the pros and cons). They can also help strengthen client self-efficacy. Furthermore, they can help create ambivalence regarding the desire to quit smoking juxtaposed with the fear of not being successful. There may also be extrinsic motivators that are helping push the client toward making a change, and counselors can remind clients of these positive influences.

Specific preparation strategies.

Alderson (2011), in his book entitled *Breathe, Freedom: A Comprehensive and Hypnotic Approach to Quitting Smoking*, recommended that clients commit to taking a few steps before quit day, a date that was generally suggested for 2 or 3 weeks after deciding to stop smoking. The reason for this was to provide enough time for the client to become maintained on appropriate medication (remember the top two medications are varenicline and bupropion SR). Bupropion SR is a great choice for smokers who have found that they experience depression when they quit smoking. If the client is only going to take NRTs, an earlier quit date is desirable (also recall the study by Anesi et al., 2017, that found most smokers do better if they quit within 1 week of beginning a smoking cessation program).

Use the following ideas with clients *before* quit day (i.e., preparation strategies) together with the ideas found in Appendix B.

1. Change brands. At the beginning of each week before quit day, change the brand of cigarettes that you smoke; pick a brand that has lower nicotine content than the brand you smoked the week before if possible.
2. Don't do anything else while smoking. Begin breaking associations between smoking and other activities (the next two points are related to this as well). Consequently, do not do anything else while smoking from now on; instead, just sit and pay attention to each puff of smoke (e.g., do not work, socialize, or converse; drink coffee; or drink alcohol while smoking).
3. Pairing breathing with relaxation. After you finish a cigarette, take three deep abdominal breaths, each time telling yourself, "Breathe freedom and relax," as you exhale.
4. Break associations. Begin to break down the associations between smoking and eating and drinking. Do not let yourself have a cigarette at least 10 min before eating and at least 10 min after you eat. Furthermore, if you drink coffee, tea, or alcohol, do not let yourself have a cigarette for at least 10 min before and after drinking the beverage.
5. Control your surroundings. If you have other smokers at home, ask them not to leave their cigarettes around the house for at least 2 weeks. If possible, ask them not to smoke around you either for at least 2 weeks.
6. Getting psychologically prepared. Psych yourself up (i.e., increase your motivation) for the fact that you will be quitting smoking on quit day. Start convincing yourself that this is the most important goal of your life. One way to do this is to write on the inside flap of your cigarette package something such as the following: **"On ____________________ (i.e., quit day), I am going to become a nonsmoker. My commitment is growing stronger each day."** Each time you want a cigarette, read this suggestion to yourself *first*. Think about it for a moment or so before you take your cigarette and begin smoking it. Remember to do point #3 after you *finish* each cigarette.
7. Get rid of ashtrays. On the day before quit day, get rid of all ashtrays.
8. Alcohol. Seriously consider not drinking alcoholic beverages during the first 2 weeks as it is highly associated with relapse.
9. Ensure that you have used up (or thrown away) any remaining cigarettes the night before quit day. If you have a few cigarettes remaining, rip these up into tiny pieces the night before quit day and throw them in the garbage.

Specific action strategies.

Similar to the previous section, the rest of Alderson's ideas for what smokers can do from quit day onward can be found in Appendix B. Like many addictions, nicotine addiction is known as a chronic, relapsing condition. Most individuals who are successful in quitting permanently have made several attempts beforehand. West (2017), for example, reported that only about 5% of unassisted quit attempts succeed for a minimum of 6 months. After the 6-month mark, the relapse rate is about 50% over subsequent years. West included a table that contained the effectiveness of various interventions. For example, with medications, varenicline and nicotine patches together with fast-acting NRT increase quit success rates by 5%–15%. Face-to-face or telephone behavioral support increases success by 3%–10%. Printed self-help materials increase success by 1%–2% only. West reported that the highest success rate occurs when face-to-face behavioral support is provided along with either varenicline or dual-form NRT. These combination methods have demonstrated up to 40% continuous abstinence rates for 52 weeks (West, 2017). Two Cochrane reviews in 2013 have indicated that adding mood management might improve cessation outcomes in smokers with current or past depression (Hartmann-Boyce, Stead, Cahill, & Lancaster, 2014). The research regarding behavioral and cognitive-behavioral therapy (CBT) will be covered later in this chapter.

Although research remains inconclusive currently, it appears that e-cigarettes might help some smokers quit or reduce their smoking (Pasquereau, Guignard, Andler, & Nguyen-Thanh, 2017; Rastegar & Fingerhood, 2016). If parents are going to smoke in their homes, it would be better if they used e-cigarettes around their children as a harm reduction strategy (Rowa-Dewar, Rooke, & Amos, 2017). So far, research is indicating that they cause less harm than smoking cigarettes (Zborovskaya, 2017).

Bernard et al. (2015) provided preliminary evidence that counseling intervention and exercise may be more beneficial to improving smoking abstinence than health education. A recent meta-analysis of mindfulness training suggested that it might play an important role in smoking cessation (Oikonomou, Arvanitis, & Sokolove, 2017). In a structured treatment program, Johnson, Garcia-Romeu, and Griffiths (2017) found that psilocybin suggested promising results in promoting long-term smoking abstinence. Other ideas for *beginning* quit day (i.e., action strategies) can be found in Appendix B.

Specific maintenance strategies and relapse prevention.

Note: Maintenance strategies and relapse prevention are also, for many, partly facilitated by regular attendance at relevant mutual support groups. A list of such mutual support groups and helpful websites is found in an upcoming section entitled Relevant Mutual Support Groups, Websites, and Videos.

A list of relapse prevention strategies can be found in Appendix C.

Motivational Interviewing

In a study of 36 smokers in South Korea who received group therapy for smoking cessation, Lee (2017) found that MI increased their motivations, whereas the group approach increased positive thoughts and confidence to quit. Conybeare (2017) found in her dissertation research with individuals who were not ready to quit smoking that MI alone led more smokers to report at follow-up that they intended to quit in the future compared with the two other experimental groups (one used behavioral intervention and MI, and the other used behavioral intervention only).

Parents who were unmotivated to quit smoking despite having an asthmatic child participated in an intensive intervention that included MI. At 6-month follow-up, they were as likely to have stopped smoking as compared with motivated parents who participated in the program (Borrelli, Endrighi, Hammond, & Dunsiger, 2017).

Krigel, Grobe, Goggin, Harris, Moreno, and Catley (2017) found that using the traditional decisional balance technique (i.e., weighing the pros and cons of quitting) to help smokers quit could be counterproductive. Krigel et al. cautioned against using this method. Instead, their research with 82 college tobacco smokers indicated that it was more helpful to focus on the perceived benefits of quitting and building a strong positive working alliance.

Peterson, Battaglia, Fehling, Williams, and Lambert-Kerzner (2017) interviewed 32 veterans with PTSD who also smoked after they completed a home telehealth and MI trial focused on smoking cessation. The respondents were highly satisfied with both methods. They stated that they found MI to be supportive, nonjudgmental, and informative.

Here is an example of how MI could be used to help an addicted individual decide that counseling might be the best first step to take in recovery. (Pertaining to Chapter 6's description of MI, the following is an example of the process called *engaging*.)

Client: Ida, I cannot thank you enough for helping me deal with my relationship breakup. I do not know what I would've done without your support.

Counselor: Thank you so much for that feedback, Ralph. You also mentioned in the first session that you have become concerned about your smoking.

Client: I really have not given that much thought since I first mentioned it. As you know, I was so preoccupied with Stacy leaving me.

Counselor: That certainly has been our focus over the past four sessions. Nonetheless, what are your thoughts currently about quitting smoking?

Client: I guess I would still like to quit. I have tried to quit smoking before, but, at best, I manage to refrain from smoking for a few days.

Counselor: Ralph, that must be so frustrating. Not being able to accomplish such an important goal on your own can really play havoc with a person's self-esteem.

Client: You know it! I just do not know if I have it in me to quit again right now.

Counselor: I understand, and I certainly do not want to rush you into anything. You have already been through so much lately.

Client: Ida, you are the greatest! You know I will come back when I am ready to quit.

Counselor: I know, Ralph. You know that, with today's methods, quitting smoking is a lot easier than it has ever been?

Client: No, I did not know that.

Counselor: If you would like, we can talk about it right now.

Client: You know, I would rather wait for a few weeks if that is okay.

Counselor: Of course it is okay! The time to quit is when you are ready, not when I'm ready for you.

Client: Thank you again. I look forward to seeing you in a few weeks.

Counselor: I look forward to that day. I already feel enthusiastic to help you overcome this bloody smoking habit.

Client: There is no doubt that I will see you soon. Bye for now!

Insight-Oriented Interventions

Shedler (2010) reviewed several meta-analyses that examined the effect size of several counseling approaches and found that psychodynamic therapy had demonstrated effectiveness with affective, personality, and substance use disorders. Lokhmotov's (2014) dissertation focused on looking at nicotine addiction within the modern psychodynamic approach called self-psychology, conceived by Heinz Kohut in Chicago between the 1960s and the 1980s. Essential to understanding this approach are the concepts of selfobject, mirroring, idealizing, alter ego/twinship, empathy, together with drives, conflicts, and complexes much like Freudian theory. A central idiom is that narcissistic vulnerabilities (i.e., threats to one's self-concept) play an important part in human suffering. The self is the center of a person's universe, and a degree of narcissism is considered healthy. Addiction is viewed as an interaction resulting from a drug and unconscious motives for using it. Some of these unconscious motives may include high neuroticism, sensation-seeking, hostility, as well as low social responsibility and self-control. Read Lokhmotov or any of the books by Kohut to get a better understanding of this interesting form of insight-focused work.

Through a psychoanalytic lens, Marcovitz (1969) described the attraction to smoking as an oral impulse that fulfills many unconscious purposes such as delineating inner boundaries, filling one's sense of emptiness, relief from fearing suffocation, respiratory erotism, and projecting the fantasized sense through exhalation. Although little reference is made to the anal aspects of smoking in the classic psychoanalytic literature, Marcovitz reminded the reader that the anal impulse in smoking is alive and well: "the droppings of ashes on clothes, rugs, and furniture, the ashtrays full of malodorous butts and dirty pipe cleaners, [and] the offensive odors of stale smoke" (p. 1074). He goes on to describe how "a cigarette in the presence of others may be a magic grasping of phallic power" (p. 1074). Interesting ideas, but not empirically testable.

Spiritual Interventions

Bailey, Slopen, Albert, and Williams (2015) used data at baseline and compared it with data 9 or 10 years later. Participants were classified as nonsmokers, persistent smokers, ex-smokers, and relapse smokers. The participants who were involved at high levels with their religion were less likely to be a persistent smoker or ex-smoker. Bailey et al. postulated that smoking cessation interventions targeted at drawing ties to religious and spiritual organizations and beliefs might result in increased effectiveness. This was not empirically tested in this study, however. Although we know that religious attendance is correlated with lower smoking prevalence (Keener, 2008), this does not extrapolate to mean that spirituality and religion are helpful to smokers who want to quit.

Gonzales et al. (2007) surveyed 104 Adult Smokers in Portland, Oregon, regarding their smoking behaviors and spiritual beliefs. Although none were attempting to quit, 78% reported that they believed using spiritual resources to quit would be helpful, and 77% reported that they were open to having providers encourage the use of spiritual resources when quitting. Gonzalez et al. concluded that especially heavy smokers might be receptive to using spiritual resources to help them stop smoking.

Nonnemaker, McNeely, and Blum (2016) studied a nationally representative sample of U.S. students in grades 7 through 12 regarding private (religious practice alone) and public (religious practice in public) religiosity and its effect on the initiation, escalation, and cessation of smoking. Private religiosity protected against beginning smoking among nonsmokers, but, in instances where smoking was initiated, it did not lead to a reduction or cessation once the young person had become nicotine addicted. On the other hand, public religiosity was related to the reduction and cessation of cigarette use among regular smokers.

Yong et al. (2013) analyzed data from 2166 Muslim Malaysian and 2463 Buddhist Thai adult smokers. Both groups reported that their religions discouraged smoking, but considerably more Buddhist Thais perceived that their society disapproved of smoking (80% compared with 25%). Among the Muslim group, religious but not societal norms affected quit attempts. By comparison, the Buddhist Thais reported a greater effect due to societal norms.

What remains unclear in the literature is the extent to which spiritual and/or religious practices can help individuals with varying degrees of TUD to stop smoking. This is an area for further research.

Cognitive-Behavioral Therapy

CBT can be facilitated using the triple column technique. It can be used both by counselors in their work with clients and by clients alone. The full instructions for using the technique are found in Chapter 6. The following are some of the cognitions that can be problematic for clients with this addiction.

Spears et al. (2017) compared mindfulness-based addiction treatment (MBAT), CBT, and usual care (UC) for smoking cessation. Participants (N = 412) were drawn from a larger study. Both the MBAT group and the CBT group were more helpful than the UC group in lowering anxiety, concentration problems, cravings, and dependence while increasing self-efficacy. Those in the MBAT group also experienced a better sense of conscious control over smoking and less anger.

CBT and personalized music-listening were equally effective in helping smokers regulate their emotions (Dingle & Carter, 2017). Individuals with severe mental disorders are estimated to lose 28 years of life, mostly due to smoking (Schuster et al., 2017). A 12-week program of smoking cessation that combined varenicline and CBT was found helpful for individuals with either schizophrenic spectrum disorders (N = 130) or bipolar disorder (N = 23) (Schuster et al., 2017). Another study focused on people with schizophrenia who were also depressed (N = 179) who entered a 12-week program of combined varenicline and behavior therapy. The program had a positive effect on reducing depression scores for completers, and 41% (N = 74) had also quit smoking for 2 or more weeks (Cather et al., 2017).

Automatic Thought or Belief	Questioning It	Healthier Thought or Belief
I cannot stand the idea of not smoking.		I can become a nonsmoker whenever I choose. I have a responsibility to take charge of my body and my health.
Smoking is the only thing that helps me relax.		Wanting to smoke is not relaxing. It makes me feel like a junkie needing another fix. There are better ways to relax than to smoke.
Smoking is an integral part of my identity.		Many identities have come and gone already in my life. It is better for my health to recreate an identity as a nonsmoker.
I will gain weight after I quit smoking.		I might gain weight if I do nothing else but quit smoking. I can decide to exercise more, eat lower-calorie foods, and/or get medication to help with weight reduction.
I have quit before and failed, so what is the point?		Most smokers have failed several times before becoming successful. If I learn the best ways to quit smoking, it will increase the likelihood that the next quit attempt will be my last.

Cooney et al. (2017) offered a 3-week smoking cessation program for individuals who were receiving outpatient treatment for alcohol use disorder. The participants who received a combination of CBT, NRT, and contingency management were the most likely to be smoking abstinent at the end of treatment. In another study (N = 103), a CBT group was compared to a control group receiving autogenic training (i.e., a type of relaxation focused on breathing while feeling warm and heavy) for smoking cessation during alcohol detoxification treatment (Mueller, Petitjean, & Wiesbeck, 2012). Although there was no difference between groups 6 months later, the takeaway for Mueller et al. (2012) was that alcohol-dependent smokers are interested in smoking interventions, even during detoxification.

RELEVANT MUTUAL SUPPORT GROUPS, WEBSITES, AND VIDEOS

Mutual Support Groups

For the Addicted Individual

Nicotine Anonymous. www.nicotine-anonymous.org

Quoted from website:

The primary purpose of Nicotine Anonymous is to help all those who would like to cease using tobacco and nicotine products in any form.

For the Partner and/or Family

These groups are intended to help family members refrain from behaviors that may trigger the addict. They also target underlying maladaptive thoughts and behaviors of the co-addict. Lastly, they focus on facilitating spiritual growth.

1. Smokefree.gov. https://smokefree.gov/help-others-quit/family-friends/how-support-your-quitter

   Quoted from website:

   Someone who feels supported is more likely to quit smoking for good. That's why friends, family members, and significant others can play a big part in helping a person become smokefree.

2. American Cancer Society. https://www.cancer.org/healthy/stay-away-from-tobacco/helping-a-smoker-quit.html

Websites

1. National Institute on Drug Abuse. https://www.drugabuse.gov/publications/research-reports/tobacco/new-frontiers-in-tobacco-research
2. Nicotine Addiction. https://www.ncbi.nlm.nih.gov/pmc/articles/PMC2928221/
3. Medical News Today. https://www.medicalnewstoday.com/articles/181299.php
4. Health Canada. https://www.canada.ca/en/health-canada/services/health-concerns/tobacco/smoking-your-body/addiction.html
5. Cancer Research UK. http://www.cancerresearchuk.org/about-cancer/causes-of-cancer/smoking-and-cancer/smoking-facts-and-evidence
6. Mayo Clinic (Nicotine Dependence). https://www.mayoclinic.org/diseases-conditions/nicotine-dependence/symptoms-causes/syc-20351584
7. http://smokehelp.org/ for smoking cessation in the United States
8. http://www.tobaccofree.com/ for smoking cessation for young people
9. http://www.infotobacco.com for smoking cessation in Canada

Videos

To view these videos, search their titles on YouTube.

1. *What Happens to Your Body • When You VAPE for a Month.*
2. *The Future of Tobacco and Nicotine | Hemant Goswami | TEDxGGDSDCollege.*
3. *Smoking | Johnathan Ross, MD | TEDxToledo.*
4. *The FDA's new role overseeing a deadly product: tobacco | Kathy Crosby | TEDxMidAtlantic.*
5. *Tobacco Dependence - causes, symptoms, diagnosis, treatment, pathology.*
6. *Smoking deconstructed | James Monsees | TEDxBrussels.*

RELEVANT PHONE APPS

Generic Addiction Apps

Note: Generic apps are described in Chapter 6.

This list is not exhaustive. New apps are continually being developed. Do an Internet search to find out the latest apps available. Most are for specific addictions but some, such as these four, are generic.

1. I Am Sober. https://play.google.com/store/apps/details?id=com.thehungrywasp.iamsober
2. Sober Time. https://play.google.com/store/apps/details?id=com.sociosoft.sobertime
3. Pocket Rehab: Get Sober & Addiction Recovery. https://play.google.com/store/apps/details?id=com.getpocketrehab.app
4. Loop Habit Tracker. https://play.google.com/store/apps/details?id=org.isoron.uhabits

Specialized Apps

1. Livestrong MyQuit Coach. https://itunes.apple.com/us/app/livestrong-myquit-coach-dare/id383122255

   Quoted from website:

   You can choose to quit smoking cold turkey or gradually decrease your daily nicotine intake at a pace that works for you.

2. Smoke Free, quit smoking now and stop for good. https://play.google.com/store/apps/details?id=com.portablepixels.smokefree&hl=en

   Quoted from website:

   This is the stop smoking app that science built. Over 20 different, evidence-based techniques to help you become—and stay—smoke free.

3. NHS Smokefree. https://www.nhs.uk/oneyou/apps#nhs-smokefree

   Quoted from website:

   Our Smokefree app can help you stop smoking by providing daily support and motivation. If you stay smokefree for the 4-week programme you're up to 5 times more likely to quit for good.

4. QuitNow! https://quitnowapp.com/en

   Quoted from website:

   QuitNow! is a proven app that engages you to quit smoking. It aims you to avoid tobacco just giving you a picture of yourself.

5. Smiling Instead of Smoking (app is currently for Windows). https://appsonwindows.com/apk/927143/

   Quoted from website:

   After conducting a content analysis of currently existing smoking cessation smartphone apps, we have developed a smartphone app [note that the smartphone app appears to be currently unavailable] to provide smoking cessation support to help smokers quit smoking.

JOURNALS AND CONFERENCES

Journals

1. *Nicotine & Tobacco Research*. https://academic.oup.com/ntr Quoted from website: "Nicotine & Tobacco Research is one of the world's few peer-reviewed journals devoted exclusively to the study of nicotine and tobacco. It aims to provide a forum for empirical findings, critical reviews, and conceptual papers on the many aspects of nicotine and tobacco, including research from the biobehavioral, neurobiological, molecular biologic, epidemiological, prevention, and treatment arenas. Along with manuscripts from each of the areas mentioned above, the editors encourage submissions that are integrative in nature and that cross traditional disciplinary boundaries. The journal is sponsored by the Society for Research on Nicotine and Tobacco (SRNT). It publishes twelve times a year."

2. *Tobacco Control: An International Journal*. https://tobaccocontrol.bmj.com/ Quoted from website: "*Tobacco Control* is an international peer review journal covering the nature and consequences of tobacco use worldwide; tobacco's effects on population health, the economy, the environment, and society; efforts to prevent and control the global tobacco epidemic through population level education and policy changes; the ethical dimensions of tobacco control policies; and the activities of the tobacco industry and its allies. Essential reading for everyone with an interest in tobacco control, including public health professionals, researchers, policy makers and educators."

Conferences

There are plenty of conferences around the world given the enormity of the crisis caused by smoking. Below are three well-known annual conferences.

1. Annual National Conference on Tobacco or Health.

   Quoted from website (Search the Internet for details):

The National Conference on Tobacco or Health (NCTOH) is one of the largest, long-standing gatherings for top United States tobacco control professionals. The convening attracts a diversity of public health professionals committed to best practices and policies to reduce tobacco use—the leading preventable cause of disease and death in the United States.

2. Annual World Conference on Tobacco or Health. Hosted by the World Health Organization. https://www.wctoh.org/

3. Annual Ottawa Conference.

   Quoted from website (search the Internet for details):

   Annual Ottawa Conference brings together health professionals seeking to gain knowledge in clinical smoking cessation. It provides the attendees with the opportunity for knowledge exchange for a variety of stakeholders (*note*: Ottawa is the capital of Canada).

COUNSELING SCENARIO

As you are reading, imagine that you are the client in this scenario. Note the areas in which the session could be improved on the part of the counselor.

Your name is Liam, a 49-year-old banking professional. You have wanted to stop smoking for the past 20 years, but you have never made a serious effort. You book an appointment with a counselor who was recommended to you by a friend. Your friend had seen Vernon for four sessions earlier because she was dealing with depression. She found Vernon very helpful. This is the beginning of your second session.

- Counselor: Good to see you again, Liam. Please come in.
- You: Thank you, Vernon.
- Counselor: Last session, I collected a reasonably thorough history from you. Thank you for providing me with that information.
- You: You are welcome.
- Counselor: I would like to take a more in-depth look at your childhood now. Tell me about any traumas that you experienced.
- You: Traumas? I actually have two loving parents, and I do not remember any trauma.
- Counselor: How then do you explain your smoking behavior?
- You: I was young and foolish. I tried so hard to keep up with my peers, and smoking seemed like the thing to do.
- Counselor: Did your parents smoke?
- You: No, although I think my dad smoked when he was younger.
- Counselor: Did you start smoking at the same age as your dad?
- You: I really don't know. I have not talked to him about that in years.
- Counselor: I see. Maybe a better approach would be to ask you about the thoughts you have about smoking.
- You: Thoughts? The only thought I have about smoking is having another smoke [chuckles].
- Counselor: [chuckles]. To what extent is depression leading you to smoke?
- You: That seems like an excellent question. Honestly, I never thought smoking had anything to do with depression. I do not remember ever being depressed.
- Counselor: Are you saying that nothing sad has ever happened to you?
- You: No, I am not saying that. When things don't work out the way I want them to, I seem able to shrug it off and carry on reasonably well.
- Counselor: I'm still not understanding why you smoke.
- You: I suppose that is a good question, but I honestly don't know. It just seems like I am addicted to it.
- Counselor: I think it is deeper than that, Liam. You are hanging onto something by continuing to smoke.
- You: Hum, I really don't know about that. I think I am just like most smokers out there who have smoked for more than 20 years.
- Counselor: It's never that straightforward, Liam.
- You: Really? I do not think there is anything special about my smoking addiction compared to other people.

- Counselor: There is. We just haven't gotten to the bottom of it yet.
- You: Wow, I didn't think I was going to need to go into my life this deeply to quit smoking.
- Counselor: Without knowing the root cause of your smoking behavior, I am concerned that the reason you have been unable to quit is that something worse could take its place that is outside of your awareness.
- You: Do you really think so? I have known several people who have quit smoking, and nothing like that seemed to happen to them.
- Counselor: But how many times have they relapsed?
- You: I do not know. I think most people have tried more than once to quit before they are entirely successful.
- Counselor: That is true, but it is true because they never got to the root cause.
- You: Isn't there some medication that would help me stop smoking?
- Counselor: I am not a physician, Liam, but are you the kind of guy that wants to take drugs the rest of your life? Isn't that the entire premise of your smoking behavior to begin with?
- You: Okay, that I really need to think about. I just don't think there's anything deep psychologically about my continuing to smoke.
- Counselor: There is, Liam. There is.

From the Client's Perspective

1. How would you feel if you were told that there is a deeper reason that you continue to smoke?
2. What is missing for you in this dialogue?
3. What would you find more helpful from a counselor in this scenario?

From the Counselor's Perspective

1. How could you develop a positive and stronger working alliance with Liam?
2. Going back to the Common Counseling Mistakes list in Chapter 6, which mistakes is the counselor making with Liam?
3. What theoretical approach is this counselor taking with Liam? What would be a better approach to take, if any, in helping someone to stop smoking?

INDIVIDUAL EXERCISES

1. Arrange an interview with someone you know who smokes. What is this person's perception of their nicotine addiction? Why does he or she continue smoking knowing about its potential to do great harm? Create a list of additional questions. Before you conclude the interview, determine what stage of change this person is at in the transtheoretical model.
2. Help a friend or family member establish, as precisely as possible, how much he or she spends yearly on cigarettes. Then brainstorm, back and forth, all the ways that each of you would spend this money right now if it were in your pocket or purse. You might have even provided a motivational intervention in doing this exercise!
3. Spend 30 min in a bingo hall, a nightclub, a casino, or any other contained space that still permits smoking. After you leave, write down the effects that this has already had on you. Focus mainly on how you feel physically, paying attention to irritation in your throat and lungs. Also, how do you and your clothes smell?

CLASSROOM EXERCISES

1. This first exercise will have a powerful effect on your students if it can be arranged. Contact the Foundation for a Smokefree America (or the American Cancer Society or the American Lung Association) and inquire about having a speaker with advanced lung cancer (or another terminal illness caused by smoking) address your class (or your college or university). Have your students prepare questions in advance to ask the speaker if time permits.

2. Show one or more YouTube videos of individuals with terminal diseases related to smoking. An excellent choice is one about Terrie Hall, an American antismoking lobbyist (visit https://www.youtube.com/watch?v=22ZXjCRY-RY). There are many other YouTube videos from which to select.
3. Break the class into two for a debate. One half takes the perspective of the tobacco industry and launches their arguments for why smoking should be permitted and given greater latitude in advertising their products. The other half of the class argues against this tobacco lobby with the facts about smoking.

CHAPTER SUMMARY

The 2017 prevalence of smoking throughout the world was estimated at 25% among males and 5.4% among females, making it the most prevalent addiction on the planet. Smoking resulted in 11.5% of all global deaths in 2015. The importance of quitting cannot be overstated. It is the number one preventable cause of premature death and preventable disease throughout the world. Every year, the United States alone loses $96.8 billion in productivity due to smoking.

Although nicotine itself is not particularly harmful, the tar, carbon monoxide, arsenic, ammonia, methanol, and butane in cigarettes create most of its disease-inducing and lethal effects. Many smokers are afraid they will gain weight when they quit smoking, and, on average, most smokers do gain between 6 and 11 pounds. Smokers should be told that this is not inevitable. To maintain their current weight, however, they will need to increase the amount of exercise they currently get and/or lower the number of calories in their diet as their body's metabolism will slow down when they quit smoking.

Most smokers begin smoking before the age of 18; over four fifths of adults who ever smoked daily began when they were children or adolescents, and more than one half of adolescents who experiment with smoking will become adult smokers. Having two smoking parents (as compared to zero or one) is associated with higher rates of nicotine dependence in adulthood.

Chronic smoking causes a myriad of health problems that reduce both the quality and likely duration of smokers' lives. The list of such physical maladies and conditions includes increased risk of blood clots, wrinkled and dry skin, hair loss and balding, erectile dysfunction in men, early menopause in women, infertility, numerous problems with newborns if the mother smoked, cardiovascular disease, respiratory illness, COPD, and various cancers. Although the leading cause of death due to smoking is coronary heart disease, lung cancer sits in second place.

Most American smokers spend more than $100,000 in their lifetimes on cigarettes and more than $2000 yearly. For most American families, quitting smoking results in substantial savings.

The primary medical treatments for smoking cessation include varenicline, bupropion SR, and NRTs. The best psychological treatments include MI, CBT, and behavioral interventions. Combined approaches result in the best prognosis. Nicotine addiction is difficult to beat, and many smokers will take up to 30 or more quit attempts before they are finally successful.

REFERENCES

Aboaziza, E., & Eissenberg, T. (2015). Waterpipe tobacco smoking: What is the evidence that it supports nicotine/tobacco dependence? *Tobacco Control: An International Journal, 24*(1), 44–53.

Agabio, R., Campesi, I., Pisanu, C., Gessa, G. L., & Franconi, F. (2016). Sex differences in substance use disorders: Focus on side effects. *Addiction Biology, 21*(5), 1030–1042.

Aguiar, M., Todo-Bom, F., Felizardo, M., Macedo, R., Caeiro, F., Mayor, R. S., & De Almeida, A. B. (2011). Four years' follow up at a smoking cessation clinic. In N. Nash (Ed.), *Yearbook of international psychiatry and behavioral neurosciences 2009* (pp. 209–219). Hauppauge, NY: Nova Biomedical Books.

Akkus, F., Treyer, V., Johayem, A., Ametamey, S. M., Mancilla, B. G., Sovago, J., . . . Hasler, G. (2016). Association of long-term nicotine abstinence with normal metabotropic glutamate receptor-5 binding. *Biological Psychiatry, 79*(6), 474–480.

Alderson, K. (2004). *Grade power: The complete guide to improving your grades through self-hypnosis.* Toronto, ON: Insomniac Press.

Alderson, K. (2011). *Breathe, freedom: A comprehensive and hypnotic approach to quitting smoking.* London, ON: Insomniac Press.

Allen, A. M., Carlson, S., Eberly, L. E., Hatsukami, D., & Piper, M. E. (2018). Use of hormonal contraceptives and smoking cessation: A preliminary report. *Addictive Behaviors, 76*, 236–242.

Alpert, H. R., Agaku, I. T., & Connolly, G. N. (2016). A study of pyrazines in cigarettes and how additives might be used to enhance tobacco addiction. *Tobacco Control: An International Journal, 25*(4), 444–450.

American Psychiatric Association (APA). (2013). *Diagnostic and statistical manual of mental disorders* (5th ed.). Washington, DC: Author.

Anesi, G. L., Halpern, S. D., Harhay, M. O., Volpp, K. G., & Saulsgiver, K. (2017). Time to selected quit date and subsequent rates of sustained smoking abstinence. *Journal of Behavioral Medicine, 40*(6), 989–997.

Anthenelli, R. M. (2014). Nicotine-related disorders. In G. O. Gabbard (Eds.), *Gabbard's treatments of psychiatric disorders* (5th ed., pp. 871–883). Arlington, VA: American Psychiatric.

Ara, A., Jacobs, W., Bhat, I. A., & McCall, W. V. (2016). Sleep disturbances and substance use disorders: A bi-directional relationship. *Psychiatric Annals, 46*(7), 408–412.

Asbridge, M., Duff, C., Marsh, D. C., & Erickson, P. G. (2014). Problems with the identification of "problematic" cannabis use: Examining the issues of frequency, quantity, and drug use environment. *European Addiction Research, 20*(5), 254–267.

Ashton, H., Millman, J. E., Telford, R., & Thompson, J. W. (1973). Stimulant and depressant effects of cigarette smoking on brain activity in man. *British Journal of Pharmacology, 48*(4), 715–717.

Attwood, A., Aveyard P., Bauld, L., Britton, J., Hajek, P., Hastings, G., . . . West, R. (2013). Tobacco. In P. M. Miller, S. A. Ball, M. E. Bates, A. W. Blume, K. M. Kampman, D. J. Kavanagh, M. E. Larimer, N. M. Petry, & P. De Witte (Eds.), *Principles of addiction: Comprehensive addictive behaviors and disorders, Vol 1* (pp. 767–776). San Diego, CA: Elsevier Academic Press.

Bagot, K. S., Wu, R., Cavallo, D., & Krishnan-Sarin, S. (2017). Assessment of pain in adolescents: Influence of gender, smoking status and tobacco abstinence. *Addictive Behaviors, 67*, 79–85.

Bailey, Z. D., Slopen, N., Albert, M., & Williams, D. R. (2015). Multidimensional religious involvement and tobacco smoking patterns over 9-10 years: A prospective study of middle-aged adults in the United States. *Social Science & Medicine, 138*, 128–135.

Bakhshaie, J., Kulesz, P. A., Garey, L., Langdon, K. J., Businelle, M. S., Leventhal, A. M., . . . Zvolensky, M. J. (2018). A prospective investigation of the synergistic effect of change in anxiety sensitivity and dysphoria on tobacco withdrawal. *Journal of Consulting and Clinical Psychology, 86*(1), 69–80.

Balch, G. I., Tworek, C., Barker, D. C., Sasso, B., Mermelstein, R. J., & Giovino, G. A. (2004). Opportunities for youth smoking cessation: Findings from a national focus group study. *Nicotine & Tobacco Research, 6*(1), 9–17.

Baribeau, D., & Araki, K. F. (2013). Intravenous bupropion: A previously undocumented method of abuse of a commonly prescribed antidepressant agent. *Journal of Addiction Medicine, 7*, 216–217.

Baskerville, N. B., Shuh, A., Wong-Francq, K., Dash, D., & Abramowicz, A. (2017). LGBTQ youth and young adult perspectives on a culturally tailored group smoking cessation program. *Nicotine & Tobacco Research, 19*(8), 960–967.

Batra, A., Petersen, K. U., Hoch, E., Andreas, S., Bartsch, G., Gohlke, H., . . . Mann, K. (2016). S3 guideline "screening, diagnostics, and treatment of harmful and addictive tobacco use". *Sucht: Zeitschrift fur Wissenschaft und Praxis, 62*(3), 139–152.

Beard, E., McNeill, A., Aveyard, P., Fidler, J., Michie, S., & West, R. (2013). Association between use of nicotine replacement therapy for harm reduction and smoking cessation: A prospective study of English smokers. *Tobacco Control, 22*, 118–122.

Bedendo, A., Andrade, A. L. M., & Noto, A. R. (2016). Neurobiology of substance abuse. In A. L. M. Andrade & D. D. Micheli (Eds.), *Innovations in the treatment of substance addiction* (pp. 17–34). Cham, Switzerland: Springer.

Benowitz, N. L. (2010). Nicotine addiction: Mechanisms of disease. *New England Journal of Medicine, 362*(24), 2295–2303.

Benowitz, N. L., Porchet, H., & Peyton, J. III. (1989). Nicotine dependence and tolerance in man: Pharmacokinetic and pharmacodynamic investigations. *Progress in Brain Research, 79*, 279–287.

Beresford, T. P., Wongngamnit, N., & Temple, B. A. (2015). Alcoholism: Diagnosis and natural history in the context of medical disease. In J. Neuberger & A. DiMartini (Eds.), *Alcohol abuse and liver disease* (pp. 23–34). Hoboken, NJ: Wiley-Blackwell.

Berg, C. J., Stratton, E., Schauer, G. L., Lewis, M., Wang, Y., Windle, M., & Kegler, M. (2015). Perceived harm, addictiveness, and social acceptability of tobacco products and marijuana among young adults: Marijuana, hookah, and electronic cigarettes win. *Substance Use & Misuse, 50*(1), 79–89.

Bernard, P., Ninot, G., Cyprien, F., Courtet, P., Guillaume, S., Georgescu, V., . . . Quantin, X. (2015). Exercise and counseling for smoking cessation in smokers with depressive symptoms: A randomized controlled pilot trial. *Journal of Dual Diagnosis, 11*(3–4), 205–216.

Bernat, J. K., Ferrer, R. A., Margolis, K. A., & Blake, K. D. (2017). US adult tobacco users' absolute harm perceptions of traditional and alternative tobacco products, information-seeking behaviors, and (mis)beliefs about chemicals in tobacco products. *Addictive Behaviors, 71*, 38–45.

Besson, M., & Forget, B. (2016). Cognitive dysfunction, affective states, and vulnerability to nicotine addiction: A multifactorial perspective. *Frontiers in Psychiatry, 7*, 1–24.

Bidwell, L. C., Balestrieri, S. G., Colby, S. M., Knopik, V. S., & Tidey, J. W. (2018). Abstinence-induced withdrawal severity among adolescent smokers with and without ADHD: Disentangling effects of nicotine and smoking reinstatement. *Psychopharmacology, 235*(1), 169–178.

Bloom, E. L., Minami, H., Brown, R. A., Strong, D. R., Riebe, D., & Abrantes, A. M. (2017). Quality of life after quitting smoking and initiating aerobic exercise. *Psychology, Health & Medicine, 22*(9), 1127–1135.

Blumenthal, D. M., & Gold, M. S. (2012). Relationships between drugs of abuse and eating. In K. D. Brownell & M. S. Gold (Eds.), *Food and addiction: A comprehensive handbook* (pp. 254–265). New York, NY: Oxford University Press.

Bold, K. W. (2017). Independent and interactive effects of real-time risk factors on later temptations and lapses among smokers trying to quit. *Dissertation Abstracts International: Section B: The Sciences and Engineering, 77*(7-B(E)). No pagination specified.

Bombard, J. M., Pederson, L. L., Koval, J. J., & O'Hegarty, M. (2009). How are lifetime polytobacco users different than current cigarette-only users? Results from a Canadian young adult population. *Addictive Behaviors, 34*(12), 1069–1072.

Boothby, C. A., Kim, H. S., Romanow, N. K., Hodgins, D. C., & McGrath, D. S. (2017). Assessing the role of impulsivity in smoking & non-smoking disordered gamblers. *Addictive Behaviors, 70*, 35–41.

Borderias, L., Duarte, R., Escario, J. J., & Molina, J. A. (2015). Addiction and other reasons adolescent smokers give to justify smoking. *Substance Use & Misuse, 50*(12), 1552–1559.

Borland, R., Cappiello, M., & Owen, N. (1997). Leaving work to smoke. *Addiction, 92*, 1361–1368.

Borrelli, B., Busch, A. M., & Trotter, D. R. M. (2013). Methods used to quit smoking by people with physical disabilities. *Rehabilitation Psychology, 58*(2), 117–123.

Borrelli, B., Endrighi, R., Hammond, S. K., & Dunsiger, S. (2017). Smokers who are unmotivated to quit and have a child with asthma are more likely to quit with intensive motivational interviewing and repeated biomarker feedback. *Journal of Consulting and Clinical Psychology, 85*(11), 1019–1028.

Brandon, T. H., & Baker, T. B. (1991). The Smoking Consequences Questionnaire: The subjective expected utility of smoking in college students. *Psychological Assessment: A Journal of Consulting and Clinical Psychology, 3*(3), 484–491.

Branstetter, S. A., Horton, W. J., Mercincavage, M., & Buxton, O. M. (2016). Severity of nicotine addiction and disruptions in sleep mediated by early awakenings. *Nicotine & Tobacco Research, 18*(12), 2252–2259.

Braverman Bronstein, A., Lomelin Gascón, J., Eugenio González, C. I., & Barrientos-Gutierrez, T. (2018). Environmental tobacco exposure and urinary cotinine levels in smoking and nonsmoking adolescents. *Nicotine & Tobacco Research, 20*(4), 523–526.

Bray, B. (2016, November 29). What counselors can do to help clients stop smoking. *Counseling Today*. Retrieved on February 13, 2019, from https://ct.counseling.org/2016/11/counselors-can-help-clients-stop-smoking/

Brennan, T. K., Levesque, A., & Riley, C. (2016). Tobacco. In P. Levounis, E. Zerbo, & R. Aggarwal (Eds.), *Pocket guide to addiction assessment and treatment* (pp. 225–241). Arlington, VA: American Psychiatric Association.

Buis, D. R., & Batjer, H. H. (2017). Aneurysm rupture: Another reason to abstain from smoking. *Neurology, 89*(13), 1320–1321.

Cahill, K., Lancaster, T., & Green, N. (2010). Stage-based interventions for smoking cessation. *Cochrane Database of Systematic Reviews, 11*, CD004492.

Carey, F. R., & Wilkinson, A. V. (2016). The biology of nicotine addiction and factors that differentiate youth who smoke from those who do not. In A. Swann, F. G. Moeller, & M. Lijffijt (Eds.), *Neurobiology of addiction* (pp. 67–86). New York, NY: Oxford University Press.

Carlson, S. C., Allen, A. M., Allen, S. S., & al'Absi, M. (2017). Differences in mood and cortisol by menstrual phase during acute smoking abstinence: A within-subject comparison. *Experimental and Clinical Psychopharmacology, 25*(5), 338–345.

Carr, A. (1999). *Easy way to stop smoking* (3rd ed.). New York, NY: Penguin Books. Available for free download from http://prdupl02.ynet.co.il/ForumFiles_2/15119301.pdf

Castillo-Rolón, D. E., Arenas-López, G., Mihailescu, S., Hernandez-Gonzalez, O., & Hernández-López, S. (2018, November). *Modulation of glutamate release by nicotine in the rostromedial tegmental nucleus (RMTg)*. Poster session presented at the Annual Meeting of Society for Neurosciences, San Diego, CA.

Cather, C., Pachas, G. N., Cieslak, K. M., & Evins, A. E. (2017). Achieving smoking cessation in individuals with schizophrenia: Special considerations. *CNS Drugs, 31*(6), 471–481.

Centers for Disease Control and Prevention (CDC). (2018a, August 9). *Cigarette smoking among adults with disabilities*. Retrieved on February 12, 2019, from https://www.cdc.gov/ncbddd/disabilityandhealth/smoking-in-adults.html

Centers for Disease Control and Prevention (CDC). (2018b, March 22). *Smoking and diabetes*. Retrieved on February 17, 2019, from https://www.cdc.gov/tobacco/campaign/tips/diseases/diabetes.html

Chaffee, B. W., Couch, E. T., & Gansky, S. A. (2017). Trends in characteristics and multi-product use among adolescents who use electronic cigarettes, United States 2011–2015. *PLoS ONE, 12*(5), 1–19.

Chaiton, M., Diemert, L., Cohen, J. E., Bondy, S. J., Selby, P., Philipneri, A., & Schwartz, R. (2016). Estimating the number of quit attempts it takes to quit smoking successfully in a longitudinal cohort of smokers. *BMJ, 6*, 1–9.

Choi, S., Rankin, S., Stewart, A., & Oka, R. (2008). Effects of acculturation on smoking behavior in Asian Americans: A meta-analysis. *Journal of Cardiovascular Nursing, 23*(1), 67–73.

Chou, S. P., Saha, T., D, Zhang, H., Ruan, W. J., Huang, B., Grant, B. F., . . . Compton, W. (2017). Prevalence, correlates, comorbidity and treatment of electronic nicotine delivery system use in the United States. *Drug and Alcohol Dependence, 178*, 296–301.

Christen, A. G., & McDonald, J. L. (1987). Smokeless tobacco country: From nicotine dependency to oral problems and cancer. *Aviation, Space, and Environmental Medicine, 58*(2), 97–104.

Chuang, C.-W. I., Sussman, S., Stone, M. D., Pang, R. D., Chou, C.-P., Leventhal, A. M., & Kirkpatrick, M. G. (2017). Impulsivity and history of behavioral addictions are associated with drug use in adolescents. *Addictive Behaviors, 74*, 41–47.

Chun, J., Haug, N. A., Guydish, J. R., Sorensen, J. L., & Delucchi, K. (2009). Cigarette smoking among opioid-dependent clients in a therapeutic community. *American Journal on Addictions, 18*(4), 316–320.

Churchill, S. A., & Farrell, L. (2017). Investigating the relationship between smoking and subjective welfare. *Journal of Behavioral and Experimental Economics, 71*, 1–12.

Clyde, M., Pipe, A., Els, C., Reid, R., & Tulloch, H. (2017). Factor structure of the Smoking Cessation Self-Efficacy Questionnaire among smokers with and without a psychiatric diagnosis. *Psychology of Addictive Behaviors, 31*(2), 162–170.

Collins, C. C., & Moolchan, E. T. (2006). Shorter time to first cigarette of the day in menthol adolescent cigarette smokers. *Addictive Behaviors, 31*(8), 1460–1464.

Connors, G. J., DiClemente, C. C., Velasquez, M. M., & Donovan, D. M. (2013). *Substance abuse treatment and the stages of change: Selecting and planning interventions* (2nd ed.). New York, NY: Guilford Press.

Conybeare, D. (2017). Fidelity of motivational interviewing with behavioral interventions for smokers who are not ready to quit. *Dissertation Abstracts International: Section B: The Sciences and Engineering, 77*(7-B(E)). No pagination specified.

Cooney, J. L., Cooper, S., Grant, C., Sevarino, K., Krishnan-Sarin, S., Gutierrez, I. A., & Cooney, N. L. (2017). A randomized trial of contingency management for smoking cessation during intensive outpatient alcohol treatment. *Journal of Substance Abuse Treatment, 72*, 89–96.

Cooper, M., Loukas, A., Harrell, M. B., & Perry, C. L. (2017). College students' perceptions of risk and addictiveness of e-cigarettes and cigarettes. *Journal of American College Health, 65*(2), 103–111.

Cosgrove, K. P. (2016). A need for longitudinal studies in the addiction field. *Biological Psychiatry, 80*(3), 174–175.

Courtemanche, C. J., Palmer, M. K., & Pesko, M. F. (2017). Influence of the flavored cigarette ban on adolescent tobacco use. *American Journal of Preventive Medicine, 52*(5), e139–e146.

Criscitelli, K., & Avena, N. M. (2016). The neurobiological and behavioral overlaps of nicotine and food addiction. *Preventive Medicine: An International Journal Devoted to Practice and Theory, 92*, 82–89.

Cross, S. J., Lotfipour, S., & Leslie, F. M. (2017). Mechanisms and genetic factors underlying co-use of nicotine and alcohol or other drugs of abuse. *American Journal of Drug and Alcohol Abuse, 43*(2), 171–185.

Dai, H., & Hao, J. (2017). Electronic cigarette and marijuana use among youth in the United States. *Addictive Behaviors, 66*, 48–54.

Daly, M. & Egan, M. (2017). Childhood cognitive ability and smoking initiation, relapse and cessation throughout adulthood: Evidence from two British cohort studies. *Addiction, 112*(4), 651–659.

Das, S., Hickman, N. J., & Prochaska, J. J. (2017). Treating smoking in adults with co-occurring acute psychiatric and addictive disorders. *Journal of Addiction Medicine, 11*(4), 273–279.

Diehl, A., & Scherbaum, N. (2008). Nicotine dependence as comorbidity of alcohol dependence—Epidemiology, etiology and therapy. *Fortschritte der Neurologie, Psychiatrie*, *76*, 14–20.

DiFranza, J. R. (2014). Commentary on Hu et al. (2014): The validity of the DSM is not a "given." *Addiction*, *109*(9), 1529–1530.

DiFranza, J. R., Savageau, J. A., Fletcher, K., Ockene, J. K., Rigotti, N. A., McNeill, A. D., Coleman, M., & Wood, C. (2002). Measuring the loss of autonomy over nicotine use in adolescents. *Archives of Pediatric and Adolescent Medicine*, *156*, 397–403.

Dingle, G. A., & Carter, N. A. (2017). Smoke into sound: A pilot randomised controlled trial of a music cravings management program for chronic smokers attempting to quit. *Musicae Scientiae*, *21*(2), 151–177.

Donaldson, E. A., Hoffman, A. C., Zandberg, I., & Blake, K. D. (2017). Media exposure and tobacco product addiction beliefs: Findings from the 2015 Health Information National Trends Survey (HINTS-FDA 2015). *Addictive Behaviors*, *72*, 106–113.

Dumont, G., Maex, R., & Gutkin, B. (2018). Dopaminergic neurons in the ventral tegmental area and their dysregulation in nicotine addiction. In A. Anticevic & J. D. Murray (Eds.), *Computational psychiatry: Mathematical modeling of mental illness* (pp. 47–84). San Diego, CA: Elsevier Academic Press.

Dunlop, S., Perez, D., Dessaix, A., & Currow, D. (2017). Australia's plain tobacco packs: Anticipated and actual responses among adolescents and young adults 2010–2013. *Tobacco Control: An International Journal*, *26*(6), 617–626.

Eguae, E. E. (2018). Factors associated with menthol cigarettes smoking among youths ages 12 to 19. *Dissertation Abstracts International: Section B: The Sciences and Engineering*, *79*(9-B(E)). No pagination specified.

Evatt, D. P., & Griffiths, R. R. (2012). Caffeine, addiction, and food consumption. In K. D. Brownell & M. S. Gold (Eds.), *Food and addiction: A comprehensive handbook* (pp. 238–243). New York, NY: Oxford University Press.

Fabian, L. A., Canlas, L. L., Potts, J., & Pickworth, W. B. (2012). Ad lib smoking of Black & Mild cigarillos and cigarettes. *Nicotine & Tobacco Research*, *14*(3), 368–371.

Falcone, M., Bernardo, L., Ashare, R. L., Hamilton, R., Faseyitan, O., McKee, S. A., . . . Lerman, C. (2016). Transcranial direct current brain stimulation increases ability to resist smoking. *Brain Stimulation*, *9*(2), 191–196.

Felman, A. (2018, January 11). Everything you need to know about nicotine. *Medical News Today*. Retrieved on February 15, 2019, from https://www.medicalnewstoday.com/articles/240820.php

Formagini, T. D. B., Gomide, H. P., Perales, J., & Colugnati, F. A. B. (2017). Prevalence and correlates of light and non-daily smoking in Brazil: Results from a nationwide representative survey. *Drug and Alcohol Dependence*, *178*, 15–19.

Fortuna, L. R., Porche, M. V., Alam, N., Douglass, K. M., & Kim, S. S. (2012). Smoking and co-occurring disorders: Implications for smoking cessation interventions for adolescents in residential addiction treatment. *Journal of Dual Diagnosis*, *8*(2), 133–139.

Foulds, J. A., & Lubman, D. I. (2017). Treating depression in patients with alcohol or drug use disorders: A need for clearer guidelines. *Australian and New Zealand Journal of Psychiatry*, *51*(7), 668–669.

Foulstone, A. R., Kelly, A. B., & Kifle, T. (2017). Partner influences on smoking cessation: A longitudinal study of couple relationships. *Journal of Substance Use*, *22*(5), 501–506.

Fu, S. S., Okuyemi, K. S., Partin, M. R., Ahluwalia, J. S., Nelson, D. B., Clothier, B. A., & Joseph, A. M. (2008). Menthol cigarettes and smoking cessation during an aided quit attempt. *Nicotine & Tobacco Research*, *10*(3), 457–462.

Garcia-Rodriguez, O., Suarez-Vazquez, R., Santonja-Gomez, F. J., Secades-Villa, R., & Sanchez-Hervas, E. (2011). Psychosocial risk factors for adolescent smoking: A school-based study. *International Journal of Clinical and Health Psychology*, *11*(1), 23–33.

Garey, L., Jardin, C., Kauffman, B. Y., Sharp, C., Neighbors, C., Schmidt, N. B., & Zvolensky, M. J. (2017). Psychometric evaluation of the Barriers to Cessation Scale. *Psychological Assessment*, *29*(7), 844–856.

Garey, L., Manning, K., Jardin, C., Leventhal, A. M., Stone, M., Raines, A. M., . . . Zvolensky, M. J. (2018). Smoking Consequences Questionnaire: A reevaluation of the psychometric properties across two independent samples of smokers. *Psychological Assessment*, *30*(5), 678–692.

Gass, J. C., Morris, D. H., Winters, J., VanderVeen, J. W., & Chermack, S. (2018). Characteristics and clinical treatment of tobacco smokers enrolled in a VA substance use disorders clinic. *Journal of Substance Abuse Treatment*, *84*, 1–8.

Gearhardt, A. N., & Corbin, W. R. (2012). Food addiction and diagnostic criteria for dependence. In K. D. Brownell & M. S. Gold (Eds.), *Food and addiction: A comprehensive handbook* (pp. 167–171). New York, NY: Oxford University Press.

Gifford, E., Tavakoli, S., Wisdom, J., & Hamlett-Berry, K. (2015). Implementation of smoking cessation treatment in VHA substance use disorder residential treatment programs. *Psychiatric Services*, *66*(3), 295–302.

Giorgi, I., Fiabane, E., Vittadini, G., Anastasi, S., Benvenuto, A., Malovini, A., . . . Ceriana, P. (2017). Outcome evaluation of an integrated treatment for comorbid alcohol and nicotine addiction: An exploratory study. *Archives of Psychiatric Nursing*, *31*(4), 429–430.

Glasser, I. (2010). Nicotine Anonymous may benefit nicotine-dependent individuals. *American Journal of Public Health*, *100*(2), 196.

Glatard, A., Dobrinas, M., Gholamrezaee, M., Lubomirov, R., Cornuz, J., Csajka, C., & Eap, C. B. (2017). Association of nicotine metabolism and sex with relapse following varenicline and nicotine replacement therapy. *Experimental and Clinical Psychopharmacology*, *25*(5), 353–362.

Global Adult Tobacco Survey Collaborative Group (2011). *Tobacco questions for surveys: A subset of key questions from the Global Adult Tobacco Survey (GATS)*. Retrieved on August 6, 2019, from https://www.who.int/tobacco/surveillance/en_tfi_tqs.pdf

Gonzales, D., Redtomahawk, D., Pizacani, B., Bjornson, W. G., Spradley, J., Allen, E., & Lees, P. (2007). Support for spirituality in smoking cessation: Results of pilot survey. *Nicotine & Tobacco Research*, *9*(2), 299–303.

Goodwin, R. D., Keyes, K. M., & Hasin, D. S. (2009). Changes in cigarette use and nicotine dependence in the United States: Evidence from the 2001-2002 wave of the National Epidemiologic Survey of Alcoholism and related conditions. *American Journal of Public Health*, *99*(8), 1471–1477.

Gorman, I. (2018). Social norm feedback in online based smoking cessation: Do actual norms matter? *Dissertation Abstracts International: Section B: The Sciences and Engineering*, *78*(10-B(E)). No pagination specified.

Gorukanti, A., Delucchi, K., Ling, P., Fisher-Travis, R., & Halpern-Felsher, B. (2017). Adolescents' attitudes towards e-cigarette ingredients, safety, addictive properties, social norms, and regulation. *Preventive Medicine, 94*, 65–71.

Gowing, L. R., Ali, R. L., Allsop, S., Marsden, J., Turf, E. E., West, R., & Witton, J. (2015). Global statistics on addictive behaviours: 2014 status report. *Global Statistics on Addiction, 110*(6), 904–919.

Gracia, R., & Shepherd, G. (2014). Cyanide poisoning and its treatment. *Pharmacotherapy, 24*(10), 1358–1365.

Grant, J., Lynskey, M., Madden, P., Nelson, E., Few, L., Bucholz, K., . . . Agrawal, A. (2015). The role of conduct disorder in the relationship between alcohol, nicotine and cannabis use disorders. *Psychological Medicine, 45*(16), 3505–3515.

Greenfield, S. F., & Weiss, R. D. (2017). Addictions—25 years later. *Harvard Review of Psychiatry, 25*(3), 97–100.

Grucza, R. A., & Bierut, L. J. (2006). Cigarette smoking and the risk for alcohol use disorders among adolescent drinkers. *Alcoholism: Clinical and Experimental Research, 30*, 2046–2054.

Grunberg, N. E. (2003). Commentary on "Tobacco Smoking: Current Concepts in Etiology and Treatment": The tobacco use crisis and mental health. *Psychiatry: Interpersonal and Biological Processes, 66*, 200–201.

Gubner, N. R., Williams, D. D., Pagano, A., Campbell, B. K., & Guydish, J. (2018). Menthol cigarette smoking among individuals in treatment for substance use disorders. *Addictive Behaviors, 80*, 135–141.

Guydish, J., Passalacqua, E., Pagano, A., Martinez, C., Le, T., Chun, J., . . . Delucchi, K. (2016). An international systematic review of smoking prevalence in addiction treatment. *Addiction, 111*(2), 220–230.

Guydish, J., Tajima, B., Pramod, S., Le, T., Gubner, N. R., Campbell, B., & Roman, P. (2016). Use of multiple tobacco products in a national sample of persons enrolled in addiction treatment. *Drug and Alcohol Dependence, 166*, 93–99.

Hair, E., Pitzer, L., Bennett, M., Halenar, M., Rath, J., Cantrell, J., . . . Vallone, D. (2017). Harnessing youth and young adult culture: Improving the reach and engagement of the truth® campaign. *Journal of Health Communication, 22*(7), 568–575.

Hammons, G. (2010). What is the biological fate of mentholated cigarette smoking? *Addiction, 105*(Suppl 1), 8–10.

Harrell, P. T., Naqvi, S. M. H., Plunk, A. D., Ji, M., & Martins, S. S. (2017). Patterns of youth tobacco and polytobacco usage: The shift to alternative tobacco products. *American Journal of Drug and Alcohol Abuse, 43*(6), 694–702.

Hartman-Boyce, J., Stead, L. F., Cahill, K., & Lancaster, T. (2014). Efficacy of interventions to combat tobacco addiction: Cochrane update of 2013 reviews. *Addiction, 109*(9), 1414–1425.

Healton, C. G., Beck, S. E., Cartwright, J., & Vallone, D. M. (2010). Prohibiting menthol in tobacco products: a policy whose time has come. *Addiction, 105*(Suppl 1), 5–7.

Heatherton, T. F., Kozlowski, L. T., Frecker, R. C., & Fagerstrom, K. O. (1991). The Fagerstrom Test for Nicotine Dependence: A revision of the Fagerstrom Tolerance Questionnaire. *British Journal of Addictions, 86*, 1119–1127.

Hebert, R. (2005). What's new in nicotine & tobacco research? *Nicotine & Tobacco Research, 7*, 1–7.

Heffner, J. L., Johnson, C. S., Blom, T. J., & Anthenelli, R. M. (2010). Relationship between cigarette smoking and childhood symptoms of inattention and hyperactivity/impulsivity in alcohol-dependent adults without attention-deficit hyperactivity disorder. *Nicotine & Tobacco Research, 12*(3), 243–250.

Heilig, M. (2015). *The thirteenth step: Addiction in the age of brain science*. New York, NY: Columbia University Press.

Henningfield, J. E., & Hartel, C. R. (1999). Scientific basis for tobacco policy: Nicotine research travails. In M. D. Glantz & C. R. Hartel (Eds.), *Drug abuse: Origins & interventions* (pp. 431–446). Washington, DC: American Psychological Association.

Herzog, T. A. (2008). Analyzing the transtheoretical model using the framework of Weinstein, Rothman, and Sutton (1998): The example of smoking cessation. *Health Psychology, 27*(5), 548–556.

Hill, S. Y., Shen, S., Wellman, J. L., Rickin, E., & Lowers, L. (2005). Offspring from families at high risk for alcohol dependence: Increased body mass index in association with prenatal exposure to cigarettes but not alcohol. *Psychiatry Research, 135*(3), 203–216.

Hodge, D. R., Andereck, K., & Montoya, H. (2007). The protective influence of spiritual-religious lifestyle profiles on tobacco use, alcohol use, and gambling. *Social Work Research, 31*, 211–219.

Hooper, M. W., Antoni, M. H., Okuyemi, K., Dietz, N. A., & Resnicow, K. (2017). Randomized controlled trial of group-based culturally specific cognitive behavioral therapy among African American smokers. *Nicotine & Tobacco Research, 19*(3), 333–341.

Hu, M.-C., Griesler, P. C., Wall, M. M., & Kandel, D. B. (2014). Reciprocal associations between cigarette consumption and DSM-IV nicotine dependence criteria in adolescent smokers. *Addiction, 109*(9), 1518–1528.

Huang, L.-L., Baker, H. M., Meernik, C., Ranney, L. M., Richardson, A., & Goldstein, A. O. (2017). Impact of non-menthol flavours in tobacco products on perceptions and use among youth, young adults and adults: A systematic review. *Tobacco Control: An International Journal, 26*(6), 709–719.

Hurt, R. T., Croghan, I. T., Schroeder, D. R., Hays, J. T., Choi, D. S., & Ebbert, J. O. (2017). Combination varenicline and lorcaserin for tobacco dependence treatment and weight gain prevention in overweight and obese smokers: A pilot study. *Nicotine & Tobacco Research, 19*(8), 994–998.

Husky, M. M., Mazure, C. M., Paliwal, P., & McKee, S. A. (2008). Gender differences in the comorbidity of smoking behavior and major depression. *Drug and Alcohol Dependence, 93*, 176–179.

Irish Cancer Society. (n.d.). *What's in a cigarette?* Retrieved January 14, 2019, from https://www.cancer.ie/reduce-your-risk/smoking/health-risks/whats-in-cigarettes#sthash.7K0A6qD2.dpbs

Jacobs, D. C. (2004). A pragmatist approach to integrity in business ethics. *Journal of Management Inquiry, 13*(3), 215–223.

Johnson, M. W., Garcia-Romeu, A., & Griffiths, R. R. (2017). Long-term follow-up of psilocybin-facilitated smoking cessation. *American Journal of Drug and Alcohol Abuse, 43*(1), 55–60.

Jones, D. M., Majeed, B. A., Weaver, S. R., Sterling, K., Pechacek, T. F., & Eriksen, M. P. (2017). Prevalence and factors associated with smokeless tobacco use, 2014–2016. *American Journal of Health Behavior, 41*(5), 608–617.

Jones, K. (2018). A culturally targeted smoking cessation/HIV medication adherence intervention for African American MSM. *Dissertation Abstracts International: Section B: The Sciences and Engineering, 78*(7-B(E)). No pagination specified.

Kandel, D. B., Hu, M.-C., & Yamaguchi, K. (2009). Sequencing of DSM-IV criteria of nicotine dependence. *Addiction, 104*(8), 1393–1402.

Karam-Hage, M., Minnix, J., & Cinciripini, P. M. (2012). Nicotine. In B. A. Johnson (Ed.), *Addiction medicine: Science and practice* (pp. 417–443). New York, NY: Springer.

Kardia, S. L. R., Pomerleau, C. S., Rozek, L. S., & Marks, J. L. (2003). Association of parental smoking history with nicotine dependence, smoking rate, and psychological cofactors in adult smokers. *Addictive Behaviors, 28*(8), 1447–1452.

Keener, J. M. (2008). Spirituality and cigarette smoking in combat theater veterans with PTSD. *Dissertation Abstracts International: Section B: The Sciences and Engineering, 68*(12-B), 8401.

Kim, S. S. (2017). A culturally adapted smoking cessation intervention for Korean Americans: Preliminary findings. *Journal of Transcultural Nursing, 28*(1), 24–31.

Kirkcaldya, B. D., Siefenb, G., Surallb, D., & Bischoff, R. J. (2004). Predictors of drug and alcohol abuse among children and adolescents. *Personality and Individual Differences, 36*(2), 247–265.

Koller, K. R., Flanagan, C. A., Day, G. E., Thomas, T. K., Smith, C. A., Wolfe, A. W., . . . Patten, C. A. (2017). Developing a biomarker feedback intervention to motivate smoking cessation during pregnancy: Phase II MAW study. *Nicotine & Tobacco Research, 19*(8), 930–936.

Korhonen, T., Broms, U., Levalahti, E., Koskenvuo, M., & Kaprio, J. (2009). Characteristics and health consequences of intermittent smoking: Long-term follow-up among Finnish adult twins. *Nicotine & Tobacco Research, 11*, 148–155.

Krigel, S. W., Grobe, J. E., Goggin, K., Harris, K. J., Moreno, J. L., & Catley, D. (2017). Motivational interviewing and the decisional balance procedure for cessation induction in smokers not intending to quit. *Addictive Behaviors, 64*, 171–178.

Kulik, M. C., & Glantz, S. A. (2017). Softening among U.S. smokers with psychological distress: More quit attempts and lower consumption as smoking drops. *American Journal of Preventive Medicine, 53*(6), 810–817.

Lauterstein, D. (2017). Early life exposure to E-cigarettes induces CNS modifications associated with adverse neurobiological and neurobehavioral outcomes. *Dissertation Abstracts International: Section B: The Sciences and Engineering, 78*(5-B(E)). No pagination specified.

Le, T. L. (2018). The influence of attachment phenomena on alcohol and tobacco use. *Dissertation Abstracts International: Section B: The Sciences and Engineering, 79*(4-B(E)). No pagination specified.

Lechner, W. V., Grant, D. M., Meier, E., Mills, A. C., Judah, M. R., & Dempsey, J. P. (2014). The influence of stress on the affective modulation of the startle response to nicotine cues. *Applied Psychophysiology and Biofeedback, 39*(3–4), 279–285.

Lee, E. J. (2017). The effect of positive group psychotherapy and motivational interviewing on smoking cessation: A qualitative descriptive study. *Journal of Addictions Nursing, 28*(2), 88–95.

Lee, K., Gilmore, A. B., & Collin, J. (2004). Editorial: Looking inside the tobacco industry: Revealing insights from the Guildford Depository. *Addiction, 99*(4), 394–397.

Lempert, L. K., & Glantz, S. (2017). Packaging colour research by tobacco companies: The pack as a product characteristic. *Tobacco Control: An International Journal, 26*(3), 307–315.

Littlewood, R. A., Claus, E. D., Wilcox, C. E., Mickey, J., Arenella, P. B., Bryan, A. D., & Hutchison, K. E. (2017). Moderators of smoking cessation outcomes in a randomized-controlled trial of varenicline versus placebo. *Psychopharmacology, 234*(23–24), 3417–3429.

Lodge, K.-M. (2016). *Smoking and people with an intellectual disability.* Retrieved on February 12, 2019, from http://www.intellectualdisability.info/physical-health/articles/smoking-and-people-with-an-intellectual-disability

Logan, C. A., Rothenbacher, D., & Genuneit, J. (2017). Postpartum smoking relapse and breast feeding: Defining the window of opportunity for intervention. *Nicotine & Tobacco Research, 19*(3), 367–372.

Lokhmotov, R. (2014). Addiction as selfobject: An integrated analysis of self psychological and neurobiological models of nicotine addiction. *Dissertation Abstracts International: Section B: The Sciences and Engineering, 74*(10-B(E)). No pagination specified.

Loree, A. M., Ondersma, S. J., & Grekin, E. R. (2017). Toward enhancing treatment for pregnant smokers: Laying the groundwork for the use of complementary and alternative medicine approaches. *Nicotine & Tobacco Research, 19*(5), 562–571.

Lotfipour, S., Ferguson, E., Leonard, G., Miettunen, J., Perron, M., Pike, G. B., . . . Paus, T. (2014). Maternal cigarette smoking during pregnancy predicts drug use via externalizing behavior in two community-based samples of adolescents. *Addiction, 109*(10), 1718–1729.

Luijten, M., Kleinjan, M., & Franken, I. H. A. (2016). Event-related potentials reflecting smoking cue reactivity and cognitive control as predictors of smoking relapse and resumption. *Psychopharmacology, 233*(15–16), 2857–2868.

Lyvers, M., Carlopio, C., Bothma, V., & Edwards, M. S. (2014). Mood, mood regulation, and frontal systems functioning in current smokers, long-term abstinent ex-smokers, and never-smokers. *Journal of Psychoactive Drugs, 46*(2), 133–139.

Ma, Y., Yuan, W., Jiang, Z., Cui, W.-Y., & Li, M. D. (2015). Updated findings of the association and functional studies of DRD2/ANKK1 variants with addictions. *Molecular Neurobiology, 51*, 281–299.

MacKillop, J., & Monti, P. M. (2007). Advances in the scientific study of craving for alcohol and tobacco. In P. M. Miller & D. J. Kavanagh (Eds.), *Translation of addictions science into practice* (pp. 189–209). New York, NY: Elsevier Science.

Macnee, C. L., & Talsma, A. (1995). Development and testing of the Barriers to Cessation Scale. *Nursing Research, 44*, 214–219.

Maharaj, K., & Ternullo, S. (2001). Using nicotine replacement therapy in treating nicotine addiction in adolescents. *Journal of School Nursing, 17*(5), 278–282.

Malone, V., Harrison, R., & Daker-White, G. (2018). Mental health service user and staff perspectives on tobacco addiction and smoking cessation: A meta-synthesis of published qualitative studies. *Journal of Psychiatric and Mental Health Nursing, 25*, 270–282.

Manning, B. J. (2017, June 1). *Global Burden of Disease publication on smoking – Lancet, May, 2017.* Retrieved on February 12, 2019, from https://www.vascularhealth.ie/2017/06/01/global-burden-of-disease-update-on-smoking-2/

Mantler, T. (2013). A systematic review of smoking youths' perceptions of addiction and health risks associated with smoking: Utilizing the framework of the health belief model. *Addiction Research & Theory, 21*(4), 306–317.

Marcovitz, E. (1969). On the nature of addiction to cigarettes. *Journal of the American Psychoanalytic Association, 17*(4), 1074–1096.

Margolis, R. D., & Zweben, J. E. (2011). *Treating patients with alcohol and other drug problems: An integrated approach* (2nd ed.). Washington, DC: American Psychological Association.

Marqueta, A., Nerin, I., Gargallo, P., & Beamonte, A. (2017). Gender differences in success at quitting smoking: Short- and long-term outcomes. *Diferencias de genero en el exito al dejar de fumar: Resultados a corto y largo plazo., 29*(1), 13–21.

Maté, G. (2008). *In the realm of hungry ghosts: Close encounters with addiction*. Toronto, ON: Vintage Books.

Mathew, A. R., Heckman, B. W., Meier, E., & Carpenter, M. J. (2017). Development and initial validation of a cessation fatigue scale. *Drug and Alcohol Dependence, 176*, 102–108.

Matthews, A. K., Cesario, J., Ruiz, R., Ross, N., & King, A. (2017). A qualitative study of the barriers to and facilitators of smoking cessation among lesbian, gay, bisexual, and transgender smokers who are interested in quitting. *LGBT Health, 4*(1), 24–33.

Mayer, B. (2014). How much nicotine kills a human? Tracing back the generally accepted lethal dose to dubious self-experiments in the nineteenth century. *Archives of Toxicology, 88*(1), 5–7.

McCann, A. (2019, January 9). *The real cost of smoking by state*. Retrieved on February 11, 2019, from https://wallethub.com/edu/the-financial-cost-of-smoking-by-state/9520/

McCaul, K. D., Hockemeyer, J. R., Johnson, R. J., Zetocha, K., Quinlan, K., & Glasgow, R. E. (2006). Motivation to quit using cigarettes: A review. *Addictive Behaviors, 31*(1), 42–56.

McDermott, K. A., Joyner, K. J., Hakes, J. K., Okey, S. A., & Cougle, J. R. (2018). Pain interference and alcohol, nicotine, and cannabis use disorder in a national sample of substance users. *Drug and Alcohol Dependence, 186*, 53–59.

McKelvey, K., & Halpern-Felsher, B. (2017). Adolescent cigarette smoking perceptions and behavior: Tobacco control gains and gaps amidst the rapidly expanding tobacco products market from 2001 to 2015. *Journal of Adolescent Health, 60*(2), 226–228.

McKelvey, K. L., Ramo, D. E., Delucchi, K., & Rubinstein, M. L. (2017). Polydrug use among urban adolescent cigarette smokers. *Addictive Behaviors, 66*, 145–150.

McKenzie, M., Olsson, C. A., Jorm, A. F., Romaniuk, H., & Patton, G. C. (2010). Association of adolescent symptoms of depression and anxiety with daily smoking and nicotine dependence in young adulthood: Findings from a 10-year longitudinal study. *Addiction, 105*(9), 1652–1659.

MedicineNet. (n.d.). *Nicotine: Tobacco addiction and abuse*. Retrieved on February 11, 2019, from https://www.medicinenet.com/nicotine/article.htm

Milkman, H. B., & Sunderwirth, S. G. (2010). *Craving for ecstasy and natural highs: A positive approach to mood alteration*. Thousand Oaks, CA: SAGE.

Moolchan, E. T. (2004). Adolescent menthol smokers: Will they be a harder target for cessation? *Nicotine & Tobacco Research, 6*(Suppl1), S93–S95.

Moolchan, E. T., Fagan, P., Fernander, A. F., Velicer, W. F., Hayward, M. D., King, G., & Clayton, R. R. (2007). Addressing tobacco-related health disparities. *Addiction, 102*(Suppl2), 30–42.

Moore, B. A. (2012). *Handbook of counseling military couples*. New York, NY: Routledge/Taylor & Francis Group.

Moran, L. V., Sampath, H., Kochunov, P., & Hong, L. (2013). Brain circuits that link schizophrenia to high risk of cigarette smoking. *Schizophrenia Bulletin, 39*(6), 1373–1381.

Morean, M. E., & Wedel, A. V. (2017). Vaping to lose weight: Predictors of adult e-cigarette use for weight loss or control. *Addictive Behaviors, 66*, 55–59.

Morojele, N. K., Brook, J. S., & Brook, D. W. (2016). Tobacco and alcohol use among adolescents in South Africa: Shared and unshared risks. *Journal of Child and Adolescent Mental Health, 28*(2), 139–152.

Morphett, K., Carter, A., Hall, W., & Gartner, C. (2016). A qualitative study of smokers' views on brain-based explanations of tobacco dependence. *International Journal of Drug Policy, 29*, 41–48.

Morphett, K., Carter, A., Hall, W., & Gartner, C. (2017). Framing tobacco dependence as a "brain disease": Implications for policy and practice. *Nicotine & Tobacco Research, 19*(7), 774–780.

Mueller, S. E., Petitjean, S. A., & Wiesbeck, G. A. (2012). Cognitive behavioral smoking cessation during alcohol detoxification treatment: A randomized, controlled trial. *Drug and Alcohol Dependence, 126*(3), 279–285.

Muller, D. P., & de Haan, L. (2017). Smoking cessation and schizophrenia. *Tijdschrift voor Psychiatrie, 59*(5), 297–301.

Musk, A. W., & De Klerk, N. H. (2003). History of tobacco and health. *Respirology, 8*, 286–290.

Nagaya, T., Takahashib, A., Yoshidab, I., & Yokoyamab, M. (1992). Biphasic effects of smoking on human serum dopamine-p-hydroxylase activity. *Toxicology Letters, 60*, 325–328.

National Institute on Drug Abuse (NIDA). (n.d.). *Tobacco and nicotine facts*. Retrieved on February 11, 2019, from https://easyread.drugabuse.gov/content/tobacco-and-nicotine-facts

Needham, B. L. (2007). Gender differences in trajectories of depressive symptomatology and substance use during the transition from adolescence to young adulthood. *Social Science & Medicine, 65*(6), 1166–1179.

Nellum, A. L. (2018). The prospective associations of stress, depression, and social support with smoking cessation and relapse among low-income pregnant women. *Dissertation Abstracts International: Section B: The Sciences and Engineering, 78*(9-B(E)). No pagination specified.

Netter, P., Muller, M. J., & Kamradik, N. B. (1994). The influence of nicotine on performance, mood, and physiological parameters as related to smoking habit, gender, and suggestibility. *Clinical Investigator, 72*, 512–518.

New Health Advisor. (2019, February). *What are the street names for tobacco?* Retrieved on February 11, 2019, from https://www.newhealthadvisor.com/street-names-for-tobacco.html

Niemela, S., Raisanen, A., Koskela, J., Taanila, A., Miettunen, J., Ramsay, H., & Veijola, J. (2017). The effect of prenatal smoking exposure on daily smoking among teenage offspring. *Addiction, 112*(1), 134–143.

Nonnemaker, J., McNeely, C. A., & Blum, R. W. (2016). Public and private domains of religiosity and adolescent smoking transitions. *Social Science & Medicine, 62*(12), 3084–3095.

Nowak, D., Jorres, R. A., & Ruther, T. (2014). E-cigarettes—Prevention, pulmonary health, and addiction. *Deutsches Arzteblatt International, 111*(20), 349–355.

Nutt, D. J., Phillips, L. D., Balfour, D., Curran, H., Dockrell, M., Foulds, J., . . . Sweanor, D. (2014). Estimating the harms of nicotine-containing products using the MCDA approach. *European Addiction Research, 20*(5), 218–225.

O'Brien, C. P. (2007). Brain development as a vulnerability factor in the etiology of substance abuse and addiction. In D. Romer & E. F. Walker (Eds.), *Adolescent psychopathology and the developing brain: Integrating brain and prevention science* (pp. 388–398). New York, NY: Oxford University Press.

O'Connell, K. A., Fears, B. A., Cook, M. R., Gerkovich, M. M., & Zechmann, A. (1991). Overcoming the urge to smoke: The strategies of long-term abstainers and late relapsers. *Psychology of Addictive Behaviors, 5*(1), 1–8.

O'Connor, R. J., Rees, V. W., Rivard, C., Hatsukami, D. K., & Cummings, K. M. (2017). Internalized smoking stigma in relation to quit intentions, quit attempts, and current e-cigarette use. *Substance Abuse, 38*(3), 330–336.

O'Gara, E., Sharma, E., Boyle, R. G., & Taylor, K. A. (2017). Exploring exclusive and poly-tobacco use among adult cigarette smokers in Minnesota. *American Journal of Health Behavior, 41*, 84–91.

Ogbonna, F. (2018). Assessing provider use of Veterans Health Administration tobacco-cessation guideline. *Dissertation Abstracts International: Section B: The Sciences and Engineering, 79*(1-B(E)). No pagination specified.

Ohlmeier, M. D., Peters, K., Kordon, A., Seifert, J., Te Wildt, B., Wiese, B., . . . Schneider, U. (2013). "Nicotine and alcohol dependence in patients with comorbid attention-deficit/hyperactivity disorder (ADHD)": Erratum. *Alcohol and Alcoholism, 48*(4), 517.

Oikonomou, M. T., Arvanitis, M., & Sokolove, R. L. (2017). Mindfulness training for smoking cessation: A meta-analysis of randomized-controlled trials. *Journal of Health Psychology, 22*(14), 1841–1850.

Okoli, C. T. C., Rayens, M. K., Wiggins, A. T., Ickes, M. J., Butler, K. M., & Hahn, E. J. (2016). Secondhand tobacco smoke exposure and susceptibility to smoking, perceived addiction, and psychobehavioral symptoms among college students. *Journal of American College Health, 64*(2), 96–103.

Okuyemi, K. S., Lawrence, D., Hammons, G., & Alexander, L. A. (2010). Use of mentholated cigarettes: What can we learn from national data sets? *Addiction, 105*(Suppl 1), 1–4.

Olfson, E., Bloom, J., Bertelsen, S., Budde, J. P., Breslau, N., Brooks, A., . . . Bierut, L. J. (2018). CYP2A6 metabolism in the development of smoking behaviors in young adults. *Addiction Biology, 23*(1), 437–447.

Ouzir, M., & Errami, M. (2016). Etiological theories of addiction: A comprehensive update on neurobiological, genetic, and behavioural vulnerability. *Pharmacology, Biochemistry and Behavior, 148*, 59–68.

Pachankis, J. E., Hatzenbuehler, M. L., & Starks, T. J. (2014). The influence of structural stigma and rejection sensitivity on young sexual minority men's daily tobacco and alcohol use. *Social Science & Medicine, 103*, 67–75.

Park, E. R., Luberto, C. M., O'Cleirigh, C., Perez, G. K., & Wilner, J. G. (2017). Smoking cessation. In A.-M. Vranceanu, J. A. Greer, & S. A. Safren (Eds.), *The Massachusetts General Hospital handbook of behavioral medicine: A clinician's guide to evidence-based psychosocial interventions for individuals with medical illness* (pp. 9–35). Totowa, NJ: Humana Press.

Park, S. H., Duncan, D. T., Shahawy, O. E., Lee, L., Shearston, J. A., Tamura, K., . . . & Weitzman, M. (2017). Characteristics of adults who switched from cigarette smoking to e-cigarettes. *American Journal of Preventive Medicine, 53*(5), 652–660.

Pasquereau, A., Guignard, R., Andler, R., & Nguyen-Thanh, V. (2017). Electronic cigarettes, quit attempts and smoking cessation: A 6-month follow-up. *Addiction, 112*(9), 1620–1628.

Patkar, A. A., Vergare, M. J., Batra, V., Weinstein, S. P., & Leone, F. T. (2003). Tobacco smoking: Current concepts in etiology and treatment. *Psychiatry: Interpersonal and Biological Processes, 66*, 183–199.

Patten, S. B., Williams, J. V. A., Lavorato, D. H., Wang, J. L., Sajobi, T. T., & Bulloch, A. G. M. (2017). Major depression and non-specific distress following smoking cessation in the Canadian general population. *Journal of Affective Disorders, 218*, 182–187.

Patterson, F., Schnoll, R. A., & Lerman, C. (2011). Nicotine. In B. A. Johnson (Ed.), *Addiction medicine: Science and practice* (Vol. 1, pp. 991–1016). New York, NY: Springer New York.

Pepper, J. K., Farrelly, M. C., & Watson, K. A. (2018). Adolescents' understanding and use of nicotine in e-cigarettes. *Addictive Behaviors, 82*, 109–113.

Perkins, K. A., Grobe, J. E., Fonte, C., Goettler, J., Caggiula, A. R., Reynolds, W. A., . . . Jacob, R. G. (1994). Chronic and acute tolerance to subjective, behavioral and cardiovascular effects of nicotine in humans. *Journal of Pharmacology and Experimental Therapeutics, 270*(2), 628–638.

Perry, B. L. (2016). Gendering genetics: Biological contingencies in the protective effects of social integration for men and women. *American Journal of Sociology, 121*(6), 1655–1696.

Peterson, J., Battaglia, C., Fehling, K. B., Williams, K. M., & Lambert-Kerzner, A. (2017). Perspectives on a home telehealth care management program for veterans with posttraumatic stress disorder who smoke. *Journal of Addictions Nursing, 28*(3), 117–123.

Pietrangelo, A., & Cherney, K. (2017). The effects of smoking on the body. *Healthline*. Retrieved on February 17, 2019, from https://www.healthline.com/health/smoking/effects-on-body#1

Prasad, S., Kaisar, M. A., & Cucullo, L. (2017). Unhealthy smokers: Scopes for prophylactic intervention and clinical treatment. *BMC Neuroscience, 18*, ArtID 70.

Prochaska, J. O., Norcross, J. C., & DiClemente, C. C. (1994). *Changing for good*. New York, NY: Avon Books.

Rastegar, D., & Fingerhood, M. (2016). *The American Society of Addiction Medicine handbook of addiction medicine*. New York, NY: Oxford University Press.

Raval, A. P., Hirsch, N., Dave, K. R., Yavagal, D. R., Bramlett, H., & Saul, I. (2011). Nicotine and estrogen synergistically exacerbate cerebral ischemic injury. *Neuroscience, 181*, 216–225.

Reitsma, M. B., Fullman, N., Ng, M., Salama, J. S., Abajobir, A., Abate, K. H., . . . Gakidou, E. (2017). Smoking prevalence and attributable disease burden in 195 countries and territories, 1990-2015: A systematic analysis from the Global Burden of Disease Study 2015. *Lancet, 389*(10082), 1885–1906.

Richter, L., Pugh, B. S., Smith, P. H., Ball, S. A. (2017). The co-occurrence of nicotine and other substance use and addiction among youth and adults in the United States: Implications for research, practice, and policy. *American Journal of Drug and Alcohol Abuse, 43*(2), 132–145.

Rios, E. L. R., Herval, A. M., Ferreira, R. C., & Freire, M. D. C. M. (2019). Prevalences of stages of change for smoking cessation in adolescents and associated factors: systematic review and meta-analysis. *Journal of Adolescent Health, 64*, 149–157.

Robinson, L. M. (2012). An integrative review of adolescent smoking cessation using the transtheoretical model of change. *Journal of Pediatric Health Care, 26*(5), 336–345.

Roditis, M., Lee, J., & Halpern-Felsher, B. L. (2016). Adolescent (mis) perceptions about nicotine addiction: Results from a mixed-methods study. *Health Education & Behavior, 43*(2), 156–164.

Rohsenow, D. J., Martin, R. A., Tidey, J. W., Colby, S. M., & Monti, P. M. (2017). Treating smokers in substance treatment with contingent vouchers, nicotine replacement and brief advice adapted for sobriety settings. *Journal of Substance Abuse Treatment, 72*, 72–79.

Rollins, K., Lewis, C., Goeckner, R., Pacheco, J., Smith, T. E., Hale, J., . . . Daley, C. M. (2017). American Indian knowledge, attitudes, and beliefs about smokeless tobacco: A comparison of two focus group studies. *Journal of Community Health: The Publication for Health Promotion and Disease Prevention, 42*(6), 1133–1140.

Rollins, K. L. (2017). A culturally tailored tobacco cessation program for American Indians: Program development. *Dissertation Abstracts International Section A: Humanities and Social Sciences*, *77*(10-A(E)). No pagination specified.

Rose, J. E., & Behm, F. M. (2017). Combination varenicline/bupro pion treatment benefits highly dependent smokers in an adaptive smoking cessation paradigm. *Nicotine & Tobacco Research*, *19*(8), 999–1002.

Rostron, B. (2013). Mortality risks associated with environmental tobacco smoke exposure in the United States. *Nicotine & Tobacco Research*, *15*(10), 1722–1728.

Rowa-Dewar, N., Rooke, C., & Amos, A. (2017). Using e-cigarettes in the home to reduce smoking and secondhand smoke: Disadvantaged parents' accounts. *Health Education Research*, *32*(1), 12–21.

Rubinstein, M. L., Rait, M. A., & Prochaska, J. J. (2014). Frequent marijuana use is associated with greater nicotine addiction in adolescent smokers. *Drug and Alcohol Dependence*, *141*, 159–162.

Saw, A., Paterniti, D., Fung, L.-C., Tsoh, J. Y., Chen, M. S., Jr., & Tong, E. (2017). Social environmental influences on smoking and cessation: Qualitative perspectives among Chinese-speaking smokers and nonsmokers in California. *Journal of Immigrant and Minority Health*, *19*(6), 1404–1411.

Scherrer, J. F., Xian, H., Lyons, M. J., Goldberg, J., Eisen, S. A., True, W. R., . . . Koenen, K. C. (2008). Posttraumatic stress disorder; combat exposure; and nicotine dependence, alcohol dependence, and major depression in male twins. *Comprehensive Psychiatry*, *49*(3), 297–304.

Schiff, H. A. (2018). Alcohol and tobacco consumption as addictive behaviors in emerging adults. *Dissertation Abstracts International: Section B: The Sciences and Engineering*, *79*(7-B(E)). No pagination specified.

Schulte, M. H. J., Goudriaan, A. E., Kaag, A. M., Kooi, D. P., van den Brink, W., Wiers, R. W., & Schmaal, L. (2017). The effect of N-acetylcysteine on brain glutamate and gamma-aminobutyric acid concentrations and on smoking cessation: A randomized, double-blind, placebo-controlled trial. *Journal of Psychopharmacology*, *31*(10), 1377–1379.

Schuster, R. M., Cather, C., Pachas, G. N., Zhang, H., Cieslak, K. M., Hoeppner, S. S., . . . Eden Evins, A. (2017). Predictors of tobacco abstinence in outpatient smokers with schizophrenia or bipolar disorder treated with varenicline and cognitive behavioral smoking cessation therapy. *Addictive Behaviors*, *71*, 89–95.

Secades-Villa, R., Olfson, M., Okuda, M., Velasquez, N., Perez-Fuentes, G., Liu, S.-M., & Blanco, C. (2013). Trends in the prevalence of tobacco use in the United States, 1991-1992 to 2004–2005. *Psychiatric Services*, *64*(5), 458–465.

Sells, J. R., Waters, A. J., & MacLean, R. R. (2017). Evaluating the influence of at-risk alcohol use on factors associated with smoking cessation: Combining laboratory and ecological momentary assessment. *Drug and Alcohol Dependence*, *179*, 267–270.

Serre, F., Fatseas, M., Denis, C., Swendsen, J., & Auriacombe, M. (2018). Predictors of craving and substance use among patients with alcohol, tobacco, cannabis or opiate addictions: Commonalities and specificities across substances. *Addictive Behaviors*, *83*, 123–129.

Shake, L. M. (2017). Exploring the emotions of smokers during the contemplation stage of smoking cessation: A multiple-case study. *Dissertation Abstracts International: Section B: The Sciences and Engineering*, *78*(5-B(E)). No pagination specified.

Shedler, J. (2010). The efficacy of psychodynamic psychotherapy. *American Psychologist*, *65*(2), 98–109.

Smith, E. A., & Malone, R. E. (2009). "Everywhere the soldier will be": Wartime tobacco promotion in the US military. *American Journal of Public Health*, *99*, 1595–1602.

Smith, P. H., Oberleitner, L. M. S., Smith, K. M. Z., & McKee, S. A. (2016). Childhood adversity interacts with adult stressful events to predict reduced likelihood of smoking cessation among women but not men. *Clinical Psychological Science*, *4*(2), 183–193.

Smith, P. H., Zhang, J., Weinberger, A. H., Mazure, C. M., & McKee, S. A. (2017). Gender differences in the real-world effectiveness of smoking cessation medications: Findings from the 2010–2011 Tobacco Use Supplement to the Current Population Survey. *Drug and Alcohol Dependence*, *178*, 485–491.

Solmi, M., Veronese, N., Sergi, G., Luchini, C., Favaro, A., Santonastaso, P., . . . Stubbs, B. (2016). The association between smoking prevalence and eating disorders: A systematic review and meta-analysis. *Addiction*, *111*, 1914–1922.

Spears, C. A., Hedeker, D., Li, L., Wu, C., Anderson, N. K., Houchins, S. C., . . . Wetter, D. W. (2017). Mechanisms underlying mindfulness-based addiction treatment versus cognitive behavioral therapy and usual care for smoking cessation. *Journal of Consulting and Clinical Psychology*, *85*(11), 1029–1040.

Sreeramareddy, C. T., Pradhan, P. M. S., Mir, I. A., & Sin, S. (2014). Smoking and smokeless tobacco use in nine South and Southeast Asian countries: Prevalence estimates and social determinants from demographic and health surveys. *Population Health Metrics*, *12*, 1–16.

Stead, L. F., & Lancaster, T. (2007, July). Interventions to reduce harm from continued tobacco use. *Cochrane Database of Systematic Reviews, Issue 3*. Art. No.: CD005231. Available for download from https://www.cochranelibrary.com/cdsr/doi/10.1002/14651858.CD005231.pub2/epdf/full

Stevenson, J. G., Oliver, J. A., Hallyburton, M. B., Sweitzer, M. M., Conklin, C. A., & McClernon, F. J. (2017). Smoking environment cues reduce ability to resist smoking as measured by a delay to smoking task. *Addictive Behaviors*, *67*, 49–52.

Stroup, A. M., & Branstetter, S. A. (2018). Effect of e-cigarette advertisement exposure on intention to use e-cigarettes in adolescents. *Addictive Behaviors*, *82*, 1–6.

Tanner, J.-A., Henderson, J. A., Buchwald, D., Howard, B. V., Henderson, P. N., & Tyndale, R. F. (2018). Relationships between smoking behaviors and cotinine levels among two American Indian populations with distinct smoking patterns. *Nicotine & Tobacco Research*, *20*, 466–473.

Tarman, V., & Werdell, P. (2014). *Food junkies: The truth about food addiction*. Toronto, ON: Dundurn.

Thrul, J., Ferguson, S. G., & Buhler, A. (2016). How do light and intermittent smokers differ from heavy smokers in young adulthood: The role of smoking restraint strategies. *Journal of Psychoactive Drugs*, *48*, 153–158.

Travaglini, L. E., Li, L., Brown, C. H., & Bennett, M. E. (2017). Predictors of smoking cessation group treatment engagement among veterans with serious mental illness. *Addictive Behaviors*, *75*, 103–107.

Tverdal, A., & Bjartveit, K. (2011). Health consequences of pipe versus cigarette smoking. *Tobacco Control: An International Journal*, *20*, 123–130.

Twyman, L., Bonevski, B., Paul, C., Bryant, J., West, R., Siahpush, M., . . . Palazzi, K. (2016). Factors associated with concurrent tobacco smoking and heavy alcohol consumption within a socioeconomically disadvantaged Australian sample. *Substance Use & Misuse*, *51*(4), 459–470.

Tynan, M. A., Polansky, J. R., Titus, K., Atayeva, R., & Glantz, S. A. (2017, July 7). Tobacco use in top-grossing movies: United States, 2010-2016. *Morbidity and Mortality Weekly Report (MMWR)*, *66*, 681–686. Retrieved on February 13, 2019, from https://www.cdc.gov/mmwr/volumes/66/wr/mm6626a1.htm?s_cid=mm6626a1_w

Tyndale, R. F. (2003). Genetics of alcohol and tobacco use in humans. *Annals of Medicine*, *35*, 94–121.

Tzelepis, F., Daly, J., Dowe, S., Bourke, A., Gillham, K., & Freund, M. (2017). Supporting aboriginal women to quit smoking: Antenatal and postnatal care providers' confidence, attitudes, and practices. *Nicotine & Tobacco Research*, *19*(5), 642–646.

U.S. Food and Drug Administration. (2018, October 18). *FDA launches new campaign: "The Real Cost" Youth E-Cigarette Prevention Campaign.* Retrieved on February 17, 2019, from https://www.fda.gov/TobaccoProducts/PublicHealthEducation/PublicEducationCampaigns/TheRealCostCampaign/ucm620783.htm

Valentine, G. W., Jatlow, P. I., Coffman, M., Nadim, H., Gueorguieva, R., & Sofuoglu, M. (2016). The effects of alcohol-containing e-cigarettes on young adult smokers. *Drug and Alcohol Dependence*, *159*, 272–276.

Valera, P., McClernon, F. J., Burkholder, G., Mugavero, M. J., Willig, J., O'Cleirigh, C., & Cropsey, K. L. (2017). A pilot trial examining African American and White responses to algorithm-guided smoking cessation medication selection in persons living with HIV. *AIDS and Behavior*, *21*(7), 1975–1984.

Vander Weg, M. W., Holman, J. E., Rahman, H., Sarrazin, M. V., Hillis, S. L., Fu, S. S., . . . Katz, D. A. (2017). Implementing smoking cessation guidelines for hospitalized veterans: Cessation results from the VA-BEST trial. *Journal of Substance Abuse Treatment*, *77*, 79–88.

Veliz, P., McCabe, S. E., McCabe, V. V., & Boyd, C. J. (2017). Adolescent sports participation, e-cigarette use, and cigarette smoking. *American Journal of Preventive Medicine*, *53*(5), e175–e183.

Vest, B. H., Kane, C., DeMarce, J., Barbero, E., Harmon, R., Hawley, J., & Lehmann, L. (2014). Outcomes following treatment of veterans for substance and tobacco addiction. *Archives of Psychiatric Nursing*, *28*, 333–338.

Waldrop, A. E., & Cohen, B. E. (2014). Trauma exposure predicts alcohol, nicotine, and drug problems beyond the contribution of PTSD and depression in patients with cardiovascular disease: Data from the Heart and Soul Study. *American Journal on Addictions*, *23*(1), 53–61.

Ward, K. D., Kedia, S., Webb, L., & Relyea, G. E. (2012). Nicotine dependence among clients receiving publicly funded substance abuse treatment. *Drug and Alcohol Dependence*, *125*(1-2), 95–102.

Ware, J. J., Tanner, J.-A., Taylor, A. E., Bin, Z., Haycock, P., Bowden, J., . . . Munafo, M. R. (2017). Does coffee consumption impact on heaviness of smoking? *Addiction*, *112*(10), 1842–1853.

Waters, E. A., Janssen, E., Kaufman, A. R., Peterson, L. M., Muscanell, N. L., Guadagno, R. E., & Stock, M. L. (2016). The relationship between young adult smokers' beliefs about nicotine addiction and smoking-related affect and cognitions. *Journal of Cancer Education*, *31*(2), 338–347.

Watson, N. L., Heffner, J. L., McClure, J. B., Mull, K. E., & Bricker, J. B. (2017). Differential prevalence of established risk factors for poor cessation outcomes among smokers by level of social anxiety. *American Journal on Addictions*, *26*(2), 176–182.

Weckler, H., Kong, G., Larsen, H., Cousijn, J., Wiers, R. W., & Krishnan-Sarin, S. (2017). Impulsivity and approach tendencies towards cigarette stimuli: Implications for cigarette smoking and cessation behaviors among youth. *Experimental and Clinical Psychopharmacology*, *25*(5), 363–372.

Wehbe, L., Ubhi, H. K., & West, R. (2018). Want, need and habit as drivers of smoking behaviour: A preliminary analysis. *Addictive Behaviors*, *76*, 135–138.

Weinberger, A. H., Franco, C. A., Hoff, R. A., Pilver, C. E., Steinberg, M. A., Rugle, L., . . . Potenza, M. N. (2015). Gambling behaviors and attitudes in adolescent high-school students: Relationships with problem-gambling severity and smoking status. *Journal of Psychiatric Research*, *65*, 131–138.

Weinberger, A. H., Platt, J. M., Smith, P. H., & Goodwin, R. D. (2017). Racial/ethnic differences in self-reported withdrawal symptoms and quitting smoking three years later: A prospective, longitudinal examination of US adults. *Nicotine & Tobacco Research*, *19*(3), 373–378.

West, J. H., Blumberg, E. J., Kelley, N. J., Hill, L., Sipan, C. L., Schmitz, K. E., . . . Hovell, M. F. (2013). The role of parenting in alcohol and tobacco use among Latino adolescents. *Journal of Child & Adolescent Substance Abuse*, *22*(2), 120–132.

West, R. (2017). Tobacco smoking: Health impact, prevalence, correlates and interventions. *Psychology & Health*, *32*(8), 1018–1036.

White, M. A., & O'Malley, S. S. (2012). Interactions between smoking, eating, and body weight. In K. D. Brownell & M. S. Gold (Eds.), *Food and addiction: A comprehensive handbook* (pp. 244–248). New York, NY: Oxford University Press.

Wilson, S. M., Pacek, L. R., Dennis, P. A., Bastian, L. A., Beckham, J. C., & Calhoun, P. S. (2017). Veterans living with HIV: A high-risk group for cigarette smoking. *AIDS and Behavior*, *21*, 1950–1955.

Woolston, C. (2019, January 1). *Smokescreen: Smoking in the movies.* Retrieved on February 13, 2019, from https://consumer.healthday.com/encyclopedia/smoking-and-tobacco-cessation-36/tobacco-and-kids-health-news-662/smoke-screen-smoking-in-the-movies-645323.html

Yeni, N., Tumay, F., Tonguc, O., Azaroglu, E., & Bozok, N. (2015). Survey on smoking, consuming alcohol, and using illicit drugs in patients with epilepsy. *Noropsikiyatri Arsivi*, *52*, 354–358.

Yong, H.-H., Savvas, S., Borland, R., Thrasher, J., Sirirassamee, B., & Omar, M. (2013). Secular versus religious norms against smoking: Which is more important as a driver of quitting behaviour among Muslim Malaysian and Buddhist Thai smokers? *International Journal of Behavioral Medicine*, *20*, 252–258.

Young, C., & Skorga, P. (2011). Stage-based interventions for smoking cessation: A review synopsis. *Public Health Nursing*, *28*(5), 441–443.

Zborovskaya, Y. (2017). E-cigarettes and smoking cessation: A primer for oncology clinicians. *Clinical Journal of Oncology Nursing*, *21*(1), 54–63.

Zvolensky, M. J., Rodriguez-Cano, R., Paulus, D. J., Kotov, R., Bromet, E., Gonzalez, A., . . . Luft, B. J. (2017). Respiratory problems and anxiety sensitivity in smoking lapse among treatment seeking smokers. *Addictive Behaviors*, *75*, 25–29.

13 Other Drug Addictions

iStock.com/monkeybusinessim

Learning Objectives

1. Learn about the impact of the ongoing war on drugs initiated by Richard Nixon.
2. Learn about stimulants, depressants (and sedative-hypnotics), hallucinogens (psychedelics), inhalants, club drugs, and prescription and over-the-counter medications.
3. Become familiar with the experience of people who take the more common drugs.
4. Learn about the medications that are helpful in treating drug addiction.
5. Discover empirically validated ways to counsel drug addicts.

CHALLENGING YOUR ASSUMPTIONS ABOUT THIS ADDICTION

1. What judgments do you make when you see someone on the street high on crack or crystal meth? To what extent do you believe that they have control over their drug use? Why do these individuals not seek out rehabilitation to get over their drug addiction once and for all?
2. What would you do if you had a teenage child who became a drug addict? What steps would you take to get your child help?
3. If you are or are becoming an addictions counselor and you had a client who kept relapsing repeatedly, what actions would you consider taking that you would see as ethical? Is it ethical for you to continue seeing a client who is *not* improving?
4. Think about illegal drugs that you have taken in the past (if any). What was it about you that kept you from becoming addicted? Alternatively, if you did become addicted to a drug, what was it about the drug that you found irresistible?
5. If you became addicted to a drug (or if you are addicted), what barriers would you (or did you) experience in seeking help for your problem? How bad would (did) your drug use have to become before you would (did) seek help?

PERSONAL REFLECTIONS

Both a family member and a very close friend became crack addicts. First my family member. "George" was raised in a middle-class home. According to George, his parents were not caring and in fact did some things that, if true, would be considered abusive. Nonetheless, George grew up to be a very successful realtor. Thanks to a condo complex that he and a friend had exclusive rights to sell, George became the only member of the family to become a millionaire at least twice over. He bought several properties, married his second wife, had another child, and appeared to be living the good life. One day unexpectedly, another family member phoned to tell me that he believed George was using drugs. The story unfolded over the ensuing months. George's wife left him, the economy tanked, and George could not maintain payments on his properties. Somewhere along the way, he had become a crack addict. I remember the day I had breakfast with him. His dad already forewarned me that George looks and acts a little "sketchy." He was indeed agitated when I met him, and likely high as well. I knew that, if I confronted him or talked about his estranged wife, he would bolt from the restaurant. A few months after our breakfast, he relocated to my city. I found out he had racked up $14,000 in traffic violations and he needed to declare bankruptcy and receive social assistance for several months.

Regarding my close friend, "Bill," we used to live together in a character home. Both of us were professionals. Although Bill and I would occasionally smoke pot together and talk, his behavior started becoming increasingly weird. I knew that he snorted cocaine occasionally with a different friend. But the expanding shift in his behavior was disturbing, and I eventually moved out. One day that I came over to visit, a mutual friend answered the door and told me that Bill was in the basement rolling naked on newsprint covered with blotches of wet paint of various colors. Reportedly Bill, who had been quite conservative, decided that this would be a fun activity. I do not question that it was fun. It's just that this was not Bill. A few weeks later when I was on vacation, I received a phone call from his parents wondering if I knew what was going on with Bill. By this point, everyone in his family had experienced his strange and unexplainable behavior. I told them that his conduct was explainable; Bill had become a crack addict. Within a couple of weeks, Bill was admitted to a residential treatment program. The day he left was the last time I ever heard from him. Perhaps because we would occasionally smoke pot together, I needed to be cut from his life. I know that this is a common recommendation provided in treatment centers and one that makes a great deal of sense, at least for a period. Our friends can act as triggers to use again. I still wonder about Bill. I genuinely hope he has managed to stay clean despite knowing that crack is one of the most addictive substances on earth, and it has one of the highest rates of relapse.

I begin this chapter thinking about Bill and George. George does not say he is in recovery, and every time he returns to the city where he used crack, he gets together with his old "friends" and crack is provided for everyone until he and his money are spent. How can two individuals so successful let their lives degenerate to this degree? How can anyone do that?

INSIDE AN ADDICTED PERSON'S MIND

Martina, Age 22

My friends and I used to sniff cleaning fluid every chance we got when I was in grade 6. I loved the dopamine rush, that feeling of being drowsy, a bit intoxicated I suppose, and lightheaded. That was only the beginning of my journey into drugs. I don't remember sniffing cleaning fluid after that year, but I went to a different school than my peers because my parents wanted me to learn Spanish. Even though my parents are terrific people, they were not very good at teaching me Spanish. I was looking forward to learning Spanish so that I could communicate better with them in their native language.

It turned out there were a lot of Hispanic kids in grade 7. I had no idea, however, that they would be into drugs, too. Perhaps not everyone but the friends I was attracted to were like myself.

It didn't take long until I was using many drugs and often more than one at a time. There was something about my peer group, and perhaps it was partly caused by the drugs themselves, that made me want to use more and more drugs. Getting booze was easy; getting drugs was even easier. There were at least two dealers I knew of that went to my school. The problem for me was that I didn't have any money for this sort of thing. My friends were great, and they shared a lot. But I could not take and not give back. I tried stealing but I wasn't good at it, and a couple of times I was nearly arrested. What was I going to do? By this point I was craving. Craving what? Mostly stimulants I suppose, but I also looked forward to using hallucinogens on the weekend.

Increasingly, however, crystal meth became my favorite drug. The high lasted longer than cocaine, and much longer than crack. After a while, however, the cravings became intense, and I needed more of the drug to feel as high as before and to keep the high going. Even though I might be okay for a couple of days, craving always took me back, and I just wanted more. I was starting to twitch after being on a weekend drug run, and thankfully my parents just assumed that I was a bit hyperactive. They weren't worried about me yet. They didn't know I was using drugs.

I needed to do something to make fast cash. I was filling out pretty good for a 13-year-old, and I had already been approached by men several times downtown. Something about the drugs I was using made me feel like it would be okay and that I would have fun. I was even feeling horny despite not having a word for it. My parents were hardworking individuals who were so against drugs. Dad didn't mind getting drunk frequently enough though. About once a week he was simply bombed and snoring in his recliner. Mom was tired and wrapped up in managing responsibilities. Regardless, I snuck out, went downtown, and tricked my way around until I had enough money to have meth for my friends and me. My grades at school began dropping rapidly as I continued this pattern, and I was missing many classes.

The school phoned my parents, and they were rightly pissed at me. The principal told them I was using drugs, and that made everything so much worse at home. I blame him for what happened because the next 3 years were torturous. I had to have my drugs, and my parents kept trying to hold me back. But, the time I was 14, they knew I was sneaking out at night time, and sometimes they were locking my door to keep me contained. My relationship with them became increasingly caustic, and I couldn't wait to move out. At age 16, I left and lived with a guy who didn't mind my sex work.

I don't know what else to say. The next 6 years were a blur as I merely went from one high to another and from one low to the next. It wasn't until I attempted suicide and spent time in rehabilitation that I learned what I had become. But, at this writing, it seems too late to change. Of course, I went through a dry spell while in rehab, but, the moment I got out, I was back on the street doing what I do best. I don't know where my life is going to head, but right now all I can think about is getting high again so I can stop thinking about how lousy I feel.

Commentary

Martina's drug use escalated until it became a full-blown addiction. Her relationship with her parents deteriorated over time due to her drug use. Drug addiction led her to enter sex work, which wouldn't likely have happened otherwise. Like most other addicts, Martina refuses to take responsibility for her behavior and instead projects blame for her behavior onto others.

Her use is having many adverse consequences and, rather than face these, she runs back to using the first chance that she gets after going through rehab. The symptoms of drug addiction that we can ascertain from Martina are (a) loss of control—exemplified by her cravings, and the amount of use and time spent using, (b) social impairment—illustrated by her school failure and interpersonal problems with family, (c) risky use—exemplified by her involvement in sex work and continuing to use despite its adverse effects, and (d) pharmacological dependence—illustrated by increased tolerance and then withdrawal symptoms when she stops using.

Discussion

1. Do you know of anyone who you suspect has become dependent on stimulants? If "yes," which symptoms noted in the commentary apply to him or her?
2. Does this person have symptoms that are not listed in the commentary? If so, what are they?
3. If you were Martina's counselor, how would you go about helping her?

COUNSELING SCENARIO

As you are reading, imagine that you *are the client in this scenario. Note the areas in which the session could be improved on the part of the counselor.*

Your name is Phoenix, a 16-year-old grade 11 student. You are popular at school, and many girls would love to date you. Your mom, however, found your stash of crack and completely freaked out. She has booked this appointment for you to see an addictions counselor. You do not believe you have a problem despite using crack every single day. You resent that your mom is forcing you to see this counselor. You do not want to have this appointment.

- You: I'm only here because my mom forced me. She is always on my back about something.
- Counselor: Your mom told me that you have been using crack. Is that correct?
- You: Yeah, a bunch of kids at my school use it.
- Counselor: So, you are not the only one who uses it. How often are you using crack, Phoenix?
- You: I just met you, and I don't think it is any of your business.
- Counselor: I understand that you think this is a private matter. Your mom is obviously concerned for you, though.
- You: She can be as concerned as she wants to be. It's not a problem for me.
- Counselor: You appear to be strongly in denial of the effect that crack is having in your life.
- You: What do you mean by that? How do you know what effect it is having?
- Counselor: Crack always affects people. Tell me about the effect it has on you.
- You: It makes me concentrate better, it gives me more confidence, and I am super popular. I want to keep it that way.
- Counselor: I can assure you that crack is not making you more popular. Give it time, and it will take you down a path of self-destruction.
- You: You don't know me! How can you say any of that?
- Counselor: Because I know, Phoenix. I know.
- You: I really don't care what you think. I never wanted to come here in the first place.
- Counselor: You seem so full of resentment. What is making you this way?
- You: You are!
- Counselor: That is not true. You just don't want to take ownership of the problem that you have developed.
- You: I have not developed a problem. Well, I do have a problem, and it's called my mother. If she got off my back, everything would be okay.
- Counselor: You want to blame your mother for your crack use?
- You: Since you put it that way, I would have to say yes. Her, my dad, and my younger sister. They all give me more than enough reason to want to use even more crack than I use.

(Continued)

(Continued)

- Counselor: You believe it is their fault that you use crack at all?
- You: Not entirely but they certainly don't help any either. They stress me out, and I am tired of it.
- Counselor: It sounds like your family may well be having a negative effect on you.
- You: Yeah. Maybe you are beginning to understand me.

From the Client's Perspective

1. How would you feel if you were being told so early in this first session that you are in denial and that it is not what is making you more popular?
2. What is missing for you in this dialogue?
3. What would you find more helpful from a counselor in this scenario?

From the Counselor's Perspective

1. What is interfering with developing a working alliance?
2. Going back to the Common Counseling Mistakes list in Chapter 6, which mistakes is the counselor making with Phoenix?
3. What advantages and disadvantages does it have in this scenario to provide interpretations based on such limited understanding of Phoenix?

Background Information

The United Nations reported that 271 million people worldwide between the ages of 15 and 64 (about 5.5% of the world's population) used a psychoactive drug in 2017. About 35 million individuals suffer from a diagnosable drug use disorder. Approximately 585,000 people died from drug use in 2017 globally (United Nations Office on Drugs and Crime, 2019), compared to 450,000 in 2015 (United Nations Office on Drugs and Crime, 2018).At least two thirds of the deaths in 2017 were due to opioids (United Nations Office on Drugs and Crime, 2019).

Although the legal use of opiates began during the American Revolutionary War (1775–1783), the recognition of uncontrolled and illegal use of addictive drugs in America is a problem that dates back only to the mid-19th century (Kandall, 2010). Physicians had a limited number of medications that they could prescribe, and opiates became the mainstay of their pharmaceutical repertoire (Kandall, 2010). Recreational use of opium coincided. A dramatic increase in cocaine use began toward the end of the 19th century. Although it was often viewed that addiction was a men's issue, between two thirds and three quarters of opium-addicted individuals were women as opium was considered the treatment of choice for "female problems" (Kandall, 2010). Cocaine was also frequently prescribed to both men and women. It was only in 1914 that President Wilson criminalized the nonmedical use of opiates and cocaine (Heyman & Mims, 2017). Before then, one could access these drugs at a nearby pharmacy or order them via mail from Sears, Roebuck and Company (Heyman & Mims, 2017). Alcohol Prohibition occurred from 1920 to 1933, and it did reduce drinking in alcoholics, perhaps mostly because of the increased cost, the risk of arrest, and effort required to obtain it (Heyman & Mims, 2017).

Substance abuse and addiction remain a substantial issue for many Americans. The National Survey of Drug Use and Health (National Institute on Drug Abuse [NIDA], 2017) is conducted annually. For example, for those between ages 18 and 25, the lifetime and past-year prevalence for the use of illicit drugs in 2016 was 56.30% and 37.70%, respectively. Disconcerting is the percentage of children (ages 12–17) who have used illegal drugs: prevalence for lifetime and past-year use is 23.0% and 15.80%, respectively (National Institute on Drug Abuse, 2017).

Illicit drug use increased in the United States between 2002 and 2013. In 2013, 24.6 million Americans aged 12 or older (9.4% of the population) had used an illicit drug in the past month, whereas, in 2002, the percentage was 8.3% (NIDA, 2015b). This percentage increase is mostly due to the rise in the use of marijuana. Nonetheless, it is estimated that 8%–10% of people 12 years of age or older in the United States are addicted to either alcohol or other drugs. This amounts to 20–22 million American children and adults (Volkow, Koob, & McLellan, 2016). The cost to the nation is enormous: a loss of more than $700 billion annually attributed to crime, lost or diminished work productivity, and healthcare (Volkow et al., 2016).

Alaskan Natives and American Indians experience some of the highest rates of drug dependence. It is believed that intergenerational trauma and grief resulting from treatment by White settlers are significant contributors to addictive disorders (Morgan & Freeman, 2009). Although stimulants remain highly controlled substances today in the United States, the Native American Church of North America is legally allowed to use mescaline and peyote (note that mescaline is a hallucinogen found within the peyote cactus) during its formal ceremonies (Csiernik, 2016).

The war on drugs in the United States that began with Richard Nixon in 1971 has *not* achieved its goal of drug use prevention (Bowen & Redmond, 2016; Werb, 2018). "The cost of drugs remains low and drugs remain widely available" (Cooper, 2015, p. 1188). Although anti-drug public service announcements have been a visible approach to deterring youth, such interventions are generally ineffective. The emphasis on fear-based deterrence, in fact, has increased drug use among youth (Werb, 2018).

The war on drugs has primarily focused on punitive approaches to drug control, which in turn have led to high incarceration rates that have affected especially low-income people of color (Bowen & Redmond, 2016). Nearly half of U.S. federal prisoners are imprisoned for drug offenses, and arrest rates for drug charges of African Americans are 2.8–5.5 times greater than the rates for White adults (Bowen & Redmond, 2016). Raids on crack houses and crackdowns have a minimal effect on reducing the availability of drugs, they may displace drug activity to other areas, and they increase drug-related violence and risk of HIV transmission (Cooper, 2015).

Increasingly other countries are adopting drug policies having a greater emphasis on harm reduction and human rights (Rehn-Mendoza, 2016). In this regard, Portugal has approved a highly controversial approach: The country decriminalized all substances in 2001. The possession of small amounts of drugs is handled through a committee staffed with social workers and other professionals who recommend treatment, community service, attendance at a drug education program, or fines. Portugal currently boasts one of the lowest rates of drug use in Europe (Bowen & Redmond, 2016; Mistral, 2016). The country has also decreased the number of new HIV cases through decriminalizing drugs (Earleywine, 2016).

When caffeine and tobacco are included, most people in the world use at least one psychoactive substance (Kosten, Newton, De La Garza, & Haile, 2014). Both drugs remain commonplace throughout the United States. Alcohol is also commonly consumed throughout the world, but, despite the known health consequences that frequently result from excessive alcohol and tobacco use over a prolonged period (Sarvet & Hasin, 2016), most individuals do not develop substance-related disorders (Kosten et al., 2014). For the minority that do, "opioids and benzodiazepines remain the most commonly misused controlled drugs" (Rastegar & Fingerhood, 2016, p. 369).

Chronic use of psychoactive drugs usually creates long-term health consequences. But even in the short term, they are responsible for increasing the number of vehicular and other accidents, suicides, assaults (at least for alcohol), and overdose (opioids and alcohol). Accidents and overdose can, of course, be fatal.

The United States Drug Enforcement Administration (DEA, n.d.) classifies a drug (i.e., Schedule I, II, III, IV, or V) depending on its acceptable medical applications and its abuse or dependency potential. Schedule I drugs are those that have no currently accepted medical use and have a high potential for abuse and/or dependency. Drugs at this highest level include heroin, lysergic acid diethylamide (LSD), 3,4-methylenedioxymethamphetamine (ecstasy), methaqualone, peyote, and marijuana (cannabis). Lobbyists are continuing their efforts to get cannabis reclassified, but the DEA has consistently rejected the idea that cannabis may have medicinal properties.

Schedule II drugs also have a high potential for abuse and can potentially create psychological or physical dependence. Consequently, although at a lower level than a Schedule I drug, these drugs are also considered dangerous. Examples include cocaine, methamphetamine, methadone, hydromorphone (Dilaudid), meperidine (Demerol), oxycodone (OxyContin), fentanyl, Dexedrine, Adderall, Ritalin, and some combination drugs with less than 15 milligrams of hydrocodone per dosage unit (Vicodin).

Schedule III drugs have a moderate to low potential for physical and psychological dependence. Examples include ketamine, anabolic steroids, testosterone, and products that contain less than 90 milligrams of codeine per dosage unit (Tylenol with codeine). Schedule IV drugs have a low potential for abuse and also a low risk of dependence. Examples include Xanax, Soma, Darvon, Darvocet, Valium, Ativan, Talwin, Ambien, and Tramadol. Schedule V drugs have a lower potential for abuse and include preparations containing small amounts of certain narcotics (note that the DEA defines *narcotics* as drugs that contain opium, opium derivatives, and their semisynthetic substitutes; see https://www.dea.gov/sites/default/files/2018-06/drug_of_abuse.pdf). Examples include Lomotil, Motofen, Lyrica, Parepectolin, and cough preparations containing less than 200 milligrams of codeine or per 100 milliliters (i.e., Robitussin AC).

Although psychoactive drugs can be loosely categorized into three main groups (i.e., depressants, stimulants, and hallucinogens; Bedendo, Andrade, & Noto, 2016), this chapter will use several additional categories, including stimulants (including cocaine/crack), depressants and sedative-hypnotics, hallucinogens (i.e., psychedelics), and inhalants. Prescription and over-the-counter medications and club drugs will also be briefly mentioned. An interesting fact regarding tolerance is that, once it develops, "it applies to all drugs in the same class" (Mistral, 2016).

Homeostasis refers to mechanisms within the body and its cells to both attain or re-establish a state of equilibrium. Like Newton's law, "for every action, there is an equal and opposite reaction," a psychoactive drug's effect on the body is comparable. Drugs that artificially stimulate the body create withdrawal effects that are close to the opposite reaction (i.e., the body experiences physical depression effects such as tiredness, exhaustion, and lethargy). On the other hand, drugs that physically depress the body create withdrawal effects that are also its opposite (i.e., the body experiences stimulation effects such as agitation, anxiety, and excitability). Keep this in mind as you learn about withdrawal effects.

Addiction is most commonly associated with (a) alcohol, (b) depressants and sedative-hypnotics including barbiturates (e.g., Seconal and Tuinal) and benzodiazepines (e.g., Valium and Librium), (c) opium, opioids, and morphine derivatives (e.g., heroin, morphine, codeine, Percodan, Demerol, and methadone), (d) stimulants (e.g., methamphetamine and cocaine), and (e) hallucinogens (LSD, PCP, and marijuana) (Milkman & Sunderwirth, 2010). These drugs are often used in various combinations. Alcoholism has a high rate of co-occurrence with nicotine addiction, for example (Milkman & Sunderwirth, 2010).

The category of *opium, opioids, and morphine derivatives* was included in the previous chapter. Previous chapters have also already covered *alcohol, cannabis*, and *nicotine addiction*. Not all drugs in each category are included in this chapter: Only the most well-known are noted. Besides the information provided here, the National Institute on Drug Abuse is an excellent and reliable source of detailed information about drugs and their effects (https://www.drugabuse.gov/drugs-abuse). Here we begin with stimulants.

Stimulants

Stimulants are drugs that speed up the body's nervous system, thereby creating a feeling of energy. They're also referred to as "uppers" because they make people feel very awake. They have an opposite effect compared with depressants. Some stimulants create dopamine (DA) surges that reach unstoppable heights, which include such drugs as cocaine/crack, amphetamines (especially crystal meth), and ecstasy (Tarman & Werdell, 2014). The flip side is that stimulant use leads to alterations in both presynaptic and postsynaptic DA function (Ashok, Mizuno, Volkow, & Howes, 2017).

The primary examples of stimulants include drugs used in the treatment of attention deficit hyperactivity disorder (ADHD) (e.g., Adderall, Ritalin, Vyvanse, Cylert), methamphetamines (crystal meth), amphetamines, methylenedioxymethamphetamine (MDMA; ecstasy), and cocaine/crack. Individuals who prefer stimulants tend to have higher tendencies for sensation-seeking, risk-taking, impulsiveness, and disinhibition (Milkman & Sunderwirth, 2010). Some people intoxicated on amphetamines become aggressive, and commission of murders and other violent offenses sometimes occurs (McKetin et al., 2014; Smith, 2013).

Timko, Moos, and Finney (2016) provided an overview of three studies that tracked the trajectories of drug users. In a study by Kertesz et al. (2012), 4301 men and women were followed for 18 years (from young adulthood to middle age) regarding their cocaine, amphetamine, and opioid use. The trajectories included nonusers (86%), early occasional users (8%), persistent occasional users (4%), and early frequent/later occasional users (3%). More than one third continued using illegal drugs into middle age. In a review of several studies with follow-up periods ranging from 3 to 33 years, remission for amphetamine users was 45%, opioid users 22%, and cocaine users 14% (Calabria et al., 2010). In a representative American study that focused on alcohol, cannabis, or cocaine dependence, remission was 91% for alcohol, 97% for cannabis, and 99% for cocaine dependence (Lopez-Quintero et al., 2010). The review by Timko et al. confirmed that the chronic, progressive course of substance use disorders (SUDs) is not inevitable.

Cocaine/crack.

Cocaine is derived from the *Erythroxylum coca* plant. It was used over 5000 years ago in religious ceremonies among ancient civilizations of South America. After Albert Niemann purified it into cocaine in 1860, it was used in various medicines and the original recipe for a new soft drink introduced in 1886: Coca-Cola (Beech & Sinha, 2011). Despite the passage of the Harrison Narcotics Tax Act in 1914, cocaine products continued to be sold over-the-counter in the United States until 1916 (Beech & Sinha, 2011).

Cocaine acts on the central nervous system (CNS) and creates elevated mood, increased activity, mental alertness, and decreased appetite. These effects are similar to those of adrenaline, which is produced naturally in the body. Many users report feeling increases in self-confidence and self-esteem, increased sex drive, improved concentration, talkativeness, and rapid respiration. Because cocaine is a vasoconstrictor and raises body temperature and heart rate, it increases the risk of stroke. High doses can also cause cardiac arrhythmia, hypothermia, seizures, and—unlike any of the other stimulants, respiratory depression. Aspiration caused by vomiting can be fatal. Larger doses can also create bizarre, erratic, paranoiac, and occasionally violent behavior (Csiernik, 2016).

Cocaine is also known as benzoylmethylecgonine or "coke." Cocaine can be snorted, freebased, ingested orally, "plugged" (inserted anally), or injected (injecting is the most intense). When snorted, cocaine reaches the brain and produces euphoria within 3–5 min. When injected, it enters the brain within 15–30 seconds.

Freebase refers to freeing the base from the salt form in which the drug is naturally found.

Crack is cocaine that has been freebased, resulting in its base form. Although cocaine powder is water-soluble, crack is not water-soluble and therefore cannot be eaten or snorted. It must be smoked to feel its effects. Crack delivers a short but intense high to smokers that can be felt within 8 seconds (Csiernik, 2016), and, because of this, it is the most addictive form of cocaine. In purer forms, crack rocks look like jagged nuggets that are off-white with a density slightly higher than candle wax. Crack sold on the streets, however, may be cut with other substances such as levamisole, a medication used to treat parasitic worm infections.

Continued use of cocaine creates dependency in the body, which comes to rely on it to maintain homeostasis. When habitual users stop using the drug, they lose the ability to feel pleasant emotions and pleasurable sensations from food, water, and sex (Csiernik, 2016). This inability to experience pleasure is called *anhedonia*. Chronic cocaine use can lead to depletion of DA in the brain, which results in serious depression, which in turn sometimes leads to suicide (Smith, 2013). Cocaine addiction is characterized by compulsive drug-seeking and frequent relapses (Beech & Sinha, 2011).

Frequent users of cocaine can experience depressant effects such as social withdrawal, sadness, decreased blood pressure, substantially lowered heart rate, and diminished psychomotor activity. Cocaine creates an anxiety disorder in some individuals, and these symptoms might not relent following cessation of use. It can also induce delirium, which refers to an acute disturbance in consciousness and cognition. Severe intoxication from cocaine might lead to seizures, irregular heartbeat, extremely high fever, and vasoconstriction that can lead to myocardial infarction, stroke, and possibly death (Beech & Sinha, 2011).

Regular users might also experience insomnia and agitation with abstinence. Cocaine use often creates chest pain, which is a frequent reason for emergency room visits (Rastegar & Fingerhood, 2016). Chronic use of cocaine or methamphetamine is associated with substantial cognitive impairments, particularly in attention, working memory, and response inhibition (Sofuoglu & Forray, 2014).

Taking cocaine and alcohol together creates interaction effects. In fact, taking the two drugs together creates a different chemical (i.e., cocaethylene) that does not otherwise exist if either drug is taken alone. Cocaethylene carries an 18- to 25-fold increase over cocaine alone in creating the risk of immediate death. Cocaine use often increases while individuals are in their late 20s and early 30s before declining (Earleywine, 2016).

In 2016, adults aged 26 years and older had the highest lifetime and past-year prevalence rates for cocaine use in the United States which were 16.60% and 1.30%, respectively. For crack, prevalence was 4.10% and 0.30%, respectively. For children (ages 12–17), cocaine prevalence was 0.90% and 0.50%, respectively; crack prevalence was 0.10% and 0.00%, respectively (National Institute on Drug Abuse, 2017).

Methamphetamine.

Methamphetamine was initially referred to as speed, and it has become a public health concern. It is also known by the names ice and glass. Although it enjoyed popularity in the 1970s, the heavy toll it took on the body made relatively common usage short-lived. However, it re-emerged as part of the rave scene. Some know it as the "poor man's cocaine" (Csiernik, 2016, p. 144). It is the most potent amphetamine (Smith, 2013).

The freebase version of methamphetamine (meth) is an oily liquid, which the body cannot absorb. The only way a user can get high from it is to smoke it. Crystal meth, on the other hand, has been converted to a water-soluble salt, and therefore it can be smoked, snorted, injected, or ingested orally, and rarely anally. The acute effects from meth generally last between 6 and 12 hours (Csiernik,

2016). Although regular users experience withdrawal symptoms upon cessation, there is not a clear-cut observable syndrome as can be found with opioids, sedatives, or alcohol withdrawal (Rastegar & Fingerhood, 2016). Many street dwellers report that using meth makes their lives more livable, at least in the short term. It is difficult to sleep on the street, and one can grow tired from hunger. Meth provides for all three: it keeps the user awake, it suppresses appetite, and it gives boundless energy (Maté, 2008).

It is often difficult for providers-in-training to understand the experiences of someone with an addiction. The following passages, composites adapted from individual stories found online, are intended to provide an "insider's" perspective on cocaine use. The effects from drugs are subjective; these portrayals are not indicative of every experience with the drug. The composites are adapted from https://www.quora.com/What-does-a-cocaine-high-feel-like.

Getting High on Snorted Cocaine

I was disappointed. There's nothing a line of cocaine could do for me that a cup of coffee couldn't. The effects were VERY similar to caffeine except that too much caffeine makes you feel jittery, but, with cocaine, you don't know when you've overdone it. Anywhere the coke touches become numb as well as most of the front center of your face. You don't know when to stop. You become talkative while making idiotic debates and conversations, and you become unable to criticize yourself. To be honest, I felt more euphoric during some concerts and video game sessions. As an alternative to trying cocaine, I might recommend that you rub some Orajel in your mouth and drink a Red Bull. It will be close enough! It is nothing special at all and overhyped as crap. I won't do it again because it isn't worth it.

Getting High on Injected Cocaine

After you inject cocaine, the first thing you feel is a cool, minty-like chill shoot down your spine and through your body. You can suddenly taste and smell the coke, and then you feel this incredible rush of pleasure that beats even an orgasm. Your pupils instantly dilate, and you feel a slight ringing in your ears that builds to a deafening roar but then fades gradually. It becomes immediately apparent why so many people get addicted to it. Even if your life was in ruins and you had no hope for the future, at that moment you will feel unbelievably happy, content, and optimistic. But that quickly ends after 20 to 30 minutes. You are going to want another hit to do it again.

Getting High From Smoking Crack

Smoking crack is a little different from injecting cocaine. You still get the same intense feeling of pleasure, but, because a rush is more gradual, you have more control over how much you smoke. Consequently, you are less likely to overdose accidentally. Depending on several factors, the comedown can be mildly annoying to quite awful. You will feel physically worn out, possibly depressed and anxious, but mostly wishing you could have another hit.

It is often difficult for providers-in-training to understand the experiences of someone with an addiction. The following passages, a composite adapted from individual stories found online, are intended to provide an "insider's" perspective on methamphetamine use. The effects from drugs are subjective; this portrayal is not indicative of every experience with the drug. The composite was adapted from http://bluelight.org/vb/threads/546582-What-was-your-first-time-trying-meth-like, http://www.bluelight.org/vb/threads/590624-Cocaine-vs-Meth, and sites no longer available.

Getting High on Crystal Meth

My first time trying meth, I just loved it! This drug is UNBELIEVABLY good. I'm not going to deny that. It was amazing, like heaven. The euphoria I felt was like nothing else. It feels like a particular part of your brain is burning hot with goodness. The high can go on for 6 or 7 hours. It made me incredibly horny and sexy.

The comedown is potentially horrendous. It kept me awake all night. Oh, and don't bother trying it unless you're happy to risk your health and your ability to make good decisions. As soon as you're out, you want more. I can understand people wanting more at ANY cost! But over time, it soon turned to hell, and I never got that high like my first time again. Meth brought me down harder and faster, and I've done all the other drugs before, but nothing else has destroyed my life quite like meth has.

Crystal Meth High Compared to a Cocaine High

I much prefer meth over cocaine due to the length of action, the intensity of euphoria, and the fact that I don't have to be redosing every half hour to an hour. Also, cocaine tends to cause much more anxiety than meth does, but I attribute this to the fact that, in me, after about 15–20 minutes I start to come down, which can last as long as the high can. Then you spend the rest of the time looking for more coke (having an eager or intense desire/craving is colloquially called "jonesing"). Meth, on the other hand, makes me feel awesome and super horny. Coke is like trying to watch a program on an airport TV, but meth is like having your own TV. But the power goes out if you keep doing meth all the time.

[For others] I prefer coke over meth. Although meth provides euphoria, it is short-lived. Cocaine keeps delivering euphoria and meth makes you feel "all sped out." Meth will keep you awake for days. You might feel so spun that you can only walk at a running pace. There is something evil about meth in that the drug has a weird presence on people. Although meth provides a good to amazing high, the comedown afterward is terrible. Try coming off a 7-day meth binge! Although cocaine is a plant derivative, meth is made by people.

Meth also increases and intensifies a person's sex drive and enhances the perception of sexual pleasure. The drug can release up to 12 times as much DA in the CNS compared to eating a favorite food, an effect, however, that dissipates with as little as 6 months of regular usage (Csiernik, 2016).

Meth use can create serious side effects, including rapid and irregular heartbeat, heart palpitations, increased blood pressure, strokes, wakefulness, insomnia, convulsions, tremors, confusion, anxiety, aggressiveness, hyperactivity, delusions of grandeur, paranoia as well as kidney, lung, and liver disorders. The meth-addicted individual experiences intense cravings and severe depression if unable to resume using (Milkman & Sunderwirth, 2010). "The usual aftermath of abusing methamphetamine is incredible hardship and suffering (Milkman & Sunderwirth, 2010, p. 172). Methamphetamine use often decreases with time from adolescence onward (Earleywine, 2016).

In 2016, adults aged 26 years and older had the highest lifetime and past-year prevalence rates for meth use in the United States, which were 6.40% and 0.60%, respectively. For children (ages 12–17), prevalence was 0.30% and 0.10%, respectively (National Institute on Drug Abuse, 2017).

Methylenedioxyamphetamine (MDA), methylenedioxymethamphetamine (MDMA; "Ecstasy"), and DOM.

MDA is often called the "love drug" (Csiernik, 2016). Low doses of MDA (60–150 mg) reportedly produce a feeling of peacefulness and emotional connectedness with others. Use of MDA has diminished with the emergence and popularity of MDMA. Although the effects of MDA and MDMA are similar, MDMA is generally milder, and its effects do not last as long (Csiernik, 2016). Both drugs are stimulants, but they also have hallucinogenic properties. Both drugs are used mostly for their hallucinogenic effect of inducing feelings of empathy. Drugs that induce empathy are referred to as *entactogens* or *empathogens* (Rastegar & Fingerhood, 2016).

MDA has more hallucinogenic effects than MDMA, but it is considered less of an empathogen. MDA is also considered more toxic than MDMA, and its effects persist for 6–10 hours. Both drugs are known as serotonin-norepinephrine-dopamine releasing agents. MDA and MDMA create euphoria, a feeling of well-being, and decreased appetite. They also cause erectile dysfunction, muscle tension (often people on these drugs grind their teeth), short-term memory loss, headaches, and, upon cessation, mild depression that can last up to a week. MDMA also causes sleep difficulties, anxiety, agitation, hypertension, perspiration, loss of appetite, heart palpitations, drug cravings, and impulsiveness (Milkman & Sunderwirth, 2010).

MDMA, commonly referred to as "ecstasy," is also referred to as a love drug. The German pharmaceutical company Merck first manufactured it in 1912 (Csiernik, 2016). MDMA is viewed as the most popular club drug among youth (Milkman & Sunderwirth, 2010).

"Molly" is a current slang term for the drug, and some believe it to be a pure form of MDMA. Given that it is illegal, however, purity is a misnomer. Molly often consists of harsher substances, typically paramethoxymethamphetamine (PMMA; Csiernik, 2016). PMMA is also a hallucinogenic stimulant.

DOM, commonly called "STP" on the streets, is chemically similar to mescaline, amphetamines, and LSD. It often led to nonfatal overdoses in the late 1960s. DOM was created initially as a treatment for schizophrenia in 1994. It is considered more potent than mescaline but less potent than LSD at the same dosage (Csiernik, 2016).

In 2016, adults aged 18–25 had the highest lifetime and past-year prevalence rates for MDMA use in the United States, which were 11.60% and 3.50%, respectively. For children (ages 12–17), prevalence was 1.20% and 0.70%, respectively (National Institute on Drug Abuse, 2017).

It is often difficult for providers-in-training to understand the experiences of someone with an addiction. The following passages, a composite adapted from individual stories found online, are intended to provide an "insider's" perspective on MDMA use. The effects from drugs are subjective; this portrayal is not indicative of every experience with the drug. The composite was adapted from http://bluelight.org/vb/threads/546582-What-was-your-first-time-trying-meth-like, https://www.quora.com/What-does-it-feel-like-to-take-MDMA-ecstasy, and sites no longer available.

Getting High From Ingesting MDMA

"Like a saccharine dream, a quest into the known, rediscovering innocence, a tribal feeling, a sense of community, a release, going outside the self, being fully human, being more alive than you've ever been, immersion, engagement." It's called ecstasy for a reason. Many regard the first time as one of life's great experiences. The feeling of happiness is tricky to express properly. After about 40 minutes to an hour, you find yourself needing to use the restroom. You look at yourself in the mirror, see the joy spread across your face, and think to yourself, "What a sexy person you are!" You might wonder if this is what true happiness feels like. Giddy with excitement and overflowing with newfound energy, you soar back to your friends (doing it alone might be disappointing). Minutes turn into hours as you talk about anything and everything. But you are still in charge of yourself; it's just that your neurotic filters have dropped away, allowing for natural self-expression. You might feel warm and flushed, but it is a pleasant sensation like sitting in front of a log fire.

You enjoy the sense of touch, closeness with others, and human connection. Every inch of your skin becomes a receptacle for pleasure, but not in a sexual way. It is more altruistic than that. If music is playing, you can truly lose yourself in the beat. It's incredible how in tune you feel with the music. You'll probably want to dance. The night is simply magical, lights are mind-blowing, and time stands still. All that matters is how happy you are.

On the opposite extreme, a small event (such as someone telling you that your increased talkativeness is slightly annoying) may cause you to sink into great despair. The next day, you might feel spacy, depressed, jittery, tired, or sluggish, but it depends on the person. You do not want to do too much of it.

Crystal Meth High Compared to an MDMA High

Comparing meth to MDMA, meth is like a "F%#K YEAH!" total rush kind of feeling and MDMA is more like an "OH MY GOD I LOVE EVERYTHING!" feeling. Although meth is the "I want to do everything in the entire world right NOW" sort of drug, MDMA is the "I want to love everything, touch everything, express my feelings to everyone" sort of drug. Although meth is more fun for getting high, MDMA is more fun for connecting with friends or making new DEEP friends. The MDMA high is more euphoric and sociable than meth. The MDMA high feels more druggish, but the meth high gives you more energy, you can concentrate more, you feel more confident, and you feel more awake. With meth, though, the environment doesn't look, sound, or feel any different.

Khat and "bath salts."

Khat is a flowering plant (i.e., *Catha edulis*) that contains the alkaloid cathinone, which is the amphetamine-like stimulant that causes excitement, diminished appetite, and euphoria. In some parts of Yemen and East Africa, Khat is used by 85% of adult males. Use of the plant is considered a fundamental aspect of social and cultural traditions in these countries (Csiernik, 2016).

"Bath salts" in the drug world are not used to create a relaxing bath. Instead, they are one of several designer drugs or legal highs that emerged in the 21st century. The name comes from instances whereby these drugs were sold disguised as true bath salts. These drugs can be ingested, snorted, smoked, or injected. The primary motive for developing these drugs was to create potent stimulants and hallucinogens that would avoid legislation (Csiernik, 2016). These substances include several different compounds such as "synthetic cannabinoids, synthetic cathinones, and piperazines, and traditional plant-based psychoactive substances, such as khat (*Catha edulis*), kratom (*Mitragyna speciosa*), and *Salvia divinorum*" (Csiernik, 2016, p. 150). The number of calls to poison centers regarding bath salts in the United States rose from 304 in 2010 to 6138 in 2011 but then decreased to 2697 in 2012, 998 in 2013, 587 in 2014, and 522 in 2015 (American Association of Poison Control Centers, 2015). Users of bath salts report experiencing headaches, heart palpitations, nausea, cold fingers, hallucinations, paranoia, panic attacks, violent behavior, heart attacks, and a long list of other adverse effects (see drugabuse.com for an extensive list).

Intoxication from bath salts has also resulted in death (National Institute on Drug Abuse, 2018c). Hundreds of pills sold as Molly capsules (remember Molly is supposed to be pure MDMA) in Florida have contained bath salts (National Institute on Drug Abuse, 2018d).

Depressants (Including Sedative-Hypnotics)

Alcohol is the best-known depressant, but there are many drugs in this class. *Sedative-hypnotics* are depressants that lower anxiety and induce sleep, and these began with the introduction of bromides in 1826. The U.S. National Survey on Drug Use and Health divides these drugs into two arbitrary categories: tranquilizers and sedatives (Rastegar & Fingerhood, 2016).

Bromides were followed by the first barbiturate in 1903 called barbital, then chloral hydrate in 1932, and meprobamate in 1955. Barbiturates are derived from barbituric acid. They are classified according to duration: (a) short-acting are used to create anesthesia, (b) intermediate-acting are oral sedatives used for sedation and sleep, and (c) long-acting are orally administered as anticonvulsants (Rastegar & Fingerhood, 2016). There are other sedative-hypnotics that have a high abuse potential, including Quaalude, chloral hydrate, and meprobamate (Smith, 2013).

Benzodiazepines quickly replaced barbiturates as the most prescribed sedative-hypnotics because they diminished anxiety and were less sedating and less risky for respiratory depression. Nonetheless, the literature regarding medical complications resulting from sedative-hypnotics is mostly focused on the use of benzodiazepines, the most serious of which include cognitive impairment and accidental injury (Rastegar & Fingerhood, 2016).

The first benzodiazepine was chlordiazepoxide (Librium), which hit the market in 1961. Benzodiazepines are also classified according to three groups: (a) those containing active metabolites (e.g., chlordiazepoxide, diazepam, flurazepam, flunitrazepam, clorazepate), (b) those which do not create active metabolites (e.g., Lorazepam, oxazepam), and (c) those which create active metabolites but have little clinical activity (e.g., alprazolam, triazolam) (Rastegar & Fingerhood, 2016).

Rohypnol and gamma-hydroxybutyrate (GHB) are depressants. Rohypnol, an intermediate-acting benzodiazepine, is a legally prescribed drug in numerous countries but not in the United States. It has become known as a "date rape drug" because it creates both sedation and amnesia. As a date rape drug, it has been added unknowingly to the drinks of victims often at a bar or party. The victims have limited or no memory of the actual assault. The sedative effects of Rohypnol are seven to 10 times stronger than Valium. Its effects appear 15–20 min after administration and typically last between 4 and 6 hours (Milkman & Sunderwirth, 2010).

GHB is the active agent in a prescription medication for narcolepsy called Xyrem (i.e., sodium oxybate). GHB is an odorless, colorless drug that can be combined with alcohol and given to unsuspecting victims before a sexual assault because of its sedative effects and its ability to create amnesia in some individuals. Besides its illegal use as a date rape drug, it is also commonly used as a club drug at raves (Rastegar & Fingerhood, 2016). It produces its clinical effects between 15 and 30 min after oral ingestion. Although the drug initially produces euphoria, this is followed by dizziness, hypersalivation, and drowsiness. More severe side effects may include nausea, seizures, unconsciousness, severe respiratory depression, and coma (Milkman & Sunderwirth, 2010).

In 2016, the highest past-year prevalence rate for tranquilizer use in the United States was among adults aged 18–25, which was 5.40%. For children (ages 12–17), prevalence was 1.70%. The highest past-year prevalence rate for sedative use in the United States was among adults aged 18–25, which was 0.70%. For children (ages 12–17), prevalence was 0.40% (National Institute on Drug Abuse, 2017).

It is often difficult for providers-in-training to understand the experiences of someone with an addiction. The following passage, a composite adapted from individual stories found online, is intended to provide an "insider's" perspective on GHB use. The effects from drugs are subjective; this portrayal is not indicative of every experience with the drug. The composite was adapted from https://www.reddit.com/r/Drugs/comments/1fsis9/from_experience_what_was_ghb_like/, https://www.quora.com/Whats-it-like-to-be-on-GHB, and http://bluelight.org/vb/archive/index.php/t-529494.html.

Getting High on GHB

After being handed a drink, this proved to be my last drink of the night, and while I'd had a couple earlier, it was nowhere near enough to cause what happened next. The last thing I remember distinctly was talking with this girl and a few others while I finished my drink. The next memory I have—well, imagine if your eyes were coated in molasses, everything dark and thick and slow-moving, and the light, what little I could see, was tinged this burnt amber hue. I was stumbling through an outdoor area filled with stools made of cut trees. All the voices were hard to hear and slurred together. I remember finally making it past the crowds of people, and then time slipped again. When I finally started to become aware of my surroundings again, it was just after dawn, and I was sitting on some steps that led to nowhere, and my car was in front of me where I'd parked it last night, thankfully. I looked around for my glasses, but couldn't find them anywhere. Finally, I decided to drive home without them—highly illegal given my license requirements, but I still couldn't reach anyone, and there was absolutely nobody on the streets. The fact that any of those things could have happened quite easily without me knowing—that's terror.

It's like drinking without the drag of alcohol, if done correctly you will not have ANY hangover on GHB, and sexual performance and experience will be heightened for both men and women. It's like MDMA but less about love and more about having sex. It's a little euphoric but not like ecstasy. Start at a low dose: the difference between a low dose and a higher one is whether you want to be lying in a pool of your vomit. GHB can be an enjoyable experience—but it can also be a f#*king nightmare of a drug!

If there was ever a drug to be scared of, this is it. Of all the drugs I've seen people f#*ked up on, nothing even comes close to f#*king people up as much as GHB. Recently, I saw a guy at a major event in my area who had the telltale sign. . . drooling on himself. Stay the hell away from G. There are plenty other fun drugs to try.

I am an experienced GHB user. GHB does indeed knock you into a profound sleep that you can entirely not wake up from or be wakened up from. The problem is, dosing is very difficult for GHB. The recreational dose is dangerously close to the overdose of GHB. GHB is a downer when combined with another depressant like alcohol; it will knock you out very quickly, and this is very dangerous: You may stop breathing, vomit, or suffocate on your tongue.

Hallucinogens (Psychedelics)

PERSONAL REFLECTION

This memory riveted in my head forever. Mom took me to the doctor's office when I was 13 for asthma. Dr. Blackstock was on the fourth floor, and, after a few minutes of sitting in his waiting room, I heard the most ear-piercing and harrowing screaming that I have ever heard in my life. Scared, I sat there, unsure what to do. Only my fear got worse as the sound got closer. Like something out of the worst horror movie, the screaming-turned-screeching echoed at what felt like 180 decibels (e.g., a rocket launch) as my doctor's office opened. Four men, each gripping an appendage of a young blonde woman fighting to flee from her own demons, entered. A few minutes later, the four men, still clutching the screaming woman, left while we all sat in the doctor's office that day, looking pale as ghosts.

When it was my turn to see Dr. Blackstock, I asked him what happened. He told me the woman had dropped too much LSD and he didn't know what to do, so he sent her together with her latched-on friends to the hospital. That was 1969. Man, did I know the drug that I would never, ever take in my life? As the years passed, I tried many other drugs, but never that one.

It came to be known as the drug to "turn on, tune in, and drop out" to, but I was never going to trust these words epitomized from the famous Harvard professor of psychology whom Richard Nixon once described as "the most dangerous man in America." Dr. Timothy Leary died, but the drug he preached about lives on.

I first became aware of PCP while I received training with police officers and correctional officers. I was a child and youth care worker, and I was supposed to be notified in advance that I was not eligible to participate, but no one informed me, and they let me stay for this 40-hour intensive training in 1979. The martial arts expert who taught the LAPD told us that, if someone were high on PCP and were also agitated and dangerous, an officer had only two choices: shoot to kill or apply the sleeper hold if possible. Individuals high on PCP in handcuffs, for example, were known to pull their hands out of handcuffs, leaving most of their skin behind. I know this sounds horrifying, but it's true. As addiction counselors, we have our hands full. We have no idea what law enforcement has to deal with, often on a daily basis.

A resurgence of interest in serotonergic hallucinogens (e.g., LSD, psilocybin, and mescaline) is occurring in the medical and psychological fields. Reiche et al. (2018) completed their systematic review and concluded that individuals with life-threatening diseases who experience symptoms of depression and anxiety benefit from administration of serotonergic hallucinogens. LSD has been used to successfully treat alcoholism "by compressing years of psychotherapy into a single, intensive, self-reflective session" (Dyck, 2015, p. 1079).

On May 5, 1953, the novelist Aldous Huxley dissolved four tenths of a gram of mescaline in water and drank it. He was under the direct supervision of his psychiatrist, Humphry Osmond. Dr. Osmond coined the term "psychedelic." Although his research was showing positive results for using LSD as a treatment for alcoholism, his work was abruptly halted in the following decade because of the backlash against the hippie counterculture (Costandi, 2014).

Johansen and Krebs (2015) used a dataset comprising 135,095 randomly selected U.S. adults, which included 19,299 psychedelic users, and compared associations between psychedelic use in mental health. They failed to find evidence that serotonergic hallucinogens create a risk factor for mental health problems. They further stated that serotonergic hallucinogens are not known to harm the brain or other body organs or lead to compulsive use. Nesvag, Bramness, and Ystrom (2015) reran the analysis from Johansen and Krebs using different statistics and also concluded that the use of serotonergic hallucinogens was not linked to mental health problems or suicidal behavior. In effect, the evidence is building that these particular hallucinogens may have therapeutic efficacy (Halberstadt, 2015).

But not every researcher agrees. Larsen (2017), who reviewed the treatment outcomes from using LSD with 151 patients in Denmark, remained skeptical. Using a retrospective design, Larsen found that 52 patients improved and 48 patients worsened with the LSD treatment. Larsen concluded that rigorous designs need to clear these drugs of having potential harms. Furthermore, Pechnick, Cunningham, and Danovitch (2014) reported that, in some cases, anxiety and depression continue for atypically long periods following hallucinogen use, and there is a link between usage and suicide attempts.

Hallucinogens, which are now also referred to as psychedelics, are the complex and diverse class of drugs that cause hallucinations, which are profound distortions in the perception of reality. Individuals under the influence may report rapid and intense emotional swings, seeing images, hearing sounds, and feeling sensations that appear real but are not. Hallucinogens' main effects are on thought, perception, and mood.

Milkman and Sunderwirth (2010) wrote that hallucinogens could be divided into two chemical groups known as tryptamines (e.g., LSD, DMT, and psilocybin) and phenethylamines (e.g., mescaline and MDMA). Note that MDMA was included previously in the Stimulant section. That is because MDMA is not easily classified as a stimulant, hallucinogen, or depressant. Primarily, however, it is considered a stimulant, and its hallucinogenic properties are rated as mild. Mescaline, on the other hand, is mostly viewed as a hallucinogen.

Drugs that boost serotonin levels are mostly hallucinogens (sometimes called serotonergic hallucinogens), including LSD, mescaline, methylene, ketamine, psilocybin ("magic mushrooms"), and PCP (Tarman & Werdell, 2014). The serotonergic hallucinogens are not generally associated with compulsive use, and they are viewed as having little to no dependence liability. More commonly, these drugs are used once or twice weekly, whereas daily use remains exceedingly rare (Pechnick et al., 2014).

In 2016, the highest lifetime and past-year prevalence rates for hallucinogen use in the United States were among adults aged 18–25, which were 17.20% and 6.90%, respectively. For children (ages 12–17), prevalence was 2.70% and 1.80%, respectively (National Institute on Drug Abuse, 2017).

Lysergic acid diethylamide (LSD).

Albert Hofmann discovered LSD-25 on April 16, 1943, at the Sandoz research laboratory in Switzerland. He was the first to experience an "acid trip." By the late 1960s, it was clear that some individuals became heavily involved with marijuana and LSD. Due to legal backlashes against hallucinogens, no human studies were conducted on them between 1972 and 1990. This began changing in 1990 as the FDA began approving studies on people (Milkman & Sunderwirth, 2010).

LSD is a clear or white, odorless, water-soluble material derived from lysergic acid, which itself is derived from the rye fungus. It is most commonly dissolved, diluted, and applied to paper or other material for oral ingestion (often called windowpanes or microdots). LSD is the most potent mood- and perception-altering drug known. Doses as small as 30 micrograms produce effects lasting between 6 and 12 hours (Milkman & Sunderwirth, 2010). Hallucinogenic effects vary from person to person and from one episode to another. The most common effects reported of LSD are perceptual distortions, but the effects are unpredictable and range from euphoria to sheer panic (Milkman & Sunderwirth, 2010). Because LSD and other hallucinogens target serotonin receptors, long-term effects include tolerance, and, in some cases, persistent psychosis and occasional "flashbacks." The use of LSD has been known to coincide with the onset of depression, which has suggested a possible causal link between depression and LSD use in young patients (Pechnick et al., 2014).

In 2016, the highest lifetime and past-year prevalence rates for LSD use in the United States were among adults 26 years and older, which were 8.30% and 3.40%, respectively. For children (ages 12–17), prevalence was 1.2% and 0.80%, respectively (National Institute on Drug Abuse, 2017).

Psilocybin ("magic mushrooms").

Recent research is finding that psilocybin can relieve symptoms of depression and anxiety (Carhart-Harris et al., 2018; Thomas, Malcolm, & Lastra, 2017). Preliminary studies are showing that psilocybin can help individuals experiencing alcohol and smoking addiction (de Veen, Schellekens, Verheij, & Homberg, 2017). When used under controlled clinical conditions, the drug can be used safely (de Veen et al., 2017). Recent research also has shown that higher doses of psilocybin produced substantial, significant positive changes over 6-month measures that looked at "interpersonal closeness, gratitude, life meaning/purpose, forgiveness, death transcendence, daily spiritual experiences, and religious faith and coping" (Griffiths et al., 2018, p. 49). Psilocybin has also been found useful in addressing the psychological suffering of the dying (Kelmendi, Corlett, Ranganathan, D'Souza, & Krystal, 2016). Although this research is encouraging, Thomas et al. (2017) cautioned that more robust clinical trials would be needed to secure FDA approval.

It is often difficult for providers-in-training to understand the experiences of someone with an addiction. The following passage, a composite adapted from individual stories found online, is intended to provide an "insider's" perspective on LSD use. The effects from drugs are subjective; this portrayal is not indicative of every experience with the drug. The composite was adapted from https://www.quora.com/What-does-it-feel-like-to-take-LSD-1, https://drugs-forum.com/threads/what-does-the-lsd-high-feel-like.5085/, and https://www.reddit.com/r/AskReddit/comments/1xzkr0/what_does_dropping_acid_feel_like_whats_your_best/.

Getting High on LSD

LSD drastically changes the way you think. Things that are funny tend to seem funnier. Some things become more difficult to comprehend and some things less. Drugs are tools, and tools are only as useful as their user. LSD is a nonspecific amplifier of unconscious information. It is a microscope for the human mind.

At lower dosages, the LSD experience is rather aesthetic. At midrange dosages, LSD becomes a more useful tool for exploring your psyche, including the unconscious parts. These dosages may give rise to transcendent states of consciousness, which means that one's identity, ego, or sense of self no longer exists. Some effects are different for everyone, and not everyone experiences ego death. It can feel like almost anything, depending mainly on the mindset you bring to the experience and the physical setting you have the experience in. High dosages allow for intense exploration of unconscious information. Difficult and intense experiences of spiritual and/or religious significance are to be expected. Bumpy rides into biographical exploration and transpersonal and perinatal experiences, all of which are fascinating, can occur. Transpersonal experiences can happen at the midrange for some people, but these will definitely happen for those who expect them at high dosages.

People who have scary experiences usually try to hold onto their psychological constructs. The usual normal state will come back unless you are predisposed to severe mental illness like schizophrenia, which you may trigger into existence with the use of psychedelics or cannabis.

A couple of weeks ago I took LSD with a close friend, an avid user. For the first hour, I didn't feel anything. By the time the burger arrived, I had started feeling some odd sensations: numbness and tingling in my limbs, a change in my visual perception (became kind of a "fish-eye" lens), and a change in my behavior—I started laughing a lot. What happened next was intense.

As I was eating my burger, my mouth and throat became numb, and eating became a challenge. Finishing it took a lot of effort and concentration on my part, but I was able to do it. My friend and I "decided" to go out for a walk. It was amazing outside. The weather was frigid, but my body didn't feel it. The cold was perceived as freshness, and it made me feel alive. Colors were extremely vivid—there was a full moon, and it looked amazing. The air seemed crystal clear. The stars sparkled. My friend and I weren't ourselves. We were two personalities walking around my small hometown. Sometimes I led, sometimes he did. It was amazing, pure, and meaningful. I felt a flow of profound thoughts and ideas flowing into my mind. I understood the purpose of life (as I see it). I understood people and animals. I understood art. When we got home, my girlfriend went to sleep, but I stayed up. This stage of the trip felt like the movie *Limitless*. I felt enlightened and wise, full of insights and revelations. I felt like a child seeing and exploring the world for the first time. Everything was new and amazing.

A lot of people talk about the good side of it. DO NOT underestimate it. It can be the most fantastic experience in the world, or it could go very differently. You will drive yourself mad if you try to comprehend everything that's happening. With the drop of the hat, it can go from the most spectacular feeling to feeling wholly and utterly helpless. It's sobering to realize how small and weak the human mind is. It can render you completely helpless. I ended up on the planet "You're F#*ked." Pink skies, purple mountains, and bright orange forever sand. A few painful events like invisible, razor sharp ice cream scoops cutting my flesh away until I dissolved to nothing. I now had a timeline-life review where every major event in my life came parading through like on a clothesline. Yep, f#*ked up.

PERSONAL REFLECTION

I used to think mushrooms were terrific. I only tried them five to 10 times, and I never took much either. After chewing a stem about 1 inch in length, I would swallow it. My moods on mushrooms shifted depending on how I felt initially and on what happened while I was high. Sometimes I was up, and sometimes I was down. The last time I ingested them created an experience I will never forget. Later in this chapter, you will read about an individual who developed spinal meningitis after substantial drug use. The individual believed that frequent use of illegal drugs brought the virus out of its ordinarily dormant state.

I did not consume mushrooms frequently at all, but, after the last occasion, the ordinarily dormant chickenpox virus, which stays with you forever, by the way, erupted 3 days after taking the mushrooms into a terribly painful case of shingles. Only people who have had shingles can appreciate the stupid pain it creates. The cause of shingles is a weakened immune system. I thought my immune system was perfectly intact as I worked out five times a week and led a balanced lifestyle.

Psilocybin (4-phosphoryloxy-N,N-dimethyltryptamine) and psilocyn (4-hydroxy-N,N-dimethyltryptamine) are naturally occurring hallucinogens produced by more than 200 species of mushrooms. Collectively, they are known as psilocybin mushrooms, abbreviated here as merely psilocybin. In 1959, it was again the Swiss chemist Albert Hofmann who isolated psilocybin from the fungus *Psilocybe mexicana*.

Psilocybin, although related to LSD chemically, is about 100 times less potent, and effects last for a shorter duration (Csiernik, 2016). These mushrooms grow in the southern and western United States. After ingestion, psilocybin is metabolized into psilocin. In turn, psilocin acts on the serotonin receptors in the brain. Effects generally last between 2 and 6 hours. The effects of psilocybin are highly variable, depending on dosage, mindset, and environment in which the drug is taken. Reported effects include euphoria, visual and mental hallucinations, distorted sense of time, perceptual changes, spiritual experiences, and possibly nausea and panic attacks. Psilocybin is viewed as having low toxicity and low harm potential. Magic mushrooms continue to be used in Indigenous New World cultures in religious and spiritual contexts.

INSIDE AN ADDICTED PERSON'S MIND

Max, Age 25

Colors seemed brighter, sounds were intensified, smells electrified, and, when I moved, WOW, it felt like I was floating. This is just another euphoric night on the dance floor. I came out earlier than most gay guys that I know. By age 13, I knew what I wanted; I knew who I was. These past 12 years have gone by amazingly fast. Where was I even four 4 years ago when I first hit up an all-night rave? I don't know. Blame that on 12 years of using magic mushrooms, I guess.

Like several regular shroom users I know, I have gone on my own hunting expeditions to find these gems growing in the wild to save cash. A few times I have ended up becoming intensely ill from swallowing the wrong kind of mushroom. They are super hard to tell apart. For the past few years, I have only bought mushrooms from a dealer, but, even then, the quality varies, and the effects seem unreliable and unpredictable. Whatever your trip, thank God it's over after a few hours. I mean, most of the time, I am just having the deepest insights and trips from taking mushrooms. Have these insights had any profound effect on my life? No, but it sure feels like it at the time. Perhaps they have helped me become more empathic, but I'm not sure.

Occasionally, however, the chips have been bad. The worst are the annoying feelings of deep discomfort and paranoia. More than a few times, I've hidden in bed with the covers pulled over my head. In the dark, I feel safer. Am I ever truly safe? There are not any long-term consequences to taking hallucinogens, at least so I have been told. I will tell you this: My weekends would not be the same without chewing a few stems on a Friday and Saturday night!

Frankly, I am still bored way too frequently. Some of my friends are telling me I should try LSD to rev things up a bit. I like to stay organic if you know what I mean. If I want to use another drug, I will smoke weed. It's just it doesn't do it for me. We all seem to have our drug of choice. Mine is mushrooms; end of story. It's Monday and I'm already looking forward to the weekend.

Commentary

Although the hallucinogens are not considered to be addictive, this does not mean they are entirely safe. Some mushroom varieties are highly toxic, for example. A 3-year-old boy living in Victoria, Canada, died from eating "death cap" mushrooms (Johnson, 2016). A mother of two died from ingesting death cap mushrooms "after 30 hours of extreme agony" (Ellicott, 2010, para. 4) in the United Kingdom. One could also die from the increased likelihood of having an accident while high on psilocybin.

Max has been ingesting psilocybin mushrooms for 12 years. The adverse consequences resulting from his use to date appear mostly to be the result of picking and consuming poisonous varieties of mushrooms. He is also frequently bored, and this may suggest that he needs to consider establishing new relationships or trying new activities.

Discussion

1. Do you know of anyone who uses hallucinogens regularly? If "yes," what have you noticed about him or her that may be drug-related?
2. What aspects of hallucinogen use are disconcerting to you?
3. If you were Max's counselor, how would you go about helping him (assuming he wanted to stop using or reduce his consumption)?

Peyote and mescaline.

Peyote is a small, spineless cactus that contains psychoactive alkaloids, especially mescaline. Consequently, mescaline is an extract of peyote, which grows naturally in Mexico and southwestern Texas. Peyote is used throughout the world, and it has an extensive history of use among Indigenous North Americans. The Indian Religious Freedom Act was modified in 1994, ensuring that the Native American Church could continue its use of peyote without facing legal ramifications (Prue, 2014)

It is often difficult for providers-in-training to understand the experiences of someone with an addiction. The following passage, a composite adapted from individual stories found online, is intended to provide an "insider's" perspective on peyote use. The effects from drugs are subjective; this portrayal is not indicative of every experience with the drug. The composite was adapted from https://www.quora.com/Psychedelic-Drugs-What-does-it-feel-like-to-be-high-on-peyote.

Getting High on Peyote

Let's put it this way: You don't eat this cactus and then go to the laundromat or Walmart! I mean this seriously. If you're gonna try it, stay away from jerks before you start looking at trees as though they are tall people. It is good to have other experienced people around you. The drug can make you nauseous, especially if you eat the white fuzz off the top of it. After the nausea, get ready for a long-lasting trip that drives into your soul. Do not underestimate the power of this cactus. It may take you into communion with God or to some other deeply spiritual place. Mindfulness becomes paramount. Have a pen or pencil handy to process the new life lessons that come to you.

After I was high, I started riding a horse. I felt such a connection to her. The colors of nature were astonishing to my eyes. I spoke, and the sound traveled, making an echo that fascinated me. I could see trees and far away some local children. I was in love with some of the trees. I fell upon a spring of water, and I wanted to get wet. The feeling was amazing. There were others with me and we headed to town. There was a tree that poured light out of it, illuminated from the inside out. Once we found a place to lodge, we turned the lights off; I close my eyes, and that is when the real trip started. There were little balls of bright colors with other little balls on the edges. The balls were moving in a synchronized way, and it was good. I sense the lamp was on and that it was attracting me to look at it. A feeling came over me that put a smile on my face. The visuals you see on this drug are important and amazing. I am soaring through time itself.

Without awareness, my mood shifted to wonderment and ease. I don't remember details from most of the day, but I do know I was in a very good place. I remember listening to Joni Mitchell's first album and the *Garden of Joy* by Jim Kweskin. The music was incredible. It remains incredible to me to this day.

Although LSD is the most potent of the hallucinogens, mescaline is the least. Mescaline was first identified by German chemist Arthur Heffter in 1897 and first synthesized in 1918 by Ernest Spath. In the phenylethylamine family, mescaline is the only alkaloid that is entirely natural, although it can be synthesized (Csiernik, 2016). The high from mescaline lasts about 12 hours, and it produces rich visual hallucinations (both open- and closed-eye visualizations), euphoria, laughter, and substantially altered states of consciousness in sufficient doses.

Ketamine (dissociative anaesthetic).

Dissociative anesthetics (e.g., ketamine and phencyclidine [PCP]) are not easily classified as these drugs also act as powerful anesthetics (i.e., depressants) and stimulants. Although these drugs are often referred to as hallucinogens, they do not produce true hallucinations. Instead, they create feelings of detachment from reality and distortions of "space, sounds, sight, and body image" (Milkman & Sunderwirth, 2010). This is why they are known as dissociative drugs.

Ketamine was developed in 1962 in the Parke-Davis laboratories and approved for use in the United States in 1970. It is used as an anesthetic for surgery and other painful procedures where the individual needs to be unconscious for only 10–15 min. It was developed as a safer alternative to PCP, and, because of its relative safety, it was used as a surgical anesthetic extensively during the Vietnam War. It does not suppress the respiratory system and aftereffects last only between 1 and 3 hours. Ketamine is also used as a date rape drug (via spiked drinks) and club drug at raves (Csiernik, 2016). Like the other drugs used for sexual assault purposes, ketamine provides pain relief, sedation, and memory loss. Ketamine is also known on the street as K, Special K, and cat Valium.

Serafini, Howland, Rovedi, Girardi, and Amore (2014) reviewed the medicinal effects of ketamine. They reported that at least 10%–20% of individuals experiencing major depressive disorder (MDD) meet the criteria for treatment-resistant depression (TRD). In the review by Serafini et al., the authors concluded that ketaimine is effective in treating both MDD and TRD. Concerns were also expressed, however, regarding the optimal dosage and frequency of administration.

Phencyclidine (PCP; "angel dust" & "zombie").

PCP is a dissociative anesthetic drug that is known to be much stronger than ketamine. It was initially made in 1926 but not introduced into the market as an anesthetic until the 1950s. In 1965, however, it was removed due to its horrifying side effects. The side effects mimic schizophrenia, even when used medicinally. Although illegal usage of the drug in the United States peaked in the 1970s, an increase in visits to emergency departments because of PCP overdose occurred between 2005 and 2011 (Bush, 2013).

PCP is not chemically related to LSD or mescaline. It creates its hallucinogenic effects by blocking the NDMA (a subtype of glutamate) neurochemical receptor site, which plays a role in pain perception, learning, memory, and emotion (Csiernik, 2016). A user may still experience memory loss and depression even following a year of abstinence (Milkman & Sunderwirth, 2010). PCP is now mostly manufactured illegally and comes in liquid, powder, or pill form. Some PCP is made legally for research purposes.

It is often difficult for providers-in-training to understand the experiences of someone with an addiction. The following passage, a composite adapted from individual stories found online, is intended to provide an "insider's" perspective on ketamine use. The effects from drugs are subjective; this portrayal is not indicative of every experience with the drug. The composite was adapted from http://www.bluelight.org/vb/threads/161600-Beginners-Guide-To-Ketamine, https://www.reddit.com/r/ketamine/comments/3rphhg/what_does_being_high_on_ketamine_feel_like/, and https://answers.yahoo.com/question/index?qid=20100531045315AAsxQ74.

Getting High on Ketamine

I would never recommend using ketamine in public; walking around can make you very sick, and more than likely you'll be falling all over the place creating all kinds of bruises. Some of my friends describe it as having similarities to being drunk but with distinctly different properties—like being "drug drunk." You are anesthetized so you kind of feel weightless and floaty. It makes you very vulnerable. Low doses make things feel lighter, like you're walking on air. Your mood is more pleasant, and you might become giggly and silly. Ketamine helps my body to move with the music in a way that is intricate, and reflective of the music that's playing, instead of just bouncing to the beat. On a medium dose, things are different. You begin to lose track of where your body begins and ends, and the feeling that you're "walking on clouds" becomes prominent. Being in a K-Hole can develop at moderate or higher doses, and it can be a good or bad experience, depending on many factors. It involves a complete loss of ego that removes your sense of self, including your personal history, your values, your opinions, etc. It feels like a movie that you're simultaneously watching and acting in.

[The following composite describes a higher dose.] I don't remember a lot of that night and don't know how we made it back home without killing ourselves. The entire drive I was coming in and out of a K-Hole, so I don't remember all the stops my friend talked about. I was paralyzed for the whole ride and vomited all over the place at a few stops along the way in front of people (I think?). When ketamine is taken outside a medical setting, the main dangers arise from the physical incapacity it produces.

It's seriously wrong for your body, it's intensely addictive, and, since it became popular, it costs more and more and is cut with more crap. My advice, not that you're asking, is to give it a miss. There are other ways to reach these places.

It is often difficult for providers-in-training to understand the experiences of someone with an addiction. The following passage, a composite adapted from individual stories found online, is intended to provide an "insider's" perspective on PCP use. The effects from drugs are subjective; this portrayal is not indicative of every experience with the drug. The composite was adapted from https://www.quora.com/What-does-it-feel-like-to-be-on-pcp, https://www.quora.com/What-is-it-like-to-do-angel-dust, http://www.businessinsider.com/here-are-the-terrifying-signs-that-somebody-is-high-on-angel-dust-2014-5, and https://answers.yahoo.com/question/index?qid=20100213213028AAzQBap.

Getting High on PCP

Once I dipped my cigarette in the wet [liquid PCP] to ensure it wasn't quite as bad as I thought it was the first time around. It was. You're incapable of completing thoughts it seems—somewhat primal emotions drive you. Both times, I was fairly reactionary and violent, even though I'm usually among the least physically combative of any group I'm in.

I was handed a PCP-laced joint back in the 1970s. It was as close as I could come to imagining a lobotomy. Higher mental functions were inaccessible, and I readily comprehended how an unarmed person on PCP could (as seemed to so often to have been the case) charge a heavily armed police officer who was aiming some serious artillery at a said person—and still do an incredible amount of damage.

This is my drug of choice without a doubt. Yet, and I mean it, there is not one day that goes by that I do not think about it; I WILL NOT EVER TOUCH IT AGAIN. PERIOD. For starters, I cannot begin to tell how many times I have literally F&@K*D myself up. I did end up overdosing. There are two types of spinal meningitis, and one of them everyone has inside of them and something has to be done to make it react or un-dormant itself. For me, it was a lot of LSD, PCP, and cocaine. This stuff is no joke. This all happened to me when I was 15 years old. I am now 48. If you are deciding to try any drug, first you should dig a 6-foot-deep hole and build a big box. 50/50 chance you will use the hole/box sooner than expected.

Stay the F#*K away from that SHIT. Pardon the language, but just DON'T! It will take you places you DO NOT want to go. It's intense. You might mutilate and eat a baby while high on PCP, but you won't remember it the next day.

The lack of pain response is what leads to the myth that PCP gives people superhuman strength.

PCP doesn't make people any stronger than they usually are. It does, however, keep them from feeling the pain that they should feel. On PCP, people have sometimes broken out of handcuffs. Usually people would feel extreme pain and experience possible wrist fractures, but they don't feel anything until the drug wears off. PCP often makes people extraordinarily sensitive to light, sound, and outside stimuli and possibly experience hallucinations. Some become psychotic. PCP users might see dragons, demons, and other things that don't exist. They might sit by themselves, stare into space, and appear to others as very tranquil and peaceful. If they hear a loud sound (such as hand clapping or a door slamming), however, or see a bright light being turned on, they might become triggered and lash out with extreme violence. Because they don't feel pain, several large people might need to restrain them, even if the PCP user is only of small to average build.

Many people in the Haight-Ashbury District of San Francisco area tried PCP, expecting an LSD-like experience. Many people were so shocked at the way they felt after taking PCP that they panicked and had terrible trips. As a result, the use of PCP was almost nonexistent in the Haight within a year after its first use.

In 2016, the highest lifetime and past-year prevalence rates for PCP use in the United States were among adults aged 26 and older, which were 2.90% and 0.00%, respectively. For children (ages 12–17), prevalence was 0.20% and 0.10%, respectively (National Institute on Drug Abuse, 2017).

Inhalants

Inhalants include various pharmacological substances that can all be readily vaporized (Shen & Chen, 2011). Widely available and frequently misused, longer-term use causes psychosocial problems, dementia, and cerebellar dysfunction. Death has also been reported and can occur through asphyxiation, suffocation, aspiration, engaging in risky behaviors, and sudden sniffing death syndrome (Shen & Chen, 2011). Inhalants include some medical anesthetics such as chloroform (no longer used in medical practice due to unpredictability), nitrous oxide ("laughing gas"), and modern volatile anesthetics (Bovill, 2008). Outside of medical uses, inhalants are used recreationally by an estimated 500,000 Americans (Rastegar & Fingerhood, 2016).

Nitrites (referred to as "poppers") are used, particularly in the gay male community, to enhance sexual performance and/or sensation. Before the discovery of the HIV virus, some researchers incorrectly hypothesized that AIDS was caused by amyl nitrite (Rastegar & Fingerhood, 2016). Like Viagra, nitrites dilate blood vessels and relax muscles. If poppers are used with Viagra, the interaction effect may prove deadly. Aside from this risk, lasting medical difficulties resulting from nitrite use are uncommon (Rastegar & Fingerhood, 2016). Physicians sometimes prescribe amyl nitrite for heart pain (Milkman & Sunderwirth, 2010).

Toluene and most of the other inhalants, except nitrites, activate DA in the brain. The rapid high that accompanies inhalant use resembles alcohol intoxication, followed by drowsiness, apathy, impaired functioning and judgment, disinhibition, lightheadedness, and belligerence (Milkman & Sunderwirth, 2010). Users may become hyperactive, agitated, and impulsive (Rastegar & Fingerhood, 2016).

In 2016, the highest lifetime and past-year prevalence rates for inhalant use in the United States were among adults aged 18–25, which were 9.80% and 1.40%, respectively. For children (ages 12–17), prevalence was 8.30% and 2.20%, respectively (National Institute on Drug Abuse, 2017).

Prescription and Over-the-Counter Medications

Addiction to prescription and over-the-counter medications has become an international concern (Bates, Cochrane, & Mackridge, 2017). In the United States and Canada, the excessive use of prescribed pharmaceuticals has come to be known as the "prescription drug crisis" (Robitaille & Collin, 2016, p. 357). But, besides the drugs that are prescribed, many pharmaceuticals that are either prescribed or available over-the-counter are used recreationally and/or abused to varying degrees. Stimulants (including decongestants), depressants, and opioids are the drug classes most likely to be abused.

When used as prescribed by a physician, stimulants help in managing ADHD and narcolepsy; depressants treat anxiety, panic, and sleep disorders; and opioids treat pain, coughing, and diarrhea (NIDA, 2018c). NIDA (2018c) warned that misusing prescription drugs can cause serious medical consequences. They are responsible for increased emergency room visits, overdose deaths, and treatment admissions. Among individuals who reported the past-year nonmedical use of one or more prescription drugs, almost 12% met criteria for prescription drug use disorder (NIDA, 2018c). Although most Americans use prescription medications responsibly, more than 20% of people aged 12 and older have reportedly used prescription drugs for nonmedical reasons at least once in their lifetime. Unintentional overdose deaths from opioids have more than quadrupled since 1999. Opioid deaths have outnumbered deaths from heroin and cocaine since 2002 (NIDA, 2018c).

In 2016, the highest past-year prevalence rate for nonmedical use of psychotherapeutic drugs (i.e., drugs used to relieve symptoms associated with anxiety, depression, or other mental disorders) in the United States was among adults aged 18–25, which was 14.50%. For children (ages 12–17), prevalence was 5.30% (National Institute on Drug Abuse, 2017).

Club Drugs

Club drugs are those used most often by teenagers and young adults in nightclubs, parties, concerts, and raves. Club drugs include cannabis, poppers, crystal meth, MDMA (ecstasy), ketamine, GHB, Rohypnol, and LSD (Herzig & Bachmann, 2017; NIDA, n.d.; Rastegar & Fingerhood, 2016). MDMA is viewed as the most popular drug among youth (Milkman & Sunderwirth, 2010). These drugs were included earlier and are listed here for quick reference purposes only.

Diagnostic and Assessment Considerations

In *DSM-5*, the section that includes drugs is called Substance-Related and Addictive Disorders. *DSM-5* encompasses 10 separate classes of drugs.[1] The details of these are quite extensive, so the reader is referred to pages 481–585 of *DSM-5* (American Psychiatric Association [APA], 2013). SUDs are defined as "a cluster of cognitive, behavioral, and physiological symptoms indicating that the individual continues using the substance despite significant substance-related problems" (APA, 2013, p. 483).

A diagnosis of a substance disorder in *DSM-5* is based on *severity* (i.e., by the number of diagnosable symptoms) as follows: (a) *mild*: 2 to 3, (b) *moderate*: 4 to 5, or (c) *severe*: 6 or more. As substance intoxication and withdrawal often involves multiple substances used simultaneously or sequentially, each diagnosis is recorded separately in *DSM-5*. Although the validity of self-reports regarding drug use is generally very good, those with severe mental illnesses (e.g., psychotic or bipolar disorders) can be especially inaccurate in providing self-report (Earleywine, 2016).

Regarding the drug categories contained in this chapter, Table 13.1 lists the subheadings under each category, followed by the DSM and ICD codes.

[1]The 10 categories include alcohol; caffeine; cannabis; hallucinogens; inhalants; opioids; sedatives, hypnotics, and anxiolytics; stimulants; tobacco; and other (or unknown) substances.

TABLE 13.1 **DSM and ICD Codes**

DSM Code	Number of Symptoms Required	ICD-10	ICD-11
Hallucinogen-Related Disorders			
Phencyclidine Use Disorder			
305.90	Mild: 2 or 3 symptoms	F16.10	
304.60	Moderate: 4 or 5 symptoms	F16.20	
304.60	Severe: 6 or more symptoms	F16.20	
Other Hallucinogen Use Disorder			
305.30	Mild: 2 or 3 symptoms	F16.10	
304.50	Moderate: 4 or 5 symptoms	F16.20	
304.50	Severe: 6 or more symptoms	F16.20	
Phencyclidine Intoxication			
292.89	Mild: 2 or 3 symptoms	Varies*	
292.89	Moderate: 4 or 5 symptoms	Varies*	
292.89	Severe: 6 or more symptoms	Varies*	
Other Hallucinogen Intoxication			
292.89	Mild: 2 or 3 symptoms	Varies*	
292.89	Moderate: 4 or 5 symptoms	Varies*	
292.89	Severe: 6 or more symptoms	Varies*	
Hallucinogen Persisting Perception Disorder			
292.89	[not rated for severity]	F16.983	
Other Phencyclidine-Induced Disorders			
N/A	[not rated for severity]	N/A	
Other Hallucinogen-Induced Disorders			
N/A	[not rated for severity]	N/A	
Unspecified Phencyclidine-Related Disorder			
292.9	[not rated for severity]	F16.99	
Unspecified Hallucinogen-Related Disorder			
292.9	[not rated for severity]	F16.99	
INHALANT-RELATED DISORDERS			
Inhalant Use Disorder			
305.90	Mild: 2 or 3 symptoms	F18.14	
304.60	Moderate: 4 or 5 symptoms	F18.24	
304.60	Severe: 6 or more symptoms	F18.24	
Inhalant Intoxication			
292.89	Mild: 2 or 3 symptoms	Varies*	

(Continued)

TABLE 13.1 (Continued)

DSM Code	Number of Symptoms Required	ICD-10	ICD-11
Hallucinogen-Related Disorders			
292.89	Moderate: 4 or 5 symptoms	Varies*	
292.89	Severe: 6 or more symptoms	Varies*	
Other Inhalant-Induced Disorders			
N/A	[not rated for severity]	N/A	
Unspecified Inhalant-Related Disorder			
292.9	[not rated for severity]	F18.99	
SEDATIVE-, HYPNOTIC-, OR ANXIOLYTIC-RELATED DISORDERS			
Sedative, Hypnotic, or Anxiolytic Use Disorder			
305.40	Mild: 2 or 3 symptoms	F13.10	Varies**
304.10	Moderate: 4 or 5 symptoms	F13.20	Varies**
304.10	Severe: 6 or more symptoms	F13.20	Varies**
Sedative, Hypnotic, or Anxiolytic Intoxication			
292.89	[not rated for severity]	Varies*	Varies**
Sedative, Hypnotic, or Anxiolytic Withdrawal			
292.0	[not rated for severity]	Varies*	Varies**
Other Sedative-, Hypnotic-, or Anxiolytic-Induced Disorders			
N/A	[not rated for severity]	N/A	Varies**
Unspecified Sedative-, Hypnotic-, or Anxiolytic-Induced Disorder			
292.9	[not rated for severity]	F13.99	Varies **
STIMULANT-RELATED DISORDERS			
Stimulant Use Disorder			
Varies*	Mild: 2 or 3 symptoms	Varies*	Varies**
Varies*	Moderate: 4 or 5 symptoms	Varies*	Varies**
Varies*	Severe: 6 or more symptoms	Varies*	Varies**
Stimulant Intoxication			
292.89	Mild: 2 or 3 symptoms	Varies*	Varies**
292.89	Moderate: 4 or 5 symptoms	Varies*	Varies**
292.89	Severe: 6 or more symptoms	Varies*	Varies**
Stimulant Withdrawal			
292.0	[not rated for severity]	Varies*	Varies**
Other Stimulant-Induced Disorders			
N/A	[not rated for severity]	N/A	Varies**
Unspecified Stimulant-Related Disorder			
292.9	[not rated for severity]	Varies*	Varies**

DSM Code	Number of Symptoms Required	ICD-10	ICD-11
Hallucinogen-Related Disorders			
OTHER (OR UNKNOWN) SUBSTANCE-RELATED DISORDERS			
Other (or Unknown) Substance Use Disorder			
305.90	Mild: 2 or 3 symptoms	F19.10	Varies**
304.90	Moderate: 4 or 5 symptoms	F19.20	Varies**
304.90	Severe: 6 or more symptoms	F19.20	Varies**
Other (or Unknown) Substance Intoxication			
292.89	Mild: 2 or 3 symptoms	Varies*	Varies**
292.89	Moderate: 4 or 5 symptoms	Varies*	Varies**
292.89	Severe: 6 or more symptoms	Varies*	Varies**
Other (or Unknown) Substance Withdrawal			
292.0	[not rated for severity]	F19.239	Varies**
Other (or Unknown) Substance-Induced Disorders			
N/A	[not rated for severity]	N/A	Varies**
Unspecified Other (or Unknown) Substance-Related Disorder			
292.9	[not rated for severity]	F19.99	Varies**

If you know the exact name of the diagnosis as it appears in *DSM-5*, you can pull up both the DSM-IV and *DSM-5* criteria for the disorder by going to *http://dsm.wikia.com/*wiki/Name of Disorder, each word separated by an underscore.

For example, to find the DSM-IV and *DSM-5* criteria for alcohol use disorder, type http://dsm.wikia.com/wiki/Alcohol_Use_Disorder

For generalized anxiety disorder, type http://dsm.wikia.com/wiki/Generalized_Anxiety_Disorder, and so forth.

*ICD-10 codes vary in many cases, depending on whether there is comorbidity with other disorders and depending on the exact type of drug under a drug class (e.g., amphetamine or cocaine in the stimulant class).

**The codes in ICD-11 are different for each specific stimulant, depressant, and hallucinogen. The complete list of codes for specific drugs and co-occurring medical conditions can be found at https://icd.who.int/ct11_2018/icd11_mms/en/release#/):

Rastegar and Fingerhood (2016) wrote that the diagnosis of SUDs is based on having at least two of 11 criteria that can be divided into four groups or clusters. These are summarized as follows:

Group I: impaired control

1. Substance use in larger amounts or over a longer period than was originally intended.
2. Persistent desire to cut down on use or multiple unsuccessful attempts at cutting down or stopping use.
3. A great deal of time is spent using a substance or recovering from its effects.
4. Intense desire to use or craving for the substance.

Group II: social impairment

5. Substance use resulting in failure to fulfill obligations at work, school, or home.
6. Substance use causing or exacerbating interpersonal problems.
7. Important social, occupational, or recreational activities given up or reduced due to substance use.

Group III: risky use

8. Recurrent use of a substance in physically hazardous situations.
9. Continued use despite negative physical or psychological consequences.

Group IV: pharmacological dependence

10. Tolerance of the effects of the substance.
11. Withdrawal symptoms with cessation of the substance. (pp. 7–8)

In the World Health Organization's *International Classification of Diseases, Version 10* (ICD-10), "mental and behavioral disorders" begin with the letter F, whereas those due to "psychoactive substance use" begin with F10–F19. Then each drug is further categorized according to the person's involvement with it as follows: acute intoxication (F1x.0), harmful use (F1x.1), or dependence syndrome (F1x.2) (Rastegar & Fingerhood, 2016).

Diagnosis and assessment may require drug testing, which should be done openly to avoid undermining the client's trust (Rastegar & Fingerhood, 2016). Urine testing is the most frequently used method to detect recent drug use. When a thorough and honest assessment of drug use is not undertaken, misdiagnosis is "alarmingly common" (Earleywine, 2016, p. 14). The American Society of Addiction Medicine (ASAM; Rastegar & Fingerhood, 2016) looks at six criteria to assess patients' drug involvement:

1. Acute intoxication and/or withdrawal potential.
2. Biomedical conditions and complications.
3. Emotional, behavioral, or cognitive conditions and complications.
4. Readiness to change.
5. Relapse, continued use, or continued problem potential.
6. Recovery/living environment. (p. 37)

Following diagnosis and assessment, ASAM (Rastegar & Fingerhood, 2016) determines the required treatment for patients. Their four choices include the following: (a) outpatient treatment, (b) intensive outpatient treatment or partial hospitalization, (c) residential treatment, or (d) intensive inpatient treatment.

Differential diagnosis.

Stimulants. Stimulant-induced disorders sometimes resemble primary mental disorders (e.g., major depressive disorder; schizophrenia, paranoid type; bipolar disorder; generalized anxiety disorder; panic disorder; APA, 2013). Counselors can distinguish stimulant intoxication from stimulant-induced disorders by severity. That is, the severity of the symptoms from intoxication exceed that of the primary mental disorders previously listed. Users of PCP or "bath salts" also need to be distinguished from those intoxicated from stimulants. The only way to distinguish stimulant use from the use of PCP or bath salts is through a urine or plasma sample focused on looking for the presence of cocaine or an amphetamine-type substance.

Depressants (including sedative-hypnotics). Individuals with disorders in this category may have symptoms that resemble primary mental disorders (e.g., generalized anxiety disorder). The slurred speech, incoordination, and other associated effects from taking depressants may be the result of another medical condition (e.g., multiple sclerosis, prior head trauma).

Hallucinogens (psychedelics). It is important to distinguish hallucinogen use from other substances such as amphetamines because hallucinogens are often used in combination with other drugs. Some people with schizophrenia exhibit paranoia, and they may come to believe that their symptoms are a consequence of hallucinogen use. It is also important to rule out panic disorder, depressive and bipolar disorders, alcohol use, sedative withdrawal, hypoglycemia and other metabolic disturbances, seizure disorder, stroke, ophthalmological disorder, and CNS tumors.

It is important to distinguish individuals with schizophrenia from those who are using hallucinogens. The way to distinguish these is that hallucinations are usually auditory in persons with schizophrenia in contrast to predominantly visual hallucinations that are created by hallucinogens (Pechnick et al., 2014).

Pechnick et al. (2014) also recommended that hallucinogen intoxication needs to be differentiated from consumption of delirium-inducing drugs (e.g., atropine-like agents), PCP, and cannabis. One atropine-like agent is from the *Datura stramonium* plant, commonly called "jimsonweed" and more rarely called "Jamestown weed." Jimsonweed is a powerful hallucinogen and deliriant. The way to distinguish jimsonweed use from other hallucinogens is that jimsonweed produces dry mouth and blurred vision. Cannabis-induced psychosis often creates drowsiness rather than the hyperalertness produced by LSD. PCP psychosis, on the other hand, is marked by neurological signs (e.g., vertical nystagmus, which is a type of involuntary eye movement whereby the eyes move rapidly and slowly on a vertical axis; ataxia, which is a lack of voluntary muscle coordination that includes abnormality of gait). Individuals experiencing psychostimulant-induced psychosis often cannot differentiate their perceptual distortions from reality, whereas LSD users are usually aware of the difference.

Inhalants. *DSM-5* cautions that unintentional inhalant exposure may result from industrial or other accidents, and it is important to distinguish this from intentional inhalant use. It is also important to ascertain if the individual is experiencing a disorder induced by inhalant use (e.g., psychotic disorder, depressive disorder, anxiety disorder, neurocognitive disorder, or other induced disorder). Inhalant use disorder must also be distinguished from other toxic, metabolic, dramatic, neoplastic, or infectious diseases that can impair central or peripheral nervous system functioning (e.g., pernicious anemia, degeneration of the spinal cord, various cognitive disorders, brain atrophy, and many nervous system disorders).

Comorbidity and co-addictions.

Individuals with co-occurring SUDs and mental disorders have poor outcomes in important quality-of-life areas, including incarceration, employment, community housing, and hospitalization (Harrison, Cousins, Spybrook, & Curtis, 2017). Earleywine (2016) wrote that there is substantial overlap between drug problems and disorders relating to impulse control, mood, anxiety, and personality. The personality disorders that are most often comorbid with substance problems are found in Cluster B (see Chapter 5), especially antisocial and borderline personality disorder. Bipolar disorder is especially associated with SUDs (Rastegar & Fingerhood, 2016). Schizophrenia is frequently associated with SUDs, particularly nicotine (Rastegar & Fingerhood, 2016). Heroin disorder is often comorbid with binge eating disorder and food addiction (Canan, Karaca, Sogucak, Gecici, & Kuloglu, 2017). Specific drug classes and comorbidity follow.

Stimulants. Stimulant disorders are often comorbid with other SUDs, particularly depressants. For example, cocaine users often use alcohol, and amphetamine-type users often use cannabis. There is also an association between stimulant disorders and posttraumatic stress disorder, antisocial personality disorder, ADHD, and gambling disorder. Those seeking help for cocaine problems often present for treatment with chest pain. Earleywine (2016) wrote that eating disorders, especially in women, are often comorbid with stimulant use as stimulant use reduces appetite.

Depressants (including sedative-hypnotics). Depressant disorders are often comorbid with alcohol use disorder, tobacco use disorder, and illicit drug use. *DSM-5* mentions that there may also be an association between depressant use and antisocial personality disorder; and depressive, bipolar, and anxiety disorders.

Hallucinogens (psychedelics). *DSM-5* informs us that teenagers and adults who have recently used ecstasy have a higher prevalence of other SUDs than those who do not use hallucinogens. Furthermore, adolescents and adults who take ecstasy are more likely than other drug users to be polydrug users. Hallucinogen users also have a higher likelihood of nonsubstance mental disorders such as anxiety, depressive, and bipolar disorders. Those who have antisocial personality disorder (but not conduct disorder) are also much more likely to be diagnosed with hallucinogen use disorder. People diagnosed with hallucinogen persisting perception disorder are more likely to experience panic disorder, alcohol use disorder, and major depressive disorder. Furthermore, hallucinogen use may unlock vulnerabilities for psychosis as well as precipitate relapse among individuals who already have a pre-existing psychotic disorder (Pechnick et al., 2014).

Inhalants. People with inhalant use disorders, at least those who present for treatment, often present with numerous other SUDs. Inhalant use disorder is commonly comorbid with adolescent conduct disorder and adult antisocial personality disorder. Inhalant users should also be screened for suicidality as this is also a frequent association.

Available Measures

Several measures can be used for assessing substance abuse. The National Institute on Drug Abuse (2018a) provides a link to many evidence-based screening tools and resource materials. Because they update this list periodically, the link may change over time. Counselors are advised to search in Google for "Chart of Evidence-Based Screening Tools for Adults and Adolescents." The Network of Alcohol and Other Drugs Agencies (Deady, 2009) created a 225-page document that reviewed assessment and outcome measures for drug and alcohol settings that contains many useful assessment instruments. The document is available for free on the Internet (see the reference for details). Following is a list of a few available measures, some of which are contained in the previously mentioned webpages (these same measures are suggested in Chapter 11):

1. Alcohol, Smoking and Substance Involvement Screening Test (ASSIST; WHO ASSIST Working Group, 2002). This questionnaire is used via face-to-face interaction with a client. It includes only seven questions, of which six are scored. This brief measure shows a good ability to discriminate among use, abuse, and dependence (Asbridge, Duff, Marsh, & Erickson, 2014). Available from http://apps.who.int/iris/bitstream/10665/44320/1/9789241599382_eng.pdf
2. Severity of Dependence Scale (SDS; Gossop et al., 1995). Measures several substances. A five-question screening tool looks at use over the past 3 months. Better used for longitudinal follow-up in quantitative studies than for individual use with clients. Available from http://www.emcdda.europa.eu/attachements.cfm/att_7364_EN_english_sds.pdf
3. Car, Relax, Alone, Forget, Friends, Trouble Inventory. "The CRAFFT is a behavioral health screening tool for use with children under the age of 21 and is recommended by the American Academy of Pediatrics' Committee on Substance Abuse for use with adolescents" (para. 1). The CRAFT and instructions for use are available from https://www.integration.samhsa.gov/clinical-practice/sbirt/adolescent_screening,_brieft_intervention_and_referral_to_treatment_for_alcohol.pdf.
4. Timeline Followback Method Assessment (TLFB). Earleywine (2016) wrote that this is an informative assessment of drug use that has proven itself to be reliable and valid over long periods in many studies. This assessment can be administered by an interviewer, self-administered, or administered by a computer. The timeline of use is within the last 7 days to 2 years before the interview date. The TLFB can be downloaded from https://cde.drugabuse.gov/instrument/d89c8e23-16e5-625a-e040-bb89ad43465d
5. Inventory of Drug Use Consequences (InDUC-2L). This is a self-report questionnaire focused on adverse consequences of drug use across several domains. It can be useful to have clients complete this to be later reviewed and discussed as part of the assessment process (Earleywine, 2016). This questionnaire and several other worthwhile assessment tools are available at no cost to counselors from the Center on Alcoholism, Substance Abuse, and Addictions (CASAA) located in New Mexico at http://casaa.unm.edu/Instruments
6. Brief Situational Confidence Questionnaire (BSCQ. In this questionnaire, clients report their confidence and sense of self-efficacy in their ability to resist alcohol and/or drug use. It is available from Nova Southeastern University at http://www.nova.edu/gsc/forms/appendix_d_brief_situational_confidence_questionnaire.pdf
7. Readiness Ruler (Rollnick, Miller, & Butler, as cited in Earleywine, 2016). The Readiness Ruler allows clients to rate their readiness to change along a continuum. A version of this that includes a description of the stages of change model is available from Zimmerman, Olsen, and Bosworth (2000) and can be accessed from https://www.aafp.org/afp/2000/0301/p1409.html
8. Drug Abuse Screening Test (DAST). There is a 20-item DAST-20 available for adults and a separate one for adolescents. There is also a DAST-10 that includes only 10 items. Harvey Skinner from York University created the DAST. A limitation of the questionnaire is that the content is obvious and clients can easily fake their results on it. The three versions of the questionnaire can be found at http://www.emcdda.europa.eu/attachements.cfm/att_61480_EN_DAST%202008.pdf
9. APA's online assessment measures. The American Psychiatric Association offers several questionnaires at no cost that can help mental health practitioners with their assessments (go to https://www.psychiatry.org/psychiatrists/practice/dsm/educational-resources/assessment-measures#Disorder). See the *DSM-5* Self-Rated Level 1 Cross-Cutting Symptom Measures (adult, ages 6–17, or ages 11–17) to get a general diagnostic picture of an individual or the specific

measure for substance use in each age category. Quoted from the webpage:

The APA is offering several "emerging measures" in Section III of *DSM–5*. These patient assessment measures were developed to be administered at the initial patient interview and to monitor treatment progress, thus serving to advance the use of initial symptomatic status and patient-reported outcome (PRO) information as well as the use of "anchored" severity assessment instruments. Instructions, scoring information, and interpretation guidelines are included. Clinicians and researchers may provide APA with feedback on the instruments' usefulness in characterizing patient status and improving patient care. . .. (para. 1)

About the Measures

These measures should be used to enhance clinical decision-making and not as the sole basis for making a clinical diagnosis. Further information on these measures can be found in *DSM–5*. (p. 1)

10. American Society of Addiction Medicine (ASAM) criteria. ASAM created its criteria from a collaboration that began in the 1980s. ASAM reports that it is the most widely used and comprehensive set for clients with addiction issues. The criteria are required in over 30 states. The ASAM criteria use six dimensions for service planning and treatment across services and levels of care. These dimensions include (a) acute intoxication and/or withdrawal potential, (b) biomedical conditions and complications, (c) emotional, behavioral, or cognitive conditions and complications, (d) readiness to change, (e) relapse, continued to use, or continued problem potential, and (f) recovery/living environment. There is a cost associated with the materials needed for the ASAM criteria. These can be purchased from https://www.asam.org/resources/the-asam-criteria. Based on several studies, Miller (2016) concluded that the ASAM criteria have failed at matching clients to levels of treatment intensity. Instead, he advocates that individuals "make informed choices from a menu of evidence-based options" (p. 94).
11. Substance Abuse Subtle Screening Inventory (SASSI). According to the website (https://www.sassi.com/), the SASSI is a brief psychological questionnaire, available in both adult and adolescent versions, that can identify people with an SUD with a high degree of accuracy. There is a fee for this instrument. When I attended an addictions session at the American Counseling Association conference in 2017, several participants said that they used this questionnaire. Its reported empirically tested accuracy is between 93% and 94% (according to https://pubs.niaaa.nih.gov/publications/AssessingAlcohol/InstrumentPDFs/66_SASSI.pdf).
12. Structured Clinical Interview for *DSM-5* (SCID-5). A general interview for diagnosis purposes (available from https://www.amazon.com/Structured-Clinical-Interview-Disorders-Scid-5-cv/dp/1585624616/ref=sr_1_1?ie=UTF8&qid=1513038044&sr=8-1&keywords=structured+clinical+interview+for+dsm-5). There is a cost for this measure.
13. Addiction Severity Index, Version 6 (ASI-6). The ASI is one of the most widely used clinical assessment instruments for individuals with SUDs. It was revised to version 6 in 2006 (McLellan, Cacciola, Alterman, Rikoon, & Carise, 2006), and it has acceptable scalability, reliability, and concurrent validity (Cacciola, Alterman, Habing, & McLellan, 2011; Thylstrup, Bloomfield, & Hesse, 2018). The ASI is a semistructured interview that addresses seven problem areas in substance-abusing clients (i.e., medical status, employment and support, drug use, alcohol use, legal status, family/social status, and psychiatric status). It takes a skilled interviewer approximately 1 hour to complete. A modified version (i.e., mASI) is now available that assesses all SUDs and gambling disorders (Denis et al., 2016).

Clinical Interview Questions

(These same questions are suggested in Chapter 11.) The modified CAGE (remember the original CAGE is a four-item test used to assess alcohol problems) can be asked as questions to help assess drug addiction:

1. Have you ever thought you should Cut down your drug or alcohol use?
2. Have you ever felt Annoyed when people have commented on your use?
3. Have you ever felt Guilty or badly about your use?
4. Have you ever used drugs or alcohol to Ease withdrawal symptoms or to avoid feeling low after using? (Melemis, 2018, para. 3)

Johns Hopkins University developed a self-test to identify alcoholism, which was adapted to include drugs as well as alcohol. The questions include

1. Do you lose time from work due to drinking or drug use?
2. Is drinking or drug use making your home life unhappy?
3. Do you drink or use drugs because you are shy with other people?
4. Is drinking or drug use affecting your reputation?
5. Have you ever felt remorse after drinking or drug use?
6. Have you gotten into financial difficulties as a result of your drinking or drug use?
7. Do you turn to lower companions and an inferior environment when drinking or using drugs?
8. Does your drinking or drug use make you careless of your family's welfare?
9. Has your ambition decreased since drinking or using drugs?
10. Do you crave a drink or a drug at a definite time daily?
11. Do you want a drink or drug the next morning?

12. Does your drinking or drug use cause you to have difficulties in sleeping?
13. Has your efficiency decreased since drinking or using drugs?
14. Is your drinking or drug use jeopardizing your job or business?
15. Do you drink or use drugs to escape from worries or troubles?
16. Do you drink or use drugs alone?
17. Have you ever had a complete loss of memory?
18. Has your physician ever treated you for drinking or drug use?
19. Do you drink or use drugs to build your self-confidence?
20. Have you ever been in a hospital or institution on account of drinking or drug use? (AddictScience.com, n.d., p. 1)

Below are a few common questions that can be asked:

1. Do you feel you must consume drugs or alcohol to get through your day?
2. Have you ever sought medical attention because of your drug and alcohol use?
3. Has your performance at school, work, or home been affected by your drug and alcohol consumption?
4. Do you constantly think about the next time you will drink alcohol or take drugs?
5. Has your drinking or drug use interfered or caused problems with your personal relationships?
6. Have you suffered from memory loss after using drugs or alcohol?
7. Do you experience withdrawal symptoms after not consuming drugs or alcohol for an extended period?
8. Do you go to extensive lengths to obtain drugs or alcohol?
9. Do you remain intoxicated for several days at a time?
10. Do you say or do things while intoxicated that you later regret while sober? (Laplante, 2018, p. 1)

Generic Names and Street "Lingo"

The number of slang terms for these drugs appears almost endless. People on the street will find new words to talk "code" so that others do not know the lingo. Consequently, the names provided here constitute a partial list and *by no means* an exhaustive one.

Stimulants.

The most common names used in the United States for cocaine include coke, blow, nose candy, snow, and yeyo. Other common names include flake, white, toot, powder, dust, big rush, pearl, candy, cola, C, big C, baseball, bump, line, rail, aunt, batman, Hubba, Bernice, Bernie, big bloke, star, stardust, and stash. In cocaine lingo, an "eight ball" refers to one eighth of an ounce of cocaine. Crack is also known as freebase, snow coke, rocks, black rocks, chemical, candy, nuggets, gravel, grit, hail, hard rock, jellybeans, cookies, dice, scrabble, purple caps, sleet, trey, tornado, and yam.

Methamphetamine was initially known as speed, and it is sometimes referred to as the "poor man's cocaine" (Csiernik, 2016, p. 144). It is also referred to as meth, crystal, crystal meth, ice, crank, jib, tina, glass, fire, and chalk.

MDMA is commonly called ecstasy and, although Molly is often referred to as a pure form of MDMA, it is often not pure and is more typically paramethoxymethamphetamine (PMMA) (Csiernik, 2016). Other terms for MDMA include Adam, beans, candy, dancing shoes, disco biscuits, doves, E-bomb, eggrolls, happy pill, hug drug, love drug, Malcolm or Malcolm X, smarties, sweets, skittles, vitamin E or vitamin X, and vowels. MDA is also known as the love drug and love trip (Csiernik, 2016). MDA is also known on the street as Sally. DOM is known as STP on the street (Csiernik, 2016). Khat is often referred to as cat, oat, Abyssinian tea, African salad, atha, and hat. Bath salts are called Arctic blast, blue silk, charge, cloud 10, hurricane Charlie, and ivory snow (Csiernik, 2016).

Depressants (including sedative-hypnotics).

Barbiturates have also been called barbs, barbies, downers, goofballs, idiot pills, sleepers, and stumblers (Csiernik, 2016). Benzodiazepines are sometimes referred to as benzos, downers, nerve pills, and tranks. GHB is most commonly referred to as "G," but other names include gamma-OH, liquid E, fantasy, Georgia Home boy, grievous bodily harm, liquid X, liquid ecstasy (it is not ecstasy), Scoop, water, Everclear, soap, salty water, and Cherry meth (it is not meth).

Hallucinogens (psychedelics).

The most common name for LSD is acid, but other frequently used names include blaze, blotter, cheer, dose, dots, flash, fry, gel, hawk, L, lightning, Lucy, microdots, paper mushrooms, purple haze, pyramid, rainbow, smilies, stars, superman, tab, ticket, trips, window, and window pane (from http://psychedelics.com/lsd/street-names-for-lsd/). Other names for psilocybin include magic mushrooms, psychedelic mushrooms, shrooms, amani, liberty cap, mushies, liberties, happies, and magics. Peyote and mescaline go by the names buttons, cactus, mesc, tops, San Pedro, half-moon, Hikori, nubs, and P.

Ketamine is called K, special K, big K, vitamin K, breakfast, cat killer, cat tranquilizer, cat valium, donkey, green, super C, horsey, jet, ket, kitkat, kitty, and super acid (Csiernik, 2016). PCP is often referred to as Angel dust, and other names include super grass, killer weed, wet, water, wack, Fry, formaldehyde, boat, Tic Tac, Zoom, Shermans, embalming fluid, ozone, wack, rocket fuel, hog, cliffhanger, goon dust, Peter Pan, lethal weapon, and kools.

Inhalants.

Each type of inhalant often has its slang or street names. For example, nitrous oxide is often called laughing gas. Amyl nitrite and butyl nitrite are called poppers, snappers, bold, or rush. Whippets refer to the nitrous oxide found in whipping cream dispensers.

Other terms for inhalants may include air blast, bagging, heart-on, highball, hippie crack, honey oil, moon gas, Satan's secret, spray, tolly, and whiteout. "Snotballs" refer to rubber cement that has been rolled into balls that are then burned while the fumes are inhaled.

The preceding makes it clear that illegal drugs are sold on the street by many names, and sometimes by the same name. It is a "buyer beware" market. We know from the opioid crisis that people do not always get what they are told or think they are being sold. Most users will not find out—if they have a second chance to find out—until it is too late.

Neuroscience

Maté (2008) noted that brain development in utero and during the childhood years remains the most important biological factor that determines if a person will be predisposed to both substance addiction and addictive behaviors. The brains of abused children, for example, have been found to be 7%–8% smaller compared to the brains of nonabused children. Smaller areas include the impulse-regulating prefrontal cortex, the corpus callosum, and, in several regions of the limbic system, dysfunction in these areas increases vulnerability to addiction (Maté, 2008).

No research supports the idea that a single gene or biological factor predicts the development of a chronic drug problem. As Earleywine (2016) indicated, some familial and behavioral factors will lead to drug problems regardless of an individual's biological constituency. There are also drugs such as the opiates that will undoubtedly lead to increases in tolerance and withdrawal irrespective of a person's biological disposition (Earleywine, 2016).

Bedendo et al. (2016) cautioned that, whereas the neurobiological bases of addiction are noteworthy, addiction should always be considered a multifactor biopsychosocial disorder. The entire dependence process cannot be explained through neuroscience alone. Although the idea that substance abuse is a brain disease continues to be questioned, neuroscience supports the theory that it is (Volkow et al., 2016). Vulnerability to drug addiction results from an interaction of several brain systems (i.e., the reward, decision-making, serotonergic, oxytocin, interoceptive insula, CRF, norepinephrine, dynorphin/KOR, orexin, vasopressin), genetic predisposition, sociocultural factors, impulsivity, and the drug types themselves (Ouzir & Errami, 2016). The effect of alcohol and other drugs results from "how they interact or interface with the brain's neurotransmitter systems" (Begun & Brown, 2014, p. 45). With chronic drug use, the brain often adapts to the presence of that drug by changing the neurotransmitter system. This may affect the production, release, reuptake, or sensitivity of neurotransmitters affected by the drug (Begun & Brown, 2014).

The next seven paragraphs are condensed and adapted from Hall and Walker (2017), whose chapter is an excellent read for counselors interested in the neuroscience of addictions. Addiction researchers study how the brain adapts to chronic drug use. They look at (a) how drugs of abuse create problems in the motivational and executive function and (b) how these deficits contribute to both chronic and compulsive drug use. One possible explanation is that drugs can trigger changes in neuroplasticity. Cocaine, for example, may alter gene expression, resulting in structural changes to the neuron's dendrites. In turn, this creates more liking and wanting for cocaine.

One lens through which to interpret this neuroplasticity is the incentive-sensitization hypothesis (ISH) of addiction. The ISH suggests that reward consists of three separate elements: wanting, liking, and learning. Liking can also be subdivided into experiencing pleasure and the objective neural or behavioral response to rewarding stimuli. According to the ISH, drugs of abuse reshape the brain systems, so they become more sensitized to the incentives provided by drugs.

Another lens through which to interpret this neuroplasticity is the opponent-process theory of acquired motivation. This model describes the vacillation between two opposing psychological mechanisms such that, after repeated exposure to a stimulus, the intensity of the initial process diminishes while that of the secondary process increases. Consequently, concerning chronic drug use, the individual becomes less sensitive to the first process (i.e., tolerance develops to the pleasurable properties of the drug) while simultaneously becoming more sensitive to the unpleasant state of withdrawal (i.e., the secondary process). In turn, allostasis (the body's ability to adjust its setpoints to maintain homeostasis) occurs as the body requires more of a drug to achieve the desired effects while at the same time avoiding the increasingly negative experience of withdrawal.

There are also epigenetic factors that occur in addiction. Epigenetic refers to gene expressions that carry over from one generation to the next but do not occur because of alterations to the DNA sequence. Epigenetic factors either engage or silence gene expression by changing chromatin structure such as adding a methyl group or removing an acetyl group. Regarding chronic drug use, the evidence is building that the engagement and silencing of gene expression create habitual behavioral and cognitive changes.

Neurotransmission, which is the transmission of nerve impulses between neurons or between a neuron and a muscle fiber or other structure, creates effects on gene expression. Some genes are acted on immediately, and others take a longer time for activation. Some of the transmissions are turned into protein products; Fos is one of the families of these proteins. The ΔFosB protein has received increasing attention in the addiction literature. It is believed to influence behavior change by altering the expression of other genes. Recent research is showing that chronic drug use creates an accumulation of ΔFosB in the nucleus accumbens, the dorsal striatum, and the prefrontal cortex to a lesser extent. This, in turn, may produce undesirable long-term impacts on neuroplasticity such as increased drug sensitivity, increased craving, and compulsive behavior. Hall and Walker (2017) noted, however, that the effect of ΔFosB is not permanent and in fact is no longer detectable 1–2 months after withdrawal.

The addiction cycle follows a binge and intoxication phase followed by withdrawal. Addiction researchers have mostly studied DA for the part it plays in reward and motivation. The primary reward circuit is known as the mesocorticolimbic DA system, which is divided into two pathways: mesolimbic and mesocortical. DA in the mesolimbic pathway (primarily in the nucleus accumbens; Rastegar & Fingerhood, 2016) leads to reward and pleasurable sensations, whereas neurons in the mesocortical pathway affect executive functions such as working memory, behavioral flexibility, and decision-making.

As drug addiction progresses, the brain's reward system becomes weakened. The motivational deficits associated with withdrawal unfold, as do the dysphoric mood states. As preoccupation and anticipation build, both craving and relapse become likely. Chronic drug use affects more than just motivation: It also impairs brain regions that exert top-down control over behavior.

For example, abnormal functioning in the insula increases both impulsivity and difficulty in identifying high-risk situations. The said brain alterations contribute to "priming" or "kindling." These terms refer to how addicted individuals rapidly return to a previous high level of use with a particular drug once they relapse (Rastegar & Fingerhood, 2016). Over time, the brain becomes less able to produce DA, and the addicted individual becomes less able to enjoy pleasure from everyday stimuli (e.g., relationships, activities) that used to be motivating and rewarding. These changes are not immediately reversed through the cessation of drug use (Volkow et al., 2016).

Drugs of abuse have different effects depending on their classification. Although depressants slow down the CNS, stimulants act in the opposite way by increasing its activity (Bedendo et al., 2016). Neurobiologically, what makes these drugs create different effects is the type of neurotransmission system involved, its particular mechanisms of action, and the brain areas that the drug affects.

Stimulants.

Cocaine and crack stimulate the CNS by blocking monoamine transporters (i.e., DA, serotonin, and noradrenaline), which are the main DA transporters. Stimulation results from the effect of the drug on different brain regions, including the ventral tegmental area, the amygdala, the hippocampus, and the frontal cortex. The neuroadaptations that result from cocaine and crack use can be extremely long-lasting, even following periods of extended abstinence. For these reasons, cocaine addiction is marked by repeated episodes of binging, withdrawal, recovery, and relapse (Beech & Sinha, 2011).

Amphetamines work differently to create an intracellular concentration of DA (Bedendo et al., 2016). Of all the drugs of abuse, amphetamines have the greatest effect on DA, and this is especially true of methamphetamine (Milkman & Sunderwirth, 2010). The damage to nerve endings of DA-producing cells caused by methamphetamine abuse lasts for at least 3 years following drug cessation because of this heightened overstimulation (Milkman & Sunderwirth, 2010).

Serotonin is a major contributor to the euphoria brought upon by MDMA use (Milkman & Sunderwirth, 2010). MDMA also increases activity in the prefrontal cortex, which is the area where higher-level brain processing happens (Csiernik, 2016). The rapid release of serotonin from nerve endings can also cause long-lasting damage to serotonin neurons (Milkman & Sunderwirth, 2010).

Depressants (including sedative-hypnotics).

Benzodiazepines bind to the GABA receptors. In turn, the drug modulates the functioning of the neuron, potentializing and prolonging the GABA effects, activating the chloride channels, increasing the number of chloride ions in the neuron, which then inhibits the neuron (Bedendo et al., 2016).

Hallucinogens (psychedelics).

Hallucinogens qualitatively work on the CNS by changing the perceptions of the individual. Hallucinogens are thought to create their effects by acting on neural circuits in the brain that rely on serotonin. Their prominent effects occur in the prefrontal cortex as well as in other areas that regulate arousal and physiological responses to stress and panic (National Institute on Drug Abuse, 2015a).

Inhalants.

The inhalants, except for nitrites, activate the brain's DA system (Milkman & Sunderwirth, 2010). Inhalants damage the myelin sheath of nerve cells, and, with chronic toluene abuse, the brain shrinks in size (Milkman & Sunderwirth, 2010).

Physical Impacts (Long-Term Use)

Chronic drug abusers experience both medical complications (Rastegar & Fingerhood, 2016) and a substantial reduction in life expectancy (Charlson et al., 2015). Taking drugs in ways that lead to a rapid and dramatic onset of effects (e.g., injection) often leads to the greatest number of problems (Earleywine, 2016). Having an SUD is also a risk factor for suicide (Lineberry & Brady, 2014). Interestingly, sometimes dramatic and even fatal sensitivity can occur when people use the same drugs in the same amount but in a different environment (Earleywine, 2016).

As one ages, alcohol and drug misuse becomes increasingly associated with many negative physical and mental health outcomes. This includes functional and cognitive impairments, compromised immune systems, and depression (Mavandadi & Oslin, 2015). Substance addiction often leads to accelerated aging processes such as a decline in brain volume and function and early beginnings of cardiac, cerebrovascular, kidney, and liver disease (Bachi, Sierra, Volkow, Goldstein, & Alia-Klein, 2017).

Drugs of abuse often cause sleep difficulties, including insomnia, hypersomnia, obstructive sleep apnea, and excessive sleepiness during day hours. Ara, Jacobs, Bhat, and McCall (2016) pointed out that it is often not recognized in substance use treatment programs that sleep problems can persist even after abstinence.

Diehl, Pillon, dos Santos, Rassool, and Laranjeira (2016) found that, in their sample of 508 Brazilian male drug users, 37.2% experienced sexual dysfunction, whereas 63.8% experienced premature ejaculation. The specific classes of drugs also lead to their own particular physical health issues.

Stimulants.

Although the most expected withdrawal symptom from stimulants is fatigue, some addicted individuals experience it as a jittery, nerve-racking, and edgy feeling (Earleywine, 2016). Interestingly, if a stimulant like cocaine or crystal meth creates a calming effect in an individual, this confirms that she or he has ADHD (Maté, 2008). Other symptoms of withdrawal include disturbed sleep, irritability, intense hunger, apathy, abdominal and muscle cramps, and moderate to severe depression. Some take to fits of violence (Csiernik, 2016).

Cocaine-related deaths have increased in the United Kingdom and the rest of Europe since the early 1990s. In the United Kingdom, 74% of the recorded deaths involve adults aged 25–44. Opioids are also involved in most of these deaths (58%; Corkery, Claridge, Goodair, & Schifano, 2017). Cocaine has anesthetic effects so, when combined with alcohol, barbiturates, or heroin, it increases the likelihood of death due to respiratory arrest (Csiernik, 2016). Cocaine-addicted individuals also appear aged compared to their peers, and their mortality is eight times higher than nonaddicted individuals of equivalent age (Csiernik, 2016).

Chronic cocaine use is associated with abnormal cardiac functioning (Mahoney, Haile, De La Garza, Thakkar, & Newton, 2017) and weakening of the immune system (Ersche & Doffinger, 2017).

Chest pain is often experienced by users and is a frequent reason for emergency room visits (Rastegar & Fingerhood, 2016). Although a 2001 systematic literature review did not find that prenatal cocaine was associated with developmentally toxic effects on children, cocaine use during pregnancy is related to an increased risk of vaginal bleeding, placental abruption, and premature labor (Rastegar & Fingerhood, 2016).

Although crystal meth is a powerfully addictive drug, most people who use it do not become addicted (Maté, 2008). Nonetheless, "there is no safe way to use crystal meth" (Maté, 2008, p. 303). Meth use predisposes people to tooth decay. Chronic meth use leads to many dental problems, a condition known as "meth mouth" (Stanciu, Glass, Muzyka, & Glass, 2017, p. 250). Although using meth can release up to 12 times more DA in the CNS compared to eating one's favorite food, the effect dissipates with sometimes as little as 6 months of regular usage (Csiernik, 2016).

MDMA use also has its own withdrawal syndrome. The sudden drop in serotonin experienced the next day may leave the user with high blood pressure, fatigue, anxiety, paranoia, and/or depression (Csiernik, 2016; Rastegar & Fingerhood, 2016). This has led to a slang expression called "Suicide Tuesdays" (Csiernik, 2016, p. 173). Using MDMA if one is taking antidepressants called MAO inhibitors is particularly dangerous. MDMA increases heart rate and blood pressure, and some myocardial infarctions have occurred in users with preexisting vascular malformations (Rastegar & Fingerhood, 2016). MDMA has led to chronic psychiatric symptoms in some users, including depression, anxiety, delusions, somatization, and psychosis (Rastegar & Fingerhood, 2016).

Depressants (including sedative-hypnotics).

With depressants, euphoria is followed by sedation, drowsiness, and sometimes seizures and unconsciousness. A coma and potentially death may result if enough of the drug is taken (Csiernik, 2016). Barbiturates often create both physical and psychological dependence, and dependency usually occurs after 2–4 weeks of regular use. The physical dependence on barbiturates is one of the most life-threatening of all drug dependencies because of the symptoms that occur shortly after cessation, most notable of which is respiratory depression (Csiernik, 2016). The benzodiazepines are much safer and rarely cause a fatal overdose. Nonetheless, benzodiazepines (e.g., Xanax or Valium) are implicated in over half of the nonfatal overdoses in Australia (Najman, McIlwraith, Kemp, & Smirnov, 2017). It is important to note that many clients who are physically dependent on sedative-hypnotics also misuse other drugs concurrently (Rastegar & Fingerhood, 2016).

Consuming GHB together with alcohol can lead to amnesia, confusion, and symptoms similar to having seizures. An overdose from GHB can cause respiratory problems, coma, or death (Csiernik, 2016).

Hallucinogens (psychedelics).

Unlike the other drugs, the primary effect of hallucinogens is not euphoria; instead, it is a disconnect from and change of perception of the physical world (Csiernik, 2016). There is no evidence that brain damage, chromosomal abnormalities, or congenital disabilities result from the use of LSD, psilocybin, or mescaline (Pechnick et al., 2014). Nonetheless, tolerance to hallucinogens develops within days (Csiernik, 2016). Hallucinogens do not appear to create physical withdrawal. Jimsonweed, on the other hand, can create circulatory collapse, coma, and even death with as little as a teaspoon of seeds (Csiernik, 2016).

Inhalants.

Some research has provided a link between the use of amyl nitrate and butyl nitrate and Kaposi's sarcoma, which is a form of cancer that affects the immune system. Inhalant use can create abdominal pains, amnesia, diarrhea, fatigue and sleepiness, headache and hangover, depressed mood, inattentiveness, irritability, incoordination, loss of appetite, and irregular or rapid heartbeat, and occasionally sudden death (Csiernik, 2016; Rastegar & Fingerhood, 2016). Asthmatics who use inhalants may experience diminished lung functioning (Rastegar & Fingerhood, 2016). Long-term effects from inhalant use can include neurological and cognitive deficits such as tremor, gait abnormality, and delirium, to name but a few (Rastegar & Fingerhood, 2016).

Mental, Emotional, and Spiritual Impacts

The amount of psychological distress caused by drug abuse and addiction can range from mild to severe. Whatever the severity, however, it can have a profoundly negative effect on a person's life. A drug-addicted individual often develops negative and unhappy thoughts together with a negative view of life. Addiction often negatively impacts their sense of self-esteem, self-worth, and self-acceptance.

Almost all drugs of abuse initially produce euphoria (Earleywine, 2016), and they are effective in alleviating the symptoms of physical or psychological distress (Rastegar & Fingerhood, 2016). But they do not solve the distress. Instead, the distress returns after the drug-taking is ceased, but, in addition to the original problem, there is often the common reaction of shame, guilt, and self-blame for the addictive behavior itself and things said and done while under the influence of the drug. Many drugs reduce inhibitions, and the addicted individual becomes likelier to engage in risky behavior. Addicted individuals are usually profoundly self-critical and hard on themselves (Maté, 2008). Drug addiction can result in emotional trauma that may persist for many years. Substance abusers also display elevated rates of alexithymia, which is a diminished ability to identify or express emotions (Earleywine, 2016).

The period that follows acute withdrawal is usually fraught with continuing difficulties. Problems dealing with the complexity of daily living (e.g., working, engaging in social relationships) and diminished problem-solving ability, memory, and learning sometimes persist over a long duration (Begun & Brown, 2014). Individuals often report problems with mood as they move through the recovery process, including irritability, anger, anxiety, and depression. This may be the result of elevated levels of norepinephrine in the extended amygdala. Norepinephrine acts as a stimulating neurotransmitter in the autonomic nervous system (Begun & Brown, 2014).

Anhedonia is also typical, which is when a person experiences a marked diminished ability to experience pleasure from naturally occurring experiences. It often persists for more than a year into the recovery process. This may result from disturbances of the DA system in areas of the brain that control motivation and reward (Begun & Brown, 2014). Continuing to think about, seek, and crave drugs also is common during the extended withdrawal process. Neurobiology suggests that this may occur from within the ventral striatum and extended amygdala (Begun & Brown, 2014). Sleep disturbances are also commonly experienced, most notably insomnia. Furthermore, a person who experiences severe insomnia during early recovery is likely to develop persistent insomnia, even in those who continue to not use their drug (Begun & Brown, 2014). Insomnia needs to be assessed and treated during the recovery process.

Heavy use of stimulants can lead to panic, generalized anxiety, mania, paranoia, and delusions (Earleywine, 2016). Psychosis and paranoia caused by cocaine is a relatively common experience for heavy users (Rastegar & Fingerhood, 2016). Meth-addicted individuals in remission experience impairments in executive functioning and impulsivity, and these deficits have a substantial impact in their everyday life (Ellis et al., 2016). The long-term effects of taking depressants can include difficulty concentrating, memory loss, confusion, diminished cognitive ability, high anxiety, and depression. Heavy use of MDMA has led to depression, anxiety, delusions, somatization, and psychosis in some individuals.

For most hallucinogens (except for cannabis), the long-term effects are only psychological (Csiernik, 2016). Nonetheless, Csiernik (2016) warned that people with mental health issues should avoid psilocybin as it can increase feelings of fear and confusion. Frequent users of LSD may experience flashbacks for months or years after cessation, which is technically known as hallucinogen persisting perception disorder (Rastegar & Fingerhood, 2016). Chronic use of LSD is also associated with amotivational syndrome, apathy, developing a passive attitude toward life, and diminished interest in the environment and social contacts (Csiernik, 2016). Hallucinogen intoxication can create symptoms of psychosis or delirium. Hallucinogen-induced psychosis has in some cases lasted from weeks to years (Pechnick et al., 2014). Long-term users of inhalants may experience disorientation, irritability, depression, and memory impairment.

Tim Stoddart (2013) wrote a non-peer-reviewed article about the possible spiritual impact of drug addiction on an individual. Spirituality is a vague term as it means different things to different people. Spiritual refers to anything that relates to the spirit or soul. Stoddart wrote that spirituality is an individual thing that is mostly about finding one's path toward inner peace and happiness. Addiction can have a devastating impact on this path. As the disease process of addiction occurs, the spiritual path becomes broken as lying to both others and oneself becomes normative to cover drug or alcohol use. Addicted individuals may be unaware of how they are hurting others, and some resort to stealing to secure their fix. Morals and values are deeply affected as the high and the search for the high become increasingly important. Even after the addicted individual quits using and becomes clean, becoming a moral person does not occur at once. Immorality is a habit that needs to be broken, and habits take time to change (Stoddart, 2013).

Psychosocial Impacts (Relationships, Career/Work, Legal, Financial)

Drug addictions are one of the most stigmatized health issues (da Silveira et al., 2018). They can profoundly change how a person interacts with the world, with resulting adverse impacts on intimate relationships, family connections, friendships, employment, educational advancement, financial issues, and legal issues. An addict's behavior typically changes: for example, an easygoing person may become prone to mood swings; aggressive outbursts; and unacceptable, extreme, or erratic behavior. Such behavior is difficult for others around them, especially when children are involved.

People struggling with drug addiction commonly lie to the people around them about their use. Once people learn to lie about one important matter, lying about other matters becomes easier, too. Addicted individuals can also become self-centered, selfish, and oblivious of the needs of others ("Social effects," n.d.). Staying in some form of relationship with an addicted individual often becomes increasingly difficult.

Drug-addicted individuals typically change their friends to those who are also drug users. In fact, one of the most consistent findings in drug research is the strong relationship between a person's drug use and concurrent use by friends (Milkman & Sunderwirth, 2010). Due to the problems that addiction creates, drug abuse is a significant predictor of homelessness (Csiernik, 2016).

Addiction is also associated with loss of employment (Beech & Sinha, 2011). Absences from work, diminished work performance, interpersonal difficulties, behavioral changes, and neglect of personal hygiene and self-care sometimes lead to job dismissal and financial ruin. Going into debt and spending often large sums of money on drugs is common. Often an intimate partner is unaware of the extent of spending. Some addicted individuals have blown large inheritances on drugs over a short period (Maté, 2008).

For some, the financial consequences lead to illegal activities that result in legal consequences. For example, drug abusers are three to four times likelier to commit a crime than nonabusers (Csiernik, 2016). Socioeconomically disenfranchised drug-addicted individuals are often unable to meet the cost of both their basic needs and illegal drugs (Luongo et al., 2017).

It is important to clarify that there is nothing about drugs that intrinsically turns a person into a criminal. Nonetheless, it is well-established that alcohol often feeds a person's internal aggression and removes barriers that thwart violence. Stimulants also have that effect on some drug users. Opioids, however, have the opposite effect by calling people down. It is when opioid-addicted individuals are in withdrawal that they are more likely to be irritable and aggressively out of desperation to secure more of their drug (Maté, 2008).

Given all of this information, drug-addicted individuals create strain in nearly all of their relationships with others, which in turn impacts their lives across all areas. Intimate relationships and marriages are strained, and many close connections end if the addiction persists unabated.

Working With Diverse Populations

Sex Differences

> We maintain that 'sex sameness' is as important as 'sex differences' when building a complete understanding of biology for both males and females . . . . By not doing so, a distorted landscape of how sex affects brain function and behavior might repeatedly be portrayed, thereby fueling the misleading (sometimes, even mischievous) notion that males and females are more different than they really are. (Sanchis-Segura & Becker, 2016, p. 1004)

Although males are more likely than females to use and abuse drugs, the gap between the sexes disappears during adolescence, and this is true for cocaine, cannabis, heroin, and the abuse of synthetic non-prescribed psychoactive drugs (Simonelli et al., 2017). Women are likelier than men to abuse prescription drugs such as tranquilizers and sedatives, whereas men are likelier to abuse illicit drugs such as cocaine and heroin (Fattore, Melis, Fadda, & Fratta, 2014).

There are sex-specific differences in how brain structures develop and function between males and females. For example, the frontal lobes reach their peak development of gray matter at 12 years of age in males but at 11 years of age in females, whereas development in the parietal lobes of gray matter is highly present at age 12 for boys and at age 10 for girls (Simonelli et al., 2017). Sex also affects SUD vulnerability rates, addiction pathways, and intervention processes and their outcomes (Simonelli et al., 2017).

Although women report initiating cocaine use at later ages compared to men, they progress quicker from first use to dependence, a phenomenon known as *telescoping* (Beech & Sinha, 2011). Furthermore, although childhood trauma is predictive of cocaine relapse in women, this finding is not replicated in men (Beech & Sinha, 2011).

Researchers have found that, in cocaine dependence, greater hyperactivity in the cortico- and striatal-limbic regions is linked to drug cues in men but to stress cues in women. This may explain why women report stress as the reason for drug use and relapse more often than men (Fattore & Melis, 2016). In outpatients who have abused cocaine and heroin, women have reported feelings of guilt after drug use and higher cravings to drug cues compared with men. Men, on the other hand, demonstrate a larger striatal DA release following amphetamine use, which may account for their higher vulnerability to stimulant use disorders. But, whereas cocaine use disorder has a higher prevalence among men than women, crack use is particularly frequent among young women and devoid of sex differences (Agabio, Campesi, Pisanu, Gessa, & Franconi, 2016). It also appears that the incidence of cocaine-induced mortality and psychosis is higher in women than in men (Agabio, Campesi, Pisanu, Gessa, & Franconi, 2016).

Whereas, in the general population, boys and men appear to be more impulsive than girls and women, among drug addicts, the opposite appears to be true (i.e., that females are more impulsive than males; Fattore & Melis, 2016). A substantial amount of evidence reveals that women are at higher risk of experiencing "alcohol-induced injury, liver disease, cardiomyopathy, myopathy, brain damages and mortality" (Agabio et al., 2016, p. 1030). Women are also more likely to experience greater side effects from heroin, marijuana, and cocaine as well as from the medications used to treat SUDs (Agabio et al., 2016). Substance-addicted women are also much more likely to experience physical and sexual abuse compared to women who are not addicted (Maté, 2008).

Adolescents and Youth

Nearly one third of the U.S. youth population (ages 12–17) used psychoactive substances in 2014, and about one fifth met criteria for having an SUD (Han, Compton, Blanco, & DuPont, 2017). Adolescents often lack insight or are unaware of the harm that drugs can cause (Rastegar & Fingerhood, 2016). The trends in their use of substances are bimodal: It is both favorable and unfavorable.

Data from 288,330 persons who participated in National Surveys on Drug Use and Health from 2002 to 2014, ages 12–17, were analyzed to ascertain trends in their use of substances and SUDs (Han et al., 2017). During this 12-year period, the 12-month prevalence of any substance use decreased by 27.1%, the 12-month prevalence of SUD decreased by 28.9%, and the ratio of dependence to abuse diminished from 2.2 to 1.6. The age at first using a substance increased from age 12.0 in 2002 to 13.1 in 2014.

The past-year prevalence of having a marijuana use disorder declined by approximately 24% between 2002 and 2013 (Grucza et al., 2016). The National Institute on Drug Abuse (2018b) reported that, whereas marijuana use by middle and high school students began to decline through the mid-2000s gradually, it has leveled, although some reports suggest it may have declined still further over the past 5 years.

This is excellent news given that the burden attributable to substance abuse and addiction begins in adolescence and young adulthood (Degenhardt, Stockings, Patton, Hall, & Lynskey, 2016). Research has shown that the pre-adolescent years (ages 10–12) remain a particularly vulnerable period for the development of longstanding substance abuse problems (Csiernik, 2016). The earlier age at which a drug is used, the higher the likelihood it will turn into drug abuse or addiction over a person's lifetime (Begun & Brown, 2014). For each year drug use is deferred, the rate of abuse and dependency drops by an additional 4%–5% (Begun & Brown, 2014).

Some teenagers are more at risk of becoming substance abusers and addicted individuals than others. Those who have trouble with emotional processing (e.g., affect regulation, alexithymia) and/or those who have greater interpersonal conflicts (e.g., underlying personality disorders) are more likely to abuse illicit drugs (El-Rasheed, ElAttar, Elrassas, Mahmoud, & Mohamed, 2017). Children and youth who experience early life stressors are at increased risk for developing SUDs (Blake, Tung, Langley, & Waterman, 2018; Yoon, Kobulsky, Yoon, & Kim, 2017). Street-involved youth are more likely to become involved in drug dealing if they are stimulant users and/or are homeless (Hepburn et al., 2016).

Although the brain continues to enlarge in size during adolescence, the more substantial changes concern its increasing interconnectedness and specialization (Giedd, 2015). Although it is believed that most effects from substance abuse are reversible in adolescents due to neuroplasticity, the risk of driving while intoxicated, increased aggressiveness, and unprotected sexual activity may lead to injuries or diseases that may result in disability or death (Begun & Brown, 2014). Furthermore, SUDs are also a leading cause of suicidality (Rastegar & Fingerhood, 2016).

The three most common substances of abuse for 12- to 17-year-olds in descending order are alcohol, tobacco, and marijuana (Herron, 2016). Inhalant use is in fourth place for this age bracket. Inhalant use is highest among teenagers and declines with age (Herron, 2016). The most commonly used inhalants in descending order are nitrous oxide, amyl nitrite, and organic compounds. Approximately half a million Americans are current inhalant users (Rastegar & Fingerhood, 2016).

Prescription drug misuse has become a growing problem in the United States (Park, Melander, & Sanchez, 2016). Parents ought to monitor drug use by their children, including the use of prescription medications. A recent longitudinal study found evidence for the importance of this advice. McCabe, Veliz, Wilens, and Schulenberg (2017) followed 8362 individuals from age 18 to age 35. The researchers found that 8.1% used prescribed stimulants and 16.7% had used them nonmedically. Although those who used them by prescription did not differ from controls, those who used them nonmedically had lower educational attainment and greater symptoms of SUDs.

Both alcohol and cannabis are associated with an increased percentage of vehicular accidents. Given that alcohol-related accidents of youth between ages 15 and 24 account for 46% of their deaths, and suicide claims another 13% (Milkman & Sunderwirth, 2010), the more "socially accepted" drugs used by today's youth remain a serious concern. Thankfully, most drug problems dissipate spontaneously as individuals move into young adulthood. The proportion of those age 24 and older who continue abusing drugs is small compared with the percentage of initial users (Csiernik, 2016).

Race and Ethnicity

Hastings (2009) stated that population growth among racial and ethnic groups is rapidly increasing in the United States. Projections are that, by 2050, a majority of the population will comprise persons from racial and ethnic minorities. There is little overall difference by race or ethnicity regarding the prevalence rate of drug use in the United States, but there are some "notable differences between groups in drug use patterns, preferences, risk factors, and reported drug consequences" (Beatty, 2010, p. 325).

Research based on the National Survey on Drug Use and Health published in 2007 found that the rates of dependency on alcohol and illicit drugs increased for Latinos and African Americans (Hastings, 2009). At the same time, the data suggest that African Americans abuse illegal drugs at a similar or lower prevalence than Whites. Research on Latinos suggests they have a high prevalence rate for substance abuse and the highest reported symptoms of dependency compared with African Americans and Whites (Hastings, 2009). African Americans and Latinos also experience more adverse consequences from substance addictions compared with Whites. This is believed to result from poverty status, education, unemployment, families in crisis, low or no insurance coverage, etc.

Data regarding Asian Americans (AA) and Native Hawaiians/Pacific Islanders (NHPI) are often aggregated because of their relatively small population size. When they are considered as a single group, AAs and NHPIs have a low prevalence of substance use and disorders. However, when data for the two groups are separated, NHPIs have a higher prevalence of substance use (alcohol, drugs) compared with AAs (Wu & Blazer, 2015). Both groups are unlikely to seek treatment, particularly for alcohol problems (Wu & Blazer, 2015).

Oh and DeVylder (2014) conducted a study about homelessness based on results from the National Latino and Asian American Survey. They found that, among Latinos, alcohol abuse or dependence were risk factors for homelessness while attending religious services more than once a week acted as a protective factor. Substance abuse was not related to homelessness for Asians.

Perceptions of racial minorities with drug addictions were skewed in documentary films between 1991 and 2008. For example, White addicted individuals were shown as individuals suffering from disease and in need of treatment, despite heavy criminal involvement. Minority addicted individuals were underrepresented, but, when they were depicted, they were highlighted with criminal narratives, which highlighted personal choice and deviance (Anderson, Scott, & Kavanaugh, 2015).

Nonpsychiatric Disabilities

More than 50 million Americans live with some form of mental or physical disability (Addiction.com, 2014). West et al. (2009) commented that people with disabilities are often overlooked in addictions research despite the extreme rates of alcoholism and other drug abuse issues that some disabled individuals experience.

The Christopher and Diana Reeve Foundation Paralysis Resource Center reported that substance abuse occurs more frequently in the disabled community than in the general population (American Addiction Centers, 2018). Those with intellectual disabilities experience disproportionate problems with substance use (Chapman & Wu, 2012; Sharma & Lakhan, 2017). A 2006 study based on admissions data from the State of Maine Treatment Data System ($N = 12{,}639$) found that persons with developmental disabilities were less likely to abuse opiates and prescription drugs than others who were in treatment (Brucker, 2008).

Reportedly more than 50% of people with traumatic brain injuries or spinal cord injuries abuse drugs or alcohol (American Addiction Centers, 2018). Individuals who are deaf or who have arthritis or multiple sclerosis have substance abuse rates double that of the general population (American Addiction Centers, 2018).

Some research from Sweden has suggested that individuals with autism spectrum disorders (ASDs) are at a higher risk of developing a substance disorder (Butwicka et al., 2017). Butwicka et al. (2017) reviewed data from 26,986 individuals diagnosed with ASD between 1973 and 2009 together with 96,557 non-ASD relatives. Those with ASD had double the risk of developing an SUD. Individuals who had both ASD and ADHD were at the highest risk of all.

Lesbian, Gay, Bisexual, and Transgender (LGBT)

Many studies have found that LGBT individuals experience addictions and substance abuse problems at a higher prevalence compared to heterosexual and cisgendered people (Chaney & Brubaker, 2014; Green, Bux, & Feinstein, 2013; Irwin, 2009; Wallace & Santacruz, 2017). A study of 215 men who have sex with men in New York City found that 78% of the participants were addicted to methamphetamine, and, of this group, over 70% were also dependent on other substances such as cocaine and ecstasy (Solomon, Halkitis, Moeller, & Pappas, 2012). Gay and bisexual men are also common ingesters of club drugs, and, for some, this is well-controlled (Naidoo, 2017).

Often transgender individuals are either excluded from research or subsumed under the sexual minority population (i.e., lesbian, gay, bisexual). When they need residential addiction treatment, they often face stigma that expresses itself in the form of social rejection and violence. They also face transphobia in residential treatment (Lyons et al., 2015).

Given the higher prevalence of addiction and substance abuse in the LGBT community, counselors are wise to routinely assess these issues when working with this population (Alderson, 2013). Underlying issues often include internalized homophobia, biphobia, and/or transphobia (Alderson, 2013).

War Veterans

Plenty of research has established the problem of SUDs in American veterans. Maté (2008) wrote that military personnel in the Vietnam War experienced lack of meaning and, together with the dangers of war itself, created a major stress factor that triggered the onset of SUDs in this population. But it appears that there is an increasing veteran population with SUDs (Carroll et al., 2016). Bohnert, Ilgen, Louzon, McCarthy, and Katz (2017) looked at the associations between SUDs and suicide for men and women receiving Veterans Health Administration care. Their sample included all recipients who were alive at the beginning of 2006 (N = 4,863,086). This data was compared to National Death Index records between 2006 and 2011. The researchers found that SUDs were all associated with significantly increased risk of suicide for both males and females. After adjusting for several factors, they found that current SUDs and increased suicide risk were especially true for women.

The evidence is accumulating that cocaine use may alter the structure and function of different systems in the brain, and the extent of recovery that will occur over time is unclear (He et al., 2018). He et al. (2018) examined 39 male military veterans who experienced different stages of cocaine addiction and long-term abstinence (1 year up to 30 years). Participants were invited to come to the Cognitive Neuroscience Imaging Center, where they were given an MRI scan. The results revealed that there were differences in both brain structure (gray matter volume) and function between cocaine users and the control group. Because of the small sample size, He et al. suggested that their results should be viewed as preliminary. The results do suggest, however, that male military veteran cocaine users remain at higher risk compared to controls for experiencing lapses in judgment and decision-making, which in turn may lead to relapse.

Soldiers who are drug addicted are more difficult to discipline and train. They demonstrate more critical attitudes toward military service obligation and are more likely to believe that it is a waste of time. Those who use drugs generally produce worse results in general and in professional military training (Jedrzejczak & Blaszczyk, 2005). Of 552 soldiers in the Polish army in 2001, over half of those who ingested drugs (total percent that used was 16.6%) believed that the drugs did not disturb their service ability (Jedrzejczak & Kocur, 2003). The most common drugs used were marijuana and amphetamine.

Medications and Other Relevant Physical Interventions

The treatment of drug addiction is challenging, and many of the approaches used today have low effectiveness, particularly when used alone. As Begun and Brown (2014) noted, "medication alone is not a sufficient treatment intervention" (p. 53). Integrated approaches to treatment are generally recommended, and these often include both medications and evidence-informed behavioral therapies (Begun & Brown, 2014).

Mendes and Prado (2016) wrote about using herbal medicines to treat drug addiction, but more clinical trials are needed to look at this as a viable avenue. Similarly, hallucinogens such as ayahuasca, ibogaine, psilocybin, LSD, and ketamine have been used for both problematic drug use and alcohol use but require further study (Heink, Katsikas, & Lange-Altman, 2017; Morgan, McAndrew, Stevens, Nutt, & Lawn, 2017).

Note that some medications are used to help manage withdrawal, others to assist in relapse prevention, and still others that deal with coexisting conditions. Not all drugs require a detoxification phase. Although medications might be significant in treating alcohol, opioids, benzodiazepines, and cocaine/crack withdrawal, other drugs like LSD, psilocybin, and amphetamines (including methamphetamine) do not produce substantial withdrawal syndromes (Andrade & Micheli, 2016). Below are medications that have found some success in assisting some people with drug addiction.

Stimulants

No medication has yet to be approved for stimulant addiction (Csiernik, 2016; Phillips, Epstein, & Preston, 2014). Consequently, treatment remains focused on behavioral interventions (Phillips et al., 2014). There is no specific treatment for a stimulant overdose, although benzodiazepines are often used to reduce agitation and phenothiazines to reduce psychotic symptoms (Rastegar & Fingerhood, 2016). Ibogaine has been used as a drug to potentially eliminate dependency on stimulants (Csiernik, 2016). Drugs that target glutamate in the brain and those with GABAergic effects hold promise but require further study (Sofuoglu & Forray, 2014). Inderal has been associated with abstinence in some highly motivated cocaine- and methamphetamine-addicted individuals (Tanguay, n.d.).

It is believed that regular use of MDMA depletes serotonin, which suggests that selective serotonin reuptake inhibitors (SSRIs, a class of antidepressants that are believed to work by inhibiting the reuptake of serotonin in the brain) may be useful as a form of replacement therapy. Some studies have indeed shown that SSRIs (i.e., fluoxetine and duloxetine) block the effects of MDMA (Rastegar & Fingerhood, 2016).

Cocaine/crack.

Medications targeting dopamine D1 and D3 receptors have been developed and tested on rodents and nonhuman primates. Unfortunately, these have not had favorable results with humans due to toxicity and several negative side effects (Galaj, Ewing, & Ranaldi, 2018).

N-Acetylcysteine is a drug that is used to treat acetaminophen overdose among other medical conditions, and it is also helpful in treating cocaine addiction and cannabis dependence (Asevedo, Mendes, Berk, & Brietzke, 2014). Other glutamatergic drugs (e.g., acamprosate, D-cycloserine, gabapentin, lamotrigine, memantine, modafinil, and topiramate) hold promise for treating both drug and behavioral addictions but require further testing (Olive, Cleva, Kalivas, & Malcolm, 2012). Antabuse is also being studied for its potential helpfulness in cocaine addiction (Soyka & Mutschler, 2016).

Ritalin, which is very similar in structure to cocaine, has proven helpful for some people with cocaine addiction (Perkins & Freeman, 2018). Although both drugs increase DA in the brain, Ritalin has slower reuptake, which reduces dependence potential. Another stimulant that is being researched for cocaine addiction is methylphenidate (Soyka & Mutschler, 2016). A drug used to treat narcolepsy called modafinil is also being researched (Soyka & Mutschler, 2016). Benzodiazepines are used with cocaine-addicted individuals who are agitated (Beech & Sinha, 2011). It is important to keep in mind that no medication has been consistently helpful in treating cocaine addiction, and no drug has been FDA approved for treating it (Soyka & Mutschler, 2016).

Methamphetamine.

In mild to moderate methamphetamine addiction, bupropion has been shown to assist in abstinence. Modafinil has also been helpful as has Concerta (Elkashef & Montoya, 2012). Naltrexone has also helped individuals with amphetamine addiction, and Lobeline has a potential benefit (Elkashef & Montoya, 2012). Dextran, Ritalin, and Provigil have shown benefit in some small drug trials (Tanguay, n.d.).

Depressants (Including Sedative-Hypnotics)

Long-term benzodiazepine users who suddenly stopped taking their drug often experience severe discomfort and even life-threatening complications. One approach used by an addiction unit is administering Flumazenil to ease the detoxification process (Faccini et al., 2016). Valium and Phenobarbital, both benzodiazepines, are used to help people with benzodiazepine withdrawal (Csiernik, 2016; Rastegar & Fingerhood, 2016). "Benzodiazepines with long half-lives are used to assist persons to withdraw from dependencies on benzodiazepines with short half-lives" (Csiernik, 2016, p. 206). Gradually reducing the dose is also a recommended protocol (Tanguay, n.d.). For those who use benzodiazepines for sleep, an alternative is to substitute medications that are less likely to cause dependence (e.g., zolpidem, melatonin, trazodone, amitriptyline, quetiapine; Andrade & Micheli, 2016).

Hallucinogens (Psychedelics)

The best treatment for most individuals high on a hallucinogen is to create a calm and supportive environment. For some, administering a benzodiazepine or other sedative may be helpful (Rastegar & Fingerhood, 2016).

Inhalants

There is no effective treatment available for acute inhalant intoxication and withdrawal (Canadian Pediatric Society, 2018). Antiarrhythmics or beta-blockers may be used to stabilize the myocardium and avoid overstimulation by catecholamines.

Club Drugs (Rohypnol, Date Rape, GHB, Flunitrazepam)

For GHB, withdrawal is similar to that of alcohol. High-dose benzodiazepines are recommended for withdrawal from it and inpatient care may be needed (Tanguay, n.d.).

Polydrug Users

Ohana et al. (2016) began a study with 121 polydrug users who volunteered, but only 64 participated for at least 1 month. The researchers tested the drug called dehydroepiandrosterone (DHEA), which is a circulating steroid hormone found naturally in the human body, to see if it would reduce relapse rates. After 16-month follow-up, relapse rates in the DHEA condition were about one third compared with the placebo group (12% versus 38%).

Some males and females around the world co-abuse benzodiazepines and methamphetamine (Spence, 2017). The benzodiazepines are used to help with the side effects of methamphetamine, but, in some cases, the addicted individual will become addicted to the benzodiazepines and will need to be careful during withdrawal. For those who abuse opioids and cocaine, psychopharmacology studies have found mixed results of medications that may prove helpful (Tanguay, n.d.). In those who abuse opioids and alcohol, buprenorphine has been found more beneficial than methadone in reducing alcohol consumption and alcohol craving (Tanguay, n.d.). Antabuse has been found helpful in those who co-abuse alcohol and cocaine (Tanguay, n.d.).

Specific Counseling Considerations

ROLEPLAY SCENARIOS

Roleplay in dyads with one of you acting as the counselor and the other as the counselee. If a roleplay is not possible, work individually in writing out a list of your suggestions.

Roleplay #1

Dalton, age 21, started using crystal meth when he was 14. He said he began his use only at parties and fell in love with this drug because of how uninhibited and sexual it made him feel. His use escalated until he dropped out of school before finishing grade 12. Although he tells you that he binges only on weekends, he is finding it challenging to organize his thoughts well enough to maintain stable employment. He is coming to you to find out how he can keep using but to find a way to focus his thoughts better so that he can work.

(Continued)

(Continued)

Roleplay #2

Ruth, age 36, came to see you because her employer has become concerned about her frequent absences. Ruth tells you that she has been enhancing her spirituality through using LSD but that sometimes her trips last longer than expected. Consequently, she finds it difficult to go to work sometimes on a Monday. She begins describing some of the effects that LSD is causing her. Ruth tells you, "I have to tell you that I have had some incredible experiences! At times, however, I feel like I am invincible and I do not experience pain. There have also been some occasions where I have felt hostile and aggressive, and I am trying to figure out where that is coming from because it is unlike me." As Ruth provides you further details, you begin to suspect that, instead of always purchasing LSD, she is sometimes buying PCP instead.

HOW WOULD AN ADDICTION COUNSELOR HELP THIS PERSON?

You are working as a professional counselor. Curt is a 20-year-old gay man. For the past 2 years, he has been a regular at nightclubs and massive gay raves known as circuit parties. He tells you that he has used every club drug at one time or another. He has recently been getting heavily into Molly, which he tells you is a "purer" form of MDMA. You are aware, however, that many drugs today sold as ecstasy or Molly do not even contain trace amounts of MDMA. Nonetheless, Curt tells you that he has been losing weight, and he is already of slight build. More disconcerting, however, is that he is beginning to suspect that a group of homophobes is following him around and taping some of his conversations. As you inquire further, there appears to be no good reason to believe that this is occurring.

Remember to view clients within their environmental contexts, keeping in mind societal, parental/familial, cultural/spiritual, and peer influences. Specifically, become aware of the impact that the following influences have and continue to have in your clients' lives: race, language, religion and spirituality, gender, familial migration history, sexual/affectional orientation, age and cohort, physical and mental capacities, socioeconomic situation and history, education, and history of traumatic experience.

1. What defines this person's environment, past and present?
2. Who is this person sitting in front of me, taking into account environmental and personal characteristics?
3. What defines the problem that he or she is presenting within their multicultural milieu?

Goals and Goal Setting

Treatment goals for either abstinence or harm reduction need to be worked out collaboratively with our clients (Blume & Logan, 2013). Regardless of the impact that a drug may be having on an individual, it is that person who still must decide (possibly in consultation with us) what he or she intends to do about drug use, misuse, or addiction. Although drugs compromise a person's free choice, no drug can force its user to consume it. Some people seem to need to hit "rock-bottom," that place where they have lost nearly everything that matters. But that is not everyone's story by any stretch. It is possible for individuals to reverse the neurobiological manifestations of addictions through their efforts (Uusitalo & van der Eijk, 2016).

It is important to know that harm reduction strategies are helpful for clients who are unwilling or unable to stop their addictive behaviors (Blume & Logan, 2013). What choices does a drug-addicted individual have? Here are their options:

1. Drug substitution. Individuals can turn to safer drugs. For example, addictiveness and physical harm are greatest for drugs like alcohol, heroin, and cocaine, and they are considered the lowest for drugs like caffeine, cannabis, and hallucinogens (Earleywine, 2016). There is no evidence that harm reduction encourages drug use (Maté, 2008).
2. Reduce use of the problem drug. Although not everyone can do this even with help, many if not most will prefer

to give this a try before deciding if abstinence is their best option (whether they are successful at achieving it or not).

3. Creating greater drug safety. This involves using the drug responsibly and/or in safer environments, for example, using hallucinogens only in the company of trusted friends. Avoiding polydrug use would be another positive strategy.

4. Avoiding simultaneous polydrug use. Following this rule alone helps reduce the number of overdoses. As Earleywine (2016) cautioned, a good rule of thumb for stimulant users is not to take an additional dose of a stimulant before recovering from the first dose.

5. Abstinence. Abstinence will likely be the goal for most people attending a mutual support group based on AA principles and for those who have decided that this is the best goal. It will also be the best choice for those who have unsuccessfully attempted (a) drug substitution, (b) reducing the use of the problem drug, (c) creating greater drug safety, and/or (d) avoiding simultaneous polydrug use, which are harm reduction strategies noted previously.

Stages of Change Strategies

The processes of change mentioned are based on those outlined by Connors, DiClemente, Velasquez, and Donovan (2013) and Prochaska, Norcross, and DiClemente (1994). The definitions for the various processes can be found in Chapter 6. Besides these processes, other strategies are included that have separate citations.

The University of Rhode Island Change Assessment Scale (URICA) is a helpful scale in determining where the client is currently regarding the stages of change model. There are 24-, 28-, and 32-item versions of the scale.

A 24-item version is published for alcohol or drug problems. The scale, however, is generic and can be easily adapted for use with other addictions. It is available with norms as a free download from https://www.guilford.com/add/miller11_old/urica.pdf.

Specific precontemplation strategies.

Please visit the section of this chapter called Relevant Mutual Support Groups, Websites, and Videos for free or low-cost information and resources that may help someone move out of precontemplation.

A very good movie about drug addiction is called *Requiem for a Dream* (2000). Another good choice is *The Basketball Diaries* (1995). A documentary available from YouTube (https://www.youtube.com/watch?v=7thZbHTvZIQ) called *Ben: Diary of a Heroin Addict* (2008) is yet another great choice.

Although people in the precontemplation phase might not be interested in reading about drug addiction, there will be those who are. Here are a few suggested books:

1. *Beyond Addiction: How Science and Kindness Help People Change* (by Jeffrey Foote, Carrie Wilkens, Nicole Kosanke, and Stephanie Higgs, 2014). This book looks at how positive reinforcement and kindness are more effective than tough-love approaches to creating a lasting recovery.

2. *Recovery: Freedom from Our Addictions* (by Russell Brand, 2017). Russell is an English comedian, actor, and radio host. His style is humorous and entertaining.

3. *Rewired: A Bold New Approach to Addiction and Recovery* (by Erica Spiegelman, 2015). This book is considered by some to be one of the best modern addiction recovery books. It includes positive affirmations and intentions together with an action-oriented approach.

4. *The Gifts of Imperfection: Let Go of Who You Think You're Supposed to Be and Embrace Who You Are* (by Brene Brown, 2010). Likely everyone should read this book because it is about self-acceptance and self-love.

5. *Spirit Junkie: A Radical Road to Self-Love and Miracles* (by Gabrielle Bernstein, 2012). This is another book about self-love, although it is presented in a very accessible way.

During the precontemplation stage, drug use has become so normalized that it is not viewed as a problem. Instead, it has become part of an addict's identity. They are resistant to changing their drug use pattern (Rastegar & Fingerhood, 2016). Cocaine-addicted individuals during the precontemplation stage believe they have the greatest control over their drug use, which is in sharp contrast to where they have the lowest perception of control during the maintenance stage (Fanton, Azzollini, Ayi, Sio, & Mora, 2013). Individuals in this stage need help in gaining insight into their behavior by the proviso of facts and information (Csiernik, 2016).

Chambers and Wallingford (2017) likened the process of addiction recovery to both going through grieving per Kubler-Ross's stages of grief and Prochaska's stages of change. Physical activity is often included as part of a treatment program for drug addicts, and Williams and Strean (2004) included a short questionnaire to ascertain at what stage of change an addicted individual is at regarding readiness for exercise. Their questions are as follows:

Circle the statement that best applies to you:

1. I currently do not exercise, and I do not intend to begin exercising within the next 6 months [i.e., precontemplation].

2. I currently do not exercise, but I intend to start within the next 6 months [i.e., contemplation].

3. I exercise some, but not regularly (three times per week, for 20 minutes or longer) [preparation].

4. I currently exercise regularly, but I have been doing so for less than 6 months [action].

5. I currently exercise regularly and have been doing so for longer than 6 months [maintenance]. (p. 91)

Specific contemplation strategies.

Individuals early in the contemplation stage are not convinced that they need to change their drug use, but at least they are considering it. Counselors can help people at this stage look at a cost-benefit analysis of their drug use to help them decide whether to make a change now. It is important to recognize that some people will stay in the contemplation stage for years. Often the best strategies involve providing nonjudgmental information and using motivational approaches, not confrontational methods, to encourage change (ideas adapted from lastingrecovery.com).

People in the contemplation stage are often ambivalent about their drug use. Although they might be thinking about making a change, they might not know how to and may not be confident in their ability. It is always best to help them find their reasons to cut down or stop their drug use. Once individuals begin to plan for changing their drug use behavior, they move into the preparation stage of change.

Specific preparation strategies.

In the preparation stage, the individual decides on what changes are needed and on what type of treatment might be helpful to create that change. This work, of course, can be facilitated with a counselor, or another individual can assist in brainstorming action plans. Goals and strategies need to be clarified in this stage. It is important not to rush the preparation stage. The counselor helps the client evaluate the problem with a greater focus on the future than on the past. The plan works best when it is created mostly by the client. Some components of the change plan might include the following:

1. Deciding whether to diminish use, practice harm reduction, or abstain altogether. Depending on the goal, the specifics of how the goal will be realized needs to be explicit (e.g., if diminishing use, how much will the use need to be reduced? What will be necessary to facilitate that reduction?).
2. Attending support groups such as Narcotics Anonymous or Cocaine Anonymous.
3. Committing to see a counselor on a regular basis.
4. Applying to a treatment program or entering a hospital for detoxification.
5. Changing the types of relationships the person has with those who are still using drugs.
6. Deciding and soliciting the support of those who will become the support network during the change process.
7. Obtaining necessary resources (i.e., securing appropriate medication).
8. Eliminating triggers (e.g., getting rid of drug paraphernalia, relocating if living with others who are current users).

Other ideas for *before* their chosen quit day (i.e., preparation strategies) can be found in Appendix B.

Specific action strategies.

Although it is important to help our clients develop hope and approach treatment with a positive attitude, it is also imperative to prepare them for potential problems that may arise with lapses and relapse remaining as normative possibilities. Lapses and relapses should not be viewed as failures but instead as temporary setbacks. We can help our clients use these as learning opportunities to determine continuing changes that need to be made to reduce the likelihood that the same high-risk situations will again lead to a return to drug use.

However, our clients face barriers in receiving treatment from counselors and other professionals. By being aware of these barriers, counselors can be better prepared to deal with clients who may need help. A meta-analysis revealed that, at least for methamphetamine abusers, the four most commonly endorsed barriers to seeking help include embarrassment and stigma, believing that treatment is unnecessary, preferring to go through withdrawal alone, and privacy concerns (Cumming, Troeung, Young, Kelty, & Preen, 2016). Besides barriers, equally disparaging is that there remains no gold-standard treatment for cocaine addiction, and even psychosocial treatments (including contingency management) have limited/short-term efficacy (Fischer et al., 2015).

Nonetheless, there are many action strategies available for drug addictions, each with varying degrees of efficacy and effectiveness. Morrison, Lin, and Gersh (2018) argued that an integrated approach is often preferable, despite the fact that most studies using integrative treatments have only concentrated on cigarette smoking, alcohol, and opiate use disorders. Recall from Chapter 6 that the integrative approach mixes mainstream therapies (i.e., psychological and pharmacological) with complementary and alternative therapies.

There are guides to assist in placing clients into the appropriate level of care. The American Society of Addiction Medicine developed criteria that are now required in over 30 states. Visit the society's website for details (https://www.asam.org/resources/the-asam-criteria). The criteria resulted from a collaboration that began in the 1980s, and they have become the most widely used and comprehensive set of guidelines. The criteria include six dimensions as follows:

1. Acute intoxication and/or withdrawal potential.
2. Biomedical conditions and complications.
3. Emotional, behavioral, or cognitive conditions and complications.
4. Readiness to change.
5. Relapse, continued use, or continued problem potential.
6. Recovery/living environment.

The National Institute on Drug Abuse offers many free manuals on treatment for drug addiction. A search engine for these can be found at https://www.drugabuse.gov/publications.

Some of the goals of the action stage often include the following:

1. Entering the level of treatment that was decided in the preparation stage. The levels of care continuum include the following: (a) support group, (b) support group plus individual therapy, (c) support group, individual therapy, and medication, (d) intensive outpatient program, (e) partial hospitalization, (f) hospitalization, and (g) residential.
2. Finding alternative sources of pleasure. Our clients will miss the highs that the preferred drug used to create, so it is important that they find other pleasurable activities. Leisure time is associated with both the prevention and treatment of problematic drug use (Lacsan, Arany, & Farkas, 2017). Recall that stimulant-addicted individuals may not be able to experience much pleasure for several months or years. It is important that stimulant-addicted clients understand this. They may need to "fake it till they make it" before real pleasure returns to them. Moderate exercise has been shown to reduce depressive

symptoms in meth-addicted individuals after 60-min sessions offered three times a week over an 8-week period (Haglund et al., 2015).

3. Learning new coping skills in place of their drug use. Drug use was often used as the panacea for every life circumstance whether stress (i.e., negative emotions) or joy (i.e., positive emotions). Life skills will be necessary to handle both the negative and positive feelings and occasions.
4. Develop and implement relapse prevention strategies. This will entail many components that were outlined in Chapter 6.
5. Learn better ways to deal with stress. Stress is recognized as the most predictable trigger for relapse (Maté, 2008).
6. Activate social support systems. These were previously decided in the preparation stage.
7. Work on bringing emotions back into a healthy balance (Maté, 2008). Addictions create false emotions—artificial highs followed by artificial downs (i.e., negative moods created by physical withdrawal instead of by life circumstances). The healthy balance of emotions refers to experiencing real positive and negative emotions that surface once substance abuse desists.
8. Modify the change plan as new issues arise or as other events suggest that revising the plan will enhance effectiveness.

Substantial literature reveals that various interventions are helpful in creating significant change with those individuals diagnosed with SUDs (Hall & Walker, 2017). Meta-analyses, for example, have shown that cognitive-behavioral therapy (CBT), motivational interviewing (MI), acceptance and commitment therapy, 12-step treatments, and contingency management are efficacious (Hall & Walker, 2017). Although these approaches are promising, the effect size from treatment generally ranges from small to medium, indicating that they are moderately effective (Hall & Walker, 2017). One of the inherent difficulties is that addictions often co-occur with other disorders (Holmes, 2017).

"Substance abusers are a heterogeneous group, necessitating different types of intervention methods" (Csiernik, 2016, p. 197). Consequently, it is important to attempt to match the client with the most appropriate counseling approach (Csiernik, 2016). Unfortunately, this is much more art at present than science. As Chapter 6 indicated, treatment method is only one factor in the process of helping people change. Other factors include the strength of the working alliance, the personality of the counselor, and the qualities of the clients themselves. Given that most addicted individuals have unresolved issues from their past, including current issues created by the clients' avoidance of past issues along with issues created by the drug addiction itself, several counseling approaches may be indicated.

Csiernik (2016) stated that a strength-based approach, which began in the United States in the 1980s, has become a contemporary focus in the addictions field. It focuses on clients' abilities, their competencies, and their resources instead of on their deficits, problems, and pathology. The six principles of this model, according to Csiernik, include the following: (a) addicted clients can fully recover, (b) the focus is on individual strengths and not deficits, (c) the community offers a plethora of resources, (d) clients direct the helping process, (e) working alliance is primary and essential, and (f) most of the work is done in the community and not in a residential center. The strength-based approach is most encapsulated in the postmodern therapies such as narrative therapy, solution-focused therapy, and collaborative therapy. Please see Chapter 6 for details.

Popular therapy approaches deal with existential issues such as aloneness, meaning and purpose in our lives, identity questions, what is appropriate behavior, and a person's obligations. Psychodynamic and psychoanalytic approaches deal with people's defenses, ego strengthening, overcoming self-criticism, and establishing stable and meaningful relationships (Csiernik, 2016).

Yoga has proven helpful for people with SUDs (Afonso, 2016) and it has been used for decades to assist with addictions (Dylan, 2014). Similarly, Vipassana meditation (mindfulness) has also been empirically validated as a method for decreasing substance abuse (Earleywine, 2016).

Eye movement desensitization and reprocessing (EMDR) has been found to reduce the intensity of substance-related imagery and craving, suggesting that EMDR may be a useful technique in addiction treatment (Littel, van den Hout, & Engelhard, 2016). Marich (2017) also wrote about how EMDR can be used in the treatment of addiction. Another technique that has shown success in reducing drug craving is systematic desensitization together with New Age relaxing music (Stamou, Chatzoudi, Stamou, Romo, & Graziani, 2016). Other art therapies have proven useful in drug addiction treatment, including music therapy (Fachner, 2017; Murphy, 2017) and dramatherapy (Krasanakis, 2017). Group counseling is also often recommended for SUD treatment (Rastegar & Fingerhood, 2016).

The Substance Abuse and Mental Health Services Administration offers many PDFs at no cost that are very helpful regarding treatment of substance abuse (see https://search.usa.gov/search/docs?affiliate=samhsa-store&dc=1415&query=TIP+42). The following are only a **few** examples you will find here:

- Substance Abuse Treatment for Persons with Co-Occurring Disorders (Treatment Improvement Protocol [TIP] 42). Quoted: "This guide gives substance use disorder treatment providers information on mental illness, substance use disorders, or both."
- Substance Abuse Treatment: Group Therapy (TIP 41). Quoted: "This guide helps counsellors improve their skills in leading group therapy sessions for substance use treatment."
- Substance Abuse Treatment for Adults in the Criminal Justice System (TIP 44).
- Detoxification and Substance Abuse Treatment (TIP 45).
- Addiction Counseling Competencies (Technical Assistance Publication Series [TAP] 21).

Although acupuncture has been studied for cocaine dependence, it has not been shown to be effective. Likewise, there is limited evidence to suggest that hypnotherapy is effective (Rastegar & Fingerhood, 2016). However, Pekala (2017) suggested that hypnotherapy may be used adjunctively to improve self-esteem and serenity, decrease anger and impulsivity, and access altered states of consciousness in a nonpharmacological way.

According to a substantial independent analysis, contingency management was the most effective psychosocial treatment for individuals with SUDs (Dutra et al., as cited in Petry, 2012). Contingency management involves creating a token economy for those with SUDs. This technique was covered in Chapter 6. Although the treatments used with adolescents are similar to those with adults, there is less evidence supporting their efficacy (Rastegar & Fingerhood, 2016). Other ideas for *beginning* their chosen quit day (i.e., action strategies) can be found in Appendix B.

Specific maintenance strategies and relapse prevention.

Note: Maintenance strategies and relapse prevention are also, for many, partly facilitated by regular attendance at relevant mutual support groups (MSGs). A list of such MSGs and helpful websites is found in an upcoming section entitled Relevant Mutual Support Groups, Websites, and Videos.

Many drug-addicted individuals are going to require long-term continuing care and relapse-prevention services (Brecht & Herbeck, 2014). There remains a propensity to relapse, even following months or years of abstinence (Chesworth & Corbit, 2017). Depending on one's definition, estimates suggest that more than 90% of addicted individuals will continue to have the potential to lapse or relapse (Csiernik, 2016). Reducing the risk of relapse is arguably the most important aspect of the maintenance stage. Research in this area often involves comparing relapse strategies. More severe users of cocaine, for example, who receive relapse prevention therapy are more likely to achieve abstinence compared with those who received interpersonal psychotherapy (Beech & Sinha, 2011).

Work is an important aspect of everyday life. In a study based on interviews with 32 opiate-addicted individuals in Sweden, work was regarded as an "indispensable tool" for remaining drug-free and for enhancing personal development (Augutis, Rosenberg, & Hillborg, 2016, p. 385). During the maintenance stage, continued efforts will need to be made to stabilize relationships and life circumstances, including work and free time (Rastegar & Fingerhood, 2016).

It is important to note that most people with SUDs do not maintain either abstinence or recovery on their first attempt (Rastegar & Fingerhood, 2016). The relapse process often occurs long before the addicted individual begins using the drug again. The three highest risk situations involve (a) anger and frustration, (b) social pressure, and (c) interpersonal temptation (Rastegar & Fingerhood, 2016). Furthermore, the relapse process often follows a predictable sequence: (a) return of denial, (b) growing isolation and defensiveness, (c) "creating" a crisis to justify the progression of symptoms, (d) becoming immobilized, (e) developing confusion and overreaction, (f) feeling depressed, (g) losing control over behavior, (h) recognizing this loss of control, and (i) relapse to using the drug (Rastegar & Fingerhood, 2016).

Becoming involved in activities, especially those which have nothing to do with possible drug use, helps improve mood and minimize lapses (Earleywine, 2016). It is important to teach clients that lapses are a part of change and to not let these become major emotional setbacks, thus creating a full relapse (Earleywine, 2016).

Csiernik (2016) stated that five strategies could be used in both the action and maintenance stages. They are as follows:

1. Reinforcement management. This is the use of reinforcements for not using the drug. Addicted individuals in recovery can reward themselves, for example, or it can be a group that recognizes their achievements.
2. Helping relationships. Having a strong therapeutic alliance with the counselor and having a buddy system (e.g., having a sponsor in an MSG) can be great sources of social support.
3. Counterconditioning. This involves substituting a healthier choice instead of taking a drug (e.g., relaxation instead of stress, assertiveness instead of following peers, nicotine replacement instead of smoking cigarettes).
4. Stimulus control. This involves eliminating cues for drug use and replacing them with cues for healthier alternatives (e.g., participating in mutual help groups, changing one's environment).
5. Social liberation. As an addicted individual becomes more involved in non-drug-related activities, they develop emotionally. Such growth allows them to consider the needs of others. In other words, they become liberated from their own selfishness. Social liberation requires that individuals become more involved in social activities, which may include advocacy and empowerment strategies for those who are marginalized.

Other ideas for relapse prevention can be found in Appendix C.

Motivational Interviewing

Although MI is generally done face-to-face in individual counseling, Jiang, Wu, and Gao (2017) did a systematic review and found that offering MI over the telephone is also effective in substance abuse treatment and prevention. A systematic review and meta-analysis has not, however, shown that MI is effective in reducing adolescent drug use (Li, Zhu, Tse, Tse, & Wong, 2016).

Rastegar and Fingerhood (2016) noted that the acronym FRAMES could be used to help remember the steps of MI. It stands for **F**eedback, **R**esponsibility, **A**dvice, **M**enu, **E**mpathy, and **S**elf-efficacy. Feedback of personal risk is a client-focused review of the problems drug use is creating. Responsibility for change is about helping clients to avoid self-blame but to know it is they who must make the change. Advice refers to clarifying that a change is needed. Menu is about providing alternatives to what the change could look like. Empathy involves demonstrating to clients that you understand the challenge before them. Self-efficacy is about encouraging and enhancing clients' views that they can change.

Furthermore, Rastegar and Fingerhood (2016) shared another useful acronym for remembering what change talk looks like: DARN-C. The following are the examples the authors used:

- Desire: Why would you want to make this change?
- Ability: How would you do it if you decided?
- Reasons: What are the reasons for change?
- Need: How important is it, and why?
- Commitment: What do you plan to do? (p. 24)

Here is an example of MI that incorporates DARN-C. (Pertaining to Chapter 6's description of MI, the following is an example of the three processes called *focusing, evoking*, and *planning*.) The client is Nathan, 36 years old.

Counselor: Hi Nathan. It's good to see you again.

Client: Thank you for seeing me on such short notice. I have been doing a lot of thinking about what we talked about last time.

Counselor: Please continue.

Client: Well, I know I need to do something about my cocaine and alcohol use. I don't know where to start, and, truthfully, whenever I do try to make a change, I always fall on my face and resort back to using.

Counselor: I know you have been dealing with this ambivalence for a long time. This is the third time I have seen you, and it has struck me that your resolve grows stronger each time. Please remind me why it is so important for you to change your use of cocaine and alcohol. [*Desire*]

Client: When I am high, I do incredibly stupid things. The last time, which was only 3 days ago, by the way, I used coke after getting drunk. I ended up spending $500 on blow and another $400 on hookers. I don't make enough money for this.

Counselor: You need to stop doing this because it costs you so much. [*Desire*]

Client: Yes, that's right.

Counselor: What other reasons do you have for wanting to make this change? [*Reasons*]

Client: I don't think my girlfriend is going to put up with much more of this.

Counselor: I can imagine this is hard on her, too. I know you have tried quitting before. How would you do it this time if you decided to quit for good? [*Ability*]

Client: That is why I am seeing you. I really don't know what to do.

Counselor: I know it is disappointing to work so hard at something and not succeed. What makes this time so important compared with your previous attempts at quitting for good? [*Need*]

Client: I don't know. I think mostly because I'm just getting fed up with the consequences of continuing. I am also pissed off that I don't feel I am in control.

Counselor: You have been down this road enough times. I understand that. The more you come up with what it is you want to do differently this time in quitting, the more you are going to take your advice and do it. What else could you try to reduce the likelihood that you are going to drink and start coke again? [*Commitment*]

Client: After I get my paycheck, I could have my girlfriend manage the finances for me and give me an allowance each week after expenses are paid. I think the key for me right now is that, if I have money around, I am going to spend it on drugs.

Counselor: You have been seeing your girlfriend for nearly 3 years. She sounds like someone you can trust. I know you have it in you to make this change, and I think, at this juncture, your idea holds a lot of merit. Is there anything else you could do to increase your chances for success this time around? [*Commitment*]

Client: I think I need to stop hanging out with my co-workers! [chuckles]

Counselor: [chuckles] In what ways would that help you, Nathan? [*Commitment*]

Client: The times I begin using is often after work on Fridays. I go out with my colleagues for beers, I drink too many, and then I go home and phone my dealer for coke. That starts a run that lasts the whole weekend.

Counselor: You have certainly made the connection between how you use your free time with colleagues and your cycle of abuse.

Client: Yes, that is true.

Counselor: How could you change this pattern? [*Commitment*]

Client: I really think my only hope is to only order soft drinks or to not join them at all after work.

Counselor: That sounds like a realistic appraisal of where you're at right now, Nathan. You are doing an excellent job of developing insight into what creates a lapse for you. Which of the two choices that you suggested regarding after work on Fridays would you want to try, if either?

Client: You know, I would really prefer not to try either at this juncture. If my girlfriend controls my allowance, that will prevent me from buying coke. Hanging out with my colleagues on Fridays is actually the highlight of my week.

Counselor: I understand. It sounds like you are committing to letting your girlfriend manage your finances until you feel stronger.

Insight-Oriented Interventions

Steinert, Munder, Rabung, Hoyer, and Leichsenring (2017) conducted a meta-analysis of 23 studies with a total of 2751 patients and concluded that psychodynamic therapy was as effective as CBT for a diverse number of mental disorders. Cristea, Cuijpers, and Naudet (2017) refuted these findings, however, by pointing out several shortcomings. Although the meta-analysis targeted various mental conditions, the studies used widely divergent measures for the disorders, thereby creating a heterogeneous mix regarding the relevance of the findings. Additionally, Steinert et al. included studies where patients were taking medications, further confounding the results.

Lightdale, Mack, and Frances (2015) stated that psychodynamic approaches could add depth to working with substance abusers, both individually and in groups. These authors also provided their own psychodynamic approach to working with addictions that include neurobiological findings.

Barrocas, Vieira-Santos, and Paixao (2016) suggested using a psychodynamic approach in both research and practice to look at the "fragile" parenting styles of those who are themselves drug addicts. These authors suggested that, even when drug use is curtailed or controlled, the parents' relational and mental abilities remain impaired, thus compromising the parent-child relationship.

Khantzian (1986) noted that early psychodynamic thinkers stressed pleasure-seeking or self-destruction in their views of addiction, whereas todays perspective focuses more on their internal emotions and their external adjustment. Khantzian also cautioned that group approaches, including MSGs, may be contraindicated for addicted individuals who experience "shame, severe social anxiety, paranoia, or depression" (p. 220). Those interested in reading more in this area are referred to the *Psychodynamics of Addiction* (Weegmann & Cohen, 2002), an edited book on the topic.

Spiritual Interventions

> *"No one saves us but ourselves.*
> *No one can, and no one may.*
> *We ourselves must walk the path:*
> *Buddhas only show the way."* (attributed to Lord Buddha)

Many church pastors are not trained in addictions despite the major problem it has become in American society (Daniels, 2016). There is plenty of research to demonstrate that spirituality promotes addiction recovery (Bliss, 2015). Also, religious or spiritual beliefs may lower the risk of substance addictions because of beliefs that support moderate use (or no use at all), association with others who moderate or abstain, and enhancement of a sense of well-being (Johnson & Kristeller, 2013).

Lee, Pagano, Johnson, and Post (2016) conducted a study of 195 adolescents with SUDs who were court-referred to residential treatment. They were assessed at intake, discharge, and 6 months later. The researchers found that those who provided greater service to others had lower levels of recidivism and relapse and experienced greater character development.

As Maté (2008) clarified, a higher power does not need to refer to a God. Instead, it can mean rising of above one's selfish ego to commit to something greater than immediate desires. An approach to counseling that integrates logotherapy, existential-humanistic therapy, narrative, CBT, and positive psychology is called meaning therapy (Wong, 2015, 2017). The motto of meaning therapy is "Meaning is all we have, Relationship is all we need" (Wong, 2015, p. 155). Meaning therapy intends to focus clients on what really matters such as "serving a higher meaning and developing loving relationships" (Wong, 2015, p. 156).

Cognitive-Behavioral Therapy

> *"The road to hell is not paved with good intentions. It is paved with the lack of intention"* (Maté, 2008, p. 362).

CBT can be facilitated using the triple column technique. It can be used both by counselors in their work with clients and by clients alone. The full instructions for using the method are found in Chapter 6. The following are some of the cognitions that can be problematic for clients with this addiction.

Automatic Thought or Belief	Questioning It	Healthier Thought or Belief
I am not responsible for my drug problem.		I am entirely responsible for my behavior. Dwelling on shame and guilt is unhelpful.
I have had so many good times while being high.		Using drugs has caused me a substantial number of adverse consequences. The initial highs can never be recaptured.
I desperately crave my drug of choice.		I am learning to take control of my behavior. My cravings will become less over time.
I feel really negative now that I am not using drugs.		My brain needs to recover, and this will take time. I am developing restraint, constraint, and strength of character.
I cannot get through the day without my drug.		I can and will get through the day. I need to focus on creating and living a new life filled with meaning and purpose.

CBT has the highest level of empirical validation as a treatment for SUDs (Carroll & Kiluk, 2017; Kiluk & Carroll, 2014). It can be offered individually and/or in group formats. CBT programs often involve contingency management and community reinforcement (Rastegar & Fingerhood, 2016). The goal of using CBT is to teach both coping and cognitive strategies to help prevent drug use (Sofuoglu & Forray, 2014). CBT is intended to teach addicted individuals when they are most likely to use drugs (i.e., high-risk situations), to avoid these situations, and to cope with their cravings (Kiluk & Carroll, 2014).

Some research has been done using computerized CBT for cocaine addiction, which has the advantage that material can be repeated as needed (Sofuoglu & Forray, 2014). Computerized behavioral interventions have been developed for computers, smartphones, and other electronic devices (Patterson Silver Wolf [Adelv Unegv Waya] et al., 2017). Several of these apps are included in the next section.

Marinchak and Morgan (2012) suggested that counselors who are behaviorally oriented need to accomplish six tasks: (a) develop a collaborative working alliance, (b) work toward enhancing patient motivation, (c) complete a functional analysis to create a thorough assessment of the client's presenting issues, (d) work with the client to develop treatment goals, (e) monitor and evaluate treatment progress, and (f) provide information for both long-term recovery and noticing early signs of relapse. Marinchak and Morgan wrote about behavioral techniques that addiction counselors can utilize. Although aversion therapy was used in the past, today techniques center on covert sensitization, cue exposure, behavioral self-control training, social skills training, contingency management, and relapse prevention (see Chapter 6 for a description of these techniques).

The recommended treatments for club drug addiction include CBT, both individual and group. Contingency management has proven effective, but the treatment of club drug addiction has proven challenging due to the young age of users and the likelihood of concurrent polysubstance abuse. Also recommended is motivational enhancement therapy and 12-step MSG facilitation (Weaver, Delos Reyes, & Schnoll, 2014).

Da Silva Roggi, da Gama, Neves, and Garcia (2015) selected 34 studies for analysis that focused on the treatment of craving using CBT. The CBT treatments focused on relapse prevention, psychoeducation, humor and stress management, MI, exposure and response prevention, relaxation techniques, and relapse prevention. Mindfulness was used in three studies. Other behavioral methods include behavioral contracting, community reinforcement, and dialectical behavior therapy (DBT; Csiernik, 2016). DBT was found to have a large effect size in helping American Indian/Alaskan Native adolescents with SUDs when it was combined with cultural, spiritual, and traditional practices (Beckstead, Lambert, DuBose, & Linehan, 2015). Acceptance and commitment therapy has also shown effectiveness with SUDs (Strosahl, 2016).

Despite the hype regarding the effectiveness of CBT, Csiernik (2016) suggested that the advantage of CBT over other counseling approaches is minor. Carroll and Kiluk (2017) concluded, however, that effect sizes for CBT are moderate, which is considered better than "minor" statistically.

Although many CBT organizations are arguably questionable, two are considered highly respectable. Most prominent are the Academy of Cognitive Therapy (https://www.academyofct.org/default.aspx) and the Association for Cognitive and Behavioral Therapies (www.abct.org). Both organizations offer solid training in CBT and provide several resources.

RELEVANT MUTUAL SUPPORT GROUPS, WEBSITES, AND VIDEOS

Mutual Support Groups

For the Addicted Individual

1. SMART Recovery—Self-Management and Recovery training. http://www.smartrecovery.org/

   Quoted from website:

   SMART Recovery is the leading self-empowering addiction recovery support group. Our participants learn tools for addiction recovery based on the latest scientific research and participate in a world-wide community which includes free, self-empowering, science-based mutual help groups.

   SMART Recovery, a non-profit corporation, was originally named the Rational Recovery Self-Help Network, and was affiliated with Rational Recovery Systems, a for-profit corporation owned by Jack Trimpey. In 1994, the non-profit changed its name to SMART Recovery, and ended all affiliation with Trimpey. This change occurred because of disagreements between Trimpey and the non-profit's board of directors about the program of recovery to be offered in the self-help groups.

2. Rational Recovery. https://rational.org

   Quoted from website:

   The combined mission of Rational Recovery Systems, Inc., is (1) to disseminate information on independent recovery from addiction through planned, permanent abstinence, (2) to make self-recovery a viable option to all addicted people everywhere, and (3) to make informed consent to addiction treatment and recovery group participation available to all addicted people.

3. LifeRing Secular Recovery. https://lifering.org/

   Quoted from website:

   LifeRing Secular Recovery is an abstinence-based, worldwide network of individuals seeking to live in recovery from addiction to alcohol or to other non-medically indicated drugs. In LifeRing, we offer each other peer-to-peer support in ways that encourage personal growth and continued learning through personal empowerment. Our approach is based on developing, refining, and sharing our own personal strategies for continued abstinence and crafting a rewarding life in recovery. In short, we are sober, secular, and self-directed.

4. Secular Organizations for Sobriety. http://www.sossobriety.org/

   Quoted from website:

   Secular Organizations for Sobriety (SOS) is a nonprofit network of autonomous, non-professional local groups, dedicated solely to helping individuals achieve and maintain sobriety/abstinence from alcohol and drug addiction, food addiction and more. Watch the award-winning short documentary about SOS! "No God at the Bottom of a Glass" is an award-winning short documentary produced by Sarah Barker of Creative Media Hub. The film tells the story of Secular Organizations for Sobriety (SOS), the brainchild of founder, James Christopher.

5. Women for Sobriety. https://womenforsobriety.org/

   Quoted from website:

   Women for Sobriety (WFS) is an organization whose purpose is to help all women find their individual path to recovery through discovery of self, gained by sharing experiences, hopes and encouragement with other women in similar circumstances. We are an abstinence-based self-help program for women facing issues of alcohol or drug addiction. Our "New Life" Program acknowledges the very special needs women have in recovery—the need to nurture feelings of self-value and self-worth and the desire to discard feelings of guilt, shame, and humiliation.

6. Cocaine Anonymous. https://ca.org/

   Quoted from website:

   Cocaine Anonymous is a Fellowship of men and women who share their experience, strength and hope with each other that they may solve their common problem and help others recover from their addiction. The best way to reach someone is to speak to them on a common level. The members of C.A. are all recovering addicts who maintain their individual sobriety by working with others. We come from various social, ethnic, economic and religious backgrounds, but what we have in common is addiction.

7. Narcotics Anonymous. https://na.org/

   Quoted from website:

   Narcotics Anonymous is a global, community-based organization with a multi-lingual and multicultural membership. NA was founded in 1953, and our membership growth was minimal during our initial twenty years as an organization. Since the publication of our Basic Text in 1983, the number of members and meetings has increased dramatically. Today, NA members hold nearly 67,000 meetings weekly in 139 countries. We offer recovery from the effects of addiction through working a twelve-step program, including regular attendance at group meetings. The group atmosphere provides help from peers and offers an ongoing support network for addicts who wish to pursue and maintain a drug-free lifestyle. Our name, Narcotics Anonymous, is not meant to imply a focus on any particular drug; NA's approach makes no distinction between drugs including alcohol. Membership is free, and we have no affiliation with any organizations outside of NA including governments, religions, law enforcement groups, or medical and psychiatric associations. Through all of our service efforts and our cooperation with others seeking to help addicts, we strive to reach a day when every addicted individual in the world has an opportunity to experience our message of recovery in their own language and culture.

For the Partner and/or Family

Nar-Anon. https://www.nar-anon.org/

Quoted from website:

The Nar-Anon Family Groups is primarily for those who know or have known a feeling of desperation concerning the addiction problem of someone very near to you. We have traveled that unhappy road too, and found the answer with serenity and peace of mind. When you come into the family group, you are no longer alone, but among true friends who understand your problem as few others could. We respect your confidence and anonymity as we know you will respect ours. We hope to give you the assurance that no situation is too difficult, and no unhappiness is too great to be overcome.

Websites

1. Treatment Approaches for Drug Addiction. https://www.drugabuse.gov/publications/drugfacts/treatment-approaches-drug-addiction
2. MedlinePlus. https://medlineplus.gov/druginformation.html
3. Signs and Symptoms of Drug Abuse. https://www.narconon.org/drug-abuse/heroin/physical-and-mental.html
4. Get Smart About Drugs. https://www.getsmartaboutdrugs.gov/drugs
5. SAMSA's National Helpline. https://www.samhsa.gov/find-help/national-helpline

Videos

To view these videos, search their titles on YouTube.

1. *What's your Story? Family, Addiction and the Brain | Dr. Melissa Vayda | TEDxHarrisburg .*
2. *Recover Out Loud: A 2018 Documentary.*
3. *Rewriting the Story Of My Addiction | Jo Harvey Weatherford | TEDxUniversityofNevada.*
4. *Drugs Inc. - Crack.*
5. *Top 10 Facts About Prescription Drug Abuse in America.*
6. *The Power of Addiction and The Addiction of Power: Gabor Maté at TEDxRio+20.*
7. *The House I Live In (2012)* [sic]. sanjie lio. This full-length documentary takes a critical look at U.S. drug policy from several perspectives.
8. *Let's quit abusing drug users* (with Dr. Carl Hart). TEDMED.

RELEVANT PHONE APPS

Generic Addiction Apps

Note: Generic apps are described in Chapter 6. This list is not exhaustive. New apps are continually being developed. Do an Internet search to find out the latest apps available. Most are for specific addictions, but some, such as these four, are generic.

1. I Am Sober. https://play.google.com/store/apps/details?id=com.thehungrywasp.iamsober
2. Sober Time. https://play.google.com/store/apps/details?id=com.sociosoft.sobertime
3. Pocket Rehab: Get Sober & Addiction Recovery. https://play.google.com/store/apps/details?id=com.getpocketrehab.app
4. Loop Habit Tracker. https://play.google.com/store/apps/details?id=org.isoron.uhabits

Specialized Apps

1. NA Meeting Search 3.6.1. For smartphones, visit https://play.google.com/store/apps/details?id=org.na.naapp&hl=en_US. For IOS, visit https://apps.apple.com/us/app/na-meeting-search/id627643748

   Quoted from website:

   This is the only recovery app based on the narcotics anonymous basic text book that you will ever need to maintain your daily reprieve. It is a perfect companion app for your 12-step program.

2. Sober Grid. https://www.sobergrid.com/

   Quoted from website:

   Sober Grid puts a free peer support network right in your pocket to aid you in your recovery. You can remain anonymous if you wish.

3. Sober Tool. http://www.sobertool.com/

   Quoted from https://www.addictionrecoveryguide.org/resources/mobile_apps

   This app is geared to relapse prevention. It teaches the user how to identify thoughts and feelings which can lead to relapse. Then it leads the user to a daily reading geared to what they are currently experiencing which helps change "relapse" thinking into "sober" thinking. It also calculates sober time and money saved staying sober. It was developed by a licensed chemical dependency counselor who personally has over 27 years of sobriety.

4. Ascent. http://ourascent.com/

   Quoted from website: Connect with peers and professional coaches in recovery, 24/7/365—straight from your phone.

5. Technology Assisted Care for Substance Use Disorders. http://sudtech.org/about/

   Quoted from website:

   Therapeutic Education System (TES)

   TES is an interactive, web-based psychosocial intervention for SUDs, grounded in:

   Community Reinforcement Approach (CRA) + Contingency Management Behavior Therapy + HIV Prevention

   Features of TES

   Consists of 65 interactive multimedia modules

   Self-directed, evidence-based program includes skills training, interactive exercises, and homework

   Audio component accompanies all module content

   Electronic reports of patient activity available

   Contingency Management Component tracks earnings of incentives dependent on some defined outcome (e.g., urine results confirming abstinence)

   New content can be readily added

   Uses incentive procedures including a virtual "fishbowl" using intermittent schedule of reinforcement based on abstinence and module completion.

6. There are also many apps for meditation, which can be helpful to people in recovery. A list of these can be found at https://www.addictionrecoveryguide.org/holistic/meditation_spirituality#apps

JOURNALS AND CONFERENCES

Journals

There are innumerable journals that publish articles about drug addictions. The following is, therefore, an incomplete list of 20 journals that publish in the addictions field. Please visit their websites for further details.

1. *Addiction Biology*. https://onlinelibrary.wiley.com/journal/13691600
2. *Addiction Research & Theory*. https://www.tandfonline.com/loi/iart20
3. *Addiction*. https://onlinelibrary.wiley.com/journal/13600443
4. *Addictive Behaviors*. https://www.journals.elsevier.com/addictive-behaviors/

5. *Addictive Disorders & Their Treatment.* https://journals.lww.com/addictiondisorders/pages/default.aspx
6. *American Journal of Drug and Alcohol Abuse.* https://www.tandfonline.com/loi/iada20
7. *American Journal on Addictions.* https://onlinelibrary.wiley.com/journal/15210391
8. *Drug and Alcohol Dependence.* https://www.journals.elsevier.com/drug-and-alcohol-dependence/
9. *Journal of Addiction Medicine.* https://journals.lww.com/journaladdictionmedicine/pages/default.aspx
10. *Journal of Addiction Research & Therapy.* https://www.omicsonline.org/addiction-research-therapy.php
11. *Journal of Addictive Diseases.* https://www.tandfonline.com/loi/wjad20
12. *Journal of Drug Abuse.* http://drugabuse.imedpub.com/
13. *Journal of Psychoactive Drugs.* https://www.tandfonline.com/toc/ujpd20/current
14. *Journal of Psychopharmacology.* http://journals.sagepub.com/home/jop/
15. *Journal of Social Work Practice in the Addictions.* https://www.tandfonline.com/loi/wswp20
16. *Journal of Substance Abuse and Alcoholism.* https://www.jscimedcentral.com/SubstanceAbuse/
17. *Journal of Substance Abuse Treatment.* https://www.journalofsubstanceabusetreatment.com/
18. *Psychology of Addictive Behaviors.* http://www.apa.org/pubs/journals/adb/index.aspx
19. *Substance Abuse.* https://www.tandfonline.com/loi/wsub20
20. *Substance Use & Misuse.* https://www.tandfonline.com/loi/isum20

Conferences

1. American Society of Addictive Medicine hosts an annual conference. Details at https://www.asam.org/education/live-online-cme/the-asam-annual-conference
2. Substance Abuse and Mental Health Services Administration lists several conferences. Details at https://www.samhsa.gov/
3. National Institute on Drug Abuse lists several conferences. Details at https://www.drugabuse.gov/news-events/meetings-events
4. OMICS International lists many conferences dealing with substance abuse, and these can be found at https://www.omicsonline.org/conferences-list/substance-abuse
5. Canadian Centre on Substance Use and Addiction. Details of conferences at https://ccsa.ca/

INDIVIDUAL EXERCISES

1. Attend an MSG meeting. At the end, ask someone you thought was interesting if you could arrange to go for a beverage to talk more about their addiction. Then ask questions about their addiction.
2. Watch a TV show about addiction. Examples include an episode of *Intervention, Breaking Bad, Nurse Jackie,* or *Shameless.* What did you think was authentic about the program? What do you believe was inaccurate or overdramatized?
3. Interview an addictions counselor who works with clients addicted to any of the drugs included in this chapter. What does the counselor find most challenging about working with this population? What does this counselor find most rewarding about working with drug addicts?

CLASSROOM EXERCISES

1. Either in small groups or as a classroom discussion, have students talk about how they would identify friends who have a mild, moderate, or severe SUD. In other words, what criteria do students use to define mild, moderate, or severe? What would they need to see in their friends that would indicate the severity of their drug abuse or addiction?
2. Create a list of keywords and, in class, read each word out loud, one at a time, and ask students to identify which drug or drugs would be most associated with that word. For example, your list could include words like nervous system arousal, rush, paranoia, memory impairment, extreme cravings, glue, methadone, dissociative anesthetic, etc.
3. Write out a list of the most common drugs in each drug category, creating a list of perhaps 20 words or so. If your list has 20 words, establish 20 groups from your class. If your list only has 10 words, then 10 groups. Have each word on a piece of paper and assign them randomly to the groups without each group knowing what the other words are. Have the groups disperse for 15 minutes, working independently of the other groups. Their task is to create

a brief skit that will highlight aspects of that drug. Likely best is if they do an improvisation. For example, for the group assigned cocaine, the group will create a brief skit that will highlight some aspects of cocaine. The skit is intended to last for only about 2 minutes. After a group performs their skit in front of the class, the class has to guess which drug has been portrayed. Each group presents until all skits have been enacted.

CHAPTER SUMMARY

Drug abuse and addictions are a worldwide phenomenon. In 2017, it was estimated that approximately 5.5% of the world's population used a psychoactive drug. Current estimates suggest that 8%–10% of people 12 years of age or older in the United States are addicted to either alcohol or other drugs. This chapter focused on *other drug addictions*, which included those not written about in separate chapters. Consequently, this chapter focused on stimulants (including cocaine/crack), depressants (and sedative-hypnotics), hallucinogens (psychedelics), inhalants, and some reference to club drugs, designer drugs, and prescription and over-the-counter medications.

The war on drugs in the United States has not achieved its goals of drug use prevention. This chapter reviewed the empirically validated treatments for *other drug addictions*, including medications and psychological approaches.

REFERENCES

Addiction.com. (2014, May 28). *Living with disability increases risk for substance abuse*. Retrieved on July 22, 2018, from https://www.addiction.com/3007/living-disability-increases-risk-substance-abuse/

AddictScience.com. (n.d.). *20-Question Addiction Questionnaire*. Retrieved on June 29, 2018, from http://www.addictscience.com/20-question-addiction-questionnaire/

Afonso, R. F. (2016). The effects of yoga on substance abuse. In A. L. M. Andrade & D. D. Micheli (Eds.), *Innovations in the treatment of substance addiction* (pp. 193–199). Cham, Switzerland: Springer International.

Agabio, R., Campesi, I., Pisanu, C., Gessa, G. L., & Franconi, F. (2016). Sex differences in substance use disorders: Focus on side effects. *Addiction Biology, 21*(5), 1030–1042.

Alderson, K. (2013). *Counseling LGBTI clients*. Thousand Oaks, CA: SAGE.

American Addiction Centers. (2018). *Drug treatment centers for the physically and mentally disabled*. Retrieved on August 3, 2018, from https://americanaddictioncenters.org/rehab-guide/physically-mentally-disabled/

American Association of Poison Control Centers. (2015, December 31). *Bath salts data*. Retrieved on June 20, 2018, from https://aapcc.s3.amazonaws.com/files/library/Bath_Salts_Web_Data_through_12.2015.pdf

American Psychiatric Association (APA). (2013). *Diagnostic and statistical manual of mental disorders* (5th ed.). Washington, DC: Author.

Anderson, T. L., Scott, B. L., & Kavanaugh, P. R. (2015). Race, inequality and the medicalization of drug addiction: An analysis of documentary films. *Journal of Substance Use, 20*, 319–332.

Andrade, A. L. M., & Micheli, D. D. (Ed.). (2016). *Innovations in the treatment of substance addiction*. Cham, Switzerland: Springer.

Ara, A., Jacobs, W., Bhat, I. A., & McCall, W. (2016). Sleep disturbances and substance use disorders: A bi-directional relationship. *Psychiatric Annals, 46*(7), 408–412.

Asbridge, M., Duff, C., Marsh, D. C., & Erickson, P. G. (2014). Problems with the identification of "problematic" cannabis use: Examining the issues of frequency, quantity, and drug use environment. *European Addiction Research, 20*(5), 254–267.

Asevedo, E., Mendes, A. C., Berk, M., & Brietzke, E. (2014). Systematic review of N-acetylcysteine in the treatment of addictions. *Revista Brasileira de Psiquiatria, 36*, 168–175.

Ashok, A. H., Mizuno, Y., Volkow, N. D., & Howes, O. D. (2017). Association of stimulant use with dopaminergic alterations in users of cocaine, amphetamine, or methamphetamine: A systematic review and meta-analysis. *JAMA Psychiatry, 74*(5), 511–519.

Augutis, M., Rosenberg, D., & Hillborg, H. (2016). The meaning of work: Perceptions of employed persons attending maintenance treatment for opiate addiction. *Journal of Social Work Practice in the Addictions, 16*(4), 385–402.

Bachi, K., Sierra, S., Volkow, N. D., Goldstein, R. Z., & Alia-Klein, N. (2017). Is biological aging accelerated in drug addiction? *Current Opinion in Behavioral Sciences, 13*, 34–39.

Barrocas, J., Vieira-Santos, S., & Paixao, R. (2016). Parenting and drug addiction: A psychodynamic proposal based on a multifactorial perspective. *Psychoanalytic Psychology, 33*, 161–178.

Bates, G., Cochrane, M., & Mackridge, A. J. (2017). The extent that health professionals suspect and address addiction to medicines in primary care: Findings from a survey in Northwest England. *Journal of Addictive Diseases, 36*(3), 147–150.

Beatty, L. A. (2010). Drug abuse research: Addressing the needs of racial and ethnic minority populations. In L. Scheier (Ed.), *Handbook of drug use etiology: Theory, methods, and empirical findings* (pp. 325–339). Washington, DC: American Psychological Association.

Beckstead, D. J., Lambert, M. J., DuBose, A. P., & Linehan, M. (2015). Dialectical behavior therapy with American Indian/Alaska Native adolescents diagnosed with substance use disorders: Combining an evidence based treatment with cultural, traditional, and spiritual beliefs. *Addictive Behaviors, 51*, 84–87.

Bedendo, A., Andrade, A. L. M., & Noto, A. R. (2016). Neurobiology of substance abuse. In A. L. M. Andrade & D. D. Micheli (Ed.), *Innovations in the treatment of substance addiction* (pp. 17–36). Cham, Switzerland: Springer.

Beech, R., & Sinha, R. (2011). Cocaine. In B. A. Johnson (Ed.), *Addiction medicine: Science and practice* (Vol. 1, pp. 397–416). New York, NY: Springer Science + Business Media.

Begun, A., & Brown, S. (2014). Neurobiology of substance use disorders and implications for treatment. In S. L. A. Straussner (Ed.), *Clinical work with substance-abusing clients* (3rd ed., pp. 39–66). New York, NY: Guilford Press.

Blake, A. J., Tung, I., Langley, A. K., & Waterman, J. M. (2018). Substance use in youth adopted from foster care: Developmental mechanisms of risk. *Children and Youth Services Review, 85*, 264–272.

Bliss, D. L. (2015). Spirituality-enhanced addiction treatment protocol: Conceptual and operational development. *Alcoholism Treatment Quarterly, 33*(4), 385–394.

Blume, A. W., & Logan, D. (2013). Harm reduction approaches. In P. M. Miller, S. A. Ball, M. E. Bates, A. W. Blume, K. M. Kampman, D. J. Kavanagh, M. E. Larimer, N. M. Petry, & P. De Witte (Eds.), *Comprehensive addictive behaviors and disorders, Vol. 3: Interventions for addiction* (pp. 633–641). San Diego, CA: Elsevier Academic Press.

Bohnert, K. M., Ilgen, M. A., Louzon, S., McCarthy, J. F., & Katz, I. R. (2017). Substance use disorders and the risk of suicide mortality among men and women in the US Veterans Health Administration. *Addiction, 112*(7), 1193–1201.

Bovill, J. G. (2008). Inhalation anaesthesia: From diethyl ether to xenon. *Handbook of Experimental Pharmacology, 182*, 121–142.

Bowen, E. A., & Redmond, H. (2016). Teaching note—No peace without justice: Addressing the United States' war on drugs in social work education. *Journal of Social Work Education, 52*(4), 503–508.

Brecht, M.-L., & Herbeck, D. (2014). Time to relapse following treatment for methamphetamine use: A long-term perspective on patterns and predictors. *Drug and Alcohol Dependence, 139*, 18–25.

Brucker, D. L. (2008). Prescription drug abuse among persons with disabilities. *Journal of Vocational Rehabilitation, 29*(2), 105–115.

Bush, D. M. (2013, November 12). Emergency department visits involving phencyclidine (PCP). *CBHSQ Report*. Rockville (MD): Substance Abuse and Mental Health Services Administration (US). Retrieved on June 22, 2018, from https://www.ncbi.nlm.nih.gov/pubmed/27656747

Butwicka, A., Langstrom, N., Larsson, H., Lundstrom, S., Serlachius, E., Almqvist, C., . . . Lichtenstein, P. (2017). Increased risk for substance use-related problems in autism spectrum disorders: A population-based cohort study. *Journal of Autism and Developmental Disorders, 47*, 80–89.

Cacciola, J. S., Alterman, A. I., Habing, B., & McLellan, A. T. (2011). Recent status scores for version 6 of the Addiction Severity Index (ASI-6). *Addiction, 106*, 1588–1602.

Calabria, B., Degenhardt, L., Briegleb, C., Vos, T., Hall, W., Lynskey. M., . . . McLaren, J. (2010). Systematic review of prospective studies investigating "remission" from amphetamine, cannabis, cocaine or opioid dependence. *Addictive Behaviors, 35*, 741–749.

Canadian Pediatric Society. (2018, February 28). *Inhalant abuse*. Retrieved on August 3, 2018, from https://www.cps.ca/en/documents/position/inhalant-abuse

Canan, F., Karaca, S., Sogucak, S., Gecici, O., & Kuloglu, M. (2017). Eating disorders and food addiction in men with heroin use disorder: A controlled study. *Eating and Weight Disorders, 22*(2), 249–257.

Carhart-Harris, R. L., Bolstridge, M., Day, C. M. J., Rucker, J., Watts, R., Erritzoe, D. E., . . . Nutt, D. J. (2018). Psilocybin with psychological support for treatment-resistant depression: Six-month follow-up. *Psychopharmacology, 235*(2), 399–408.

Carroll, J. F. X., Hall, C. E., Kearse, R., Mooney, M., Potestivo, J., & Forman, N. (2016). Meeting the treatment needs of veterans with substance use disorders. *Alcoholism Treatment Quarterly, 34*, 354–364.

Carroll, K. M., & Kiluk, B. D. (2017). Cognitive behavioral interventions for alcohol and drug use disorders: Through the stage model and back again. *Psychology of Addictive Behaviors, 31*, 847–861.

Chambers, R. A., & Wallingford, S. C. (2017). On mourning and recovery: Integrating stages of grief and change toward a neuroscience-based model of attachment adaptation in addiction treatment. *Psychodynamic Psychiatry, 45*(4), 451–474.

Chaney, M. P., & Brubaker, M. (2014). The impact of substance abuse and addiction in the lives of gay men, adolescents, and boys. In M. M. Kocet (Ed.), *Counseling gay men, adolescents, and boys: A strengths-based guide for helping professionals and educators* (pp. 109–128). New York, NY: Routledge/Taylor & Francis Group.

Chapman, S. L. C., & Wu, L.-T. (2012). Substance abuse among individuals with intellectual disabilities. *Research in Developmental Disabilities, 33*(4), 1147–1156.

Charlson, F., Baxter, A., Dua, T., Degenhardt, L., Whiteford, H., & Vos, T. (2015). Excess mortality from mental, neurological and substance use disorders in the Global Burden of Disease Study 2010. *Epidemiology and Psychiatric Sciences, 24*(2), 121–140.

Chesworth, R., & Corbit, L. H. (2017). Recent developments in the behavioural and pharmacological enhancement of extinction of drug seeking. *Addiction Biology, 22*(1), 3–43.

Connors, G. J., DiClemente, C. C., Velasquez, M. M., & Donovan, D. M. (2013). *Substance abuse treatment and the stages of change: Selecting and planning interventions* (2nd ed.). New York, NY: Guilford Press.

Cooper, H. L. F. (2015). War on drugs policing and police brutality. *Substance Use & Misuse, 50*(8–9), 1188–1194.

Corkery, J. M., Claridge, H., Goodair, C., & Schifano, F. (2017). An exploratory study of information sources and key findings on UK cocaine-related deaths. *Journal of Psychopharmacology, 31*(8), 996–1014.

Costandi, M. (2014). A brief history of psychedelic psychiatry. *Psychologist, 27*(9), 714–715.

Cristea, I. A., Cuijpers, P., & Naudet, F. (2017). Equivalence of psychodynamic therapy to other established treatments: Limited supporting evidence and clinical relevance. *American Journal of Psychiatry, 174*, 1122–1123.

Csiernik, R. (2016). *Substance use and abuse: Everything matters* (2nd ed.). Toronto, ON: Canadian Scholar's Press.

Cumming, C., Troeung, L., Young, J. T., Kelty, E., & Preen, D. B. (2016). Barriers to accessing methamphetamine treatment: A systematic review and meta-analysis. *Drug and Alcohol Dependence, 168*, 263–273.

Daniels, G. T. (2016). A faith-infused, addiction recovery model of pastoral care to help reduce the epidemic of substance addiction; an urban ministry prototype in Raleigh, North Carolina. *Dissertation Abstracts International Section A: Humanities and Social Sciences, 76*(12-A(E)). No pagination specified.

Da Silva Roggi, P. M., da Gama, M. F. N., Neves, F. S., & Garcia, F. (2015). Update on treatment of craving in patients with addiction using cognitive behavioral therapy. *Clinical Neuropsychiatry: Journal of Treatment Evaluation, 12*(5), 118–127.

Da Silveira, P. S., Casela, A. L. M., Monteiro, E. P., Ferreira, G. C. L., de Freitas, J. V. T., Machado, N. M., . . . Ronzani, T. M. (2018).

Psychosocial understanding of self-stigma among people who seek treatment for drug addiction. *Stigma and Health*, *3*(1), 42–52.

Deady, M. (2009). Review of screening, assessment and outcome measures for drug and alcohol settings. *Network of Alcohol and Other Drugs Agencies*. Retrieved on June 28, 2018, from http://www.drugsandalcohol.ie/18266/1/NADA_A_Review_of_Screening%2C_Assessment_and_Outcome_Measures_for_Drug_and_Alcohol_Settings.pdf

Degenhardt, L., Stockings, E., Patton, G., Hall, W. D., & Lynskey, M. (2016). Substance use in young people 1: The increasing global health priority of substance use in young people. *Lancet Psychiatry*, *3*(3), 251–264.

Denis, C., Fatseas, M., Beltran, V., Serre, F., Alexandre, J.-M., Debrabant, R., . . . Auriacombe, M. (2016). Usefulness and validity of the modified Addiction Severity Index: A focus on alcohol, drugs, tobacco, and gambling. *Substance Abuse*, *37*(1), 168–175.

De Veen, B. T. H., Schellekens, A. F. A., Verheij, M. M. M., & Homberg, J. R. (2017). Psilocybin for treating substance use disorders? *Expert Review of Neurotherapeutics*, *17*(2), 203–212.

Diehl, A., Pillon, S. C., dos Santos, M. A., Rassool, G., & Laranjeira, R. (2016). Sexual dysfunction and sexual behaviors in a sample of Brazilian male substance misusers. *American Journal of Men's Health*, *10*(5), 418–427.

Dyck, E. (2015). LSD: A new treatment emerging from the past. *Canadian Medical Association Journal*, *187*(14), 1079–1080.

Dylan, A. (2014). Noble Eightfold Path and Yoga (NEPY): A group for women experiencing substance use challenges. *Social Work With Groups: A Journal of Community and Clinical Practice*, *37*(2), 142–157.

Earleywine, M. (2016). *Substance use problems* (2nd ed.). Ashland, OH: Hogrefe.

Elkashef, A., & Montoya, I. (2012). Pharmacotherapy of addiction. In J. C. Verster, K. Brady, M. Galanter, & P. Conrod (Eds.), *Drug abuse and addiction in medical illness: Causes, consequences and treatment* (pp. 107–119). New York, NY: Springer Science + Business Media.

Ellicott, C. (2010, March 18). Mother died in agony after eating death cap mushrooms she thought were edible. *Daily Mail*. Retrieved on December 16, 2018, from https://www.dailymail.co.uk/news/article-1258895/Mother-died-eating-death-cap-mushrooms-picked-Botanic-Gardens.html

Ellis, C., Hoffman, W., Jaehnert, S., Plagge, J., Loftis, J. M., Schwartz, D., & Huckans, M. (2016). Everyday problems with executive dysfunction and impulsivity in adults recovering from methamphetamine addiction. *Addictive Disorders & Their Treatment*, *15*(1), 1–5.

El-Rasheed, A. H., ElAttar, K. S., Elrassas, H. H., Mahmoud, D. A. M., & Mohamed, S. Y. (2017). Mood regulation, alexithymia, and personality disorders in adolescent male addicts. *Addictive Disorders & Their Treatment*, *16*(2), 49–58.

Ersche, K. D., & Doffinger, R. (2017). Inflammation and infection in human cocaine addiction. *Current Opinion in Behavioral Sciences*, *13*, 203–209.

Faccini, M., Leone, R., Opri, S., Casari, R., Resentera, C., Morbioli, L., . . . Lugoboni, F. (2016). Slow subcutaneous infusion of flumazenil for the treatment of long-term, high-dose benzodiazepine users: A review of 214 cases. *Journal of Psychopharmacology*, *30*(10), 1047–1053.

Fachner, J. (2017). Retraining of drug reward, music cues and state-dependent recall in music therapy. *Music and Medicine*, *9*(1), 8–14.

Fanton, M. C., Azzollini, S. C., Ayi, J. A., Sio, A. G., & Mora, G. E. (2013). Perception of control over cocaine use and stages of change. *Psychology of Addictive Behaviors*, *27*, 841–847.

Fattore, L., & Melis, M. (2016). Sex differences in impulsive and compulsive behaviors: A focus on drug addiction. *Addiction Biology*, *21*, 1043–1051.

Fattore, L., Melis, M., Fadda, P., & Fratta, W. (2014). Sex differences in addictive disorders. *Frontiers in Neuroendocrinology*, *35*(3), 272–284.

Fischer, B., Blanken, P., Da Silveira, D., Gallassi, A., Goldner, E. M., Rehm, J., . . . Wood, E. (2015). Effectiveness of secondary prevention and treatment interventions for crack cocaine abuse: A comprehensive narrative overview of English-language studies. *International Journal on Drug Policy*, *26*, 352–363.

Galaj, E., Ewing, S., & Ranaldi, R. (2018). Dopamine D1 and D3 receptor polypharmacology as a potential treatment approach for substance use disorder. *Neuroscience and Biobehavioral Reviews*, *89*, 13–28.

Giedd, J. N. (2015). Adolescent neuroscience of addiction: A new era. *Developmental Cognitive Neuroscience*, *16*, 192–193.

Gossop, M., Darke, S., Griffiths, P., Hando, J., Powis, B., Hall, W., & Strang, J. (1995). The severity of dependence scale (SDS): Psychometric properties of the SDS in English and Australian samples of heroin, cocaine and amphetamine users. *Addiction*, *90*, 607–614.

Green, K. E., Bux, D. A., Jr., & Feinstein, B. A. (2013). Lesbian, gay, bisexual, and transgender individuals. In B. S. McCrady & E. E. Epstein (Eds.), *Addictions: A comprehensive guidebook* (2nd ed., pp. 819–835). New York, NY: Oxford University Press.

Griffiths, R. R., Johnson, M. W., Richards, W. A., Richards, B. D., Jesse, R., MacLean, K. A., . . . Klinedinst, M. A. (2018). Psilocybin-occasioned mystical-type experience in combination with meditation and other spiritual practices produces enduring positive changes in psychological functioning and in trait measures of prosocial attitudes and behaviors. *Journal of Psychopharmacology*, *32*(1), 49–69.

Grucza, R. A., Agrawal, A., Krauss, M. J., Bongu, J., Plunk, A. D., Cavazos-Rehg, P. A., & Bierut, L. J. (2016). Declining prevalence of marijuana use disorders among adolescents in the United States, 2002 to 2013. *Journal of the American Academy of Child & Adolescent Psychiatry*, *55*, 487–494.

Haglund, M., Ang, A., Mooney, L., Gonzales, R., Chudzynski, J., Cooper, C. B., . . . Rawson, R. A. (2015). Predictors of depression outcomes among abstinent methamphetamine-dependent individuals exposed to an exercise intervention. *American Journal on Addictions*, *24*(3), 246–251.

Halberstadt, A. L. (2015). Recent advances in the neuropsychopharmacology of serotonergic hallucinogens. *Behavioural Brain Research*, *277*, 99–120.

Hall, S. B., & Walker, K. D. (2017). Clinical neuroscience of substance use disorders. In T. A. Field, L. K. Jones, & L. A. Russell-Chapin (Eds.), *Neurocounseling: Brain-based clinical approaches* (pp. 149–164). Alexandria, VA: American Counseling Association.

Han, B., Compton, W. M., Blanco, C., & DuPont, R. L. (2017). National trends in substance use and use disorders among youth. *Journal of the American Academy of Child & Adolescent Psychiatry*, *56*(9), 747–754.

Harrison, J., Cousins, L., Spybrook, J., & Curtis, A. (2017). Peers and co-occurring research-supported interventions. *Journal of Evidence-Informed Social Work, 14*(3), 201–215.

Hastings, J. F. (2009). Cross-cultural issues in substance addiction research including Black Americans and Latinos. In A. Browne-Miller (Ed.), *The Praeger international collection on addictions, Vol 1: Faces of addiction, then and now* (pp. 17–35). Santa Barbara, CA: Praeger/ABC-CLIO.

He, Q., Huang, X., Turel, O., Schulte, M., Huang, D., Thames, A., . . . Yih-Ing, H. (2018). Presumed structural and functional neural recovery after long-term abstinence from cocaine in male military veterans. *Progress in Neuro-Psychopharmacology & Biological Psychiatry, 84*, 18–29.

Heink, A., Katsikas, S., & Lange-Altman, T. (2017). Examination of the phenomenology of the ibogaine treatment experience: Role of altered states of consciousness and psychedelic experiences. *Journal of Psychoactive Drugs, 49*(3), 201–208.

Hepburn, K., Barker, B., Nguyen, P., Dong, H., Wood, E., Kerr, T., & DeBeck, K. (2016). Initiation of drug dealing among a prospective cohort of street-involved youth. *American Journal of Drug and Alcohol Abuse, 42*(5), 507–512.

Herron, A. J. (2016). Inhalants. In P. Levounis, E. Zerbo, & R. Aggarwal (Eds.), *Pocket guide to addiction assessment and treatment* (pp. 155–169). Arlington, VA: American Psychiatric.

Herzig, D. A., & Bachmann, S. (2017). Cannabis and clubbing: Relevance of cannabis and polydrug use in the clubbing culture today. In V. R. Preedy (Ed.), *Handbook of cannabis and related pathologies: Biology, pharmacology, diagnosis, and treatment* (pp. 171–179). San Diego, CA: Elsevier Academic Press.

Heyman, G. M., & Mims, V. (2017). What addicts can teach us about addiction: A natural history approach. In N. Heather & G. Segal (Eds.), *Addiction and choice: Rethinking the relationship* (pp. 385–408). New York, NY: Oxford University Press.

Holmes, A. (2017). Drug addictions: New insight into causes, comorbidity and potential treatments. *Genes, Brain & Behavior, 16*(1), 5–7.

Irwin, T. W. (2009). Substance use disorders among sexual-minority women. In K. T. Brady, S. E. Back, & S. F. Greenfield (Ed.), *Women and addiction: A comprehensive handbook* (pp. 475–489). New York, NY: Guilford Press.

Jedrzejczak, M. & Blaszczyk, J. (2005). Attitudes of soldiers taking drugs to military service, training, and discipline. *Military Medicine, 170*, 691–695.

Jedrzejczak, M., & Kocur, J. (2003). Threat of drug addiction in the army. *Psychiatria Polska, 37*(3), 511–518.

Jiang, S., Wu, L., & Gao, X. (2017). Beyond face-to-face individual counseling: A systematic review on alternative modes of motivational interviewing in substance abuse treatment and prevention. *Addictive Behaviors, 73*, 216–235.

Johansen, P.-O., & Krebs, T. S. (2015). Psychedelics not linked to mental health problems or suicidal behavior: A population study. *Journal of Psychopharmacology, 29*(3), 270–279.

Johnson, L. (2016, October 12). Three-year-old Victoria boy dies from poisonous "death" mushroom. *CBC News*. Retrieved on December 16, 2018, from https://www.cbc.ca/news/canada/british-columbia/death-cap-mushroom-victoria-boy-poisoned-1.3802245

Johnson, T. J., & Kristeller, J. L. (2013). Spirituality and addiction. In P. M. Miller, S. A. Ball, M. E. Bates, A. W. Blume, K. M. Kampman, D. J. Kavanagh, M. E. Larimer, N. M. Petry, & P. De Witte (Eds.), *Comprehensive addictive behaviors and disorders, Vol. 1: Principles of addiction* (pp. 283–291). San Diego, CA: Elsevier Academic Press.

Kandall, S. R. (2010). Women and drug addiction: A historical perspective. *Journal of Addictive Diseases, 29*(2), 117–126.

Kelmendi, B., Corlett, P., Ranganathan, M., D'Souza, C., & Krystal, J. H. (2016). The role of psychedelics in palliative care reconsidered: A case for psilocybin. *Journal of Psychopharmacology, 30*(12), 1212–1214.

Kertesz, S., Khodneva, Y., Richman, J., Tucker, J., Safford, M., Jones, B., . . . Pletcher, M. (2012). Trajectories of drug use and mortality outcomes among adults followed over 18 years. *Journal of General Internal Medicine, 27*(7), 808–816.

Khantzian, E. J. (1986). A contemporary psychodynamic approach to drug abuse treatment. *American Journal of Drug and Alcohol Abuse, 12*(3), 213–222.

Kiluk, B. D., & Carroll, K. M. (2014). Illegal drug use. In S. G. Hofmann, D. J. A. Dozois, W. Rief, & J. A. J. Smits (Eds.), *The Wiley handbook of cognitive behavioral therapy* (Vols. 1–3, pp. 1339–1358). Hoboken, NJ: Wiley-Blackwell.

Kosten, T. R., Newton, T. F., De La Garza, R., II, & Haile, C. N. (2014). Substance-related and addictive disorders. In R. E. Hales, S. C. Yudofsky, & L. W. Roberts (Eds.), *The American Psychiatric Publishing textbook of psychiatry* (6th ed., pp. 735–813). Arlington, VA: American Psychiatric.

Krasanakis, S. (2017). Dramatherapy and drug addiction treatment. *Dramatherapy, 38*(1), 53–58.

Lacsan, K., Arany, Z., & Farkas, A. (2017). The role of leisure in prevention and treatment of addiction. In Z. Benko, I. Modi, & K. Tarko (Eds.), *Leisure, health and well-being: A holistic approach* (pp. 115–120). New York, NY: Palgrave Macmillan.

Laplante, C. (2018). *What are drug addiction assessments for? Project Know*. Retrieved on June 29, 2018, from https://www.projectknow.com/research/assessment/

Larsen, J. K. (2017). LSD treatment in Scandinavia: Emphasizing indications and short-term treatment outcomes of 151 patients in Denmark. *Nordic Journal of Psychiatry, 71*(7), 489–495.

Lee, M. T., Pagano, M. E., Johnson, B. R., & Post, S. G. (2016). Love and service in adolescent addiction recovery. *Alcoholism Treatment Quarterly, 34*, 197–222.

Li, L., Zhu, S., Tse, N., Tse, S., & Wong, P. (2016). Effectiveness of motivational interviewing to reduce illicit drug use in adolescents: A systematic review and meta-analysis. *Addiction, 111*, 795–805.

Liang, H.-J., Lin, Y., Zhang, C., Ungvari, G. S., & Tang, W.-K. (2016). Drug addiction: A global challenge. *East Asian Archives of Psychiatry, 26*(2), 43–44.

Lightdale, H. A., Mack, A. H., & Frances, R. J. (2015). Psychodynamic psychotherapy. In M. Galanter, H. D. Kleber, & K. T. Brady (Eds.), *The American Psychiatric Publishing textbook of substance abuse treatment* (5th ed., pp. 365–383). Arlington, VA: American Psychiatric Publishing.

Lineberry, T. W., & Brady, K. T. (2014). Suicide and substance use disorders. In S. H. Koslow, P. Ruiz, & C. B. Nemeroff (Eds.), *A concise guide to understanding suicide: Epidemiology, pathophysiology, and prevention* (pp. 117–122). New York, NY: Cambridge University Press.

Littel, M., van den Hout, M. A., & Engelhard, I. M. (2016). Desensitizing addiction: Using eye movements to reduce the intensity of substance-related mental imagery and craving. *Frontiers in Psychiatry, 7*, 1–11.

Lopez-Quintero, C., Hasin, D. S., Pérez de los Cobos, J., Pines, A., Wang, S., Grant, B. F., & Blanco, C. (2010). Probability and predictors of remission from life-time nicotine, alcohol, cannabis or cocaine dependence: Results from the National Epidemiologic Survey on Alcohol and Related Conditions. *Addiction, 106*, 657–669.

Luongo, N. M., Dong, H., Kerr, T. H., Milloy, M. J. S., Hayashi, K., & Richardson, L. A. (2017). Income generation and attitudes towards addiction treatment among people who use illicit drugs in a Canadian setting. *Addictive Behaviors, 64*, 159–164.

Lyons, T., Shannon, K., Pierre, L., Small, W., Krusi, A., & Kerr, T. (2015). A qualitative study of transgender individuals' experiences in residential addiction treatment settings: Stigma and inclusivity. *Substance Abuse Treatment, Prevention, and Policy, 10*(1), 1–6.

Mahoney, J. J., III, Haile, C. N., De La Garza, R., II, Thakkar, H., & Newton, T. F. (2017). Electrocardiographic characteristics in individuals with cocaine use disorder. *American Journal on Addictions, 26*(3), 221–227.

Marich, J. (2017). EMDR therapy and the recovery community: Relational imperatives in treating addiction. In M. Nickerson (Ed.), *Cultural competence and healing culturally based trauma with EMDR therapy: Innovative strategies and protocols* (pp. 279–293). New York, NY: Springer.

Marinchak, J. S., & Morgan, T. J. (2012). Behavioral treatment techniques for psychoactive substance use disorders. In S. T. Walters & F. Rotgers (Eds.), *Treating substance abuse: Theory and technique* (3rd ed., pp. 138–166). New York, NY: Guilford Press.

Maté, G. (2008). *In the realm of hungry ghosts: Close encounters with addiction*. Toronto, ON: Vintage Books.

Mavandadi, S., & Oslin, D. W. (2015). Substance-related and addictive disorders. In D. C. Steffens, D. G. Blazer, & M. E. Thakur (Eds.), *The American Psychiatric Publishing textbook of geriatric psychiatry* (5th ed., pp. 459–489). Arlington, VA: American Psychiatric Publishing.

McCabe, S. W., Veliz, P., Wilens, T. E., & Schulenberg, J. E. (2017). Adolescents' prescription stimulant use and adult functional outcomes: a national prospective study. *Journal of the American Academy of Child & Adolescent Psychiatry, 56*(3), 226–233.

McKetin, R., Lubman, D. I., Najman, J. M., Dawe, S., Butterworth, P., & Baker, A. L. (2014). Does methamphetamine use increase violent behaviour? Evidence from a prospective longitudinal study. *Addiction, 109*(5), 798–806.

McLellan, A. T., Cacciola, J. C., Alterman, A. I., Rikoon, S. H., & Carise, D. (2006). The Addiction Severity Index at 25: Origins, contributions and transitions. *American Journal on Addictions, 15*, 113–124.

Melemis, S. M. (2018, June 12). Substance abuse quiz: Are you addicted to drugs or alcohol? *Addiction and Recovery*. Retrieved on June 29, 2018, from https://www.addictionsandrecovery.org/addiction-self-test.htm

Mendes, F. R., & Prado, D. d. R. (2016). Use of herbal medicine to treat drug addiction. In A. L. M. Andrade & D. D. Micheli (Eds.), *Innovations in the treatment of substance addiction* (pp. 51–68). Cham, Switzerland: Springer International.

Milkman, H. B., & Sunderwirth, S. G. (2010). *Craving for ecstasy and natural highs: A positive approach to mood alteration*. Thousand Oaks, CA: SAGE.

Miller, W. R. (2016). Sacred cows and greener pastures: Reflections from 40 years in addiction research. *Alcoholism Treatment Quarterly, 34*(1), 92–115.

Mistral, W. (2016). From substance use to addiction. In W. Mistral (Ed.), *Integrated approaches to drug and alcohol problems: Action on addiction* (pp. 3–15). New York, NY: Routledge/Taylor & Francis Group.

Morgan, C., McAndrew, A., Stevens, T., Nutt, D., & Lawn, W. (2017). Tripping up addiction: The use of psychedelic drugs in the treatment of problematic drug and alcohol use. *Current Opinion in Behavioral Sciences, 13*, 71–76.

Morgan, R., & Freeman, L. (2009). The healing of our people: Substance abuse and historical trauma. *Substance Use & Misuse, 44*(1), 84–98.

Morrison, M. F., Lin, K., & Gersh, S. (2018). Addictions: Evidence for integrative treatment. In D. A. Monti & A. B. Newberg (Eds.), *Integrative psychiatry and brain health* (2nd ed., pp. 1–22). New York, NY: Oxford University Press.

Murphy, K. M. (2017). Music therapy in addictions treatment: A systematic review of the literature and recommendations for future research. *Music and Medicine, 9*(1), 15–23.

Naidoo, D. (2017). 'What helps to keep it under control?': Studying the experiences of gay/bisexual men who take drugs on a controlled basis when clubbing. *Counselling Psychology Review, 32*(1), 16–25.

Najman, J. M., McIlwraith, F., Kemp, R., & Smirnov, A. (2017). When knowledge and experience do not help: A study of nonfatal drug overdoses. *Journal of Addiction Medicine, 11*(4), 280–285.

National Institute on Drug Abuse (NIDA). (2015a, February). *How do hallucinogens (LSD, psilocybin, peyote, DMT, and ayahuasca) affect the brain and body?* Retrieved on July 1, 2018, from https://www.drugabuse.gov/publications/hallucinogens-dissociative-drugs/how-do-hallucinogens-lsd-psilocybin-peyote-dmt-ayahuasca-affect-brain-body

National Institute on Drug Abuse (NIDA). (2015b, June). *Nationwide trends*. Retrieved on June 25, 2018, from https://www.drugabuse.gov/publications/drugfacts/nationwide-trends

National Institute on Drug Abuse (NIDA). (2017). *National Survey of Drug Use and Health*. Retrieved on June 25, 2018, from https://www.drugabuse.gov/national-survey-drug-use-health

National Institute on Drug Abuse (NIDA). (2018a). *Chart of evidence-based screening tools for adults and adolescents*. Retrieved on June 28, 2018, from https://www.drugabuse.gov/nidamed-medical-health-professionals/tool-resources-your-practice/screening-assessment-drug-testing-resources/chart-evidence-based-screening-tools-adults

National Institute on Drug Abuse (NIDA). (2018b, January). *Marijuana*. Retrieved on August 9, 2019, from https://d14rmgtrwzf5a.cloudfront.net/sites/default/files/1380-marijuana.pdf

National Institute on Drug Abuse (NIDA). (2018c, January). *Misuse of prescription drugs*. Retrieved on June 23, 2018, from https://www.drugabuse.gov/publications/research-reports/misuse-prescription-drugs/summary

National Institute on Drug Abuse (NIDA). (2018d, February). *What are synthetic cathinones?* Retrieved on August 3, 2018, from https://www.drugabuse.gov/publications/drugfacts/synthetic-cathinones-bath-salts

National Institute on Drug Abuse (NIDA). (n.d.). *Club drugs*. Retrieved on June 23, 2018, from https://www.drugabuse.gov/drugs-abuse/club-drugs

Nesvag, R., Bramness, J. G., & Ystrom, E. (2015). The link between use of psychedelic drugs and mental health problems. *Journal of Psychopharmacology, 29*(9), 1035–1040.

Oh, H. Y., & DeVylder, J. E. (2014). Mental health correlates of past homelessness in Latinos and Asians. *Community Mental Health Journal, 50*(8), 953–959.

Ohana, D., Maayan, R., Delayahu, Y., Roska, P., Ponizovsky, A. M., Weizman, A., . . . Yechiam, E. (2016). Effect of dehydroepiandrosterone add-on therapy on mood, decision making and subsequent relapse of polydrug users. *Addiction Biology, 21*, 885–894.

Olive, M. F., Cleva, R. M., Kalivas, P. W., & Malcolm, R. J. (2012). Glutamatergic medications for the treatment of drug and behavioral addictions. *Pharmacology, Biochemistry and Behavior, 100*, 801–810.

Ouzir, M., & Errami, M. (2016). Etiological theories of addiction: A comprehensive update on neurobiological, genetic and behavioural vulnerability. *Pharmacology, Biochemistry and Behavior, 148*, 59–68.

Park, N. K., Melander, L., & Sanchez, S. (2016). Nonmedical prescription drug use among Midwestern rural adolescents. *Journal of Child & Adolescent Substance Abuse, 25*, 360–369.

Patterson Silver Wolf (Adelv Unegv Waya), D. A., Hughes, M., Maher, N., Shen, Y., Shore-Fitzgerald, C., & Wang, Y. (2017). Computerized behavioral interventions: Current products and recommendations for substance use disorder treatment. *Journal of Social Work Practice in the Addictions, 17*, 339–351.

Pechnick, R. N., Cunningham, K. A., & Danovitch, I. (2014). Hallucinogen-related disorders. In G. O. Gabbard (Ed.), *Gabbard's treatments of psychiatric disorders* (5th ed., pp. 829–839). Arlington, VA: American Psychiatric Publishing.

Pekala, R. J. (2017). Addictions and relapse prevention. In G. R. Elkins (Ed.), *Handbook of medical and psychological hypnosis: Foundations, applications, and professional issues* (pp. 443–451). New York, NY: Springer.

Perkins, F. N., & Freeman, K. B. (2018). Pharmacotherapies for decreasing maladaptive choice in drug addiction: Targeting the behavior and the drug. *Pharmacology, Biochemistry and Behavior, 164*, 40–49.

Petry, N. M. (2012). *Contingency management for substance abuse treatment: A guide to implementing evidence-based practice*. New York, NY: Routledge/Taylor & Francis Group.

Phillips, K. A., Epstein, D. H., & Preston, K. L. (2014). Psychostimulant addiction treatment. *Neuropharmacology, 87*, 150–160.

Prochaska, J. O., Norcross, J. C., & DiClemente, C. C. (1994). *Changing for good*. New York, NY: Avon Books.

Prue, B. (2014). Prevalence of reported peyote use 1985-2010 effects of the American Indian Religious Freedom Act of 1994. *American Journal on Addictions, 23*(2), 156–161.

Rastegar, D., & Fingerhood, M. (2016). *The American Society of Addiction Medicine handbook of addiction medicine*. New York, NY: Oxford University Press.

Rehn-Mendoza, N. (2016). Shades of grey: Are we making progress in international drug policies? *Nordic Studies on Alcohol and Drugs, 33*(3), 223–224.

Reiche, S., Hermle, L., Gutwinski, S., Jungaberle, H., Gasser, P., & Majic, T. (2018). Serotonergic hallucinogens in the treatment of anxiety and depression in patients suffering from a life-threatening disease: A systematic review. *Progress in Neuro-Psychopharmacology & Biological Psychiatry, 81*, 1–10.

Robitaille, C., & Collin, J. (2016). Prescription psychostimulant use among young adults: A narrative review of qualitative studies. *Substance Use & Misuse, 51*(3), 357–369.

Sanchis-Segura, C., & Becker, J. B. (2016). Why we should consider sex (and study sex differences) in addiction research. *Addiction Biology, 21*, 995–1006.

Sarvet, A. L., & Hasin, D. (2016). The natural history of substance use disorders. *Current Opinion in Psychiatry, 29*(4), 250–257.

Serafini, G., Howland, R. H., Rovedi, F., Girardi, P., & Amore, M. (2014). The role of ketamine in treatment-resistant depression: A systematic review. *Current Neuropharmacology, 12*(5), 444–461. Retrieved on December 16, 2018, from https://www.ncbi.nlm.nih.gov/pmc/articles/PMC4243034/

Sharma, M., & Lakhan, R. (2017). Substance abuse among people with intellectual disabilities: Areas of future research. *Journal of Alcohol and Drug Education, 61*(2), 3–6.

Shen, Y.-C., & Chen, S.-F. (2011). Clinical aspects of inhalant addiction. In B. A. Johnson (Ed.), *Addiction medicine: Science and practice* (Vol. *1*, pp. 525–532). New York, NY: Springer Science + Business Media.

Simonelli, A., Parolin, M., Mapelli, D., Cristofalo, P., Cimino, S., & Cerniglia, L. (2017). Cognitive functioning, clinical profile and life events in young adults addicted to drugs. Does being a girl make a difference? *Clinical Neuropsychiatry: Journal of Treatment Evaluation, 14*(3), 226–238.

Smith, R. L. (2013). The major substances of abuse and the body. In P. Stevens & R. L. Smith (Eds.), *Substance abuse counseling: Theory and practice* (5th ed., pp. 51–97). New York, NY: Pearson.

Social effects of an addiction—drug addiction. (n.d.). Medic8. Retrieved on July 5, 2018, from http://www.medic8.com/drug-addiction/social-effects.html

Sofuoglu, M., & Forray, A. (2014). Stimulant-related disorders. In G. O. Gabbard (Ed.), *Gabbard's treatments of psychiatric disorders* (5th ed., pp. 859–869). Arlington, VA: American Psychiatric Publishing.

Solomon, T. M., Halkitis, P. N., Moeller, R.W., & Pappas, M. K. (2012). Levels of methamphetamine use and addiction among gay, bisexual, and other men who have sex with men. *Addiction Research & Theory, 20*, 21–29.

Soyka, M., & Mutschler, J. (2016). Treatment-refractory substance use disorder: Focus on alcohol, opioids, and cocaine. *Progress in Neuro-Psychopharmacology & Biological Psychiatry, 70*, 148–161.

Spence, A. L. (2017). Polydrug use: The differential effects of alprazolam and oxazepam on methamphetamine- and cocaine-related behaviors. *Dissertation Abstracts International: Section B: The Sciences and Engineering, 77*(11-B(E)). No pagination specified.

Stamou, V., Chatzoudi, T., Stamou, L., Romo, L., & Graziani, P. (2016). Music-assisted systematic desensitization for the reduction of craving in response to drug-conditioned cues: A pilot study. *Arts in Psychotherapy, 51*, 36–45.

Stanciu, C. N., Glass, M., Muzyka, B. C., & Glass, O. M. (2017). "Meth mouth": An interdisciplinary review of a dental and psychiatric condition. *Journal of Addiction Medicine, 11*(4), 250–255.

Steinert, C., Munder, T., Rabung, S., Hoyer, J., & Leichsenring, F. (2017). Psychodynamic therapy: As efficacious as other empirically supported treatments? A meta-analysis testing equivalence of outcomes. *American Journal of Psychiatry, 174*(11), 943–953.

Stoddart, T. (2013, May 8). Addiction: A disease of spirituality. *Sober Nation*. Retrieved on July 4, 2018, from https://sobernation.com/addiction-a-disease-of-spirituality/

Strosahl, K. (2016). Pain is inevitable, but suffering is optional. *Psychologist, 29*(8), 632–633.

Tanguay, R. L. (n.d.). *Pharmacological treatment for substance-based addictions*. Retrieved on July 23, 2018, from http://www.addictionday.ca/handouts/Theatre/Morning%201/Final%20CSAM%20copy%20Tanguay.pdf

Tarman, V., & Werdell, P. (2014). *Food junkies: The truth about food addiction*. Toronto, ON: Dundurn.

Thomas, K., Malcolm, B., & Lastra, D. (2017). Psilocybin-assisted therapy: A review of a novel treatment for psychiatric disorders. *Journal of Psychoactive Drugs*, *49*(5), 446–455.

Thylstrup, B., Bloomfield, K., & Hesse, M. (2018). Incremental predictive validity of the Addiction Severity Index psychiatric composite score in a consecutive cohort of patients in residential treatment for drug use disorders. *Addictive Behaviors*, *76*, 201–207.

Timko, C., Moos, R. H., & Finney, J. W. (2016). The course of substance use disorders: Trajectories, endpoints, and predictors. In E. J. Bromet (Ed.), *Long-term outcomes in psychopathology research: Rethinking the scientific agenda* (pp. 53–76). New York, NY: Oxford University Press.

United Nations Office on Drugs and Crime. (2018, June). Executive summary: Conclusions and policy implications. *World Drug Report 2018*. Retrieved on August 9, 2019, from https://www.unodc.org/wdr2018/en/exsum.html

United Nations Office on Drugs and Crime. (2019, June). *Home page*. Retrieved on July 18, 2019, from https://www.unodc.org/unodc/en/frontpage/2019/June/world-drug-report-2019_-35-million-people-worldwide-suffer-from-drug-use-disorders-while-only-1-in-7-people-receive-treatment.html

United States Drug Enforcement Administration. (n.d.). *Drug schedules*. Retrieved on August 3, 2018, from https://www.dea.gov/druginfo/ds.shtml

Uusitalo, S., & van der Eijk, Y. (2016). Scientific and conceptual flaws of coercive treatment models in addiction. *Journal of Medical Ethics: Journal of the Institute of Medical Ethics*, *42*(1), 18–21.

Volkow, N. D., Koob, G. F., & McLellan, A. T. (2016). Neurobiologic advances from the brain disease model of addiction. *New England Journal of Medicine*, *374*, 363–371.

Wallace, B. C., & Santacruz, E. (2017). Addictions and substance abuse in the LGBT community: New approaches. In R. Ruth & E. Santacruz (Eds.), *LGBT psychology and mental health: Emerging research and advances* (pp. 153–175). Santa Barbara, CA: Praeger/ABC-CLIO.

Weaver, M., Delos Reyes, C., & Schnoll, S. (2014). Club drug addiction. In G. O. Gabbard (Ed.), *Gabbard's treatments of psychiatric disorders* (5th ed., pp. 851–858). Arlington, VA: American Psychiatric Publishing.

Weegmann, M., & Cohen, R. (Eds.). (2002). *The psychodynamics of addiction*. Hoboken, NJ: Wiley.

Werb, D. (2018). Post-war prevention: Emerging frameworks to prevent drug use after the War on Drugs. *International Journal of Drug Policy*, *51*, 160–164.

West, S. L., Graham, C. W., & Cifu, D. X. (2009). Alcohol and other drug problems and persons with disabilities: A new light on an often overlooked problem. *Alcoholism Treatment Quarterly*, *27*, 238–241.

WHO ASSIST Working Group. (2002). The Alcohol, Smoking and Substance Involvement Screening Test (ASSIST): Development, reliability and feasibility. *Addiction*, *97*(9), 1183–1194.

Williams, D. J., & Strean, W. B. (2004). Physical activity as a helpful adjunct to substance abuse treatment. *Journal of Social Work Practice in the Addictions*, *4*, 83–100.

Wong, P. T. P. (2015). Meaning therapy: Assessments and interventions. *Existential Analysis*, *26*(1), 154–167.

Wong, P. T. P. (2017). Meaning-centered approach to research and therapy, second wave positive psychology, and the future of humanistic psychology. *Humanistic Psychologist*, *45*, 207–216.

Wu, L., & Blazer, D. (2015). Substance use disorders and comorbidities among Asian Americans and Native Hawaiians/Pacific Islanders. *Psychological Medicine*, *45*(3), 481–494.

Yoon, S., Kobulsky, J. M., Yoon, D., & Kim, W. (2017). Developmental pathways from child maltreatment to adolescent substance use: The roles of posttraumatic stress symptoms and mother-child relationships. *Children and Youth Services Review*, *82*, 271–279.

Zimmerman, G. L., Olsen, C. G., & Bosworth, M. F. (2000). A 'stages of change' approach to helping patients change behavior. *American Family Physician*, *61*(5), 1409–1416.

PART III

Recognized Behavioral Addictions

14 Gambling Addiction

iStock.com/skyn

Learning Objectives

1. Learn about the history of gambling.
2. Become familiar with the qualities and characteristics of compulsive gamblers.
3. Be able to define gambling disorder (GD) and know how to diagnose it.
4. Become informed about the possible consequences that could result from excessive gambling.
5. Discover best practices in counseling individuals with GD.

CHALLENGING YOUR ASSUMPTIONS ABOUT THIS ADDICTION

1. Often individuals with GD will stop gambling on their own. In what ways, if any, does knowing this challenge *your* definition of addiction?
2. The legal age to gamble varies from state to state and, in some cases, by the type of gambling. Should there be a uniform age? Why or why not? (see https://www.worldcasinodirectory.com/gambling_age_chart.htm to compare legal gambling age, state by state).
3. Before reading the chapter, what images come into your mind when you think of a compulsive gambler? What does this person look like? Is your image of a male or a female? What characterizes their personality?
4. If you have never gambled, what has kept you from this activity? If you have gambled, to what extent? Which gambling activities have you participated in, and why? Which gambling activities have you avoided, and why?
5. According to the *New York Times* (https://www.nytimes.com/2016/01/13/us/powerball-odds.html), the chance of winning the Powerball jackpot is estimated at 1 in 292.2 million. The same source reports that your chance of being hit by lightning is 1 in 1.19 million. Given the remote chances of winning the Powerball, are *you* likely to purchase these tickets? Why or why not?

PERSONAL REFLECTIONS

"Ligaya,"[1] my first spouse, has a stepfather who is a compulsive gambler. I met him in about 1984, and, even then, he was spending much of the family income on horse races, poker, and mahjong. Many times, Ligaya bailed him out from his gambling debts. If not, he and my now deceased ex-mother-in-law would not have been eating, plus they would have been living on the street. Now he is with a new wife, and I have already heard through the grapevine that his gambling has nearly crippled their relationship.

My first experience with a casino was in Reno when I was 20 years old. I lasted about 5 minutes before being asked to leave. I never won more than $100 in my life, but, in reviewing my gambling, I have likely spent about $3000 in total. I know that some blackjack players used to make money by using counting techniques but go to Vegas now and most blackjack tables are using six decks or continuous shuffle machines! Good luck on counting that many decks.

A little gambling can be fun, but what leads someone to spend an entire paycheck on what amounts to little more than pure luck in most cases? What draws people in so pervasively? We all know we have bills to pay, so what happens in compulsive gamblers' minds that makes them think the "rules of living" do not pertain to them? These are the questions that fill my mind as I begin researching and writing this chapter.

Background Information

> My friends and I were about 100 yards from the stage. I left to get more beer and heard a distinct "Pop! Pop! Pop!" sound. I thought it was just the sound guy messing up. Within seconds, people started screaming, "Run!" But I stood there stunned, not knowing what to do. People were running, diving under tables, and jumping over things. I felt numb. But then I got shot in the arm. Bullets everywhere and raining down from above the crowd. Someone else saved my life as I heard him get shot in the back. Blood everywhere. (Route 91 Harvest Festival, Las Vegas, October 1, 2017)[2]

The perpetrator in the Las Vegas shooting, Stephen Paddock, experienced gambling addiction, according to media reports (Weinstock, 2018). Although this was never fully substantiated, Weinstock (2018) commented that the incident does raise questions about the potentially disastrous consequences that can result from addictions. Weinstock wrote about how feelings of isolation, despondency, suicidality, perceptions of injustice, disregard for the

---

[1]All the names of actual people in this book have been changed. I choose the name Ligaya as it means happiness in Tagalog. Isagani, in Tagalog, means a rich and bountiful harvest.

[2][Depiction adapted from reports found at https://www.usatoday.com/story/news/nation-now/2017/10/02/blood-all-over-elevator-las-vegas-shooting-survivors-recall-attack-own-words/724924001/ and https://www.washingtonpost.com/news/post-nation/wp/2018/05/16/im-not-gonna-lay-here-and-just-get-shot-survivors-describe-the-terror-and-chaos-of-las-vegas-massacre/?utm_term=.2efacc6d7de6]

rights of others, and the lethality of owning several high-powered automatic rifles might lead someone to kill en masse. As you will learn in this chapter, gambling disorder (GD) frequently co-occurs with personality disorders, and, of these, narcissistic and antisocial personality disorder are at the top of the list (Dowling et al., 2015).

Gambling and betting have been around since ancient times (Gobet & Schiller, 2014). Historical forms of gambling were zero-sum games that helped redistribute items among the members of a community (Clark, 2017). These included cockfights in the Indus Valley and dice games dating around 2000 BC (Gobet & Schiller, 2014). Gambling was also popular in Egypt and the Roman Empire, even among emperors like Augustus and Nero. Records also show people betting their entire fortune—or even their liberty—in India and Germany (Gobet & Schiller, 2014).

Gambling became especially popular in the late 19th and early 20th centuries (Wardle, 2015). During this time, countries like the United States would swing from virtually total prohibition on gambling to widespread acceptance (Rash & Petry, 2017). Recessions prompted this in the 1920s and 1930s in which the government needed to fund social programs. Hence, in the 1930s, American states began to legalize games such as bingo and horseracing. Another example is the creation of the British National Lottery in 1994, which gave gambling a government endorsement (Wardle, 2015). The subsequent British Gambling Act further deregulated and liberalized gambling opportunities (Wardle, 2015). Lotteries are now one of the most common forms of gambling and the least harmful (Costes, Kairouz, Monson, & Eroukmanoff, 2018). Some countries, such as Sweden and Russia, still have systematic bans on gambling, which has led to the creation of uncontrolled illegal markets (Airas, 2014).

For much of Western history, excessive gambling was seen as a moral problem (Welsh, Jones, Pykett, & Whitehead, 2014). However, after Edmund Bergler (1943) published *The Gambler: A Misunderstood Neurotic* and argued that compulsive gambling was an illness needing medical treatment, views on excessive gambling began to change. Finally, in 1980, pathological gambling was classified as an impulse control disorder (ICD) in the DSM-III. Antisocial behavior and crime were included as indicators of problematic gambling but were subsequently removed in the fifth edition (Gobet & Schiller, 2014). Gambling was also changed to a behavioral addiction due to its similarities with substance use disorders (SUDs; Welsh et al., 2014). Today, gambling addiction is the most well-understood behavioral addiction (Hodgins & Petry, 2016). The South Oaks Gambling Screen (SOGS) and its revision, SOGS-R, are the most common measures of problem gambling (Gobet & Schiller, 2014).

Gambling is a lucrative industry, raking in $34 billion for American casinos (Grant & Odlaug, 2014). It is a worldwide phenomenon, being common in such countries as the United States, the United Kingdom, Australia, Switzerland, and Hong Kong. This availability is amplified by the advent of Internet gambling in 1996 (Gobet & Schiller, 2014). Last but not least, smartphones and other portable media devices have permitted gambling to cross into a whole new market of consumers (Armstrong, Rockloff, Browne, & Li, 2018).

Gambling disorder is defined as "the presence of persistent and recurrent patterns of gambling behavior that result in clinically significant impairment or distress. These typically impact the domains of financial, personal, marital/familial, employment, legal, and social functioning" (Burckhardt & Blaszczynski, 2017, p. 166). Addicted gamblers are more likely to be younger, male, ethnic, unmarried, have lower education, more adverse childhood experiences, and engage in more tobacco and alcohol use than low-risk gamblers (Van Patten, Weinstock, & McGrath, 2018). An Austrian study also found that gamblers may have poor mental health, have grown up with a single parent, have parents with addiction problems, and belong to the working class (Buth, Wurst, Thon, Lahusen, & Kalke, 2017). In the United States, non-Caucasians experience higher prevalence of disordered gambling than Caucasians (Cookman & Weatherly, 2016).

Problem/pathological gamblers may gamble regularly or irregularly. Of 214 patients entering treatment for gambling, 28% reported gambling episodes that were regular and alternating, whereas 32% reported irregular and intermittent gambling (Cowlishaw, Nespoli, Jebadurai, Smith, & Bowden-Jones, 2018). The irregular episodic gamblers had lower levels of problem gambling severity and comorbidity. For gamblers who win more than they lose, the detrimental effect of gambling is more in the loss of time (Griffiths, 2011).

The Internet has been suggested to be a more problematic medium of gambling than offline gambling environments (Griffiths & Kuss, 2015). The nature of the Internet allows for addictive factors like anonymity, convenience, escape, dissociation/immersion, accessibility, high event frequency, interactivity, disinhibition, simulation, and associability (Griffiths, 2015). Internet gamblers, compared to non-Internet gamblers, highly endorse gambling preoccupation and escapism. As well, nonsports Internet gamblers are likely to have higher levels of debt than their offline counterparts (Estevez et al., 2017).

Furthermore, Internet gamblers have a higher prevalence and severity of problem gambling (Baggio, Dupuis, Berchtold, Spilka, Simon, & Studer, 2017). Most online gamblers also gamble offline, and each type has its own profile (Hing, Russell, & Browne, 2017). For example, online poker players play significantly more, but live poker players have considerably longer gambling sessions (Barrault & Varescon, 2016). Hence, time spent gambling and the diversity of gambling formats are better predictors of problem gambling than the online/offline dichotomy (Baggio, Dupuis, Berchtold, Spilka, Simon, & Studer, 2017). Nevertheless, the profile of the typical Internet gambler is male, young, single, educated, and employed in professional or managerial positions (Griffiths & Kuss, 2015).

Online gambling machines are continually being improved to make them more appealing (Adams & Wiles, 2017). Offline environments are also set up in a certain way to encourage gambling behavior. The tightly clumped layout of certain gambling areas discourages social interaction, encourages uninterrupted and solitary play via dimmed lighting, and provides no social tables, factors that are oriented toward heavy and problematic gambling (Adams & Wiles, 2017). Not surprisingly, addicted gamblers care less about the company they share than regular gamblers, and they prefer larger venues (Rockloff, Moskovsky, Thorne, Browne, & Bryden, 2017)

Slot machine players may enter a state of absorption wherein they become entirely occupied by the game and forget everything else; researchers call this state *dark flow* (Dixon et al., 2019). Dixon et al. (2019) found that these slot machine players lacked mindfulness in other contexts and were prone to depression, whereas during dark flow they experienced positive affect.

Some gamblers are *chasers* (i.e., people who continue to gamble to recoup losses) whereas others are not. Chasers score higher on maladaptive personality dimensions than do nonchasers (Nigro, Ciccarelli, & Cosenza, 2018b). Chamberlain, Stochl, Redden, Odlaug, and Grant (2017) found that chasing losses distinguished recreational gamblers from problem gamblers, whereas endorsement of social, financial, or occupational losses due to gambling distinguished pathological gamblers from the other groups. Gamblers who chase tend to have poorer decision-making performance than other gamblers (Nigro, Ciccarelli, & Cosenza, 2018a).

Individuals with GD have significant deficits in cognitive flexibility, attentional set-shifting, and attentional bias (van Timmeren, Daams, van Holst, & Goudriaan, 2018). The strength of cognitive biases accounts for much of the variance in pathological gambling, with stronger cognitive biases indicating more severe gambling problems (Tani, Gori, & Ponti, 2018). Most recreational gamblers view gambling as a game of chance, whereas "Problem gamblers believe that they will win" (Semmell, as cited in Xu & Harvey, 2014, p. 61). For these reasons, addicted gamblers have diminished decision-making abilities (Schiller & Gobet, 2014).

Compared to recreational gamblers, GD patients score higher in positive and negative urgency (Navas et al., 2017). This means that addicted gamblers act impulsively whether they are in a highly positive or negative mood state (Lindberg, Clark, & Bowden-Jones, 2014). Hence, compulsive gamblers have poor inhibitory control over their gambling behavior (Chowdhury, Livesey, Blaszczynski, & Harris, 2017). Indeed, impulsivity is key to several behavioral addictions (Bodor, Tomic, Ricijas, Zoricic, & Filipcic, 2016; Lutri et al., 2018).

Addicted gamblers also score higher in discounting, reward sensitivity, the intensity of gambling-related cognitions, and perseverance (Navas et al., 2017). Discounting means that individuals with GD tend to choose smaller immediate rewards over larger delayed rewards (Yakovenko & Hodgins, 2014).

Sévigny and Ladouceur (2003) coined the concept *double switching* where players switch off their rational beliefs while gambling and switch them back on afterward (Lindberg, Clark, & Bowden-Jones, 2014). Passanisi, Craparo, and Pace (2017) have dubbed these irrational thoughts "magical thinking." Some gambling-related cognitive biases include

1. The overall belief that one is lucky (Cowie et al., 2017).
2. The gambler's fallacy, a false belief that sequences of random events tend to self-correct (Gobet & Schiller, 2014). In other words, a big win is bound to happen after a losing streak.
3. The related "hot hand," a belief in streaks of good or bad luck (Gobet & Schiller, 2014).
4. The illusion of control, when gamblers behave as if they have control despite gambling being a situation of chance (Campitelli & Speelman, 2014).
5. The illusion of expertise, when gamblers think they have more skill than they actually do (Campitelli & Speelman, 2014).
6. Unrealistic optimism, in which gamblers overestimate the chances of something good happening and underestimate the chances of adverse events (Gobet & Schiller, 2014).

Many individuals may not accurately perceive any transitions in their gambling, likely due to these gambling fallacies and dissonant feelings (Mutti-Paker et al., 2017). The quicker a person progresses from first gambling to GD, the longer the duration of the addiction (Medeiros, Redden, Chamberlain, & Grant, 2017). Worldwide, the mean age of onset for GD is 11.5 years (Korpa & Papadopoulou, 2013).

Having a financially focused self-concept (i.e., viewing money as a domain of self-worth) is more predictive of disordered gambling severity than other known predictors (Tabri, Wohl, Eddy, & Thomas, 2017). Interestingly, a study by Lemon, Kmiec, and Roland-Levy (2017) found that recreational gamblers fear losing money, whereas probable pathological gamblers fear losing the game, as losing the game would be an affront to their ego.

Pathological gamblers, compared to healthy controls, tend to have low or high loss aversion (Takeuchi et al., 2016). Well-being decreases as the severity of GD increases (Farrell, 2018). Like others suffering from addiction, they also have decreased empathy (Tomei, Besson, & Grivel, 2017).

Addicted gamblers internalize actual or anticipated public stigma until it becomes self-stigma, which may prevent them from seeking treatment (Hing & Russell, 2017a). Self-stigma increases with female gender and older age, which are doubly associated with GD (Hing & Russell, 2017b). One study of 2000 Australian adults found that social stigma against GD included social distancing, emotional reactions, and status loss/discrimination. Problem gambling was seen to be caused by bad character and to be disruptive (Hing, Russel, & Gainsbury, 2016).

Not many problem gamblers seek treatment (Grant & Odlaug, 2014). If they do seek treatment, it is usually for a mental health disorder rather than for gambling itself (Rash & Petry, 2017). However, a significant proportion of problem/pathological gamblers appear to recover without treatment (Petry, 2015).

One study of undergraduate gamblers and nongamblers found that the honesty-humility dimension on the HEXACO model of personality was associated with nongambling (McGrath, Neilson, et al., 2018). Social support from others and a sense of coherence (that one's environment is manageable and meaningful) are also protective factors against developing GD (Langham, Russell, Hing, & Gainsbury, 2017; Rasanen, Lintonen, Tolvanen, & Konu, 2016).

GD is not a homogenous illness, and causality has not been determined for many of the risk factors (Geel & Fisher, 2015). Indeed, problem gambling appears to be transitory and episodic—gamblers move in and out of clinical thresholds concerning their life circumstances (Godinho, Kushnir, Hodgins, Hendershot, & Cunningham, 2018).

Still, theories abound regarding the causes of problem gambling. One of these is the pathways model, which suggests three developmental pathways to problem gambling: behaviorally conditioned (BC), emotionally vulnerable (EV), and biologically vulnerable (BV) gamblers (Allami et al., 2017). BC gamblers have been conditioned either by a big win or via social gambling. EV gamblers compensate or distract themselves from another emotional problem such as depression or anxiety. Lastly, BV gamblers have are thought to have a genetic predisposition to addictive behavior. This type has been replaced in some studies by the term antisocial-impulsivist (AI) gamblers (Geel & Fisher, 2015; Moon, Lister, Milosevic, & Ledgerwood, 2017). AI gamblers have the highest rates of antisocial personality disorder, attention deficit hyperactivity disorder (ADHD) symptoms, impulsivity, and risk-taking among the pathway types.

One of the key causes of continual gambling is escapism. Gamblers play to draw their attention away from negative emotions and worries. Loneliness and lack of social activities can be triggers for some addicted gamblers—especially females—to gamble since many forms of gambling are in social contexts (Dhillon, 2015; Richard, Baghurst, Faragher, & Stotts, 2017). For men, gambling may help them escape boredom, especially sensation-seeking gambling like horse-racing bets (Smith & Shah, 2015). People may also start gambling compulsively after playing social casino games; these individuals tend to be male, younger, more involved in the game, and have higher levels of problem gambling severity (Gainsbury, Russell, King, Delfabbro, & Hing, 2016).

Once gambling problems begin, the negative consequences perpetuate the behavior as gamblers try to escape their new problems. For instance, gamblers may feel shame at their behavior and will keep gambling to cope with this negative feeling (Schlagintweit, Thompson, Goldstein, & Stewart, 2017). Also, the more a gambler loses, the more significant the potential win becomes (Smith & Shah, 2015). Gambling increases when the monetary payout increases, but this relationship is moderated by debt (Quilty, Lobo, Zack, Crew-Brown, & Blaszczynski, 2016).

Children of problem gamblers are more than 10 times likelier to develop gambling problems, too, possibly due to the gambling expectancies and motives passed down to them by their parents (Dowling et al., 2018). Adolescents may also take up gambling if they believe their peers are gambling (Zhai et al., 2017).

Other risk factors for young people include low levels of parental bonding, learning difficulties, and lack of connection to a school community (Anastassiou-Hadicharalambous & Essau, 2015). For adolescents, low conformity, low self-discipline, boredom, and excitability are also linked to problem gambling. Lastly, instant gratification games are strongly associated with the number of games played (Parodi, Dosi, Zambon, Ferrari, & Muselli, 2017).

Another risk factor for the development of GD is adverse childhood experiences (ACEs). People who experience three or more types of ACEs are significantly more likely to develop disordered gambling compared to people with no history of ACEs (Poole, Kim, Dobson, & Hodgins, 2017). Addicted gamblers who experienced ACEs are more likely to be female, have more severe gambling symptoms, and have co-occurring mood and anxiety disorders (Shultz et al., 2016). Childhood maltreatment also tends to be intergenerational. Limited data has shown that problem gamblers are more likely to physically abuse or neglect their children, leading to a cycle of abuse (Lane et al., 2016).

Hence, traumatic stress plays a role in the development of GD (Green, Nahhas, Scoglio, & Elman, 2017). Furthermore, emotional dysregulation was found to be a mediator between ACEs and GD (Poole et al., 2017), whereas an Italian study found that pathological dissociative symptoms mediated between childhood trauma and gambling problems (Imperatori et al., 2017). Alexithymia and difficulties in emotion regulation appear to be key factors linked to GD (Elmas, Cesur, & Oral, 2017). Alexithymia is associated with pathological gambling in strategic gamblers (usually males), but depression is more associated with GD in nonstrategic gamblers (usually females; Bonnaire et al., 2017).

Lastly, cognitive distortions play a large part in GD (Hahmann, 2016; Schiller & Gobet, 2014). For instance, losses disguised as wins (LDWs) increase the likelihood that a person will continue betting (Leino et al., 2016). Also, Tabri, Will Shead, and Wohl (2017) found that people with a financially focused self-concept were more influenced by relative deprivation (mediated by delay discounting), leading to disordered gambling.

Noncompulsive gambling does offer some benefits to players. Social casino games are often free to play, and they can provide hours of entertainment (Wohl, Salmon, Hollingshead, & Kim, 2017). Wohl et al. (2017) stated that playing such games may act as a proxy for addicted gamblers. Casinos bring certain benefits to a community such as increased personal incomes for some; improvement in a city's financial power, landscape, infrastructure, and facilities; and increased entertainment and recreation facilities (Penny Wan, Li, & Kong, 2011). College students in one study reported that gambling offered them social enhancement, more money, and positive changes in affect (Wickwire et al., 2007). Hope and Havir (2002) found that older Americans (ages 65–74) had fun gambling and enjoyed its social benefits. These elders were well aware of the danger signs of GD. The Internet is also replete with purported benefits emanating from gambling.

On the other hand, there are also drawbacks from noncompulsive gambling. Gamblers can end up spending a lot of time and money on an activity designed to have more people lose than win. Penny Wan et al. (2011) mentioned the reduction of public leisure and green spaces, increased traffic problems, higher dropout rates among students, increases in crime and GD, increased need for counseling services, and, for some, deteriorating quality of life. The prevalence of gambling in general—and GD in particular—is positively correlated with the number of legal types of gambling in a state. States that have had legal lotteries or casinos the longest have higher rates of GD (Welte, Tidwell, Barnes, Hoffman, & Wieczorek, 2016). Penny Wan et al. concluded that the disadvantages of gambling outweighed the benefits. This is a value judgment, and, of course, not everyone would agree.

Gambling is a common activity, with participation of between 60% and 80% of people from developed countries. Data from a Canadian national survey in 2002 pegged the overall gambling rate at 76% for people 15 and over, Australian surveys reported adult rates of 69–86% between 1999 and 2009, and an American national study found rates of 82% for respondents aged 18 and over in 2002 (Gobet & Schiller, 2014).

The number of people experiencing gambling-related harm is greater than the number who misuse Class A drugs (Roaf, 2015). It is estimated that between 1% and 3% of the world population gambles problematically, although rates as high as 5.8% have been found by studies in certain countries (Calado & Griffiths, 2016; George & Bowden-Jones, 2015). In the United States, problem gambling affects between 6 and 9 million people directly (Lewis, Black, & McMullen, 2016). It is much more prevalent in prison populations than in the general population worldwide; for instance, American prisoners are five to 10 times more likely to be problem gamblers (Turner et al., 2017).

Studies from Western countries suggest that 60%–80% of youth aged 13–17 partake in some form of gambling at least once a year (Anastassiou-Hadicharalambous & Essau, 2015; Ricijas, Hundric, Huic, Kranzelic, 2016). About 3%–6% of these youth display characteristics of pathological gambling (Anastassiou-Hadicharalambous & Essau, 2015).

In the United States, the rate of addicted gambling was estimated to be 0.2%–12.3% for youth (Truong, Moukaddam, Toledo, &

Onigu-Otite, 2017). Ipsos MORI (2009) found that 1% of British youth aged 11–15 had gambled on the Internet for money in the past 7 days (as cited in Griffiths, 2015). Alarmingly, one Canadian study from Quebec found that 13% of youth aged 12–19 were probably addicted gamblers (Gobet & Schiller, 2014).

College-age students have a high prevalence of GD (Martin, Nelson, & Gallucci, 2016; McKinley, Luo, Wright, & Kraus, 2016; Zhao, Marchica, Derevensky, & Shaffer, 2017). GD is also more prevalent in online poker players compared to other gamblers (Moreau, Chabrol, & Chauchard, 2016). However, purely online gamblers are relatively rare since many of them also gamble offline (Griffiths & Kuss, 2015).

Older adults make up a large proportion of gamblers—and pathological/problem gamblers—in the United States and Canada (Anderson, Rempusheski, & Leedy, 2018; Elton-Marshall et al., 2018). Like women (and many older gamblers are women, as previously discussed), older adults may use gambling as a means to escape anxiety and depression caused by deteriorating health and social support (Parke, Griffiths, Pattinson, & Keatley, 2018). Indeed, studies have shown that psychological satisfaction is inversely related to gambling behavior among seniors (Dennis, Davis, Chang, & McAllister, 2017).

Diagnostic and Assessment Considerations

GD is found on pages 585–589 of *DSM-5* (APA, 2013). It is the first behavioral addiction to be included in *DSM-5* within the section called Substance-Related and Addictive Disorders. Although the *DSM-5* criteria for substance-related disorders include 11 criteria, the criteria for GD contains only nine. Similar to substance disorders in *DSM-5*, GD is diagnosed by *severity* (i.e., by the number of diagnosable symptoms) as follows: (a) *mild*: 4 to 5, (b) *moderate*: 6 to 7, or (c) *severe*: 8 or 9.

Petry (2015) indicated that gamblers who meet fewer than four criteria in *DSM-5* but who are still experiencing gambling problems are often referred to as "problem gamblers" (p. 124). However, problem gambling of GD is also viewed as a synonym in the published literature. Research based on *DSM-5* criteria will help provide consistency among the results found in gambling studies.

The overall diagnostic criteria for GD are "Persistent and recurrent problematic gambling behavior leading to clinically significant impairment or distress, as indicated by the individual exhibiting four (or more) of the following in a 12-month period" (APA, 2013, p. 585). The specific criteria include (a) needing to increase the amount of gambling to achieve the same excitement as earlier, (b) becomes irritable or restless when attempts are made to reduce or stop gambling, (c) unsuccessful and repeated efforts have been to control, diminish, or stop gambling, (d) frequent preoccupation with gambling, (e) frequently gambles when feeling negative emotional states such as anxiety and depression, (f) frequently returns to "chase losses" (i.e., attempt to win back what was previously lost), (g) lies to others to minimize their involvement in gambling, (h) gambling has created relationship, job, educational, or career difficulties, and (i) asks and receives money from others to pay for debts caused by gambling.

There is a secondary criterion as well for GD. The disorder must not be the result of a manic episode.

You also specify if GD is episodic or persistent, and whether it is in *early remission*, meaning between 3 months and 12 months, or in *sustained remission*, which requires 12 months or longer. The *DSM-5* codes are the same for the varying degrees of severity, so it is important to specify if the severity is *mild, moderate*, or *severe*. See Table 14.1 for the DSM and ICD codes:

Several studies that demonstrated common effects, clinical course, and neurobiological features among GD and SUDs are what led to the inclusion of GD into the addictions section of

TABLE 14.1 DSM and ICD Codes

DSM Code	Number of Symptoms Required	ICD-10	ICD-11
312.31	Mild: 4 or 5 symptoms	F63.0	Varies*
312.31	Moderate: 6 or 7 symptoms	F63.0	Varies*
312.31	Severe: 8 or 9 symptoms	F63.0	Varies*

*The gambling codes in ICD-11 vary substantially as evident from the following (this is a complete list for gambling):

#	Specific entity	Specific ICD-11 Code
1	Hazardous gambling or betting (includes betting and gambling)	QE21
2	Gambling disorder, unspecified	6C50.Z
3	Problems related to primary support group, including family circumstances, unspecified (includes problems related to gambling in the family)	QE70.Z
4	Gambling disorder, predominantly online	6C50.1
5	Gambling disorder, predominantly offline	6C50.0

DSM-5 (Bullock & Potenza, 2015; Clark, 2015; O'Brien, 2015). Grant, Odlaug, and Chamberlain (2017) reviewed baseline data collected on individuals with GD from 2001 to 2016. The total sample included 574 adults with 12.7% mild, 32.1% moderate, and 55.2% severe GD using *DSM-5* criteria. Grant et al. found that the mild cases were clearly distinguished from the moderate and severe cases, but the moderate and severe cases were not clearly differentiated. In other words, this study suggests that it may be difficult to distinguish moderate from severe GD using *DSM-5* criteria.

A later study by Grant and associates (Stinchfield et al., 2016), however, found *DSM-5* to provide more accurate diagnoses of GD over DSM-IV criteria. Research based on eight datasets from Canada, the United States, and Spain (*n* = 3247) revealed that *DSM-5* criteria for GD resulted in satisfactory reliability, validity, and classification accuracy. Compared to DSM-IV, there was also a reduction of false-negative errors using *DSM-5* criteria (Stinchfield et al., 2016).

During the initial assessment, Kaspar (2015) noted that counselors should gather as much information regarding both the history of the gambling behavior and the current gambling behavior. It is likely that other people have been affected by the clients' gambling by the time you see them for an assessment. Consequently, it is important to ascertain the impacts the clients' gambling has had on other people. Also, Kaspar wrote that it is critical to ascertain the client's motivation to change.

Pfund et al. (2017) found that, in a sample of 69 disordered gamblers, a score of 16 or higher on the Beck Depression Inventory II (BDI-II) predicted an elevation on at least one scale of a well-known psychopathology test (i.e., MMPI-2). Consequently, the researchers suggested that addiction counselors use the BDI-II as a screen for psychological distress and the co-occurrence of psychopathology.

Differential Diagnosis

As stated in the previous section, a trained mental health professional does not diagnose GD if an individual is experiencing a manic episode (APA, 2013). This is because manic episodes involve a loss of judgment.

DSM-5 stresses that it is important to distinguish between professional and social gambling from GD. Professional gambling is defined as where "the risks are limited and discipline is central" (APA, 2013, p. 589). Gambling is often comorbid with antisocial personality disorder among other personality disorders, and, if criteria are met for both disorders, they should both be diagnosed.

There are medical conditions that can create excessive gambling behaviors. *DSM-5* noted that those taking dopaminergic medications, such as required by those with Parkinson's disease, may increase the desire to gamble. If the medication is stopped and the gambling behavior follows, a diagnosis of GD is not given.

It is possible that other medical conditions contribute to GD. For example, Tondo, De Marchi, Terazzi, Sacchetti, and Cantello (2017) reported the case of a 55-year-old man who developed GD. Disordered gambling was followed by agitation, disinhibition, euphoric feelings, dysthymia, and binge eating. At the researchers' clinic, 2 years later he was given a diagnosis of "probable behavioral variant frontotemporal dementia presenting with a psychiatric symptom" (p. 62). When a client presents with atypical features, GD may be masking an underlying medical condition.

Comorbidity and Co-Addictions

In their scoping review of comorbidity in people with GD, Yakovenko and Hodgins (2018) found that few studies have looked at the mechanisms of comorbidity and instead have focused merely on prevalence rates. Furthermore, Yakovenko and Hodgins reported that there is a lack of treatment evaluation studies focused on dual-diagnosis individuals.

DSM-5 noted that individuals with GD are often in poor overall health, and such conditions as tachycardia and angina are more common with them than in the general population. Most individuals with GD have at least one co-occurring psychological condition, and many have multiple disorders (Martyres & Townshend, 2016). Individuals with GD experience higher rates of comorbidity with psychiatric disorders, including SUDs, depressive disorders, anxiety disorders, and personality disorders (APA, 2013). In Vaddiparti and Cottler's (2017) review, GD was most often associated with the cluster B personality disorders (this cluster includes antisocial personality disorder, borderline personality disorder, histrionic personality disorder, and narcissistic personality disorder). Medeiros and Grant (2018) found that GD is commonly comorbid with obsessive-compulsive personality disorder.

The rates of personality disorder among individuals with GD are higher when using self-report instruments (87%–93%) compared to semistructured interviews (25%–61%) (Gaston, 2015). Kessler et al. (as cited in Gaston, 2015) found the prevalence of anxiety disorder among addicted gamblers to be 60.3%, phobias to be 52.2%, panic disorder to be 21.9%, generalized anxiety disorder to be 16.6%, and PTSD to be 14.8%. Ledgerwood and Petry (as cited in Geel & Fisher, 2015) reported the prevalence of PTSD to be higher and in the range of 12.5%–29%. Grubbs, Chapman, Milner, Gutierrez, and Bradley (2018) also found links between GD and PTSD.

Individuals with GD have a high rate of suicidality; Ronzitti et al. (2017) found that 46% of 903 addicted gamblers seeking treatment reported current suicidal ideation. A UK study (*N* = 122) found that having comorbid mental health issues was more influential than gambling severity in leading to increased suicidality (Roberts, Smith, Bowden-Jones, & Cheeta, 2017).

Bipolar disorder is frequently comorbid with GD (Varo et al., 2019). Rodriguez-Monguio, Errea, and Volberg (2017) analyzed data from 2009 to 2013 in Massachusetts (*N* = 869 patients) and found that the most common co-occurring disorders with GD were anxiety disorders (28%), mood disorders (26%), and SUDs (18%). In their sample of 515 male disordered gamblers, Mann et al. (2017) found that 88% of the gamblers were nicotine addicted and 28% were addicted to alcohol. GD is also correlated with intimate partner violence (Roberts et al., 2018).

GD is positively correlated with impulsivity (Savvidou et al., 2017) and emotional dysregulation (Jauregui, Estevez, & Urbiola, 2016). Unsurprisingly, ADHD is more common in individuals with GD (Peter et al., 2016). Having alexithymia is also related to gambling severity (Noel et al., 2018).

Lanteri et al. (2018) concluded that drug-induced GD is an underreported condition. As previously noted by *DSM-5*, dopaminergic agonists are most commonly implicated (taken for Parkinson's disease), the worst of which is pramipexole currently. Lastly, some research has found a relationship between individuals with traumatic brain injury and GD, particularly among those who experience psychological distress, hazardous drinking, and lower educational levels (Turner et al., 2019).

Available Measures

The addiction counselor has plenty of choices when it comes to using screening tools for GD. The following is only a sample of what is available.

1. South Oaks Gambling Screen (SOGS; Lesieur & Blume, 1987). The SOGS remains the most commonly used screening tool for assessing GD (Gobet & Schiller, 2014; Kaspar, 2015). It is a 20-item self-administered questionnaire that was based on DSM-III diagnostic criteria. The questionnaire has been criticized for placing too much emphasis on the financial aspects of gambling, and it may produce false positives in individuals within lower socioeconomic groups (Kaspar, 2015). The questionnaire was developed at the Gambling Treatment Team at South Oaks Hospital in Long Island, New York (Gobet & Schiller, 2014). There is a revised version that only includes 18 items available online from the South Oaks Hospital website (http://www.south-oaks.org/files/South_Oaks_Gambling_Screen.pdf).
2. Canadian Problem Gambling Index (CPGI; Ferris & Wynne, 2001). The CPGI has become increasingly popular (Clark, 2015). Although the original CPGI contained 33 items, the revised Problem Gambling Severity Index (PGSI) only includes nine items. The Canadian Consortium for Gambling Research (2017) recommended that a score of 1–4 on the PGSI indicates low-risk gambling, whereas 5–7 indicates moderate-risk gambling (a nine-item Likert-scale version of the PGSI with scoring interpretation is available from https://learn.problemgambling.ca/PDF%20library/assessment-pgsi-en.pdf).
3. Metacognitions about Gambling Questionnaire (MGQ; Caselli et al., 2018). This is a 10-item questionnaire, and participants respond using a 4-point Likert scale (i.e., do not agree, agree slightly, agree moderately, and agree very much). It has good psychometric properties as well as predictive and divergent validity (Caselli et al., 2018).
4. Gambling Pathways Questionnaire (GPQ; Nower & Blaszczynski, 2017). Nower and Blaszczynski (2017) tested their questionnaire on 1176 gamblers attending treatment centers in Canada, the United States, and Australia. The authors suggested that their 48-item questionnaire would take about 10 min to complete (the questionnaire with scoring is found in the appendix of their article). The instrument has excellent internal consistency and good to high reliability, and factor analysis revealed that it measures the three subtypes of gamblers theorized in the pathways model, that is, Cluster 1 (Behaviorally Conditioned Subtype), Cluster 2 (Emotionally Vulnerable Subtype), and Cluster 3 (Antisocial, Impulsive Risk-Taking Subtype).
5. South Oaks Gambling Screen Revised for Adolescents (SOGS-RA). This version of the SOGS is for use with adolescents. Anastassiou-Hadicharalambous and Essau (2015) noted that it is the most widely used screen for teenagers. It contains 12 items (available from http://www.ncpgambling.org/files/NPGAW/SOGS_RA.pdf).
6. Canadian Adolescent Gambling Inventory (CAGI; Wiebe, Wynne, Stinchfield, & Tremblay 2007). In their review of screening tools for gambling in adolescents, Edgren et al. (2016) stated that the CAGI was the only one developed specifically for teenagers. Edgren et al. concluded that, of the instruments examined psychometrically, the CAGI demonstrated low response bias and good applicability. Factor analysis revealed a four-factor solution, called psychological consequences, social consequences, financial consequences, and loss of control. The researchers found that one of its subscales (i.e., 9-item Gambling Problem Severity) was optimal for classification purposes (the full inventory is available from https://prism.ucalgary.ca/bitstream/handle/1880/48158/CAGI_Phase_III_Report_e.pdf?sequence=1&isAllowed=y).

Clinical Interview Questions

The Minnesota Impulse Disorders Interview was revised to make it compatible with *DSM-5* criteria for GD (Chamberlain & Grant, 2018). The interview has good concurrent validity and discriminant validity and excellent test-retest reliability (the article by Chamberlain & Grant, 2018, is available from https://www.sciencedirect.com/science/article/pii/S0165178117315925).

Gamblers Anonymous (n.d.) also has 20 questions that can be answered by individuals who think they might have a gambling problem. The psychometric properties of these questions were investigated by Toneatto (2008) and found to have good internal consistency and validity (i.e., concurrent, convergent, and predictive). The 20 questions can be administered and scored online (http://www.gamblersanonymous.org/ga/content/20-questions). Increasing severity of problematic gambling occurs with scores of 7 and higher. Toneatto suggested that a score of 14 or higher more accurately captures pathological gambling as defined in DSM-IV.

Generic Names and Street "Lingo"

Several terms are used in the literature in referring to GD. These include problem gambling, problematic gambling, disordered gambling, pathological gambling, compulsive gambling, addictive gambling, and at-risk gambling. Gobet and Schiller (2014) wrote that GD has also been referred to as "ludomania" (p. 3). Franklin (2014) indicated that GD is often called "the secret addiction" (p. 294) because of how hidden the behavior often is from family and friends.

Neuroscience

The central neurological hypothesis regarding GD is that altered activity is occurring in different brain areas compared to nonproblematic gamblers and nongamblers (Conversano et al., 2012; Quintero, 2016). Abnormalities occur in frontal lobe activation, which then projects into the frontal lobe (Conversano et al., 2012). Problematic gamblers can be distinguished from casual gamblers through differences in brain activation, amount of brain gray matter, the size of specific brain structures, the extent of previous cerebral damage, and abnormal EEGs (Quintero, 2016).

Regarding brain activation, Miedl, Fehr, Meyer, and Herrmann (2010) found that blood oxygen levels differed markedly between pathological gamblers and casual gamblers in the thalamus, superior temporal, and inferior frontal brain regions. Problematic gamblers also had a different activation pattern in the frontoparietal brain. Fuentes et al. (2015) found that, compared to controls, pathological gamblers had a smaller thalamus, hippocampus, and putamen. Koehler, Hasselmann, Wustenberg, Heinz, and Romanczuk-Seiferth (2015) found higher gray matter volume in the ventral striatum and anterior prefrontal cortex among pathological gamblers compared to the control group.

Brain dysfunctions have been found in individuals with GD in the insula, the frontal lobe, several areas of the cortex (e.g., orbitofrontal, prefrontal, dorsolateral prefrontal, ventrolateral prefrontal, and orbitofrontal cortex), the frontotemporolimbic matrix, the frontotemporal area, and the ventral striatum (Quintero, 2016). Pathological gamblers also experienced cerebrum impairment and more EEG irregularities compared to a control group (Quintero, 2016).

Dopamine has played a central role in investigations of neurochemical abnormalities in individuals with GD given its important function in SUDs (Clark et al., 2013). Biochemical dysfunctions occur in individuals with GD, particularly with the neurotransmitters dopamine, serotonin, and norepinephrine and opioid systems (Conversano et al., 2012). Potenza (2013) described the effect of these neurochemicals on compulsive gamblers. Dopamine provides reinforcement, serotonin leads to behavioral initiation and behavioral cessation (i.e., the impulse component), norepinephrine acts to excite and arouse gambling behavior, and the opioid system creates a feeling of pleasure and increases urges to gamble. Potenza also stated that cortisol is released in response to stress in gamblers, and so is glutamate, which serves to increase compulsiveness and cognitive inflexibility.

As mentioned earlier, overall, GD is believed to activate the same regions of the brain as do SUDs (Fauth-Buhler, Mann, & Potenza, 2017). Fauth-Buhler et al. (2017) concurred with APA's (2013) decision to reclassify GD as an addiction (and not as an ICD). The reasons stated by Fauth-Buhler et al. are as follows:

> The existence of similar diagnostic characteristics; the high co-morbidity rates between the disorders; their common reward-related aspects (positive reinforcement: behaviors are pleasurable at the beginning which is not the case for ICDs); the findings that the same brain structures are involved in PG and SADs [Substance-Related and Addictive Disorders], including the ventral striatum and the overlap in pharmacological and behavioral treatments . . . Research on compulsivity suggests a relationship with PG and SAD, particularly in later stages of the disorders. (p. 893)

Conversano et al. (2012) recognized that GD is both an ICD and a "'drugless' SUD or 'behavioral addiction'" (p. 140). Pathological gamblers exhibit impaired decision-making, which prevents them from considering or acting upon the negative consequences of their behavior, and irrational beliefs that lead them to overestimate their chances of winning (Conversano et al., 2012).

Physical Impacts (Long-Term Use)

Compulsive gambling is associated with many adverse health consequences such as tachycardia, angina, cirrhosis, and other liver diseases (Milkman & Sunderwirth, 2010); however, these consequences could have been the result of alcohol use disorder (AUD), which is frequently comorbid with GD (Cowlishaw & Kessler, 2016). The best research we have concerning the health consequences of pathological gambling was based on the 2001–2002 National Epidemiologic Survey on Alcohol and Related Conditions (NESARC; Morasco et al., 2006). Morasco et al. (2006) analyzed data from 43,093 adults (18 years+) and found that compulsive gamblers were more likely to have received a diagnosis for tachycardia, cirrhosis, and other liver diseases. These effects remained even *after* the researchers controlled for alcohol and substance dependence (including nicotine), age, gender, ethnicity, marital status, body mass index, and mood and anxiety disorders.

There is a relationship between pathological gambling and increased suicidality (Stein, Pretorius, Stein, & Sinclair, 2016). The type of gambling might be a variable as Bischof et al. (2016) found that electronic gambling machines in gambling halls and bars were most associated with suicidal events, and not casino games or betting on sports.

Mental, Emotional, and Spiritual Impacts

Williams, Grisham, Erskine, and Cassedy (2012) compared 56 pathological gamblers with a mixed clinical comparison group (MCCG; $N = 50$) and a healthy control group (HCG; $N = 49$). The pathological gamblers reported less emotional awareness than the HCG and reported less ability to use emotion-regulation strategies than the other two groups. Grant and Odlaug (2014) stated that GD is related to substantial impairment in functioning socially and occupationally. GD commonly co-occurs with mood and anxiety disorders, but it is not known if one causes the other (Grant & Odlaug, 2014). Stressful events often trigger pathological gambling, but stress also follows gambling losses (Elman, Tschibelu, & Borsook, 2010).

Blaszczynski and Nower (2002) suggested that anxiety and worry are the consequences of gambling and not the cause of it. That is not always the case, however. In their study, Parke, Griffiths, Pattinson, and Keatley (2018) found that GD may develop in vulnerable individuals who are escaping anxiety and depression. Also, as GD increases, an individual's sense of well-being diminishes (Farrell, 2018). Land-based gamblers experienced greater psychological distress, self-acknowledged need for treatment, and help-seeking behaviors compared with gamblers who strictly gambled online ($N = 4594$; Blaszczynski, Russell, & Gainsbury, 2016).

Some pathological gamblers might have psychological vulnerability (e.g., personality and mood) that impacts the severity of their GD (Levesque, Sévigny, Giroux, & Jacques, 2018). Shame and guilt are common among individuals with GD, but shame particularly follows a recent loss (Yi & Kanetkar, 2011). Pathological gamblers are less accurate regarding the amount of regret they anticipate having if they make a losing bet compared with social gamblers (Tochkov, 2012).

The impact of religiosity on gambling behavior appears equivocal. In Mutti-Packer, Hodgins, Williams, and Thege's (2017) study, religiosity acted as a static protective factor against the severity of problem gambling, but it may not play a role in predicting future severity. Most research suggests that having religious beliefs deters believers from gambling (Beyerlein & Sallaz, 2017). This also appears to be true for adolescents (Casey et al., 2011).

However, Lam (2006) analyzed the adult data from the 1999 American National Gambling Impact Study Commission (N = 2,947) and found that faith did not affect gambling participation. Furthermore, when gambling does occur, the severity of GD is related to the extent that religious individuals believe in gambling fallacies such as thinking that faith and their higher power will help them win in gambling, which has random outcomes (Kim, Shifrin, Sztainert, & Wohl, 2018).

Psychosocial Impacts (Relationships, Career/Work, Legal, Financial)

Compulsive gamblers report intrusive thoughts that interfere with their functioning both at home and work (Grant & Odlaug, 2014). Their preoccupation with gambling can lead to absenteeism and inefficiency at work (Binde, 2016). Across several studies, Kaspar (2015) stated that between 21% and 36% of problem gamblers seeking treatment had lost a job due to gambling.

Financial problems are common, leading to such outcomes as bankruptcy, failing to pay credit cards and bank loans, and mortgage foreclosures (Grant & Odlaug, 2014). The need for money leads some compulsive gamblers into the theft of money or goods from work or other settings, leading to potential legal difficulties (Binde, 2016). Mestre-Bach et al. (2018) compared treatment-seeking gamblers (N = 382) with a sample that had a history of illegal acts (N = 103) and a sample with no criminal record (N = 279). The pathological gamblers with a history of unlawful acts experienced greater severity of both GD and gambling-related debts. In a study reported by Kaspar (2015), more than 50% of the participants attending Gamblers Anonymous admitted to engaging in criminal acts to fund their gambling.

GD often creates or worsens existing problems with an intimate other, and it diminishes intimacy and trust with family members (Grant & Odlaug, 2014). Intimate partners often feel anger, resentment, depression, loneliness, and/or isolation from the addicted gambler (Velleman, Cousins, & Orford, 2015). In Velleman et al.'s (2015) study of wives, feelings of helplessness, confusion, and several physical maladies were reported. Many intimate others consider leaving (or do leave) their relationship when involved with a disordered gambler (Velleman et al., 2015).

Family members in the household of a compulsive gambler report high degrees of anxiety, fear, isolation, moodiness, anger, frustration, irritability, and shock (Velleman et al., 2015). Children are often caught in the middle of family tensions around excessive gambling behaviors. Also, the children raised in a family with someone who experiences GD are likely to develop gambling problems themselves (Velleman et al., 2015). The children of addicted gamblers are more inclined to develop impulse control problems, depression, low self-esteem, have a history of physical and sexual abuse, lower parental bonding, less monitoring and supervision, and learning difficulties compared to families without an addicted parent (Anastassiou-Hadicharalambous & Essau, 2015). Another study found that having a parent who is a problem gambler predicted ADHD behaviors in children (Carbonneau, Vitaro, Brendgen, & Tremblay, 2018)

The partners of addicted gamblers sometimes experience another physical impact: intimate partner violence (IPV). In waves 1 and 2 of the NESARC (N = 25,631), GD was associated with increased odds of IPV perpetration by both males and females (Roberts et al., 2018). As Roberts et al. (2018) stated, however, it is important to realize that the relationship between gambling and violence is complex because there are often co-occurring mental health and substance use disorders that are affecting compulsive gamblers simultaneously.

Australia's Productivity Commission estimated that every problem gambler affects between five and 10 other people (Gobet & Schiller, 2014). Unsurprisingly, addicted gamblers often lose friends because of their gambling (Yakovenko & Hodgins, 2014).

Working With Diverse Populations

Sex Differences

Little sex-specific research has been conducted on GD internationally (Dhillon, 2015). However, it is known that more men gamble—and become addicted to gambling—than women do (Estevez, Jauregui, Sanchez-Marcos, Lopez-Gonzalez, & Griffiths, 2017). This is historically due to the socialization of women and gambling being a "man's game." Gambling is now available to both sexes, and more women are consequently gambling (Dhillon, 2015). Lifetime GD among women is estimated to be between 0.4% and 2.0% and problem gambling to be between 1.3% and 2.3% (Rash & Petry, 2017).

Women are more likely than men to become problem gamblers if they are both homemakers and working women, probably due to gendered expectations surrounding work and family life (van der Maas, 2016). Athletes, particularly male athletes in team sports, develop problem gambling more often than the general population (Rhind, O'Brien, Jewett, & Greenlees, 2014). Furthermore, a strong association was found between problem gambling and problem gaming among university athletes (Hakansson, Kentta, & Akesdotter, 2018).

Compared to men, women progress to GD more quickly (Ronzitti, Lutri, Smith, Clerici, & Bowden-Jones, 2016), start gambling at a later age (Dhillon, 2015), and gamble for a shorter time before seeking treatment (Rash & Petry, 2017). Women also gamble a higher percentage of their incomes compared to men, likely due to the wage disparity between the sexes (Rash & Petry, 2017; Beaulac et al., 2017). This means they may play until all their money is lost (Dhillon, 2015; Karter, 2015). Indicators of problem gambling are similar overall between the two sexes, with a few exceptions: Emotional distress is more commonly reported among females, whereas aggressive behavior toward gambling devices and other people is more common among males (Delbaffro, Thomas, & Armstrong, 2018).

Because women have a higher risk for DSM Axis I disorders, they appear to experience other disorders before the onset of problem gambling, whereas for men it is the opposite (Haw & Holdsworth, 2016). Female problem gamblers are more likely than males to report comorbid mood and anxiety disorders, whereas men are more likely to report comorbid alcohol or drug use disorders (Ronzitti, Lutri, Smith, Clerici, & Bowden-Jones, 2016).

More than in men, GD in women is driven by stress, depression, and anxiety, with gambling being used as a form of self-medication. Where men become addicted to the high of risky gambling, women become addicted to the escapism (Dhillon, 2015; Karter, 2015; O'Brien, 2015). It is not surprising then that men prefer strategic games and women prefer nonstrategic games like slot machines and bingo (Dhillon, 2015; Rash & Petry, 2017). These nonstrategic games comprise a low level of skill and high level of absorption that allow women to reach a "zone" or "bubble" where they are in a world of their own (Karter, 2015). Likewise, because online gambling has a lesser social aspect than land-based gambling (in bingo halls, for example), female online gamblers are more prone to unhealthy gambling than their offline counterparts (Karter, 2015).

Women are more likely than men to report negative impacts on relationships due to gambling (Dhillon, 2015) and to feel psychological distress due to quarrels with their partners (Koschel, Lindenmeyer, & Heinrichs, 2017). They may lie about their gambling problem rather than face their loved ones (Karter, 2015). Furthermore, women feel guilt, shame, and self-stigma due to their gambling behavior compared with men (Dhillon, 2015). Self-stigma in females is compounded by their (usually) older age, higher problem gambling severity, greater use of secrecy, and lower self-esteem (Hing & Russell, 2017). In comparison, one study of French male gamblers found males more likely to score higher on self-esteem and perceived quality of life than female gamblers (Bonnaire, Kovess, Guignard, Richard, Du-Roscoat, & Beck, 2016).

Women are likely to report internal and external barriers to treatment for problem gambling (Kaufman, Nielsen, & Bowden-Jones, 2017) and often seek general instead of specialized services (Beaulac et al., 2017). Female gamblers usually seek treatment more than their male counterparts (Rash & Petry, 2017). One study of New Zealanders, however, found that male gamblers were more likely than females to access treatment after contacting a helpline (Kim, Hodgins, Bellringer, & Abbott, 2016).

According to Karter (2015), the first 4 weeks of recovery are the hardest for women. They are vulnerable to replacing their addiction with another absorbing activity, like Facebook, eBay, or playing *The Sims*. Women also suffer from withdrawal symptoms during this time such as cravings, overeating (or its opposite), nausea, sleep problems, and headaches. Research suggests that women may prefer women-only treatment groups to co-ed groups like Gamblers Anonymous (Dhillon, 2015).

Adolescents and Youth

The rate of problem gambling among adolescents is higher than it is in adults, sitting somewhere between 0.2% and 12.3% (Milkman & Sunderwirth, 2010; Truong, Moukaddam, Toledo, & Onigu-Otite, 2017). As in the adult population, adolescent gambling is associated with the male sex, ethnic minority, and the presence of other addictive disorders (Simmons, Whelan, Meyers, & Wickwire, 2016). It is also linked to "positive gambling attitudes, higher levels of gambling involvement, ineffective coping strategies and unhelpful parenting practices" (Dixon et al., 2016, p. 42), although more research should be done on exactly how each factor impacts adolescent gambling (Derevensky, 2016).

As in other addictions, impulsivity is a major personality trait related to gambling addiction. Impulsivity among adolescents may manifest as delinquent behavior (violent or nonviolent), alcohol consumption (sometimes mixed with energy drinks), or tobacco use, all of which are linked to problem gambling (Buja et al., 2017; Kryszajtys et al., 2018; Vieno et al., 2018).

One study of Hong Kong adolescents found that low self-control and social strain predicted problem gambling (Cheung, 2016). Another study of male adolescents in Germany found similar results and reported that many adult gamblers started as adolescents (Giralt et al., 2018). Youth who partake in simulated gambling games are prone to begin monetary gambling, and some develop GD eventually (Armstrong, Rockloff, Browne, & Li, 2018).

Both perceived excessive peer gambling and family gambling are associated with problem/pathological gambling in youth (Zhai et al., 2017). Ho (2017) found that living in a gambling-permissive culture, where gambling is viewed as entertainment, and both parents and society are supportive of gambling, enables problem gambling among adolescents. It is worth noting here that the United Kingdom permits children under the age of 16 to gamble on slot machines (Franklin, 2014). Also, having a dismissive attachment style could predispose an adolescent toward gambling (Terrone et al., 2018). Lastly, immigrant status and living with only one biological or adoptive parent increased the chances of GD in one Italian study (Canale et al., 2017).

Parents influence their children's access to and participation in gambling activities. However, this influence is declining with the rise of digital online gambling; adolescents' participation in online activities tends to be unsupervised compared to offline activities (King & Delfabbro, 2016). McBride (2016) found that online gamblers (versus nongamblers) were more likely to play video games, and video game players (versus nonplayers) were more likely to gamble, suggesting an overlap between the two populations.

Race and Ethnicity

Two characteristics of problem gamblers transcend ethnicity: impulsivity and negative feelings (Van Slyke, 2017). Caucasians appear to have a lower rate of gambling problems compared to non-Caucasians (Cookman & Weatherly, 2016; Geel & Fisher, 2015). Based on a random-digit telephone survey of 2631 U.S. residents between August 1999 and October 2000, African Americans living in disadvantaged neighborhoods who either smoked or were alcohol dependent were the most likely to report GD (Welte, Wieczorek, Barnes, & Tidwell, 2006). Quintero (2016) also concluded that African Americans had a higher likelihood of experiencing gambling problems than White individuals. Using data from the NESARC (N = 32,316; 13% Black, 87% White), Barry, Stefanovics, Desai, and Potenza (2011b)[3] found that African American adults were more likely to report GD than White participants.

[3]Note that the entire sample in this survey included 43,093 respondents. African American households and Hispanic households were intentionally oversampled.

Gambling is also more prevalent among Native populations in countries such as the United States, Australia, and Canada, although prevalence rates have not been studied in depth (Bond et al., 2017; Williams, Belanger, & Prusak, 2016). One study using NESARC data found that, compared to other ethnicities, Native Americans were the least likely to report non-low-frequency gambling and the most likely to report low-risk gambling (Kong, Smith, Pilver, Hoff, & Potenza, 2016). There was also a stronger correlation between problem gambling severity and past-year psychiatric disorders.

According to another study done by Barnes, Welte, and Tidwell (2017), neighborhood disadvantage has a greater effect on gambling for Native Americans than it does for the rest of the U.S. population. In Canada, GD was found to be higher in cities were Indigenous individuals were in the majority (Williams, Belanger, & Prusak, 2016). Another study of Canadian Cree found that 20.6% were moderate/high-risk gamblers and 3.2% were in the highest PG category (Gill, Heath, Derevensky, & Torrie, 2016).

According to the 2010 BGPS, British problem gamblers were more likely to be from Asian or Asian-British ethnic groups (Wardle, 2015). Ethnic Chinese individuals have higher rates of gambling-related harm likely due to their beliefs in luck, which can cause gambling-related cognitive biases (Geel & Fisher, 2015; Lim & Rogers, 2017). In one study of college gamblers, Asian participants gambled less frequently than Caucasians or Hispanics but had a larger prevalence of problematic gambling and at-risk gambling criteria than any other ethnicity (Rinker, Rodriguez, Krieger, Tackett, & Neighbors, 2016). In a study of Chinese, Korean, and White American college students, gambling problems were highly comorbid with AUDs in Chinese- and White American men but only moderately comorbid in Korean American men (Luczak & Wall, 2016). No relationship between AUDs and gambling problems was found in women (Luczak & Wall, 2016).

Some data have also suggested that GD is prevalent among Hispanic individuals in the United States (Campos et al., 2016; Quintero, 2016). Barry, Stefanovics, Desai, and Potenza (2011b)[4] used data from the NESARC (N = 31,830; 13% Hispanic, 87% White) and found that Hispanic adults were more likely to report GD than White participants.

Nonpsychiatric Disabilities

The disability most associated with GD is Parkinson's disease (PD). Individuals with PD are more likely to become problematic gamblers because of dopaminergic agonist agents used to treat PD. ICDs—including gambling disorder—show up in about 17% of PD patients on dopamine agonists (Voon et al., 2017). This relationship between dopamine agonists and problem gambling in PD patients provides evidence for the reward deficiency model of gambling (Olley, Blaszczynski, & Lewis, 2015).

PD patients have more "functional" profiles than other patients seeking behavioral addiction treatment; that is, they are less impulsive and have more typical personality traits (Sauvaget et al., 2017). However, individuals with PD and PG perform worse on gambling tasks such as the IOWA Gambling Task (Balconi, Angioletti, Siri, Meucci, & Pezzoli, 2018) and may have more severe depressive and anxious symptoms than PD patients with other ICDs or no ICDs (Pontieri et al., 2015).

ADHD is also linked to GD as noted previously (Carbonneau, Vitaro, Brendgen, & Tremblay, 2018). Also, case studies have shown that the onset of frontotemporal dementia may cause problem gambling (Cimminella, Ambra, Vitaliano, Iavarone, & Garofalo, 2015; Tondo, De Marchi, Terazzi, Sacchetti, & Cantello, 2017).

Lesbian, Gay, Bisexual, and Transgender (LGBT)

Research on the LGBT community and gambling addiction is currently lacking. Nevertheless, one study found that, compared to heterosexual men, gay and bisexual men with GD were more likely to be single, have an ICD, and/or have an SUD (Grant & Potenza, 2006). In an online survey of 605 individuals (51% women; 11% nonheterosexual), Broman and Hakansson (2018) found that, whereas problem gaming and Internet use were more prevalent among nonheterosexual respondents, problem gambling did not differ between the heterosexual and the nonheterosexual participants.

War Veterans

Veterans across the globe have elevated rates of GD compared to the general population (Dighton, Roberts, Hoon, & Dymond, 2018; Whiting et al., 2016). In one study of over 3000 American veterans, the rate of recreational gambling was found to be 35.1% and problem gambling to be 2.2% (Stefanovics, Potenza, & Pietrzak, 2017).

Problem gambling among veterans is associated with substance use, anxiety, depressive disorders, physical or sexual trauma, minority group status, and trauma burden (Stefanovics et al., 2017). Compared to alcohol or cocaine misusers, veterans who were problematic gamblers scored higher on impulsivity and inability to resist craving but not on sensation-seeking (Castellani & Rugle, 1995). Whiting et al. (2016) also found a higher instance of PTSD, traumatic brain injury, general harassment during deployment, lower social support, and more stressful life events postdeployment in veterans with problem gambling.

From studying admitted patients at the Brecksville Veterans Administration Medical Center, Kausch (2003a) found that 66.4% of pathological gamblers had a lifetime history of substance abuse/dependence, and the onset of substance dependence preceded pathological gambling in most of the cases. An earlier study reported that about one third of veterans in VA hospital substance abuse units had comorbid pathological gambling (Daghestani, Elena, & Crayton, 1996). Kausch (2003b) also found that 39.5% of gambling patients at the Louis Stokes VA Medical Center reported having made a suicide attempt at some point in their lives, with 64% of those attempts related to gambling. Elderly veteran gamblers are just as likely as younger gamblers to have a lifetime history of suicidal ideation (Kausch, 2004).

GD is linked to symptoms of PTSD, making veterans susceptible to this behavioral addiction (Grubbs, Chapman, Milner, Gutierrez, & Bradley, 2018). One study found that 34% of pathological gambling treatment-seekers had PTSD (Ledgerwood & Petry, 2006). PTSD appears to exacerbate the symptoms of compulsive gambling. For example, a study of community adults found

[4]Ibid.

that compulsive gamblers who did not have PTSD had better psychological health, less co-occurring disorders, and less suicidality than adults with only PTSD or PTSD/PG (Najavits, Meyer, Johnson, & Korn, 2011). Furthermore, remission from pathological gambling among Native Americans and Hispanic veterans is linked to the absence of a current Axis I diagnosis, especially PTSD (Westermeyer et al., 2006).

Around 10% of Native American veterans have had GD in their lifetime (Westermeyer, Canive, Gerrard, Thuras, & Thompson, 2005). Among this population, lifetime nicotine dependence is associated with various lifetime disorders including pathological gambling (Dickerson, O'Mallye, Canive, Thuras, & Westermeyer, 2009).

Still, more research is needed regarding veterans from racial and ethnic minorities. Most studies have relied on samples that are primarily White, older, and male (Levy & Tracy, 2018). Furthermore, there is a need for more research among veterans in community settings. Only a small proportion of veterans receive care through VA medical centers (Levy & Tracy, 2018).

Medications and Other Relevant Physical Interventions

The U.S. Food and Drug Administration (FDA) has not yet approved any medication for GD (Grant & Chamberlain, 2017). Grant and Chamberlain (2017) indicated that the problem has been that treatments for GD have produced an unusually high placebo effect. To test this, Grant and Chamberlain assigned placebo to 152 GD participants. Of this group, 51% showed a significant clinical response! What distinguished them from the group that did not improve? The placebo responders stayed in treatment longer, were likelier to state that enjoyment was a trigger for gambling, and were less likely to report that boredom or loneliness were triggers for gambling. Grant and Chamberlain concluded that what predicted the placebo response was strikingly different compared with other mental illnesses.

Nonetheless, various medications are being tested and used. Choi et al. (2017) provided a succinct review of drug treatments. The drug categories that are being used include (a) anticraving agents, (b) antidepressants, and (c) mood stabilizers. The anticraving agents include opioid receptor antagonists like naltrexone and nalmefene. In individuals with GD, they can diminish urges to gamble and increase periods of abstinence. A meta-analysis of pharmacotherapy for GD was based on 14 trials with 1024 participants (Bartley & Bloch, 2013). Bartley and Bloch (2013) found that opioid antagonists demonstrated a small effect size compared to placebo. Other medications tested had nonsignificant effect sizes. Consequently, they concluded that current trials provide limited support for the use of pharmacological agents in treating GD. In a study of 101 participants, Kovanen et al. (2016) concluded that naltrexone might not provide additional benefit to GD patients who are already receiving psychosocial support.

The selective serotonin reuptake inhibitors (SSRIs) were among the earliest drugs tested for GD (Choi et al., 2017). Several studies reported that fluvoxamine was helpful, yet another study did not replicate those results. Similar equivocal results have been found with other SSRIs.

Mood stabilizers have been used for individuals with GD (Choi et al., 2017). Nonetheless, small sample sizes limit the generalizability of findings.

Other medications have also been tried (Choi et al., 2017). Bupropion has been used to treat various addictive disorders, for example. Tests have shown it to have equivocal results. Other drugs that have been tested that have provided equivocal findings or results based on very small samples include olanzapine, ecopipam, N-acetylcysteine (NAC), memantine, and amantadine for those with PD.

Brito et al. (2017) tested topiramate (a medication used to treat epilepsy and prevent migraines) with 30 pathological gamblers seeking treatment. Half received topiramate and half received a placebo. Results showed that topiramate was superior to placebo in reducing gambling craving, time and money spent on gambling, and cognition distortions and in promoting social adjustment.

Two other studies have suggested effective treatment with aripiprazole or agomelatine. A case study by Peterson and Forlano (2017) found aripiprazole (a dopamine partial agonist) effective. Agomelatine (an atypical antidepressant) was provided to 17 men and five women for 8 weeks. Egorov (2017) concluded that agomelatine was effective for GD.

Jayan's (2015) conclusions regarding the pharmacotherapy of GD summarizes well the current state of the field:

> Pharmacological management of PG [pathological gambling] may be useful, but the evidence is limited by small sample sizes, attrition rates, and minimal follow-up data. There are discrepancies about researchers' definitions of positive responses to treatment, limiting comparisons across studies. There is no agreement as to which drug is most effective in treating gambling behavior as medication is often linked to the comorbid symptom of the patient. The side effects of these drugs are not always included in the studies. Owing to the high rates of comorbidity between depression and PG, it is worthwhile to conduct further research on the role of antidepressants in gambling. (p. 228)

There are some treatment protocols concerning individuals with GD who have a co-occurring disorder. Although these studies remain rare, Dowling, Merkouris, and Lorains (2016) included in their review the use of naltrexone for comorbid AUDs, N-acetylcysteine in tobacco support programs, lithium for bipolar disorder, and escitalopram for comorbid anxiety disorders.

Gay et al. (2017) assigned 22 individuals to either the treatment group or a placebo group.

They then delivered a single session of repetitive transcranial magnetic stimulation of the prefrontal cortex. Gay et al. concluded that it was effective in reducing cue-induced craving to gamble. Dickler et al. (2018) used transcranial direct current stimulation (TDCS) over the dorsolateral prefrontal cortex in patients with GD (N = 16; assigned to either treatment or sham condition). Dickler et al. measured neural metabolite levels. The researchers concluded that TDCS could modulate GABA levels in these individuals. You might recall from Chapter 3 that GABA has an inhibitory effect on the CNS, thereby producing tranquil feelings.

Sauvaget et al. (2018) conducted a similar study with TDCS but included a sham control group. Their results indicated that the sham condition was as effective as the TDCS condition. Consequently, Sauvaget et al. concluded that there is a strong placebo effect operating with TDCS. Despite this, the researchers were convinced that TDCS "remains a promising therapeutic method" (p. 126).

INSIDE AN ADDICTED PERSON'S MIND

Penny, Age 65

I would be lying if I didn't tell you how much I looked forward to retirement over the past 10 years. Now I'm retired, and I had no idea I would be this miserable. I live in South Dakota, which was one of the first states to legalize video lottery terminals (VLTs). I don't know exactly when they arrived, but I started playing them in the early 1990s. My bets began with quarters, but now I typically play the maximum bet the stupid machine can handle! How can anyone love these machines when they take far more from you than they ever give back? It seems ridiculous telling you this. I used to sit in front of those machines more nights than not, often for hours at a stretch. It's surprising when I look back that I didn't lose my job at some point because so many mornings I would arrive at work, tired as hell from the night before, and I could hardly concentrate on the bookkeeping before me. Never did I get much of an education, by the way. I was hired straight out of high school to help some locals do their income tax. Always pretty good at numbers, it seemed natural that I would get hired for this work.

I married Steve in 1999, but he only stayed with me for 2 years. I was deeply in love with him, but he wanted to build a secure future. So did I, of course. I tried several times to cut down on gambling, but I could never stay off them (i.e., the VLTs) for more than a day. Even then, I felt shaky, tense, and angry.

After 2 years, Steve told me that I was not building a future. . . I was digging his grave! He said that I was squandering all the money that he was trying to save for us. I told him that I rarely spent more than 5 dollars playing VLTs, but he knew differently. So, I did what any woman in love would do: I begged for him to stay. I told him that my luck was about to turn around and I would pay back everything. He did not believe me as he drove away in that damn red Pontiac. I cried until I made my way back to my best friend (i.e., my VLTs). Yes, I even hugged my VLT one night—well, I mean after drinking a few pints. I am not really that crazy.

How do I tell you that, even when I'm not gambling, I'm spending most of my time thinking about winning back what I lost the night before? Oh, I have had my big wins. Times when I have played the maximum bets, I've taken home over a $1000. You know I heard of some woman in Canada who won about $1.2 million playing on a progressive VLT. Boy, would it be great to know her secret!

But you do not want to know about the losses. After tax, I earn about $1500 every 2 weeks. That isn't much these days. After expenses, I have about $500 to the good, and then I go and gamble about $900 worth on my tiring habit! I cannot stop. Most of my friends have either died or moved. My two older brothers and I do not see eye-to-eye, so I am alone 99% of the time since I retired. What do I do? I feel miserable if I cannot distract myself in front of a VLT.

My situation is getting worse daily. My bank phoned me a few days back to say I had reached the maximum on my line of credit. Credit card companies are sending their collectors after me, and yesterday a Sheriff came to my door! He said I have a month to pay one of these bills or he would haul me off to jail. Jail is sounding pretty good right now. Maybe that's what I need to stop gambling.

Commentary

Penny demonstrates eight of the nine diagnostic symptoms found in *DSM-5* for GD, placing her in the severe range. The eight criteria that she meets are (a) needing to increase the amount of gambling to achieve the same excitement as earlier, (b) becomes irritable or restless when attempts are made to reduce or stop gambling, (c) unsuccessful and repeated efforts have been made to control, diminish, or stop gambling, (d) frequent preoccupation with gambling, (e) frequently gambles when feeling negative emotional states such as anxiety and depression, (f) frequently returns to "chase losses" (i.e., attempt to win back what was previously lost), (g) lies to others to minimize her involvement in gambling, and (h) gambling has created relationship, job, educational, or career difficulties. The only criterion that she hasn't met is asking and receiving money from others to pay for debts caused by gambling. If you asked her, and if she told you the truth, you would likely find out that she has done this before as well.

Discussion

1. How many of your friends and family members gamble? How many would you say are casual gamblers and how many are pathological gamblers?
2. Looking at the criteria for GD listed in *DSM-5*, what criteria do you think should be added or deleted from their list of nine criteria? On what basis do you believe that?
3. If you were Penny's counselor, how would you go about helping her?

Specific Counseling Considerations

ROLEPLAY SCENARIOS

Roleplay in dyads with one of you acting as the counselor and the other as the counselee. If roleplay is not possible, work individually in writing out a list of your suggestions.

Roleplay #1

Aiguo, age 59, arrives for his appointment with his wife, Howin. You bring the two of them into your office. They share with you that they were both born in mainland China and they only emigrated to the United States 5 years ago. Howin begins the session, "I can't stand living with Aiguo anymore! Every paycheck, he is at the casino and spends most if not all his money. I have told him to stop doing this repeatedly, but he disobeys me every time. If it were not for the fact that I work hard in the restaurant, our bills would never get paid." Aiguo tries to comfort Howin in the session and tells both of you that she has grossly exaggerated his gambling.

Roleplay #2

Jacqueline was very excited when she turned 19 6 months ago. In Alabama, that allowed her to enter casinos and hopefully make some "hard cash," as she described it. Winning, however, has remained elusive, and Jaclyn has become desperate. Last night, she pulled out her father's Visa card from his wallet and took off with it to the casino. She knew his PIN in case she needed it. In the session, she told you that she was convinced that she had perfected her new blackjack strategy. Instead of winning back her losses as she anticipated, she spent over $2000 using Dad's credit card. She has come to see you because she does not know how to tell her dad what happened. You find out that her father has physically assaulted Jacqueline one or more times in the recent past.

HOW WOULD AN ADDICTION COUNSELOR HELP THIS PERSON?

You are working as a professional counselor. Your next appointment walks into your office uninvited and unannounced, but on time, for his first session with you. Before you have time to respond, he says, "Which seat do I take?" Feeling caught off guard, you ask him to sit down in your client chair. He introduces himself as Dr. Derek Smith, age 41, and he tells you that he is a well-known naturopath. He then begins describing his problem before you have a chance to open your mouth. "To cut to the chase, I am a gambling addict. My wife left me a year ago because of it, which has only made my gambling worse. I do not know how to stop."

As you begin to get his history, he cuts you off and says, "I do not need you to know everything about my life. I want help now, and if you cannot provide it, I will seek out the services of someone who can." As the conversation ensues, you increasingly get a sense that Derek is narcissistic yet you are still expected to help him at your agency.

Remember to view clients within their environmental contexts, keeping in mind societal, parental/familial, cultural/spiritual, and peer influences. Specifically, become aware of the impact that the following influences have and continue to have in your clients' lives: race, language, religion and spirituality, gender, familial migration history, sexual/affectional orientation, age and cohort, physical and mental capacities, socioeconomic situation and history, education, and history of traumatic experience.

1. What defines this person's environment, past and present?
2. Who is this person sitting in front of me, taking into account environmental and personal characteristics?
3. What defines the problem that he or she is presenting within their multicultural milieu?

Goals and Goal Setting

There is controversy over whether total abstinence from gambling is always a necessary goal (Gobet & Schiller, 2014). Gambling is transitory and episodic for many gamblers, meaning that at times they reach clinical thresholds for gambling disorder while at other times do not (Godinho, Kushnir, Hodgins, Hendershot, & Cunningham, 2018). Godinho et al. (2018) stated that life events could act as motivators that contribute to change over time in gambling behavior. They studied 204 adult problem gamblers who wanted to reduce or quit their gambling. Over 12 months, gamblers who experienced positive events were most likely to exhibit gambling reductions over time. Gamblers who experienced adverse events experienced smaller reductions in gambling, and some increased in gambling severity.

In working collaboratively with clients to help ascertain their goals regarding their gambling behavior, it is important to share with them such research findings. In some cases, the intimate partner will be the one that pushes hard for the gambler to cease gambling forever. Compulsive gamblers themselves may instead want to try moderating their gambling behavior.

Many places in the world have implemented responsible gambling (RG) programs to reduce gambling-related adverse consequences. They are noted here as some of them can be adapted to clients who wish to reduce the amount of time and/or money that they spend on gambling. Individual suggestions are found in square brackets after each area. Ladouceur, Shaffer, Blaszczynski, and Shaffer (2017) conducted a synthesis of the empirical evidence and concluded that five areas constitute best practice currently (note that these programs have demonstrated only some effectiveness):

1. Self-exclusion programs. In these programs, compulsive gamblers voluntarily ban themselves from gambling establishments. Many of these programs are poorly utilized, and breaches are common. Furthermore, there is currently minimal evidence for their long-term benefit. Nonetheless, it is considered an evidence-based practice. [Clients can choose to ban themselves from places nearby that make it too easy for them to gamble.]
2. Development of algorithms to identify behavioral characteristics. Some studies have looked at algorithms that predict problem gambling. One example is that players who engage in more than two types of gambling within a month and who wager varying amounts are considered at-risk players. [Clients can self-monitor their gambling behavior to establish a baseline and learn the variables surrounding their gambling patterns.]
3. Limit setting. This tool enables gamblers to preset either monetary and/or time limits to their gambling activity (e.g., pressing a button for how long you wish to gamble, broken into 15-min increments). [Clients can decide to gamble for a given period and then leave the establishment. They might set their alarm on their cell phone and only allow themselves one "snooze."]
4. Responsible gambling machine features. The machine itself may provide warnings at specified intervals to players. Messages that appear in the middle of the screens are most impactful. [If the machine does not have these features, the client can have some warnings typed on paper and commit to taking one out of his/her back pocket/purse every 10 min and place it in front of the machine's screen for a few seconds before deciding whether to continue gambling.]
5. Employees training. Employees are taught to recognize problem gambling behavior and to approach customers exhibiting these behaviors. Unsurprisingly, staff have difficulty doing this because of feeling awkward, embarrassed, and apprehensive. [Clients can learn to continue self-monitoring so they and their counselors can see their gambling patterns that need modifying.]

Following are a few ideas to consider if moderation is the goal:

- Taking breaks in play can help gamblers stay within their gambling limit (Roaf, 2015).
- Restricting access to cash within the venue (Roaf, 2015).
- Set a dollar limit and a time limit each time you gamble (Petry, 2015).
- Leave checks, ATM cards, and credit cards at home (Petry, 2015).
- Take your winnings home (Petry, 2015).
- Remember that the odds of losing always outweigh the odds of winning; otherwise stakeholders would not be earning so much money from lotteries and gambling (Petry, 2015).
- Limit opportunities to gamble (Smith & Shah, 2015).
- Leave home later but commit to returning home within a specified period. Spend less time gambling.
- Break associations between triggers and gambling behavior (Smith & Shah, 2015).
- Use cognitive strategies to challenge irrational beliefs regarding gambling (Smith & Shah, 2015).
- Implement interventions aimed at reducing impulsivity (Smith & Shah, 2015).
- Learn coping strategies such as problem-solving skills (Smith & Shah, 2015).
- Develop mindfulness skills to create greater calmness (Smith & Shah, 2015).
- Become involved in activities that produce pleasure and allow for mastery. These can alleviate boredom and reduce stress (Smith & Shah, 2015).
- Use physical exercise to generate endorphin release (Smith & Shah, 2015).
- Deal successfully with interpersonal problems and solve ongoing conflicts (Smith & Shah, 2015).
- Gamble for fun and not for money (Petry, 2015).
- Gamble only what you can afford to lose (Petry, 2015).

- If needed, phone the National Problem Gambling Helpline at 1-800-522-4700 (https://www.ncpgambling.org/help-treatment/national-helpline-1-800-522-4700/). (Miers, 2014).

If the goal is total abstinence from gambling, the next few sections of this chapter will help guide you in developing an appropriate treatment program with your clients. Remember that collaborating with them throughout the process of their recovery will provide the best help you can offer.

Stages of Change Strategies

The processes of change mentioned are based on those outlined by Connors, DiClemente, Velasquez, and Donovan (2013) and Prochaska, Norcross, and DiClemente (1994). The definitions for the various processes can be found in Chapter 6. Besides these processes, other strategies are included that have separate citations.

The University of Rhode Island Change Assessment Scale (URICA) is a helpful scale in determining where the client is currently regarding the stages of change model. There are 24-, 28-, and 32-item versions of the scale. Petry (2005) established the reliability and validity of the URICA for gamblers seeking treatment.

A 24-item version is published for alcohol or drug problems. The scale, however, is generic and can be easily adapted for use with other addictions. It is available with norms as a free download from https://www.guilford.com/add/miller11_old/urica.pdf.

Hodgins (2001) tested 37 recovered problem gamblers to find out which processes in the stages of change model were most used by the participants. The processes that were used most often were cognitive-experiential. These included self-reevaluation, environmental reevaluation, dramatic relief, and self-liberation. The processes that were used least often were reinforcement management and social liberation (see Chapter 6 for an explanation of the different processes).

Specific precontemplation strategies.

Most Hollywood movies glorify gambling, focusing on its exciting aspects (not helpful to pathological gamblers). The following movies may assist addicted gamblers to reflect on their gambling behaviors:

1. *High Roller: The Stu Ungar Story* (also called *Stuey*). (2003). Captures Stu's rise to the top in the gambling world, followed by his dramatic fall.
2. *The Gambler* (1974). This film looks at the devasting effect that gambling has on the main character (Jeffrey, 1996).

There are many books on the topic of gambling. Some that clients may find helpful to read include the following:

1. *The Unbelievable TRUTH About Gambling Addiction: New Discoveries and Rapid Recovery Techniques* (by Michael Chatha, 2019). The author argues that gambling is not a disease or illness but, instead, a treatable condition.
2. *Gambling, Gambling, Gone* (by Lance Libel, 2018). Quoted from Amazon.com's description: "A young problem gambler's true story of denial, acceptance and a lifelong trial to quit gambling for good. An eye-opening novel focused around the hidden dangers of gambling."
3. *All Bets Are Off: Losers, Liars, and Recovery From Gambling Addiction* (by Arnie Wexler, Sheila Wexler, and Steve Jacobson, 2015). Quoted from Amazon.com's description: "[Arnie] Wexler's gripping narrative leads us through the dungeon of a compulsive gambler's world—chasing the big win and coming up with empty pockets—and how his addiction drove him and his wife, Sheila, to the edge of life. With help, they managed to escape, and together they have devoted themselves to helping others with the problem they know so well."
4. *Overcoming Your Pathological Gambling: Workbook* (by Robert Ladouceur and Stella Lachance, 2012). Quoted from Amazon.com's description: "*Overcoming Your Pathological Gambling* is written by researchers who have spent over two decades studying the psychology of gambling. This book represents the treatment they have found to be most effective at controlling the urge to gamble, understanding the true nature of gambling games, and preventing future gambling problems. Intended for use in conjunction with supervised therapy, this workbook includes various self-assessments and exercises designed to help you reach the ultimate goal of complete abstinence from gambling."
5. *Taking Back Your Life: Women and Problem Gambling* (by Diane Rae Davis. 2009). Quoted from Amazon.com's description: "Up-to-date, guided support to help women with a gambling problem achieve the rewards of a hopeful life, free of addiction."

Kushnir, Godinho, Hodgins, Hendershot, and Cunningham (2016) demonstrated that it is not merely a matter of how motivated compulsive gamblers are to change: It is also about whether their desire is intrinsically or extrinsically motivated. Their hypothesis aligns with self-determination theory (SDT), which is a theory suggesting that people are more motivated to change when their desire is internal instead of externally motivated by others. Kushnir et al. found support for SDT. In other words, compulsive gamblers are likelier to want to change if they have decided to do so for their reasons and not because others are requesting that they change.

Soberay, Grimsley, Faragher, Barbash, and Berger (2014) tested 71 problem and pathological gamblers seeking treatment (43 men, 28 women; age range = 21–71 years). Soberay et al. (2014) found that the individuals who were in the precontemplation stage were the most likely to have severe GD yet they reported having few gambling problems. The researchers suggested that it was a likely result of denial experienced by compulsive gamblers in this stage.

As noted by DiClemente, Story, and Murray (2000), compulsive gamblers in the precontemplation stage need to create a decisional balance (i.e., have more reasons to change than reasons to continue) for either modifying or stopping their gambling behavior. Movement through the stages of change are typically more cyclical than linear (DiClemente et al., 2000).

Adolescent problematic gamblers need to be convinced that their gambling is causing them problems. This is the first step for them in their change process (DiClemente et al., 2000). DiClemente et al. (2000) recommended that motivational interviewing (MI) is best suited for this stage with teenagers.

The Centre for Addiction and Mental Health (CAMH; 2019) offered several precontemplation strategies for helping to motivate individuals with GD. The following is an adapted list:

- Share information about gambling addiction.
- Discuss both the positive and negative aspects of addictive gambling.
- Encourage clients to talk objectively about their gambling behavior.
- Work at creating emotional tension within the client regarding their gambling behavior.
- Recommend that clients attend information sessions.
- Encourage clients to practice leaving their credit and debit cards at home and only gambling with cash.
- Request that clients make a list of the people most and least affected by their gambling behavior. Once the list is complete, help them understand how others are being negatively impacted by their gambling.
- Explore with clients how they would know if their gambling has become a problem. What warning signs would occur?
- Talk about clients' past attempts at changing and what they found most helpful.

CAMH (2013–2018) provided some great ideas for how friends and family can assist addicted gamblers (see https://www.problemgambling.ca/gambling-help/support-for-families/stages-of-change.aspx). Ideas are provided for each stage.

Specific contemplation strategies.

DiClemente et al. (2000) noted that the purpose of the contemplation stage is to create and nurture a commitment to change. CAMH (2019) offered suggestions for helping to do this with compulsive gamblers as follows:

- Work at increasing clients' emotional arousal concerning their gambling.
- Encourage clients to reflect on the impact gambling has on their lives.
- Avoid creating resistance by "rolling" with clients' ambivalence regarding change.
- Encourage clients to focus on the positive aspects of changing their addictive gambling behavior.
- Suggest to clients that they begin monitoring their gambling behavior.
- Consider encouraging clients to attend a mutual support group.
- Suggest that clients plan outings with friends or family that do not involve gambling.
- Ask clients to pay attention to the impact that their gambling has on others.
- Help clients align their gambling behaviors with their personal values.
- Instill hope with clients by focusing on the fact that change is possible.
- Work with clients to create a list of possible barriers and collaboratively develop strategies for overcoming those barriers.

Specific preparation strategies.

In the preparation stage, the primary intent is to create an action plan (DiClemente et al., 2000). CAMH (2019) provided the following ideas to help clients get ready for change:

- Assist clients in increasing their support network. This might include attending mutual support groups or becoming involved in other supportive communities.
- Collaboratively help clients develop their change plan in alignment with the SMART acronym. SMART stands for creating goals that are **S**pecific, **M**easurable, **A**chievable **R**ealistic, and **T**imely (and in sync with the desired result).
- Help clients expand their lifestyle beyond the plans for making changes to their gambling behavior.
- Encourage clients to become involved in meaningful activities.
- Praise clients regarding their decision to change.
- Explore with clients alternative ways to deal with their money (e.g., have another trusted person assist with managing finances).

In helping clients build their change plan, it is beneficial to look at why they gamble, including emotional, behavioral, and cognitive triggers. Moon, Lister, Milosevic, and Ledgerwood (2017), for example, looked at coping reasons for gambling, childhood trauma, risk-taking, impulsivity, ADHD, and boredom. Clients' change plans should include how they will deal with high-risk situations. Other ideas for *before* their chosen quit day (i.e., preparation strategies) can be found in Appendix B.

Specific action strategies.

Gambling problems often diminish or resolve over time, regardless of whether treatment is provided (Petry, Rash, & Alessi, 2016). Also, few addicted gamblers seek formal treatment (Grant & Odlaug, 2014). When treatment (including counseling) is sought, dropout rates are high, particularly with those experiencing comorbidity (Maniaci et al., 2017). In a study of 846 treatment-seeking pathological gamblers in the United Kingdom, Ronzitti, Soldini, Smith, Clerici, and Bowden-Jones (2017) found that predictors of pretreatment dropping out included being younger and use of drugs. Likewise, having a family history of GD, having a lower score on the Problem Gambling Severity Index, and being a smoker were associated with in-treatment dropout. Mailing a letter based on MI techniques and a reminder phone call to individuals with GD can increase attendance at the first counseling session (Pfund, Whelan, Peter, & Meyers, 2018).

Grant and Odlaug (2014) surmised that some studies have shown that up to 20 sessions are needed to treat individuals with GD, whereas other efficacious studies have been much briefer. For example, a single web-based intervention was effective at reducing problem gambling (Rodda, Lubman, Jackson, & Dowling, 2017). Single-session face-to-face interventions have also demonstrated effectiveness with up to 12 months follow-up (Toneatto, 2016). Consequently, more treatment does not always mean greater benefits (Petry, 2015).

CAMH (2013–2018) reminded addicted gamblers that the action stage could take a lot of time and energy. If relapses occur, they should be viewed as learning opportunities. CAMH (2019) recommended that, during the action stage, the following should occur:

- Support and encourage increased self-confidence, self-reliance, and self-determination.
- Focus clients on implementing substitute activities instead of gambling.
- Assist clients in implementing coping strategies, create a plan for dealing with high-risk situations as part of a relapse prevention plan, and teach them ways of managing urges. Strategies include teaching clients to substitute urges, thoughts, and impulses with realistic thoughts and self-talk, redirecting their fantasies toward what really happens after gambling behavior occurs, and refocusing on their goals and values.
- Provide reassurance that thinking about gambling and wanting to gamble is common, especially at this stage.
- Ensure that clients are aware of the cycle of behavior change, which often includes relapse.
- Help clients develop a recovery plan for if or when relapse occurs.
- Encourage clients to give themselves rewards for making both small and big progress.
- Suggest and collaborate with clients to determine if they wish to apply for voluntary self-exclusion from particular casinos or other gambling establishments.
- Suggest and collaborate with clients regarding installing GamBlock (see https://www.gamblock.com/) on their computer and cell phone. This app blocks access to online gambling.
- Suggest and encourage clients to include their support network by telling friends and family members of the change they are making.
- Begin working with other issues (e.g., finances, legal problems, relationship issues).

Dwyer, Piquette, Buckle, and McCaslin (2013) suggested using journaling with women who experience GD as both a data collection method and as a therapeutic technique. Their results indicated that it could be a useful counseling tool.

Online gambling is common in youth, many of whom are already indicating problematic gambling. In a sample of 1200 young Finnish Internet users (age range = 15–25 years), Sirola, Kaakinen, and Oksanen (2018) found that over half (54.33%) of the respondents who had visited online gambling sites were gamblers who were either at-risk or were likely compulsive gamblers. In working with GD in youth, it is important to assess for online gambling, and counsel if evident.

GD is often comorbid with depression. Bucker, Bierbrodt, Hand, Wittekind, and Moritz (2018) randomly assigned 140 pathological gamblers to either a control condition or an online intervention for depression ("Deprexis"; see https://deprexis.com/). After 8 weeks, participants in the treatment condition experienced a significant reduction in depression scores. Linnet, Jeppsen Mensink, de Neergaard Bonde, and Winterdahl (2017) highlighted the importance of providing integrated treatment when working with individuals with GD and comorbid conditions.

Petry, Ginley, and Rash (2017) systematically reviewed treatments for problem gambling. They concluded that cognitive-behavioral therapy (CBT) either alone or combined with MI demonstrated both short-term and long-term benefits. The researchers also found that counselor contact generally improved outcomes better than entirely self-directed interventions.

Another important and interesting work was a meta-analysis done by Goslar, Leibetseder, Muench, Hofmann, and Laireiter (2017). Goslar et al. were interested in determining the efficacy of face-to-face versus entirely self-directed interventions. They found 27 studies with a total sample of 3879 participants. The effect sizes were substantially higher for face-to-face intervention.

As is true of the other addictions, individual counseling is only one of several modalities. Group, couples, and family counseling approaches are also prominent. When 106 patients with comorbid PTSD and pathological gambling were asked what treatment modality they preferred, individual counseling was rated higher than group counseling (Najavits, 2011). Dowling, Smith, and Thomas (2007) also provided cautionary results in their study of 56 female pathological gamblers assigned to either a CBT group treatment or individual counseling. Dowling et al. found that, at 6 months follow-up, 92% and 60% of the gamblers assigned to individual or group treatment, respectively, no longer met the criteria for pathological gambling. Consequently, in this study, individual counseling offered better results at the 6-month mark. If women are going to receive group counseling, one study found that they preferred participating in an all-woman group compared with a co-ed group (Piquette & Norman, 2013).

Group approaches have generally adhered to CBT techniques (Gomez-Pena et al., 2012; Harris & Mazmanian, 2016; Jimenez-Murcia et al., 2015). In running a group, Adkins, Taber, and Russo (1985) suggested that having pathological gamblers in a group write a biography and then delivering it orally to the group was "a powerful tool" (quoted from the title).

Regarding couples counseling for pathological gambling, Tremblay et al. (2018) found that participants enjoyed couples counseling more than individual therapy. Congruence couples therapy (CCT) has been used when one partner has GD (George & Bowden-Jones, 2015; Yakovenko & Hodgins, 2014). CCT is a structured 12-session program that addresses "social isolation, low self-esteem, childhood trauma, coping skills, depression and anxiety" (Yakovenko & Hodgins, 2014, p. 241). Jimenez-Murcia et al. (2017) compared two groups ($N = 675$) and found that pathological gamblers who went to sessions with a concerned significant other had higher attendance, less dropout, and fewer relapses at 3-month follow-up than those who attended alone. On the other hand, the involvement of a concerned family member can also adversely affect a client's response to treatment (Jimenez-Murcia et al., 2015).

Family counseling has shown to have some merit in counseling for GD, but a substantial problem remains given the lack of substantiating evidence provided in most studies (Yakovenko &

Hodgins, 2014). Grant and Chamberlain (2018) reported on two studies using the Community Reinforcement and Family Therapy (CRAFT) model. Although the self-help program appeared to garner positive effects, a counselor was needed to train family members regarding the implementation of the techniques. Another study found limited support for using the CRAFT approach as an individual modality for treatment-resistant GD (Nayoski & Hodgins, 2016).

Internet-based interventions have also become popular due to their lower costs and equivalent efficacy to face-to-face interventions (Casey et al., 2017; Chebli, Blaszczynski, & Gainsbury, 2016; Choi et al., 2017). These can be delivered over a computer or smartphone. Many of these programs translate conventional treatments to online delivery (e.g., CBT). Canale et al. (2016) offered an Internet intervention for preventing at-risk gambling among high school students. Some positive results were found at the 2-month follow-up. A follow-up period of more than 2 months is needed if valid conclusions are to be drawn regarding the impact of prevention and treatment efforts.

Personalized feedback interventions (PFIs) have also demonstrated success with both excessive alcohol consumption and problematic gambling (Marchica & Derevensky, 2016). PFIs can be delivered over the computer or smartphones or via email. They consist of providing (a) a summary of a person's gambling pattern, (b) an overview of the adverse consequences of the behavior, (c) provision of information, and (d) a review of moderation techniques (Marchica & Derevensky, 2016).

Grant and Odlaug (2014) commented that there is no evidence to support using residential treatment for GD. Based on questionnaires, however, Ledgerwood and Arfken (2017) found that most counselors ($N = 30$) and problem gamblers ($N = 93$) in their Michigan sample reported that they wanted to have higher levels of care available to them. About 42% of the problem gamblers reported they would either "probably" or "definitely" attend residential treatment. Other ideas for *beginning* their chosen quit day (i.e., action strategies) can be found in Appendix B.

Specific maintenance strategies and relapse prevention.

Note: Maintenance strategies and relapse prevention are also, for many, partly facilitated by regular attendance at relevant mutual support groups. A list of such mutual support groups and helpful websites is found in an upcoming section entitled Relevant Mutual Support Groups, Websites, and Videos.

The maintenance stage occurs as an addicted gambler maintains behavioral change over a substantial period (DiClemente et al., 2000) of about 6 months (CAMH, 2013–2018). CAMH (2019) made several suggestions to counselors for this stage:

- Encourage clients to use their support system to maintain change efforts.
- Have clients measure their progress using a timeline.
- Suggest that clients follow their relapse prevention plan and continue to identify new high-risk situations (HRSs) and barriers that hamper their progress. Help clients develop additional strategies or ways of managing HRSs and barriers.
- Help clients with other problematic behaviors that emerge now that they are no longer gambling.
- Assist clients in identifying other areas that warrant growth such as other aspects of psychological and spiritual wellness.
- Focus on other life areas that remain affected (e.g., relationships, physical health, career).
- Encourage daily journaling to capture thoughts, feelings, and events that trigger them.
- Help foster development and achievement of long-term goals.

Other ideas for relapse prevention can be found in Appendix C.

Motivational Interviewing

Petry (2015) noted that both MI and motivational enhancement therapy were originally designed to treat problem and pathological gambling. Often MI is used before or in conjunction with CBT. Petry summarized several studies attesting to the effectiveness of MI. Even a single session of MI can suffice to reduce gambling in at least some gamblers (Petry, 2015). Nonetheless, several studies have found mixed results regarding its efficacy as a brief treatment (Yakovenko & Hodgins, 2014). Richard, Baghurst, Faragher, and Stotts (2017) wrote that MI is an appropriate treatment for working with problem gamblers from culturally diverse backgrounds. A Cochrane review (Cowlishaw et al., 2012) concluded that MI might have some benefits in the treatment of GD but the results should be viewed as preliminary. Regardless, MI remains useful as a method for creating a strong positive working alliance (Southern & Hilton, 2015).

Here is an example of how MI could be used with an individual with problem gambling (Pertaining to Chapter 6's description of MI, the following is an example of all four processes called *engaging, focusing, evoking*, and *planning*.) The client is Elsie, a 21-year-old theater student.

Counselor: Come in, Elsie. It is a pleasure to meet you.
Client: Thank you, Jaxon.
Counselor: What brings you to see me today?
Client: My parents are deeply concerned about me. I don't think it's a big deal, but they do. I have been playing a lot of casino games on my iPhone.
Counselor: I see. I know some casino games are free while others cost money. What type of games are you playing?
Client: Well, I began by playing free games... but now... they are costing me... money.
Counselor: I hear the hesitation in your voice, Elsie.
Client: [a few tears forming in her eyes] Ah, I wasn't aware of that.
Counselor: It's okay. Please help yourself to the Kleenex.
Client: [more tears] I don't know why I am crying. My parents have exaggerated this all to hell. It makes me angry.
Counselor: For some reason, your parents' reaction is bothering you.
Client: Yes, that's true. I usually get along with them very well. I don't know why this is bothering me so much in fact.
Counselor: I can hear the respect that you have for your parents and what you just said.

Client: [more tears start flowing again] Yeah . . . yes.
Counselor: Sometimes it can seem that we are not living up to our parents' expectations.
Client: I think it is more than that. I don't think I have wanted to look at my gambling seriously.
Counselor: What leads you to believe that?
Client: I have spent a lot of money on this [says sheepishly].
Counselor: You are aware that you've already spent more than you thought you would on gambling.
Client: [tears up again] Ah, yes, that is entirely true. I guess I haven't wanted to look at this behavior. I feel so embarrassed.
Counselor: I can tell, Elsie, and I completely understand. It's hard not living up to your parents' expectations but even harder is not living up to your own.
Client: [now bawling and so choked up she cannot speak for a few seconds] Please help me.
Counselor: You can bet on it! I am here for you. Tell me why you want to make this change so badly.
Client: I didn't even know I wanted to make a change before I sat down. How can you tell?
Counselor: Everything in your voice and your tears have told me how much you want to regain control.
Client: Are you psychic? That's exactly how I feel right now.
Counselor: I don't think I am psychic, Elsie, but I am good at understanding people who want to change.
Client: What should I do?
Counselor: I do not think I am the best person to answer that. What would *you* like to do?
Client: I want to stop gambling. I don't want to have a continuing conflict with my parents.
Counselor: You want to stop both gambling and the conflicts.
Client: Yes! I want this now before I change my mind.
Counselor: I understand. Would it be okay if we look at things you could do to help start this change now?
Client: Absolutely! Thank you so much, Jaxon. I had no idea at the start of this session that I needed to change my behavior.

Insight-Oriented Interventions

Gobet and Schiller (2014) wrote that, whereas psychoanalytical and psychodynamic therapies are appropriate counseling options for GD, there are methodological weaknesses in published studies on the topic (e.g., no control group, selection bias). Empirical data has not supported its efficacy (Gobet & Schiller, 2014).

Adam (2016) stated that, from his experience as a psychoanalyst, pathological gamblers are rarely interested in embarking in "sustained dialogue" (p. 189). Rosenthal (2008) reviewed the research regarding psychodynamic psychotherapy in the treatment of pathological gambling. He stated that there had not been a single randomized controlled study; however, he found eight positive outcome studies that were described as eclectic, with half of those seeming to utilize psychodynamic methods. Rosenthal concluded that the evidence warrants a clinical trial for psychodynamic therapy for pathological gambling.

An earlier publication by Rosenthal and Rugle (1994) outlined one aspect of psychodynamic therapy with pathological gamblers. To assist with promoting abstinence, Rosenthal and Rugle suggested five strategies: breaking through denial, confronting the gamblers' defenses, interrupting the cycle of chasing losses, identifying reasons for gambling, and motivating clients to become active in their treatment. Reasons for gambling noted by Rosenthal and Rugle included having a "spectacular" need for success, rebelliousness and anger, freedom from dependency, social acceptance (e.g., gamblers receive perks like casino employees remembering their names, lighting their cigarettes, bringing them a drink), an escape from painful affects, and the competitiveness of gambling.

Rugle and Rosenthal (1994) outlined some of the common transferences and countertransferences that occur when working with pathological gamblers. Both could act as obstacles, or they could serve as mechanisms for understanding clients' conflicts, defenses, and reasons for gambling.

Potenza (2005) reviewed the book entitled *The Psychodynamics and Psychology of Gambling: The Gambler's Mind, Volume I* by Mikal Aasyed and surmised that the book is useful for counselors interested in understanding the psychodynamics underlying gambling. Given the current state of empirical evidence regarding the treatment of GD, however, using psychoanalytic and psychodynamic approaches cannot be viewed as best practice.

Spiritual Interventions

In a New Zealand study (n = 244), Clarke et al. (2006) found that the 148 problem gamblers in their sample were three times likelier than the nonproblem gamblers to endorse the belief that gambling provides hope and an opportunity for a better life. In Gamblers Anonymous and various treatment programs (N = 100), pathological gamblers reported that religious experiences and spiritual transcendence were significant and predictive of subjective well-being (Walsh, 2002).

Religious individuals are more prone to having gambling fallacies, believing that a higher power can influence their luck (Kim et al., 2018). Counselors should be aware of this potential fallacy. Kim et al. (2018) suggested that education may reduce these false beliefs among people of faith. Kim et al. did not suggest alternate ways of addressing these fallacies such as perhaps through spiritual counseling or CBT.

CCT includes the four dimensions of intrapsychic, interpersonal, intergenerational, and universal-spiritual (Lee, 2015). Part of the counseling focus is in helping couples rebuild their spiritual resources as congruence is hypothesized to occur only after the four dimensions are aligned (Lee, 2015). Mariann, Andras, Zsolt, Eva, and Zsolt (2014) wrote about using a bio-psycho-socio-spiritual approach in their work in Hungary.

Lee, Ghandour, Takache, and Martins (2014) provided questionnaires to 570 students at the American University of Beirut in 2010. About 12% were probably pathological gamblers.

The link between alcohol abuse and gambling was stronger among Christians than Muslims in the sample, but, conversely, Muslims had a higher likelihood of engaging in various gambling behaviors that were comorbid with illegal drug use and cigarette use. In a study of 2631 U.S. residents (Welte, Barnes, Wieczorek, & Tidwell, 2004), Catholics were more likely to have gambled (92%) compared with Protestants (78%). Elderly Protestants reported the lowest likelihood of gambling (55%)

Interest in Buddhist-derived interventions (BDIs) for treating GD has grown (Shonin, Van Gordon, & Griffiths, 2013). Shonin et al. (2013) suggested that studies regarding its efficacy have been impeded by a shortage of trained BDI clinicians and inadequate provision of both BDIs and dedicated gambling interventions by service providers.

If counselors are thinking of referring clients to Gamblers Anonymous (GA), they should be aware that they are regarded as more secular than other 12-step fellowships (Ferentzy, Skinner, & Antze, 2010). GA is arguably more pragmatic in its focus on emphasizing abstinence and dealing with debts (Ferentzy et al., 2010). Despite this, even ardently secular GA members interviewed favored the Serenity Prayer in this fellowship (Ferentzy et al., 2010).

Cognitive-Behavioral Therapy

CBT can be facilitated using the triple column technique. It can be used both by counselors in their work with clients and by clients alone. The full instructions for using the technique are found in Chapter 6. The following are some of the cognitions that can be problematic for clients with this addiction.

Automatic Thought or Belief	Questioning It	Healthier Thought or Belief
Gambling makes me forget about my problems.		I am better off to engage in problem-solving to resolve my issues.
I cannot imagine giving up gambling.		I need to develop other interests instead of gambling.
I have to win back what I lost.		Chasing losses will not bring back what I lost. It is time to stop gambling completely and make money in ways that are guaranteed.
The more times I lose means I will soon be having a big win.		The odds of losing are always higher than the odds of winning. If this were not true, casinos would not be in business. Casinos make huge profits!
I have a deep feeling inside that I will win today.		Feelings do not affect the odds of winning. The odds of losing are always higher than the odds of winning.

The goal of using CBT with pathological gamblers is to help clients become aware of their cognitive distortions and then raise doubt about the validity of their beliefs and distortions (Yakovenko & Hodgins, 2014). CBT is the most widely researched treatment for GD (Petry, 2015), but how effective is it? Cowlishaw et al. (2012) meta-analyzed 14 studies in their Cochrane review (N = 1245), which focused on psychological therapies for pathological and problem gambling. CBT was found effective 0–3 months posttreatment, with effect sizes that ranged from medium (when defined as financial loss from gambling) to very large (when defined as gambling symptom severity). Consequently, we know that CBT is effective for GD over the short-term and that long-term durability remains uncertain.

Few studies have reported long-term benefits from CBT used for GD (Yakovenko & Hodgins, 2014). In fact, systematic reviews have found that the effect sizes from CBT generally decrease at 6 months follow-up (Yakovenko & Hodgins, 2014).

CBT for GD includes cognitive restructuring, psychoeducation, helping clients understand their gambling urges, and irrational cognition awareness training (Grant & Odlaug, 2014). "Behavioural outcome literature suggests that techniques based on exposure, relaxation and direct behaviour modification may be effective in treating gambling disorders" (Yakovenko & Hodgins, 2014, p. 235). Other behavioral techniques used in CBT with GD include stimulus control, problem-solving, relapse prevention, use of alternative behaviors, identification of gambling triggers, and social skills training (Grant & Odlaug, 2014; Lindberg, Clark, & Bowden-Jones, 2014). Imaginal desensitization that includes MI is also effective over 6 months follow-up (Grant, Donahue, Odlaug, & Kim, 2011). An 8-week stress management program for GD was found effective in decreasing stress, depression, and anxiety and in improving life satisfaction and daily routine (Linardatou, Parios, Varvogli, Chrousos, & Darviri, 2014). In a study of 84 Chinese participants assigned to either a control group or a cognitive-behavioral intervention (CBI), Zhuang et al. (2018) found that the CBI condition was effective in decreasing gambling severity, gambling-related cognitions, negative psychological states, and money spent on gambling up to their 6-month follow-up period.

Chretien, Giroux, Goulet, Jacques, and Bouchard (2017) completed a systematic review focused on cognitive restructuring for changing gambling-related thoughts. They focused their review on 39 studies out of the total 2607 studies. Exposure, whether in imagination or in vivo, was the most frequently used technique to help identify gambling-related thoughts. Preliminary studies also support virtual reality exposure. Bouchard et al. (2017) provided some confirmation in their experiment regarding the viability of using virtual reality and CBT with pathological gamblers.

Mansueto et al. (2016) compared 69 pathological gamblers at their first hospital admission with a matched sample of 58 controls from the general population. The pathological gamblers showed higher degrees of comorbid symptomatology and metacognition. Metacognition refers to having stable knowledge and beliefs about one's own thought processes and includes two components: (a) having knowledge about cognition and (b) regulation of cognition. Given their findings, Mansueto et al. surmised that therapy based on changing metacognitions (called metacognitive therapy) might lead to reductions in pathological gambling by challenging clients' erroneous beliefs regarding their own thinking. Helping clients to develop greater sensitivity to losing at gambling while concurrently diminishing their expectancy of having a positive outcome from it might also be a valuable CBT technique (Rossini-Dib, Fuentes, & Tavares, 2015).

Internet-based CBT (I-CBT) has demonstrated effectiveness. Casey et al. (2017) randomly selected 174 problem gamblers into either a waitlist control, I-CBT, or an active comparison group consisting of monitoring, feedback, and support (I-MFS). Both the I-CBT and the I-MFS groups reduced their gambling severity. The I-CBT group also experienced greater positive treatment effects when it came to reducing gambling urges, cognitions, stress, and life satisfaction. The gains made in treatment were stable throughout the 12-month follow-up.

Mladenovic, Lazetic, Lecic-Tosevski, and Dimitrijevic (2015) wrote about offering integrative-systemic counseling (ISC) in a hospital setting. They described ISC as an integration of family therapy and CBT with some elements of psychodynamic, existential, and pharmacotherapy. Extended group treatment continues for 2 years. Mladenovic et al. stated that they had offered this approach for the past 10 years. At 1-year follow-up, they boasted effectiveness exceeding 90%. This was not a randomized trial, and there was no control group. Consequently, it may just be that the pathological gamblers who attend their program are highly motivated to begin with (given their continuance for 2 years). Given that gamblers are frequent dropouts from other treatment programs, their results might be an artifact of the rare type of gambler that they attract.

RELEVANT MUTUAL SUPPORT GROUPS, WEBSITES, AND VIDEOS

Mutual Support Groups

For the Addicted Individual

1. Gamblers Anonymous (GA). http://www.gamblersanonymous.org/ga/

   Quoted from website:

   Gamblers Anonymous is not allied with any sect, denomination, politics, organization or institution; does not wish to engage in any controversy; neither endorses nor opposes any cause. Our primary purpose is to stop gambling and to help other compulsive gamblers do the same.

   Ferentzy, Skinner, and Antze (2009) noted that, regarding the fourth step, GA members write a financial inventory alongside the moral one. Often the fourth step and the ninth step (i.e., making amends) occur early in the program and earlier steps are addressed later (Ferentzy et al., 2009). As mentioned earlier, GA tends to be more pragmatic than other 12-step programs where abstinence from gambling and dealing with debts take priority (Ferentzy et al., 2010). McGrath, Kim, Hodgins, Novitsky, and Tavares (2018) stated that GA "is the most widely available form of support for disordered gambling" (p. 1423).

2. SMART Recovery. https://www.smartrecovery.org/addiction-recovery/gambling-addiction/

   Quoted from website:

   SMART Recovery's potential effectiveness for assisting individuals to find relief from gambling addiction is supported by research.

3. Freedom from Problem Gambling (self-help workbook; available in several languages). http://www.uclagamblingprogram.org/treatment/workbook.php

   Quoted from website:

   This self-help workbook will help you understand your gambling behavior, why you gamble, how it may have become a problem, and will teach you ways to help stop or reduce your gambling.

For the Partner and/or Family

1. National Problem Gambling Helpline. https://www.ncpgambling.org/help-treatment/national-helpline-1-800-522-4700/

   Quoted from website:

   Offers a confidential, 24-hour helpline for problem gamblers or their family members in the U.S. Call 1-800-522-4700. (NCPG).

2. Personal Financial Strategies for the Loved Ones of Problem Gamblers (PDF). http://www.calproblemgambling.org/wp-content/uploads/2012/06/Personal-Financial-Strategies-for-the-Loved-Ones-of-Problem-Gamblers-1.pdf

   Quoted from website:

   The National Council on Problem Gambling operates the National Problem Gambling Helpline Network (1-800-522-4700). The network is a single national access point to local resources for those seeking help for a gambling problem. The network consists of 28 call centers which provide resources and referrals for all 50 states, Canada and the US Virgin Islands. Help is available 24/7 and is 100% confidential.

Websites

1. *Psychology Today*. https://www.psychologytoday.com/us/conditions/gambling-disorder-compulsive-gambling-pathological-gambling

2. *Scientific American*. https://www.scientificamerican.com/article/how-the-brain-gets-addicted-to-gambling/

3. Helpguide.org. https://www.helpguide.org/articles/addictions/gambling-addiction-and-problem-gambling.htm

4. Mayo Clinic. Compulsive Gambling. https://www.mayoclinic.org/diseases-conditions/compulsive-gambling/symptoms-causes/syc-20355178

5. Gamblers Anonymous. 20 Questions. http://www.gamblersanonymous.org/ga/content/20-questions

6. Segal, J., Smith, M., & Robinson, L. (2018, November). Gambling addiction and problem gambling: How to stop gambling and regain control of your life. HelpGuide.org. Retrieved on from https://www.helpguide.org/articles/addictions/gambling-addiction-and-problem-gambling.htm?pdf=12393

Videos

To view these videos, search their titles on YouTube.

1. *Understanding Joy: The Devastation of a Gambling Addiction.*
2. *The fall and rise of a gambling addict | Justyn Rees Larcombe | TEDxRoyalTunbridgeWells.*
3. *All Bets Are Off* (Documentary, 2018), dir. Baz Ashmawy. [not on YouTube].
4. *Treating Addiction Against All Odds: Henrietta Bowden-Jones at TEDMEDLive Imperial College 2013.*
5. *Gambling on Addiction: How Governments Rely on Problem Gamblers - The Fifth Estate.*

RELEVANT PHONE APPS

Generic Addiction Apps

Note: Generic apps are described in Chapter 6.

This list is not exhaustive. New apps are continually being developed. Do an Internet search to find out the latest apps available. Most are for specific addictions but some, such as these four, are generic.

1. I Am Sober. https://play.google.com/store/apps/details?id=com.thehungrywasp.iamsober
2. Sober Time. https://play.google.com/store/apps/details?id=com.sociosoft.sobertime
3. Pocket Rehab: Get Sober & Addiction Recovery. https://play.google.com/store/apps/details?id=com.getpocketrehab.app
4. Loop Habit Tracker. https://play.google.com/store/apps/details?id=org.isoron.uhabits

Specialized Apps

1. Barred Online Gambling App Self Exclusion Tool. https://play.google.com/store/apps/details?id=com.appmakr.onlinegamblingaddiction

   Quoted from website:

   If gambling is taking over your life, [or] if you have problems, use this app, it is free. It provides information on how to make physical barriers to stop gambling, including getting barred from gambling websites using the apps self-exclusion system by contacting over 425 gambling websites to request self-exclusion using a medical reason which cannot be undone.

2. Gambling Therapy. https://play.google.com/store/apps/details?id=com.gamblingtherapy

   Quoted from website:

   The Gambling Therapy app has been designed to help those that are struggling with problem gambling by providing easy to access information and straightforward tools.

3. Mobile Monitor Your Gambling & Urges (MYGU). http://www.problemgambling.ca/gambling-help/mygu-getmobile/

   Quoted from website:

   Research has shown that people who keep track of their gambling behavior are more successful when they try to quit or reduce their gambling!

4. GamBlock. One subscribes to this service for a fee. https://www.gamblock.com/

   Quoted from website:

   GamBlock blocks access to online gambling.

JOURNALS AND CONFERENCES

Journals

The first two journals focus specifically on gambling. The other four journals frequently publish articles about gambling:

1. *Journal of Gambling Studies*. Quoted from website: "The *Journal of Gambling Studies* is an interdisciplinary forum for research and discussion of the many and varied aspects of gambling behavior, both controlled

and pathological. Coverage extends to the wide range of attendant and resultant problems, including alcoholism, suicide, crime, and a number of other mental health concerns. Articles published in this journal span a cross-section of disciplines including psychiatry, psychology, sociology, political science, criminology, and social work." https://link.springer.com/journal/10899

2. *International Gambling Studies*. Quoted from website: "International Gambling Studies is a peer-reviewed interdisciplinary journal in gambling studies. Launched by a team of international experts with a commitment to the highest scholarly standards, *International Gambling Studies* adopts a transnational and comparative approach to the challenges posed by the global expansion of gambling in the 21st century." https://www.tandfonline.com/toc/rigs20/current
3. *American Journal on Addictions*. Quoted from website: "The *American Journal on Addictions* is the official journal of the American Academy of Addiction Psychiatry (AAAP), and provides a forum for the dissemination of information in the extensive field of addiction, including topics ranging from codependence to genetics, epidemiology to dual diagnostics, etiology to neuroscience, and much more." https://onlinelibrary.wiley.com/journal/15210391
4. *Journal of Behavioral Addictions*. Quoted from website: "The aim of the journal is to create a forum for the scientific information exchange with regard to behavioral addictions. The journal is a broad focused interdisciplinary one that publishes manuscripts on different approaches of non-substance addictions, research reports focusing on the addictive patterns of various behaviors, especially disorders of the impulsive-compulsive spectrum, and also publishes reviews in these topics. Coverage ranges from genetic and neurobiological research through psychological and clinical psychiatric approaches to epidemiological, sociological and anthropological aspects." https://akademiai.com/loi/2006
5. *Psychology of Addictive Behaviors*. Quoted from website: "*Psychology of Addictive Behaviors*® publishes peer-reviewed original articles related to the psychological aspects of addictive behaviors. The journal includes articles on the following topics:
   - alcohol use and alcohol use disorders
   - drug use and drug use disorders
   - smoking and nicotine use and disorders
   - eating disorders, and
   - other addictive behaviors"

   https://www.apa.org/pubs/journals/adb/
6. *Addictive Behaviors*. Quoted from website: "*Addictive Behaviors* is an international peer-reviewed journal publishing high quality human research on addictive behaviors and disorders since 1975. The journal accepts submissions of full-length papers and short communications on substance-related addictions such as the abuse of alcohol, drugs and nicotine, and behavioral addictions involving gambling and technology. We primarily publish behavioral and psychosocial research but our articles span the fields of psychology, sociology, psychiatry, epidemiology, social policy, medicine, pharmacology and neuroscience." https://www.journals.elsevier.com/addictive-behaviors/

Conferences

There are many conferences devoted to gambling and GD. Do an Internet search to find local and "one-off" conferences.

1. National Council on Problem Gambling Annual Conference. https://www.ncpgambling.org/national-conference/
2. National Center for Responsible Gaming (NCRG) Conference. Check http://www.ncrg.org/ for details.
3. International Gambling Conference. https://www.internationalgamblingconference.com/

COUNSELING SCENARIO

As you are reading, imagine that you are the client in this scenario. Note the areas in which the session could be improved on the part of the counselor.

Your name is Caleb, a 26-year-old African American living in New Orleans. You have worked in maintenance at the Morial Convention Center since finishing high school. To get to your job, you usually walk by Harrah's casino. The casino has always fascinated you with its alluring neon lights. On your 21st birthday, you were more excited about going to Harrah's than anywhere else. You remember your first night there, embracing every magical moment. You even walked out of there with an extra $200 in your pocket! Five years later, however, your life is in shambles. The bright lights have dulled as you continue reflecting on the deep debts that will take you years to pay back. Nightly you have prayed for the big win, but your favorite game of craps pretty much sums up your life—crap and more crap. You decide to meet with Tiana, an African American addictions counselor.

- Counselor: Hello Caleb, please come in.
- You: Thanks, Tiana.
- Counselor: From the intake forms, I know a lot about your problem already. Tell me how you think I might help you today.
- You: I just cannot resist going into the casino after work. Lord knows how much I pray to win back even a fraction of what I have lost, but I keep losing big money. This makes me so depressed that, on my days off, I sometimes spend most of my time in bed.
- Counselor: Wow, you sure got the gambling bug. Have you been doing this for 5 years already?
- You: Pretty much. I think I quit once when I was in the hospital with pneumonia [begins chuckling].
- Counselor: [no response] How much do you owe right now?
- You: It is close to $50,000 spread across four credit cards.
- Counselor: How much do you earn in your job?
- You: A little more than $42,000 a year.
- Counselor: How much total payment are you making each month on your credit cards?
- You: Exactly $1000.
- Counselor: It sure sounds like bankruptcy is your best choice right now.
- You: I can't do that, Tiana. My parents taught me to pay back everything I owe in this life. We are all Baptists.
- Counselor: Doesn't matter. You are in way over your head right now, Caleb. Won't be long until you have creditors phoning you at all hours of the day and night.
- You: I certainly have thought about bankruptcy, but I know that is not the right thing to do in my case.
- Counselor: What makes you so special, Caleb?
- You: Nothing. It is more about what makes me humble.
- Counselor: I see. I imagine it will take you 10 years to pay all this back, and a ton of it will be interest.
- You: It doesn't matter. I am not about to compromise what I believe.
- Counselor: Okay, okay—I get it. So, here's your homework. Here are some sheets to figure out your budget. Bring it back completed next week.
- You: I will complete these, but what can I do to stop gambling now? I was at the casino again last night and dropped another $300!
- Counselor: Start by banning yourself at that casino. Go there and tell them you are not to be let in under any circumstances.
- You: They usually only take a glancing look at my ID. I do not think that will help much.
- Counselor: How about locking yourself in your basement?
- You: [chuckles] My parents might go for that!
- Counselor: Seriously, then, let's have you cut up your credit cards. Pull them out and here are a pair of scissors.
- You: Wow, I don't think I can do that right now. I need some time to think through this.
- Counselor: I didn't think you were ready to make a serious change regarding your gambling.

From the Client's Perspective

1. How would you feel if you received this kind of help from Tiana?
2. What is missing for you in this dialogue?
3. What would you find more helpful from a counselor in this scenario?

From the Counselor's Perspective

1. What is interfering with developing a strong working alliance?
2. Going back to the Common Counseling Mistakes list in Chapter 6, which mistakes is the counselor making with Caleb?
3. Some online calculators can assist you with determining how long it will take for your clients (and yourself) to pay back a credit card debt, and it will determine exactly how much interest you will pay (see https://www.thecalculatorsite.com/finance/calculators/credit-card-payment-calculators.php). Spend a few seconds to determine precisely how long it will take Caleb to pay back his credit card debt. Assume Caleb is paying, on average, 19% interest. Some websites tell you how much interest is added to most credit cards (see https://www.valuepenguin.com/average-credit-card-interest-rates). How could you use results from the online calculator to be of help to Caleb?

INDIVIDUAL EXERCISES

1. Talk to people that you know who gamble. If possible, find people who are involved in different kinds of gambling (e.g., slot machines, poker, horse races, lotteries). What enjoyment do they derive from gambling? Find out their definition of pathological gambling. Do they see any signs of addiction within themselves?
2. Attend a mutual support group meeting for compulsive gamblers. Be sure to request permission ahead of time from the organization to attend, given that many meetings are reserved for those who are addicted.
3. Spend time learning about how to develop a budget for yourself. Then create your budget and stick to it over the next 2 weeks. What was most difficult about sticking to your budget, and what was easiest? How could you apply what you learned to working with individuals with GD?

CLASSROOM EXERCISES

1. Separate your class into five groups. Assign each group to slot machine, poker, horse race, lottery, or bingo. Now have the five groups debate what they would believe to be the addictive qualities of their assigned form of gambling. Also, have them debate which form would likely be the most addictive and why.
2. Invite one or more speakers from Gamblers Anonymous to speak to your class. Have the speakers tell their stories of gambling addiction. Ensure that the class has prepared questions in advance for the speakers.
3. For this exercise, you need a computer and a projector. Bring up a free gambling site such as https://www.vegasworld.com/fx/?env=fxhome. It takes a little time to load before you choose an avatar. Play a few of the free games in class and lead a discussion. Here are some sample questions to ask your class:
   A. Do you believe that designers of this game have ulterior motives besides "teaching" people how to enjoy gambling? If you think there are ulterior motives, what are they?
   B. What aspects of these games might some people find addicting?
   C. What do you see as your risk factors in gambling? What steps should you take to minimize or neutralize these factors?

CHAPTER SUMMARY

Gambling has been around since ancient times, but it did not especially grow in popularity until the late 19th and early 20th centuries. Today's gambler faces new possibilities for gambling such as glitzy slot machines and online venues, all designed to "seduce" people into spending more. For some, the allure is overpowering, and addiction results. Chasing one's losses is common in individuals with gambling disorder (GD), and so are several cognitive distortions such as believing that one is "lucky," that big wins are likely to follow a stream of losses, that one has control in games that are rigged to ensure the house mostly wins, and that one has greater skill than is evident.

Few pathological gamblers seek treatment, and there is a high dropout rate even when they do initiate help-seeking. Also, many problem and pathological gamblers recover without treatment. GD is a heterogeneous condition, so predicting who will become a compulsive gambler is challenging. There are likely different pathways to becoming a problem or pathological gambler. There may be a genetic predisposition toward addictive behavior. Escapism, avoiding negative emotions and worries, loneliness, lack of social activities, boredom, sensation-seeking, risk-taking, impulsivity, and compulsivity are just some of the reasons that some people gamble excessively.

Most people can enjoy gambling without it leading to negative consequences, and between 60% and 80% of people from developed countries have gambled at some point during their lifetime. Problematic and pathological gambling, on the other hand, is estimated at between 1% and 3% of the world's population.

GD is the first behavioral addiction to become recognized in *DSM-5*. GD has been found to have similar neurological correlates to alcohol and substance use disorders. Several physical, mental, emotional, spiritual, legal, financial, career/work, and relationship consequences that might result from compulsive gambling were noted.

The FDA has not approved any medication for GD at this writing. Nonetheless, several medications are being tested and used. Several counseling interventions were identified in the chapter. Evidence-based counseling includes primarily CBT and MI. Gamblers Anonymous (GA) is the most widely available form of help for disordered gamblers. Unlike the other 12-step programs, GA tends to be more pragmatic with its primary focus on abstinence and dealing with debts.

REFERENCES

Adam, R. (2016). Psychoanalytical reflections about a case of gambling [Reflexions psychanalytiques a partir d'un cas d'addiction au jeu]. *Cliniques mediterraneennes: Psychanalyse et Psychopathologie Freudiennes, 93*, 189–201.

Adams, P. J., & Wiles, J. (2017). Gambling machine annexes as enabling spaces for addictive engagement. *Health & Place, 43*, 1–7.

Adkins, B. J., Taber, J. I., & Russo, A. M. (1985). The spoken autobiography: A powerful tool in group psychotherapy. *Social Work, 30*, 435–439.

Airas, A. (2014). Behind the scenes of creating the tool for responsible games. In F. Gobet & M. Schiller (Eds.), *Problem gambling: Cognition, prevention and treatment* (pp. 107–126). New York, NY: Palgrave Macmillan.

Allami, Y., Vitaro, F., Brendgen, M., Carbonneau, R., Lacourse, E., & Tremblay, R. E. (2017). A longitudinal empirical investigation of the pathways model of problem gambling. *Journal of Gambling Studies, 33*, 1153–1167.

American Psychiatric Association (APA). (2013). *Diagnostic and statistical manual of mental disorders* (5th ed.). Washington, DC: Author.

Anastassiou-Hadicharalambous, X., & Essau, C. A. (2015). Young people and problem gambling. In H. Bowden-Jones & S. George (Eds.), *A clinician's guide to working with problem gamblers* (pp. 182–194). New York, NY: Routledge.

Anderson, T. L., Rempusheski, V. F., & Leedy, K. N. (2018). Casino gambling and the family: Exploring the connections and identifying consequences. *Deviant Behavior, 39*, 1109–1119.

Armstrong, T., Rockloff, M., Browne, M., & Li, E. (2018). An exploration of how simulated gambling games may promote gambling with money. *Journal of Gambling Studies, 34*, 1165–1184.

Baggio, S., Dupuis, M., Berchtold, A., Spilka, S., Simon, O., & Studer, J. (2017). Is gambling involvement a confounding variable for the relationship between internet gambling and gambling problem severity? *Computers in Human Behavior, 71*, 148–152.

Balconi, M., Angioletti, L., Siri, C., Meucci, N., & Pezzoli, G. (2018). Gambling behavior in Parkinson's disease: Impulsivity, reward mechanism and cortical brain oscillations. *Psychiatry Research, 270*, 974–980.

Barnes, G. M., Welte, J. W., & Tidwell, M.-C. O. (2017). Gambling involvement among Native Americans, blacks, and whites in the United States. *American Journal on Addictions, 26*, 713–721.

Barrault, S., & Varescon, I. (2016). Online and live regular poker players: Do they differ in impulsive sensation seeking and gambling practice? *Journal of Behavioral Addictions, 5*(1), 41–50.

Barry, D. T., Stefanovics, E. A., Desai, R. A., & Potenza, M. N. (2011b). Gambling problem severity and psychiatric disorders among Hispanic and white adults: Findings from a nationally representative sample. *Journal of Psychiatric Research, 45*(3), 404–411.

Bartley, C. A., & Bloch, M. H. (2013). Meta-analysis: Pharmacological treatment of pathological gambling. *Expert Review of Neurotherapeutics, 13*(8), 887–894.

Beaulac, E., Andronicos, M., Lesage, A., Robert, M., Larochelle, S., & Seguin, M. (2017). The influence of gender on the help-seeking behaviour of gamblers [Quelle est l' influence du genre dans la recherche de soins chez les joueurs?]. *Journal of Gambling Issues, 35*, 101–124.

Bergler, E. (1943). The gambler: A misunderstood neurotic. *Journal of Criminal Pathology, 4*, 379–393.

Beyerlein, K., & Sallaz, J. J. (2017). Faith's wager: How religion deters gambling. *Social Science Research, 62*, 204–218.

Binde, P. (2016). Gambling-related embezzlement in the workplace: A qualitative study. *International Gambling Studies, 16*(3), 391–407.

Bischof, A., Meyer, C., Bischof, G., John, U., Wurst, F. M., Thon, N., . . . Rumpf, H.-J. (2016). Type of gambling as an independent risk factor for suicidal events in pathological gamblers. *Psychology of Addictive Behaviors, 30*(2), 263–269.

Blaszczynski, A., & Nower, L. (2002). A pathways model of problem and pathological gambling. *Addiction, 97*(5), 487–499.

Blaszczynski, A., Russell, A., & Gainsbury, S., & Hing, N. (2016). Mental health and online, land-based and mixed gamblers. *Journal of Gambling Studies, 32*(1), 261–275.

Bodor, D., Tomic, A., Ricijas, N., Zoricic, Z., & Filipcic, I. (2016). Impulsiveness in alcohol addiction and pathological gambling. *Alcoholism and Psychiatry Research, 52*(2), 149–158.

Bond, K. S., Dart, K. M., Jorm, A. F., Kelly, C. M., Kitchener, B. A., & Reavley, N. J. (2017). Assisting an Australian Aboriginal and Torres Strait Islander person with gambling problems: A Delphi study. *BMC Psychology, 5*, 1–8.

Bonnaire, C., Barrault, S., Aite, A., Cassotti, M., Moutier, S., & Varescon, I. (2017). Relationship between pathological gambling, alexithymia, and gambling type. *American Journal on Addictions, 26*(2), 152–160.

Bonnaire, C., Kovess, V., Guignard, R., Richard, J.-B., Du-Roscoat, E., & Beck, F. (2016). Life events, substance use, psychological distress, and quality of life in male and female French gamblers. *Annals of Clinical Psychiatry, 28*(4), 263–279.

Bouchard, S., Robillard, G., Giroux, I., Jacques, C., Loranger, C., St-Pierre, M., . . . Goulet, A. (2017). Using virtual reality in the treatment of gambling disorder: The development of a new tool for cognitive behavior therapy. *Frontiers in Psychiatry, 8*, 1–10.

Brito, A. M. C., de Almeida Pinto, M. G., Bronstein, G., Carneiro, E., Faertes, D., Fukugawa, V., . . . Tavares, H. (2017). Topiramate combined with cognitive restructuring for the treatment of gambling disorder: A two-center, randomized, double-blind clinical trial. *Journal of Gambling Studies, 33*, 249–263.

Broman, N., & Hakansson, A. (2018). Problematic gaming and internet use but not gambling may be overrepresented in sexual minorities—A pilot population web survey study. *Frontiers in Psychology, 9*, 1–6.

Bucker, L., Bierbrodt, J., Hand, I., Wittekind, C., & Moritz, S. (2018). Effects of a depression-focused internet intervention in slot machine gamblers: A randomized controlled trial. *PLoS ONE, 13*(6), 1–22.

Buja, A., Lion, C., Scioni, M., Vian, P., Genetti, B., Vittadello, F., . . . Baldo, V. (2017). SOGS-RA gambling scores and substance use in adolescents. *Journal of Behavioral Addictions, 6*, 425–433.

Bullock, S., & Potenza, M. N. (2015). Pharmacological treatments. In H. Bowden-Jones & S. George (Eds.), *A clinician's guide to working with problem gamblers* (pp. 134–162). New York, NY: Routledge.

Burckhardt, R., & Blaszczynski, A. (2017). Gambling. In J. Fitzgerald (Ed.), *Foundations for couples' therapy: Research for the real world* (pp. 166–175). New York, NY: Routledge/Taylor & Francis.

Buth, S., Wurst, F. M., Thon, N., Lahusen, H., & Kalke, J. (2017). Comparative analysis of potential risk factors for at-risk gambling, problem gambling and gambling disorder among current gamblers—Results of the Austrian representative survey 2015. *Frontiers in Psychology*, *8*, 1–11.

Calado, F., & Griffiths, M. D. (2016). Problem gambling worldwide: An update and systematic review of empirical research (2000–2015). *Journal of Behavioral Addictions*, *5*(4), 592–613.

Campitelli, G., & Speelman, C. (2014). Expertise and the illusion of expertise in gambling. In F. Gobet & M. Schiller (Eds.), *Problem gambling: Cognition, prevention and treatment* (pp. 41–60). New York, NY: Palgrave Macmillan.

Campos, M. D., Camacho, A., Pereda, K., Santana, K., Calix, I., & Fong, T. W. (2016). Attitudes towards gambling, gambling problems, and treatment among Hispanics in Imperial County, CA. *Journal of Gambling Studies*, *32*(3), 985–999.

Canadian Consortium for Gambling Research. (2017). *Canadian Problem Gambling Index*. Retrieved on April 6, 2019, from http://www.ccgr.ca/en/projects/canadian-problem-gambling-index.aspx

Canale, N., Vieno, A., Griffiths, M. D., Borraccino, A., Lazzeri, G., Charrier, L., . . . Santinello, M. (2017). A large-scale national study of gambling severity among immigrant and non-immigrant adolescents: The role of the family. *Addictive Behaviors*, *66*, 125–131.

Canale, N., Vieno, A., Griffiths, M. D., Marino, C., Chieco, F., Disperati, F., . . . Santinello, M. (2016). The efficacy of a web-based gambling intervention program for high school students: A preliminary randomized study. *Computers in Human Behavior*, *55*(Part B), 946–954.

Carbonneau, R., Vitaro, F., Brendgen, M., & Tremblay, R. E. (2018). The intergenerational association between parents' problem gambling and impulsivity-hyperactivity/inattention behaviors in children. *Journal of Abnormal Child Psychology*, *46*, 1203–1215.

Caselli, G., Fernie, B., Canfora, F., Mascolo, C., Ferrari, A., Antonioni, M., . . . Spada, M. M. (2018). The Metacognitions about Gambling Questionnaire: Development and psychometric properties. *Psychiatry Research*, *261*, 367–374.

Casey, D. M., Williams, R. J., Mossiere, A. M., Schopflocher, D. P., el-Guebaly, N., Hodgins, D. C., . . . Wood, R. T. (2011). The role of family, religiosity, and behavior in adolescent gambling. *Journal of Adolescence*, *34*(5), 841–851.

Casey, L. M., Oei, T. P. S., Raylu, N., Horrigan, K., Day, J., Ireland, M., & Clough, B. A. (2017). Internet-based delivery of cognitive behaviour therapy compared to monitoring, feedback and support for problem gambling: A randomised controlled trial. *Journal of Gambling Studies*, *33*(3), 993–1010.

Castellani, B., & Rugle, L. (1995). A comparison of pathological gamblers to alcoholics and cocaine misusers on impulsivity, sensation seeking, and craving. *International Journal of the Addictions*, *30*, 275–289.

Centre for Addiction and Mental Health (CAMH). (2013-2018). *The stages of change*. Retrieved on April 9, 2019, from https://www.problemgambling.ca/gambling-help/support-for-families/stages-of-change.aspx

Centre for Addiction and Mental Health (CAMH). (2019, January 16). *Transtheoretical model (stages of change)*. Retrieved on April 9, 2019, from https://learn.problemgambling.ca/eip/stages-of-change

Chamberlain, S. R., & Grant, J. E. (2018). Minnesota Impulse Disorders Interview (MIDI): Validation of a structured diagnostic clinical interview for impulse control disorders in an enriched community sample. *Psychiatry Research*, *265*, 279–283.

Chamberlain, S. R., Stochl, J., Redden, S. A., Odlaug, B. L., & Grant, J. E. (2017). Latent class analysis of gambling subtypes and impulsive/compulsive associations: Time to rethink diagnostic boundaries for gambling disorder? *Addictive Behaviors*, *72*, 79–85.

Chebli, J.-L., Blaszczynski, A., & Gainsbury, S. M. (2016). Internet-based interventions for addictive behaviours: A systematic review. *Journal of Gambling Studies*, *32*(4), 1279–1304.

Cheung, N. W. T. (2016). Social strain, self-control, and juvenile gambling pathology: Evidence from Chinese adolescents. *Youth & Society*, *48*(1), 77–100.

Choi, S.-W., Shin, Y.-C., Kim, D.-J., Choi, J.-S., Kim, S., Kim, S.-H., . . . Youn, H. (2017). Treatment modalities for patients with gambling disorder. *Annals of General Psychiatry*, *16*, 1–8.

Chowdhury, N. S., Livesey, E. J., Blaszczynski, A., & Harris, J. A. (2017). Pathological gambling and motor impulsivity: A systematic review with meta-analysis. *Journal of Gambling Studies*, *33*, 1213–1239.

Chretien, M., Giroux, I., Goulet, A., Jacques, C., & Bouchard, S. (2017). Cognitive restructuring of gambling-related thoughts: A systematic review. *Addictive Behaviors*, *75*, 108–121.

Cimminella, F., Ambra, F. I., Vitaliano, S., Iavarone, A., & Garofalo, E. (2015). Early-onset frontotemporal dementia presenting with pathological gambling. *Acta Neurologica Belgica*, *115*, 759–761.

Clark, L. (2015). Neurobiology of pathological gambling. In H. Bowden-Jones & S. George (Eds.), *A clinician's guide to working with problem gamblers* (pp. 53–74). New York, NY: Routledge.

Clark, L. (2017). Decision-making in gambling disorder: Understanding behavioral addictions. In J.-C. Dreher & L. Tremblay (Eds.), *Decision neuroscience: An integrative perspective* (pp. 339–347). San Diego, CA: Elsevier Academic Press.

Clark, L., Averbeck, B., Payer, D., Sescousse, G., Winstanley, C. A., & Xue, G. (2013). Pathological choice: The neuroscience of gambling and gambling addiction. *Journal of Neuroscience*, *33*, 17617–17623.

Clarke, D., Tse, S., Abbott, M., Townsend, S., Kingi, P., & Manaia, W. (2006). Religion, spirituality and associations with problem gambling. *New Zealand Journal of Psychology*, *35*(2), 77–83.

Connors, G. J., DiClemente, C. C., Velasquez, M. M., & Donovan, D. M. (2013). *Substance abuse treatment and the stages of change: Selecting and planning interventions* (2nd ed.). New York, NY: Guilford Press.

Conversano, C., Marazziti, D., Carmassi, C., Baldini, S., Barnabei, G., & Dell'Osso, L. (2012). Pathological gambling: A systematic review of biochemical, neuroimaging, and neuropsychological findings. *Harvard Review of Psychiatry*, *20*, 130–148.

Cookman, M. L., & Weatherly, J. N. (2016). Investigating possible effects of ethnicity and age on gambling as an escape. *Journal of Gambling Studies*, *32*(2), 499–509.

Costes, J.-M., Kairouz, S., Monson, E., & Eroukmanoff, V. (2018). Where lies the harm in lottery gambling? A portrait of gambling practices and associated problems. *Journal of Gambling Studies*, *34*, 1293–1311.

Cowie, M. E., Stewart, S. H., Salmon, J., Collins, P., Al-Hamdani, M., Boffo, M., . . . Wiers, R. W. (2017). Distorted beliefs about luck and skill and their relation to gambling problems and gambling behavior in Dutch gamblers. *Frontiers in Psychology*, *8*, 1–12.

Cowlishaw, S., & Kessler, D. (2016). Problem gambling in the UK: Implications for health, psychosocial adjustment and health care utilization. *European Addiction Research*, *22*(2), 90–98.

Cowlishaw, S., Merkouris, S., Dowling, N., Anderson, C., Jackson, A., & Thomas, S. (2012). Psychological therapies for pathological and problem gambling. *Cochrane Database of Systematic Reviews*, *11*, 1–91.

Cowlishaw, S., Nespoli, E., Jebadurai, J. K., Smith, N., & Bowden-Jones, H. (2018). Episodic and binge gambling: An exploration and preliminary quantitative study. *Journal of Gambling Studies, 34*, 85–99.

Daghestani, A. N., Elenz, E., & Crayton, J. W. (1996). Pathological gambling in hospitalized substance abusing veterans. *Journal of Clinical Psychiatry, 57*(8), 360–363.

Delfabbro, P., Thomas, A., & Armstrong, A. (2018). Gender differences in the presentation of observable risk indicators of problem gambling. *Journal of Gambling Studies, 34*, 119–132.

Dennis, C. B., Davis, T. D., Chang, J., & McAllister, C. (2017). Psychological vulnerability and gambling in later life. *Journal of Gerontological Social Work, 60*, 471–486.

Derevensky, J. L. (2016). Youth gambling problems. In Y. Kaminer (Ed.), *Youth substance abuse and co-occurring disorders* (pp. 307–336). Arlington, VA: American Psychiatric.

Dhillon, J. (2015). Women and gambling. In H. Bowden-Jones & S. George (Eds.), *A clinician's guide to working with problem gamblers* (pp. 172–181). New York, NY: Routledge.

Dickerson, D. L., O'Malley, S. S., Canive, J., Thuras, P., & Westermeyer, J. (2009). Nicotine dependence and psychiatric and substance use comorbidities in a sample of American Indian male veterans. *Drug and Alcohol Dependence, 99*, 169–175.

Dickler, M., Lenglos, C., Renauld, E., Ferland, F., Edden, R. A., Leblond, J., & Fecteau, S. (2018). Online effects of transcranial direct current stimulation on prefrontal metabolites in gambling disorder. *Neuropharmacology, 131*, 51–57.

DiClemente, C. C., Story, M., & Murray, K. (2000). On a roll: The process of initiation and cessation of problem gambling among adolescents. *Journal of Gambling Studies, 16*, 289–313.

Dighton, G., Roberts, E., Hoon, A. E., & Dymond, S. (2018). Gambling problems and the impact of family in UK armed forces veterans. *Journal of Behavioral Addictions, 7*, 355–365.

Dixon, M. J., Gutierrez, J., Stange, M., Larche, C. J., Graydon, C., Vintan, S., & Kruger, T. B. (2019). Mindfulness problems and depression symptoms in everyday life predict dark flow during slots play: Implications for gambling as a form of escape. *Psychology of Addictive Behaviors, 33*, 81–90.

Dixon, R. W., Youssef, G. J., Hasking, P., Yucel, M., Jackson, A. C., & Dowling, N. A. (2016). The relationship between gambling attitudes, involvement, and problems in adolescence: Examining the moderating role of coping strategies and parenting styles. *Addictive Behaviors, 58*, 42–46.

Dowling, N., Smith, D., & Thomas, T. (2007). A comparison of individual and group cognitive-behavioural treatment for female pathological gambling. *Behaviour Research and Therapy, 45*(9), 2192–2202.

Dowling, N. A., Cowlishaw, S., Jackson, A. C., Merkouris, S. S., & Francis, K. L., & Christensen, D. R. (2015). The prevalence of comorbid personality disorders in treatment-seeking problem gamblers: A systematic review and meta-analysis. *Journal of Personality Disorders, 29*(6), 735–754.

Dowling, N. A., Merkouris, S. S., & Lorains, F. K. (2016). Interventions for comorbid problem gambling and psychiatric disorders: Advancing a developing field of research. *Addictive Behaviors, 58*, 21–30.

Dowling, N. A., Oldenhof, E., Shandley, K., Youssef, G. J., Vasiliadis, S., Thomas, S. A., . . . Jackson, A. C. (2018). The intergenerational transmission of problem gambling: The mediating role of offspring gambling expectancies and motives. *Addictive Behaviors, 77*, 16–20.

Dwyer, S. C., Piquette, N., Buckle, J. L., & McCaslin, E. (2013). Women gamblers write a voice: Exploring journaling as an effective counseling and research tool. *Journal of Groups in Addiction & Recovery, 8*, 36–50.

Edgren, R., Castren, S., Makela, M., Portfors, P., Alho, H., & Salonen, A. H. (2016). Reliability of instruments measuring at-risk and problem gambling among young individuals: A systematic review covering years 2009-2015. *Journal of Adolescent Health, 58*(6), 600–615.

Egorov, A. Y. (2017). The use of agomelatine (Valdoxan) in the treatment of gambling: A pilot study. *Neuroscience and Behavioral Physiology, 47*(7), 795–798.

Elman, I., Tschibelu, E., & Borsook, D. (2010). Psychosocial stress and its relationship to gambling urges in individuals with pathological gambling. *American Journal on Addictions, 19*(4), 332–339.

Elmas, H. G., Cesur, G., & Oral, E. T. (2017). Alexithymia and pathological gambling: The mediating role of difficulties in emotion regulation. *Turk Psikiyatri Dergisi, 28*(1), 1–7.

Elton-Marshall, T., Wijesingha, R., Sendzik, T., Mock, S. E., van der Maas, M., McCready, J., . . . Turner, N. E. (2018). Marital status and problem gambling among older adults: An examination of social context and social motivations. *Canadian Journal on Aging, 37*, 318–332.

Estevez, A., Jauregui, P., Sanchez-Marcos, I., Lopez-Gonzalez, H., & Griffiths, M. D. (2017). Attachment and emotion regulation in substance addictions and behavioral addictions. *Journal of Behavioral Addictions, 6*(4), 534–544.

Farrell, L. (2018). Understanding the relationship between subjective wellbeing and gambling behavior. *Journal of Gambling Studies, 34*, 55–71.

Fauth-Buhler, M., Mann, K., & Potenza, M. N. (2017). Pathological gambling: A review of the neurobiological evidence relevant for its classification as an addictive disorder. *Addiction Biology, 22*, 885–897.

Ferentzy, P., Skinner, W., & Antze, P. (2009). Gamblers Anonymous and the 12 steps: How an informal society has altered a recovery process in accordance with the special needs of problem gamblers. *Journal of Gambling Issues, 23*, 42–65.

Ferentzy, P., Skinner, W., & Antze, P. (2010). The Serenity Prayer: Secularism and spirituality in Gamblers Anonymous. *Journal of Groups in Addiction & Recovery, 5*, 124–144.

Ferris, J., & Wynne, H. (2001, February 19). *The Canadian Problem Gambling Index: Final report.* Retrieved on April 6, 2019, from http://www.ccgr.ca/en/projects/resources/CPGI-Final-Report-English.pdf

Franklin, T. (2014). Life as a compulsive gambler: A first-hand account. In F. Gobet & M. Schiller (Eds.), *Problem gambling: Cognition, prevention and treatment* (pp. 289–310). New York, NY: Palgrave Macmillan.

Fuentes, D., Rzezak, P., Pereira, F. R., Malloy-Diniz, L. F., Santos, L. C., Duran, F. L. S., . . . Gorenstein, C. (2015). Mapping brain volumetric abnormalities in never-treated pathological gamblers. *Psychiatry Research: Neuroimaging, 232*(3), 208–213.

Gainsbury, S. M., Russell, A. M. T., King, D. L., Delfabbro, P., & Hing, N. (2016). Migration from social casino games to gambling: Motivations and characteristics of gamers who gamble. *Computers in Human Behavior, 63*, 59–67.

Gamblers Anonymous. (n.d.). *20 questions: Are you a compulsive gambler?* Retrieved on April 18, 2019, from www.gamblersanonymous.org/ga/content/20-questions

Gaston, R. L. (2015). Psychiatric co-morbidity in gambling. In H. Bowden-Jones & S. George (Eds.), *A clinician's guide to working with problem gamblers* (pp. 75–89). New York, NY: Routledge.

Gay, A., Boutet, C., Sigaud, T., Kamgoue, A., Sevos, J., Brunelin, J., & Massoubre, C. (2017). A single session of repetitive transcranial magnetic stimulation of the prefrontal cortex reduces cue-induced craving in patients with gambling disorder. *European Psychiatry*, *41*, 68–74.

Geel, A., & Fisher, R. (2015). Aetiology of problem gambling. In H. Bowden-Jones & S. George (Eds.), *A clinician's guide to working with problem gamblers* (pp. 28–38). New York, NY: Routledge.

George, S., & Bowden-Jones, H. (2015). Family interventions in gambling. In H. Bowden-Jones & S. George (Eds.), *A clinician's guide to working with problem gamblers* (pp. 163–171). New York, NY: Routledge.

Gill, K. J., Heath, L. M., Derevensky, J., & Torrie, J. (2016). The social and psychological impacts of gambling in the Cree communities of Northern Quebec. *Journal of Gambling Studies*, *32*(2), 441–457.

Giralt, S., Muller, K. W., Beutel, M. E., Dreier, M., Duven, E., & Wolfling, K. (2018). Prevalence, risk factors, and psychosocial adjustment of problematic gambling in adolescents: Results from two representative German samples. *Journal of Behavioral Addictions*, *7*, 339–347.

Gobet, F., & Schiller, M. (2014). Introduction. In F. Gobet & M. Schiller (Eds.), *Problem gambling: Cognition, prevention and treatment* (pp. 1–38). New York, NY: Palgrave Macmillan.

Godinho, A., Kushnir, V., Hodgins, D. C., Hendershot, C. S., & Cunningham, J. A. (2018). Betting on life: Associations between significant life events and gambling trajectories among gamblers with the intent to quit. *Journal of Gambling Studies*, *34*, 1391–1406.

Gomez-Pena, M., Penelo, E., Granero, R., Fernandez-Aranda, F., Alvarez-Moya, E., Santamaria, J. J., . . . Jimenez-Murcia, S. (2012). Correlates of motivation to change in pathological gamblers completing cognitive-behavioral group therapy. *Journal of Clinical Psychology*, *68*, 732–744.

Goslar, M., Leibetseder, M., Muench, H. M., Hofmann, S. G., & Laireiter, A.-R. (2017). Efficacy of face-to-face versus self-guided treatments for disordered gambling: A meta-analysis. *Journal of Behavioral Addictions*, *6*, 142–162.

Grant, J. E., & Chamberlain, S. R. (2017). The placebo effect and its clinical associations in gambling disorder. *Annals of Clinical Psychiatry*, *29*(3), 167–172.

Grant, J. E., & Chamberlain, S. R. (2018). Caffeine's influence on gambling behavior and other types of impulsivity. *Addictive Behaviors*, *76*, 156–160.

Grant, J. E., Donahue, C. B., Odlaug, B. L., & Kim. S. W. (2011). A 6-month follow-up of imaginal desensitization plus motivational interviewing in the treatment of pathological gambling. *Annals of Clinical Psychiatry*, *23*(1), 3–10.

Grant, J. E., & Odlaug, B. L. (2014). Diagnosis and treatment of gambling disorder. In K. P. Rosenberg & L. C. Feder (Eds.), *Behavioral addictions: Criteria, evidence, and treatment* (pp. 35–59). San Diego, CA: Academic Press.

Grant, J. E., Odlaug, B. L., & Chamberlain, S. R. (2017). Gambling disorder, *DSM-5* criteria and symptom severity. *Comprehensive Psychiatry*, *75*, 1–5.

Grant, J. E., & Potenza, M. N. (2006). Sexual orientation of men with pathological gambling: Prevalence and psychiatric comorbidity in a treatment-seeking sample. *Comprehensive Psychiatry*, *47*, 515–518.

Green, C. L., Nahhas, R. W., Scoglio, A. A., & Elman, I. (2017). Posttraumatic stress symptoms in pathological gambling: Potential evidence of anti-reward processes. *Journal of Behavioral Addictions*, *6*, 98–101.

Griffiths, M. (2011). Gambling addiction on the Internet. In K. S. Young & C. Nabuco de Abreu (Eds.), *Internet addiction: A handbook and guide to evaluation and treatment* (pp. 91–111). Hoboken, NJ: John Wiley & Sons.

Griffiths, M. (2015). Remote gambling: An overview of Internet gambling, mobile phone gambling and interactive television gambling. In H. Bowden-Jones & S. George (Eds.), *A clinician's guide to working with problem gamblers* (pp. 195–218). New York, NY: Routledge.

Griffiths, M. D., & Kuss, D. J. (2015). Online addictions: Gambling, video gaming, and social networking. In S. S. Sundar (Ed.), *The handbook of the psychology of communication technology* (pp. 384–403). Hoboken, NJ: Wiley-Blackwell.

Grubbs, J. B., Chapman, H., Milner, L., Gutierrez, I. A., & Bradley, D. F. (2018). Examining links between posttraumatic stress and gambling motives: The role of positive gambling expectancies. *Psychology of Addictive Behaviors*, *32*, 821–831.

Hahmann, T. E. (2016). Moderate-risk and problem slot machine gamblers: A typology of gambling-related cognitions. *Journal of Gambling Issues*, *34*, 140–155.

Hakansson, A., Kentta, G., & Akesdotter, C. (2018). Problem gambling and gaming in elite athletes. *Addictive Behaviors Reports*, *8*, 79–84.

Harris, N., & Mazmanian, D. (2016). Cognitive behavioural group therapy for problem gamblers who gamble over the internet: A controlled study. *Journal of Gambling Issues*, *33*, 170–188.

Haw, J., & Holdsworth, L. (2016). Gender differences in the temporal sequencing of problem gambling with other disorders. *International Journal of Mental Health and Addiction*, *14*(5), 687–699.

Hing, N., Russell, A. M., & Browne, M. (2017). Risk factors for gambling problems on online electronic gaming machines, race betting and sports betting. *Frontiers in Psychology*, *8*, 1–15.

Hing, N., & Russell, A. M. T. (2017a). How anticipated and experienced stigma can contribute to self-stigma: The case of problem gambling. *Frontiers in Psychology*, *8*, 1–11.

Hing, N., & Russell, A. M. T. (2017b). Psychological factors, sociodemographic characteristics, and coping mechanisms associated with the self-stigma of problem gambling. *Journal of Behavioral Addictions*, *6*(3), 416–424.

Hing, N., Russell, A. M. T., & Gainsbury, S. M. (2016). Unpacking the public stigma of problem gambling: The process of stigma creation and predictors of social distancing. *Journal of Behavioral Addictions*, *5*(3), 448–456.

Ho, K.-w. (2017). Risk factors of adolescent pathological gambling: Permissive gambling culture and individual factors. *Deviant Behavior*, *38*(5), 533–548.

Hodgins, D. C. (2001). Processes of changing gambling behavior. *Addictive Behaviors*, *26*(1), 121–128.

Hodgins, D. C., & Petry, N. M. (2016). The world of gambling: The National Gambling Experiences series. *Addiction*, *111*(9), 1516–1518.

Hope, J., & Havir, L. (2002). You bet they're having fun! Older Americans and casino gambling. *Journal of Aging Studies*, *16*, 177–197.

Imperatori, C., Innamorati, M., Bersani, F. S., Imbimbo, F., Pompili, M., Contardi, A., & Farina, B. (2017). The association among childhood trauma, pathological dissociation and gambling severity in casino gamblers. *Clinical Psychology & Psychotherapy*, *24*, 203–211.

Ipsos MORI. (2009). *British Survey of Children, the National Lottery and Gambling 2008-09: Report of a quantitative survey*. London, England: National Lottery Commission.

Jauregui, P., Estevez, A., & Urbiola, I. (2016). Pathological gambling and associated drug and alcohol abuse, emotion regulation, and anxious-depressive symptomatology. *Journal of Behavioral Addictions*, *5*(2), 251–260.

Jayan, R. (2015). Pharmacotherapy of gambling. *Addictive Disorders & Their Treatment, 14*, 220–229.

Jeffrey, D. (1996). *Going for broke: The depiction of compulsive gambling in Hollywood films* (Master's thesis). Retrieved from Proquest. (EP30396).

Jimenez-Murcia S., Granero, R., Fernandez-Aranda, F., Arcelus J., Aymami, M. N., Gomez-Pena, M., . . . Menchon, J. M. (2015). Predictors of outcome among pathological gamblers receiving cognitive behavioral group therapy. *European Addiction Research, 21*, 169–178.

Jimenez-Murcia, S., Tremblay, J., Stinchfield, R., Granero, R., Fernandez-Aranda, F., Mestre-Bach, G., . . . Menchon, J. M. (2017). The involvement of a concerned significant other in gambling disorder treatment outcome. *Journal of Gambling Studies, 33*(3), 937–953.

Karter, L. (2015). *Working with women's groups for problem gambling: Treating gambling addiction through relationship*. London, England: Routledge.

Kaspar, P. (2015). Pathological gambling: Screening, diagnosis and assessment. In H. Bowden-Jones & S. George (Eds.), *A clinician's guide to working with problem gamblers* (pp. 104–122). New York, NY: Routledge.

Kaufman, A., Nielsen, J. D. J., & Bowden-Jones, H. (2017). Barriers to treatment for female problem gamblers: A UK perspective. *Journal of Gambling Studies, 33*(3), 975–991.

Kausch, O. (2003a). Patterns of substance abuse among treatment-seeking pathological gamblers. *Journal of Substance Abuse Treatment, 25*(4), 263–270.

Kausch, O. (2003b). Suicide attempts among veterans seeking treatment for pathological gambling. *Journal of Clinical Psychiatry, 64*(9), 1031–1038.

Kausch, O. (2004). Pathological gambling among elderly veterans. *Journal of Geriatric Psychiatry and Neurology, 17*, 13–19.

Kim, H. S., Hodgins, D. C., Bellringer, M., & Abbott, M. (2016). Gender differences among helpline callers: Prospective study of gambling and psychosocial outcomes. *Journal of Gambling Studies, 32*(2), 605–623.

Kim, H. S., Shifrin, A., Sztainert, T., & Wohl, M. J. A. (2018). Placing your faith on the betting floor: Religiosity predicts disordered gambling via gambling fallacies. *Journal of Behavioral Addictions, 7*(2), 401–409.

King, D. L., & Delfabbro, P. H. (2016). Adolescents' perceptions of parental influences on commercial and simulated gambling activities. *International Gambling Studies, 16*(3), 424–441.

Koehler, S., Hasselmann, E., Wustenberg, T., Heinz, A., & Romanczuk-Seiferth, N. (2015). Higher volume of ventral striatum and right prefrontal cortex in pathological gambling. *Brain Structure & Function, 220*, 469–477.

Kong, G., Smith, P. H., Pilver, C., Hoff, R., & Potenza, M. N. (2016). Problem-gambling severity and psychiatric disorders among American-Indian/Alaska native adults. *Journal of Psychiatric Research, 74*, 55–62.

Korpa, T. N., & Papadopoulou, P. V. (2013). Clinical signs and symptoms of addictive behaviors. *International Journal of Child and Adolescent Health, 6*(4), 369–376.

Koschel, O., Lindenmeyer, J., & Heinrichs, N. (2017). Pathological gambling: Couple relationship and gender. *Pathologisches Glucksspielen: Partnerschaft und Geschlecht., 63*(3), 145–156.

Kovanen, L., Basnet, S., Castren, S., Pankakoski, M., Saarikoski, S. T., Partonen, T., . . . Lahti, T. (2016). A randomised, double-blind, placebo-controlled trial of as-needed naltrexone in the treatment of pathological gambling. *European Addiction Research, 22*, 70–79.

Kryszajtys, D. T., Hahmann, T. E., Schuler, A., Hamilton-Wright, S., Ziegler, C. P., & Matheson, F. I. (2018). Problem gambling and delinquent behaviours among adolescents: A scoping review. *Journal of Gambling Studies, 34*, 893–914.

Kushnir, V., Godinho, A., Hodgins, D. C., Hendershot, C. S., & Cunningham, J. A. (2016). Motivation to quit or reduce gambling: Associations between self-determination theory and the transtheoretical model of change. *Journal of Addictive Diseases, 35*, 58–65.

Ladouceur, R., Shaffer, P., Blaszczynski, A., & Shaffer, H. J. (2017). Responsible gambling: A synthesis of the empirical evidence. *Addiction Research & Theory, 25*, 225–235.

Lam, D. (2006). The influence of religiosity on gambling participation. *Journal of Gambling Studies, 22*, 305–320.

Lane, W., Sacco, P., Downton, K., Ludeman, E., Levy, L., & Tracy, J. K. (2016). Child maltreatment and problem gambling: A systematic review. *Child Abuse & Neglect, 58*, 24–38.

Langham, E., Russell, A. M. T., Hing, N., & Gainsbury, S. M. (2017). Sense of coherence and gambling: Exploring the relationship between sense of coherence, gambling behaviour and gambling-related harm. *Journal of Gambling Studies, 33*(2), 1–24.

Lanteri, P. F., Leguia, A., Dolade, N. G., Garcia, G. C., & Figueras, A. (2018). Drug-induced gambling disorder: A not so rare but underreported condition. *Psychiatry Research, 269*, 593–595.

Ledgerwood, D. M., & Arfken, C. L. (2017). Assessing the need for higher levels of care among problem gambling outpatients. *Journal of Gambling Studies, 33*(4), 1263–1275.

Ledgerwood, D. M., & Petry, N. M. (2006). Posttraumatic stress disorder symptoms in treatment-seeking pathological gamblers. *Journal of Traumatic Stress, 19*, 411–416.

Lee, B. K. (2015). Towards a relational framework for pathological gambling (Part II): Congruence. *Journal of Family Therapy, 37*, 103–118.

Lee, G. P., Ghandour, L. A., Takache, A. H., & Martins, S. S. (2014). Investigating the association between strategic and pathological gambling behaviors and substance use in youth: Could religious faith play a differential role? *American Journal on Addictions, 23*, 280–287.

Leino, T., Torsheim, T., Pallesen, S., Blaszczynski, A., Sagoe, D., & Molde, H. (2016). An empirical real-world study of losses disguised as wins in electronic gaming machines. *International Gambling Studies, 16*(3), 470–480.

Lemoine, J., Kmiec, R., & Roland-Levy, C. (2017). Characterization of controlled gamblers and pathological gamblers using the social representation theory. *European Review of Applied Psychology / Revue Europeenne de Psychologie Appliquee, 67*(1), 13–23.

Lesieur, H. R., & Blume, S. B. (1987). The South Oaks Gambling Screen (SaGS): A new instrument for the identification of pathological gamblers. *American Journal of Psychiatry, 144*(9), 1184–1188.

Levesque, D., Sévigny, S., Giroux, I., & Jacques, C. (2018). Psychological vulnerability and problem gambling: The mediational role of cognitive distortions. *Journal of Gambling Studies, 34*, 807–822.

Levy, L., & Tracy, J. K. (2018). Gambling disorder in veterans: A review of the literature and implications for future research. *Journal of Gambling Studies, 34*(4), 1205–1239.

Lewis, L., Black, P. L., & McMullen, K. (2016). Problem gambling: "Behind the eight ball." *Journal of Social Work Practice in the Addictions, 16*(3), 290–305.

Lim, M. S. M., & Rogers, R. D. (2017). Chinese beliefs in luck are linked to gambling problems via strengthened cognitive biases: A mediation test. *Journal of Gambling Studies, 33*, 1325–1336.

Linardatou. C., Parios, A.,Varvogli, L., Chrousos, G., & Darviri, C. (2014). An 8-week stress management program in pathological gamblers: A pilot randomized controlled trial. *Journal of Psychiatric Research*, *56*, 137–143.

Lindberg, A., Clark, L., & Bowden-Jones, H. (2014). Impulsivity and cognitive distortions in problem gambling: Theory and application. In F. Gobet & M. Schiller (Eds.), *Problem gambling: Cognition, prevention and treatment* (pp. 252–286). New York, NY: Palgrave Macmillan.

Linnet, J., Jeppsen Mensink, M., de Neergaard Bonde, J., & Winterdahl, M. (2017). Treatment of gambling disorder patients with comorbid depression. *Acta Neuropsychiatrica*, *29*, 356–362.

Luczak, S. E., & Wall, T. L. (2016). Gambling problems and comorbidity with alcohol use disorders in Chinese-, Korean-, and White-American college students. *American Journal on Addictions*, *25*(3), 195–202.

Lutri, V., Soldini, E., Ronzitti, S., Smith, N., Clerici, M., Blaszczynski, A., & Bowden-Jones, H. (2018). Impulsivity and gambling type among treatment-seeking disordered gamblers: An explorative study. *Journal of Gambling Studies*, *34*, 1341–1354.

Maniaci, G., La Cascia, C., Picone, F., Lipari, A., Cannizzaro, C., & La Barbera, D. (2017). Predictors of early dropout in treatment for gambling disorder: The role of personality disorders and clinical syndromes. *Psychiatry Research*, *257*, 540–545.

Mann, K., Lemenager, T., Zois, E., Hoffmann, S., Nakovics, H., Beutel, M., . . . Fauth-Buhler, M. (2017). Comorbidity, family history and personality traits in pathological gamblers compared with healthy controls. *European Psychiatry*, *42*, 120–128.

Mansueto, G., Pennelli, M., De Palo, V., Monacis, L., Sinatra, M., & De Caro, M. F. (2016). The role of metacognition in pathological gambling: A mediation model. *Journal of Gambling Studies*, *32*(1), 93–106.

Marchica, L., & Derevensky, J. L. (2016). Examining personalized feedback interventions for gambling disorders: A systematic review. *Journal of Behavioral Addictions*, *5*(1), 1–10.

Mariann, T., Andras, T., Zsolt, F., Eva, G., & Zsolt, P. (2014). Traditional form—Revised material: Minnesota model from the viewpoint of the up-to-date psychological approaches. *Pszichoterapia*, *23*(3), 158–164.

Martin, R. J., Nelson, S. E., & Gallucci, A. R. (2016). Game on: Past year gambling, gambling-related problems, and fantasy sports gambling among college athletes and non-athletes. *Journal of Gambling Studies*, *32*(2), 567–579.

Martyres, K., & Townshend, P. (2016). Addressing the needs of problem gamblers with co-morbid issues: Policy and service delivery approaches. *Journal of Gambling Issues*, *33*, 68–81.

McBride, J. (2016). Gambling and video game playing among youth. *Journal of Gambling Issues*, *34*, 156–178.

McGrath, D., Kim, H., Hodgins, D., Novitsky, C., & Tavares, H. (2018). Who are the anonymous? Involvement and predictors of Gamblers Anonymous attendance among disordered gamblers presenting for treatment. *Journal of Gambling Studies*, *34*(4), 1423–1434.

McGrath, D. S., Neilson, T., Lee, K., Rash, C. L., & Rad, M. (2018). Associations between the HEXACO model of personality and gambling involvement, motivations to gamble, and gambling severity in young adult gamblers. *Journal of Behavioral Addictions*, *7*(2), 392–400.

McKinley, C. J., Luo, Y., Wright, P. J., & Kraus, A. (2016). Problem gambling messages on college counseling center websites: An over-time and cross-country comparison. *Journal of Gambling Studies*, *32*(1), 307–325.

Medeiros, G. C., & Grant, J. E. (2018). Gambling disorder and obsessive-compulsive personality disorder: A frequent but understudied comorbidity. *Journal of Behavioral Addictions*, *7*, 366–374.

Medeiros, G. C., Redden, S. A., Chamberlain, S. R., & Grant, J. E. (2017). Gambling disorder: Association between duration of illness, clinical, and neurocognitive variables. *Journal of Behavioral Addictions*, *6*(2), 194–202.

Mestre-Bach, G., Steward, T., Granero, R., Fernandez-Aranda, F., Talon-Navarro, M. T., Cuquerella, A., . . . Jimenez-Murcia, S. (2018). Gambling and impulsivity traits: A recipe for criminal behavior? *Frontiers in Psychiatry*, *9*, 1–10.

Miedl, S. F., Fehr, T., Meyer, G., & Herrmann, M. (2010). Neurobiological correlates of problem gambling in a quasi-realistic blackjack scenario as revealed by fMRI. *Psychiatry Research: Neuroimaging*, *181*(3), 165–173.

Miers, D. (2014). Implementing a social responsibility agenda in the regulation of gambling in Great Britain. In F. Gobet & M. Schiller (Eds.), *Problem gambling: Cognition, prevention and treatment* (pp. 188–218). New York, NY: Palgrave Macmillan.

Milkman, H. B., & Sunderwirth, S. G. (2010). *Craving for ecstasy and natural highs: A positive approach to mood alteration*. Thousand Oaks, CA: SAGE.

Mladenovic, I., Lazetic, G., Lecic-Tosevski, D., & Dimitrijevic, I. (2015). Treatment of pathological gambling-integrative systemic model. *Psychiatria Danubina*, *27*(1), 107–111.

Moon, M., Lister, J. J., Milosevic, A., & Ledgerwood, D. M. (2017). Subtyping non-treatment-seeking problem gamblers using the pathways model. *Journal of Gambling Studies*, *33*, 841–853.

Morasco, B. J., Pietrzak, R. H., Blanco, C., Grant, B. F., Hasin, D., & Petry, N. M. (2006). Health problems and medical utilization associated with gambling disorders: Results from the National Epidemiologic Survey on Alcohol and Related Conditions. *Psychosomatic Medicine*, *68*(6), 976–984.

Moreau, A., Chabrol, H., & Chauchard, E. (2016). Psychopathology of online poker players: Review of literature. *Journal of Behavioral Addictions*, *5*(2), 155–168.

Mutti-Packer, S., Hodgins, D. C., Williams, R. J., & Thege, B. K. (2017). The protective role of religiosity against problem gambling: Findings from a five-year prospective study. *BMC Psychiatry*, *17*, 1–10.

Mutti-Packer, S., Kowatch, K., Steadman, R., Hodgins, D. C., el-Guebaly, N., Casey, D. M., . . . Smith, G. J. (2017). A qualitative examination of factors underlying transitions in problem gambling severity: Findings from the Leisure, Lifestyle, & Lifecycle Project. *Addiction Research & Theory*, *25*(5), 424–431.

Najavits, L. M. (2011). Treatments for PTSD and pathological gambling: What do patients want? *Journal of Gambling Studies*, *27*, 229–241.

Najavits, L. M., Meyer, T., Johnson, K. M., & Korn, D. (2011). Pathological gambling and posttraumatic stress disorder: A study of the co-morbidity versus each alone. *Journal of Gambling Studies*, *27*, 663–683.

Navas, J. F., Billieux, J., Perandres-Gomez, A., Lopez-Torrecillas, F., Candido, A., & Perales, J. C. (2017). Impulsivity traits and gambling cognitions associated with gambling preferences and clinical status. *International Gambling Studies*, *17*(1), 102–124.

Nayoski, N., & Hodgins, D. C. (2016). The efficacy of individual Community Reinforcement and Family Training (CRAFT) for concerned significant others of problem gamblers. *Journal of Gambling Issues*, *33*, 189–212.

Nigro, G., Ciccarelli, M., & Cosenza, M. (2018a). Tempting fate: Chasing and maladaptive personality traits in gambling behavior. *Psychiatry Research*, *267*, 360–367.

Nigro, G., Ciccarelli, M., & Cosenza, M. (2018b). The illusion of handy wins: Problem gambling, chasing, and affective decision-making. *Journal of Affective Disorders*, *225*, 256–259.

Noel, X., Saeremans, M., Kornreich, C., Bechara, A., Jaafari, N., & Fantini-Hauwel, C. (2018). On the processes underlying the relationship between alexithymia and gambling severity. *Journal of Gambling Studies*, *34*, 1049–1066.

Nower, L., & Blaszczynski, A. (2017). Development and validation of the Gambling Pathways Questionnaire (GPQ). *Psychology of Addictive Behaviors*, *31*, 95–109.

O'Brien, K. L. (2015). A qualitative study of the development and maintenance of pathological gambling in females: And making the choice to recover. *Dissertation Abstracts International Section A: Humanities and Social Sciences*, *77*(3-A(E)). No pagination specified.

Olley, J., Blaszczynski, A., & Lewis, S. (2015). Dopaminergic medication in Parkinson's disease and problem gambling. *Journal of Gambling Studies*, *31*, 1085–1106.

Parke, A., Griffiths, M., Pattinson, J., & Keatley, D. (2018). Age-related physical and psychological vulnerability as pathways to problem gambling in older adults. *Journal of Behavioral Addictions*, *7*, 137–145.

Parodi, S., Dosi, C., Zambon, A., Ferrari, E., & Muselli, M. (2017). Identifying environmental and social factors predisposing to pathological gambling combining standard logistic regression and logic learning machine. *Journal of Gambling Studies*, *33*, 1121–1137.

Passanisi, A., Craparo, G., & Pace, U. (2017). Magical thinking and decision-making strategies among late adolescent regular gamblers: A mediation model. *Journal of Adolescence*, *59*, 51–58.

Penny Wan, Y. K., Li, X. C., & Kong, W. H. (2011). Social impacts of casino gaming in Macao: A qualitative analysis. *Tourism: An International Interdisciplinary Journal*, *59*(1), 63–82.

Peter, S. C., Whelan, J. P., Ginley, M. K., Pfund, R. A., Wilson, K. K., & Meyers, A. W. (2016). Disordered gamblers with and without ADHD: The role of coping in elevated psychological distress. *International Gambling Studies*, *16*(3), 455–469.

Peterson, E., & Forlano, R. (2017). Partial dopamine agonist-induced pathological gambling and impulse-control deficit on low-dose aripiprazole. *Australasian Psychiatry*, *25*, 614–616.

Petry, N. M. (2005). Stages of change in treatment-seeking pathological gamblers. *Journal of Consulting and Clinical Psychology*, *73*, 312–322.

Petry, N. M. (2015). Psychosocial treatments for problem and pathological gambling. In H. Bowden-Jones & S. George (Eds.), *A clinician's guide to working with problem gamblers* (pp. 123–133). New York, NY: Routledge.

Petry, N. M., Ginley, M. K., & Rash, C. J. (2017). A systematic review of treatments for problem gambling. *Psychology of Addictive Behaviors*, *31*, 951–961.

Petry, N. M., Rash, C. J., & Alessi, S. M. (2016). A randomized controlled trial of brief interventions for problem gambling in substance abuse treatment patients. *Journal of Consulting and Clinical Psychology*, *84*, 874–886.

Pfund, R. A., Whelan, J. P., Greenburg, J. E., Peter, S. C., Wilson, K. K., & Meyers, A. W. (2017). Psychological distress as an indicator of co-occurring psychopathology among treatment-seeking disordered gamblers. *Journal of Gambling Studies*, *33*, 907–918.

Pfund, R. A., Whelan, J. P., Peter, S. C., & Meyers, A. W. (2018). Can a motivational letter increase attendance to psychological treatment for gambling disorder? *Psychological Services*, [Online First Publication, October 1]. No pagination specified.

Piquette, N., & Norman, E. (2013). An all-female problem-gambling counseling treatment: Perceptions of effectiveness. *Journal of Groups in Addiction & Recovery*, *8*, 51–75.

Pontieri, F. E., Assogna, F., Pellicano, C., Cacciari, C., Pannunzi, S., Morrone, A., . . . Spalletta, G. (2015). Sociodemographic, neuropsychiatric and cognitive characteristics of pathological gambling and impulse control disorders NOS in Parkinson's disease. *European Neuropsychopharmacology*, *25*, 69–76.

Poole, J. C., Kim, H. S., Dobson, K. S., & Hodgins, D. C. (2017). Adverse childhood experiences and disordered gambling: Assessing the mediating role of emotion dysregulation. *Journal of Gambling Studies*, *33*, 1187–1200.

Potenza, M. N. (2005). Review of *The Psychodynamics and Psychology of Gambling: The Gambler's Mind*, Volume *I*. *American Journal on Addictions*, *14*, 489–490.

Potenza, M. N. (2013). Neurobiology of gambling behaviors. *Current Opinion in Neurobiology*, *23*, 660–667.

Prochaska, J. O., Norcross, J. C., & DiClemente, C. C. (1994). *Changing for good*. New York, NY: Avon Books.

Quilty, L. C., Lobo, D. S. S., Zack, M., Crewe-Brown, C., & Blaszczynski, A. (2016). Hitting the jackpot: The influence of monetary payout on gambling behaviour. *International Gambling Studies*, *16*(3), 481–499.

Quintero, G. C. (2016). A biopsychological review of gambling disorder. *Neuropsychiatric Disease and Treatment*, *13*, 51–60.

Rasanen, T., Lintonen, T., Tolvanen, A., & Konu, A. (2016). The role of social support in the association between gambling, poor health and health risk-taking. *Scandinavian Journal of Public Health*, *44*(6), 593–598.

Rash, C. J., & Petry, N. M. (2017). Gambling disorder impacts homeless to affluent women in the US. In H. Bowden-Jones & F. Prever (Eds.), *Gambling disorders in women: An international female perspective on treatment and research* (pp. 52–62). New York, NY: Routledge/Taylor & Francis.

Rhind, D. J. A., O'Brien, K., Jewett, S., & Greenlees, I. (2014). Problem gambling among athletes in the United Kingdom. In F. Gobet & M. Schiller (Eds.), *Problem gambling: Cognition, prevention and treatment* (pp. 127–139). New York, NY: Palgrave Macmillan.

Richard, K., Baghurst, T., Faragher, J. M., & Stotts, E. (2017). Practical treatments considering the role of sociocultural factors on problem gambling. *Journal of Gambling Studies*, *33*, 265–281.

Ricijas, N., Hundric, D. D., Huic, A., & Kranzelic, V. (2016). Youth gambling in Croatia—Frequency of gambling and the occurrence of problem gambling. *Kriminologija & Socijalna Integracija*, *24*(2), 48–72.

Rinker, D. V., Rodriguez, L. M., Krieger, H., Tackett, J. L., & Neighbors, C. (2016). Racial and ethnic differences in problem gambling among college students. *Journal of Gambling Studies*, *32*(2), 581–590.

Roaf, E. (2015). Gambling and public health. In H. Bowden-Jones & S. George (Eds.), *A clinician's guide to working with problem gamblers* (pp. 15–27). New York, NY: Routledge.

Roberts, A., Landon, J., Sharman, S., Hakes, J., Suomi, A., & Cowlishaw, S. (2018). Gambling and physical intimate partner violence: Results from the National Epidemiologic Survey on Alcohol and Related Conditions (NESARC). *American Journal on Addictions*, *27*, 7–14.

Roberts, K. J., Smith, N., Bowden-Jones, H., & Cheeta, S. (2017). Gambling disorder and suicidality within the UK: An analysis investigating mental health and gambling severity as risk factors to suicidality. *International Gambling Studies*, *17*, 51–64.

Rockloff, M., Moskovsky, N., Thorne, H., Browne, M., & Bryden, G. (2017). Electronic gaming machine (EGM) environments: Market segments and risk. *Journal of Gambling Studies, 33*, 1139–1152.

Rodda, S. N., Lubman, D. I., Jackson, A. C., & Dowling, N. A. (2017). Improved outcomes following a single session web-based intervention for problem gambling. *Journal of Gambling Studies, 33*, 283–299.

Rodriguez-Monguio, R., Errea, M., & Volberg, R. (2017). Comorbid pathological gambling, mental health, and substance use disorders: Health-care services provision by clinician specialty. *Journal of Behavioral Addictions, 6*, 406–415.

Ronzitti, S., Lutri, V., Smith, N., Clerici, M., & Bowden-Jones, H. (2016). Gender differences in treatment-seeking British pathological gamblers. *Journal of Behavioral Addictions, 5*(2), 231–238.

Ronzitti, S., Soldini, E., Smith, N., Clerici, M., & Bowden-Jones, H. (2017). Gambling disorder: Exploring pre-treatment and in-treatment dropout predictors. A UK study. *Journal of Gambling Studies, 33*(4), 1277–1292.

Ronzitti, S., Soldini, E., Smith, N., Potenza, M. N., Clerici, M., & Bowden-Jones, H. (2017). Current suicidal ideation in treatment-seeking individuals in the United Kingdom with gambling problems. *Addictive Behaviors, 74*, 33–40.

Rosenthal, R. J. (2008). Psychodynamic psychotherapy and the treatment of pathological gambling. *Revista Brasileira de Psiquiatria, 30*, S41–S50.

Rosenthal, R. J., & Rugle, L. J. (1994). A psychodynamic approach to the treatment of pathological gambling: I. Achieving abstinence. *Journal of Gambling Studies, 10*(1), 21–42.

Rossini-Dib, D., Fuentes, D., & Tavares, H. (2015). A naturalistic study of recovering gamblers: What gets better and when they get better. *Psychiatry Research, 227*, 17–26.

Rugle, L. J., & Rosenthal, R. J. (1994). Transference and countertransference reactions in the psychotherapy of pathological gamblers. *Journal of Gambling Studies, 10*(1), 43–65.

Sauvaget, A., Bulteau, S., Guilleux, A., Leboucher, J., Pichot, A., Valriviere, P., . . . Grall-Bronnec, M. (2018). Both active and sham low-frequency rTMS single sessions over the right DLPFC decrease cue-induced cravings among pathological gamblers seeking treatment: A randomized, double-blind, sham-controlled crossover trial. *Journal of Behavioral Addictions, 7*, 126–136.

Sauvaget, A., Jimenez-Murcia, S., Fernandez-Aranda, F., Granero, R., Grall-Bronnec, M., Victorri-Vigneau, C., . . . Menchon, J. M. (2017). A comparison of treatment-seeking behavioral addiction patients with and without Parkinson's disease. *Frontiers in Psychiatry, 8*, 1–6.

Savvidou, L. G., Fagundo, A. B., Fernandez-Aranda, F., Granero, R., Claes, L., Mallorqui-Baque, N., . . . Jimenez-Murcia, S. (2017). Is gambling disorder associated with impulsivity traits measured by the UPPS-P and is this association moderated by sex and age? *Comprehensive Psychiatry, 72*, 106–113.

Schiller, M. R. G., & Gobet, F. R. (2014). Cognitive models of gambling and problem gambling. In F. Gobet & M. Schiller (Eds.), *Problem gambling: Cognition, prevention and treatment* (pp. 74–103). New York, NY: Palgrave Macmillan.

Schlagintweit, H. E., Thompson, K., Goldstein, A. L., & Stewart, S. H. (2017). An investigation of the association between shame and problem gambling: The mediating role of maladaptive coping motives. *Journal of Gambling Studies, 33*, 1067–1079.

Sévigny, S., & Ladouceur, R. (2003). Gamblers' irrational thinking about chance events: the 'double switching' concept. *International Gambling Studies, 3*(2), 149–161.

Shonin, E., Van Gordon, W., & Griffiths, M. D. (2013). Buddhist philosophy for the treatment of problem gambling. *Journal of Behavioral Addictions, 2*, 63–71.

Shultz, S. K., Shaw, M., McCormick, B., Allen, J., & Black, D. W. (2016). Intergenerational childhood maltreatment in persons with DSM-IV pathological gambling and their first-degree relatives. *Journal of Gambling Studies, 32*(3), 877–887.

Simmons, J. L., Whelan, J. P., Meyers, A. W., & Wickwire, E. M. (2016). Gambling outcome expectancies and gambling behavior among African-American adolescents: Gender as a moderating variable. *Journal of Gambling Studies, 32*(1), 205–215.

Sirola, A., Kaakinen, M., & Oksanen, A. (2018). Excessive gambling and online gambling communities. *Journal of Gambling Studies, 34*, 1313–1325.

Smith, N., & Shah, S. (2015). Cognitive-behavioural models of problem gambling. In H. Bowden-Jones & S. George (Eds.), *A clinician's guide to working with problem gamblers* (pp. 39–52). New York, NY: Routledge.

Soberay, A. D., Grimsley, P., Faragher, J. M., Barbash, M., & Berger, B. (2014). Stages of change, clinical presentation, retention, and treatment outcomes in treatment-seeking outpatient problem gambling clients. *Psychology of Addictive Behaviors, 28*, 414–419.

Southern, S., & Hilton, K. (2015). Pathological gambling. In R. L. Smith (Ed.), *Treatment strategies for substance and process addictions* (pp. 149–176). Alexandria, VA: American Counseling Association.

Stefanovics, E. A., Potenza, M. N., & Pietrzak, R. H. (2017). Gambling in a national U.S. veteran population: Prevalence, socio-demographics, and psychiatric comorbidities. *Journal of Gambling Studies, 33*, 1099–1120.

Stein, G. N., Pretorius, A., Stein, D. J., & Sinclair, H. (2016). The association between pathological gambling and suicidality in treatment-seeking pathological gamblers in South Africa. *Annals of Clinical Psychiatry, 28*(1), 43–50.

Stinchfield, R., McCready, J., Turner, N. E., Jimenez-Murcia, S., Petry, N. M., Grant, J., . . . Winters, K. C. (2016). Reliability, validity, and classification accuracy of the *DSM-5* diagnostic criteria for gambling disorder and comparison to DSM-IV. *Journal of Gambling Studies, 32*(3), 905–922.

Tabri, N., Will Shead, N., & Wohl, M. J. A. (2017). Me, myself, and money II: Relative deprivation predicts disordered gambling severity via delay discounting, especially among gamblers who have a financially focused self-concept. *Journal of Gambling Studies, 33*, 1201–1211.

Tabri, N., Wohl, M. J. A., Eddy, K. T., & Thomas, J. J. (2017). Me, myself and money: Having a financially focused self-concept and its consequences for disordered gambling. *International Gambling Studies, 17*, 30–50.

Takeuchi, H., Kawada, R., Tsurumi, K., Yokoyama, N., Takemura, A., Murao, T., . . . Takahashi, H. (2016). Heterogeneity of loss aversion in pathological gambling. *Journal of Gambling Studies, 32*(4), 1143–1154.

Tani, F., Gori, A., & Ponti, L. (2018). Cognitive distortions and gambling behaviors: Which comes first? Analyzing the relationship between superstitious beliefs and pathological gambling. *Clinical Neuropsychiatry: Journal of Treatment Evaluation, 15*(2), 77–82.

Terrone, G., Musetti, A., Raschielli, S., Marino, A., Costrini, P., Mossi, P., . . . Vincenzo, C. (2018). Attachment relationships and internalization and externalization problems in a group of adolescents with pathological gambling disorder. *Clinical Neuropsychiatry: Journal of Treatment Evaluation, 15*(1), 66–74.

Tochkov, K. (2012). No regrets? Mood and the anticipation of emotions in problem gambling. *International Gambling Studies, 12*, 39–53.

Tomei, A., Besson, J., & Grivel, J. (2017). Linking empathy to visuospatial perspective-taking in gambling addiction. *Psychiatry Research, 250*, 177–184.

Tondo, G., De Marchi, F., Terazzi, E., Sacchetti, M., & Cantello, R. (2017). Frontotemporal dementia presenting as gambling disorder: When a psychiatric condition is the clue to a neurodegenerative disease. *Cognitive and Behavioral Neurology, 30*, 62–67.

Toneatto, T. (2008). Reliability and validity of the Gamblers Anonymous 20 questions. *Journal of Psychopathology and Behavioral Assessment, 30*(1), 71–78.

Toneatto, T. (2016). Single-session interventions for problem gambling may be as effective as longer treatments: Results of a randomized control trial. *Addictive Behaviors, 52*, 58–65.

Tremblay, J., Dufour, M., Bertrand, K., Blanchette-Martin, N., Ferland, F., Savard, A.-C., . . . Cote, M. (2018). The experience of couples in the process of treatment of pathological gambling: Couple vs. individual therapy. *Frontiers in Psychology, 8*, 1–14.

Truong, A., Moukaddam, N., Toledo, A., & Onigu-Otite, E. (2017). Addictive disorders in adolescents. *Psychiatric Clinics of North America, 40*, 475–486.

Turner, N. E., McAvoy, S., Ferentzy, P., Matheson, F. I., Myers, C., Jindani, F., . . . Malat, J. (2017). Addressing the issue of problem gambling in the criminal justice system: A series of case studies. *Journal of Gambling Issues, 35*, 74–100.

Turner, N. E., McDonald, A. J., Ialomiteanu, A. R., Mann, R. E., McCready, J., Millstone, D., . . . Cusimano, M. D. (2019). Moderate to severe gambling problems and traumatic brain injury: A population-based study. *Psychiatry Research, 272*, 692–697.

Vaddiparti, K., & Cottler, L. B. (2017). Personality disorders and pathological gambling. *Current Opinion in Psychiatry, 30*, 45–49.

Van der Maas, M. (2016). An exploration of gender differences in the relationship between work family conflict and gambling problems. *International Gambling Studies, 16*(1), 156–174.

Van Patten, R., Weinstock, J., & McGrath, A. B. (2018). Health outcomes in individuals with problem and pathological gambling: An analysis of the 2014 North Carolina Behavioral Risk Factor Survey System (BRFSS). *Journal of Gambling Studies, 34*, 297–306.

Van Slyke, J. K. (2017). Examining the role of ethnicity, socioeconomic status, and setting in gambling expectancies and behavior among men. *Dissertation Abstracts International: Section B: The Sciences and Engineering, 77*(11-B(E)). No pagination specified.

Van Timmeren, T., Daams, J. G., van Holst, R. J., & Goudriaan, A. E. (2018). Compulsivity-related neurocognitive performance deficits in gambling disorder: A systematic review and meta-analysis. *Neuroscience and Biobehavioral Reviews, 84*, 204–217.

Varo, C., Murru, A., Salagre, E., Jimenez, E., Sole, B., Montejo, L., et al. (2019). Behavioral addictions in bipolar disorders: A systematic review. *European Neuropsychopharmacology, 29*, 76–97.

Velleman, R., Cousins, J., & Orford, J. (2015). Effects of gambling on the family. In H. Bowden-Jones & S. George (Eds.), *A clinician's guide to working with problem gamblers* (pp. 90–103). New York, NY: Routledge.

Vieno, A., Canale, N., Potente, R., Scalese, M., Griffiths, M. D., & Molinaro, S. (2018). The multiplicative effect of combining alcohol with energy drinks on adolescent gambling. *Addictive Behaviors, 82*, 7–13.

Voon, V., Napier, T. C., Frank, M. J., Sgambato-Faure, V., Grace, A. A., Rodriguez-Oroz, M., . . . Fernagut, P.-O. (2017). Impulse control disorders and levodopa-induced dyskinesias in Parkinson's disease: An update. *Lancet Neurology, 16*, 238–250.

Walsh, J. M. (2002). Spirituality and recovery from pathological gambling. *Dissertation Abstracts International: Section B: The Sciences and Engineering, 62*(9-B), 4241.

Wardle, H. (2015). Gambling behaviour in Britain: Evidence from the British Gambling Prevalence Survey series. In H. Bowden-Jones & S. George (Eds.), *A clinician's guide to working with problem gamblers* (pp. 2–14). New York, NY: Routledge.

Weinstock, J. (2018). Call to action for gambling disorder in the United States. *Addiction, 113*, 1156–1158.

Welsh, M., Jones, R., Pykett, J., & Whitehead, M. (2014). The "problem gambler" and socio-spatial vulnerability. In F. Gobet & M. Schiller (Eds.), *Problem gambling: Cognition, prevention and treatment* (pp. 156–187). New York, NY: Palgrave Macmillan.

Welte, J. W., Barnes, G. M., Wieczorek, W. F., & Tidwell, M.-C. (2004). Gambling participation and pathology in the United States—A sociodemographic analysis using classification trees. *Addictive Behaviors, 29*, 983–989.

Welte, J. W., Tidwell, M.-C. O., Barnes, G. M., Hoffman, J. H., & Wieczorek, W. F. (2016). The relationship between the number of types of legal gambling and the rates of gambling behaviors and problems across U.S. states. *Journal of Gambling Studies, 32*(2), 379–390.

Welte, J. W., Wieczorek, W. F., Barnes, G. M., & Tidwell, M.-C. O. (2006). Multiple risk factors for frequent and problem gambling: Individual, social, and ecological. *Journal of Applied Social Psychology, 26*(6), 1548–1568.

Westermeyer, J., Canive, J., Garrard, J., Thuras, P., & Thompson, J. (2005). Lifetime prevalence of pathological gambling among American Indian and Hispanic American veterans. *American Journal of Public Health, 95*, 860–866.

Westermeyer, J., Canive, J., Thuras, P., Kim, S. W., Crosby, R., Thompson, J., & Garrard, J. (2006). Remission from pathological gambling among Hispanics and Native Americans. *Community Mental Health Journal, 42*, 537–553.

Whiting, S. W., Potenza, M. N., Park, C. L., McKee, S. A., Mazure, C. M., & Hoff, R. A. (2016). Investigating veterans' pre-, peri-, and post-deployment experiences as potential risk factors for problem gambling. *Journal of Behavioral Addictions, 5*(2), 213–220.

Wickwire, E. M., Jr., Whelan, J. P., West, R., Meyers, A., McCausland, C., & Leullen, J. (2007). Perceived availability, risks, and benefits of gambling among college students. *Journal of Gambling Studies, 23*, 395–408.

Wiebe, J., Wynne, H., Stinchfield, R., & Tremblay J. (2007, November). *The Canadian Adolescent Gambling Inventory (CAGI): Phase II final report.* Ottawa, ON: Canadian Centre on Substance Abuse. Retrieved on April 6, 2019, from http://dspace.ucalgary.ca/bitstream/1880/48157/1/CAGI_Phase_2_Report-English.pdf

Williams, A. D., Grisham, J. R., Erskine, A., & Cassedy, E. (2012). Deficits in emotion regulation associated with pathological gambling. *British Journal of Clinical Psychology, 51*(2), 223–238.

Williams, R. J., Belanger, Y. D., & Prusak, S. Y. (2016). Gambling and problem gambling among Canadian urban Aboriginals. *Canadian Journal of Psychiatry / La Revue canadienne de psychiatrie, 61*(11), 724–731.

Wohl, M. J. A., Salmon, M. M., Hollingshead, S. J., & Kim, H. S. (2017). An examination of the relationship between social casino gaming and gambling: The bad, the ugly, and the good. *Journal of Gambling Issues, 35*, 1–23.

Xu, J., & Harvey, N. (2014). The hot hand fallacy and the gamblers fallacy: What are they and why do people believe in them? In F. Gobet & M. Schiller (Eds.), *Problem gambling: Cognition, prevention and treatment* (pp. 61–73). New York, NY: Palgrave Macmillan.

Yakovenko, I., & Hodgins, D. C. (2014). Treatment of disordered gambling. In F. Gobet & M. Schiller (Eds.), *Problem gambling: Cognition, prevention and treatment* (pp. 221–251). New York, NY: Palgrave Macmillan.

Yakovenko, I., & Hodgins, D. C. (2018). A scoping review of co-morbidity in individuals with disordered gambling. *International Gambling Studies, 18*, 143–172.

Yi, S., & Kanetkar, V. (2011). Coping with guilt and shame after gambling loss. *Journal of Gambling Studies, 27*, 371–387.

Zhai, Z. W., Yip, S. W., Steinberg, M. A., Wampler, J., Hoff, R. A., Krishnan-Sarin, S., & Potenza, M. N. (2017). Relationships between perceived family gambling and peer gambling and adolescent problem gambling and binge-drinking. *Journal of Gambling Studies, 33*(4), 1169–1185.

Zhao, Y., Marchica, L., Derevensky, J. L., & Shaffer, H. J. (2017). The scope, focus and types of gambling policies among Canadian colleges and universities. *Canadian Psychology/Psychologie canadienne, 58*(2), 187–193.

Zhuang, X. Y., Wong, D. F. K., Ng, T. K., Jackson, A. C., Dowling, N. a., & Lo, H. H.-m. (2018). Evaluating the effectiveness of an integrated cognitive-behavioural intervention (CBI) model for male problem gamblers in Hong Kong: A matched-pair comparison design. *Journal of Gambling Studies, 34*, 969–985.

15 Internet-Related Addictions

INTERNET ADDICTION, INTERNET GAMING DISORDER, AND SOCIAL MEDIA ADDICTION

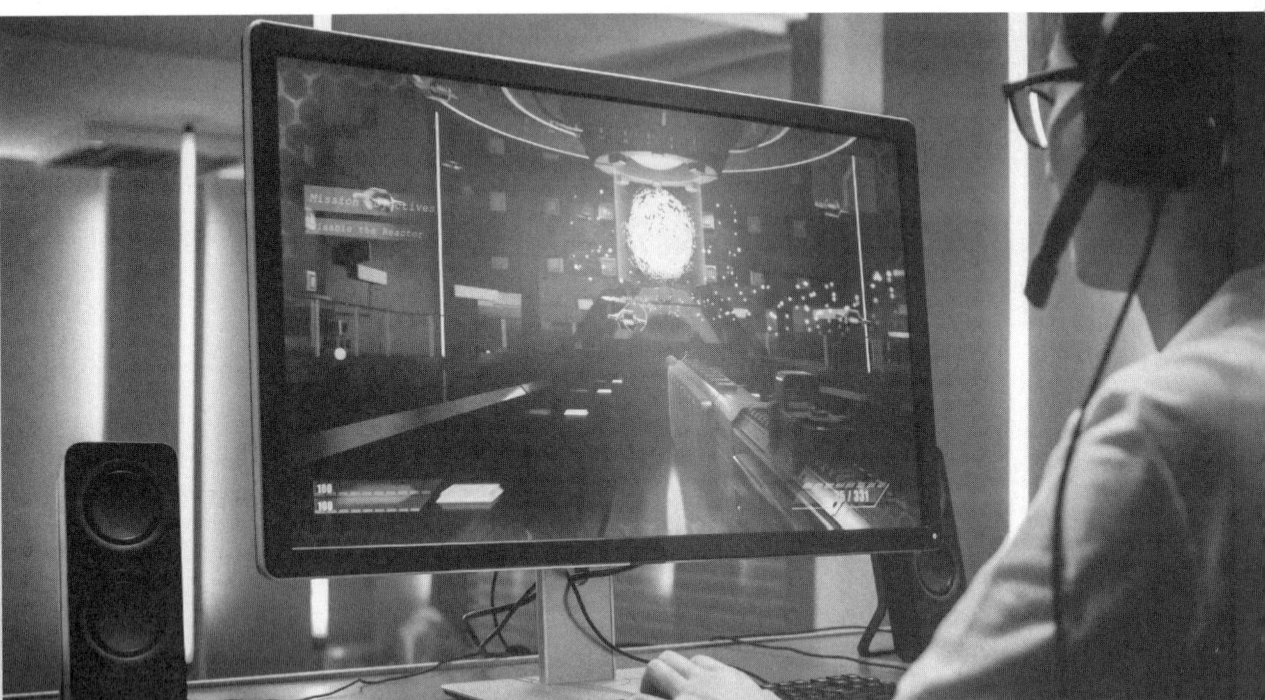

iStock.com/gorode

Learning Objectives

1. Learn about addictions to the Internet, to gaming, and to social media.
2. Become aware of section 7 in *DSM-5* and Internet gaming disorder's place in it.
3. Be able to discern excessive use of electronic devices from addictive use and hikikomori.
4. Become familiar with the common comorbidities with Internet-based addictions.
5. Discover the most effective methods for treating Internet-based addictions.

CHALLENGING YOUR ASSUMPTIONS ABOUT THIS ADDICTION

1. If you had a son or daughter who became addicted to the Internet or Internet gaming, what steps would you first take to try and either control or stop this behavior? What would you do if that didn't work?
2. If you have a profile on Facebook or another social media platform, think about the times you had an emotional reaction to something that was said or done in response to one of your posts. What did you do in response to your reactions in each instance? How different might it have looked if the social interaction had occurred in the real world instead of the virtual one? How might the outcome have differed?
3. If you found yourself unemployed or otherwise unable to work, what other activities could you engage in besides spending excessive amounts of time in Internet-based activities? In what ways could you use Internet-based activities to help you and in what ways could they hinder you?
4. What thoughts do you have when you see teenagers together that appear so preoccupied with their cell phones that they do not interact with each other?
5. In what ways do the Internet, Internet games, and social media benefit society, and in what ways do they hurt us?

PERSONAL REFLECTIONS

Long before the Internet existed, my mother had become a television addict. It became worse after my father died in 1966. Until her death in 2016, there would hardly be a time you would visit where she wasn't sitting in front of the television. When I was a child and teenager, we ate our dinners consistently off TV folding-tray tables so we could watch the latest serials. Our favorite shows then were *Bewitched*, the *Beverly Hillbillies, Gilligan's Island, Get Smart, I Dream of Jeannie*, the *Partridge Family*, the *Munsters*, and the *Ed Sullivan Show*.

It strikes me that, unlike with my upbringing, most teenagers today do not watch much television. Instead, I see their hands curled up with a phone texting or a controller, engrossed in their device in a way like we never engaged in television. Ride the bus or commuter train in cities today and observe many if not most teenagers and young adults mesmerized by their cell phone and sit in a coffee shop and see the strew of laptops, notebooks, and tablets. Enter a kid's or teenager's basement (or even worse, their bedroom) and see the array of wires and connections to ensure contact is always an icon away.

Sure, growing up, I didn't want to use the washroom except during commercials. I didn't want to be interrupted either during TV viewing, but it wasn't like any of us were in intense concentration, or, if we missed a minute, the world might end. A lost minute in some games does mean the world ends, and the eruption it creates produces a virtual setback in life.

Then there were the "visits" I used to have with James, who would phubb me half the time I was there. I didn't even know what that word meant then: all I knew is that I thought his behavior was rude and offensive.

So now my son plays video games until the wee hours of the morning. I remember his intense interest beginning at about age 15, when I would catch him looking at pop-ups on the computer screen. Oh, the joys of our early home computers. But have those joys been replaced by something far more sinister? Beyond our worry about drugs, should parents also begin scrutinizing where and how much their kids are involved with today's electronic devices? We are now living in a postmodern world, and this chapter tells the story of another worry that is far more covert but equally insidious as drug abuse. I call this new nightmare *Internet-based addictions*.

INSIDE AN ADDICTED PERSON'S MIND

Eugene, Age 18

Hey, my friends usually call me Gene, so you can, too. My parents keep trying to force me to see a shrink, but I don't need one. What I need is for them to leave me alone. For the most part, I have been successful. I have a small room in my parent's basement right next to the furnace. In the past, I had to tell both my mom and dad to get out as they would knock on my door and then barge in before I could even say if I wanted them to enter or not. They are such freaks. They don't do that anymore. My dad said he couldn't stand the smell anymore and told me to start taking a shower at least once a week. But I don't listen to what he says—he doesn't understand how busy I am trying to stay at my level in the online games that I play. Yeah, my room is my castle. Maybe I would come out more often if it wasn't for my parents' attitude and pressure. They say I should spend more time with friends and I'm tired of explaining that I do. I have hundreds of friends that I talk to every day through my video games. It is sad that none of them live in Denver. Sometimes I do wish that I could meet one or more of them, but it's not my fault that they live so far away.

Every day I seem to dislike my parents even more. I would move out, but I dropped out of high school in grade 11, and I don't have a job. I've looked at a few posts online, but they all seem demeaning or disgusting. I refuse to work at a fast food restaurant, and I'm not going to sweep floors either. My dad's a successful lawyer, and I expect something decent as well.

For the last 6 months or so, I only come out of my bedroom to use the washroom and grab some food from upstairs. Don't think that I just play video games because I don't. I'm always listening to tunes and chatting with my online friends, too. My life is balanced except, yeah, I should get more exercise. My hands and arms get plenty of exercise trying to keep up with the fast pace of some of these games, mind you. I even notice my heart beat fast, so I guess I'm getting an aerobic rush from playing with this intensity.

I know I have to start getting out more, and I will do that soon. The games are not giving me the same rush as they did earlier. I am beginning to feel a bit claustrophobic, but, to tell you the truth, I feel even worse after I leave here.

Commentary

As you will learn in this chapter, Eugene would be diagnosed with a condition called *hikikomori*, a new word with Japanese origins. Eugene demonstrates several symptoms of Internet addiction. These include the following: (a) denial of having a problem, (b) projecting blame onto his parents, (c) excessive amounts of time gaming, (d) only making online friends whom he has never met, (e) experiencing several negative consequences, (f) tolerance, (g) anger and irritability, and (h) anxiety. There may be other diagnosable conditions in Eugene's case, but more details would be required.

Discussion

1. Do you know of anyone who you suspect has become dependent on playing online games? If "yes," which symptoms noted in the commentary apply to him or her?
2. Does this person have symptoms that are not listed in the commentary? If so, what are they?
3. If you were Eugene's counselor, how would you go about helping him?

COUNSELING SCENARIO

As you are reading, imagine that you are the client in this scenario. Note the areas in which the session could be improved on the part of the counselor.

Your name is Roger, a 19-year-old student working on an apprenticeship for heavy-duty mechanics. You are finding it hard to study, and you are not sure why this is happening. Like your friends, you play video games with abandon for hours on end, especially on weekends. But you are sure that is not the problem because your friends are students, too, and they are doing well in school. You believe that, if you knew the reason for your study problems, you could become a more effective student. You go to see a counselor at your technical institute. Her name is Hallie, a woman who appears to be close to retirement age. She takes you into her office, tells you where to sit, and then she sits on the other side of a large wide desk, staring at you.

- Counselor: Roger, what can I help you with today?
- You: Thank you for seeing me, Hallie. I am having trouble studying and keeping up with my classes.
- Counselor: Do you know how to study, Roger?
- You: I think so. I just don't seem able to stick with it for any period.
- Counselor: Do you think you may have attentional problems with or without hyperactivity?
- You: Truthfully, I never gave that idea any thought.
- Counselor: How many hours a day do you study?
- You: That is my problem I think. I am lucky if I study for one hour a day.
- Counselor: Why aren't you studying more? You should study two hours for every one hour of class time.
- You: Are you serious? That would mean I should be studying 30 hours or more each week!
- Counselor: What's wrong with that, Roger?
- You: I don't have that kind of time in a week.
- Counselor: Maybe you should be making that amount of time available for school. Why aren't you taking your success seriously?
- You: I am serious about doing well in school, Hallie. I don't know what I am doing wrong.
- Counselor: I am telling you what you are doing wrong. You need to study 30 hours a week!
- You: I came to you to try and understand the reason why I don't study enough.
- Counselor: How many excuses do you want to make for yourself, Roger?
- You: I often feel too tired to study. I don't get enough sleep.
- Counselor: Come on, Roger. Tell me what the solution is to that.
- You: I don't know, pills?
- Counselor: I don't think you are taking any of this seriously.
- You: I have to say, I am feeling even worse than when I came here today. I am having trouble pulling it together.
- Counselor: Stop feeling and start doing. Your time is better spent studying at this point. Finals will be coming up in a couple of weeks, and I doubt that you are going to pass any of your exams.
- You: Thanks for the vote of confidence.
- Counselor: You're welcome. Is there anything else you want to talk to me about today?
- You: No, absolutely not. You have been more than helpful.
- Counselor: Good. I want to see you again in a week.
- You: [you are thinking, "Over my dead body!"] Okay, but right now I have to run to class. Goodbye.
- Counselor: Okay [Hallie does not get out of her chair to see you to the door].

From the Client's Perspective

1. How would you feel if your counselor sat behind a desk the entire session?
2. What is missing for you in this dialogue?
3. What would you find more helpful from a counselor in this scenario?

From the Counselor's Perspective

1. What is interfering with developing a working alliance?
2. Going back to the Common Counseling Mistakes list in Chapter 6, which mistakes is the counselor making with Roger?
3. If you were the counselor, how would you go about conducting a proper assessment of the problem?

Background Information

The Internet, as we know it today, began in 1969 in the United States. This high-speed network was built as an experiment by the U.S. Department of Defense. It linked hundreds of universities, research laboratories, and defense contractors. Today, "the Internet refers to a collection of networks connected by routers" (Schell, 2016, p. 1).

"Over the last 15 years, the number of Internet users has increased by 1,000%" (Kuss & Lopez-Fernandez, 2016, p. 143). Approximately 40% of the world's population now uses the Internet, and six times more people use it daily compared to a decade ago (Kuss & Billieux, 2017). Earlier statistics reported in 2008 suggested that nearly 71% of Americans have regular access to the Internet (Watson, 2015), and as many as 80% of Internet users lose track of time and space (Greenfield, 2011). Studies have reported that people feel less inhibited when online (Greenfield, 2011).

The Entertainment Software Association (ESA; http://www.theesa.com/) annually surveys more than 4000 American households, including the most frequent gamers within each household about their habits and attitudes. Their most salient findings from the 2017 report include the following:

1. At least one member of American households plays video games regularly.
2. The average gamer is 35 years old and those who are 18 or older represent 72% of those who play video games.
3. Adult women constitute 31% of those who play video games compared to 18% of boys under age 18.
4. 71% of parents believe that video games have a positive effect on their children.

The 2017 ESA report also reported that the video game industry contributed $11.7 billion to the U.S. gross domestic product and resulted in the employment of 65,678 Americans and $30.4 billion in consumer spending. The report also highlighted that this is an increase from $23.5 billion in 2015. Gaming has become a major industry in the United States. Milkman and Sunderwirth (2010) reported that online games had exceeded "the motion picture industry in terms of dollars spent" (p. 194). Worldwide, statistics published in 2013 suggested that video games are a $93 billion industry (Griffiths, Kiraly, Pontes, & Demetrovics, 2015).

The origin of the idea that the Internet could be addicting for some people began as a joke. In 1996, Dr. Ivan Goldberg, a New York psychiatrist, commented satirically about the rigidity of the diagnoses in DSM-IV. In his parody of DSM, he created a fictional problem that he called "Internet addiction disorder" (Watson, 2015). Goldberg was surprised as he began receiving several posts from people who felt they or others met the criteria for the disorder. The first person to write about Internet addiction as a legitimate disorder was Dr. Kimberly Young at the annual convention of the American Psychological Association in 1996 (Watson, 2015). Young has continued to be a leading researcher in this area. Dr. Young herself wrote that the concept of Internet addiction began as a "pet project" in her one-bedroom apartment (Young, 2017). Young (2017) commented that today the question is how young is considered too young for children to use the Internet. She wrote that, according to research published in 2013, "more than 30% of children under the age of 2 have used a tablet or smartphone" (Young, 2017, p. 230).

Griffiths (2016) argued that the first reference to video game addiction occurred in 1983 (see Soper & Miller, 1983). Between 2000 and 2010, about 60 empirical studies were published that dealt with various aspects of Internet gaming addiction (Griffiths, Kiraly, Pontes, & Demetrovics, 2015). Facebook, which is the most successful social networking site, was first created for Harvard students in 2004. It has more than 1.19 billion users, and, of these, 50% enter the site daily (Griffiths, Kuss, & Demetrovics, 2014).

"Internet addiction is characterized by excessive or poorly controlled preoccupations, urges or behaviours regarding computer use and internet access that lead to impairment or distress" (Shaw & Black, 2008, p. 353). A simpler and more accurate definition would be compulsive Internet use that results in negative consequences. Some gamers, for example, play for many hours but do not experience negative results from doing so. The amount of time one plays is something people can easily rectify on their own. The hallmark of addiction is the loss of control that addicted individuals experience.

Although the exact nature of Internet addiction remains controversial, researchers agree that it is growing in prevalence globally (Watson, 2015; Young & de Abreu, 2011), and several researchers argue that it is mainly a problem in Asian countries (Tateno et al., 2016). Although Chinese youth used poetry, music, and sports to express their feelings in the past, they now reportedly use electronic games and other web-oriented programs (Young, Yue, & Ying, 2011). Internet gaming has been researched more than the other Internet addictions, and *DSM-5* has included *Internet gaming disorder* (IGD) in their appendix as a possible diagnosable condition following further research.

The question that continues under debate is whether there is one Internet addiction or several related ones. Kimberly Young (1999) was one of the first to study Internet addictions, and she advanced the idea that there are five different types: (a) computer game addiction, (b) cybersex addiction, (c) cyber-relationship addiction (i.e., online relationship addiction), (d) information overload (i.e., addiction to surfing the web), and (e) net compulsions (e.g., online gambling addiction, online shopping addiction).

Other researchers, however, view each Internet addiction as part of a greater whole. Griffiths and Kuss (2015), for example, wrote that some use the term "Internet spectrum addiction disorder" (p. 393). Earlier, Griffiths argued that it is important "to distinguish between addictions *to* the Internet and addictions *on* the Internet (Griffiths, as cited in Griffiths & Kuss, 2015, p. 385).

Research to date, however, has not determined if a spectrum exists or whether there are different types of Internet addiction. For example, Sigerson, Li, Cheung, and Cheng (2017) tested 1001 U.S. adults (56% female, mean age = 35 years) and found that their confirmatory factor analysis indicated there was a common dimension to Internet addiction, thus supporting a spectrum approach. On the other hand, results from a large nationally representative sample of adolescent gamers (N = 2073, mean age = 16.4 years, 68.4% male) found that IGD was distinct from Internet addiction disorder (Kiraly et al., 2014).

Given that IGD is found in *DSM-5* as a condition requiring further study, it will be included in this chapter as a separate possible diagnosis. Furthermore, given that many Internet users utilize it primarily for social media purposes, social media addiction will also be briefly described. Internet searching addiction (or what Young previously called *information overload*) appears to be extremely rare, has been described only in case studies, and therefore will just be briefly mentioned in this chapter. The two Internet addictions that do not fit elsewhere in this book include Internet gaming and social networking addiction. These two addictions will be the primary focus of this chapter. Online pornography addiction is seen as one expression of a sexual addiction, and that is covered in Chapter 16. Likewise, online gambling addiction is primarily about gambling, so it is included in Chapter 14.

Griffiths (2016) reported that studies published before 2000 had methodological shortcomings and furthermore that gaming has evolved significantly over the last 10 years. Consequently, he does not recommend that much focus be placed on studies published before 2000 except those that pertain to the medical and health consequences of excessive video game playing. Consequently, this chapter will also focus on studies published on or after 2000.

Internet Addiction

Johnson and Keane (2017) cautioned against medicalizing individuals who have trouble controlling their online activities.

These authors preferred to understand these activities within their specific social context. This social constructionist view, however, does not appear to be the dominant discourse at present. Instead, the published literature is mostly from a clinical psychological perspective.

Young (2011) theorized that Internet addiction follows four different but interdependent stages. These four stages are as follows:

Stage 1: Rationalization (e.g., "The computer helps me to relax").

Stage 2: Regret (e.g., "I'm not getting any studying done").

Stage 3: Abstinence (e.g., "I will never play a video game again").

Stage 4: Relapse (e.g., "It looks like I'm right back where I started").

Although intuitively it might not seem that anyone would get addicted to searching for information on the Internet, perhaps like people who were called "bookworms" in the past, but some people do become addicted to surfing the Internet (Watson, 2015). Their practice of "aimless wandering" (Watson, 2015, p. 298) can consume many hours. The behavior is not considered problematic unless they become unable to control the number of hours that they spend on the Internet and that they experience negative consequences from it, such as neglect of work and social life and relationship difficulties (Griffiths & Kuss, 2015).

Griffiths and Kuss (2015) suggested that those addicted *to* the Internet will most often use Internet chat rooms, an activity that would not occur if it weren't for the Internet. Their view is that these behaviors would not happen if the Internet did not exist. Griffiths and Kuss wrote that addiction *to* the Internet affects only a tiny percentage of users.

Although many people may use the Internet excessively, most are not addicted as measured by addiction criteria (Griffiths & Kuss, 2015). Research to date has also been criticized in that the measures used do not measure severity, there is no temporal dimension, there is a tendency to overestimate the prevalence of problems, and the content of Internet use is not included (Griffiths & Kuss, 2015). Consequently, this section is focused on studies reporting something akin to generic Internet addiction but, in actuality, these individuals may be addicted to something specific to their Internet use.

Research has shown that several negative emotional states are both associated with and predictive of Internet addiction (Gervasi et al., 2017). When severe enough, some of the following would also be considered comorbid conditions: (a) anxiety, attachment anxiety, health anxiety (i.e., *hypochondriasis*; Jia & Jia, 2016; McNicol & Thorsteinsson, 2017; Scimeca et al., 2017; Younes et al., 2016), (b) depression (Estevez, Urbiola, Iruarrizaga, Onaindia, & Jauregui, 2017; Taymur et al., 2016), and (c) loneliness (Flood, 2016; Zeng, Ye, Hu, & Ma, 2016).

The list of personality traits associated with and predictive of Internet addiction is much longer. These include the following: aggressive (Aboujaoude, 2017), disagreeable (Kayis et al., 2016), disinhibited (Gervasi et al., 2017), emotionally dependent (Estevez, Urbiola, Iruarrizaga, Onaindia, & Jauregui, 2017), impulsive (Shokri, Potenza, & Sanaeepour, 2017), narcissistic (Aboujaoude, 2017), perfectionistic (Taymur et al., 2016), alexithymic (Lyvers, Karantonis, Edwards, & Thorberg, 2016), socially inept (Flood, 2016), low self-esteem (Estevez, Urbiola, Iruarrizaga, Onaindia, & Jauregui, 2017), introverted (Kayis et al., 2016), and neurotic (Kayis et al., 2016). Other traits that may predict a later Internet addiction include having a low degree of openness to new experiences (Kayis et al., 2016), low conscientiousness (Kayis et al., 2016), procrastination (Anam ul & Rafiq, 2016), and psychoticism (Ni, Qian, & Wang, 2017). Inability to regulate emotional states and handle distress is also associated with Internet addiction (Akbari, 2017). Current research suggests that resilience can act as a buffer from developing Internet addiction (Robertson, Yan, & Rapoza, 2018).

Greenfield (2011) commented that the rewarding aspects of the Internet contribute to its addictive nature. Greenfield wrote that, in behavioral terms, the Internet provides a variable ratio reinforcement schedule, which is known for its high resistance to extinction.

Griffiths (2011) outlined several reasons that help maintain online behaviors. His list includes accessibility, affordability, anonymity, convenience, escape, immersion and dissociation, disinhibition, event frequency, interactivity, simulation, and associability. He further stated that disinhibition is one of the Internet's key appeals, as it is indisputable that people become less inhibited on the Internet. Young (2011) noted that problematic Internet use results from interpersonal difficulties (e.g., introversion, having social problems). Many Internet-addicted individuals do not communicate well in face-to-face settings (Young, 2011). Those who are chronically lonely and socially anxious may predispose individuals to become addicted to the Internet (Caplan & High, 2011).

A study with 632 university students revealed that seeking social support as a form of coping with stress is associated with Internet addiction (Odaci & Celik, 2017). The Internet also provides an escape valve for people to forget about their problems and their everyday worries (Watson, 2015). Those who continue using it to escape their problems may be more at risk of developing an Internet addiction. Young, Yue, and Ying (2011) argued that, like alcoholics, Internet-addicted individuals use the Internet to dull their pain. Eidenbenz (2011) stated that the Internet is not the cause of Internet addiction but instead is a symptom of having a primary disorder such as depression or a personality disorder.

In a study of 828 middle school students in China, those who had at least one harsh parent were more likely to become dependent on the Internet (Wang & Qi, 2017). Attachment style has also been studied in a sample of 245 participants. Those participants measured to have an insecure attachment style were more likely to develop pathological Internet usage compared to those with secure attachments. Those with an ambivalent attachment style, however, were even more likely to become addicted to the Internet (Eichenberg, Schott, Decker, & Sindelar, 2017).

The exact prevalence of Internet addiction in the United States is unknown due to problems with definition and the different measures (Karim & Chaudhri, 2012). In a recent survey of students attending 25 schools (N = 2022), the prevalence of problematic Internet use was found to be 14.2% among males and 10.1% among females. The highest prevalence was among 15-year-old males and 14-year-old females (Vigna-Taglianti et al., 2017). A 12-month longitudinal study with 8286 Chinese secondary school students found that the prevalence and incidence of Internet addiction were 16.0% and 11.1%, respectively, at baseline (Lau, Gross, Wu, Cheng,

& Lau, 2017). In an even larger sample of Spanish adolescents (N = 40,955), the prevalence of problematic Internet use was 16.3% (Gomez, Rial, Brana, Golpe, &Varela, 2017).

In Jordan, the prevalence of severe Internet addiction in a sample of youth aged 12–18 years (n = 716) was 6.3% (Malak, Khalifeh, & Shuhaiber, 2017). Mihara et al. (2016) measured the prevalence of problematic Internet use in adolescents in Japan. Using a nationwide sample including 100,050 students randomly selected from junior and senior high schools, the estimated prevalence was 6.2% in males, 9.8% in females, and 7.9% in total. Other studies find a higher percentage in males over females (e.g., 12.3% in males and 4.9% in females in 5249 grade 7 to grade 12 students in Anhui province, China; Chen et al., 2016).

The differences in percentages found in different studies are likely the result of the use of various measuring instruments and perhaps cultural nuances as well. Nonetheless, overall these percentages fit well with Young's (as cited in Watson, 2015) estimate that 6%–15% of the general population exhibits symptoms of Internet addiction that may require clinical intervention. Data from two large cross-sectional school-based studies conducted in 2009/2010 and 2011/2012 in five European countries confirmed the problematic Internet use is increasing among European adolescents (two samples with total N = 15,597, approximately 55% female, approximate mean age = 15 years; Kaess et al., 2016).

Internet Gaming Disorder

Most people have entered an arcade at some time in their life to play video games and flip over some pinball. Like computers, these games eventually ended up in households in the form of game consoles. The three most popular consoles include Sony's PlayStation, Microsoft's Xbox, and Nintendo (Statista, 2018b). Each of these has versions designed for online play (e.g., Microsoft's Xbox Live, Sony's PlayStation Network, Nintendo's Nintendo Wi-Fi Connection, Nintendo Network). Online games today can be played from virtually any electronic media device.

More than 70% of gamers prefer to play online as opposed to offline, and online players spend more time at it (Kiraly, Nagygyorgy, Griffiths, & Demetrovics, 2014). Unsurprisingly, online gamers are more likely to develop problematic use (Kiraly, Nagygyorgy, Griffiths, & Demetrovics, 2014). Lemmens and Hendriks (2016) examined nine videogame genres to review their addictive potential. They found that, compared to offline games, online games had a much stronger correlation with IGD.

Lewis (2017) estimated that there are 19 million online gamers worldwide. A recent online survey of 4374 online players (mean age = 21 years, 91% male, 66% single) provides some valuable insights (Nagygyorgy et al., as cited in Griffiths, 2016). The average weekly game time was reported as between 7 hours (10%) and more than 42 hours (also 10%). Most gamers played between 15 and 27 hours a week (35%). Also, 16% of the surveyed players played professionally, which meant they played in competitions and earned money.

Playing video games is not inherently pathological by any stretch. According to Pontes and Griffiths (2017), there is a substantial body of literature that shows several positive outcomes from gaming in moderation. Gaming can lead to an improvement in prosocial behaviors andenhance life satisfaction and it can lower the level of internalizing and externalizing problems in children and adolescents. Gaming can also predict creativity. It can lead to increased selective attention and help prevent cognitive decline in seniors. Games can also be used for educational, medical, and therapeutic reasons. Sioni, Burleson, and Bekerian (2017) wrote that Internet gaming provides opportunities for people to connect socially that and the games can enhance self-esteem.

A recent study based on interviews with 20 participants and an analysis of survey data (N = 3629) found that highly involved video game players (i.e., intense gaming involvement) experience the greatest psychosocial benefits from their engagement in gaming. This included more positive play experiences and a greater sense of social inclusion and support (Snodgrass et al., 2018). Again, it is critical to establish that highly engaged players are not necessarily individuals experiencing IGD.

Types of games.

Gamers can indulge in a wide variety of games across a range of game genres. Three of the most popular genres include role-playing games (RPGs), first-person shooter (FPS) games, and real-time strategy (RTS) games (Statista, 2018a). The three genres mentioned are the most frequently associated with IGD (Eichenbaum, Kattner, Bradford, Gentile, & Green, 2015; Na et al., 2017).

1. Massively multiplayer online role-playing games (MMORPGs, or simply RPGs). Popular examples include World of Warcraft, Guild Wars, EverQuest, and Final Fantasy.

   Blinka and Smahel (2011) described some of the features of these games and the people who play them. These games create a virtual world and allow players to explore and create an alternate reality that expands continually. The games have no end, and they continue to exist after the player logs off. In fact, if the player is absent for an extended period, they become out of touch and lose their influence and power in the virtual world. Over time, the player's avatar gains experience and obtains better equipment. Equipment gradually becomes obsolete, and therefore a player needs to continue playing to acquire new equipment. Online gaming is a social activity, and, in fact, solo play is not encouraged. There is an emphasis on communication and cooperation with other players.

   The average age of MMORPG players is around 25 years. Adult players outnumber adolescent players. Most of the gamers are men. The average age of a female player is 32. Statistics suggest that up to 11% of players spend over 40 hours per week playing video games and that 80% of players play over 8 hours in one session at least occasionally. Furthermore, adolescent players will play the game for approximately 2 years and adult players for 27 months (Blinka & Smahel, 2011).

   Hussain, Williams, and Griffiths (2015) sampled 1167 gamers to find out about their gaming motivations. The analysis revealed that the main motivations for playing MMORPGs included socializing, exploring, and novelty-seeking.

   Arguably the most significant difference between these games and other computer games is that MMORPGs are played for 25 hours per week on average compared to other games where the percentage of people playing more than 20 hours a week is only 6% (Blinka & Smahel, 2011). Also, in other games, most people play less than 6 hours per week (84%; Blinka & Smahel, 2011).

Individuals with poor self-esteem find these games very appealing as they provide rapid relief. Players of these games will often daydream about the game, their characters, and various scenarios within the game itself. Those who become addicted individuals may be motivated by a desire to express a full self, something they may lack in reality (Blinka & Smahel, 2011).

Not all MMORPGs are games per se. Second Life, for example, is a simulation game that is often viewed by players as a "second life" (Blinka & Smahel, 2011, p. 73).

2. Massively multiplayer online first-person shooter (MMOFPS, or simply FPS games). Popular examples include Wolfenstein 3D, Doom, Duke Nukem 3D, Descent, and Marathon.

   These are action games in which the player uses a single avatar from a first-person perspective. They require good reaction time and attention abilities and can be played either cooperatively or competitively. The player typically oversees large troops and/or territories, fights and battles, or creates alliances with other players. Players can establish status in the game and garner esteem from other players.

3. Massively multiplayer online real-time strategy games (MMORTS, or simply RTS games). Popular examples include StarCraft and Age of Empires.

   These games have been a staple since the mid-1990s. They are typically played on a PC and require the use of the mouse and keyboard controls. The player will often assume the role of the general, king, or some other figurehead and lead an army into combat while ensuring that adequate resources are maintained to continue the fight. The games are often situated in a science fiction or fantasy universe.

Lemmens and Hendriks (2016) had 1921 respondents report on the video games that they played. The respondents were divided into two groups. One group received the IGD survey with dichotomous response categories (i.e., "yes" or "no"), and the other group responded with a 6-point Likert scale (range from *never* to *almost daily*). Respondents reported playing 3272 video games for which 2720 could be assigned to one of nine genres (in order of how often these games were reported): (a) action/adventure, (b) sports, (c) RPGs, (d) strategy, (e) simulation, (f) puzzle, (g) shooter, (h) racing, and (i) fighting. Players spent the most *time* playing shooters followed by action/ adventure with RPGs in third place. The four most popular games were Call of Duty, FIFA, Candy Crash Saga, and the Sims. After performing multiple linear regressions, Lemmens and Hendriks found that the games most associated with IGD were in descending order: (a) RPGs, (b) shooter, (c) action, and (d) simulation. Although puzzle and action games are popular yet weakly related to IGD, RPGs are not very popular yet are strongly related to IGD. Some genres of games appear to have a higher addiction potential. Lemmens and Hendriks reported neither on how they constructed the IGD scale nor on the limitations of their study.

The most popular game in 2018 was reportedly Fortnite Battle Royale (Campbell, 2018). Campbell (2018) reported 25 reasons that the game became such a hit. His reasons were categorized into the following main headings: (a) the game is eminently shareable, (b) it has a smart design, (c) it is easy and free of cost, (d) it has depth and sophistication, and (e) it provides a way for friends to interact throughout the world.

Addictive potential.

Using the results from four survey studies ($N = 18{,}932$), Przybylski, Weinstein, and Murayama (2017) found that, among those who played games, more than two out of three reported no symptoms of IGD. The authors concluded that only a small percentage of the general population (between 0.3% and 1.0%) might qualify for a diagnosis. They also concluded that online games are significantly less addictive than gambling.

Distinguishing between highly engaged players and addicted individuals is essential. Lehenbauer-Baum and Fohringer (2017) surveyed 577 participants (mean age 24.38 years, 77.1% male). In the sample, 93.7% was considered high-level players (level 85—at the time this was the highest level in World of Warcraft). They found that addicted players spent on average 31.31 hours per week playing games compared to those who were classified as highly engaged players, who played for 22.19 hours per week. Only 3.1% were addicted according to scores on the Internet Addiction Scale.

Errity et al. (2016) stated that the controversy surrounding video game behavior boils down to two questions:

1. Does playing for excessive lengths of time classify as an addiction or is it over-enthusiastic behavior—i.e., is the behavior pathological or problematic?
2. Does playing (violent) video games have a genuine and lasting effect on (aggressive) behavior in real life? (p. 264)

After 25 years of research on violent video games, there is no evidence to support a strong causal link between video game use and acts of violence. Empirical evidence to date provides mixed results (Elson & Ferguson, as cited in Errity et al., 2016).

A qualitative study of nine people seeking treatment for Internet gaming addiction revealed reasons that they played despite experiencing negative consequences (Beranuy, Carbonell, & Griffiths, 2013). Their reasons fit into three central themes: (a) entertainment, (b) escapism, and/or (c) online friendships.

In a study of 394 participants (50% male), social connection and approval were strong motivators for gamers to play, especially for those who reported symptoms of social phobia (Sioni, Burleson, & Bekerian, 2017). Consequently, gaming-addicted individuals do make more new, online friends compared with nonaddicted individuals (Chrismore, Betzelberger, Bier, & Camacho, 2011).

Another study found that problematic gamers had higher motivation to socialize, achieve, and immerse themselves compared to the nonproblematic players (Khan & Muqtadir, 2016). In a sample of 630 adult gamers, 4% screened positive for IGD (King, Herd, & Delfabbro, 2018). What distinguished the addicted individuals from the nonaddicted individuals was that the addicted individuals were motivated by wealth (achieving in-game rewards of increasing rarity, novelty, or quantity), achievement (pursuing activities with increased complexity, difficulty, or uniqueness), and inadequacy (needing to correct a perceived insufficiency, inability, or progress; King et al., 2018).

Similar to the previous section focused on generic Internet addiction, many studies have focused on personality qualities or factors that may predict the development of IGD. It is essential to keep in mind that these are correlational studies and therefore cannot reveal causation. The earlier one begins playing online games, the more likely symptoms of IGD will develop (Beard, Haas, Wickham, & Stavropoulos, 2017). Compared to nonaddicted individuals, Internet gaming-addicted individuals are more likely to

1. Be impulsive and have an impaired ability to postpone rewards (Nuyens et al., 2016).
2. Avoid social interactions presumably because of having fears of social rejection (Weinstein, Abu, Timor, & Mama, 2016).
3. Be socially inhibited and have low emotional intelligence (Griffiths & Kuss, 2015).
4. Have diminished emotional stability (Kiraly, Nagygyorgy, Griffiths, & Demetrovics, 2014).
5. Report lower life satisfaction (Kiraly, Nagygyorgy, Griffiths, & Demetrovics, 2014).
6. Experience state anxiety, trait anxiety, social anxiety, dysfunctional attachment to others, and overdependency (Mehroof & Griffiths, 2010; Skarupova & Blinka, 2016; Vanzoelen & Caltabiano, 2016).
7. Have trait anhedonia (i.e., the inability to experience pleasure from typically enjoyable activities) (Guillot et al., 2016).
8. Have low self-esteem and low self-worth (Flood, 2016).
9. Play to avoid negative moods and everyday problems (Ballabio et al., 2017; Cross, 2017).
10. Procrastinate (Yeh et al., 2017).
11. Display impaired and/or risky decision-making ability (Yao, Chen, et al., 2015; Yao, Wang, et al., 2015).
12. Be neurotic (Mehroof & Griffiths, 2010).
13. Display aggressiveness, hostility, and diminished agreeableness (Griffiths & Kuss, 2015).
14. Show diminished self-control (Griffiths & Kuss, 2015).
15. Present with avoidant, schizoid, schizotypal, and/or narcissistic tendencies (Griffiths & Kuss, 2015; Schimmenti, Infanti, Badoud, Laloyaux, & Billieux, 2017).

When gaming-addicted individuals cannot play, they are often consumed by thoughts, fantasies, and daydreams about gaming instead of doing what is expected of them (Kiraly, Nagygyorgy, Griffiths, & Demetrovics, 2014). If they cannot play, they become increasingly restless, irritable, and moody (Kiraly, Nagygyorgy, Griffiths, & Demetrovics, 2014). Internet gaming addiction develops gradually (Kiraly, Nagygyorgy, Griffiths, & Demetrovics, 2014).

Although playing for escapism is related in some studies to gaming-addicted individuals (Ballabio et al., 2017; Cross, 2017), a recent dissertation using 5 years of cross-sectional data from the Korean Video Gaming Survey found that escapism was not an important motivator for gaming-addicted individuals (Lee, 2018).

Anderson (2017) identified eight factors, which he calls gaming mechanics, that make a game potentially addictive. In his view, not all games are equally addictive. He believed that the more gaming mechanics and amount of each mechanic a specific game includes, the higher its addictive potential. Some games are designed so that a person cannot play them without using all of the addictive mechanics. The example Anderson provided here is World of Warcraft. The following are the eight gaming mechanics followed by a brief description of each:

1. Level grinding. This refers to the playing time required to perform repetitive tasks to progress through the game. The most common example is killing the same set of opponents repeatedly to gain experience or gold.
2. Twitch. This refers to high-speed gameplay that distinguishes victory from defeat. These games move at a heart-pounding pace.
3. Guilds and leagues. These capitalize on social motivation. A league is where gamers enter tiers of competition against one another or as a guild involves players teaming up to achieve common goals.
4. Social status. This becomes another way to build social status besides guilds and leagues. Gaming platforms like Xbox Live have found ways to connect players in communities even when they are not playing together online.
5. Fantasy alter egos. Although some video games allow the player to assume only a predetermined role, others will enable the player to create a character carefully. Anderson (2017) believed that gamers might create a character that compensates for the things that they are not and/or play out fantasies of being the object of their desires.
6. Long gaming epochs. A gaming epoch is the amount of time required before the status quo changes from the start of a given gaming episode. In other words, this is the point at which gamers know they are better off when they began playing the game on a particular day. Once reached, this is often a good place to end the game for today.
7. Interrupted flow. Flow is a state that is attained when someone becomes completely absorbed in an activity that leads to enhanced vitality, awareness, and fulfillment. Several factors need to be present to qualify as a flow experience. These include having challenging goals, needing intense concentration, feeling intrinsic rewards, feeling serene, feeling timeless, getting immediate feedback, knowing the task is challenging but doable, feeling personal control over the situation and outcome, becoming unaware of physical needs (e.g., you could continue without sleeping or eating), and the activity creates complete focus toward itself.
8. Infinity. The unfolding game can seem hypnotic, and, as one anticipates an end, there is none. The game is open-ended and continues indefinitely.

Eidenbenz (2011) hypothesized that gamers immerse themselves in fighting heroic battles because they have no voice in their own families. There appears to be no empirical research currently to support this opinion.

A recent manuscript reported prevalence results from national surveys of gaming disorder/addiction (Saunders et al., 2017). Saunders et al. (2017) reported prevalence rates of 10%–15% among young people in several Asian countries and prevalence rates of 1%–10% in some Western countries. In a nationally representative sample of 12- to 25-year olds in Germany ($N = 1531$), the prevalence of IGD was 5.7%, which rose to 7% when a sensitivity analysis was conducted. The prevalence was higher in males than in females: 8.4% versus 2.9%, respectively.

Social Media Addiction

Ozer (2015) stated that, since 2008, the use of social networking sites now constitutes the highest proportion of time spent on the Internet. Social networking has become big business. Leading the pack is Facebook, with 1.4 billion people logging onto it daily (Noyes, 2018). It constitutes the biggest social networking site globally. Also high on the list are YouTube, Twitter, Instagram, LinkedIn, Reddit, VK, Tumblr, Pinterest, Google+, Flickr, Meetup, and MySpace, to name a few.

These sites facilitate social interaction among both people who are familiar and those who are strangers. Interestingly, when it comes to communicating with strangers, less than 2% of individuals believe that others are honest in online venues, particularly when it comes to appearance (90%) and to a lesser extent gender (55%) (sample comprising 272 American adults, average age = 32 years; Drouin, Miller, Wehle, & Hernandez, 2016)! A frequent comment made was that "everyone lies on the Internet" (Drouin et al., 2016, p. 134).

Even when looking at Facebook sites of familiar people, a type of deception occurs. People post photos and commentary that create an impression that their lives are better than they are (de Vries & Kuhne, 2015). In a Danish study involving 1095 participants, about half were assigned to a control group (i.e., use Facebook as usual) and the other half to the experimental group (i.e., do not use Facebook for a week). The researchers found that the group that didn't use Facebook for a week reported higher life satisfaction than the control group (Tromholt, Lundby, Andsbjergand, & Wiking, 2015).

There is no question that social networking sites have provided an unprecedented opportunity for people to stay in touch who otherwise wouldn't. It has also created a haven for those who prefer online social interaction. There is evidence that social networking sites promote identity development by providing a virtual laboratory where individuals can learn independence and social skills and try on different identities while at the same time receive peer acceptance and improve their sense of self-worth (Tzavela & Mavromati, 2013).

Nonetheless, social media has created an unprecedented fear of missing out (FOMO). In fact, FOMO was added to the Oxford English Dictionary in 2013, which is defined as an "anxiety that an exciting or interesting event may currently be happening elsewhere, often aroused by posts seen on social media" (from https://en.oxforddictionaries.com/definition/fomo). Three quarters of young adults experience FOMO (Przybylski, Murayama, DeHaan, & Gladwell, 2013), and research has shown that FOMO makes people feel worse about themselves (Przybylski et al., 2013).

For some, the drive to stay in touch with others is itself so intoxicating that addiction results. Griffiths, Kuss, and Demetrovics (2014) described three models to explain social media addiction. The cognitive-behavioral model emphasized maladaptive cognitions that become amplified by environmental factors, which in turn lead to compulsive or addictive social networking behavior. The social skills model underscored the notion that addicted individuals lack social skills and therefore prefer online communication to face-to-face communication, which over time leads to addictive behavior. The socio-cognitive model underlined the expectation of deriving a positive outcome together with having good Internet skills that are not self-regulated, which then becomes compulsive or addictive over time. Each of these models may help explain the acquisition of social media addiction in some individuals.

Who is most likely to become a social media addict? Social media-addicted individuals are more likely to be younger, female, single, and narcissistic; have neurotic tendencies and lower self-esteem; and fear missing out on something if they don't stay on top of what's occurring in their electronic social universe (Andreassen, Pallesen, & Griffiths, 2017; Blackwell, Leaman, Tramposch, Osborne, & Liss, 2017).

As mentioned, narcissism is associated with social media addiction, although the type of narcissism implicated is equivocal. The study of narcissism has benefited from recent studies demonstrating that there are two types: grandiose and vulnerable. *Grandiose narcissism*, also referred to as "overt," is displayed by an arrogant person with high self-esteem who needs and seeks admiration by others. *Vulnerable narcissism*, also referred to as either "covert" or "hypersensitive," is characterized as a defensive and insecure style of grandiosity displayed by a shy, shame-prone, insecure person who has low self-esteem and is hypersensitive to the evaluation of others (Casale, Fioravanti, & Rugai, 2016).

A study of 535 students suggested that vulnerable narcissism is more likely to lead to problematic social networking use than to grandiose narcissism (Casale, Fioravanti, & Rugai, 2016). A more recent study by Casale and Fioravanti (2018) did not find a relationship between vulnerable narcissism and Facebook addiction. Instead, they found Facebook addiction was associated with grandiose narcissism but that this was entirely mediated by the need for admiration and the need to belong. This would suggest that admiration and needing to belong explain social media addiction more than narcissism itself.

In a study of 590 undergraduate students, those who felt shame were more likely to experience problematic social networking site use (Casale & Fioravanti, 2017). Personality traits of high extraversion and low conscientiousness are also predictive of having addictive tendencies to social media (Griffiths & Kuss, 2015).

A study from Serbia ($N = 2014$) found that people with lower self-esteem, lower sense of self-efficacy, and higher introversion were more likely to report social networking addiction (Milosevic-Dordevic & Zezelj, 2014). In the Czech Republic, youth between ages 12 and 26 ($N = 394$) were more at risk of social networking addiction if they had more online friends, preferred online communication, and spent more time online (Smahel, Brown, & Blinka, 2012). In a group of 499 Chinese college students, individuals who scored high on psychological resilience were less likely to report problematic social networking use (Hou et al., 2017).

The prevalence of social media addiction is currently unknown. Griffiths and Kuss (2015) reviewed the results from several studies and reported a wide variation, from 1.6% to 34% prevalence.

Facebook.

Although Facebook use can improve one's psychological well-being, too much time spent on it is associated with lower self-esteem. Furthermore, over time, Facebook seems to have an adverse effect on subjective well-being, thereby reducing life satisfaction (Young, Kuss, Griffiths, & Howard, 2017). Some researchers distinguish between active Facebook use (i.e., using it to communicate with others) and passive Facebook use (using it for its content, such as viewing other people's photos). Research suggests that active use decreases feelings of loneliness and passive use increases them (Young, Kuss, Griffiths, & Howard, 2017).

Sofiah, Zobidah, Bolong, and Osman (as cited in Griffiths, Kuss, & Demetrovics, 2014) surveyed 380 female university students, aged 19–28 years, in Malaysia regarding their motives for using Facebook. The five motivations included social interaction, passing time, entertainment, companionship, and communication. The researchers also found that there was a relationship between these motives and Facebook addiction: passive time was most predictive followed by entertainment and communication motives. Other reasons for using Facebook reported in the literature include affection, fashion, sharing problems, social information, information-seeking, escape, and professional advancement (Young, Kuss, Griffiths, & Howard, 2017).

It is not merely a matter of how much time a person spends on Facebook that is problematic. In a study of 489 respondents, having symptoms of Facebook addiction was not associated with the amount of time spent on it (Muench, Hayes, Kuerbis, & Shao, 2015). The authors suggested that intervention needs to be targeted at the addict's underlying loss of control.

A study in India of 100 postgraduate students found that loneliness was associated with Facebook addiction (Shettar, Karkal, Kakunje, Mendonsa, & Chandran, 2017). Using Facebook as a means of escapism is also associated with addiction (Young, Kuss, Griffiths, & Howard, 2017). In two Polish studies of 631 and 452 participants, respectively, results indicated that excessive Facebook use was associated with lower scores on conscientiousness, openness to experience, and emotional stability (Blachnio & Przepiorka, 2016b). In another study of 284 participants by Blachnio and Przepiorka (2016a), those who are most resistant to Facebook addiction were able to resist impulses or temptations, were more self-disciplined, and did not focus on negative emotions.

Mobile phones.

Approximately 40% of young adults use their cell phones for more than 4 hours a day (Young & de Abreu, 2011). The use of mobile phones by children and adolescents has dramatically increased (Shin, 2017). A published case study reported a young woman named "Anette" who used her cell phone for about 8 hours every day (Kormendi, Brutoczki, Vegh, & Szekely, 2016).

The cell phone behavior of some individuals has created a new word in our vocabulary: "nomophobia" (Flood, 2016). *Nomophobia* is a term that refers to the fear of not having access to a usable cell phone (e.g., rundown battery, out of range of a cell tower, forgetting or losing the cell phone). One can only imagine the dark fear that pervades the mind of someone who is addicted to their cell phone. Another new term that has entered the scene due to smartphones is "phubbing." *Phubbing* refers to "snubbing someone in a social setting by concentrating on one's phone instead of talking to the person directly" (Chotpitayasunondh & Douglas, 2016, p. 9).

Smartphone addiction in children and adolescents may be a consequence of personality traits (e.g., low self-esteem, loneliness, negative emotions), social reasons (e.g., lack of parental support), and technological factors (e.g., advanced gaming technology, high-resolution screens) (Shin, 2017). Other studies have shown that smartphone-addicted individuals score higher on anxiety, narcissism, and neuroticism (Hussain, Griffiths, & Sheffield, 2017; Pearson & Hussain, 2015). Addicted smartphone users have lower levels of conscientiousness, openness, and emotional stability, and they tend to be younger (Hussain, Griffiths, & Sheffield, 2017). In their review of 23 peer-reviewed papers, Elhai, Dvorak, Levine, and Hall (2017) found that problematic smartphone use was associated in these studies with anxiety, chronic stress, depression, and low self-esteem. Duke and Montag (2017) surveyed 262 participants and found that smartphone addiction had a substantially adverse effect on productivity in both the home and workplace.

The prevalence of social media addiction and smartphone addiction has been measured in several studies. Using a nationally representative Hungarian sample of 5961 adolescents, the Bergen Social Media Addiction Scale revealed that 4.5% scored in the at-risk category (Banyai et al., 2016). In a study of 490 middle school students, 128 (26.61%) of these adolescents were deemed to be at high risk of smartphone addiction (Lee et al., 2018). In a 2016 study of 1441 undergraduate students attending a medical college in China, it was ascertained that the prevalence of smartphone addiction among participants was 29.8% (30.3% in males, 29.3% in females; Chen et al., 2017). Lopez-Fernandez (2017) found lower rates of smartphone addiction in his sample of 281 Spanish and 144 Francophone Belgian adults (i.e., 12.5% and 21.5%, respectively).

Diagnostic and Assessment Considerations

Internet addiction.

As Suler (2004) aptly described it, Internet addictions are as problematic as the degree to which they disrupt a person's ability to function in the real world. Although the controversy surrounding diagnostic criteria for IGD remains strong, disagreement regarding a generic Internet addiction is even more contentious. Musetti et al. (2016) insisted that the construct of generic Internet addiction is "too broad and generic to be explicative for a diagnosis" (p. 1). Starcevic and Billieux (2017) argued that the umbrella term "Internet addiction" is adequate because it overlooks differences among the plethora of online activities, whereas Kuss, Griffiths, and Pontes (2017) focused their discussion on distinguishing between IGD and generic Internet addiction.

Kimberly Young was arguably the first to suggest criteria for generic Internet addiction in a paper that she presented at the American Psychological Association convention in 1996 (Watson, 2015). Her criteria were based on a modified version of the then-current DSM criteria for pathological gambling. Internet addiction was defined by Young as five or more of the following symptoms:

1. Preoccupied with the Internet (i.e., salience).
2. Needing more time on the Internet to get the same degree of satisfaction required earlier (i.e., tolerance).
3. Unsuccessful attempts to cut down use (i.e., loss of control).

4. Feeling restless or irritable when attempting to cut back (i.e., withdrawal).
5. Being online much longer than intended (i.e., salience).
6. Engaging in secretive behaviors/lying about online pursuits (i.e., deception).
7. Subjective distress or dysfunction in consequence of this behavior (i.e., continuing despite harmful consequences).
8. Using the Internet to self-medicate (i.e., using it to escape or cope with problems).

One other criterion suggested by Tao (as cited in Rosenberg, O'Connor, & Carnes, 2014) was a loss of interest in non-Internet activities. Watson (2015) wrote that criteria for Internet addiction generally involves aspects of excessive use, withdrawal symptoms, tolerance, and adverse consequences. Young, Yue, and Ying (2011) included three criteria that a Chinese organization included in a 2005 report: (a) believing that it would be easier to self-actualize online than in real life, (b) experiencing dysphoria or depression when unable to access the Internet, and (c) hiding one's actual usage time from family members.

Griffiths (2005) also created criteria that could be used for diagnosing either Internet addiction or Internet gaming addiction. These six criteria have been described in Chapter 3. I will only mention them here: salience, mood change, tolerance, withdrawal symptoms, conflict, and relapse and reinstatement.

Internet gaming disorder.

It is important to remember that intense video gaming is not, in and of itself, an issue requiring intervention. Based on their sample of 5222 (mean age = 22.2 years) online gamers, Kiraly, Toth, Urban, Demetrovics, and Maraz (2017) concluded that the length of time engaged in gaming is not a reliable predictor of its being problematic. In the same year, however, Lehenbauer-Baum and Fohringer (2017) concluded that gaming-addicted individuals spend on average 31.31 hours per week playing games, whereas highly engaged players spend only 22.19 hours per week. Griffiths and Kuss (2015) had clarified earlier that problematic use is about spending too much time and energy in gaming, but it is also about feeling euphoria, experiencing tolerance, being in denial, and having a preference for online relationships. Griffiths and Kuss also emphasized that the core criteria of addiction involve conflict, withdrawal symptoms, relapse, reinstatement, and behavioral salience. At the same time, they delegated cognitive salience, tolerance, and euphoria to a peripheral level of importance.

Hajela and Love (2017) surmised that APA's decision to discard the idea of generic Internet addiction in favor of basing a diagnosis on one of its subtypes (i.e., IGD) is creating more confusion. But it is not just APA. The World Health Organization has included gaming disorder in ICD-11 (see Table 15.1). Bean, Nielsen, van Rooij, and Ferguson (2017) cautioned against this, claiming that there is some research that indicates the idea of video game addiction is not a stable concept and that clinical impairment might be quite low.

Along these lines, Kardefelt-Winther (2014) tested a theory of compensatory Internet use that excessive online gamers do so to cope with psychosocial problems. Of the total sample of 898 online players, 196 had to be excluded from the analysis due to missing data. His final sample included 702 participants (age range = 14–60, 89% male). The results from his study supported the theory, and Kardefelt-Winther concluded that excessive online gaming is not a mental disorder as proposed in *DSM-5* but is instead a coping method for dealing with life problems. Conversely, Mann, Kiefer, Schellekens, and Dom (2017) argued that, although most of the so-called behavioral addictions are not addictions at all, there are two exceptions: gambling and gaming disorder.

TABLE 15.1 DSM and ICD Codes

DSM Code	Number of Symptoms Required	ICD-10	ICD-11
None	Severity not established	N/A	6C51*
None	Severity not established	N/A	6C51*
None	Severity not established	N/A	6C51*

*The gaming codes in ICD-11 mostly begin with 6C51, as follows:

#	Specific Entity	Specific ICD-11 Code
1	Gaming disorder, unspecified	6C51.Z
2	Hazardous gaming	QE22
3	Gaming disorder, predominantly online	6C51.0
4	Gaming disorder, predominantly offline	6C51.1

IGD can be found on pages 795–797 in Section III (i.e., Emerging Measures and Models) of *DSM-5* (APA, 2013). As is true for other substance disorders contained in DSM, in contrast to DSM-IV, a diagnosis distinguishing between *substance abuse* and *substance dependence* no longer occurs. Instead, a substance disorder is diagnosed by *severity* (i.e., by the number of diagnosable symptoms) as follows: (a) *mild*: 2 to 3, (b) *moderate*: 4 to 5, or (c) *severe*: 6 or more. *DSM-5* includes 11 listed criteria with two specifiers.

The overall diagnostic criteria for IGD is "persistent and recurrent use of the Internet to engage in games, often with other players, leading to clinically significant impairment or distress" (APA, 2013, p. 795).

The specific criteria include five or more of the following:

1. Becoming preoccupied with Internet gaming (i.e., salience).
2. Experiencing withdrawal symptoms when not playing (i.e., withdrawal).
3. Experiencing tolerance (i.e., tolerance).
4. Making unsuccessful attempts to control use (i.e., relapse/loss of control).
5. Developing a loss of interest in previous activities (i.e., conflict).
6. Continuing use despite knowing it causes problems (i.e., conflict).
7. Deceiving others (i.e., conflict).

8. Playing games on the Internet to avoid negative feelings (i.e., mood modification).
9. Experiencing the loss or jeopardization of a substantial relationship, job, education, or career in consequence of Internet gaming (i.e., conflict).

Gamers have their view of what makes for an Internet gaming addict. Colder Carras et al. (2018) led two focus groups at a video game convention and asked participants to submit suggestions for signs of gaming addiction. The strongest agreement between their suggested criteria and the proposed *DSM-5* criteria for IGD included usage creating harm, functional impairment, continuing to use despite problems, unsuccessful attempts to control gaming, and loss of interest in previous activities.

Social media addiction.

Carbonell and Panova (2017) argued that there is not enough empirical evidence to claim that social networking addiction exists. They emphasized that it is important to distinguish between true addictive disorders and appealing activities like use of social networking sites. They believed that to do so is to undermine the severity of psychiatric disorders. Their warning has not been enough to deter others from creating criteria for at least what in the colloquial has come to be known as social media or social networking addiction.

Griffiths, Kuss, and Demetrovics (2014) included the criteria that Griffiths developed in 2005 regarding his six core components of addiction and applied these to social networking addiction. Examples of each follow:

1. Salience. Social networking becomes their most important activity and dominates their thinking.
2. Mood modification. The subjective experience of either feeling aroused (e.g., a buzz or high) or calm (e.g., escape or numbing) through use.
3. Tolerance. The amount of time spent on social networking increases.
4. Withdrawal symptoms. If unable to social network, addicted individuals may experience shakiness, moodiness, or irritability.
5. Conflicts. The addicted individual may experience interpersonal conflicts, conflicts between networking and doing other activities, or intrapsychic conflicts (e.g., feeling a loss of control, belief they are spending too much time on it).
6. Relapse. The addicted individual returns to previous levels of use after having slowed down for a period.

Lin et al. (2016) proposed the following criteria for smartphone addiction:

I. Criterion A. Criterion A concerns maladaptive use of smartphones that leads to significant impairment or distress within the same 3-month period. Three or more of the following symptoms have to be present:
   1. Repeated failure to resist the impulse to use the smartphone.
   2. Feeling dysphoric, anxious, and/or irritable after a period of not using it (i.e., withdrawal).
   3. Using for longer than intended.
   4. Continuing desire and/or unsuccessful attempts to stop or reduce usage.
   5. Excessive time devoted to either using or quitting the smartphone.
   6. Continued use despite having negative consequences (e.g., recurring physical or psychological problem from overuse).

II. Criterion B. Criterion B concerns functional impairment, and two or more of the following symptoms must be present:
   1. Continued use despite the occurrence of persistent or recurrent physical or psychological problems.
   2. Continuing to use in physically hazardous situations (e.g., while driving, crossing the street) or experiencing other negative impacts in one's daily life.
   3. Continued use leading to impairment in social relationships, academic achievement, or at work.
   4. Continued use causes substantial subjective distress or consumes excessive amounts of time.

III. Criterion C. The excessive smartphone use is not better accounted for by obsessive-compulsive disorder or bipolar I disorder.

Differential Diagnosis

Korpa and Papadopoulou (2013) stated that whether Internet addiction is a primary disorder or a secondary disorder remains controversial among researchers. If it is a primary disorder, it means that it is not due to another cause. If it is a secondary disorder, it means that it results from a psychiatric condition (i.e., it is "second," or *caused by*, the primary psychiatric disorder). On the other hand, as in the case of exercise addiction, it may be that both exist—that is, both the primary and the secondary form of Internet addiction.

Internet addiction has several features in common with impulse-control, obsessive-compulsive disorders, and substance abuse (Watson, 2015). The main difference between obsessive-compulsive disorder and addictive behaviors is that the compulsive behavior of addicted individuals brings pleasure to the individual and does not itself result in personal distress (Watson, 2015), whereas someone with obsessive-compulsive disorder is genuinely bothered by their continued compulsive behavior and engaging and it does not bring pleasure, only temporary relief from anxiety.

Wolfling, Beutel, Dreier, and Muller (2015) studied 368 individuals seeking treatment for Internet addiction who were also screened for bipolar spectrum disorders. In their sample, 30.9% also experienced bipolar disorders. This study tells us that these two conditions can be comorbid, but it also suggests that symptoms of Internet addiction may occur during a manic or hypomanic episode. For a differential diagnosis, if the symptoms of Internet addiction dissipate following adequate treatment for the manic or hypomanic symptoms, then only bipolar disorder would be coded and not Internet addiction. Furthermore, *DSM-5* (APA, 2013) mentions that using the Internet that does *not* involve playing online games (e.g., generic Internet addiction, social media addiction) is not analogous to IGD.

Comorbidity and Co-Addictions

Internet addiction is often comorbid with other psychological conditions (Younes et al., 2016). Some have suggested that the comorbidity rate is as high as 86% (Bernardi & Pallanti, 2009).

Korpa and Papadopoulou (2013) stated that, in adolescents, both pathological gambling and excessive Internet use usually occur with another psychiatric disorder. Internet addiction is related to depression, eating disorders, autism, attention deficit hyperactivity disorder (ADHD), and substance use disorders (Canan, 2016; Jorgenson, Hsiao, & Yen, 2016; Moore, 2017; Wang, Yao, Zhou, Liu, & Lv, 2017). Similar findings are being found in other countries (de Vries, Nakamae, Fukui, Denys, & Narumoto, 2018).

In addition to these, IGD is associated with social phobia and panic disorder (Griffiths, Kiraly, Pontes, & Demetrovics, 2015). A large-scale study of 23,533 adults (mean age = 35.8 years) found that video game addiction and social media addiction were related to ADHD, obsessive-compulsive disorder, anxiety, and depression (Andreassen et al., 2016).

In a sample of 786 participants between ages 18 and 35 (mean age = 23.7 years), more than 20% of the sample experienced problematic Internet use. Compared to the nonproblematic users, the problematic users had higher scores in all the personality disorder clusters, nonadaptive coping measures, and depressive symptoms (Laconi, Vigouroux, Lafuente, & Chabrol, 2017). The association of Internet addiction and personality disorders has also been found in other studies: borderline (Lu et al., 2017) and schizotypal (Truzoli, Osborne, Romano, & Reed, 2016).

Internet-addicted individuals have a higher likelihood of experiencing insomnia, anxiety, depression, stress, and self-esteem issues (Younes et al., 2016). All of the previous findings should alert counselors to do a thorough assessment when working with individuals presenting with Internet addictive behavior.

Available Measures

Internet addiction.

Assessing for Internet addiction is done through client self-report (Watson, 2015). Young (as cited in Watson, 2015) suggested that four triggers should be assessed that are related to excessive Internet use: (a) applications, (b) feelings, (c) cognitions, and (d) life events. Usage is often confined to one or two applications, and these act as the first trigger. Feelings or emotions are also involved in Internet addiction and need to be assessed. People often use the Internet as a form of psychological escape and thoughts, and cognitions also need to be and considered. Lastly, experiencing traumatic or stressful life events that exceed one's coping abilities may foster excessive Internet use.

Janikian (2013) suggested that, with adolescents, information should be gathered from multiple sources. She recommended that the interview be conducted with the teenage client first before collecting information from parents. Besides history taking and doing a mental status examination, questions should be asked about alcohol and drug use and family history of addiction as well. Psychological comorbidity needs to be assessed.

As stated earlier, agreement on the exact nature of Internet addiction has not yet occurred. Consequently, there are various instruments available, and each may be measuring something different to some extent. The measures listed here include some of the newest ones that are available as well as some that are frequently used by researchers.

1. Diagnostic Classification Test for Internet Addiction (DCT-IA; Tu, Gao, Wang, & Cai, 2017). This test was designed with what the authors referred to as "cutting-edge psychometric theory" (Tu et al., 2017, p. 1). It is also based on the *DSM-5*. The authors claim that it differs from traditional questionnaires in that it can simultaneously generate general diagnostic information and detailed symptom criteria-level information. The DCT-IA provides accurate and valid information.

2. Internet Disorder Scale (IDS-15; Pontes & Griffiths, 2017). This test is based on the nine *DSM-5* criteria for IGD. It has demonstrated construct validity as assessed by factorial, convergent, and discriminant validity. Participants can be classified as low addiction risk, medium addiction risk, and high addiction risk.

   Janikian (2013) reviewed several tests, and these are as follows along with her assessment of them:

3. Internet Addiction Test (IAT). This test by Kimberley Young is an expanded version of her original eight-item diagnostic questionnaire. This is a 20-item test with answers provided on a 5-point Likert scale. It measures the extent of an individual's involvement with the Internet, the degree of preoccupation, loss of control, extent of lying about use, and general functioning. It has acceptable psychometric properties. According to Weinstein, Curtiss Feder, Rosenberg, & Dannon (2014), it is the most commonly used questionnaire in research and practice. This test is a valid and reliable measure of Internet addiction.

   The IAT is available from http://huibee.com/wordpress/wp-content/uploads/2013/11/GLOBALADDICTION-Scales-InternetAddictionTest.pdf

4. Generalized Problematic Internet Use Scale (GPIUS). This scale by Caplan has 29 items. Exploratory factor analysis revealed it has seven factors: mood change, perceived social benefits, adverse outcomes related to Internet use, compulsive use, excessive online time, withdrawal symptoms, and perceived social control. The scale has high internal consistency and construct validity. It has been further revised and updated.

5. Internet Addiction Scale (IAS). This is a 36-item, 5-point Likert scale based on the seven substance dependence criteria included in DSM-IV and two additional criteria (i.e., mood modification and salience) recommended by Griffiths. It has high internal consistency and measures one factor relating to the negative consequences of excessive Internet use. It has been criticized for using substance dependence criteria, as most researchers view it as a behavioral addiction.

6. Problematic Internet Usage Scale (PIUS). This is a 33-item, 5-point Likert scale. It measures three factors: negative consequences, social benefit/social comfort, and excessive use. The scale has high internal consistency, test-retest reliability, and split-half reliability.

7. Problematic Internet Use Questionnaire (PIUQ). This is an 18-item, 5-point Likert scale constructed by modifying Young's Internet addiction test. The questionnaire has three subscales based on factor analysis: obsession, neglect scale, and control disorder. It has high internal consistency and high test-retest reliability. The article describing this questionnaire is available at no charge from https://www.academia.edu/527999/The_three-factor_model_of_Internet_addiction_The_development_of_the_Problematic_Internet_Use_Questionnaire?auto=download

Internet gaming disorder.

The number of questionnaires and scales measuring IGD has expanded exponentially since *DSM-5* included it as a potential diagnosis for further study. Following further research, it is likely that some of these scales will disappear and others will be revised shortly. The following are some of the newest published scales:

1. Internet Gaming Disorder Scale-Short-Form (IGDS9-SF). Pontes, Stavropoulos, and Griffiths (2017) wrote that the IGDS9-SF had been used throughout the world to assess IGD behaviors. Although there is one factor in this instrument, there are also cross-cultural differences among the United States, India, and the United Kingdom. Please refer to Pontes et al. to read about these differences. The longer version (i.e., IGD-20 Test) is also a psychometrically robust tool (Pontes & Griffiths, 2017).

   A short version (IGDS9-SF) is available from https://www.halleypontes.com/igds9sf/

2. Screening Tool for Excessive Gamers. The online tool was created by On-line Gamers Anonymous (questions are available from http://www.olganon.org/self_tests_on_gaming_addiction). They offer several questions, but the essential one is: "Is excessive gaming affecting your real life in a negative way?"

3. Videogame Addiction Scale for Children (VASC; Yilmaz, Griffiths, & Kan, 2017). This questionnaire of 21 items was constructed following a factor analysis, which suggested that the instrument has four factors. The four factors include self-control, reward/reinforcement, problems, and involvement.

4. Metacognitions about Online Gaming Scale (Spada & Caselli, 2017). This scale has good psychometric properties in addition to predictive and divergent validity.

5. Internet Gaming Disorder Test (IGDT-10; Kiraly et al., 2017). This 10-item test measures IGD using definitions contained in *DSM-5*. The test has demonstrated validity, reliability, and suitability for use in future research.

6. Electronic Gaming Motives Questionnaire (Myrseth, Notelaers, Strand, Borud, & Olsen, 2017). Designed to measure motivation for gaming. The test has good internal consistency, and the confirmatory factor analysis indicated that it measures enhancement, coping, and social and self-gratification motives.

7. Behavioral Addiction Measure for Video Gaming (BAM-VG: Sanders & Williams, 2016). The BAM-VG has good internal consistency and 1-month test-retest reliability. It also has demonstrated criterion-related validity and construct validity.

Social media addiction.

Several instruments have also been designed recently to measure various aspects of social media addiction. Some of these instruments include the following:

1. Bergen Facebook Addiction Scale (Andreassen, Torsheim, Brunborg, & Pallesen, 2012). This is one of the most psychometrically sound scales currently available (Griffiths, Kuss, & Demetrovics, 2014). It also appears to be the one that is most commonly used in research. Griffiths et al. (2014) suggested that switching the term from Facebook to social networking might be worthwhile to researchers. Available from https://newatlas.com/bergen-facebook-addiction-scale/22460/ or https://psychcentral.com/quizzes/facebook-addict-quiz/ for a self-scoring version.

2. Facebook Addiction Test (F-AT; Dantlgraber, Wetzel, Schutzenberger, Stieger, & Reips, 2016). This test has both a long form and a short form. The long form is available from http://www.techaddiction.ca/facebook-addiction-test-symptoms.html

3. Problematic Facebook Use Scale. Marino, Vieno, Altoe, and Spada (2017) found that this scale was useful in assessing problematic Facebook use among male and female young adults and adolescents. The authors' original article is available from https://www.researchgate.net/publication/312538169_Factorial_validity_of_the_Problematic_Facebook_Use_Scale_for_adolescents_and_young_adults

4. Problematic Tinder Use Scale (PTUS; Orosz, Toth-Kiraly, Bothe, & Melher, 2016). Both a 12-item and a six-item version were tested. The six-item version was found to have appropriate reliability and factor structure. The authors concluded it is suitable and reliable to for measuring problematic Tinder use. The authors' original article is available from https://akademiai.com/doi/abs/10.1556/2006.5.2016.016

   The six-item version is available as a free download from https://www.researchgate.net/publication/305656114_Problematic_Tinder_Use_Scale_Appendix

5. Social Media Disorder Scale (van den Eijnden, Lemmens, & Valkenburg, 2016). This is a nine-item scale that has shown good structural, convergent, and criterion validity. It also has good internal consistency and sufficient test-retest reliability. The authors' original article is available from https://www.sciencedirect.com/science/article/pii/S0747563216302059

6. Smartphone Addiction Inventory (SPAI, Pavia, Cavani, Di Blasi, & Giordano, 2016; SPAI-SF; Lin, Pan, Lin, & Chen, 2017). The SPAI is a 26-item instrument. The short form replicates the longer version regarding its four-factor model measuring compulsive behavior, functional impairment, withdrawal, and tolerance. The authors' original article is available from http://journals.plos.org/plosone/article?id=10.1371/journal.pone.0098312

   The short form in English, Spanish, and French is available from http://www.uclep.be/wp-content/uploads/pdf/Pub/Lopez_AB_2016.pdf
7. Smartphone Overuse Screening Questionnaire (SOS-Q; Lee et al., 2017). This screening instrument has good internal consistency and moderate test-retest reliability. It can be used as a primary and supplementary measure in a variety of settings.

Clinical Interview Questions

Internet addiction.

The questionnaires and scales listed in the previous section comprise mostly questions that could be asked in a clinical interview.

Young (2011) suggested the following questions:

1. When did you first begin to use the Internet?
2. How many hours per week do you currently spend online (for nonessential use)?
3. What applications do you use on the Internet (specific site/groups/games visited)?
4. How many hours per week do you spend using each application?
5. How would you rank order each application from most to least important? (1 = first, 2 = second, 3 = third, etc.)?
6. What do you like most about each application? What do you like least?
7. How has the Internet changed your life?
8. How do you feel when you log offline?
9. What problems or consequences have stemmed from your Internet use? (If these are difficult for the client to describe, have the client keep a log near the computer in order to document such behaviors for the next week's session.)
10. Have others complained about how much time you spend online?
11. Have you sought treatment for this condition before? If so, when? Have you had any success? (p. 25)

Young (2011) also offered several questions for evaluating social problems. These are as follows:

1. Have you been honest about your Internet habit with your friends and family?
2. Have you ever created an online persona?
3. Did you develop an identity or persona online?
4. Have there been online activities that you kept secret or thought others would not approve of?
5. Have online friends disrupted real-life relationships?
6. If so, who (husband, wife, parent, friend) and how were they impacted?
7. Does Internet use disrupt your social or work relationships? If so, how?
8. What other ways has Internet use impacted your life? (p. 30)

Internet gaming disorder.

Bargeron and Hormes (2017) examined nine questions based on *DSM-5* diagnostic criteria. They are as follows:

1. Over time, have you been spending much more time thinking about playing video games, learning about video-game playing, or planning the next opportunity to play?
2. Do you need to spend more and more time and/or money on video games in order to feel the same amount of excitement?
3. Have you tried to play video games less often or for shorter periods of time but were unsuccessful?
4. Do you become restless or irritable when attempting to cut down or stop playing video games?
5. Have you played video games as a way of escaping from problems or bad feelings?
6. Have you ever lied to family or friends about how much you play video games?
7. Have you ever stolen a video game from a store or a friend, or have you ever stolen money in order to buy a video game?
8. Do you sometimes skip tasks in order to spend more time playing video games?
9. Have you ever done poorly on a school assignment or test because you spent too much time playing video games? (p. 391)

Social media addiction.

Using the six components of addiction described by Griffiths (2005), Roberts (2015) offered six questions that can be helpful in identifying social media addiction. These have been adapted to include a scaling component with each question. These could be asked as they are written, or you could ask your clients to scale these on a scale from 0 (*not at all*) to 10 (*all the time*):

1. To what extent is social media use heavily integrated into your daily routine (i.e., salience)?
2. To what extent do you find yourself spending progressively more time on social media to get the same satisfaction (i.e., tolerance)?

3. To what extent do you rely on social media as a source of excitement or to cope with boredom or loneliness (i.e., euphoria)?
4. To what extent do you feel the need to use social media, and do you feel edgy or anxious when you cannot (i.e., withdrawal)?
5. To what extent have your attempts to quit or reduce social media use failed (i.e., relapse)?
6. To what extent does social media cause problems in your life or conflicts with loved ones? (I.e., conflict)?

Generic Names and Street "Lingo"

Internet addiction.

Internet addiction also goes by several names. These include the following: compulsive Internet use, pathological Internet use, Internet dependence (Yau, Derevensky, & Potenza, 2016), information technology addictions (Sigerson, Li, Cheung, & Cheng, 2017), technological addiction (Griffiths & Kuss, 2015), Internet use disorder, cyberspace addiction, online addiction, high Internet dependency, problematic Internet usage (Watson, 2015), problematic Internet use (Korpa & Papadopoulou, 2013), Internet addiction disorder, technical addictions (Karim & Chaudhri, 2012), Internet abuse, Internet-enabled behavior, virtual addiction, Internet-enabled compulsive behavior (Greenfield, 2011), Internet overuse, Internet misuse, and Internet/computer addiction (Chrismore, Betzelberger, Bier, & Camacho, 2011).

Internet gaming disorder.

Terms in this category include the following: problem video game playing, problematic online game use or gaming, video game addiction, pathological video game use or gaming, online gaming addiction, Internet gaming addiction, and IGD (Griffiths, Kiraly, Pontes, & Demetrovics, 2015).

Social media addiction.

Other terms here include the following: Facebook addiction disorder, SNS Addiction disorder (Griffiths, Kuss, & Demetrovics, 2014), digital media compulsion (Greenfield, 2011), Internet-communication disorder (Wegmann & Brand, 2016), and social networking disorder or addiction.

Neuroscience

Numerous neurobiological studies have been done over the past years regarding Internet addiction and Internet use disorder (Park, Han, & Roh, 2017). Park, Han, and Roh (2017) reviewed the results of 84 major studies concerning the neuroscience of what other researchers have called Internet addiction, Internet use disorder, and IGD. Park et al. included studies that dealt with typical neurobiological methods, including

1. Neuroimaging and neurophysiologic methods.
   A. Structural magnetic resonance imaging (sMRI; e.g., voxel-based morphometry [VBM] and diffusion tensor imaging [DTI]).
   B. Functional magnetic resonance imaging (fMRI).
   C. Nuclear imaging (e.g., positron emission tomography [PET] and single photon emission computed tomography [SPECT]).
2. Neurophysiologic studies using electroencephalogram (EEG).

Without going into detail about these 84 studies, Park et al. (2017) surmised that Internet use disorder is associated with structural and functional impairments within the orbitofrontal cortex, dorsolateral prefrontal cortex, anterior cingulate cortex, and posterior cingulate cortex. Collectively these regions deal with reward, motivation, memory, and cognitive control. They also found that Internet use disorder is associated with decreased gray matter density and brain areas associated with impulsivity and craving. Park et al. also clarified that, whereas early neurobiological research suggested that Internet use disorder had many similarities with substance use disorders, recent research indicates that there are differences in their biological an psychological markers.

D'Hondt and Maurage (2017), however, concluded in their recent systematic review of 14 electrophysiological studies that Internet addiction has features similar to other addictions. They mostly focused on its joint hypo-activation of the reflective system (i.e., decreased executive control abilities) and hyperactivation of the automatic-affective system (i.e., excessive emotional processing of addiction-related cues).

Kim and Han (2015) also summarized the literature and concluded that playing video games, mainly action video games, improves visuospatial attention and speed of processing of tasks. Furthermore, extensive video game use is related to the frontoparietal network. A genetic predisposition to problematic Internet and video game use has also been postulated, and this may consist of an insufficient number of dopamine receptors or inadequate amounts of serotonin and dopamine. In response, these individuals would need to play more to derive the same degree of pleasure. Problematic Internet and video game use appear to have abnormal reward processing in corticolimbic circuits in common with substance abuse. Kim and Han's overall conclusion was that problematic Internet and video game use appear similar to the neurobiological characteristics that underpin impulse control disorders and substance dependence.

Weinstein, Livny, and Weizman's (2017) review of the current literature led to similar conclusions. The evidence they reviewed suggested that the structural and functional changes concerning reward and craving in IGD are similar to that which occurs in substance use disorders. Weinstein et al. concluded that IGD should be classified as an impulse control disorder or as an obsessive-compulsive disorder.

Readers who are interested in understanding the neural basis of video gaming in mostly nonaddicted individuals are referred to a recent review by Palaus, Marron, Viejo-Sobera, and Redolar-Ripoll (2017). These authors provided a systematic review of 116 articles, 100 of which looked at functional data and 22 that measured structural brain changes (note that there was some overlap between the two areas).

Neurobiological studies on social media addiction have begun as well. A recent study utilized 50 random university students (25 in the experimental group and 25 and the control group) who reported varying degrees of excessive social media use (He, Turel, Brevers, & Bechara, 2017).

The authors concluded that excessive social media use is associated with GMV reduction in the bilateral amygdala and possibly the striatum as well. Volume differences were not found in the prefrontal regions, however. Another study of 68 college students (34 in the control group and 34 in the experimental group) found evidence of altered brain structure with those who overused mobile phones (Wang et al., 2016).

Physical Impacts (Long-Term Use)

One of the proposed criteria listed in *DSM-5* for IGD is withdrawal symptoms. King, Kaptsis, Delfabbro, and Gradisar (2016) used a qualitative study to gather written responses from 24 participants (mean age = 24.6 years). Only nine of the 24 met the criteria for IGD. Overall, "the participants' reactions to gaming abstinence could be broadly characterized as boredom and a drive for mental stimulation" (King et al., 2016, p. 488). Although the results of this study should be seen as only suggestive, the authors questioned whether a true withdrawal syndrome occurs when gaming-addicted individuals stop playing.

Most studies, however, do report withdrawal symptoms, and these seem to apply to the various Internet addictions. Much of these results, however, are based on correlational studies. For example, a frequent finding is that adults with Internet addiction have greater difficulty initiating and maintaining sleep and, as a result, are functionally impaired the next day (Bhandari et al., 2017; Kim et al., 2017; Zhang et al., 2017). Problematic social media use with adolescents also coincides with poor sleep habits, which in turn is associated with poor school experiences (Vernon, Barber, & Modecki, 2015). A question, of course, is which came first: sleep problems leading to greater Internet use or greater Internet use leading to sleep problems? The direction of causality remains unknown currently.

Children between ages 9 and 16 in nine European countries (N = 368) were asked in focus groups and interviews about what they perceived as being most negative or problematic with Internet and technology use. The children reported physical health symptoms that included eye problems, headaches, not eating, and tiredness (Smahel, Wright, & Cernikova, 2015).

Kaptsis, King, Delfabbro, and Gradisar (2016) conducted the most comprehensive review to date of withdrawal symptoms for those with IGD. They evaluated a total of 34 studies, including 10 qualitative studies, 17 research reports, and seven treatment studies. They concluded that the available evidence on withdrawal is underdeveloped currently. The most common withdrawal symptoms reported were irritability and restlessness following termination of gaming.

Kim, Kim, and Jee (2015) tested 110 Chinese International Students in Korea for smartphone addiction. They found that smartphone-addicted individuals did not walk as much as nonaddicted individuals and thus concluded that smartphone addiction might have adverse health consequences due to lack of physical activity.

Griffiths and Kuss (2015) summarized the findings from several studies and reported that several health and medical consequences may occur as a result of excessive gaming. Their list included epileptic seizures; auditory hallucinations; obesity; wrist, neck, and/or elbow pain and repetitive strain injuries; blisters, calluses, sore tendons, and numbness of fingers; hand-arm vibration syndrome; and psychosomatic challenges. Griffiths (2016) added a few more: visual hallucinations, enuresis, encopresis, and tenosynovitis, which is also called "Nintendinitis." Kuss and Billieux (2017) suggested that the health problems relating to Internet addictions are typically associated with substance addictions.

Mental, Emotional, and Spiritual Impacts

Some Internet-addicted individuals spend between 20 and 80 hours a week on the Internet (Carli & Durkee, 2016). Carli and Durkee (2016) concluded that these addicted individuals frequently experience anxiety, social isolation, depression, and despair; other researchers have found similar symptoms (Griffiths, 2016; Nuyens, Kuss, Lopez-Fernandez, & Griffiths, 2017; Romano et al., 2017). Cerniglia et al. (2017) focused on Internet-addicted adolescents and reported that they often suffer a loss of control, anger, distress, social withdrawal, and conflicts with family. As in the previous section, it is important to remember that these are correlational studies and do not ascertain causation or directionality.

Video game-addicted individuals generally have poorer mental health, cognitive functioning, and impulse control than nonaddicted individuals (Nuyens, Kuss, Lopez-Fernandez, & Griffiths, 2017; Stockdale & Coyne, 2018). Those who use smartphones excessively may also experience social problems and depression (Kim, Kim, & Jee, 2015).

Griffiths (2016) included studies showing that gaming-addicted individuals experience increased stress, inattention, and aggressive/oppositional behavior; less psychological well-being, loneliness, and verbal memory performance; maladaptive cognitions and coping strategies; and increased suicidal ideation compared to nonaddicted individuals. Current studies also support these results: psychological distress (Saquib et al., 2017), narcissism and diminished self-esteem (Pantic et al., 2017), psychological inflexibility and experiential avoidance (Chou et al., 2017), increased depression (Bhandari et al., 2017; Stockdale & Coyne, 2018), anxiety (Stockdale & Coyne, 2018), maladaptive cognitions (Forrest, King, & Delfabbro, 2017), impaired cognitive processing (Nuyens, Kuss, Lopez-Fernandez, & Griffiths, 2017), greater impulsivity (Aboujaoude, 2017), and possibly impaired empathy (Jiao, Wang, Peng, & Cui, 2017).

A new word that has entered the Japanese vocabulary is *hikikomori* (Stip, Thibault, Beauchamp-Chatel, & Kisely, 2016, p. 1). This is a condition that affects mostly adolescents or young adults. These individuals isolate themselves from the world by locking themselves in their bedrooms for days, months, or years. They leave their bedrooms only to deal with pressing bodily needs. Although the condition was first described in Japan, cases have now been described from around the globe. Stip et al. (2016) also wrote that, although most of these individuals have a diagnosable mental disorder, this is not always the case.

A recent meta-analysis including 23 studies with a total of 13,929 participants (60.7% females; mean age = 21.93 years) focused on problematic Facebook use. The analysis revealed a positive correlation between psychological distress and problematic Facebook use and a negative correlation between problematic Facebook use and psychological distress and well-being (Marino, Gini, Vieno, & Spada, 2018). A recent review of 65 articles also reported that Facebook addiction was associated with anxiety, depression, body image and disordered eating, and other mental health problems (Frost & Rickwood, 2017).

Spirituality and/or religion appear to reduce the likelihood of developing Internet addiction. Those who read the Bible more frequently use social networking sites less often than those who don't (Miller, Mundey, & Hill, 2013). Furthermore, highly religious individuals are less likely to use social networking sites and less likely to visit them frequently (Smith & Snell, 2009).

In a study of 5990 young men, a stronger belief in God was associated with playing video games less frequently and lower scores on a game addiction scale (Braun, Kornhuber, & Lenz, 2016). Charlton, Soh, Ang, and Chew (2013) found a negative relationship between religiosity and Internet addiction for females across the four religions that they studied (i.e., Islam, Hinduism, Buddhism, and Christianity). However, this was not found for the males in their sample.

Psychosocial Impacts (Relationships, Career/Work, Legal, Financial)

Researchers are aware that not all studies find the same results. The first study mentioned here, a dissertation, is a good example of sound longitudinal research that found different results from most studies. Liu (2015) used data from three waves of the nationally representative Longitudinal Study of Adolescent Health (i.e., 1994–1995, 1996, 2001–2002). Liu defined heavy video and computer gaming as at least 21 hours per week usage with additional cutoffs recorded at over 35 hours, 42 hours, and 56 hours. Although playing these games for 21 hours or more per week during adolescence was correlated with a diminished likelihood of high school completion, playing them for 35 hours or more per week was related to having a higher likelihood of reporting better health 5 years later, less likelihood of using marijuana, and more total years of education. Individuals playing for 42 hours or more per week were more likely to have better self-reported health 5 years later, were less likely to use marijuana, and were less likely to have conduct disorder. The only adverse outcome was that they were more likely to experience depression. Liu's study highlights that it is impossible to have a single cutoff point for what constitutes the amount of heavy gaming that will lead to long-term negative consequences.

Studies using cross-sectional designs suggest that adverse impacts on relationships result from Internet addictions (Milkman & Sunderwirth, 2010). Greenfield (2011) reported that, in France, 50% of divorces had some Internet or social media issue attached to them. In adolescence, having insecure attachment appears to be predictive of problematic Internet use in both sexes (Reiner et al., 2017). Adolescents who are addicted to the Internet often suffer social withdrawal and family conflicts (Cerniglia et al., 2017). Cerniglia et al. (2017) argued that Internet use can be seen as addictive when it replaces genuine real-life sociability. In these cases, the Internet-addicted individual has developed relationships in the virtual world that have replaced the ones they have in real life (Eidenbenz, 2011).

In a survey of 100 students, the students themselves wrote that the dark side of social networking is that communicating with friends and family is occurring increasingly through technology at the expense of personal contact (Wiederhold, 2016). Karim and Chaudhri (2012) reported that the most likely individuals to become addicted to the Internet are marginalized socially to some extent and/or have difficulty interacting in real-life social situations. Furthermore, spending too much time on the Internet can have a negative impact on one's social development, thereby creating social inadequacies and producing social anxiety (Milkman & Sunderwirth, 2010).

Lacking social skills is significantly associated with gaming addiction (You, Kim, & Lee, 2017). Stockdale and Coyne (2018) tested 1205 young adults (mean age = 20.32 years, 48.85% male) to find 87 video game-addicted individuals (in their sample) who were then matched with another 87 who served as the control group. The addicted individuals felt more socially isolated from the nonaddicted individuals.

Excessive video gaming can lead to other psychosocial consequences. Some individuals sacrifice work, education, and hobbies for video gaming (Griffiths, 2016). Some studies report that school performance in grade school and college is negatively impacted by the amount of time addicted individuals spend on the Internet (Busch, Laninga-Wijnen, Petrus Schrijvers, & De Leeuw, 2017; Schmitt & Livingston, 2015). A study based on 370 high school students, however, found that the correlation between game addiction and academic achievement was negligible (Sahin, Gumus, & Dincel, 2016).

A significant predictor of Internet addiction in college students (N = 1173, 62.1% males, mean age = 19.65 years) in China was the quality of parent-child relationships among other psychological factors (Chi, Lin, & Zhang, 2016). A systematic review (14 studies) found that poorer quality parent-child relationships are associated with increased severity of problematic gaming (Schneider, King, & Delfabbro, 2017).

Working With Diverse Populations

Sex Differences

Reiner et al. (2017) tested a similarly large sample of adolescents (N = 2410; 1307 girls, 1103 boys) between ages 12 and 18 and found that problematic Internet use and social media use were more prevalent in boys. The researchers found that insecure peer attachment was predictive of developing problematic Internet use in both sexes. Several studies besides this one have reported that adolescent and young adult males have a more significant problem with Internet use than females (Chrismore, Betzelberger, Bier, & Camacho, 2011; Garcia-Oliva & Piqueras, 2016; Waqas et al., 2016).

Laconi, Vigouroux, Lafuente, and Chabrol (2017) tested 786 participants between ages 18 and 35. More than 20% of the sample consisted of problematic Internet users. Regression analysis highlighted that problematic Internet use was primarily explained by (1) personality traits, (2) psychological variables, and (3) depressive symptoms. The authors then went on to elaborate on some of the sex differences that their study and other studies have found. Women are more prone to using the Internet for social activities, whereas men have a greater preference for solitary online activities. Men are more likely to be involved in video games, gambling, and cybersex. Although depressive symptoms often appear to be a preexisting condition that becomes exacerbated through problematic Internet use, depressive symptoms in the study of Laconi et al. had a more significant impact on women compared to men.

A large sample of 4852 participants (51.71% males) revealed that problematic Internet use was significantly lower for females.

Nonetheless, there was a stronger association for females between life satisfaction and problematic Internet use. The authors concluded that there is a different threshold for males and females regarding the negative effects of subjective well-being on problematic Internet use (Lachmann, Sariyska, Kannen, Cooper, & Montag, 2016).

A high rate of personality disorders has been found in individuals with Internet addiction (Wu, Ko, & Lane, 2016). In their sample of 556 college students (341 females), Wu et al. (2016) found that the males with Internet addiction had a higher frequency of narcissistic personality disorder and that the females had a higher frequency of borderline, narcissistic, avoidant, or dependent personality when compared to those without Internet addiction.

A study of 1441 Chinese undergraduate students found that the prevalence of smartphone addiction was comparable for males and females (30.3% in males, 29.3% in females; Chen et al., 2017). A smaller study of 448 college students from South Korea found that being female was a risk factor for smartphone addiction, however (Choi et al., 2015). Visconte (2017) found, in her dissertation of 295 Facebook users, that females reported having significantly more Facebook friends than did males. Kimpton et al. (2016) also found a higher prevalence of Facebook addiction in female university students, whereas gaming addiction had a higher prevalence in males.

Adolescents and Youth

There is a high comorbidity between IGD and psychiatric disorders in adolescents (Vadlin, Aslund, Hellstrom, & Nilsson, 2016). In a study of 996 of Italian adolescents (240 males, 756 females; mean age = 16.47 years, SD = 4.85), Di Nicola et al. (2017) found that addictive behaviors in adolescents (these researchers also looked at other addictions) were associated with higher likelihood of dissociative processes, anhedonia, alexithymia, and impulsivity. A longitudinal study of 354 adolescents (mean age = 13.9 years, 48.9% boys) followed over 12 months found that attentional problems, social vulnerability, and having lesser life satisfaction uniquely and interactively predicted increases in IGD symptoms (Peeters, Koning, & van den Eijnden, 2018).

Adolescents with attention problems, particularly those who are socially vulnerable and unhappy with life, are more likely to develop problematic gaming behaviors (Peeters, Koning, & van den Eijnden, 2018). Having decreased self-esteem, shyness, and having difficulty with emotional regulation are related to problematic Internet use in adolescents (Li, 2018; Li, Newman, Li, & Zhang, 2016; Spada & Marino, 2017). Adolescent Internet-addicted individuals are likelier to display lower levels of self-care compared with nonaddicted individuals (McNicol & Thorsteinsson, 2017). Social skill deficits, having greater anxiety, and feeling lonely are also associated with Internet addiction in adolescents (Chou et al., 2017; Stavropoulos et al., 2017; Vigna-Taglianti et al., 2017). Poorer grades, academic performance, and school satisfaction are often found in studies looking at Internet addiction in teenagers (Busch et al., 2017; Vernon, Barber, & Modecki, 2015). Adolescent obesity and Internet addiction are also correlated (Eliacik et al., 2016).

Rosenkranz, Muller, Dreier, Beutel, and Wolfling (2017) tested a representative sample of 5667 adolescents aged 12–19. Similar to the findings from studies involving young adults, they found that chatting and social networking were most strongly predictive of problematic Internet use in girls, whereas gaming was the most reliable predictor in boys. In a study of 1095 adolescents ages 12–14, adolescents with IGD reported less social support, lower health-related quality of life, and more friends only known through the Internet compared to those without IGD (Wartberg, Kriston, & Kammerl, 2017). A large study of 9733 adolescents revealed that the degree of online communication was an important factor; those who were very socially active online reported fewer symptoms of gaming addiction (Carras et al., 2017).

A cross-sectional study in seven European countries had a total sample size of 13,284 adolescents (53% female; mean age = 15.8 years). The researchers found that Internet addiction among adolescents was most frequently associated with a lower educational level of the parents, earlier age at first use of the Internet, and greater use of social networking sites and gaming sites (Tsitsika et al., 2014).

A study of 701 male adolescents (mean age = 15.6 years) determined that the more genres of video games played, the greater were the number of negative consequences caused by gaming (Donati, Chiesi, Ammannato, & Primi, 2015). Male teenagers who are sensation seekers and who are impulsive are more likely to become online gaming addicted individuals (Hu, Zhen, Yu, Zhang, & Zhang, 2017; Tian et al., 2018).

Race and Ethnicity

Research from the Pew Research Center (Anderson, 2015) found that about half of U.S. adults (49%) report playing video games. Whites, Blacks, and Hispanics are equally likely to say they have done so, but Blacks and Hispanics tend to play video games more frequently than Whites. Blacks are somewhat more likely to have favorable views of video games and less likely to say they are a waste of time compared to Whites and Hispanics. Hispanics, more than Whites and Blacks, are more likely to identify themselves as gamers and to see a link between violent video games and actual violence. Blacks are more likely than Whites to say that video games portray minority groups poorly.

Mak et al. (2014) surveyed 5366 adolescents between ages 12 and 18 from six Asian countries (i.e., China, Hong Kong, Japan, South Korea, Malaysia, Philippines). The authors concluded that Internet addiction is common among adolescents in Asian countries and that it is the highest in the Philippines.

Although most studies about Internet addictions have occurred in Southeast Asia, where the concern is seen as a severe mental health problem (Mak et al., 2014), studies have not distinguished Internet-related symptoms among people of different races or ethnicities. Studies that have focused on prevalence have suggested that rates are unusually high with Asian adolescents and young adults. Yates, Gregor, and Haviland (2012) tested 1470 college students (62.9% female, mean age = 19.13 years) and found that the males and Asian students reported higher levels of problematic Internet use compared to females and those of other ethnoracial groups. Data from 260 adolescents (175 Chinese, 61 Malay, 14 Indian, and 10 Other) who presented at an addiction treatment center revealed that those diagnosed with IGD were more likely to be of Chinese ethnicity (Ong, Peh, & Guo, 2016).

Nonpsychiatric Disabilities

There is only one published study to date focused on Internet addiction and nonpsychiatric disabilities. Questionnaires were completed by 216 youth with intellectual disabilities, and it was found that they had higher rates of excessive use of both the Internet and cell phones compared with 410 young people without disabilities (Jenaro et al., 2018).

Lesbian, Gay, Bisexual, and Transgender (LGBT)

Every individual who was sent to a national transgender health service in the United Kingdom over a 12-month period was invited to take part in a study measuring several psychiatric symptoms but also gaming behavior. In total, 240 people participated with 154 (62.9%) describing themselves as current gamers. Less than 1% scored as having IGD, however (Arcelus et al., 2017).

Some studies have been conducted looking at gay males and cybersex addiction, but these are not covered in this chapter. Please refer to Chapter 16 regarding sex addiction.

War Veterans

There is only one study in this category. Myrseth, Olsen, Strand, and Borud (2017) investigated gaming addiction among conscripts. Their sample consisted of 1017 conscripts (80.3% men). Of this group, 4.8% were addicted to gaming. Addicted gamers had higher scores on boredom, loneliness, depression, and anxiety compared with nonproblem gamers and nongamers.

Another study's findings may have applicability to war veterans who have experienced trauma. Contractor, Frankfurt, Weiss, and Elhai (2017) recruited 347 participants and assessed them for problematic smartphone use and PTSD symptoms. Their results suggested that problematic smartphone use was associated with adverse effect and arousal among individuals exposed to trauma.

Medications and Other Relevant Physical Interventions

Currently, no medications for Internet addictions are approved by the U.S. Food and Drug Administration (FDA). In a 12-week double-blind trial, 15 patients received bupropion and 15 escitalopram. Depressive symptoms and IGD symptoms in both groups were improved after the treatment. Bupropion showed greater effectiveness in reducing impulsivity and attentional problems (Nam, Bae, Kim, Hong, & Han, 2017). Comparable results were found in a similar study with the same two medications (Song et al., 2016).

In 86 adolescents with ADHD who were also diagnosed with problematic online gaming, Park, Lee, Sohn, and Han (2016) found that both atomoxetine and methylphenidate reduced the severity of IGD symptoms. This reduction was correlated with reduced impulsivity. In their review of pharmacological treatments for Internet addictions, Camardese, Leone, Walstra, Janiri, and Guglielmo 2015) found that, when they pooled the data from 49 subjects, escitalopram, bupropion, and methylphenidate were the only medications that had demonstrated effectiveness. They cautioned, however, that the research base currently remains scant.

Specific Counseling Considerations

ROLEPLAY SCENARIOS

Roleplay in dyads with one of you acting as the counselor and the other as the counselee. If roleplay is not possible, work individually in writing out a list of your suggestions.

Roleplay #1

You are a school counselor, and Aida, age 14, comes to see you. Her teacher sent her to see you because Aida has been missing classes, she is always on her smartphone when she does show up, and she is often seen crying by other students. Aida tells you that she posted a joke on Facebook and nearly a dozen of her "friends" took offense to it. As she explains, they not only unfriended her, but some went so far as to block her. Aida feels devastated by the rejection. As you begin helping her accept that not everyone will agree with everything that she posts, you start to find out about the extent of her Facebook usage. Aida checks for Facebook every few minutes to find out if anybody is saying anything about her. Aida tells you that, when people like her posts, it no longer gives her a rush. However, if they make a negative comment, she is increasingly bothered by it. She tells you that she could not imagine stopping her use of Facebook.

Roleplay #2

Lucas, age 31, was sent to you for counseling by his employer. He has worked there for 5 years, but his work performance has deteriorated over the past 10 months. The employer's referral tells you that Lucas was a "peppy-full-of-life" person before this. Coworkers are often finding him asleep at his desk, and, when they talk to him, he is often yawning and appearing disinterested in conversation. When you go out to greet Lucas in the waiting room, you find him snoring and annoying other clients. Once Lucas is in your office and begins talking, he tells you that he has a sleep problem. Within minutes you find out that he is playing World of Warcraft until 4 a.m. or later most nights of the week.

HOW WOULD AN ADDICTION COUNSELOR HELP THIS PERSON?

You are working as a professional counselor. Allen, age 12, is brought to see you by his mother, Mary. Mary is a devout Pentecostal Christian who appears to be about 35 years old. Mary tells you that she cannot keep Allen from going onto the Internet to play games, visit pornographic sites, search for trivial information, chat with friends, and, when not doing that, play with his Xbox.

Mary tells you that she has been praying for her son endlessly for the past year. She and her husband, Aldrich, have tried grounding him, sending him to his room for timeouts, taking away his Xbox for hours at a time, and even scolding. Nothing seems to work. When he is not closely supervised, Allen gets onto any electronic device that is available. If he is closely supervised, he tries to get out to be with friends and uses their devices. When he is grounded, he appears to become so depressed that Mary becomes concerned that she is psychologically harming him. She is at her wit's end and has come to you for help.

Remember to view clients within their environmental contexts, keeping in mind societal, parental/familial, cultural/spiritual, and peer influences. Specifically, become aware of the impact that the following influences have and continue to have in your clients' lives: race, language, religion and spirituality, gender, familial migration history, sexual/affectional orientation, age and cohort, physical and mental capacities, socioeconomic situation and history, education, and history of traumatic experience.

1. What defines this person's environment, past and present?
2. Who is this person sitting in front of me, taking into account environmental and personal characteristics?
3. What defines the problem that he or she is presenting within their multicultural milieu?

Goals and Goal Setting

Below are just a few ideas regarding goals and goal setting:

- Self-imposed abstinence from computer use and/or Internet access (Weinstein, Curtiss Feder, Rosenberg, & Dannon, 2014).
- Stop gaming altogether (Eidenbenz, 2011).
- Moderate Internet use (Young, 2011). This could be accomplished through stimulus control procedures (e.g., leaving work earlier instead of staying on the Internet, putting Post-it notes on the monitor, shutting off the computer before making a meal; Eidenbenz, 2011).
- Implement the "reset program." This involves taking an extended electronic "fast" followed by individualized screen management (Dunckley, 2017).
- Learn coping strategies for dealing with cravings (King, Kaptsis, Delfabbro, & Gradisar, 2016).
- Get together with friends or make new ones instead of socializing online.
- Have or use a cell phone that allows or provides only for phone calls and text messages.
- Delete Facebook account or use stimulus control to reduce usage.

Stages of Change Strategies

The processes of change mentioned are based on those outlined by Connors, DiClemente, Velasquez, and Donovan (2013) and Prochaska, Norcross, and DiClemente (1994). The definitions for the various processes can be found in Chapter 6. Besides these processes, other strategies are included that have separate citations.

The University of Rhode Island Change Assessment Scale (URICA) is a helpful scale for determining where a client is currently at regarding the stages of change model. There are 24-, 28-, and 32-item versions of the scale. A 24-item version is published for alcohol or drug problems. The scale, however, is generic and can be easily adapted for use with other addictions. It is available with norms as a free download from https://www.guilford.com/add/miller11_old/urica.pdf.

Specific precontemplation strategies.

Only one empirical study has been conducted looking at the transtheoretical model of behavior change and computer gaming. Teoh and Tan (2010) tested 112 students (36 girls, 75 boys, age range 12–17) in Singapore. They found a positive correlation between the precontemplation phase and a scale revealing that teenagers are likely to make decisions based on the cost of quitting games (as contrasted to the advantages of stopping). The researchers also found that self-efficacy (particularly symptom management and interpersonal skills) was a good predictor of whether these youth would move into the contemplation phase.

Based on these findings, counselors might do well to help young clients develop better interpersonal skills and focus on symptom reduction before later dealing with assisting them to develop greater awareness of their Internet addiction. Then if the counselor helped them focus on the cost of quitting these games, adolescents might realize that the price is minimal.

Several books are available from Amazon.com that deal with video game addiction and Internet addiction. A recommended book for parents is *How to Help Children Addicted to Video Games: A Guide for Parents* by Dr. Brent Conrad (available as an instant download from http://www.techaddiction.ca/children-addicted-to-video-games.html).

Two movies might be of interest to counselors who want to better understand the appeal of video games to players. These movies may or may not be helpful for addicted individuals to watch. The first is called *King of Kong: A Fistful of Quarters* (1 hr, 22 min) produced as an American documentary in 2007. Attempts to become the new champion of the arcade game called Donkey Kong. The film has been critically acclaimed. Currently, a free version is available on YouTube at https://www.youtube.com/watch?v=fc-P8Kyvnz4.

The other movie produced as an American documentary in 2007 is called *Second Skin*. It follows the lives of seven people as they enter the world of MMORPGs. The film is available for purchase; however, the official trailer (1 min, 25 sec) it is worth watching and is available at https://www.youtube.com/watch?v=wWM-DTQWvN4.

BBC's Panorama produced two videos about video game addiction, parts 1 and 2. Part 1 is available at https://www.youtube.com/watch?v=R83287N6kFg and part 2 at https://www.youtube.com/watch?v=pE-5sm_Iqts.

Other videos are included in the later section of this chapter called Relevant Mutual Support Groups, Websites, and Videos. Another approach that may help someone get out of the precontemplation phase is attending mutual support groups such as On-Line Gamers Anonymous or Media Addicts Anonymous.

As in other addictions, helping relationships (i.e., counselor, family, friends) at this stage should focus on providing encouragement and support. People in this stage are not ready for action and pushing them to make change will be frustrating and futile.

Specific contemplation strategies.

The Teoh and Tan's (2010) study mentioned in the previous section found that, when it came to the contemplation, action, and maintenance phases, gamers considered the benefits of quitting gaming (i.e., pros of changing behavior) as having become more important to their change efforts. Based on these findings, counselors might do well to focus on how they deal with other addicted individuals in the contemplation phase: that is, helping clients to see the advantages of reducing or quitting their problematic Internet behavior. Some clients will also be ready to do more extensive reading about the negative consequences that result from Internet addiction. As with other addictions, emotional arousal can be facilitated by having clients talk about how their addiction is hurting them. Clients are more likely to be willing to attend a mutual support group at this stage. Helping relationships should continue focusing on support.

Kuss (2017) interviewed five adult gamers receiving help for excessive Internet use from an outpatient treatment center and found that they had limited insight into their need for counseling. Their reaching out for help followed an awareness that they had lost connection to reality. She also explained that they needed "substantial triggers" to seek help (e.g., losing a job, conflicts with family and/or friends, having a strong desire to become free of the game). Kuss suggested that counselors may need to work with gaming-addicted individuals to increase their internal motivation for change.

Specific preparation strategies.

Hartney (2018) offered several suggestions as to the things that can be done during the preparation stage that could be applied to any addiction. Her ideas are as follows:

1. Determine what the goal is (i.e., cut down, reduce harm, or quit altogether).
2. Acquire necessary resources (e.g., parental controls for Internet use, cell phone without data).
3. Get rid of triggers (e.g., only have a computer at school or work, delete Facebook account).
4. Ensure adequate supports are in place (e.g., tell friends and family what you intend to do and solicit their support).
5. If necessary, change the living situation (e.g., moving to a different location; more likely to be required for some people facing substance addictions).

Other preparation strategies might include

1. Self-monitoring (i.e., tracking the amount of time spent on the Internet, gaming, or using social media).
2. Blocking problematic Internet sites.
3. Take a complete break from the problematic technology device.
4. Limit amount of time (e.g., set a timer, check email only one to three times a day).

The counselor's role during the preparation stage continues to primarily focus on helping clients evaluate their problem and assist in creating commitment toward change. As mentioned in other chapters, the plan of action is most likely followed when it is constructed mainly by the client. Some suggested goals were included earlier in the section of this chapter called Goals and Goal Setting. Other ideas for *before* their chosen quit day (i.e., preparation strategies) can be found in Appendix B.

Specific action strategies.

Internet addiction. During the action stage, counselors can help clients take initial steps toward change with the attitude of experimenting to see what level of intervention might be required. For example, before taking further steps, clients might find out that they can first self-monitor and then limit the amount of time they spend on their problematic technology device, thereby relinquishing the need to take more drastic measures. As Young, Yue, and Ying (2011) suggested, the most appropriate treatment goal for Internet addiction in most cases is moderated and controlled use.

The published scientific literature paints a somewhat discouraging picture regarding how little we know about how to treat Internet addiction and IGD. Zajac, Ginley, Chang, and Petry (2017) conducted a systematic review of treatments for the two disorders, finding 13 that focused on treatments for IGD and 13 on Internet addiction. The results of their review highlighted a shortage of well-designed treatment outcome studies and little evidence to support the effectiveness of any particular treatment. Similar results were found from a review of 30 treatment studies for IGD (King et al., 2017). The review by King et al. (2017) concluded that the trials (a) lacked consistency in definition, diagnosis, and measurement, (b) lacked necessary randomization and blinding, (c) failed to provide adequate controls, and (d) provided insufficient information regarding recruitment dates, effect sizes, and sample characteristics.

Despite the lack of carefully controlled studies, several researchers and writers have claimed success using a multitude of methods. Korea has developed and implemented a nationwide screening system for Internet addiction. Cho (2015) described interventions used in South Korea to treat adolescents. Cho recommended four steps in sequence: (a) begin with an initial assessment, (b) use motivational interviewing (MI) techniques, (c) deal with the immediate and practical issues first before dealing with more profound concerns later, and (d) provide relapse management strategies. Individual counseling strategies are broken down into three phases:

1. Initial phase. The steps here include creating rapport, assessment, MI, and then helping the client recognize the problem and set goals.
2. Middle phase. These next steps depend on Korea's classification of addict subtypes. For the stimulus-seeking type, they recommend self-regulation training. The depressive type receives a cognitive-behavioral therapy (CBT) approach to treat depression. The weak peer relationship type receives social skills training. All clients in the middle phase receive help for changing their irrational thoughts on Internet use, time planning, finding replacement activities in place of Internet use, coping skills, career planning, etc.
3. Final phase. During this phase, maintaining a supportive environment continues while the counselors and clients plan for relapse and evaluation.

Cho (2015) also elaborated on their 8-week group counseling program. Each group would include seven or eight participants. The treatment is based on the transtheoretical model and CBT. Home visits may also occur, particularly for those who are socially withdrawn or are disconnected from social services for other reasons. The goal is to bring these youth into the counseling office. Some additional approaches used in Korea include residential programs such as intensive "school" or "camp." The last choice is hospitalization for seriously addicted clients.

Chun, Shim, and Kim (2017) provided a more favorable review of treatments for Internet addiction among Korean adolescents. Based on 70 studies, the researchers found that interventions for treating Internet addiction were effective (total effect size = 1.838). Integrative therapy appeared to be more effective than CBT and reality therapy. The authors concluded the best treatment to date involves integrative therapy offered in groups with nine to 12 participants for 8 or more weeks.

Khazaei, Khazaei, and Ghanbari-H. (2017) evaluated the efficacy of a group-based positive psychology (PP) intervention in treating Internet addiction. As they explained, PPs "refer to individual/group-based treatment methods that increase positive emotions and can enhance social relationships of individual(s)" (Khazaei et al., 2017, p. 304). A sample of 48 Internet-addicted university students was randomly assigned to either the experimental group or the control group (24 in each). The researchers found that PP was an effective method for treating Internet addiction. The treatment helped to mitigate Internet use and improved the quality of social relationships with members of the experimental group.

Kuss and Lopez-Fernandez (2016) conducted a systematic review of 46 relevant studies. Regarding treatment, they found 10 studies that met their criteria. The most common approach used to treat Internet addiction was CBT, usually offered on a one-on-one basis. The CBT programs were provided for a duration of eight to 28 sessions. The topics covered included the following:

1. Identifying the Internet application that was problematic.
2. Focusing on control issues (e.g., impulsivity, self-management).
3. Teaching healthy communication skills.
4. Increasing Internet awareness to online content and relationships developed on the Internet.
5. Learning to recognize the addictive behavior and discontinue it.
6. Other elements (e.g., career planning, marital discord, factors underlying Internet abuse).

In four of the five studies that included group therapy, the Internet-addicted individuals and family groups were treated simultaneously. The CBT modalities used were called multimodal school-based group, multifamily group therapy, traditional family therapy, and a multilevel intervention model (Kuss & Lopez-Fernandez, 2016). Details of these interventions are found in Kuss and Lopez-Fernandez (2016). Interestingly, the treatment studies that included a control group reported varying results. The Internet overuse was the same between the experimental and control groups in two studies, and, furthermore, only two of the four experimental studies found that psychological therapy was effective (Kuss & Lopez-Fernandez, 2016).

Several variations of family therapy approaches are highly recommended in the literature for young people dealing with IGD. These include brief strategic family therapy, systemic family therapy, and multidimensional family therapy (Day, 2017; Eidenbenz, 2011; Young, 2017).

Chrismore, Betzelberger, Bier, and Camacho (2011) argued that group counseling was the preferred modality. Cho (2015) wrote that group counseling acts as a support group for clients, which they need because of their fragile identities. Cho stated that this is important because a perceived lack of peer approval is one of the main precipitators of adolescent Internet addiction.

Six studies reviewed by Kuss and Lopez-Fernandez (2016) focused on combined therapy. CBT was again among the most common psychological therapy. One study reviewed combined CBT, MI, and an on-the-job lifestyle training program. The program included eliciting and strengthening motivation to change, picking a treatment goal, learning self-control, avoiding relapse, and coping skills. The treatment was successful in reducing Internet use, increasing social contacts, providing structure, encouraging different ways to use free time, and developing positive beliefs.

Watson (2015) summarized techniques that Kimberley Young suggested in several of her writings that were helpful in working with Internet-addicted individuals. These include the following:

1. Practicing the opposite. The opposite of having clients access the Internet whenever they want to is to restrict usage to the times where Internet activities are necessary. Counselors would work with clients to achieve this goal.
2. Establish visible reminders. Setting a timer or other reminders to get offline.
3. Setting achievable goals. Rather than encouraging clients to stop Internet use altogether, they might be helped to reduce their time online gradually.
4. Writing or typing reminder cards. Clients write what they will lose if they continue with their problematic Internet usage.
5. Writing or typing a personal inventory. Clients make a list of activities or responsibilities that were neglected because of their excessive Internet use. Then steps can be taken to ensure these activities are no longer overlooked.
6. Seeking out social support. This might involve participating in a support group or spending time with understanding friends and family.
7. Participating in group therapy with those who have been marginalized. This serves to rebuild relationships with friends and/or family who have been affected by the Internet addict.

Other therapies that have been either suggested or tried for Internet addiction include logotherapy (Didelot, Hollingsworth, & Buckenmeyer, 2012; Storey, 2017), community-based interventions (Markle, 2017), mindfulness-based techniques (Gamez-Guadix & Calvete, 2016; Li et al., 2017), narrative therapy (Graham, 2014), reality therapy (Yao et al., 2017), and acupuncture combined with a psychological intervention (Weinstein, Feder, Rosenberg, & Dannon, 2014).

Young and de Abreu (2011) claimed that a complete recovery requires overcoming the underlying issues that led to the Internet addiction in the first place. Young (2011) suggested that Internet-addicted individuals need to make amends with people they have neglected or rejected as well as to make a full recovery. Cho (2015) recommended social skills training, whereas Chun (2016) suggested that interventions need to focus on improving the self-esteem of addicted adolescents. Other ideas for *beginning* their chosen quit day (i.e., action strategies) can be found in Appendix B.

Internet gaming disorder. The previous interventions also apply to those experiencing IGD and social media addiction. In addition to these, there are a few suggestions explicitly made for IGD.

Eidenbenz (2011) recommended that counselors (and parents) show interest in the game in which the child or adolescent addicted individual plays to build and maintain a relationship. It is often the only topic the young person wants to talk about with any interest (Kiraly, Nagygyorgy, Griffiths, & Demetrovics, 2014). Eidenbenz suggested entering the young person's world by asking questions such as the following:

1. "What level do you play at?
2. What kind of avatar do you have?
3. Do you have multiple avatars? Are you in a guild or a clan?
4. What status does the clan have and how many of you are there?
5. How many raids do you do per week and when do you do them?" (p. 254)

A study tested the effect of using a manualized therapy for video game addiction in 12 males (ages 14–18). The results were varied with therapists rating only a moderate treatment response in only six of the 12 youth (Pallesen, Lorvik, Bu, & Molde, 2015). Other ideas for *beginning* their chosen quit day (i.e., action strategies) can be found in Appendix B.

Social media addiction. Romo et al. (2017) tested 1423 teenagers from the Paris region (mean age = 15.1 years) focused on pathological social networking use. They claimed that their literature review established the efficacy of CBT to help adolescents with problems relating to social network use. They also drew particular attention to the idea that prematurely labeling young people with a diagnosis of social media addiction could cause significant stigma.

Gupta, Arora, and Gupta (as cited in Griffiths, Kuss, and Demetrovics, 2014) suggested some strategies for counselors to help manage and treat Facebook addiction. Their ideas included the following:

1. Learn to recognize the symptoms of Facebook addiction.
2. Begin questioning the actions you are taking on Facebook.
3. Record exactly how much time you spend on Facebook.
4. Decide for yourself what is of value to you on Facebook.
5. Determine a specific time of the day to visit the site.
6. Give up Facebook for a particular event and monitor how you manage.

7. Consider turning off email notifications.
8. Think about ways to enable smarter use of Facebook in the future.
9. Do not get caught up in trying to increase your number of friends.
10. Avoid clichéd and automatic Facebook reactions (e.g., instead of "I'll Facebook you," try other phrases such as "See you soon").
11. When you think about going on to Facebook, meditate instead.

Other ideas for *beginning* their chosen quit day (i.e., action strategies) can be found in Appendix B.

Specific maintenance strategies and relapse prevention.

Note: Maintenance strategies and relapse prevention are also, for many, partly facilitated by regular attendance at relevant mutual support groups. A list of such mutual support groups and helpful websites is found in an upcoming section entitled Relevant Mutual Support Groups, Websites, and Videos.

There are no novel relapse prevention strategies for Internet addictions per se, but, given that many addicted individuals are children or adolescents who are underage, parents continue to have a responsibility to supervise their children's electronic usage. Counselors are advised to use Appendix C with their clients as these contain many relapse prevention strategies.

Motivational Interviewing

MI has also been used to help in the treatment of Internet addictions (Chele, Macarie, & Stefanescu, 2013; Tsitsika, Janikian, Greydanus, Omar, & Merrick, 2013; Young, 2011). Poddar, Sayeed, and Mitra (2015) applied motivational enhancement therapy (MET) to a case involving a 14-year-old boy addicted to gaming. Kuss and Lopez-Fernandez (2016) described MET for IGD as consisting of three steps: (a) contemplation stage (i.e., building rapport and case formulation), (b) preparation stage (i.e., psychoeducation, relaxation techniques, cost-benefit analysis of gaming addiction), and (c) contract stage (contract among the patient, a parent, and the counselor; focus on behavior modification of gaming, reducing time spent online, and promoting healthy activities). The MET manual as applied to alcohol problems is available at no cost from https://pubs.niaaa.nih.gov/publications/ProjectMatch/match02.pdf.

Here is an example of how MI could be used to help an addicted individual decide that counseling might be the best first step to take in recovery. The client is 13-year-old Cowan, a Native American child, and this is the first session. (Pertaining to Chapter 6's description of MI, the following is an example of the process called *engaging*.)

Counselor: Welcome, Cowan. It is a pleasure to meet you finally.

Client: I don't want to be here. I just want to be left alone [staring at the ground the entire time]. I didn't do anything wrong.

Counselor: I know you didn't do anything wrong. Your mother wanted me to see you because she says you are sometimes spending more than 20 hours a week on Facebook. How many friends do you have on Facebook, Cowan?

Client: I'm not telling you anything. The last time I talked to a counselor I was placed in child custody for a week.

Counselor: Boy, I can't imagine how that must've felt. Nothing like that ever happened to me when I was your age. We grew up poor, that's about it. You felt let down by that counselor.

Client: Yeah, I guess so. I don't think you people understand us.

Counselor: That is true. Not all of the White counselors understand how difficult it is to grow up without a lot of money and sometimes face discrimination, too. I want you to know that I admire you, Cowan, because you likely have a lot more friends than I do on Facebook. I only have 30 friends.

Client: Yeah, you are a loser! [says while still staring at the ground]

Counselor: [chuckles] Yep, I bet you have a lot more Facebook friends than I do. Who is your favorite friend?

Client: I don't really have a favorite friend. I've never even met most of my Facebook friends before. Sometimes I just randomly invite strangers.

Counselor: I never thought about doing that! Has that been a good way to get more Facebook friends?

Client: Yes, it has. I now have more friends than anyone in grade 7 at my school!

Counselor: Cowan, that is a real accomplishment! To be number one at something must feel really good.

Client: It does. It is the only thing that I am proud of.

Counselor: Having many friends is something to be proud of. It's a wonderful thing when you can talk to people about the stuff that bothers you or the stuff that matters.

Client: Well, I don't really talk to any of these people in any deep sort of way. I don't have a lot to say if the truth is known.

Counselor: I am fascinated by how hard you are trying to be connected to other people out there.

Client: Hum, thank you. Hum, can I have a Kleenex? [tears in his eyes]

Insight-Oriented Interventions

Langenbach and Schutte (2012) focused on traumatic experiences in patients' childhood as the cause of Internet addiction. In a study based on 27 consecutive cases (14–23 years, mean age = 17.5 years) to an outpatient program at a mental hospital, 60% of the adolescents displayed unconscious conflicts in their identity development, autonomy, and economic self-sufficiency. These adolescents were also deemed to have regressive psychic development and to have close dysfunctional relationships with their mothers.

Several studies in languages other than English have described psychoanalytic or psychodynamic approaches to helping

Internet-addicted individuals. A therapeutic model, called the Adolescent Psychotherapy Q-Set (APQ), was developed in Italy for adolescents experiencing several disorders, one of which is Internet addiction. It integrates psychoanalysis and developmental psychopathology. Di Lorenzo, Maggiolini, and Suigo (2014) asked 30 psychotherapists with an average of 14 years of experience to rate their practice with adolescents. The psychotherapists indicated that APQ is a useful tool that describes the therapy process with adolescents. Only the abstract is in English, and details of this method were not included.

Gojkovic (2011) reported that 10 Internet-addicted adolescents in Serbia-Croatia, who also experienced social and school phobia, were successfully treated using a psychodynamic approach. Only the abstract is in English, and the the article itself is in Serbo-Croatian.

A case study from Germany focused on a computer-game-addicted adolescent. Gerlach and Traxl (2015) focused on the psychodynamics regarding the impact of infantile and current relationship experiences on relationships with both family and peers. The authors concluded that psychodynamic conflict dominated online computer-game addiction. Psychodynamic approaches in Germany have focused on real relationships that might be viewed as frightening or depreciatory and virtual identities that might appear to be seductively controllable (Bilke-Hentsch, Sorychta, & Hellenschmidt, 2011).

An article from Pakistan tested 522 medical and dental students and found that 32 (6.1%) reported severe problems with Internet usage (Waqas et al., 2016). Scores on the Internet addiction test were negatively related to sublimation but positively correlated with projection, denial, autistic fantasy, passive aggression, and displacement.

Perrella and Caviglia (2017) used a sample of 153 adolescents (age range = 14–17 years) to ascertain specific relational patterns (i.e., object relations) and self-esteem. Problematic Internet use was not related to a particular object relations model, but it was related to having self-esteem issues. The authors concluded that psychodynamic research on Internet addiction should focus on self-esteem.

Games like World of Warcraft can be interpreted psychodynamically as a grand adventure that everyday life cannot deliver (Essig, 2012). Essig (2012) referred to this as "simulation entrapment" (p. 1175). Perhaps as Deeble (2008) theorized in her dissertation, excessive World of Warcraft use could be seen as users' attempts to make sense of their experience and find meaning in life.

Schimmenti and Caretti (2017) proposed a new construct called video-terminal dissociative trance (VDT). They defined VDT as a syndrome characterized by several symptoms in the area of addiction, regression, and an individual's dissociation regarding their use of the computer and its applications. Their conclusions suggested that VDT may involve a disturbance in one's state of consciousness, identity, and memory. Regarding dissociation, they concluded that an Internet addict's identity becomes replaced by a new virtual identity.

Li (2016) wrote about the psychodynamic factors underlying excessive social networking. Li described social networking as an extension of one's social self but organized in a way that is more controllable than what one can do in real life. Although these platforms are rewarding, they also induce much anxiety. Li went on to suggest that the addictive quality involves the "collapse of dialectical space and . . . defensive use of [it]" (Li, 2016, p. 91).

Spiritual Interventions

As reported in the earlier section of this chapter dealing with spiritual impacts, spirituality and/or religion appears to help buffer the likelihood of becoming an Internet addict. Sandoz (2004) claimed that our culture today encourages people to seek comfort from things rather than from other individuals. He suggested that one preventative measure is to spend time with family each week by interacting in playful ways. By developing family rituals, Sandoz suggested it would help to build emotional growth but, more important, it would help create a strong spiritual foundation among the family members.

Cognitive-Behavioral Therapy

CBT can be facilitated using the triple column technique. It can be used both by counselors in their work with clients and by clients alone. The full instructions for using the method are found in Chapter 6. The following are some of the cognitions that can be problematic for clients with Internet addictions. Note that the word "Internet" can be substituted for "online gaming," "Facebook," or any of the other specific addictions under this heading.

Automatic Thought or Belief	Questioning It	Healthier Thought or Belief
I can't function without the Internet.		I need to create a "real life" besides what the Internet provides.
I am worthless offline, but online I am someone.		My worth is independent of my status on the Internet. Every person, including me, has worth.
The Internet is the only place I will be respected.		I will develop respect in real life after I develop better social skills and acquire real friends.
I need to get on the Internet so I can stop thinking about my problems.		I need to deal constructively with my problems so they are either resolved or become more manageable.
I wish I didn't spend so much time online.		I need to plan and then take action to reduce my excessive Internet use.

As noted in the previous section called Specific Action Strategies, CBT has been extensively used to treat Internet addictions. Winkler, Dörsing, Rief, Shen, and Glombiewski (2013) concluded from their meta-analysis that preliminary results suggest that CBT outperforms other psychological treatments regarding the amount of time spent on the Internet. Young created her brand of CBT for Internet addiction (CBT-IA; Young & Brand, 2017), which involved the three phases of behavior modification, cognitive restructuring, and harm reductions. CBT-IA was shown to be helpful in reducing symptoms, changing unhealthy cognitions, and managing personal and situational factors related to symptoms (Young & Brand, 2017).

Watson (2015) provided a succinct summary of the three phases of CBT-IA:

1. Phase 1: behavioral modification. The counselor asks clients to keep a journal of their Internet use for 1–2. Clients keep track of the times they access the Internet, precipitating events, duration of time spent online, and consequences of their Internet usage. Once the baseline is established of problematic Internet behavior, the counselor and client work together to eradicate the questionable behavior.
2. Phase 2: cognitive restructuring. This phase follows typical CBT protocols. Internet-addicted individuals may do so because they believe the Internet is the only place where happiness will be found or that no one in the world loves or respects them.
3. Phase 3: harm reduction therapy. Counselors and clients work together to achieve two goals: identify the underlying issues that created the problem in the first place and then develop healthier coping strategies.

In a sample of 465 Australian adults (84% male, mean age = 26.2 years), Forrest, King, and Delfabbro (2017) found that four beliefs typified Internet gaming-addicted individuals:

1. Perfectionism. Wanting to be the best at particular games.
2. Cognitive salience. Thoughts about not being able to function without video games and ruminating about games when not playing.
3. Regret. Feeling personally responsible when negative consequences occur in the game and feeling the need to play less.
4. Behavioral salience. Thoughts about needing to repeat some of the activities in the game as well as thoughts about the amount of time invested.

Through their analysis, Forrest et al. found that that cognitive salience and regret were the most important thoughts in problematic gamers longitudinally, followed by perfectionism. Problematic gaming may also have underlying cognitions dealing with gaining social acceptance, self-esteem, and self-acceptance (Forrest, King, & Delfabbro, 2016) and escapism from thinking about real-life problems (Taquet, Romo, Cottencin, Ortiz, & Hautekeete, 2017).

For anyone planning to run a group based on CBT principles, de Abreu and Sampaio Goes (2011) provided a thorough description of their program. Their program includes many of the best techniques of CBT practice.

RELEVANT MUTUAL SUPPORT GROUPS, WEBSITES, AND VIDEOS

Mutual Support Groups

For the Addicted Individual

1. On-Line Gamers Anonymous. http://www.olganon.org/welcome-recovering-gamers

   Quoted from website:

   We're a community of people who have a desire to stop gaming. Many of us have stories like yours. When we came here we were desperate, afraid, depressed. Today, many of us have successfully stayed away from games for weeks, months and years.

2. Media Addicts Anonymous. http://mediaanonymous.org/

   Quoted from website:

   Media Anonymous™ is a fellowship of individuals who share their experience, strength and hope with each other that they may solve their common problem and help others to recover from the effects of media addiction or dependency.

   The only requirement for membership is a desire to stop compulsive bottom line behavior in relation to Media.

3. Emotions Anonymous (EA). http://emotionsanonymous.org/

   Quoted from website:

   Emotions Anonymous is an international fellowship of men and women who desire to improve their emotional well-being. EA members come together in weekly meetings for the purpose of working toward recovery from any sort of emotional difficulties. EA members are of diverse ages, races, economic status, social and educational backgrounds. The only requirement for membership is a desire to become well emotionally. . . . We also offer phone and skype groups if there are no face to face groups in your area—but you can always start one!

For the Partner and/or Family

These groups are intended to help family members refrain from behaviors that may trigger the addict. They also target underlying maladaptive thoughts and behaviors of the co-addict. Lastly, they focus on facilitating spiritual growth.

OLG-Anon. http://www.olganon.org/welcome-family-and-loved-ones

Quoted from website:

The olganon.org website supports:

1. The OLGA fellowship (recovering excessive/addicted gamers)
2. The OLG-Anon fellowship (friends and family of excessive gamers)
3. Outreach (press/media, professionals, the public service division that educates about the "dark-side" of gaming.)

Websites

1. Internet gaming addiction: Current perspectives. https://www.ncbi.nlm.nih.gov/pmc/articles/PMC3832462/
2. Internet Addiction. https://www.addictions.com/internet/
3. Internet Gaming Disorder vs. Internet Addiction Disorder. https://www.psychologytoday.com/blog/in-excess/201607/internet-gaming-disorder-vs-internet-addiction-disorder
4. Internet addiction is Sweeping America, affecting millions. https://www.cnbc.com/2017/08/29/us-addresses-internet-addiction-with-funded-research.html
5. Tech Addiction: Effective Help for Video Game and Computer Addiction. http://www.techaddiction.ca/
6. Online Social Network Site Addiction: A Comprehensive Review. https://link.springer.com/article/10.1007/s40429-015-0056-9
7. 7 Telltale Signs of Facebook Addiction. https://www.hongkiat.com/blog/facebook-addiction-signs/

   115 Mind-Boggling Facts You Never Knew About Social Media. https://azaharmedia.com/social-media-facts-infographic/
8. Smartphone Addiction. Tips For Breaking Free of Compulsive Smartphone Use https://www.helpguide.org/articles/addictions/smartphone-addiction.htm

Videos

To view these videos, search their titles on YouTube.

1. *What you need to know about internet addiction | Dr. Kimberly Young | TEDxBuffalo.*
2. *What you are missing while being a digital zombie | Patrik Wincent | TEDxStockholm.*
3. *Shosh Shlam on Internet Addicts in 'Web Junkie': VICE Meets.*
4. *Connected, but alone? | Sherry Turkle.*
5. *Is Social Media Hurting Your Mental Health? | Bailey Parnell | TEDxRyersonU.*
6. *Quit social media | Dr. Cal Newport | TEDxTysons.*
7. *Psychologist Discusses Facebook Addiction.*

RELEVANT PHONE APPS

Generic Addiction Apps

Note: Generic apps are described in Chapter 6.

This list is not exhaustive. New apps are continually being developed. Do an Internet search to find out the latest apps available. Most are for specific addictions but some, such as these four, are generic.

1. I Am Sober. https://play.google.com/store/apps/details?id=com.thehungrywasp.iamsober
2. Sober Time. https://play.google.com/store/apps/details?id=com.sociosoft.sobertime
3. Pocket Rehab: Get Sober & Addiction Recovery. https://play.google.com/store/apps/details?id=com.getpocketrehab.app
4. Loop Habit Tracker. https://play.google.com/store/apps/details?id=org.isoron.uhabits

Specialized Apps

1. AppDetox. App Blocker for Digital Detox. https://play.google.com/store/apps/details?id=de.dfki.appdetox&hl=en

   Quoted from website:

   Get more social time for your life, block apps and spent less time on the phone!

2. Net Nanny. https://get.netnanny.com/netnanny/?pid=3&utm_source=bing&utm_medium=cpc&utm_campaign=Brand%20-%20NonUS%20-%20CoreTerm&utm_term=net%20nanny&utm_content=Brand_NetNanny_Term_Exact

   Quoted from website:

   Be in control of your Internet. Set Filtering for 18 categories of online content to either block, warn, or allow for view.

3. Freedom. https://alternativeto.net/software/macfreedom/

   Quoted from website:

   Freedom is an application that disables networking on an Apple computer for up to eight hours at a time. At the end of your selected offline period, Freedom re-enables your network, restoring everything as normal.

4. Cold Turkey. https://alternativeto.net/software/cold-turkey/

   Quoted from website:

   Cold Turkey is a productivity program that you can use to temporarily block yourself off of popular social media sites, addicting websites and games so that you can get your work done.

5. Social Fever. https://play.google.com/store/apps/details?id=com.systweak.social_fever&hl=en

   Quoted from website:

   - Let's [*sic*] you limit app usage by setting timers
   - Let's [*sic*] you track your cell phone usage for better understating of what is 'wise usage'
   - Keeps tabs on how many times you unlocked the phone
   - Monitors app over usage and shows a pop-up message.

6. Quality Time—My Digital Diet. https://play.google.com/store/apps/details?id=com.zerodesktop.appdetox.qualitytime&hl=en

   Quoted from website:

   QualityTime is a fun, visually engaging and easy-to-use Android app that allows you to monitor and get real time reports on how much time you spend on your smartphone and on your favorite apps.

7. StayOnTask. https://play.google.com/store/apps/details?id=valavg.stayontask

   Quoted from website:

   Added option that adjusts the timer so that it will interrupt you less often when you're "On Task" and more often when you've been loafing.

   RealizD. http://www.realizd.com/ Quoted from website:

   Do you think that your're spending a lot of time in front of your devices and want to reduce the screen time? Maybe you want to address phone addiction and start a digital diet right now? RealizD is a professionally designed app created specifically for monitoring your [. . .] use at all times. It's a high quality tool that delivers a great user experience via controls, alerts, graphics, insights and stats alongside many others.

JOURNALS AND CONFERENCES

Journals

1. *Computers in Human Behavior*. Quoted from the website: "*Computers in Human Behavior* is a scholarly journal dedicated to examining the use of computers from a psychological perspective." https://www.journals.elsevier.com/computers-in-human-behavior/

2. *Cyberpsychology, Behavior, and Social Networking*. Quoted from website: "The premier peer-reviewed journal for authoritative research on understanding the social, behavioral, and psychological impact of today's social networking practices, including Twitter, Facebook, and internet gaming and commerce." https://home.liebertpub.com/publications/cyberpsychology-behavior-and-social-networking/10/overview

3. *International Journal of Cyber Behavior, Psychology and Learning*. Quoted from website: [Focusing] "on cyber behavior, psychology, and learning, IJCBPL encourages the exploration of emerging areas in cyber learning such as online social communication, individual differences, cognitive and metacognitive learning, etc. to generate deep understanding about the behavior, information processing, and psychological orientations of online learners. https://www.igi-global.com/journal/international-journal-cyber-behavior-psychology/1182

Other journals that frequently publish in the areas of Internet-based addictions include *Journal of Behavioral Addictions, Addictive Behaviors, Addictive Behaviors Reports, Addiction Research & Theory, Psychiatry Research*, and *Frontiers in Psychiatry*.

Conferences

1. International Society of Internet Addiction. This society hosts an annual conference. Details at https://isiaweb.wordpress.com/

2. International Conference on Behavioral Addictions. The fifth International conference was held in Cologne, Germany, and many of the keynote speakers were experts on Internet addiction. The exact website changes every year so do a Google search for details.

3. International Congress of Technology Addiction. Their fourth Congress was held in 2017. Details at http://technologyaddiction.org/en/
4. American Society of Addictive Medicine (ASAM) Annual Conference. A generic conference offered each year. Details at https://www.asam.org/education/live-online-cme/the-asam-annual-conference
5. National Conference on Addiction Disorders. This conference is touted as the country's "premier annual event" (para. 1; https://www.theaddictionconference.com/), held in both the east and the west (NCAD East, NCAD West). See website for details.

INDIVIDUAL EXERCISES

1. Begin by thinking about your use of the Internet, including gaming and social media. Approximately how much time per week are you engaged in one of these activities? How would you distinguish between healthy use and excessive use for yourself?
2. Interview someone who you know who is heavily involved in gaming. After asking her or him a series of questions about usage, ask yourself if this person gave any indication of meeting one or more criteria for Internet addiction or IGD. Which symptoms were present, and which were not?
3. For one night, involve yourself excessively in some aspect of Internet use. Do something that you have not done before. If you are a gamer, focus instead on Internet searching, Facebook, or your cellular phone. If you are not a gamer, immerse yourself in a game, perhaps with someone who is. What aspects of yourself could you see becoming addicted to that activity? What is it that prevents you from becoming an Internet addict?

CLASSROOM EXERCISES

1. Read the chapter by Doan, Yung, Cazares, and Klam (2017) about future careers regarding IGD and Internet addiction. Which careers would be a good choice for you, and why would you pick them? Which careers would not be chosen by you, and why not?
2. Ask someone to present in class who self-identifies as an Internet addict, a gaming addict, or a social media addict. Before the individual presents, create a list of questions to ask him or her. Which criteria for addiction does this person meet, and which do they not?
3. In groups of four, discuss friends and family that each person knows who displays some signs or symptoms of Internet addiction, IGD, or social media addiction. What additional signs or symptoms would be necessary before your group would think this person is an addict?

CHAPTER SUMMARY

In the same year that Neil Armstrong said "That's one small step for [a] man, one giant leap for mankind" as he landed on the moon, the Internet as we know it today was born. Most of us are aware of many of the benefits the Internet has brought to us, but along with this advancement has come a new form of problematic behavior: Internet-based addictions. *Internet addiction* is compulsive Internet use that results in negative consequences. Although the diagnosis remains controversial, everyone agrees that it's growing in prevalence globally. In this chapter, Internet-based addictions included a generic Internet addiction, IGD (a potential diagnosis found in the appendix of *DSM-5*), and social media addiction (e.g., Facebook, cell phones). Like other addictions, hallmarks of Internet-based addictions are a loss of control, continuing to use despite harmful consequences, subjective distress or dysfunction resulting from this behavior, using it to escape or cope with problems, loss of interest in non-Internet activities, and experiencing psychological withdrawal effects when the Internet or the device is unavailable.

Comorbidity with Internet-based addictions is as high as 86%. Although no specific medications for Internet addictions have been approved by the FDA currently, psychological approaches have shown varying degrees of effectiveness. Treatments often involve CBT, CBT-IA, MI, group counseling, and family counseling.

REFERENCES

Aboujaoude, E. (2017). The Internet's effect on personality traits: An important casualty of the "Internet addiction" paradigm. *Journal of Behavioral Addictions, 6*, 1–4.

Akbari, M. (2017). Metacognitions or distress intolerance: The mediating role in the relationship between emotional dysregulation and problematic internet use. *Addictive Behaviors Reports, 6*, 128–133.

American Psychiatric Association (APA). (2013). *Diagnostic and statistical manual of mental disorders* (5th ed.). Washington, DC: Author.

Anam-ul, M., & Rafiq, N. (2016). Exploring the relationship of personality, loneliness, and online social support with interned addiction and procrastination. *Pakistan Journal of Psychological Research*, *31*(1), 93–117.

Anderson, M. (2015, December 15). Views on gaming differ by race, ethnicity. *Pew Research Center*. Retrieved on March 31, 2018, from http://www.pewresearch.org/fact-tank/2015/12/17/views-on-gaming-differ-by-race-ethnicity/

Anderson, R. (2017). Understanding video game mechanics as a tool in creating a sustainable relationship with digital media. In J. D. Christenson & A. N. Merritts (Eds.), *Family therapy with adolescents in residential treatment: Intervention and research* (pp. 49–70). Cham, Switzerland: Springer.

Andreassen, C. S., Billieux, J., Griffiths, M. D., Kuss, D. J., & Demetrovics, Z., . . . Pallesen, S. (2016). The relationship between addictive use of social media and video games and symptoms of psychiatric disorders: A large-scale cross-sectional study. *Psychology of Addictive Behaviors*, *30*, 252–262.

Andreassen, C. S., Pallesen, S., & Griffiths, M. D. (2017). The relationship between addictive use of social media, narcissism, and self-esteem: Findings from a large national survey. *Addictive Behaviors*, *64*, 287–293.

Andreassen, C. S., Torsheim, T., Brunborg, G. S., & Pallesen, S. (2012). Development of a Facebook Addiction Scale. *Psychological Reports*, *110*, 501–517.

Arcelus, J., Bouman, W. P., Jones, B. A., Richards, C., Jimenez-Murcia, S., & Griffiths, M. D. (2017). Video gaming and gaming addiction in transgender people: An exploratory study. *Journal of Behavioral Addictions*, *6*, 21–29.

Ballabio, M., Griffiths, M. D., Urban, R., Quartiroli, A., Demetrovics, Z., & Kiraly, O. (2017). Do gaming motives mediate between psychiatric symptoms and problematic gaming? An empirical survey study. *Addiction Research & Theory*, *25*, 397–408.

Banyai, F., Zsila, A., Kiraly, O., Maraz, A., Elekes, Z., Griffiths, M. D., . . . Demetrovics, Z. (2016). Problematic social media use: Results from a large-scale nationally representative adolescent sample. *PLoS ONE*, *12*(1). Retrieved from http://ovidsp.ovid.com/ovidweb.cgi?T=JS&PAGE=reference&D=psyc13&NEWS=N&AN=2017-03915-001.

Bargeron, A. H., & Hormes, J. M. (2017). Psychosocial correlates of internet gaming disorder: Psychopathology, life satisfaction, and impulsivity. *Computers in Human Behavior*, *68*, 388–394.

Bean, A. M., Nielsen, R. K. L., van Rooij, A. J., & Ferguson, C. J. (2017). Video game addiction: The push to pathologize video games. *Professional Psychology: Research and Practice*, *48*, 378–389.

Beard, C. L., Haas, A. L., Wickham, R. E., & Stavropoulos, V. (2017). Age of initiation and internet gaming disorder: The role of self-esteem. *Cyberpsychology, Behavior, and Social Networking*, *20*, 397–401.

Beranuy, M., Carbonell, X., & Griffiths, M. D. (2013). A qualitative analysis of online gaming addicts in treatment. *International Journal of Mental Health and Addiction*, *11*, 149–161.

Bernardi, S, & Pallanti, S. (2009). Internet addiction: A descriptive clinical study focusing on comorbidities and dissociative symptoms. *Comprehensive Psychiatry*, *50*(6), 510–516.

Bhandari, P. M., Neupane, D., Rijal, S., Thapa, K., Mishra, S. R., & Poudyal, A. K. (2017). Sleep quality, internet addiction and depressive symptoms among undergraduate students in Nepal. *BMC Psychiatry*, *17*, 1–8.

Bilke-Hentsch, O., Sorychta, H., & Hellenschmidt, T. (2011). Psychodynamics and conflicts in male adolescent Internet addicted patients. *Sucht: Zeitschrift fur Wissenschaft und Praxis*, *57*, 9–15.

Blachnio, A., & Przepiorka, A. (2016a). Dysfunction of self-regulation and self-control in Facebook addiction. *Psychiatric Quarterly*, *87*, 493–500.

Blachnio, A., & Przepiorka, A. (2016b). Personality and positive orientation in Internet and Facebook addiction. An empirical report from Poland. *Computers in Human Behavior*, *59*, 230–236.

Blackwell, D., Leaman, C., Tramposch, R., Osborne, C., & Liss, M. (2017). Extraversion, neuroticism, attachment style and fear of missing out as predictors of social media use and addiction. *Personality and Individual Differences*, *116*, 69–72.

Blinka, L., & Smahel, D. (2011). Addiction to online role-playing games. In K. S. Young & C. Nabuco de Abreu (Eds.), *Internet addiction: A handbook and guide to evaluation and treatment* (pp. 73–90). Hoboken, NJ: John Wiley & Sons.

Braun, B., Kornhuber, J., & Lenz, B. (2016). Gaming and religion: The impact of spirituality and denomination. *Journal of Religion and Health*, *55*, 1464–1471.

Busch, V., Laninga-Wijnen, L., Petrus Schrijvers, A. J., & De Leeuw, J. R. J. (2017). Associations of health behaviors, school performance and psychosocial problems in adolescents in The Netherlands. *Health Promotion International*, *32*, 280–291.

Camardese, G., Leone, B., Walstra, C., Janiri, L., & Guglielmo, R. (2015). Pharmacological treatment of Internet addiction. In C. Montag & M. Reuter (Eds.), *Internet addiction: Neuroscientific approaches and therapeutical interventions* (pp. 151–165). New York, NY: Springer Science + Business Media.

Campbell, C. (2018, March 30). *Why is Fortnite Battle Royale so wildly popular?* Retrieved on December 16, 2018, from https://www.polygon.com/fortnite-battle-royale/2018/3/30/17177068/why-is-fortnite-popular

Canan, F. (2016). The relationship between Internet addiction and eating disorders. *Eating and Weight Disorders*, *21*, 137–138.

Caplan, S. E., & High, A. C. (2011). Online social interaction, psychosocial well-being, and problematic Internet use. In K. S. Young & C. Nabuco de Abreu (Eds.), *Internet addiction: A handbook and guide to evaluation and treatment* (pp. 35–53). Hoboken, NJ: John Wiley & Sons.

Carbonell, X., & Panova, T. (2017). A critical consideration of social networking sites' addiction potential. *Addiction Research & Theory*, *25*, 48–57.

Carli, V., & Durkee, T. (2016). Pathological use of the Internet. In D. Mucic & D. M. Hilty (Eds.), *e-Mental health* (pp. 269–288). Cham, Switzerland: Springer International.

Carras, M. C., Van Rooij, A. J., Van de Mheen, D., Musci, R., Xue, Q.-L., & Mendelson, T. (2017). Video gaming in a hyperconnected world: A cross-sectional study of heavy gaming, problematic gaming symptoms, and online socializing in adolescents. *Computers in Human Behavior*, *68*, 472–479.

Casale, S., & Fioravanti, G. (2017). Shame experiences and problematic social networking sites use: An unexplored association. *Clinical Neuropsychiatry: Journal of Treatment Evaluation*, *14*(1), 44–48.

Casale, S., & Fioravanti, G. (2018). Why narcissists are at risk for developing Facebook addiction: The need to be admired and the need to belong. *Addictive Behaviors*, *76*, 312–318.

Casale, S., Fioravanti, G., & Rugai, L. (2016). Grandiose and vulnerable narcissists: Who is at higher risk for social networking addiction? *Cyberpsychology, Behavior, and Social Networking*, *19*, 510–515.

Cerniglia, L., Zoratto, F., Cimino, S., Laviola, G., Ammaniti, M., & Adriani, W. (2017). Internet addiction in adolescence: Neurobiological, psychosocial and clinical issues. *Neuroscience and Biobehavioral Reviews, 76*(Part A), 174–184.

Charlton, J. P., Soh, P. C.-H., Ang, P. H., & Chew, K.-W. (2013). Religiosity, adolescent Internet usage motives and addiction: An exploratory study. *Information, Communication & Society, 16*, 1619–1638.

Chele, G. E., Macarie, G., & Stefanescu, C. (2013). Management of Internet addictive behaviors in adolescents. *International Journal of Child and Adolescent Health, 6*(4), 443–453.

Chen, B., Liu, F., Ding, S., Ying, X., Wang, L., & Wen, Y. (2017). Gender differences in factors associated with smartphone addiction: A cross-sectional study among medical college students. *BMC Psychiatry, 17*, 1–9.

Chen, Y., Kang, Y., Gong, W., He, L., Jin, Y., Zhu, X., & Yao, Y. (2016). Investigation on Internet addiction disorder in adolescents in Anhui, People's Republic of China. *Neuropsychiatric Disease and Treatment, 12*, 2233–2236.

Chi, X., Lin, L., & Zhang, P. (2016). Internet addiction among college students in China: Prevalence and psychosocial correlates. *Cyberpsychology, Behavior, and Social Networking, 19*, 567–573.

Cho, E. (2015). Therapeutic interventions for treatment of adolescent Internet addiction: Experiences from South Korea. In C. Montag & M. Reuter (Eds.), *Internet addiction: Neuroscientific approaches and therapeutical interventions* (pp. 167–181). New York, NY: Springer Science + Business Media.

Choi, S.-W., Kim, D.-J., Choi, J.-S., Ahn, H., Choi, E.-J., Song, W.-Y., . . . Youn, H. (2015). Comparison of risk and protective factors associated with smartphone addiction and Internet addiction. *Journal of Behavioral Addictions, 4*(4), 308–314.

Chotpitayasunondh, V., & Douglas, K. M. (2016). How "phubbing" becomes the norm: The antecedents and consequences of snubbing via smartphone. *Computers in Human Behavior, 63*, 9–18.

Chou, W.-P., Lee, K.-H., Ko, C.-H., Liu, T.-L., Hsiao, R. C., Lin, H. F., & Yen, C.-F. (2017). Relationship between psychological inflexibility and experiential avoidance and internet addiction: Mediating effects of mental health problems. *Psychiatry Research, 257*, 40–44.

Chrismore, S., Betzelberger, E., Bier, L., & Camacho, T. (2011). Twelve-step recovery in inpatient treatment for Internet addiction. In K. S. Young & C. Nabuco de Abreu (Eds.), *Internet addiction: A handbook and guide to evaluation and treatment* (pp. 205–222). Hoboken, NJ: John Wiley & Sons.

Chun, J. (2016). Effects of psychological problems, emotional dysregulation, and self-esteem on problematic internet use among Korean adolescents. *Children and Youth Services Review, 68*, 187–192.

Chun, J., Shim, H., & Kim, S. (2017). A meta-analysis of treatment interventions for Internet addiction among Korean adolescents. *Cyberpsychology, Behavior, and Social Networking, 20*, 225–231.

Colder Carras, M., Porter, A. M., Van Rooij, A. J., King, D., Lange, A., Carras, M., & Labrique, A. (2018). Gamers' insights into the phenomenology of normal gaming and game "addiction": A mixed methods study. *Computers in Human Behavior, 79*, 238–246.

Connors, G. J., DiClemente, C. C., Velasquez, M. M., & Donovan, D. M. (2013). *Substance abuse treatment and the stages of change: Selecting and planning interventions* (2nd ed.). New York, NY: Guilford Press.

Contractor, A. A., Frankfurt, S. B., Weiss, N. C., & Elhai, J. D. (2017). Latent-level relations between *DSM-5* PTSD symptom clusters and problematic smartphone use. *Computers in Human Behavior, 72*, 170–177.

Cross, N. A. (2017). The relationship of online gaming addiction with motivations to play and craving. *Dissertation Abstracts International: Section B: The Sciences and Engineering, 78*(2-B(E)). No pagination specified.

Dantlgraber, M., Wetzel, E., Schutzenberger, P., Stieger, S., & Reips, U.-D. (2016). Simple construct evaluation with latent class analysis: An investigation of Facebook addiction and the development of a short form of the Facebook Addiction Test (F-AT). *Behavior Research Methods, 48*, 869–879.

Day, I. (2017). A family systems approach to the understanding and treatment of internet gaming disorder. *Family Journal, 25*, 264–270.

De Abreu, C. N., & Sampaio Goes, D. (2011). Psychotherapy for Internet addiction. In K. S. Young & C. N. de Abreu (Eds.), *Internet addiction: A handbook and guide to evaluation and treatment* (pp. 155–171). Hoboken, NJ: John Wiley & Sons.

Deeble, L. (2008). Problematic Internet use and the "World of Warcraft"—Addiction linked to a quest for meaning. *Dissertation Abstracts International: Section B: The Sciences and Engineering, 69*(3-B), 1949.

De Vries, D. A., & Kuhne, R. (2015). Facebook and self-perception: Individual susceptibility to negative social comparison on Facebook. *Personality and Individual Differences, 86*, 217–221.

De Vries, H. T., Nakamae, T., Fukui, K., Denys, D., & Narumoto, J. (2018). Problematic internet use and psychiatric co-morbidity in a population of Japanese adult psychiatric patients. *BMC Psychiatry, 18*, 1–10.

D'Hondt, F., & Maurage, P. (2017). Electrophysiological studies in internet addiction: A review within the dual-process framework. *Addictive Behaviors, 64*, 321–327.

Didelot, M. J., Hollingsworth, L., & Buckenmeyer, J. A. (2012). Internet addiction: A logotherapeutic approach. *Journal of Addictions & Offender Counseling, 33*, 18–33.

Di Lorenzo, M., Maggiolini, A., & Suigo, V. (2014). A developmental perspective of adolescent psychotherapy. An Italian study with the Adolescent Psychotherapy Q-Set. *Psichiatria e Psicoterapia, 33*(4), 343–365.

Di Nicola, M., Ferri, V. R., Moccia, L., Panaccione, I., Strangio, A. M., Tedeschi, D., . . . Janiri, L. (2017). Gender differences and psychopathological features associated with addictive behaviors in adolescents. *Frontiers in Psychiatry, 8*, 1–10.

Doan, A. P., Yung, K., Cazares, P., & Klam, W. P. (2017). Internet gaming disorder and Internet addiction disorder: Future careers in research, education, and treatment. In M. M. Maheu, K. P. Drude, & S. D. Wright (Eds.), *Career paths in telemental health* (pp. 53–61). Cham, Switzerland: Springer.

Donati, M. A., Chiesi, F., Ammannato, G., & Primi, C. (2015). Versatility and addiction in gaming: The number of video-game genres played is associated with pathological gaming in male adolescents. *Cyberpsychology, Behavior, and Social Networking, 18*(2), 129–132.

Drouin, M., Miller, D., Wehle, S. M. J., & Hernandez, E. (2016). Why do people lie online? "Because everyone lies on the Internet." *Computers in Human Behavior, 64*, 134–142.

Duke, E., & Montag, C. (2017). Smartphone addiction, daily interruptions and self-reported productivity. *Addictive Behaviors Reports, 6*, 90–95.

Dunckley, V. L. (2017). Electronic screen syndrome: Prevention and treatment. In K. S. Young & C. N. de Abreu (Eds.), *Internet addiction in children and adolescents: Risk factors, assessment, and treatment* (pp. 213–242). New York, NY: Springer.

Eichenbaum, A., Kattner, F., Bradford, D., Gentile, D. A., & Green, C. (2015). Role-playing and real-time strategy games associated with greater probability of internet gaming disorder. *Cyberpsychology, Behavior, and Social Networking, 18*(8), 480–485.

Eichenberg, C., Schott, M., Decker, O., & Sindelar, B. (2017). Attachment style and Internet addiction: An online survey. *Journal of Medical Internet Research, 19*(5), 316–324.

Eidenbenz, F. (2011). Systemic dynamics with adolescents addicted to the Internet. In K. S. Young & C. Nabuco de Abreu (Eds.), *Internet addiction: A handbook and guide to evaluation and treatment* (pp. 245–266). Hoboken, NJ: John Wiley & Sons.

Elhai, J. D., Dvorak, R. D., Levine, J. C., & Hall, B. J. (2017). Problematic smartphone use: A conceptual overview and systematic review of relations with anxiety and depression psychopathology. *Journal of Affective Disorders, 207*, 251–259.

Eliacik, K., Bolat, N., Kocyigit, C., Kanik, A., Selkie, E., Yilmaz, H., . . . Dundar, B. N. (2016). Internet addiction, sleep and health-related life quality among obese individuals: A comparison study of the growing problems in adolescent health. *Eating and Weight Disorders, 21*(4), 709–717.

Errity, A., Rooney, B., & Tunney, C. (2016). Gaming. In I. Connolly, M. Palmer, H. Barton, & G. Kirwan (Eds.), *An introduction to cyberpsychology* (pp. 257–270). New York, NY: Routledge/Taylor & Francis.

Essig, T. (2012). The addiction concept and technology: Diagnosis, metaphor, or something else? A psychodynamic point of view. *Journal of Clinical Psychology, 68*, 1175–1184.

Estevez, A., Urbiola, I., Iruarrizaga, I., Onaindia, J., & Jauregui, P. (2017). Emotional dependency in dating relationships and psychological consequences of Internet and mobile abuse. *Anales de Psicologia, 33*(2), 260–268.

Flood, C. (2016). Abnormal cyberpsychology and cybertherapy. In I. Connolly, M. Palmer, H. Barton, & G. Kirwan (Eds.), *An introduction to cyberpsychology* (pp. 153–166). New York, NY: Routledge/Taylor & Francis.

Forrest, C. J., King, D. L., & Delfabbro, P. H. (2016). The measurement of maladaptive cognitions underlying problematic video-game playing among adults. *Computers in Human Behavior, 55*(Part A), 399–405.

Forrest, C. J., King, D. L., & Delfabbro, P. H. (2017). Maladaptive cognitions predict changes in problematic gaming in highly-engaged adults: A 12-month longitudinal study. *Addictive Behaviors, 65*, 125–130.

Frost, R. L., & Rickwood, D. J. (2017). A systematic review of the mental health outcomes associated with Facebook use. *Computers in Human Behavior, 76*, 576–600.

Gamez-Guadix, M., & Calvete, E. (2016). Assessing the relationship between mindful awareness and problematic Internet use among adolescents. *Mindfulness, 7*, 1281–1288.

Garcia-Oliva, C., & Piqueras, J. A. (2016). Experiential avoidance and technological addictions in adolescents. *Journal of Behavioral Addictions, 5*(2), 293–303.

Gerlach, M., & Traxl, B. (2015). "What I don't appreciate in real life": Online role playing game addiction of an adolescent—Case study. *Praxis der Kinderpsychologie und Kinderpsychiatrie, 64*, 460–479.

Gervasi, A. M., La Marca, L., Lombardo, E. M. C., Mannino, G., Iacolino, C., & Schimmenti, A. (2017). Maladaptive personality traits and Internet addiction symptoms among young adults: A study based on the alternative *DSM-5* model for personality disorders. *Clinical Neuropsychiatry: Journal of Treatment Evaluation, 14*(1), 20–28.

Gojkovic, J. (2011). School phobia and Internet addiction disorder in adolescents. *Socijalna Psihijatrija, 39*(4), 235–242.

Gomez, P., Rial, A., Brana, T., Golpe, S., & Varela, J. (2017). Screening of problematic internet use among Spanish adolescents: Prevalence and related variables. *Cyberpsychology, Behavior, and Social Networking, 20*, 259–267.

Graham, J., Jr. (2014). Narrative therapy for treating video game addiction. *International Journal of Mental Health and Addiction, 12*(6), 701–707.

Greenfield, D. (2011). The addictive properties of Internet usage. In K. S. Young & C. Nabuco de Abreu (Eds.), *Internet addiction: A handbook and guide to evaluation and treatment* (pp. 135–153). Hoboken, NJ: John Wiley & Sons.

Griffiths, M. (2011). Gambling addiction on the Internet. In K. S. Young & C. Nabuco de Abreu (Eds.), *Internet addiction: A handbook and guide to evaluation and treatment* (pp. 91–111). Hoboken, NJ: John Wiley & Sons.

Griffiths, M. D. (2005). A 'components' model of addiction within a biopsychosocial framework. *Journal of Substance Use, 10*, 191–197.

Griffiths, M. D. (2016). Gaming addiction and internet gaming disorder. In R. Kowert & T. Quandt (Eds.), *The video game debate: Unravelling the physical, social, and psychological effects of digital games* (pp. 74–93). New York, NY: Routledge/Taylor & Francis.

Griffiths, M. D., Kiraly, O., Pontes, H. M., & Demetrovics, Z. (2015). An overview of problematic gaming. In E. Aboujaoude & V. Starcevic (Eds.), *Mental health in the digital age: Grave dangers, great promise* (pp. 27–45). New York, NY: Oxford University Press.

Griffiths, M. D., & Kuss, D. J. (2015). Online addictions: Gambling, video gaming, and social networking. In S. S. Shyam (Ed.), *The handbook of the psychology of communication technology* (pp 384–403). Hoboken, NJ: Wiley-Blackwell.

Griffiths, M. D., Kuss, D. J., & Demetrovics, Z. (2014). Social networking addiction: An overview of preliminary findings. In K. P. Rosenberg & L. Curtiss Feder (Eds.), *Behavioral addictions: Criteria, evidence, and treatment* (pp. 119–141). San Diego, CA: Elsevier Academic Press.

Guillot, C. R., Bello, M. S., Tsai, J. Y., Huh, J., Leventhal, A. M., & Sussman, S. (2016). Longitudinal associations between anhedonia and internet-related addictive behaviors in emerging adults. *Computers in Human Behavior, 62*, 475–479.

Hajela, R., & Love, T. (2017). Addiction beyond substances: What's up with the DSM? *Sexual Addiction & Compulsivity, 24*, 11–22.

Hartney, E. (2018, March 19). *The stages of change model of overcoming addiction.* Retrieved on April 3, 2018, from https://www.verywellmind.com/the-stages-of-change-model-of-overcoming-addiction-21961

He, Q., Turel, O., Brevers, D., & Bechara, A. (2017). Excess social media use in normal populations is associated with amygdala-striatal but not with prefrontal morphology. *Psychiatry Research: Neuroimaging, 269*, 31–35.

Hou, X.-L., Wang, H.-Z., Guo, C., Gaskin, J., Rost, D. H., & Wang, J.-L. (2017). Psychological resilience can help combat the effect of stress on problematic social networking site usage. *Personality and Individual Differences, 109*, 61–66.

Hu, J., Zhen, S., Yu, C., Zhang, Q., & Zhang, W. (2017). Sensation seeking and online gaming addiction in adolescents: A moderated mediation model of positive affective associations and impulsivity. *Frontiers in Psychology, 8*, 1–8.

Hussain, Z., Griffiths, M. D., & Sheffield, D. (2017). An investigation into problematic smartphone use: The role of narcissism, anxiety, and personality factors. *Journal of Behavioral Addictions, 6*, 378–386.

Hussain, Z., Williams, G. A., & Griffiths, M. D. (2015). An exploratory study of the association between online gaming addiction and enjoyment motivations for playing massively multiplayer online role-playing games. *Computers in Human Behavior, 50*, 221–230.

Janikian, M. (2013). Assessment of Internet addictive behavior. *International Journal of Child and Adolescent Health, 6*(4), 391–398.

Jenaro, C., Flores, N., Cruz, M., Perez, M. C., Vega, V., & Torres, V. A. (2018). Internet and cell phone usage patterns among young adults with intellectual disabilities. *Journal of Applied Research in Intellectual Disabilities, 31*, 259–272.

Jia, R., & Jia, H. H. (2016). Maybe you should blame your parents: Parental attachment, gender, and problematic Internet use. *Journal of Behavioral Addictions, 5*, 524–528.

Jiao, C., Wang, T., Peng, X., & Cui, F. (2017). Impaired empathy processing in individuals with internet addiction disorder: An event-related potential study. *Frontiers in Human Neuroscience, 11*, 1–10.

Johnson, N. F., & Keane, H. (2017). Internet addiction? Temporality and life online in the networked society. *Time & Society, 26*, 267–285.

Jorgenson, A. G., Hsiao, R. C.-J., & Yen, C.-F. (2016). Internet addiction and other behavioral addictions. *Child and Adolescent Psychiatric Clinics of North America, 25*(3), 509–520.

Kaess, M., Parzer, P., Brunner, R., Koenig, J., Durkee, T., Carli, V., . . . Wasserman, D. (2016). Pathological internet use is on the rise among European adolescents. *Journal of Adolescent Health, 59*(2), 236–239.

Kaptsis, D., King, D. L., Delfabbro, P. H., & Gradisar, M. (2016). Trajectories of abstinence-induced Internet gaming withdrawal symptoms: A prospective pilot study. *Addictive Behaviors Reports, 4*, 24–30.

Kardefelt-Winther, D. (2014). Meeting the unique challenges of assessing Internet gaming disorder. *Addiction, 109*(9), 1568–1570.

Karim, R., & Chaudhri, P. (2012) Behavioral addictions: An overview. *Journal of Psychoactive Drugs, 44*(1), 5–17.

Kayis, A. R., Satici, S. A., Yilmaz, M. F., Simsek, D., Ceyhan, E., & Bakioglu, F. (2016). Big five-personality trait and internet addiction: A meta-analytic review. *Computers in Human Behavior, 63*, 35–40.

Khan, A., & Muqtadir, R. (2016). Motives of problematic and nonproblematic online gaming among adolescents and young adults. *Pakistan Journal of Psychological Research, 31*(1), 119–138.

Khazaei, F., Khazaei, O., & Ghanbari-H., B. (2017). Positive psychology interventions for internet addiction treatment. *Computers in Human Behavior, 72*, 304–311.

Kim, K., Lee, H., Hong, J. P., Cho, M. J., Fava, M., Mischoulon, D., . . . Jeon, H. J. (2017). Poor sleep quality and suicide attempt among adults with internet addiction: A nationwide community sample of Korea. *PLoS ONE, 12*(4), 1–13.

Kim, S.-E., Kim, J.-W., & Jee, Y.-S. (2015). Relationship between smartphone addiction and physical activity in Chinese international students in Korea. *Journal of Behavioral Addictions, 4*, 200–205.

Kim, S. M., & Han, D. H. (2015). Neurobiological aspects of problematic Internet and video game use. In E. Aboujaoude & V. Starcevic (Eds.), *Mental health in the digital age: Grave dangers, great promise* (pp. 69–85). New York, NY: Oxford University Press.

Kimpton, M., Campbell, M., Weigin, E. L., Orel, A., Wozencroft, K., & Whiteford, C. (2016). The relation of gender, behavior, and intimacy development on level of Facebook addiction in emerging adults. *International Journal of Cyber Behavior, Psychology and Learning, 6*, 56–67.

King, D. L., Delfabbro, P. H., Wu, A. M. S., Doh, Y. Y., Kuss, D. J., Pallesen, S., . . . Hiroshi, S. (2017). Treatment of Internet gaming disorder: An international systematic review and CONSORT evaluation. *Clinical Psychology Review, 54*, 123–133.

King, D. L., Herd, M. C. E., & Delfabbro, P. H. (2018). Motivational components of tolerance in internet gaming disorder. *Computers in Human Behavior, 78*, 133–141.

King, D. L., Kaptsis, D., Delfabbro, P. H., & Gradisar, M. (2016). Craving for internet games? Withdrawal symptoms from an 84-h abstinence from Massively Multiplayer Online gaming. *Computers in Human Behavior, 62*, 488–494.

Kiraly, O., Nagygyorgy, K., Griffiths, M. D., & Demetrovics, Z. (2014). Problematic online gaming. In K. P. Rosenberg & L. Curtiss Feder (Eds.), *Behavioral addictions: Criteria, evidence, and treatment* (pp. 61–97). San Diego, CA: Academic Press.

Kiraly, O., Toth, D., Urban, R., Demetrovics, Z., & Maraz, A. (2017). Intense video gaming is not essentially problematic. *Psychology of Addictive Behaviors, 31*, 807–817.

Kormendi, A., Brutoczki, Z., Vegh, B. P., & Szekely, R. (2016). Smartphone use can be addictive? A case report. *Journal of Behavioral Addictions, 5*, 548–552.

Korpa, T. N., & Papadopoulou, P. V. (2013). Clinical signs and symptoms of addictive behaviors. In A. Tsitsika, M. Janikian, D. E. Greydanus, H. A. Omar, & J. Merrick (Eds.), *Internet addiction: A public health concern in adolescence* (pp. 3–14). Hauppauge, NY: Nova Science.

Kuss, D. J. (2017). "I can't do it by myself": An IPA of clients seeking psychotherapy for their MMORPG addiction. In Information Resources Management Association (Ed.), *Gaming and technology addiction: Breakthroughs in research and practice* (Vol. *1*, pp. 566–599). Hershey, PA: Information Science Reference/ IGI Global.

Kuss, D. J., & Billieux, J. (2017). Technological addictions: Conceptualisation, measurement, etiology and treatment. *Addictive Behaviors, 64*, 231–233.

Kuss, D. J., Griffiths, M. D., & Pontes, H. M. (2017). Chaos and confusion in *DSM-5* diagnosis of Internet Gaming Disorder: Issues, concerns, and recommendations for clarity in the field. *Journal of Behavioral Addictions, 6*, 103–109.

Kuss, D. J., & Lopez-Fernandez, O. (2016). Internet addiction and problematic Internet use: A systematic review of clinical research. *World Journal of Psychiatry, 6*(1), 143–176.

Lachmann, B., Sariyska, R., Kannen, C., Cooper, A., & Montag, C. (2016). Life satisfaction and problematic internet use: Evidence for gender specific effects. *Psychiatry Research, 238*, 363–367.

Laconi, S., Vigouroux, M., Lafuente, C., & Chabrol, H. (2017). Problematic Internet use, psychopathology, personality, defense and coping. *Computers in Human Behavior, 73*, 47–54.

Langenbach, M., & Schutte, J. (2012). Online addiction as an attempt to compensate traumatic experiences. *Sucht: Zeitschrift fur Wissenschaft und Praxis, 58*, 195–202.

Lau, J. T. F., Gross, D. L., Wu, A. M. S., Cheng, K.-m., & Lau, M. M. C. (2017). Incidence and predictive factors of Internet addiction among Chinese secondary school students in Hong Kong: A longitudinal study. *Social Psychiatry and Psychiatric Epidemiology, 52*, 657–667.

Lee, H.-K., Kim, J.-H., Fava, M., Mischoulon, D., Park, J.-H., Shim, E.-J., . . . Jeon, H. J. (2017). Development and validation study of the Smartphone Overuse Screening Questionnaire. *Psychiatry Research, 257*, 352–357.

Lee, J., Sung, M.-J., Song, S.-H., Lee, Y.-M., Lee, J.-J., Cho, S.-M., . . . Shin, Y.-M. (2018). Psychological factors associated with smartphone addiction in South Korean adolescents. *Journal of Early Adolescence, 38*(3), 288–302.

Lee, Y. (2018). Exploring the role of escapism in the DSM-V criteria for internet gaming disorder: A meta-analytic investigation. *Dissertation Abstracts International Section A: Humanities and Social Sciences, 79*(1-A(E)). No pagination specified.

Lehenbauer-Baum, M., & Fohringer, M. (2017). Internet gaming disorder: A deeper look into addiction vs. high engagement. In Information Resources Management Association (Ed.), *Gaming and technology addiction: Breakthroughs in research and practice* (Vol. 1, pp. 1–15). Hershey, PA: Information Science Reference/IGI Global.

Lemmens, J. S., & Hendriks, S. J. F. (2016). Addictive online games: Examining the relationship between game genres and internet gaming disorder. *Cyberpsychology, Behavior, and Social Networking, 19(4)*, 270–276.

Lewis, M. S. (2017). Massively multiplayer online roleplaying gaming: Motivation to play, player typologies, and addiction. *Dissertation Abstracts International: Section B: The Sciences and Engineering, 78*(4-B(E)). No pagination specified.

Li, T. C. W. (2016). Psychodynamic factors behind online social networking and its excessive use. *Psychodynamic Psychiatry, 44*, 91–104.

Li, W., Garland, E. L., McGovern, P., O'Brien, J. E., Tronnier, C., & Howard, M. O. (2017). Mindfulness-oriented recovery enhancement for internet gaming disorder in U.S. adults: A stage I randomized controlled trial. *Psychology of Addictive Behaviors, 31*, 393–402.

Li, X. (2018). Cumulative risk and Chinese adolescent problematic internet use: The mediating role of self-esteem. *Dissertation Abstracts International: Section B: The Sciences and Engineering, 79*(1-B(E)). No pagination specified.

Li, X., Newman, J., Li, D., & Zhang, H. (2016). Temperament and adolescent problematic Internet use: The mediating role of deviant peer affiliation. *Computers in Human Behavior, 60*, 342–350.

Lin, Y.-H., Chiang, C.-L., Lin, P.-H., Chang, L.-R., Ko, C.-H., Lee, Y.-H., & Lin, S.-H. (2016). Proposed diagnostic criteria for smartphone addiction. *PLoS ONE, 11*(11), 1–11.

Lin, Y.-H., Pan, Y.-C., Lin, S.-H., & Chen, S.-H. (2017). Development of short-form and screening cutoff point of the Smartphone Addiction Inventory (SPAI-SF). *International Journal of Methods in Psychiatric Research, 26*(2), 1–6.

Liu, C. (2015). Long term effects of video and computer game heavy use on health, mental health and education outcomes among adolescents in the U.S. *Dissertation Abstracts International Section A: Humanities and Social Sciences, 76*(6-A(E)). No pagination specified.

Lopez-Fernandez, O. (2017). Short version of the Smartphone Addiction Scale adapted to Spanish and French: Towards a cross-cultural research in problematic mobile phone use. *Addictive Behaviors, 64*, 275–280.

Lu, W.-H., Lee, K.-H., Ko, C.-H., Hsiao, R. C., Hu, H.-F., & Yen, C.-F. (2017). Relationship between borderline personality symptoms and Internet addiction: The mediating effects of mental health problems. *Journal of Behavioral Addictions, 6*, 434–441.

Lyvers, M., Karantonis, J., Edwards, M. S., & Thorberg, F. A. (2016). Traits associated with internet addiction in young adults: Potential risk factors. *Addictive Behaviors Reports, 3*, 56–60.

Mak, K.-K., Lai, C.-M., Watanabe, H., Kim, D.-I., Bahar, N., Ramos, M., . . . Cheng, C. (2014). Epidemiology of Internet behaviors and addiction among adolescents in six Asian countries. *Cyberpsychology, Behavior, and Social Networking, 17*(11), 720–728.

Malak, M. Z., Khalifeh, A. H., & Shuhaiber, A. H. (2017). Prevalence of Internet Addiction and associated risk factors in Jordanian school students. *Computers in Human Behavior, 70*, 556–563.

Mann, K., Kiefer, F., Schellekens, A., & Dom, G. (2017). Behavioural addictions: Classification and consequences. *European Psychiatry, 44*, 187–188.

Marino, C., Gini, G., Vieno, A., & Spada, M. M. (2018). The associations between problematic Facebook use, psychological distress and well-being among adolescents and young adults: A systematic review and meta-analysis. *Journal of Affective Disorders, 226*, 274–281.

Marino, C., Vieno, A., Altoe, G., & Spada, M. M. (2017). Factorial validity of the Problematic Facebook Use Scale for adolescents and young adults. *Journal of Behavioral Addictions, 6*, 5–10.

Markle, T. (2017). The FITSC-IA model: A community-based approach. In K. S. Young & C. N. de Abreu (Eds.), *Internet addiction in children and adolescents: Risk factors, assessment, and treatment* (pp. 257–282). New York, NY: Springer.

McNicol, M. L., & Thorsteinsson, E. B. (2017). Internet addiction, psychological distress, and coping responses among adolescents and adults. *Cyberpsychology, Behavior, and Social Networking, 20*, 296–304.

Mehroof, M., & Griffiths, M. D. (2010). Online gaming addiction: The role of sensation seeking, self-control, neuroticism, aggression, state anxiety, and trait anxiety. *Cyberpsychology, Behavior, and Social Networking, 13*, 313–316.

Mihara, S., Osaki, Y., Nakayama, H., Sakuma, H., Ikeda, M., Itani, O., . . . Higuchi, S. (2016). Internet use and problematic Internet use among adolescents in Japan: A nationwide representative survey. *Addictive Behaviors Reports, 4*, 58–64.

Milkman, H. B., & Sunderwirth, S. G. (2010). *Craving for ecstasy and natural highs: A positive approach to mood alteration*. Thousand Oaks, CA: SAGE.

Miller, B., Mundey, P., & Hill, J. (2013). Faith in the age of Facebook: Exploring the links between religion and social network site membership and use. *Sociology of Religion, 74*, 227–253.

Milosevic-Dordevic, J. S., & Zezelj, I. L. (2014). Psychological predictors of addictive social networking sites use: The case of Serbia. *Computers in Human Behavior, 32*, 229–234.

Moore, D. (2017). Internet and gaming addiction in youth on the autism spectrum: A particularly vulnerable population. In K. S. Young & C. N. de Abreu (Eds.), *Internet addiction in children and adolescents: Risk factors, assessment, and treatment* (pp. 83–100). New York, NY: Springer.

Muench, F., Hayes, M., Kuerbis, A., & Shao, S. (2015). The independent relationship between trouble controlling Facebook use, time spent on the site and distress. *Journal of Behavioral Addictions, 4*, 163–169.

Musetti, A., Cattivelli, R., Giacobbi, M., Zuglian, P., Ceccarini, M., Capelli, F., . . . Castelnuovo, G. (2016). Challenges in Internet addiction disorder: Is a diagnosis feasible or not? *Frontiers in Psychology, 7*, 1–8.

Myrseth, H., Notelaers, G., Strand, L. A., Borud, E. K., & Olsen, O. K. (2017). Introduction of a new instrument to measure motivation for gaming: The electronic gaming motives questionnaire. *Addiction, 112*, 1658–1668.

Myrseth, H., Olsen, O. K., Strand, L. A., & Borud, E. K. (2017). Gaming behavior among conscripts: The role of lower psychosocial well-being factors in explaining gaming addiction. *Military Psychology, 29*, 128–142.

Na, E., Choi, I., Lee, T.-H., Lee, H., Rho, M.-J., Cho, H., . . . Kim, D.-J. (2017). The influence of game genre on Internet gaming disorder. *Journal of Behavioral Addictions*, *6*, 248–255.

Nam, B., Bae, S., Kim, S. M., Hong, J. S., & Han, D. H. (2017). Comparing the effects of bupropion and escitalopram on excessive internet game play in patients with major depressive disorder. *Clinical Psychopharmacology and Neuroscience*, *15*, 361–368.

Ni, X., Qian, Y., & Wang, Y. (2017). Factors affecting pathological Internet use among Chinese university students. *Social Behavior and Personality*, *45*, 1057–1068.

Noyes, D. (2018, March 14). *The top 20 valuable Facebook statistics – Updated March 2018*. Retrieved on March 20, 2018, from https://zephoria.com/top-15-valuable-facebook-statistics/

Nuyens, F., Deleuze, J., Maurage, P., Griffiths, M. D., Kuss, D. J., & Billieux, J. (2016). Impulsivity in Multiplayer Online Battle Arena gamers: Preliminary results on experimental and self-report measures. *Journal of Behavioral Addictions*, *5*(2), 351–356.

Nuyens, F., Kuss, D. J., Lopez-Fernandez, O., & Griffiths, M. D. (2017). The experimental analysis of problematic video gaming and cognitive skills: A systematic review. *Journal de Therapie Comportementale et Cognitive*, *27*, 110–117.

Odaci, H., & Celik, C. B. (2017). Internet dependence in an undergraduate population: The roles of coping with stress, self-efficacy beliefs, and sex role orientation. *Journal of Educational Computing Research*, *55*, 395–409.

Ong, R. H. S., Peh, C. X., & Guo, S. (2016). Differential risk factors associated with adolescent addictive disorders: A comparison between substance use disorders and Internet/gaming addiction. *International Journal of Mental Health and Addiction*, *14*, 993–1002.

Orosz, G., Toth-Kiraly, I., Bothe, B., & Melher, D. (2016). Too many swipes for today: The development of the Problematic Tinder Use Scale (PTUS). *Journal of Behavioral Addictions*, *5*, 518–523.

Ozer, I. (2015). Facebook addiction, intensive social networking site use, multitasking, and academic performance among university students in the United States, Europe, and Turkey: A multigroup structural equation modeling approach. *Dissertation Abstracts International Section A: Humanities and Social Sciences*, *76*(5-A(E)). No pagination specified.

Palaus, M., Marron, E. M., Viejo-Sobera, R., & Redolar-Ripoll, D. (2017). Neural basis of video gaming: A systematic review. *Frontiers in Human Neuroscience*, *11*, 1–40.

Pallesen, S., Lorvik, I. M., Bu, E. H., & Molde, H. (2015). An exploratory study investigating the effects of a treatment manual for video game addiction. *Psychological Reports*, *117*, 490–495.

Pantic, I., Milanovic, A., Loboda, B., Blachnio, A., Przepiorka, A., Nesic, D., . . . Ristic, S. (2017). Association between physiological oscillations in self-esteem, narcissism and internet addiction: A cross-sectional study. *Psychiatry Research*, *258*, 239–243.

Park, B., Han, D. H., & Roh, S. (2017). Neurobiological findings related to Internet use disorders. *Psychiatry and Clinical Neurosciences*, *71*, 467–478.

Park, J. H., Lee, Y. S., Sohn, J. H., & Han, D. H. (2016). Effectiveness of atomoxetine and methylphenidate for problematic online gaming in adolescents with attention deficit hyperactivity disorder. *Human Psychopharmacology: Clinical and Experimental*, *31*, 427–432.

Pavia, L., Cavani, P., Di Blasi, M., & Giordano, C. (2016). Smartphone Addiction Inventory (SPAI): Psychometric properties and confirmatory factor analysis. *Computers in Human Behavior*, *63*, 170–178.

Pearson, C., & Hussain, Z. (2015). Smartphone use, addiction, narcissism, and personality: A mixed methods investigation. *International Journal of Cyber Behavior, Psychology and Learning*, *5*, 17–32.

Peeters, M., Koning, I., & van den Eijnden, R. (2018). Predicting Internet Gaming Disorder symptoms in young adolescents: A one-year follow-up study. *Computers in Human Behavior*, *80*, 255–261.

Perrella, R., & Caviglia, G. (2017). Internet addiction, self-esteem, and relational patterns in adolescents. *Clinical Neuropsychiatry: Journal of Treatment Evaluation*, *14*(1), 82–87.

Poddar, S., Sayeed, N., & Mitra S. (2015). Internet gaming disorder: Application of motivational enhancement therapy principles in treatment. *Indian Journal of Psychiatry*, *57*, 100–101.

Pontes, H. M., & Griffiths, M. D. (2017). New concepts, old known issues: The *DSM-5* and Internet gaming disorder and its assessment. In Information Resources Management Association (Ed.), *Gaming and technology addiction: Breakthroughs in research and practice* (Vol. 1, pp. 883–898). Hershey, PA: Information Science Reference/IGI Global.

Pontes, H. M., Stavropoulos, V., & Griffiths, M. D. (2017). Measurement invariance of the Internet Gaming Disorder Scale-Short-Form (IGDS9-SF) between the United States of America, India and the United Kingdom. *Psychiatry Research*, *257*, 472–478.

Prochaska, J. O., Norcross, J. C., & DiClemente, C. C. (1994). *Changing for good*. New York, NY: Avon Books.

Przybylski, A., Murayama, K., DeHaan, C. R., & Gladwell, V. (2013). Motivational, emotional, and behavioural correlates of fear of missing out. *Computers in Human Behaviour*, *29*(4), 1841–1848.

Przybylski, A. K., Weinstein, N., & Murayama, K. (2017). Internet gaming disorder: Investigating the clinical relevance of a new phenomenon. *American Journal of Psychiatry*, *174*, 230–236.

Reiner, I., Tibubos, A. N., Hardt, J., Muller, K., Wolfling, K., & Beutel, M. E. (2017). Peer attachment, specific patterns of Internet use and problematic Internet use in male and female adolescents. *European Child & Adolescent Psychiatry*, *26*, 1257–1268.

Roberts, J. A. (2015). *Too much of a good thing: Are you addicted to your smartphone?* Austin, TX: Sentia.

Robertson, T. W., Yan, Z., & Rapoza, K. A. (2018). Is resilience a protective factor of internet addiction? *Computers in Human Behavior*, *78*, 255–260.

Romano, M., Roaro, A., Re, F., Osborne, L. A., Truzoli, R., & Reed, P. (2017). Problematic internet users' skin conductance and anxiety increase after exposure to the internet. *Addictive Behaviors*, *75*, 70–74.

Romo, L., Saleh, D., Scanferla, E., Coeffec, A., Cheze, N., & Taquet, P. (2017). Can cognitive and behavioral therapy be adapted for the problematic use of social network? *Journal de Therapie Comportementale et Cognitive*, *27*, 99–109.

Rosenberg, K. P., O'Connor, S., & Carnes, P. (2014). Sex addiction: An overview. In K. P. Rosenberg & L. Curtiss Feder (Eds.), *Behavioral addictions: Criteria, evidence, and treatment* (pp. 215–236). San Diego, CA: Elsevier Academic Press.

Rosenkranz, T., Muller, K. W., Dreier, M., Beutel, M. E., & Wolfling, K. (2017). Addictive potential of Internet applications and differential correlates of problematic use in Internet gamers versus generalized Internet users in a representative sample of adolescents. *European Addiction Research*, *23*, 148–156.

Sahin, M., Gumus, Y. Y., & Dincel, S. (2016). Game addiction and academic achievement. *Educational Psychology*, *36*, 1533–1543.

Sanders, J. L., & Williams, R. J. (2016). Reliability and validity of the Behavioral Addiction Measure for video gaming. *Cyberpsychology, Behavior, and Social Networking*, *19*, 43–48.

Sandoz, J. (2004). Internet addiction. *Annals of the American Psychotherapy Association, 7*(1), 34.

Saquib, N., Saquib, J., Wahid, A., Ahmed, A. A., Dhuhayr, H. E., Zaghloul, M. S., . . . Al-Mazrou, A. (2017). Video game addiction and psychological distress among expatriate adolescents in Saudi Arabia. *Addictive Behaviors Reports, 6*, 112–117.

Saunders, J. B., Hao, W., Long, J., King, D. L., Mann, K., Fauth-Buhler, M., . . . Poznyak, V. (2017). Gaming disorder: Its delineation as an important condition for diagnosis, management, and prevention. *Journal of Behavioral Addictions, 6*, 271–279.

Schell, B. H. (2016). *Online health and safety: From cyberbullying to internet addiction*. Santa Barbara, CA: Greenwood Press/ABC-CLIO.

Schimmenti, A., & Caretti, V. (2017). Video-terminal dissociative trance: Toward a psychodynamic understanding of problematic Internet use. *Clinical Neuropsychiatry: Journal of Treatment Evaluation, 14*(1), 64–72.

Schimmenti, A., Infanti, A., Badoud, D., Laloyaux, J., & Billieux, J. (2017). Schizotypal personality traits and problematic use of massively-multiplayer online role-playing games (MMORPGs). *Computers in Human Behavior, 74*, 286–293.

Schmitt, Z. L., & Livingston, M. G. (2015). Video game addiction and college performance among males: Results from a 1 year longitudinal study. *Cyberpsychology, Behavior, and Social Networking, 18*(1), 25–29.

Schneider, L. A., King, D. L., & Delfabbro, P. H. (2017). Family factors in adolescent problematic Internet gaming: A systematic review. *Journal of Behavioral Addictions, 6*, 321–333.

Scimeca, G., Bruno, A., Crucitti, M., Conti, C., Quattrone, D., Pandolfo, G., . . . Muscatello, M. R. A. (2017). Abnormal illness behavior and Internet addiction severity: The role of disease conviction, irritability, and alexithymia. *Journal of Behavioral Addictions, 6*, 92–97.

Shaw, M., & Black, D. W. (2008). Internet addiction: definition, assessment, epidemiology and clinical management. *CNS Drugs, 22*(5), 353–365.

Shettar, M., Karkal, R., Kakunje, A., Mendonsa, R. D., & Chandran, V. V. M. (2017). Facebook addiction and loneliness in the post-graduate students of a university in southern India. *International Journal of Social Psychiatry, 63*, 325–329.

Shin, Y. M. (2017). Smartphone addiction in children and adolescents. In K. S. Young & C. N. de Abreu (Eds.), *Internet addiction in children and adolescents: Risk factors, assessment, and treatment* (pp. 29–45). New York, NY: Springer.

Shokri, O., Potenza, M. N., & Sanaeepour, M. H. (2017). A preliminary study suggesting similar relationships between impulsivity and severity of problematic Internet use in male and female Iranian college students. *International Journal of Mental Health and Addiction, 15*, 277–287.

Sigerson, L., Li, A. Y.-L., Cheung, M. W.-L., & Cheng, C. (2017). Examining common information technology addictions and their relationships with non-technology-related addictions. *Computers in Human Behavior, 75*, 520–526.

Sioni, S. R., Burleson, M. H., & Bekerian, D. A. (2017). Internet gaming disorder: Social phobia and identifying with your virtual self. *Computers in Human Behavior, 71*, 11–15.

Skarupova, K., & Blinka, L. (2016). Interpersonal dependency and online gaming addiction. *Journal of Behavioral Addictions, 5*, 108–114.

Smahel, D., Brown, B. B., & Blinka, L. (2012). Associations between online friendship and Internet addiction among adolescents and emerging adults. *Developmental Psychology, 48*, 381–388.

Smahel, D., Wright, M. F., & Cernikova, M. (2015). The impact of digital media on health: Children's perspectives. *International Journal of Public Health, 60*, 131–137.

Smith, C., & Snell, P. (2009). *Souls in transition: The religious and spiritual lives of emerging adults*. New York, NY: Oxford University Press.

Snodgrass, J. G., Bagwell, A., Patry, J. M., Dengah, H. J. F., II, Smarr-Foster, C., Van Oostenburg, M., & Lacy, M. G. (2018). The partial truths of compensatory and poor-get-poorer internet use theories: More highly involved videogame players experience greater psychosocial benefits. *Computers in Human Behavior, 78*, 10–25.

Song, J., Park, J. H., Han, D. H., Roh, S., Son, J. H., Choi, T. Y., . . . Lee, Y. S. (2016). Comparative study of the effects of bupropion and escitalopram on internet gaming disorder. *Psychiatry and Clinical Neurosciences, 70*, 527–535.

Soper, W. B., & Miller, M. J. (1983). Junk-time junkies: An emerging addiction among students. *School Counselor, 31*(1), 40–43.

Spada, M. M., & Caselli, G. (2017). The Metacognitions about Online Gaming Scale: Development and psychometric properties. *Addictive Behaviors, 64*, 281–286.

Spada, M. M., & Marino, C. (2017). Metacognitions and emotion regulation as predictors of problematic Internet use in adolescents. *Clinical Neuropsychiatry: Journal of Treatment Evaluation, 14*(1), 59–63.

Starcevic, V., & Billieux, J. (2017). Does the construct of Internet addiction reflect a single entity or a spectrum of disorders? *Clinical Neuropsychiatry: Journal of Treatment Evaluation, 14*(1), 5–10.

Statista. (2018a). *Genre breakdown of video game sales in the United States in 2016*. Retrieved on March 19, 2018, from https://www.statista.com/statistics/189592/breakdown-of-us-video-game-sales-2009-by-genre/

Statista. (2018b). *Video game console sales worldwide for products total lifespan as of September 2017 (in million units)*. Retrieved on March 19, 2018, from https://www.statista.com/statistics/268966/total-number-of-game-consoles-sold-worldwide-by-console-type/

Stavropoulos, V., Gomez, R., Steen, E., Beard, C., Liew, L., & Griffiths, M. D. (2017). The longitudinal association between anxiety and Internet addiction in adolescence: The moderating effect of classroom extraversion. *Journal of Behavioral Addictions, 6*, 237–247.

Stip, E., Thibault, A., Beauchamp-Chatel, A., & Kisely, S. (2016). Internet addiction, Hikikomori syndrome, and the prodromal phase of psychosis. *Frontiers in Psychiatry, 7*, 1–8.

Stockdale, L., & Coyne, S. M. (2018). Video game addiction in emerging adulthood: Cross-sectional evidence of pathology in video game addicts as compared to matched healthy controls. *Journal of Affective Disorders, 225*, 265–272.

Storey, L. (2017). Prisoners of the web: Utilizing logotherapy for the dehumanizing consequences of Internet addiction. *International Forum for Logotherapy, 40*(1), 16–23.

Suler, J. (2004). Computer and cyberspace "addiction." *International Journal of Applied Psychoanalytic Studies, 1*, 359–362.

Taquet, P., Romo, L., Cottencin, O., Ortiz, D., & Hautekeete, M. (2017). Video game addiction: Cognitive, emotional, and behavioral determinants for CBT treatment. *Journal de Therapie Comportementale et Cognitive, 27*, 118–128.

Tateno, M., Teo, A. R., Shirasaka, T., Tayama, M., Watabe, M., & Kato, T. A. (2016). Internet addiction and self-evaluated attention-deficit hyperactivity disorder traits among Japanese college students. *Psychiatry and Clinical Neurosciences, 70*(12), 567–572.

Taymur, I., Budak, E., Demirci, H., Akdag, H. A., Gungor, B. B., & Ozdel, K. (2016). A study of the relationship between internet addiction, psychopathology and dysfunctional beliefs. *Computers in Human Behavior, 61*, 532–536.

Teoh, L. S. C., & Tan, A.-G. (2010). A study of the transtheoretical model of behaviour change in computer gaming. *Ricerche di Psicologia, 33*(1), 141–155.

Tian, M., Tao, R., Zheng, Y., Zhang, H., Yang, G., Li, Q., & Liu, X. (2018). Internet gaming disorder in adolescents is linked to delay discounting but not probability discounting. *Computers in Human Behavior, 80*, 59–66.

Tromholt, M., Lundby, M., Andsbjergand, K., & Wiking, M. (2015). The Facebook experiment: Does social media affect the quality of our lives? Happiness Research Institute. Retrieved on May 30, 2018, from https://www.happinessresearchinstitute.com/copy-of-publications-1

Truzoli, R., Osborne, L. A., Romano, M., & Reed, P. (2016). The relationship between schizotypal personality and internet addiction in university students. *Computers in Human Behavior, 63*, 19–24.

Tsitsika, A., Janikian, M., Greydanus, D. E., Omar, H. A., & Merrick, J. (2013). Internet addiction: A public health concern in adolescence. In A. Tsitsika, M. Janikian, D. E. Greydanus, H. A. Omar, & J. Merrick (Eds.). *Internet addiction: A public health concern in adolescence*. Hauppauge, NY: Nova Science.

Tsitsika, A., Janikian, M., Schoenmakers, T. M., Tzavela, E. C., Olafsson, K., Wojcik, S., . . . Tzavara, C. (2014). Internet addictive behavior in adolescence: A cross-sectional study in seven European countries. *Cyberpsychology, Behavior, and Social Networking, 17*, 528–535.

Tu, D., Gao, X., Wang, D., & Cai, Y. (2017). A new measurement of internet addiction using diagnostic classification models. *Frontiers in Psychology, 8*, 1–9.

Tzavela, E. C., & Mavromati, F. M. (2013). Online social networking in adolescence: Associations with development, well-being and internet addictive behaviors. *International Journal of Child and Adolescent Health, 6*(4), 411–420.

Vadlin, S., Aslund, C., Hellstrom, C., & Nilsson, K. W. (2016). Associations between problematic gaming and psychiatric symptoms among adolescents in two samples. *Addictive Behaviors, 61*, 8–15.

Van den Eijnden, R. J. J. M., Lemmens, J. S., & Valkenburg, P. M. (2016). The Social Media Disorder Scale. *Computers in Human Behavior, 61*, 478–487.

Vanzoelen, D., & Caltabiano, M. L. (2016). The role of social anxiety, the behavioural inhibition system and depression in online gaming addiction in adults. *Journal of Gaming and Virtual Worlds, 8*, 231–245.

Vernon, L., Barber, B. L., & Modecki, K. L. (2015). Adolescent problematic social networking and school experiences: The mediating effects of sleep disruptions and sleep quality. *Cyberpsychology, Behavior, and Social Networking, 18*, 386–392.

Vigna-Taglianti, F., Brambilla, R., Priotto, B., Angelino, R., Cuomo, G., & Diecidue, R. (2017). Problematic internet use among high school students: Prevalence, associated factors and gender differences. *Psychiatry Research, 257*, 163–171.

Visconte, S. R. (2017). Personality traits related to problematic Facebook use. *Dissertation Abstracts International: Section B: The Sciences and Engineering, 78*(5-B(E)). No pagination specified.

Wang, B.-q., Yao, N.-q., Zhou, X., Liu, J., & Lv, Z.-t. (2017). The association between attention deficit/hyperactivity disorder and Internet addiction: A systematic review and meta-analysis. *BMC Psychiatry, 17*, 1–12.

Wang, M., & Qi, W. (2017). Harsh parenting and problematic Internet use in Chinese adolescents: Child emotional dysregulation as mediator and child forgiveness as moderator. *Computers in Human Behavior, 77*, 211–219.

Wang, Y., Zou, Z., Song, H., Xu, X., Wang, H., Uquillas, F. d., & Huang, X. (2016). Altered gray matter volume and white matter integrity in college students with mobile phone dependence. *Frontiers in Psychology, 7*, 1–10.

Waqas, A., Rehman, A., Malik, A., Aftab, R., Allah Yar, A., Allah Yar, A., & Rai, A. B. S. (2016). Exploring the association of ego defense mechanisms with problematic internet use in a Pakistani medical school. *Psychiatry Research, 243*, 463–468.

Wartberg, L., Kriston, L., & Kammerl, R. (2017). Associations of social support, friends only known through the Internet, and health-related quality of life with Internet gaming disorder in adolescence. *Cyberpsychology, Behavior, and Social Networking, 20*, 436–441.

Watson, J. C. (2015). Internet addiction. In R. L. Smith (Ed.), *Treatment strategies for substance and process addictions* (pp. 293–311). Alexandria, VA: American Counseling Association.

Wegmann, E., & Brand, M. (2016). Internet-communication disorder: It's a matter of social aspects, coping, and Internet-use expectancies. *Frontiers in Psychology, 7*, 1–13.

Weinstein, A., Abu, H. B., Timor, A., & Mama, Y. (2016). Delay discounting, risk-taking, and rejection sensitivity among individuals with Internet and video gaming disorders. *Journal of Behavioral Addictions, 5*, 674–682.

Weinstein, A., Curtiss Feder, L., Rosenberg, K. P., & Dannon, P. (2014). Internet addiction disorder: Overview and controversies. In K. P. Rosenberg & L. Curtiss Feder (Eds.), *Behavioral addictions: Criteria, evidence, and treatment* (pp. 99–117). San Diego, CA: Academic Press.

Weinstein, A., Livny, A., & Weizman, A. (2017). New developments in brain research of internet and gaming disorder. *Neuroscience and Biobehavioral Reviews, 75*, 314–330.

Wiederhold, B. K. (2016). Social media sites, part 1: The dark side. *Cyberpsychology, Behavior, and Social Networking, 19*(3), 157.

Winkler, A., Dörsing, B., Rief, W., Shen, Y., & Glombiewski, J. A. (2013). Treatment of internet addiction: A meta-analysis. *Clinical Psychology Review, 33*, 317–329.

Wolfling, K., Beutel, M. E., Dreier, M., & Muller, K. W. (2015). Bipolar spectrum disorders in a clinical sample of patients with Internet addiction: Hidden comorbidity or differential diagnosis? *Journal of Behavioral Addictions, 4*, 101–105.

Wu, J. Y.-W., Ko, H.-C., & Lane, H.-Y. (2016). Personality disorders in female and male college students with internet addiction. *Journal of Nervous and Mental Disease, 204*, 221–225.

Yao, Y.-W., Chen, P.-R., Li, C.-s. R., Hare, T. A., Li, S., Zhang, J.-T., . . . Fang, X.-Y. (2017). Combined reality therapy and mindfulness meditation decrease intertemporal decisional impulsivity in young adults with Internet gaming disorder. *Computers in Human Behavior, 68*, 210–216.

Yao, Y.-W., Chen, P.-R., Li, S., Wang, L.-J., Zhang, J.-T., Yip, S. W., . . . Fang, X.-Y. (2015). Decision-making for risky gains and losses among college students with Internet gaming disorder. *PLoS ONE, 10*(1), 1–10.

Yao, Y.-W., Wang, L.-J., Yip, S. W., Chen, P.-R., Li, S., Xu, J., . . . Fang, X.-Y. (2015). Impaired decision-making under risk is associated with gaming-specific inhibition deficits among college students with Internet gaming disorder. *Psychiatry Research, 229*, 302–309.

Yates, T. M., Gregor, M. A., & Haviland, M. G. (2012). Child maltreatment, alexithymia, and problematic Internet use in young adulthood. *Cyberpsychology, Behavior, and Social Networking, 15*, 219–225.

Yau, Y. H. C., Derevensky, J. L., & Potenza, M. N. (2016). Pathological preoccupation with the Internet. In Y. Kaminer (Ed.), *Youth substance abuse and co-occurring disorders* (pp. 337–349). Arlington, VA: American Psychiatric.

Yeh, Y.-C., Wang, P.-W., Huang, M.-F., Lin, P.-C., Chen, C.-S., & Ko, C.-H. (2017). The procrastination of internet gaming disorder in young adults: The clinical severity. *Psychiatry Research, 254*, 258–262.

Yilmaz, E., Griffiths, M. D., & Kan, A. (2017). Development and validation of Videogame Addiction Scale for Children (VASC). *International Journal of Mental Health and Addiction, 15*, 869–882.

You, S., Kim, E., & Lee, D. (2017). Virtually real: Exploring avatar identification in game addiction among massively multiplayer online role-playing games (MMORPG) players. *Games and Culture: A Journal of Interactive Media, 12*, 56–71.

Younes, F., Halawi, G., Jabbour, H., El Osta, N., Karam, L., Hajj, A., & Khabbaz, L. R. (2016). Internet addiction and relationships with insomnia, anxiety, depression, stress and self-esteem in university students: A cross-sectional designed study. *PLoS ONE, 11*(9), 1–13.

Young, K. (1999, January). Internet addiction: symptoms, evaluation and treatment. In L. VandeCreek & T. Jackson (Eds.), *Innovations in clinical practice: A source book, Vol. 17* (pp. 19–31). Sarasota, FL: Professional Resource Press.

Young, K. S. (2011). Clinical assessment of Internet-addicted clients. In K. S. Young & C. N. de Abreu (Eds.), *Internet addiction: A handbook and guide to evaluation and treatment* (pp. 19–34). Hoboken, NJ: John Wiley & Sons.

Young, K. S. (2017). The evolution of internet addiction. *Addictive Behaviors, 64*, 229–230.

Young, K. S., & Brand, M. (2017). Merging theoretical models and therapy approaches in the context of Internet Gaming Disorder: A personal perspective. *Frontiers in Psychology, 8*, 1–12.

Young, K. S., & de Abreu, C. N. (2011). Closing thoughts and future implications. In K. S. Young & C. N. de Abreu (Eds.), *Internet addiction: A handbook and guide to evaluation and treatment* (pp. 267–273). Hoboken, NJ: John Wiley & Sons.

Young, K. S., Yue, X. D., & Ying, L. (2011). Prevalence estimates and etiologic models of Internet addiction. In K. S. Young & C. N. de Abreu (Eds.), *Internet addiction: A handbook and guide to evaluation and treatment* (pp. 3–17). Hoboken, NJ: John Wiley & Sons.

Young, N. L., Kuss, D. J., Griffiths, M. D., & Howard, C. J. (2017). Passive Facebook use, Facebook addiction, and associations with escapism: An experimental vignette study. *Computers in Human Behavior, 71*, 24–31.

Zajac, K., Ginley, M. K., Chang, R., & Petry, N. M. (2017). Treatments for Internet gaming disorder and Internet addiction: A systematic review. *Psychology of Addictive Behaviors, 31*, 979–994.

Zeng, W., Ye, K., Hu, Y., & Ma, Z.-w. (2016). Explicit self-esteem, loneliness, and pathological Internet use among Chinese adolescents. *Social Behavior and Personality, 44*, 965–972.

Zhang, M. W. B., Tran, B. X., Huong, L. T., Hinh, N. D., Nguyen, H. L. T., Tho, T. D., . . . Ho, R. C. M. (2017). Internet addiction and sleep quality among Vietnamese youths. *Asian Journal of Psychiatry, 28*, 15–20.

PART IV

Controversial Behavioral Addictions

Chapters 16 through 21 are *not* included in *DSM-5*. One or more of these might eventually be recognized as behavioral addictive disorders in the DSM system, but, currently, there is insufficient evidence for their inclusion. Nonetheless, a great deal of research is occurring in these areas, and behind each one are several researchers who would like to see their addiction become officially recognized. In the interim, you will likely see clients in practice who experience one or more of these addictions, and that is why I have included them.

16 Sex Addiction

iStock.com/Rap

Learning Objectives

1. Be able to discern the difference between having a high sex drive and having a sexual addiction.
2. Become familiar with some proposed diagnostic criteria for the DSM classification system.
3. Learn about the 11 categories of potentially addictive sexual behaviors.
4. Learn about the characteristics of individuals experiencing sex addiction.
5. Discover ways to counsel individuals addicted to sex by helping them develop healthy sex lives.

CHALLENGING YOUR ASSUMPTIONS ABOUT THIS ADDICTION

1. What kinds of judgments would you make of a friend or family member who became known as a sex addict? What moral judgments would you attach to their behavior?
2. If you found yourself unable to stop thinking about sex and then acted on your urges, what would you do to help yourself?
3. If you became aware that your adolescent son or daughter were watching a great deal of pornography, how would you handle it? What kind of talk might help him or her diminish this behavior, and what kind of talk might exasperate it?
4. What do you think would be an effective treatment for individuals with sex addiction who are addicted to having sex with children (i.e., a pedophile)? How might these methods be helpful for other types of individuals addicted to sex?
5. Based on your readings so far, what do you think might be the cause of sexual addiction?

PERSONAL REFLECTIONS

I have known Carl for nearly 20 years. More than once, he has referred to himself as a sex addict. The most obvious sign of this to me was when I used to visit him; he would sometimes be texting women to hook up with for more than half the time we were together! He would also abruptly ask me to leave his home because a sex date would be arriving momentarily. The plain rudeness of these behaviors beckoned a confrontation. Although I hoped that our friendship would persist, there was also the gnawing feeling that the ensuing challenge might end it. I was especially aware of this possibility with Carl. Over the past few years, I have seen him become increasingly aggressive in his interactions with others—including myself.

He told me years ago that he has never been in a relationship. I was shocked. How can someone, now age 64, have never experienced a sustained intimate relationship with someone?

Carl continues hooking up on a regular basis. I have known for a while that he uses alcohol, cocaine, crack, and crystal meth to help lure young women into his bed and accentuate the pleasure of his sexual encounters. Last night I saw him, and, at the end of our visit, he asked for $400, which would have been added to his current debt of $1200. Instead, I replied "NO" because I knew how the money would be spent.

So I have asked myself many questions over the years. Is Carl's growing aggressiveness a symptom of his addiction? Furthermore, I query the age-old "chicken and the egg" question: Which came first, the drug use or the sexual addiction? If Carl stopped using drugs, would the sexual addiction dissipate? Is there *really* a condition that could be called sexual addiction, and, if so, what distinguishes it from someone who just happens to enjoy lots of sex?

Background Information

Accounts of "excessive" sexual behavior (including masturbation) have been documented since the 18th century (Kafka, 2010). Burlew and Barton (2002) reported that the term "sexual addiction," however, was not invented until a chapter of Alcoholics Anonymous coined it in the 1970s. A different source suggested that, in 1978, Orford (as cited in Kafka, 2014) wrote about excessive sexual behavior as being synonymous with addiction. Regardless of its origin, Patrick Carnes (1983) popularized the concept with his publication, *Out of the Shadows: Understanding Sexual Addiction*.

The DSM system acknowledged that excessive sexual behavior that was disturbing to the individual could be classified in DSM-III as "Psychosexual Disorder Not Otherwise Specified." In DSM-III-R, the name was changed to "Sexual Disorders Not Otherwise Specified," and for the first time DSM acknowledged that excessive sexual behavior could take a nonparaphilic[1] form. However, the nonparaphilic aspect was deleted in DSM-IV and IV-R because of insufficient empirical evidence, and the original DSM-III criteria for "Sexual Disorders Not Otherwise Specified" was reintroduced (Kafka, 2010). *DSM-5* changed the name of sexual disorders to sexual dysfunctions, and they do not include sexual addiction either because of insufficient empirical evidence (APA, 2013).

[1]A *paraphilia* "denotes any intense and persistent sexual interest other than sexual interest in genital stimulation or preparatory fondling with phenotypically normal, physically mature, consenting human partners" (APA, 2013, p. 685). *Nonparaphilic*, then, refers to normative sexual interest in another consenting mature human partner.

Today, the American Society of Addiction Medicine and the International Classification of Diseases acknowledge the existence of sexual addiction, whereas psychiatric organizations (e.g., American Psychiatric Association, American Academy for Addiction Psychiatry) remain skeptical (Rosenberg, O'Connor, & Carnes, 2014). Although the diagnosis of sexual addiction remains controversial, there is no dispute that something akin to it has been increasingly observed and studied over the past 30 years (Riemersma & Sytsma, 2013).

Research remains in its infancy regarding sexual addiction (Kraus, Voon, & Potenza, 2016), and several writers have defined it differently. A criticism sometimes launched relates to the social judgment embedded in deciding what is deemed healthy sexuality. Those people with high sex drives might be labeled as having "hypersexual disorder," for example, which fails to recognize the wide range of "normal" human sexuality (Tepper, Owens, Coleman, & Carnes, 2007). If someone enjoys lots of sexual stimulation, why should it be labeled as a disorder?

Naming behavior as hyper- or hyposexual does not take into account cultural differences—in some cultures, high sexual activity (or low sexual activity) may be normative, so those falling on either end could be pathologized. For example, a Swedish study (Langstrom & Hanson, 2006) found that high-frequency sexual behavior with a stable partner was related to good psychological functioning. Having high levels of sexual activity might also be therapeutic for some individuals. Some cybersex addicts have commented on its benefits, such as (a) exploring one's sexuality, (b) learning to become less inhibited, and (c) learning new sexual techniques (Jiang, Huang, & Tao, 2013). Similarly, watching erotic visual stimuli (i.e., visual stimuli involving mutual sexual activity between consenting adults, contrasted with pornography, which includes nonconsensual, assaultive, violent, or otherwise demeaning sexual activity) may be helpful to some people by lowering their propensity toward sexual aggression (Hald, Seaman, & Linz, 2014).

However, sexual addiction, like the other addictions covered in this textbook, is primarily about lack of control (Bancroft, 2013). The term *sexual addiction* will be defined herein "as a disorder characterized by compulsive sexual behavior [including obsessive thoughts, fantasies, and urges] that results in tolerance, escalation, withdrawal, and a loss of volitional control despite negative consequences (Riemersma & Sytsma, 2013, p. 308; bracketed section added). Although it can refer to both paraphilic or nonparaphilic varieties (Wood, 2013), this chapter will restrict the discussion to nonparaphilic sexual addiction (note that the paraphilic forms are addressed in *DSM-5*).

Derbyshire and Grant (2015) reviewed the research in sexual addiction (they called it *compulsive sexual behavior*) and concluded that the disorder is likely heterogeneous. There are several features to it that may or may not be present in any one individual. These characteristics include sexual thoughts, fantasies, behaviors, and urges that are repetitive, preoccupying, intrusive, distressing, and impulsive (Derbyshire & Grant, 2015; Garcia & Thibaut, 2010; Kraus et al., 2016). The course of sexual addiction in adults is viewed as being chronic and progressive (De Crisce, 2013). Many if not most sex addicts have co-occurring psychiatric conditions and/or other addictions (Kraus et al., 2016).

Often the intentions and actions of self and others are sexualized by the individual addicted to sex (IAS) so that even hugs have sexual connotations. When they see an attractive person, they may have trouble moving on as most people do (Laaser, 2004). Some cannot stop obsessing about sex, despite their best efforts, and many will feel compelled to act on their urges (Griffin-Shelley, 1993b).

Sexual addiction generally begins in adolescence, and most presenting for treatment will have experienced several outlets for their hypersexuality over their lifetimes (Kafka, 2014). Some of the common outlets include excessive masturbation, telephone sex, visiting strip clubs, pornography use, cybersex, and sexual behavior with consenting adults (Weinstein, 2014).

Many in relationships will prefer increasingly "unconventional sexual activities" (Kafka, 2014, p. 285) to having sex with their partner. Excessive masturbation and having sex with multiple partners are two behaviors that are often reported as leading to relationship, social, and occupational difficulties (Kor, Fogel, Reid, & Potenza, 2013).

In his sample of nearly 1000 sex addicts, Carnes (1991) found that most nearly all sex addicts agree that most of their time is spent in obsessing about sex and sexual fantasies. Despite their preoccupation with sex, sex addicts are not good at actually having sex. Sexual difficulties are common, including "premature ejaculation, erectile dysfunction, anorgasmia, and sexual anorexia (extended periods when the IAS has no sexual activity)" (Rosenberg, Carnes, & O'Connor, 2014, p. 85).

Many sexual addicts need increasing amounts or varieties of sexual experiences over time (i.e., tolerance) (Griffin-Shelley, 1993b). Danger and the unknown are part of the excitement for sex addicts (Carnes, 1991). Sex addicts are typically the most secretive of addicts, largely due to their shame and guilt regarding their behavior (Griffin-Shelley, 1993b). Many can keep their addiction secretive for years.

IASs often do not "fit" the common stereotype of what IASs look like. They are often gentle and kind individuals who care deeply for others (Laaser, 2004). But, like other addicted individuals, they are two selves: the addict self and the healthy self, both of whom are kept separate from the other (Schaeffer, 2009). The other side of the IAS is self-centered after which they become "cold, manipulative, detached, and harsh" (Griffin-Shelley, 1993b, p. 13).

Although sex addicts may be the life of the party, no one knows them: they have plenty of acquaintances but few if any friends (Laaser, 2004). Sex addicts have an intimacy disorder, and they experience a great deal of loneliness (Griffin-Shelley, 1993b). They have a deep fear of intimacy, and they are incapable of creating it (Heilakka, 1993; Martin, 1989). Their sexual partners are merely sex objects, nondescript entities fulfilling their selfish motives (Kaufman, 1993). They believe that sexual activity is their only way to fulfill their needs for love and affection, but it never provides that to them (Martin, 1989). Consequently, they become increasingly dissatisfied with any sexual relationship, and no amount of sex is ever enough (Schaeffer, 2009). However, sex has become their way of dealing with ongoing emotional pain (Laaser, 2004).

Carnes has studied sex addicts since 1985 (Tepper et al., 2007), and he has classified their behaviors into 10 categories:

1. Fantasy sex. The sexual fantasies and planning for a sexual liaison are more important than having sex itself.
2. Seductive role sex. The excitement of the chase and risk-taking are central. This can be heightened by having many sexual partners.
3. Voyeuristic sex. The focus is on visual stimulation, including watching erotica.

4. Exhibitionist sex. Attracting attention to the body or sexual parts for arousal.

5. Paying for sex. Payment and searching for a sex worker creates excitement.

6. Trading sex. Arousal is attached to gaining control of others through sexual activity.

7. Intrusive sex. Excitement follows the violation of boundaries without resulting repercussions.

8. Anonymous sex. Sex that involves no obligations or commitments of any sort.

9. Pain exchange sex. Arousal occurs through specific sex scripts or humiliation and shame.

10. Exploitive sex. Arousal is based on having sex with vulnerable individuals.

11. Masturbation. Individuals can also become addicted to excessive masturbation. (Griffin-Shelley, 1993b)

Carnes (1983) suggested that sex addicts experience their addiction as a four-phase cycle: *preoccupation, ritualization, compulsive sexual behavior*, and *despair*. First, the IAS becomes preoccupied with their particular expression of sex, an activity that may consume hours unto itself. Then they experience their particular ritual that adds to their excitement, such as turning on the computer to view erotica. During these two phases, the IAS may report that they are in a trance-like state, outside of their usual level of consciousness. Next comes the actual sexual behavior, and this is followed by feelings of despair after they are done. Sexual acting out occurs most often during periods of stress (Kafka, 2014).

Due to the rapid growth of the Internet, sexual addiction may now have a rapid onset (Riemersma & Sytsma, 2013), and concern has been raised that it may disrupt the "normal neurochemical, sexual, and social development in youth" (Riemersma & Sytsma, 2013, p. 306). Sex is the most frequently searched term on the Internet (Crossan, 2014), and approximately 200 sex-related websites are added daily (Tepper et al., 2007). Internet pornography is addictive for some individuals (Bancroft, 2013), and cybersex addicts typically spend between 15 and 25 hours a week watching sexual material (Schaeffer, 2009). Jiang et al. (2013) suggested that the Internet may facilitate cybersex addiction because it can be "intoxicating, isolating, integral, inexpensive, imposing, and interactive" (p. 814). It also provides anonymous, convenient, and accessible experiences for users (Crossan, 2014).

Although Kafka (2014) has reported that the cause of sexual addiction is unknown, every researcher and writer on the topic suggests it is usually the result of childhood abuse (e.g., Burlew & Barton, 2002; Campbell & Stein, 2016; Cohen, 2015; Delmonico & Griffin, 2015; Griffee et al., 2014) and insecure attachments (anxious and avoidant) (Crossan, 2014) to caregivers (Jore, Green, Adams, & Carnes, 2016; Riemersma & Sytsma, 2013; Rosenberg, O'Connor, & Carnes, 2014). Carnes (1991) also found that two thirds of sex addicts were parented in families that were rigid and disengaged.

In Carnes's (1991) research with 1000 sex addicts, he found that 97% had experienced emotional abuse, 72% were victims of physical abuse, and 81% had been sexually abused. The sex addicts who went on to molest children had been emotionally abused the most severely (Carnes, 1991). Those who have experienced multiple forms of abuse are also more likely to develop sex addiction (Kuhn, 2014).

The fantasy created by sex addiction is thought to satisfy deep emotional and spiritual needs for belonging (Laaser, 2004). The IAS believes that sex will fulfill their need for love and belonging (Laaser, 2004). Berry and Berry (2014) postulated that hypersexual behavior might represent a means of defending the individual against difficult thoughts and feelings.

Beveridge (2015) stated that young people seeking counseling for sex addiction might not have experienced childhood abuse. Rather, it may have developed opportunistically as a result of availability to extreme and sometimes shocking material. As noted earlier, rapid-onset sexual addiction has occurred in consequence of the ease of exposure to sexual imagery via Internet technology (Riemersma & Sytsma, 2013).

As in other addictions, neuroscience has also provided an explanation for the etiology of sex addiction. This will be covered later.

It is commonly thought that sex addiction affects between 3% and 6% of the adult population in the United States (Campbell & Stein, 2016; Woehler, Giordano, & Hagedorn, 2018). The only representative sample conducted to generate estimates comprised 32-year-olds (N = 940) in New Zealand. The researchers found that close to 13% of men and 7% of women reported having sexual fantasies, urges, or behavior that they felt were out of control for the past year. Few in the sample believed, however, that these experiences had interfered with their lives (3.8% of men, 1.7% of women; Skegg, Nada-Raja, Dickson, & Paul, 2010).

In a sample of young adults, an epidemiological study estimated prevalence at 2% (Odlaug et al., 2013). In a sample of 136 male and 99 female undergraduate students, Giordano and Cecil (2014) found that 16.2% of the men and 11.1% of the total sample scored in the "hypersexual" range. Carnes (Tepper et al., 2007) reported that nearly 1% of Internet users experience a severe problem with cybersex, resulting in neglect of their life activities.

Diagnostic and Assessment Considerations

In ICD-11, sex addiction is called *compulsive sexual behavior disorder* (code 6C72). Kafka (2010) proposed criteria for what he called *hypersexuality disorder* (HD) for inclusion in *DSM-5*. Kafka viewed HD as "primarily a nonparaphilic sexual desire disorder with an impulsivity component" (p. 377). As noted earlier, the *DSM-5* committee rejected HD as a diagnosis due to insufficient empirical evidence. Nonetheless, Kafka (2014) suggested that HD can be considered an impulsivity disorder, and he recommended that clinicians could code it in *DSM-5* as "Other Specified Disruptive, Impulse-Control, and Conduct Disorder: hypersexual disorder" (see APA, 2013, p. 479).

Rosenberg, O'Connor, and Carnes (2014, pp. 218-220) summarized criteria for sexual addiction-related diagnoses offered independently by Ariel Goodman, Patrick Carnes, and Martin Kafka. These are outlined in Table 16.1.

A perusal of Table 16.1 reveals the overlap of the diagnoses and the areas where they differ. Another criterion could include *denial*, which can be defined here as "some way of convincing yourself that it's okay to do what you're doing" (Burlew & Barton, 2002, p. 266).

TABLE 16.1 Three Diagnostic Classifications for Sexual Addiction (Adapted)

Criteria	Goodman	Carnes	Kafka
Required Duration	12 months	12 months	6 months
Required Number of Symptoms	3+ from list of 7	3+ from list of 10 plus B criteria	4+ from list of 5 plus B, C, and D criteria
List of Symptoms Include	1. Unsuccessful reduction of behavior 2. Great deal of time spent 3. Tolerance 4. Withdrawal 5. Greater use than intended 6. Other activities given up or reduced 7. Use continues despite having other physical or psychological problems that may contribute to the sexual behavior	A. 1. Unsuccessful reduction of behavior 2. Great deal of time spent 3. Tolerance 4. Withdrawal 5. Greater use than intended 6. Other activities given up or reduced 7. Preoccupation 8. Interferes with other important functions (e.g., social, financial) 9. Continuance despite what is contained in the previous point (point #8) 10. Recurrent failure to resist the sexual impulses B. Creates significant consequences (e.g., loss of job, partner)	A. 1. Unsuccessful reduction of behavior 2. Great deal of time spent 3. Repetitive engaging in behavior due to negative mood states 4. Repetitive engaging in behavior due to stressful life events 5. Repetitive engaging despite harm to self or others B. Creates significant consequences (personal distress or impairment) in important functions (e.g., loss of job, partner) C. Not due to other mental disorder or drug use D. Age 18+ (with specifiers regarding type of sexual behavior and if in remission)

Differential Diagnosis

Sexual addiction needs to be distinguished from obsessive-compulsive disorder (OCD). Although OCD thoughts often have sexual content, they generally occur with negative mood without accompanying sexual arousal (Bancroft, 2013). The negative mood associated with OCD often leads to a decline in sexual arousal ability. Furthermore, individuals with OCD score high on measures of harm avoidance, in contrast to sex addicts who score high on measures of risk-taking (Grant & Odlaug, 2012).

Individuals with hypersexual behavior may be experiencing a different mental disorder, so they should be screened for another *DSM-5* axis I (i.e., clinical syndromes) and axis II (i.e., personality disorders) diagnoses (Cantor & Sutton, 2015). Alternatively, they may have a physiological disease that produces hypersexual behavior, such as "dementia, traumatic brain injury, Tourette's syndrome, Parkinson's Disease, and others" (Delmonico & Griffin, 2015, p. 244).

Another condition that was considered for inclusion in *DSM-5* is called persistent genital arousal disorder, a condition in women associated with overwhelming episodes of intense genital arousal with symptoms returning within a few hours in many cases. The arousal, however, is not accompanied by sexual desire (the strength of which is the cardinal problem with sex addicts) (Cohen, 2015), and consequently is viewed as distinct from sexual addiction (Bancroft, 2013).

Comorbidity and Co-Addictions

Multiple addictions are so common with sex addicts that Carnes, Murray, and Charpentier (2005) coined the term *addiction interaction disorder*. They speculated that "addictions do more than coexist. They, in fact, interact, reinforce, and become part of one another. They, in effect, become packages" (p. 87). A common interaction disorder is that existing among sexual addiction, cocaine use, and alcohol abuse (Rawson, Washton, Domier, & Reiber, 2002). Drugs like "methamphetamine, poppers, cocaine, and crack . . . can extend masturbating and sexual sprees for hours" (Beveridge, 2015, p. 42). Laaser (2004) reported that nearly 50% of sex addicts are also alcoholics. More recently, Elmquist, Shorey, Anderson, and Stuart (2016) concluded that studies suggest comorbidity rates with substance abuse of 40%–60%.

In a sample of 225 problem gamblers, 19.6% also experienced sexual addiction (Grant & Steinberg, 2005). Dubrow (1993) wrote that, of the female sex and love addicts that she has worked with, food or compulsive eating were common co-addictions. In Carnes' (1991) sample, 83% reported concurrent addictions.

Attention deficit hyperactivity disorder is often associated with taking sexual risks, particularly cybersex, which may indicate an increased propensity to become sexually addicted (Rosenberg, Carnes, & O'Connor, 2014). A report by Kafka and Hennen (1999) found that 72% of patients with hypersexual disorder reported mood disorders, 38% anxiety disorders, and 40% substance abuse. Co-morbidity with DSM Axis I disorders may be somewhere between 80% (Black, Kehrberg, Flumerfelt, & Schlosser, 1997) and 100% (Raymond, Coleman, & Miner, 2003). A meta-analysis (N = 95 studies) conducted by Rooney, Tulloch, and Blashill (2018) established that depression and anxiety are most strongly associated with sexual compulsivity (SC). Sex addiction has also been associated with affect dysregulation, impulsivity, loneliness, low self-worth (Rosenberg, O'Connor, & Carnes, 2014), sexual dysfunctions, medical problems, attention deficit disorder, and posttraumatic stress disorder (PTSD; Delmonico & Griffin, 2015).

A relationship between sex addiction and Axis II disorders (i.e., paranoid, passive-aggressive, and narcissistic personality disorder) has also been found (Black et al., 1997; Raymond et al., 2003). Other comorbidities include antisocial, borderline, avoidant, dependent, and obsessive-compulsive personality disorder (Campbell & Stein, 2016). Interviews with 132 male sex addicts (aged 20–66) screened on the SCID-II Personality Questionnaire suggested potential personality disorders in 92% of the sample, but only 17% met full criteria for a personality disorder (Carpenter, Reid, Garos, & Najavits, 2013). There is also a relationship between compulsive sexual behaviors and aggressive attitudes, physical aggression, and verbal aggression (Elmquist et al., 2016).

Available Measures

Carnes and Wilson (2002) recommended that a thorough assessment of sexual addiction should include the following components: (a) a structured interview, (b) self-report screening instruments, and (c) collateral corroboration. Because of the high comorbidity rates with other mental disorders, Delmonico and Griffin (2015) suggested that clients should be administered several psychological tests such as the Minnesota Multiphasic Personality Inventory-2 (for psychopathology), Millan Clinical Multiaxial Inventory-III (for personality disorders), Psychopathy Checklist-Revised (for antisocial personality disorder), Test of Variable Tension (for attention deficit), Beck Anxiety Inventory, and Beck Depression Inventory-II. If depression is substantial, they also recommended the Scale for Suicide Ideation.

Of the measures reviewed by Womack et al. (2013), two stood out as measuring all aspects of the HD criteria proposed by Kafka (2010). One was the Hypersexual Disorder Diagnostic Clinical Interview (Reid et al., 2012), and the other was the Hypersexual Disorder Questionnaire (Reid et al., 2012). There are also checklists that serve as warning signs of cybersex addiction (Jiang, Huang, & Tao, 2013).

Perhaps the best known self-report measure was developed by Carnes, Green, and Carnes (2010), a 45-item inventory called the Sexual Addiction Screening Test-Revised (SAST-R). The test has good reliability with alphas between 0.85 and 0.95 (Hook, Hook, Davis, Worthington, & Penberthy, 2010). A quick screening instrument comprising six items from the SAST-R was developed called the PATHOS, and it was also found to have good internal consistency (0.77–0.94). The cutoff score is 3. These items can be found in Table 16.2.

The number of instruments developed that measure some aspect of hypersexual behavior is numerous: Womack, Hook, Ramos, Davis, and Penberthy (2013), for example, reviewed 32 measures. A few were also reviewed in Southern, Ellison, and Hagwood (2015). Here is a sample of some of the available measures:

1. Sexual Addiction Screening Test-Revised (separate versions for men and women). A 25-item test developed from the original SAST. Scores range from 0 to 25 with a cutoff score of 6 or greater indicating sexual addiction. Available from https://www.sexualrecovery.com/resources/self-tests/

TABLE 16.2 PATHOS Items

1. Do you often find yourself preoccupied with sexual thoughts? (Preoccupied)
2. Do you hide some of your sexual behavior from others? (Ashamed)
3. Have you ever sought help for sexual behavior you did not like? (Treatment)
4. Has anyone been hurt emotionally because of your sexual behavior? (Hurt)
5. Do you feel controlled by your sexual desire? (Out of control)
6. When you have sex, do you feel depressed afterward? (Sad)

Source: From Rosenberg, O'Connor, and Carnes (2014, p. 221)

2. Compulsive Sexual Behavior Inventory. A 28-item scale that produces a total score and three subscale scores, which include Control (*sexual behavior*), Abuse (*past history*), and Violence (*experiences of violence*). A five-point Likert scale is used. Higher scores indicate a lower probability of sexual addiction.
3. Sexual Compulsivity Scale. A 10-item scale produces a score that measures the "insistent, repetitive, intrusive, and unwanted urge to perform specific acts often in a ritualized or routine fashion" (Hook et al., 2010, p. 242). A four-point Likert-type scale is used ranging from 1 (not at all like me) to 4 (very much like me). The cutoff score of 24 indicates possible problems with sexual addiction. Available from http://chipcontent.chip.uconn.edu/chipweb/documents/Research/K_SexualCompulsivityScale.pdf
4. Sex Addicts Anonymous Questionnaire. A-16 item scale designed from the questionnaire used by 12-step Sex Addicts Anonymous Groups. Scores range from 0 to 32, with higher scores indicating sexual addiction. The 16-item version is printed on pages 116–117 in Mercer's (1998) assessment of this instrument. A 12-item version is available from https://saa-recovery.org/IsSAAForYou/SelfAssessment/
5. Sexual Symptom Assessment Scale. A 12-item scale scored using a five-point Likert scale. Total scores range from 0 to 48, with higher scores indicating sexual addiction. It samples both subjective (How strong were your urges?) and objective symptoms (How much time did you spend engaging in problematic sexual behaviors?). Available from http://www.pathwaysinstitute.net/S-SAS.pdf
6. Internet Sex Screening Test. A 25-item scale used to measure online sexual addiction. The five subscales include online sexual compulsivity, online sexual behavior-social, online sexual behavior-isolated, online sexual spending, and interest in online sexual behavior.

A total score of affirmative answers ranges from 0 to 25, with higher scores indicative of sexual addiction. The self-scored scale is available from https://www.recoveryzone.com/tests/sex-addiction/ISST/index.php. A 34-item test by the same name is available from http://www.internetbehavior.com/pdf/isst.pdf

7. Compulsive Sexual Behavior Consequences Scale. A 21-item scale with two versions: one assesses lifetime consequences, and the other assesses consequences in the last 90 days. It uses a five-point Likert scale ranging from 0 to 4 and producing totals from 0 to 84. Higher scores indicate more consequences of addiction.
8. Tonigan, J. S., & Miller, W. R. (2002). The Inventory of Drug Use Consequences (InDUC): Test-retest stability and sensitivity to detect change. *Psychology of Addictive Behaviors, 16*, 165–168.
9. Online Pornography Test. This is a 12-item test that focuses on online pornography. Available from http://virtual-addiction.com/online-pornography-test/
10. Several tests for many different mental disorders including various addictions are available from http://www.healthyplace.com/psychological-tests/, http://www.mental-health-today.com/tests/ , and http://www.dangardnermd.com/screening-tests.html

Clinical Interview Questions

Woody (as cited in Southern et al., 2015) suggested that the clinical interview should include questions focused on the sex addicts' (a) variety of sexual behaviors, (b) behaviors that create distress and their context, (c) incongruence between their behavior and their values, (d) sexual and relationship history, (e) use of substances currently, and (f) readiness to receive treatment. Woody also recommended that the interview include the partner or a family member, if available, to corroborate the addict's disclosures.

Burlew and Barton (2002) offered 10 questions (note that these were adapted from two other writers) that can assist in determining if one is experiencing sexual addiction and/or romantic relationship addiction (the topic of the next chapter). These questions are as follows:

1. Do you, or others who know you, find that you are overly preoccupied or obsessed with sexual activity [love relationships]?
2. Do you ever find yourself compelled to engage in sexual [love relationship] activity in response to stress, anxiety, or depression?
3. Have serious problems developed as a result of your sexual [or love relationship] behavior, such as job or relationship loss, contracting or spreading sexually transmitted diseases or other illness, experiencing or causing injuries, or getting charged with sexual offenses?
4. Do you feel guilt and shame about some of your sexual [or love relationship] behaviors?
5. Do you fantasize or engage in any unusual or what some would consider to be "deviant" sexual behavior [love fantasies]?
6. Do you find yourself constantly searching or "scanning" the environment for a potential sexual [or love] partner (or an opportunity to engage in behavior perceived as sexually oriented)?
7. Do you ever find yourself sexually [or romantically] obsessed with someone (or some thing) who is not interested in you or does not even know you?
8. Do you think your pattern of masturbation (or any other behavior perceived as sexually oriented and/or motivated) is excessive, driven, or dangerous?
9. Have you had numerous love [or sex] relationships (or sexually oriented experiences) that were short-lived, intense, and unfulfilling?
10. Do you feel a constant need for sex or expressions of love in your sexual [or love] relationships? (p. 266–267)

Generic Names and Street "Lingo"

Sexual addiction has come to be known by many names, several of which are reflective of the many ways this behavior has been viewed historically and today. In the past, for example, sexual addiction might have been called erotomania, nymphomania (for females), satyriasis (for men), Don Juanism, hyper libido, and erotophilia (Burlew & Barton, 2002). Some terms had a particularly disparaging ring to them, such as sexual deviant, womanizer, dirty old man, whore, slut, fallen woman, harlot, sin, and pervert (Schaeffer, 2009; Southern et al., 2015).

Contemporary terms include sexual addiction, hypersexuality or HD, hyperphilia, compulsive sexual behavior, sexual compulsion, atypical impulse control disorder, obsessive-compulsive disorder, sexual desire disorder, problematic sexual behavior, paraphilia or paraphilia-related disorder, nonparaphilic related disorder, and sexual dependence (Burlew & Barton, 2002; Campbell & Stein, 2016; Delmonico & Griffin, 2015; Lord, 1993; Southern et al., 2015).

Neuroscience

Sexual arousal and orgasm appear to be mediated by the mesolimbic reward system: this includes the striatum, medial prefrontal cortex, and orbitofrontal cortex (Kor et al., 2013). A study by Voon et al. (2014) compared 19 people with compulsive sexual behavior (CSB) with 19 healthy volunteers using functional magnetic resonance imaging (fMRI). Those with CSB compared to the controls displayed greater activation of the dorsal anterior cingulate, ventral striatum, and amygdala in response to cue-related sexual desire. Dopamine may contribute to CSB—those taking dopamine replacement therapies for Parkinson's disease have increased rates of CSB and other impulsive control disorders (Weintraub et al., 2010). Voon et al. (2014) suggested that their results are suggestive and not definitive regarding the neuroscience of sexual addiction.

Fantasy (including sexual fantasies) can produce chemicals called catecholamines (a group of amines that includes dopamine, epinephrine, and norepinephrine) in the pleasure areas of the brain, and this can have a narcotic-like effect (Laaser, 2004). Carnes (1991) noted that endorphins (a group of hormones/peptides that create an analgesic effect) are also released during sex.

Although the dopaminergic reward system can explain the drive underlying sexual addiction, "it cannot explain the object of the addiction" (Cohen, 2015, p. 144). As explained earlier, the belief is that premature sexual stimulation—particularly childhood sexual abuse—directs the addiction toward sex as opposed to other addictive possibilities (Cohen, 2015).

Physical Impacts (Long-Term Use)

Hypersexual behavior can lead to the transmission of sexually transmitted diseases (Delmonico & Griffin, 2015). There is also concern regarding the high comorbidity between sex addiction and alcohol and drug abuse (Benotsch, Kalichman, & Pinkerton, 2001). Beveridge (2015) stated that, when sex addicts attempt to give up their hypersexual behavior, they go into physical withdrawal, which includes symptoms like headaches and flulike symptoms. Some engage in a multitude of activities and become exhausted and burned out, and this, in turn, may lead to a variety of physical illnesses and symptoms (Laaser, 2004). Compulsive masturbators sometimes damage their genitalia. Some attempt suicide (Carnes, 1991; Laaser, 2004).

Carnes (1991) provided the most complete list of physical symptoms that may occur when an IAS is in withdrawal. He reported the following as being very common: dizziness, body aches, headaches, sleeplessness, and extreme restlessness. Other possible symptoms include fatigue, shakes, high sexual arousal, low sexual arousal, increased food appetite, genital sensitivity, itchy skin, chills, sweats, nausea, shortness of breath, and rapid heartbeat. Many addicts who had also recovered from a drug addiction reported that the sex addiction was more difficult to overcome (Carnes, 1991).

Mental, Emotional, and Spiritual Impacts

Laaser (2004) expressed it simply: "Most sex addicts experience devastating shame and believe they are totally worthless" (p. 24). Several studies have suggested a strong linkage between negative emotional states (especially shame) and SC (Petrican, Burris, & Moscovitch, 2015). Because addictive sex is often "illicit, stolen, or exploitive" (Carnes, 1991, p. 254), it produces feelings of shame and the feeling of being unlovable. It often reenacts their childhood abuse, creating feelings of dissociation within themselves (Carnes, 1991).

Sex addicts are often lonely and isolated (Laaser, 2004). They think about sex constantly, which consumes a great deal of mental energy in the process (Laaser, 2004). Laaser (2004) maintained that fantasy is used by sex addicts in their unsuccessful attempts to satisfy deep emotional and spiritual needs: they also use having sex as an unsuccessful means of coping with this pain (Burlew & Barton, 2002).

Carnes (1991) listed several of the emotional costs experienced by sex addicts. In descending order of reported frequency, the list includes lowered self-esteem, strong guilt and shame, substantial isolation and loneliness, extreme hopelessness and despair, acting contrary to one's personal values and beliefs, feeling like two different people, feeling emotionally exhausted, having strong fears about one's own future, emotional instability, and loss of life goals. More than half of hospital admissions for sex addicts are because of clinical depression (Carnes, 1991).

Psychosocial Impacts (Relationships, Career/Work, Legal, Financial)

Carnes (1991) found that, in his sample of sex addicts, 10 losses were especially painful. In descending order of priority, the list includes (note that five of the top six have to do with relationships): loss of primary relationships, loss of children (including abortions, death, and custody), loss of important friends, unavailability to children, financial losses, guilt from hurting others, loss of productivity and creativity, career and job losses, loss of integrity (including compromising personal values), and loss of self-esteem. The active IAS places sex as a higher priority than family, friends, hobbies, and work (Carnes, 1991).

Nearly 60% of sex addicts have faced financial problems, and 58% have engaged in illegal activities (Schaeffer, 2009). Sexual offenses become likelier as the addiction progresses and individuals take increasingly higher risks (e.g., exhibitionism, voyeurism, prostitution, child pornography; Delmonico & Griffin, 2015).

Cybersex addicts also face emotional, social, job, and financial consequences, and sometimes legal issues result from involvement with children or adolescents (Jiang et al., 2013). The time spent on their addiction means that they are less available to the family (Jiang et al., 2013).

Working With Diverse Populations

Sex Differences

Hypersexuality among women remains an understudied phenomenon (Carvalho, Guerra, Neves, & Nobre, 2015; Dhuffar & Griffiths, 2014). Georgianna (2015) conducted a literature review of experimental, correlational, and case studies with samples greater than 20 per group where the sample was separated by sex. Georgianna found that women were more likely to develop sex addiction if they (a) were exposed to developmental stressors, (b) had difficulty in regulating affect, (c) experienced comorbid addictions, (d) lacked relationship skills, and (e) were involved in sex work. Women are more likely than men to engage in fantasy sex and sadomasochism and to become involved in sex work (Kuzma & Black, 2008). In one online study of 988 women, hypersexuality was characterized by "impersonal sexual activity" (Klein, Rettenberger, & Briken, 2014, p. 1974).

Women who act out sexually tend to have related mental health disorders such as depression and bipolar disorder (Dubrow, 1993). They are also likely to experience attachment disorder (Southern et al., 2015). Kaplan and Krueger (2010) estimated that between 8% and 20% of hypersexual individuals are female.

Because cybersex is accessible, anonymous, and affordable, studies suggest that about equal numbers of men and women become addicted (Southern et al., 2015). About 60% of individuals who search for the term *adult sex* on the Internet are female (Delmonico & Griffin, 2015).

Adolescents and Youth

The research regarding sexual addiction in teenagers is meager (De Crisce, 2013), but it is believed that they can become addicted to sex (Griffin-Shelley, 1995; Lundrigan, 2004). Efrati (2018) found that adolescents who feel shame regarding their CSB reported a greater likelihood of requesting professional help than those who reported little or no shame. Carol (2009) reported on a group specifically for adolescent sex addicts in Houston.

Sex addiction develops during childhood, adolescence, or young adulthood (Griffee et al., 2014; Kuzma & Black, 2008), often in response to "sex abuse experiences and poor family environment" (Perera, Reece, Monahan, Billingham, & Finn, 2009, p. 131). Early exposure to pornography, however, has not been linked to SC (Stulhofer, Jelovica, & Ruzic, 2008). As reported earlier, Giordano and Cecil (2014) found that 11.1% of students (16.2% of males) were hypersexual in their college sample.

Race and Ethnicity

One study (Becerra, Robinson, & Balkin, 2011) found a small effect size between ethnically diverse men who embrace traditional views of masculinity and online sexual addiction (n = 1441; 11.5% African American, 3.7% Asian Indian, 56.9% Caucasian, 17.2% Hispanic, 0.2% Pacific Islander, 0.7% Middle Eastern, 6.9% Multiracial, and 1% Other Ethnicities). The practical significance of the findings was questioned by the authors. Robinson (1999) suggested that sexual addiction in African American men may be a response to PTSD, resulting from historical attributions related to slavery, racism, and discrimination.

Jardin, Garey, Sharp, and Zvolensky (2016) sampled 758 racially/ethnically diverse college students (N = 758; 16.2% African American, 51.5% Hispanic, 24.9% Asian, and 7.4% Other Races) and found partial support for their hypothesis that SC is linked to sexual-health risk behaviors. Their finding is in sync with other research that suggests sexual behavior is often used by ethnic minorities as a means of coping with stress (Stevens-Watkins, Brown-Wright, & Tyler, 2011).

Nonpsychiatric Disabilities

There is no published literature about sex addiction and disabilities. This is noted here so that both students and practitioners are aware of the current lack of research in this area.

Lesbian, Gay, Bisexual, and Transgender (LGBT)

Kort (2004) argued that gay male teenagers are at a high risk of becoming sex addicts because of "covert cultural sexual abuse" (p. 287). Grant and Potenza (2006) studied pathological gambling and comorbidity and found that 59% of gay or bisexual men experienced a lifetime prevalence rate of compulsive sexual behaviors compared to heterosexual men. In a sample of 86 sexually compulsive men in Brazil (26% gay, 17% bisexual, 57% heterosexual), the gay and bisexual men were more likely to report that casual sex and sex with multiple casual partners was problematic for them (de Tubino Scanavino et al., 2013). Co-diagnosis of a mood disorder predicted higher SC scores (de Tubino Scanavino et al., 2013).

Sexual addiction is more likely to result in men who have sex with men who are bored, have fewer social connections, and who dissociate while engaging in excessive online sexual activities (Chaney & Chang, 2005). In a sample of 172 gay male couples (N = 344), high levels of SC in one or both partners was associated with negative sexual communication and sexual satisfaction (Starks, Grov, & Parsons, 2013).

A sample of 305 gay and bisexual men revealed that those who have not disclosed their sexual identities to their mothers are more likely to experience compulsive sexuality (Chaney & Burns-Wortham, 2015). Gay and bisexual men who experience substantial internalized homonegativity or emotion dysregulation are also more likely to become sex addicts in consequence of the resulting anxiety and depression (Pachankis et al., 2015).

Gay men are also more likely to have experienced cybersex compared to heterosexual men (Jiang et al., 2013). Some research suggests that lesbian and bisexual women gravitate toward chat room use as their preferred online activity compared to gay and bisexual men (Green, Carnes, Carnes, & Weinman, 2012). Lastly, gay and bisexual men are substantially likelier to experience SC compared to lesbian and bisexual women (Kelly, Bimbi, Nanin, Izienicki, & Parsons, 2009).

War Veterans

The only study that has researched war veterans was conducted by Smith et al. (2014). They administered surveys to male military veterans at baseline (N = 258), 3 months (N = 194), and 6 months (N = 136) to look at the prevalence and factors associated with CSB. At baseline, 16.7% of the sample reported CSB. The factors that were significant were PTSD severity, childhood sexual trauma, and age. Men with CSB were more likely to be older (M = 37.2 years, SD = 15). PTSD symptoms were most strongly associated with CSB.

Medications and Other Relevant Physical Interventions

Kafka (2014) reported that he had had experience using pharmaceuticals with over 500 males with HD. He has found that the following medications are often helpful with both nonparaphilic and paraphilic HD: mood stabilizers, antidepressants, opiate antagonists (like naltrexone), and the orally administered anti-androgen medroxyprogesterone—alone or in various combinations. Two antidepressants with demonstrated effectiveness include Bupropion and Celexa (Southern et al., 2015). Although selective serotonin reuptake inhibitors can improve mood and inhibit the sexual response, anti-androgen drugs may produce negative moods (Bancroft, 2013). Nonaddictive anxiolytics such as Buspirone (Buspar) may be useful as well (Rosenberg, O'Connor, & Carnes, 2014). Bancroft (2013) noted that pharmaceuticals should be used together with cognitive-behavioral therapy (CBT).

INSIDE AN ADDICTED PERSON'S MIND

Jorge, Age 39

I have lived in Atlanta for 25 years. My parents emigrated from Veracruz, Mexico, when I was 14. After a few months of living in the US., my padre bought me my first laptop. I already knew several of the sites I wanted to visit, thanks to a few friends. Surprisingly, a large number of the sites offered pornography for free. Before long, I would spend hours a day searching for greater varieties of porn that would keep me stimulated while I did what every teen does while watching it. One day my mamá walked in on me, and I could have died. She looked shocked, and as she turned and walked out quietly, I continued sitting there, feeling enormous guilt and shame.

Raised as a good Catholic, I wasn't sure if what I was doing was okay. So I tried stopping it, but I couldn't for some reason. I mean, I guess I could have if I tried really hard, but masturbation without the porn wasn't enjoyable anymore. I felt frustrated, but I kept on jacking off to this stuff, and only after I came did the familiar guilt and shame creep back in.

Over time, the porn "phase" passed, and I started using Craigslist to arrange hookups. I began with two or three of these a week. Lately, I have been stressed at work (I am now an accountant with a large firm), and I have five to seven hookups every week. Along with that, I have brought back porn into my repertoire. Thinking about sex and having sex is taking upward of 25 hours a week! Man, if I was getting paid for all that time, I could afford a new Mercedes. My wife, Josefina, of 14 years knows something is up: She no longer believes I work until 9 five days a week. But she doesn't excite me anymore—sex with her became boring soon after our first child. So it stopped.

Josefina has learned, however, to keep shut about such matters. She was raised to believe that married men can have a mistress so long as they keep providing for the family, which I have done. That doesn't mean she likes it, but she is supposed to stay quiet about it. But what if she knew that, instead of having a mistress, I was jumping from one stranger to the next? What if she knew I watched more porn than most people watch television or play video games in a week?

I know I am doing wrong, but whenever I try to stop, my mood drops to a level that scares me. I start thinking about quitting my job, leaving my wife and children, even committing suicide. The only thing that seems to elevate my mood are fantasies about sex and then enacting some of them. I need more sex than anyone can provide me. . . yet I feel so alone in all of this. I am a miserable skunk, and I don't deserve Josefina or anyone else. I am so tired at work from all of these shenanigans that my performance is rapidly deteriorating. For the first time, I am truly afraid, but I am too embarrassed to let anyone know.

Commentary

For Jorge, extramarital sex has become increasingly important, and it is having consequences for him. He experiences severe mood swings when he tries to stop his behavior, and sexual intimacy has ended with his wife. He does not confide in his wife either and feels alone. Consequently, he has created emotional distance from her. He uses strangers as sex objects: they are merely for his fleeting pleasure. He is experiencing decreased productivity at work, which may lead to consequences. Jorge appears unable to express his emotions to anyone, so, instead, he keeps riding a roller coaster with no beginning and no end.

Discussion

1. Do you know of anyone who you suspect has become dependent on sexual imagery (e.g., pornography) and/or behavior? If "yes," which symptoms noted in the commentary apply to him or her?
2. Does this person have symptoms that are not listed in the commentary? If so, what are they?
3. If you were Jorge's counselor, how would you go about helping him?

Specific Counseling Considerations

ROLEPLAY SCENARIOS

Roleplay in dyads, with one of you acting as the counselor and the other as the counselee. If a roleplay is not possible, work individually in writing out a list of your suggestions.

Roleplay #1

Briana, age 35, describes herself as a nymphomaniac. She thinks about having sex constantly and finds her thoughts so distracting that her work as a photographer is hampered by her daydreaming and sexualizing of attractive men and women. On a given night, she will go to pickup bars and attempt to have sex with one guy and then return to the bar to have sex with a second man. She tells you that she feels compelled to do this behavior most nights of the week. When she tries to stay home, she reports feeling overwhelmed with sadness and anxiety.

Roleplay #2

Eduardo, age 42, impresses as a suave businessman of Spanish descent. He has already lost several jobs for having sex with a close employee—often one of the secretaries. You are a female counselor in this scenario, and Eduardo stares at your breasts the entire first session. He seems to be getting excited as he talks about many of his sexual conquests. He tries to find sexual innuendo in everything you say to him. You also learn of a relationship history marked by frequent cheating behaviors and sexual affairs. Eduardo is again single after being caught having sex with two women by his girlfriend Rosalinda, a sultry 17-year-old. As Eduardo is leaving your office, he asks you out on a date.

HOW WOULD AN ADDICTION COUNSELOR HELP THIS PERSON?

You are working as a professional counselor. You go out to the waiting room and see Sean, age 29, sitting quietly in the corner. He is handsome with a slim, muscular look, and you think it odd that he has his shirt undone nearly to his navel. You immediately notice scratch marks on his chest. Once in your office, he tells you that he thinks he has "crossed the line." A long history is shared with you of excessive use of hardcore pornography and frequent visits to the restroom where he works to "relieve" himself. He reports that he spends a great deal of time engaged in sexual fantasy, which has become increasingly violent and nonconsensual. Yesterday, he awoke feeling as if he were in a trance—this was a feeling that had just started to develop occasionally. He decided to leave his shirt at home and take a drive in his convertible. He knew where to head. He drove along Ocean Drive and noticed a gorgeous young blonde dressed in a bikini. Sean tells you that he became instantly overwhelmed with lust by the sight of her. He pulled over a block in front of her and waited. As she got close, he got outside and charmed her into getting a ride with him. He knew she wanted it. Once in the car, Sean drove past where she wanted to get let off until he came to a treed area. Then the threat was uttered loudly, "Either give me head or I'll kill you right here!" He said the young woman looked terrified, but she complied. After a few minutes, he wanted more, and he ripped open her blouse and began feeling her up. It was then that she raked her nails across his chest as hard as she could. Sean, enraged, pushed her out of the car, backed up a sufficient distance so she could not get his license number, and sped away. Sean appeared incredibly relaxed and calm as he told his story to you. You are sitting there wondering if you should report him to the police.

Remember to view clients within their environmental contexts, keeping in mind societal, parental/familial, cultural/spiritual, and peer influences. Specifically, become aware of the impact that the following influences have and continue to have in your clients' lives: race, language, religion and spirituality, gender, familial migration history, sexual/affectional orientation, age and cohort, physical and mental capacities, socioeconomic situation and history, education, and history of traumatic experience.

1. What defines this person's environment, past and present?
2. Who is this person sitting in front of me, taking into account environmental and personal characteristics?
3. What defines the problem that he or she is presenting within their multicultural milieu?

Goals and Goal Setting

Most clinicians and mutual support groups recommend a period of abstinence initially for sex addicts early in their recovery followed by learning to control their undesirable sexual activities (Burlew & Barton, 2002; Carnes, 1991). Burlew and Barton (2002) remind counselors that it will take time for clients to develop a healthy sexuality. Some appropriate goals for counseling clients with sex addiction include the following:

- Provide a comprehensive assessment that may span several weeks (Carnes & Lee, 2014; Delmonico & Griffin, 2015).
- Establish safety (Carnes & Lee, 2014).
- Create a strong working alliance (Carnes & Lee, 2014).
- Distinguish those who have value conflicts with their sexuality from those who have become compulsive about their sexuality (Tepper et al., 2007).
- Assess for high-risk situations and establish a behavioral plan to help prevent the occurrence of undesirable sexual activities (Goodman, 1993).
- Teach coping strategies for managing urges (Goodman, 1993).
- Learn and reframe slips to help prevent relapse (Goodman, 1993).
- Integrate sexuality into one's life as a healthy element (Heilakka, 1993; Tepper et al., 2007).
- Address low self-esteem, shame, and guilt (Zmuda, 2014).
- Address co-morbid conditions (Delmonico & Griffin, 2015).
- Teach cognitive-behavioral techniques to minimize compulsiveness (e.g., don't carry large amounts of money for purchasing pornography, use thought-stopping methods, and identify rituals around sexual behavior; Delmonic & Griffin, 2015).
- Do not expect perfection . . . relapse is part of the process (Delmonico & Griffin, 2015).

Stages of Change Strategies

The processes of change mentioned are based on those outlined by Connors, DiClemente, Velasquez, and Donovan (2013) and Prochaska, Norcross, and DiClemente (1994). The definitions for the various processes can be found in Chapter 6. Besides these processes, other strategies are included that have separate citations.

The University of Rhode Island Change Assessment Scale (URICA) is a helpful scale in determining where client is currently at regarding the stages of change model. There are 24-, 28-, and 32-item versions of the scale. A 24-item version is published for alcohol or drug problems. The scale, however, is generic and can be easily adapted for use with other addictions. It is available with norms as a free download from https://www.guilford.com/add/miller11_old/urica.pdf.

Specific precontemplation strategies.

Please visit the section of this chapter called Relevant Mutual Support Groups, Websites, and Videos for free or low-cost information and resources that may help someone move out of precontemplation.

Suggested readings here include the following books:

- Carnes, P. (1991). *Don't call it love: Recovery from sexual addiction.* Toronto, ON: Bantam Books.
- Carnes, P. (2009). *Out of the shadows: Understanding sexual addiction* (3rd ed.). Center City: Hazelden.
- Hall, P. (2012). *Understanding and treating sex addiction: A comprehensive guide for people who struggle with sex addiction and those who want to help them.* New York, NY: Routledge.
- Weiss, R. (2015). *Sex addiction 101: A basic guide to healing from sex, porn, and love addiction.* Deerfield Beach, FL: HCI Books.

Some movies that may help a client move into the next stage are *Shame* (2011), *Don Jon* (2013), *Thanks for Sharing* (2012), and *Looking for Mr. Goodbar* (1977). Counselors can help sex addicts by creating interest and concern regarding their problematic behaviors. Helping clients emote regarding their sex addiction may trigger self-re-evaluation and environmental re-evaluation regarding the impact and consequences their unhealthy behaviors have on self and others.

Specific contemplation strategies.

Once clients are willing to consider that a sex addiction problem is evident, continuing to focus on their problem(s) and themselves is indicated. As clients continue to experience and express their feelings about their issues and possible solutions, motivation builds. If the client is willing to journal, this is an ideal time to begin. Bibliotherapy and films noted in the previous section may be helpful here, too. Ambivalence toward change is common in this stage, so motivational interviewing (MI) is recommended.

Prochaska et al. (1994) recommended having clients make their own "propaganda" and using imagination as possible motivators (e.g., visualizing oneself without the problem, imagining the money saved and what can be done with it instead). They also suggested that collecting data would be helpful. Self-monitoring by recording baseline behaviors is an example. Some other ideas suggested by Prochaska et al. include doing a functional analysis, such as the ABCs of rational emotive behavior therapy (i.e., antecedents-behavior-consequences). Also, clients need to ask difficult questions such as: "What are you willing to sacrifice in order to have a better life and better health?" Creating a new self-image is needed. Soliciting the support of significant others is helpful at every stage of the change process.

Specific preparation strategies.

Clients need to decide when to make the impending change and face the anticipatory anxiety that may result. The preparation stage is primarily about deciding when to make the change and making the commitment to change. Similar to getting ready for major surgery, clients need to psychologically prepare for this major event that is about to occur (Prochaska et al., 1994). Counselors can help with this process by guiding clients through guided-imagery exercises and talking through the client's apprehension. It is helpful if they go public with this date by telling significant others who act as their support throughout the change process. Important others need to be told to neither nag nor keep asking how the client is doing.

Stimulus control is an important process during the preparation stage (Connors et al., 2013). This is done by having clients eliminate triggers as much as possible from their life spaces (e.g., throw away pornographic materials, restrict computer usage or access, get rid of 1-900 numbers, delete phone numbers of sex workers).

During this stage, you work with the client to create a detailed plan of action. Instead of engaging in compulsive sexual activity, what other activities will take their place? How will the client deal with urges? What strategies will be used to minimize negative emotional states? Will regularly attending a mutual support group be included in the plan? The more the client creates the plan, the greater the likelihood it will be followed in the action stage (Prochaska et al., 1994). Other ideas for *before* their chosen quit day (i.e., preparation strategies) can be found in Appendix B.

Specific action strategies.

Wordecha et al. (2018) stated that binge pornography use together with masturbation is one of the most common behaviors that lead males to seek treatment for sex addiction. The following are suggestions made by several writers that may be helpful to counselors working with sex addicts. Note that there are currently no carefully conducted studies in the area of treatment for sex addiction (Hook, Reid, Penberthy, Davis, & Jennings, 2014; Rosenberg, Carnes, & O'Connor, 2014). Instead, treatment approaches established for other addictions are recommended, including individual counseling, cognitive-behavioral interventions, dialectical behavior techniques to reduce cravings, group counseling, family counseling, insight-focused counseling to identify causes, exercise and nutrition, treatment of comorbid addictions and mental health issues, 12-step programs, and psychopharmacology (Rosenberg, Carnes, & O'Connor, 2014).

Riemersma and Sytsma (2013) recommended trauma-focused and attachment work, based on the high percentage of sex addicts that have been physically, sexually, and emotionally abused as children. Eye movement desensitization and reprocessing has shown some promise for dealing with trauma with sex addicts (Delmonico & Griffin, 2015). Beveridge (2015) argued that young people experiencing sexual addiction might not have come from abusive pasts, however. Instead, Beveridge maintained that an addiction to pornography might have occurred serendipitously following repeated viewings of "extreme and shocking material" (p. 49) together with the concomitant isolation created by solitary viewing.

Wood (2013) posed the question, "Why is insight not enough to enable someone to gain self-control?" (p. 151). Wood maintained that, for change to occur, sex addicts need to experience both the terror underlying their addiction and something akin to its opposite (i.e., that addiction can be both sufferable and controllable). Laaser (2004) commented on how fear of the unknown future prevents the IAS from recovering. Griffin-Shelley (1993a) suggested that the most effective counseling involves having sex addicts be exposed to that which they fear the most. Benfield (2018) created an attachment-based approach to working with IASs, based on the repeated finding that sex addiction is correlated with having an insecure attachment style.

Laaser (2004) recommended that sex addicts do the following during the first weeks and months of recovery: (a) have a schedule of men or women who agree once every day or more, (b) make a list of all the good things in their lives and focus on resulting positive affirmations (using the AA edict, "Fake it till you make it"), (c) stop all sexual behaviors (including masturbation) for at least 90 days, and (d) confront the abuse (if it occurred earlier) but not necessarily the abuser. As Laaser noted, there are various ways to confront abuse, such as expressing emotions in counseling, going through imaginal desensitization, write letters that might never be sent, and/or roleplay confrontation in session.

Although a period of abstinence is recommended in the literature (Carnes, 1991; Laaser, 2004), the goal for sex addicts, as it is for food addicts, is to control undesirable compulsive sexual behaviors (Burlew & Barton, 2002). Burlew and Barton (2002) recommended existential counseling with the goals of finding meaning through living authentically, taking responsibility for choices made in life, developing I-Thou relationships (i.e., respectful relationships that acknowledge but do not objectify others), and appreciating the fleeting nature of one's life.

Work focused on identity development and how to function in intimate relationships is likely indicated (Tepper et al., 2007). Carnes (Tepper et al., 2007) asked 190 sex addicts what treatments they considered to be the most helpful, and they came up with (in order of most helpful to least) the following: (a) a higher power, (b) couples-based 12-step group, (c) friendship support, (d) individual counseling, (e) celibacy period, (f) a sponsor, (g) exercise and nutrition, (h) 12-step group, (i) supportive partner, (j) outpatient group counseling, (k) family counseling, and (l) hospital aftercare. Carnes (1991) noted that sex addicts need to work on their beliefs, attitudes, and distorted thinking and to own their vulnerabilities of being "human, ordinary, not unique" (p. 198). Both Carnes and the addicts he interviewed also recommended that, during recovery, addicts work on creating appropriate boundaries with others, accept that life is not perfect, and remind oneself that things will change. It is critical that sex addicts learn to be genuinely intimate with others and accept both themselves and others (Carnes, 1991). Interrupting the cycle of addiction as outlined by Carnes is indicated (i.e., preoccupation, ritualization, acting out, despair). Spiritual exploration and growth may need to be included (Riemersma & Sytsma, 2013).

Additional suggested interventions include psychoeducation, crisis intervention (De Crisce (2013), and social skills training—including conversational, conflict resolution, assertiveness, and attention skills (Riemersma & Sytsma, 2013). Coleman et al. (2018) recommended using their model of intervention that they called the "integrative biopsychosocial and sex positive model of impulsive/compulsive sexual behavior (ICSB), its ecological conceptualization, and multifaceted approach to treatment of ICSB" (p. 125). Couples counseling might also be required to deal with the necessary healing for partners (Riemersma & Sytsma, 2013).

Other treatment approaches that have some empirical support include acceptance and commitment therapy and experiential psychotherapy (Campbell & Stein, 2016). Some research suggests that sex addicts lack mindfulness, so mindfulness training may prove helpful (Campbell & Stein, 2016). Imaginal desensitization was found in one study to be as effective as convert sensitization in reducing sexually compulsive behaviors (McConaghy & Armstrong, as cited in Kafka, 2014).

A key modality in helping sex addicts recover is group counseling (Campbell & Stein, 2016; Southern et al., 2015). It provides opportunities for "disclosure, self-expression, accountability, and closeness" (Southern et al., 2015, p. 195).

Carnes, Delmonico, and Griffin (2000) developed an intervention called the concentric circles exercise to assist sex addicts in becoming clear on what healthy sexuality looks like. It is explained in the following:

> Draw three circles, one each inside the other (like a bullseye). The client then places any sexual behaviors they are avoiding (known as their "bottom line behaviors") in the center circle. The second ring represents "yellow light" behaviors that may or may not be acceptable depending on your state of emotional or mental health. These yellow-light behaviors may include behaviors that are still being determined as healthy or unhealthy and may include triggers that may lead towards bottom line behaviors. Finally, the outer circle includes healthy behaviors they know they can practice as part of their healthy sexuality. This exercise provides clients with a visual image of behaviors that are both healthy and unhealthy. (Delmonico & Griffin, 2015, p. 247)

Other ideas for *beginning* their chosen quit day (i.e., action strategies) can be found in Appendix B.

Specific maintenance strategies and relapse prevention.

Note: Maintenance strategies and relapse prevention are also, for many, partly facilitated by regular attendance at relevant mutual support groups. A list of such mutual support groups and helpful websites is found in an upcoming section entitled Relevant Mutual Support Groups, Websites, and Videos.

Goodman (1993) sets goals with clients to help prevent the beginning of addictive behavior (slips), and, if the behavior does recur, to keep the slip from moving into relapse. Goodman focused on the following: (a) risk recognition, i.e., when is the behavior most likely to occur, (b) coping with urges, and (c) reframing slips and learning from them. As all addictive substances and behaviors result in a dopamine release, Reed (2000) recommended that sex addicts engage in a variety of activities that release dopamine. Reed suggested that addicts create or engage in (note that most of these could pertain to any addiction)

1. Variety in one's life so that excitement occurs.
2. Wonder, curiosity, and surprise as uncertainty releases dopamine.
3. Romantic mood states as they trigger good memories.
4. Pleasurable sensations through smell, sound, touch, and taste.
5. Good sex.
6. Laughter and playfulness.
7. Excitement.
8. Novel activities.
9. Good and fair arguments to resolve disagreements.
10. Activities that evoke romantic feelings in one's partner.
11. Sensual activities.
12. Emotional intimacy.

Carnes (1991) noted that becoming emotionally overwhelmed is most commonly linked with relapse as addicts use their addiction to cope with pain. He recommended that counselors use a three-phase method to build a relapse strategy:

1. Ask the client for a description of the ideal sexual fantasy to enact. This provides insight into the sexual script that underlies the addiction. The underlying dynamics can then be resolved through counseling.
2. The client imagines and documents all of the consequences that would result from enacting the ideal sexual fantasy. This begins to "spoil" the fantasy.
3. Have the client imagine what he or she will do if a slip occurs. Working with this, the counselor and client create an "exit strategy" to stop the cycle of addiction from occurring again. Carnes noted that the exit strategy often takes the form of a written contract between the counselor, or sponsor, and the client.

Other ideas for relapse prevention can be found in Appendix C.

Motivational Interviewing

Southern et al. (2015) noted that MI is useful in helping sexual addicts prepare for either recovery or treatment. MI is useful as well for establishing a strong working alliance. Here is an example of how MI could be used to help an IAS decide that counseling might be the best first step to take in recovery. (Pertaining to Chapter 6's description of MI, the following is an example of the process called *planning*.)

Client: I have certainly appreciated this session with you, Dr. Paul. I am not sure what the next step should look like, however, in overcoming my excessive use of pornography.

Counselor: It is really good to see, Cliff, that you have decided to do something about it.

Client: Well, I cannot carry on the way that I'm going. I am 21 years old, and I have never been on a date. I am very lonely.

Counselor: You have mentioned your loneliness several times. Would you like to look at some ways that you could go about overcoming your porn addiction and perhaps also strategies for reducing or overcoming your loneliness?

Client: Yes, I would like that very much.

Counselor: I would be very willing to work with you individually on this issue. We also have a group for clients experiencing sexual addiction in its many forms. We usually recommend that you begin with some individual work before moving into the group, but it is your choice. Many people also benefit from attending a mutual support group of some kind. There are several that I could recommend to you.

Client: As you know, Dr. Paul, I am a very shy individual. I think going to a group or a mutual support group would be difficult for me right now. Not to mention that I am so embarrassed by my problem. How many sessions would I be able to see you for?

Counselor: At our clinic, Cliff, we have a six-session limit. Let's see how you're doing at the end of that before we decide together what the next step might look like. Would that be okay with you?

Client: I think that would be an excellent place to start. Thank you.

Insight-Oriented Interventions

Little is written about the use of psychoanalytic or psychodynamic approaches to dealing with sex addiction. Instead, some have offered opinions regarding underlying considerations. Craparo (2014) advanced the notion that sexual addiction results from dissociation of dysregulated emotions, or what Dubrow-Eichel (1993) referred to as a "disowning of parts of the self (splits in the self)" (p. 130). This fragmentation was believed to occur in response to shame. Soon after orgasm, the individual would feel this shame doubled (Dubrow-Eichel, 1993). Crossan (2014) also viewed sex addiction as resulting from escape or avoidance of strong negative feelings. Both Crossan and Beveridge (2015) stated that sex addicts use sex to self-sooth the stress resulting from life struggles.

Laaser (2004) wrote that addicts need to become aware of the abuse that they experienced in childhood for pent-up anger toward the abuse and the abuser to be released. Until then, Laaser did not believe that healing could occur. Following the anger, Laaser maintained, the IAS needs to confront the abuser. Given that not all sex addicts have been abused, this advice may be inappropriate for the majority of sex addicts, perhaps especially the piece regarding confronting the abuser. As mentioned earlier, counseling offers several strategies that can be used to deal with the trauma that does not directly involve the perpetrator.

Another interpretation of sex addiction was offered by Gerevich, Treuer, Danics, and Herr (2005). In treating a 61-year-old male with sexual addiction, they framed the addiction as a means by which their client projected a masculine identity, which resulted from identification with his father.

Spiritual Interventions

Grubbs and Hook (2016), in their introduction to a special issue about religiosity and sexual addiction, stated that "recent research has linked religious belief to higher levels of self-perceived sexual addiction" (p. 156). These authors wrote that the findings seem surprising because having strong religious convictions is often associated with prohibiting pornography and other potentially addictive behaviors (Grubbs & Hook, 2016). This negative perception, however, may be the result of religious individuals having less tolerance of behaviors associated with sexual addiction such as pornography (Karaga, Davis, Choe, & Hook, 2016). In their review of the research on this topic, Karaga et al. (2016) concluded that hypersexuality and religion/spirituality are correlated inversely, meaning that higher levels of religiosity are associated with lower levels of compulsive sexual behaviors.

Giordano and Cecil (2014) sampled 235 college students and found that those who did not have a sense of purpose and meaning, and those who engaged in negative religious coping, were more likely to struggle with compulsive sexual behaviors. Negative religious coping refers to engaging in religious beliefs and behaviors that are associated with diminished health and well-being. In contrast, positive religious coping refers to having a secure relation with God and spiritual beliefs that lead to enhanced health and well-being. Such associated behaviors include seeking help from one's spiritual leaders or community and having a deep sense of spiritual connectedness and purpose. These findings tentatively suggest that helping sex addicts embrace spirituality and find meaning and purpose may be helpful in reducing SC.

Certainly, some writers believe that the path to recovery from sexual addiction will occur through spiritual means (Carnes, 1991; Laaser, 2004). Wagner's (2009) case study provided some evidence that her client "Steve" was helped through spiritual interventions (namely use of forgiveness, Christian visualization, and self-acceptance) and schema-focused therapy (SFT). Wagner explained that SFT is an integration of CBT, gestalt, object relations, and psychoanalytic methods. Partners of sex addicts (N = 92) have also reported that spiritual practices were helpful to their recovery and mental health (Pollard, Hook, Corley, & Schneider, 2014).

Laaser (2004) stressed that sex addicts need to let go of their "selfish needs and desires" (p. 125) and, in so doing, experience a spiritual awakening. Laaser, however, did not believe that most addicts would ever be "cured." Lord (1993) wrote that sex addicts who meditate/pray and who accept a higher power have vastly different neurochemical events occurring compared to those who are actively pursuing their addictions.

Heilakka (1993), from a secular perspective, wrote that discovering real intimacy (which may have spiritual components) leads to self-knowledge and feelings of self-worth. Carnes (1991) summarized the advice that sex addicts provided regarding how to develop a spiritual life. The addicts recommended that other sex addicts (a) use the 12 steps, (b) find others who will share their spiritual experiences, (c) disentangle religion from spirituality, (d) get into nature, (e) make some effort daily, (f) look for ways to promote self-reflection, (g) surrender by admitting your powerlessness and letting go, and (h) heal the split between your sexual and spiritual sides.

Cognitive-Behavioral Therapy

CBT can be facilitated using the triple column technique. It can be used both by counselors in their work with clients and by clients alone. The full instructions for using the technique are found in Chapter 6. The following are some of the cognitions that can be problematic for clients with this addiction.

Automatic Thought or Belief	Questioning it	Healthier Thought or Belief
I am a bad and unworthy person.		My strengths and weaknesses do not define my self-worth. We are equal as humans, and I am a human. I can choose to do good deeds.

Automatic Thought or Belief	Questioning it	Healthier Thought or Belief
The person I am is unlovable.		I too deserve to be happy, and, despite my faults, I am a lovable person.
I will never get my needs met from other people.		Once I learn how, I can get my social needs met by others.
My most important need is sex.		Sex can certainly be pleasurable, but I can certainly live without it. Many people choose to be celibate, and they survive. Plus, I can introduce sex into a romantic relationship when the time is right.
I will never have a life partner if I have to rely on my social skills.		I can learn to improve my dating and relationship skills. They are skills after all.

The left column was adapted from Martin (1989, p. 17). Martin (1989) claimed that the beliefs in the left column have been found to be almost always present in the cognitions of addicts.

Miles, Cooper, Nugent, and Ellis (2016) reviewed treatments for sex addicts. They concluded that most of the treatments evaluated included modified cognitive-behavioral methods as well as expressive (i.e., art therapy and psychodrama combined with CBT) and exposure techniques (i.e., EMDR). All studies reviewed had several methodological weaknesses.

Cognitive-behavioral strategies can be useful in diminishing compulsive sexual behaviors. Delmonico and Griffin (2015) provided several examples: (a) don't carry large amounts of cash to purchase pornographic materials, (b) use thought-stopping methods, and (c) identify and alter rituals regarding sexual behavior.

CBT can be used to identify and change the thoughts, emotions, and behaviors that perpetuate compulsive sexual behaviors (Cohen, 2015). Specifically, it can help clients identify and better address the triggers that lead to these behaviors. For example, permission-granting thoughts (e.g., "It is okay if I have this affair") lead clients to engage in the behaviors by weakening their resistance. Alternative thoughts (e.g., "I vowed to stay faithful") can help build clients' resolve to abstain from the behavior. Also, CBT can focus on the negative consequences of the sexual behaviors, which helps strengthen self-restraint (Cohen, 2015).

RELEVANT MUTUAL SUPPORT GROUPS, WEBSITES, AND VIDEOS

Mutual Support Groups

For the Addicted Individual

1. Sexaholics Anonymous (SA). http://www.sa.org/

   Quoted from website:

   Sexaholics Anonymous is a fellowship of men and women who share their experience, strength, and hope with each other that they may solve their common problem and help others to recover. The only requirement for membership is a desire to stop lusting and become sexually sober. There are no dues or fees for SA membership; we are self-supporting through our own contributions. SA is not allied with any sect, denomination, politics, organization, or institution; does not wish to engage in any controversy; neither endorses nor opposes any causes. Our primary purpose is to stay sexually sober and help others to achieve sexual sobriety. Sexaholics Anonymous is a recovery program based on the principles of Alcoholics Anonymous and received permission from AA to use its Twelve Steps and Twelve Traditions in 1979.

   We have a solution. We don't claim it's for everybody, but for us, it works. If you identify with us and think you may share our problem, we'd like to share our solution with you (Sexaholics Anonymous, last sentence, page 2). In defining sobriety, we do not speak for those outside Sexaholics Anonymous. We can only speak for ourselves. Thus, for the married sexaholic, sexual sobriety means having no form of sex with self or with persons other than the spouse. In SA's sobriety definition, the term "spouse" refers to one's partner in a marriage between a man and a woman. For the unmarried sexaholic, sexual sobriety means freedom from sex of any kind. And for all of us, single and married alike, sexual sobriety also includes progressive victory over lust (Sexaholics Anonymous, pp. 191–192). The only requirement for SA membership is a desire to stop lusting and become sexually sober according to the SA sobriety definition. Any two or more sexaholics gathered together for SA sobriety according to SA sobriety definition may call themselves an SA group.

   Meetings that do not adhere to and follow Sexaholics Anonymous' sobriety statement as set forth in the foregoing Statement of Principle adopted by the General Delegate Assembly in 2010 are not SA meetings and shall not call themselves SA meetings.

2. Sex Addicts Anonymous (SAA). https://saa-recovery.org/

Quoted from website:

An Invitation to Recovery

We found in each other what we could find nowhere else: people who knew the depth of our pain. Together we found hope and the care of a loving Higher Power. Our commitment is to help others recover from sexual addiction, just as we have been helped.— Sex Addicts Anonymous, p. 2.

Looking for help?

If you believe you have a problem with sex addiction (or are wondering if you might) and you want to change your behavior, we recommend that you find and attend a meeting of Sex Addicts Anonymous as soon as possible. We have found that the path to recovery begins with meetings. You may attend as many meetings as you like, and they are free of charge. The only requirement is a desire to stop your addictive sexual behavior. You may find a list of meetings here. We wish you well in your recovery.

About SAA

As a fellowship of recovering addicts, Sex Addicts Anonymous offers a message of hope to anyone who suffers from sex addiction. Through long and painful experience, we came to realize that we were powerless over our sexual thoughts and behaviors and that our preoccupation with sex was causing progressively severe adverse consequences for us, our families, and our friends. Despite many failed promises to ourselves and attempts to change, we discovered that we were unable to stop acting out sexually by ourselves. Many of us came to this realization when we started attending SAA meetings. In that setting we heard stories similar to ours and realized that recovery from our problem was possible. We learned through the SAA Fellowship that we were not hopelessly defective. The basic principles of recovery practiced by SAA are found in the Twelve Steps and Twelve Traditions of Alcoholics Anonymous. Although we are not affiliated with AA or with any other organization or agency, we are, indeed, grateful for permission to modify and apply the Steps and Traditions to sex addiction, making recovery possible for us.

SAA Convention Recordings available in mp3 format

Many members of the fellowship have found our convention speaker and workshop CDs to be a valuable resource in their recovery. The ISO is pleased to announce the immediate availability of downloadable mp3 audio files.

The mp3 downloads can be purchased online from the SAA Store. These files may be played on almost any portable music device or computer.

After your online purchase is complete, you will receive an e-mail order receipt containing the links to download each recording that you have purchased. (Please keep in mind that each file is very large and may take considerable time to download).

3. Sex and Love Addicts Anonymous (SLAA). https://www.slaafws.org/

Quoted from website:

You are not alone.

Sex and Love Addicts Anonymous, or S.L.A.A., is a program for anyone who suffers from an addictive compulsion to engage in or avoid sex, love, or emotional attachment. We use the Twelve Steps and Twelve Traditions adapted from Alcoholics Anonymous to recover from these compulsions. The following behaviors have been experienced by members.

- Having few healthy boundaries, we become sexually involved with and/or emotionally attached to people without knowing them.
- Fearing abandonment and loneliness, we stay in and return to painful, destructive relationships. . . .
- We confuse love with neediness, physical and sexual attraction, pity and/or the need to rescue or be rescued.
- We sexualize stress, guilt, loneliness, anger, shame, fear and envy. . . .
- To avoid feeling vulnerable, we may retreat from all intimate involvement . . . Excerpts from the Twelve Characteristics of Sex and Love Addiction ©1985

You may be experiencing one or all of these characteristics, but only you can decide for sure if S.L.A.A. is right for you. To help you make this decision, it is suggested that you complete the 40 Questions for Self-Diagnosis. If you answer yes to any combination of these questions and think you may be struggling with sex and love addiction, you are welcome in S.L.A.A.

Now What?

You have already taken a big step in seeking information about the program of S.L.A.A. If you believe this program is for you, the next thing to do is find out if there is a meeting in your area. Gathering with other sex and love addicts at an S.L.A.A. meeting is the primary way we learn how to get sober and maintain recovery. There are no dues, fees, or registration process to attend a meeting, only voluntary contributions. By giving and receiving support from others like us, we not only have a better chance of recovering, but we also begin to learn how to engage with people in a non-addictive way.

An essential piece of literature to help you start and stay with the program is the S.L.A.A. Basic Text. This book contains information about discovering the illness, beginning recovery, defining sobriety, the Twelve Steps of S.L.A.A. and contains personal stories of others who have gone from addiction to recovery. There are also pamphlets that can be of great help. These include the Welcome pamphlet, An Introduction to Sex and Love Addicts Anonymous, Suggestions for Newcomers, Questions Beginners Ask, and Addiction and Recovery. The Twelve Step program of S.L.A.A. has helped many of us break free from the grip of sex and love addiction. You Are Not Alone.

4. Sexual Compulsives Anonymous (SCA). http://www.sca-recovery.org/

   Quoted from website:

   Sexual Compulsives Anonymous is a fellowship of men and women who share their experience, strength and hope with each other, that they may solve their common problem and help others to recover from sexual compulsion. The only requirement for membership is a desire to stop having compulsive sex. There are no dues or fees for SCA membership; we are self-supporting through our own contributions. SCA is not allied with any sect, denomination, politics, organization, or institution; does not wish to engage in any controversy; neither endorses nor opposes any causes.

   Our primary purpose is to stay sexually sober and to help others to achieve sexual sobriety. Members are encouraged to develop their own sexual recovery plan, and to define sexual sobriety for themselves. We are not here to repress our God-given sexuality, but to learn how to express it in ways that will not make unreasonable demands on our time and energy, place us in legal jeopardy—or endanger our mental, physical or spiritual health.

5. Sexual Recovery Anonymous (SRA). http://sexualrecovery.org/

   Quoted from website:

   Welcome to the website of Sexual Recovery Anonymous (SRA), a fellowship of men and women who share their experience, strength and hope with each other that they may solve their common problem—sexual addiction—and help others to recover.

   Our program offers a path of recovery from sex addiction. Like all addictions, sex addiction interferes with the life process, and can even be life-threatening. SRA offers a way to stop compulsive sexual behavior through practicing the Twelve Steps and Twelve Traditions. The list of statements in the section Do I Belong in SRA? will help you decide if you are addicted. This Website is also for the family members and friends of the sex addict who want to better understand sex addiction and where help can be obtained.

   This website provides a starting point for the person who suffers from compulsive obsessive sexual addiction and wishes to find release from this destructive behavior. The website is also for the helping professional who wants to become better acquainted with the SRA 12- Step program.

   To purchase SRA's book, Stories of Recovery from Members of Sexual Recovery Anonymous, please click here.

6. Sex Addiction Support Groups. Note that most of these incorporate Christian ideology: http://porn-free.org/support_groups.htm

For the Partner and/or Family

These groups are intended to help family members refrain from behaviors that may trigger the addict. They also target underlying maladaptive thoughts and behaviors of the co-addict. Lastly, they focus on facilitating spiritual growth.

1. Codependents of Sex Addicts (COSA). http://www.cosa-recovery.org/

   Quoted from website:

   COSA is a Twelve Step recovery program for men and women whose lives have been affected by compulsive sexual behavior. Adapted from Alcoholics Anonymous and Al-Anon, COSA is a program for our spiritual development, no matter what our religious beliefs. As we meet to share our experience, strength, and hope while working the Twelve Steps, we grow stronger in spirit. We begin to lead our lives more serenely and in deeper fulfillment, little by little, one day at a time. Only in this way can we be of help to others. (COSA is in no way affiliated with Circles of Support and Accountability).

2. Co-Dependents Anonymous (CODA). http://coda.org/

   Quoted from website:

   Welcome to Co-Dependents Anonymous, a fellowship of men and women whose common purpose is to develop healthy relationships. The only requirement for membership is a desire for healthy and loving relationships.

3. Recovering Couples Anonymous (RCA). http://www.recovering-couples.org/

   Quoted from website:

   Welcome to Recovering Couples Anonymous. Ours is a fellowship of recovering couples. We suffer from many addictions and dysfunctions, and we share our experience, strength, and hope with each other that we may solve our common problems and help other recovering couples restore their relationships. The only requirement for membership is the desire to remain committed to each other and to develop new intimacy. There are no dues or fees for membership; we are self-supporting through our own contributions. We are not allied with any organization. We do not wish to engage in any controversy, neither endorse nor oppose any causes. Although there is no organizational affiliation between Alcoholics Anonymous and our fellowship, we are based on the principles of AA. Our primary purpose is to stay committed in loving and intimate relationships and to help other couples achieve freedom from dysfunctional relationships.

4. S-Anon International Family Groups (S-Anon). http://www.sanon.org/

   Quoted from website:

   Hope & Help for Family & Friends of Sexaholics

   S-Anon is a program of recovery for those who have been affected by someone else's sexual behavior. S-Anon is based on the Twelve Steps and the Twelve Traditions of Alcoholics Anonymous. The primary purpose of S-Anon is to recover from the effects upon us of another person's sexaholism, and to help families and friends of sexaholics. Read more about S-Anon's purpose.

   For the Newcomer

   Welcome to S-Anon! Let us assure you that no matter what feelings you may be having right now, other members of S-Anon have felt similar emotions. Meetings are a vital part of the S-Anon program, providing us with the opportunity to identify and confirm common problems and to hear the experience, strength and hope of others. If this is your first contact with a Twelve-Step program, you may have some questions about meetings and how our group works. Read more about S-Anon meetings. Throughout the year, S-Anon conventions are held at the area, state, regional, national, and international levels. View a list of upcoming international conventions and other S-Anon events.

   For the Teenager

   S-Ateen is a Twelve Step program for teenagers who have been affected by the sexual behavior of a relative or friend. The meetings follow S-Anon's Twelve Steps and Twelve Traditions. S-Ateen meetings are conducted separately from those of S-Anon, and are guided by adult S-Anon sponsors. Read more about S-Ateen's purpose.

5. CoSex and Love Addicts Anonymous (COSLAA). http://coslaa.org/

   Quoted from website:

   COSLAA is a 12-step support group for the recovery of family, friends, and significant others whose lives have been affected by their relationship with someone addicted to sex and love. COSLAA, also known as CO-Sex and Love Addicts Anonymous, reaches out to the suffering individual, 18 years or older, regardless of sexual orientation, gender, or relationship status. COSLAA meetings have a united purpose of mutual aid to those affected by another's sex and love addiction, but who are not sex addicts themselves.

   COSLAA is a closed fellowship and not an intergroup with any sex addiction recovery group. COSLAA is the corresponding 12 step family group for SLAA, and is cooperative in referring sex addicted calls to that group. COSLAA reserves the right to screen newcomer calls to help match appropriate group assignment. COSLAA offers a safe and confidential recovery fellowship for members who have been affected by another's sexually addictive behaviors, such as visits to strip clubs, obsessive use of pornography, internet sex, voyeurism, phone sex, and serial infidelity. The only requirement for membership is a desire to stop living out a pattern of codependency to someone who is sexually addicted. We diligently protect members' anonymity and we are self-supporting through our own contributions. We are not affiliated with any other organizations, movements, or causes, and we are neither religious nor secular. We believe that sex and love addiction is a family illness. By looking at our own attitudes and behaviors, we can find a new way of life that will allow us to be happier. We do this by practicing the 12 steps and traditions of COSLAA, defining our own bottom lines in dealing with the disease, and developing a relationship with a power greater than ourselves. COSLAA Help Line for newcomers is 860-456-0032.

Websites

1. Elements Behavioral Health. http://www.cybersexualaddiction.com/treatment-for-sexual-addiction/

2. Association for the Treatment of Sexual Abusers (ATSA). http://www.atsa.com/

   Quoted from website:

   The Association for the Treatment of Sexual Abusers is an international, multi-disciplinary organization dedicated to making society safer by preventing sexual abuse. ATSA promotes sound research, effective evidence-based practice, informed public policy, and collaborative community strategies that lead to the effective assessment, treatment, and management of individuals who have sexually abused or are at risk to abuse. ATSA's members include treatment providers, researchers and educators, victims' rights advocates, law enforcement and court officials, and representatives of many other stakeholder groups. The core values that guide ATSA are professional excellence, community safety, collaboration, and advocacy. ATSA promotes the philosophy that empirically based assessment, practice, management, and policies enhance community safety, reduce sexual recidivism, protect victims and vulnerable populations, transform the lives of those caught in the web of sexual violence, and illuminate paths to prevent sexual abuse.

3. International Institute for Trauma & Addiction Professionals (IITAP). https://www.iitap.com/

   Quoted from website:

   IITAP's research is one of the reasons that our certifications are highly sought after in the sexual addiction community. IITAP also hosts a valuable website for sex addicts themselves at https://www.sexhelp.com/am-i-a-sex-addict/

4. Society for the Advancement of Sexual Health (SASH). http://www.sash.net/

   Quoted from website:

   The Society for the Advancement of Sexual Health (SASH) is a nonprofit organization dedicated to promoting sexual health and addressing the escalating consequences of problematic sexual behaviors affecting individuals, families and communities. Seeking collaboration among clinical, educational, legal, policy, and research professionals, SASH advocates a multifactorial approach to address problematic sexual behaviors, further research and to promote sexual health in general.

5. Internet Behavior Consulting, Cybersex Addiction and Online Sex Offender Resources (IBConsulting). http://www.internetbehavior.com/

6. Relativity (formerly the Sexual Recovery Institute). https://www.sexualrecovery.com/sexual-addiction/

7. Your Brain on Porn. https://www.yourbrainonporn.com/

Videos

To view these videos, search their titles on YouTube.

1. *The Science of Porn Addiction – Gabes Story.*
2. *The Science of Pornography Addiction (SFW).*
3. *Are You A Hurting Partner of a SA with Carol the Coach.* [This video is not on YouTube; you'll find it on BlogTalkRadio from Sex Help with Carol the Coach.]
4. *Dr. Patrick Carnes, Leading Sex Addiction Expert, Video Interview.*
5. Ex-Porn Star Shelley Lubben, *The Truth Behind the Fantasy of Porn - PornHarms.com briefing.*
6. *How to Treat Sex Addiction: Sexual Addiction Treatment with Dr. Clark.*
7. *Kids access porn sites at 6, begin flirting online at 8.* [This video is not on YouTube; you'll find it on USA TODAY, published May 14, 2013.]
8. *Sex Addicts' Dark World.*
9. *Sex Addiction Informational Video.*
10. *Spouses of Sex Addicts Informational Video.*

RELEVANT PHONE APPS

Generic Addiction Apps

[*Note*: Generic apps are described in Chapter 6.

This list is not exhaustive. New apps are continually being developed. Do an Internet search to find out the latest apps available. Most are for specific addictions but some, such as these four, are generic.

1. I Am Sober. https://play.google.com/store/apps/details?id=com.thehungrywasp.iamsober
2. Sober Time. https://play.google.com/store/apps/details?id=com.sociosoft.sobertime
3. Pocket Rehab: Get Sober & Addiction Recovery. https://play.google.com/store/apps/details?id=com.getpocketrehab.app
4. Loop Habit Tracker. https://play.google.com/store/apps/details?id=org.isoron.uhabits

Specialized Apps

1. Brainbuddy: Quit Porn Fever Porn & Masturbation Addiction

   https://itunes.apple.com/us/app/brainbuddy-porn-masturbation/id726780077?mt=8

   Quoted from website:

   HOW BRAINBUDDY WORKS

   A. Check in Each Evening

   Your daily checkup learns from you and tracks your progress, mood and habits so you reboot fast, effectively and permanently.

B. 24/7 Protection

Based on over 3000 hours of patient study, Brainbuddy monitors the factors that lead to dopamine cravings and protects you from porn relapse.

C. Daily Missions

Each day you receive a new mission card. Every mission you complete rewires your brain to seek out healthy sources of dopamine, instead of unsatisfying porn.

D. Quests

From one day to one year, build up your willpower one quest at a time.

E. Rewiring Exercises

Depending on your mood, Brainbuddy will often prescribe specialized exercises that destroy addiction pathways, freeing you from porn cravings. Permanently.

F. Know Yourself to Conquer Yourself

Track your progress, learn about your strengths and weaknesses, and see just how far you've come.

G. Level Up Your Life

Rebooting your brain has immense psychological and physical benefits. Brainbuddy unlocks achievements as your brain, body and life get better.

2. Sex Addiction

   https://play.google.com/store/apps/details?id=com.andromo.dev529751.app503111

   Quoted from the website:

   In this application, we will help you to learn step by step How to Have Sex: [Includes 53 topics].

3. List of several apps for IPhone

   https://ios.lisisoft.com/s/sex-addiction.html

JOURNALS AND CONFERENCES

Journals

1. *Sexual Addiction & Compulsivity: The Journal of Prevention & Treatment*. Published by the Society for the Advancement of Sexual Health (SASH). The Journal is included with a membership to SASH. http://www.sash.net/journal-and-listserv-member-resources/#myaccount

2. *Sexual Offender Treatment*. Published by the International Association for the Treatment of Sexual Offenders (IATSO). http://sexual-offender-treatment.org/

   Quoted from website:

   Welcome to the journal *Sexual Offender Treatment*, the official journal of the International Association for the Treatment of Sexual Offenders.

   Sexual Offender Treatment is an international peer reviewed journal open to all scientists and practitioners researching sexual abuse. We welcome all contributions that enhance or illuminate relevant practice and science. For further information and guidelines for authors please visit the association's homepage http://sexual-offender-treatment.org/

Conferences

1. SASH hosts an annual conference, and this can be found at http://www.sash.net/sash-annual-conference-program/

2. The Association for the Treatment of Sexual Addiction and Compulsivity (ATSAC) hosts a conference. For details visit https://10times.com/atsac or their home page at https://atsac.org.uk/

COUNSELING SCENARIO

As you are reading, imagine that you are the client in this scenario. Note the areas in which the session could be improved on the part of the counselor.

Your name is Sabrina, a 52-year-old woman working in the mortgage department at a bank. You have jumped from one short-term relationship to the next through your entire adulthood. Whether you are currently single or attached, you continue seeing guys on the side because your sexual appetite is "insatiable." When you aren't having sex, you are thinking about it. You have taken young guys on unaffordable holidays with you because they were hot and good in bed. But the bank you work for is wondering how you will ever pay back the low-interest loan it has given you as an employee perk. Now you know it is time to get help, and you see a counselor.

- You: Men are users. They use you for sex, they use you for money, and then they are spiteful when you leave them.

- Counselor: It sounds like you have had some trying times with men.
- You: Trying times? Like you would not believe!
- Counselor: Please tell me about some of these times.
- You: Well, for example, I just got back from Barbados, and the only appreciation Trevor ever showed was when we returned. He said "thank you," and that was it. He didn't even stay the night.
- Counselor: It felt like Trevor used you. You were hurt and disappointed.
- You: Yes! You understand that. But to go back to your parents the night of our return after I spent a month's salary on him?
- Counselor: You spent a good amount of money on him, and you expected more from him. Is Trevor a bit younger than yourself?
- You: Well, he is 22 years old. He is old enough to know what he wants.
- Counselor: Why are you dating someone so young?
- You: Why not? If you look as good as I do, then why not enjoy a younger guy?
- Counselor: Your behavior is disgusting. Do you think your average looks entitles you to enslave young guys to your narcissistic wishes?

From the Client's Perspective

1. How would you feel if the counselor began with you in this way?
2. What is missing for you in this dialogue?
3. What would you find more helpful from a counselor in this scenario?

From the Counselor's Perspective

1. What is interfering with developing a working alliance?
2. Going back to the Common Counseling Mistakes list in Chapter 6, which mistakes is the counselor making with Sabrina?
3. As the counselor, what direction could you take that might be more helpful to the client?
4. What else would you want to know before you begin thinking that Sabrina might be a sex addict?

INDIVIDUAL EXERCISES

1. Talk to someone you believe has a strong sex drive. How does he or she differentiate having a strong sex drive from having a sex addiction? What are the strengths and challenges of having a strong sex drive? Have your interviewee comment on whether it matters whether it is a man or a woman who has the strong sex drive.
2. Spend some time alone reflecting on what characteristics you have that resemble some qualities of being a sex addict. How do these qualities differentiate you from those who have a sexual addiction?
3. Consider watching the movie *Shame*, which is about a man who is a sex addict. What do you find most interesting about the character portrayed in the movie and his behavior?

CLASSROOM EXERCISES

1. Split the class into two and have a debate. One side takes the position that there is no such thing as a sex addiction, and the other side takes the view that sex addiction does exist. At the end of the debate, have a member of each team write the key points on the board supporting that team's perspective.
2. In dyads or triads, discuss whether you believe sex addiction belongs in the next version of DSM. Why or why not?
3. Begin a roleplay where one of you is the client with a sexual addiction and one of you is the counselor. After hearing about the problem, how would you, as the counselor, help this individual?

CHAPTER SUMMARY

Sex addiction does not currently exist in DSM. This is because there is currently insufficient empirical evidence to support it as a separate diagnosis. Nonetheless, there are many supporters of the concept, and it certainly has become a popular concept in everyday discourse. Patrick Carnes, in his research, found that sex addicts experience their addiction in a four-phase cycle: *preoccupation, ritualization, compulsive sexual behavior*, and *despair*. He also classified their behaviors into 10 categories, including fantasy sex, seductive role sex, voyeuristic sex, exhibitionist sex, paying for sex, trading sex, intrusive sex, anonymous sex, pain exchange sex, and exploitive sex. An 11th category can be added to the list that includes compulsive masturbation.

Regardless of whether one believes that sex addiction exists, sex is the most frequently searched term on the Internet. It is currently thought that between 3% and 6% of the adult population in the United States experiences a sex addiction. There are several instruments that can be used to measure various aspects of hypersexual behavior. This chapter referred to 17 of these instruments. Several clinical interview questions were also included as well as various strategies for helping people experiencing dysfunction akin to a sex addiction.

Most writers on the topic of sex addiction believe that the origin of sex addiction, much as writers in the next chapter, begins in childhood. Most sex addicts have reported a childhood replete with varying forms of neglect and/or abuse (emotional, physical, and/or sexual abuse). The worse and more varied the abuse, the worse the addiction.

REFERENCES

American Psychiatric Association (APA). (2013). *Diagnostic and statistical manual of mental disorders* (5th ed.). Washington, DC: Author.

Bancroft, J. (2013). Sexual addiction. In P. M. Miller, S. A. Ball, M. E. Bates, A. W. Blume, K. M. Kampman, D. J. Kavanagh, M. E. Larimer, N. M. Petry, & P. De Witte (Eds.), *Comprehensive addictive behaviors and disorders, Vol. 1: Principles of addiction* (pp. 855–861). San Diego, CA: Academic Press.

Becerra, M. D., Robinson, C., & Balkin, R. (2011). Exploring relationships of masculinity and ethnicity as at-risk markers for online sexual addiction in men. *Sexual Addiction & Compulsivity, 18*(4), 243–260.

Benfield, J. (2018). Secure attachment: An antidote to sex addiction? A thematic analysis of therapists' experiences of utilizing attachment-informed treatment strategies to address sexual compulsivity. *Sexual Addiction & Compulsivity, 25*(1), 12–27.

Benotsch, E., Kalichman, S. C., & Pinkerton, S. D. (2001). Sexual compulsivity in HIV-positive men and women: Prevalence, predictors, and consequences of high-risk behaviors. *Sexual Addiction & Compulsivity, 8*(2), 83–99.

Berry, M. D., & Berry, P. D. (2014). Mentalization-based therapy for sexual addiction: Foundations for a clinical model. *Sexual and Relationship Therapy, 29*(2), 245–260.

Beveridge, J. (2015). A tangled web: Internet pornography, sexual addiction, and the erosion of attachment. In L. Cundy (Ed.), *Love in the age of the Internet: Attachment in the digital era* (pp. 31–52). London, England: Karnac Books.

Black, D. W., Kehrberg, L. L. D., Flumerfelt, D. L., & Schlosser, S. S. (1997). Characteristics of 36 subjects reporting compulsive sexual behavior. *The American Journal of Psychiatry, 152*, 243–249.

Burlew, L. D., & Barton, A. (2002). Counseling for sexual compulsion/addiction/dependence (SCAD). In L. D., Burlew & D. Capuzzi (Eds.), *Sexuality counseling* (pp. 257–284). Hauppauge, NY: Nova Science.

Campbell, M. M., & Stein, D. J. (2016). Hypersexual disorder. In N. Petry (Ed.), *Behavioral addictions: DSM-5 and beyond* (pp. 101–123). New York, NY: Oxford University Press.

Cantor, J. M., & Sutton, K. S. (2015). Paraphilia, gender dysphoria, and hypersexuality. In P. H. Blaney, R. F. Krueger, & T. Millon (Eds.), *Oxford textbook of psychopathology* (3rd ed., pp. 589–614). New York, NY: Oxford University Press.

Carnes, P. (1983). *Out of the shadows: Understanding sexual addiction.* Minneapolis, MN: CompCare.

Carnes, P. (1991). *Don't call it love: Recovery from sexual addiction.* Toronto, ON: Bantam Books.

Carnes, P., Green, B., & Carnes S. (2010). The same yet different: Refocusing the Sexual Addiction Screening Test (SAST) to reflect orientation and gender. *Sexual Addiction & Compulsivity, 17*(1), 7–30.

Carnes, P. J., Delmonico, D. L., & Griffin, E. J. (2000). *In the shadows of the net: Breaking free of compulsive online sexual behavior.* Center City, MN: Hazelden.

Carnes, P. J., Murray, R. E., & Charpentier, L. (2005). Bargains with chaos: Sex addicts and addiction interaction disorder. *Sexual Addiction & Compulsivity, 12*(2–3), 79–120.

Carnes, P. J., & Wilson, M. (2002). The sexual addiction assessment process. In P. J. Carnes & K. M. Adams (Eds.), *Clinical management of sex addiction* (pp. 3–19). New York, NY: Routledge.

Carnes, S., & Lee, M. A. (2014). Picking up the pieces: Helping partners and family members survive the impact of sex addiction. In K. P. Rosenberg & L. Curtiss Feder (Eds.), *Behavioral addictions: Criteria, evidence, and treatment* (pp. 267–284). San Diego, CA: Academic Press.

Carol, A. R. (2009). The history of meetings for teen sex addicts in Houston. *Sexual Addiction & Compulsivity, 16*(2), 168–171.

Carpenter, B. N., Reid, R. C., Garos, S., & Najavits, L. M. (2013). Personality disorder comorbidity in treatment-seeking men with hypersexual disorder. *Sexual Addiction & Compulsivity, 20*(1–2), 79–90.

Carvalho, J., Guerra, L., Neves, S., & Nobre, P. J. (2015). Psychopathological predictors characterizing sexual compulsivity in a nonclinical sample of women. *Journal of Sex & Marital Therapy, 41*(5), 467–480.

Chaney, M. P., & Burns-Wortham, C. M. (2015). Examining coming out, loneliness, and self-esteem as predictors of sexual compulsivity in gay and bisexual men. *Sexual Addiction & Compulsivity, 22*(1), 71–88.

Chaney, M. P., & Chang, C. Y. (2005). A trio of turmoil for internet sexually addicted men who have sex with men: Boredom proneness, social connectedness, and dissociation. *Sexual Addiction & Compulsivity, 12*(1), 3–18.

Cohen, L. J. (2015). Sex addiction: The fire down below. In M. S. Ascher & P. Levounis (Eds.), *The behavioral addictions* (pp. 137–152). Arlington, VA: American Psychiatric Publishing.

Coleman, E., Dickenson, J. A., Girard, A., Rider, G. N., Candelario-Perez, L. E., Becker-Warner, R., . . . Munns, R. (2018). An integrative biopsychosocial and sex positive model of understanding and treatment of impulsive/compulsive sexual behavior. *Sexual Addiction & Compulsivity, 25*, 125–152.

Connors, G. J., DiClemente, C. C., Velasquez, M. M., & Donovan, D. M. (2013). *Substance abuse treatment and the stages of change: Selecting and planning interventions* (2nd ed.). New York, NY: Guilford Press.

Craparo, G. (2014). The role of dissociation, affect dysregulation, and developmental trauma in sexual addiction. *Clinical Neuropsychiatry: Journal of Treatment Evaluation, 11*(2), 86–90.

Crossan, C. (2014). Technology, attachment, and sexual addiction. In R. Gill (Ed.), *Addictions from an attachment perspective: Do broken bonds and early trauma lead to addictive behaviours?* (pp. 111–118). London, England: Karnac Books.

De Crisce, D. (2013). Sexual addiction and hypersexual behaviors in adolescents. In R. Rosner (Ed.), *Clinical handbook of adolescent addiction* (pp. 362–376). Hoboken, NJ: Wiley-Blackwell.

Delmonico, D. L, & Griffin, E. J. (2015). Sexual compulsivity: Diagnosis, assessment, and treatment. In K. M. Hertlein, G. R. Weeks, & N. Gambescia, Nancy (Eds.), *Systemic sex therapy* (2nd ed., pp. 235–254). New York, NY: Routledge/Taylor & Francis.

Derbyshire, K. L., & Grant, J. E. (2015). Compulsive sexual behavior: A review of the literature. *Journal of Behavioral Addictions, 4*(2), 37–43.

De Tubino Scanavino, M., Ventuneac, A., Abdo, C. H. N., Tavares, H., Amaral, M. L. S., Messina, B., . . . Parsons, J. T. (2013). Compulsive sexual behavior and psychopathology among treatment-seeking men in Sao Paulo, Brazil. *Psychiatry Research, 209*(3), 518–524.

Dhuffar, M. K., & Griffiths, M. D. (2014). Understanding the role of shame and its consequences in female hypersexual behaviours: A pilot study. *Journal of Behavioral Addictions, 3*(4), 231–237.

Dubrow, L. (1993). Women's issues in addiction recovery. In E. Griffin-Shelley (Ed.), *Outpatient treatment of sex and love addicts* (pp. 87–100). Westport, CT: Praeger/Greenwood.

Dubrow-Eichel, S. K. (1993). The cultural context of sex and love addiction recovery. In E. Griffin-Shelley (Ed.), *Outpatient treatment of sex and love addicts* (pp. 113–135). Westport, CT: Praeger/Greenwood.

Efrati, Y. (2018). Adolescents with a disposition toward compulsive sexual behavior: The role of shame in willingness to seek help and treatment. *Sexual Addiction & Compulsivity, 25*(1), 28–45.

Elmquist, J., Shorey, R. C., Anderson, S., & Stuart, G. L. (2016). The relation between compulsive sexual behaviors and aggression in a substance-dependent population. *Journal of Aggression, Maltreatment & Trauma, 25*(1), 110–124.

Garcia, F. D., & Thibaut, F. (2010). Sexual addictions. *American Journal of Drug and Alcohol Abuse, 36*(5), 254–260.

Georgianna, S. (2015). Addressing risk factors associated with women's sexually compulsive behaviors through psycho-education and self-leadership development. *Sexual Addiction & Compulsivity, 22*(4), 314–343.

Gerevich, J., Treuer, T., Danics, Z., & Herr, J. (2005). Diagnostic and psychodynamic aspects of sexual addiction appearing as a non-paraphiliac form of compulsive sexual behaviour. *Journal of Substance Use, 10*(4), 253–259.

Giordano, A. L., & Cecil, A. L. (2014). Religious coping, spirituality, and hypersexual behavior among college students. *Sexual Addiction & Compulsivity, 21*(3), 225–239.

Goodman, A. (1993). Diagnosis and treatment of sexual addiction. *Journal of Sex & Marital Therapy, 19*(3), 225–247.

Grant, J. E., & Odlaug, B. L. (2012). In J. E. Grant & M. N. Potenza (Eds.), *The Oxford handbook of impulse control disorders* (pp. 47–55). New York, NY: Oxford University Press.

Grant, J. E., & Potenza, M. N. (2006). Sexual orientation of men with pathological gambling: Prevalence and psychiatric comorbidity in a treatment-seeking sample. *Comprehensive Psychiatry, 47*, 515–518.

Grant, J. E., & Steinberg, M. A. (2005). Compulsive sexual behavior and pathological gambling. *Sexual Addiction & Compulsivity, 12*(2–3), 235–244.

Green, B. A., Carnes, S., Carnes, P. J., & Weinman, E. A. (2012). Cybersex addiction patterns in a clinical sample of homosexual, heterosexual, and bisexual men and women. *Sexual Addiction & Compulsivity, 19*(1–2), 77–98.

Griffee, K., O'Keefe, S. L., Beard, K. W., Young, D. H., Kommor, M. J., Linz, T. D., . . . Stroebel, S. S. (2014). Human sexual development is subject to critical period learning: Implications for sexual addiction, sexual therapy, and for child rearing. *Sexual Addiction & Compulsivity, 21*(2), 114–169.

Griffin-Shelley, E. (1993a). Conclusions. In E. Griffin-Shelley (Ed.), *Outpatient treatment of sex and love addicts* (pp. 137–152). Westport, CT: Praeger/Greenwood.

Griffin-Shelley, E. (1993b). Sex and love addiction: Definition and overview. In E. Griffin-Shelley (Ed.), *Outpatient treatment of sex and love addicts* (pp. 5–19). Westport, CT: Praeger/Greenwood.

Griffin-Shelley, E. (1995). Adolescent sex and relationship addicts. *Sexual Addiction & Compulsivity, 2*(2), 112–127.

Grubbs, J. B., & Hook, J. N. (2016). Religion, spirituality, and sexual addiction: A critical evaluation of converging fields. *Sexual Addiction & Compulsivity, 23*(2–3), 155–166.

Hald, G. M., Seaman, C., & Linz, D. (2014). Sexuality and pornography. In D. L. Tolman, L. M. Diamond, J. A. Bauermeister, W. H. George, J. G. Pfaus, & L. M. Ward (Eds.), *APA handbook of sexuality and psychology, Vol. 2: Contextual approaches* (pp. 3–35). Washington, DC: American Psychological Association.

Heilakka, S. (1993). Integrating sex therapy and addiction recovery. In E. Griffin-Shelley (Ed.), *Outpatient treatment of sex and love addicts* (pp. 101–111). Westport, CT: Praeger/Greenwood.

Hook, J. N., Hook, J. P., Davis, D. E., Worthington, E. L., Jr., & Penberthy, J. K. (2010). Measuring sexual addiction and compulsivity: A critical review of instruments. *Journal of Sex & Marital Therapy, 36*(3), 227–260.

Hook, J. N., Reid, R. C., Penberthy, J. K., Davis, D. E., & Jennings, D. J. (2014). Methodological review of treatments for nonparaphilic hypersexual behavior. *Journal of Sex & Marital Therapy, 40*(4), 294–308.

Jardin, C., Garey, L., Sharp, C., & Zvolensky, M. J. (2016). Acculturative stress and risky sexual behavior: The roles of sexual compulsivity and negative affect. *Behavior Modification, 40*(1–2), 97–119.

Jiang, Q., Huang, X., & Tao, R. (2013). Internet addiction: Cybersex. In P. M. Miller, S. A. Ball, M. E. Bates, A. W. Blume, K. M. Kampman, D. J. Kavanagh, M. E. Larimer, N. M. Petry, & P. De Witte (Eds.), *Comprehensive addictive behaviors and disorders, Vol. 1: Principles of addiction* (pp. 809–818). San Diego, CA: Academic Press.

Jore, J., Green, B., Adams, K., & Carnes, P. (2016). Attachment dysfunction and relationship preoccupation. *Sexual Addiction & Compulsivity, 23*(1), 56–90.

Kafka, M. P. (2010). Hypersexual disorder: A proposed diagnosis for DSM-V. *Archives of Sexual Behavior, 39*(2), 377–400.

Kafka, M. P. (2014). Nonparaphilic hypersexuality disorders. In Y. M. Binik & K. S. K. Hall (Eds), *Principles and practice of sex therapy* (5th ed., pp. 280–304). New York, NY: Guilford Press.

Kafka, M. P., & Hennen, J. (1999). The paraphilia-related disorders: An empirical investigation of nonparaphilic hypersexuality disorders in 206 outpatient males. *Journal of Sex and Marital Therapy, 25*, 305–319.

Kaplan, M. S., & Krueger, R. B. (2010). Diagnosis, assessment, and treatment of hypersexuality. *Journal of Sex Research, 47*(2–3), 181–198.

Karaga, S., Davis, D. E., Choe, E., & Hook, J. N. (2016). Hypersexuality and religion/spirituality: A qualitative review. *Sexual Addiction & Compulsivity, 23*(2–3), 167–181.

Kaufman, J. (1993). Group process issues in men's groups. In E. Griffin-Shelley (Ed.), *Outpatient treatment of sex and love addicts* (pp. 65–85). Westport, CT: Praeger/Greenwood.

Kelly, B. C., Bimbi, D. S., Nanin, J. E., Izienicki, H., & Parsons, J. T. (2009). Sexual compulsivity and sexual behaviors among gay and bisexual men and lesbian and bisexual women. *Journal of Sex Research, 46*(4), 301–308.

Klein, V., Rettenberger, M., & Briken, P. (2014). Self-reported indicators of hypersexuality and its correlates in a female online sample. *Journal of Sexual Medicine, 11*(8), 1974–1981.

Kor, A., Fogel, Y. A., Reid, R. C., & Potenza, M. N. (2013). Should hypersexual disorder be classified as an addiction? *Sexual Addiction & Compulsivity, 20*(1–2), 27–47.

Kort, J. (2004). Covert cultural sexual abuse of gay male teenagers contributing to etiology of sexual addiction. *Sexual Addiction & Compulsivity, 11*(4), 287–300.

Kraus, S. W., Meshberg-Cohen, S., Martino, S., Quinones, L. J., & Potenza, M. N. (2015). Treatment of compulsive pornography use with naltrexone: A case report. *American Journal of Psychiatry, 172*(12), 1260–1261.

Kraus, S. W., Voon, V., & Potenza, M. N. (2016). Neurobiology of compulsive sexual behaviour: Emerging science. *Neuropsychopharmacology, 41*, 385–386.

Kuhn, A. D. (2014). Risk factors for sexual addiction among adult children of alcoholic parents. *Dissertation Abstracts International: Section B: The Sciences and Engineering*, 75(3-B(E)). No pagination specified.

Kuzma, J. M., & Black, D. W. (2008). Epidemiology, prevalence, and natural history of compulsive sexual behavior. *Psychiatric Clinics of North America, 31*(4), 603–611.

Laaser, M. R. (2004). *Healing the wounds of sexual addiction*. Grand Rapids, MI: Zondervan.

Langstrom, N., & Hanson, R. K. (2006). High rates of sexual behavior in the general population: Correlates and predictors. *Archives of Sexual Behavior, 35*(1), 37–52.

Lord, W. (1993). A diagnostic proposal with neurochemical underpinnings. In E. Griffin-Shelley (Ed.), *Outpatient treatment of sex and love addicts* (pp. 21–38). Westport, CT: Praeger/Greenwood.

Lundrigan, S. (2004). Integrating addictions-based approaches in the treatment of adolescent sexual offenders. *Sexual Addiction & Compulsivity, 11*(4), 301–324.

Martin, G. L. (1989). Relationship, romance, and sexual addiction in extramarital affairs. *Journal of Psychology and Christianity, 8*(4), 5–25.

Mercer, J. T. (1998). Assessment of the sex addicts anonymous questionnaire: Differentiating between the general population, sex addicts, and sex offenders. *Sexual Addiction & Compulsivity, 5*(2), 107–117.

Miles, L. A., Cooper, R. L., Nugent, W. R., & Ellis, R. A. (2016). Sexual addiction: A literature review of treatment interventions. *Journal of Human Behavior in the Social Environment, 26*(1), 89–99.

Odlaug, B. L., Lust, K., Schreiber, L. R. N., Christenson, G., Derbyshire, K., Harvanko, A., . . . Grant, J. E. (2013). Compulsive sexual behavior in young adults. *Annals of Clinical Psychiatry, 25*(3), 193–200.

Pachankis, J. E., Rendina, H. J., Restar, A., Ventuneac, A., Grov, C., & Parsons, J. T. (2015). A minority stress-emotion regulation model of sexual compulsivity among highly sexually active gay and bisexual men. *Health Psychology, 34*(8), 829–840.

Perera, B., Reece, M., Monahan, P., Billingham, R., & Finn, P. (2009). Childhood characteristics and personal dispositions to sexually compulsive behavior among young adults. *Sexual Addiction & Compulsivity, 16*(2), 131–145.

Petrican, R., Burris, C. T., & Moscovitch, M. (2015). Shame, sexual compulsivity, and eroticizing flirtatious others: An experimental study. *Journal of Sex Research, 52*(1), 98–109.

Pollard, S. E., Hook, J. N., Corley, M. D., & Schneider, J. P. (2014). Support utilization by partners of self-identified sex addicts. *Journal of Sex & Marital Therapy, 40*(4), 339–348.

Prochaska, J. O., Norcross, J. C., & DiClemente, C. C. (1994). *Changing for good*. New York, NY: Avon Books.

Rawson, R. A., Washton, A., Domier, C. P., & Reiber, C. (2002). Drugs and sexual effects: Role of drug type and gender. *Journal of Substance Abuse Treatment, 22*(2), 103–108.

Raymond, N. C. C., Coleman, E., & Miner, M. H. (2003). Psychiatric comorbidity and compulsive/impulsive traits in compulsive sexual behavior. *Comprehensive Psychiatry, 44*, 370–380.

Reed, S. J. (2000). Shame and hope in sexual addiction. *Journal of Ministry in Addiction & Recovery, 7*(1), 9–17.

Reid, R. C., Carpenter, B. N., Hook, J. N., Garos, S., Manning, J. C., Gilliland, R., . . . Fong, T. (2012). Report of findings in a *DSM-5* field trial for hypersexual disorder. *Journal of Sexual Medicine, 9*(11), 2868–2877.

Riemersma, J., & Sytsma, M. (2013). A new generation of sexual addiction. *Sexual Addiction & Compulsivity, 20*(4), 306–322.

Robinson, D. W. (1999). Sexual addiction as an adaptive response to post-traumatic stress disorder in the African American community. *Sexual Addiction & Compulsivity, 6*(1), 11–22.

Rooney, B. M., Tulloch, T. G., & Blashill, A. J. (2018). Psychosocial syndemic correlates of sexual compulsivity among men who have sex with men: A meta-analysis. *Archives of Sexual Behavior, 47*, 75–93.

Rosenberg, K. P., Carnes, P., & O'Connor, S. (2014). Evaluation and treatment of sex addiction. *Journal of Sex & Marital Therapy, 40*(2), 77–91.

Rosenberg, K. P., O'Connor, S., & Carnes, P. (2014). Sex addiction: An overview. In K. P. Rosenberg & L. Curtiss Feder (Eds.), *Behavioral addictions: Criteria, evidence, and treatment* (pp. 215–236). San Diego, CA: Academic Press.

Schaeffer, B. (2009). *Is it love or is it addiction?* (3rd ed.). Center City, MN: Hazelden.

Skegg, K., Nada-Raja, S., Dickson, N., & Paul, C. (2010). Perceived "out of control" sexual behavior in a cohort of young adults from the Dunedin multidisciplinary health and development study. *Archives of Sexual Behavior, 39*(4), 968–978.

Smith, P. H., Potenza, M. N., Mazure, C. M., Mckee, S. A., Park, C. L., & Hoff, R. A. (2014). Compulsive sexual behavior among male military veterans: Prevalence and associated clinical factors. *Journal of Behavioral Addictions, 3*(4), 214–222.

Southern, S., Ellison, D., & Hagwood, M. (2015). Sexual addiction. In R. L. Smith (Ed.), *Treatment strategies for substance and process addictions* (pp. 177–206). Alexandria, VA: American Counseling Association.

Starks, T. J., Grov, C., & Parsons, J. T. (2013). Sexual compulsivity and interpersonal functioning: Sexual relationship quality and sexual health in gay relationships. *Health Psychology, 32*(10), 1047–1056.

Stevens-Watkins, D., Brown-Wright, L., & Tyler, K. (2011). Brief report: The number of sexual partners and race-related stress in African American adolescents: Preliminary findings. *Journal of Adolescence, 34*, 191–194.

Stulhofer, A., Jelovica, V., & Ruzic, J. (2008). Is early exposure to pornography a risk factor for sexual compulsivity? Findings from an online survey among young heterosexual adults. *International Journal of Sexual Health, 20*(4), 270–280.

Tepper, M. S., Owens, A. F., Coleman, E., & Carnes, P. (2007). Current controversies in sexual health: Sexual addiction and compulsion. In A. F. Owens & M. S. Tepper (Eds.), *Sexual health: Vol. 4. State-of-the-art treatments and research* (pp. 349–363). Westport, CT: Praeger Publishers/Greenwood.

Voon, V., Mole, T. B., Banca, P., Porter, L., Morris, L., Mitchell, S., . . . Irvine, M. (2014). Neural correlates of sexual cue reactivity in individuals with and without compulsive sexual behaviours. *PLoS ONE, 9*(7), ArtID e102419.

Wagner, J. (2009). Sexual Steve: A schema-focused, spiritually based approach. *Journal of Psychology and Christianity, 28*(3), 275–279.

Weinstein, A. (2014). Sexual addiction or hypersexual disorder: Clinical implications for assessment and treatment. *Directions in Psychiatry, 34*(3), 185–195.

Weintraub, D., Koester J., Potenza, M. N., Siderowf, A. D., Stacy, M., Voon, V., . . . Lang, A. E. (2010). Impulse control disorders in Parkinson disease: A cross-sectional study of 3090 patients. *Archives of Neurology, 67*(5), 589–595.

Woehler, E. S., Giordano, A. L., & Hagedorn, W. B. (2018). Moments of relational depth in sex addiction treatment. *Sexual Addiction & Compulsivity, 25*, 153–169.

Womack, S. D., Hook, J. N., Ramos, M., Davis, D. E., & Penberthy, J. K. (2013). Measuring hypersexual behavior. *Sexual Addiction & Compulsivity, 20*(1–2), 65–78.

Wood, H. (2013). The nature of the addiction in "sex addiction" and paraphilias. In M. Bower, R. Hale, & H. Wood (Eds.), *Addictive states of mind* (pp. 151–173). London, England: Karnac Books.

Wordecha, M., Wilk, M., Kowalewska, E., Skorko, M., Lapinski, A., & Gola, M. (2018). "Pornographic binges" as a key characteristic of males seeking treatment for compulsive sexual behaviors: Qualitative and quantitative 10-week-long diary assessment. *Journal of Behavioral Addictions, 7*, 433–444.

Zmuda, N. (2014). Assessment and treatment of co-occurring substance use disorders and process addictions: Eating disorders, pathological gambling, and sexual addiction. In S. L. A. Straussner (Ed.), *Clinical work with substance-abusing clients* (3rd ed., pp. 520–536). New York, NY: Guilford Press.

17 Romantic Relationship Addiction

iStock.com/Syl

Learning Objectives

1. Be able to discern the difference between healthy love and romantic relationship addiction.
2. Learn about the two types of romantic relationship (RR) addiction.
3. Become aware of proposed diagnostic criteria for the DSM classification system.
4. Learn the characteristics of individuals experiencing the two forms of RR addiction.
5. Discover ways to counsel RR addicts and help them break free from feelings of inadequacy and interpersonal dependency.

CHALLENGING YOUR ASSUMPTIONS ABOUT THIS ADDICTION

1. To what extent would you find yourself being judgmental of clients who are overly dependent on their romantic partner? What is it about your own past that would help explain your reactions?
2. How frustrated would you feel if a woman with young children is unwilling to leave her physically abusive husband? How might you intervene to help convince her that leaving is in her and her children's best interest?
3. Imagine that you are in an addictive relationship. No matter what you do, you cannot stop thinking about your romantic partner for more than a few minutes. What strategies would you undertake to help reduce the amount of time you ruminate about your partner?
4. Some RR addicts end relationships once the infatuation fades sufficiently. Would it be better to help these clients find ways to keep the "magic" alive, or would it be better to help them settle for the new feelings that are not so dramatic? Which approach would be better, and why?
5. Imagine you have a 16-year-old sister who has become involved with a 25-year-old who is manipulating her to have sex. You know that this person has served time in jail for sexual assault against minors. How would you go about persuading her to leave this guy?

PERSONAL REFLECTIONS

You may recall from the Preface that I had started smoking pot again after my spouse left me. I was devastated by that loss, and, in retrospect, I realized I had been interpersonally addicted from the start of the relationship. I was compelled to send countless text messages when I felt any sign of rejection, however minute. If there were any delay in the reply, I became highly anxious and agitated, unable to concentrate or work. None of my other relationships in life have had that quality, except one—that was the first person I fell in love with romantically. It seems as though we repeat relationship patterns until we learn something about ourselves that leads us to enact similar dynamics again. Even then, we might need to be forever cautious about whom we allow into our heart.

What leads a person to *crave* another individual? What causes someone to get involved with another, whatever the consequences? When is love healthy, and when is it addictive? These questions beckon an answer as I explore romantic relationship addiction.

Background Information

Many writers have referred to romantic relationship (RR) addiction by the term *love addiction* (Earp, Wudarczyk, Foddy, & Savulescu, 2017). I have purposefully stayed away from it, as it potentially compromises the definition of romantic love, which, as many of you know, can itself feel addictive at times. Craving to see the person again for whom you have romantic feelings is common, as is pining for him or her when absence sets you apart (Acevedo & Aron, 2014; Sukel, 2012). Romantic love can be construed as a natural addiction (Fisher, Xu, Aron, & Brown, 2016). Fisher (2014) described romantic love as something that evolved 4.4 million years ago, and it was meant to help humans bond with one partner before subsequently raising children together. The occurrence of romantic love has been reflected in art and scriptures for several millennia (Acevedo & Aron, 2014). Romantic love has also been documented in every culture (Reynaud, Karila, Blecha, & Benyamina, 2010), and so has the feeling of being lovesick (Timmreck, 1990). The concept of RR addiction has widespread acceptance by addiction counselors and those in recovery, whereas many therapists remain skeptical (Briggie & Briggie, 2015). Some conceptualize it within existing frameworks such as "attachment disorder, borderline personality disorder, separation anxiety disorder, and posttraumatic stress disorder" (Briggie & Briggie, 2015, p. 153). Some who are rejected by their lovers never recover, their wounds continuing to hurt over their life span (Timmreck, 1990).

Briggie and Briggie (2015) asked self-identified RR addicts about what it was they most craved. One group craved the euphoria that accompanies a new romance, whereas the other group craved the security of a lifetime relationship. Briggie and Briggie compared these two groups to the two phases of healthy love: attraction and attachment, respectively. RR addicts attracted to the high they experience in a new relationship is something I referred to as the "chasing the dragon syndrome" (Alderson, 2012, p. 251), a term that is also used to describe the chase made by heroin addicts to get higher by heating and inhaling the substance. Such RR addicts are prone to ending and starting new relationships in their search for yet another experience of euphoria. They are afraid of being trapped or consumed by a relationship (Diamond, 1991). Martin (1989) suggested that these people are "in love with the *idea* of romance" (p. 7).

Those who are addicted to attachment will stay in the relationship despite the negative consequences that result. Briggie and Briggie (2015) provided the examples of tolerating domestic violence, affairs, abuse, and theft. These individuals are afraid of being abandoned (Diamond, 1991).

What, then, is a definition of RR addiction? There is neither a recognized definition of it nor a diagnosis in *DSM-5*. Nonetheless, I will borrow a generic definition for RR addiction from Briggie and Briggie (2015) that encompasses the two varieties:

> The maladaptive craving for, and pursuit of, romantic relationships to experience a euphoric high or powerful sense of security and worth that will tranquilize one's loneliness and related affective distress. Craving and pursuit continues despite causing harm and negative consequences. (p. 154)

RR attraction addiction will be defined as an obsessive and compulsive need to feel euphoria toward another, followed by ending of the relationship once the euphoria diminishes sufficiently. *RR attachment addiction* will be defined as an obsessive and compulsive need for attachment toward the other, which persists despite ongoing distress and negative consequences (Diamond, 1991; Reynaud et al., 2010; Schaeffer 2009). Most writers have not distinguished between RR attraction and attachment addiction, and it is unclear if the same dynamics apply to both types.

As with all addictions, there are similarities between RR addiction and drug addiction (Reynaud et al., 2010). These include the following:

1. Constant craving. Unabated desire to be with the person when absent from him or her.
2. Intoxication. Feelings of euphoria when with or in communication with the other.
3. Withdrawal. Experiencing anxiety, desperation, panic, negative mood, sleep disturbance, and reduced or inability to feel pleasure when apart from the other, worsening as duration increases or in response to the relationship ending. Halpern (1982) wrote that the relationship ending could create greater agony than that experienced by either alcoholics or drug addicts. The pain can drive the individual addicted to romantic relationship attachment (IRRA) back into the addictive relationship, despite its unhealthiness. In the RR attracted addict, the desperation drives the individual into the search for a quick replacement.
4. Clinically significant impairment or distress. Compromised functioning or distress (possibly suffering) as a result of being in a relationship with the other.
5. Ongoing negative consequences. Negative consequences persist through the duration of the relationship.

The RR-addicted individual has become overly dependent on the other person (Feeney & Noller, 1990; Wright & Wright, 1991) in an attempt to "relieve emotional pain and fill a perceived inner void" (Diamond, 1991, p. 167). Those who are in an RR addictive relationship are thought to have learned mistaken ways of interacting (Bireda, 1990), and they struggle with true intimacy (Burlew & Barton, 2002). Kaufman (1993) believed that RR addiction was characterized by a deep alienation from and distrust of the partner. Halpern (1982), on the other hand, wrote about the love and commitment that are often found in addictive relationships. The hallmark for him of RR addiction was that the addicted person is unable to freely choose their partner. Instead, the addict is compulsively driven to enter into the relationship with the other.

Halpern (1982) also distinguished between nonaddictive losses (i.e., loss of love) and that which follows the end of an addictive relationship. In nonaddictive losses, the person recovers slowly, followed by sad acceptance and healing. With RR addicts, however, there is a feeling of freedom and accomplishment following the mourning period.

As mentioned earlier, it is important to distinguish healthy love, which can sometimes feel like an addiction, from unhealthy RR addiction. In a healthy relationship, "one's self-development is not abandoned" (Simon, 1982, p. 253). Mature love allows both people to grow (Noller, 1996; Sussman, 2010; Tosone, 2002), as mutual growth and fulfillment is one of the purposes of the relationship (Bireda, 1990). Healthy relationships bring out the best in us (Halpern, 1982). They begin from a place of self-love, instead of from a perceived void characteristic of those prone to addictive relationships (Bireda, 1990). It is exemplified by people being secure in their attachments to others with little fear of abandonment (Noller, 1996; Tosone, 2002). If the relationship ends, despite how painful this might be, the person is soon able to once again stand up, enjoy life, and thrive (Halpern, 1982). Curtis (as cited in Sussman, 2010) suggested that healthy love includes needing, giving, romance, and companionship. Healthy lovers can maintain intimacy, passion, and commitment toward one another (Tosone, 2002).

In contrast, RR addicts are consumed by obsessive thoughts around clinginess and potential unfaithfulness, possessiveness, uncertainty, and other anxieties (Sussman, 2010). RR addicts feel "a sense of incompleteness, emptiness, despair, and sadness that he or she seeks to remedy by connecting with another. Developmental issues have not been satisfactorily resolved" (Bireda, 1990, p. 5). There is the idea that RRs are magical, and the loved one is idolized (Tosone, 2002) as a "higher power" (Mellody, Wells Miller, & Miller, 2003, p. 13). Instead of providing an opportunity for mutual growth, the RR addict is absorbed in the partner, relegating their growth to a lesser status (Tosone, 2002). The addict appears to love "the other too much while loving the self too little" (Bireda, 1990, p. 3).

Several writers believe that insecure or anxious attachments in childhood or childhood trauma experiences predispose individuals to become RR addicts (Briggie & Briggie, 2015; Diamond, 1991; Griffin-Shelley, 1993; Schaeffer, 2009). This results in a perennial longing for attachment, which Halpern (1982, p. 14) called "attachment hunger." They may also come from families with rigid rules but who fail to express much emotion (Griffin-Shelley & Griffin-Shelley, 1993). Their motivation to get involved in relationships represents an urgent search to find love, a desperation that keeps at bay "their only true source of love—themselves" (Wright & Wright (1991, p. 169). Their sense of self-worth is derived from how others see them, and consequently many become people-pleasers (Diamond, 1991).

Some RR addicts appear to display their addictive behaviors only within some relationships (Sukel, 2012), whereas others demonstrate a repetitive pattern of addictive relationships (Mellody et al., 2003). The addictive components may appear early in the relationship, or they may develop over time. A life that once seemed colorful and bright becomes "empty, grey, unattractive, and uninteresting" (Reynaud et al., 2010, p. 263). Generally, the RR addict underestimates the effect the other is having on him or her (Reynaud et al., 2010) and denies the extent of their dependency needs (Griffin-Shelley, 2009). Even when IRRAs know the relationship is unhealthy, they are unable to detach (Bireda, 1990), whereas the RR attraction addicts are compelled to start and end relationships, regardless of how functional they may be.

RR addicts may also be sex addicts (the topic of the previous chapter), but not always (Sussman, 2010). Griffin-Shelley (2009) believed that both RR and sex addicts are filled with shame. To help offset their perceived deficiencies, their involvement with and expectations of others become excessive (Bireda, 1990).

Prevalence rates for RR addiction are unknown. Peele and Brodsky (2015) claimed that it is perhaps the most common form of addiction but that it remains the least recognized kind.

Diagnostic and Assessment Considerations

Although there is no official diagnosis of RR addiction in both *DSM-5* and ICD-11, the research base is currently insufficient to include it. Nonetheless, Reynaud et al. (2010) proposed criteria. Reynaud et al. cautioned that "there is a risk of misunderstanding and 'overmedicalizing' persons with such disorders" (p. 266):

A maladaptive or problematic pattern of love relation leading to clinically significant impairment or distress is manifested by three (or more) of the following (occurring at any time in the same 12-month period for the first five criteria): (source: DSM-IV)

1. Existence of a characterized withdrawal syndrome in the absence of the loved one, by significant suffering and a compulsive need for the other.
2. Considerable amount of time spent on this relation (in reality or in thought).
3. Reduction in important social, professional, or leisure activities.
4. Persistent desire or fruitless efforts to reduce or control [this] relation.
5. Pursuit of the relation despite the existence of problems created by this relation.
6. Existence of attachment difficulties (see section 3.5 of DSM-IV for more clarification), as manifested by either of the following:
   (a) repeated exalted amorous relationships without any durable period of attachment;
   (b) repeated painful amorous relationships, characterized by insecure attachment." (p. 263)

More recently, Redcay and Simonetti (2018) suggested 11 criteria for love addiction that are subsumed under four factors (i.e., impaired control [criteria 1–4], life impairment [criteria 5, 6, 8, and 9], disregard for the partner's behavior [criterion 7], and preventing or reducing undesirable or unbearable emotions [criteria 10 and 11]. These include the following:

1. Desire to stop or reduce contact or end a relationship.
2. Inability to control, reduce, or stop contact.
3. Experiencing frequent preoccupation regarding caring for or worrying about the partner.
4. Feeling intense desires and urge to continue contact.
5. Relationship interferes with fulfilling major obligations.
6. Continues contact despite the problems the relationship has created for oneself (e.g., emotional problems, financial difficulties).
7. Continues contact despite the problems the partner creates in the relationship (e.g., infidelity, substance abuse).
8. Relies heavily on advice from others or disregards advice to end the relationship.
9. Lies to others to conceal the extent of contact or intensity of involvement.
10. Initial euphoria that began early in the relationship becomes replaced by having undesirable or unbearable emotions when the partner is not present.
11. Returns to the relationship when feeling distressing and negative emotions.

Differential Diagnosis

Regarding differential diagnosis, RR addiction needs to be distinguished from separation anxiety disorder (American Psychiatric Association [APA], 2013), which is about having "excessive fear or anxiety concerning separation from home or attachment figures" (p. 191). Although an IRRA will likely experience separation anxiety, the emotions extend beyond anxiety and fear concerning separation. Another related disorder is dependent personality disorder (DPD), which is "a pervasive and excessive need to be taken care of that leads to submissive and clinging behavior and fears of separation" (APA, 2013, p. 675). Again, although some with RR attachment addiction would also have DPD, individuals with RR attachment addiction (IRR-AAs) are often themselves the caregivers, and RR attachment addiction might not occur in every RR. IRR-AAs would not fit the diagnosis for either of these *DSM-5* diagnoses.

Furthermore, it is important to differentiate between RR addictions and personality disorders. Some with either RR attraction or attachment addiction may also be experiencing borderline personality disorder (BPD), which is defined as a "pervasive pattern of instability of interpersonal relationships, self-image, and affects, and marked impulsivity that begins by early adulthood and is present in a variety of contexts" (APA, 2013, p. 663). It seems likely that those with BPD also experience RR addiction, but the reverse is not necessarily true. BPD is pervasive, and it affects the person across a "variety of contexts," only one of which is within the interpersonal domain.

Individuals experiencing histrionic personality disorder experience "pervasive and excessive emotionality and attention-seeking behavior" (APA, 2013, p. 667). These individuals often feel underappreciated, particularly when they are not the center of attention. They are also typically lively and dramatic and, in being so, they draw attention to themselves. In contrast, there is no requirement that individuals with RR addiction experience a need to be the center of attention or to draw attention to themselves. Similarly, individuals with narcissistic personality disorder are grandiose, they need to be admired, and they lack empathy for others. There is no requirement that individuals with RR addiction should be grandiose, require admiration, or lack empathy.

Comorbidity and Co-Addictions

As noted in the previous section, RR addicts may also experience separation anxiety disorder, dependent personality disorder, or borderline personality disorder. They are also more likely than nonaddicts to experience depression, anxiety (Sussman, 2010), and substance abuse (Acevedo & Aron, 2014).

Available Measures

One of the best validated and often-used measures of romantic love (Acevedo & Aron, 2014), which may provide insights regarding RR addiction, is the Passionate Love Scale (Hatfield & Sprecher, 1986; available from https://theanatomyoflove.com/relationship-quizzes/the-passionate-love-scale/). It is a 30-item Likert scale with ratings from 1 (*not at all true*) to 9 (*definitely true*). Another is the Love Attitudes Scale (LAS) (Hendrick & Hendrick, 1986; available from http://fetzer.org/sites/default/files/images/stories/pdf/selfmeasures/Different_Types_of_Love_LOVE_ATTITUDES.pdf). It is a 42-item Likert Scale, with ratings from 1 (*strongly agree*) to 5 (*strongly disagree*). The LAS is based on the love theory from Lee (1973).

Bireda (1990) offers both a relationship analysis and an Inventory of Addictive Thoughts and Behaviors in her book, *Love Addiction: A Guide to Emotional Independence*. There are also several inventories available on the Internet, including the following:

1. A 40-question "yes-no" questionnaire from the Augustine Fellowship, which is part of Sex and Love Addicts Anonymous. It is available from https://chicagointerslaa.files.wordpress.com/2014/07/the_40_questions_of_slaa.pdf
2. A 25-question "yes-no" inventory from G. Mattox, available from http://mattoxpsychotherapy.com/wp-content/uploads/2013/10/LoveAddictionScreeningTest.pdf
3. A 24-item test called the Love Addiction Inventory (Costa, Barberis, Griffiths, Benedetto, & Ingrassia, 2019) was recently published that fits a theoretical model of addiction proposed earlier by Mark Griffiths, one of the authors of the test. The publication by Costa et al. (2019) reported its prelimary findings only.
4. A 32-item inventory, with three choices per question (*hardly ever, some of the time, most of the time*), that is Web scored, available from http://www.allthetests.com/quiz12/quiz/1108596251/Are-You-a-Love-Addict

Clinical Interview Questions

Peele and Brodsky (2015) provided six questions that offer insight as to whether one is in a healthy relationship or one that has elements of RR addiction:

1. Does each lover have a secure belief in their own value?
2. Are the lovers improved by the relationship? By some measure outside of the relationship are they better, stronger, more attractive, more accomplished, or more sensitive individuals? Do they value the relationship for this very reason?
3. Do the lovers maintain serious interests outside the relationship, including other meaningful personal relationships?
4. Is the relationship integrated into, rather than being set off from, the totality of the lovers' lives?
5. Are the lovers beyond being possessive or jealous of each other's growth and expansion of interest?
6. Are the lovers also friends? Would they seek each other out if they should cease to be primary partners? (p. 98)

A seventh question by Germaine Greer (as quoted in Peele & Brodsky, 2015, p. 99) is, "Do I want my love to be happy more than I want him [or her] to be with me?"

Generic Names and Street "Lingo"

The most common name for RR addiction is love addiction. Briggie and Briggie (2015) listed several other names, including codependent, relationship obsession, romantic obsession, and maladaptive romantic love. Albert Ellis, not always known for his kind use of words with clients, used the expression "love slob" (Weinrach et al., 2001).

Neuroscience

Studies using functional magnetic resonance imaging (fMRI) have shown that romantic love activates the reward system region (namely, the ventral tegmental area, caudate nucleus, and putamen) (Acevedo & Aron, 2014) of the brain in a way similar to drug addictions (Fisher, 2014). The ventral tegmental area is located near the base of the brain, and it generates feelings of pleasure and motivation. Dopamine, which is the neurotransmitter released when one is in love, is manufactured here it creates the euphoric state (Fisher, 2014). Norepinephrine is also released, and it serves to stimulate the sympathetic nervous system, thus creating excitement (Schaeffer, 2009). Phenethylamine is also released in the brain (Milkman & Sunderwirth, 2010); it's a substance that is found in chocolate!

Interestingly, serotonin levels drop in the early stages of love to levels close to those experiencing obsessive-compulsive disorders (Reynaud et al., 2010). Dopamine and serotonin work in reverse with each other: as one increases, the other drops (Sukel, 2012).

The caudate nucleus is found in both hemispheres of the brain, and each is shaped like a shrimp. It combines the intensity of romantic passion with complex emotions and thoughts about the loved one. The putamen is found at the base of the forebrain, and, together with the caudate nucleus, forms the dorsal striatum. It mainly functions to regulate movements and affects learning.

Physical Impacts (Long-Term Use)

When RR addicts (and those in romantic love) are in the peak of their euphoric high, they may constantly daydream about their lover and feel prone to exaggerated laughter. They may feel butterflies in the stomach, feel weak in the knees, and have sweaty palms, loss of appetite, and elevated heart rate (Sukel, 2012). The peak may feel a bit like obsessive-compulsive disorder (Sukel, 2012).

If the relationship ends, the withdrawal effects from RR addiction (and love) may include disturbed sleep and appetite, agitation, low energy level, and loss of pleasure in usual activities (Griffin-Shelley, 1993). Some may write letters continuously or stalk the individual (Timmreck, 1990). Others may look for a new relationship immediately to fill the void and act as a replacement (Timmreck, 1990). The somatic symptoms may last between 2 and 6 weeks (Griffin-Shelley, 1993).

Mental, Emotional, and Spiritual Impacts

Griffin-Shelley (1993) suggested that the worst part of the withdrawal from a relationship that has ended is the psychological side. "Most addicts experience intense feelings of tension, anxiety, anger, irritability, sadness, emptiness, boredom, hopelessness, helplessness, and depression" (Griffin-Shelley, 1993, p. 10). Other possible feelings include stressed, isolated, confused, rejected, vulnerable, and obsessed (Timmreck, 1990). Panic and grief-stricken can also be added to the list (Briggie & Briggie, 2015) as well as suicidal tendencies (Acevedo & Aron, 2014) and feelings of betrayal (Schaeffer, 2009).

Most people in love who have been jilted experience a tough time emotionally, and it is unclear if the RR addict feels worse than nonaddicts. Presumably so, as the emptiness felt by an addict extends beyond the loss of the loved one to the loss of one's self-esteem and self-worth as well.

Most people need to know why the relationship ended, as it may be unclear or misunderstood (Timmreck, 1990). Fisher (2014) suggested that the rejected person goes through two stages. In the protest stage, the rejected person tries to win back the lover, whereas, in the resignation/despair stage, the rejected person gives up hope and slides into despair.

Spiritually, the end of a relationship can constitute the loss of deep connection and inspiration, with the resulting loss of purpose and meaning (Acevedo & Aron, 2014). It can be experienced as a sacred loss or desecration (Hawley & Mahoney, 2013; Krumrei, Mahoney, & Pargament, 2009).

Psychosocial Impacts (Relationships, Career/Work, Legal, Financial)

RR addicts are unlikely to make a good choice of romantic partner because the feeling underlying their addiction is what matters (Briggie & Briggie, 2015). For the RR attraction addict, it is the high that accompanies a new relationship, and, for the IRRA, it is the fictionalized promise of a relationship that will last forever under any circumstances. If a partner is not wisely chosen, relationship problems are more likely to arise (Bireda, 1990). RR addicts are usually attracted to those who are (a) emotionally unavailable, (b) needy, or (c) validating (Bireda, 1990). These characteristics alone are insufficient for a suitable mate.

Furthermore, RR addicts overfocus their attention on the romantic partner. A relationship is meant to "enhance your life, rather than to *be* your life" (Bireda, 1990, p. 123). As Bireda (1990) noted, it is a mistaken notion to believe that you must have a relationship to be happy. It is also highly unlikely that one relationship can provide for all of a partner's needs, which is why it is important to have other relationships (i.e., friends, relatives, acquaintances) to provide for some of these.

All addictions can have an impact at work as the neediness they create can interfere with job search and job productivity. As noted in the previous section, RR addicts experience a plethora of emotional lability, and this can lead to spillover into one's career (Diamond, 1991). Absenteeism is also common. The obsessiveness and compulsiveness of RR addiction consume time, energy, and resources. The pain that this creates, along with emotional lability, is also difficult for most people to conceal indefinitely.

Financial loss may result from the expenses incurred in consequence of RR addiction (Sussman, 2010). Because RR addicts will do almost anything to maintain a relationship, regardless of how unhealthy it might be, some will commit theft or other crimes to keep the relationship intact (Briggie & Briggie, 2015). When a fantasized relationship has not developed or an actual relationship has ended, crimes of passion may occur, including stalking behavior and homicide.

Working With Diverse Populations

Sex Differences

Although men are more likely to experience romantic love early in a relationship, women may experience stronger feelings of romantic love over time (Sussman, 2010). Stalking is more common among women in love compared to men (Purcell, Pathe, & Mullen, 2001).

Women are more prone to RR attachment addiction, just as men are more prone to RR attraction addiction (Diamond, 1991). Although men are likely to have greater difficulty committing to a relationship, women have a more difficult time leaving one that has deteriorated (Tosone, 2002). Dubrow (1993) suggested that RR-addicted women tend to be diagnosed with mental health problems, such as depression or bipolar disorder, instead of RR addiction. Many of the women who were referred to Dubrow's therapy group had become involved in criminal behavior because their partners had requested it, despite these women being generally law-abiding citizens.

Adolescents and Youth

It is a common experience to be rejected by someone who was passionately loved. In a study published in 1993, Baumeister (as cited in Fisher, 2014) found that 93% of both sexes in an American college sample had been rejected, whereas 95% had rejected someone else who felt deep romantic love for them. In a current nationwide study of 486 young people pursuing a college education, 9.5%

reported having problems with either sex or RR addiction (Laudet, Harris, Kimball, Winters, & Moberg, 2015). Griffin-Shelley (1995) stated that adolescents could become as easily addicted to relationships as to nicotine, alcohol, and drugs, and he also found about 10% of adolescents in an inpatient setting were addicted to either sex or relationships.

Race and Ethnicity

There is no published literature about RR addiction and race/ethnicity. This is noted here so that both students and practitioners are aware of the current lack of research in this area.

Nonpsychiatric Disabilities

There is no published literature about RR addiction and disabilities. This is noted here so that both students and practitioners are aware of the current lack of research in this area.

Lesbian, Gay, Bisexual, and Transgender (LGBT)

Alderson (2012) wrote about the "chasing the dragon" syndrome in LGBT individuals, which is comparable to RR attraction addiction. He hypothesized that, although consciously these people want a committed relationship, they continue to sabotage relationships early without generally understanding the reasons. The underlying reasons were postulated to result from low self-esteem, which was then further compounded by internalized homophobia, biphobia, or transphobia.

War Veterans

There is no published literature about RR addiction and veterans. This is noted here so that both students and practitioners are aware of the current lack of research in this area.

Medications and Other Relevant Physical Interventions

Although there are no physical interventions specifically targeted at RR addiction (Briggie & Briggie, 2015), Fisher (2014) suggested antidepressants may be indicated for those experiencing rejection. Briggie and Briggie (2015) postulated that medications targeted at lust, attraction, and attachment might be helpful, too, including naltrexone (for lust), obsessive-compulsive medications (for anti-attraction), and oxytocin/dopamine antagonists (for anti-attachment).

INSIDE AN ADDICTED PERSON'S MIND

Julia, Age 44

Several of my friends warned me about Frank when we first started dating. I saw the same signs as they did, and I knew they were right. But that didn't change how I felt then or now. I simply knew Frank was the man for me. On the surface, there is nothing special about him. At 49 years of age, he is reasonably attractive, intelligent, successful, has children, is six feet tall, weighs 170 pounds. . . and did I mention married? Yes, Frank is still married, and, yes, he still lives with Carla, his wife of 20-plus years. He was open about this from the start, though, and I respect his honesty. He told me that he and Carla were on the rocks, and he was planning to leave her as soon as he could afford his own apartment. He also has a temper, and, when he flares, he calls me names that hurt. He has done this numerous times over the 15 months we have dated, but I know his work as a mortgage broker takes its toll. I understand his moods, and I know he doesn't mean anything he says when he is angry.

So my friends are on me because they believe he is abusive and that he will never leave his wife. They don't understand why I remain in this relationship. He did break up with me a month ago, and I thought I would go insane. The text messages, the phone calls, the heavy breathing, even the insults—all of it ended that day. I went berserk. I could not eat, sleep, work out, be alone, watch TV, or do anything that mattered. I felt worthless. All I could think about is, "What is wrong with me?" "Why won't he call?" "I can't live without him!" "I must have him in my life!" "I will never find anyone like him again!" The screaming in my head was unbearable, and the Ativan barely kept me alive. I started driving to his place when I knew he would get home from work, sitting in my car, making sure I wasn't seen. I wanted to run over and hug him and not let him go until he took me back. It took every bit of restraint not to do that. Instead, I left messages on his phone, and I was either hysterical, begging him to come back, or filled with rage and doing my best to show restraint. I hated him for torturing me. I couldn't let him see how bad it was for me, but I imagine he was getting a pretty good idea.

So he did come back after that, and I promised to be everything he needed. I promised to be patient until he could leave his wife. I promised to give him all the sex he could ever want. I promised not to upset him. He shrugged his shoulders, and told me, "I love you." My heart melted at that moment. I never heard this enough, not from anyone actually. I needed him to love me—he was, after all, all I had that mattered. Friends come and go, but Frank, he will be there for me from now on!

That was until 2 days ago. We never fought, I lived up to all my promises, and I did everything right. BUT HE HASN'T CALLED ME IN 2 DAYS! I am crawling on the floor from taking too many Ativan and sucking back whiskey neat. I CAN'T STAND IT ANYMORE! He won't return any of my messages—I am terrified. What did I do wrong?

Commentary

Julia demonstrates several of the symptoms of romantic relationship addiction. Apart from symptoms, which will be discussed later, the notable themes in Julia's case include the following: (a) inadequate discernment of a potential mate, (b) reliance on emotionality over reason, (c) willingness to tolerate abuse, (d) taking on more than 50-50 responsibility for the relationship, (e) feeling worthless and incomplete, (f) feeling unloved and unlovable, (g) turning the love object into a God-like figure, (h) desperation, (i) anxiety, (j) craving, (k) severe withdrawal effects, (l) projecting blame for her own feelings, (m) engaging in self-destructive behavior, and (n) engaging in stalking behavior. Julia had unwittingly surrendered control to another person, one whom she came to believe was more deserving and more important than herself.

Discussion

1. Do you know of anyone who you suspect has become dependent on relationships? If "yes," which symptoms noted in the commentary apply to him or her?
2. Does this person have symptoms that are not listed in the commentary? If so, what are they?
3. If you were Julia's counselor, how would you go about helping her?

Specific Counseling Considerations

ROLEPLAY SCENARIOS

Roleplay in dyads with one of you acting as the counselor and the other as the counselee. If a roleplay is not possible, work individually in writing out a list of your suggestions.

Roleplay #1

Mark, age 35, is a White man who has dated 12 women over the past year. Each relationship has lasted 3 weeks at most. He broke up with 10 of these women, and the other two ended it, suggesting that he was not the type who would be faithful. When he is not dating, he feels desperately alone, and he fills his time with mindless pursuits. This is only marginally successful, as he continues struggling with low self-esteem and a feeling that no one will ever want to commit to him. You find out that his longest relationship ever lasted 6 months. He never felt that he could get enough of her, and she was often unavailable due to other commitments. Mark, however, believed she was seeing other guys. He had started attending a Sex and Love Addicts Anonymous meeting in his community, but he was unsure he belonged there.

Roleplay #2

Belinda, a 22-year-old African American, began seeing Juan 26 months ago. Early into it she felt that she could not get away from his "mesmerizing nature." Juan was 35 and well-established in his career. But Belinda was first attracted to his manly looks and his near perfect beauty. Within a month of the start of the relationship, Juan would say things to her that hurt. He would insinuate that she was promiscuous, calling her derogatory names that no one else ever called her. He also treated her roughly in bed, sometimes biting and leaving marks that would last for weeks. Belinda knew deep down that Juan was not right for her, and she wanted to end it. However, she could not bring herself to do so. Instead, she feared constantly that he would end up leaving her instead.

HOW WOULD AN ADDICTION COUNSELOR HELP THIS PERSON?

You are working as a professional counselor. Aaron, a man of Chinese descent, age 42, enters your office and breaks down immediately. He is profusely apologetic, telling you that such a display of emotion is not acceptable in his cultural upbringing. The story unfolds of a person who has craved deep connection with another person since he can remember. Aaron tells you that his parents are very aloof, and he can recall times when he was crying, and he was told to shut up or go to bed. After several failed relationships, he has been with Cheryl, a wild White woman of 24 years of age, for the past 4 years. He tells you about how he has compromised most of his principles to be with her. She has had numerous sexual encounters with other men while being intoxicated since being with Aaron. She also smokes pot in front of him and expects that he will accept it because "this is the way I am." Aaron has tried to accept all of these things about her that hurt him, but it has created great stress for him to try and do so. Nonetheless, creating harmony is important to him, and he has tolerated all of her behavior. When she is out having a good time with other men, his heart sinks so low he wonders about killing himself. But he has learned to keep this to himself, as he learned to keep his feelings private growing up. The thought of losing Cheryl was catastrophic to Aaron, and, in keeping with his deepest fears, she left him for another man a week ago. Since then, Aaron cannot stop his emotional outbursts. His feelings of loneliness, desperation, anxiety, and depression are leading him to seriously consider suicide. You find out he has a revolver and bullets at home.

Remember to view clients within their environmental contexts, keeping in mind societal, parental/familial, cultural/spiritual, and peer influences. Specifically, become aware of the impact that the following influences have and continue to have in your clients' lives: race, language, religion and spirituality, gender, familial migration history, sexual/affectional orientation, age and cohort, physical and mental capacities, socioeconomic situation and history, education, and history of traumatic experience.

1. What defines this person's environment, past and present?
2. Who is this person sitting in front of me, taking into account environmental and personal characteristics?
3. What defines the problem that he or she is presenting within their multicultural milieu?

Goals and Goal Setting

Griffin-Shelley (2009) commented that love addicts are challenging to treat and that helping them can be lengthy (perhaps 5–8 years!). Some appropriate goals for counseling clients with RR addiction include the following:

- Develop realistic expectations of relationships (Briggie & Briggie, 2015).
- Learn to balance the interest and investment in oneself and one's partner (Briggie & Briggie, 2015).
- Develop an independent identity, including having one's own set of interests, friends, and obligations (Briggie & Briggie, 2015).
- Learn to become honest (Briggie & Briggie, 2015).
- Learn to trust (Briggie & Briggie, 2015).
- Establish and maintain one's limits and boundaries (Briggie & Briggie, 2015).
- Focus on healing childhood trauma (Schaeffer, 2009).
- Learn to take responsibility for making oneself feel happy, worthy, and deserving of love (Bireda, 1990).
- Increase belief regarding one's value, attractiveness, and desirability (Bireda, 1990).
- Challenge unhealthy beliefs and behaviors (Bireda, 1990).
- Learn to accept and approve of oneself (Bireda, 1990).
- Appreciate one's uniqueness and personal qualities (Bireda, 1990).
- Learn how to become playful (Bireda, 1990).
- Learn to enjoy spending time without your partner (Bireda, 1990).
- Relinquish the notion that you can change him or her (Bireda, 1990).
- Become aware of what triggers you in the relationship (Bireda, 1990).

- Learn about one's relationship patterns (Bireda, 1990).
- Live in the present (Bireda, 1990).
- Learn when to end a relationship and when to hang in (Bireda, 1990).
- Learn other ways to meet psychological dependency needs (Griffin-Shelley, 1993).
- Find ways to manage cravings for a particular person or a new relationship (Griffin-Shelley, 1993).

Stages of Change Strategies

The processes of change mentioned are based on those outlined by Connors, DiClemente, Velasquez, and Donovan (2013) and Prochaska, Norcross, and DiClemente (1994). The definitions for the various processes can be found in Chapter 6. Besides these processes, other strategies are included that have separate citations.

The University of Rhode Island Change Assessment Scale (URICA) is a helpful scale in determining where the client is currently at regarding the stages of change model. There are 24-, 28-, and 32-item versions of the scale. A 24-item version is published for alcohol or drug problems. The scale, however, is generic and can be easily adapted for use with other addictions. It is available with norms as a free download from https://www.guilford.com/add/miller11_old/urica.pdf.

Specific precontemplation strategies.

Please visit the section of this chapter called Relevant Mutual Support Groups, Websites, and Videos for free or low-cost information and resources that may help someone move out of precontemplation.

Many individuals in the precontemplation stage are unable to see their problems clearly if they can see them at all. Consciousness raising here includes bibliotherapy. Two suggested books are *Facing Love Addiction: Giving Yourself the Power to Change the Way You Love* (Mellody et al., 2003) and *Is It Love or Is It Addiction?* (Schaeffer, 2009). Self-liberation (i.e., self-awareness in this stage) might also result from attending one of the mutual support groups, the most popular of which is Sex and Love Addicts Anonymous. However, most RR addicts at this stage will likely resist attending a meeting.

Counselors can also help RR addicts by creating interest and concern regarding the problematic relationship. Encouraging RR addicts to look at the pros and cons of their relationship patterns and/or their addictive relationship may be useful, as well as looking at the impact it has on others.

Helping relationships (i.e., counselor, family, friends) at this stage should focus on providing encouragement and support. People in this stage are not ready for action, and attempts at pushing the RR addict will be futile.

Specific contemplation strategies.

Emotional arousal is one of the strategies that can be used at this stage. Clients are likely already experiencing a plethora of overwhelming emotions, so the focus may be on helping them make connections to RR addiction. If they are not currently experiencing emotions, simply talking about the pain their relationship style causes ought to create arousal. Listening to music or watching movies that emphasize romantic love and focusing on specific memories will also arouse feelings.

Consciousness raising will occur through self-monitoring of the problematic thoughts and feelings that surface and of the dysfunctional behaviors that follow. Self-re-evaluation involves the emotional and cognitive appraisal of the problem and oneself, so focusing on how the RR addiction helps and hurts them may be productive. Attending a meeting of SLAA is more likely to occur at either this stage or in later stages.

Helping relationships during this stage should continue focusing on support. Other important aspects here include listening and providing feedback.

Specific preparation strategies.

During the preparation stage, the counselor continues to help the client evaluate the problem, but with greater emphasis on the future than on the troubled past. The primary goal of this stage is to create commitment toward changing. Helping the client establish goals and deciding upon how these will be attained becomes the main focus.

The plan of action works best when it is constructed primarily by the client. Some suggested goals that could be used here are included in the earlier section of this chapter called Goals and Goal Setting.

Regarding helping relationships, it is sometimes helpful to go public with the change project. Regardless, it is still helpful to have support from others. The client should encourage others to refrain from asking how he or she is doing and to avoid nagging.

Fisher (2014) recommended that rejected lovers should remove all items that remind them of the other. Her list included "cards, photos, and memorabilia" (pp. 256–257). Other ideas for *before* their chosen quit day (i.e., preparation strategies) can be found in Appendix B.

Specific action strategies.

Besides the ideas mentioned here, the remainder of this chapter is primarily about action strategies. It does not make sense to rely on a single technique in the action stage (Prochaska et al., 1994). Prochaska et al. (1994) recommended countering, environmental control, and reward during this stage. The following writers have elaborated these as they pertain to RR addiction.

Fisher (2014) recommended that rejected lovers avoid contact with the other because any kind of reminder is likely to delay the healing process. She also mentioned that a combination of talk therapy and short-term antidepressant medication might be the best treatment. Also, encourage clients to stay busy and thereby distract themselves. Some activities that could be encouraged include signing up for courses, participating in meditation or exercise, and developing friendships of a nonsexual kind (Sussman, 2010). Also suggested was to spend time in new environments to encourage healthier experiences (Fisher, as cited in Sussman, 2010).

Timmreck (1990) suggested that counselors instruct clients to stop masturbating while thinking of the other, especially thoughts relating to sexual experiences. Clients should also focus on creating a support system and use guided healthy self-talk.

Group counseling is also recommended (Griffin-Shelley, 2018). One Brazilian study found that a group of eight RR addicts reported lessened "love-addicted" feelings after 18 sessions (Lorena, Sophia, Mello, Tavares, & Ziberman, as cited in Sussman, 2010).

No comparison group was reported in the study. Sussman (2010) suggested that use of psychodrama may reduce illusions regarding romantic partners and help understand one's feeling toward others. Group work might also help individuals learn how to engage in healthy RRs, which may be "less exciting but more rewarding in the long run" (Sussman, 2010, p. 41). Psychoeducational groups are also suggested, and they may be viewed as less threatening than group therapy (Griffin-Shelley, 1993). Griffin-Shelley (1993) recommended that RR addicts be placed in same-sex groups to help avoid triggering addictive love fantasies.

Helping relationships during the action stage should include spending time together with family and friends. The goal should be to seek support for life. Other ideas for *beginning* their chosen quit day put a halt to relationship addiction (i.e., action strategies) and can be found in Appendix B.

Specific maintenance strategies and relapse prevention.

Note: Maintenance strategies and relapse prevention are also, for many, partly facilitated by regular attendance at relevant mutual support groups. A list of such mutual support groups and helpful websites is found in an upcoming section entitled Relevant Mutual Support Groups, Websites, and Videos.

Regarding processes of change, the strategies here include keeping a healthy distance from those who trigger RR addictive feelings, creating a new and healthy lifestyle, and checking your thinking to ensure that negative thoughts are minimized. Helping relationships may include having a sponsor one can call (if the client has become a member of SLAA) for when addictive feelings resurface and perhaps helping someone else who is experiencing RR addiction.

Relapse becomes less likely once RR addicts have learned insight into their sense of incompleteness and dependency with its roots in early childhood. This awareness needs to be accompanied by a developing sense of their own identity and feeling of wholeness. Once they feel like an equal to everyone else, and they develop a support network of several people who care about them, they learn to develop authentic intimacy with others. They are then ready to enter into healthy RRs.

Continuing attendance at Sex and Love Addicts Anonymous may be important as well. In such groups, RR addicts learn to (a) take care of their own needs, (b) trust and accept others, and (c) feel comfortable being alone (Sussman, 2010). Furthermore, SLAA provides an ongoing support network. Reynaud et al. (2010) reported that more men attend for sexual addiction instead of RR addiction, whereas the reverse is true for women.

As is commonly thought, time does heal the pain from broken relationships (Fisher, 2014). For the IRRA, it is also about committing to refuse to enter or remain in unhealthy RRs again. For the RR attraction addict, it is the reverse: that is, it is about staying in relationships that prove to be healthy. Other ideas for relapse prevention can be found in Appendix C.

Motivational Interviewing

Sussman (2010) believed that motivational interviewing might help RR addicts understand their maladaptive romantic relationships with others. One example provided is that clients may learn that they express themselves ambiguously regarding trust and intimacy. A solution might be to take more time before entering relationships. (Pertaining to Chapter 6's description of motivational interviewing, the following is an example of the process called *planning*.)

Here is an example regarding the desperate loneliness that RR addicts experience:

Client: I can't stand it when I don't see Bryan for more than a few hours. I know he is busy, but I feel completely abandoned and desperate.

Counselor: I remember you saying the last session that you want to learn to become more comfortable when you are by yourself.

Client: That is correct. I know my feelings are irrational.

Counselor: Tell me about how you see your feelings as irrational.

Client: Well, I can't expect Bryan to be constantly at my beck and call. I mean, he has a life of his own, too!

Counselor: You certainly acknowledge that Bryan also has a life separate from your own.

Client: Yes, that's true. But I can hardly cope when we are apart.

Counselor: I understand that this is challenging to you. But you also implied that you do cope to some extent. How do you do that?

Client: Sometimes I phone a friend, and that helps.

Counselor: So you have learned that talking to friends is helpful. What else has proven helpful?

Client: Sometimes I just try and relax. Then I stop thinking about Bryan for a few minutes.

Counselor: You have talked to friends and spent time relaxing. Both have helped you deal with your loneliness.

Client: Yes, but it's not enough.

Counselor: You acknowledge that you need to do more to manage your alone time.

Insight-Oriented Interventions

Briggie and Briggie (2015) recommended psychodynamic counseling because an effective working alliance does much to promote insight followed by behavior change. Loving others is a projection of how people feel about themselves, and several writers have noted that RR addicts have difficulty with self-love (Hutchison, 2007; Schaeffer, 2009; Versaevel, 2011). The theory most frequently advanced is that they were deprived of unconditional love and/or bonding in childhood (Halpern, 1982; Schaeffer, 2009; Smaldino, 1991), so they are now re-enacting their earlier emotional traumas (Schaeffer, 2009; Simon, 1982). Consequently, those so afflicted find that, without a significant other, they feel unlovable in a life without meaning and purpose (Schaeffer, 2009). Addictive love then becomes necessary for survival itself (Schaeffer, 2009).

Although it may take a major life event for clients to recognize their RR addiction (Schaeffer, 2009), counselors may be instrumental in helping clients explore the nature of their relationships to help them develop this insight. Making connections of current emotional traumas caused by relationship issues to early ones may help clients become aware of and make sense of their relationship patterns (Halpern, 1982).

Attachment theory is also important here. A study by Feeney and Noller (1990) looked at attachment style and forms of love with 374 college students. Those who were securely attached reported stable family and love relationships. Avoidant students had a mistrust of people and reported fewer love experiences. Those who were anxious-ambivalent had the least stable relationships, and they were also the most dependent. Those who are anxious-ambivalent are inclined to become the most obsessive in relationships (Hutchison, 2007), which is a defining feature of RR addiction.

Spiritual Interventions

Bireda (1990) believed that RR addicts need to learn to self-validate, which she wrote consists of three steps: accepting oneself, appreciating oneself, and acting lovingly toward oneself. Besides treating oneself lovingly, she claimed that a "complete life is one that is happy, satisfying, and fulfilling *with* or *without* a partner" (p. 141). Finding meaning and purpose in life, whether alone or in a relationship with someone, is about spirituality.

"People in a state of meditation or prayer *and* who accept a Higher Power (God), seem to have profoundly different neurobiochemical events going on in their brains than people who are actively involved in addiction" (Lord, 1993; *italics added*). Mellody et al. (2003) suggested that RR addicts often make people their Higher Power, which they suggested was at the heart of RR addiction. The dependency on people associated with RR addiction may be one that can be transferred to a Higher Power. As Halpern (1982) noted, feeling a connection to all living things, to all of humankind, or to a Supreme Being can be helpful coping aids. Every 12-step program is based on spiritual principles, and attending one of these groups may facilitate spiritual healing.

Cognitive-Behavioral Therapy

Cognitive-behavioral therapy can be facilitated using the triple column technique. It can be used both by counselors in their work with clients and by clients alone. The full instructions for using the technique are found in Chapter 6. The following are some of the cognitions that can be problematic for clients with this addiction.

Automatic Thought or Belief	Questioning it	Healthier Thought or Belief
I can't stand it if my partner gets upset with me.		It may be temporarily uncomfortable if my partner's upset with me, but I will be okay.
I don't deserve to get what I want or need in a relationship.		My wants and needs are valid, and I deserve to get my wants and needs met in a relationship.
In a relationship, I should be willing to sacrifice my own needs for my partner.		It is essential to recognize and communicate my needs to my partner; sacrificing my needs does not foster a healthy relationship based on equality.
If this relationship comes to an end, it will destroy me.		I may experience painful emotions if the relationship ends, but I will ultimately be okay. I am not defined by this one relationship.
Say no or setting limits with my partner is a selfish thing to do.		Setting limits and saying no are important ways to protect both myself and the relationship.

Beliefs and thoughts listed in the previous table were adapted from Briggie and Briggie (2015, p. 169).

Halpern (1982) suggested that, if clients are unable to make a complete break from the person to whom they are addicted, they might be helped if they take a temporary separation and allow themselves to experience the painful emotions. Halpern also offered several writing exercises, such as keeping a relationship log and writing memos to oneself (e.g., writing advice to oneself). Other writing techniques are discovering one's relationship patterns (i.e., looking at the relationship characteristics of those with whom one has been in a relationship) and making connections (i.e., write out negative feelings that are triggered by thinking about breaking up with the current partner and making connections to earliest relationship memories). Other ideas suggested by Halpern include deep-breathing exercises for when the client loses a sense of self when alone and thought-stopping and distraction techniques.

Mellody et al. (2003) recommended that RR addicts correct their distorted thinking regarding seeing the other as the all-important "Higher Power." RR addicts need to be reminded that all people are "perfectly imperfect" (p. 117).

Lovelyjune (2011) stipulated that RR addicts believe there is a void inside them that only another person can fill. This distortion needs to be corrected. There is no void within: instead, the empty feeling represents a part of oneself. She advocated that the RR addict should spend time alone while experiencing the empty feeling and over time learn to accept that the feeling is simply a flaw, similar to having a crooked nose or another slight defect in appearance. One's perception of oneself as incomplete is wrong, fostered again from a flawed childhood, not from a flawed personhood.

RELEVANT MUTUAL SUPPORT GROUPS, WEBSITES, AND VIDEOS

Mutual Support Groups

For the Addicted Individual

1. Sex and Love Addicts Anonymous (SLAA; http://www.slaafws.org/).

   Quoted from website:

   YOU ARE NOT ALONE.

   Sex and Love Addicts Anonymous, or S.L.A.A., is a program for anyone who suffers from an addictive compulsion to engage in or avoid sex, love, or emotional attachment. We use the Twelve Steps and Twelve Traditions adapted from Alcoholics Anonymous to recover from these compulsions. The following behaviors have been experienced by members.

   Having few healthy boundaries, we become sexually involved with and/or emotionally attached to people without knowing them.

   Fearing abandonment and loneliness, we stay in and return to painful, destructive relationships. . . .

   We confuse love with neediness, physical and sexual attraction, pity and/or the need to rescue or be rescued.

   We sexualize stress, guilt, loneliness, anger, shame, fear and envy. . . .

   To avoid feeling vulnerable, we may retreat from all intimate involvement . . .

   Excerpts from the Twelve Characteristics of Sex and Love Addiction ©1985

   You may be experiencing one or all of these characteristics, but only you can decide for sure if S.L.A.A. is right for you. To help you make this decision, it is suggested that you complete the 40 Questions for Self-Diagnosis. If you answer yes to any combination of these questions and think you may be struggling with sex and love addiction, you are welcome in S.L.A.A.

   Now What?

   You have already taken a big step in seeking information about the program of S.L.A.A. If you believe this program is for you, the next thing to do is find out if there is a meeting in your area. Gathering with other sex and love addicts at an S.L.A.A. meeting is the primary way we learn how to get sober and maintain recovery. There are no dues, fees, or registration process to attend a meeting, only voluntary contributions. By giving and receiving support from others like us, we not only have a better chance of recovering, but we also begin to learn how to engage with people in a non-addictive way.

   An essential piece of literature to help you start and stay with the program is the S.L.A.A. Basic Text. This book contains information about discovering the illness, beginning recovery, defining sobriety, the Twelve Steps of S.L.A.A. and contains personal stories of others who have gone from addiction to recovery. There are also pamphlets that can be of great help. These include the Welcome pamphlet, An Introduction to Sex and Love Addicts Anonymous, Suggestions for Newcomers, Questions Beginners Ask, and Addiction and Recovery.

   The Twelve Step program of S.L.A.A. has helped many of us break free from the grip of sex and love addiction. You Are Not Alone.

2. Love Addicts Anonymous group (http://loveaddicts.org/). Only some locales have this particular mutual support group.

   Some of their headings include "40 Questions: Are You a Love Addict?," "Recovery for Love Addicts," "Does LAA Work?," "Typical Kinds of Love Addicts," "Stories of Recovery," and "LAA Textbook."

Peele and Brodsky (2015) are skeptical of the 12-step approach to relationship problems. They maintain that such groups are ineffective. This opinion is not shared by others who write about RR addiction, however.

For the Partner and/or Family

These groups are intended to help family members refrain from behaviors that may trigger the addict. They also target underlying maladaptive thoughts and behaviors of the co-addict. Lastly, they focus on facilitating spiritual growth.

CoSex and Love Addicts Anonymous (COSLAA). http://coslaa.org/ [described in Chapter 16].

Websites

1. Sex Addiction Symptoms, Causes, and Effects. http://www.psychguides.com/guides/sex-addiction-symptoms-causes-and-effects/
2. What Is Sexual Addiction? By Michael Herkov, Ph.D. https://psychcentral.com/lib/what-is-sexual-addiction/
3. Is Sex Addiction Real? By Matt McMillen. http://www.webmd.com/sexual-conditions/features/is-sex-addiction-real#1

Videos

To view these videos, search their titles on YouTube.

1. *What is Sex Addiction? 5 Symptoms of Addiction.* Andrea Cairella.

   Quoted from website:

   In today's video, you'll learn what are the 5 possible causes of sex addiction and how to recognize the 5 symptoms of addiction.

A. What Is Sex Addiction? Sexual addiction is best described as a progressive intimacy disorder characterized by compulsive sexual thoughts and acts. Like all addictions, it negatively impacts the addict and the family members as the disorder progresses and the addictive behaviors intensify.

B. Symptoms of Addiction-According to the Diagnostic and Statistical Manual of Psychiatric Disorders, the symptoms of sex addiction are: a) distress about a pattern of repeated sexual relationships involving a succession of lovers who are experienced by the individual only as things to be used, b) compulsive searching for multiple partners, c) compulsive fixation on an unattainable partner, d) compulsive masturbation, compulsive love relationships and/or compulsive sexuality in a relationship, e) extensive use of pornography, phone sex, cyber sex or other illegal activities like sex with a prostitute or fellow sex addicts.

C. What Causes Sex Addiction? a) one theory is that since antidepressants and other psychotropic medications have proven effective in treating some people with sex addiction, some suggest that biochemical abnormality or other brain changes increase risk; b) other studies indicate that food, drug abuse and sexual interests share a common pathway within our brains' survival and reward systems; which thus short circuits the area of reason and sends a signal that compulsive sexual behavior is necessary for survival; c) people addicted to sex get a sense of euphoria and use sexual activity to seek pleasure, avoid unpleasant feelings or respond to outside stressors, d) research also has found that sex addicts often come from dysfunctional families (i.e. addiction present at home or parents rigid and uncaring); e) and are more likely than non-sex addicts to have been abused.

2. *We Need to Talk About Sex Addiction | Paula Hall | TEDxLeamingtonSpa.*

   Quoted from website:

   Sex addiction affects young and old, rich and poor, male and female. Paula Hall shares what we can do about it, even if we don't suffer from it ourselves. Paula Hall (UKCP Reg, BACP Acc, COSRT Acc, ATSAC) has been working in the field of Sex Addiction for over 10 years and is author of *Understanding & Treating Sex Addiction* (Routledge 2013). *Sex Addiction—The Partner's Perspective* (Routledge 2015). She has also been published in a number of academic journals and within the professional press. Paula was a founder member of ATSAC and served as Chair for three years and is currently on the board of SASH. In addition to working with individuals and couples, she developed the Hall Recovery Course which is available around the UK and also under licence in Denmark and Holland and provides residential programmes for both people with addiction and partners. She has spoken at conferences in the UK, Europe and in the US on behalf of ESSM, UKCP, BACP, ATSAC, UKESAD and The International Sex Addiction Conference. This talk was given at a TEDx event using the TED conference format but independently organized by a local community. Learn more at http://ted.com/tedx

3. *Dr. Patrick Carnes, Leading Sex Addiction Expert, Video Interview.*

RELEVANT PHONE APPS

Generic Addiction Apps

Note: Generic apps are described in Chapter 6.

This list is not exhaustive. New apps are continually being developed. Do an Internet search to find out the latest apps available. Most are for specific addictions, but some, such as these four, are generic.

1. I Am Sober. https://play.google.com/store/apps/details?id=com.thehungrywasp.iamsober
2. Sober Time. https://play.google.com/store/apps/details?id=com.sociosoft.sobertime
3. Pocket Rehab: Get Sober & Addiction Recovery. https://play.google.com/store/apps/details?id=com.getpocketrehab.app
4. Loop Habit Tracker. https://play.google.com/store/apps/details?id=org.isoron.uhabits

Specialized Apps

There are no apps specifically for RR addiction. There are apps for those in healthy love relationships and for those wishing to maintain a long-distance relationship. A few of these can be found at the following websites:

1. https://rumorscity.com/2015/02/06/5-best-love-apps-for-couples-on-iphone-ipad-and-android/

   They list five apps as follows: Avocado, Snapchat, Couple, Between, and LoveByte.

2. https://www.buzzfeed.com/chelseypippin/17-apps-everyone-in-a-long-distance-relationship-needs?utm_term=.pkAOjpz1EV#.ijd2G04jBE

   In addition to those listed previously, other apps they list include Without, TouchRoom, TheIceBreak, LokLok, Skype Qik, Sesame, Klikaklu, Cartolina, Touchnote, Long Distance, Path, HeyTell, Dreamdays, and We-Connect.

JOURNALS AND CONFERENCES

There are no journals specifically dedicated to RR addiction. Articles often appear in journals committed to marriage and the family. Some journals that carry articles in this area include *Journal of Marriage and Family, Journal of Sex & Marital Therapy, Personal Relationships, Families in Society, Contemporary Family Therapy, Journal of Personality and Social Psychology, Personality and Individual Differences, Psychological Reports*, and *Sexual Addiction & Compulsivity*.

Two international conferences on love and sex addiction were offered in 2013 and 2014 (http://www.usjt.com/Conferences/2014/2nd-Intl-Conference-On-Sex-and-Love-Addiction/). The annual conference of the Association for Addiction Professionals pertains to all addictions (https://www.naadac.org/annualconference), as does the Australian and New Zealand addictions conference (http://addictionaustralia.org.au/). This is only a partial list of conferences, and many are at the state level. Interested individuals should check online for upcoming conferences in this area.

COUNSELING SCENARIO

As you are reading, imagine that you are the client in this scenario. Note the areas in which the session could be improved on the part of the counselor.

Your name is Frank, a 22-year-old student at a 4-year college. Susan, your girlfriend of 18 months, has just broken up with you, and you feel shattered. Three weeks later, you are still finding it difficult to function. You are worried that you may need to withdraw from this term if you don't pull it together, so you make an appointment to see a guidance counselor at the school. After providing her background information, the session continues:

- You: I can't stop thinking about her—it's driving me mad!
- Counselor: How so, Frank?
- You: I am unable to sleep at night, I cannot study without having intrusive thoughts, and I feel jittery.
- Counselor: It sounds like you are suffering from love addiction. I have seen at least three other students this week alone with this condition.
- You: Love addiction? What's that?
- Counselor: Well, you are addicted to her just like some students get addicted to drugs. You are an addict, Frank.
- You: I am? But this is the only serious relationship I have ever had!
- Counselor: Doesn't matter—you're messed up over her . . . right?

From the Client's Perspective

1. How would you feel if you were given this "diagnosis"?
2. What is missing for you in this dialogue?
3. What would you find more helpful from a counselor in this scenario?

From the Counselor's Perspective

1. What is interfering with developing a working alliance?
2. Going back to the Common Counseling Mistakes list in Chapter 6, which mistakes is the counselor making with Frank?
3. As the counselor, what else would you like to know before assuming it is a form of romantic relationship addiction?
4. What negative effect might the label have for a client of this age?

INDIVIDUAL EXERCISES

1. Talk to someone you believe has had or is in an addictive relationship. How does he or she see the benefits and drawbacks of the relationship? Does he or she see the relationship as addictive, and, if so, what aspects of the relationship are addictive?
2. Spend some time alone reflecting on what aspects of relationships you find addicting to one extent or another. What do you need to watch out for to protect yourself accordingly?
3. Listen to five current songs with content focused on romantic love. Which lyrics speak to healthy romantic love, and which are more reflective of RR addiction?

CLASSROOM EXERCISES

1. In dyads or triads, discuss a relationship you were in that you believe had some addictive qualities to it. Describe these addictive qualities. Defend your position that, overall, it was or was not an addictive relationship.
2. In dyads or triads, discuss whether you believe RR addiction belongs in the next version of DSM. Why or why not?
3. Begin a roleplay where one of you is the client with RR addiction and one of you is the counselor. After hearing about the problem, how would you, as the counselor, help this individual?

CHAPTER SUMMARY

Some writers have declared that all romantic love is an addiction, but, to distinguish between the two, the term RR addiction is used in this chapter instead of the more commonly used term, love addiction. There are two kinds of RR addiction, based on the stage at which healthy love becomes compromised: the attraction and the attachment phase. RR attraction addiction represents an obsessive and compulsive need to feel euphoria toward another, followed by ending of the relationship once the euphoria diminishes sufficiently. RR attachment addiction represents an obsessive and compulsive need for attachment toward the other and persists despite ongoing distress and negative consequences.

Writers who focus on RR addiction maintain that its origins are in early childhood, and, due to an anxious-ambivalent style of parental nurturing, the child, in turn, becomes anxious-ambivalent in subsequent relationships. Healing from RR addiction occurs after the addict develops insight into this childhood connection, followed by cognitive restructuring and behavioral intervention. Prevalence rates for RR addiction are unknown, but Peele and Brodsky (2015) advanced the idea that it is possibly the most common form of addiction.

REFERENCES

Acevedo, B. P., & Aron, A. P. (2014). Romantic love, pair-bonding, and the dopaminergic reward system. In M. Mikulincer & P. R. Shaver (Eds.), *Mechanisms of social connection: From brain to group* (pp. 55–69). Washington, DC: American Psychological Association.

Alderson, K. (2012). *Breaking out II: The complete guide to building a positive LGBTI identity*. London, ON: Insomniac Press.

American Psychiatric Association (APA). (2013). *Diagnostic and statistical manual of mental disorders* (5th ed.). Washington, DC: Author.

American Society of Addiction Medicine. (2011, April 12). *Definition of addiction*. Retrieved on December 15, 2018, from https://www.asam.org/quality-practice/definition-of-addiction

Bireda, M. R. (1990). *Love addiction: A guide to emotional independence*. Oakland, CA: New Harbinger.

Briggie, A., & Briggie, C. (2015). Love addiction: What's love got to do with it? In M. S. Ascher & P. Levounis (Eds.), *The behavioral addictions* (pp. 153–173). Arlington, VA: American Psychiatric Publishing.

Burlew, L. D., & Barton, A. (2002). Counseling for sexual compulsion/addiction/dependence (SCAD). In L. D., Burlew & D. Capuzzi, David (Eds.), *Sexuality counseling* (pp. 257–284). Hauppauge, NY: Nova Science.

Connors, G. J., DiClemente, C. C., Velasquez, M. M., & Donovan, D. M. (2013). *Substance abuse treatment and the stages of change: Selecting and planning interventions* (2nd ed.). New York, NY: Guilford Press.

Costa, S., Barberis, N., Griffiths, M. D., Benedetto, L., & Ingrassia, M. (2019). The love addiction inventory: Preliminary findings of the development process and psychometric characteristics. *International Journal of Mental Health and Addiction*. Advance online publication.

Diamond, J. (1991). Looking for love in all the wrong places. In N. Van Den Bergh (Ed.), *Feminist perspectives on addictions* (pp. 167–180). New York, NY: Springer.

Dubrow, L. (1993). Women's issues in addiction recovery. In E. Griffin-Shelley (Ed.), *Outpatient treatment of sex and love addicts* (pp. 87–100). Westport, CT: Praeger/Greenwood.

Earp, B. D., Wudarczyk, O. A., Foddy, B., & Savulescu, J. (2017). Addicted to love: What is love addiction and when should it be treated? *Philosophy, Psychiatry, & Psychology*, *24*, 77–92.

Feeney, J. A., & Noller, P. (1990). Attachment style as a predictor of adult romantic relationships. *Journal of Personality and Social Psychology*, *58*(2), 281–291.

Fisher, H. E. (2014). The tyranny of love: Love addiction—An anthropologist's view. In K. P. Rosenberg & L. Curtiss Feder. (Eds.), *Behavioral addictions: Criteria, evidence, and treatment.* (pp. 237–265). San Diego, CA: Academic Press.

Fisher, H. E., Xu, X., Aron, A., & Brown, L. L. (2016). Intense, passionate, romantic love: A natural addiction? How the fields that investigate romance and substance abuse can inform each other. *Frontiers in Psychology*, *7*, 1–10.

Griffin-Shelley, E. (1993). Conclusions. In E. Griffin-Shelley (Ed.), *Outpatient treatment of sex and love addicts* (pp. 137–152). Westport, CT: Praeger/Greenwood.

Griffin-Shelley, E. (1995). Adolescent sex and relationship addicts. *Sexual Addiction & Compulsivity*, *2*(2), 112–127.

Griffin-Shelley, E. (2009). Ethical issues in sex and love addiction treatment. *Sexual Addiction & Compulsivity*, *16*(1), 32–54.

Griffin-Shelley, E. (2018). The importance of group psychotherapy for sex and love addiction recovery. In T. Birchard & J. Benfield (Eds.), *The Routledge international handbook of sexual addiction* (pp. 181–189). New York, NY: Routledge/Taylor & Francis.

Griffin-Shelley, E., & Griffin-Shelley, H. (1993). Using individual and group therapy in recovery. In E. Griffin-Shelley (Ed.), *Outpatient treatment of sex and love addicts* (pp. 39–64). Westport, CT: Praeger/Greenwood.

Halpern, H. M. (1982). *How to break your addiction to a person*. New York, NY: Bantam.

Hatfield, E., & Sprecher, S. (1986). Measuring passionate love in intimate relations. *Journal of Adolescence*, *9*(4), 383–410.

Hawley, A. R., & Mahoney, A. (2013). Romantic breakup as a sacred loss and desecration among Christians at a state university. *Journal of Psychology and Christianity*, *32*(3), 245–260.

Hendrick, C, & Hendrick, S. (1986). A theory and method of love. *Journal of Personality and Social Psychology*, *50*(2), 392–402.

Hutchison, R. (2007). The role of unconscious guilt in obsessive love relationships. *Dissertation Abstracts International: Section B: The Sciences and Engineering*, *68*(1-B), 624.

Kaufman, J. (1993). Group process issues in men's groups. In E. Griffin-Shelley (Ed.), *Outpatient treatment of sex and love addicts* (pp. 65–85). Westport, CT: Praeger/Greenwood.

Krumrei, E. J., Mahoney, A., & Pargament, K. I. (2009). Divorce and the divine: The role of spirituality in adjustment to divorce. *Journal of Marriage and Family*, *71*(2), 373–383.

Laudet, A. B., Harris, K., Kimball, T., Winters, K. C., & Moberg, D. P. (2015). Characteristics of students participating in collegiate recovery programs: A national survey. *Journal of Substance Abuse Treatment*, *51*, 38–46.

Lee, J. A. (1973). *The colors of love: An exploration of the ways of loving*. Don Mills, ON: New Press.

Lord, W. (1993). A diagnostic proposal with neurochemical underpinnings. In E. Griffin-Shelley (Ed.), *Outpatient treatment of sex and love addicts* (pp. 21–38). Westport, CT: Praeger/Greenwood.

Lovelyjune. (2011). *Filling the "void."* Retrieved on May 7, 2016, from https://thelovelyaddict.com/2011/01/07/filling-the-void/

Martin, G. L. (1989). Relationship, romance, and sexual addiction in extramarital affairs. *Journal of Psychology and Christianity*, *8*(4), 5–25.

Mellody, P., Wells Miller, A., & Miller, J. K. (2003). *Facing love addiction: Giving yourself the power to change the way you love*. New York, NY: HarperOne.

Milkman, H. B., & Sunderwirth, S. G. (2010). *Craving for ecstasy and natural highs: A positive approach to mood alteration*. Thousand Oaks, CA: SAGE.

Noller, P. (1996). What is this thing called love? Defining the love that supports marriage and family. *Personal Relationships*, *3*(1), 97–115.

Peele, S., & Brodsky, A. (2015). *Love and addiction* (2nd ed.). New York, NY: Taplinger.

Prochaska, J. O., Norcross, J. C., & DiClemente, C. C. (1994). *Changing for good*. New York, NY: Avon Books.

Purcell, R., Pathe, M., & Mullen, P. E. (2001). A study of women who stalk. *American Journal of Psychiatry*, *158*, 2056–2060.

Redcay, A., & Simonetti, C. (2018). Criteria for love and relationship addiction: Distinguishing love addiction from other substance and behavioral addictions. *Sexual Addiction & Compulsivity*, *25*, 80–95.

Reynaud, M., Karila, L., Blecha, L., & Benyamina, A. (2010). Is love passion an addictive disorder? *American Journal of Drug and Alcohol Abuse*, *36*(5), 261–267.

Schaeffer, B. (2009). *Is it love or is it addiction?* (3rd ed.). Center City, MN: Hazelden.

Simon, J. (1982). Love: Addiction or road to self-realization, a second look. *The American Journal of Psychoanalysis*, *42*(3), 253–263.

Smaldino, C. (1991). Desperate worship: A view of love addiction. In A. Smaldino (Ed.), *Psychoanalytic approaches to addiction* (pp. 80–95). Philadelphia, PA: Brunner/Mazel.

Sukel, K. (2012). *Dirty minds: How our brains influence love, sex, and relationships*. New York, NY: Free Press.

Sussman, S. (2010). Love addiction: Definition, etiology, treatment. *Sexual Addiction & Compulsivity*, *17*(1), 31–45.

Timmreck, T. C. (1990). Overcoming the loss of a love: Preventing love addiction and promoting positive emotional health. *Psychological Reports*, *66*(2), 515–528.

Tosone, C. (2002). Women and relationship addiction. In S. L. A. Straussner & S. Brown (Eds.), *The handbook of addiction treatment for women* (pp. 170–186). San Francisco, CA: Jossey-Bass.

Versaevel, C. (2011). Affective dependency and psychiatry: A discord. La dependance affective et la psychiatrie: Une mesentente. *L'Encephale: Revue de psychiatrie clinique biologique et therapeutique*, *37*(1), 25–32.

Weinrach, S. G., Ellis, A., MacLaren, C., DiGiuseppe, R., Vernon, A., Wolfe, J., . . . Backx, W. (2001). Rational emotive behavior therapy successes and failures: Eight personal perspectives. *Journal of Counseling & Development*, *79*(3), 259–268.

Wright, P. H., & Wright, K. D. (1991). Codependency: Addictive love, adjustive relating, or both? *Contemporary Family Therapy: An International Journal*, *13*(5), 435–454.

18 Food Addiction

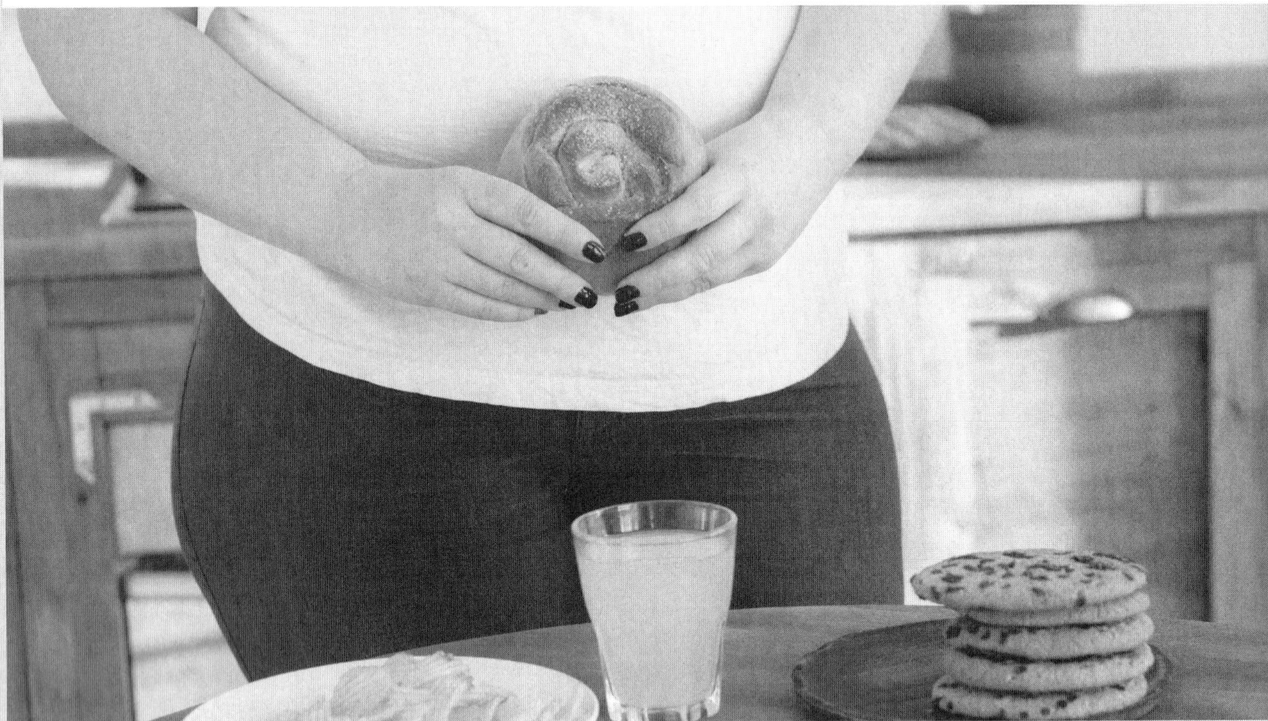

iStock.com/Vadym Petroche

Learning Objectives

1. Learn about the overlap and distinguishing features of food addiction from the three eating disorder diagnoses found in DSM.
2. Become familiar with the foods implicated in having an addictive component for some individuals.
3. Become informed about the causes of food addiction.
4. Become aware of the consequences of overweight and obesity.
5. Discover ways to counsel individuals addicted to food that will not leave them feeling hungry.

CHALLENGING YOUR ASSUMPTIONS ABOUT THIS ADDICTION

1. If you were to discover that most obese individuals are food addicts, in what ways would your judgments be less harsh and in what ways would your judgments be perhaps more punitive?
2. Most people have had food cravings from time to time to varying degrees. What was the most difficult food craving that you ever faced and how did you overcome it? What feelings would develop within you if you found you could not stop the food craving and the consumption of that food?
3. Most people who lose weight on a diet regain that weight. Why do you think that occurs? What would help people sustain their weight loss?
4. What steps, if any, should the food industry and/or government take to educate people about food addiction and to help prevent it from becoming a problem with certain individuals?
5. If you had (or have) a grossly obese child who continued to help himself or herself to unhealthy foods in your house, what would you do to help curtail that behavior? What would you do if your attempts were unsuccessful?

PERSONAL REFLECTIONS

Back when I was 22, I became friends with my roommate's morbidly obese cousin, whom I will name "Petunia." Petunia was my age, and she grew up in a town 90 miles away. Her father was treasurer of the bible college there, and, unsurprisingly, she was raised as a strict evangelical Christian. I remember visiting her family in that town once and was surprised by the fact that they had no television, and radio was permitted only for listening to the news. I asked Petunia about that, and, according to her, it was because the TV contained too much material that was anti-Christian, and so did many of the songs on the radio.

Over the ensuing months, we became good friends. I remember the day she phoned me to say that her father forbade her from seeing me again. When asked why she said it was because of the content in a movie I took her to at a local theater. Obviously Petunia told her dad that I took her to *Cruising*, a 1980 crime film starring Al Pacino. I assume she told her dad that it was a serial killer who targeted gay men, and some of the footage was in a gay leather bar. I was shocked due to my ignorance of the sensitivities that directed her life and that of her family. I phoned her dad, apologized profusely, and asked for forgiveness. He did not want his daughter hurt or corrupted, and, after a brief but emotional conversation, he reversed his decision. Perhaps that struck Petunia as chivalrous because, without my ever knowing about it for 20 years, she fell in love with me . . . a love she never disclosed. Our friendship waned over time, however, without reason other than I had moved on, I guess.

In 2004, while I was in Vancouver, Canada, to research a clothing-optional beach, I received a call from Petunia's brother informing me that she was dying from cancer. She wanted to see me while in hospital. I hadn't seen Petunia in years, but, more important, I was so messed up from smoking cannabis all the time that I assumed I would make it there eventually. Three weeks later, I learned of her death. It took me a year after becoming clean from cannabis that I even realized how sad I was over her death, but especially the shame and guilt over not visiting her at the bedside. But addicts *have* to forgive themselves or they will not heal.

I was told Petunia would eat voluminous amounts of food when she was alone, and she was alone a lot. She was never in a consummate relationship. I was told she went to a "fat farm," which I assume meant enrolling an intensive program somewhere to help her lose weight. I was told it was unsuccessful.

Was Petunia a food addict? Is every obese person a food addict? How does food addiction differ from the existing eating disorders? I was curious to learn about this diagnosis of which I was only vaguely aware.

Background Information

When I stop and ask myself, "What am I really hungry for?" the answer is always, "I'm hungry for balance, I'm hungry to do something other than work. . . . [Y]our work and obligations have become a substitute for life, then you have no one else to blame. Only you can take the reins back. (Oprah Winfrey, as cited in Tarman & Werdell, 2014, p. 19)

Like most other behavioral addictions, most of us can relate to food addiction to some extent. Cravings, like other aspects of addiction, are on a continuum, and most people have had times where they crave a certain food (Hill, 2012). Chocolate remains the most craved food (Milkman & Sunderwirth, 2010), and it accounts for about one half of food cravings (Hill, 2012). The most common craving for men, however, includes savory foods such as snacks, meats, and takeaway items (Hill, 2012).

Food craving, binge eating, and compulsive eating contribute to the construct of food addiction, a perspective that has received unanimous acceptance (Davis and Carter, 2009). Still, some have hypothesized that food addiction *causes* chronic overeating, binge eating, and obesity (Corsica & Pelchat, 2010). Regardless, it is important to clarify from the outset that food addiction can occur alone. It does not necessarily accompany binge eating disorder (BED) or result in obesity (Wiss & Brewerton, 2017). But, because becoming overweight or obese is often the catalyst for a client to seek help, it will be addressed throughout this chapter.

Obesity is defined as having a body mass index (BMI) of over 30 kg/m^2 (Tarman & Werdell, 2014). It has reached "pandemic proportions" worldwide (Wiss, Criscitelli, Gold, & Avena, 2017, p. 19), and the United States is no exception. Obesity continues to be a major public health issue in the United States, and the prevalence in children continues to grow (Wiss et al., 2017). Approximately one third of American adults over age 20 are overweight, and, if obesity rates continue to rise, 51% of all U.S. adults will be obese by 2030, and nearly all African American women will be obese by 2034 (Blumenthal & Gold, 2012). Obesity is already considered the second leading cause of death in the United States (Dimitrijevic, Popovic, Sabljak, Skodric-Trifunovic, & Dimitrijevic, 2015). Like alcohol and tobacco, obesity is more common among poor individuals than wealthy ones(Blumenthal & Gold, 2012). Furthermore, "we have no cure for obesity; it is a chronic relapsing medical problem" (Blumenthal, Dupont, & Gold, 2012, p. 322).

About 90% of Americans believe they are overweight, and a third want to lose 15 pounds or more (Milkman & Sunderwirth, 2010). Dieting in the United States is a $46-billion-a-year industry. It is estimated that $92.6 billion is spent annually on the health consequences of those who are overweight and obese, a figure that represents over 9% of health expenditures in the United States (Milkman & Sunderwirth, 2010). Obesity, like regular tobacco use, remains one of the leading causes of preventable illness in the United States (Avena & Hoebel, 2012).

According to Gallup's annual November Health and Healthcare Survey (Norman, 2017), the average weight of men and women in the United States between 2013 and 2017 was 195 and 158 pounds, respectively. Currently, 52% of American men and women state that they want to lose weight, but only 25% are actively trying to do so. Slof-Op 't Landt et al. (2017) conducted a large-scale study of 31,636 participants (60.2% women; age 13–98 years) in the Netherlands to look at the prevalence of dieting. Women between 35 and 65 years (56.6%–63%) and men between 45 and 65 years (31.7%–31.9%) were the most frequent dieters. The prevalence of fearing weight gain was highest in women between 16 and 25 (73.2%–74.3%) and men between 25 and 55 (43.2%–46.1%).

The first article about food addiction that is indexed in PsycINFO is by Randolph (1956). Randolph wrote that addiction, which he construed as an allergy, could result from frequently consumed foods. Randolph (1947) had written earlier about the contribution of this "allergy" in the development and persistence of obesity. His list included coffee, eggs, milk, and corn. Current research does *not* suggest that any of these are potentially addictive foods. The individual who is considered the founder of food addiction *research* is Mark Gold, followed by several of his colleagues (Brownell & Gold, 2012a).

The concept of food addiction remains controversial (Brewerton, 2017; Vella & Pai, 2017) and it does not appear in DSM. Nonetheless, the construct has gained momentum in both professional and lay circles (Cullen et al., 2017; Ruddock, Field, & Hardman, 2017; Wiss et al., 2017). Kirschenbaum and Krawczyk (2018) argued that food addiction does not exist and that it can be viewed instead as depressed binge eating. Kirschenbaum and Krawczyk suggested that the concept of food addiction can do more harm than good by encouraging professionals and obese individuals "to view food addiction as a cause of obesity" (p. 227). Leigh and Morris (2018) concurred, stating that it remains unclear if food addiction is distinct from BED behaviorally and neurobiologically.

Wiss et al. (2017) maintained that research supports the idea that certain foods are addictive, referred to by several writers as *highly palatable foods* (HPFs) (Blumenthal & Gold, 2012; Tarman & Werdell, 2014; Wiss et al., 2017). HPFs include foods that are highly processed with added fats and/or refined carbohydrates such as sugar (Polk, Schulte, Furman, & Gearhardt, 2017). The single largest source of sugar for most individuals is purportedly from sweetened beverages (Yau, Gottlieb, Krasna, & Potenza, 2014). Salt is also implicated as addictive, and those who ingest excessive amounts are more likely to become obese, experience hypertension, and contract several other diseases (Soto-Escageda et al., 2016). Particular food types might create different moods: sugar provides an energy rush, flour creates sedation, and high-fat dairy produces calming feelings (Ifland, Sheppard, & Wright, 2012).

One of the controversies surrounding food addiction is whether it warrants a separate diagnosis from the three known eating disorders (EDs) (i.e., anorexia nervosa, bulimia nervosa (BN), and BED). Although researchers like Wiss et al. (2017) maintain that it deserves a separate diagnosis, others like Brewerton (2017) contend that the concept is a proxy for other diagnoses. Davis (2017) acknowledged the mounting evidence of addictive symptomatology for some individuals to certain foods, but she also commented on food addiction's overlapping features with other conditions. There is a high degree of overlap between a new diagnosis in *DSM-5* (i.e., BED) and food addiction, for example (Schulte, Grilo, & Gearhardt, 2016). Other research supports an even stronger link between BN and food addiction while simultaneously revealing that food addiction has distinctive elements from both BED and BN (Gearhardt, Boswell, & White, 2014). Meule, Rezori, and Blechert (2014) concluded that, because of the overlap, food addiction symptoms would diminish alongside BN symptoms.

There are politics in diagnosis, and Rogers (2017) warned that "blaming excessive eating on food addiction could be counterproductive" (p. 182), as it may trivialize other more serious addictions. Another concern is that excessive eaters may rationalize their overeating and fail to take corrective action because they label their behavior as an addiction, thereby making an external attribution (Hardman et al., 2015). In other words, by attributing their eating to addiction, they may avoid taking responsibility for it (Ruddock & Hardman, 2018). Also, being labeled as an obese person addicted to food may become yet another stigmatized identity (DePierre, Puhl, & Luedicke, 2014).

Gold and Shriner (2013) provided the most thorough working definition of food addiction, including features that distinguish it from normal eating behavior:

> Food addiction represents a pervasive and enduring pattern of both food perception and food-related behavior (leading to either excessive food ingestion or aversion) whose dual valence (i.e., perception and behavior) biases

> interaction with food in harmful and unhealthy ways. Such a biasing and unhealthy valence toward food continue, despite knowledge of its harmful consequences. Food addicts usually present both a tolerance (i.e. a need to increase participation in their harmful relationships with food over space and time) as well as a form of withdrawal (i.e. an inability to escape their addiction with food without suffering undue anxiety, craving, or other adverse neurochemical reactivity [which may include depression or anger]) when deprived of access to addictive foods. This latter emotional and behavioral reactivity must reliably occur during efforts to either alter or disrupt the food addict's harmful and maladaptive pattern of eating. (p. 787)

Despite Gold and Shriner's (2013) comprehensive definition, Imperatori et al. (2016) concluded after their review of food addiction that it is *transnosographic* meaning that the concept traverses across several diseases, with the highest prevalence in BN. Nonetheless, both Imperatori et al. and Brewerton (2017) surmised that the comorbidity between food addiction and other EDs suggests a worse condition, so a diagnosis of food addiction is useful for both assessment and treatment.

Behind the notion of food addiction is the hypothesis that it may be one cause of obesity (Liu, von Deneen, Kobeissy, & Gold, 2010). It has been likened to drug addiction (Blass, 2012) in that there are neuropsychological links with both substance-related disorders and EDs (these will be discussed in the section on neuroscience). In some regards, addiction to food is more complex than addiction to substances because one cannot live without food (Blumenthal & Gold, 2012).

Self-perceived female individuals with food addiction (IAFs) (N = 31) in one study experienced food as more rewarding, and they were more likely to overeat compared to 29 nonaddicts (Ruddock et al., 2017). These results were recently replicated (Schulte, Sonneville, & Gearhardt, 2019). An earlier study found that individuals who scored as IAFs on the Yale Food Addiction Scale (YFAS) had higher scores on all food craving subscales (except for a scale measuring anticipation of positive reinforcement from eating) compared to nonaddicts (N = 616, 75.8% female; Meule & Kubler, 2012).

IAFs have reported two different patterns: One type often eats throughout the day (i.e., episodic binging), and the other binges episodically (Ifland et al., 2012). Tarman and Werdell (2014) suggested that an IAF goes through four developmental stages, including (a) progressive loss of control, (b) weight gain followed by periodic dieting, (c) behaviors specific to addiction (e.g., hoarding and/or stealing of particular foods, finishing other people's food), and (d) awareness of loss of control and medical consequences.

How much might an IAF eat in one sitting? Tarman and Werdell (2014) described a typical binge for one woman with food addiction. It included "six bagels with butter, a stack of pancakes with syrup, a large cheese omelette with sausage, half a dozen doughnuts, three candy bars, a bowl of sugared cereal with whole milk, a McDonald's meal of hamburger and fries, and a pint of ice cream" (p. 144).

Lemeshow et al. (2018) used the data from two large-scale studies (N= 58,625 and 65,063) to look at aspects of food addiction in female nurses in the United States. They found that eating red/processed meats, low/no-fat snacks and desserts, and low-calorie beverages was associated with food addiction. Conversely, consumption of refined grains, sugar-sweetened drinks, fruits, vegetables, and legumes was inversely related. These findings support the literature that has found that simple carbohydrates are less associated with food addiction.

We know that obesity can be caused by some health conditions and some medications, including hypothyroidism, Cushing's syndrome, polycystic ovarian syndrome, corticosteroids, and anti-epileptic medications (Davis, Edge, & Gold, 2014). Genetic and hormonal conditions can also play a role, in addition to stress and emotional factors (Davis et al., 2014; Lagrotte & Foster, 2012). Whether psychological or physiological factors play the bigger role in obesity remains debatable (Maté, 2008; Milkman & Sunderwirth, 2010). But what causes food addiction?

In a recent study (Hardy, Fani, Jovanovic, & Michopoulos, 2018), 229 women were assessed for no addiction, a substance use disorder (SUD) only, or a food addiction only (N = 117, 70, and 42, respectively). The woman with an SUD or food addiction exhibited more symptoms of depression, posttraumatic stress disorder (PTSD), emotional dysregulation, impulsivity, and difficulty in accomplishing goals compared to those with no addiction. The women with SUD exhibited higher levels of trauma in both childhood and adulthood compared to either the IAFs or the nonaddicts.

Childhood trauma *is*, however, considered a major risk factor for the onset of food addiction and obesity (Imperatori et al., 2016). A recent Brazilian study of 7639 individuals revealed that early psychological and sexual abuse was common in the 4.3% of the sample who scored as IAFs (Nunes-Neto et al., 2018).

There is considerable evidence that high uncontrollable stress, chronic stress, and negative emotions are related to food addiction (Blumenthal & Gold, 2012; Bourdier et al., 2018; Sinha, 2012). An inability to regulate especially strong emotions is implicated in food addiction (Innamorati et al., 2017; Pivarunas & Conner, 2015). In a 2017 survey, 77% of the members (N= 648) had received some kind of treatment for medical, psychological, and/or spiritual help before attending Overeaters Anonymous (2018) .

Several studies have found personality qualities or characteristics that are associated with food addiction. One of the consistent traits that has emerged in research is that individuals high in impulsivity are more likely to become IAFs (Gearhardt & Corbin, 2012c; Murphy, Stojek, & MacKillop, 2014; VanderBroek-Stice, Stojek, Beach, vanDellen, & MacKillop, 2017) and/or alcoholics (Gearhardt & Corbin, 2012c). The tendency to act impulsively when under duress is referred to as having *high negative urgency*, and it is the most frequently measured trait associated with food addiction (Pivarunas & Conner, 2015; Wolz et al., 2016; Wolz, Granero, & Fernandez-Aranda, 2017). IAFs also struggle more with focusing on long-term goals compared to those with other EDs (Wolz et al., 2016).

A cluster analysis based on 80 obese women with food addiction found that five personality tendencies were prominent: (a) depressed, (b) anxious, (c) controlling, (d) addictive, and (e) caretaking (i.e., nurturant while independent) (Kayloe, 1993). Kabat-Zinn (2013) postulated that food could become a crutch for people who are anxious and depressed. Feeling empty inside leads people to fill the void (Kabat-Zinn, 2013; Tarman & Werdell, 2014).

There is one reported positive quality ascribed to obesity. Obese individuals are rarely indulged in other addictions. They smoke fewer cigarettes and use fewer illicit drugs compared to every other population (Blumenthal & Gold, 2012). It is possible that IAFs are less likely to become addicted to cocaine (Dietrich et al., 2012). This, however, is quite speculative, as the study by Dietrich et al.

(2012) was focused on mice, and the researchers found that mice that are not interested in food are more likely to ingest cocaine.

Obesity is more common in psychiatric populations. It is related to premature morbidity of between 25 and 30 years (Ifland et al., 2012). Obese individuals are more likely to die in accidents due to complications. They have an increased likelihood of contracting several diseases and conditions, including hypertension, heart disease, diabetes, respiratory illnesses, and back and joint problems (Milkman & Sunderwirth, 2010). Obese men suffer from colon, rectal, and prostate cancers, and obese women experience more cancerous tumors of the ovaries, uterine lining, and the breasts postmenopause (Milkman & Sunderwirth, 2010).

Estimates suggest that between one third and three quarters of the population is on a diet at any given moment, but only between 1% and 10% keep off their lost weight after a year (Tarman & Werdell, 2014). The prevalence of food addiction has been mostly calculated in research using the YFAS. Results from the scale suggest that 37% of obese individuals have a food addiction (Tarman & Werdell, 2014). In a study of 353 participants, 11.4% of normal-weight people were diagnosed with food addiction (Gearhardt et al., as cited in Dimitrijevic et al., 2015). In the Nurses' Health Study with a combined sample size of 123,688, the prevalence of food addiction was 5.4% (Lemeshow et al., 2018). In the Brazilian sample of 7639 noted earlier, the prevalence was 4.32% (Nunes-Neto et al., 2018). Food addiction in Canada reportedly affects nearly 5% of adults (Pedram, Zhai, Gulliver, Zhang, & Sun, 2017). In the Netherlands, 2.6% of a sample of 2653 adolescents between ages 14 and 21 met the criteria for food addiction (Mies et al., 2017).

Diagnostic and Assessment Considerations

The American Society of Addiction Medicine (ASAM) includes food in its definition of addiction (see https://www.asam.org/quality-practice/definition-of-addiction). Tarman and Werdell (2014) noted that this occurred in 2011 after ASAM redefined addictions as a brain disorder. ICD-11 included diagnosis called food hypersensitivity, unspecified (code 4A85.2Z) and other specified food hypersensitivity (code 4A85.2Y).

According to research by Gearhardt and others (as cited in Dimitrijevic et al., 2015), the three most common symptoms of food addiction in adults are

1. Persistent desire or failure to reduce food intake.
2. Continuing to eat excessively despite its harmful consequences.
3. Much time spent in trying to reduce the amount eaten and in recovery from overeating.

The most common symptoms of food addiction in children reportedly are

1. Consuming excessive amounts of food over an extended duration.
2. Unsuccessful efforts made in attempting to reduce the amount eaten.
3. Continuing to eat excessively despite its harmful consequences.

Although BED is viewed as a behavioral addiction to food (Zmuda, 2014), data suggest that it is a different condition from food addiction (Yau et al., 2014). Yau et al. (2014), for example, noted that factors related to binge-eating, such as negative affect and eating disorder psychopathology, are not predictive of the frequency of binge-eating, whereas higher food addiction scores are related to an increased frequency of binge-eating. One study found that 57% of a sample of individuals with BED also met criteria for food addiction, indicating that there is considerable overlap between the two conditions (Gearhardt, White, et al., 2012). Werdell (2012) considered food addiction to be a "chemical dependency on food" (p. 354). Gearhardt and Corbin (2012b) indicated that the most commonly diagnosed ED [likely referring to DSM-IV or DSM-IV-TR] is Eating Disorder Not Otherwise Specified, and it is not clear what the relationship of this diagnosis is to food addiction.

Gearhardt, Corbin, and Brownell (2016) recently revised their YFAS, and criteria were adapted by Moore, Sabino, Koob, and Cottone (2017) to reflect a DSM style. Severity ratings were similar to *DSM-5* for addictions (i.e., mild: 2 to 3, moderate: 4 to 5, and severe: 6 or more). Here are the criteria they offered for food addiction:

Clinically significant impairment or distress AND 2 or more of the following criteria:

1. Consumed more (larger amount and for a longer period) than planned.
2. Unable to cut down or stop.
3. Great deal of time spent.
4. Important activities given up or reduced.
5. Use despite knowledge of physical/emotional consequences.
6. Tolerance (increase in amount, decrease in effect).
7. Withdrawal (symptoms, substance taken to relieve withdrawal).
8. Craving or strong desire.
9. Failure in role obligation.
10. Use despite interpersonal/social consequences.
11. Use in physically hazardous situations. (p. 1377)

Differential Diagnosis

Wolz et al. (2017) found in their study of 315 patients that what distinguished IAFs from those with other EDs was their impulsivity triggered by experiencing negative mood states. Zmuda (2014) acknowledged the co-morbidity of EDs and sSUDs. Consequently, the reverse may also be true (i.e., also assess for SUD in clients with an ED, perhaps especially those who would be classified as IAFs).

Tarman and Werdell (2014) maintained that many people diagnosed with BED are IAFs. They go on to explain that what should lead physicians (and counselors) to suspect food addiction is the cravings and obsessions that clients have for certain highly palatable foods (usually sugar and fat). BED is primarily defined by recurring episodes of binge eating but without the measures that anorexics and bulimics take to compensate (e.g., purging, extreme dieting; Grilo, 2012). In one study, between 43% and 50% of those with BED did not meet criteria for food addiction, and 30% of the binge eaters did not score in the food addiction range (Yau et al., 2014). This study suggests that BED and food addiction are highly related yet separate diagnoses. Bak-Sosnowska's (2017) study found that BED could be distinguished from food addiction based on (a) the function of food, (b) reaction to food that is unavailable, (c) coping mechanisms with excessive eating and body image, (d) tolerance, (e) withdrawal symptoms, and (f) how excessive eating is related to other areas of life.

Another similarity between binge eating and food addiction is their association with emotional dysregulation (Eichen, Chen, Boutelle, & McCloskey, 2017). According to DSM-IV criteria, between 1.1% and 1.9% of the general population experience BED (Agh et al., 2015). One important distinguishing feature between food addiction and BED is that, although food intake may be rapid, it is not always large. A BED diagnosis requires food intake that is voluminous (Fattore, Melis, Fadda, & Fratta, 2014).

In a study of 26 women with current BN compared to 20 who had remitted BN and 63 controls, all patients with current BN received a diagnosis of food addiction, whereas only six with remitted BN did. None in the control group received a food addiction diagnosis (Meule et al., 2014). This study suggests that BN and food addiction also share many similarities.

Comorbidity and Co-Addictions

Wang, Volkow, and Fowler (2012) reported on the co-morbidity between attention-deficit hyperactivity disorder (ADHD) in overweight children, adolescents, and adults. A recent review found similar co-morbidity between ADHD and several behavioral addictions, including food addiction (Karaca, Saleh, Canan, & Potenza, 2017). Brunault et al. (2018) also found that adults with ADHD were at greater risk of food addiction.

It is hypothesized that obesity and binge eating may be related to food addiction (Carter, Van Wijk, & Rowsell, 2019; Davis et al., 2014). The relationship between substance abuse disorders and EDs was mentioned in the previous section (Zmuda, 2014). Research has found correlations between food addiction and other eating disorders, depression, bipolar disorder, skin picking disorder, and early psychological and sexual abuse (de Vries & Meule, 2016; Hardy et al., 2018; Nunes-Neto et al., 2018).

Men with heroin use disorder are co-morbid with both BED and food addiction (Canan, Karaca, Sogucak, Gecici, & Kuloglu, 2017). Gambling addicts with food addiction have poorer emotional and psychological states compared to those without this co-morbidity (Jimenez-Murcia et al., 2017).

Available Measures

The gold standard in the measurement of food addiction is the YFAS. It has been extensively studied, it has sound psychometric properties, and it is the most widely used scale in research. Consequently, it is the first scale that is briefly described:

1. Yale Food Addiction Scale (YFAS). This is the most commonly used standardized scale today. It was constructed by Ashley Gerhardt in 2008 (Gearhardt & Corbin, 2012a). The scale contains 25 items, including dichotomous and Likert-type questions. The test "is based upon the *DSM-IV-TR* diagnostic criteria for substance dependence as applied to eating behavior" (Gearhardt & Corbin, 2012a, p. 282). It also has good test-retest reliability over 18 months (Pursey, Collins, Stanwell, & Burrows, 2016). A downloadable version of the YFAS, the YFAS for Children, the modified shorter version of the YFAS, and the instructions are available from http://fastlab.psych.lsa.umich.edu/yale-food-addiction-scale/
2. Addiction Severity Index (ASI). According to Ifland et al. (2012), this index is the gold standard for assessing the severity of addiction. It has been validated for several addictions across cultures. It is now in its sixth edition (Cacciola, Alterman, Habing, & McLellan, 2011).
3. Food Craving Questionnaire. These two questionnaires, one measuring *state* and the other measuring *trait* food cravings, have demonstrated reliability and validity (see Moreno, Rodriguez, Fernandez, Tamez, & Cepeda-Benito, 2008).
4. Obsessive Compulsive Eating Scale (Niemiec, Boswell, & Hormes, 2016). This test is based on the well-validated Obsessive Compulsive Drinking Scale. The test has excellent internal consistency and good convergent and criterion validity.
5. Weight Efficacy Lifestyle Questionnaire-Short Form. This questionnaire measures long-term adherence to increased physical activity and reduction of consumed calories (Ames, Heckman, Diehl, Grothe, & Clark, 2015). It is a psychometrically sound measure of eating self-efficacy.
6. Loss of Control Over Eating Scale. Results from this new test were significantly correlated with eating problems, general levels of distress, functional impairment, and general levels of self-control (Latner, Mond, Kelly, Haynes, & Hay, 2014).
7. Several eating questionnaires are also available from http://www.ucl.ac.uk/iehc/research/behavioural-science-health/resources/questionnaires/eating-behaviour-questionnaires

Clinical Interview Questions

Food Addicts in Recovery Anonymous (visit https://www.foodaddicts.org/am-i-a-food-addict) offered the following 20 questions that can be asked of potential IAFs (note that, similar to other 12-step websites, this group writes that, if a person answers yes to any of the questions, he or she might be a food addict; Tarman and Werdell, 2014, suggested that answering yes to four or more questions means the respondent is likely a food addict):

Quoted from website:

1. Have you ever wanted to stop eating and found you just couldn't?
2. Do you think about food or your weight constantly?
3. Do you find yourself attempting one diet or food plan after another, with no lasting success?
4. Do you binge and then "get rid of the binge" through vomiting, exercise, laxatives, or other forms of purging?

5. Do you eat differently in private than you do in front of other people?
6. Has a doctor or family member ever approached you with concern about your eating habits or weight?
7. Do you eat large quantities of food at one time (binge)?
8. Is your weight problem due to your "nibbling" all day long?
9. Do you eat to escape from your feelings?
10. Do you eat when you're not hungry?
11. Have you ever discarded food, only to retrieve and eat it later?
12. Do you eat in secret?
13. Do you fast or severely restrict your food intake?
14. Have you ever stolen other people's food?
15. Have you ever hidden food to make sure you have "enough"?
16. Do you feel driven to exercise excessively to control your weight?
17. Do you obsessively calculate the calories you've burned against the calories you've eaten?
18. Do you frequently feel guilty or ashamed about what you've eaten?
19. Are you waiting for your life to begin "when you lose the weight"?
20. Do you feel hopeless about your relationship with food?

In describing the story of "Christine," another question was suggested by Tarman and Werdell (2014) that could be asked of IAFs after their weight is ascertained: "How do you feel about that number?" Given that many IAFs experienced childhood trauma (Imperatori et al., 2016), questions about childhood abuse would be pertinent as well.

Generic Names and Street "Lingo"

Other terms that are sometimes used in place of food addiction include eating addiction (Hebebrand et al., 2014; Korpa & Papadopoulou, 2013), compulsive overeating (Davis & Carter, 2009; Zmuda, 2014), food use disorder (Nolan, 2017), addictive-like eating (Schulte, Potenza, & Gearhardt, 2017), and refined food addiction (Ifland et al., 2012).

Neuroscience

The leading cause of overweight and obesity is overeating (Ferrario, 2017). But why do some people find it so hard to stop eating compulsively? The hypothalamus and its circuits are believed to be the main brain areas responsible for the body's regulation of weight (Wang et al., 2012). The regulators of energy in the body also come into play in moderating the pleasure derived from food, including leptin, insulin, orexin, and ghrelin (Yau et al., 2014).

Naturally occurring opioids and dopamine are involved in how much an individual enjoys highly palatable foods (Davis et al., 2014). Dopamine can increase appetite, whereas acetylcholine lessens it toward the end of a meal (Wang et al., 2012). Sugar has a strong and direct influence on the dopamine system (De Jong, Vanderschuren, & Adan, 2016), and bingeing on it daily creates steady dopamine release into the nucleus accumbens (Wang et al., 2012). Other neurotransmitters involved in eating behaviors include acetylcholine, gamma-aminobutyric acid, serotonin, cannabinoids, and glutamine (Wang et al., 2012).

One hypothesis for why obesity occurs is that the obese may experience food as less rewarding and therefore eat more to increase the satisfaction they derive from food (Wang et al., 2012). Another hypothesis is that the obese experience a hyperresponsivity of mesolimbic and mesocortical circuits to food cues (Yokum & Stice, 2012). It is believed that the regular consumption of highly palatable food results in long-standing changes to the stress and reward pathways in an attempt for the body to regain homeostasis (Sinha, 2012).

Recently, Contreras-Rodriguez, Martin-Perez, Vilar-Lopez, and Verdejo-Garcia (2017) concluded that "obesity is linked to alterations in the functional connectivity of dorsal striatal networks relevant to food craving and weight gain. These neural alterations are associated with habit learning and thus compatible with the food addiction model of obesity" (p. 789). Addiction vulnerability may also be associated with dysregulated brain endocannabinoid (eCB) signaling because of its effect on stress responsivity, negative emotional states, and food cravings (Parsons & Hurd, 2015). Obese individuals in most studies experience reduced availability in the D2 receptor (D2R) sites and dopamine transport availability (Davis et al., 2014). A recent study, however, did not find a difference in D2R availability between obese and nonobese subjects. Instead, the researchers likened obesity to opioid addiction more than to other addictions (Karlsson et al., 2015).

Brownell and Gold (2012b) postulated that food addiction could affect vast numbers of people. The rewarding aspects of food occur through several systems in the brain, including the nucleus accumbens, the ventral pallidum in the ventral striatum, the ventral tegmental area, the prefrontal cortex, the hippocampus, and the amygdala (Davis et al., 2014). Davis et al. (2014) suggested that these areas are the same as those found in SUDs.

Epigenetics might also contribute to a predisposition toward obesity. "Epigenetics refers to the regulation of genomic functions like gene expression independent of DNA sequence, such as potentially reversible chemical modifications occurring on the DNA and/or histones leading to chromatin remodelling and histone modification, inducing alteration in gene expression" (Davis et al., 2014, p. 194). There is currently limited support for the notion that food addiction and drug addiction share similar genetic roots (Cornelis et al., 2016). The underlying genes in food addiction, however, remain mostly unknown (Pedram et al., 2017).

According to Moore et al. (2017), The main systems involved in compulsive eating include the following:

> (1) the basal ganglia, (2) the extended amygdala, and (3) the prefrontal cortex. The basal ganglia . . . consist of multiple subcortical nuclei, such as the nucleus accumbens (NAc), which is involved in the rewarding

and reinforcing effects of food, and the dorsal striatum, which is involved in instrumental learning and habitual behavior. The basal ganglia contribute to habitual overeating that can arise from maladaptive habit formation processes. The extended amygdala . . . is a basal forebrain composite structure encompassing the central nucleus of the amygdala (CeA), the bed nucleus of the stria terminalis (BNST), and a transition area in the medial and caudal portions of the NAc. The brain stress systems in the extended amygdala mediate overeating to relieve a negative emotional state that emerges from withdrawal processes. Prefronto-cortical regions . . . include the medial prefrontal (mPFC, comprised of dorsolateral (dlPFC) and ventromedial (vmPFC) regions), anterior cingulate (ACC), and orbitofrontal (OFC) cortices; these areas control cognitive functions such as decision-making and response inhibition through interactions with subcortical structures such as the basal ganglia and the extended amygdala. Dysfunctions in the PFC are hypothesized to underlie overeating despite aversive consequences, reflecting failures in inhibitory control over behavior. (p. 1376)

Physical Impacts (Long-Term Use)

A substantial consequence of having a food addiction is a greatly increased likelihood of becoming overweight or obese. For example, multiple longitudinal studies have found a positive relationship between sugar-sweetened beverages and weight gain in both children and adults (Ebbeling, Willett, & Ludwig, 2012).

Diets high in fat and sugar cause several health conditions, including type 2 diabetes, cancer, and heart disease (Gearhardt & Corbin, 2012b). Obesity is associated with even more medical conditions. For example, obesity is associated with metabolic and endocrine complications, hormonal level disruptions, circulation difficulties, organ system failure and diseases, asthma, osteoarthritis, nonalcoholic fatty liver disease and liver cirrhosis, heart disease, hypertension, diabetes, malignancies, mechanical difficulties, and surgical complications (Blumenthal & Gold, 2012; Dimitrijevic et al., 2015; Tarmen & Werdell, 2014). Tarmen and Werdell (2014) stated that there are always medical consequences to those in the later stages of food addiction, with a shortened expected life expectancy of between 5 and 10 years. Obesity, on the other hand, is associated with diminished life expectancy of between 25 and 30 years (Ifland et al., 2012).

Cravings can impair working memory, which can in turn negatively impact effective decision-making (Monti & Ray, 2012). Accident-related deaths and complications are about twice as high for obese individuals (Ifland et al., 2012).

Both tolerance and withdrawal occur in IAFs, and high rates of relapse occur (Gearhardt & Corbin, 2012b). Particularly sugar can cause withdrawal symptoms akin to opiate withdrawal (Davis & Carter, 2009). Some of the observed withdrawal symptoms include "fatigue, dizziness, irritability, depression, fainting spells, insomnia, night sweats, suicidal tendencies, shaking, crying spells, poor memory, mood swings, temper outbursts, indigestion, and headache" (Werdell, 2012, p. 356). Tarman and Werdell (2014) suggested that detoxification from highly palatable foods only lasts between 1 and 4 weeks.

Mental, Emotional, and Spiritual Impacts

Obese IAFs experience a high prevalence of social anxiety (Abdollahi & Talib, 2015). They tend to have a worse body image compared to normal-weight individuals, and some become so preoccupied with their-weight that they avoid social situations (Asthana, 2010).

Individuals who diet are afraid of weight gain (Slof-Op 't Landt et al., 2017). Unsurprisingly, IAFs live with anxiety regarding the consequences of overeating. After a food binge, IAFs feel guilty, shameful, anxious, and depressed (Dimitrijevic et al., 2015; Ruddock & Hardman, 2018; Tarman & Werdell, 2014).

Werdell (2012) claimed that IAFs in the late stage develop a false sense of self. Wardell also stated that denial is a common symptom of IAFs. Binge eating, similar to smoking, provides an escape from feeling negative emotions (White & O'Malley, 2012). Ifland et al. (2012) stated that IAFs are also prone to maladaptive behaviors, including lying, hiding, stealing, manipulating, blaming, shaming, threatening, and even violence. They may also be overly dramatic and act like martyrs (Ifland et al., 2012).

Psychosocial Impacts (Relationships, Career/Work, Legal, Financial)

The public stigmatizes IAFs (DePierre et al., 2014). "For all ages, the impact of being 'fat' cannot be overstated" (Ifland et al., 2012, p. 351). In an experiment where women of varying weights were assigned to either a condition where half thought they were being videotaped in giving a speech about why they would make good dating partners and half did not, weight stigma had a substantial impact on overweight people, creating stress, increased blood pressure, and poorer performance on a cognitive task (Major, Eliezer, & Rieck, 2012). In one study, heavier women were rated as less attractive and as having less vitality by men (heavier men were not rated as less desirable by women, however; Boyes & Latner, 2009). Being heavier has a more negative effect on women than on men (Stake & Lauer, 1987).

Both heavier girls and boys are less likely to date compared to their lighter counterparts (Cawley, Joyner, & Sobal, 2006). Another study found that, for White girls and for Black girls who had college-educated mothers, those who were heavier had a lower likelihood of dating (Halpern, Udry, Campbell, & Suchindran, 1999).

Obese individuals experience psychological distress, stigmatization, and discrimination in work settings (Asthana, 2010; Flint et al., 2016; Henry & Kollamparambil, 2017). They are viewed as having less potential for success and leadership compared to those who are of typical weight (Flint et al., 2016). Heavier men face more interpersonal discrimination than nonheavy men (Ruggs, Hebl, & Williams, 2015), and evaluators rate products more negatively if sold by heavier men and women (Ruggs et al., 2015).

Not only do obese people face discrimination at work, but they are also shamed, blamed, and teased by family, friends, and health professionals alike (Rand et al., 2017), and, at least for adult women, this is associated with a reduction in self-esteem (Matz, Foster, Faith, & Wadden, 2002). IAFs lessen the amount of time they spend with friends and family to either consume more food or to recover from how it makes them feel (Gearhardt & Corbin, 2012b).

A meta-analysis revealed that having heavier weight is associated with having lower self-esteem (Miller & Downey, 1999). Having high self-esteem, on the other hand, acts as a moderator between interpersonal difficulties and the psychological distress that obese individuals experience (Salerno et al., 2015).

Working With Diverse Populations

Sex Differences

As noted in the previous section, heavier women face greater stigma and discrimination compared to men in both their relationships and in employment. Women with food addiction encounter more difficulties with emotional regulation and symptoms of depression and PTSD than non-food-addicted women (Hardy et al., 2018). Hardy et al. (2018) concluded that women with food addiction experience psychological characteristics similar to those with SUDs.

In an experiment where subjects watched a sad video of a child who died from cancer (thereby inducing a sad mood), women with food addiction spent more time attending to unhealthy food images while attention to healthy food choices decreased; there was no difference for non-IAFs in their attention to images (Frayn, Sears, & von Ranson, 2016). This experiment shows that negative mood states are associated with greater attention to unhealthy, highly palatable foods in food-addicted women.

Research has consistently demonstrated that women are more likely than men to experience food cravings (Rodriguez-Martin & Meule, 2015). Food cravings result from specific mood states and can be triggered by environmental cues (Rodriguez-Martin & Meule, 2015). Women are also slightly more likely than men to be obese (Fattore et al., 2014).

Adolescents and Youth

Lee and Gibbs (2013) stated that adolescent obesity in low- and middle-income countries had become an increasingly urgent issue. The statistics shared earlier also reflect the importance of dealing with childhood and adolescent obesity in the United States.

In children (ages 5–12), food addiction is associated with higher BMIs (Burrows et al., 2017). Symptoms of food addiction are highly correlated with childhood overeating, uncontrolled eating, emotional eating, preoccupation with food, and overconcern about body size (Merlo, Klingman, Malasanos, & Silverstein, 2009). Excessive overeating in children was related to both proximity and high palatability to food in a study by Laurent and Sibold (2016). As with adults, poor emotional regulation may also contribute to obesity in adolescence due to the eating of unhealthy foods (Orihuela, Mrug, & Boggiano, 2017).

Food addiction occurs at much higher rates in adolescents receiving psychiatric inpatient care compared to community samples of children, teenagers, and adults (Albayrak et al., 2017). In a sample of 50 adolescents attending a weight-loss hospital, 19 received a food addiction diagnosis. These teens did not differ from the other 31 on measures of BMI, age, and gender. The adolescent IAFs reported more days of bingeing, more frequent food cravings, higher amounts of overall eating, more depression, greater attentional and hyperactivity symptoms, and more concern about weight and shape compared to the nonaddicted group (Meule, Hermann, & Kubler, 2015).

In a sample of 181 obese African American adolescents, about 10% met criteria on the Yale Food Addiction Scale for Children (YFAS-C) for food addiction with highest scores on objective binge episodes. The strongest association between the nutrients examined in the study and YFAS-C scores was with trans fats, which is most frequently found in highly processed foods (Schulte, Jacques-Tiura, Gearhardt, & Naar, 2017).

Mies et al. (2017) sampled 2653 Dutch youth, ages 14–21, for food addiction. They found it was correlated with smoking, alcohol use, cannabis use, and sugar intake. Because adolescents are vulnerable to developing numerous addictions, Boyd, Harris, and Knight (2012) strongly encouraged clinicians to screen for these as part of routine practice and to deliver brief interventions as needed.

Race and Ethnicity

Bucchianeri et al. (2016) had a large population-based sample of teens (N = 2793: M = 14.4 years) of varying racial/ethnic groups participating in Eating and Activity in Teens, 2010. The sample was divergent both racially/ethnically (81%) and socioeconomically (54% low or low-middle income). In total, 29.0% were African American, 19.9% Asian, 18.9% White, 16.9% Hispanic, 3.7% Native American, and 11.6% were mixed race or other race (46.8% boys and 53.2% girls). Body dissatisfaction (BD) was dissimilar among groups; Asian American girls and boys experience the highest degree of BD. African American boys had the weakest association between body dissatisfaction and dieting/disordered eating.

In a cross-sectional survey about health behaviors including food addiction, 2.8% of 1067 low-income women (ages 18–40) obtained a diagnosis of food addiction. The prevalence did not vary by race/ethnicity, age group, education, income, or BMI (Berenson, Laz, Pohlmeier, Rahman, & Cunningham, 2015).

As a large number of IAFs also have a diagnosis of BED, the results of a study by Lydecker and Grilo (2016) may be applicable. Research clinicians completed structured interviews with 195 men and 560 women to arrive at a diagnosis of BED, and these participants then completed self-report measures. In total, 121 self-identified as Black, 54 as Hispanic, and 580 as White. The Black participants presented for treatment with the highest BMIs, but the White and Hispanic participants reported greater depression.

Nonpsychiatric Disabilities

Obesity and food addiction are not the same things (Davis & Carter, 2009), but they are strongly linked. There are no studies that specifically look at food addiction among disabled individuals, so the focus here is the relationship between obesity and disability. But is obesity itself a disability? The European Court of Justice ruled in 2014 that severe forms of obesity fall under disability protection legislation (Luck-Sikorski & Riedel-Heller, 2017). Luck-Sikorski and Riedel-Heller (2017) surveyed 1000 obese individuals in Germany regarding whether they thought obesity should itself be considered a disability. In the analysis, 38.2% agreed that it should, and heavier participants expressed more support for this opinion.

Surveys in the United States have indicated higher prevalence rates of obesity in intellectually challenged adults (Fisher, Hardie, Ranjan, & Peterson, 2017; Hoey et al., 2017). In the retrospective study of 40 adults with intellectual disability, the "prevalence of overweight, obese, and morbidly obese was 28%, 58%, and 23%, respectively" (Fisher et al., 2017, p. 387). Hoey et al. (2017) also found very high rates of overweight (28.2%) and obesity (46.8%) with 131 intellectually disabled participants (age 16–64). Many in the sample also had poor diet quality (e.g., excess of fats and sugar).

Obesity is more prevalent in intellectually challenged and developmentally delayed children (Bennett, Kolko, Chia, Elliott, & Kalarchian, 2017). Children with physical disabilities also are at high risk of becoming obese (McPherson et al., 2016). Children with autism spectrum disorders experience increased risk of becoming overweight or obese (Corvey, Menear, Preskitt, Goldfarb, & Menachemi, 2016). Cook, Li, and Heinrich (2015) used a nationally representative sample of 45,987 youth in the United States to establish that youth who have both a learning disability (LD) and ADHD are more likely to become obese, and those with only ADHD or LD are less likely to meet recommended physical activity levels.

Lee et al. (2016) analyzed a data set of 8032 individuals between ages 11 and 21 and found that youth who were developing obesity or had persistent obesity during adolescence had an increased likelihood of disability in young adulthood. Obese adults are more likely to experience lost time, illness, and disability in the workplace compared to those with a healthy BMI (Nowrouzi et al., 2016).

Elderly individuals in the United States who were both obese and receiving activity of daily living (ADL) assistance were compared to normal weight older adults in a retrospective study (N = 5612) to ascertain caregiving. The obese elderly individuals with disabilities were given less help to get out of bed and walk both inside and outside compared to the normal weight older individuals (Ankuda et al., 2017). The study was unable to ascertain whether caregivers knowingly or unwittingly provided more attention to normal weight elders who are not disabled.

Lesbian, Gay, Bisexual, and Transgender (LGBT)

Rainey, Furman, and Gearhardt (2018) found that, in a convenience sample of 356 participants (43.3% sexual minority), sexual minorities had nearly double the prevalence of food addiction (16.9%) compared to the heterosexual contingent (8.9%). Harassment by heterosexual individuals was claimed to be the cause of the increased food addiction, whereas being self-compassionate was concluded to be a protective factor. In a study of 642 male veterans of which 24 identified as gay or bisexual, the sexual minority group exhibited more ED symptoms on the YFAS than the heterosexual men, despite there being no difference between the two groups regarding BMI (Bankoff, Richards, Bartlett, Wolf, & Mitchell, 2016).

Although there is currently no study that looks at food addiction in transgender individuals, Duffy, Henkel, and Earnshaw (2016) stated that there is emerging research that suggests EDs may be more common in individuals who identify as transgender. In their online study, Duffy et al. found that none of their 84 transgender participants reported having had a positive experience with clinicians concerning treatment for their EDs.

War Veterans

Mitchell and Wolf (2016) noted that there is a positive correlation between PTSD and food addiction in the extant research. In a sample of primarily older male (N = 642) and female (N = 55) veterans who had been exposed to trauma, structural equation modeling revealed that PTSD was associated with EDs and food addiction symptoms. This suggests that PTSD is a risk factor for both EDs and food addiction. As noted in the previous section, sexual minority male veterans are also at higher risk for ED and food addiction (Bankoff et al., 2016).

Medications and Other Relevant Physical Interventions

Treatments for food addiction remain sparse (Yau et al., 2014). Treatments for obesity, on the other hand, are frequently reported in the literature. Many drugs that were initially approved were later withdrawn because of either safety concerns or poor efficacy (Davis et al., 2014).

Some medications proven helpful in promoting weight loss include dopamine reuptake inhibitors (e.g., bupropion), opioid antagonists (e.g., naltrexone), or other drugs combined that moderate dopamine activity (e.g., zonisamide and topiramate) (Wang et al., 2012). Bupropion, however, does not help individuals keep their weight off over the long term (Blumenthal & Gold, 2012). The only drug as of 2012 shown to promote weight loss and maintain diminished weight gain over more than 3 months is Rimonabant, which is a cannabinoid antagonist (Blumenthal & Gold, 2012). Davis et al. (2014) reported that two other approved medications include Lorcaserin and Qsymia.

Stimulants continue to be used as a pharmacological treatment for obesity (e.g., Phentermine; Blumenthal & Gold, 2012), but, because these drugs can be abused, they are not prescribed to patients with a history of drug abuse. Currently, the only drug approved by the U.S. Food and Drug Administration for the long-term management of obesity is Orlistat (Rosen & Aronne, 2012). According to Rosen and Aronne (2012), the drug that is most commonly used is Phentermine. Topiramate can help reduce food cravings (Davis et al., 2014).

Bariatric surgery is recommended in the literature as a long-term weight loss approach for those with a BMI of greater than 40 kg/m^2 or greater than 35 kg/m^2 if there are comorbidities (Davis et al., 2014). There are two main procedures for bariatric surgery that involve either restrictive or malabsorptive procedures (Davis et al., 2014). Details of these procedures can be found within the references in this section.

Although bariatric surgery is considered effective by many accounts, expected weight loss is 15% or more of initial weight (Davis et al., 2014; Vetter, Faulconbridge, Williams, & Wadden, 2012). Some individuals regain a substantial amount of weight several years following bariatric surgery (Vetter et al., 2012). Nearly 60% regain their weight by the 5-year mark (Tarman & Werdell, 2014).

Furthermore, such procedures are expensive and are associated with significant risks. These include, for example, gastric dumping syndrome, malnutrition from absorption difficulties, and an increased risk of bone fractures (Davis et al., 2014). About 22% of those who undergo gastric banding will require a subsequent surgery (Vetter et al., 2012). In a survey of 1900 bariatric surgery patients, alcohol abuse increased in the second year after gastric bypass surgery (Tarman & Werdell, 2014).

On a positive note, Sevincer, Konuk, Bozkurt, and Coskun (2016) tested 166 bariatric patients ($N = 166$ total; 38 male, 128 female) before surgery and 6 months and 12 months later. The researchers found that 57.8% of the preoperative participants met criteria for food addiction. At 6 and 12 months following surgery, however, the percentage of those who continued to have measured food addiction dropped to 7.2% and 13.7%, respectively. Food addiction decreased substantially following bariatric surgery. There was no difference between the weight lost when the addicted group was compared to the non-food-addicted group, however, which led the authors to conclude that follow-up studies should continue for 2 years instead of only 12 months.

INSIDE AN ADDICTED PERSON'S MIND

Joe, Age 36

I'm sure my story is the same as everyone else out there who is obese. At my last weigh-in, I was 324 pounds. Just a bit heavy given that I am only 5' 10". If there were one word to describe how I feel it would be disgusted. But it is more than that. Most of the time I don't want to look at myself in the mirror. I dread going to buy clothes, and even worse is when I go out to eat. People stare at what I order and at what I have on my plate. I notice they don't do that with everyone. Nope, they do it only with fat people. Maybe I would do the same if I wasn't one of them, but I have to tell you, every one of those looks hurts me more than you know. It makes me want to eat even more, and, usually, I do. I liken it to people living up to the stereotypes that others have of them. I have suspected that happens with many of our Indigenous peoples and gay folk.

I even tried jogging last summer but couldn't stand the ridicule, especially from smart-mouthed teenagers. Not to mention it was very hard on my knees and ankles. If you wonder why you don't see many overweight and obese people in aerobics classes or even at gyms for that matter, it is for those reasons. The heat of the workout pales in comparison to the heat of other people's judgment, ridicule, and that look that kills.

Was I always this heavy? No, I surely wasn't. Growing up I was just like other kids around me. But I grew up in a very judgmental and for the most part unloving family. My dad could never say anything nice to me or my two siblings. We were constantly berated. Why? I think dad just hated his job and took out his stress on us. He used to yell at Mom a fair amount as well. I don't know if I can blame anyone, however, for my obesity. I ended up this way, and it's simply what I have to deal with now.

I think about food all the time, but I wouldn't say that it is hunger that drives my eating. It's more that I feel empty inside, lonely, and for some reason desperate. Eating seems to relieve all that. I do my best to keep snacks down to a minimum, and I do pretty well at it. I rarely eat more than four chocolate bars between 9 and 5 pm and a few Twinkies.

It's another story after I get home, however. I cannot tell you how many times I have bought a 14-inch cheesecake and devoured it over the course of an evening. Of course, I have tried every diet. They don't work. After 2 days of dieting, I feel like I am going to rage, like someone on 'roids. I keep trying to control my eating, but look at me: a athetic mess of a human being.

I feel completely ashamed that I cannot stop eating all the crap I shove down my face nightly. It's at a point where I only go to food stores that have self-serve checkouts so I can avoid the cashier that notices when I buy cheesecake two or three times a week. Sometimes I try very hard to stop eating like this so, instead, I buy pizzas, steaks, rotisserie chickens, pizza pops, and a few fruits and vegetables. My work is exhausting, and so I seem to rarely get around to cooking the vegetables: instead, they rot in my fridge. Occasionally I'll have a banana with breakfast, but most of the fruit goes bad as well.

It doesn't matter what I buy. If I buy steak, I'll eat three of them at nighttime when I get home from work.

If I buy a rotisserie chicken, I eat the whole thing and go for two pizzas on top of it. A few hours later when I'm feeling devastated over how much I've eaten, I go out and buy a gallon of ice cream and finish most of it when I get home. Even then, what I crave is cheesecake.

I sleep poorly most nights because of indigestion and occasional severe heartburn. The next morning, I also feel horrible, usually shaky and often anxious. Once I sit down and eat a pound of bacon and eight or more eggs, the shakiness subsides. But I still feel anxious. I can't get out of my head the results from my last physical. My doctor said if I keep eating like this, I will surely bring on premature death. Deep down, I guess that's what I want. Better than this premature life I live.

Commentary

Joe presents many of the symptoms of both binge eating disorder and food addiction. Like most IAFs, he is obsessed with food and eats compulsively. Joe has told us that there is a substantial emotional component to his excessive eating. He has also tried unsuccessfully many times to reduce his eating of highly palatable foods. But he is drawn to those foods and prefers them greatly over the healthy alternatives of fruits and vegetables. His self-esteem has also suffered a great deal because of his weight and his inability to control this part of his life.

Discussion

1. Do you know of anyone who you suspect has become dependent on food? If "yes," which symptoms noted in the commentary apply to him or her?
2. Does this person have symptoms that are not listed in the commentary? If so, what are they?
3. If you were Joe's counselor, how would you go about helping him?

Specific Counseling Considerations

ROLEPLAY SCENARIOS

Roleplay in dyads with one of you acting as the counselor and the other as the counselee. If roleplay is not possible, work individually in writing out a list of your suggestions.

Roleplay #1

Gloria, age 25, came to see you because of problems she is having with her live-in boyfriend Jim, age 32. They met 3 years ago when Gloria was 170 pounds. She is 5'5" tall. Over the past 3 years, Gloria gained 80 pounds. She tells you that Jim was not happy about this, to begin with, but, on the weekend, he said he was going to leave if she gained another pound. Gloria confides in you that she cannot stop herself from eating and that she feels very vulnerable hearing this right now as her mother passed away just 5 weeks ago. As you talk to her, you discover that she has always had trouble regulating her emotions.

Roleplay #2

Ralph, age 48, came in to see you sounding very distraught. He just found out from his oncologist that he likely only has 6 months to live. His doctor told him that his cancer is related to the fact that Ralph weighs nearly 500 pounds. Ralph is insistent on going out with dignity and part of this for him is to gain control of his compulsive eating. Ralph is single, never married, and reports that he has only one close friend who lives 180 miles away. His parents are both deceased, and his 31-year-old sister, Diane, will have nothing to do with him. When you ask him about this, he tells you that this is because he always hoarded food and, when he lived with Diane for 2 years, his eating became so out of control that she put a lock on the fridge door. In a moment of emotional desperation, Ralph yanked so hard on it that it came off its hinges and needed to be replaced. As he did not have the money at the time, Diane ended up paying for it. Reportedly Diane has never forgiven him for that incident.

HOW WOULD AN ADDICTION COUNSELOR HELP THIS PERSON?

You are working as a professional counselor. You receive a phone call from Alice, a social worker from the local psychiatric ward of a nearby hospital. Alice asked you if you would be prepared to work with Eugene. Eugene is a 55-year-old morbidly obese unemployed accountant, and he was taken to the hospital by police 3 weeks ago. Eugene had attempted suicide through carbon monoxide, but luckily his wife found him minutes before brain damage occurred. He was completely despondent when he first entered the psychiatric ward, but now he is being released. You agree to work with Eugene. You soon find out that he has not worked in over 2 years despite improvements in the economy. Eugene tells you that he believes his inability to find employment comes down to discrimination against men of his age who are, in his words, "grossly fat and slovenly." Although it quickly becomes apparent that Eugene is still mildly to moderately depressed, he is motivated to receive counseling from you. As you collect his history, you discover that he has been obese since early childhood and that he presents all the symptoms of food addiction. Eugene is also concerned for his two children, both of whom are already sizably overweight.

Remember to view clients within their environmental contexts, keeping in mind societal, parental/familial, cultural/spiritual, and peer influences. Specifically, become aware of the impact that the following influences have and continue to have in your clients' lives: race, language, religion and spirituality, gender, familial migration history, sexual/affectional orientation, age and cohort, physical and mental capacities, socioeconomic situation and history, education, and history of traumatic experience.

1. What defines this person's environment, past and present?
2. Who is this person sitting in front of me, taking into account environmental and personal characteristics?
3. What defines the problem that he or she is presenting within their multicultural milieu?

Goals and Goal Setting

Unlike most of the other addictions in this book, one cannot live without food, so complete "abstinence" from eating is not a possibility. Tarman and Werdell (2014) offered several appropriate goals for a food addict. These include the following:

- Stop eating your favorite foods, such as doughnuts, croissants, ice cream, or whatever.
- Learn to view your favorite foods as drugs.
- Give up sugar.
- Give up saturated fats.
- Stop drinking sugar-laced soda.
- Abstain from all trigger foods.
- Minimize consumption of *all* processed foods.
- Don't give in to thinking that giving into craving even once is okay.
- Remember that dieting is often harder each time you begin again.
- Learn to refuse any unhealthy or calorie-rich food offered to you.
- Switch to foods with a low glycemic index such as cauliflower and broccoli.
- Disengage from one food at a time if needed. Some find it easier to give up all trigger foods at once.
- As addictions are all related, monitor yourself for indications that another addiction is growing as your food addiction is diminishing. If you are cross-addicted, consider stopping all of your addictions. Give up your addictions in the order in which they will kill you.
- Consider switching food addiction to a "positive addiction." Examples might include running 5 miles a day or knitting scarves.
- Learn adaptive coping skills and how to manage uncomfortable emotions.
- Become involved in a 12-step program or support group.

Some of the specialized programs for food addiction include the following (Tarman & Werdell, 2014):

- ACORN Food Dependency Recovery Services (details can be found at https://foodaddiction.com/). [Note that Phil Werdell, co-author of this citation, is the co-founder of ACORN.]

- Shades of Hope in Buffalo Gap, Texas (details can be found at http://shadesofhope.com/).
- Kay Sheppard at Kay's Place, Palm Bay, Florida (details can be found at https://kaysheppard.com/).
- The COR food recovery program, offered by the Retreat, Wayzata, Minnesota (details can be found at http://cormn.org/?utm_source=adCenter&utm_medium=CPC&utm_campaign=SearchLocal).
- Rebecca's House, Lake Forest, California (details can be found at http://www.rebeccashouse.org/).
- Turning Point, Tampa, Florida (details can be found at https://www.tpoftampa.com).
- Milestones in Recovery, Cooper City, Florida (details can be found at https://www.milestonesprogram.org/).

Stages of Change Strategies

The processes of change mentioned are based on those outlined by Connors, DiClemente, Velasquez, and Donovan (2013) and Prochaska, Norcross, and DiClemente (1994). The definitions for the various processes can be found in Chapter 6. Besides these processes, other strategies are included that have separate citations.

The University of Rhode Island Change Assessment Scale (URICA) is a helpful scale for determining where the client is currently at regarding the stages of change model. There are 24-, 28-, and 32-item versions of the scale. A 24-item version is published for alcohol or drug problems. The scale, however, is generic and can be easily adapted for use with other addictions. It is available with norms as a free download from https://www.guilford.com/add/miller11_old/urica.pdf.

Specific precontemplation strategies.

Please visit the section of this chapter called Relevant Mutual Support Groups, Websites, and Videos for free or low-cost information and resources that may help someone move out of precontemplation.

Food Addicts in Recovery Anonymous offer several stories of teens and young adults in recovery (go to https://www.foodaddicts.org/downloads/food_addiction_stories_of_teens_and_twenties_in_recovery-final_12_0801_readonly.pdf). Like attending a 12-step group, hearing or reading about the stories of others can help move a person from precontemplation to contemplation. Bing.com lists several videos that might be helpful as well (go to https://www.bing.com/videos/search?q=movies+about+food+addiction+or+food+addicts&qpvt=movies+about+food+addiction+or+food+addicts&FORM=VQFRML).

Looking at a healthy food plan allows clients to make internal comparisons to their eating patterns. Food Addicts Anonymous offers their FAA Food Plan (go to https://www.foodaddictsanonymous.org/faa-food-plan). Providing a copy of the YFAS may be another helpful method of helping clients develop early insight into their problem. Watching a 2004 movie called *Lbs.* (trailer can be found at https://www.youtube.com/watch?v=69ZDSkE8Nzk), which is both a comedy and a drama, might also increase awareness.

Specific contemplation strategies.

The strategies for dealing with contemplation include emotional arousal, consciousness-raising, self-re-evaluation, and helping relationships. Regarding emotional arousal, attending a 12-step meeting might increase one's sense of urgency in deciding to gain control as a food addict. Also, having clients think about how their weight issue has affected them may increase their emotional arousal.

Consciousness-raising may be fostered through looking at the negative consequences of being overweight or obese, which may include its impact on physical health, emotional health, relationships, and employment. Another idea is for clients to attend a Weight Watchers meeting or Jenny Craig meeting as a way of increasing awareness.

Self-re-evaluation helps clients look at both sides of an issue. Having clients both compare and contrast the benefits and drawbacks of being overweight or obese might be helpful here. As with other addictions, helping relationships during this stage focus on gaining and sustaining support from significant others.

Specific preparation strategies.

Remember that the primary goal of the preparation stage is to help clients create commitment toward changing. Working with the client to establish goals and collaboratively decide on how these will be achieved is the main focus. Some suggested goals were included in the earlier section of the chapter called Goals and Goal Setting. Removing highly palatable foods from one's home is also advisable, as is ensuring that there is an ample supply of healthy foods.

As with other addictions, "going public" with the change project often provides deeper commitment to goal attainment. It is worth suggesting to clients that they place affirmations and slogans in common areas, perhaps especially on or around the fridge and food cupboards/pantries. Some examples of this include the following:

- Eat un-processed foods.
- I will increasingly enjoy healthy foods.
- Sugar and fats are the enemies.
- I am succeeding at my goal.
- I am worth it!

Other ideas for *before* their chosen quit day (i.e., preparation strategies) can be found in Appendix B.

Specific action strategies.

A longitudinal study that began with 90 women who were overweight or obese completed a 7- month weight loss intervention. Only 86 completed follow-up surveys 12 and 24 months later following the end of treatment. Participants who lost at least 10% of their initial weight and maintained their weight loss were defined as successful. At the end of 24 months, 27 participants (31.3%) were successful, and 59 (68.6%) were not. What distinguished the two groups was that the successful women experienced greater weight reduction during the weight loss intervention, they had lower scores on disinhibition (i.e., overconsuming food in response to stimuli such as emotions or alcohol), and they had lower scores on food addiction (Sawamoto et al., 2017).

Cattivelli et al. (2015) argued that acceptance and commitment therapy would be helpful in dealing with the symptoms of food addiction. The authors reported that this approach is often used to promote healthier lifestyles and improve psychological well-being in many different contexts that include addictions. Similarly, Hirsch (2008) found that using logotherapy was useful with one patient with food addiction. According to Werdell (2012), efficacious treatments for food addiction need to address five components, including "physical craving, loss of control, withdrawal, tolerance or progression, and biochemical denial" (p. 355).

Davis and Carter (2009) recommended stimulus control techniques (e.g., limit the availability of highly palatable foods) and cue exposure with response prevention (CERP). The way CERP works is by repeatedly presenting relevant food cues (e.g., foods that an IAF finds most appealing) but preventing the response, which is eating. CERP has been well-established in various small-scale studies with binge eaters and substance abusers. Davis and Carter remarked that the typical cognitive-behavioral therapy (CBT) model recommends including binge foods into one's daily meal plan but, from an addiction perspective, this is contraindicated. Although many writers and researchers like Davis and Carter recommend that IAFs avoid highly palatable foods on a permanent basis, this remains debatable, and further research is needed to establish the best approach to both promote and sustain recovery from food addiction (Setnick, as cited in Yau et al., 2014).

Other behavior modification techniques may prove helpful as well. Yau et al. (2014) included the following: (a) don't engage in other activities while eating, (b) throw out leftovers, (c) write out a grocery list, (d) avoid shopping when hungry, (e) eat single-serving foods, (f) buy foods that require preparation, (g) carry limited amounts of money, (h) eat meals with others, and (i) brush teeth after eating.

Weinstein, Zlatkes, Gingis, and Lejoyeux (2015) conducted a longitudinal study with 60 women who participated in Compulsive Eating Anonymous, which is one of the 12-step programs. They measured food craving, anxiety, depression, and self-efficacy at the beginning of the program, after 1 year, and after 5 years. Following 5 years, the participants had lower scores on anxiety and depression. However, this change was not noted in measures of food addiction or self-efficacy.

Carlisle, Buser, and Carlisle (2012) wrote about working with children who are IAFs. They suggested that eating patterns are taught to children by their parents, which means that targeting the parents' eating habits may be beneficial. Solution-focused brief therapy, motivational interviewing, and providing education about self-regulation were three suggested approaches to assisting in this work with parents.

Grilo (2012) reported that interpersonal psychotherapy (IPT) and dialectical behavior therapy have proven helpful for treating BED. These approaches might also be helpful for food addiction (Yau et al., 2014). However, neither approach produced weight loss. IPT is an approach that combines elements of psychodynamic psychotherapy and CBT approaches. The focus is usually on the connection between current symptoms and interpersonal problems (Yau et al., 2014).

Yau et al. (2014) recommended family therapy focused on the relationship between family members and significant others. Yau et al. suggested three foci for family therapy: (a) dealing with family disruption, stresses, and losses, (b) minimizing enabling behaviors, and (c) rectifying poor child-rearing practices and lack of monitoring by parents.

Wansink (2012) described how portion size influences how much people eat. One strategy related to this is to eat off smaller plates. For example, 4 ounces of meat on a 12-inch plate looks small compared to the same 4 ounces on a 6-inch plate. Another suggestion was to use small spoons to serve or to eat from a bowl. Wansink noted how the size of dinner plates increased from 1900 to 2010. Furthermore, the greater the variety of foods available, the more people will pick from several, thereby eating more than if fewer choices were available. Consequently, avoiding buffets is a good idea.

Dimitrijevic et al. (2015) suggested several interventions for IAFs including the following:

- Become aware of the signals that trigger unhealthy eating and avoid these triggers.
- Eat only when true hunger is felt. On a scale of 0 (starvation) to 10 (overeating), avoid either extreme and eat when at a 2 or 3 and stop when feeling satiated (5 or 6).
- Do not use food to deal with emotional distress; instead, use constructive coping strategies.
- Become informed about the impact of food processing and marketing on your food choices.
- Engage in regular exercise. Exercise increases the number of dopamine receptors in the brain.

Besides dopamine, research has also found that exercise helps to stabilize mood and promote sleep (Blumenthal et al., 2012). One study found little communality among 5000 Americans who had lost at least 30 pounds and kept this weight off for a year with a further weight loss totaling 70 pounds maintained over 6 years. One striking similarity, however, was these individuals exercised for an average of 1 hour per day (Gorman, 2004).

Additional ideas offered by writers/researchers include the following:

- "Eat food, mostly plants, not too much" (Pollan, as cited in Kabat-Zinn, 2013, p. 522).
- Drinking green tea or green tea extract can promote weight loss and reduce weight regain (Evatt & Griffiths, 2012).
- Mindful eating can help create separation of emotions from hunger and reduce the amount of food consumed in a binge (Epel, Tomiyama, & Dallman, 2012).
- Consider eliminating all sugar, flour (Rosenberg, 2012), processed foods, trans fats, hydrogenated fats, and artificial sweeteners (Yau et al., 2014).
- Avoid caffeine and liquid calories as these are associated with cravings (Yau et al., 2014).
- When invited out for dinner, bring your own prepared meal with you (Rosenberg, 2012).
- Consider fasting for one day each week, allowing yourself only water. It will reduce the desire for sugar (Neufeld, as cited in Milkman & Sunderwirth, 2010).
- Find alternative sources of reward other than eating and food (Davis & Carter, 2009).

The research focused on the benefit of nutrition counseling for food addicts remains limited (Yau et al., 2014), and most weight-loss approaches have been ineffective with IAFs (Davis et al., 2014). Individuals have a "setpoint," which means that their body's metabolism slows down or speeds up to maintain a constant weight (Milkman & Sunderwirth, 2010). Furthermore, most studies find that people regain the weight they lost on diets over the long term, and some end up even heavier (Milkman & Sunderwirth, 2010). On a positive note, however, changing one's lifestyle comprehensively can slow down, arrest, and even reverse the progression of heart disease and early-stage prostate cancer (Kabat-Zinn, 2013).

Nonetheless, no one denies the benefit of sticking with a healthy meal plan. Below are just a few examples of meal plans and/or recipes:

- https://robbwolf.com/what-is-the-paleo-diet/meal-plans-shopping-guides/
- https://www.verywellfit.com/an-example-of-a-healthy-balanced-meal-plan-2506647
- http://www.eatingwell.com/category/4286/meal-plans/
- https://www.healthyeating.org/Healthy-Eating/Meals-Recipes/Meal-Planner
- https://www.healthymealplans.com/
- http://www.personal-nutrition-guide.com/free-meal-plans.html

It is important to remember that true recovery for addiction comes from a very deep place. Addiction is a general condition, and the best results are going to occur by "working the program" (Blumenthal et al., 2012, p. 325). This refers to maintaining a commitment to change through the program however it is constructed, but it is also about working on the underlying mental, emotional, and spiritual issues that have triggered this addiction in the first place (Werdell, 2012).

Werdell (2012) stated that there is little emphasis on food addiction prevention at the national level in the United States. Furthermore, there are few clinicians trained to work with those in the later stages of food addiction (Werdell, 2012). The only in-depth experiential training program in the United States is offered by Werdell's ACORN Food Dependency and Recovery Services (go to https://foodaddiction.com/) and no degree programs are currently offered.

Tarman (2016) opined that the scarcity of food addiction counselors "borders on criminal" (para. 3). She recommended that counselors who want to specialize in food addiction should pursue a master's degree and then specialize in food addiction. The only internationally accredited food addiction counseling program offered in the world so far is the International Food Addiction Counselor Training program. It is held online with 18 weekly lessons and includes assignments, a final project, and examinations (see http://infact.is/ for details). Other ideas for *beginning* their chosen quit day (i.e., action strategies) can be found in Appendix B.

Specific maintenance strategies and relapse prevention.

Note: Maintenance strategies and relapse prevention are also, for many, partly facilitated by regular attendance at relevant mutual support groups. A list of such mutual support groups and helpful websites is found in an upcoming section entitled Relevant Mutual Support Groups, Websites, and Videos.

One of the strategies for preventing relapse is maintaining awareness of "red flags" (Tarman & Werdell, 2014, p. 176). Some examples of these include if the IAF begins keeping food secrets; daydreams about food; begins to pity self and feels jealous of others who can eat whatever they want; feels impatient, exhausted, or irritable; or begins to slip in their recovery routines (e.g., self-care, eating highly palatable foods). Another caution is not to allow the food addiction to become a different addiction. Relapse studies reveal that the most common precipitators of relapse are both negative and positive emotional states (Mason & Higley, 2012). Learning to deal with stress is essential to helping prevent relapse in all addictions (Mason & Higley, 2012). Other ideas for relapse prevention can be found in Appendix C.

Motivational Interviewing

As you may recall, the four processes of motivational interviewing including engaging, focusing, evoking, and planning. (Pertaining to Chapter 6's description of motivational interviewing, the following is an example of the process called *focusing*.)

Client: Given my history, it certainly makes sense that I have acted as a food addict for the last 20 years, Richard.
Counselor: I am glad to see that you are ready to take responsibility for this, Omar.
Client: Yes, but I don't know where to start.
Counselor: How would you feel if we work together on this?
Client: I would like that very much.
Counselor: What do you think will work for you, Omar?
Client: I honestly don't know. That's why I am coming to see you I guess.
Counselor: Ha-ha, that is certainly understandable. I know how overwhelming this must seem, given your struggle with this for so many years. What might even a small step look like for you?
Client: Well, perhaps I could stop eating at fast food outlets.
Counselor: That is an excellent suggestion! How difficult do you think that would be?
Client: I have never tried to do this before so I'm not sure.
Counselor: It certainly sounds like a very good idea that you could start with. Besides this, what other change might you be able to start now?
Client: I was hoping that you could give me some ideas here.
Counselor: Okay, I will certainly do my best. You mentioned to me that you nearly always go to bed on a full stomach. Can you imagine what changing that might look like?
Client: For starters, I think I'll have to clean out just about everything in my fridge! I know I'm saying that half jokingly but I'm serious.
Counselor: I know you are, and you are very brave to realize that some major changes need to occur for you. I'm guessing what you are saying is that you will need to do some rearranging of your eating habits.

Insight-Oriented Interventions

Although "addiction is a pressing issue for psychoanalysis" (Johnson, 2003, p. 29), there is little work that has been done on it since the 1970s. Perhaps one reason this has occurred is due to the continuing discovery of the impact of neuroscience in addictive processes. Johnson (2003) wrote that a neuropsychoanalytic approach is needed today.

Neuropsychoanalysis is the integration of psychoanalysis (mind) and biology (body), a field that focuses on the impact of damage to various cerebral structures on personality, motivation, and complex emotions (Johnson, 2003). Johnson (2003) pressed for more work to be done in this area in not only substance addictions but also in behavioral addictions, including food addiction.

Spiritual Interventions

Tonkin's (2006) dissertation compared results from nine women who attended a 16-week obesity intervention using CBT and another nine who attended CBT that also contained a spiritual component. There were no differences between the two groups regarding weight loss on any outcome measure. Tonkin concluded that, despite this, CBT plus spirituality might be attractive to some participants. In another dissertation, participants used spiritual recovery to gain freedom from food addiction (Ortigara Crego, 2007).

A study focused on 2378 African Americans in central Mississippi who measured higher on varying measures of spirituality did not differ in weight from those who scored lower. However, spirituality did reduce the likelihood of African Americans having lower energy intake, less alcohol use, and less likelihood of lifetime smoking. In another study using the same dataset, Bruce, Beech, Griffith, and Thorpe (2016) found in 105 12- to 19-year-old African American males that those who practiced daily spirituality were more likely to attempt to lose weight than those who were less spiritually oriented.

In a study of 102 women (19–57 years), Strenger, Schnitker, and Felke (2016) found that participants who had an insecure-anxious attachment to God had an increase in emotional eating due to sociocultural pressures. Similarly, Pirutinsky, Rosmarin, and Holt (2012) found in a sample of 212 Jewish participants that religious coping buffered maladaptive eating.

There is no question that some individuals find that spirituality replaces the void left when they stop doing their addictive behavior (Tarman & Werdell, 2014). Many addicts find this support in their commitment to 12-step programs, particularly when they have enough "clean time" to be able to help others who are struggling similarly by acting as a sponsor (Tarman & Werdell, 2014). As Tarman and Werdell (2014) noted, "the spiritual dimension of the twelve-step fellowships is the single biggest reason members claim they are able to remain abstinent over the long term" (p. 197).

Cognitive-Behavioral Therapy

> "As with any chronic illness, we rarely have an opportunity to cure, but we do have an opportunity to treat the patient with respect. Such an experience may be the greatest gift that [we] can give an obese patient" (Stunkard, as cited in Lagrotte & Foster, 2012, pp. 293–294)

CBT can be facilitated using the triple column technique. It can be used both by counselors in their work with clients and by clients alone. The full instructions for using the technique are found in Chapter 6. The following are some of the cognitions that can be problematic for clients with this addiction.

Automatic Thought or Belief	Questioning It	Healthier Thought or Belief
I am so fat and ugly.		I need to love myself as I am so that I have the compassion to work on achieving my goals.
I can get away with eating my favorite food just one last time.		I need to accept that I am a food addict, and that means I need to avoid my trigger foods.
I'm so upset I just need to eat.		When I'm upset, I will focus on mindfulness, meditation, relaxation, exercise, and healthy thinking.
The void I feel is overwhelming.		I am already a whole and complete person, but I will constructively address my needs of which I am becoming increasingly aware.
I think about food all the time.		I will think about healthy food choices and expand my thoughts to include other goals and topics.

There are currently no guidelines for CBT with food addiction (Yau et al., 2014). Several behavioral interventions, however, have been recommended. Some of these regarding stimulus control were noted earlier.

The following ideas are suggested by Lagrotte and Foster (2012). As a general rule, the more a counselor talks during a session, the less effective the session will be for the client. Clients need to become aware of antecedent events (i.e., cues) that trigger unhealthy food choices and overeating. Helping clients become aware of these triggers and learn new responses to them is therefore important. Much of this work comes under the rubric of classical conditioning. The idea is to disconnect the "antecedents (times, places, activities, emotions, and people) from unwanted behaviors" (Lagrotte & Foster, 2012, p. 290).

Behavioral goals are very specific. Some appropriate goals include the following:

- Walk five times a week.
- Increase meal duration by 10 minutes.
- Decrease the number of self-derogatory statements.

Once goals are specified, clients are provided help to identify factors that will either hinder or help facilitate achieving their goals. For example, if watching television leads to overeating, then changing where one eats to a different location will help weaken the link.

Given that individuals receiving meal replacements achieve greater weight reduction than those who do not, this suggests that increasing structure may improve weight loss. Studies have shown that self-monitoring (e.g., maintain food and activity records) and physical activity are consistently correlated with better weight control both in the short and long term. Despite the positive efforts that can be made by clients and counselors alike, "it is important to note that the most frequent outcome of weight loss treatment is weight regain" (Lagrotte &Foster, 2012, p. 293).

CBT is a well-established treatment for BED. It has been shown to improve self-concept, reduce depression, and reduce body-image dissatisfaction (Yau et al., 2014). The three main aspects of doing CBT with EDs include (a) having clients keep diaries of what they eat and antecedents to eating these foods, (b) identifying unhealthy perceptions about food and body image (e.g., "I'm so fat and ugly"), and (c) removing cues that promote unhealthy perceptions (e.g., remove scales and mirrors) (Milkman & Sunderwirth, 2010).

DBT is used to treat BED either individually or in groups to teach mindfulness, distress tolerance skills, and emotional regulation (Yau et al., 2014). Part of teaching these skills is showing individuals how to embrace or accept challenging situations instead of trying to fight them (Yau et al., 2014). CBT and DBT, however, did not lead to significant weight loss for BED patients (Yau et al., 2014). The National Institute Health and Care Excellence (NICE) recommends CBT-ED, which is an adapted version of CBT focused on EDs (its guidelines can be found at https://www.nice.org.uk/guidance/ng69/chapter/Recommendations#treating-binge-eating-disorder).

RELEVANT MUTUAL SUPPORT GROUPS, WEBSITES, AND VIDEOS

Mutual Support Groups

For the Addicted Individual

1. Food Addicts in Recovery Anonymous (FA). https://www.foodaddicts.org/

   Quoted from website:

   Food Addicts in Recovery Anonymous (FA) offers relief from the symptoms of eating disorders and guidance on living in recovery.

2. Food Addicts Anonymous. http://www.foodaddictsanonymous.org/about

   Quoted from website:

   Food Addicts Anonymous is an organization that believes that Food Addiction is a biochemical disorder that occurs at a cellular level and therefore cannot be cured by willpower or by therapy alone.

3. Food Addiction Support Group. https://www.dailystrength.org/group/food-addiction

   The group's website says that it currently has about 900 members.

For the Partner and/or Family

These groups are intended to help family members refrain from behaviors that may trigger the addict. They also target underlying maladaptive thoughts and behaviors of the co-addict. Lastly, they focus on facilitating spiritual growth.

1. Food Addicts in Recovery Anonymous (FA) encourages partners and/or family members to attend a meeting to learn more about their fellowship. https://www.foodaddicts.org/family-friends

2. Co-Dependents Anonymous (CoDA). http://coda.org/

   Quoted from website:

   Welcome to Co-Dependents Anonymous, a fellowship of men and women whose common purpose is to develop healthy relationships. The only requirement for membership is a desire for healthy and loving relationships.

3. Communicating With Someone Who Has an Addiction. This website is not a group but is a helpful resource for the partner and/or family. https://www.verywell.com/how-to-talk-to-an-addict-22012

Websites

1. Food Addiction Institute. https://foodaddictioninstitute.org/
2. Addictions.com. https://www.addictions.com/food/
3. ACORN Food Dependency Services. https://foodaddiction.com/resources/
4. Healthline / Food Addiction. https://www.healthline.com/health/addiction/food#overview1
5. Eating Disorder HOPE. https://www.eatingdisorderhope.com/information/food-addiction
6. Huffington Post, Food Addiction: Could it explain why 70 percent of Americans are fat? https://www.huffingtonpost.com/dr-mark-hyman/food-addiction-could-it-e_b_764863.html

Videos

To view these videos, search their titles on YouTube.

1. *Food Addiction: Inside Food Addicts in Recovery Anonymous - The Feed.*

2. *Freaky Eaters | Sugar Addict (Full Episode) | Only Human.*
3. *The Science of Addictive Food.*
4. *Obsessed: My Addiction to Food and My Journey to Health | Diane Smith | TEDxSpringfield.*
5. *Hooked, Hacked, Hijacked: Reclaim Your Brain from Addictive Living: Dr. Pam Peeke at TEDxWallStreet.*

RELEVANT PHONE APPS

Generic Addiction Apps

Note: Generic apps are described in Chapter 6.

This list is not exhaustive. New apps are continually being developed. Do an Internet search to find out the latest apps available. Most are for specific addictions but some, such as these four, are generic.

1. I Am Sober. https://play.google.com/store/apps/details?id=com.thehungrywasp.iamsober
2. Sober Time. https://play.google.com/store/apps/details?id=com.sociosoft.sobertime
3. Pocket Rehab: Get Sober & Addiction Recovery. https://play.google.com/store/apps/details?id=com.getpocketrehab.app
4. Loop Habit Tracker. https://play.google.com/store/apps/details?id=org.isoron.uhabits

Specialized Apps

1. CraveMASTER. http://appcrawlr.com/ios/cravemaster#authors-description

   Quoted from website:

   CraveMASTER's underlying principles are based on 15 years of Mind-Body Medicine research and development . . .
2. Food Addiction Calendar. https://itunes.apple.com/US/app/id1112385170?mt=8

   Quoted from website:

   Food addiction calendar helps you notice that you are addicted to food, and helps you stay accountable for when you let yourself become a victim of binge eating. Use food addiction calendar to stop eating obscene amounts of food and lower your risk for many diseases.
3. Food Addiction Self Help Handbook: Overcoming. https://appadvice.com/app/food-addiction-self-help-handbook-overcoming/1165182587

   Quoted from website:

   Tutorial Video: Step by step guide and coaching to help you obtain in-depth understanding and knowledge.

JOURNALS AND CONFERENCES

Journals

There is no journal dedicated to food addiction currently. Articles about food addiction can be found in generic addiction journals, journals dealing with EDs, and nutrition journals. The following are a few of these:

1. *Appetite*. Quoted from website:

   Appetite is an international research journal specializing in cultural, social, psychological, sensory and physiological influences on the selection and intake of foods and drinks. It covers normal and disordered eating and drinking and welcomes studies of both human and non-human animal behavior toward food. Appetite publishes research reports, reviews and commentaries. Thematic special issues appear regularly. From time to time the journal carries abstracts from professional meetings. https://www.journals.elsevier.com/appetite/
2. *Eating Behaviors*. Quoted from website:

   Eating Behaviors is an international peer-reviewed scientific journal publishing human research on the etiology, prevention, and treatment of obesity, binge eating, and eating disorders in adults and children. Studies related to the promotion of healthy eating patterns to treat or prevent medical conditions (e.g., hypertension, diabetes mellitus, cancer) are also acceptable. Two types of manuscripts are encouraged: (1) Descriptive studies establishing functional relationships between eating behaviors and social, cognitive, environmental, attitudinal, emotional or biochemical factors; (2) Clinical outcome research evaluating the efficacy of prevention or treatment protocols.

   While theoretical orientations are diverse, the emphasis of the journal is primarily empirical. That is, sound experimental design combined with valid, reliable assessment and evaluation procedures are a requisite for acceptance. Uncontrolled clinical demonstrations and case studies are not accepted for publication. A limited number of reviews are published. https://www.journals.elsevier.com/eating-behaviors/

3. *Journal of Addictive Medicine*. https://journals.lww.com/journaladdictionmedicine/pages/default.aspx

4. *Journal of Addiction and Prevention*.

   https://ca.linkedin.com/in/journal-of-addiction-and-dependence-1a5266102

5. *International Journal of Eating Disorders*.

   http://onlinelibrary.wiley.com/journal/10.1002/(ISSN)1098-108X/homepage/ProductInformation.html

6. *Addiction*.

   http://addictionjournal.org/

Conferences

1. The World Academy of Science, Engineering and Technology (https://waset.org/) advertises several conferences across many disciplines, including the International Conference on Eating Disorders, Disordered Eating and Food Addiction. Their description of the 2018 conference was as follows (quoted from website):

   The 20th International Conference on Eating Disorders, Disordered Eating and Food Addiction aims to bring together leading academic scientists, researchers and research scholars to exchange and share their experiences and research results on all aspects of Eating Disorders, Disordered Eating and Food Addiction. It also provides a premier interdisciplinary platform for researchers, practitioners and educators to present and discuss the most recent innovations, trends, and concerns as well as practical challenges encountered and solutions adopted in the fields of Eating Disorders, Disordered Eating and Food Addiction.

2. The Food Addiction Institute organizes educational events including conferences. For details visit https://foodaddictioninstitute.org/

   Quoted from website:

   The Food Addiction Institute is an educational institution. Our priority is to reach out to healthcare and allied health providers who serve patients or clients who are or may be addicted to (dependent on) one or more foods or to volume eating.

   We provide up to date information about initial screening, diagnosis and treatment.

   We also provide information to those afflicted with food addiction (substance dependency).

   We refer them to sources of information, support and appropriate professional assistance.

   All webinars to date can be viewed by clicking links on their website.

COUNSELING SCENARIO

As you are reading, imagine that you are the client in this scenario. Note the areas in which the session could be improved on the part of the counselor.

Your name is Elvia, age 21, and you are in the final year of college. Your family emigrated to the United States from Mexico about 6 years ago, and you continue to identify as mostly Mexican in your worldview. You have struggled with weight since you were beginning school at age 6. It is March and now seems like a good time to begin focusing on losing weight. Your appointment is with Rebecca, a middle-aged counselor who strikes you as impeccably dressed.

- You: Wow, I just have to complement you on that amazing suit you are wearing. You look awesome in it!
- Counselor: Thank you, Elvia. I bought it at Nordstrom's just last week.
- You: I wish I could afford to buy from there.
- Counselor: I likely paid too much for it, but I had my eye on it for months. What would you like to talk about today?
- You: My weight. I weigh 210 pounds, and at 5' 3", I need to do something about it.
- Counselor: Let me begin by suggesting that you join my gym for no-impact aerobic classes. They have a great instructor there.
- You: Really? Where do you go?
- Counselor: It's an exclusive club . . . I can probably get you a membership for less than $200 per month.
- You: I cannot afford that! I'm living off my parents as it is.
- Counselor: Well, how important is losing this weight to you?

- You: A lot. I want to start dating, but I don't feel I can until I lose at least 60 pounds. I just can't afford a gym like that.
- Counselor: That is too bad. I want you to start walking for 2 hours a day then.
- You: Two hours? You know after a full day at school, a few hours of homework, helping my mom cook dinner, do my chores, and spend time with my younger brother, I don't have any time left!
- Counselor: You certainly are busy, Elvia. Tell me about your eating habits.
- You: I have learned to eat smaller meals many times a day. Most of my meals include tortillas, queso, either carne or pollo, and salsa.
- Counselor: How many meals do you eat a day?
- You: Usually three, but I snack a lot—it depends on how depressed I feel.
- Counselor: Okay, well first off then, let's have you cut out the snacks. Furthermore, cut out the tortillas and cheese and use low-calorie bread without butter.
- You: Hummmm, I don't know. My mama makes my meals for me, and I cannot tell her what to buy.
- Counselor: You certainly have a lot of excuses. Can't you see that your mom is an enabler? Have you thought of talking to her assertively?
- You: Well, in my family, you don't talk back to Mama. I will try to get more exercise and cut down on my snacking.
- Counselor: Very good. You won't be depressed after you lose your excess weight.

From the Client's Perspective

1. How would you feel if you had met with this counselor?
2. What is missing for you in this dialogue?
3. What would you find more helpful from a counselor in this scenario?

From the Counselor's Perspective

1. What is interfering with developing a working alliance?
2. Going back to the Common Counseling Mistakes list in Chapter 6, which mistakes is the counselor making with Elvia?
3. As counselor, what else would you like to know before giving advice?
4. What cultural differences are not being respected?

INDIVIDUAL EXERCISES

1. Obese IAFs deal both with the psychological consequences of being an addict and the physical implications of excess weight. Most people of normal weight have little idea how difficult it is to live each day carrying so many extra pounds. In this experiential exercise, get a sense of this by wearing a heavy backpack for several hours. The impact of this extra weight will be especially felt if you decide to do some climbing and other forms of aerobic exercise while wearing the backpack.
2. With permission, talk to one of more obese individuals who would be interested to find out if their obesity may be partly or fully caused by food addiction. Have them complete the YFAS before looking at the results together. Then lead a discussion about the concept of food addiction. Do your interviewees believe food addiction exists? Why or why not?
3. Watch the 21-minute YouTube video called *Freaky Eaters* with a friend (go to https://www.youtube.com/watch?v=smBgwCmXhY8). Kelly eats only cheesy potatoes—she is revolted by other foods. After watching the video, talk with your friend about the similarities and differences between Kelly's eating habits and your own.

CLASSROOM EXERCISES

1. Have the class split into two: half the class takes the perspective that food addiction exists, and the other half takes the opposing view. Allow the debate to continue until all reasons for and against seeing compulsive eating as an addiction have been expressed. Have a team member write the stated reasons of its side on the board.

2. In small groups of three or four, have groups discuss one of the following topics: (a) what could the food industry do to discourage food addiction?, (b) what could the government do to help prevent food addiction?, or (c) what could families do (parents and siblings) to help each other avoid becoming addicted to certain foods?

3. As a class or again in small groups, lead a discussion about ways that healthy foods can be more appealing to eat. Be as specific as possible. Consider which spices can bring out richer flavors in fruits and vegetables, for example. Mexican Americans and Asian Indians may have several examples to offer here.

CHAPTER SUMMARY

Like other addictions, food addiction is characterized by loss of control, cravings, tolerance, withdrawal, and negative consequences. Neuroscience has revealed that circuitry and neurotransmitters are involved in food addiction in a way similar to how they're involved in substance addiction. As is true of other addictions, a high percentage of IAFs have suffered varying traumas in childhood. They continue to experience difficulty controlling stress and negative emotions as they mature into adulthood.

What makes food addiction challenging to break is the fact that people need to eat, unlike in the case of substance addictions. The literature identifies only certain foods, however, as having addictive properties. These are referred to as highly palatable foods, and they are processed foods that usually contain unhealthy amounts of sugars and fats.

Food addiction is not currently listed in DSM. Instead, presently there are three EDs included: anorexia nervosa, BN, and BED. Although food addiction has qualities in common with these three EDs, it is also a distinct disorder. There are thought to be two different types of IAFs. One type often eats throughout the day, and the other binges on food episodically. Although many IAFs are overweight or obese, and food addiction is hypothesized to be one of the causes of obesity, many are also of normal weight.

REFERENCES

Abdollahi, A., & Talib, M. A. (2015). Sedentary behaviour and social anxiety in obese individuals: The mediating role of body esteem. *Psychology, Health & Medicine*, *20*, 205–209.

Agh, T., Kovacs, G., Pawaskar, M., Supina, D., Inotai, A., & Voko, Z. (2015). Epidemiology, health-related quality of life and economic burden of binge eating disorder: A systematic literature review. *Eating and Weight Disorders*, *20*(1), 1–12.

Albayrak, O., Focker, M., Kliewer, J., Esber, S., Peters, T., de Zwaan, M., & Hebebrand, J. (2017). Eating-related psychopathology and food addiction in adolescent psychiatric inpatients. *European Eating Disorders Review*, *25*(3), 214–220.

Ames, G. E., Heckman, M. G., Diehl, N. N., Grothe, K. B., & Clark, M. M. (2015). Further statistical and clinical validity for the Weight Efficacy Lifestyle Questionnaire-Short form. *Eating Behaviors*, *18*, 115–119.

Ankuda, C. K., Harris, J., Ornstein, K., Levine, D. A., Langa, K. M., & Kelley, A. S. (2017). Caregiving for older adults with obesity in the United States. *Journal of the American Geriatrics Society*, *65*, 1939–1945.

Asthana, H. S. (2010). Obesity and psychological distress: A growing health problem. *Social Science International*, *26*(2), 179–192.

Avena, N. M., & Hoebel, B. G. (2012). Bingeing, withdrawal, and craving. In K. D. Brownell & M. S. Gold (Eds.), *Food and addiction: A comprehensive handbook* (pp. 206–213). New York, NY: Oxford University Press.

Bak-Sosnowska, M. (2017). Differential criteria for binge eating disorder and food addiction in the context of causes and treatment of obesity. *Psychiatria Polska*, *51*(2), 247–259.

Bankoff, S. M., Richards, L. K., Bartlett, B., Wolf, E. J., & Mitchell, K. S. (2016). Examining weight and eating behavior by sexual orientation in a sample of male veterans. *Comprehensive Psychiatry*, *68*, 134–139.

Bennett, E. A., Kolko, R. P., Chia, L., Elliott, J. P., & Kalarchian, M. A. (2017). Treatment of obesity among youth with intellectual and developmental disabilities: An emerging role for telenursing. *Western Journal of Nursing Research*, *39*, 1008–1027.

Berenson, A. B., Laz, T. H., Pohlmeier, A. M., Rahman, M., & Cunningham, K. A. (2015). Prevalence of food addiction among low-income reproductive-aged women. *Journal of Women's Health*, *24*(9), 740–744.

Blass, E. M. (2012). Psychogenetic and ontogenetic contributions to today's obesity quagmire. In K. D. Brownell & M. S. Gold (Eds.), *Food and addiction: A comprehensive handbook* (pp. 172–177). New York, NY: Oxford University Press.

Blumenthal, D. M., & Gold, M. S. (2012). Relationships between drugs of abuse and eating. In K. D. Brownell & M. S. Gold (Eds.), *Food and addiction: A comprehensive handbook* (pp. 254–265). New York, NY: Oxford University Press.

Blumenthal, K., Dupont, R. L., & Gold, M. S. (2012). Treatment of alcohol and drug dependence in 2011 and relevance to food addiction. In K. D. Brownell & M. S. Gold (Eds.), *Food and addiction: A comprehensive handbook* (pp. 318–328). New York, NY: Oxford University Press.

Bourdier, L., Orri, M., Carre, A., Gearhardt, A. N., Romo, L., Dantzer, C., & Berthoz, S. (2018). Are emotionally driven and addictive-like eating behaviors the missing links between psychological distress and greater body weight? *Appetite*, *120*, 536–546.

Boyd, J. W., Harris, S. K., & Knight, J. R. (2012). Screening and brief interventions for the addiction syndrome: Considering the vulnerability of adolescence. In H. Shaffer, D. A. LaPlante, & S. E. Nelson (Eds.), *APA addiction syndrome handbook, Vol. 2: Recovery, prevention, and other issues* (pp. 169–194). Washington, DC: American Psychological Association.

Boyes, A. D., & Latner, J. D. (2009). Weight stigma in existing romantic relationships. *Journal of Sex & Marital Therapy, 35*(4), 282–293.

Brewerton, T. D. (2017). Food addiction as a proxy for eating disorder and obesity severity, trauma history, PTSD symptoms, and comorbidity. *Eating and Weight Disorders, 22*(2), 241–247.

Brownell, K. D., & Gold, M. S. (2012a). Acknowledgments. In K. D. Brownell & M. S. Gold (Eds.), *Food and addiction: A comprehensive handbook* (p. x). New York, NY: Oxford University Press.

Brownell, K. D., & Gold, M. S. (2012b). Introduction. In K. D. Brownell & M. S. Gold (Eds.), *Food and addiction: A comprehensive handbook* (pp. xxiii–xxv). New York, NY: Oxford University Press.

Bruce, M. A., Beech, B. M., Griffith, D. M., & Thorpe, R. J., Jr. (2016). Spirituality, religiosity, and weight management among African American adolescent males: The Jackson Heart KIDS Pilot Study. *Behavioral Medicine, 42*(3), 183–189.

Brunault, P., Frammery, J., Montaudon, P., De Luca, A., Hankard, R., Ducluzeau, P. H., . . . Ballon, N. (2018). Adulthood and childhood ADHD in patients consulting for obesity is associated with food addiction and binge eating, but not sleep apnea syndrome. *Appetite, 136*, 25–32.

Bucchianeri, M. M., Fernandes, N., Loth, K., Hannan, P. J., Eisenberg, M. E., & Neumark-Sztainer, D. (2016). Body dissatisfaction: Do associations with disordered eating and psychological well-being differ across race/ethnicity in adolescent girls and boys? *Cultural Diversity and Ethnic Minority Psychology, 22*(1), 137–146.

Burrows, T., Skinner, J., Joyner, M. A., Palmieri, J., Vaughan, K., & Gearhardt, A. N. (2017). Food addiction in children: Associations with obesity, parental food addiction and feeding practices. *Eating Behaviors, 26*, 114–120.

Cacciola, J. S., Alterman, A. I., Habing, B., & McLellan, A. T. (2011). Recent status scores for version 6 of the Addiction Severity Index (ASI-6). *Addiction, 106*, 1588–1602.

Canan, F., Karaca, S., Sogucak, S., Gecici, O., & Kuloglu, M. (2017). Eating disorders and food addiction in men with heroin use disorder: A controlled study. *Eating and Weight Disorders, 22*(2), 249–257.

Carlisle, K. L., Buser, J. K., & Carlisle, R. M. (2012). Childhood food addiction and the family. *Family Journal, 20*(3), 332–339.

Carter, J. C., Van Wijk, M., & Rowsell, M. (2019). Symptoms of 'food addiction' in binge eating disorder using the Yale Food Addiction Scale version 2.0. *Appetite, 133*, 362–369.

Cattivelli, R., Pietrabissa, G., Ceccarini, M., Spatola, C. A., Villa, V., Caretti, A., . . . Castelnuovo, G. (2015). ACTonFOOD: Opportunities of ACT to address food addiction. *Frontiers in Psychology, 6*, ArtID 396.

Cawley, J., Joyner, K., & Sobal, J. (2006). Size matters: The influence of adolescents' weight and height on dating and sex. *Rationality and Society, 18*(1), 67–94.

Connors, G. J., DiClemente, C. C., Velasquez, M. M., & Donovan, D. M. (2013). *Substance abuse treatment and the stages of change: Selecting and planning interventions* (2nd ed.). New York, NY: Guilford Press.

Contreras-Rodriguez, O., Martin-Perez, C., Vilar-Lopez, R., & Verdejo-Garcia, A. (2017). Ventral and dorsal striatum networks in obesity: Link to food craving and weight gain. *Biological Psychiatry, 81*(9), 789–796.

Cook, B. G., Li, D., & Heinrich, K. M. (2015). Obesity, physical activity, and sedentary behavior of youth with learning disabilities and ADHD. *Journal of Learning Disabilities, 48*, 563–576.

Cornelis, M. C., Flint, A., Field, A. E., Kraft, P., Han, J., Rimm, E. B., & van Dam, R. M. (2016). A genome-wide investigation of food addiction. *Obesity, 24*(6), 1336–1341.

Corsica, J. A., & Pelchat, M. L. (2010). Food addiction: True or false? *Current Opinion in Gastroenterology, 26*(2), 165–169.

Corvey, K., Menear, K. S., Preskitt, J., Goldfarb, S., & Menachemi, N. (2016). Obesity, physical activity and sedentary behaviors in children with an autism spectrum disorder. *Maternal and Child Health Journal, 20*, 466–476.

Cullen, A. J., Barnett, A., Komesaroff, P. A., Brown, W., O'Brien, K. S., Hall, W., & Carter, A. (2017). A qualitative study of overweight and obese Australians' views of food addiction. *Appetite, 115*, 62–70.

Davis, A. A., Edge, P. J., & Gold, M. S. (2014). New directions in the pharmacological treatment of food addiction, overeating, and obesity. In K. P. Rosenberg & L. Curtiss Feder (Eds.), *Behavioral addictions: Criteria, evidence, and treatment* (pp. 185–213). San Diego, CA: Academic Press.

Davis, C. (2017). A commentary on the associations among 'food addiction', binge eating disorder, and obesity: Overlapping conditions with idiosyncratic clinical features. *Appetite, 115*, 3–8.

Davis, C., & Carter, J. C. (2009). Compulsive overeating as an addiction disorder. A review of theory and evidence. *Appetite, 53*(1), 1–8.

De Jong, J. W., Vanderschuren, L. J. M. J., & Adan, R. A. H. (2016). The mesolimbic system and eating addiction: What sugar does and does not do. *Current Opinion in Behavioral Sciences, 9*, 118–125.

DePierre, J. A., Puhl, R. M., & Luedicke, J. (2014). Public perceptions of food addiction: A comparison with alcohol and tobacco. *Journal of Substance Use, 19*(1–2), 1–6.

De Vries, S.-K., & Meule, A. (2016). Food addiction and bulimia nervosa: New data based on the Yale Food Addiction Scale 2.0. *European Eating Disorders Review, 24*(6), 518–522.

Dietrich, M. O., Bober, J., Ferreira, J. G., Tellez, L. A., Mineur Y. S., Souza, D. O., . . . Horvath, T. L. (2012). AgRP neurons regulate development of dopamine neuronal plasticity and nonfood-associated behaviors. *Nature Neuroscience, 15*(8), 1108–1110.

Dimitrijevic, I., Popovic, N., Sabljak, V., Skodric-Trifunovic, V., & Dimitrijevic, N. (2015). Food addiction-diagnosis and treatment. *Psychiatria Danubina, 27*(1), 101–106.

Duffy, M. E., Henkel, K. E., & Earnshaw, V. A. (2016). Transgender clients' experiences of eating disorder treatment. *Journal of LGBT Issues in Counseling, 10*(3), 136–149.

Ebbeling, C. B., Willett, W. C., & Ludwig, D. S. (2012). The special case of sugar-sweetened beverages. In K. D. Brownell & M. S. Gold (Eds.), *Food and addiction: A comprehensive handbook* (pp. 147–153). New York, NY: Oxford University Press.

Eichen, D. M., Chen, E., Boutelle, K. N., & McCloskey, M. S. (2017). Behavioral evidence of emotion dysregulation in binge eaters. *Appetite, 111*, 1–6.

Epel, E. S., Tomiyama, A. J., & Dallman, M. F. (2012). Stress and reward: Neural networks, eating, and obesity. In K. D. Brownell & M. S. Gold (Eds.), *Food and addiction: A comprehensive handbook* (pp. 266–272). New York, NY: Oxford University Press.

Evatt, D. P., & Griffiths, R. R. (2012). Caffeine, addiction, and food consumption. In K. D. Brownell & M. S. Gold (Eds.), *Food and addiction: A comprehensive handbook* (pp. 238–243). New York, NY: Oxford University Press.

Fattore, L., Melis, M., Fadda, P., & Fratta, W. (2014). Sex differences in addictive disorders. *Frontiers in Neuroendocrinology, 35*, 272–284.

Ferrario, C. R. (2017). Food addiction and obesity. *Neuropsychopharmacology, 42*(1), 361–362.

Fisher, K., Hardie, T. L., Ranjan, S., & Peterson, J. (2017). Utilizing health records to characterize obesity, comorbidities, and health-care services in one human service agency in the United States. *Journal of Intellectual Disabilities, 21*, 387–400.

Flint, S. W., Cadek, M., Codreanu, S. C., Ivic, V., Zomer, C., & Gomoiu, A. (2016). Obesity discrimination in the recruitment process: "You're not hired"! *Frontiers in Psychology, 7*, ArtID 647.

Frayn, M., Sears, C. R., & von Ranson, K. M. (2016). A sad mood increases attention to unhealthy food images in women with food addiction. *Appetite, 100*, 55–63.

Gearhardt, A. N., Boswell, R. G., & White, M. A. (2014). The association of "food addiction" with disordered eating and body mass index. *Eating Behaviors, 15*(3), 427–433.

Gearhardt, A. N., & Corbin, W. R. (2012a). Clinical assessment of food and addiction. In K. D. Brownell & M. S. Gold (Eds.), *Food and addiction: A comprehensive handbook* (pp. 281–284). New York, NY: Oxford University Press.

Gearhardt, A. N., & Corbin, W. R. (2012b). Food addiction and diagnostic criteria for dependence. In K. D. Brownell & M. S. Gold (Eds.), *Food and addiction: A comprehensive handbook* (pp. 167–171). New York, NY: Oxford University Press.

Gearhardt, A. N., & Corbin, W. R. (2012c). Interactions between alcohol consumption, eating, and weight. In K. D. Brownell & M. S. Gold (Eds.), *Food and addiction: A comprehensive handbook* (pp. 249–253). New York, NY: Oxford University Press.

Gearhardt, A. N., Corbin, W. R., & Brownell, K. D. (2016). Development of the Yale Food Addiction Scale Version 2.0. *Psychology of Addictive Behaviors, 30*(1), 113–121.

Gearhardt, A. N., White, M. A., Masheb, R. M., Morgan, P. T., Crosby, R. D., & Grilo, C. M. (2012). An examination of the food addiction construct in obese patients with binge eating disorder. *International Journal of Eating Disorders, 45*(5), 657–663.

Gold, M. S., & Shriner, R. L. (2013). Food addictions. In P. M. Miller, A. W. Blume, D. J. Kavanagh, K. M. Kampman, M. E. Bates, M. E. Larimer, N. M. Petry, P. De Witte, & S. A. Ball (Eds.), *Comprehensive addictive behaviors and disorders, Vol. 1: Principles of addiction* (pp. 787–795). San Diego, CA: Elsevier Academic Press.

Gorman, C. (2004, June 7). America's obesity crisis: Weight loss—The secrets of their success. *Time*. Retrieved on May 29, 2018, from http://content.time.com/time/subscriber/printout/0,8816,994396,00.html

Grilo, C. M. (2012). Treatment of binge eating disorder. In K. D. Brownell & M. S. Gold (Eds.), *Food and addiction: A comprehensive handbook* (pp. 329–335). New York, NY: Oxford University Press.

Halpern, C. T., Udry, J. R., Campbell, B., & Suchindran, C. (1999). Effects of body fat on weight concerns, dating, and sexual activity: A longitudinal analysis of Black and White adolescent girls. *Developmental Psychology, 35*(3), 721–736.

Hardman, C. A., Rogers, P. J., Dallas, R., Scott, J., Ruddock, H. K., & Robinson, E. (2015). "Food addiction is real." The effects of exposure to this message on self-diagnosed food addiction and eating behaviour. *Appetite, 91*, 179–184.

Hardy, R., Fani, N., Jovanovic, T., & Michopoulos, V. (2018). Food addiction and substance addiction in women: Common clinical characteristics. *Appetite, 120*, 367–373.

Hebebrand, J., Albayrak, O., Adan, R., Antel, J., Dieguez, C., de Jong, J., . . . Dickson, S. L. (2014). "Eating addiction," rather than "food addiction," better captures addictive-like eating behavior. *Neuroscience and Biobehavioral Reviews, 47*, 295–306.

Henry, J., & Kollamparambil, U. (2017). Obesity-based labour market discrimination in South Africa: A dynamic panel analysis. *Journal of Public Health, 25*, 671–684.

Hill, A. J. (2012). The psychology of food cravings. In K. D. Brownell & M. S. Gold (Eds.), *Food and addiction: A comprehensive handbook* (pp. 226–230). New York, NY: Oxford University Press.

Hirsch, B. Z. (2008). Treating food addiction with logotherapy. *International Forum for Logotherapy, 31*(1), 3–8.

Hoey, E., Staines, A., Walsh, D., Corby, D., Bowers, K., Belton, S., . . . Sweeney, M. R. (2017). An examination of the nutritional intake and anthropometric status of individuals with intellectual disabilities: Results from the SOPHIE study. *Journal of Intellectual Disabilities, 21*, 346–365.

Ifland, J., Sheppard, K., & Wright, H. T. (2012). From the front lines: The impact of refined food addiction on well-being. In K. D. Brownell & M. S. Gold (Eds.), *Food and addiction: A comprehensive handbook* (pp. 348–353). New York, NY: Oxford University Press.

Imperatori, C., Fabbricatore, M., Vumbaca, V., Innamorati, M., Contardi, A., & Farina, B. (2016). Food addiction: Definition, measurement and prevalence in healthy subjects and in patients with eating disorders. *Rivista di Psichiatria, 51*(2), 60–65.

Innamorati, M., Imperatori, C., Harnic, D., Erbuto, D., Patitucci, E., Janiri, L., . . . Fabbricatore, M. (2017). Emotion regulation and mentalization in people at risk for food addiction. *Behavioral Medicine, 43*(1), 21–30.

Jimenez-Murcia, S., Granero, R., Wolz, I., Bano, M., Mestre-Bach, G., Steward, T., . . . Fernandez-Aranda, F. (2017). Food addiction in gambling disorder: Frequency and clinical outcomes. *Frontiers in Psychology, 8*, ArtID 473.

Johnson, B. (2003). Commentary on "Understanding Addictive Vulnerability." *Neuro-Psychoanalysis, 5*(1), 29–34.

Kabat-Zinn, J. (2013). *Full catastrophe living: Using the wisdom of your body and mind to face stress, pain, and illness* (Rev. ed.). New York, NY: Bantam.

Karaca, S., Saleh, A., Canan, F., & Potenza, M. N. (2017). Comorbidity between behavioral addictions and attention deficit/hyperactivity disorder: A systematic review. *International Journal of Mental Health and Addiction, 15*(3), 701–724.

Karlsson, H. K., Tuominen, L., Tuulari, J. J., Hirvonen, J., Parkkola, R., Helin, S., . . . Nummenmaa, L. (2015). Obesity is associated with decreased micro-opioid but unaltered dopamine D2 receptor availability in the brain. *Journal of Neuroscience, 35*(9), 3959–3965.

Kayloe, J. C. (1993). Food addiction. *Psychotherapy: Theory, Research, Practice, Training, 30*(2), 269–275.

Kirschenbaum, D. S., & Krawczyk, R. (2018). The food addiction construct may do more harm than good: Weight controllers are athletes, not addicts. *Childhood Obesity, 14*, 227–236.

Korpa, T. N., & Papadopoulou, P. V. (2013). Clinical signs and symptoms of addictive behaviors. In A. Tsitsika, M. Janikian, D. E. Greydanus, H. A. Omar, & J. Merrick (Eds.), *Internet addiction: A public health concern in adolescence* (pp. 3–14). Hauppauge, NY: Nova Science.

Lagrotte, C. A., & Foster, G. D. (2012). Behavioral treatments for obesity. In K. D. Brownell & M. S. Gold (Eds.), *Food and addiction: A comprehensive handbook* (pp. 290–295). New York, NY: Oxford University Press.

Latner, J. D., Mond, J. M., Kelly, M. C., Haynes, S. N., & Hay, P. J. (2014). The Loss of Control over Eating Scale: Development and psychometric evaluation. *International Journal of Eating Disorders, 47*(6), 647–659.

Laurent, J. S., & Sibold, J. (2016). Addictive-like eating, body mass index, and psychological correlates in a community sample of preadolescents. *Journal of Pediatric Health Care, 30*, 216–223.

Lee, A., & Gibbs, S. E. (2013). Neurobiology of food addiction and adolescent obesity prevention in low- and middle-income countries. *Journal of Adolescent Health, 52*, S39–S42.

Lee, H., Pantazis, A., Cheng, P., Dennisuk, L., Clarke, P. J., & Lee, J. M. (2016). The association between adolescent obesity and disability incidence in young adulthood. *Journal of Adolescent Health, 59*, 472–478.

Leigh, S.-J., & Morris, M. J. (2018). The role of reward circuitry and food addiction in the obesity epidemic: An update. *Biological Psychology, 131*, 31–42.

Lemeshow, A. R., Rimm, E. B., Hasin, D. S., Gearhardt, A. N., Flint, A. J., Field, A. E., & Genkinger, J. M. (2018). Food and beverage consumption and food addiction among women in the Nurses' Health Studies. *Appetite, 121*, 186–197.

Liu, Y., von Deneen, K. M., Kobeissy, F. H., & Gold, M. S. (2010). Food addiction and obesity: Evidence from bench to bedside. *Journal of Psychoactive Drugs, 42*(2), 133–145.

Luck-Sikorski, C., & Riedel-Heller, S. G. (2017). Obesity as a disability—A representative survey of individuals with obesity from Germany. *Disability and Health Journal, 10*, 152–156.

Lydecker, J. A., & Grilo, C. M. (2016). Different yet similar: Examining race and ethnicity in treatment-seeking adults with binge eating disorder. *Journal of Consulting and Clinical Psychology, 84*(1), 88–94.

Major, B., Eliezer, D., & Rieck, H. (2012). The psychological weight of weight stigma. *Social Psychological and Personality Science, 3*(6), 651–658.

Mason, B. J., & Higley, A. E. (2012). Human laboratory models of addiction. In K. D. Brownell & M. S. Gold (Eds.), *Food and addiction: A comprehensive handbook* (pp. 14–19). New York, NY: Oxford University Press.

Maté, G. (2008). *In the realm of hungry ghosts: Close encounters with addiction*. Toronto, ON: Vintage Books.

Matz, P. E., Foster, G. D., Faith, M. S., & Wadden, T. A. (2002). Correlates of body image dissatisfaction among overweight women seeking weight loss. *Journal of Consulting and Clinical Psychology, 70*, 1040–1044.

McPherson, A. C., Ball, G. D. C., Maltais, D. B., Swift, J. A., Cairney, J., Knibbe, T. J., . . . Krog, K. (2016). A call to action: Setting the research agenda for addressing obesity and weight-related topics in children with physical disabilities. *Childhood Obesity, 12*, 59–69.

Merlo, L. J., Klingman, C., Malasanos, T. H., & Silverstein, J. H. (2009). Exploration of food addiction in pediatric patients: A preliminary investigation. *Journal of Addiction Medicine, 3*, 26–32.

Meule, A., Hermann, T., & Kubler, A. (2015). Food addiction in overweight and obese adolescents seeking weight-loss treatment. *European Eating Disorders Review, 23*, 193–198.

Meule, A., & Kubler, A. (2012). Food cravings in food addiction: The distinct role of positive reinforcement. *Eating Behaviors, 13*(3), 252–255.

Meule, A., Rezori, V., & Blechert, J. (2014). Food addiction and bulimia nervosa. *European Eating Disorders Review, 22*(5), 331–337.

Mies, G. W., Treur, J. L., Larsen, J. K., Halberstadt, J., Pasman, J. A., & Vink, J. M. (2017). The prevalence of food addiction in a large sample of adolescents and its association with addictive substances. *Appetite, 118*, 97–105.

Milkman, H. B., & Sunderwirth, S. G. (2010). *Craving for ecstasy and natural highs: A positive approach to mood alteration*. Thousand Oaks, CA: SAGE.

Miller, C. T., & Downey, K. T. (1999). A meta-analysis of heavyweight and self-esteem. *Personality and Social Psychology Review, 3*, 68–84.

Mitchell, K. S., & Wolf, E. J. (2016). PTSD, food addiction, and disordered eating in a sample of primarily older veterans: The mediating role of emotion regulation. *Psychiatry Research, 243*, 23–29.

Monti, P. M., & Ray, L. A. (2012). The study of craving and its role in addiction. In K. D. Brownell & M. S. Gold (Eds.), *Food and addiction: A comprehensive handbook* (pp. 53–58). New York, NY: Oxford University Press.

Moore, C. F., Sabino, V., Koob, G. F., & Cottone, P. (2017). Pathological overeating: Emerging evidence for a compulsivity construct. *Neuropsychopharmacology, 42*, 1375–1389.

Moreno, S., Rodriguez, S., Fernandez, M. C., Tamez, J., & Cepeda-Benito A. (2008). Clinical validation of the trait and state versions of the Food Craving Questionnaire. *Assessment, 15*(3), 375–387.

Murphy, C. M., Stojek, M. K., & MacKillop, J. (2014). Interrelationships among impulsive personality traits, food addiction, and Body Mass Index. *Appetite, 73*, 45–50.

Niemiec, M. A., Boswell, J. F., & Hormes, J. M. (2016). Development and initial validation of the Obsessive Compulsive Eating Scale. *Obesity, 24*(8), 1803–1809.

Nolan, L. J. (2017). Is it time to consider the "food use disorder?" *Appetite, 115*, 16–18.

Norman, J. (2017, November 22). Americans weigh more, but shun "overweight" label. *Gallup News*. Retrieved on February 2, 2018, from http://news.gallup.com/poll/222578/americans-weigh-shun-overweight-label.aspx

Nowrouzi, B., Gohar, B., Nowrouzi-Kia, B., Mintsopoulos, V., Mcdougall, A., Jordan, G., . . .Tremblay, A. (2016). Lost-time illness, injury and disability and its relationship with obesity in the workplace: A comprehensive literature review. *International Journal of Occupational Medicine and Environmental Health, 29*(5), 749–766.

Nunes-Neto, P. R., Kohler, C. A., Schuch, F. B., Solmi, M., Quevedo, J., Maes, M., . . . Carvalho, A. F. (2018). Food addiction: Prevalence, psychopathological correlates and associations with quality of life in a large sample. *Journal of Psychiatric Research, 96*, 145–152.

Orihuela, C. A., Mrug, S., & Boggiano, M. M. (2017). Reciprocal relationships between emotion regulation and motives for eating palatable foods in African American adolescents. *Appetite, 117*, 303–309.

Ortigara Crego, L. M. (2007). The experience of a spiritual recovery from food addiction: A heuristic inquiry (Clark Moustakas). *Dissertation Abstracts International: Section B: The Sciences and Engineering, 67*(7-B), *2007*, 4112.

Overeaters Anonymous. (2018). *2017 membership survey report*. Retrieved on August 15, 2019, from https://oa.org/files/pdf/OA-Membership-Survey-2017.pdf

Parsons, L. H., & Hurd, Y. L. (2015). The endocannabinoid system: Endocannabinoid signalling in reward and addiction. *Nature Reviews Neuroscience, 16*(10), 579–594.

Pedram, P., Zhai, G., Gulliver, W., Zhang, H., & Sun, G. (2017). Two novel candidate genes identified in adults from the Newfoundland population with addictive tendencies towards food. *Appetite, 115*, 71–79.

Pirutinsky, S., Rosmarin, D. H., & Holt, C. L. (2012). Religious coping moderates the relationship between emotional functioning and obesity. *Health Psychology, 31*(3), 394–397.

Pivarunas, B., & Conner, B. T. (2015). Impulsivity and emotion dysregulation as predictors of food addiction. *Eating Behaviors, 19*, 9–14.

Polk, S. E., Schulte, E. M., Furman, C. R., & Gearhardt, A. N. (2017). Wanting and liking: Separable components in problematic eating behavior? *Appetite, 115*, 45–53.

Prochaska, J. O., Norcross, J. C., & DiClemente, C. C. (1994). *Changing for good*. New York, NY: Avon Books.

Pursey, K. M., Collins, C. E., Stanwell, P., & Burrows, T. L. (2016). The stability of 'food addiction' as assessed by the Yale Food Addiction Scale in a non-clinical population over 18-months. *Appetite, 96*, 533–538.

Rainey, J. C., Furman, C. R., & Gearhardt, A. N. (2018). Food addiction among sexual minorities. *Appetite, 120*, 16–22.

Rand, K., Vallis, M., Aston, M., Price, S., Piccinini-Vallis, H., Rehman, L., . . .Kirk, S. F. L. (2017). "It is not the diet; it is the mental part we need help with." A multilevel analysis of psychological, emotional, and social well-being in obesity. *International Journal of Qualitative Studies on Health and Well-being, 12*(1), ArtID 36.

Randolph, T. G. (1947). Masked food allergy as a factor in the development and persistence of obesity. *Proceedings of the Central Society for Clinical Research (Annual Meeting), 20*, 85.

Randolph, T. G. (1956). The descriptive features of food addiction: addictive eating and drinking. *Quarterly Journal of Studies on Alcohol, 17*, 198-224.

Rodriguez-Martin, B. C., & Meule, A. (2015). Food craving: New contributions on its assessment, moderators, and consequences. *Frontiers in Psychology, 6*, ArtID 21.

Rogers, P. J. (2017). Food and drug addictions: Similarities and differences. *Pharmacology, Biochemistry and Behavior, 153*, 182–190.

Rosen, O., & Aronne, L. J. (2012). Pharmacotherapy for obesity: Current and future treatments. In K. D. Brownell & M. S. Gold (Eds.), *Food and addiction: A comprehensive handbook* (pp. 303–309). New York, NY: Oxford University Press.

Rosenberg, A. (2012). Food and addiction: A personal story. In K. D. Brownell & M. S. Gold (Eds.), *Food and addiction: A comprehensive handbook* (pp. 360–363). New York, NY: Oxford University Press.

Ruddock, H. K., Field, M., & Hardman, C. A. (2017). Exploring food reward and calorie intake in self-perceived food addicts. *Appetite, 115*, 36–44.

Ruddock, H. K., & Hardman, C. A. (2018). Guilty pleasures: The effect of perceived overeating on food addiction attributions and snack choice. *Appetite, 121*, 9–17.

Ruggs, E. N., Hebl, M. R., & Williams, A. (2015). Weight isn't selling: The insidious effects of weight stigmatization in retail settings. *Journal of Applied Psychology, 100*, 1483–1496.

Salerno, L., Lo Coco, G., Gullo, S., Iacoponelli, R., Caltabiano, M. L., & Ricciardelli, L. A. (2015). Self-esteem mediates the associations among negative affect, body disturbances, and interpersonal problems in treatment-seeking obese individuals. *Clinical Psychologist, 19*, 85–95.

Sawamoto, R., Nozaki, T., Nishihara, T., Furukawa, T., Hata, T., Komaki, G., & Sudo, N. (2017). Predictors of successful long-term weight loss maintenance: A two-year follow-up. *BioPsychoSocial Medicine, 11*, ArtID 14.

Schulte, E. M., Grilo, C. M., & Gearhardt, A. N. (2016). Shared and unique mechanisms underlying binge eating disorder and addictive disorders. *Clinical Psychology Review, 44*, 125–139.

Schulte, E. M., Jacques-Tiura, A. J., Gearhardt, A. N., & Naar, S. (2017). Food addiction prevalence and concurrent validity in African American adolescents with obesity. *Psychology of Addictive Behaviors*. No pagination specified.

Schulte, E. M., Potenza, M. N., & Gearhardt, A. N. (2017). A commentary on the "eating addiction" versus "food addiction" perspectives on addictive-like food consumption. *Appetite, 115*, 9–15.

Schulte, E. M., Sonneville, K. R., & Gearhardt, A. N. (2019). Subjective experiences of highly processed food consumption in individuals with food addiction. *Psychology of Addictive Behaviors, 33*, 144–153.

Sevincer, G. M., Konuk, N., Bozkurt, S., & Coskun, H. (2016). Food addiction and the outcome of bariatric surgery at 1-year: Prospective observational study. *Psychiatry Research, 244*, 159–164.

Sinha, R. (2012). Stress and addiction: A brief overview. In K. D. Brownell & M. S. Gold (Eds.), *Food and addiction: A comprehensive handbook* (pp. 59–66). New York, NY: Oxford University Press.

Slof-Op't Landt, M. C. T, van Furth, E. F., van Beijsterveldt, C. E. M., Bartels, M., Willemsen, G., de Geus, E. J., . . . Boomsma, D. I. (2017). Prevalence of dieting and fear of weight gain across ages: A community sample from adolescents to the elderly. *International Journal of Public Health, 62*, 911–919.

Soto-Escageda, J. A., Estanol-Vidal, B., Vidal-Victoria, C. A., Michel-Chavez, A., Sierra-Beltran, M. A., & Bourges-Rodriguez, H. (2016). Does salt addiction exist? *Salud Mental, 39*(3), 175–181.

Stake, J. E., & Lauer, M. L. (1987). The consequences of being overweight: A controlled study of gender differences. *Sex Roles, 17*(1–2), 31–47.

Strenger, A. M., Schnitker, S. A., & Felke, T. J. (2016). Attachment to God moderates the relation between sociocultural pressure and eating disorder symptoms as mediated by emotional eating. *Mental Health, Religion & Culture, 19*(1), 23–36.

Tarman, V. (2016, April 30). Buyer beware: Training programs for food addiction counselling (Part I). *Addictions Unplugged*. Retrieved on February 8, 2018, from https://addictionsunplugged.com/2016/04/30/buyer-beware-training-programs-for-food-addiction-counselling1/

Tarman, V., & Werdell, P. (2014). *Food junkies: The truth about food addiction*. Toronto, ON: Dundurn.

Tonkin, K. M. (2006). Obesity, bulimia, and binge-eating disorder: The use of a cognitive behavioral and spiritual intervention. *Dissertation Abstracts International: Section B: The Sciences and Engineering, 67*(1-B), 563.

VanderBroek-Stice, L., Stojek, M. K., Beach, S. R. H., vanDellen, M. R., & MacKillop, J. (2017). Multidimensional assessment of impulsivity in relation to obesity and food addiction. *Appetite, 112*, 59–68.

Vella, S.-L., & Pai, N. (2017). What is in a name? Is food addiction a misnomer? *Asian Journal of Psychiatry, 25*, 123–126.

Vetter, M. L., Faulconbridge, L. F., Williams, N. N., & Wadden, T. A. (2012). Surgical treatments for obesity. In K. D. Brownell & M. S. Gold (Eds.), *Food and addiction: A comprehensive handbook* (pp. 310–317). New York, NY: Oxford University Press.

Wang, G.-J., Volkow, N. D., & Fowler, J. S. (2012). Dopamine deficiency, eating, and body weight. In K. D. Brownell & M. S. Gold (Eds.), *Food and addiction: A comprehensive handbook* (pp. 185–193). New York, NY: Oxford University Press.

Wansink, B. (2012). Specific environmental drivers of eating. In K. D. Brownell & M. S. Gold (Eds.), *Food and addiction: A comprehensive handbook* (pp. 159–164). New York, NY: Oxford University Press.

Weinstein, A., Zlatkes, M., Gingis, A., & Lejoyeux, M. (2015). The effects of a 12-step self-help group for compulsive eating on measures of food addiction, anxiety, depression, and self-efficacy. *Journal of Groups in Addiction & Recovery*, *10*(2), 190–200.

Werdell, P. (2012). From the front lines: A clinical approach to food and addiction. In K. D. Brownell & M. S. Gold (Eds.), *Food and addiction: A comprehensive handbook* (pp. 354–359). New York, NY: Oxford University Press.

White, M. A., & O'Malley, S. S. (2012). Interactions between smoking, eating, and body weight. In K. D. Brownell & M. S. Gold (Eds.), *Food and addiction: A comprehensive handbook* (pp. 244–248). New York, NY: Oxford University Press.

Wiss, D. A., & Brewerton, T. D. (2017). Incorporating food addiction into disordered eating: The disordered eating food addiction nutrition guide (DEFANG). *Eating and Weight Disorders*, *22*(1), 49–59.

Wiss, D. A., Criscitelli, K., Gold, M., & Avena, N. (2017). Preclinical evidence for the addiction potential of highly palatable foods: Current developments related to maternal influence. *Appetite*, *115*, 19–27.

Wolz, I., Granero, R., & Fernandez-Aranda, F. (2017). A comprehensive model of food addiction in patients with binge-eating symptomatology: The essential role of negative urgency. *Comprehensive Psychiatry*, *74*, 118–124.

Wolz, I., Hilker, I., Granero, R., Jimenez-Murcia, S., Gearhardt, A. N., Dieguez, C., . . . Fernandez-Aranda, F. (2016). "Food addiction" in patients with eating disorders is associated with negative urgency and difficulties to focus on long-term goals. *Frontiers in Psychology*, *7*, 61.

Yau, Y. H. C., Gottlieb, C. D., Krasna, L. C., & Potenza, M. N. (2014). Food addiction: Evidence, evaluation, and treatment. In K. P. Rosenberg & L. Curtiss Feder (Eds.), *Behavioral addictions: Criteria, evidence, and treatment* (pp. 143–184). San Diego, CA: Academic Press.

Yokum, S., & Stice, E. (2012). Genes and reward circuitry as predictors of eating and weight gain. In K. D. Brownell & M. S. Gold (Eds.), *Food and addiction: A comprehensive handbook* (pp. 194–199). New York, NY: Oxford University Press.

Zmuda, N. (2014). Assessment and treatment of co-occurring substance use disorders and process addictions: Eating disorders, pathological gambling, and sexual addiction. In S. L. A. Straussner (Ed.), *Clinical work with substance-abusing clients* (3rd ed.) (pp. 520–536). New York, NY: Guilford Press.

19 Exercise Addiction

iStock.com/anou

Learning Objectives

1. Learn to distinguish between the two types of exercise addiction.
2. Become able to distinguish between healthy exercising and unhealthy exercising.
3. Learn about the various diagnostic criteria that have been suggested by researchers.
4. Learn about the current scales and inventories used to measure exercise addiction.
5. Discover the recommended methods for treating compulsive exercisers.

CHALLENGING YOUR ASSUMPTIONS ABOUT THIS ADDICTION

1. If your 17-year-old teenage son or daughter began spending 30 hours a week at the gym, and in doing so began failing in school, what actions would you take to encourage moderation of exercise? If your first approach didn't work, what would you try next?
2. Without knowing much about exercise addiction yet, what would you suspect likely causes it?
3. Exercise addiction is not in *DSM-5*. What reasons would you suspect are behind its exclusion?
4. What factors in society might lead some people to exercise far more than is healthy for them?
5. What judgments would you make regarding someone who appears to be super toned and yet at the same time sickly?

PERSONAL REFLECTIONS

I used to wonder if my friend "Jake" was an exercise addict. Going to the gym always seemed like his highest priority. The jobs he worked never seemed to matter to him much, and he was often unemployed, but, if he missed a workout, that seemed like a huge deal. When he was between jobs, he would be at the gym even more often.

Especially when he was young, Jake was a very good-looking man. He had a look that most women would find very hot, not to mention his blonde hair and German blue eyes. I have found it strange over the last 20 years of knowing him that I continue to run into people that "remember him at the gym." Interestingly, he hasn't even worked out at the same gym! Jake is someone you would notice.

Jake is the kind of person you never get to know. I remember a mutual friend who called him "delightfully superficial" at one point to his face. I thought that would've bothered him, but it appeared to have had little to no effect. For the past 10 years, he has lived with a much older well-off woman. Ever since, he has not worked but instead has tended to household duties, including all outdoor work, cooking, acting as the host at dinner parties, cleaning, and laundry. In many ways, his life appears boring to me. But the one thing he still can talk about is his time at the gym.

So, as I begin writing this chapter, I ask myself, "Is Jake an exercise addict?" What would I need to know about him to answer that question fully, or do I already know enough to provide that label? Seriously, I have questioned whether there is even such a thing as exercise addiction. Would an Olympic athlete, for example, qualify as an exercise addict? Don't they need to push themselves beyond what most humans endure to achieve greatness in the world of elite competitive sport? I know that I will always admire Olympic athletes, so these questions become even more challenging to me. I am sure you have thoughts about this as well before you begin fully engaging in reading and studying this chapter.

Background Information

The benefits of healthy exercising are enormous and include enhancements to quality of life, health, aesthetics, performance, and rehabilitation from both physical and psychological illnesses (Esteves, dos Santos Nose, & de Mello, 2016). People who exercise regularly report an improvement in affect, and those who are depressed will often experience a reduction in their symptoms in a period of 8–16 weeks (Williams & Marcus, 2012). Likewise, a lack of exercise is related to having higher levels of anxiety and depression (Weinstein, Maayan, & Weinstein, 2015). Estimates from Great Britain suggest that about 14% of the population attends a gym (Lichtenstein, Hinze, Emborg, Thomsen, & Hemmingsen, 2017).

The American College of Sports Medicine (2011) published four guidelines recommending the intensity and frequency of exercise that adults should attain each week. Americans should engage in

1. Aerobic activity 5 days a week for at least 30 minutes per day. The activity needs to increase the heart rate and respiration.
2. Weight training or another form of resistance training that targets each muscle group 2 or 3 days a week.
3. Stretching and flexibility exercises that target each muscle group 2 or 3 days a week.
4. Neuromotor training (i.e., functional fitness) for 30 minutes 2 or 3 days a week. Some examples include yoga and balancing exercises.

Similarly, the Canadian Society for Exercise Physiology recommended that healthy adults between ages 18 and 64 should engage in at least 150 minutes of moderate (5 or 6 on a scale of 0–10) to vigorous (7–8 on the same scale) aerobic exercise per week for a minimum of at least 10 minutes but in total at least 30 minutes a day five times a week (Landolfi, 2013). Even a single session of exercise has a positive effect on body image (Beres, Czegledi, & Babusa, 2017). Regular exercise is immensely helpful to alcoholics and drug addicts for both treatment and relapse prevention (Damian & Mendelson, 2017; Giesen, Zimmer, & Bloch, 2016; Haglund et al., 2015; Weinstock, Farney, Elrod, Henderson, & Weiss, 2017).

Excessive exercise does not impair executive functioning either. Instead, obligatory exercisers experience increased cognitive functioning (Ryu, Kim, Kwon, Kim, & Kim, 2016).

The pursuit of the "runner's high" is elusive for many, however. Many endurance athletes report never experiencing it and others report experiencing it but not during every exercise session. For those who have very low activity levels, research has shown that these individuals find exercise to be aversive (Williams & Marcus, 2012).

On the other end of the spectrum appear to be those individuals who can never get enough exercise. For individuals addicted to exercise, what was once a positive activity becomes a negative one (Kerulis, 2015). The discerning distinction is between people who are committed to exercise and those who become addicted to it (Petitpas, Brewer, & Van Raalte, 2015). That is the topic of this chapter.

The concept of exercise addiction has been written about since only the 1970s, when awareness grew that there can be negative consequences to excessive exercising (Berczik et al., 2014). In the mid-1970s, Glasser coined the term *positive addiction* to describe the positive effects emanating from physical exercise. Morgan (1979) questioned the concept because case studies had revealed that excessive exercise could lead to physical injury and other negative consequences in one's personal life. Morgan argued that the concept of exercise addiction was viable given the evidence.

Like all behavioral addictions except gambling, exercise addiction does not appear in *DSM-5* (Dakwar, 2015). Furthermore, there remains controversy regarding whether addictive processes are involved with even some problematic exercisers (Dakwar, 2015).

Exercise addiction is defined as a "multidimensional maladaptive pattern of exercise, leading to clinically significant impairment or distress" (Kerulis, 2015, p. 263). A compulsive exerciser will continue exercising despite experiencing physical injury, inconvenience, work consequences, lack of time for other activities, marital strain, and other disruptions in one's life (Landolfi, 2013).

The motivations for committed exercisers and addicted exercisers differ. Committed exercisers do so mostly for extrinsic rewards, and they do not suffer withdrawal when they are unable to exercise. Addicted exercisers, on the other hand, do so more often for intrinsic rewards, and they experience substantial feelings of deprivation when they cannot exercise (Landolfi, 2013).

The first major consideration in ascertaining exercise addiction is whether it is the primary problem (i.e., primary exercise addiction [PEA]) or whether it is a result of other psychological conditions (i.e., secondary exercise addiction [SEA]). SEA, for example, is common with people experiencing anorexia nervosa or bulimia nervosa (Berczik et al., 2014). In the case of PEA, the motive is commonly focused on avoiding something negative, although the reasons may be unknown to the individual. In SEA, the motivation is to lose weight (Berczik et al., 2014). In Cunningham, Pearman, and Brewerton's (2016) study of 1497 adults (608 men, 885 women, 4 other), they elucidated the difference between PEA and SEA. They concluded that SEA is related more to compulsivity and PEA is associated more with addiction.

As is true in most other addictions, exercise addiction symptomatology includes salience, mood modification, tolerance, withdrawal symptoms, personal conflict, and relapse (Berczik et al., 2014). Addicted exercisers don't just want to do the behavior—they feel *compelled* to exercise.

Similar to drug addiction, compulsive exercise becomes an avoidance or escape from unpleasant or painful feelings (Berczik et al., 2014). In research involving 684 students (age range: 18–25 years), addicted exercisers used exercise to deal with negative affect states, including negative urgency, positive urgency, and sensation-seeking (Kotbagi, Morvan, Romo, & Kern, 2017). Excitement-seeking and achievement-striving were also found in another study (Lichtenstein, Christiansen, Elkit, Bilenberg, & Stoving, 2014).

Addicted exercisers experience a craving for physical training that leads to compulsive excessive exercise (Lichtenstein et al., 2017). They experience withdrawal symptoms when they cannot exercise. In a small-scale study that compared eight male runners with exercise addiction and 10 in a control group, a withdrawal period was sustained for 2 weeks. The exercise addiction group showed increases in depression, anger, confusion, and fatigue, and a less vigorous mood at all time periods evaluated (Antunes et al., 2016). Furthermore, recreational exercisers who are at high risk of exercise addiction report more symptoms of depression and emotional stress compared with those not at risk (Lichtenstein, Nielsen, Gudex, Hinze, & Jorgensen, 2018).

Using Delphi methodology (e.g., a method involving consensus building among experts), MacFarlane, Owens, and Cruz (2016) found that there was consensus that excessive exercise is an addiction including some aspects of perfectionism, obsessive-compulsiveness, and hedonism (i.e., compensating for feeling diminished self-worth, reducing negative affect, and withdrawal). Hill, Robson, and Stamp (2015) tested 248 gym members (age range: 18–75 years) and found that self-oriented perfectionism and perfectionistic self-presentational styles were important predictors of exercise addiction. These findings suggest that, besides exhibiting trait perfectionism, compulsive exercisers are committed to portraying an image of perfection. A study that compared an exercise-addicted group ($N = 41$) and a control group ($N = 80$) also found that the addicted group scored higher on perfectionism but that this was not as high as those with eating disorders (Lichtenstein, Christiansen, et al., 2014). Exercise addiction is also correlated with narcissism (Miller & Mesagno, 2014).

Similar to individuals with eating disorders, addicted exercisers have a negative or distorted body image (de la Torre, 1995). They have higher levels of body dissatisfaction compared with individuals who are not addicted to exercise (Lichtenstein, Griffiths, Hemmingsen, & Stoving, 2018). Those who strongly identify as exercisers experience a high degree of social physique anxiety (e.g., anxiety about showing one's body publicly), and they are at increased risk for exercise addiction (Cook et al., 2015). These findings were not found, however, in a study comparing competitive and noncompetitive runners. The competitive runners were more likely to be addicted exercisers compared with the noncompetitive runners, but they did not exhibit more social physique anxiety. Furthermore, there were no significant differences between the females and males (Smith, Wright, & Winrow, 2010). Many addicted exercisers are afraid of aging (de la Torre, 1995). In their study of 25 runners who were at risk of exercise addiction, Di Lodovico, Dubertret, and Ameller (2018) found that the at-risk group were likelier to be younger women who began running to lose weight more often than the 136 runners not at risk in their sample.

Both obsessive and harmonious passion are predictors of exercise addiction, with obsessive passion being the strongest predictor (Kovacsik et al., 2018; Parastatidou, Doganis, Theodorakis, & Vlachopoulos, 2014). In a study of 398 recreational endurance exercisers (381 men, 17 women, ages 18–60), psychological inflexibility was a contributing factor in explaining exercise addiction (Alcaraz-Ibanez, Aguilar-Parra, & Alvarez-Hernandez, 2018). Orthorexic eating (i.e., individuals who are obsessed with eating foods that they only consider healthy) is also related to an increase in exercise addiction symptomatology (Oberle, Watkins, & Burkot, 2017).

Male amateur triathletes (*N* = 93; age range: 25–43 years) in Spain showed addictive potential, especially in those focused on long distances (Valenzuela & Arriba-Palomero, 2017). Youngman (2008) researched 1285 male and female triathletes (age range: 18–70) in Olympic, Half-Ironman, and Ironman competitions and found that 20% are at risk for exercise addiction, 79% exhibited some signs of exercise addiction, and only 1% were asymptomatic. Female triathletes were at greater risk for exercise addiction than the male triathletes. A study of 72 male and 20 female runners and 60 male and 30 female exercisers revealed that, the longer one is involved in physical activity, the higher the scores on exercise addiction (Furst & Germone, 1993). Elite athletes appear to be at particular risk of exercise addiction (Szabo, De La Vega, Ruiz-Barquin, & Rivera, 2013).

Some weight trainers become dependent on exercise. Research done in Adelaide, South Australia, with 101 men (age range: 18–67 years) found that weight trainers had three different motives for exercising, including mood control, physique anxiety, and personal challenge. Of these motives, personal challenge and mood control were the most related to exercise addiction (Emini & Bond, 2014).

In a study with a small sample size (12 addicted exercisers, 12 nonaddicts, 12 nonexercisers), the addicted exercisers did not differ from the nonaddicted exercisers in extraversion, although both exercise groups were more extraverted than the group who didn't exercise (Mathers & Walker, 1999). Andreassen et al. (2013) found different results regarding extraversion in addicted exercisers, however.

Andreassen et al. (2013) had 218 university students complete questionnaires that measured seven different behavioral addictions and the five-factor model of personality. The results suggested that exercise addiction has a positive relationship with neuroticism, extraversion, and conscientiousness but has an inverse relationship with agreeableness. Di Lodovico et al. (2018) also found that exercise addiction was associated with neuroticism. Basson (2001) studied 339 runners between the ages of 19 and 65 and found that exercise addiction was correlated with having a rigid, inflexible personality style. Basson also found that there was an association between addiction to running and interpersonal difficulties.

Unsurprisingly, addicted exercisers may enter scholastic programs that pertain to their addiction. Nuzzo, Schindler, and Ryan (2013) tested 419 undergraduate students in a midsize northeastern university in the United States and found that exercise science students had more symptoms of exercise addiction than those in other programs.

Four causes of exercise addiction were proposed by Berczik et al. (2014). These included the thermogenic regulation hypothesis, the catecholamine hypothesis, the cognitive appraisal hypothesis, and the affect regulation hypothesis. The thermogenic regulation hypothesis is based on the idea that, because body temperature increases with intense physical exercise, the warmth in the body becomes associated with a relaxed state and reductions in anxiety. Consequently, exercise becomes rewarded, thereby leading eventually to excessive exercise. The catecholamine hypothesis is based on the finding that levels of circulating catecholamines increase following exercise. According to the hypothesis, catecholamine levels increase in the brain, which leads to improved mood and affect, which also plays a role in the reward system (which, in turn, can lead to excessive exercise). The cognitive appraisal hypothesis suggests that excessive exercisers use exercise to cope with stress. Over time, the individual learns to both depend on and need exercise (Berczik et al., 2014). The idea behind the affect regulation hypothesis is that exercise has two effects on mood: (a) it improves one's general mood state and (b) it diminishes negative feelings like "guilt, irritability, sluggishness, and anxiety associated with missed exercise or training sessions" (Berczik et al., 2014, p. 329). However, the positive mood-enhancing effects from exercise are temporary, and, over time, increasing amounts of exercise are needed to experience the same mood-enhancing effects.

McNamara and McCabe (2012) developed a biopsychosocial model to explain the results from their study of 234 elite Australian athletes. They hypothesized that their biopsychosocial model would include the following factors: (a) biological factors (i.e., body mass index), (b) social forces (i.e., coach and teammate pressure, sociocultural pressure), and (c) psychological processes (i.e., self-esteem, training beliefs). These results supported the idea that at-risk athletes had greater BMIs, greater pressure from coaches and teammates, and more maladaptive exercise beliefs. The at-risk group did not experience lower self-esteem, however. In fact, high self-esteem can act as a positive predictor of exercise addiction when body shame is controlled (Ertl et al., 2018).

Adams (2013) suggested that, because exercise has a positive connotation, this could be a causative factor in exercise addiction. As Adams stated, however, there is no empirical evidence supporting this hypothesis currently.

In the general population, the prevalence of exercise addiction runs at about 0.3%–0.5% (Egorov & Szabo, 2013). Consequently, exercise addiction is considered rare. The prevalence of exercise addiction in adolescents, however, may be substantially higher. Villella et al. (2011) measured it to be 8.5% in their sample of 2853 high school students. In their study of 471 high-risk samples of students, ages 11–20, Lichtenstein, Griffiths, et al. (2018) found a prevalence rate for exercise addiction of 4.0% for school athletes, 8.7% in those attending fitness classes, and 21% in those with eating disorders.

Among regular exercisers, the prevalence of exercise addiction appears to be in the 1%–5% range (Williams & Marcus, 2012). Using the Exercise Dependence Scale, Maselli, Gobbi, Probst, and Carraro (2018) tested 427 people engaged in endurance sports (END), aesthetic sports (AES), team sports, or fitness activities. They found a prevalence range of between 7% (i.e., AES) and 12.9% (i.e., END) but differences among the four groups were not statistically significant. The highest prevalence is found among elite athletes. For example, McNamara and McCabe (2012) found that 34% scored in the range of exercise addiction in their sample of 234 elite Australian athletes.

Athletes on teams might be most likely to become addicted exercisers because team sport cultures overtly and covertly encourage "machismo" (i.e., a strong or aggressive form of pride; Bible, n.d.). Anyone who feels pressure to stay in shape, particularly at any cost, demonstrates a risk for developing exercise addiction (Stubblefield, 2016).

In a sample of 179 cyclists (M = 32.47 years), the prevalence of being at risk for PEA and SEA was 8.24% and 1.18%, respectively (Cook & Luke, 2017). A convenience sample of 603 regular crossfitters (*CrossFit* is a group of "boot camp" type fitness facilities where participants focus on varied movements done at high intensity) who participated in an online survey revealed that 5% of them were addicted exercisers with the highest risk in young males (Lichtenstein & Jensen, 2016).

Diagnostic and Assessment Considerations

As mentioned earlier, the diagnosis of exercise addiction remains controversial, and it does not appear in *DSM-5*. ICD-11, however, includes effects of strenuous physical exercise, unspecified (code NF06.Z) and other specified effects of strenuous physical exercise (code NF06.Y).

Weinstein and Weinstein (2016) noted that excessive exercise had been described by some as either an addiction or as a form of obsessive-compulsiveness. Obsessions are persistent thoughts, ideas, or images that preoccupy a person's mind, whereas compulsions are repeated behaviors precipitated by strong urges. Also, there is no consensus on the final diagnostic criteria for exercise addiction (Berczik et al., 2014). Nonetheless, several criteria have been suggested in the literature.

Freimuth, Moniz, and Kim (2011) advanced a four-phase model that may help to distinguish healthful exercising from exercise addiction. This model may be particularly helpful for those working with athletes (Kerulis, 2015).

1. Phase 1. This phase describes healthful exercising that adds to the quality of one's life.
2. Phase 2. In this phase, individuals are at risk of developing exercise problems. They begin to exercise to reduce anxiety and other mood states as opposed to using exercise as an intrinsic reward.
3. Phase 3. In this phase, exercise begins to become an issue. Individuals begin organizing their day around exercise, and negative consequences such as relationship problems emerge.
4. Phase 4. This is the phase of exercise addiction. Individuals keep exercising despite injuries, and they become unable to fulfill daily life expectations.

Adams (2013) surmised that a diagnosis of exercise addiction requires the following:

1. Exercising daily without taking days off.
2. Experiencing illnesses or injuries as a result of exercise is likely.
3. The exercise is done for intense and long durations.
4. A substantial amount of time is spent planning and thinking about exercise.
5. The individual exercises at the same time or in the same way most days (i.e., stereotypical exercising).
6. Experiences irrational thoughts and feelings when exercising is thwarted.
7. Withdrawal symptoms are experienced, such as mood swings, dry mouth, and aches and pains.

de Coverley Veale (1987) was the first to propose diagnostic criteria, which he based on criteria for alcohol dependence. He referred to the condition as exercise dependence. His criteria included the following:

1. A stereotypical pattern of exercise that occurs once or more daily.
2. The individual gives increasing importance to exercise over other activities (i.e., salience).
3. Tolerance to the amount of exercise increases over the years.
4. Withdrawal symptoms occur when exercise is halted.
5. Withdrawal symptoms are either relieved or avoided by continuing to exercise.
6. Having awareness of a compulsion to exercise.
7. Return to the previous pattern of exercise soon following a period of abstinence from it.

   Associated Features

8. Continuing to exercise despite having developed a serious physical disorder or the individual continues exercising despite negative consequences to relationships or employment.
9. Intentionally losing weight through dieting as a way of improving performance.

The following four paragraphs are adapted from Adams's (2013) summary of the criteria for exercise addiction of several others. First, Ogden, Veale, and Summers (1997) proposed separate criteria for what they called primary exercise dependence and secondary exercise dependence. Their criteria were as follows:

1. Primary exercise dependence
   a. A stereotypical pattern of exercise that is followed once or more daily.
   b. The individual gives increasing priority to exercise over other activities (i.e., salience).
   c. The amount of exercise performed increases over the years (i.e., tolerance).
   d. Upon cessation of exercise negative symptoms develop (i.e., withdrawal).
   e. Symptoms of withdrawal are relieved or avoided upon resuming exercise.

   f. Having awareness of the need to exercise expressed as a compulsion.
   g. Following a period of abstinence, a rapid return to the previous pattern of exercise and withdrawal should abstinence again occur.

2. Secondary exercise dependence

   Same as primary exercise dependence but with the inclusion of an eating disorder.

Second, Bamber, Cockerill, Rodgers, and Carroll (2003) also created criteria for primary and secondary exercise dependence. Their criteria were as follows:

1. Primary exercise dependence
   a. Impaired functioning (in at least two of the following areas):
      - Psychological. Ruminating or having intrusive thoughts about exercise.
      - Social and occupational. Making exercise more important than social activities or becoming unable to work.
      - Physical. Exercise either causes or aggravates an injury or health condition, yet the individual continues exercising despite its harmful consequences.
      - Behavioral. The excessive exercise is stereotyped and inflexible.
   b. Withdrawal (as evidenced in one or more of the following areas):
      - Experiencing a substantial negative response toward having to change or interrupt exercise habits.
      - Persistent desire and or unsuccessful attempts to control or reduce exercise.
2. Secondary exercise dependence
   - Same as primary exercise dependence but with the inclusion of an eating disorder. The following associated features are indicative but not definitive:
   - Increasing amount of exercise required (i.e., tolerance).
   - A substantial amount of exercise required or exercising at least every day.
   - Exercising by oneself.
   - Lying to others about the amount of exercising or keeping it a secret (i.e., deception).
   - Denying that exercise is a problem (i.e., insight).

Third, Hausenblas and Symons-Downs (2002a) suggested the following diagnostic criteria:

Clinically significant distress or impairment as manifested by three or more of the following symptoms:

1. Increased amounts of exercise needed to achieve the desired effect or experiencing a diminished effect from continuing the same amount of exercise (i.e., tolerance).
2. Withdrawal symptoms experienced when not exercising or continuing to exercise to avoid withdrawal symptoms (i.e., withdrawal).
3. Exercising more and over longer periods than intended (i.e., loss of intention).
4. Persistent desire or inability to cut down or control exercise (i.e., lack of control).
5. Spending a great deal of time in activities related to obtaining exercise (i.e., time).
6. Less time spent doing social, occupational, or recreational activities (i.e., reduction in other activities).
7. Continuing to exercise despite knowledge of having a physical or psychological problem that worsens from excessive exercise (i.e., continuance).

Fourth, Terry, Szabo, and Griffiths (2004) created the following criteria for exercise addiction:

1. Salience. Exercise becomes the most important activity in the person's life and dominates their thinking (rumination and cognitive distortions), feelings (cravings), and social behavior.
2. Mood modification. Exercising creates a "buzz" or "high" or a feeling of "escape" or "numbing."
3. Tolerance. Increasing amounts of exercise are required to create the same effect as before.
4. Withdrawal symptoms. Unpleasant feelings or physical effects when the exercise is discontinued or reduced. Examples include moodiness, irritability, and the shakes.
5. Conflict. Internal conflict, conflict between the addict and others, or conflict between choosing exercise over performing other activities.
6. Relapse. The tendency to revert to previous levels of excessive activity following a period of exercise reduction.

Differential Diagnosis

The counselor's first task is to determine whether the client is experiencing PEA or SEA. In the case of SEA, the eating disorder or substance addiction will be prominent. Berczik et al. (2014) wrote that exercise addiction would need to be distinguished from obsessive-compulsive disorder (OCD). Both addicted exercisers and those with OCD crave exercise and feel substantial distress when they are unable to exercise. The distinguishing feature is that the addict exercises to reduce negative moods and release endorphins, whereas those with OCD exercise in response to their obsessions. Furthermore, exercise addiction includes both addictive and compulsive features, and they can exist in both a primary and a secondary form (Lichtenstein et al., 2017).

Besides OCD, it is important to ascertain if the client is exercising excessively in response to a personality disorder (Berczik et al., 2014). In that case, the personality disorder will need to be treated for symptom remission. An example here might be individuals with a narcissistic personality disorder who exercise to make themselves feel superior to others.

Comorbidity and Co-Addictions

Most of the literature concerning comorbidity focuses on the combination of exercise addiction and eating disorders (Lichtenstein et al., 2017). Some researchers have even speculated that the two conditions cannot exist separately from each other, thereby suggesting that PEA does not exist (Lichtenstein et al., 2017). The percentage of people with eating disorders who also exercise excessively is estimated at between 39% and 48% (Lichtenstein et al., 2017).

Although a recent literature review found comorbidity between many behavioral addictions and attention deficit hyperactivity disorder (ADHD), there was no study that found comorbidity between exercise addiction and ADHD (Karaca, Saleh, Canan, & Potenza, 2017). Exercise addiction is often comorbid with depressive and anxiety problems (Berczik et al., 2014).

Muscle dysmorphia (MD) may be comorbid with exercise addiction. Those who experience this disorder see their bodies as both small and weak even though they may look to others as normal or even highly muscular (Foster, Shorter, & Griffiths, 2015). This condition is considered a type of body dysmorphic disorder in the *DSM-5*. Currently little is known about MD (Lichtenstein et al., 2017). Some hypothesize that MD should itself be classified as an addiction (Foster et al., 2015).

Comorbid personality traits can include perfectionism, neuroticism, narcissism, high extraversion, and low agreeableness (Lichtenstein et al., 2017). Andreassen et al. (2013) also found in their study that conscientiousness was also related to exercise addiction.

Some of the addictions that have been found to co-occur with exercise addiction include nicotine, alcohol, illicit drugs, shopping, sex, and work addictions (Freimuth et al., 2011). A study from Paris, however, found that addicted exercisers smoke less than nonaddicts (Lejoyeux, Avril, Richoux, Embouazza, & Nivoli, 2008). Some addictions that have been found to coexist with exercise addiction in adolescents include gambling, shopping, Internet, and work addiction (Villela et al., as cited in Lichtenstein et al., 2017). Lichtenstein et al. (2017) concluded that about one third of individuals with exercise addiction are also addicted to something else.

Available Measures

As Kerulis (2015) noted, some of the following instruments have not been validated. Furthermore, self-report questionnaires and scales may create misleading results, as they better reflect the risk of developing the disorder rather than providing an actual diagnosis (Szabo & Egorov, 2016). It is recommended that counselors collect additional information through observations, self-reports, and other assessment tools. The first two questionnaires are psychometrically sound, and they have proven to be similar in sensitivity and reliability (Egorov & Szabo, 2013).

1. Exercise Dependence Scale-21 (EDS-21; Symons-Downs, Hausenblas, & Niggs, 2004). This scale is also known as the EDS-R (revised). It is a 21-item scale based on diagnostic criteria for alcohol dependence. The scale has been used in several exercise settings (Lichtenstein et al., 2017). Available from http://www.personal.psu.edu/dsd11/EDS/EDS21Manual.pdf
2. Exercise Addiction Inventory (EAI; Terry et al., 2004). This is a six-item inventory that has good psychometric properties cross-culturally (Lichtenstein et al., 2017). Available from http://fastatforty.blogspot.mx/2010/03/are-exercise-addict.html
3. Exercise Dependence Questionnaire (EDQ; Ogden et al., 1997). The EDQ has 29 items on a 7-point Likert scale. This scale has been used in several studies, and it is considered by its authors to be both reliable and valid (Kerulis, 2015; Lichtenstein et al., 2017).
4. Exercise Beliefs Questionnaire (EBQ; Loumidis & Wells, 1998). This is a 21-item scale that looks at unhealthy beliefs about the consequences of not exercising.
5. Obligatory Exercise Questionnaire (OEQ; Thompson & Pasman, 1991). This is a 21-item questionnaire measuring a range of exercise behavior. Available from http://jkthompson.myweb.usf.edu/oeqweb.htm
6. Commitment to Exercise Scale (Davis, Brewer, & Ratusny, 1993). This provides a measure of compulsive thinking and pathology for those who continue exercising despite injuries.
7. Bodybuilding Dependency Scale (Smith, Hale, & Collins, 1998). This is a scale that measures exercise dependence in bodybuilders.
8. Running Addiction Scale (RAS; Chapman & De Castro, 1990). The RAS is an 11 item 5-point Likert scale. The RAS has good psychometric properties (Lichtenstein et al., 2017).
9. Exercise Dependence Interview (EDI; Bamber, Cockerill, & Carroll, 2000). This is a unique measure of both compulsive eating and exercising with good reliability and validity.

Clinical Interview Questions

Besides the questions asked in the previous inventories, a few additional questions may help ascertain a client's relationship with exercise. Warner and Griffiths (2006) completed a qualitative analysis of exercise addiction, and an adaptation of their four questions may be useful. The revised questions are as follows:

1. Tell me about a positive experience you have had with exercise.
2. Describe for me a negative experience you have had with exercise.
3. What is the driving force behind your exercise?
4. To what extent do you use exercise as a way of dealing with difficult areas of your life?

The following list of questions that a counselor or physician may ask to help ascertain if the client/patient is a compulsive exerciser is quoted from Hausenblas, Schreiber, and Smoliga (2017, p. 2):

Determine if the patient seems to be engaging in excessive exercise:

- How often do you exercise?
- How long is your typical workout?

Explore the patient's motivation for exercise behaviors:

- Why do you exercise?
- What are your goals that you hope to achieve through your exercise routine? How did you decide on the exercise routine your currently perform?

Determine if the patient is responsive to physical cues to reduce exercise when necessary:

- How do you know when you have exercised too much or reached your limit?
- If you feel you have done too much, what do you do to ensure that you recover properly?
- How do you know when you are ready to resume your normal exercise routine?
- When you have been ill or injured, do you continue to exercise? If so, how do you modify your training to accommodate the illness or injury?

Determine if exercise behaviors are interfering with other important aspects of life:

- Does your exercise schedule frequently conflict with your work, school, family, or social obligations or interests?
- If so, what do you feel are the consequences of these conflicts?

Establish the patient's emotional connection to exercise.

- How do you feel when you are unable to exercise or have to modify your exercise routine?

Determine if the patient balances exercise with other leisurely activities:

- Do you engage in any other activities in your free time?

Lee (2014) created a list of questions to assess a person's state of powerlessness and unmanageability. Pertinent questions are adapted for exercise addiction (note that these questions could be used with other addictions):

1. What pain or fear do you associate with stopping (or moderating) your exercise routine?
2. What pleasure do you get from your exercise routine?
3. What will it cost you if you do not stop your exercise routine?
4. What are the benefits you could gain by stopping your exercise routine?
5. How has your exercise routine placed your important relationships in jeopardy?
6. Have you lost self-respect and/or reputation due to your exercise routine? If yes, how?
7. Has your exercise routine made your home life unhappy? If yes, how?
8. Has your exercise routine caused any injury or illness? If yes, what?
9. Do you turn to the type of people who enable you to continue your exercise routine?
10. What aspects of your exercise routine do your loved ones, friends, family, or business associates object to the most?
11. List examples of what you have done in the past to fix, control, or change your exercise pattern.
12. If this issue is such an important area in your life that needs to be changed, why hasn't it changed?

Generic Names and Street "Lingo"

The terms for exercise addiction have also varied over the last 40 years. It is not clear whether these are truly synonyms or whether they have slightly different meaning. Nonetheless, the words that appear include compulsive exercise, exercise dependence, running addiction (Lichtenstein et al., 2017), negative addiction (Petitpas et al., 2015), morbid exercising, compulsory exercising, compulsive exercising (Adams, 2013), obligatory exercising, exercise abuse, compulsive exercise (Berczik et al., 2012), and running anorexics (de Coverley Veale, 1987). Lichtenstein et al. (2017) recommended that it be called *exercise addiction* because the word *addiction* contains the ideas of both compulsion and dependence.

Neuroscience

Adams (2013) described several of the neurobiological explanations offered in the literature for exercise addiction. This section is adapted from his description.

Early explanations of the neurobiological correlates and antecedents to exercise addiction focused on the endogenous opioid systems. This was based on the idea that exercisers could achieve a "runner's high." There is, however, little evidence to support this hypothesis. It is unlikely that sufficient levels of beta-endorphins could cross the blood-brain barrier to have an appreciable effect. For example, mice that have been run excessively have not shown posthumously much activation of the opiate systems.

Another explanation is referred to as the "sympathetic arousal" theory. This suggests that modifications to how epinephrine and norepinephrine are utilized in the brain may be sufficient to create exercise dependence. The hypothesis is that regular exercising enhances metabolism efficiency, which results in a reduction of these catecholamines. So, the fitter one would become, the lower the catecholamine levels, resulting in lower arousal. To return the arousal level to a normal range, the individual would need to exercise at higher intensities and for longer durations. Although this theory sounds conceptually appealing, there have been no studies to date to support it (Adams, 2013).

The leading neurobiological theory is that exercise creates modifications to the mesolimbic dopamine system (MDS). The MDS is the pathway in the midbrain that includes the nucleus accumbens and the ventral tegmental area. These areas have been described in earlier chapters. Released dopamine creates seductively positive feelings in some people. An increase in dopamine levels, unfortunately, reduces the availability of postsynaptic dopamine receptors. In this way, the body can maintain homeostasis. *Homeostasis* refers to the mechanism by which an organism maintains internal stability. Once there are fewer dopamine receptors, a reduced but healthy regime of exercise will no longer result in the same intensity of a dopamine high to which the exercise addict has become accustomed.

The problem for exercise addicts only results, then, if the person attempts to reduce the behavior (e.g., exercise) that is creating the high levels of dopamine that are now required to maintain a "normal" mood state and level of arousal. In turn, this results in strong cravings for the person to return to previous exercise levels, which by this time have become excessive. Furthermore, when the depletion of dopamine becomes severe enough, the person is no longer able to experience pleasure in any life area without returning to the previous intensity of exercise (note that this same pattern occurs with any addictive behavior or substance). The word for this inability to experience pleasure is *anhedonia*. There is a substantial body of research in both animal and human studies to support the dopaminergic modification theory (Adams, 2013).

Physical Impacts (Long-Term Use)

Addicted exercisers continue to push their bodies physically despite physical injury or the development of other physical illnesses. Some of these injuries are incurred through overuse. People between ages 45 and 55 years who walk and run several hours a week have a greater risk of developing osteoarthritis than those who are less active physically (Lichtenstein et al., 2017).

Overtraining is a serious consequence of exercise addiction. It results from not giving the body enough rest between exercise sessions. The result of overtraining includes damage to the "musculoskeletal, endocrine, cardiovascular, reproductive, and immune systems" (Adams, 2013, p. 833). Overtraining can also create permanent damage to one's reproductive system, and anecdotal reports suggest it may even result in chronic fatigue syndrome (Adams, 2013).

Respiratory problems and heart attacks may result from overdoing it physically. Those who are striving to lose or gain weight may become addicted to yet something else in turn, such as pills and steroids (Mulvay, 2016).

Mental, Emotional, and Spiritual Impacts

A recent study of 1439 participants found that 6.5% of them identified as amateur competitive exercisers. Those who scored in the exercise addiction range experienced lower self-esteem and diminished subjective well-being compared to those who were not addicted to exercise (Menczel et al., 2017). A study with Chinese college students found that addicted exercisers also reported diminished subjective well-being but also increased levels of state anxiety and depression (Li, Nie, & Ren, 2015).

Faigin, Pargament, and Abu-Raiya (2014) conducted a longitudinal study with 90 freshmen college students. They found that those who experienced spiritual struggles had higher scores on measures of 11 out of 14 addiction domains including exercise addiction.

Adams (2013) reported that withdrawal symptoms might include mood swings, aches and pains, and dry mouth. In a group of 18 runners (8 addicted exercisers and 10 nonaddicted exercisers), after 2 weeks of not exercising, the addicted exercisers displayed symptoms of depression, confusion, anger, fatigue, and negative mood (Antunes et al., 2016). Other symptoms of withdrawal may include guilt, irritability, nervousness, tension, anxiety, and lethargy (Avril, Nivoli, & Lejoyeux, 2007).

Psychosocial Impacts (Relationships, Career/Work, Legal, Financial)

Compulsive exercise can lead to serious financial problems and problems at school and work and in relationships (Menczel et al., 2017). As increasing amounts of time are needed to exercise, the addict withdraws time and energy from other areas of life, including social and romantic relationships and recreational activities, as well as work and school (Adams, 2013). Many addicts, according to anecdotal reports, exercise more than 3 hours a day (Adams, 2013). Increasingly, motivation diminishes to engage in activities that are unrelated to exercise.

Working With Diverse Populations

Sex Differences

Studies focused on the prevalence of exercise addiction are equivocal. Some studies suggest that men are at higher risk, and other studies suggest that women are (Davis, 2000; Hausenblas & Symons Downs, 2002b; Miller & Mesagno, 2014; Pierce, Rohaly, & Fritchley, 1997).

In a sample of 1497 adults (608 men, 885 women, 4 other), men and women were found to be equally at risk for exercise addiction. Of the total sample, 21 participants (1.4%) scored high for PEA, whereas 75 (5.0%) scored high for SEA. The researchers found that men were at greater risk of developing PEA, whereas women were more at risk of SEA (Cunningham et al., 2016). Kjelsas and Augestad (2003) found in their sample of 236 female and 226 male competitive runners that women were more likely than men to exercise for stress relief and to improve their mood and physical appearance. Women who are unable to exercise report more cravings and nervousness compared with men (Fattore, Melis, Fadda, & Fratta, 2014).

Adolescents and Youth

Given that adolescence is a time of vulnerability, interventions aimed at teenagers showing signs of addiction are needed (Boyd, Harris, & Knight, 2012). A recent Italian study of high school students (N = 996; M = 240, F = 756) found that the prevalence of what the authors called maladaptive physical exercise was 6.2% (Di Nicola et al., 2017). In their sample of 2853 high school students, Villella et al. (2011) found a prevalence of exercise addiction to be 8.5%.

Parents who have eating disorders are likelier to have children who experience binge eating and compulsive exercise symptoms (Lydecker & Grilo, 2016). A study of 417 male and female adolescents between ages 14 and 16 completed questionnaires, and it was found that those involved in sports reported higher levels of compulsive exercise than those who were nonsport participants (Goodwin, Haycraft, & Meyer, 2016).

A study of 572 adolescents found that the compulsive exercisers had difficulty with emotional regulation, a finding similar to that found in adults who are addicted exercisers (Goodwin, Haycraft, & Meyer, 2014). In 1488 male and female adolescents, ages 12 to 14 years, compulsive exercise was most strongly associated with the drive for thinness and perfectionism, as well as obsessive-compulsiveness (Goodwin, Haycraft, Willis, & Meyer, 2011).

To understand the results of this next study, it is important to understand the four types of extrinsic motivation: external regulation, introjected regulation, identification, and integrated regulation. External regulation is about engaging in behavior to achieve externally provided rewards or satisfy external pressures (e.g., If I finish the race I get a medallion). Introjected regulation is about internalizing external controls, which results in self-imposed pressures to avoid feeling guilt or anxiety (e.g., I continue running to keep others believing that I am a good runner). Identification creates motivation by accepting that the behavior is beneficial, as it will result in personally valued outcomes (e.g., I continue exercising because I know it is good for me). Integrated regulation is about valuing a goal (or regulation) so that taking action is viewed as personally important (e.g., I run because I find it personally meaningful).

Symons-Downs, Savage, and DiNallo (2013) tested a sample of 805 teenagers (mean age = 15 years, 46% girls). In the teens displaying primary exercise dependence symptoms, integrated regulation (boys and girls), introjected regulation (boys and girls), and external regulation (boys only) were substantial determinants of their symptoms. Consequently, these three forms of external motivation may be causative factors in exercise addiction in adolescents.

Many children display high levels of body dissatisfaction, including boys and preschoolers (Cohane & Pope, 2001; McCabe & Ricciardelli, 2004; Tatangelo, McCabe, Mellor, & Mealey, 2016). Body dissatisfaction is a major risk factor for developing an eating disorder. Denial of having an eating disorder is common in adolescents (Levallius, Collin, & Birgegard, 2017). A study of 3116 girls and 139 boys from an eating disorder database revealed that 36% experienced compulsive exercising, but, when those in denial of having an eating disorder were included, the percentage increased to 44% (Levallius et al., 2017). The authors concluded that it is important to screen adolescents carefully because of the impact of their denial. One study found that supervised exercise, however, provided psychological benefits (i.e., reduced anxiety and depression and an increase in positive affect) to teenagers experiencing anorexia nervosa (Noetel et al., 2016).

Race and Ethnicity

Petitpas et al. (2015) hypothesized that nationality, race, and ethnicity might influence how and whether exercise addiction is experienced and expressed. To date, little research has been done in this area. There is some evidence suggesting that Asian American males might be more prone to binge eating and report greater body image concerns compared with men of other races and ethnicities (Kelly, Cotter, Tanofsky-Kraff, & Mazzeo, 2015). Compulsive exercise is also particularly high among Asian American men who binge eat (Kelly et al., 2015).

Nonpsychiatric Disabilities

There is no published literature about exercise addiction and nonpsychiatric disabilities. This is noted here so that both students and practitioners are aware of the current lack of research in this area.

Lesbian, Gay, Bisexual, and Transgender (LGBT)

Brewster, Sandil, DeBlaere, Breslow, and Eklund (2017) tested a sample of 326 sexual minority men. Together with other findings, the researchers found that striving to gain muscularity was related to compulsive exercising. A similar study conducted by Velez, Breslow, Brewster, Cox, and Foster (2016) utilized a national sample of 304 transgender men. They found that, among other constructs, compulsive exercise was correlated directly with only the internalization of sociocultural standards of attractiveness.

War Veterans

There is no published literature about exercise addiction and veterans. This is noted here so that both students and practitioners are aware of the current lack of research in this area.

Medications and Other Relevant Physical Interventions

There are no empirically supported medical treatments for PEA. There are medical treatments for SEA that involve treating the primary condition (e.g., eating disorders, bipolar disorder).

Di Nicola et al. (2010) found that 12 weeks of quetiapine (i.e., Seroquel) administration eliminated the compulsive buying and exercise addiction of a 47-year-old Caucasian man who also had bipolar I disorder. There are no approved medications for anorexia nervosa. For a review of medications that have been tried, see Frank and Shott (2016).

For those with bulimia nervosa, there are effective treatments for the metabolic abnormalities caused by purging (known as pseudo Bartter syndrome) (Mascolo, McBride, & Mehler, 2016). The U.S. Food and Drug Administration approved lisdexamfetamine (e.g., Vyvanse) for the treatment of moderate to severe binge eating disorder (BED) in adults (Fornaro et al., 2016). The drug continues to be scrutinized, however, due to adverse side effects and high discontinuation rates (Fornaro et al., 2016). Gianini, Broft, and Devlin (2016) wrote about the treatment of eating disorders. Antidepressants are the most-studied medications for the treatment of bulimia nervosa. For individuals with BED who are overweight or obese, the FDA-approved medications for weight loss include lorcaserin (e.g., Belviq), naltrexone-bupropion (e.g., Contrave), orlistat (e.g., Alli, Xenical), and phentermine-topiramate (e.g., Qsymia) (Gianini et al., 2016).

INSIDE AN ADDICTED PERSON'S MIND

Chloe, Age 32

I guess you could say that I have suffered from depression for many years. About a year ago, I went to the emergency room, and they asked me more questions about my eating habits than they did about my moods! I know I am slim because I take really good care of myself. I am 5' 3" tall, and I weigh just under 100 pounds. Okay, I admit, perhaps I do look overly thin, but I do eat a normal amount of food. Their questions led me to think that they thought I was anorexic or bulimic. I have never had an eating disorder in my life, but for some reason, they didn't seem to believe me. They offered me an antidepressant, but I don't believe in taking medications. So, I left the hospital that day feeling really frustrated.

I am glad they didn't ask me about exercise. Some people might think that my exercise routine is excessive, and I don't need hospital staff telling me otherwise. I am a very determined individual, and exercise is the only thing that makes me feel good about myself. I don't believe that going to the gym for 20 hours a week and aerobics classes at night five nights a week is over-the-top at all for someone who used to be 20 pounds overweight.

I became serious about exercise when I was 14 years old. It is mostly what I think about because it does me so much good—even fantasizing about it improves my mood. My parents were killed in a car crash 18 years ago. I still think about them a lot, and it upsets me a great deal, but when I'm exercising, I can push everything out of my mind and focus instead on the next repetition.

I inherited quite a bit of money following my parents' death. Today I live alone in a very swank apartment. I don't think I will ever have to work, which is a good thing because I don't know how I would fit work into my very busy schedule. I barely have enough time as it is for Lisa and Amanda, my only two friends that have time during the day to get together for the odd coffee or lunch. They sometimes ask me why I don't have time for them later in the day, but I don't think it is any of their business to know about my aerobics classes. They wouldn't understand how painful it is for me to miss one of my classes. Besides, I want to get my money's worth out of my gym membership that includes unlimited aerobic classes.

I have found over the last couple of years that my Achilles tendons seem to be bothering me increasingly, but thankfully I know what to do about it. I have been working steadily at strengthening the muscles around the tendons by doing tons of calf raises. A trainer at the gym told me I was doing too much exercise and he told me I should stop doing leg exercises until my tendons fully heal. But he doesn't understand how badly I feel if I cannot keep up the pace.

Commentary

Chloe demonstrates many symptoms of being an exercise addict. These include the following:

1. Chloe exercises an enormous number of hours per week yet is not training for an athletic event (i.e., compulsiveness).
2. Chloe's excessive exercise began around the time she was traumatized after suddenly losing both parents (i.e., personal conflict).
3. Exercising is the only thing that makes her feel better (i.e., mood modification).
4. She thinks about exercise all the time (i.e., obsessiveness).
5. She minimizes the time spent in close relationships to exercise more (i.e., salience).
6. She continues to exercise despite injury to her Achilles tendons (i.e., ignoring negative consequences).
7. She is in denial of having a problem with excessive exercise (i.e., denial).
8. She avoids telling people about her excessive exercise (i.e., secretiveness).

Discussion

1. Do you know of anyone who you suspect has become dependent on exercise? If "yes," which symptoms noted in the commentary apply to him or her?
2. Does this person have symptoms that are not listed in the commentary? If so, what are they?
3. If you were Chloe's counselor, how would you go about helping her?

Specific Counseling Considerations

ROLEPLAY SCENARIOS

Roleplay in dyads with one of you acting as the counselor and the other as the counselee. If a roleplay is not possible, work individually in writing out a list of your suggestions.

Roleplay #1

Dar, a 56-year-old Asian-Indian Realtor, came to see you upon the recommendation of his physician. Dar had a heart attack nearly 6 years ago, and he tells you that it nearly killed him. His entire family would visit him in the hospital, and they looked deeply concerned. Dar interpreted this as believing that they thought he would pass away.

As you look at Dar, however, you see what appears to be a very healthy person in front of you, but Dar tells you that he used to be 80 pounds heavier. He has been pushing himself to win something he calls a beach body contest. As you talk to Dar, you find out that he thinks about exercise all the time and that he has missed a lot of real estate sales because he refuses to shortchange his workouts by leaving it before a minimum of 2 hours have passed. You also find out that his wife died 2 years ago from a heart attack, and you suspect that his grief remains very severe. You determine in your assessment that Dar does not have any other psychological or psychiatric problem in his life currently.

Roleplay #2

Beth, age 21, works part-time as a retail salesperson. Your first session with her is a telephone intake call. Beth seems like a reluctant caller, and she tells you that she is phoning because her mother is forcing her to take some action. Beth doesn't think there is anything wrong with her other than she doesn't earn enough money in her current job. She tells you, however, that she exercises 7 days a week for durations of 90 minutes each, and she does this two or three times a day. Beth tells you that her mother simply doesn't understand what it is like to be 21 years old today and the demands made by guys in online dating.

You set up your live counseling session with Beth for 2 days later. When you go out to the waiting room to bring her to your office, you are struck that she looks to be about 5' 4" and likely weighs less than 90 pounds.

HOW WOULD AN ADDICTION COUNSELOR HELP THIS PERSON?

You are working as a professional counselor. You have always been a sports enthusiast yourself, and you recognize Mason when he comes to your office, but you cannot remember the context of why he seems familiar. You are struck by his amazing upper body muscularity and his good looks. He tells you that he used to be an Olympic gymnast and he won a silver medal a few years ago in his only Olympic competition. Since then, he has not qualified with USA Gymnastics to compete again at the Olympic level. Mason is now 30 years old, and his presenting concern is that he has been getting depressed increasingly because his leg development is not in proportion to his upper body development. Although you do not say anything to Mason, you do notice that his upper body does seem much larger in proportion to his lower body.

You find out that he exercises aerobically and with weights for several hours a day. He also tells you that he has not worked since the Olympics. As you inquire further, he tells you that his shoulder joints have been permanently damaged from the years of practice on the rings. Despite this, however, in the gym, he tries hard to lift the heaviest weights he can in both bench press and military press. He also performs squats with 400 pounds and leg presses with 600 pounds or more during his leg days, which are 4 days a week. He repeats his leg workout at least twice a day during these four leg days. Mason has not suffered any leg injuries to date, and he tells you that he intends to keep squatting and doing leg presses with increasing amounts of weight.

During one of his training days 6 months ago, he dislocated his shoulder while doing military presses. His physician told him that it is likely he is going to suffer severe arthritis in both shoulders if he does not slow down his exercise routine. Mason is not concerned, however, and he intends to continue exercising as he is doing. He said he is mostly wanting to see you to get over the depression he feels at not accomplishing his leg goals in the gym.

Remember to view clients within their environmental contexts, keeping in mind societal, parental/familial, cultural/spiritual, and peer influences. Specifically, become aware of the impact that the following influences have and continue to have in your clients' lives: race, language, religion and spirituality, gender, familial migration history, sexual/affectional orientation, age and cohort, physical and mental capacities, socioeconomic situation and history, education, and history of traumatic experience.

1. What defines this person's environment, past and present?
2. Who is this person sitting in front of me, taking into account environmental and personal characteristics?
3. What defines the problem that he or she is presenting within their multicultural milieu?

Goals and Goal Setting

Heather Hausenblas, one of the leading experts in exercise addiction, stated that the goal of counseling is to help clients recognize their addictive behavior and moderate their extreme exercise routines (Howard, 2017). Hausenblas went on to explain that it is not the amount of exercise that is the issue. When elite athletes become injured through overuse, they take time off until sufficient healing has occurred. Addicted exercisers, on the other hand, have a very difficult time doing that (Howard, 2017).

The goals that follow apply to most if not all addictions including exercise addiction (adapted from "Drug and Alcohol," n.d.) :

- Work on overcoming the character flaws that left them susceptible to addiction (e.g., impulsiveness, perfectionism).
- Learn to deal with positive and especially negative emotions in healthy ways.
- Rebuild relationships that have been hurt by the addiction.
- Focus on finding important and meaningful things to do in life.
- Regain those things that were lost due to addiction.

SMART is an acronym that is useful in goal setting. The acronym SMARTER adds two additional characteristics as follows (adapted from "Drug and Alcohol," n.d.):

1. Specific. Ensure that the goal is clear and unambiguous (e.g., I will go to the gym only three times a week).
2. Measurable. Progress can be determined only if the goal is measurable (e.g., Each time I go to the gym, I will exercise for only 60 minutes).
3. Attainable. The goal needs to be achievable and realistic (e.g., On a scale of 0–10, I will exercise at a level of 5 or 6).
4. Relevant. The goal has to make sense to the client (e.g., Exercising only once a week will not likely seem reasonable to someone who has been exercising 7 days a week).
5. Timely. The goal can be achieved within a certain timeline (e.g., I will exercise only once a week for 6 weeks until my injury has healed).
6. Evaluate. Deciding how attainment of the goal will be measured and deciding how often to measure it (e.g., I will keep a log every day of how much time I am spending exercising and review this log every Sunday).
7. Reevaluate. Occasionally it is important to ascertain if the approach being used to reach the goal is working and to adjust as necessary (e.g., After reviewing my log for one month, it is clear that I need to reduce the amount of exercise I do still further. I will now set my goal to exercise for only 45 minutes when I visit the gym).

Stages of Change Strategies

The processes of change mentioned are based on those outlined by Connors, DiClemente, Velasquez, and Donovan (2013) and Prochaska, Norcross, and DiClemente (1994). The definitions for the various processes can be found in Chapter 6. Besides these processes, other strategies are included that have separate citations.

The University of Rhode Island Change Assessment Scale (URICA) is a helpful scale in determining where a client is currently at regarding the stages of change model. There are 24-, 28-, and 32-item versions of the scale. A 24-item version is published for alcohol or drug problems. The scale, however, is generic and can be easily adapted for use with other addictions. It is available with norms as a free download from https://www.guilford.com/add/miller11_old/urica.pdf.

Specific precontemplation strategies.

Please visit the section of this chapter called Relevant Mutual Support Groups, Websites, and Videos for free or low-cost information and resources that may help someone move out of precontemplation.

Suggested bibliotherapy is a book entitled *The Truth About Exercise Addiction: Understanding the Dark Side of Thinspiration* (Schreiber & Hausenblas, 2017). The book receives nearly a five-star rating from Amazon.com.

Most addicts in precontemplation are not ready to attend a mutual support group, but some will go if they are accompanied. Recoveries Anonymous has been in existence for 34 years, and it is are open to people experiencing a plethora of different addictions. The group also focuses on exercise addiction (visit http://www.r-a.org/i-exercise-addicts.htm#.WpbD_0xFzE0). Its website provides a substantial amount of free information. Addicts can also find nearby meetings (where available). Although there is mention of an Exercise Addicts Anonymous meeting (i.e., http://www.exerciseaddictsanonymous.org/), it does not appear that this group has flourished currently. There is, however, an Online Exercise Addiction Support Group (visit https://exercise-addiction.supportgroups.com/).

A person in precontemplation can be encouraged to look at the pros and cons of continuing their excessive exercise behavior. Most will already be experiencing negative consequences by the time they book an appointment to see you.

Specific contemplation strategies.

The published literature to date does not offer suggestions to help facilitate this stage with addicted exercisers. Consequently, the ideas offered here are somewhat speculative.

Helping clients look at the negative consequences caused by their exercise addiction may be helpful in creating an emotional response, particularly if those consequences have been substantial. If addicts can make the connection between their excessive exercise and relationship difficulties, for example, they are more apt to consider modifying their compulsiveness. Helping clients talk about the pain that their addiction is causing them is key in the contemplation phase.

Consciousness-raising is often best facilitated through self-monitoring of the thoughts and feelings associated with continuing the addictive behavior. For example, how do compulsive exercisers truly feel as they are pushing themselves through the pain associated with overuse injuries? As they listen intensely to what their body is telling them, they may become aware of how destructive exercise has become for them.

Self-re-evaluation occurs when addicted exercisers begin assessing the costs and benefits of continuing their compulsive behavior. As mutual support groups are at a fledgling stage of development currently, there may not be a group where clients live that they can attend. It is often recommended, however, that attending any 12-step meeting will help facilitate change as the steps are the same across meetings that deal with different addictions. As with other addictions, helping relationships at this stage focus on supporting the addict with making the desired change.

Specific preparation strategies.

The primary goal of the preparation stage is to help the client develop commitment toward change and to create a plan of action. Although there is little literature on the treatment of exercise addiction, Hausenblas et al. (2017) stated that the goal is not to prevent clients from working out but instead it is to help them recognize their addictive behavior and reduce their rigidity around exercise. These authors also suggested that early assessment may help clients not progress to developing either an eating disorder or a physical problem related to excessive exercise.

A preparation strategy might include having clients meet with fitness professionals to design an appropriate training routine and to relearn how to use internal sensations to monitor whether the exercise is helping or hurting (Hausenblas et al., 2017). For competitive athletes, they may want to work with their coaches and allied staff (e.g., athletic trainers, physiotherapists) to come to understand how fatigue from excessive exercise will diminish their performance. Orthopedics may be required if clients have already sustained injuries from excessive exercise, and dietitians may need to assist if weight has become a concern (Hausenblas et al., 2017). Other ideas for *before* their chosen quit day (i.e., preparation strategies) can be found in Appendix B.

Specific action strategies.

Addicted exercisers are typically ambivalent about changing and score low on measures of compliance (Lichtenstein et al., 2017). Adams and Kirkby (1998) found that their respondents treated exercise addiction with (a) education regarding overtraining consequences, (b) recommending different training activities, and (c) referral for counseling/psychotherapy. Psychological methods are the most recommended for treating exercise addiction (Lichtenstein et al., 2017).

Adams, Miller, and Kraus (2003) recommended that treatment consist of the following: (a) identifying triggers for the compulsive behavior, (b) teaching about the health benefits of exercising in moderation, (c) helping the client develop a self-management strategy, and (d) teaching coping strategies. Cognitive and behavioral strategies are typical recommendations (Lichtenstein et al., 2017). Motivational interviewing (MI) is also recommended, but no treatment methods have been sufficiently empirically validated (Berczik et al., 2014). Hausenblas et al. (2017) also recommended dialectical behavior therapy to better manage mood disturbances.

Mulvay (2016) suggested that addicted exercisers should seek out the support of significant others and reconnect with friends who don't work out at a gym. Mulvay also recommended developing new hobbies, practicing healthier eating, and putting as much energy into recovery as one did into exercise.

Kerulis (2015) wrote that both inpatient and outpatient programs could be helpful to addicted exercisers. Some considerations here mentioned included severity, time availability, and finances. Inpatient programs may run 14–21 days (Kerulis, 2015). Other ideas for *beginning* a chosen quit day (i.e., action strategies) can be found in Appendix B.

Specific maintenance strategies and relapse prevention.

Note: Maintenance strategies and relapse prevention are also, for many, partly facilitated by regular attendance at relevant mutual support groups. A list of such mutual support groups and helpful websites is found in an upcoming section entitled Relevant Mutual Support Groups, Websites, and Videos.

The published literature is silent on this phase. One can speculate that, once the issues underlying exercise addiction are dealt with and a moderate exercise program has been implemented, little else may be required. But there is no research that speaks to maintenance strategies for exercise addiction currently. Some generic ideas for relapse prevention can be found in Appendix C.

Motivational Interviewing

As problems with compliance are documented in the literature on addicted exercisers, MI has been suggested as a treatment strategy (Lichtenstein et al., 2017). This is the third session that Bobby, age 18, is having with his counselor. (Pertaining to Chapter 6's description of MI, the following is an example of the process called *evoking*.)

Client: After having had two sessions with you, Ralph, I don't think I want to change anything at all regarding my exercise and fitness goals. I am an appropriate weight for my height, so all this hype about my exercise program seems overboard to me.

Counselor: I certainly understand, Bobby, why you might not want to alter anything about your life. You are of average weight, and you are doing well in your job.

Last week you did, however, bring up a few reasons that you think your exercise program might be excessive. Remind us both again of what those reasons were.

Client: Well, my family doctor told me that, if I keep doing what I'm doing, I will likely develop arthritis when I'm older. But I'm only 18, and that just seems like too far away for me to think about.

Counselor: So, you don't want to think about your future right now. Nonetheless, your physician has given you a warning about what may happen if you continue on your present course. I sure wouldn't want to push you to do anything that you don't want to do.

Client: Yes, I know, I know. You're probably the most understanding counselor I have ever talked to before. I know you would like me to slow down on my exercise, too. I guess I'm quite worried that, if I do, I will gain weight and I will have a harder time finding a girlfriend.

Counselor: Yeah, I can appreciate that that is a concern at your age. Thank you for the compliment, by the way. I'm glad you find it easy to talk to me about things that matter in your life.

Client: Do you think I should be concerned about what the doctor said?

Counselor: You know, Bobby, that is really up to you how you want to live your life. I know you enjoy exercising a great deal and that it takes up a lot of your time every week. You've told me that you don't always know how you're going to find time to date someone. And then there is what your doctor has told you about the consequences that can happen if you keep exercising the way that you are. I certainly hear your reservation about making a change right now. I also know that you want to do what's right for yourself.

Client: That's right! You really do get it. I don't have time to date because I'm in the gym for all of my free time.

Counselor: You told me in the first session that you were feeling a lot of loneliness, and also that you really would like to have a girlfriend but that you are not finding time to date because of the high expectations you place on yourself regarding fitness and weight control.

Client: Correct—how am I supposed to do it all?

Counselor: Sometimes it can seem like it is difficult to shuffle priorities. To what extent do you think that is true in your case?

Client: Totally. I didn't think I had any priorities to tell you the truth. But I am lonely, I do want a girlfriend, and I don't know how to fit it all in.

Counselor: Can I add that you also want to be healthy and live a long life without pain?

Client: I cannot deny that. I just don't know where to start.

Counselor: I know. All of this can seem overwhelming. How to balance work with your home life. How to balance an appropriate amount of exercise while maintaining sufficient time to date someone. By the sounds of it, you are ready to start dating. Have you met anyone that you would like to ask out?

Client: Not yet, but I did put up a profile on Plenty of Fish the other night, and already 10 girls have responded to me. One of them looks really sweet.

Counselor: That was quick, Bobby! Young women obviously see you as attractive in so many ways. You're off to a better start than I was at your age.

Client: I just wish I had some confidence like you do. Don't know why that doesn't seem to be there already. I suspect it might be part of the reason I spend so much time in the gym. I want to look super hot so the girls will think I'm okay.

Counselor: It looks like a lot of girls think you're okay. I can certainly help you develop greater confidence. We can even talk about how to initiate the first date. How does that sound?

Client: That sounds awesome. You are simply the best, Ralph!

Insight-Oriented Interventions

Emini and Bond (2014) sampled 101 men between ages 18 and 67 who were active weight trainers. About 18% ($N = 18$) of the sample scored high on the Bodybuilding Dependence Scale (i.e., more than one standard deviation above the mean). Results suggested that bodybuilding dependence was a result of and a way of coping with stress that manifested as aggression.

Krueger (2001), writing from a psychoanalytic perspective, suggested that compulsive exercise may represent inadequate ego development resulting from a lack of integration between mind and body and as a defensive maneuver against painful feelings. Krueger defined ego development as a sense of self that is cohesive, distinctive, and accurate.

Automatic Thought or Belief	Questioning It	Healthier Thought or Belief
I need to keep exercising excessively to feel good about myself.		I will learn to develop positive self-esteem independent of how much I exercise.
If I stop exercising like this, I will gain weight.		Weight gain is better managed through eating a healthy diet than through excessive exercise.
I have to lose weight fast.		It is healthy to lose weight gradually.
I exercise to keep my mind off my unresolved issues or my current stress.		I will seek help to work through my unresolved issues and to learn to cope better with stress.
I should keep exercising despite my exercise-induced injury.		I need to follow medical advice regarding my injury for optimal healing to occur.

Taken together, a counselor may find it fruitful to help clients learn to become assertive with others and learn strategies for coping better with stress. One way of helping clients cope better with stress would be teaching them to recognize painful feelings and to deal with these in healthier ways, such as what is taught in dialectical behavior therapy. Krueger's (2001) speculation, if accurate, may also lead counselors to help clients develop a stronger and more accurate sense of self.

Spiritual Interventions

There is no published literature about exercise addiction and spiritual interventions.

Cognitive-Behavioral Therapy

Cognitive-behavioral therapy (CBT) can be facilitated using the triple column technique. It can be used both by counselors in their work with clients and by clients alone. The full instructions for using the technique are found in Chapter 6. The following are some of the cognitions that can be problematic for clients with this addiction.

Although Lichtenstein et al. (2017) recommended CBT because it has received empirical validation for treating other behavioral addictions, currently there are no empirically validated studies that have adequately demonstrated its effectiveness. On the other hand, enhanced cognitive-behavioral therapy (CBT-E) is a well-known and empirically supported treatment for eating disorders (Danielsen, Ardal Rekkedal, Frostad, & Kessler, 2016). CBT-E has been developed over the last decade, and it takes a "transdiagnostic approach." Its assumption is that cognitions such as overevaluating body shape and weight are common to all eating disorders. CBT-E is a structured 20-session intervention, and it requires delivery by one counselor. Using a CD-ROM was found in one study to be an effective medium for delivering CBT to individuals with bulimia nervosa (Murray et al., 2007).

McNamara and McCabe (2012) tested 234 elite Australian athletes and found 34% of them were classified as exercise dependent. Their exercise beliefs were measured using the Exercise Beliefs Questionnaire. The exercise-dependent group reported more beliefs that there would be severe consequences physically, mentally, and socially if they did not continue their excessive exercise routines. This suggests indirectly that CBT might be helpful in modifying these beliefs.

RELEVANT MUTUAL SUPPORT GROUPS, WEBSITES, AND VIDEOS

Mutual Support Groups

For the Addicted Individual

1. Recoveries Anonymous. http://www.r-a.org/i-exercise-addicts.htm#.WpbD_0xFzE0

   Quoted from website:

   R.A. is a Twelve Step program. We have no dues or fees. We are here for those who want a full recovery from compulsive exercise—but despite their best efforts, have yet to find a full recovery from compulsive exercise—and for their family and friends.

2. Addictions.com. https://exercise-addiction.supportgroups.com/welcome

For the Partner and/or Family

These groups are intended to help family members refrain from behaviors that may trigger the addict. They also target underlying maladaptive thoughts and behaviors of the co-addict. Lastly, they focus on facilitating spiritual growth.

Co-Dependents Anonymous. http://coda.org/

Quoted from website:

We welcome you to Co-Dependents Anonymous, a program of recovery from codependence, where each of us may share our experience, strength, and hope in our efforts to find freedom where there has been . . .

Websites

1. Clarifying Exercise Addiction: Differential Diagnosis, Co-occurring Disorders, and Phases of Addiction. https://www.ncbi.nlm.nih.gov/pmc/articles/PMC3210598/
2. Exercise Addiction: Causes, Risk Factors and Symptoms. https://www.healthline.com/health/exercise-addiction#overview1
3. Orthorexia, Excessive Exercise & Nutrition. https://www.eatingdisorderhope.com/information/orthorexia-excessive-exercise
4. Exercise Addiction 101. https://www.addiction.com/addiction-a-to-z/exercise-addiction/exercise-addiction-101/
5. Exercise Addiction. https://www.unm.edu/~lkravitz/Article%20folder/exerciseaddictionLK.html

Videos

To view these videos, search their titles on YouTube.

1. *Addicted to Exercise.* CBS. Dr. Jennifer Ashton.

2. *Addicted to Working Out.*
3. *Exercise Addiction: When Fitness Becomes a Dangerous Obsession.*
4. *Joe Rogan – What It Takes to Be an Ultra Marathon Runner.*
5. *The SAD TRUTH of Becoming an Olympic Athlete.*

RELEVANT PHONE APPS

Generic Addiction Apps

Note: Generic apps are described in Chapter 6.

This list is not exhaustive. New apps are continually being developed. Do an Internet search to find out the latest apps available. Most are for specific addictions, but some, such as these four, are generic.

1. I Am Sober. https://play.google.com/store/apps/details?id=com.thehungrywasp.iamsober
2. Sober Time. https://play.google.com/store/apps/details?id=com.sociosoft.sobertime
3. Pocket Rehab: Get Sober & Addiction Recovery. https://play.google.com/store/apps/details?id=com.getpocketrehab.app
4. Loop Habit Tracker. https://play.google.com/store/apps/details?id=org.isoron.uhabits

Specialized Apps

There do not appear to be apps specifically designed for exercise addiction currently. Do periodic Internet searches as new apps are constantly under development.

JOURNALS AND CONFERENCES

Journals

There are no journals specifically dedicated to exercise addiction currently. The first three journals listed, however, publish a significant number of articles about exercise addiction, and a description of each is included. The remaining sports medicine journals listed publish some manuscripts in this area.

1. *International Journal of Mental Health and Addiction.* Quoted from website: "The *International Journal of Mental Health & Addiction* offers a forum for up-to-date information and developments in mental health and addiction-related research, policy, phenomenology, literature, and treatment . . . We publish 4 times a year." http://www.springer.com/public+health/journal/11469
2. *Journal of Behavioral Addictions.* Quoted from website: "The aim of the journal is to create a forum for the scientific information exchange with regard to behavioral addictions . . . [focuses] on the addictive patterns of various behaviors, especially disorders of the impulsive-compulsive spectrum, and also publishes reviews in these topics." http://akademiai.com/loi/2006
3. *Journal of Behavioral Medicine.* Quoted from website: "The Journal of Behavioral Medicine is a broadly conceived interdisciplinary publication devoted to furthering understanding of physical health and illness through the knowledge and techniques of behavioral science." https://link.springer.com/journal/10865
4. *Sports Medicine Training and Rehabilitation.*
5. *Medicine and Science in Sports & Exercise.*
6. *British Journal of Sports Medicine.*
7. *Journal of Sports Medicine and Physical Fitness.*
8. *The International Journal of Sport Science.*

Conferences

There are no conferences that specifically deal with exercise addiction presently. Conferences that may have sessions concerning it include some of the following (note that, in several cases, links are not provided as the conference website changes annually):

1. Sport Science Conferences. For a list of these visit http://www.topendsports.com/study/conferences/index.htm
2. International Conference on Kinesiology and Exercise Sciences. https://10times.com/conference-kinesiology-exercise
3. International Conference on Qualitative Research in Sport and Exercise. http://qrse.org/
4. International Conference on Sports and Exercise Science
5. International Conference on Exercise, Sports & Health
6. International Conference on Exercise and Fitness
7. International Conference on Exercise, Metabolism, Weight Loss and Health

COUNSELING SCENARIO

As you are reading, imagine that you are the client in this scenario. Note the areas in which the session could be improved on the part of the counselor.

Your name is Jayden, a 16-year-old jock who plays middle linebacker in high school football. You are very popular with the girls in your school, and you have plenty of friends. You are the first to admit that your early years were challenging. Your dad was an alcoholic, and he never seemed to have any time for you. When he did spend time with you, he seemed nasty and disinterested. You remember many times he would scream and shout for no reason other than he was drunk and acting out due to his addiction. At least you know you are not addicted to anything.

Nevertheless, you have been suffering several injuries, particularly lower back distress due to the number of times you have been tackled. Your coach has seen the way you grimace in pain throughout most of the season. After asking you twice to take time off from playing, you refused adamantly. Consequently, he sent you to the high school counselor, Marguerite. This is now your second session with her.

- You: Hi, Marguerite.
- Counselor: Hi, Jayden. I'm glad you came back. You seemed disgruntled as you left my office 3 weeks ago.
- You: I guess you didn't tell me anything I wanted to hear. I just can't stop playing football. I am one of the best players out there.
- Counselor: I know this is hard for you. The coach, however, is insisting that you do not come back for the rest of the season.
- You: I do not buy that for one minute! He has no right to stop me from playing.
- Counselor: Actually, he does have the right. He *is* the coach. Last session I told you to go and talk to him. The coach told me that you did not follow up with him.
- You: That's right. I'm not going to suck up to him just because he has it out for me. Why are you talking to the coach without my permission? I thought this was supposed to be confidential.
- Counselor: School counselors here have the right to talk to anyone they please.
- You: Well then, how do you expect me to trust you?
- Counselor: Jayden, I told you what to do last session. I expected you to do it.
- You: Since when did you become my mother?
- Counselor: Your attitude is not helping the situation. I also told you to stop exercising for the past 3 weeks to let your body recover. Did you do it?
- You: No, of course not. I'm not going to let myself become weaker. That will just ensure that I am not allowed to play football.
- Counselor: You didn't talk to the coach and you didn't stop exercising.
- You: Yeah, what's your point?
- Counselor: I am telling you how to resolve this problem. Before next session, go talk to the coach. Furthermore, do not exercise until your injuries have fully healed.
- You: Right. I am so glad you know what I need right now.
- Counselor: I do know. I have worked with a lot of our school's athletes over the years.
- You: And I bet none of them amounted to anything!
- Counselor: Good bye, Jayden. See you again in 3 weeks.

From the Client's Perspective

1. How would you feel if you were treated this way by Marguerite?
2. What is missing for you in this dialogue?
3. What would you find more helpful from a counselor in this scenario?

From the Counselor's Perspective

1. What is interfering with developing a working alliance?
2. Going back to the Common Counseling Mistakes list in Chapter 6, which mistakes are the counselor making with Jayden?
3. What negative effect might this approach have on the client?

INDIVIDUAL EXERCISES

1. Create a list of 10 questions before interviewing someone you know who exercises a lot. What symptoms, if any, does this person have that would be reflective of someone with an exercise addiction? If you have time, also interview someone who seems to have an exercise addiction and ask your same 10 questions of this person.
2. Apply the same criteria to exercise addiction that are used to diagnose drug addiction as outlined in Chapter 13. Which criteria apply, and which criteria do not?
3. Spend time doing more exercise in an activity than you normally do. Then make a journal entry describing all symptoms you felt during the exercise and following the exercise that informs you that you did more exercise than usual. How do your body and mind let you know that you have engaged in excessive exercise given your current fitness level?

CLASSROOM EXERCISES

1. Invite a coach to your classroom who works with elite athletes. Have the class contribute a list of questions to ask him or her in advance of the class. Focus on getting the coach's perspective on training athletes who show signs and symptoms of exercise addiction. Also, find out in what ways coaching at this level both contributes to and deters athletes from becoming addicted to exercise.
2. Break the class into dyads or triads. Have half of the groups discuss all the health benefits that derive from getting adequate exercise. Focus the other half of the groups on discussing the various consequences that can result from exercise addiction. Ask all groups to be as specific as possible and then have a member of each group write these on the board.
3. Before the next class, ask students to do some Internet research to find out the names of celebrities, famous people, or elite athletes who have openly discussed having symptoms of exercise addiction. Also ask the class to write some details of what that celebrity has shared in the media regarding this. Alternatively, give your students a list of names of celebrities, famous people, and elite athletes who have discussed exercise addiction in the media and ask them to bring to class some of the details to share in a class discussion on this topic (e.g., Madonna, Sarah Jessica Parker, Tara Palmer-Tomkinson, Neil McAndrew, Renée Zellweger, and Heidi Montag). The details might include examples of their exercise regimes, their lifestyles, which may or may not promote exercise addiction, and any personality characteristics that may leave the individual vulnerable to becoming an exercise addict.

CHAPTER SUMMARY

The benefits of healthy exercising are enormous, but, for many active runners, the "runner's high" remains elusive. But some vulnerable individuals seem to become addicted to exercise, sometimes in pursuit of the neurochemical changes that may occur in their brain. Other addicts exercise excessively in an unsuccessful attempt to resolve inner conflicts or as a means of coping with current stressors. Exercise addiction has been written about since the 1970s. It was once thought to be a positive addiction, but further study has shown that its negative consequences can be substantial in a person's life. Exercise addiction does not currently appear in *DSM-5*.

Some symptoms of exercise addiction include (a) exercising an enormous number of hours per week despite the negative consequences, (b) exercising to modify mood, (c) obsessing about exercise, (d) compulsively engaging in exercise, (e) making exercise more important than other areas of life, including relationships, (f) continuing to exercise despite overuse injuries, (g) experiencing withdrawal symptoms when not exercising, and (h) possibly remaining in denial and keeping excessive exercise a secret. There are two kinds of exercise addiction. PEA occurs when exercise is the primary problem, and SEA results from other psychological conditions such as eating disorders.

Addicted exercisers may display aspects of perfectionism, obsessive compulsiveness, hedonism, and narcissism. Research with university students has shown that exercise addiction is positively correlated with neuroticism, extraversion, and conscientiousness but is inversely related to agreeableness. Addicted exercisers are often noncompliant in recovery efforts. They tend to have a negative or distorted body image, and they display a high degree of social physique anxiety. Many are afraid of aging. The prevalence of exercise addiction is estimated at between 0.3% and 0.5% of the general population. The prevalence is higher among regular exercisers but particularly among elite athletes.

Addicted exercisers are often noncompliant during recovery efforts. The goal of counseling is to help them recognize their addictive behavior and moderate their extreme exercise patterns. Worthy goals include improving their character flaws, learning to deal with both positive and negative emotions, rebuilding relationships, focusing on important and meaningful pursuits, and regaining other aspects of life that were lost due to the addiction. MI, CBT, and dialectical behavior therapy have been recommended as treatment strategies, but none have been empirically validated sufficiently.

REFERENCES

Adams, J. (2013). Exercise dependence. In P. M. Miller, S. A. Ball, M. E. Bates, A. W. Blume, K. M. Kampman, D. J. Kavanagh, M. E. Larimer, N. M. Petry, & P. De Witte (Eds.), *Comprehensive addictive behaviors and disorders, Vol. 1: Principles of addiction* (pp. 827–835). San Diego, CA: Elsevier Academic Press.

Adams, J., & Kirkby, R. J. (1998). Exercise dependence: A review of its manifestation, theory and measurement. *Sports Medicine Training and Rehabilitation, 8*(3), 265–276.

Adams, J. M., Miller, T. W., & Kraus, R. F. (2003). Exercise dependence: Diagnostic and therapeutic issues for patients in psychotherapy. *Journal of Contemporary Psychotherapy, 33*, 93–107.

Alcaraz-Ibanez, M., Aguilar-Parra, J. M., & Alvarez-Hernandez, J. F. (2018). Exercise addiction: Preliminary evidence on the role of psychological inflexibility. *International Journal of Mental Health and Addiction, 16*, 199–206.

American College of Sports Medicine. (2011). Quantity and quality of exercise for developing and maintaining cardiorespiratory, musculoskeletal, and neuromotor fitness in apparently healthy adults: Guidance for prescribing exercise. *Medicine and Science in Sports & Exercise, 43*, 1334–1359.

Andreassen, C. S., Griffiths, M. D., Gjertsen, S. R., Krossbakken, E., Kvam, S., & Pallesen, S. (2013). The relationships between behavioral addictions and the five-factor model of personality. *Journal of Behavioral Addictions, 2*(2), 90–99.

Antunes, H. K. M., Leite, G. S. F., Lee, K. S., Barreto, A. T., Santos, R. V. T. d., Souza, H. d. S., . . . de Mello, M. T. (2016). Exercise deprivation increases negative mood in exercise-addicted subjects and modifies their biochemical markers. *Physiology & Behavior, 156*, 182–190.

Avril, M., Nivoli, F., & Lejoyeux, M. (2007). Exercise dependence. *Alcoologie et Addictologie, 29*(2), 143–153.

Bamber, D., Cockerill, I. M., & Carroll, D. B. J. (2000). The pathological status of exercise dependence. *British Journal of Sports Medicine, 34*(2), 125–132.

Bamber, D. J., Cockerill, I. M., Rodgers, S., & Carroll, D. (2003). Diagnostic criteria for exercise dependence in women. *British Journal of Sports Medicine, 37*(5), 393–400.

Basson, C. J. (2001). Personality and behaviour associated with excessive dependence on exercise: Some reflections from research. *South African Journal of Psychology, 31*(2), 53–59.

Berczik, K., Griffiths, M. D., Szabo, A., Kurimay, T., Urban, R., & Demetrovics, Z. (2014). Exercise addiction. In K. P. Rosenberg & L. Curtiss Feder (Eds.), *Behavioral addictions: Criteria, evidence, and treatment* (pp. 317–342). San Diego, CA: Elsevier Academic Press

Berczik, K., Szabo, A., Griffiths, M. D., Kurimay, T., Kun, B., Urban, R., & Demetrovics, Z. (2012). Exercise addiction: Symptoms, diagnosis, epidemiology, and etiology. *Substance Use & Misuse, 47*(4), 403–417.

Beres, A., Czegledi, E., & Babusa, B. (2017). Effects of a single aerobic exercise session on body image. *Mentalhigiene es Pszichoszomatika, 18*(1), 84–104.

Bible, A. (n.d.). Athletes on teams might be more likely to become addicts. Here's why. *Men's Journal.* Retrieved on December 15, 2018, from https://www.mensjournal.com/health-fitness/athletes-teams-might-be-more-likely-become-addicts-heres-why/

Boyd, J. W., Harris, S. K., & Knight, J. R. (2012). Screening and brief interventions for the addiction syndrome: Considering the vulnerability of adolescence. In H. Shaffer, D. A. LaPlante, & S. E. Nelson (Eds.), *APA addiction syndrome handbook, Vol. 2: Recovery, prevention, and other issues* (pp. 169–194). Washington, DC: American Psychological Association.

Brewster, M. E., Sandil, R., DeBlaere, C., Breslow, A., & Eklund, A. (2017. "Do you even lift, bro?" Objectification, minority stress, and body image concerns for sexual minority men. *Psychology of Men & Masculinity, 18*(2), 87–98.

Chapman, C. L., & De Castro, J. M. (1990). Running addiction: Measurement and associated psychological characteristics. *Journal of Sports Medicine and Physical Fitness, 30*(3), 283–290.

Cohane, G. H., & Pope, H. G., Jr. (2001). Body image in boys: A review of the literature. *International Journal of Eating Disorders, 29*(4), 373–379.

Connors, G. J., DiClemente, C. C., Velasquez, M. M., & Donovan, D. M. (2013). *Substance abuse treatment and the stages of change: Selecting and planning interventions* (2nd ed.). New York, NY: Guilford Press.

Cook, B., Karr, T. M., Zunker, C., Mitchell, J. E., Thompson, R., Sherman, R., . . . Crosby, R. D. (2015). The influence of exercise identity and social physique anxiety on exercise dependence. *Journal of Behavioral Addictions, 4*(3), 195–199.

Cook, B., & Luke, R. (2017). Primary and secondary exercise dependence in a sample of cyclists. *International Journal of Mental Health and Addiction, 15*(2), 444–451.

Cunningham, H. E., Pearman, S., III, & Brewerton, T. D. (2016). Conceptualizing primary and secondary pathological exercise using available measures of excessive exercise. *International Journal of Eating Disorders, 49*(8), 778–792.

Dakwar, E. (2015). Problematic exercise: A case of alien feet. In M. S. Ascher & P. Levounis (Eds.), *The behavioral addictions* (pp. 29–42). Arlington, VA: American Psychiatric Publishing.

Damian, A. J., & Mendelson, T. (2017). Association of physical activity with alcohol abuse and dependence in a nationally-representative U.S. sample. *Substance Use & Misuse, 52*(13), 1744–1750.

Danielsen, Y. S., Ardal Rekkedal, G., Frostad, S., & Kessler, U. (2016). Effectiveness of enhanced cognitive behavioral therapy (CBT-E) in the treatment of anorexia nervosa: A prospective multidisciplinary study. *BMC Psychiatry, 16*(1), 1–14.

Davis, C. (2000). Exercise abuse. *International Journal of Sport Psychology, 31*(2), 278–289.

Davis, C., Brewer, H., & Ratusny, D. J. (1993). Behavioral frequency and psychological commitment: Necessary concepts in the study of excessive exercising. *Journal of Behavioral Medicine, 16*, 611–628.

De Coverley Veale, D. M. (1987). Exercise dependence. *British Journal of Addiction, 82*(7), 735–740.

De la Torre, J. (1995). Mens sana in corpore sano, or exercise abuse? Clinical considerations. *Bulletin of the Menninger Clinic, 59*(1), 15–31.

Di Lodovico, L., Dubertret, C., & Ameller, A. (2018). Vulnerability to exercise addiction, socio-demographic, behavioral and psychological characteristics of runners at risk for eating disorders. *Comprehensive Psychiatry, 81*, 48–52.

Di Nicola, M., Ferri, V. R., Moccia, L., Panaccione, I., Strangio, A. M., Tedeschi, D., . . . Janiri, L. (2017). Gender differences and psychopathological features associated with addictive behaviors in adolescents. *Frontiers in Psychiatry, 8*, ArtID 256.

Di Nicola, M., Martinotti, G., Mazza, M., Tedeschi, D., Pozzi, G., & Janiri, L. (2010). Quetiapine as add-on treatment for bipolar I disorder with comorbid compulsive buying and physical exercise addiction. *Progress in Neuro-Psychopharmacology & Biological Psychiatry, 34*(4), 713–714.

Drug and Alcohol Rehab in Thailand. (n.d.). Retrieved on February 26, 2018, from http://alcoholrehab.com/addiction-recovery/goal-setting-for-recovery/

Egorov, A. Y., & Szabo, A. (2013). The exercise paradox: An interactional model for a clearer conceptualization of exercise addiction. *Journal of Behavioral Addictions, 2*(4), 199–208.

Emini, N. N., & Bond, M. J. (2014). Motivational and psychological correlates of bodybuilding dependence. *Journal of Behavioral Addictions, 3*(3), 182–188.

Ertl, M. M., Longo, L. M., Groth, G. H., Berghuis, K. J., Prout, J., Hetz, M. C., & Martin, J. L. (2018). Running on empty: High self-esteem as a risk factor for exercise addiction. *Addiction Research & Theory, 26*, 205–211.

Esteves, A. M., dos Santos Nose, P. D. R., & de Mello, M. T. (2016). Physical exercise and treatment of addiction. In A. L. M. Andrade & D. De Micheli (Eds.), *Innovations in the treatment of substance addiction* (pp. 201–211). Cham, Switzerland: Springer International.

Faigin, C. A., Pargament, K. I., & Abu-Raiya, H. (2014). Spiritual struggles as a possible risk factor for addictive behaviors: An initial empirical investigation. *International Journal for the Psychology of Religion, 24*(3), 201–214.

Fattore, L., Melis, M., Fadda, P., & Fratta, W. (2014). Sex differences in addictive disorders. *Frontiers in Neuroendocrinology, 35*(3), 272–284.

Fornaro, M., Solmi, M., Perna, G., De Berardis, D., Veronese, N., Orsolini, L., Gananca, L., & Stubbs, B. (2016). Lisdexamfetamine in the treatment of moderate-to-severe binge eating disorder in adults: Systematic review and exploratory meta-analysis of publicly available placebo-controlled, randomized clinical trials. *Neuropsychiatric Disease and Treatment, 12*, ArtID 1827–1836.

Foster, A. C., Shorter, G. W., & Griffiths, M. D. (2015). Muscle dysmorphia: Could it be classified as an addiction to body image? *Journal of Behavioral Addictions, 4*(1), 1–5.

Frank, G. K. W., & Shott, M. E. (2016). The role of psychotropic medications in the management of anorexia nervosa: Rationale, evidence and future prospects. *CNS Drugs, 30*(5), 419–442.

Freimuth, M., Moniz, S., & Kim, S. R. (2011). Clarifying exercise addiction: Differential diagnosis, co-occurring disorders, and phases of addiction. *International Journal of Environmental Research and Public Health, 8*, 4069–4081.

Furst, D. M., & Germone, K. (1993). Negative addiction in male and female runners and exercisers. *Perceptual and Motor Skills, 77*(1), 192–194.

Gianini, L., Broft, A., & Devlin, M. (2016). Treatment of binge eating, including bulimia nervosa and binge-eating disorder. In B. T. Walsh, E. Attia, D. R. Glasofer, & R. Sysko (Eds.), *Handbook and assessment and treatment of eating disorders* (pp. 279–295). Arlington, VA: American Psychiatric Association.

Giesen, E. S., Zimmer, P., & Bloch, W. (2016). Effects of an exercise program on physical activity level and quality of life in patients with severe alcohol dependence. *Alcoholism Treatment Quarterly, 34*(1), 63–78.

Goodwin, H., Haycraft, E., & Meyer, C. (2014). Emotion regulation styles as longitudinal predictors of compulsive exercise: A twelve month prospective study. *Journal of Adolescence, 37*(8), 1399–1404.

Goodwin, H., Haycraft, E., & Meyer, C. (2016). Disordered eating, compulsive exercise, and sport participation in a UK adolescent sample. *European Eating Disorders Review, 24*(4), 304–309.

Goodwin, H., Haycraft, E., Willis, A.-M., & Meyer, C. (2011). Compulsive exercise: The role of personality, psychological morbidity, and disordered eating. *International Journal of Eating Disorders, 44*(7), 655–660.

Haglund, M., Ang, A., Mooney, L., Gonzales, R., Chudzynski, J., Cooper, C. B., . . . Rawson, R. A. (2015). Predictors of depression outcomes among abstinent methamphetamine-dependent individuals exposed to an exercise intervention. *American Journal on Addictions, 24*(3), 246–251.

Hausenblas, H. A., Schreiber, K., & Smoliga, J. M. (2017, April 26). Addiction to exercise. *BMJ*. doi:10.1136/bmj.j1745

Hausenblas, H. A., & Symons Downs, D. (2002a). Exercise dependence: A systematic review. *Psychology of Sport and Exercise, 3*, 89–123.

Hausenblas, H. A., & Symons Downs, D. (2002b). Relationship among sex, imagery, and exercise dependence symptoms. *Psychology of Addictive Behaviors, 16*(2), 169–172.

Hill, A. P., Robson, S. J., & Stamp, G. M. (2015). The predictive ability of perfectionistic traits and self-presentational styles in relation to exercise dependence. *Personality and Individual Differences, 86*, 176–183.

Howard, J. (2017, May 9). *When exercise shifts from a healthy habit to an unhealthy addiction.* Retrieved on February 26, 2018, from https://edition.cnn.com/2017/05/09/health/exercise-addiction-explainer/index.html

Karaca, S., Saleh, A., Canan, F., & Potenza, M. N. (2017). Comorbidity between behavioral addictions and Attention Deficit/Hyperactivity Disorder: A systematic review. *International Journal of Mental Health and Addiction, 15*(3), 701–724.

Kelly, N. R., Cotter, E. W., Tanofsky-Kraff, M., & Mazzeo, S. E. (2015). Racial variations in binge eating, body image concerns, and compulsive exercise among men. *Psychology of Men & Masculinity, 16*(3), 326–336.

Kerulis, M. (2015). Exercise addiction. In R. L. Smith (Ed.), *Treatment strategies for substance and process addictions* (pp. 263–276). Alexandria, VA: American Counseling Association.

Kjelsas, E., & Augestad, L. B. (2003). Gender differences in competitive runners and their motive for physical activity. *European Journal of Psychiatry, 17*(3), 157–171.

Kotbagi, G., Morvan, Y., Romo, L., & Kern, L. (2017). Which dimensions of impulsivity are related to problematic practice of physical exercise? *Journal of Behavioral Addictions, 6*(2), 221–228.

Kovacsik, R., Griffiths, M. D., Pontes, H. M., Soos, I., Vega, R., Ruiz-Barquin, R., . . . Szabo, A. (2018). The role of passion in exercise addiction, exercise volume, and exercise intensity in long-term exercisers. *International Journal of Mental Health and Addiction*. No pagination specified.

Krueger, D. W. (2001). Body self: Development, psychopathologies, and psychoanalytic significance. *Psychoanalytic Study of the Child, 56*, 238–259.

Landolfi, E. (2013). Exercise addiction. *Sports Medicine, 43*(2), 111–119.

Lee, A. (2014, January 28). *20 questions to assess your powerlessness & unmanageability*. Retrieved on February 19, 2018, from http://terminallyforgetful.com/20-powerlessness-unmanageability/

Lejoyeux, M., Avril, M., Richoux, C., Embouazza, H., & Nivoli, F. (2008). Prevalence of exercise dependence and other behavioral addictions among clients of a Parisian fitness room. *Comprehensive Psychiatry, 49*(4), 353–358.

Levallius, J., Collin, C., & Birgegard, A. (2017). Now you see it, now you don't: Compulsive exercise in adolescents with an eating disorder. *Journal of Eating Disorders, 5*, ArtID 9.

Li, M., Nie, J., & Ren, Y. (2015). Effects of exercise dependence on psychological health of Chinese college students. *Psychiatria Danubina, 27*(4), 413–419.

Lichtenstein, M. B., Christiansen, E., Elklit, A., Bilenberg, N., & Stoving, R. K. (2014). Exercise addiction: A study of eating disorder symptoms, quality of life, personality traits and attachment styles. *Psychiatry Research, 215*(2), 410–416.

Lichtenstein, M. B., Griffiths, M. D., Hemmingsen, S. D., & Stoving, R. K. (2018). Exercise addiction in adolescents and emerging adults—Validation of a youth version of the Exercise Addiction Inventory. *Journal of Behavioral Addictions, 7*, 117–125.

Lichtenstein, M. B., Hinze, C. J., Emborg, B., Thomsen, F., & Hemmingsen, S. D. (2017). Compulsive exercise: Links, risks and challenges faced. *Psychology Research and Behavior Management, 10*, ArtID 85-95.

Lichtenstein, M. B., & Jensen, T. T. (2016). Exercise addiction in CrossFit: Prevalence and psychometric properties of the Exercise Addiction Inventory. *Addictive Behaviors Reports, 3*, 33–37.

Lichtenstein, M. B., Larsen, K. S., Christiansen, E., Stoving, R. K., & Bredahl, T. V. G. (2014). Exercise addiction in team sport and individual sport: Prevalences and validation of the exercise addiction inventory. *Addiction Research & Theory, 22*(5), 431–437.

Lichtenstein, M. B., Nielsen, R. O., Gudex, C., Hinze, C., J., & Jorgensen, U. (2018). Exercise addiction is associated with emotional distress in injured and non-injured regular exercisers. *Addictive Behaviors Reports, 8*, 33–39.

Loumidis K. S., & Wells, A. (1998). Assessment of beliefs in exercise dependence: The development and preliminary validation of the Exercise Beliefs Questionnaire. *Personality and Individual Differences, 25*(3), 553–567.

Lydecker, J. A., & Grilo, C. M. (2016). Fathers and mothers with eating-disorder psychopathology: Associations with child eating-disorder behaviors. *Journal of Psychosomatic Research, 86*, 63–69.

MacFarlane, L., Owens, G., & Cruz, B. D. P. (2016). Identifying the features of an exercise addiction: A Delphi study. *Journal of Behavioral Addictions, 5*(3), 474–484.

Mascolo, M., McBride, J., & Mehler, P. S. (2016). Effective medical treatment strategies to help cessation of purging behaviors. *International Journal of Eating Disorders, 49*(3), 324–330.

Maselli, M., Gobbi, E., Probst, M., & Carraro, A. (2018). Prevalence of primary and secondary exercise dependence and its correlation with drive for thinness in practitioners of different sports and physical activities. *International Journal of Mental Health and Addiction*. No pagination specified.

Mathers, S., & Walker, M. B. (1999). Extraversion and exercise addiction. *Journal of Psychology: Interdisciplinary and Applied, 133*(1), 125–128.

McCabe, M. P., & Ricciardelli, L. A. (2004). Body image dissatisfaction among males across the lifespan: A review of past literature. *Journal of Psychosomatic Research, 56*(6), 675–685.

McNamara, J., & McCabe, M. P. (2012). Striving for success or addiction? Exercise dependence among elite Australian athletes. *Journal of Sports Sciences, 30*(8), 755–766.

Menczel, Z., Griffiths, M. D., Vingender, I., Eisinger, A., Farkas, J., Magi, A., . . . Demetrovics, Z. (2017). Exercise dependence in amateur competitors and non-competitor recreational exercisers. *International Journal of Mental Health and Addiction, 15*(3), 580–587.

Miller, K. J., & Mesagno, C. (2014). Personality traits and exercise dependence: Exploring the role of narcissism and perfectionism. *International Journal of Sport and Exercise Psychology, 12*(4), 368–381.

Morgan, W. P. (1979). Negative addiction in runners. *Physician and Sportsmedicine, 7*, 57–70.

Mulvay, M. (2016). *Exercise addiction: How to overcome it?* Retrieved on February 15, 2018, from http://www.inspirational-quotes-and-thoughts.com/exercise-addiction.html

Murray, K., Schmidt, U., Pombo-Carril, M.-G., Grover, M., Alenya, J., Treasure, J., & Williams, C. (2007). Does therapist guidance improve uptake, adherence and outcome from a CD-ROM based cognitive-behavioral intervention for the treatment of bulimia nervosa? *Computers in Human Behavior, 23*, 850–859.

Noetel, M., Miskovic-Wheatley, J., Costa, D., Crosby, R. D., Hay, P., Kohn, M., . . . Touyz, S. (2016). Exercise for the compulsive exercisers? An exploratory study in adolescent inpatients with anorexia nervosa. *Advances in Eating Disorders, 4*(3), 264–276.

Nuzzo, J. L., Schindler, C. L., & Ryan, W. J. (2013). Exercise dependence symptoms in a sample of exercise science students in the United States. *International Journal of Mental Health and Addiction, 11*(5), 611–618.

Oberle, C. D., Watkins, R. S., & Burkot, A. J. (2017). Orthorexic eating behaviors related to exercise addiction and internal motivations in a sample of university students. *Eating and Weight Disorders, 23*(1), 67–74.

Ogden, J., Veale, D., & Summers, Z. (1997). The development and validation of the Exercise Dependence Questionnaire. *Addiction Research, 5*(4), 343–355.

Parastatidou, I. S., Doganis, G., Theodorakis, Y., & Vlachopoulos, S. P. (2014). The mediating role of passion in the relationship of exercise motivational regulations with exercise dependence symptoms. *International Journal of Mental Health and Addiction, 12*(4), 406–419.

Petitpas, A. J., Brewer, B. W., & Van Raalte, J. L. (2015). Exercise dependence: Too much of a good thing. In A. J. Petipas, B. W. Brewer, & J. L. Van Raalte (Eds.), *Doing exercise psychology* (pp. 275–285). Champaign, IL: Human Kinetics.

Pierce, E. F., Rohaly, K. A., & Fritchley, B. (1997). Sex differences on exercise dependence for men and women in a marathon road race. *Perceptual and Motor Skills, 84*(3, Pt 1), 991–994.

Prochaska, J. O., Norcross, J. C., & DiClemente, C. C. (1994). *Changing for good*. New York, NY: Avon Books.

Rouse, W. (2015, August 3). *Eminem says he 'replaced addiction with exercise' after ballooning to 230 lbs*. Retrieved on February 15, 2018, from http://people.com/celebrity/eminem-i-replaced-addiction-with-exercise/

Ryu, K., Kim, Y., Kwon, M., Kim, H., & Kim, J. (2016). The frontal executive function in exercise addicts, moderate exercisers, and exercise avoiders. *American Journal on Addictions, 25*(6), 466–471.

Schreiber, K., & Hausenblas, H. H. (2017). *The truth about exercise addiction: Understanding the dark side of thinspiration*. Lanham, MD: Rowman & Littlefield.

Smith, D., Hale, B. D., & Collins, D. (1998). Measurement of exercise dependence and bodybuilders. *Journal of Sports Medicine and Physical Fitness, 38*(1), 66–74.

Smith, D., Wright, C., & Winrow, D. (2010). Exercise dependence and social physique anxiety in competitive and non-competitive runners. *International Journal of Sport and Exercise Psychology, 8*(1), 61–69.

Stevens, E. C. (n.d.). *Are you addicted to exercise? The tell-tale signs*. Retrieved on February 21, 2018, from https://breakingmuscle.com/fitness/are-you-addicted-to-exercise-the-tell-tale-signs

Stubblefield, H. (2016, June 29). Exercise addiction. *Healthline*. Retrieved on December 15, 2018, from https://www.healthline.com/health/exercise-addiction

Symons-Downs, D., Hausenblas, A. H., & Nigg, C.R. (2004). Factorial validity and psychometric examination of the Exercise Dependence Scale-Revised. *Measurement in Physical Education and Exercise Science, 8*, 183–201.

Symons-Downs, D., Savage, J. S., & DiNallo, J. M. (2013). Self-determined to exercise? Leisure-time exercise behavior, exercise motivation, and exercise dependence in youth. *Journal of Physical Activity & Health, 10*(2), 176–184.

Szabo, A., De La Vega, R., Ruiz-Barquin, R., & Rivera, O. (2013). Exercise addiction in Spanish athletes: Investigation of the roles of gender, social context and level of involvement. *Journal of Behavioral Addictions, 2*(4), 249–252.

Szabo, A., & Egorov, A. Y. (2016). Exercise addiction. In A. M. Lane (Ed.), *Sport and exercise psychology* (2nd ed., pp. 178–208). New York, NY: Routledge/Taylor & Francis.

Tatangelo, G., McCabe, M., Mellor, D., & Mealey, A. (2016). A systematic review of body dissatisfaction and sociocultural messages related to the body among preschool children. *Body Image, 18*, 86–95.

Terry, A., Szabo, A., & Griffiths, M. D. (2004). The exercise addiction inventory: A new brief screening tool. *Addiction Research and Theory, 12*(5), 489–499.

Thompson, J. K., & Pasman, L. (1991). The Obligatory Exercise Questionnaire. *Behavior Therapist, 14*, 137.

Valenzuela, P. L., & Arriba-Palomero, F. (2017). Risk of exercise addiction among male amateur triathletes and its relationship with training variables. *RICYDE. Revista internacional de Ciencias del Deporte / The International Journal of Sport Science, 13*, 162–171.

Velez, B. L., Breslow, A. S., Brewster, M. E., Cox, R., Jr., & Foster, A. B. (2016). Building a pantheoretical model of dehumanization with transgender men: Integrating objectification and minority stress theories. *Journal of Counseling Psychology, 63*(5), 497–508.

Villella, C., Martinotti, G., Di Nicola, M., Cassano, M., La Torre, G., Gliubizzi, M. D., . . . Conte, G. (2011). Behavioural addictions in adolescents and young adults: Results from a prevalence study. *Journal of Gambling Studies, 27*(2), 203–214.

Warner, R., & Griffiths, M. D. (2006). A qualitative thematic analysis of exercise addiction: An exploratory study. *International Journal of Mental Health and Addiction, 4*(1), 13–26.

Weinstein, A., Maayan, G., & Weinstein, Y. (2015). A study on the relationship between compulsive exercise, depression and anxiety. *Journal of Behavioral Addictions, 4*(4), 315–318.

Weinstein, A., & Weinstein, Y. (2016). Exercise addiction: Diagnosis, psychobiological mechanisms, and treatment. In N. M. Petry (Ed.), *Behavioral addictions: DSM-5 and beyond* (pp. 157–170). New York, NY: Oxford University Press.

Weinstock, J., Farney, M. R., Elrod, N. M., Henderson, C. E., & Weiss, E. P. (2017). Exercise as an adjunctive treatment for substance use disorders: Rationale and intervention description. *Journal of Substance Abuse Treatment, 72*, 40–47.

Williams, D. M., & Marcus, B. H. (2012). Exercise addiction and aversion: Implications for eating and obesity. In K. D. Brownell & M. S. Gold (Eds.), *Food and addiction: A comprehensive handbook* (pp. 336–341). New York, NY: Oxford University Press.

Youngman, J. D. (2008). Risk for exercise addiction: A comparison of triathletes training for Sprint-, Olympic-, Half-Ironman, and Ironman-distance triathletes. *Dissertation Abstracts International: Section B: The Sciences and Engineering, 68*(12-B), 8421.

20 Shopping Addiction

iStock.com/pixelrainst

Learning Objectives

1. Learn about the dynamics underlying shopping addiction.
2. Become familiar with the common symptoms of shopping addiction.
3. Be able to differentially diagnose shopping addiction and know its comorbidities.
4. Become informed about the controversy regarding how to classify shopping addiction.
5. Discover the most effective methods for treating shopping addicts.

CHALLENGING YOUR ASSUMPTIONS ABOUT THIS ADDICTION

1. What judgments do you make of individuals who spend more money than they make? What judgments do you make of yourself when you have done the same thing on occasion?
2. To what extent do you believe that shopping addiction exists in contrast to believing that it is simply a bad habit?
3. How much should the practice of overspending be blamed on advertisers and how much should be blamed on addicted consumers, and why?
4. If you found that your spending had become uncontrollable, what steps would you take before seeking the help of a counselor? At what point do you believe it would be necessary to reach before you would see a counselor for excessive spending?
5. Before reading this chapter, do you think that individual, group, or family counseling would be the most effective in helping shopping addicts? What assumptions are you making in arriving at that decision?

PERSONAL REFLECTIONS

I remember hearing about the over 1000 reported pairs of shoes owned by Imelda Marcos, widow of the late former Filipino dictator, Ferdinand Marcos. She once worked as a fashion designer and model, so perhaps many of the shoes were given to her. Regardless, hearing of this made me think of what I imagined a shopping-addicted individual would look like.

The closest person I have ever known whom I thought might be a shopping-addicted individual is my ex-wife. She was an impulse buyer (and perhaps still is) and would sometimes come home with hundreds of dollars worth of merchandise. She was rarely a bargain shopper either. Full price, and a big price at that!

The question I had, of course, was how she was going to pay for everything. She earned decent money, but she was by no means rich. She and I are still very good friends, and she would be horrified to read what I have written here. I know that she continues to spend a great deal of money, and she sometimes laments to me as to how she will pay for everything. My first thought is, "Why buy these things in the first place?"

When we separated, our line of credit was maxed out at $15,000. I knew most of this debt belonged to her. As I begin researching this chapter, I wonder if she really was, or is, addicted to shopping. Is there even such a thing as a true shopping addict? Let's find out.

Background Information

Marketing methods are effective in selling a host of products, including many things that become the focus of one's addiction. For most people around the world, shopping constitutes a leisure activity that can reduce the stress of a bad day or give a person the confidence he or she needs to face an upcoming special event (Frazier, 2015). Although about one third of the general population experiences shopping impulses from time to time (Lejoyeux & Weinstein, 2013), a smaller percentage of people find their urges to shop irresistible and uncontrollable. This chapter is about them.

In the early part of the 20th century, a German psychiatrist by the name of Emile Kraepelin coined the term oniomania to describe his patients whom he saw as "buying maniacs" (Frazier, 2015). "Onios" is a Greek word that means "for sale." Around that time, Eugen Bleuler viewed the condition as a type of monomania or instinctual impulse (Lejoyeux & Weinstein, 2013). It was not until the mid-1980s, however, that research began on this condition (Dittmar, 2004).

But the classification of shopping addiction remains hotly debated. Is it a mood disorder, an aspect of obsessive-compulsiveness, or an impulse control disorder (Tavares, Lobo, Fuentes, & Black, 2008)? Frazier (2015) noted that some still argue that it is a moral problem, not a medical one, and, consequently, does not belong in DSM.

Although Frazier (2015) referred to the condition as "compulsive buying disorder," her definition captures the important components of shopping addiction. Fraser's definition is "an impulse-control disorder that is characterized by impulsive drives and compulsive behaviors to buy unneeded things that cause personal distress, impair social and job functioning, and cause financial issues" (p. 278). Comparable to other addicts, shopping-addicted individuals have a very difficult time stopping their behavior (Lejoyeux & Weinstein, 2013).

Shopping addiction is chronic and prevalent worldwide (Tavares et al., 2008). Black, Shaw, and Allen (2016) began with a sample of 26 participants, and 17 of them were interviewed 5 years later. At follow-up, they ranged in age from 23 to 67 (mean age = 44 years). Spending had decreased for eight, stayed the same for five, and increased for four participants. Consequently, nine of the 17 participants at follow-up continued to experience symptoms of shopping addiction.

Zhang, Brook, Leukefeld, De La Rosa, and Brook (2017) conducted a study of 548 (53% female, mean age = 43.0 years) residents in New York counties. Their analysis found that compulsive buying is associated with diminished quality of life. Zhang et al. concluded that shopping-addicted individuals are both consciously and unconsciously troubled deeply by their compulsive behavior. As they dug into the reasons, they discovered that lower quality of life could be explained by the materialistic beliefs of the shopping addicts. Other studies have found that shopping-addicted individuals are highly materialistic (Islam, Wei, Sheikh, Hameed, & Azam, 2017; Lejoyeux & Weinstein, 2013; Lo & Harvey, 2012). They will buy items simply to impress others (Lejoyeux & Weinstein, 2013).

Racine, Kahn, and Hollander (2014) argued that materialism is the strongest predictor of compulsive buying disorder. Their rationale was that those who place substantial importance on having goods to bring happiness would generally feel less happy and more insecure, thereby making them more suggestible to messages put forth by advertisers.

Although nonaddicted individuals also enjoy shopping, Lejoyeux and Weinstein (2013) shared that the two best distinctions between normal buyers and shopping-addicted individuals are (a) negative consequences of the behavior and (b) the purchased items are not used as much as expected. Individuals who become addicted to shopping are preoccupied with buying and they experience uncontrollable impulses to spend (Frasier, 2015). Shopping-addicted individuals often engage in their behavior alone (Frasier, 2015). There are three core addictive features underlining compulsive buying: irresistible impulses, loss of control, and continuing to purchase excessively despite negative consequences (Dittmar, 2004; Fong, Reid, & Parhami, 2012). Several studies have found that female shopping-addicted individuals most often purchase clothes, shoes, and accessories, whereas men buy automotive items, electronic items, and gadgets (Dittmar, 2004; Fong et al., 2012; Frazier, 2015).

Compulsive buyers typically are in a negative mood state before shopping, which leads to a more positive mood for a while shortly after their purchases (Marino, Ertelt, Mitchell, & Lancaster, 2012). This positive mood state, however, is short-lived after they realize they cannot afford the items. More specifically, feelings of anxiety, boredom, depression, anger, and self-critical thoughts often precede a buying spree within a shopping-addicted individual (Korpa & Papadopoulou, 2013). They will often experience a craving to buy clothes or another item, many of which they will not use after their purchase (Lejoyeux & Weinstein, 2013).

While planning, hunting, and shopping, shopping-addicted individuals feel excitement and relief (Dittmar, 2004; Fong et al., 2012). These feelings often shift, however, to dejection, deep shame, regret, embarrassment, and/or guilt once they get home (Dittmar, 2004; Fong et al., 2012), a phenomenon that some call "buyer's remorse" (Milkman & Sunderwirth, 2010, p. 146). Shopping-addicted individuals will often lie about their purchases and may hide their new acquisitions from significant others (Marino et al., 2012). Most spend over $100 on a typical spending spree (Marino et al., 2012).

The "typical" shopping-addicted individual is often described as younger (Dittmar, 2004). Racine et al. (2014) stated that most are in their early 20s, whereas Marino et al. (2012) stated that they tend to be middle-aged. Studies have suggested that shopping-addicted individuals are more likely to be impulsive (Jung, 2017; Nicolai, Daranco, & Moshagen, 2016), have an external locus of control (Taylor, Klontz, & Lawson, 2017), experience diminished self-esteem and pathological narcissism (Biolcati, 2017; Zerach, 2016), and be confused about their identity (Claes, Muller, & Luyckx, 2016; Sharif & Khanekharab, 2017).

Many shopping-addicted individuals find returning items also to be rewarding (Fong et al., 2012). For those who don't return items, hoarding behavior may result (Marino et al., 2012). Shopping-addicted individuals who hoard are more likely to experience comorbid conditions, so compulsive buyers who hoard are often seen as having a more serious condition than those who do not (Marino et al., 2012).

Most shopping-addicted clients will describe their shopping experiences as providing them a "high," "buzz," or "rush" (Lejoyeux & Weinstein, 2013). In a qualitative study of nine women, Sohn and Choi (2014) found that their compulsive buying participants experienced five sequential phases: (a) filling emptiness through shopping, (b) ignoring overexpenditures, (c) experiencing debt, (d) impulse buying, and (e) feeling that they cannot stop. Karim and Chaudhri (2012) suggested that the disorder has four phases: anticipation, preparation, shopping, and spending.

Caplan and Profit (2004) argued that many shopping-addicted individuals suffer from depression and that calling them out as having a compulsive shopping disorder trivializes their condition. Although depression may be a causal factor in shopping addiction for some individuals, it can also be the result of it. Millions of shopping-addicted individuals become depressed while they face unmanageable debt (Baker, Moschis, Rigdon, & Fatt, 2016). Baker et al. (2016) found in a sample of 492 young adults that peer communications during their formative years were linked to both the obsessive-compulsive and impulse-control aspects of compulsive buying in early adulthood.

Several models have been used to explain compulsive shopping. Some view it as an addictive disorder, an impulse-control disorder, an obsessive-compulsive disorder (OCD), or part of a larger psychiatric disorder (Fong et al., 2012). Neuropsychological models have not been established yet (Fong et al., 2012). Hartston (2012) postulated that the hyperstimulating marketing techniques used today and rapid accessibility facilitated by the Internet contribute to the addictive nature of shopping. For example, Lo, Lin, and Hsu (2016) included in their article the most effective sales promotion stimuli and a checklist for web designers.

Zhang et al. (2017) reported that the prevalence of shopping addiction in the United States is 5.5% of men and 6.0% of women. Maraz et al. (2015) measured compulsive buying behavior by testing three different instruments in a nationally representative sample of 2710 Hungarians and a sample of 1447 shopping mall customers. The prevalence of compulsive buying disorder was 1.85% in the general population but 8.7% in the shopping mall customers. A study of 1448 university students in Galicia, Spain, found that 7.4% experienced compulsive buying (Villardefrancos & Otero-Lopez, 2016).

The most comprehensive study of prevalence was conducted by Maraz, Griffiths, and Demetrovics (2016). They pooled 40 studies that offered 49 prevalence estimates from 16 countries (N = 32,000). They found that the pooled prevalence of compulsive buying behavior was 4.9%. It was higher in university students (8.3%) and shopping-specific samples (16.2%). Maraz et al. concluded that prevalence is roughly 5%, but there is a large variation among samples.

Diagnostic and Assessment Considerations

Frazier (2015) noted that shopping addiction is not in *DSM-5*, and those meeting the criteria for compulsive buying disorder are often diagnosed with impulse-control disorder not elsewhere classified. Although the *DSM-5* Task Force considered compulsive buying as an obsessive-compulsive spectrum disorder, they considered it inappropriate because of its different phenomenology, the absence of a familial history of OCD, and its differential response to treatment (Hussain, Guanci, Raza, & Ostrovsky, 2015). Compulsive buying-shopping disorder does appear in ICD-11, together with other specified impulse control disorders (code 6C7Y).

McElroy, Keck, Pope, Smith, and Strakowski (1994) developed diagnostic criteria for compulsive buying disorder. Their criteria are the most frequently cited in the literature. The criteria are as follows:

1. Frequent preoccupation with shopping or intrusive, irresistible, "senseless" buying impulses.
2. Clearly buying more than is needed or can be afforded.
3. Distress related to buying behavior.
4. Significant interference with work or social functioning (quoted with minor modifications from Frazier, 2015, p. 283).

Marino et al. (2012) adapted the criteria of McElroy et al. (1994) as follows:

1. Maladaptive preoccupation with buying or shopping, or maladaptive buying or shopping impulses on behavior, as indicated by at least one of the following:
   a. Frequent preoccupation with buying or impulses to buy that are experienced as irresistible, intrusive, and/or senseless.
   b. Frequent buying of more than can be afforded, frequent buying of items that are not needed, "or" shopping for longer periods of time than intended.
2. The buying preoccupations, impulses, or behaviors cause marked distress, are time-consuming, significantly interfere with social or occupational functioning, or result in financial problems (e.g., bankruptcy).
3. The excessive buying or shopping behavior does not occur exclusively during periods of hypomania or mania. (p. 650)

Another potential criterion suggested by Karim and Chaudhri (2012) is that some compulsive buyers demonstrate increasing tolerance over time. In other words, they feel that they need to buy more to feel the same degree of euphoria as experienced previously.

Jung and Yi (2016) surveyed 809 individuals who frequently experienced buying lapses. They concluded that their findings supported the case for differentiating between moderate-risk buyers and full-fledged compulsive buyers. They hypothesized that moderate-risk buyers would hold significantly higher materialistic values than noncompulsive buyers while exhibiting significantly less depressive symptoms and covert narcissism than full-fledged compulsive buyers. What differentiated the two groups was that moderate-risk buyers had fewer buying lapses. They also had fewer negative feelings before experiencing buying lapses and hid purchases less frequently.

Differential Diagnosis

First and foremost, "shopping addiction must be distinguished from normal buying impulse" (Lejoyeux & Weinstein, 2013, p. 850). Spontaneous urges to buy are a common phenomenon in today's consumer-driven world. Lejoyeux and Weinstein (2013) suggested that counselors look at the differences between what a client intended to buy before entering a store and what he or she ended up buying. The shopping-addicted individual will consistently buy more than intended.

Before making a diagnosis of shopping addiction, other diagnoses must first be ruled out. These include bipolar disorder, OCD, and depression or a personality disorder (Fong et al., 2012). To rule out bipolar disorder, when a person is in a manic or hypomanic episode of bipolar disorder, the individual lacks insight into compulsive buying behavior (Frazier, 2015). Shopping-addicted individuals are well aware of what they are doing when shopping excessively.

Although there is overlap among OCD, hoarding, and shopping addiction, there are some important distinctions. Fong et al. (2012) noted that compulsive shoppers find the shopping process to be ego-syntonic, which means that their behavior feels neither out of character nor distressing while it is occurring. Instead, the shopping experience is rewarding and results in a positive mood state. In contrast, those having OCDs and hoarding disorders relieve tension or minimize anxiety because of the belief that something undesirable will occur if the behavior is not repeatedly enacted.

Comorbidity and Co-Addictions

Racine et al. (2014) concluded that the more severe the compulsive shopping behavior, the higher the rate of psychiatric comorbidity. Shopping addiction is frequently comorbid with mood disorders, eating disorders, substance use disorders, other impulse control disorders, and personality disorders (Hussain et al., 2015; Zhang, Brook, Leukefeld, & Brook, 2016). The comorbidity between compulsive buying behavior and mood disorders ranges from 28% to 95% (Marino et al., 2012). Particularly, depression is frequently cited as comorbid with compulsive shopping behaviors (Bani-Rshaid & Alghraibeh, 2017; Thomas, Al-Menhali, & Humeidan, 2016).

Obsessive-compulsive personality disorder, avoidant personality disorder, and borderline personality disorder are associated with shopping addiction (Maraz, Urban, & Demetrovics, 2016; Marino et al., 2012). Some have identified a link between kleptomania and compulsive buying disorder and possibly with gambling disorder (Cuzen & Stein, 2014; Marino et al., 2012).

Anxiety disorders are also frequently comorbid (Platania, Castellano, Santisi, & Di Nuovo, 2017). Some studies have found features in common between compulsive buying and hoarding (Marino et al., 2012).

Available Measures

There are several scales that can be used by counselors. Here is a list of some of them:

1. Bergen Shopping Addiction Scale (Andreassen et al., 2015). The authors of the scale tested the items on 23,537 participants with a mean age of 35.8 years. The factor structure of the scale is acceptable, and it has strong internal consistency. It is the first scale to look at shopping addiction within an addiction paradigm.

   Available at https://psychology-tools.com/bergen-shopping-addiction-scale/

2. Online Shopping Addiction Scale (Zhao, Tian, & Xin, 2017). This is an 18-item scale that can be used to understand the phenomenon among young adults.

3. Compulsive Online Shopping Scale (COSS; Manchiraju, Sadachar, & Ridgway, 2017). This is another newly developed scale measuring online shopping addiction.

4. Compulsive Buying Scale. This scale, developed by Faber and O'Guinn (1992), is based on the criteria of McElroy et al. (1994). It is a 7-item Likert scale. Racine et al. (2014) claimed that this is one of the most commonly used scales in the United States. Its focus is mainly on financial control. The scale correctly classifies 88% of individuals tested (Hussain et al., 2015).

   Available at http://www.shopaholicnomore.com/wp-content/uploads/2011/02/Faber-and-OGuinn-Compulsive-Buying-Scale.pdf

5. Compulsive Buying Scale (Edwards, 1993). This is 13-item scale. Factor analysis revealed five factors: the tendency to spend, compulsion/drive to spend, feelings of joy about shopping and spending, dysfunctional spending, and postpurchase guilt.

6. Compulsive Buying Measurement Scale (Valence, d'Astous, & Fortier, 1988). This scale includes 16 items that measure for dimensions (e.g., tendency to spend, feeling the urge to shop and buy, postpurchase guilt, and family environment). Available at http://www.shopaholicnomore.com/wp-content/uploads/2011/02/Valence-Scale-with-scoring-11-item2.pdf

7. Klontz Money Behavior Inventory (KMBI; Taylor, Klontz, & Britt, 2015). The KMBI "is a standalone, multi-scale measure than can screen for the presence of eight distinct money disorders" (Taylor et al., 2015, p. 14).

8. Richmond Compulsive Buying Scale (RCBS; Ridgway, Kukar-Kinney, & Monroe, 2008). According to the authors, the RCBS measures both OCD and impulse-control disorders. It has a strong theoretical foundation and good psychometric properties and it can be applied to general consumer populations (Ridway et al., 2008).

   Available at http://www.shopaholicnomore.com/wp-content/uploads/2011/02/Ridgway-formatted-by-Nancy-with-scoring-and-ref.pdf

9. Minnesota Impulsive Disorder Interview (Christenson, Faber, & de Zwaan, 1994). The interview assesses several impulse-control disorders. The compulsive buying screen includes four questions with five subsections. There are no published data available regarding its validity and reliability (Frazier, 2015).

10. Yale-Brown Obsessive-Compulsive Scale—Shopping Version (Monahan, Black, & Gabel, 1996). It is a modified version of the Yale-Brown Obsessive-Compulsive Scale. It consists of 10 items. The scale has high internal consistency and good interrater reliability (Frazier, 2015).

Clinical Interview Questions

In addition to the questions contained in the various questionnaires and scales noted in the previous section, Racine et al. (2014) offered two general screening questions for counselors: (a) "Do you feel overly preoccupied with shopping and spending?" and (b) "Do you ever feel that your shopping behavior is excessive, inappropriate, or uncontrolled?" The authors also suggested that a positive response to these questions should be followed by additional questions regarding each answer.

Generic Names and Street "Lingo"

Shopping addiction has several different names in the literature. These include the following: money disorders (Taylor et al., 2017), pathological shopping addiction (Lejoyeux & Weinstein, 2013), oniomania, shopaholism, compulsive spending, compulsive buying, compulsive shopping (Fong et al., 2012), addictive buying, compulsive consumption, excessive buying, uncontrolled buying, spendaholisim, buying maniac (Frazier, 2015), pathological shopping, compulsive buying disorder (Hussain et al., 2015), compulsive shopping disorder (Black et al., 2016), compulsive buying disorder (Tavares et al., 2008), pathological buying (Trotzke, Starcke, Muller, & Brand, 2015), and online shopping addiction (Jiang, Zhao, & Li, 2017).

Neuroscience

There is currently insufficient research to suggest that compulsive buying disorder has a genetic component (Racine et al., 2014). Researchers suspect that addiction and compulsive buying affect the same parts of the brain because increased tolerance has been observed (Karim & Chaudhri, 2012). Raab, Elger, Neuner, and Weber (2011) compared 26 noncompulsive buyers and 23 compulsive buyers during their performance on the Saving Holdings or Purchase task. They were shown 100 products with its price, and participants had to decide if they would purchase the product. Results found significant differences in brain activity between the two groups. Compulsive buyers experienced more activity in the parts of their brain that control arousal mechanisms. However, there was no difference in the decision-making part of the brain.

In a small-scale study with 26 persons with compulsive buying disorder and 32 controls, Black, Shaw, McCormick, Bayless, and Allen (2012) had their participants take a battery of tests, including a comprehensive neuropsychological test battery. They did not find a pattern of neuropsychological deficits between the two groups.

Racine et al. (2014) stated that shopping, like substances, could lead to dopamine release in the brain. Individuals with Parkinson's disease receive dopamine agonists, compounds that activate dopamine receptors. Studies have shown that these individuals then develop a higher prevalence of four behavioral addictions: binge eating, compulsive shopping, hypersexuality, and pathological gambling (Gendreau & Potenza, 2014).

When the frequent hyperstimulation of the dopamine release system occurs, lasting changes to the dopamine reward pathways may result. This process is called neuroadaptation, and it is a distinctive feature of addiction (Racine et al., 2014). The individual then needs to engage in the activity more to derive the same euphoric rush.

Physical Impacts (Long-Term Use)

Although most addictions have long-term physical effects on an individual, shopping addiction appears to be an exception. Although withdrawal symptoms are usually touted as one indication that a person is addicted to something, the only withdrawal symptoms reported in the literature are psychological and psychosocial ones (Lejoyeux & Weinstein, 2013). These are covered in the next two sections.

Mental, Emotional, and Spiritual Impacts

Villardefrancos and Otero-Lopez (2016) tested 1448 university students in Galicia, Spain. They found that 108 scored as compulsive buyers, whereas 1340 were noncompulsive buyers. The compulsive buyers scored significantly higher regarding psychological distress symptoms (i.e., anxiety, depression, obsession-compulsion, hostility, and somatization).

Shopping-addicted individuals often rely on shopping to boost their mood (Clark & Calleja, 2008), but what it triggers is an emotional roller coaster. They begin their shopping spree after experiencing negative emotions (e.g., anxiety, anger, negative thoughts), followed by several positive emotions (e.g., happiness, euphoria), while later experiencing guilt, remorse, and shame (Racine et al., 2014).

Negative emotions are often the trigger for our relapse with shopping addicts. In the 5-year follow-up study of Black et al. (2016), the main triggers for returning to compulsive shopping were boredom, sadness, depression, frustration, anger, and stress.

Psychosocial Impacts (Relationships, Career/Work, Legal, Financial)

Studies that have looked at the consequences of shopping addiction cite large financial debts (53%), inability to pay their debts (41%), legal issues (8%), and criminal issues (8%) (Frazier, 2015). Regardless of their income, most shopping-addicted individuals will face serious economic difficulties (Racine et al., 2014).

Many shopping-addicted individuals also experience familial and occupational problems. They may borrow money from family and friends and face disapproval and negative remarks from both (Lejoyeux & Weinstein, 2013). Like gambling addicts, they make promises to repay large amounts of money, and, over time, some will become rejected and alienated from significant others. Some lie and steal to continue shopping (Lejoyeux & Weinstein, 2013). The compulsiveness of the disorder is glaring as one realizes that losing one's job, ruining a good relationship or marriage, interpersonal strains with one's children, and legal difficulties do not always halt this behavior (Racine et al., 2014).

Working With Diverse Populations

Sex Differences

You might recall reading earlier that Zhang et al. (2017) reported a prevalence of shopping addiction in the United States at 5.5% of men and 6.0% of women. Furthermore, several studies have reported that female shopping-addicted individuals most often purchase clothes, shoes, and accessories, whereas men buy automotive items, electronic items, and gadgets (Dittmar, 2004; Fong et al., 2012; Frazier, 2015).

Studies typically report a higher proportion of shopping addiction in women (Granero et al., 2016; Hussain et al., 2015; Korpa & Papadopoulou, 2013). In a sample of 359 Brazilians, for example, being female was associated with compulsive buying (Leite & Silva, 2016). In the large-scale study ($N = 23{,}537$ participants) that reported the creation of the Bergen Shopping Addiction Scale, Andreassen et al. (2015) reported that females scored higher on their measure than males.

A sex difference was recently noted in a study by Gallagher, Watt, Weaver, and Murphy (2017). Gallagher et al. sampled 437 undergraduate students (78% females, age range = 17–41, mean age = 18.39 years) at a Canadian university and found that females were more likely to report impulsive spending followed by guilt, and the males were more likely to report having negative feelings about shopping.

Marino et al. (2012) wrote that women are more likely to be diagnosed with shopping addiction because they most often play the shopping role in families. Women are also more likely to admit that they enjoy shopping compared with men (Fattore, Melis, Fadda, & Fratta, 2014).

Adolescents and Youth

Little research has focused on young consumers, and this includes shopping addiction in adolescents (Roberts & Roberts, 2012). Roberts and Roberts (2012) found that compulsive buying was a common coping strategy for dealing with stress for both male and female seventh graders, aged 12–13 ($N = 82$, 46 girls, 36 boys). In a sample of 1329 adolescents from a public high school in the midwestern United States (mean age = 14.7, 55% female), Manoli and Roberts (2012) found that having too much or too little time for life's many activities was associated with having both a lessened sense of well-being and greater compulsive buying tendencies.

Based on their sample of 129 undergraduates attending an Australian university, Weaver, Moschis, and Davis (2011) concluded that one's experiences and circumstances during the adolescent years are related to both compulsive buying and materialistic beliefs in early adulthood. A study by Roberts, Manolis, and Tanner (2008) had earlier found that parents and especially peers play an important role in shaping adolescent materialism and compulsive buying practices.

Race and Ethnicity

In a study of 373 obstetrics/gynecology patients, Sansone, Chang, Jewell, and Marion (2013) looked at compulsive buying and body mass index in both White women and African American women. They found that compulsive buying was related to increasing body mass index and adulthood, but this was especially true for White women. Race does not play a substantial role in the relationship between childhood trauma and compulsive buying, however (Sansone, Chang, Jewell, & Rock, 2013).

Nonpsychiatric Disabilities

The only study in this section is noted subsequently in the section about war veterans. It concerns traumatic brain injury and compulsive buying tendencies.

Lesbian, Gay, Bisexual, and Transgender (LGBT)

Grant et al. (2014) tested a sample of 2108 students (mean age = 22.6 years, age range = 18–58, 41.8% male), but only 2011 participants were included in the analysis due to missing data. Of this group, 112 (5.6%, $N = 60$, 53.6% female) defined as lesbian, gay, bisexual, or queer (LGBQ). The heterosexual students and the LGBQ students did not differ demographically. Grant et al. wrote that the LGBQ students reported significantly more problems with compulsive buying.

War Veterans

The two studies reported here did not deal specifically with veterans. However, one concerns posttraumatic stress disorder (PTSD), and the other deals with moderate to severe traumatic brain injury, both of which can result from combat.

Fontenelle et al. (2012) analyzed 106 patients who developed OCD after PTSD (note that this group was called posttraumatic OCD), 41 patients who developed OCD before PTSD, and 810 OCD patients without any history of PTSD. Posttraumatic OCD was correlated with compulsive buying disorder.

Caregivers of 74 patients with traumatic brain injury were asked to provide a subjective assessment regarding the patients' impulsivity and their tendency toward compulsive buying. Their caregivers reported that both impulsivity and compulsive buying tendencies increased following the brain injury (Rochat, Beni, Billieux, Annoni, & Van der Linden, 2011).

Medications and Other Relevant Physical Interventions

Sepede, Di Iorio, Sarchione, Fiori, and Di Giannantonio (2017) reported a single case study where a 60-year-old woman with a severe form of compulsive buying disorder showed good clinical improvement while taking a combination of bupropion and mirtazapine. High-dose naltrexone (100–200 mg/day) reduced urges to shop and shopping behavior in three patients (Grant, 2003).

Antidepressants and mood stabilizers are often prescribed to shopping-addicted individuals (Frazier, 2015). In a study of 24 subjects with a shopping addiction, Koran, Bullock, Hartston, Elliott, and D'Andrea (2002) found that 17 participants reported that they were much improved while taking 60 mg of citalopram daily for the 12 weeks of the study. Frazier (2015) noted that a limitation of the study was that it did not exclude participants suffering from depression.

Soares, Fernandes, and Morgado (2016) provided a systematic review of 21 studies regarding the pharmacological treatment of compulsive buying disorder. The review covered antidepressants, mood stabilizers, opioid antagonists, and second-generation antipsychotics. The authors concluded that "there is no evidence to propose a specific pharmacologic agent for compulsive buying disorder" (p. 281).

INSIDE AN ADDICTED PERSON'S MIND

Liam Age 35

My wife, Anna, can see the look of horror on my face when I open the American Express bill. She says gently with concern in her voice, "Is everything all right, Liam?" I said, of course, that I was just surprised my new buzz saw was not on it. I could tell she didn't believe me, but she also knew better than to ask about my spending. I earn good money, and I can pay my bills, thank you very much. But when I look at this one, even I'm not sure. I didn't tell Anna that the buzz saw was actually on the bill, but so was the new sound system for the basement, the heater for the garage, the new fridge that makes ice cubes that hasn't arrived yet, best seats in the house for their very last, I'm sure, Rolling Stones concert (yes, I'm taking her but it will be a surprise), and the airline tickets to see them in London. Thank God my Visa and MasterCard bill have not arrived yet . . . I was on a roll last month!

I would like to say last month was an exception, but it wasn't. Anna doesn't know that my three credit cards are maxed out, and I now owe nearly $100,000. I am honest with her about everything else, but this is something that gives me no pride. I've thought about cutting up the credit cards several times, but she would find out about it. I should be able to stop this nonsense, but I told myself this a year ago and what has changed? Nothing has changed.

She doesn't know anything about my finances, but this month she is going to find out. I will need to ask her to cover the mortgage. I would rather tell her I had terminal cancer! Asking her for money isn't fair because she works a two-bit job for $10 an hour. Somehow, I don't think I can bring myself to ask her for money. Last night I didn't sleep at all as I pondered what I should do. Seeing this bill is just messing with my head. I can't explain what happened next.

I find out that I was rushed to the hospital later that day. Anna told me she got home from work early and found me unconscious. Apparently, I've been in a coma for the last 3 days. Perhaps I was always impulsive and reckless, but the look of worry on her face made even me cry. And men don't cry. More than ever I knew that she loves me, and for some reason that hit me hard. I must be a terrible planner. She should never have found me in the car in the garage with the engine running. My brother-in-law, Robert, was supposed to find me at about 4 p.m., and I can't stand him.

Frankly, I didn't want ever to have to face her again. How can I tell her what I have been doing these past few months? I've been keeping most of what I have purchased in a locked room in the basement, and she knows that this is my man cave and she stays out of it. If she had ever opened that door, she could not have entered anyway because it is so stuffed with merchandise. I even have a few gifts for her that I thought I would give her eventually but not all at once. I don't want to spoil her, after all. My head feels fuzzy, and I'm having trouble thinking clearly. I guess that's what exhaust fumes do to you. Now what am I going to do? I am a complete piece of crap. I cannot live like this any longer.

Commentary

Liam demonstrates the classic symptoms of shopping addiction. The notable themes apparent in Liam's case include the following: (a) excessive and compulsive spending, (b) buying merchandise that will never get used, (c) hiding merchandise from his wife, (d) lying to his wife about his spending, (e) feelings of deep shame and guilt, (f) feelings of desperation and hopelessness, (g) feelings of worthlessness, and (h) crippling financial debt. Liam has lost control, and the negative consequences of his spending have become so immense that he attempted suicide to permanently escape his problems.

Discussion

1. Do you know of anyone who you suspect has become dependent on shopping? If "yes," which symptoms noted in the commentary apply to him or her?
2. Does this person have symptoms that are not listed in the commentary? If so, what are they?
3. If you were Liam's counselor, how would you go about helping him?

Specific Counseling Considerations

ROLEPLAY SCENARIOS

Roleplay in dyads with one of you acting as the counselor and the other as the counselee. If roleplay is not possible, work individually in writing out a list of your suggestions.

Roleplay #1

Harold, age 20, came to see you and appears to be in a state of panic. He is in his second year of university, which is located a few hundred miles away from his parents' home. His dad started an education savings plan for Harold soon after he was born. Harold tells you that the certificate has hung in his bedroom for his entire life. He knew he was going to university; there was no question about that. What is in question, however, is that it is only 3 weeks into the term and Harold has already spent the entire scholarship allotment for

(Continued)

(Continued)

this academic year. You find out he has spent this money on frivolous expenditures.

Roleplay #2

Priscilla, age 28, works in high fashion. It appears obvious to you at first that she is a very successful young woman who has been working in Manhattan for the past 4 years. Given the clothes and jewelry she is wearing, you would assume she is earning well over $200,000 a year. A few minutes into the session, however, she tells you that she earns only $40,000 per annum. After she asked for the second raise in a year, her boss fired her. You find out that she was also missing a lot of time at work to shop for clothes and she was spending work time on the Internet doing online shopping. Now Priscilla is wondering how she will pay back the $60,000 debt she has acquired.

HOW WOULD AN ADDICTION COUNSELOR HELP THIS PERSON?

You are working as a professional counselor. Teresa, age 46, comes to see you with her husband, Heintz. Teresa met Heintz in Germany 8 years ago. They soon married and immigrated to the United States. Heintz begins the session, "SHE HAS SPENT EVERY CENT I EVER HAD!" He is practically screaming these words at you. As you begin collecting background information, you discover that Heintz was a manager in a prestigious factory in Germany where he earned top dollar. When the two of them moved to Albuquerque, Heintz said he had over €500,000 in his bank account. Teresa reluctantly confirmed this amount, looking very sheepish and appearing as though she wants to hide from both you and him.

Remember to view clients within their environmental contexts, keeping in mind societal, parental/familial, cultural/spiritual, and peer influences. Specifically, become aware of the impact that the following influences have and continue to have in your clients' lives: race, language, religion and spirituality, gender, familial migration history, sexual/affectional orientation, age and cohort, physical and mental capacities, socioeconomic situation and history, education, and history of traumatic experience.

1. What defines this person's environment, past and present?
2. Who is this person sitting in front of me, taking into account environmental and personal characteristics?
3. What defines the problem that he or she is presenting within their multicultural milieu?

Goals and Goal Setting

Engs (2010) focused some of her research efforts on studying shopping addiction. She offered several ideas that could be set as goals. Her ideas verbatim are as follows:

- Pay for purchases by cash, check, debit card.
- Make a shopping list and only buy what is on the list.
- Destroy all credit cards except one to be used for emergency only.
- Avoid discount warehouses. Allocate only a certain amount of cash to be spent if you do visit one.
- "Window shop" only after stores have closed. If you do "look" during the day, leave your wallet at home.
- Avoid phoning in catalog orders and don't watch TV shopping channels.
- If you're traveling to visit friends or relatives, have your gifts wrapped and call the project finished; people tend to make more extraneous purchases when they shop outside their own communities.
- Take a walk or exercise when the urge to shop comes on.
- If you feel out of control, you probably are. Seek counseling or a support group such as Debtors Anonymous. (p. 1)

Other possible goals include the following:

- Get help with budgeting.
- Meet with a bankruptcy trustee or credit counseling agency if debts have become unmanageable.
- Practice mindfulness.
- Have someone else in the household do the shopping.
- Have someone else in the household manage the finances.

Stages of Change Strategies

The processes of change mentioned are based on those outlined by Connors, DiClemente, Velasquez, and Donovan (2013) and Prochaska, Norcross, and DiClemente (1994). The definitions for the various processes can be found in Chapter 6. Besides these processes, other strategies are included that have separate citations.

The University of Rhode Island Change Assessment Scale (URICA) is a helpful scale for determining where clients are currently at regarding the stages of change model. There are 24-, 28-, and 32-item versions of the scale.A 24-item version is published for alcohol or drug problems. The scale, however, is generic and can be easily adapted for use with other addictions. It is available with norms as a free download from https://www.guilford.com/add/miller11_old/urica.pdf.

Specific precontemplation strategies.

Please visit the section of this chapter called Relevant Mutual Support Groups, Websites, and Videos for free or low-cost information and resources that may help someone move out of precontemplation.

There is a 2009 American romantic comedy that may help increase awareness of shopping addiction called *Confessions of a Shopaholic*. Regarding bibliotherapy, there are three recommended books:

1. Flanders, C. (2018). *The Year of Less: How I Stopped Shopping, Gave Away My Belongings, and Discovered Life Is Worth More Than Anything You Can Buy in a Store.*
2. Cruz, J. (2015). *Compulsive Shopping Solution: How to Overcome Compulsive Shopping and Spending Addiction for Good.*
3. Lincoln, C. (2014). *Shopping Addiction: The Ultimate Guide for How to Overcome Compulsive Buying and Spending.*

Self-liberation (i.e., self-awareness in this stage) might also result from attending one of the mutual support groups. The three that cater to shopping-addicted individuals are Debtors Anonymous, Recoveries Anonymous, and Spenders Anonymous.

Specific contemplation strategies.

Clients in contemplation feel ambivalent about change. Prochaska and Norcross (2001) suggested that these feelings of ambivalence and the conflicts between their addiction and their values should be explored at this stage. Counselors should also normalize ambivalent feelings in their clients and make the discrepancies explicit between their values and their actions. There are no specific strategies mentioned in the published literature regarding this stage and shopping addiction.

Specific preparation strategies.

Prochaska and Norcross (2001) noted that clients in this stage need help on strengthening their commitment toward change. Providing clients a list of options for treatment, for example, is helpful, followed by helping clients decide on the treatment that is best for them. Having clients publicly announce to others their plan for change is also recommended.

Hamm (2014) offered a few ideas for shopping-addicted individuals that could be implemented during the preparation phase:

1. Remove your cash flow. Ideas here include leaving credit cards at home and taking only a small amount of cash when shopping.
2. Decide to avoid shopping situations for an indeterminate period.
3. Rely on others to shop for you.
4. Review your shopping mistakes and find your triggers. Some questions to ask yourself include why it happened, what antecedents led up to your overspending, what feelings you had at the time, if there was any external reason for excessive spending, and if there was a website that increased your desires.
5. Seek out the services of a financial therapist or money coach.

Other ideas for *before* a chosen quit day (i.e., preparation strategies) can be found in Appendix B.

Specific action strategies.

Hague, Hall, and Kellett (2016) reviewed the quality of treatment studies focused on shopping addiction. In total, 29 articles met their inclusion criteria, but only 17 dealt with psychotherapy. Of the 29 studies, only five had been tested with a high degree of methodological rigor. Based on their review, the authors concluded that group psychotherapy was the most promising treatment for compulsive buying disorder. I will come back to group interventions later.

Frazier (2015) concluded that a consensus on effective treatment for shopping addiction had not been reached. There is a lack of empirical evidence regarding psychotherapy's effectiveness with compulsive buying.

Perhaps more disconcerting, Racine et al. (2014) surmised that treatments for all addictions "have not been overwhelmingly effective" (p. 287). Racine et al. expressed concern that applying the traditional treatment approaches to buying addiction might not be the most helpful approach.

Despite the "hard line" taken by the previous researchers, Hussain et al. (2015) and most others have suggested that cognitive-behavioral therapy (CBT) is effective. Leite, Pereira, Nardi, and Silva (2014) found 1659 references on the topic of shopping addictions, and, after their screening, 23 articles were selected for their review. They found that, other than case studies and clinical trials, the only studies that revealed a successful response to treatment were CBT-based. Hussain et al. (2015) wrote that studies have shown that dialectical behavior therapy is also a promising treatment.

The emphasis on treatment is to establish healthy purchasing habits, restructure maladaptive and unhealthy thoughts, develop healthy coping skills, and overcome negative feelings related to excessive shopping (Fong et al., 2012). Clients also need help with learning effective problem-solving relapse prevention techniques (Marino et al., 2012). Couples counseling may be indicated because the financial consequences of shopping addiction impact intimate relationships (Frazier, 2015).

Based on their study of 98 college students, Jiang et al. (2017) concluded that interventions focused on teaching self-control are important for online shopping addicts. Another study found that compulsive buyers do engage in self-control, but they differ from noncompulsive buyers in how they apply self-control mechanisms (Horvath, Buttner, Belei, & Adiguzel, 2015).

Given that shopping-addicted individuals tend to be highly materialistic, Villardefrancos and Otero-Lopez (2016) recommended the treatment should focus on reducing the importance clients assign to money and possessions. Along these lines, Herziger et al. (2017) recommended that some clients could be taught to embrace voluntary minimalism, which is a lifestyle choice based on reduced consumption. Herziger et al. outlined a program based on promoting voluntary minimalism. Lam and Lam (2017) wrote about the importance of providing financial counseling as part of the treatment protocol.

As mentioned at the outset of this section, group therapy is touted by many as the treatment of choice for shopping addiction. Burgard and Mitchell (2000) and Benson, Eisenach, Abrams, and van Stolk-Cooke (2014) provided details of their respective 12-week and 10-week group treatment for compulsive buying. Mitchell (2011a, b) included his compulsive buying disorder group treatment manual. Group work can reduce addicts' feelings of shame and denial. Members also feel understood and supported by others experiencing the same addiction (Lejoyeux & Weinstein, 2013). Frazier (2015) suggested four reasons that researchers believe group therapy is effective: (a) groups diminish feelings of aloneness, (b) group members receive feedback from other members, (c) group members know how the others think and feel so members take more responsibility, and (d) the group allows members to see and experience the different stages of recovery. Racine et al. (2014) suggested that learning how to reject shopping urges might be the most important skill learned in these groups. Bendtsen and Johnsson (2013) reported on the possibility that screening and intervention for addictions, including group counseling, may be deliverable online as this would be cost-effective given the magnitude of addiction problems. Other ideas for *beginning* their chosen quit day (i.e., action strategies) can be found in Appendix B.

Specific maintenance strategies and relapse prevention.

Note: Maintenance strategies and relapse prevention are also, for many, partly facilitated by regular attendance at relevant mutual support groups. A list of such mutual support groups and helpful websites is found in an upcoming section entitled Relevant Mutual Support Groups, Websites, and Videos.

Besides mutual support or therapy groups, Vasiliu and Vasile (2017) also recommended joining a "simplicity circle." The Environmental Research Foundation (see http://rachel.org/?q=en/node/145) defined *simplicity circles* as being

> part of the "voluntary simplicity movement," a movement that encourages people to simplify their external lives while enriching their inner lives. Simplicity Circles are groups of people who gather together and help one another simplify their lives. Simplicity Circles are small—generally four to eight people—and are structured to allow for participation and learning. (p. 1)

A simplicity circle study guide is available online at no cost (see Heath, 2000).

Anticipating difficulties and having a plan in place for high-risk situations is a very helpful relapse-prevention strategy. Counselors can also help clients by affirming their resolve and their self-efficacy. Other ideas for relapse prevention can be found in Appendix C.

Motivational Interviewing

The group therapy approach used by Benson et al. (2014) includes components involving motivational interviewing (MI), among other well-known methods (i.e., psychodynamic counseling, CBT, dialectical behavior therapy, mindfulness, and acceptance and commitment therapy). A case report also found that shopping addiction was successfully treated with MI, imaginal desensitization, and naltrexone (Donahue, Odlaug, & Grant, 2011). The design of the study makes it impossible to know the extent to which each of the three approaches was individually therapeutic. Pertaining to Chapter 6's description of MI, the following is an example of the process called focusing. The client's name is Christy, age 44. This is a segment from the second session.

Counselor: Christy, I find it helpful if my clients begin their sessions by providing a summary of what they were able to take away from the previous session. Would it be okay if I ask you to do that?

Client: Sure, I can try. I felt like we spent our time mostly on you getting to know me and getting to understand why I spend the way that I do. You also asked me at the end of the last session to think about what kind of a change I would like to make regarding my spending habits.

Counselor: Thank you for that overview. That is my recollection as well. Would you like to pick up then from where we left off the last session, or would you like to begin today somewhere else?

Client: Well, I know I could spend a lot of time talking about what a terrible week I had and how I ended up spending yet another thousand dollars that I don't have. Not sure how useful that would be, however.

Counselor: I can tell how troubling it is to you, Christy, as you become increasingly aware this problem has been costing you a lot of money that you don't have. I know that paying back all of this money is going to be difficult for you.

Client: It sure is! I can't believe I've let the problem get to this point. It makes me feel sick inside.

Counselor: I understand that sinking feeling. I feel in your words just how motivated you are now do something about this problem. You feel like you've let it go on already too long. Thank goodness you came in to see me before perhaps your spending gets even worse.

Client: I was thinking the same thing myself. Obviously, I cannot stop shopping entirely. I live alone, as you know. I don't have any family here that I can count on, and I would be too embarrassed to tell any of my friends that I need their help.

Counselor: This certainly has been an embarrassing problem for you. Would it be okay if we begin to explore what your goal will be regarding your shopping habits?

Client: Yes, I feel ready for that.

Counselor: That's great to hear, Christy. You have such a positive attitude about all of this.

Client: Well, I'm not sure I would go that far! But thank you for believing in me.

Counselor: You're welcome. As you said, you cannot stop shopping completely. You need to find ways to reduce and control your spending. Tell me about some of the alternatives that you can think of, regardless of how bad the ideas seem to you. In other words, I don't want you to judge each idea but instead to brainstorm possible ways that you could shop in a limited way as you move forward.

Client: I think it would make a lot of sense if I chop up my credit cards. I'm serious. I am continually spending money that I don't have because I have lots of credit, despite the fact I am getting calls now almost weekly from collection agencies asking me to make payments on some of these bills. I really don't know what else I could do.

Counselor: Would it be okay if I help you come up with a few additional ideas?

Client: Yes, of course.

Counselor: Besides cutting up your credit cards, what else could you do before you leave your home to ensure that you will be unable to overspend?

Client: I could just take enough money for what I need to buy. The problem is, I don't always know what I need to buy before I get to the store and see what they are selling.

Counselor: It sounds like you don't know what you need until you find out what is out there. Is that what you are saying, Christy?

Client: Hum, yes, I think that's what I said, but I'm not sure I like how it sounds.

Counselor: What do you find troubling about that?

Client: It makes it sound like I buy things just on impulse. Crap, that is part of my problem, isn't it?

Counselor: I'm certainly hearing that you may have done this more than once before!

Client: [chuckles] Yes, I can certainly confess to that!

Counselor: [chuckles along with Christy] It sounds like that one struck a nerve, hey? What could you do before you leave home to reduce the likelihood of impulse shopping?

Insight-Oriented Interventions

Racine et al. (2014) suggested that the main focus of treatment for people with compulsive buying disorder should be to understand why they engage in these behaviors. Often compulsive shoppers have an inadequate sense of self, low self-esteem, and negative perceptions of self. Marcinko, Bolanca, and Rudan (2006) found that the combination of psychodynamic psychotherapy and fluvoxamine was helpful in treating two female patients with a shopping addiction. An earlier study reported how psychoanalytic psychotherapy was helpful to a 26-year-old female graduate student to help her overcome bulimia, kleptomania, and compulsive shopping (Schwartz, 1992).

In Zerach's (2016) study of 204 Israeli adults (97 males, mean age = 45.86 years), compulsive buying was associated with narcissistic grandiosity, narcissistic vulnerability, materialism, and feelings of emptiness. Each of these suggests possible applications for a psychodynamic approach. Psychodynamic psychotherapy is also one of the components of Benson et al.'s (2014) 12-week group therapy for shopping addicts.

Chatterjee and Farkas (1992) suggested dynamics in spending addiction. They viewed money as a displacement, representing affection, security, love, and possibly an identity. Krueger (1988) theorized that compulsive shopping might be an attempt to regulate the effect of having a fragmented sense of self and to re-establish a balance between self and object.

Jejoyeux, Ades, and Solomon (1997) construed uncontrolled buying as a "derivative of unconscious wishes for sexual adventure" (p. 1477). According to Fugua (as cited in Chatterjee & Farkas, 1992, p. 614), "The major psychoanalytic view has always linked money with feces in our repressed mental life." Lawrence (1990) provided a psychoanalytic interpretation of compulsive shopping in women. Lawrence began by suggesting that the excessive shopping was a way to nurture the self that was not provided elsewhere in the woman's environment. Her analysis then went deeper into earlier notions promoted by Sigmund Freud that are today considered sexist notions of penis envy and castration regret for an organ that never existed.

There is a branch of financial counseling called psychodynamic financial therapy. Some of this work analyzes the person's early experiences and how they result in "money scripts" that drive excessive shopping (Klontz, Britt, & Archuleta, 2015).

Spiritual Interventions

There is no published literature about shopping addiction and spirituality, other than that which is included in all AA-based mutual support groups.

Cognitive-Behavioral Therapy

CBT can be facilitated using the triple column technique. It can be used both by counselors in their work with clients and by clients alone. The full instructions for using the technique are found in Chapter 6. The following are some of the cognitions that can be problematic for clients with this addiction.

Automatic Thought or Belief	Questioning It	Healthier Thought or Belief
I need to spend more than what is on my shopping list.		It is critical that I purchase only what is on my shopping list.
Shopping is the only thing that makes me feel better.		I will learn several different ways to deal constructively with my negative moods.
I cannot live without having several credit cards.		I can live without any credit cards if I cannot control my spending.
It is critical that I keep up or surpass what other people have.		I do not need a lot of items to live happily. It is time I become less materialistic.
I cannot return any merchandise to the merchant.		I will learn to become assertive so that I can return merchandise that I do not need promptly.

As noted earlier, Leite et al. (2014) found in their systematic review that only CBT revealed successful response to treatment. Muller, Mitchell, and de Zwaan (2015) specified that it was group CBT that was effective. Brandtner and Serralta (2016) reported, based on a Psychotherapy Process Q-Set, that therapist factors (i.e., empathy and responsiveness), patient factors (i.e., collaboration), relationship factors (i.e., working alliance), and technical factors (i.e., providing support and appropriate homework) were the main contributing factors in patients reporting positive changes from receiving CBT for compulsive buying.

Despite the evidence reporting effectiveness of CBT, Granero et al. (2017) estimated the short-term effectiveness of individually administered CBT to 97 patients. Granero et al. reported the following: (a) 27.8% poor adherence to the program, (b) 47.4% relapse, and (c) 46.4% dropout rate. The authors suggested that future interventions using CBT should view the approach multidimensionally with focus on patients' sex, comorbidity, and personality trait profiles.

Kellett and Bolton (2009) provided details of their four-phase model of treating compulsive buying through CBT. The four phases include looking at antecedents, triggers, the purchasing behavior itself, and postpurchase cognitions, emotions, and behaviors. This article is a very worthy resource.

The cognitive component of CBT involves identifying and modifying thoughts and feelings related to buying. Counselors can encourage clients to keep a daily self-monitoring diary of their shopping cravings. Lejoyeux and Weinstein (2013) recommended that they keep track of what they purchased, the amount of time spent shopping, and the amount of money spent. Lejoyeux and Weinstein wrote that, through CBT, clients learn that the euphoria they feel in purchasing is an illusion. The counselor also helps to teach problem-solving skills and to focus on other behaviors that are less impulsive and more constructive. The authors also recommended "exposition experiments" (p. 851), such as going into shops, not buying anything, and then leaving. Clients are also encouraged to find other sources of pleasure and to find other ways of releasing tension. Hodgins and Peden (2008) recommended that compulsive buying be treated through common CBT techniques such as "covert sensitization, exposure and response prevention, stimulus control, cognitive restructuring, and relapse prevention" (p. S31).

Below are common cognitions expressed by shopping addicts:

- If I have any money left at the end of the pay period, I just have to spend it.
- As soon as I enter a shopping center, I have an irresistible urge to go into a shop and buy something.
- Bought things even though I couldn't afford them.
- I sometimes feel that something inside pushed me to go shopping.
- Felt others would be horrified if they knew of my spending habits.
- When I have money, I cannot help but spend part or all of it. (the preceding is quoted from Dittmar, 2004, p. 424)
- I'm not paying for this right now.
- I can afford this next month.
- I can pay off this credit card with another card. (the preceding is quoted from Marino et al., 2012, p. 651)
- Thinking that buying will compensate for and alleviate negative feelings.
- Thinking that things bought will create emotional security and attachment.
- Believing that every item is unique and that if it is not purchased a special opportunity will be lost.
- Having a sense of personal responsibility for each item purchased. (the preceding is quoted from Frazier, 2015, p. 285)

RELEVANT MUTUAL SUPPORT GROUPS, WEBSITES, AND VIDEOS

Mutual Support Groups

For the Addicted Individual

1. Debtors Anonymous. http://www.debtorsanonymous.org/

   Marino et al. (2012) noted that Debtors Anonymous had helped shopping-addicted individuals with debt management. Unfortunately, they also noted that the group can be found in only a limited number of locations.

   Quoted from website:

   Debtors Anonymous offers hope for people whose use of unsecured debt causes problems and suffering in their lives and the lives of others.

2. Recoveries Anonymous (RA). http://www.r-a.org/i-compulsive-shopping.htm#.WirbEExFy70

   Quoted from website:

   Welcome to Recoveries Anonymous. R.A. is a Twelve Step program. We have no dues or fees. We are here for those who want a full recovery from compulsive shopping—but despite their best efforts, have yet to find a full recovery from compulsive shopping—and for their family and friends.

3. Spenders Anonymous. http://www.spenders.org/home.html

   Quoted from their website:

   Spenders Anonymous is a community of women and men sharing our experience, strength and hope as we work toward clarity in our relationship with money.

For the Partner and/or Family

These groups are intended to help family members refrain from behaviors that may trigger the addict. They also target underlying maladaptive thoughts and behaviors of the co-addict. Lastly, they focus on facilitating spiritual growth.

Co-Dependents Anonymous (CoDA). http://coda.org/

Quoted from website:

Welcome to Co-Dependents Anonymous, a fellowship of men and women whose common purpose is to develop healthy relationships. The only requirement for membership is a desire for healthy and loving relationships.

Websites

1. A review of compulsive buying disorder. https://www.ncbi.nlm.nih.gov/pmc/articles/PMC1805733/
2. Compulsive Spending / Shopping. https://www.goodtherapy.org/learn-about-therapy/issues/compulsive-shopping
3. The Shopaholic: When Shopping Becomes an Illness.

   https://www.psychologytoday.com/us/blog/the-intelligent-divorce/201407/the-shopaholic
4. Shopping Addiction 101. https://www.addiction.com/addiction-a-to-z/shopping-addiction/shopping-addiction-101/
5. Ways to Combat an Online Shopping Addiction. https://money.usnews.com/money/blogs/my-money/2014/12/02/5-ways-to-combat-an-online-shopping-addiction

Videos

To view these videos, search their titles on YouTube.

1. *Can You Be Addicted to Shopping?? | Kati Morton.*
2. *What compels a shopping addict to buy?* Habit Doc.
3. *Meet the Experts- Compulsive Buying Disorder With Dr. April Benson PhD.*
4. *Shopping Addiction - 7 Signs & 7 Solutions || SugarMamma.TV.*
5. *Retail therapy or addicted to shopping? 01.07.15, Chrissy B Show.*

RELEVANT PHONE APPS

Generic Addiction Apps

Note: Generic apps are described in Chapter 6.

This list is not exhaustive. New apps are continually being developed. Do an Internet search to find out the latest apps available. Most are for specific addictions, but some, such as these four, are generic.

1. I Am Sober. https://play.google.com/store/apps/details?id=com.thehungrywasp.iamsober
2. Sober Time. https://play.google.com/store/apps/details?id=com.sociosoft.sobertime
3. Pocket Rehab: Get Sober & Addiction Recovery. https://play.google.com/store/apps/details?id=com.getpocketrehab.app

4. Loop Habit Tracker. https://play.google.com/store/apps/details?id=org.isoron.uhabits

Specialized Apps

There are more apps available to help you spend *more* than there are to help you spend *less*! According to Newton (2013), shopping addiction has "soared" because of the apps that encourage online spending. Nevertheless, there are a few apps that help consumers become better at budgeting and simultaneously become more aware of their spending habits.

1. Spending Tracker. https://play.google.com/store/apps/details?id=com.mhriley.spendingtracker&hl=en_US and https://apps.apple.com/us/app/spending-tracker/id548615579

   Quoted from website:

   Spending Tracker is the easiest and most user friendly expense manager app in the store. The simple fact is, by tracking your spending you will be able to stick to a budget and therefore SAVE MONEY. So download it for free, enter your expenses and income, and have instant control over your spending!

2. Easy Spending – Money Tracker and Budget Planner (I-Phone only). https://itunes.apple.com/us/app/easy-spending-money-tracker-budget-planner/id459019300?mt=8

   Quoted from website:

   It's a simple and convenient finance tracker that provides the most powerful and convenient daily money management for iPhone and iPad, that neatly tracks all your cash flow between different accounts . . .

3. Mint. https://www.mint.com/

   Quoted from website:

   It's all coming together. When you're on top of your money, life is good. We help you effortlessly manage your finances in one place.

4. Good budget. https://goodbudget.com/

   Quoted from website:

   Spend, save, and give toward what's important in life.

JOURNALS AND CONFERENCES

Journals

There are currently no journals specifically dedicated to shopping addiction. Journals that have frequently published in this area include clinical psychology journals, particularly *Comprehensive Psychiatry* and *Psychiatry Research*. The *Journal of Behavioral Addictions* publishes shopping addiction manuscripts, as does *Frontiers in Psychology*. The *Financial Counseling and Planning* journal also publishes the odd article about shopping addiction.

Conferences

There are currently no conferences specifically dedicated to shopping addiction. This is apt to change as awareness increases. In the interim, there are several generic conferences about addictions that may have sessions dealing with shopping addiction. A list of these follows:

1. International Conference on Behavioral Addictions. The website advertising this conference changes annually. Search in Google for their latest offering.
2. World Congress on Addictive Disorders & Addiction Therapy. Search in Google for their latest offering.
3. Addiction Therapy Conference. https://addictiontherapy.conferenceseries.com/
4. American Society of Addiction Medicine (ASAM). ASAM hosts an annual conference. Check website for current details. https://www.asam.org/
5. International Conference on Addiction Research & Therapy. http://addiction.alliedacademies.com/

COUNSELING SCENARIO

As you are reading, imagine that you are the client in this scenario. Note the areas in which the session could be improved on the part of the counselor.

Your name is Holly, a 19-year-old working full-time at Starbucks. You were so excited when you received your first credit card just after your 19th birthday 7 months ago. Since then, you've been able to acquire another four credit cards at local department stores. It didn't take you long to learn that your $11 an hour job doesn't stretch very far when it comes to paying bills. Already you owe nearly $9000, and you have no idea how you got there so fast. You haven't dared to tell your parents about this or your younger brother. You go to see a counselor at a free agency:

- Counselor: How can I help you today, Holly?
- You: Well, I, I owe a couple of hundred dollars to a friend. He wants me to repay the money, but on my low salary, I don't seem to have enough after expenses.
- Counselor: That is a common problem at your age. I know what you can do. You simply pay him back in installments. How much could you afford to give him every paycheck?
- You: Honestly, ahem, maybe $30.
- Counselor: What's his name, Holly?
- You: Ahem, I'm not sure he would want me to give you his name, but it's Allen.
- Counselor: Thank you. Hand me your phone.
- You: Whaaat?
- Counselor: You heard me. Give me your telephone.
- You: [You hand the counselor your phone]
- Counselor: Okay, what is Allen's number?
- You: Why do you need that?
- Counselor: You will see. What is his number?
- You: Ahhh, 995-802-5430.
- Counselor: [dials number] Hello, Allen? This is Mrs. Peters, a friend of Holly's. I understand she owes you $200 and she is having trouble paying you. Would it be okay if she arranges to pay you $30 every 2 weeks when she gets paid? [pause] I told you I am Mrs. Peters. I am trying to help her deal with her debts. [pause] Hello, hello? He hung up!
- You: I don't think you should have done that, Mrs. Peters! I should be the one to decide how to deal with my debt.
- Counselor: Holly, you came to see me for help. Can you not see that is what I'm doing here?
- You: [gulps] Well, I haven't been fully honest with you.
- Counselor: [gasps] What do you mean?
- You: Well, I owe more than $200, and it's not to Allen. I more like $9000, and it's to five different credit card companies.
- Counselor: Why didn't you tell me that in the first place? Are you trying to make me look like a fool?
- You: I am so sorry. I am just so ashamed of myself.
- Counselor: As you should be, Holly. I don't see the point in deceiving a counselor when you're asking me for help. Do you?
- You: No, I am terribly sorry.
- Counselor: That's good. Now hand me your credit cards and let's begin working on this problem.
- You: [reluctantly hand Mrs. Peters your credit cards]
- Counselor: [reaches under her desk for her scissors] No worries at all anymore, Holly [she cuts up the cards in front of you]. Once your bills arrive, come back to see me, and I will help you take care of a sensible repayment plan.
- You: I CAN'T BELIEVE YOU JUST DID THAT!!!
- Counselor: Too much drama, Holly. You are just like my teenage daughter. I'll see you again soon after you've gotten a grip on your emotions.

From the Client's Perspective

1. How would you feel if you were treated this way?
2. Which ethics have been violated by Mrs. Peters (see Chapter 2)?
3. What would you find more helpful from a counselor in this scenario?

From the Counselor's Perspective

1. What is interfering with developing a working alliance?
2. Going back to the Common Counseling Mistakes list in Chapter 6, which mistakes is the counselor making with Holly?
3. Mrs. Peters mentions her daughter. What is the defense mechanism called when a counselor treats someone in a way that reminds them of another person they know? How can counselors reduce the likelihood that this will occur in their practice?

INDIVIDUAL EXERCISES

1. Think about times when you have spent more money than you intended or you have looked at a credit card bill and wondered how you are going to pay it off. What feelings did you have associated with that experience? What did you do to deal with those feelings? How different do you think that would look if you were a shopping addict?
2. Interview someone who defines as a shopaholic or shopping addict. Ask him or her the same questions as those listed in question 1. How is this person's experience the same as and different from your own?
3. Many of the YouTube videos about shopping-addicted individuals portray a young, good-looking woman who appears to be fun-loving and carefree. If these were the only exposures you had of compulsive shoppers, what stereotypes would you develop of shopping addicts? After reading this chapter, in what ways would some of these stereotypes apply to a good number of shopping-addicted individuals, and in what ways would they not?

CLASSROOM EXERCISES

1. Take the class to a large shopping center. Before arriving, provide them instructions regarding the assignment. In groups of two or three with notebooks or an electronic device in hand, have students record observations regarding how the stores and services have arranged their businesses to make themselves more appealing to shoppers. At the next class, have each group present to the class or write on the board what techniques or methods were used by the businesses to increase the likelihood of product purchase. Alternatively, lead a discussion with the class concerning the exercise and what they learned. How might a shopping-addicted individual find these techniques or methods more enticing than a typical shopper would?
2. Have students create their own collage either with images cut out of magazines or downloaded images from the Internet. The images selected are to represent what the student would most want right now if she or he could afford it. Have the students present their collage either to the class or to a smaller group, sharing why each item has significance to them. The final part of their presentation is telling the other students how they would acquire these items right now if they were a shopping-addicted individual and how they would feel after making all of these purchases, both in the short term and in the long term.
3. Play one or more of the videos listed in the section of this chapter called Relevant Mutual Support Groups, Websites, and Videos. Afterward, lead a discussion regarding what students learned from the video(s). Which aspects of the video(s) did students find believable and well-represented, and which aspects produced a different reaction? Overall, what were the reactions of your students to the video(s)?

CHAPTER SUMMARY

It remains debatable if shopping addiction is a mood disorder, a type of obsessive-compulsiveness, or an impulse control disorder. Regardless of how it is classified, it affects 5% or more of the population, and it can result in insurmountable debt. The case of Liam demonstrated many of the classic symptoms of shopping addiction, including (a) excessive and compulsive spending, (b) buying merchandise that will never get used, (c) hiding merchandise, (d) lying about his spending, (e) feelings of deep shame and guilt, (f) feelings of desperation and hopelessness, (g) feelings of worthlessness, and (h) crippling financial debt. Shopping-addicted individuals have lost control, and they experienced adverse consequences from continuing their excessive and compulsive spending.

The high that accompanies shopping is soon replaced by a devastating low as shopping-addicted individuals realize they cannot afford what they just purchased. Many are materialistic, pathological narcissists who experience diminished self-esteem and confusion about their identity. Comorbidity is common with shopping addiction. Depression is the most common comorbid condition, and it can be either an antecedent or a consequence of the disorder. Although most addictions have long-term physical effects on individuals, shopping addiction appears to be the exception. The emotional, psychosocial, and financial effects, however, can be devastating.

Currently, there are no pharmacological treatments recommended for shopping addiction. Empirical evidence regarding psychotherapy's effectiveness is also limited, but the most promising treatments appear to be group-based, cognitive-behavioral, or a combination of several treatment modalities.

REFERENCES

Andreassen, C. S., Griffiths, M. D., Pallesen, S., Bilder, R. M., Torsheim, T., & Aboujaoude, E. (2015). The Bergen Shopping Addiction Scale: Reliability and validity of a brief screening test. *Frontiers in Psychology*, *6*, 1–11.

Baker, A. M., Moschis, G. P., Rigdon, E. E., & Fatt, C. K. (2016). Linking family structure to impulse-control and obsessive-compulsive buying. *Journal of Consumer Behaviour*, *15*(4), 291–302.

Bani-Rshaid, A. M., & Alghraibeh, A. M. (2017). Relationship between compulsive buying and depressive symptoms among males and females. *Journal of Obsessive-Compulsive and Related Disorders*, *14*, 47–50.

Bendtsen, P., & Johnsson, K. (2013). Internet screening and intervention programs. In P. M. Miller, S. A. Ball, M. E. Bates, A. W. Blume, K. M. Kampman, D. J. Kavanagh, M. E. Larimer, N. M. Petry, & P. De Witte (Eds.), *Comprehensive addictive behaviors and disorders, Vol. 3: Interventions for addiction* (pp. 655–664). San Diego, CA: Elsevier Academic Press.

Benson, A. L., Eisenach, D., Abrams, L., & van Stolk-Cooke, K. (2014). Stopping overshopping: A preliminary randomized controlled trial of group therapy for compulsive buying disorder. *Journal of Groups in Addiction & Recovery*, *9*, 97–125.

Biolcati, R. (2017). The role of self-esteem and fear of negative evaluation in compulsive buying. *Frontiers in Psychiatry*, *8*, 1–8.

Black, D. W., Shaw, M., & Allen, J. (2016). Five-year follow-up of people diagnosed with compulsive shopping disorder. *Comprehensive Psychiatry*, *68*, 97–102.

Black, D. W., Shaw, M., McCormick, B., Bayless, J. D., & Allen, J. (2012). Neuropsychological performance, impulsivity, ADHD symptoms, and novelty seeking in compulsive buying disorder. *Psychiatry Research*, *200*, 581–587.

Brandtner, M., & Serralta, F. B. (2016). Cognitive-behavioral therapy for compulsive buying: A systematic case study. *Psicologia: Teoria e Pesquisa*, *32*, 181–188.

Burgard, M., & Mitchell, J. E. (2000). Group cognitive-behavioral therapy for buying disorder. In A. Benson (Ed.), *I shop, therefore I am: Compulsive buying and the search for self* (pp. 367–397). New York, NY: Jason Aronson.

Caplan, P. J., & Profit, W. E. (2004). Some future contenders. In P. J. Caplan & L. Cosgrove (Eds.), *Bias in psychiatric diagnosis* (pp. 249–253). Lanham, MD: Jason Aronson.

Chatterjee, P., & Farkas, K. J. (1992). Spending behaviors: Implications for human service practitioners. *Families in Society*, *73*(10), 613–622.

Christenson, G. A., Faber, R. J., & de Zwann, M. (1994). Compulsive buying: Descriptive characteristics and psychiatric comorbidity. *Journal of Clinical Psychiatry*, *55*, 5–11.

Claes, L., Muller, A., & Luyckx, K. (2016). Compulsive buying and hoarding as identity substitutes: The role of materialistic value endorsement and depression. *Comprehensive Psychiatry*, *68*, 65–71.

Clark, M., & Calleja, K. (2008). Shopping addiction: A preliminary investigation among Maltese university students. *Addiction Research & Theory*, *16*(6), 633–649.

Connors, G. J., DiClemente, C. C., Velasquez, M. M., & Donovan, D. M. (2013). *Substance abuse treatment and the stages of change: Selecting and planning interventions* (2nd ed.). New York, NY: Guilford Press.

Cuzen, N. L., & Stein, D. J. (2014). Behavioral addiction: The nexus of impulsivity and compulsivity. In K. P. Rosenberg & L. Curtiss Feder (Eds.), *Behavioral addictions: Criteria, evidence, and treatment* (pp. 19–34). San Diego, CA: Elsevier Academic Press.

Dittmar, H. (2004). Understanding and diagnosing compulsive buying. In R. H. Coombs (Ed.), *Handbook of addictive disorders: A practical guide to diagnosis and treatment* (pp. 411–450). Hoboken, NJ: John Wiley & Sons.

Donahue, C. B., Odlaug, B. L., & Grant, J. E. (2011). Compulsive buying treated with motivational interviewing and imaginal desensitization. *Annals of Clinical Psychiatry*, *23*(3), 226–227.

Edwards, E.A. (1993). Development of a new scale for measuring compulsive buying behaviour. *Financial Counseling and Planning*, *4*, 67–85.

Engs, R. (2010). *How can I manage compulsive shopping and spending addiction (shopoholism)?* Retrieved on April 17, 2018, from http://www.indiana.edu/~engs/hints/shop.html

Faber, R. J., & O'Guinn, T. (1992). Money changes everything: Compulsive buying from a biopsychosocial perspective. *American Behavioral Science*, *35*, 809–819.

Fattore, L., Melis, M., Fadda, P., & Fratta, W. (2014). Sex differences in addictive disorders. *Frontiers in Neuroendocrinology*, *35*(3), 272–284.

Fong, T. W., Reid, R. C., & Parhami, I. (2012). Behavioral addictions: Where to draw the lines? *Psychiatric Clinics of North America*, *35*(2), 279–296.

Fontenelle, L. F., Cocchi, L., Harrison, B. J., Shavitt, R. G., do Rosario, M. C., Ferrao, Y. A., . . . Torres, A. R. (2012). Towards a post-traumatic subtype of obsessive-compulsive disorder. *Journal of Anxiety Disorders*, *26*, 377–383.

Frazier, K. (2015). Compulsive buying/shopping addiction. In R. L. Smith (Ed.), *Treatment strategies for substance and process addictions* (pp. 277–291). Alexandria, VA: American Counseling Association.

Gallagher, C. E., Watt, M. C., Weaver, A. D., & Murphy, K. A. (2017). "I fear, therefore, I shop!" Exploring anxiety sensitivity in relation to compulsive buying. *Personality and Individual Differences*, *104*, 37–42.

Gendreau, K. E., & Potenza, M. N. (2014). Detecting associations between behavioral addictions and dopamine agonists in the Food & Drug Administration's Adverse Event database. *Journal of Behavioral Addictions*, *3*(1), 21–26.

Granero, R., Fernandez-Aranda, F., Bano, M., Steward, T., Mestre-Bach, G., del Pino-Gutierrez, A., . . . Jimenez-Murcia, S. (2016). Compulsive buying disorder clustering based on sex, age, onset and personality traits. *Comprehensive Psychiatry*, *68*, 1–10.

Granero, R., Fernandez-Aranda, F., Mestre-Bach, G., Steward, T., Bano, M., Aguera, Z., . . . Jimenez-Murcia, S. (2017). Cognitive behavioral therapy for compulsive buying behavior: Predictors of treatment outcome. *European Psychiatry*, *39*, 57–65.

Grant, J. E. (2003). Three cases of compulsive buying treated with naltrexone. *International Journal of Psychiatry in Clinical Practice*, *7*, 223–225.

Grant, J. E., Odlaug, B. L., Derbyshire, K., Schreiber, L. R. N., Lust, K., & Christenson, G. (2014). Mental health and clinical correlates in lesbian, gay, bisexual, and queer young adults. *Journal of American College Health*, *62*, 75–78.

Hague, B., Hall, J., & Kellett, S. (2016). Treatments for compulsive buying: A systematic review of the quality, effectiveness and progression of the outcome evidence. *Journal of Behavioral Addictions*, *5*, 379–394.

Hamm, T. (2014, September 30). 5 *Strategies for defeating a shopping addiction: A shopaholic's guide to make the 'I-just-have-to-have-this' impulse go away*. Retrieved on April 17, 2018, from https://money.usnews.com/money/blogs/my-money/2014/09/30/5-strategies-for-defeating-a-shopping-addiction

Hartston, H. (2012). The case for compulsive shopping as an addiction. *Journal of Psychoactive Drugs*, *44*(1), 64–67.

Heath, F. (Ed.). (2000). *Live simply: A Simplicity Circle study guide for the Waterloo region*. Waterloo, ON: Live Simply Project. Retrieved on April 18, 2018, from file:///C:/Users/Kevin%20Alderson/Desktop/live-simply%20-simplicity%20circle%20manual.pdf

Herziger, A., Benzerga, A., Berkessel, J., Dinartika, N. L., Franklin, M., Steinnes, K. K., & Sundstrom, F. (2017). A study protocol for testing the effectiveness of user-generated content in reducing excessive consumption. *Frontiers in Psychology*, *8*, 1–10.

Hodgins, D. C., & Peden, N. (2008). Cognitive-behavioral treatment for impulse control disorders. *Revista Brasileira de Psiquiatria*, *30*, S31–S40.

Horvath, C., Buttner, O. B., Belei, N., & Adiguzel, F. (2015). Balancing the balance: Self-control mechanisms and compulsive buying. *Journal of Economic Psychology*, *49*, 120–132.

Hussain, N., Guanci, N., Raza, M., & Ostrovsky, D. (2015). Shopping addiction: If the shoe fits, buy it in every color! In M. S. Ascher & P. Levounis (Eds.), *The behavioral addictions* (pp. 175–186). Arlington, VA: American Psychiatric.

Islam, T., Wei, J., Sheikh, Z., Hameed, Z., & Azam, R. I. (2017). Determinants of compulsive buying behavior among young adults: The mediating role of materialism. *Journal of Adolescence*, *61*, 117–130.

Jejoyeux, M., Ades, J., & Solomon, J. (1997). "Phenomenology and psychopathology of uncontrolled buying": Reply. *American Journal of Psychiatry*, *154*(10), 1477–1478.

Jiang, Z., Zhao, X., & Li, C. (2017). Self-control predicts attentional bias assessed by online shopping-related Stroop in high online shopping addiction tendency college students. *Comprehensive Psychiatry*, *75*, 14–21.

Jung, J. (2017). Impact of motives on impulsivity and compulsivity in compulsive buying behavior. *Social Behavior and Personality*, *45*(5), 705–718.

Jung, J., & Yi, S. (2016). The case for moderate-risk buyers: An empirical investigation. *Psychiatry Research*, *240*, 300–307.

Karim, R., & Chaudhri, P. (2012). Behavioral addictions: An overview. *Journal of Psychoactive Drugs*, *44*, 5–17.

Kellett, S., & Bolton, J. (2009). Compulsive buying: A cognitive-behavioral model. *Clinical Psychology and Psychotherapy*, *16*, 83–89.

Klontz, B. T., Britt, S. L., & Archuleta, K. L. (Eds.). (2015). *Financial therapy: Theory, research, and practice*. Cham, Switzerland: Springer International.

Koran, L. M., Bullock, K. D., Hartston, H. J., Elliott, M. A., & D'Andrea, V. (2002). Citalopram treatment of compulsive shopping: An open-label study. *Journal of Clinical Psychiatry*, *63*(8), 704–708.

Korpa, T. N., & Papadopoulou, P. V. (2013). Clinical signs and symptoms of addictive behaviors. In A. Tsitsika, M. Janikian, D. E. Greydanus, H. A. Omar, & J. Merrick (Eds.), *Internet addiction: A public health concern in adolescence* (pp. 3–14). Hauppauge, NY: Nova Science.

Krueger, D. W. (1988). On compulsive shopping and spending: A psychodynamic inquiry. *American Journal of Psychotherapy*, *42*(4), 574–584.

Lam, L. T., & Lam, M. K. (2017). The association between financial literacy and problematic internet shopping in a multinational sample. *Addictive Behaviors Reports*, *6*, 123–127.

Lawrence, L. (1990). The psychodynamics of the compulsive female shopper. *American Journal of Psychoanalysis*, *50*(1), 67–70.

Leite, P. L., Pereira, V. M., Nardi, A. E., & Silva, A. C. (2014). Psychotherapy for compulsive buying disorder: A systematic review. *Psychiatry Research*, *219*(3), 411–419.

Leite, P. L., & Silva, A. C. (2016). Psychiatric and socioeconomic aspects as possible predictors of compulsive buying behavior. *Trends in Psychiatry and Psychotherapy*, *38*(3), 141–146.

Lejoyeux, M., & Weinstein, A. (2013). Shopping addiction. In P. M. Miller, S. A. Ball, M. E. Bates, A. W. Blume, K. M. Kampman, D. J. Kavanagh, M. E. Larimer, N. M. Petry, & P. De Witte (Eds.), *Comprehensive addictive behaviors and disorders, Vol. 1: Principles of addiction* (pp. 847–853). San Diego, CA: Elsevier Academic Press.

Lo, H.-Y., & Harvey, N. (2012). Effects of shopping addiction on consumer decision-making: Web-based studies in real time. *Journal of Behavioral Addictions*, *1*(4), 162–170.

Lo, L. Y.-S., Lin, S.-W., & Hsu, L.-Y. (2016). Motivation for online impulse buying: A two-factor theory perspective. *International Journal of Information Management*, *36*(5), 759–772.

Manchiraju, S., Sadachar, A., & Ridgway, J. L. (2017). The Compulsive Online Shopping Scale (COSS): Development and validation using panel data. *International Journal of Mental Health and Addiction*, *15*(1), 209–223.

Manolis, C., & Roberts, J. A. (2012). Subjective well-being among adolescent consumers: The effects of materialism, compulsive buying, and time affluence. *Applied Research in Quality of Life*, *7*, 117–135.

Maraz, A., Eisinger, A., Hende, B., Urban, R., Paksi, B., Kun, B., . . . Demetrovics, Z. (2015). Measuring compulsive buying behaviour: Psychometric validity of three different scales and prevalence in the general population and in shopping centres. *Psychiatry Research*, *225*(3), 326–334.

Maraz, A., Griffiths, M. D., & Demetrovics, Z. (2016). The prevalence of compulsive buying: A meta-analysis. *Addiction*, *111*(3), 408–419.

Maraz, A., Urban, R., & Demetrovics, Z. (2016). Borderline personality disorder and compulsive buying: A multivariate etiological model. *Addictive Behaviors*, *60*, 117–123.

Marcinko, D., Bolanca, M., & Rudan, V. (2006). Compulsive buying and binge eating disorder—Case vignettes. *Progress in Neuro-Psychopharmacology & Biological Psychiatry*, *30*, 1542–1544.

Marino, J. M., Ertelt, T. W., Mitchell, J. E., & Lancaster, K. (2012). Compulsive buying. In B. A. Johnson (Ed.), *Addiction medicine: Science and practice (vols 1 and 2)* (pp. 649–660). New York, NY: Springer Science + Business Media.

Martinez-Novoa, L. M. (2017). Consumed by consumption: A phenomenological exploration of the compulsive clothing buying experience. *Dissertation Abstracts International Section A: Humanities and Social Sciences*, *78*(6-A(E)). No pagination specified.

McElroy, S. L., Keck, P. E., Pope, H. G., Smith, J. M. R., & Strakowski, S. M. (1994). Compulsive buying: A report of 20 cases. *Journal of Clinical Psychiatry*, *55*(6), 242–248.

Milkman, H. B., & Sunderwirth, S. G. (2010). *Craving for ecstasy and natural highs: A positive approach to mood alteration*. Thousand Oaks, CA: SAGE.

Mitchell, J. E. (2011a). Compulsive buying disorder group treatment manual. In A. Muller & J. E. Mitchell (Eds.), *Compulsive buying:*

Clinical foundations and treatment (pp. 169–278). New York, NY: Routledge/Taylor & Francis Group.

Mitchell, J. E. (2011b). Therapist's guide to the treatment manual. In A. Muller & J. E. Mitchell (Eds.), *Compulsive buying: Clinical foundations and treatment* (pp. 161–168). New York, NY: Routledge/Taylor & Francis Group.

Monahan, P., Black, D. W., & Gabel, J. (1996). Reliability and validity of a scale to measure change in persons with compulsive buying. *Psychiatry Research, 64*, 59–67.

Muller, A., Mitchell, J. E., & de Zwaan, M. (2015). Compulsive buying. *American Journal on Addictions, 24*, 132–137.

Newton, P. (2013, July 10). *Shopping addiction soars with mobile shopping apps*. Retrieved on August 16, 2019, from https://au.lifestyle.yahoo.com/shopping-addictions-soar-with-mobile-shopping-apps-17959311.html

Nicolai, J., Daranco, S., & Moshagen, M. (2016). Effects of mood state on impulsivity in pathological buying. *Psychiatry Research, 244*, 351–356.

Platania, S., Castellano, S., Santisi, G., & Di Nuovo, S. (2017). Personality correlates of the tendency to compulsive shopping. [Italian]. Correlati di personalita della tendenza allo shopping compulsivo. *Giornale Italiano di Psicologia, 44*(1), 137–155.

Prochaska, J. O., & Norcross, J. C. (2001). *Summary: Stages of change, objectives, strategies*. Retrieved April 17, 2018, from https://www.bing.com/search?q=contemplation+strategies+for+%22shopping+addiction%22&qs=n&form=QBRE&sp=-1&pq=contemplation+strategies+for+%22shopping+addiction%22&sc=0-49&sk=&cvid=7427B3460DDF46A1AF86451121045853

Prochaska, J. O., Norcross, J. C., & DiClemente, C. C. (1994). *Changing for good*. New York, NY: Avon Books.

Raab, G., Elger, C. E., Neuner, M., & Weber, B. (2011). The neural basis of compulsive buying. In A. Muller & J. E. Mitchell (Eds.), *Compulsive buying: Clinical foundations and treatment* (pp. 63–86). New York, NY: Routledge/Taylor & Francis.

Racine, E., Kahn, T., & Hollander, E. (2014). Compulsive buying disorder. In K. P. Rosenberg & L. Curtiss Feder (Eds.), *Behavioral addictions: Criteria, evidence, and treatment* (pp. 285–315). San Diego, CA: Elsevier Academic Press.

Ridgway, N. M., Kukar-Kinney, M., & Munroe, K. B. (2008). An expanded conceptualization and a new measure of compulsive buying. *Journal of Consumer Research, 35*(4), 622–639.

Roberts, J. A., Manolis, C., & Tanner, J. F. (Jeff), Jr. (2008). Interpersonal influence and adolescent materialism and compulsive buying. *Social Influence, 3*, 114–131.

Roberts, J. A., & Roberts, C. (2012). Stress, gender and compulsive buying among early adolescents. *Young Consumers, 13*, 113–123.

Rochat, L., Beni, C., Billieux, J., Annoni, J.-M., & Van der Linden, M. (2011). How impulsivity relates to compulsive buying and the burden perceived by caregivers after moderate-to-severe traumatic brain injury. *Psychopathology, 44*, 158–164.

Sansone, R. A., Chang, J., Jewell, B., & Marion, B. E. (2013). Compulsive buying: Relationship with body mass index. *Obesity, 21*, E86–E87.

Sansone, R. A., Chang, J., Jewell, B., & Rock, R. (2013). Childhood trauma and compulsive buying. *International Journal of Psychiatry in Clinical Practice, 17*, 73–76.

Schwartz, H. J. (1992). Psychoanalytic psychotherapy for a woman with diagnoses of kleptomania and bulimia. *Hospital & Community Psychiatry, 43*(2), 109–110.

Sepede, G., Di Iorio, G., Sarchione, F., Fiori, F., & Di Giannantonio, M. (2017). Bupropion augmentation in a case of compulsive buying disorder. *Clinical Neuropharmacology, 40*, 189–191.

Sharif, S. P., & Khanekharab, J. (2017). Identity confusion and materialism mediate the relationship between excessive social network site usage and online compulsive buying. *Cyberpsychology, Behavior, and Social Networking, 20*(8), 494–500.

Soares, C., Fernandes, N., & Morgado, P. (2016). A review of pharmacologic treatment for compulsive buying disorder. *CNS Drugs, 30*(4), 281–291.

Sohn, S.-H., & Choi, Y.-J. (2014). Phases of shopping addiction evidenced by experiences of compulsive buyers. *International Journal of Mental Health and Addiction, 12*(3), 243–254.

Tavares, H., Lobo, D. S. S., Fuentes, D., & Black, D. W. (2008). Compulsive buying disorder: A review and a case vignette. *Revista Brasileira de Psiquiatria, 30*(Suppl1), S16–S23.

Taylor, C. D., Klontz, B. T., & Britt, S. L. (2015). Internal consistency and convergent validity of the Klontz Money Behavior Inventory (KMBI). *Journal of Financial Therapy, 6*(2), 14–31.

Taylor, C. D., Klontz, B. T., & Lawson, D. R. (2017). Money disorders and locus of control: Implications for assessment and treatment. *Journal of Financial Therapy, 8*(1), ArtID 8.

Thomas, J., Al-Menhali, S., & Humeidan, M. (2016). Compulsive buying and depressive symptoms among female citizens of the United Arab Emirates. *Psychiatry Research, 237*, 357–360.

Trotzke, P., Starcke, K., Muller, A., & Brand, M. (2015). Pathological buying online as a specific form of Internet addiction: A model-based experimental investigation. *PLoS ONE, 10*(10), 1–17.

Valence, G., d'Astous, A., & Fortier, L. (1988), Compulsive buying: Concept and measurement. *Journal of Consumer Policy, 11*, 419–433.

Vasiliu, O., & Vasile, D. (2017). Compulsive buying disorder: A review of current data. *International Journal of Economics and Management Systems, 2*, 134–137.

Villardefrancos, E., & Otero-Lopez, J. M. (2016). Compulsive buying in university students: Its prevalence and relationships with materialism, psychological distress symptoms, and subjective well-being. *Comprehensive Psychiatry, 65*, 128–135.

Weaver, S. T., Moschis, G. P., & Davis, T. (2011). Antecedents of materialism and compulsive buying: A life course study in Australia. *Australasian Marketing Journal (AMJ), 19*, 247–256.

Zerach, G. (2016). The mediating role of emptiness and materialism in the association between pathological narcissism and compulsive buying. *International Journal of Mental Health and Addiction, 14*(4), 424–437.

Zhang, C., Brook, J. S., Leukefeld, C. G., & Brook, D. W. (2016). Associations between compulsive buying and substance dependence/abuse, major depressive episodes, and generalized anxiety disorder among men and women. *Journal of Addictive Diseases, 35*, 298–304.

Zhang, C., Brook, J. S., Leukefeld, C. G., De La Rosa, M., & Brook, D. W. (2017). Compulsive buying and quality of life: An estimate of the monetary cost of compulsive buying among adults in early midlife. *Psychiatry Research, 252*, 208–214.

Zhao, H., Tian, W., & Xin, T. (2017). The development and validation of the online shopping addiction scale. *Frontiers in Psychology, 8*, 1–9.

21 Work Addiction

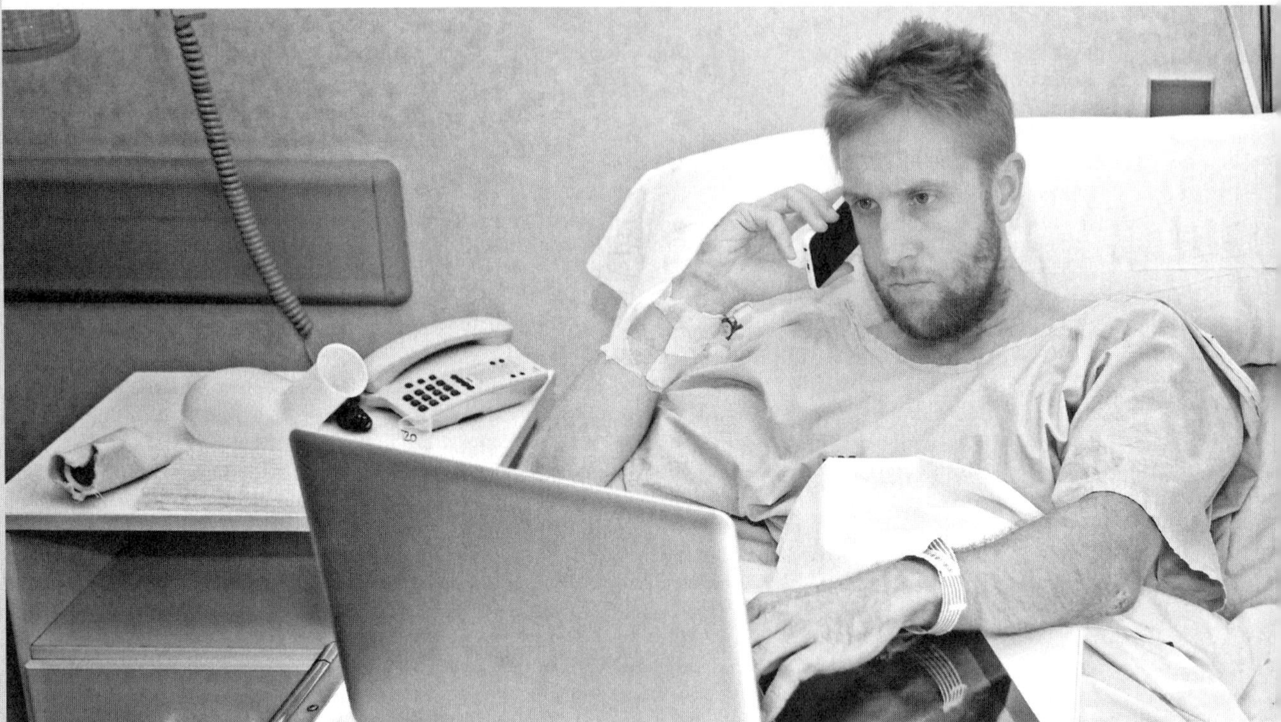

iStock.com/OcusFo

Learning Objectives

1. Be able to differentiate workaholism from other types of heavy work investment.
2. Learn the characteristics of work-addicted individuals from a recent meta-analysis.
3. Become familiar with the adverse consequences that result from workaholism.
4. Become aware of diagnostic criteria for work addiction.
5. Learn about schema-focused therapy and other recommended methods for counseling work addicts.

CHALLENGING YOUR ASSUMPTIONS ABOUT THIS ADDICTION

1. Work-addicted individuals are often in denial that heavy work involvement is causing them difficulties. What factors do you believe contribute to this propensity to stay in denial?
2. In what ways are work-addicted individuals rewarded in society for their extreme work ethic?
3. Think of people you know who work excessively. What consequences have you noticed they experience as a result of working so many hours?
4. How would you talk a friend out of being a workaholic? What difficulties would you have in broaching this topic with her or him?
5. If you ever found yourself having to spend too much time at work, what steps would you take to reduce your working hours? What would you do if your boss were the one forcing you to work long hours, but you needed the job because it was your first one out of college or university and you needed the experience and employer reference?

PERSONAL REFLECTIONS

Two examples come to mind as I think about individuals I have known who have worked long hours. One of my favorite colleagues, whom I will call Ben, typically worked 60 to 70 hours a week, and he maintained this since the day he started. He often looked tired but persisted nonetheless to not only become a full professor sooner than most but to take on additional administrative duties on top of his self-chosen heavy workload. A few years into his tenure, I remember when he would nearly lose his voice after talking for a few minutes. It was as though he could no longer project his voice, making it difficult to hear him in a meeting but even worse for students to listen to him teach. Ben had other health issues as the years passed, but his loss of voice was the one that seemed most dysfunctional. I don't know if Ben would be called a workaholic. What I did know is that he rarely dated and had few friends despite his outward kindness and gentleness.

The second example of someone I thought might be a workaholic scared me. Soon after I was promoted to full professorship, I was at the photocopy machine and started talking to a colleague I will call Heidi. Expecting to hear the typical "Congratulations!" I was shocked instead to hear, "After I became a full professor, the administration tore me apart in my subsequent biennial appraisal. There was no salary increase following the promotion, yet I was expected to work much harder and longer based on the results of that report." There was no celebration in her voice. Instead, it felt like an agonizing discontent from an exhausted individual. I was already working hard enough, I thought. I knew from long ago that some people live to work and others work to live. It no longer felt as if I could live in the middle of these two ideologies. Months later I ran into Heidi in the elevator at about 9:30 p.m. I came back to my office to pick up a few things and she was just leaving. She seemed like a deer caught in the headlights as she told me that she usually works till 11 p.m. 6 days a week but was too tired tonight and so she decided to leave early. I wondered what kind of a life she has at home, knowing that she is at work by 9 a.m. at least on weekdays. Heidi was working 70 to 80 hours a week, twice as much as most typical jobs.

Both examples have led me to wonder what defines a workaholic. In both cases, the hard work of these individuals was rewarded at the University. In fact, as I read a draft document outlining expectations of full professors, I commented that they were so excessive in every area of evaluation that no one could attain these lofty expectations. It seemed to me that employers love employees who will sacrifice almost everything for their jobs.

Are workaholics simply people who work longer hours than most of us because they are highly competitive and/or people who internalize the expectations of others to a greater extent? Are they perhaps individuals who enjoy their work more than most of us? I was indeed interested to find out as I began research for this chapter.

Background Information

Work is important for several reasons, some of which include providing meaning and purpose to life, improving self-esteem, building status, developing a sense of accomplishment, contributing to society, paying bills, and creating a "nest egg" of savings for retirement. Work also helps people structure their days, form identities, and establish and develop relationships (Andreassen, 2015). Several studies have shown that people rank work as second in importance only to family, and, even after winning the lottery, 85%

of Americans continue to work (Shamai, 2015). For some people, however, work becomes pathological.

Work addiction is usually called "workaholism" both in the vernacular and in the published literature. The term workaholism was introduced into the English language by Oates in either 1968 (Shimazu, Kubota, & Bakker, 2015) or 1971 (Aziz & Uhrich, 2014), depending on the source. Oates described it as a compulsive need to work relentlessly. Although employers often see workaholics as desirable hires, researchers are aware of the harmful effects work addiction has on both the employee and the organizations that hire them (Aziz & Uhrich, 2014).

Despite this awareness of its harmful consequences, workaholism continues to lack a consensus regarding its definition, classification, or acceptance of the concept (Andreassen, 2015). There remains little written about workaholism, which is surprising given the amount of interest in the topic (Aziz & Burke, 2015). Another concept related to work addiction is work engagement, and Kahn in 1990 is considered to have been the first to discuss it (Clark, Michel, & Stevens, 2015).

The average number of work hours engaged in annually has diminished substantially since the mid-1800s when working days were often between 10 and 16 hours for 6 days a week (Harpaz, 2015). Today, the average number of working hours in most modern countries is between 30 and 40 per week (Shamai, 2015). A heavy worker now works approximately 50 hours per week or more, and a common full-time worker works less than 50 hours per week (Shamai, 2015).

Studies are consistently finding that dual-income families work harder than they used to (Stier & Sella-Dotan, 2015). In the 1970s, the percentage of professional women who worked 50 hours a week or more was 6%. By the late 2000s, it had more than doubled to 14% (Stier & Sella-Dotan, 2015). The increased percentage of men increased only from 34% to 38% during this period (Stier & Sella-Dotan, 2015). Work demands have similarly increased, including increases in the amount of effort required and the pace of work (Stier & Sella-Dotan, 2015).

As with other behavioral addictions excluding gambling, debate continues as to whether work addiction ought to be called an addiction as it lacks a physiological cause (Porter, 2015). Killinger (2011) defined a *workaholic* as "a work-obsessed individual who gradually becomes emotionally crippled and addicted to power and control in a compulsive drive to gain approval and public recognition of success" (para. 3). Although this definition has merit, it suggests too many hypothesized *causal* relationships for it to be parsimonious. For example, it has not been demonstrated that *all* workaholics are addicted for reasons of power and control to gain approval and recognition (note, however, that it does apply to *some*).

One of the most trusted forms of research in the social sciences is a *meta-analysis*, which is a statistical analysis based on the results of several similar empirical studies. Clark, Michel, Zhdanova, Pui, and Baltes (2016) conducted the only meta-analysis done to date on workaholism. Their results are substantial, and they will be reviewed shortly. They defined *workaholism* "as an addiction to work that leads to many negative individual, interpersonal, and organizational outcomes" (p. 1836).

Researchers differ in believing whether workaholics need to experience a low level of job satisfaction before receiving a diagnosis or if the opposite is true (i.e., that they need to greatly enjoy their work) (Clark et al., 2016). Some have also argued that workaholism is a form of obsessive-compulsive personality disorder that merely finds its expression at work (Naughton, as cited in Aziz & Burke, 2015).

Although researchers continue to grapple with coming to a consensus regarding the definition of workaholism, most agree that it involves the idea that workaholics work longer and harder than those who are not addicted to work (Clark et al., 2016). Snir and Harpaz (2015) introduced the concept of *heavy work investment* (HWI), which includes dimensions of both working long hours and making heavy effort. Although some researchers define extreme work hours as requiring 61 or more hours of work per week, many use a 48-hour cutoff point that is in line with a 1993 European Directive (Snir & Harpaz, 2015).

Astakhova and Hogue (2014) developed a typology of HWI. Their model distinguished among three general types of HWI (i.e., workaholic HWI [W-HWI], situational HWI [S-HWI], and pseudo-HWI [P-HWI]), which interacted with biopsychosocial factors to create nine presentations of HWI. The psychosocial factors included one's culture, which in turn affects the biological, psychological, and social presentation of work. Astakhova and Hogue theorized that the W-HWI type would be most associated with biological factors, which in turn could lead to compulsive behaviors such as the inability or reluctance to refrain from work.

Snir and Harpaz (2015) advanced their theory of HWI. According to Snir and Harpaz, there are different types of HWI, of which workaholism constitutes one type. There are dispositional heavy work investors (HWIs) and situational HWIs. Situational HWIs need to work long hours because of external pressures. These demands might be permanent or temporary. Constitutional HWIs are intrinsically motivated to work long hours, and there are two types. Devoted heavy workers have a passion for their work and are heavily engaged in it, which results from internal, controllable, and stable predictors. Workaholics, on the other hand, have an addiction to work, which results from internal, uncontrollable, and stable predictors. According to Harpaz and Snir's theory, workaholics are not in control of their HWI and consequently are most prone to developing negative consequences from their HWI. Although work-engaged individuals generally report positive outcomes, workaholics mostly experience negative consequences (Taris, Van Beek, & Schaufeli, 2015).

There is both empirical support and lack of support for aspects of Snir and Harpaz's (2015) theory. Midje, Nafstad, Syse, and Torp (2014) found in their study of 118 participants that workaholics with HWI were also more likely than nonworkaholics to have mental health problems. Grebot, Olivier, Berjot, Girault-Lidvan, and Duprez (2017) tested 155 business professionals and managers (56 women, 99 men) and found that neuroticism, having anxious-depressive tendencies and feeling vulnerable to stress, differentiated what they called "real" workaholics from enthusiastic HWIs. Other research supports the idea that heavy work engagement and workaholism are different constructs (Mazzetti, Schaufeli, & Guglielmi, 2018).

Results from a nationally representative cross-sectional survey of employees in Norway (N = 1608; mean age = 45.2 years; age range = 21–60) did not support one aspect of Snir and Harpaz's (2015) theory, however (Keller, Spurk, Baumeler, & Hirschi, 2016). Keller et al. (2016) found that workaholism increased where workers reported having *high* control rather than low control over their work. Workaholism was also related to experiencing high work demands, role conflict, and negative acts at work (e.g., pressure from the boss, competition from colleagues). Individuals were more vulnerable to workaholism if the work environment was competitive (Keller et al., 2016).

Workaholism is correlated negatively with job satisfaction and job performance but associated positively with intention to change jobs. Work engagement, on the other hand, is associated positively with job satisfaction and job performance but correlated negatively with a desire to change jobs (van Beek, Taris, Schaufeli, & Brenninkmeijer, 2014).

Workaholics tend to be perfectionists who have irrational beliefs regarding failure and performance expectations (Falco et al., 2017). A recent study found that having low self-esteem led to workaholism; workaholism, in turn, led to working more hours that were associated with feeling stressed at work; and working more hours led to still greater stress (Aziz, Zamary, & Wuensch, 2018).

Now coming back to the meta-analysis conducted by Clark et al. (2016). They analyzed 89 articles that included 68 published and 21 unpublished studies. Combined these represent 97 independent samples. The researchers found that workaholism was associated with the following personality qualities: perfectionism, nondelegation, type A personality, trait negative affect, state negative affect, and extraversion. Type A personalities are found in individuals who are ambitious, competitive, impatient, irritable, aggressive, and quick-tempered (Shamai, 2015). Individuals with a type B personality, on the other hand, demonstrate few of these characteristics (Shamai, 2015).

Clark et al. (2016) found that workaholism was associated with work environments where employees had little control over their work and where the work itself was ambiguous. Workaholics were more likely to (a) have reached managerial status, (b) be overloaded by their work role, (c) experience work role conflict, (d) receive support for their hard work from a supervisor, (e) be overly involved at work (e.g., excessive work engagement), and (f) enjoy work.

The positive outcome from workaholism included increased career prospects (Clark et al., 2016). The negative consequences, however, were numerous. Clark et al. (2016) found the following were associated with workaholism: (a) increased job stress, (b) counterproductive work behaviors, (c) marital disaffection, (d) work-life conflict, (e) lower life satisfaction, (f) burnout, (g) emotional exhaustion, (h) cynicism, (i) depersonalization, (j) diminished work satisfaction, (k) poor family satisfaction/functioning, (l) worse physical health, and (m) worse emotional/mental health.

Overall, Clark et al. (2016) found that the most robust relationships were between workaholism and HWI, followed next by job stress, perfectionism, and marital disaffection. This provided support for the idea that workaholics are not driven because of financial or family needs: they are driven instead by some internal compulsion. Workaholism was related to neither self-esteem nor increased levels of performance or job satisfaction in their meta-analysis.

Workaholics are more likely found in specific occupations (e.g., surgeons, lawyers) (Aziz & Burke, 2015). Many of these individuals are without question highly devoted and passionate toward their work. The prevalence of passion varies among occupations. Teachers rank highly, with 90% of them reporting that they are passionate about their work, whereas 78% of managers, professionals, and white-collar workers report feeling passionate (Houlfort, Vallerand, & Laframboise, 2015).

Interestingly, some students develop a form of work addiction called *study addiction*. The Bergen Study Addiction Scale was created as a measure of this and was administered to 218 and 993 Polish students in the author's first attempt to demonstrate its psychometric properties (Atroszko, Andreassen, Griffiths, & Pallesen, 2015). Students may also be interested in learning that the evidence from several studies suggests that multitasking is inefficient. Research finds that multitasking leads to poor performance on every task that is being juggled (Kabat-Zinn, 2013).

The cause of work addiction is likely reflected in the findings of Clark et al.'s (2016) meta-analysis; however, a meta-analysis cannot answer questions of causation because it is a type of correlational research. Nonetheless, the causes of work addiction are thought to result from an interaction of individual dispositions (e.g., personality traits as found in Clark et al., 2016), sociocultural factors (e.g., stressful or dysfunctional childhood and family experiences, competitive work environment), and behavioral reinforcement (e.g., classical conditioning, operant conditioning, and social learning theory; Shimazu, Kubota & Bakker, 2015).

Killinger (as cited in Aziz & Burke, 2015) suggested that perfectionism leads to a compulsive desire to become successful and project a successful persona. Aziz and Burke (2015) postulated that perfectionism might be a precursor of obsessive-compulsiveness. Obsessions are persistent thoughts, ideas, or images that preoccupy a person's mind, whereas compulsions are repeated behaviors precipitated by strong urges.

Having rigid personal beliefs predicted working compulsively in a sample of 191 participants followed for 6 months in a two-wave longitudinal survey (van Wijhe, Peeters, & Schaufeli, 2014). Comparable with other addictions, working becomes a coping strategy for stress (Andreassen, 2015). Clark, Michel, and Stevens (2015) suggested that workaholics are "driven to work because of an inner compulsion or to resolve an ego depletion" (p. 191).

Adult children of workaholics are more likely to become workaholics themselves (Snir & Harpaz, 2015). This predisposition to work addiction could result from several or all the reasons stated previously. This finding might also suggest a biological or genetic heritable factor.

The prevalence of workaholism in Andreassen, Nielsen, Pallesen, and Gjerstad's (2019) nationally representative cross-sectional survey in Norway ($N = 1608$) was 7.3%. In another nationally representative survey ($N = 1124$) of employees in Norway conducted by Andreassen et al. (2014), the prevalence of workaholism was 8.3%. Among college-educated individuals, the workaholism prevalence was reported to be between 8% and 17.5% in a literature review article (Sussman, 2012). Golden (2015) suggested that about 30% of workers in North America self-define as workaholics. Stier and Sella-Dotan (2015) reported that the percentage of professional women who work at least 50 hours a week has more than doubled in the United States between the 1970s and the late 2000s (i.e., from 6% to 14%, respectively). The percentage increase in men is much less (i.e., from 34% to 38%, respectively). Snir (2015b) estimated that 22% of the global workforce works more than 48 hours per week.

Diagnostic and Assessment Considerations

Work addiction is not included in either *DSM-5* or ICD-11. Diagnostic criteria for work addiction is embedded within assessment instruments designed to measure it. The only instrument that includes the core addiction criteria advanced by Griffiths (2005), according to Quinones and Griffiths (2015), is the Bergen Work Addiction Scale (BWAS). Consequently, this is the only one that will be presented in this section in addition to Griffiths' components model.

Cecilie Andreassen and colleagues (Andreassen, Griffiths, Hetland, & Pallesen, 2012) created the BWAS. The BWAS is free for everyone to use without stipulations. Respondents are asked to answer seven questions using a 5-point Likert scale (1 = never, 2 = rarely, 3 = sometimes, 4 = often, 5 = always). The authors suggested that the scoring of *often* or *always* on at least four of the seven items *may* suggest that a person is a work addict. The seven questions are as follows:

How often during the last year have you

1. Thought of how you could free up more time to work? (i.e., salience).
2. Spent much more time working than initially intended? (i.e., tolerance).
3. Worked in order to reduce feelings of guilt, anxiety, helplessness and depression? (i.e., mood modification).
4. Been told by others to cut down on work without listening to them? (i.e., relapse).
5. Become stressed if you have been prohibited from working? (i.e., withdrawal).
6. Deprioritized hobbies, leisure activities, and exercise because of your work? (i.e., conflict).
7. Worked so much that it has negatively influenced your health? (i.e., problems). (p. 269)

The BWAS was constructed to include Griffiths' (2005) components model together with a question about health consequences (i.e., "problems," Andreassen et al., 2012). Griffiths (2014) elaborated on his six components as they relate to workaholism as follows:

1. Salience. This occurs when work becomes an individual's most important life activity. Even when they are not at work, workaholics constantly think about work.
2. Mood modification. Work creates either arousal or feelings of escape or numbing.
3. Tolerance. Workaholics gradually increase the amount of time they spend working each day.
4. Withdrawal symptoms. Workaholics experience the shakes or varying degrees of unpleasant mood states when they are ill or on holidays.
5. Conflict. Workaholics create conflicts with other people around them who are concerned about the amount of time they spend work.
6. Relapse. Even when workaholics reduce their working hours, they often return to their previous levels as they lose control.

Differential Diagnosis

Quinones, Griffiths, and Kakabadse (2016) conducted an exploratory two-wave longitudinal study with 244 participants who used the Internet as part of their employment. They found that workaholism was unrelated to compulsive Internet use. In other words, work addiction and compulsive Internet use are two different phenomena.

It is important that clinicians differentiate between work addiction and other types of HWIs (Snir & Harpaz, 2015). As mentioned earlier, some people need to work extensively because it is a requirement of their job either temporarily or permanently (i.e., situational HWIs). Work-addicted individuals must also be distinguished from devoted heavy workers (i.e., a dispositional HWI) who are passionate about their work and who are also heavily engaged in it. Remember that workaholics mostly experience negative consequences from their compulsive work frenzy and that their addiction stems from internal and uncontrollable factors.

Andreassen, Griffiths, Sinha, Hetland, and Pallesen (2016) conducted the most extensive study ever done on the topic of workaholism, which included 16,426 working Norwegian adults. Griffiths (2016), who was the second author of the study, provided insights as to other diagnoses that are sometimes comorbid with work addiction or that need to be distinguished from it. This discussion here will focus on the latter. Individuals with attention deficit hyperactivity disorder (ADHD) may present as work-addicted individuals because their impulsiveness and concentration difficulties may necessitate that they work long hours to accomplish what their colleagues complete within regular working hours. Griffiths hypothesized that, because people with ADHD may fail in other aspects of life, they may become particularly driven to prove themselves at work.

Work addiction also needs to be distinguished from obsessive-compulsive disorder (OCD). Individuals with OCD may have a high need to arrange things in particular ways, have a strong need to control, and obsess over details to the point of impaired functioning. Remember that "OCD is characterized by the presence of obsessions and/or compulsions" (APA, 2013, p. 235). Consequently, OCD is a much more pervasive disorder than work addiction, which means that OCD will affect other areas of life besides work. Furthermore, when OCD is successfully treated, the obsessions and/or compulsions dissipate or diminish substantially, in which case work addiction symptoms would also subside correspondingly, thereby substantiating that OCD was the cause of the compulsive work behavior. Links have also been drawn between anxiety and/or depression and addictions, and it is, therefore, important to ensure that the work-addictive symptoms are not a consequence of these disorders (Griffiths, 2016).

Comorbidity and Co-Addictions

As mentioned in the previous section, the largest study done regarding workaholism focused on comorbidity between workaholism and psychiatric disorders. The study included 16,426 working Norwegian adults (Andreassen et al., 2016). Griffiths (2016) noted other diagnoses that are sometimes comorbid with work addiction. Griffiths reported that workaholics scored higher on *all* psychiatric symptoms compared with nonworkaholics. He reported the following rates of comorbidity:

- 32.7% met ADHD criteria (12.7% among nonworkaholics).
- 25.6% met OCD criteria (8.7% among nonworkaholics).

- 33.8% met anxiety criteria (11.9% among nonworkaholics).
- 8.9% met depression criteria (2.6% among nonworkaholics). (para. 3)

Available Measures

Clark et al. (2016) wrote that the three most commonly used scales to measure work addiction include the Workaholism Battery (Spence & Robbins, 1992), the Work Addiction Risk Test (WART; Robinson, 1989), and the Dutch Workaholism Scale (DUWAS; Schaufeli, Shimazu, & Taris, 2009). Of these, Quinones and Griffiths (2015) stated, the Workaholism Battery is arguably the most extensively used test. Besides these three tests, three others are included:

1. Workaholism Battery (Spence & Robbins, 1992). Spence and Robbins thought of workaholism as a trait-based multidimensional construct consisting of enjoyment, drive, and work involvement. Their original tests comprised 25 items. The term *enjoyment* was eventually dropped from the construct of a workaholic, instead replaced with the term *engaged*. Furthermore, empirical studies have not confirmed the three-dimensional structure of the 25-item scale (Quinones & Griffiths, 2015). The scale was subsequently revised by McMillan, Brady, O'Driscoll, and Marsh (2012).
2. Work Addiction Risk Test (WART; Robinson, 1989). Quinones and Griffiths (2015) suggested that this is likely the second most widely used test of workaholism. This 25-item scale consists of five subscales: (a) compulsive tendencies, (b) control, (c) impaired communication/self-absorption, (d) inability to delegate, and (e) self-worth. Studies that have measured its psychological properties have consistently failed to support the existence of these five components.
3. Dutch Workaholism Scale (DUWAS; Schaufeli et al., 2009). The authors developed the test to measure two dimensions: working excessively and working compulsively. Other researchers found that only two of the nine items assessed compulsive tendencies and most items measured excessive work. The test also reportedly may lead to interpretation confusion based on factor analysis (Quinones & Griffiths, 2015).
4. Bergen Work Addiction Scale (BWAS; Andreassen et al., 2012). Quinones and Griffiths (2015) argued that the BWAS is theoretically and psychometrically sound. It was validated on more than 12,000 individuals. The BWAS was included earlier under the heading Diagnostic and Assessment Considerations.
5. Workaholism Analysis Questionnaire (WAQ; Aziz, Uhrich, Wuensch, & Swords, 2013). The WAQ is a 29-item self-report measure of workaholism scored on a 5-point Likert scale, ranging from 1 (strongly disagree) to 5 (strongly agree). It has demonstrated internal reliability, convergent validity, concurrent validity, discriminant validity, and content validity. It also measures work-life imbalance.
6. Workaholic Test. This is a 25-item quiz that is scored online. This quiz appears on the Healthyplace.com website. The site claims that it "is the largest consumer mental health site on the net." Site authors also write that their quizzes are for entertainment purposes but that they *may* have a possible educational use. Despite this caveat, responses to this quiz may suggest workaholic tendencies. It is available at https://www.healthyplace.com/psychological-tests/stress-workaholic-test

Clinical Interview Questions

Shamai (2015) suggested one way to determine how central work is in a person's life. The lottery question is based on removing the rationale of necessity to work so that a person's psychological commitment to work can be ascertained. The question could be asked as follows: *If you won a substantial lottery and no longer needed to work, would you continue to do so anyway?* Arvey et al. (as cited in Shamai, 2015) found that 85% of American lottery winners continued working after they won a lottery.

Robinson (1998) included 10 indicators that are suggestive of work addiction. I have modified these by turning them into the following 10 questions:

1. To what extent do you need to hurry and stay busy?
2. How much control do you need over your work?
3. What aspects of perfectionism define your work style?
4. How are your relationships affected by your work?
5. How often do you find that you binge on work?
6. How easy is it for you to relax and have fun?
7. To what degree have you found that you have forgotten conversations or trips because you are either exhausted or preoccupied with work?
8. To what extent do you consider yourself impatient and irritable?
9. How adequate do you feel as a person and what effect does your work have on this?
10. To what extent do you practice either self-care or self-neglect?

Generic Names and Street "Lingo"

Work addiction is also referred to as compulsive work addiction and workaholism in the published literature. There are no other words or expressions used to describe this condition currently.

Neuroscience

There are currently no published studies that address the neuroscience of work addiction. This is an area that will no doubt be investigated soon if such research is not already under way.

Physical Impacts (Long-Term Use)

Work addiction can be fatal. The Japanese word *Karoshi* refers to death from overwork, and the phenomenon is recognized internationally. Most who succumb often work between 3000 and 3500 hours a year. Working 14-hour days is not uncommon. Death results from subarachnoid hemorrhage or myocardial infarction (Snir & Harpaz, 2015). "It is believed that tens of thousands of Japanese become seriously ill or die from overwork each year" (Harpaz, 2015, p. 363). Fassel (as cited in Shamai, 2015) viewed workaholism as a progressive, fatal disease. Working more than even 8 hours a day increases the risk of accidents (Wagstaff & Sigstad Lie, 2011). If a job requires working 12 hours a day, it doubles the risk of being in an accident compared to working only 8 hours a day (Harpaz, 2015).

Long working hours are associated with poor lifestyle choices and habits such as heavy smoking, excessive alcohol consumption, poor diet, sleep disorders, and lack of exercise (Harpaz, 2015). Workaholics also consume more caffeine than nonworkaholics (Salanova et al., 2016). They are more prone to psychosomatic complaints and disabling back pain (Shimazu, Kubota, & Bakker, 2015).

Workaholics have insufficient time to recover from their excessive work, which leaves them emotionally and/or cognitively exhausted over time (Shimazu, Kubota, & Bakker, 2015). In other words, they burn out but continue working despite what their bodies and minds are telling them.

Mental, Emotional, and Spiritual Impacts

Clark et al. (2016) found in their meta-analysis that work addiction was associated with feelings of psychological distress, pressure at work, guilt, anxiety, and work-life conflict. Workaholics were more likely to experience poorer emotional and mental health.

Work addiction is also related to increased depression (Shimazu, Kubota, & Bakker, 2015), anger, disappointment at work (Clark, Michel, & Stevens, 2015), irritability, shame (Taris et al., 2015), diminished life satisfaction (Shimazu, Schaufeli, Kamiyama, & Kawakami, 2015), and career dissatisfaction (Snir, 2015a).

Psychosocial Impacts (Relationships, Career/Work, Legal, Financial)

A common adverse effect resulting from work addiction is having family and relationship problems (Quinones & Griffiths, 2015). Work addiction reduces both the workaholic's and the partner's family satisfaction (Bakker, Shimazu, Demerouti, Shimada, & Kawakami, 2014) and marital satisfaction (Levy, 2015). The children of HWIs are more likely to be overweight or obese (Harpaz, 2015).

At work, workaholism can damage organizational performance and should, therefore, be a concern for companies and corporations (Midje et al., 2014). Workaholism is also related to intention to change jobs (Molino, Bakker, & Ghislieri, 2016), suggesting that some excessive workers will end up quitting to resume employment elsewhere. Further, as stated earlier, workaholics are more likely to suffer physical, emotional, and psychological illness, thereby leading to an increase in employee absence. Due to exhaustion, workaholics are more likely to be involved in car and work accidents, thus leading to possible disasters, environmental hazards, and legal problems (Harpaz, 2015).

Working With Diverse Populations

Sex Differences

Clark, Beiler, and Zimmerman (2015) suggested that workaholic women are under additional pressures compared to workaholic men. The reasons for this have more to do with gender differences than sex differences. Clark et al. suggested that these pressures are because of the conflict that some women experience between their drive to work and traditional gender roles that expect women to be particularly committed to their families. Husbands who work long hours are more likely to have wives who experience less marital satisfaction, whereas wives who work long hours are more likely to find that both they and their husbands experience diminished marital quality (Barnett, Gareis, & Brennan, 2009).

A recent study suggests that women may be more likely to become workaholics than men (Beiler-May, Williamson, Clark, & Carter, 2017). Women were found less likely to report items relating to workaholism than men, which leads to contamination of study results (Beiler-May et al., 2017). Furthermore, work-addicted women may experience more negative consequences than men because of societal gender norms and gender roles (Clark, Beiler, & Zimmerman, 2015).

Adolescents and Youth

A study conducted in Poland found that parents who had demanding attitudes and were inconsistent in their parenting style had the most significant effect on shaping "pathological attitudes" toward work (Lewandowska-Walter & Wojdylo, 2011, p. 35). The researchers observed that adolescents with a tendency to become work-addicted individuals came from families who were highly perfectionistic and who demonstrated conditional love.

Race and Ethnicity

There is no published literature about work addiction and race/ethnicity. This is noted here so that both students and practitioners are aware of the current lack of research in this area.

Nonpsychiatric Disabilities

There is no published literature about work addiction and nonpsychiatric disabilities. This is noted here so that both students and practitioners are aware of the current lack of research in this area.

Lesbian, Gay, Bisexual, and Transgender (LGBT)

There is no published literature about work addiction and LGBT. This is noted here so that both students and practitioners are aware of the current lack of research in this area.

War Veterans

There is no published literature about work addiction and veterans. This is noted here so that both students and practitioners are aware of the current lack of research in this area.

Medications and Other Relevant Physical Interventions

There is no published literature regarding medications or other physical interventions to treat work addiction. This is noted here so that both students and practitioners are aware of the current lack of research in this area.

INSIDE AN ADDICTED PERSON'S MIND

Ray, Age 60

When I was in my late teens and early 20s, I used to change jobs a lot. It did not look good on my résumé, but I was having a lot of fun. I married Natalia when I was 26 years old. We had a fantastic marriage. Natalia was everything I ever wanted in a woman and in a wife. We were planning on having a family when everything came to a halt Saturday, February 23, 1980. While driving home from a party, I lost control of the vehicle on a patch of snow and ice. I saw the pole in front of us and did my best to swerve, but I smashed directly into it on the passenger side, killing my wife instantly. I was in the hospital for a week with only minor injuries. I don't want to ever think about that experience again, but I am repeatedly haunted in my dreams.

I would have to say I stopped living that day. I started placing all my energies into my career as a stockbroker. After a few years the money was rolling in, and I was finally a success! I had so many clients that I was the talk of my colleagues. But, over time, my colleagues wanted less and less to do with me. They found me obnoxious, irritable, and so driven that they couldn't compete. I know deep down they were extremely envious, and I was a threat to them. When my company promoted me, several of my colleagues quit in protest. My boss said that they told him that they could not work with me because I was a narcissistic perfectionist. Anger seethed inside me to hear that! I was not a narcissist; I simply liked to be in control. Of course, I did some dating after Natalia died. I even married again in 1989. But Tina was no comparison to Natalia. By this time, I was working 70 hours a week, and Tina insisted that I spend more time with her. The fact is, when I did spend time with her, all I could think about was Natalia. I needed to be at work to protect myself from these feelings. I don't know if you'll understand any of this, but I simply could not bear to have much free time as my mind would fill with remorse, shame, and despair.

I don't particularly enjoy being a stockbroker, by the way, but it is better than my sickening thoughts. In 1993, Tina left me for another man. I was hurt by this and buried myself even further into work to avoid thinking that I might also be a failure. The last 5 years, however, have been the worst. My physician said the stress of my job is going to kill me. I have high blood pressure, diabetes, and my quick anger will likely lead to an early grave if I don't change my lifestyle and lose at least 50 pounds. I thanked him for his advice, but I wasn't interested in hearing it. I'm going to continue working hard because it is the only thing that makes me feel good inside. I don't care what my doctor thinks. He doesn't have to live inside my tortured mind.

Commentary

Ray demonstrates many of the qualities of a work addict. Like so many addicts, Ray uses his addiction to avoid facing his life problems. Accordingly, additional life problems surmount, and they create several adverse consequences. Ray has developed many of the personality qualities of a work-addicted individual as well. He has developed a type A personality, which is irritable, narcissistic, perfectionistic, and controlling. At the same time, he is filled with remorse, shame, despair, and guilt. The result of working long hours has resulted in several health issues, including obesity. Ray has become unable to sustain friendly relations with colleagues or maintain an intimate relationship because of his absorption in work and his neglect of other life commitments.

Discussion

1. Do you know of anyone who you suspect has become dependent on work? If "yes," which symptoms noted in the commentary apply to him or her?
2. Does this person have symptoms that are not listed in the commentary? If so, what are they?
3. If you were Ray's counselor, how would you go about helping him?

Specific Counseling Considerations

ROLEPLAY SCENARIOS

Roleplay in dyads with one of you acting as the counselor and the other as the counselee. If a roleplay is not possible, work individually in writing out a list of your suggestions.

Roleplay #1

Lance, age 19, was brought in to see you by his parents, Scott and Ruth. Lance is in his second year of college, and he later hopes to get into architecture. His parents have become increasingly concerned for their son. When he is not in class, he is studying. According to Scott and Ruth, Lance stays up most nights until 3 a.m. working on his classes. You discover that Lance is taking a BA in art literature, and he is only in four classes (i.e., 12 hours of class time per week). Scott said that he believes Lance rewrites his notes when he gets home from college, and then he rewrites them at least three more times. Lance speaks up and tells you that he rewrites his notes as he finds it the best way to study for exams. Ruth chimes in, noting that Lance has above-average ability and intelligence and he is not involved in any alcohol or drug use. More worrisome to her, she reports, he is not involved in anything!

Roleplay #2

Kay, age 38, comes to you for help. As you call her into your office, you notice that she walks like a woman who is elderly: Her gait is cautious, unsteady, and slow. Her face looks pale, and her cheeks are gaunt. More than anything, it is her eyes that appear sunken and lifeless. She tells you that she seems profoundly depressed and exhausted but does not understand why. You ask about her free time and her interests, and you are shocked to hear that she doesn't have any leisure interests or activities. Instead, Kay tells you about how she is trying to climb the corporate ladder by working 80 to 90 hours a week.

HOW WOULD AN ADDICTION COUNSELOR HELP THIS PERSON?

You are working as a professional counselor. Nyoko, age 51, recently emigrated from Tokyo, Japan, with her husband, Daiki. She is fluent in English. Nyoko looks overwhelmed and distraught as she tells you that Daiki has already begun having an affair here in Cupertino, California. She tells you that they left Japan partly because of this cheating behavior, which has been ongoing for several years. You ask her when the cheating began and find out it started around the same time that Nyoko began working as a senior manager in a computer manufacturing firm. She felt fortunate when she was given a comparable position at Apple. Since becoming an executive, Nyoko has needed to work typically 70 hours a week. Now that she has started a new position, she suspects she will need to work even more than that to be competitive. She does not know how she can win Daiki back, but she wants him to return to her and remain faithful. As you talk to her, you do not get a sense that she is entirely genuine with you. Your intuition tells you that she sees her husband more as a possession than as a person she deeply loves.

Remember to view clients within their environmental contexts, keeping in mind societal, parental/familial, cultural/spiritual, and peer influences. Specifically, become aware of the impact that the following influences have and continue to have in your clients' lives: race, language, religion and spirituality, gender, familial migration history, sexual/affectional orientation, age and cohort, physical and mental capacities, socioeconomic situation and history, education, and history of traumatic experience.

1. What defines this person's environment, past and present?
2. Who is this person sitting in front of me, taking into account environmental and personal characteristics?
3. What defines the problem that he or she is presenting within their multicultural milieu?

Goals and Goal Setting

In most cases, abstinence from work is not a possibility for a work addict. What are appropriate goals? In many cases, the workaholic will be in denial. Consequently, goals will need to be established collaboratively based on where the client is regarding the stages of change. Here are some relevant goals:

1. Do a cost-benefit analysis regarding the consequences of excessive work. Helping clients assess the consequences of work addiction may help motivate them to create balance in their lives.
2. Build a life outside of work. This can include any life area such as developing friendships, nurturing existing relationships, time with one's spouse and children, recreational activities, hobbies, sports, etc.
3. Explore childhood experience that may have led to the development of rigid beliefs and behaviors that have created perfectionism and type A personality traits.
4. Look at other reasons that explain why the client overworks. Is the client concerned about the boss's expectations? What is driving the compulsive work pattern?
5. Focus on diminishing type A personality traits. Some examples here include anger management, arousal reduction methods, and mindfulness meditation.
6. Teach assertiveness training. A workaholic may have trouble saying "no," and learning to do so may be needed to free up time for physical health, emotional well-being, spirituality, etc.
7. Focus on core dysfunctional beliefs, such as "I am only as good as my accomplishments" or "I must do things perfectly to have self-worth."
8. Create boundaries between work and home life. Help the client establish healthy boundaries between these two areas.
9. Teach ways of becoming more effective during the hours spent at work. The intent here is to get more work done in less time.
10. Instruct the client on delegation skills. Focus on teaching the client to offload some of the work demands on others.
11. Encourage the client to take regular vacations. Holiday time helps people become aware of other interests they have or interests that they can develop. One idea here is to book a holiday at an all-inclusive vacation resort that offers many scheduled and diversified activities throughout the day. Clients can be encouraged to participate in several of these to become aware of what they find enjoyable.

Stages of Change Strategies

The processes of change mentioned are based on those outlined by Connors, DiClemente, Velasquez, and Donovan (2013) and Prochaska, Norcross, and DiClemente (1994). The definitions for the various processes can be found in Chapter 6. Besides these processes, other strategies are included that have separate citations.

The University of Rhode Island Change Assessment Scale (URICA) is a helpful scale for determining where a client is currently at regarding the stages of change model. There are 24-, 28-, and 32-item versions of the scale. A 24-item version is published for alcohol or drug problems. The scale, however, is generic and can be easily adapted for use with other addictions. It is available with norms as a free download from https://www.guilford.com/add/miller11_old/urica.pdf.

Specific precontemplation strategies.

Like other addicts, workaholics are often the last to know that they have a problem. Famous contemporary movie actor James Franco struggled with work addiction. There are several stories about this on the Internet (e.g., https://people.com/movies/james-franco-on-his-moment-of-crisis-while-battling-work-addiction/).

Three books receive 5-star ratings on the topic of work addiction. These include the following:

1. Marcus Felix (2014). *Life Balance for Workaholic—Let's Put Down Your Work for a While, Relax Yourself From Stress and Enjoy Your Life* (Kindle edition). This might be a helpful beginning book as it is only 17 pages and one can read the book for free on Kindle.
2. Alexia H. (2018). *When It's Never Enough: Daily Reflections of a Work Addict*. One of the most recent books on the topic is 209 pages.
3. Michael Grossman and Robin Johnson (2017). *Someone's Got to Do the Work Around Here: Overcoming Workaholism*. A mutual support book of 154 pages.

Regarding mutual support groups following the 12-step tradition, there is Recoveries Anonymous (http://www.r-a.org/i-work-addiction.htm#.WxfzzPZFy70) and Workaholics Anonymous (http://www.workaholics-anonymous.org/). Self-Management and Recovery Training (SMART) is an alternative that is based on a secular and scientific approach. It incorporates cognitive-behavioral therapy (CBT) (particularly rational emotive behavior therapy), motivational interviewing (MI), and motivational enhancement therapy (see https://www.smartrecovery.org/).

Specific contemplation strategies.

Workaholics may be afraid to work less for fear of adverse consequences. Helping them create a cost-benefit analysis may help them realize that the bigger cost results from leading a grossly unbalanced life. It is important to distinguish among the various forms of HWI because working long hours itself is not the problem—the compulsive aspect of workaholism (when the job or career do not require such a work style) together with leading an unbalanced life indefinitely becomes the issue. Please see other chapters for ideas focused on fostering emotional arousal, consciousness-raising, self-re-evaluation, and helping relationships.

Specific preparation strategies.

Helping the client establish goals is the hallmark of the preparation stage. Some suggested goals that could be used here are included in the earlier section of this chapter called Goals and Goal Setting. For work addicts, this might also include creating a daily schedule that incorporates home-work balance. Due to their perfectionistic tendencies, workaholics might also enjoy keeping a daily record of their work activities so that they can self-monitor their efficiency and their productiveness while working fewer hours. Other ideas for *before* their chosen quit day (i.e., preparation strategies) can be found in Appendix B.

Specific action strategies.

Based on the results of their two studies (Study 1, $N = 465$; Study 2, $N = 780$), Gillet, Morin, Cougot, and Gagne (2017) recommended that counselors help workaholics reduce emotional dissonance, need thwarting, and socially prescribed perfectionism. *Need thwarting* occurs when one's need for competence is thwarted because of feeling either oppressed or despised, which results in diminished self-worth.

Van Wijhe et al. (2014) conducted a two-wave longitudinal (T1 and T2) survey study with a 6-month time interval with 191 participants. The researchers found that having rigid personal beliefs at T1 predicted working compulsively at T2, and working compulsively at T1 predicted exhaustion at T2. Consequently, the study suggests, intervention focused on cognitive restructuring of rigid personal beliefs may be beneficial to either preventing exhaustion and/or for treating workaholism. Rational emotive behavior therapy has been recommended to change the irrational beliefs of workaholics and social skills training to teach support-seeking skills (Shimazu, Kubota, & Bakker, 2015). Porter (2015) suggested that affect regulation and cognitive control are effective methods in treating workaholism. It is important that work-addicted individuals be taught to achieve a balance between work and other activities (Harpaz, 2015). Workaholics need to learn to care for their health and well-being rather than only responding to the needs of others.

Addiction.com (2009) offered a few helpful recommendations to workaholics that counselors can apply in their treatment: (a) uncover the reasons for the overwork, (b) change the way that workaholics relate to subordinates (e.g., stop micromanaging), (c) explore the roots of work addiction that may have begun in childhood, (d) learn to become more effective at work, (e) learn to delegate, (f) establish reconnections with family, (g) disconnect from work by letting go of cell phones and laptops during leisure time, and (h) take vacations.

Mindfulness-based interventions have recently been found helpful in treating workaholism. Van Gordon et al. (2017) allocated male and female workaholics ($N = 73$) to either a meditation awareness training (MAT) group or a waiting-list control group. Compared to the control group, the MAT group demonstrated fewer symptoms of workaholism, greater job satisfaction, and less psychological distress. Van Gordon, Shonin, Zangeneh, and Griffiths (2014) had recommended that organizations wanting to improve the mental health of their employees adopt mindfulness-based interventions. It was suggested that mindfulness training might transfer the locus of control from external work conditions to internal processes.

Research has found the most important factor that fosters work engagement is supervisor support (Caesens, Stinglhamber, & Luypaert, 2014). Caesens et al. (2014) recommended that organizations train their supervisors to be supportive of employees and to have regular meetings with them. Regarding workaholism, the study by Caesens et al. found that having support from coworkers was negatively related to workaholism. Supervisors were also encouraged to promote coworker support so that employees would build a robust social network.

Managerial staff should prevent workaholic employees from working when they feel sick (Mazzetti, Vignoli, Schaufeli, & Guglielmi, 2017). Organizations would also be well advised to discourage developing a culture focused on HWI due to its relationship with both workaholism and burnout (Moyer, Aziz, & Wuensch, 2017). Other ideas for *beginning* their chosen quit day (i.e., action strategies) can be found in Appendix B.

Specific maintenance strategies and relapse prevention.

Note: Maintenance strategies and relapse prevention are also, for many, partly facilitated by regular attendance at relevant mutual support groups. A list of such mutual support groups and helpful websites is found in an upcoming section entitled Relevant Mutual Support Groups, Websites, and Videos.

Porter (2015) stated that there are two aspects of self-efficacy that are important in relapse prevention: (a) which tasks addicted individuals feel confident to attempt and (b) how long they will continue at each task. Porter mentioned that high relapse rates are common but that having a strong sense of self-efficacy reduces the likelihood.

Just as substance-addicted individuals who become abstinent may become workaholics, the opposite is also true. Workaholics, like other addicted individuals, need to become resilient. As one website states, "Life is not a sprint, it is a marathon" (from https://www.relapseprevention.co.za/dealing-with-workaholism/). The same website suggested that the key to resilience is to work at something really hard, but then stop and recover before trying again. Resilience is about recharging, not enduring. Other ideas for relapse prevention can be found in Appendix C.

Motivational Interviewing

Here is an example of how MI could be used to engage a referred work-addicted individual. (Pertaining to Chapter 6's description of MI, the following is an example of the process called *engaging*.)

Client: I do not know why my boss told me that I have to see you. This is crazy. I have so much work to do, and this is a waste of my time.

Counselor: It certainly doesn't seem like you needed to come here from your point of view.

Client: Hey, I'm sorry. I don't mean to sound like a jerk. But really, I am in the middle of a major project, and I don't feel I have time for this.

Counselor: I understand, Ted. It's hard to get away when you feel so pressured to get something accomplished.

Client: Yes, it does sound like you understand. I don't know why my boss sent me to you.

Counselor: Would it help you if I gave you the reason that he told me that he wanted me to see you?

Client: Well, I guess so. I think I know what you're going to say.

Counselor: I believe it's always helpful for clients if they'd first tell me the reason they think they have been referred. Would that be okay with you?

Client: I guess so. I believe my boss thinks that I work too much.

Counselor: I wonder why he might think that?

Client: I work at least 60 hours a week for starters. My job is just about the only thing I think about. It is also driving me crazy, by the way. The boss has these incredibly high expectations, and yet he dares to tell me that I work too hard! That sounds like a definition of insanity to me.

Counselor: That does sound like a double-edged sword.

Client: It is. He keeps assigning more and more projects to me even though I do not have time for the ones currently on my plate.

Counselor: It sounds overwhelming. Just hearing you speak makes me tired.

Client: [chuckles] I can imagine. This job really is too much for me, but I do not know what to do about it.

Counselor: Perhaps you would let me be of assistance to you in this regard. Would that be okay?

Client: Absolutely. Thank you for listening to me complain. Even my wife is fed up with me.

Insight-Oriented Interventions

Molino et al. (2016) found that workaholism was related to working in a suboptimal work environment in their sample of 617 Italian workers. Consequently, one insight for both counselors and clients is that the work environment is sometimes a causative factor. Negative emotions play an important role in sustaining work addiction, and helping clients develop insight regarding this may prove helpful (van Wijhe, Peeters, Schaufeli, & Ouweneel, 2013).

Rohrlich (1981) described the dynamics of work addiction. Rohrlich wrote that the work-addicted individual is a creature of the aggressive instinct. The addicted individual controls the environment and manipulates through ulterior motives, always moving toward a goal. Based on his therapeutic work, Rohrlich outlined categories of addicted individuals based on their particular dynamics. Note that *none* of these subtypes has subsequently been empirically validated in research. Nonetheless, the subtypes have some heuristic value in revealing that different reasons may motivate work addicts. His classification scheme was as follows:

1. Angry, hostile work addicts. Instead of expressing hostility in their relationships, they displace this by compulsively "attacking" and "wrestling with" their projects at work.
2. Ashamed work addicts. These individuals have very low self-esteem, and they feel recognized and approved by the corporation. They seek love through their work.
3. Competitive work addicts. These individuals use work to gain power and "win the game." They seek respect through their work.
4. Defensive work addicts. Rohrlich believed that these addicts' compulsion was usually situational and time-limited. Defensive work-addicted individuals try to protect themselves from feeling emotional stress. Work, consequently, acts as a defense away from their present experience.
5. Friendless, lonely work addicts. Their motive is to be accepted by their colleagues. Their work environment gives them the illusion of friendships and family despite contact with colleagues rarely occurring outside of work.
6. Guilt-written work addicts. The more these individuals work, the more their needs to be punished are met.
7. Latent homosexual work addicts. Rohrlich believed that these were men with unconscious homosexual desires to be penetrated and dominated.
8. Sexually impotent or frustrated work addicts. This referred to sexually impotent men who enjoyed fantasies of conquest from being flirtatious at work. Sexually frustrated women, on the other hand, enjoy secret "affairs" with men through their flirtations at work.
9. Narcissistic work addicts. These individuals had early life experiences that created deep personal insecurities. They work compulsively to undo their sense of inadequacy.
10. Obsessive work addicts. These people are obsessed with neatness, orderliness, and structure. This obsession is satisfied through their complete immersion in work.
11. Passive-dependent work addicts. These individuals' needs are taken care of by the structure of their work. They take orders from their boss and from their tasks.
12. Pre-or postpsychotic work addicts. Rohrlich described here the boundaries and structure that work provides for people with schizophrenia. Without entrenchment in work, they develop symptoms of depersonalization and derealization.
13. Pseudo- or escapist work addicts. These individuals use work to escape from intolerable personal situations.

Spiritual Interventions

Fry and Cohen (2009) wrote about spiritual leadership in organizations. They suggested that organizations should recognize that excessive work demands encourage workaholism and they would do well to adopt a higher set of ethical principles and values. Fry and Cohen referred to these as comparable to altruistic love in spiritual leadership theory. How to accomplish this remains speculative, however. The authors encouraged more research in this area; however, they did suggest offering internal groups or prayer space, on-site chaplains, and surveying employees periodically to facilitate openness to spirituality and religion.

Lipsenthal (2003) focused on the need for physicians to create greater balance in their lives through a combination of physical well-being, emotional health, learning, personal growth, and spiritual growth. Lipsenthal recommended that physicians give themselves an hour per week to read and learn. They should also accept that they do not know everything (i.e., become less perfectionistic in their thinking): they can look up information for patients after their appointments and email it to them. Furthermore, they should stop "bitching, moaning, and whining" (p. 248) and instead accept that change is inevitable and not to let it upset them. Become forgiving of making errors and learn from them. Lipsenthal also recommended that physicians attend religious services and encouraged them to balance their lives and receive support from their community. Give love and notice how it leads to receiving more love. "We are not held back by the love we didn't receive in the past, but by the love we're not extending in the present" (Marianne Williamson, as cited in Lipsenthal, 2003, p. 249).

Cognitive-Behavioral Therapy

CBT can be facilitated using the triple column technique. It can be used both by counselors in their work with clients and by clients alone. The full instructions for using the technique are found in Chapter 6. The following are some of the cognitions that can be problematic for clients with this addiction.

There are currently no randomized controlled studies focused on the treatment of workaholism (Andreassen, 2015). Proposed recommendations, however, include CBT and rational emotive behavior therapy.

Bamber (2006) described the use of a schema-focused approach in working with a 28-year-old nurse who was a burned-out workaholic. Schema-focused therapy was developed by Jeffrey Young (1994). Young had initially worked closely with Aaron Beck, the founder of cognitive therapy. *Early maladaptive schemas* (EMSs) are "broad pervasive themes or patterns regarding oneself and one's relationships that are dysfunctional to a significant degree, which are developed during childhood or adolescence and are elaborated throughout one's lifetime" (Bamber, 2004, p. 425).

The schemas are triggered when individuals find themselves in environments similar to their childhood environment. Once triggered, intense negative emotions resurface. Because these schemas are at the core of a person's beliefs, they are difficult to change. Schema-focused therapy (SFT) is broad and integrative, and, like CBT, it is structured, systematic, and specific. It combines interpersonal, affective, experiential, and psychodynamic techniques within a CBT framework. Attachment theory informs the approach. Some examples of schemas include beliefs like "I am unlovable," "I am a failure," and "I am never going to be good enough."

Several schemas are sometimes combined into a "schema mode" to make treatment more manageable. A *schema mode* is an enduring part of self that has not been fully integrated with other parts of the self. Young suggested that most schema modes fit into one of four headings: (a) child modes (e.g., angry child, vulnerable child), (b) maladaptive parent modes (e.g., punitive parent, demanding parent), (c) maladaptive coping modes (e.g., compliant surrender, detached protector, overcompensation modes), and (d) healthy adult modes (e.g., nurturing, validating, affirmative) (Bamber, 2004). Schema mode therapy (SMT) is focused on "re-parenting," whereby the counselor helps the client develop the healthy adult mode. Imagery is one of the primary experiential techniques in SMT. SFT and SMT are not separate approaches, but SMT is viewed as a more advanced component of schema work.

Falco et al. (2017) concluded from their study that interventions designed to prevent (and treat) workaholism should focus on perfectionistic work-related irrational beliefs, particularly those focused on failure and performance demands. These are amenable to CBT.

Automatic Thought or Belief	Questioning It	Healthier Thought or Belief
I must do my work perfectly, or I will face consequences.		I will strive to be competent and realistic regarding work expectations.
I need to be appreciated by my colleagues.		Although appreciation would be nice, I do not need it to succeed in my job.
I am a worthless human being.		I have as much worth as every other human being.
Work is the only thing that gives my life meaning and purpose.		I need to balance my life and find other sources of meaningfulness.
I am flooded with negative emotions when I am not working.		It is time that I get help to become a contented person who mostly experiences positive emotions.

RELEVANT MUTUAL SUPPORT GROUPS, WEBSITES, AND VIDEOS

Mutual Support Groups

For the Addicted Individual

1. Workaholics Anonymous. http://www.workaholics-anonymous.org/

   Quoted from website:

   Workaholics Anonymous is a fellowship of individuals who share their experience, strength, and hope with each other that they may solve their common problems and help others to recover from workaholism.

2. Recoveries Anonymous. http://www.r-a.org/i-work-addiction.htm#.WxfzzPZFy70

   Quoted from website:

   R.A. is a Twelve Step program. We have no dues or fees. We are here for those who want a full recovery from a work addiction—but despite their best efforts, have yet to find a full recovery from a work addiction—and for their family and friends.

For the Partner and/or Family

These groups are intended to help family members refrain from behaviors that may trigger the addict. They also target underlying maladaptive thoughts and behaviors of the co-addict. Lastly, they focus on facilitating spiritual growth.

Work-Anon Fellowship (a program of recovery for friends and family of workaholic). http://work-anon.blogspot.com/

Websites

1. Work Addiction. H
2. How to Break Your Addiction to Work. https://hbr.org/2016/05/how-to-break-your-addiction-to-work
3. Are you a workaholic? https://www.stylist.co.uk/life/are-you-a-workaholic-bergen-work-addiction-scale-tests-symptoms/51217
4. Work Addiction and "Workaholism." https://www.psychologytoday.com/us/blog/in-excess/201802/work-addiction-and-workaholism
5. Workaholism: An overview and current status of the research. https://www.ncbi.nlm.nih.gov/pmc/articles/PMC4117275/

Videos

To view these videos, search their titles on YouTube.

1. *TEDxSydney - Nigel Marsh - Work Life Balance is an Ongoing Battle.*
2. *Stop overworking yourself: Jochen Menges at TEDxCambridgeUniversity.*
3. *Being a Workaholic Is Unhealthy & Unproductive.* David Pakman Show.
4. *The Difference Between Running and Running Free | Diana Wu David | TEDxWanChai.*

RELEVANT PHONE APPS

Generic Addiction Apps

Note: Generic apps are described in Chapter 6.

This list is not exhaustive. New apps are continually being developed. Do an Internet search to find out the latest apps available. Most are for specific addictions, but some, such as these four, are generic.

1. I Am Sober. https://play.google.com/store/apps/details?id=com.thehungrywasp.iamsober
2. Sober Time. https://play.google.com/store/apps/details?id=com.sociosoft.sobertime
3. Pocket Rehab: Get Sober & Addiction Recovery. https://play.google.com/store/apps/details?id=com.getpocketrehab.app
4. Loop Habit Tracker. https://play.google.com/store/apps/details?id=org.isoron.uhabits

Specialized Apps

Note: The following apps are not specialized for work addiction. Instead, they offer ways of reducing stress, setting goals, or keeping track of work hours.

1. Headspace for IPhone: Meditation. https://itunes.apple.com/us/app/headspace-meditation/id493145008?mt=8

   Quoted from website:

   Headspace is the simple way to reframe stress. Sleep trouble? Meditation creates the ideal conditions for a good night's rest. Relax with guided meditations and mindfulness techniques that bring calm, wellness and balance to your life in just a few minutes a day.

2. Headspace for Androids: Meditation & Mindfulness. https://play.google.com/store/apps/details?id=com.getsomeheadspace.android&hl=en

   Quoted from website:

   The Headspace app teaches you how to meditate and live mindfully. You can use it at work, at home or anywhere else. There are exercises on everything from managing anxiety and stress to breathing, sleep, happiness, calm and focus.

3. Strides Habit Tracker. https://itunes.apple.com/us/app/strides-habit-tracker/id672401817?mt=8

   Quoted from website:

   Track all your Goals & Habits in one flexible free app. With Strides you can track anything, because it's more than a habit tracker—it's also a SMART goal tracker with reminders to hold you accountable and charts to keep you motivated, all on iPhone, iPad & Web.

4. HoursTracker. http://www.hourstrackerapp.com/

   Quoted from website:

   Clock in and clock out as you work or enter start and stop times yourself. HoursTracker groups your entries by day, week, or month, so you can easily see how you spend your time week to week or across jobs.

JOURNALS AND CONFERENCES

Journals

There are no journals specifically dedicated to work addiction. However, articles often appear in management and occupational/organizational journals such as the following:

1. *Journal of Managerial Psychology*. Quoted from website:

   The *Journal of Managerial Psychology* (JMP) has a unique focus on the psychological and social understanding and impact of management in organizations. The journal concerns itself with application of theory and practice of managerial psychology. http://www.emeraldgrouppublishing.com/products/journals/journals.htm?id=jmp

2. *Journal of Management*. Quoted from website:

   Journal of Management (JOM) peer-reviewed and published bi-monthly, is committed to publishing scholarly empirical and theoretical research articles that have a high impact on the management field as a whole. JOM covers domains such as business strategy and policy, entrepreneurship, human resource management, organizational behavior, organizational theory, and research methods. http://journals.sagepub.com/home/jom/

3. *Journal of Behavioral and Applied Management*. Quoted from website:

   The *Journal of Behavioral and Applied Management* (JBAM ISSN 1930 0158) is the completely on-line academic publication of the Institute of Behavioral and Applied Management (IBAM) http://www.ibam.com/. IBAM created the Journal to provide an international outlet for its contributors and members in support of its mission. https://jbam.scholasticahq.com/about

Other journals that publish articles about work addiction include *Journal of Occupational and Organizational Psychology, Journal of Occupational and Environmental Medicine, International Journal of Workplace Health Management, Work & Stress, Human Resource Management, European Journal of Work and Organizational Psychology, Scandinavian Journal of Psychology,* and the *Scandinavian Journal of Work, Environment, & Health.*

Conferences

Finding a conference about work addiction will be a "hit and miss" search currently. Some generic addiction conferences will have one or more presentations about work addiction. I suggest checking out the following:

1. International Congress of the International Commission on Occupational Health - Work Organization and Psychosocial Factors (ICOH-WOPS) Scientific Committee. http://www.icohweb.org/site/events.asp
2. Global Conference on Addiction and Behavioral Health. https://addiction-behavioral-conferences.magnusgroup.org/
3. International Conference on Addiction Therapy & Clinical Reports. https://scientificfederation.com/

COUNSELING SCENARIO

As you are reading, imagine that you are the client in this scenario. Note the areas in which the session could be improved on the part of the counselor.

Your name is Audrey, a 49-year-old senior partner in a law firm. You began practicing law at age 24 after "whizzing" your way through law school. Working 80 hours a week paid off as you became a senior partner by the time you were 39 years old. Surprisingly, even to yourself, you have often been working more than 80 hours a week despite having several junior members to whom you could delegate most of this work. You don't think other people can do the work as well as you. On the advice of other senior partners, you decide to book an appointment with a counselor.

- Counselor: Hello, Audrey; please come in. Sit wherever you're comfortable.
- You: Thank you, Darlene [she sits as far away from the window as possible]. I find the sunlight hurts my eyes. I don't get much of it because of the long hours I work.
- Counselor: Hmmm, I see. Please tell me what you would like to talk about today.
- You: I honestly don't want to talk at all because I don't see where there is a problem. I am a senior partner in a law firm, and my two other partners insisted that I meet with you.
- Counselor: They must be really concerned about you then.
- You: I guess so, but I don't agree with them.
- Counselor: So, what led to them wanting you to see me?
- You: They said I appear unhappy, burned out, miserable, and antagonistic. In other words, they want to control my life. They think I should date, but I don't want to, and they think I should work less, and I don't want to. Essentially, they are trying to control me.
- Counselor: How much do you work in an average week?
- You: Maybe 80 to 90 hours.
- Counselor: Perhaps if you only worked 70 hours a week your partners would leave you alone.
- You: That certainly sounds reasonable to me; however, my partners believe that I should not be working more than 40 hours a week at this stage in my career.
- Counselor: Maybe they just don't understand you. Work is important to you, and you have every right to work long hours. Is there any good reason why you should only work 40 hours a week?
- You: My partners think I need to balance my life. I never spend any time outdoors, and my physician is worried about me. I was recently diagnosed with rectal cancer, and the specialist said it likely developed because I never eat properly. I will need surgery in a couple of months, but I intend to bring a lot of work with me while I recover in the hospital.
- Counselor: You certainly are dedicated. I also work 70 hours a week, and as a result, I own a beautiful house overlooking the ocean. I do not know of other counselors who could afford what I have.
- You: I couldn't agree with you more! Hard work pays off, and idleness is a waste of time.
- Counselor: Other people don't understand hard workers like us. If you reduce your working hours to 70 hours a week, you will have an extra 10 hours to take better care of yourself.
- You: That is certainly what I want to hear, but I do not think it will satisfy my partners.
- Counselor: At your stage in your career, does it really matter what they think?
- You: Your words are music to my ears. That is exactly how I feel. Thank you so much for supporting me in all of this. I just wish they would leave me alone.
- Counselor: I'm sure you know how to get them off your back.
- You: I do in fact. Thank you, Darlene! You don't know how much help you have been.
- Counselor: Audrey, I am so glad I could be here for you.

From the Client's Perspective

1. How did Audrey feel at the end of this session? Is her "feeling" a good indication of the counselor's helpfulness?
2. What is missing for you in this dialogue?
3. What would you find more helpful from a counselor in this scenario?

From the Counselor's Perspective

1. When is colluding with a client harmful to counseling practice?
2. Going back to the Common Counseling Mistakes list in Chapter 6, which mistakes is the counselor making with Audrey?
3. What other ways could the counselor have acted that would have still built a positive working alliance?

INDIVIDUAL EXERCISES

1. Prepare a list of questions and interview someone who you believe is a work addict. After conducting the interview, ask yourself whether this individual would fulfill the criteria for work addiction as outlined in this chapter. Is he or she a situational heavy work investor (HWI) or a dispositional HWI? If the person is a dispositional HWI, how do you distinguish a devoted, passionate worker from a workaholic one?
2. It is typical that, when a major project is completed, a person's parasympathetic nervous system is activated as the sympathetic nervous system takes a break. In turn, this temporarily weakens the immune system, often leaving a person more vulnerable to contracting a host of different illnesses, including the common cold. Now think about an occasion that you needed to dedicate a great deal of time and effort on a certain project. Perhaps a major school assignment comes to mind. After your major project was completed, what negative symptoms did you experience? If this heavy work investment had continued for months or years, what permanent symptoms do you think it might have created in you?
3. Wait for a time when you have a lot of work on your plate. Now spend a day acting like a workaholic. Begin working at 8:30 or 9:00 a.m. and work for a minimum of 12 hours, allowing yourself only two short breaks and a 30-minute lunch. Maintain concentrated effort and do not allow yourself much time at all to drift or daydream. After your 12-hour "shift," write down your thoughts and feelings as if it were a journal entry. Be as detailed as possible in writing about your experience of HWI. Share your experience with someone else in the class who has completed the same individual exercise.

CLASSROOM EXERCISES

1. Watch the videos mentioned earlier about work addiction in class followed by a discussion of what students have learned from watching these videos. Which qualities can students relate to concerning work addiction? Which qualities can they not?
2. Certain work qualities have defined each generation. Here is a listing of the most recent generations (note that years are approximate as there are no definitive date ranges):
   a. Interbellum Generation: Born between 1901 and 1913.
   b. Greatest Generation: This included the veterans who fought in World War II. They were born between World War I and the mid-1920s (between 1910 and 1924).
   c. Silent Generation: Born roughly between 1925 and 1945.
   d. Baby Boom Generation: Born just after World War II (between 1946 and 1964). This generation was characteristically considered part of the counterculture of the 1960s.
   e. Generation X: Born after the baby boom ended (from the early to mid-1960s to the late 1970s: 1965–1979).
   f. Generation Y: Also known as the Generation Next or the Millennials. Born between 1980s and the mid-1990s (between 1980 and 1994). Sometimes nicknamed the "Peter Pan" generation for having a reputation of deferring their passage into adulthood (Aziz, Chaney, & Raines, 2015).
   g. Generation Z: Born between 1995 and 2012.
   h. Gen Alpha: Born between 2013 and 2025.

   Assign the class proportionately to each of these eight generations and form the respective eight groups. Each group then works together to research what work qualities defined their assigned generation before presenting these in class. Alternatively, one could host a discussion in class regarding what each group learned. Which group worked the hardest or is expected to? Which group worked the least or is expected to?
3. Invite a lawyer to class to talk about their work expectations and the number of hours he or she works each week. Have the class prepare some questions in advance to also ask the presenter.

CHAPTER SUMMARY

In this chapter, you learned that work is of central importance in the lives of Americans. Some people need to work long hours because it is a long-term expectation of their career (e.g., lawyer, surgeon), a short-term requirement for a specific project, or a dispositional quality within themselves. Dispositional heavy-work investors are either of the devoted type or the workaholic type. Workaholics have an addiction to work, which results from internal, uncontrollable, and stable predictors. To some extent, it also appears that workaholics are sometimes "bred" by experiencing high work demands, pressure from bosses, competition from colleagues, and other undesirable work environment factors.

Oates described workaholism as a compulsive need to work relentlessly. Although employers often saw workaholics as desirable employees, the research is showing that work-addicted individuals experience adverse consequences that also impact their organizations negatively. Workaholics are often perfectionists who have irrational beliefs regarding failure and performance expectations. They usually have type A personalities, they experience negative affect both dispositionally and situationally, and they find it difficult to delegate work responsibilities to others. The long work hours combined with the stress it they create for workaholics bring about numerous negative consequences such as work-life conflict, diminished life satisfaction, burnout, emotional exhaustion, reduced work satisfaction, poor family satisfaction/functioning, and worse physical, emotional, and mental health. The prevalence of workaholism is roughly between 7% and 8%.

Several scales and tests have been developed to measure work addiction. Although treatments for workaholism have not been thoroughly researched, they appear to be effective. Treatments include MI, CBT, and schema-focused therapy.

REFERENCES

Addiction.com. (2009, November 11). *Are you a workaholic?* Retrieved on June 5, 2018, from https://www.addiction.com/3014/workaholic/

American Psychiatric Association (APA). (2013). *Diagnostic and statistical manual of mental disorders* (5th ed.). Washington, DC: Author.

Andreassen, C. S. (2015). Workaholism: The concept and its assessment. In I. Harpaz & R. Snir (Eds.), *Heavy work investment: Its nature, sources, outcomes, and future directions* (pp. 68–97). New York, NY: Routledge.

Andreassen, C. S., Griffiths, M. D., Hetland, J., Kravina, L., Jensen, F., & Pallesen, S. (2014). The prevalence of workaholism: A survey study in a nationally representative sample of Norwegian employees. *PLoS ONE*, *9*(8), 1–10.

Andreassen, C. S., Griffiths, M. D., Hetland, J., & Pallesen, S. (2012). Development of a work addiction scale. *Scandinavian Journal of Psychology*, *53*, 265–272.

Andreassen, C. S., Griffiths, M. D., Sinha, R., Hetland, J., & Pallesen, S. (2016). The relationships between workaholism and symptoms of psychiatric disorders: A large-scale cross-sectional study. *PLoS ONE*, *11*(5), 1–19.

Andreassen, C. S., Nielsen, M. B., Pallesen, S., & Gjerstad, J. (2019). The relationship between psychosocial work variables and workaholism: Findings from a nationally representative survey. *International Journal of Stress Management*, *26*(1), 1–10.

Astakhova, M., & Hogue, M. (2014). A heavy work investment typology: A biopsychosocial framework. *Journal of Managerial Psychology*, *29*(1), 81–99.

Atroszko, P. A., Andreassen, C. S., Griffiths, M. D., & Pallesen, S. (2015). Study addiction—A new area of psychological study: Conceptualization, assessment, and preliminary empirical findings. *Journal of Behavioral Addictions*, *4*(2), 75–84.

Aziz, S., & Burke, R. J. (2015). Personality factors, workaholism, and heavy work investment. In I. Harpaz & R. Snir (Eds.), *Heavy work investment: Its nature, sources, outcomes, and future directions* (pp. 31-46). New York, NY: Routledge.

Aziz, S., Chaney, K., & Raines, J. (2015). Workaholism in a dynamic workforce. In I. Harpaz & R. Snir (Eds.), *Heavy work investment: Its nature, sources, outcomes, and future directions* (pp. 249–266). New York, NY: Routledge.

Aziz, S., & Uhrich, B. (2014). The causes and consequences of workaholism. In R. J. Burke & D. A. Major (Eds.), *Gender in organizations: Are men allies or adversaries to women's career advancement?* (pp. 171–190). Northampton, MA: Edward Elgar.

Aziz, S., Uhrich, B., Wuensch, K. L., & Swords, B. (2013). The Workaholism Analysis Questionnaire: Emphasizing work-life imbalance and addiction in the measurement of workaholism. *Journal of Behavioral and Applied Management*, *14*(2), 71–86.

Aziz, S., Zamary, S., & Wuensch, K. (2018). The endless pursuit for self-validation through attainment: An examination of self-esteem in relation to workaholism. *Personality and Individual Differences*, *121*, 74–79.

Bakker, A. B., Shimazu, A., Demerouti, E., Shimada, K., & Kawakami, N. (2014). Work engagement versus workaholism: A test of the spillover-crossover model. *Journal of Managerial Psychology*, *29*(1), 63–80.

Bamber, M. (2004). "The good, the bad and defenceless Jimmy": A single case study of schema mode therapy. *Clinical Psychology and Psychotherapy*, *11*, 425–438.

Bamber, M. R. (2006). *CBT for occupational stress in health professionals: Introducing a schema focused approach*. New York, NY: Routledge.

Barnett, R. C., Gareis, K. C., & Brennan, R. T. (2009). Reconsidering work time: A multivariate longitudinal within-couple analysis. *Community, Work & Family*, *12*(1), 105–133.

Beiler-May, A., Williamson, R. L., Clark, M. A., & Carter, N. T. (2017). Gender bias in the measurement of workaholism. *Journal of Personality Assessment*, *99*(1), 104–110.

Caesens, G., Stinglhamber, F., & Luypaert, G. (2014). The impact of work engagement and workaholism on well-being: The role of work-related social support. *Career Development International*, *19*(7), 813–835.

Clark, M. A., Beiler, A. A., & Zimmerman, L. M. (2015). Examining the work-family experience of workaholic women. In M. Mills (Ed.), *Gender and the work-family experience: An intersection of two domains* (pp. 313–327). Cham, Switzerland: Springer.

Clark, M. A., Michel, J. S., & Stevens, G. W. (2015). Affective reactions and subsequent consequences of heavy work investments. In I. Harpaz & R. Snir (Eds.), *Heavy work investment: Its nature, sources, outcomes, and future directions* (pp. 187–203). New York, NY: Routledge.

Clark, M. A., Michel, J. S., Zhdanova, L., Pui, S. Y., & Baltes, B. B. (2016). All work and no play? A meta-analytic examination of the correlates and outcomes of workaholism. *Journal of Management*, *42*(7), 1836–1873.

Connors, G. J., DiClemente, C. C., Velasquez, M. M., & Donovan, D. M. (2013). *Substance abuse treatment and the stages of change: Selecting and planning interventions* (2nd ed.). New York, NY: Guilford Press.

Falco, A., Dal Corso, L., Girardi, D., De Carlo, A., Barbieri, B., Boatto, T., . . . Schaufeli, W. B. (2017). Why is perfectionism a risk factor for workaholism? The mediating role of irrational beliefs at work. *TPM-Testing, Psychometrics, Methodology in Applied Psychology, 24*(4), 583–600.

Fry, L., & Cohen, M. P. (2009). Spiritual leadership as a paradigm for organizational transformation and recovery from extended work hours cultures. *Journal of Business Ethics, 84*(2), 265–278.

Gillet, N., Morin, A. J. S., Cougot, B., & Gagne, M. (2017). Workaholism profiles: Associations with determinants, correlates, and outcomes. *Journal of Occupational and Organizational Psychology, 90*, 559–586.

Golden, L. (2015). Distinctions between overemployment, overwork, workaholism, and heavy investments in work time. In I. Harpaz & R. Snir (Eds.), *Heavy work investment: Its nature, sources, outcomes, and future directions* (pp. 140–170). New York, NY: Routledge.

Grebot, E., Olivier, M., Berjot, S., Girault-Lidvan, N., & Duprez, M. (2017). Personality and workaholism. *Annales Medico-Psychologiques, 175*, 528–535.

Griffiths, M. (2014, July 18). *Is 'workaholism' really a genuine addiction?* Retrieved on May 30, 2018, from https://www.rehabs.com/pro-talk-articles/is-workaholism-really-a-genuine-addiction/

Griffiths, M. D. (2005). A 'components' model of addiction within a biopsychosocial framework. *Journal of Substance Use, 10*, 191–197.

Griffiths, M. D. (2016, December 1). *Workaholism and psychiatric disorders: Is there a relationship between work addiction and OCD, ADHD and depression?* Retrieved on June 3, 2018, from https://www.psychologytoday.com/us/blog/in-excess/201612/workaholism-and-psychiatric-disorders

Harpaz, I. (2015). Epilogue: The current state of heavy work investment and future developments. In I. Harpaz & R. Snir (Eds.), *Heavy work investment: Its nature, sources, outcomes, and future directions* (pp. 361–373). New York, NY: Routledge.

Houlfort, N., Vallerand, R. J., & Laframboise, A. (2015). Heavy work investment: The role of passion. In I. Harpaz & R. Snir (Eds.), *Heavy work investment: Its nature, sources, outcomes, and future directions* (pp. 47–67). New York, NY: Routledge.

Kabat-Zinn, J. (2013). *Full catastrophe living: Using the wisdom of your body and mind to face stress, pain, and illness* (rev. ed.). New York, NY: Bantam.

Keller, A. C., Spurk, D., Baumeler, F., & Hirschi, A. (2016). Competitive climate and workaholism: Negative sides of future orientation and calling. *Personality and Individual Differences, 96*, 122–126.

Killinger, B. (2011, December 15). *Understanding the dynamics of workaholism: "Are you a workaholic?"* Retrieved on June 4, 2018, from https://www.psychologytoday.com/us/blog/the-workaholics/201112/understanding-the-dynamics-workaholism

Levy, D. V. (2015). Workaholism and marital satisfaction among female professionals. *Family Journal, 23*(4), 330–335.

Lewandowska-Walter, A., & Wojdylo, K. (2011). Ex post perception of parental attitudes of people with a tendency to workaholism. [Polish]. Spostrzeganie ex post postaw rodzicow przez osoby z tendencj do uzaleziania sie od pracy. *Studia Psychologiczne, 49*(2), 35–52.

Lipsenthal, L. (2003). Find balance, let go of blame. *Complementary Health Practice Review, 8*(3), 246–250.

Mazzetti, G., Schaufeli, W. B., & Guglielmi, D. (2018). Are workaholism and work engagement in the eye of the beholder? A multirater perspective on different forms of working hard. *European Journal of Psychological Assessment, 34*, 30–40.

Mazzetti, G., Vignoli, M., Schaufeli, W. B., & Guglielmi, D. (2017). Work addiction and presenteeism: The buffering role of managerial support. *International Journal of Psychology*. No pagination specified.

McMillan, L. H. W., Brady, E. C., O'Driscoll, M. P., & Marsh, N. V. (2002). A multifaceted validation study of Spence and Robbins' (1992) workaholism battery. *Journal of Occupational and Organizational Psychology, 75*, 357–368.

Midje, H. H., Nafstad, I. T., Syse, J., & Torp, S. (2014). Workaholism and mental health problems among municipal middle managers in Norway. *Journal of Occupational and Environmental Medicine, 56*(10), 1042–1051.

Molino, M., Bakker, A. B., & Ghislieri, C. (2016). The role of workaholism in the job demands-resources model. *Anxiety, Stress & Coping: An International Journal, 29*(4), 400–414.

Moyer, F., Aziz, S., & Wuensch, K. (2017). From workaholism to burnout: Psychological capital as a mediator. *International Journal of Workplace Health Management, 10*, 213–227.

Porter, G. (2015). Is work addiction a proper label for high work investment habits? In I. Harpaz & R. Snir (Eds.), *Heavy work investment: Its nature, sources, outcomes, and future directions* (pp. 303–321). New York, NY: Routledge.

Prochaska, J. O., Norcross, J. C., & DiClemente, C. C. (1994). *Changing for good*. New York, NY: Avon Books.

Quinones, C., & Griffiths, M. D. (2015). Addiction to work: A critical review of the workaholism construct and recommendations for assessment. *Journal of Psychosocial Nursing and Mental Health Services, 53*(10), 48–59.

Quinones, C., Griffiths, M. D., & Kakabadse, N. K. (2016). Compulsive Internet use and workaholism: An exploratory two-wave longitudinal study. *Computers in Human Behavior, 60*, 492–499.

Robinson, B. E. (1989). *Work addiction*. Deerfield Beach, FL: Health Communications.

Robinson, B. E. (1998). The workaholic family: A clinical perspective. *American Journal of Family Therapy, 26*, 65–75.

Rohrlich, J. B. (1981). The dynamics of work addiction. *Israel Journal of Psychiatry and Related Sciences, 18*(2), 147–156.

Salanova, M., Lopez-Gonzalez, A. A., Llorens, S., del Libano, M., Vicente-Herrero, M. T., & Tomas-Salva, M. (2016). Your work may be killing you! Workaholism, sleep problems and cardiovascular risk. *Work & Stress, 30*(3), 228–242.

Schaufeli, W. B., Shimazu, A., & Taris, T. W. (2009). Being driven to work excessively hard, the evaluation of a two-factor measure of workaholism in the Netherlands and Japan. *Cross-Cultural Research, 43*, 320–348.

Shamai, O. (2015). The relationship between heavy work investment and employees' happiness. In I. Harpaz & R. Snir (Eds.), *Heavy work investment: Its nature, sources, outcomes, and future directions* (pp. 204–222). New York, NY: Routledge.

Shimazu, A., Kubota, K., & Bakker, A. B. (2015). How workaholism affects employees and their families. In I. Harpaz & R. Snir (Eds.), *Heavy work investment: Its nature, sources, outcomes, and future directions* (pp. 171–186). New York, NY: Routledge.

Shimazu, A., Schaufeli, W. B., Kamiyama, K., & Kawakami, N. (2015). Workaholism vs. work engagement: The two different predictors of future well-being and performance. *International Journal of Behavioral Medicine, 22*(1), 18–23.

Snir, R. (2015a). Bring your parents to the job interview: Intergenerational similarity in (heavy) work investment. In I. Harpaz & R. Snir (Eds.), *Heavy work investment: Its nature, sources, outcomes, and future directions* (pp. 342–360). New York, NY: Routledge.

Snir, R. (2015b). Introduction—Workaholism, HWI subtypes, and beyond: Towards a general model of work investment. In I. Harpaz & R. Snir (Eds.), *Heavy work investment: Its nature, sources, outcomes, and future directions* (pp. xxvii–xxxviii). New York, NY: Routledge.

Snir, R., & Harpaz, I. (2015). A general model of heavy work investment: Introduction. In I. Harpaz & R. Snir (Eds.), *Heavy work investment: Its nature, sources, outcomes, and future directions* (pp. 3–30). New York, NY: Routledge.

Spence, J. T., & Robbins, A. S. (1992). Workaholics: Definition, measurement, and preliminary results. *Journal of Personality Assessment, 58*, 160–178.

Stier, H., & Sella-Dotan, A. (2015). Work-family balance in the era of intensive work. In I. Harpaz & R. Snir (Eds.), *Heavy work investment: Its nature, sources, outcomes, and future directions* (pp. 225–248). New York, NY: Routledge.

Sussman, S. (2012). Workaholism: A review. *Journal of Addictive Research & Therapy, Suppl. 6*(1), 4120. Retrieved on May 29, 2018, from https://www.ncbi.nlm.nih.gov/pmc/articles/PMC3835604/

Taris, T., Van Beek, I., & Schaufeli, W. (2015). The beauty versus the beast: On the motives of engaged and workaholic employees. In I. Harpaz & R. Snir (Eds.), *Heavy work investment: Its nature, sources, outcomes, and future directions* (pp. 121–139). New York, NY: Routledge.

Van Beek, I., Taris, T. W., Schaufeli, W. B., & Brenninkmeijer, V. (2014). Heavy work investment: Its motivational make-up and outcomes. *Journal of Managerial Psychology, 29*(1), 46–62.

Van Gordon, W., Shonin, E., Dunn, T. J., Garcia-Campayo, J., Demarzo, M. M. P., & Griffiths, M. D. (2017). Meditation awareness training for the treatment of workaholism: A controlled trial. *Journal of Behavioral Addictions, 6*, 212–220.

Van Gordon, W., Shonin, E., Zangeneh, M., & Griffiths, M. D. (2014). Work-related mental health and job performance: Can mindfulness help? *International Journal of Mental Health and Addiction, 12*(2), 129–137.

Van Wijhe, C. I., Peeters, M. C., & Schaufeli, W. B. (2014). Enough is enough: Cognitive antecedents of workaholism and its aftermath. *Human Resource Management, 53*(1), 157–177.

Van Wijhe, C., Peeters, M., Schaufeli, W., & Ouweneel, E. (2013). Rise and shine: Recovery experiences of workaholic and nonworkaholic employees. *European Journal of Work and Organizational Psychology, 22*(4), 476–489.

Wagstaff, A. S., & Sigstad Lie, J.-A. (2011). Shift and night work and long working hours: A systematic review of safety implications. *Scandinavian Journal of Work, Environment, & Health, 37*, 173–185.

Young, J. E. (1994). *Cognitive therapy for personality disorders: A schema-focused approach* (Rev. ed.). Sarasota, FL: Professional Resource Press/Professional Resource Exchange.

PART V

Summary and Conclusions

22 Summary and Conclusions

iStock.com/yan

Learning Objectives

1. Be able to summarize the main learnings from this textbook.
2. Recall the seriousness of substance abuse disorders and the opioid crisis and understand the pros and cons regarding the decriminalization of illegal drugs.
3. Learn a metaphor for addictions and its definition.
4. Be able to summarize risk factors and protective factors.
5. Become familiar (or refamiliar) with what counselors bring to the table.

Beautiful

The first snow
Fell softly
One flake at a time
So quietly
Even the leaves
Stopped whispering.
By daybreak
The postcard was painted.
I want to utter every word
Think every thought
As gently as the brush
That stroked this winter canvas.
I want the landscape
Of my life
To be quiet
And beautiful.

—Ronna Jeyne
December 3, 2018

(Used with permission)

PERSONAL REFLECTIONS

Paraphrasing Lao Tzu, writing this textbook has been the journey of a thousand miles. The serious writing of it began 18 months ago, and, since then, I have worked on it most days for 6 hours or more. I am not complaining, however. This is my *magnum opus*, which is a term I learned from my 21-year-old friend. It means "the greatest achievement of an artist or writer" (Merriam-Webster, 2019b). I sincerely hope that it has been worth the effort, but only you, the reader, can be its final judge.

The American Psychiatric Association now views autistic and addictive disorders as residing on a continuum, which are referred to as spectrum disorders (Shea, 2018). No two addictions are exactly alike. But neither are individuals in any other respect. The most remarkable present-day examples of this are found in DNA analysis or, if at the airport, fingerprint and retina scanning. Besides biological and genetic differences, no two people have grown up in precisely the same environment or had the same experiences. If it is true that everyone can become addicted, it will surely look different if it is you compared to me.

Although it makes eminently good sense to prevent addictions and mental disorders, the task is far more complicated than it might appear. First, you need to understand all the possible causes, but it is experimentally impossible to isolate every probable factor and test this longitudinally without other possible causes being present (McNeece & Madsen, 2012). Similarly, given that the origins of addiction are different for every individual, how do you create a prevention program that can impact all the combinations and permutations of what sustains the addiction in every person? Also, what duration of "prevention" will be needed to maximize the effect, and for how long will you need to use "outcome measures" to demonstrate that the prevention program has produced sustainable results?

The ultimate prevention effort is one that keeps individuals from even engaging in unlawful psychoactive substance use (UPSU) indefinitely. Given that addictions are generally worse and of longer duration the earlier they begin in a person's life, prevention that slows down the initiation of UPSU is also of great benefit. Addictive behaviors are different. Some behaviors cannot be avoided (e.g., food, exercise) or should likely not be avoided once they become developmentally appropriate (e.g., Internet use, sex, love, shopping, work). It is only when these potentially addictive behaviors cross a certain threshold that they become problematic. The reasons that this occurs for a small percentage of individuals have to do with risk factors (summarized shortly), and prevention efforts need to focus on reducing this risk.

Illegal drug use is on the rise globally. Approximately 275 million people (ages 15–64) worldwide used drugs one or more times in 2016 (United Nations, 2018). The war on drugs in the United States is not working, and, in addition to alcohol and substance addiction, many Americans are battling behavioral addictions. In Chapter 1, some estimated that, when behavioral addictions are included, about 47% of American adults are affected by addiction in any given year (Carnes, 1991; Sussman, Lisha, & Griffiths, 2011). "In 2015 and 2016, for the first time in half a century, life expectancy in the United States of America declined for two consecutive years. A key factor was the increase in unintentional injuries, which include overdose deaths" (United Nations, 2018, p. 23). Although car crashes used to be the number-one cause of accidental deaths in the United States, drug overdoses have now assumed first place (Katz, 2017). Fentanyl deaths alone increased by 540% between 2013 and 2016 (Katz, 2017). Just between 2000 and 2015, more than 500,000 Americans died from drug overdoses (Lee, 2018).

Over 50% of the opioids prescribed in the United States are to individuals with underlying mental disorders (Lee, 2018). Treatment of these mental disorders is needed if these individuals are to have at least a reasonable chance of recovery (Lee, 2018).

Is it time to recommend that substance-addicted individuals switch to safer drugs? Earleywine (2016) stressed that this practice is especially controversial, despite our knowledge that some drugs are substantially safer than others (cp barbiturates and benzodiazepines). If safer drugs will not work, what about providing the drug in specialized medical clinics that are safe and clean? Csiernik (2016) described heroin-assisted treatment, where heroin-addicted individuals receive their fix knowing that it does not contain fentanyl. Maté (2008), a well-known physician who treated hardcore drug-addicted individuals in Vancouver, Canada, espoused the view that "a rational stance toward drug addiction would be the decriminalization of all substance dependence" (p. 302). As he suggested, drugs are not themselves the cause of addiction. Remember that veterans serving in Vietnam had high rates of heroin use (34%) and heroin dependence (20%), yet only 1% became re-addicted in the first year after their return to the United States (Hall & Weier, 2017).

Decriminalization remains highly controversial in most parts of the world, and with good reason. Portugal decriminalized personal use of all illicit drugs in July 2001 (Hughes & Stevens, 2012). Selling of these drugs, however, remained as criminal offenses (Hughes & Stevens, 2012). Has decriminalization been "a resounding success or a disastrous failure" (Hughes & Stevens, 2012, the title of their article)? Although Hughes and Stevens (2010) argued that decriminalization did not lead to ***major*** increases in drug use, and Goncalves, Lourenco, and Silva (2015) stated that the social cost of drugs went down 12% in the first 5 years following decriminalization and 18% in the first 11 years, these findings have been deeply criticized by Coelho (2015).

As Coelho (2015) explained, although drug-induced deaths decreased from 369 in 1999 to 152 in 2003, they rose to 314 in 2007. Between 2001 and 2007, drug consumption in Portugal increased by a total of 4.2% in absolute terms (Coelho, 2015). Drug use increases over that 6-year period were noted in cannabis use (12.4%–17%; ages 15–34), cocaine (1.3%–2.8%; ages 15–34), ecstasy (1.4%–2.6%; ages 15–34), and heroin (0.7%–1.1%; ages 15–64) (Coelho, 2015). Furthermore, the number of drug-related homicides has increased by over 40% since drugs were decriminalized, and rates of HIV and AIDS did not decrease (Coelho, 2015).

Decriminalization allows for medically supervised dispensing when it is needed (Maté, 2008). Although we can hope and pray that medication-assisted treatment (MAT) will solve the opioid crisis, most individuals prescribed MAT do not continue taking it and end up resuming their injection opioid use (Lee, 2018). Perhaps if only "medical use" of these drugs (meaning that only appropriately trained physicians prescribe them) were decriminalized on a limited and experimental basis, it could be subjected to randomized treatment trials (including some additional tests required for FDA approval) and sociopsychological studies measuring the impact of proposed medical decriminalization on non-illicit-drug-using members of society. Recall from Chapter 10 that the FDA never approved cannabis for medical use because it was never subjected to the agency's 12 stages of drug testing (Miller & Oberbarnschiedt, 2017). Without randomized treatment trials, medical, psychological, and addiction counseling professionals might remain poorly informed, ill-informed, or uninformed regarding best practice.

Why do some people, but not most people, become addicted to substances and/or excessive behaviors? Before looking at risk factors, a metaphor might shed some light.

A Metaphor for Addictions

iStock.com/Aleksandr Kondratov

Imagine what the photo would look like if the traffic circle (also called a roundabout) were congested with vehicles but it was never cleared of snow during the winter months. Sometimes using a roundabout is the quickest way to get home, but, if you don't know that the one you intend to use is never cleared of snow, you might be headed for an ordeal.

Those of you who have spent your lives in the South may have trouble imagining what this is like, which itself is a fitting metaphor for individuals who do not understand addictions. Although it can be explained to you, it might still be difficult to fully comprehend unless you have been there yourself. A similar analogy might be trying to describe what riding a roller coaster is like instead of getting on it and experiencing it for yourself. I have been on roundabouts many times, winter included, and I'm going to do my best to help you understand it.

The Metaphor

First, here are the factors at play in navigating a roundabout and what they metaphorically represent:

1. Risk Factor 1 (RF-1). **Not understanding addiction.** Represented by not knowing the rules of a roundabout (e.g., yield to all vehicles already in the roundabout, be in the correct lane to exit, do not drive beside an oversize vehicle, drive slowly).
2. Risk Factor 2 (RF-2). **Denial.** Represented by continuing to believe that it is fun continuing to drive in the rut.
3. Risk Factor 3 (RF-3). **Experiencing consequences.** Represented by driving dangerously and its sequelae. If you keep driving in circles, your vehicle and tires begin showing signs of wear and tear.
4. Risk Factor 4 (RF-4). **Duration and intensity of your addiction.** Represented by the length of time you have been driving in the rut.
5. Risk Factor 5 (RF-5). **Psychological/physical vulnerability to addiction.** Represented by vehicles that sit low and/or do not have four-wheel drive.
6. Risk Factor 6 (RF-6). **Relapse.** Represented by returning to the uncleared roundabout.
7. Protective Factor 1 (PF-1). **Personal skills and resources.** Represented by your driving ability.
8. Protective Factor 2 (PF-2). **Low vulnerability to addiction.** Represented by driving a truck with four-wheel drive.
9. Protective Factor 3 (PF-3). **Your support network.** Represented by receiving road assistance from others.
10. Recovery Factor 1 (RCF-1). **Wanting help**. Represented by wanting but struggling to get out of the rut and, once out, getting your vehicle to the correct exit lane safely.
11. Recovery Factor 2 (RCF-2). **Getting help.** Represented by getting your vehicle in for repairs.
12. Recovery Factor 3 (RCF-3). **Best practice versus getting help with less demonstrated effectiveness.** Represented by the different exits leaving the roundabout, but only one provides the most direct route home. Nonetheless, any of the exits will eventually lead you home if you steer yourself in the right direction.

When a busy traffic circle is never cleaned of snow, ridges form (these create ruts) as vehicles continue driving over the same tread marks left by other vehicles. It can be difficult to drive out of the ridges or ruts, but this depends on the type of vehicle you are driving. This is an excellent place to begin the metaphor.

The first time you drive into a roundabout can feel intimidating. First thing you'll notice is that the traffic is heading counterclockwise. Especially when entering one that has four lanes, who has the right of way? Traffic already in the traffic circle has the right of way. When there is more than one lane, do not enter the roundabout until all lanes are clear. The important thing is always to drive slowly (20 mph or less is recommended).

Individuals heading into addiction usually don't know how to navigate the roundabout (i.e., RF-1). Once they enter, they become stuck driving in the innermost circle, and they become afraid of leaving it. They don't know how to get out either, so they keep driving round and round (still RF-1). For a while, and perhaps for a long while, they convince themselves that they enjoy the sensations that come from driving in a circle (RF-2).

They begin driving at different speeds. When they are driving fast, they don't realize how much their driving has become dangerous to themselves and others (RF-3). Amazingly, some can drive fast for a long time before serious consequences occur, but, eventually, the results strike with an alarming vengeance. If they drive too long, their vehicle develops mechanical problems, or the tread wears out on the tires, making driving even more treacherous (RF-3). Even at this stage, the sooner they get out (RCF-1), the sooner they can take their vehicle in for repairs (RCF-2).

At any point, they might decide they are ready to leave the roundabout (RCF-1). This is where they might encounter more problems than they anticipated. If they knew how to drive in the roundabout, they would know what to do (PF-1), but, if they don't know, they might be surprised to find out how stuck they are because the longer you drive in a rut, the deeper it gets (RF-4).

An important factor here depends on the vehicle they are driving. If they are driving a truck, particularly one with four-wheel drive, they can engage all wheels and drive safely out of the rut (PF-2). Some vehicles, however, sit low to the ground, and they are incapable of driving out of the rut. Different vehicles are not sitting as low, but they cannot get out because they only have rear- or front-wheel drive (RF-5). However, if they call for a tow truck or are pulled by a good Samaritan with a four-wheel-drive truck, they can get out of the rut and leave the traffic circle (PF-3). Regardless of which way they get out of the roundabout, they still need to know which exit to take that will get them home the quickest (RCF-3). Although they can still get home if they take the wrong exit, it will take longer.

Some people, however, keep using the same rutted roundabout, each time expecting a different outcome. But, unless you change your low-riding vehicle without four-wheel drive to a truck that has it, the result will be the same (RF-6).

Even if you are driving a truck with four-wheel drive, you still must watch that you do not hit other vehicles when you leave the innermost circle. Furthermore, you cannot directly exit the roundabout from the innermost circle. Instead, you must change lanes and get out to the third or fourth circle to exit (RCF-1). If you try to leave too quickly without looking, you may well end up in a collision (RF-3). So, the best way to get out of a four-lane roundabout is to (a) know the rules, (b) have a truck with four-wheel drive, (c) drive out of the rut or get a tow, (d) know the best exit to get home, and (e) exit the roundabout using the correct lane(s).

What Is Addiction in This Metaphor?

Addiction is being in a rut while finding yourself driving in circles. Why does anyone ever leave the rut? It seems likely that, when the protective factors (the "catalysts") exceed the risk factors (the "hindrances"), there might develop enough momentum to try recovery. Knowing that relapse is the norm, it is likely that addicted persons will enter the roundabout several times in their lifetime before they get out once and for all (if they are fortunate).

Risk Factors

We do know that a lot of factors are correlated (or associated) with addiction. Although we cannot ascertain causation from correlational studies, these factors provide us with substantial evidence regarding etiology. The factor that repeatedly appears in the literature concerns the considerable role that parents and/or guardians have in the child and adolescent development of addicted individuals. The textbook highlighted many of these studies and summations of this research (e.g., MacKillop & Ray, 2018; Maté, 2008; Milkman & Sunderwirth, 2010). Overall, addictions most commonly flourish when children and adolescents are exposed to abuse (i.e., physical, mental, emotional, sexual, verbal, spiritual), neglect, and/or trauma. Mistreated children develop increased vulnerability to a host of physical and mental disorders, including addiction (Delima & Vimpani, 2011; McCrory & Viding, 2015). MacKillop and Ray (2018) wrote that the critical period for the development of an addiction is from adolescence to young adulthood (ages 13–25). As Chapter 3 highlighted, every theory of addiction offers a partial explanation for why addiction afflicts particular people, and their explanations range from the purely psychological to the purely genetic and biological.

Why would anyone continue re-engaging in behaviors that hurt self and/or others? Someone always pays the price in addiction (Maté, 2008). Addicted individuals are thought to re-engage in their repetitive and destructive behavior because (a) they anticipate deriving a positive effect from their addictive behavior, (b) the addictive behavior produces an initial rush of pleasure, and (c) there is ongoing pressure to be part of a group that engages themselves in the addictive behavior (Witkiewitz & Marlatt, 2007).

Addicted individuals experience a lot of irrational fears, and they constantly worry (Maté, 2008). Pyszczynski (2004) stated that most people experience fear and anxiety as intolerable, and, given this, they will do almost anything to avoid these emotions. Pyszczynski went further as he introduced terror management theory. When people are afraid, their cultural worldviews and self-esteem rely heavily on consensual validation from others, which in turn serves to lower their existential anxiety. When addicted individuals decide to become clean, they come face-to-face with this anxiety as their reference group, their "friends," are often other addicts.

Maté (2008) brought attention to the emptiness that addicted individuals typically feel, which he believed is at the core of addictive behavior. It is a void that nothing or anyone adequately fills. Escaping into addictive behavior can provide temporary relief from this pain. Maté also suggested that addicted individuals are unable to maintain emotional boundaries between themselves and others and consequently absorb the emotional states that others are experiencing.

Although Maté (2008) argued that all addictions emanate from psychological pain, this appears to be an overstated idea given that there are many roads to addiction. Some individuals in persistent physical pain become addicted to opioids. Matteliano, St. Marie, Oliver, and Coggins (2014) explained that living with persistent pain often creates feelings of "depression, fear, loss, and anxiety, leading to feelings of hopelessness, helplessness, and spiritual crisis" (p. 391). Together, these become risk factors for addiction.

Polyaddictions and comorbidity with other mental disorders are so common in addicted individuals that they are now the norm, not the exception (Miller, 2016). These problems are not always secondary to addiction either (Miller, 2016). Polyaddiction and comorbidity constitute significant risk factors. Both make quitting and remaining clean of addictive behaviors more difficult. Today, the consensus is that both should be treated simultaneously and not consecutively, as generally thought in the past (Miller, 2016).

In their study of homeless men, Sumerlin and Norman (1992) found that, if men lived on the street for 4 years or longer, they were likely to adopt a positive identity as a homeless person and to have become complacent about their living situation. Similarly, the longer one is involved in an addiction, the higher the likelihood that maladaptive patterns have become entrenched as a way of life and a major source of self-identification (May, 1988; Wright & Allen, 2008). When addicted individuals try to stop their addictive behavior, the "negative and destructive customs that had come to be a part of everyday living" (Wright & Allen, 2008, p. 231) need to be replaced by healthier customs. In other words, most addicted individuals will need to create an entirely different lifestyle compared with whichever they are accustomed.

It is important to remember that, as counselors, we are often asking clients to make wide-reaching changes. Ask yourself the question: How difficult would it be for you to change your entire lifestyle? To what extent would you be satisfied or dissatisfied if most of your ways of living had to change? Making such changes can feel like a colossal expectation to addicted individuals.

Protective Factors

One of the most crucial protective factors is having intimacy and feeling a sense of belonging (Maté, 2008; Milkman & Sunderwirth, 2010). Johann Hari makes this his central point in his YouTube video, watched by nearly 6 million viewers, called *Everything You Think You Know About Addiction is Wrong* (see https://www.youtube.com/watch?v=PY9DcIMGxMs). Humans need to feel nurtured, trusted, and supported, and connectedness with others creates the "foundation for health and well-being" (Milkman & Sunderwirth, 2010, p. 7).

Griffin-Shelley (2018) wrote that actively addicted individuals are self-centered and quoted a saying from AA as an exemplar: "I want what I want when I want it" (p. 184). Furthermore, they are engulfed with secrecy, shame, guilt, and self-hatred (Griffin-Shelley, 2018). Intimacy requires responsibility, and, in assuming this interpersonal responsibility, the shame, guilt, and self-hatred felt by addicted individuals can lessen (May, 1988). It is for reasons of developing intimacy and closeness that group counseling is often ideally suited for addicted clients (Griffin-Shelley, 2018).

Another protective factor occurs as addicted individuals develop a well-rounded life (Timko, Moos, & Finney, 2016). Besides becoming clean, recovery requires that addicted people build a productive life while striving to reach their potential (Timko et al., 2016). Mediocrity is insufficient (Deramus, 2011). They need to focus on their health and good citizenship (Timko et al., 2016). An addict's life needs to be lived differently (Deramus, 2011).

Cloninger (2013) found that people are healthiest, happiest, and most fulfilled when they are high in the character traits of self-directedness, cooperativeness, and self-transcendence. Self-transcendence "is the essence of existence" (Frankl, 1966, p. 104). It is where individuals can entirely devote themselves to another person, work, cause, or activity (Frankl, 1966). Within or alongside self-transcendence is spirituality, and, as you read in Chapters 9 through 21, having spiritual and/or religious beliefs generally acts as a buffer against addiction (Krause, Pargament, Ironson, & Hill, 2017; Miller, 2016).

Farrell (2018) found that subjective well-being diminishes as gambling disorder worsens. Presumably, having a personal sense of well-being needs to increase when one is in recovery. This brings us to the next point.

Besides developing a balanced life, addicted individuals need to change their way of looking at life (Tarman & Werdell, 2014). The cup is both half-empty and half-full, but focusing on the former leads to wanting and craving, whereas concentrating on the latter leads to appreciation, serenity, and peace of mind (Tarman & Werdell, 2014). Addicted people would do well to reflect once a day on something that touched them (R. Jevne, personal communication, December 3, 2018).

May (1988) surmised that five qualities lead to good intention: "honesty, dignity, community, responsibility, and simplicity" (p. 165). Honesty is about accepting one's addictiveness, dignity is about self-respect and believing that one is worthy of receiving it from others, community is about involving others in the addicted person's struggle with false attachment (i.e., attachment to the addictive substance or behavior), responsibility is about recognizing and upholding commitments to others, and simplicity comes down to two words: *Stop It* (May, 1988). You might be reminded of actor Bob Newhart in his *Stop It* video (https://www.youtube.com/watch?v=Ow0lr63y4Mw). Although May's definition of simplicity might seem overly, for lack of a better word, *simplistic*, virtually nothing changes in addicted persons' lives until they decide to stop doing their addiction (as you know, in some less-severe cases of addiction, moderation can be achieved).

Being resilient or developing resiliency is a protective factor (Tait, 2013). Resiliency is "the ability to persist in the face of challenges and bounce back from adversity" (Tait, 2013, p. 291). Studies have found that resiliency increases when the following attitudes and skills are present: (a) optimism and hope, (b) self-efficacy, (c) strong self-regulation skills, (d) problem-solving skills, (e) adaptability, (f) self-regulation, (g) sense of humor, (h) easy temperament, (i) close relationships among family members, (j) low discord between parents, and (k) warm and structured parenting style (names of attitudes and skills quoted from Tait, 2013, p. 291).

A quality that will serve addicted persons well is courage. "It has never been a question of can you change . . . Of course you can! It has always been a question of will you change. Well, will you?" (Markson, as cited in Deramus, 2011, p. 104). Merriam-Webster (2019a) defined courage as "mental or moral strength to venture, persevere, and withstand danger, fear, or difficulty." Addicted individuals need to face their fear of what life will be like without their addictive substance or behavior.

Besides needing courage, individuals (whether addicted or not) who want to be successful in life, need to develop certain qualities. Alderson (2004) created the "success formula" to reflect his experience and reading of psychology for over 30 years. The formula is as follows: Success = B^2 P^2 where B-squared stands for *Belief* and *Balance* and P-squared stands for *Passion* and *Persistence*. Graphically, the success formula is represented in Figure 22.1.

Along the left side of the figure is an upward arrow that signifies that each of these attributes can be developed in our lives to an optimal level. Success is theorized to become likelier as each attribute is further developed (Alderson, 2004).

Exercise has been clearly demonstrated to improve physical and mental health (Milkman & Sunderwirth, 2010). During exercise, animal studies have shown, serotonin, dopamine, and norepinephrine are released, all of which contribute to calm, pleasant, and positive feelings (Milkman & Sunderwirth, 2010). Regular exercise is both a buffer against addiction and an essential component of treatment for those who are in recovery from it.

Besides exercise, Milkman and Sunderwirth (2010) examined several other natural high alternatives, which they called "the cutting edge of mood alteration" (p. 299). These include such activities as those that involve the meaningful engagement of talents, including self-expression, self-focus, aesthetic discovery, and collective harmony. Collective harmony includes mental exercise, people closeness, spiritual involvement, and helping others (Milkman & Sunderwirth, 2010). Other natural highs outlined by Milkman and Sunderwirth included the effect garnered from cognitive-behavioral therapy (CBT), the maintenance of close and intimate relationships, relaxation, mindfulness, meditation, and developing good eating habits.

Counseling Considerations

You have learned throughout this textbook that CBT and motivational interviewing are repeatedly found to be the empirically supported treatments that have accumulated the largest and strongest evidence base. Furthermore, the biopsychosocial model has gained prominence in the field (Fattore, Melis, Fadda, & Fratta, 2014; MacKillop & Ray, 2018; Sugaya, Shirasaka, Takahashi, & Kanda, 2019). This is understandable given that most of the theories covered in Chapter 3, with the exception of the biopsychosocial approach, are stand-alone theories that have never been integrated.

Speaking of integration, Miller (2016) wrote that addiction treatment today is less segregated than it used to be from mental health and healthcare services. Despite these attempts, health professionals have generally received little training regarding how to treat substance use disorders (SUDs). This is disappointing, given that SUDs constitute the second-most-common mental health diagnosis after depression (Miller, 2016).

Another type of integration stands before us today: integrative counseling, which is also called integrative therapy or integrative psychotherapy. It intends to combine different therapeutic tools and approaches to best fit the needs of the individual client. Integrative counselors also combine mainstream therapies with those developed in complementary and alternative therapies (Morrison, Lin, & Gersh, 2018). As noted in Chapter 6, integrative therapies might include acupuncture, yoga, exercise, mindfulness, hypnosis, biofeedback, neurofeedback, music and art therapy, and herbal therapies. A book focused on integrated approaches with drug and alcohol problems was written by Mistral (2016).

FIGURE 22.1 The success formula.

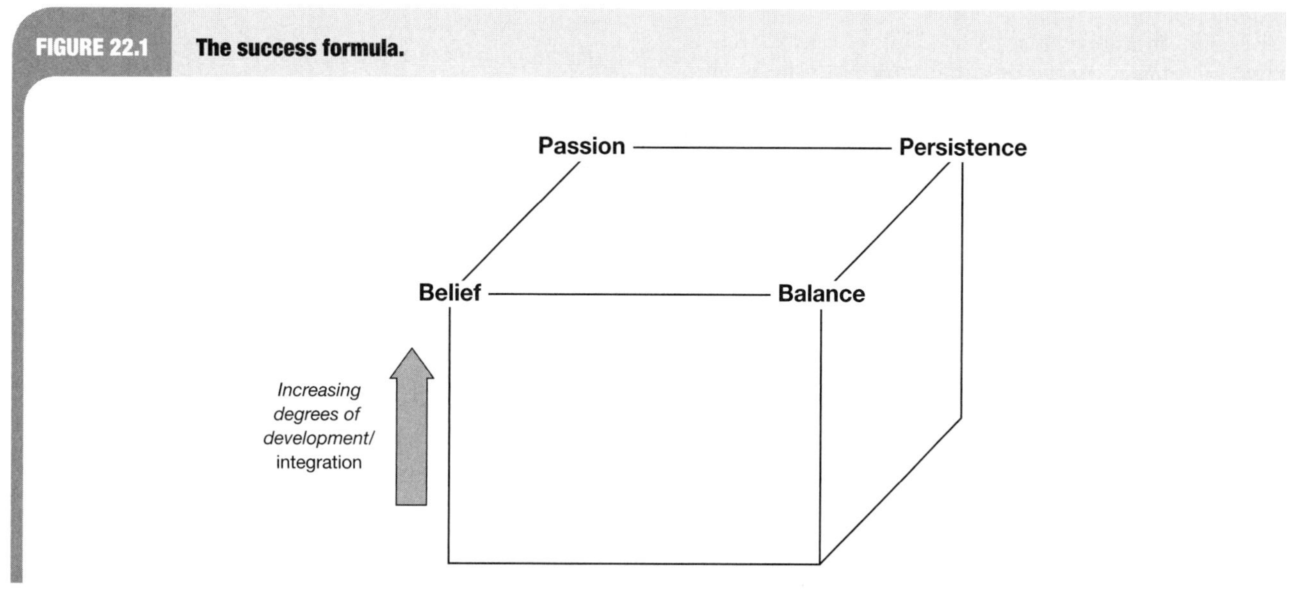

Source: Reprinted from Alderson, K., 2004, from *Grade power: The complete guide to improving your grades through self-hypnosis*. Used with permission.

The Internet age has also shaped new treatment approaches that rely on technology. Today, there are several computer-based and smartphone-based behavioral interventions for alcohol use disorder (AUD; Campbell, Lawrence, & Perry, 2018) and every addiction (see Chapters 9 through 21). Although their efficacy remains questionable in most cases (Campbell et al., 2018), research by You et al. (2017) demonstrated the usefulness of a Bluetooth breathalyzer for participants with AUDs. Research is well under way, and results are encouraging. Technology provides low-cost help, and it can reach a lot of people who otherwise might not seek treatment.

What Counselors Bring to the Table

Counseling is arguably the noblest profession. It requires that we build the finest personal qualities and rise to the highest moral principles and ideals. These are not easy aspirations or goals; however, our efforts are richly rewarded. There are scarce things comparable to the feeling evoked when we witness change in our clients. Counseling is one of the few fields that allow clients the opportunity to be honest and real: These are, in fact, an expectation of clients. It begins with modeling, and we can model only what we have actualized.

Counseling, by definition, is a strengths-based approach to helping people. Although there is an appreciation that we all have problems, and some more serious than others, counselors embrace the philosophy that all people have equal worth. Our work with clients is not "we" juxtaposed with "they"; it is "us." We are just in different places than our clients are.[1] It doesn't matter what problems have surfaced in their lives or their duration and/or intensity. More problems do not mean being worth less as a person; they just mean having more challenges to either face or deny.

Each time we see a client, we are reminded that it could be us sitting in the other chair, and, in many if not most cases, we *have* sat in the other chair one or more times in our lives. "Wounded healers" often make the best counselors, so long as the wounds are no longer bleeding (Gladding & Alderson, 2019). If we have developed empathy and compassion for ourselves, we can project these to our addicted clients, who are often struggling with shame and guilt. Our clients are deeply in need of self-compassion.

Working in addictions brings us into the heart and soul of the human condition. Advertising and marketing imply that near perfection is attainable if we purchase the right products or services. Research conducted on Facebook (Wright, White, & Obst, 2018), Tinder (Ward, 2017), and other social networks (Schroeder & Cavanaugh, 2018) reminds us that people are motivated to provide overly positive impressions of themselves . . . even when it requires outright lying. Real-life encounters operate similarly, whether they are about dazzling an employer (Levashina, 2018) or a stranger or potential mate (Zuckerman et al., 1999).

Addicted individuals remind us that these attempts are façades. There is no perfection in the human condition. Like others, addicted individuals do their best to make the "best impression" by minimizing and denying the ultimate assault to their self-esteem (i.e., admitting that their free will and free choice have become compromised by their addiction). By the time this has become evident to themselves or others, the shards of shattered glass have already cut wounds into many areas of their lives. The adverse consequences, now palpable, tell the story of human suffering.

As Miller (2016) and Timko et al. (2016) have taught us, it is essential to stay humble in our work with clients. Regardless of how much you know, and you probably know more than your clients, the fact remains that many people experiencing SUDs and addictive behaviors recover without anyone's help. This speaks to the incredible intestinal fortitude that can develop when someone knows that he or she needs to change. The person who has the answers is the one "sitting right there across from you" (Miller, 2016, p. 108). "The myth that treatment is necessary for recovery has no empirical support" (Humphreys, 2015, p. 1024). Just as there are multiple pathways to addiction, there are numerous pathways to long-term recovery (White & Nicolaus, 2005). Counseling is only one of those pathways, and research informs us that even the setting (i.e., outpatient or residential) matters little regarding treatment efficacy (Smith & Garcia, 2013).

Miller (2016) recommended that we offer clients something that will benefit them in the very first session or, for that matter, in the very first contact. Although you may begin with an intake, after a while, you can ask the question, "Tell me something about what is happening so that perhaps I can help you right now."

In some cases, counselors might help clients achieve the most significant change of all: a fundamental change in one's philosophy and approach to life. Although the word *metanoia* is often used to describe this kind of radical shift when it occurs through religious conversion, this is only one example. Existential questions eventually beckon for an answer. Viktor Frankl first wrote *Man's Search for Meaning* in 1946, which chronicled his time spent in concentration camps during World War II. In that book, Frankl provided a brief introduction to logotherapy, which is a therapy based on the notion that searching for meaning is a fundamental and primary motivational force within human beings. Clara Hill (2018) wrote that interest in the meaning of life is surging in psychology today. As Maté (2008) noted, meaning is generally found in pursuits that extend beyond the self.

In closing, remember that, as you look into your addicted client's eyes and see whatever it is that you see, it is not what's in front of your nose that matters but what's behind it. Our effectiveness will largely rest not on how much we know or how much we learn about our clients. Instead, it will depend more on what you bring to the table. I am not just referring to unconditional positive regard, empathy, and congruence (Rogers, 1957); I am referring to the entire being of your humanity. I have shared my reflections in every chapter of this textbook. Now give heed: "What are your reflections?"

If we think of our lives as a book partly written, the chapter that we co-author with our clients will also demonstrate that perfection in living is a fiction. Working one's way out of addiction is challenging. It is our role, however, to tap into our clients' amazing yet hidden inner resources. Their self-efficacy, free will, and integrity are hiding. Once something or someone (perhaps themselves) helps move them to the contemplation stage of change, the once-hidden now peeks around the corner to remind them that hope's glimmer is real. The potential for human growth that can be imagined can also be realized.

[1] When this is not the case, it means we need to get help and suspend our practice temporarily if required.

REFERENCES

Alderson, K. (2004). *Grade power: The complete guide to improving your grades through self-hypnosis.* Toronto, ON: Insomniac Press.

Campbell, E. J., Lawrence, A. J., & Perry, C. J. (2018). New steps for treating alcohol use disorder. *Psychopharmacology, 235*, 1759–1773.

Carnes, P. (1991). *Don't call it love: Recovery from sexual addiction.* Toronto, ON: Bantam Books.

Cloninger, C. R. (2013). What makes people healthy, happy, and fulfilled in the face of current world challenges? *Mens Sana Monograph, 11*, 16–24.

Coelho, M. P. (2015). Drugs: The Portuguese fallacy and the absurd medicalization of Europe. *Motricidade, 11*(2), 3–15.

Csiernik, R. (2016). *Substance use and abuse: Everything matters* (2nd ed.). Toronto, ON: Canadian Scholars Press.

Delima, J., & Vimpani, G. (2011). The neurobiological effects of childhood maltreatment: An often overlooked narrative related to the long-term effects of early childhood trauma? *Family Matters, 89*, 42–52.

Deramus, T. (2011). *The secret addiction: Overcoming your marijuana dependency.* Montgomery, TX: SMA International.

Earleywine, M. (2016). *Substance use problems* (2nd ed.). Ashland, OH: Hogrefe.

Farrell, L. (2018). Understanding the relationship between subjective wellbeing and gambling behavior. *Journal of Gambling Studies, 34*(1), 55–71.

Fattore, L., Melis, M., Fadda, P., & Fratta, W. (2014). Sex differences in addictive disorders. *Frontiers in Neuroendocrinology, 35*(3), 272–284.

Frankl, V. E. (1966). Self-transcendence as a human phenomenon. *Journal of Humanistic Psychology, 6*(2), 97–106.

Gladding, S. T., & Alderson, K. G. (2019). *Choosing the right counselor for you.* Alexandria, VA: American Counseling Association.

Goncalves, R., Lourenco, A., & Silva, S. N. D. (2015). A social cost perspective in the wake of the Portuguese strategy for the fight against drugs. *International Journal of Drug Policy, 26*(2), 199–209.

Griffin-Shelley, E. (2018). The importance of group psychotherapy for sex and love addiction recovery. In T. Birchard & J. Benfield (Eds.), *The Routledge international handbook of sexual addiction* (pp. 181–189). New York, NY: Routledge/Taylor & Francis.

Hall, W., & Weier, M. (2017). Lee Robins' studies of heroin use among US Vietnam veterans. *Addiction, 112*, 176–180.

Hill, C. E. (2018). Future directions. In C. E. Hill (Eds.), *Meaning in life: A therapist's guide* (pp. 194–204). Washington, DC: American Psychological Association.

Hughes, C. E., & Stevens, A. (2010). What can we learn from the Portuguese decriminalization of illicit drugs? *British Journal of Criminology, 50*, 999–1022.

Hughes, C. E., & Stevens, A. (2012). A resounding success or a disastrous failure: Re-examining the interpretation of evidence on the Portuguese decriminalisation of illicit drugs. *Drug and Alcohol Review, 31*, 101–113.

Humphreys, K. (2015). Addiction treatment professionals are not the gatekeepers of recovery. *Substance Use & Misuse, 50*(8–9), 1024–1027.

Katz, J. (2017, September 2). The first count of fentanyl deaths in 2016: Up 540% in three years. *New York Times.* Retrieved on March 19, 2019, from https://www.nytimes.com/interactive/2017/09/02/upshot/fentanyl-drug-overdose-deaths.html

Krause, N., Pargament, K. I., Ironson, G., & Hill, P. (2017). Religious involvement, financial strain, and poly-drug use: Exploring the moderating role of meaning in life. *Substance Use & Misuse, 52*, 286–293.

Lee, J. C. (2018). The opioid crisis is a wicked problem. *American Journal on Addictions, 27*, 51.

Levashina, J. (2018). Evaluating deceptive impression management in personnel selection and job performance. In R. Rogers & S. D. Bender (Eds.), *Clinical assessment of malingering and deception* (4th ed., pp. 530–551). New York, NY: Guilford Press.

MacKillop, J., & Ray, L. A. (2018). The etiology of addiction: A contemporary biopsychosocial approach. In J. MacKillop, G. A. Kenna, L. Leggio, & L. A. Ray (Eds.), *Integrating psychological and pharmacological treatments for addictive disorders: An evidence-based guide* (pp. 32–53). New York, NY: Routledge/Taylor & Francis.

Maté, G. (2008). *In the realm of hungry ghosts: Close encounters with addiction.* Toronto, ON: Vintage Books.

Matteliano, D., St. Marie, B. J., Oliver, J., & Coggins, C. (2014). *Pain Management Nursing, 15*(1), 391–405.

May, G. G. (1988). *Addiction and Grace: Love and spirituality in the healing of addictions.* New York, NY: HarperCollins.

McCrory, E. J., & Viding, E. (2015). The theory of latent vulnerability: Reconceptualizing the link between childhood maltreatment and psychiatric disorder. *Development and Psychopathology, 27*(2), 493–505.

McNeece, C. A., & Madsen, M. D. (2012). Preventing alcohol and drug problems. In C. A. McNeece & D. M. DiNitto (Eds.), *Chemical dependency: A systems approach* (4th ed., pp. 171–199). Upper Saddle River, NJ: Pearson.

Milkman, H. B., & Sunderwirth, S. G. (2010). *Craving for ecstasy and natural highs: A positive approach to mood alteration.* Thousand Oaks, CA: SAGE.

Miller, N. S., & Oberbarnschiedt, T. (2017). Current medical and legal status for smoked "medical marijuana" and addiction. *Psychiatric Annals, 47*(6), 335–340.

Miller, W. R. (2016). Sacred cows and greener pastures: Reflections from 40 years in addiction research. *Alcoholism Treatment Quarterly, 34*(1), 92–115.

Merriam-Webster. (2019a). *Definition of courage.* Retrieved on April 15, 2019, from https://www.merriam-webster.com/dictionary/courage

Merriam-Webster. (2019b). *Definition of magnum opus.* Retrieved on April 15, 2019, from https://www.merriam-webster.com/dictionary/magnum%20opus

Mistral, W. (Ed.) (2016). *Integrated approaches to drug and alcohol problems: Action on addiction.* New York, NY: Routledge.

Morrison, M. F., Lin, K., & Gersh, S. (2018). Addictions: Evidence for integrative treatment. In D. A. Monti & A. B. Newberg (Eds.), *Integrative psychiatry and brain health* (2nd ed., pp. 1–22). New York, NY: Oxford University Press.

Pyszczynski, T. (2004). What are we so afraid of? The terror management theory perspective on the politics of fear. *Social Research, 71*(4), 827–848.

Rogers, C. (1957). The necessary and sufficient conditions of therapeutic personality change. *Journal of Consulting Psychology, 21*(2), 95–103.

Schroeder, A. N., & Cavanaugh, J. M. (2018). Fake it 'til you make it: Examining faking ability on social media pages. *Computers in Human Behavior, 84*, 29–35.

Shea, M. (2018, September 26). Should addiction be treated as a spectrum disorder like autism? *New York Post*. Retrieved on March 20, 2019, from https://nypost.com/2018/09/26/should-addiction-be-treated-as-a-spectrum-disorder-like-autism/

Smith, R. L., & Garcia, E. E. (2013). Treatment setting and treatment planning. In P. Stevens & R. L. Smith (Eds.), *Substance abuse counseling: Theory and practice* (5th ed., pp. 155–187). New York, NY: Pearson.

Sugaya, N., Shirasaka, T., Takahashi, K., & Kanda, H. (2019). Biopsychosocial factors of children and adolescents with Internet gaming disorder: A systematic review. *BioPsychoSocial Medicine, 13*, 1–16.

Sumerlin, J. R., & Norman, R. L., Jr. (1992). Self-actualization and homeless men: A known-groups examination of Maslow's hierarchy of needs. *Journal of Social Behavior and Personality, 7*(3), 469–481.

Sussman, S., Lisha, N., & Griffiths, M. (2011). Prevalence of the addictions: A problem of the majority or the minority? *Evaluation & the Health Professions, 34*(1), 3–56.

Tait, C. (2013). Working with selected populations: Treatment issues and characteristics. In P. Stevens & R. L. Smith (Eds.), *Substance abuse counseling: Theory and practice* (5th ed., pp. 287–310). New York, NY: Pearson.

Tarman, V., & Werdell, P. (2014). *Food junkies: The truth about food addiction*. Toronto, ON: Dundurn.

Timko, C., Moos, R. H., & Finney, J. W. (2016). The course of substance use disorders: Trajectories, endpoints, and predictors. In E. J. Bromet (Ed.), *Long-term outcomes in psychopathology research: Rethinking the scientific agenda* (pp. 53–76). New York, NY: Oxford University Press.

United Nations. (2018, June). *World Drug Report 2018: Global overview of drug demand and supply—Latest trends, cross-cutting issues*. Retrieved on April 18, 2019, from https://www.unodc.org/wdr2018/prelaunch/WDR18_Booklet_2_GLOBAL.pdf

Ward, J. (2017). What are you doing on Tinder? Impression management on a matchmaking mobile app. *Information, Communication & Society, 20*(11), 1644–1659.

White, W., & Nicolaus, M. (2005). Styles of secular recovery. *Counselor, 6*(4), 58–61.

Witkiewitz, K. A., & Marlatt, G. A. (2007). High-risk situations: Relapse as a dynamic process. In K. A. Witkiewitz & G. A. Marlatt (Eds.), *Therapist's guide to evidence-based relapse prevention* (pp. 19–33). London, England: Academic Press.

Wright, E. J., White, K. M., & Obst, P. L. (2018). Facebook false self-presentation behaviors and negative mental health. *Cyberpsychology, Behavior and Social Networking, 21*(1), 40–49.

Wright, S. E., & Allen, J. B. (2008). A cultural transformation approach in the group treatment of addiction. In L. VandeCreek & J. B. Allen (Eds.), *Innovations in clinical practice: Focus on group, couples, & family therapy* (pp. 219–234). Sarasota, FL: Professional Resource Press/Professional Resource Exchange.

You, C.-W., Chen, Y.-C., Chen, C.-H., Lee, C.-H., Kuo, P.-H., Huang, M.-C., & Chu, H.-H. (2017). Smartphone-based support system (SoberDiary) coupled with a Bluetooth breathalyser for treatment-seeking alcohol-dependent patients. *Addictive Behaviors, 65*, 174–178.

Zuckerman, M., Miserandino, M., Bernieri, F., Manusov, V., Axtell, R. E., Wiemann, . . . Gallois, C. (1999). Creating impressions and managing interaction. In L. K. Guerrero, J. A. DeVito, & M. L. Hecht (Eds.), *The nonverbal communication reader: Classic and contemporary readings* (2nd ed., pp. 379–422). Prospect Heights, IL: Waveland Press.

Epilogue

iStock.com/focusstock

You might recall from the Preface that I hoped this book would be the most exciting, provocative, enlightening, and practical text that you ever read on the subject. Now only you can judge whether I succeeded. If you have ideas for how you think this textbook could be improved in the next edition, please let me know. Email me at alderson@ucalgary.ca. I will reply with at least a "Thank you!" by the way. I sincerely appreciate your feedback.

You have explored with me the many addictions that currently face societies around the world. We can no longer blindside the cry that lies quietly stifled, lurking somewhere inside the psyche of addicted individuals. Denial is a defense mechanism that keeps us from facing painful truths. The fear is that owning this truth will create an emotional cripple while becoming devastated with profound anxiety and depression.

Yet there is an interesting paradox that occurs in addiction, and that is that facing the truth with courage is always better than running from it in fear. There is no place to hide. Lies only lead to darkness, but honesty liberates a person into the light. May you always live your life in the light, and, as you do, let it shine on all persons you work with who still need to find their way.

*****

Perfect Reflections

The hurts and pains etched in your face,
You are this, and you are that,
Open wounds that have not healed,
Surely imperfect,
Surely flawed,
Needing time for deeper reflections.

The mirror shows compelling lies,
Of your soul always wanting,
Always craving,
Needing more,
Yet having less,
Than your twisted reflections.

Many years wasted,
Trying to be someone else,
Wanting to be smarter,
Wanting to be popular,
Wanting to be thinner,
Always wanting different reflections.

After all,
Your good and bad are as one,
While your truth resides somewhere in between,
No need to feel sorry,
No need to feel lacking,
Just accept these honest reflections.

One night like no other,
A miracle happens,
You wake feeling relieved,
Because the pain inside you,
Retreated behind night's darkness,
Showing now happier reflections.

Within your uniqueness,
Having less is having more,
Because more of someone or something else,
Means less of you,
So today shine some light and learn to love,
Your perfect reflections.

— Kevin Alderson
June 12, 2017

Appendix A

2016 CACREP ADDICTION COUNSELING STANDARDS

(From Section 5: Entry-Level Specialty Areas for Addiction Counseling, pp. 20–21.)

Students who are preparing to specialize as addiction counselors are expected to possess the knowledge and skills necessary to address a wide range of issues in the context of addiction counseling, treatment, and prevention programs as well as in a more-broad mental health counseling context. Counselor education programs with a specialty area in addiction counseling must document where each of the lettered standards listed is covered in the curriculum.

#	Standard	Location in Proposal*
1.	Foundations	
	a. History and development of addiction counseling	1
	b. Theories and models of addiction related to substance use as well as behavioral and process addictions	3
	c. Principles and philosophies of addiction-related self-help	7
	d. Principles, models, and documentation formats of biopsychosocial case conceptualization and treatment planning	3, 6–8
	e. Neurological, behavioral, psychological, physical, and social effects of psychoactive substances and addictive disorders on the user and significant others	4, 9–21
	f. Psychological tests and assessments specific to addiction counseling	8–21
2.	Contextual Dimensions	
	a. Roles and settings of addiction counselors	1
	b. Potential for addictive and substance use disorders to mimic and/or co-occur with a variety of medical and psychological disorders	5, 8
	c. Factors that increase the likelihood for a person, community, or group to be at risk for or resilient to psychoactive substance use disorders	TH
	d. Regulatory processes and substance abuse policy relative to service delivery opportunities in addiction counseling	2
	e. Importance of vocation, family, social networks, and community systems in the addiction treatment and recovery process	TH
	f. Role of wellness and spirituality in the addiction recovery process	TH
	g. Culturally and developmentally relevant education programs that raise awareness and support addiction and substance abuse prevention and the recovery process	TH
	h. Classifications, indications, and contraindications of commonly prescribed psychopharmacological medications for appropriate medical referral and consultation	9–21
	i. Diagnostic process, including differential diagnosis and the use of current diagnostic classification systems, including the *Diagnostic and Statistical Manual of Mental Disorders* (DSM) and the *International Classification of Diseases* (ICD)	5, 8–21
	j. Cultural factors relevant to addiction and addictive behavior	TH
	k. Professional organizations, preparation standards, and credentials relevant to the practice of addiction counseling	1
	l. Legal and ethical considerations specific to addiction counseling	2
	m. Record keeping, third party reimbursement, and other practice and management considerations in addiction counseling	2

#	Standard	Location in Proposal*
3.	Practice	
	a. Screening, assessment, and testing for addiction, including diagnostic interviews, mental status examination, symptom inventories, and psychoeducational and personality assessments	8, 9–21
	b. Assessment of biopsychosocial and spiritual history relevant to addiction	8–21
	c. Assessment for symptoms of psychoactive substance toxicity, intoxication, and withdrawal	8–21
	d. Techniques and interventions related to substance abuse and other addictions	6, 7
	e. Strategies for reducing the persisting negative effects of substance use, abuse, dependence, and addictive disorders	TH
	f. Strategies for helping clients identify the effects of addiction on life problems and the effects of continued harmful use or abuse and the benefits of a life without addiction	TH
	g. Evaluating and identifying individualized strategies and treatment modalities relative to clients' stage of dependence, change, or recovery	TH
	h. Strategies for interfacing with the legal system and working with court-referred clients	2

*Numbers represent chapter numbers; TH = throughout.

Appendix B

GENERIC PREPARATION AND ACTION STRATEGIES

[If Currently Using/Engaging in Addictive Behavior]

Before Quit Day

1. Secure appropriate medications (where appropriate).
2. Set your quit day.
3. Break associations. Begin to break down the associations between your addiction and doing anything else.
4. Get psychologically prepared (e.g., keep reminding yourself of quit day and how you feel after you have mastered remaining clean).
5. Change product (only if you are a smoker, change to a different brand for a couple of weeks before quit day).
6. Control your surroundings. Who affects you? Others at home? Peers?
7. Enlist support (see Support Agreement on last page).
8. Practice assertive behaviors. Begin to practice saying *no* when people offer you your substance or provide you the circumstances to engage in addictive behavior. Do so firmly but kindly.
9. Consider using self-hypnosis or a form of meditation to relax and focus on your goals. Self-hypnosis or meditation are excellent and quick methods of relaxation and focused attention for working on a goal, whether it be quitting your addiction or nearly anything else (e.g., weight control, improved self-esteem).
10. Download telephone app(s). Download one or two apps appropriate to your addiction onto your cell phone.

Beginning Quit Day

1. Do not allow yourself your substance or addictive behavior . . . ever. A relapse usually occurs when addicted individuals believe they can handle "just one" or do their addictive behavior "just once."
2. Positive attitude. Learn to view the process of quitting your addiction as a positive experience and improve your mental attitude regarding it. For the next several weeks, think of yourself as a special person and that you deserve to enjoy yourself immensely for deciding to quit. See the positive in everything you do.
3. Most important life goal. Think of this as the most crucial goal of your life. If you think about it, you may realize that, without question, it is. The quality of your life is contingent upon the quality of your physical, emotional, mental, and spiritual health.
4. Reward yourself systematically. One of the most important reasons that people continue their addiction is that they find it rewarding in a certain way. Perhaps you feel it helps you relax or gives you a temporary "lift." The message to your subconscious mind has been "My [ADDICTION] is pleasurable and good." That message is a half-truth if not an outright lie. Now that you have decided to stop, it is essential that you give your subconscious mind a different message. You accomplish this by rewarding yourself daily for not doing your addiction. At the simplest level, this is done by praising yourself repeatedly throughout the day and by concentrating on a feeling of accomplishment and achievement. It is also helpful to give yourself tangible or concrete rewards, such as enjoying a warm bath, spending time with a loved one, or buying some new clothes.
5. Dealing with urges and trigger situations. Refer to and use the strategies that are included later in this handout. Always keep these pages in your pocket or purse for several weeks for easy reference.
6. Positive affirmations. Write one of the following suggestions on a piece of paper or cardboard when you're at home. Make it into a poster for yourself. Read it five times before you fall asleep and five times when you awaken. Read it slowly, meaningfully, and reflectively. Concentrate on what it means to you and create a feeling of accomplishment.
   a. "I feel tremendous satisfaction and a sense of freedom by not enacting my [ADDICTION]."
   b. "I am determined *never* to use (or do) my [ADDICTION] again, and my powers of control are increasing progressively."
7. Short-term financial incentive. Save the money you would otherwise spend on your addiction by putting it aside somewhere conspicuous before you go to bed. Spend it on *yourself* after 1 or 2 weeks. Have fun with it—you would have wasted it anyway as an addicted individual in a much more harmful way.

8. Long-term financial incentive. Establish for yourself a long-term reward for not using (or doing) your addiction. The best idea is to continue saving the money you used to spend on your addiction by placing this daily amount in a piggy bank at home each evening before you go to bed. Save this for 6 months to a year and then use this money to take a vacation.

9. Do not envy other addicts! Remember: They envy you for quitting, just as you used to envy them before you decided to stop. You are not being deprived of anything; you are reclaiming what you lost since you started your addiction: your freedom, your health, your money, your self-confidence, your peace of mind, your energy, etc.

Appendix C

RELAPSE PREVENTION HANDOUTS FOR CLIENTS

Relapse Prevention Email Forms

I ask clients to complete the first few pages and return them to me before our next appointment. I review this information before their next session, and I ask clients to always keep these pages with them for a few weeks, so they can read these whenever they feel like relapsing. The forms and ideas contained in this appendix are adapted from the following sources:

Cofta-Woerpel, L., Wright, K. L., & Wetter, D. W. (2007). Smoking cessation 3: Multicomponent interventions. *Behavioral Medicine, 32*(4), 135–149.

Dodgen, C. E. (2005). *Nicotine dependence: Understanding and applying the most effective treatment interventions.* Washington, DC: American Psychological Association.

McCaul, K. D., Hockemeyer, J. R., Johnson, R. J., Zetocha, K., Quinlan, K., & Glasgow, R. E. (2006). Motivation to quit using cigarettes: A review. *Addictive Behaviors, 31*(1), 42–56.

McEwen, A., Hajek, P., McRobbie, H., & West, R. (2006). *Manual of smoking cessation: A guide for counsellors and practitioners.* Malden, MA: Blackwell.

Pbert, L., Luckmann, R., & Ockene, J. K. (2004). Smoking cessation treatment. In L. J. Haas (Ed.), *Handbook of primary care psychology* (pp. 527–549). New York: Oxford University Press.

Instructions for Clients

Please complete the following forms and return a copy to me ***before*** our next appointment if possible (scan and email back to me, fax it to me, or bring it with you to our next session).

Reasons for Quitting Your Addiction

Place a number in the last column that best represents the importance of each reason to you (1 = very unimportant, 2 = unimportant, 3 = important, 4 = very important, 5 = extremely important). Add to the list if you have other reasons for quitting not listed here. After completion, write your reasons in *your* handwriting on the next page in order of priority (i.e., list most important reason first, followed by second most important, and so forth). It is better to be more specific than general (e.g., "respiratory problems" instead of "health reasons"). Add in other reasons you are quitting that are not listed in the rows at the end.

#	Reason	1–5
1	Health reasons (e.g., given medical advice to stop, concerned about my health, increase my longevity, feel better physically, reduce the likelihood of future illness, improve my physical performance)	
2	Physical complaints (e.g., stomach distress, liver problems, respiratory, decreased lung functioning, headaches, hangovers, blackouts, personal discomfort)	
3	Social and familial reasons (e.g., responsibility to others, family pressure, encouraged by friends and family, intimate partner has asked me to quit, provide a healthier example for kids, eliminate the effect on others, someone close to me died)	
4	Personal beliefs (e.g., sick of this addiction, I have developed a deep conviction to stop, become more self-disciplined, I am addicted and I need to begin recovery)	
5	Expense (e.g., cost, save money, plan for a holiday, plan for retirement)	
6	Regaining control (e.g., self-control, take control over life)	
7	Aesthetic reasons (e.g., lost its appeal, appearance, wrinkles, weight gain, weight loss)	
8	Spiritual reasons (e.g., compromises my religious or spiritual beliefs)	
9	Education (e.g., learned how harmful this addiction is to my well-being, reading research reports has opened my eyes)	
10	Statistics (e.g., mortality and morbidity statistics)	
11	Legislation (e.g., illegal, too restricted by laws)	
12	Other reason?	

#	Reason	1–5
13	Other reason?	
14	Other reason?	
15	Other reason?	

My Reasons for Quitting or Not Using/Doing

From the preceding list, now write out your reasons for quitting, listing the most important reason first and then listing the remainder of your reasons in descending order of importance to you. You will be asked to always keep this list with for the several weeks following quit day. It is best to be as specific as possible in creating your list.

1. ______________________________
2. ______________________________
3. ______________________________
4. ______________________________
5. ______________________________
6. ______________________________
7. ______________________________
8. ______________________________
9. ______________________________
10. ______________________________

Assessing and Coping With Your High-Risk Situations

It is important to have a strategy for dealing with situations in which you used to do your addiction. These are commonly called *high-risk situations*, because these situations used to be associated with your addiction. Use the three categories called ACE strategies: **A**void, **C**ope, **E**scape. These stand for

1. Avoid. As your first defense, try avoiding stressful situations, using friends, places where people use (or do) your addiction, and other activities associated with it.
2. Cope. If you can't avoid the situation or activity, attempt to cope with the resulting urges by following the suggestions on the handout called "Overcoming a Desire for My Addiction."
3. Escape. If you can't avoid or cope, your best option is to escape the situation or activity. For example, if someone starts using around you and asking them to stop is not an option, leave the situation, at least for right now.

To help you get in touch with your own high-risk situations, do the following:

1. Reflect on the times you quit in the past. What triggered you again? List the reason in the left column.
2. What are events, situations, or activities that you strongly associate with your addiction? List these in the left column.
3. For the next 3 weeks before our second session, pay attention to the events, situations, or activities in which you do your addiction. Continue listing these as well.
4. In the right column, write out what your plan is to avoid your addiction in each scenario. Remember to pick from the ACE strategies; also use pages 10–16 for ideas.

	Event, Situation, or Activity Associated With My Addiction or Past Relapses	Specific ACE Strategies I Plan on Using to Successfully Deal With It
1		
2		
3		
4		
5		
6		
7		
8		
9		
10		

(Continued)

(Continued)

Your Strategies for Dealing With Urges

Which of the other interventions listed on the separate handout will *you* use if you feel urges to use (or do) your addiction? Also, feel free to add some of your own here:

Relapse Prevention Handouts

Most of these ideas were adapted from the references noted in the previous section of this appendix. I provide clients a copy of these ideas to assist them in their relapse prevention.

High-Risk Relapse Situations

The following are situations where individuals become likelier to relapse:

- Arguing with intimate partner or family members.
- Stressing from pressure at work.
- Experiencing special holidays (e.g., Christmas, New Year's Eve).
- Grieving the loss of someone close to me.
- Experiencing a lapse (i.e., after using/doing once).
- Enjoying holidays.
- Attending a "permissive" event with other addicted individuals present.
- Hurting emotionally.
- Rejoicing and celebrating when feeling positive emotions.

The following pages provide many examples of strategies you can use to help avoid a *lapse* (i.e., a slip that occurs once) or a *relapse* (i.e., where your *slip* returns to your previous pattern of addiction).

Overcoming a Desire for My Addiction

During the first few weeks, you are struggling not only with a psychological habit but, in many cases of substance addiction, physical withdrawal as well. Consequently, having a desire to lapse or relapse is common. You do not need to succumb to this, however. A progressive approach is recommended in overcoming a desire for your addiction.

Kick the crap out of most urges by using Dr. Alderson's *BAMMs!* approach. BAMMs! is an acronym that stands for the first five steps in overcoming an urge or craving. The steps are

1. **B** (step 1) = Breathe. Take three deep abdominal breaths, each time telling yourself, "Breathe freedom and relax," as you exhale.
2. **A** (step 2) = Affirmations. Whenever you want to do your addiction, a suggestion enters your mind (e.g., "I'd sure like to use (or do) [ADDICTION]." "I have to have (or do) it." I'll die without it"). Overcome this thought by telling yourself a positive affirmation, such as
   a. "I am in recovery now, and I'm feeling better every day as a result."
   b. I am determined not to do my addiction, and my desire for it is becoming less and less."

   This is also an excellent time to use one of your reasons for quitting as a positive affirmation. For example,

   a. "I won't use (or do) [ADDICTION] because it is damaging my health."
   b. I won't use (or do) [ADDICTION] because my children would view me as a weak person for continuing it."
3. **M** (step 3) = Massage. Massage either your dominant hand or ear lobe on your dominant side for a couple of minutes.
4. **M** (step 4) = Muscle contraction (simultaneous). Contract all of your muscles at once. Hold the contraction for 20 seconds before relaxing . . . now notice the contrast. Repeat if necessary.
5. **s!** (step 5) = Stillness technique (hint: begin with inverse Hand Lock). Sit or stand quietly, create stillness, concentrating on abdominal breathing and mindfulness (i.e., awareness of all sensations in the present, nonjudgmental attitude toward whatever you are thinking or feeling). This is a variation of BrainGym's (http://braingym.org/) hook-up technique without involving the crossing of the ankles (see child 24-second child demo at https://www.youtube.com/watch?v=OOMHz-HS4yY or 2.5-min adult demo at https://www.youtube.com/watch?v=5XL13jJUDig).

   If *bamming* your urge hasn't conquered it, then it's time to further kick the crap out of it. Do any of the following (these are not listed in any particular order).

In the table that follows, list the activities you will use if *your* urges require further intervention:

6. Attend a mutual support meeting (if there is one for your addiction).
7. Use the following strategies: stop thinking about the addiction, remind yourself that you do not want to go through this again, exercise, snack on something healthy, work hard, chew gum, exercise, snack, avoid thinking about your addiction, read or write, talk to a friend or family member, engage in a favorite activity, put something in your hand such as a rubber band or squeeze a rubber ball, do something good for yourself, encourage yourself, take a bath or shower, stretch, doodle, chew on hard vegetables, clean your glasses, play sports, bicycle, jog, do something nice for someone else, drink water, drink fruit juice, take a walk, or think of negative consequences.
8. Practice any of the forms of self-hypnosis and allow yourself to merely enter a peaceful meditative state. Self-hypnosis can be used to help yourself accomplish practically any goal.
9. Accept the urge and ride it out the way you would "surf a wave." The urge is telling you to feed it your addiction, but your resolve to be clean is stronger. Nothing can force you to embrace the enemy.

Strategies for Coping With Withdrawal

Withdrawal symptom	Strategy
Cravings/urges	Distract yourself. Remember that urges will pass. Tell yourself positive self-talk. Practice deep breathing. Leave the situation. Call a supportive friend, family member, or sponsor.
Irritability	Practice deep breathing. Do something pleasurable. Have a hot bath or shower.
Increased hunger	Make yourself a survival package (cinnamon sticks, gum, vegetables). Drink lots of water and low-calorie drinks.
Difficulty concentrating	Go for a brisk walk. Give yourself time to get ready to do your task. Simplify your schedule. Take frequent breaks.
Depression/sadness	Plan some pleasurable events. Talk to a good friend or family member. Be kind to yourself. Talk to yourself positively. Provide yourself with plenty of rest. Reward yourself for quitting your addictive behavior.
Sleep disturbance	Ensure that you get enough sleep at night. Learn to pace yourself. Ask help from others.

More Ways to Cope With Urges

Behaviors

1. Spend a weekend alone.
2. Focus time on yourself.
3. Avoid stressful situations.
4. Avoid tempting situations where you used to use (or do) your addiction.
5. Avoid friends who use (or do) your addiction.
6. Scream to let go of tension.
7. Change places of relaxation at home (favorite chair, etc.).
8. Get support from someone else who stopped.
9. Arrange a wager with a friend as a motivator.

Thoughts

1. Desire a longer life.
2. Think about being around for a grandchild.
3. Improving your health.
4. How much better you will feel shortly.
5. Notice that you already feel better.
6. Think about the adverse consequences of your addiction.
7. Reflect on or read about others who have suffered impairment from the same addiction.
8. How quitting makes important people in your life happier.
9. The pride that your family feels for achieving this goal.
10. My children will know if I use (or do) my addiction and be disgusted.
11. Think about other things on which you can spend your money.
12. Remember how much money your addiction cost you.

13. Reflect on the money that you are saving by not doing your addiction.
14. Notice positive changes in your emotions and feelings.
15. Think about the disgusting aspects of your addiction.
16. Consider how tired you are regarding your addiction.
17. Remember that the addiction created more problems than it solved.
18. Think about how your addiction made you feel worse over time.
19. Remind yourself that you don't want to do your addiction.
20. Tell yourself that you don't need your [ADDICTION].
21. Remember the reasons that you decided to stop.
22. Use your willpower.
23. Tell yourself, "I'm an addicted person in recovery."
24. Creative a visualization of yourself as a recovered addicted individual.
25. Tell yourself that you can do it.
26. Focus on the feeling of accomplishment because you have remained abstinent.
27. Remind yourself that the urges will dissipate over time.
28. Maintain a positive attitude.
29. If I use (or do) my addiction once, I might relapse.
30. Concentrate on how guilty you would feel if you lapsed or relapsed.

The Freedom From Addiction Support Agreement

I am planning to quit [NAME OF ADDICTION] ________ on ________.

I would appreciate your support during the first month of this goal. I don't want you to monitor my ______________ [NAME OF ADDICTION] or act like a therapist to me. Instead, just be supportive and encouraging.

I am taking this attempt very seriously by using the best methods. I will be following this program carefully.

I would appreciate it if you can help me with this as follows:

1. Encouraging me in my attempt.
2. Listening to me if I need to talk to you to help lessen an urge.
3. Avoiding using (or doing) this addiction in front of me if it is something you also use (or do).
4. Avoiding offering me my substance or opportunity to engage in my addictive behavior.

Please avoid doing the following:

1. Taking any responsibility for what I do.
2. Punishing me or being critical of me.
3. Harping or lecturing me if I struggle and experience a lapse.

______________________ ______________________

My Signature Your Signature

Appendix D

MENTAL STATUS EXAMINATION

Richard Lakeman (1995). Used with permission. (http://testandcalc.com/Richard/resources/Teaching_Resource_Mental_Status_Examination.pdf)

The mental health status examination (MSE) forms one component of the assessment of an individual. It augments other assessment components such as the history of the presenting complaint and provides cues as to what more detailed assessment needs to take place (e.g., cognitive assessment or psychometric testing). Although aspects of the person's history remain static (although open to revision), the mental status of an individual is dynamic.

The MSE provides a way to structure data about aspects of the individual's mental functioning. It typically follows a specific form followed by all health professionals with observations recorded under headings.

Some data can be obtained informally or while obtaining other components of the person's history. However, some questioning is usually needed.

It may be necessary to include some technical terms when writing up the MSE, but where possible verbatim accounts of the person's speech and thought content should be used. For example, "Mr. X was convinced that the CIA were observing his every move by satellite and claimed that invisible aliens had told him so" is far more informative than "Mr. X suffered from auditory hallucinations and secondary delusions."

The MSE has the following general elements, which are further divided into subheadings: (a) general appearance, (b) psychomotor behavior, (c) mood and affect, (d) speech, (e) cognition, (f) thought patterns, and (g) level of consciousness. There is some variability in how the MSE is structured. It takes a considerable amount of skill and practice to obtain the information required.

Mental Status Examination (Lakeman, 1995)

	Area	Descriptors
1	General Appearance	
	Appearance in relation to age	Does the person appear to be younger or older than the chronological age?
	Accessibility	Friendly, co-operative, hostile, alert, confused, eye contact, rapport, indifferent, etc.
	Body build	Tall, short, thin, obese. Provide a weight and height.
	Clothing	Appropriate to age, season, setting and occasion? Clean, neat, tidy, meticulous, worn, properly worn? Are the colors worn: bright, dull, drab?
	Cosmetics	Worn/applied properly, carefully or carelessly?
	Hygiene and grooming	Does the person appear clean, dirty, unbathed? Meticulous? Is hair neat, dirty, well groomed?
	Odor	Perspiration, alcohol, stool, or vaginal odor? Cologne, shaving lotion?
	Facial expression	Note whether the person appears sad, perplexed, worried, fearful, scowling, excited, elated, preoccupied, bored, suspicious, smiling, responsive, interested, animated, blank, dazed, or tense.
	Eye contact	Indirect, fixed, fleeting, glaring, darting, no contact.
2	Psychomotor Behavior	
	Gait	Brisk, slow, hesitant, propulsive, shuffling, dancing, normal, ataxic, uncoordinated.
	Handshake	Firm weak, warm, cool, resistant, heavy, refused, prolonged, seductive.

(Continued)

(Continued)

	Area	Descriptors
	Abnormal movements	Grimaces, tics, twitches, foot tapping, hand wringing, ritualistic behavior, mannerisms, posturing, nail biting, chewing movements, echopraxia.
	Posture	Stooped, relaxed, stiff, shaky, slouched, bizarre mannerisms, posturing, crouching, erect.
	Rate of movements	Hyperactive, slow, retarded, agitated.
	Coordination of movements	Awkward, clumsy, agile, falling easily.
3	Mood and Affect	
	Appropriateness of affect	Appropriate or inappropriate to situation. Congruous/incongruous.
	Range of affect	Lively, flat, normal, blunted, superficial, constricted.
	Stability of affect	Stable, labile.
	Attitude toward counselor during encounter	Frank, open, warm, fearful, suspicious, hostile, angry, evasive, playful, seductive, guarded, friendly, pleasant, ingratiating, negative, shy, overly familiar, cooperative, withdrawn.
	Specific mood or feelings observed or reported	Sadness, irritability, anger, fear, regret, elation, miserable, puzzled, optimistic, pessimistic, hopelessness, depressed.
	Anxiety level	Rate as mild, moderate, severe, panic.
4	Speech	
	Rate of speech	Rapid, slow, ordinary.
	Flow of speech	Hesitant, expansive, rambling, halting, stuttering, lilting, jerky, long pauses, forgetful.
	Intensity of volume	Loud, soft, ordinary, whispered, yelling, inaudible.
	Clarity	Clear, slurred, mumbled, lisping, rambling, relevant, incoherent.
	Liveliness	Lively, dull, monotonous, normal, intense, pressured, explosive.
	Quantity	Responds only to questions, offers information, scant, mute, verbose, repetitive.
5	Cognition	
	Attention and concentration	Sufficient, deficient, easily distractible, short span of attention, poor or adequate concentration, preoccupation. Serial 7s test. Months of year backward.
	Memory (short term and long term)	Poor or average for recent events of last few hours or days; poor or average for remote events of the past year. Family birthdays, country capitals, 5-minute recall of name and address. Digit span tests.
	Abstraction	Concrete thinking, able to think abstractly.
	Insight into illness	Complete denial; recognizes there is a problem, but projects blame; both intellectual and emotional awareness. Perception of Illness.
	Orientation	Time, place, and person.
	Judgment	Impulsive behavior with examples. Able to come to appropriate conclusions; unrealistic decisions.
6	Thought Patterns	
	Clarity	Coherent, incoherent, cloudy, confused, vague.
	Relevance/logic	Logical, illogical, relevant, or irrelevant to the topic being discussed.

	Area	Descriptors
	Flow	Excited, a flight of ideas, tangentiality, poverty of thought, word salad, clang associations, slow, normal or rapid reactions to questions, doubting, indecision, loose association, blocking, perseveration, spontaneous, continuity of thought. Any of the following types of disorder noted? a. Blocking: a sudden interruption of thought or speech. b. Mutism: refusal to speak. c. Echolalia: meaningless repetition of the nurse's words. d. Neologisms: new words formed to express ideas. e. Flight of ideas: skipping from one topic to another in fragmented, often rapid fashion. f. Perseveration: involuntary repetition of the answer to a previous question in response to a new question. g. Word salad: a mixture of words and phrases lacking comprehensive meaning or coherence. h. Pressure of speech: talking quickly and in such a way that interruption is difficult. i. Tangential speech: train of thought and response that misses the question asked/person never gets to the point. j. Circumstantiality: being incidental and irrelevant in stating details.
	Content	Rhymes, puns, suicidal ideation, unreality, delusions, illusions, hallucinations, ideas of reference, compulsions, obsessions, phobias, preoccupations, ideas of reference, paranoid ideation, homicidal ideation, depersonalization. Is the thought content consistent with reality? a. Obsessions: unwanted, recurring thoughts. b. Delusions: persistent false beliefs not in keeping with the person's culture or education (e.g., grandeur, persecution). Grandiose: unrealistic exaggeration of own importance. Persecutory: belief that one is being singled out for attack or harassment. c. Influential: Active influence: belief that one can control others through one's thoughts. Passive influence: belief that others can control the person. Somatic: total misinterpretation of physical symptoms. Nihilistic: belief in the nonexistence of self, others, or the world. Others: delusions of sin, guilt. d. Ideas of reference: incorrect interpretation of casual incidents and external events as being directed toward the self. e. Hallucinations: false sensory perceptions without external stimuli (e.g., auditory, visual, olfactory, gustatory, tactile, kinesthetic).
7	Level of consciousness	Totally unresponsive, responsive to painful stimuli only, responsive to touch, responsive to verbal stimuli only.

Index

Note: Page references followed by (table) indicate a table and page references followed by (figure) indicate an illustrated figure.